Boatowner's Mechanical and Electrical Manual
Third Edition

How to Maintain, Repair, and Improve Your Boat's Essential Systems

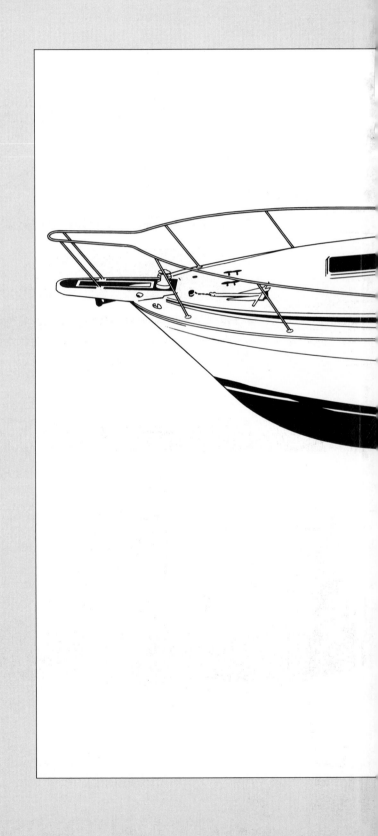

Third Edition

Boatowner's Mechanical and Electrical Manual

Nigel Calder

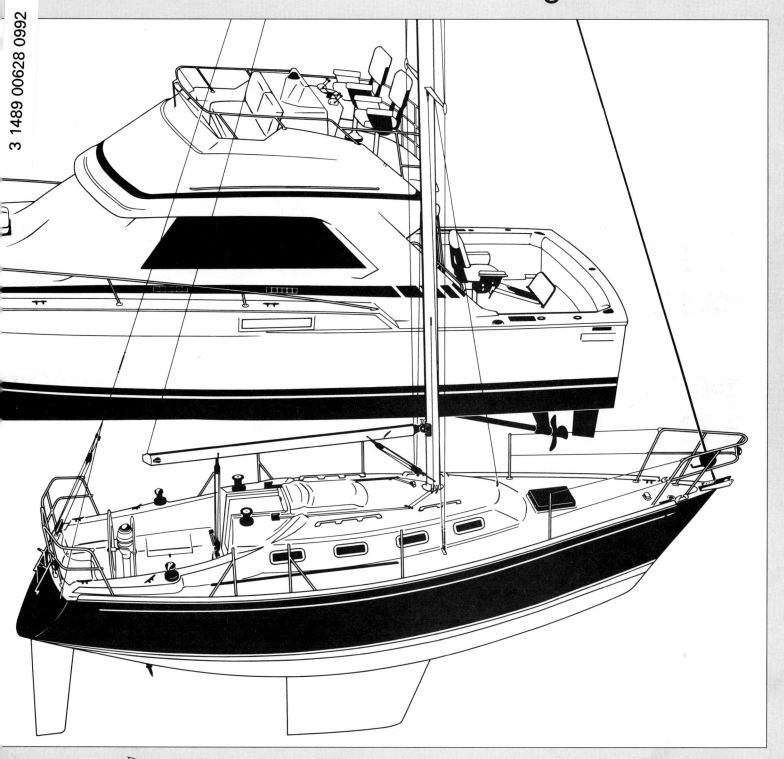

International Marine / McGraw-Hill
Camden, Maine • New York • Chicago • San Francisco • Lisbon • London • Madrid • Mexico
City • Milan • New Delhi • San Juan • Seoul • Singapore • Sydney • Toronto

Other Books by Nigel Calder

The Cruising Guide to the Northwest Caribbean: The Yucatan Coast of Mexico, Belize, Guatemala, Honduras, and the Bay Islands of Honduras
Cuba: A Cruising Guide
How to Read a Nautical Chart: A Complete Guide to the Symbols, Abbreviations, and Data Displayed on Nautical Charts
Marine Diesel Engines: Maintenance, Troubleshooting, and Repair, 2nd edition
Nigel Calder's Cruising Handbook: A Compendium for Coastal and Offshore Sailors
Refrigeration for Pleasureboats: Installation, Maintenance, and Repair
Repairs at Sea

The McGraw·Hill Companies

10 QVR/QVR 12

© 1996, 2005 by Nigel Calder

All rights reserved. The publisher takes no responsibility for the use of any of the materials or methods described in this book, nor for the products thereof. The name "International Marine" and the International Marine logo are trademarks of The McGraw-Hill Companies. Printed in the United States of America.

Library of Congress Cataloging-in-Publication Data
Calder, Nigel.
  Boatowner's mechanical and electrical manual : how to maintain, repair, and improve your boat's essential systems / Nigel Calder. — 3rd ed.
      p.   cm.
  Includes index.
  ISBN 0-07-143238-8 (hardcover : alk. paper)
  1. Boats and boating—Maintenance and repair—Handbooks, manuals, etc. 2. Boats and boating—Electric equipment—Maintenance and repair—Handbooks, manuals, etc. I. Title.
  VM322.C35 2005
  623.8'5'00288—dc22   2004027315

Questions regarding the content of this book should be addressed to
International Marine
P.O. Box 220
Camden, ME 04843
www.internationalmarine.com

Questions regarding the ordering of this book should be addressed to
The McGraw-Hill Companies
Customer Service Department
P.O. Box 547
Blacklick, OH 43004
Retail customers: 1-800-262-4729
Bookstores: 1-800-722-4726

DEDICATION

To Pippin and Paul:
May this book hasten the day when you
take over the maintenance of the boat.

Contents

List of Troubleshooting Charts

List of Tables

Preface and Acknowledgments to the Third Edition

Over time, the audience for this book has evolved. The first edition was written for hardcore cruising sailors. It paid scant attention to such things as the voluntary boatbuilding standards promulgated by the American Boat and Yacht Council (ABYC) in the United States, and none whatsoever to the legally enforceable standards then being developed by the International Standards Organization (ISO) in Europe. But then I found that in addition to cruisers, the book was being used by a significant number of marine professionals—surveyors, designers, and boatbuilders. So, for the second edition I not only added a considerable amount of new material, but I also "cleaned up" the book from a standards-compliance perspective.

Ten years later I find the book is now widely used by marine professionals all over the world. At the same time, the ISO has substantially expanded the scope of its standards. Meanwhile, much of my original audience of cruising sailors has become far better educated and sophisticated with respect to technical matters, and is capable of acting upon considerably more-complex information. At the other end of the spectrum, a new generation of sailors, many with minimal experience and limited technical knowledge, has taken up cruising. Powerboaters of all stripes have begun to use the book. As a backdrop to these developments, the systems found on almost all boats have become increasingly sophisticated.

These changes have created a major challenge in terms of defining the audience for this third edition and in determining the level of detail and complexity that should be included. One thing, however, has not changed—the primary objective of meeting the needs of cruising sailors, both those with considerable experience as well as neophytes. Within this general framework, I have also sought to meet the needs of industry professionals.

In order to satisfy these somewhat divergent objectives, I have retained most of the structure of the original book, because it has seemed to work so well over the years and is already familiar to hundreds of thousands of readers. However, I have added considerably more detail than in previous editions, and slotted in numerous new sections (e.g., a whole new chapter on boats with more-complex electrical systems requirements, and new sections on lighting technologies, air-conditioning, watermakers, and bow thrusters). Overall, the book has expanded by about 40%.

In places, the level of detail will get a little overwhelming for the beginning reader (especially some of the electrical stuff), but I encourage perseverance; if your boat has the kinds of systems discussed in this book, you need to grapple with the issues and subjects I cover. For the professionals (and for the rest of us, because the world we live in becomes ever more legalistic), I have added many more explicit references to ABYC and ISO standards. Finally, given that all of this book, except for the sections dealing with spars, standing rigging, and sail reefing devices, is as applicable to most powerboats as it is to sailboats, I have made some minor reorganization of the last chapters, relegating the few specifically sailboat subjects to the last chapter.

At the end of the day, the overall goal remains the same as ever, which is to provide the reader, whoever he or she may be, with information that will enable the systems on a boat to be designed, installed, and maintained in a manner that will minimize aggravation and maximize the enjoyment of boating.

In addition to the literally hundreds of individuals and companies who have aided me with earlier editions (see the Preface to the Second Edition), with this edition I have once again received assistance from a large number of people. In particular, I would like to thank: Ewen Thomson, Richard Cohen, Gregory Dash, and Abdel Mousa for their input on lightning; the folks at Xantrex (battery chargers, inverters, and systems monitors), Bill Montgomery of Balmar (alternators and DC generators), and Thane Lanz of Analytic Systems (DC-to-DC converters); Bill Owra (Everfair Enterprises) and Andy Kruse (Southwest Windpower) for wind generator feedback; Craig Whitworth of the Electrical Apparatus Service Association; Mark Matousec and his successors at Taylorbrite, Kinder Woodcock (Imtra), James Creveling (Nichia), and Ken James (Deep Creek Enterprises) for their help on lighting, especially LEDs; Ben Landis (Volvo) and Greg Eck (Yanmar); Kevin Woody (PYI), Michael Adler (VariProp), Chuck Angle (Flex-O-Fold), and Doug Rose (Volvo Penta) for input on propellers, and Ken Nigel (Shaft Lok) on shaft locks; Rob Warren (Frigoboat), Bengt Stenvinkel (Isotherm), and Kevin Alston (Glacier Bay) for a great deal of technical input on refrigeration; Steve Rollins (Sea Recovery) and Bill Edinger (Spectra) for help with watermakers; John Curry (Hydrovane) and Hans Bernwall (Scanmar) for updating me on wind vanes; Steve Loutrel (Navtec) for information on rod rigging; and Tony Jones (Lewmar) for feedback on the sections on winches and windlasses.

Peter Jacops (European Certification Bureau) and the staff at the ABYC have helped with numerous inquiries concerning ISO and ABYC standards. My participation in the ABYC's Electrical Project Technical Committee has given me access to many of the brightest and most energetic brains in the business, which has been of inestimable value.

There are many others who have helped in both large and small ways. My thanks to all of you. And then there is, as always, the crew at International Marine, especially Molly Mulhern, Janet Robbins, and Margaret Cook—and illustrator Jim Sollers; it is always a pleasure to work with you.

NIGEL CALDER
Maine, May 2005

Preface and Acknowledgments to the Second Edition

In the six years since I wrote the first edition of this book there have been significant changes in boat systems, particularly electrical systems, which would, in themselves, have been justification for a second edition. But in addition to this, the success of the first edition has established me as a professional technical writer. This has not only afforded me the luxury of studying the subjects covered in this book full time, but has also brought me into contact with many of the smartest and most innovative people in the boating equipment world, which has greatly improved my understanding of a number of complex issues. As a result, for this second edition I felt it necessary to rewrite much of the first half of the book, and significant sections of the second half. The text has grown by at least 20%, with numerous new illustrations, troubleshooting charts, and tables. The result is a volume that I feel is, both in small ways and large, far superior to the first edition.

In the course of writing this new edition, I have corresponded with, and received help from, literally dozens of boat and equipment manufacturers and individuals. Some have devoted considerable amounts of time and resources to reviewing and correcting draft chapters; others have shown me their plant and equipment or helped in other ways. I am especially indebted (in no particular order) to Alan Fitzpatrick of Marine and General Battery, Rick Proctor of the Cruising Equipment Company, David Smead of Ample Technology, Bob Ajeman of Professional Mariner, Paul Michaelcyck of Ancor, Chuck Hawley at West Marine, Jack Honey of Marine Technology, David Potter of Kemp Spars, Julian Whitlock of Whitlock Steering Systems, Gordan Lyall of Simpson Lawrence, Michael Adler of Adler Barbour, Kevin Alston of Glacier Bay, Jack Durrant of Ampair, Bill Owra of Everfair Enterprises, John Surrette of Rolls Battery Co., Tom Hale and Lysle Gray at the American Boat and Yacht Council, Dick Troberg of Fluke, Wally Ivison of Norseman Marine, Don Kavenagh, associate editor of *Ocean Navigator* magazine, Bob Loeser, Professors Geoffrey Swain and Harry Lipsitt, experts in corrosion, and Ron Colby.

The following companies have also provided information and support: ABI, ACDelco, Allcraft Corporation, Allison Marine Transmissions, American Insulated Wire Corp., Ampair, Aquadrive, Arco, Atlantic/Trident Solar Products, Auto-Helm, Automate, Balmar, Barient, Barlow, Battery Council International, Beckson Marine, Bertram Yacht, Blakes Lavac Taylors, Blue Sea Systems, BorgWarner Corporation, Brookes and Gatehouse, C. H. Corporation, Camper and Nicholson, Carol Cable Co., Caterpillar Tractor Co., Cetrek/Navstar, Climate Control Inc., CPT Inc., Danforth, Danfoss, Dart Union Co., Delco Remy, Detroit Diesel, Dole Refrigerating Co., Don Allen Co., Edson International, Force 10, Forespar, Four Seasons, Frigoboat, Frigomatic, Furuno, Furlex, Garrett Automotive Products Co., Givens Buoy, Gougeon Brothers, Groco, Grunert Refrigeration, Guest, Halyard Marine Ltd., Hamilton Ferris, Harken, Hart Systems Inc., Heart Interface, Henderson Pumps, Holset Engineering Co., Hood Yacht Systems, Hurth, Hydrovane Yacht Equipment Ltd., Interstate Batteries, ITT/Jabsco, Kenyon Marine, Kohler Corporation, L. Q. Moffit, Lasdrop Shaft Seal, Leeward Rigging, Lewmar Marine, Lirakis Safety Harness Inc., Loos and Co., Lucas Marine, Paul Luke and Sons, Lunaire Marine, Mansfield Sanitary, Marine Power Ltd., Marine Vane Gear Ltd., Marlec, Mars Electronics, Martec, Max-Prop, MDC, Mercantile Manufacturing, Metalmast Marine, Micrologic, Morse Controls, Munster Simms Engineering Ltd. (now Whale), Navico, Navstar, Navtec, Newmar, Nicro Fico, NMEA, Norseman/Gibb, Onan, Parker Hannifin Corporation, Parker Industrial, PDC Labs International, Perkins Engines Ltd., Plastimo, Profurl, PYI, Raritan, Raytheon Marine Co., Rolls Battery Engineering, RVG, S and F Tool Co., Sailomat, Sailtec, Sanden International, Schaefer, Sea Frost, Sea Inc., SeaLand Technology, Shaft Lok Inc., Shakespeare, Shipmate Stove Division, Signet Marine, Solar Power Corporation, Southwire Company, SpaCreek Inc., Sta-Lok, Stowe, Stream Stay, Surrette Storage Battery Co., Tartan Marine Co., Taylor's Para-Fin, Tecumseh, Trace Engineering, Tracor Instruments, Universal Enterprises, VDO Marine, Vernay Products, Wagner Marine, Walker and Sons, Wallas Marin, Westerbeke Generators, Whale, Whitlock Steering Systems, Wilcox-Crittenden, Wolter Systems, and York.

My editors at International Marine have been as helpful as ever. Jim Sollers, illustrator extraordinaire, has done an astounding job interpreting my rough sketches. Molly Mulhern, the International Marine art and production director, has shown great patience with the rest of us and somehow kept the manuscript and illustrations organized and on schedule.

So you see, although it is my name on the cover, this book is really a collective effort. My thanks to everyone.

NIGEL CALDER
Maine, September 1995

Introduction

In the past two or three decades, boat equipment has taken a quantum leap in complexity. It is no longer possible to keep things operating with a monkey wrench, hammer, and grease gun. More and more equipment needs specialized servicing, and the cost of professional help is going through the roof. While the public may think that boatowners are rich, in reality most are middle-income salary earners who strain their budgets to support their boating habit. The boatowner of today with limited funds needs a good working knowledge of all systems aboard, the ability to keep up with maintenance, and the means to troubleshoot and repair a broad range of breakdowns.

This book is intended to make these three objectives a realistic possibility with respect to the basic equipment found on most modern, midsized boats, both power and sail. In developing its contents, the biggest problem I have had is in deciding where to draw the line between what a talented amateur in a jam can reasonably be encouraged to undertake, and leading people into trouble. Since I have a high regard for most people's capabilities, I have gone well beyond the information typically available to the general boating public.

I have taken great pains to ensure the accuracy of this book. All information is given in good faith. Nevertheless, I must caution the reader: If you are in any doubt about what you are doing, leave things alone! I cannot accept liability for any damage or injuries arising from the reader's attempts to follow the procedures in this book. If you wreck a piece of equipment, sink the boat, or hurt yourself, the responsibility has to be yours.

Now that I've gotten that off my chest, a word on how to use this book. There are four distinct levels at which it can be useful:

- Many maintenance problems and equipment failures are the result of inadequate or improper installations. A quick skimming of the book, skipping over the detailed sections on equipment repair, may well highlight a number of potential difficulties on your boat and enable you to take corrective action before something goes wrong. This is especially relevant for anyone buying a new boat. Proper liaison with the boatbuilder can eliminate most built-in problems at a fraction of the cost of a later cure.

- When buying new equipment, a review of the pertinent section(s) will give you an idea of what can go wrong. Although I don't recommend one brand name over another, I can arm you with appropriate questions to ask about any brand. This may save a lot of grief later.

- Routine maintenance is covered in some detail in each chapter with an annual haulout (winterizing) summary in Appendix A.

- When equipment does malfunction or break down, the list of troubleshooting charts on page viii and the index will point you to the relevant sections on troubleshooting and repair.

After reading this book, boatowners may think that maintenance and repair is a full-time job in itself. Sometimes it does seem like that. But in reality, most routine maintenance procedures take little time. The key is to be methodical and organized. And keep in mind that boat equipment likes to be used frequently. In the marine environment, more things seize up from lack of use than from being used. Your boat will be least troublesome if you get the maintenance done, and then go out on the water as often as possible.

Happy Boating!

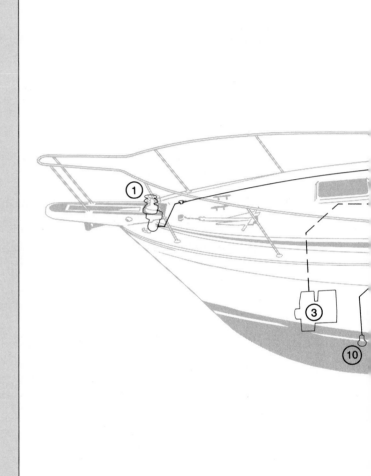

CHAPTER 1

FIGURE 1-1. These two representative boats illustrate just how complicated the electrical system of an average modern pleasure boat has become. *(Jim Sollers)*

———— 12 VDC

— — — — — 120 VAC

(1) anchor windlass
(2) macerator pump
(3) air conditioner
(4) engine instruments, radios, navigation instruments
(5) engine starter switch
(6) distribution panel
(7) battery isolation switch
(8) 120 VAC shoreside receptacle
(9) bilge pump
(10) sump pump
(11) batteries
(12) air-conditioning compressor
(13) blower
(14) starter motor
(15) refrigerator
(16) water heater
(17) head pump
(18) cabin lights
(19) navigation lights
(20) pressure water pump

Establishing a Balanced Battery-Powered Electrical System

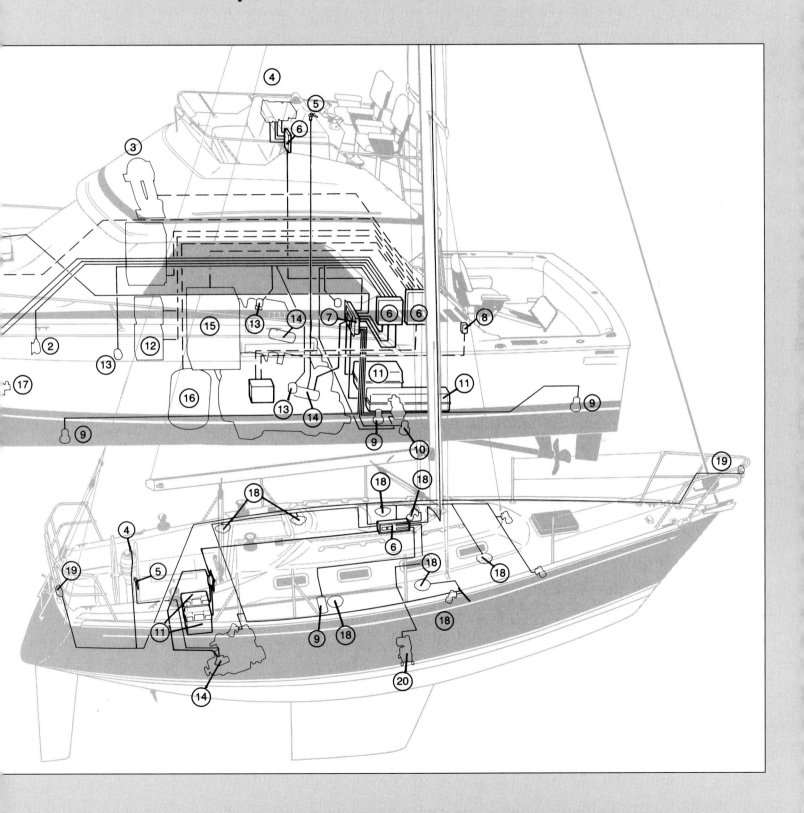

Introduction

Today's pleasure boats have become increasingly dependent on electricity. Very few engines can be started without it; an increasing number of boatowners can't navigate without it; and a lot of toilets can't even be flushed without it! While the explosive growth of electrical and electronic equipment over the past decade or two has brought about a revolution in comfort and ease of boat handling, electrical malfunctions have become the most common maintenance problem aboard boats, especially those with aging, hodgepodge, or jury-rigged electrical circuits.

The marine environment is a terrible place for electricity. To be trouble free, electrical circuits must be installed with great care and to the highest standards—topics that are dealt with in Chapter 4. But no matter how carefully an electrical installation is carried out, the entire system must be properly balanced in the first place, or it will soon become a source of endless problems and a constant drain on the pocketbook.

Because of improperly set up systems, many boatowners repeatedly find themselves with dead batteries, outright battery failures, and lengthy charging times. Fixing immediate problems does nothing to resolve the overall imbalance in the system, guaranteeing that the next difficulty is just around the corner. A large number of boats come straight off the production line with these potential problems built in. Thus the first requirement for electrical problem solving and repair is to understand the peculiar needs of a boat's DC electrical system and to make sure the overall system is in balance. This chapter takes a look at these general considerations; Chapter 2 looks at more complex systems; and Chapter 3 deals with detailed maintenance, troubleshooting, and repair procedures for specific pieces of DC electrical equipment. Although I focus on 12-volt systems, all information is equally applicable to 24 or 32 volts.

The Peculiarities of Boats

Consider first an automobile. A 12-volt battery provides the energy to crank a starter motor, normally for just a second or two, after which the engine fires up and the alternator cuts in. The alternator subsequently supplies all the car's electrical needs, plus an extra margin to replace the energy the starter motor withdrew from the battery. The car's electrical system runs on the power supplied by the alternator, not that supplied by the battery. Although starter motors use a tremendous amount of energy, they do so for a very brief period of time, and thus pull next

to nothing from a battery. For example, a 400 amp starter motor (a large starter motor) would consume 400 amp-hours of energy in 1 hour, but cranking it for 15 seconds (which is far longer than normal) drains the battery by only $400/(4 \times 60) = 1.66$ amp-hours, which is not very much! (The distinction between amps and amp-hours is drawn on page 13.) This drain is replenished by the alternator in just a few minutes. Under normal use, a car battery is almost always fully charged, and the batteries do very little work. This holds true for almost all cars, regardless of size, electrical complexity, or use. (The exceptions are some *hybrids* in which the engine shuts down when stationary in traffic, and the car systems temporarily run off the batteries.) In general, the only variable from one car to another is the capacity of the alternator—cars with high electrical loads need bigger alternators.

Contrast this first with a sailboat. The average boat spends most of its time in a slip. Periodically the owner cranks the engine, motors out of the slip, shuts the engine down, and goes sailing. Apart from the time spent motoring, the boat's electrical system runs directly off the battery. The battery will be discharged more deeply than an automobile battery, while the engine will be run far less than an automobile engine, providing minimal charging time.

Now consider the average powerboat. The engine will be run for longer periods of time than a sailboat's, with usage patterns often similar to those of an automobile. But even so, many powerboats, especially cruising boats (notably trawler yachts), will have extended periods when the engine is shut down, and the boat's electrical system is running off the batteries. Although larger powerboats may have a 24-hour-a-day generating capability, with a battery charger left permanently on so that battery service closely resembles that of an automobile, this scenario is not necessarily the norm (and in any case, is often a poor way to design a system—see Chapter 2). An increasing number of boatowners with onboard AC generators and substantial power requirements are discovering that with a DC-to-AC inverter (see Chapter 6), they can shut down their generators for most of the day, enjoying peace and quiet while on the hook and saving money at the same time. In this case too, battery use closely resembles that of cruising sailboats.

What this all adds up to is that in contrast to automotive use, at some point in time almost all boats run their DC systems off the battery, deeply discharging it. As a result, the working environment for all the major DC system com-

ESTABLISHING A BALANCED BATTERY-POWERED ELECTRICAL SYSTEM

ponents—the battery, alternator, and voltage regulator—is very different from that found in the automotive field, and yet, primarily for reasons of cost, it has been customary to use transplanted automotive equipment in marine applications with little or no modification. Not surprisingly, this leads to numerous problems, most of which have their origins in the limitations of existing battery technology. To see why this is so, and how to correct problems, we need to delve into this technology.

Batteries

How They Work

A battery is composed of one or more *cells* (Figures 1-2A and 1-2B). Each cell contains alternating negative and positive *plates*, between which are plate *separators* (insulators). All the negative plates are connected together, as are all the positive plates. Each plate has a *grid* configuration, and within the grid is bonded the plate's *active material* (Figure 1-3). The grid provides the physical structure for the plate and the means for conducting electrons in and out of the plate. The active material is the substance that produces the electrons.

When fully charged, the active material in the negative plates is pure *sponge lead*; in the positive plates, it is *lead dioxide*. The plates are placed in contact with a solution of sulfuric acid (the *electrolyte*). As a battery discharges, the acid from the electrolyte combines with the active material in the battery plates, forming *lead sulfate* and water, the latter diluting the acid solution. When a battery is charged, water is driven

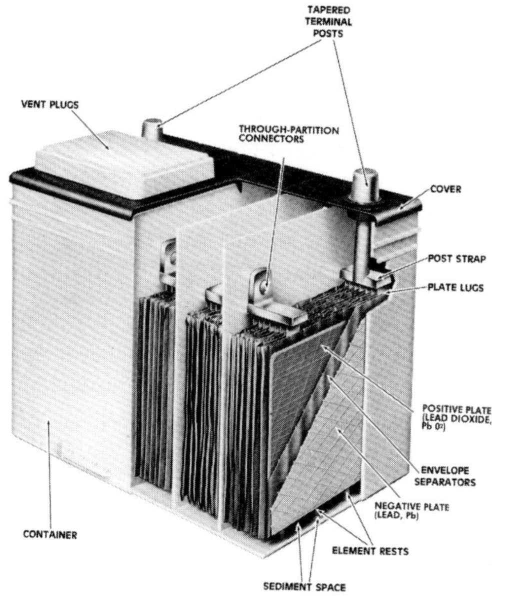

FIGURE 1-2B. Trojan deep-cycle battery construction. Similar to the automotive battery, except that everything is more heavy duty, with considerably more lead, and therefore capacity, in a given volume. *(Trojan)*

FIGURE 1-3. Negative battery plates with some of the active material removed to reveal the plate grid. Note the surface of the plate is slightly eroded away in places due to sloughing off of active material as the battery ages.

FIGURE 1-2A. Typical automobile-type battery construction. There are six cells; within each is a series of alternating negative and positive plates, each one isolated from its neighbors by intervening insulators, called separators. The plates are immersed in a sulfuric acid solution. The negative plates are connected with each other and with the negative terminal; the positive plates are collectively connected with the positive terminal. *(Battery Council International)*

from the acid solution, increasing the strength of the electrolyte, while the used portion of the plate material that formed the lead sulfate is reconverted to active material.

The formula describing this process, for those who are interested, is as follows:

$$PbO_2 + Pb + 2H_2SO_4 \leftrightarrow 2PbSO_4 + 2H_2O.$$

Voltage, capacity, and rate of discharge/ recharge. Regardless of plate size, construction, or numbers of plates in an individual cell, any charged lead-acid cell will produce a voltage of around 2.1 volts. This is simply the voltage that results from placing lead dioxide and lead in sulfuric acid. (Cells using other metals and electrolytes have different voltages; for more on this phenomenon see the section on galvanic corrosion in Chapter 5.)

What is not built into the cell chemistry is the *capacity* of a cell (how many electrons the cell can store), how fast the cell can deliver these electrons when connected to a load, and how fast it can be charged.

Crudely speaking, capacity is a function of the amount of lead in a cell—the greater the weight of lead dioxide and lead paste, the greater the storage capacity. A large, thick plate will produce the same voltage as a small, thin plate, but will store many times more electrons.

The ability of a plate to give up its stored energy depends on the ability of the acid in the electrolyte to react with the active material in the plate. The active material is made porous so that the acid can filter (diffuse) through the plate, allowing water to percolate out and fresh acid to percolate in during discharges, and the reverse to happen during charges. The thicker the plate and the denser the active material, the slower the process of percolation, and as a result, the slower a battery will give up its stored energy, and the slower it can be charged.

When a battery is put under a heavy load, the electrolyte will first react with the accessible (surface) areas of the plates. But once these have given up their stored energy, the rate at which electrons can be released from the inner areas of the plates slows down, causing the voltage to fall off. This does not necessarily mean that the battery is dead. If you rest it, allowing time for the water to diffuse out of the plates and fresh acid to filter in, the voltage will recover as fresh areas of active material are brought into service. This is why, if a car is cranked until the battery dies and then left for a short period of time, the battery will frequently recover and crank the engine again—the acid has diffused to unused portions of the plates, providing a fresh burst of energy.

When it comes time to charge, the charging current will first reconvert to active material the lead sulfates most accessible to the electrolyte— that is, those on the surface of the plates. This can be done relatively quickly. Thereafter the rate of charge will be limited by the speed with which acid can filter out of the active material and water can filter in as the charging progresses. It is this diffusion rate that determines the *charge acceptance rate* of a battery. Thick-plate, high-density-active-material batteries have a lower charge acceptance rate than thin-plate, low-density-active-material batteries.

Electrolyte Variations

The electrolyte in a battery may take different forms. These differences, in turn, will affect the nature of the battery's construction. The principal variations are:

Wet or flooded electrolyte. The traditional battery has a liquid electrolyte and is known as a *wet*, or *flooded-electrolyte*, battery. During periods of charging, particularly the final stages of charging, some of the charging current breaks down the water in the electrolyte into its component parts of hydrogen and oxygen, which then bubble out of the electrolyte—the battery is said to *boil* or *gas*—lowering the level of the electrolyte. This water must periodically be replaced by topping off the battery cells with distilled water via removable vent caps.

Much of this water loss can be prevented by fitting Hydrocaps (from Hydro-Cap, 305-696-2504). These devices contain a catalyst that causes the hydrogen and oxygen to recombine into water. However, because they tend to trap heat in the battery, Hydrocaps have to be used with caution on the kinds of fast-charging systems I will be discussing later in this chapter. In general, when they are most needed—on systems that are driven hard and experience significant water loss—they should not be used. They should *never* be used when *equalizing* or *conditioning* a battery (see later); if not removed, they can get hot enough to melt. (Anytime a Hydrocap is too hot to hold, it is being used in an inappropriate application and should be removed; on the other hand, if it does not get warm during the final stages of charging, it is not working.)

Another device that reduces water loss is the Water Miser Safety Vent Cap (made by Kyocera Solar, www.kyocerasolar.com, and available from many alternative energy suppliers), a replacement battery cap that contains polymer beads. The beads cause some of the condensates driven out of a battery to recondense and drip back in, typically reducing water loss by about 30%. A Water Miser Cap can be left in place when equalizing.

Note that the battery plate grids in wet batteries have small amounts of antimony added to the lead during their manufacture. Antimony strengthens the grid and helps to lock the active material in the grid (which reduces shedding—see below), but it has the undesirable side effect of intensifying gassing during charging, and it promotes internal *galvanic currents* within a battery, which slowly discharge the battery when it is left idle (a process known as self-discharge).

Gelled electrolyte. In a *gel-cell*, the electrolyte is in the form of a gel with the consistency of soft candle wax. During manufacture this gel is pasted onto the battery plates and separators, which are then packed tightly together (Figure 1-4). During discharges and charges, the active material in the battery reacts with the gel in immediate contact; however, there is not the same fluid movement within the electrolyte as in a wet battery. As a result, the battery plates must be kept relatively thin to achieve adequate diffusion of the gel around them. In use, the gel can develop voids or cracks that leave areas of the plates dry and result in a progressive loss of capacity.

The gel cannot be replaced during service, so gelled batteries cannot be topped off. They are built as sealed no-maintenance units. Because they cannot be topped off, it is essential to minimize gassing during charging, since this would cause the electrolyte to dry out (it leaves a powder) and the battery to fail. Several methods are used to keep gassing to a minimum:

1. Charge voltage is carefully controlled to prevent overcharging.
2. The antimony used to reinforce conventional battery plates is replaced with calcium. The resulting plate grid is not as strong, but is far less prone to gassing or self-discharge.
3. Some batteries are allowed to build up a certain amount of internal pressure. Under pressure, small amounts of hydrogen and oxygen produced during charges will recombine into water and be absorbed into the electrolyte (as a result, these batteries are sometimes called *recombinant*). Excessive charging, however, will cause excessive amounts of hydrogen and oxygen to be produced, so recombinant batteries always have pressure relief valves to vent excess gases. For this reason, gel-cell batteries are also sometimes called SVR (sealed valve regulated) or VRLA (valve regulated lead acid) batteries. Anytime venting takes place, the electrolyte is drying out and battery life is being reduced (Figure 1-5).

FIGURE 1-4. Paste-like consistency of the electrolyte in a gel-cell battery.

FIGURE 1-5. A dried-out gel-cell battery. This battery froze when in a discharged state, splitting the battery case and causing the electrolyte to dry out over time. (Unlike a wet-cell battery that would have lost all its electrolyte and failed immediately, this gel-cell battery only slowly ceased to function as the electrolyte dried out.)

Note that many so-called maintenance-free batteries are in reality nothing more than wet batteries with excess electrolyte contained in partially sealed cases. During service the excess electrolyte is slowly used up. Because there is no way to top off these batteries, once the plates begin to dry out they are doomed. So it is important to distinguish between these batteries and a true no-maintenance battery—i.e., an SVR or VRLA, recombinant, gelled-electrolyte battery.

Starved, or absorbed, electrolyte. A starved or absorbed electrolyte battery, generally known as an AGM—absorbed glass mat—battery, is a variation of an SVR/VRLA battery, in which the electrolyte is held in place by the capillary action of a sponge-like mass of matted glass fibers (Figure 1-6). The principal difference from a gel-cell is that the electrolyte is in a liquid, not a gelled, state. This liquid state enhances electrolyte migration in and out of the battery plates and minimizes void formation. The result is improved performance when confronted with high charges and discharges and extremely cold environments.

Modes of Failure

With these basic facts in hand, we can understand the main reasons why batteries fail. Such an understanding is essential to designing DC systems that will be free from premature failure, and in troubleshooting problem systems. The principal causes of failure are:

Shedding of the active plate material. When a battery is discharged and charged, the chemical processes in the plates—converting sponge lead and lead dioxide to lead sulfate and

FIGURE 1-6. An AGM battery. Fiberglass mats between the battery plates hold the electrolyte by capillary action.

back again—tend to weaken the bond between the active material and the plate grids. Every time a battery is discharged, some of the active material is loosened and shed from the grid, reducing the overall capacity of the battery (Figure 1-7). This is the normal aging process and will eventually result in complete battery failure, either through material building up in the base of the battery until it reaches the level of the plates and shorts them out (Figure 1-8), or through the loss of so much active material from the plates that the battery no longer has the capacity to carry out its tasks. (Note that in recent years, more and more batteries have been built with envelope plate separators, which are sealed on the sides and bottom, so that any shed material remains in the envelope. This reduces the incidence of plate shorting, but not the shedding itself.)

The extent to which a battery will shed its active material in a given situation is almost entirely a matter of its internal construction. Thin-plate, low-density-active-material batteries

FIGURE 1-7. Erosion of the active material from the surface of battery plates.

FIGURE 1-8. A severe case of shedding. The positive plate grids in this battery have been entirely eaten away through galvanic corrosion as a result of repeated overcharging. This has allowed the active material to fall to the base of the battery.

are far more susceptible to damage than thick-plate, high-density-active-material batteries. The process of shedding is accelerated by deep discharges, high rates of discharge and charge, the sloshing of the electrolyte around the plates when a boat is pounding in a seaway, and in the case of liquid-electrolyte batteries, by gassing during periods of overcharge, which will wash active material out of the plates. Gel-cells and AGMs, with their tightly packed plates, resist shedding to a much greater extent than liquid-electrolyte batteries, and when it does occur, the shed material tends to become trapped in the gel rather than fall to the base of the battery.

Sulfation. The lead sulfate formed in the battery plates during discharges is initially soft and relatively easy to reconvert into active material through battery charging. If a battery is left in a discharged state, however, the sulfate hardens into crystals that prove increasingly difficult to reconvert into active material (Figure 1-9). This effectively reduces battery capacity and slowly kills the battery—a process known as *sulfation*. Sulfation can occur in several different ways: leaving a battery discharged for a prolonged time; persistent undercharging so that a percentage of the battery's active material is always left uncharged; and failing to charge the inner areas of thick plates or plates with dense active material (a variant of undercharging). In addition, idle batteries slowly self-discharge and sulfate over time, at a rate largely determined by whether the plates have antimony- or calcium-reinforced grids and by the ambient temperature (the higher the temperature, the faster the rate of discharge). Gel-cells and AGMs have a slower rate of sulfation than other batteries. This is due to the recombination of oxygen—the presence of which accelerates sulfation in other batteries—into water and its reabsorption into the gel/electrolyte.

Overcharging. Overcharging can be just as damaging as undercharging, since it leads to gassing. If this results in water loss and the lost water is not replaced, sooner or later the plates dry out. Gel-cells and AGMs are particularly susceptible to damage. They have less electrolyte than wet-cells to begin with, and there is no way to replace lost electrolyte. Once active material is allowed to dry out, it is permanently lost.

During overcharges, galvanic activity within a battery also attacks the positive plate grids, causing them to deteriorate, reducing their current-carrying capability, and finally disintegrating them completely (Figures 1-10A and 1-10B). The grids in thin-plate batteries fail much sooner than those in thick-plate batteries.

FIGURE 1-9. A close-up of sulfated active material. For photographic purposes, some of the sulfates have been dislodged and turned on end to show that the sulfation is not just a surface phenomenon.

FIGURES 1-10A AND 1-10B. Persistent overcharging has destroyed the positive plate grids in this battery to the point that the active material no longer has any supporting structure.

Buckling of battery plates. A battery has an internal resistance that increases as the battery comes up to charge. As with any resistance, the more current driven through it, the warmer it gets. The normal result of excessively high rates of charge is that the battery heats up internally until the plates distort, shorting out adjoining plates and killing the battery.

Automotive (Cranking) Versus Deep-Cycle Batteries

From the foregoing we can see why automotive batteries are a bad choice in many marine applications. Automotive batteries are designed for engine starting, which requires the rapid release of a tremendous burst of energy. To make this possible, these batteries have many thin plates containing low-density active material. This maximizes the plate surface area and minimizes the diffusion time of acid through the plates. These construction features accelerate the rate at which the charge can be withdrawn from the battery.

But thin plates and low-density active material cannot handle repeated deep discharges and recharges (known as *cycling*). With each cycle some of the active material literally falls out of the plate grids. This is of little concern in automotive (cranking) use, since the batteries are rarely discharged more than a few percent, so very little shedding occurs. But in marine use, where repeated deep discharges are common, automotive batteries can quickly fall apart internally, a process accelerated by any pounding at sea. In fact, poorly constructed automotive batteries fail in as little as a dozen complete discharge/recharge cycles, while even the better-quality ones are unlikely to survive more than 30 to 40 such cycles. (On some boats, this may be just one month's cruising!) At the other end of the spectrum, the flimsy plate grids in automotive batteries cannot tolerate much overcharging during charging cycles without disintegrating.

A *deep-cycle* battery (also known as a *traction* battery) is needed for cycling applications. Deep-cycle batteries have much thicker plates, stronger grids, denser active material, heavier plate separators, and generally tougher construction than automotive (cranking) batteries. There is still some shedding of active material from the plates with every discharge cycle, but nowhere near as much as from thin-plate batteries. *Deep-cycle batteries tolerate repeated discharges in a way that no automotive battery can.* The heavier

grids also withstand considerable abuse during charging.

Life cycles (cycle life). The differences between automotive and deep-cycle batteries are matters of degree (thicker plates, stronger grids, heavier separators, a tougher case, etc.) rather than fundamental differences in design. Thus, there is no clear dividing line between them. Some high-quality automotive batteries are built as well as some cheap deep-cycle batteries. It is not possible simply to rely on a manufacturer's description of a battery as "deep-cycle" when determining its quality (Figures 1-11A and 1-11B). From a technical perspective, the key in judging one battery against another is *life cycles*, i.e., the number of times a battery can be pulled down to a certain level of discharge and then recharged before it fails (Figure 1-12).

Unfortunately for the consumer, there are a number of different ways of testing for life cycles, producing radically different results. When assessing life cycles, it is important to make sure apples are compared with apples. The three key factors are:

1. The rate at which a battery is discharged relative to its overall capacity. Typically, the discharge rate is either 20% of the rated capacity (meaning a 100 amp-hour battery is discharged at a rate of 20 amps; this is known as the C5 rate because the battery is fully discharged in 5 hours), or 5% of the rated capacity (a 100 amp-hour battery is discharged at a rate of 5 amps; this is known as the C20 rate because

FIGURE 1-11A. The effects of cycling on battery plates. This series of positive plates, each containing a different density of lead dioxide, has been subjected to 136 discharge/recharge cycles. Number 1 is typical of lightweight automotive batteries. Number 6 is from a top-of-the-line deep-cycle battery. Note the almost total loss of plate material from the former while the latter is virtually intact. The densities of lead dioxide (grams per cubic inch) in each plate are as follows: #1, 50; #2, 55; #3, 60; #4, 65; #5, 70; #6, 75. *(Surrette America)*

ESTABLISHING A BALANCED BATTERY-POWERED ELECTRICAL SYSTEM

top of plate

FIGURE 1-11B. Three batteries with similar external case sizes, all described as "marine deep cycle" by their manufacturers. Note the differences in internal construction—the one on the right has half again as much active material as the one on the left. Buying batteries is very much a case of "buyer beware."

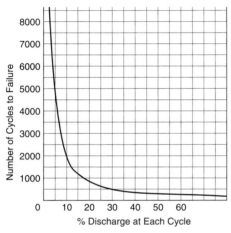

FIGURE 1-12. Life cycles as a function of depth of discharge at each cycle.

the battery is fully discharged in 20 hours). The higher the rate of discharge, the *more* life cycles a battery will have (this is counterintuitive), so a battery tested at the C5 rate will have many more life cycles than when tested at the C20 rate.

2. The termination voltage of the test. The lower this voltage, the more discharged a battery is at the termination of each cycle, and consequently, the tougher the test and the fewer the life cycles. Typically, but not always, 10.5 volts is used as the termination voltage for a 12-volt battery.

3. The definition of battery "death." This may be when battery capacity has been reduced to 80% of its rated capacity, or it may be as low as 50% of rated capacity. The lower the remaining capacity used to define death, the greater the number of life cycles.

Given the different test parameters used to develop much published data, you have to look

carefully at the small print, if present (it is often missing), and even then, it is hard to make objective comparisons between batteries. Furthermore, all test data are developed in the laboratory, which does not even come close to replicating typical (if there is such a thing) life in a boat. For example, no laboratory test is going to replicate the sloshing in a seaway of the electrolyte in a liquid-electrolyte battery, and the impact it has on washing the active material out of the plates of a deeply discharged battery (the plate material is at its most vulnerable when in the discharged state). At the end of the day, unfortunately, anecdotal information on how different batteries hold up should probably be given as much weight as the published test data. (I would like to provide some better "science" than this, but from the consumer's perspective, it is not readily available.)

Batteries for marine use. If a battery will be used *solely* for engine cranking and *immediately recharged by an engine-driven alternator*—in other words, if its usage will more or less replicate automotive use—an automotive cranking-type battery is perfectly adequate. To avoid premature plate disintegration under the rigorous conditions found at sea, especially the pounding that takes place from time to time, use a good-quality, heavy-duty cranking battery. Its capacity should be at least as great as the cold cranking amps (see the Battery Capacity Ratings sidebar) specified in the engine's manual.

For all other applications, you should assume that the batteries will be cycled at some time, especially batteries that will be used for house as opposed to engine-cranking service. These should be good-quality, deep-cycle batteries. The question then is, which is the better deep-cycle battery for marine applications—a wet-cell, gel-cell, or AGM?

Wet-Cells Versus Gel-Cells and AGMs

In the first (1989) edition of this book, I recommended top-of-the-line wet-cells over gel-cells for cycling applications. This judgment was based on the then considerably higher cost, amp-hour for amp-hour, of the recently introduced Prevailer gel-cells and my doubts about their ability to stand up to heavy cycling in marine use. By the time of the second (1996) edition, with the Prevailers manufactured under license in the United States, their cost had fallen into line with top-quality wet-cells, while they had withstood marine service well. Now we have a number of good gel-cell options, and more recently AGM batteries have been introduced, notably the Lifeline battery.

The following discussion pertains only to the best deep-cycle batteries, such as (in North America) for wet-cells the Trojan (www.trojan battery.com), Rolls (www.rollsbattery.com), and Surrette (www.rollsbattery.com); for gel-cells the Deka (www.eastpenn-deka.com), West Marine (www.westmarine.com), and similar batteries; and for AGMs the Lifeline (www.concordebat tery.com), and Optima (www.optimabatteries. com). These and similar batteries are available in the UK and Europe. The discussion will prove a useful way to recapitulate much of the preceding material on batteries.

Wet-cells. Wet-cell deep-cycle batteries get their long cycling life from heavy, antimony-reinforced plate grids; thick plates with high-density active material; multiple plate separators; and very rugged cases. If properly cared for, these batteries can be cycled *thousands* of times. But this powerful cycling performance is paid for not only in cost—the batteries are several times more expensive than an automotive battery—but also with a loss of performance in other respects.

The thick plates and dense active material slow the rate of acid diffusion through the battery and thus the rate at which a charge can be withdrawn or replaced. Anytime these batteries are placed under a high load (such as when cranking an engine), the battery voltage tends to fall off. Aside from cranking applications, this voltage drop is particularly significant with DC-to-AC inverter use (see Chapter 6); depending on the inverter, some loads (notably microwaves) will suffer a significant loss of performance as battery voltage declines.

Short-term high loads take the charge off the battery plate surfaces. Long-term lower loads (such as lights) drain a battery steadily over a number of hours, giving it time to equalize internally, which drains the charge from less-accessible plate areas as well as the surface areas. When it comes time to recharge, these inaccessible inner plate areas must also be recharged, which requires enough time for the electrolyte to diffuse in and out. If charging times are limited, the battery will not be fully charged—some of the lead sulfates formed in the inner plate areas when the battery was discharged will remain. These will slowly crystallize until no amount of normal charging will reconvert them to active plate material—the battery will become sulfated.

In other words, *the very steps taken to reduce damage from cycling—increasing plate thickness and density—increase the chances of damage from sulfation!* To prevent sulfation, extended charging times are periodically needed. If this necessitates running an engine solely for battery-charging purposes, the cost of ownership of these batteries is higher than for other battery types.

There is another problem with wet-cell batteries. The antimony used to reinforce the plate grids causes minute discharge currents within the battery itself. These currents will steadily *self-discharge* an unused battery. If the battery is not regularly recharged, the lead sulfates forming in the plates will harden, resulting in a permanent loss of capacity. *The search for maximum cycling strength increases the chances of damage from sulfation.*

To minimize damage from sulfation, a wet-cell deep-cycle battery must be periodically returned to a full charge and then given a *controlled overcharge*—a process known as *equalization* or *conditioning*. The purpose of this overcharge is to soften up hardened sulfates and put them back into active service. It is done by charging the battery at around 3% to 5% of its rated amp-hour capacity (i.e., 3 to 5 amps for a 100 Ah battery) until the battery voltage is driven to between 15.0 and 16.2 volts (for a 12-volt battery). During this period, the battery must be isolated from all loads, since these high voltages can damage sensitive electronic equipment. Equalization requires specialized equipment and takes several hours. I discuss it in more detail in Chapter 3 on page 84.

All wet-cell batteries tend to gas to a certain extent as they approach full charge. A battery subjected to an equalization charge will bubble away steadily like a simmering cook pot! Explosive (hydrogen and oxygen) and harmful (arsine and stabine) gases are given off, corrosive vapors are vented from the filler caps, and the battery uses water, necessitating regular refills to replace what is lost. None of these consequences is desirable.

In short, wet-cell deep-cycle batteries have

Battery Capacity Ratings

Battery capacity is defined in three different ways: amp-hours, reserve capacity (or minutes), and cold cranking amps.

Amp-hours rate capacity in terms of the number of amp-hours (Ah) that can be pulled from a battery at 80°F/26.7°C, at a relatively slow rate of discharge, before it dies (i.e., its voltage falls below 1.75 volts per cell, which is 10.5 volts for a 12-volt battery). In the United States, the discharge period is normally 20 hours; in the UK, 10 hours. This means that a battery rated at 100 Ah is capable of delivering 5 amps for 20 hours in the United States (known as the C20 rate), or 10 amps for 10 hours in the UK (known as the C10 rate). Shorter time periods are sometimes used, notably 5 hours on some deep-cycle batteries (known as the C5 rate).

Because of limitations in the rate of acid diffusion through its plates, *the faster a battery is discharged, the smaller the portion of its overall capacity it can deliver before its voltage falls to the threshold level.* In other words, a battery has a lower Ah capacity at higher rates of discharge (Figure 1-13A). If a typical U.S.-rated, 100 Ah, liquid-electrolyte battery (C20 rate) is discharged at a rate of 10 amps (the C10 rate), it will deliver only 84 Ah before its voltage falls to the threshold level, whereas a UK-rated, 100 Ah, liquid-electrolyte battery (C10 rate) will deliver the full 100 Ah at this rate. Put another way, a 100 Ah, C10-rated battery has a greater capacity than a 100 Ah, C20-rated battery. *When comparing battery ratings, make sure the same rating period has been used.*

Reserve capacity (or *minutes*) is an automotive industry rating that is increasingly used with marine batteries. If a car's alternator dies, the whole electrical load (which at night includes lights) will be thrown on the battery. The reserve capacity tells us how long, in minutes, a battery at a temperature of 80°F/26.7°C will sustain a certain load before its voltage falls below 1.75 volts per cell (10.5 volts for a 12-volt battery). The normal rating load is 25 amps, but sometimes other amperages are used. *For valid battery comparisons, you must use the same load.*

Cold cranking amps (CCA) rate engine-cranking ability. As temperatures decrease, it takes more energy to crank an engine, while at the same time batteries have less available power (Figures 1-13B and 1-13C). The standard U.S. cold-cranking rating assumes a cold day (0°F/–17.8°C) and a recalcitrant engine that needs to be cranked for 30 seconds. It tells us the maximum discharge rate (in amps) the battery can deliver to the starter motor without falling below 1.2 volts per cell (7.2 volts for a 12-volt battery). Lately, *marine* cold cranking amps have been introduced, in which it is assumed the temperature is 32°F/0°C, which inflates the CCA figure. In Europe, different parameters may be used. In the UK, the British Standard Rate is based on a temperature of 0°F/–17.8°C, but with cranking sustained for 180 seconds down to a final terminal voltage of 1.0 volt per cell. The International Electrotechnical Commission (IEC) rating is at the same temperature, but with cranking sustained for 60 seconds down to a final terminal voltage of 1.4 volts per cell. Once again, *when making battery comparisons, see that the same test methods are used.*

Note: An *amp (ampere)* is a measure of the *rate of flow* of electric current. It represents a specified number of electrons passing a given point every second, in the same way that gallons per minute in fluid systems represent a certain volume of fluid passing a given point in 1 minute.

An *amp-hour* (abbreviated to *Ah*) is a measure of the *quantity* of electric current. One Ah is the total number of electrons that will pass a given point if a current of 1 amp is sustained for 1 hour. It says nothing about the rate of flow, since the same number of electrons could be supplied by a 60 amp current for 1 minute or a 3,600 amp current for 1 second. In the same way, 100 gallons of water could be supplied by a 1 gallon/minute pump running for 100 minutes or a 100 gallon/minute pump running for 1 minute.

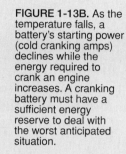

FIGURE 1-13B. As the temperature falls, a battery's starting power (cold cranking amps) declines while the energy required to crank an engine increases. A cranking battery must have a sufficient energy reserve to deal with the worst anticipated situation.

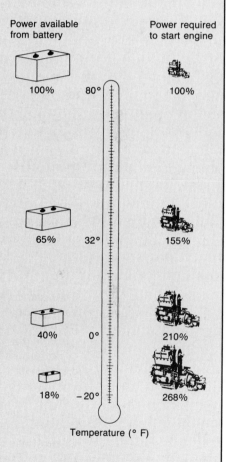

Power available from battery | Temperature (° F) | Power required to start engine

100% — 80° — 100%
65% — 32° — 155%
40% — 0° — 210%
18% — –20° — 268%

Temperature (° F)

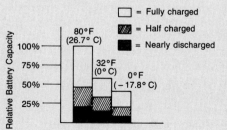

FIGURE 1-13A. Battery capacity as a function of the rate of discharge: 100 Ah battery, U.S. (20-hour) rating. *(Battery Council International)*

Rate of Discharge (amps) — 44 Ah, 54 Ah, 70 Ah, 84 Ah, 100 Ah — Hours: 1 2 5 10 15 20

= Fully charged
= Half charged
= Nearly discharged

FIGURE 1-13C. The effects of temperature and state of charge on battery capacity. *(Battery Council International)*

Relative Battery Capacity — 80°F (26.7° C), 32°F (0° C), 0°F (–17.8° C) — 100%, 75%, 50%, 25%

their problems. The gel-cells and AGMs minimize these problems, but not without introducing drawbacks of their own, which deserve a little investigation.

Gel-cells and AGMs. Gel-cells and AGMs have less electrolyte. As we discussed earlier (page 7), during construction the separators and plates are saturated with the electrolyte and then tightly packed together. Since the movement of electrolyte in and out of the plates is not the same as in a wet battery, the plates must be thinner. Close spacing of multiple, thinner plates lowers the internal resistance, which allows gel-cells and AGMs to be discharged and recharged rapidly but at the (theoretical) expense of longevity. In terms of absolute cycle life, gel-cell and AGM deep-cycle batteries fall somewhere between a cranking battery and a top-quality, wet-cell deep-cycle battery.

In practice, because of their slow charge acceptance rate (the time it takes for the acid to diffuse through the thick plates), wet-cell batteries are frequently not fully charged and as a result slowly sulfate. *Given equal charging time, gel-cells and AGMs, with their higher charge acceptance rate, will be more fully charged. This may well result in a higher cycle life for the gel-cell or AGM.*

Gel-cells and AGMs use plate grids in which the lead has been strengthened by alloying it with calcium rather than antimony. The result is a less rugged grid, but one that has a far lower rate of internal self-discharge—many times below that of a wet-cell battery. These weaker grids are another factor contributing to the theoretically shorter cycle life. On the other hand, *if a wet-cell is allowed to lose its charge and sulfate, it will never live up to expectations, whereas a gel-cell or AGM can sit unattended for months without suffering damage.* Once again, in a given set of circumstances, *this may well result in a higher cycle life for the gel-cell or AGM.* Furthermore, the tightly packed plates and separators in a gel-cell, and especially an AGM, resist vibration and motion better than a wet-cell, especially one that is well discharged—the sloshing of the wet-cell electrolyte in a seaway can wash the active material out of the plate grids.

The ability of a gel-cell or AGM to give up its charge rapidly means that under heavy loads the battery voltage will hold up better than that of a wet-cell. If the battery is to be used for cranking or with a DC-to-AC inverter, a smaller-capacity gel-cell or AGM will do as well as a larger-capacity wet-cell.

I mentioned that wet-cell batteries benefit from periodic controlled overcharges, which require specialized charging equipment. *For gel-cells and AGMs, any charging regimen that causes sustained gassing, resulting in loss of electrolyte, spells death.* Gel-cells and AGMs are sealed, maintenance-free batteries that cannot be opened and topped off. Periods of sustained overcharging will cause them to dry out and fail (Figure 1-14).

As a result, gel-cells and AGMs need carefully regulated charging devices, but not specialized charging equipment. Given correct regulation, in contrast to the wet-cells they have minimal venting of gases, no corrosive vapors, and no required maintenance.

Making the right choice. Much more could be said about wet-cells versus gel-cells and AGMs, but we already have enough information to settle the main questions (see Table 1-1). The first point to note is that *with proper charging and maintenance, a top-quality, wet-cell deep-cycle battery will have a longer service life in a cycling application than any gel-cell or AGM.* In terms of battery cost per amp-hour of energy delivered, the wet-cells will be *considerably* cheaper. However, and this is a big however, *these batteries are rarely charged or maintained properly,* with the result that very few live up to their potential. What is more, because of the relatively low charge acceptance rate of these batteries, *if an engine has to be run solely for battery charging,*

FIGURE 1-14. A dried-out gel-cell as a result of overcharging. The liquid has been driven out of the electrolyte, leaving a dry powder.

TABLE 1-1. Summary of Pros and Cons of Different Battery Technologies

Wet-Cells	SVR/VRLA Batteries
Potentially longer life at lower battery cost	Potentially higher battery cost/shorter life
Tolerant of abuse, including overcharges	Sensitive to overcharging
Slow recharging; if charge times are limited, the total cost of the energy produced can be relatively high	Faster recharging; if charge times are limited, this helps reduce the total cost of the energy produced
Need periodic equalization	No equalization required
Equalization requires specialized regulator	Specialized regulator advised
Gassing occurs near full charge; explosion risk	No gassing in normal circumstances
Terminal voltage falls under heavy loads	Terminal voltage holds up better
Position-sensitive	Not position-sensitive; can even be upside down
Will vent chlorine gas if submerged	Can be submerged safely
High rate of self-discharge	Low rate of self-discharge
Require regular maintenance	Little maintenance

by the time the engine-running costs are factored into the overall cost equation, the cost per amp-hour of energy delivered is generally *higher* than that of a gel-cell or AGM, often considerably higher. And of course absolute cycle life, and the cost per amp-hour delivered, are not the only issues.

If a boat will be left unattended for months at a time without the batteries being charged, as so many are, the lower self-discharge rate of a gel-cell or AGM battery will almost certainly make it the better choice. And if the owner habitually neglects even minimal battery maintenance, as so many do, the maintenance-free gel-cell or AGM is once again the best option. Plus, the voltage on a gel-cell or AGM holds up better under high-load discharges. The gel-cell or AGM gives off no explosive gases or corrosive fumes in normal use, and it cannot spill acid into the bilges if the boat is well-heeled or knocked down. In short, the typical sailor (one who uses his or her boat infrequently and does not have sophisticated charging devices with equalization capability) will find gel-cells or AGMs hard to beat *as long as charging devices are properly regulated.*

On the other hand, when an owner does take care of batteries, has the devices to adequately charge them, can afford the necessary charging time, does not allow the batteries to self-discharge over long periods, and does not mind the maintenance, wet-cell batteries give a longer cycle life at less cost. But it is the rare owner who meets these conditions.

Note: I am often asked which is better in marine cycling applications, a gel-cell or an AGM. East Penn, a high-end manufacturer of both gel-cells and AGMs, has cycle life data showing a greater life expectancy for gel-cells regardless of the depth of discharge (see Table 1-2). Concorde (the manufacturer of Lifeline AGM batteries) challenges this, and in real life you will sometimes find anecdotal evidence that AGMs do better. I have seen no data adequate to make a definitive judgment. However, it is worth noting that AGMs tend to have a lower internal resistance. This means they can be charged faster, which reduces engine-running times if the engine is run solely for battery charging, and thus reduces the overall cost of maintaining the batteries.

Golf-cart batteries. Finally, golf-cart batteries should be mentioned. These are constructed similarly to wet-cell deep-cycle batteries and have similar operating characteristics. They do not have as high a cycle life, but on the other hand they take a charge a little faster, are far more readily available, and are considerably cheaper. In terms of amp-hours per dollar in cycling applications, in some applications (notably for liveaboard cruisers), they may well be the best value for the money of *any* battery on the market.

Other lead-acid batteries. The Optima battery is a variation on AGM technology. It has tightly packed, spirally wound plates that have a low internal resistance, allowing them to accept high recharge rates and to pack a tremendous cranking punch into a small envelope with a

TABLE 1-2. Life Cycles Versus Depth of Discharge for East Penn Gel-Cells and AGMs

Capacity Withdrawn at Each Cycle	Gel-Cell Life Cycles	AGM Life Cycles
10%	3,800	3,100
25%	1,500	925
50%	650	370
80%	390	200
100%	300	150

(Courtesy East Penn)

high tolerance for vibration. Consequently, the Optima may be useful in certain applications. Currently, these batteries are not available in large-capacity units, so their utility in terms of building up sizable house banks on a boat is limited.

At the time of writing (2005), a new generation of AGM batteries has been launched under the Meridian name (Figure 1-15; www.meridian marine.com) with a higher power density than existing batteries (i.e., a greater battery capacity for a given battery size), while a new type of battery using carbon fiber in its internal construction is entering the marketplace. On paper both look good, with higher power-to-weight ratios than conventional lead-acid batteries, high charge acceptance and discharge rates, and good cycle life. They are worth tracking.

Nicads—The Ultimate Battery

Nickel-cadmium batteries are virtually indestructible, with a life span of up to 25 years. They will accept a fast charge right up to full capacity and maintain a high discharge voltage until almost dead. They can be discharged completely flat, left shorted out indefinitely, and still be recharged without damage! When idle, they have an extremely low rate of self-discharge. But amp-hour for amp-hour they are bulkier and far more costly than any lead-acid battery, and for these reasons (together with the fact that they are hard to find), they are rarely used in boats. They also operate at different voltages than lead-acid batteries, and as a result, require different charging voltages. If a boat is kept for the life of the

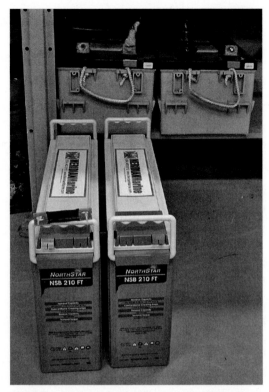

FIGURE 1-15. The two Meridian batteries in the foreground have the same nominal Ah capacity as the two conventional AGM batteries in the background. *(Meridian)*

batteries and nicads can be afforded, they will pay for themselves as long as an appropriate voltage regulator is used. After a number of years, the electrolyte will deteriorate and need replacing; therefore, consult the manufacturer.

Getting Down to Specifics

Determining the type of battery to be used in marine applications is just the first step in evaluating a DC system. Earlier I referred to average sail- and powerboats, when in reality there is no such thing as an average boat. Some have shoreside power and a permanently connected battery charger in their slip, while others cruise and anchor out for months at a time with little or no engine-running time. Some have auxiliary generators running 24 hours a day, keeping the boat's batteries constantly topped off, while others have solar panels and wind generators providing intermittent sources of power, and so on. No two boats—even identical production-line boats—end up with the same equipment, experience the same usage, or have the same electrical needs. *When discussing boat electrical*

systems, it is not possible to deal in the same kinds of generalities that can be applied to cars. Every boat must be treated as a unique entity with the peculiar requirements of its electrical system evaluated in relation to its usage.

There are four steps to take in such an evaluation:

1. Calculate the power requirements of the boat.
2. Provide the necessary battery storage capacity.
3. Install adequate charging capabilities.
4. Establish correct voltage regulation levels to maintain system harmony.

All four interact, but for clarity, they are treated separately here. The following sections focus broadly on the needs of a midsized cruising boat—sail or power—that has a moderate electrical load and relies on its batteries to supply power for extended periods of time. In Chapter 2, I use the information developed to investigate strategies for meeting the needs of boats with higher electrical loads. But regardless of the overall systems design, when evaluating the DC side, you will need to take what follows into consideration.

Calculating Power Requirements

Overall power needs are normally calculated on a 24-hour (daily) basis on the assumption that, away from the dock, the batteries will be recharged daily. For some boats, 24 hours may not be an appropriate interval, but it is easily adjusted. For example, if a generating device is run every 12 hours, divide by 2, or to determine the power needs for 3 days, multiply by 3.

All electrical appliance loads are rated in either *watts* or *amps*—a 100-watt lightbulb, a 3 amp electric motor. The magnitude of the current flowing through an appliance is measured in amps, and the work done by that current is measured in watts. The rating will be in the manufacturer's installation bulletin or on a label attached to the equipment. When adding up loads on an electrical system, it does not matter if you use watts or amps, just as long as the choice is consistent. (However, it is generally easier to use amps for DC systems because equipment is rarely rated in watts. If you have an accurate digital ammeter in the boat's distribution panel or a DC systems monitor, you can measure the current draw of any piece of equipment by turning the equipment on and noting the change in the meter reading). In any case, watts and amps are easily interchangeable since watts = volts × amps, and amps = watts/volts.

Most boats have 12-volt systems, but some do not. The following examples can readily be converted to 24 or 32 volts by substituting the appropriate voltage.

Let's say we have a 25-watt lightbulb on a 12-volt system, and we want to know our load in amps. How many amps is this?

Amps = 25 watts/12 volts = 2.08 amps.

Perhaps our DC refrigeration unit has a 7 amp, 12-volt motor. How many watts does it draw?

Watts = 7 amps × 12 volts = 84 watts.

The first step, then, in calculating our daily load is to list all the onboard electrical equipment and convert the power needs into either watts or amps (Table 1-3). This includes any AC loads that will be run off the DC system via a DC-to-AC inverter (see Chapter 6). The next

TABLE 1-3. Typical Power Consumption of Electrical Loads (12 Volts)

Equipment	Consumption
Anchor light	1.0 amp
Anchor windlass	40–300 amps
Autopilot	⅓–30 amps
Bilge blower	2.5 amps
Bilge pump	5.0 amps
Cabin fan	0.2–1.0 amp
Cabin light (incandescent)	1.5–3.5 amps
CD player/stereo	1.0 amp on up (depending on amplification)
Chart plotter	0.5–3.0 amps
Depth sounder	0.1–0.5 amp
Fluorescent light	0.7–1.8 amps
Freshwater pump	5.0 amps
GPS	0.5–1.0 amp
Knotmeter	0.1 amp
Laptop computer	5.0 amps
Loran	1.0–1.5 amps
Masthead light	1.0–1.7 amps
Radar	4.0–8.0 amps
Refrigerator (typical)	5.0–7.0 amps
Running lights (port, starboard, and stern)	3.0 amps
Spotlight	10.0 amps
Spreader lights	8.0 amps
SSB (receive)	1.5–2.0 amps
(transmit)	25–35 amps
Strobe light	0.7 amp
VHF (receive)	0.7–1.5 amps
(transmit)	5.0–6.0 amps
Wind speed indicator	0.1 amp

step is to estimate the normal daily usage, in hours or fractions of an hour (e.g., 6 minutes = 0.1 hour), for each piece of equipment. Then multiply the load for each piece by duration of use and add the items to determine the *total daily load*, expressed in *watt-hours* or *amp-hours*. (For these calculations, it is not necessary to understand the definition of watt-hours and amp-hours. The important point is to grasp the method by which the figures are derived.)

The energy consumption analysis should be conducted for two different conditions—passage-making and "on the hook"—with the higher number used to size the DC system. On modern boats, this is commonly passagemaking because of the load imposed by an autopilot, a radar, navigation electronics, navigation lights at night, and so on. On the hook, the greatest load is typically the refrigeration system.

We have answered the first question, how much power does our boat demand each day?

TABLE 1-4. Daily Power Requirements (12 Volts) of a Hypothetical Cruising Boat Anchored Off a Bahamian Beach

Equipment	Rating	Hours of Use (in 24 hours)	Total Load (in 24 hours)
6 lights	1.5 amps each	2 hours each = 12	18 amp-hours
1 refrigeration compressor	5 amps	10 hours	50 amp-hours
Masthead navigation lights	1.5 amps	8 hours	12 amp-hours
2 fans	1 amp each	5 hours each = 10	10 amp-hours
VHF radio, CD player, etc.	2 amps total	5 hours total	10 amp-hours
		TOTAL	100 amp-hours

Notes:
1. Power consumption will vary enormously according to the boat's intended cruising area. Refrigeration and fan usage in northern climates will be a fraction of that in the tropics.
2. Large items of occasional and short-term use, such as an electric anchor windlass, can in most instances be ignored, since they have little impact on the overall picture. On the rare occasions when sustained use is required, as when breaking out a deeply embedded anchor, the engine can be run during operation to provide a charging backup.
3. This example is for a boat with modest and simple electrical needs. It does not include inverter-based loads. Boats with larger and more complex needs are explored in Chapter 2.

The sample system in Table 1-4 has a daily load of 100 Ah. The next question we must resolve is how much battery storage capacity do we need to meet this demand?

Providing the Necessary Capacity

The required battery capacity is intimately related to the interval between charges. A boat such as our sample boat in Table 1-4, which uses an engine-driven alternator as its principal means of battery charging and restricts engine usage to once a day, must be capable of storing and delivering the desired 100 Ah between charges. This is a typical usage pattern for a cruising boat—sail or power—that spends much of its time at anchor. However, a boat with onboard power sources equal to its demand, such as a boat that uses the main engine continuously, runs a battery charger off a constantly operating auxiliary generator, has large banks of solar panels, or has a wind- or water-driven generator, is in a position similar to an automobile—the battery is primarily for engine starting. The main engine, auxiliary generator, solar panels, or wind generator supply the boat's electrical needs and keep the battery topped off.

As solar panels, wind generators, and intermittently used auxiliary generators (both AC and DC) become more popular and widespread, most boats fall somewhere between these two extremes. But you must always remember that the sun may not shine for days, the wind may fade away, and auxiliary generators may break down. At other times these charging sources may not meet all the electrical demands, and the battery will become a power source. When determining battery capacity, and to ensure an adequate margin for all eventualities, it is often best to omit such charging sources from the calculation. Therefore assume recharging will take place from the alternator alone and predicate

recharge intervals and consumption between charges on anticipated engine-running intervals.

So how much battery capacity do we need to deliver our 100 Ah a day? The answer is determined by three variables:

The depth to which the batteries are discharged. This is extremely important. Assuming a 100 Ah daily consumption, if we plan to discharge our batteries 100% at each cycle, a 100 Ah battery will meet our immediate needs, but will leave no emergency reserve for engine starting. However, no battery should ever be fully discharged. This applies to deep-cycle batteries just as much as to automotive batteries. Repeated 100% discharge of any battery, even the best deep-cycle battery, will drastically shorten its life (refer back to Figure 1-12).

But if we do not fully discharge a battery, we cannot utilize its full capacity. If we need 100 Ah, and we intend to discharge the battery only to the 50% level, we will need a 200 Ah battery. Bigger batteries last longer, but they cost more, weigh more, and take up more space. Somewhere we must find the balance between battery size and the degree of discharge in daily use (i.e., battery life). With deep-cycle batteries, this is normally done at around the 50% level of discharge. We try to set up our total electrical system so the battery is not discharged beyond 50% of its capacity in normal use. Occasional discharge to 80% or so can then be taken in stride.

The extent to which the batteries are routinely recharged. A discharged battery can be recharged relatively rapidly to around 70% to 80% of its fully charged level. At this time the surface areas of the plates—those areas most accessible to the electrolyte—will have been recharged while the inner plate areas will be lagging behind. The acid and water will require time to diffuse in and out of the plates. Beyond the 70% to 80% level of charge, a battery's *charge acceptance rate* slows dramatically—the rate of charge must be tapered off sharply or battery damage will result (see the sidebar on page 31). *It takes hours to bring a battery up the last 20% to a full charge*; the thicker and denser the plate material, the longer it takes.

The lower a battery's state of charge, the greater the charging current it will accept. If our sole objective was to put back a given amount of energy taken out of a battery as fast as possible, we would cycle the battery from, say, 10% charged to 40% charged, using just 30% of its nominal capacity. Given a 100 Ah demand, we would need a battery bank with a capacity of 333 Ah. At a 10% state of charge, the battery would accept a charging current of up to 100% of its rated capacity. If our charging device had a high enough output, we could put back the 100 Ah in well under an hour. The batteries, however, would fail quite rapidly from cycling stresses and sulfation. This is why we try to limit discharges to around the 50% level.

At a 50% level of discharge, a battery's charge acceptance rate will diminish to somewhere between 25% to 40% of its rated capacity, depending on battery type. As it becomes more fully charged, this charge acceptance rate will decline some more. Because of this declining charge acceptance rate, and given that charging time is at a premium on most boats, it makes no sense in normal use to bring batteries back beyond the 80% level of charge, with the caveat that at least periodically we bring the battery to a full charge, so as to arrest incipient sulfation. (If it is a wet-cell battery, we must also periodically apply an equalization charge—see page 84.) This scenario leaves us discharging to the 50% level and recharging to the 80% level. As a result, *our regular, usable storage capacity is once again reduced to just 30% of overall battery capacity.* Recharge times will be from 1 to 2 hours (depending on battery type).

This target range in terms of battery state of charge—cycling from 80% of charge down to 50% and back—has come to be known as the Mid-Capacity Rule. It represents a general prescription that balances battery life with recharge times and cost (battery cost plus the running expenses of an engine used for battery charging) *in a situation when recharge times are limited* (resulting in the engine being run solely for battery charging). It is important to remember this latter aspect. If recharge times are not limited, the batteries will always last longer if they are kept more fully charged. Although interestingly enough, data from the Trojan Battery Company show that the greatest number of lifetime amphours will be delivered by a battery cycled to

TABLE 1-5. Cycle Life of Trojan Industrial Batteries

Depth of Discharge at Each Cycle	Number of Cycles to Failure	Amp-Hours Delivered During Life (per 100 Ah of battery capacity)
10%	6,200	62,000
20%	5,200	104,000
30%	4,400	132,000
40%	3,700	148,000
50%	2,900	145,000
60%	2,400	144,000
70%	2,000	140,000
80%	1,700	136,000

around the 60% level of charge (see Table 1-5, but bear in mind that these numbers are only illustrative of the test battery in this particular laboratory test).

The age factor. Over time a battery ages, losing capacity and performance. This results primarily from sulfation and/or the progressive shedding of active plate material. In order to take account of this aging process, it is customary to build an allowance—a fudge factor—into battery sizing calculations. Twenty percent is a fair ballpark figure.

Sizing a battery bank. Where does this leave us? *To support our hypothetical boat's 100 Ah daily consumption, taking a conservative approach and utilizing only 30% of battery capacity, we need 333 Ah of battery capacity. Adding in a 20% fudge factor, we need 400 Ah of battery capacity.* This is approximately the capacity of two 8D-sized batteries wired in parallel (see below), which in point of fact is an excellent combination for most of today's electrically loaded midsize boats. (The designation "8D" refers only to the external dimensions of the battery; it says nothing about its all-important internal construction.)

If we are a little less conservative and are using top-of-the-line deep-cycle batteries, we might decide to discharge these batteries to 30% of capacity before recharging, in which case we would need a battery capacity of only 250 Ah to meet a 100 Ah daily demand. However, this would be a *minimum*, leaving almost nothing in reserve, and would substantially reduce battery life compared with a battery discharged to 50% of capacity. (See Table 1-5 and Figure 1-12. Note that while the table and figure generally agree on the overall relationship between depth of discharge and life cycles, they differ on the specific relationship; this is not an error but the result of looking at different batteries from different manufacturers.)

A final piece of the battery-capacity calculation

is to estimate the highest sustained load which the battery is likely to be subjected to (generally a DC-to-AC inverter running at full output) and ensure that this is no more than 25% of the rated capacity of the battery bank. If the inverter load exceeds this, protect the batteries from potential damage caused by high-rate discharges (which can heat the plates and buckle them) by increasing the size of the battery bank.

Series and parallel. In the example above, we are using two 8D batteries. When you include more than one battery in an electrical system, you can hook each battery into the boat's circuits independently via a suitable battery isolation switch (see pages 37–38), or you can connect them all together to boost output, either in *series* or *parallel*.

To make a series connection, tie the positive post of one battery to the negative post of another and then use the remaining positive terminal on one and negative terminal on the other to make the connection to the boat's circuits (Figure 1-16).

When in series, *the total amp-hour capacity of the two batteries together remains the same as the amp-hour rating of either one, but the output voltage is doubled.* In our example, with two 200 Ah, 12-volt batteries, a series connection would still give us a 200 Ah capacity, but at 24 volts. *Note: Never connect 12-volt batteries in series on a 12-volt electrical system—the resulting high voltage will damage equipment.*

To make a *parallel* connection, tie together the positive posts on two or more batteries and also tie together the negative posts. Then connect the boat's circuit to these combined positive and negative posts (Figure 1-17).

Paralleling batteries leaves the system voltage unchanged, but doubles the amp-hour capacity. Connecting two 200 Ah, 12-volt batteries in parallel produces only 12 volts, but has a 400 Ah capacity. *Connecting additional batteries in parallel increases system capacity at a given voltage.* The Ah capacity of all the paralleled batteries is added to find the system's total Ah capacity.

Both series and parallel connections are often made where a large storage capacity is needed but single batteries would be too cumbersome to handle. Typically in a 12-volt system, two 6-volt batteries are placed in series to give 12 volts, and then another two 6-volt batteries, also in series,

---

Scaling Back Demand

Batteries are large and heavy (over 1 cubic foot and close to 200 pounds for approximately 200 amp-hours of capacity at 12 volts). In some cases, the battery capacity necessary to support the desired lifestyle is unacceptably heavy and/or bulky for the boat (particularly if it is a lightweight, fast cruiser). In this case, the maximum acceptable battery size and weight must be determined, and *the system brought into balance* (battery capacity = 2.5 to 4 × maximum likely load between charges) by shortening the interval between charging times and/or reducing demand.

The following load reduction strategies should be considered:

- **Air-conditioning:** In most cases, you can eliminate the need for air-conditioning with proper awning, wind scoop, and ventilation design. Otherwise a generator is a necessity, in which case when the generator is running, you can use it to charge the batteries and run the DC equipment, greatly reducing the necessary "holdover" capacity of the DC system.

- **Refrigeration:** This is the greatest energy consumer on smaller yachts in a warm climate. Reduce the icebox volume to improve the insulation. Also consider vacuum-based superinsulation. Check the drains and seals for heat infiltration. Use a more efficient con-

densing unit (e.g., water cooled). For more on refrigeration choices, see Chapter 11.

- **Autopilot:** An autopilot is a significant energy consumer on long passages. Balance the boat to reduce the load and use a wind vane instead.

- **Radar:** This is another significant energy consumer when passagemaking. Turn off the radar or put it on standby when you don't need it.

- **Cabin lighting:** Turn off the lights when you don't need them! Replace incandescent and halogen lighting with fluorescent.

- **Anchor and navigation lights:** Replace with LED lights (see Chapter 7). Add a photoelectric cell to the anchor light.

- **Fans:** Replace higher-energy fans with lower-energy units (such as those manufactured by Hella [www.hella.com] or Hotwire [www.svhotwire.com]).

- **Electric toilet:** Replace with a manual toilet.

- **Microwave:** Limit microwave use to those times when energy is in plentiful supply (e.g., when tied to a dock and using shore power, or when motorsailing, or operating a generator).

are connected in parallel with the first two to double the capacity while maintaining 12 volts (Figure 1-18).

It is sometimes stated that paralleling batteries is a poor practice because if a cell fails in one battery it may drag down the other batteries, and also that small circulating currents between the batteries will increase their rate of self-discharge. The argument is that the only way to build up large-capacity 12-volt systems is to use two high-capacity 6-volt batteries in series. If the 6-volt batteries become too heavy to handle, the use of six individual 2-volt cells, connected in series, is advocated.

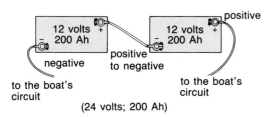

FIGURE 1-16. Series connection. The Ah capacity is unchanged from a single battery's capacity, but output voltage is doubled. Twelve-volt batteries should never be connected in series on a 12-volt electrical system—the resulting high voltage will damage equipment.

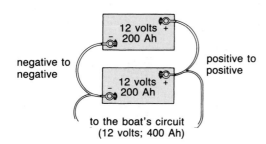

FIGURE 1-17. Parallel connection. Output voltage remains the same as that of the individual batteries, but Ah capacity is doubled.

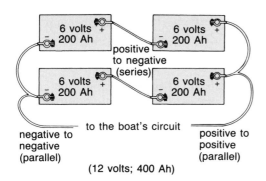

FIGURE 1-18. Series/parallel connection. In this example, each pair of 6-volt batteries connected in series delivers 12 volts, while connecting the pairs in parallel doubles system capacity. Thus this array achieves the same effect as two 12-volt batteries in parallel, but permits the use of high-capacity 6-volt batteries, which are individually lighter and easier to handle than high-capacity 12-volt batteries.

As a general rule of thumb, if you choose to parallel batteries, it is best to keep the number of batteries as low as possible (i.e., parallel a small number of large-capacity batteries rather than a large number of small-capacity batteries), but you should not have any concerns about paralleling them as a mechanism to increase the capacity of a battery bank. If one cell in one battery goes bad, it will not cause a catastrophic failure of the whole bank, whereas a cell failure in a series connection will. What is more, with good instrumentation (see later in this chapter), you will be able to detect cell failure and remove the offending battery from the paralleled system with no effect other than a loss of capacity. However, if a cell fails in a series connection, and you remove the offending battery, the system voltage will drop by either 6 or 2 volts (depending on whether you have 6-volt or 2-volt batteries in series).

At the time of writing, higher-voltage DC systems (currently up to 144 volts but with voltages as high as 800 soon to be tested), particularly for electric propulsion, are starting to be introduced. To achieve these voltages, numerous batteries are wired in series (twelve 12-volt batteries for 144 volts). This raises a number of issues, which I address in Chapter 2.

Installation considerations with large battery banks. With larger battery banks, a number of installation issues that are important from a safety and/or life expectancy perspective are commonly overlooked, notably:

- In both series and parallel connections, all batteries should be the same make, age, and type. In a series installation, they also have to be the same size (Ah capacity), but this is not necessary in a parallel installation.

- In a series installation, if one battery fails, you have to replace all the batteries. If a battery fails in a parallel installation, you simply remove it and use the rest of the batteries until they also fail, at which time you can replace them all.

- When you have two or more batteries paralleled, make the positive connection to the boat's circuits at the positive terminal on the battery at one end of the bank, and make the negative connection to the boat's circuits at the negative terminal on the battery at the other end of the bank (i.e., not off the same battery as the positive connection). This ensures that all batteries get discharged and recharged equally (Figure 1-19).

- With large, paralleled battery banks, if possible, wire the boat's distribution circuits to the positive and negative terminals at the opposite ends of the bank to those used for the charging circuits. This will create some degree of separation between the charging and distribution circuits, which will help keep unwanted voltage spikes and interference out of the distribution circuits (in effect, the batteries act as a filter; Figure 1-20).

- In a series/parallel setup, it is an excellent practice to cross-connect the positives and negatives on the individual 6-volt batteries, or 2-volt cells, as shown in Figure 1-21. This minimizes differences in the way the batteries work and perform.

- To avoid premature aging, keep batteries cool. Every 10°F/6°C temperature rise above 68°F/20°C shortens the cycle life by almost half; therefore, install batteries in well-ventilated, cool locations (for more on battery boxes, see Chapter 3). When installing multiple batteries in a bank, make sure you leave air spaces between them to encourage heat dissipation.

- *It is not acceptable to expand battery banks by wiring in additional batteries in a different physical location.* The reason is that the batteries will be at different ambient temperatures, which will cause them to discharge and

FIGURE 1-22. The aftermath of a battery explosion caused by a combination of overcharging and a spark from a non-ignition-protected switch.

recharge unequally, which will further exacerbate the temperature differences. Aside from the fact that these differences will prematurely age the batteries, in a worst-case scenario of high-load discharges and fast recharges (quite common on boats), the batteries can be driven into a dangerous condition known as *thermal runaway* (more on this later), which can lead to an explosion.

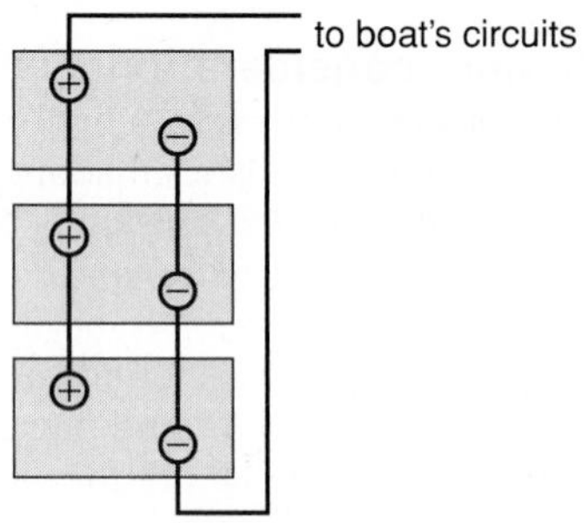

- Anytime discharge or charge rates for a battery bank approach or exceed 200 amps at 12 volts (100 amps at 24 volts) for sustained periods of time, a considerable amount of heat will be generated. You should consider using forced air ventilation for the battery bank to dissipate this heat. (Some European standards require forced air ventilation anytime batteries are connected to a charging device with a power output that exceeds 2 kW, i.e., 167 amps at 12 volts or 83 amps at 24 volts). Place the fan in the air inlet to the battery box rather than the outlet to minimize the risk of igniting the hydrogen given off by the batteries. The fan should be ignition protected (Figure 1-22).

- The voltage regulator for any high-output charging device should include temperature sensing *at the batteries* (more on this later) so that if the batteries heat up, the charge rate is tapered off.

- Large battery banks with high-rate charges and discharges should only be installed in accommodation spaces if the battery box is sealed and fitted with ventilation to the boat's exterior.

Installing Adequate Charging Capabilities

A while back, I worked on a sailboat used extensively for cruising that had seen minimal engine running and therefore minimal battery-charging time. Its frugal electrical system worked well for

FIGURE 1-19. Wiring paralleled batteries so that the positive and negative feeds to the loads come off opposite ends of the battery bank.

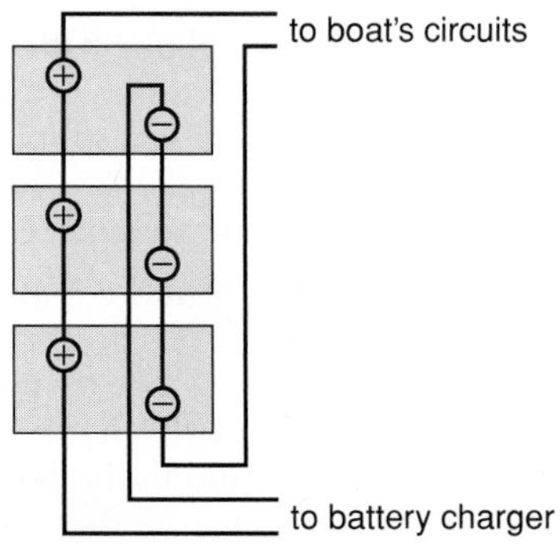

FIGURE 1-20. Paralleled batteries wired the same as in Figure 1-19, with the positive and negative feeds to a battery charger connected at the opposite ends of the bank from the positive and negative feeds to the loads.

FIGURE 1-21. Cross-connections between paralleled batteries in a series/parallel configuration. These cross-connections will minimize differences in the way in which the batteries work and perform.

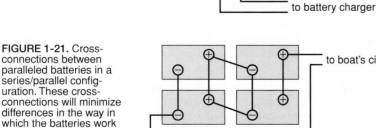
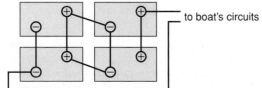

ESTABLISHING A BALANCED BATTERY-POWERED ELECTRICAL SYSTEM

years, then it changed hands. The new owner installed a small, poorly insulated 12-volt refrigeration unit. The batteries died. The owner concluded that he had insufficient battery capacity and added another battery. This too died. He added two more, and these died! I removed five miscellaneous batteries from the boat, scattered around in different lockers.

Regardless of how much battery capacity a boat has, if the charging devices are not putting back what is being taken out, the batteries eventually must go dead. The solution to this boat's problem was not more batteries, but a more-efficient refrigerator and *more charging capability.* Since the primary source of battery charging for this boat, as for almost all boats, was an engine-driven alternator, the question became, what size alternator did the boat need, and how should it be regulated?

Sizing an alternator. When engine-running time is extended, or the depth of discharge of batteries is minimal, a relatively small alternator is all that is needed—the typical 50 to 60 amp model that comes with the engine fitted to most boats will be more than adequate. The situation is similar to an automotive application, where the function of the alternator is to handle the car's electrical load and top off the battery, which typically is discharged no more than 5%.

But when, as is so often the case on a boat, engine-running time must be kept to a minimum, while at the same time the batteries are deeply discharged, the alternator must be large enough to get the charging job done as quickly as possible. In this case, *the determining factor in sizing the alternator is normally the maximum current the batteries can absorb without damage,* i.e., the *charge acceptance rate* of the batteries.

A battery discharged 50% or more will readily accept a charge rate in excess of 25% of its rated capacity; that is, a 100 Ah battery will accept a charge of 25 amps or more. But as the battery starts to come up to charge, its charge acceptance rate declines. If the alternator continues to pump in a heavy amperage, the battery will begin to heat up and gas. By the time a battery is up to 70% to 80% of full charge, its charge acceptance rate will be down to no more than 10% to 15% of its rated capacity, and thereafter declines rapidly. Thin-plate cranking batteries, gel-cells, and AGMs can be charged faster than thick-plate, liquid-electrolyte deep-cycle batteries because the rate of electrolyte diffusion through the plates is higher (at a 50% state of charge, the charge acceptance rate may be as high as 40%), but there is still a limit to how fast charging can proceed without battery damage.

In order to keep charging times to a minimum,

we need to be able to take advantage of the high charge acceptance rates at low states of battery charge. Thus, assuming discharges to the 50% state of charge, an alternator should have an amperage output of anywhere from 25% to 40% of the total Ah rating of the batteries it will be charging. To this we must add the boat's DC load while the engine is running. (This load may be quite high, particularly with some heavy-duty DC refrigeration units, and when running AC equipment off a DC-to-AC inverter. See later in this chapter and also Chapter 6.)

We need to distinguish real alternator output from *rated* output. An alternator is normally given an SAE (Society of Automotive Engineers) rating that describes its maximum output at a given temperature—77°F/25°C—and speed of rotation. But when operating, the alternator will heat up, causing its output to decline by as much as 25%. What is more, in automotive use a typical alternator puts out at full load for just a few minutes (after engine cranking) and then its output tapers off. *Many automotive alternators cannot be run continuously at full load in high ambient temperatures* (such as those found in engine rooms on boats in the tropics) *without burning up.* But this is precisely what we want our alternator to do when we try to bring a large-capacity, deeply discharged battery bank back to full charge in the shortest possible time.

We require an alternator that is capable of continuously producing its full rated output at temperatures up to 200°F/93°C—what is known in the United States as a *KKK-rated alternator* (Figure 1-23). For long life, even continuously rated marine alternators are best run at less than 100% of full output. To keep an alternator below its full output, an additional fudge factor of 25% should be built in when sizing it.

Where does this leave us? In the case of our

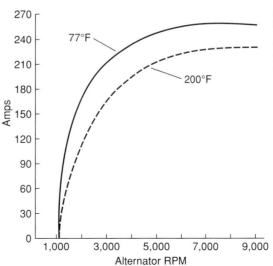

FIGURE 1-23. Power curves for a large-frame, 160 amp SAE-rated, 130 amp hot-rated alternator. *(Powerline Division of Hehr International Inc.)*

two 8Ds, with a total capacity of 400 Ah, we should start with a minimum hot-rated 100 amp alternator (25% of 400), add 25% to keep the alternator below continuous maximum output (bringing us to 125 amps), and then add in the DC load when the engine is running (which may well bring us to more than 150 amps).

High-output alternators come in a *small frame*, which is interchangeable with most automotive alternators, and a *large frame*, which may be hard to mount in some circumstances. As of this writing, small-frame 12-volt alternators are available with hot-rated outputs up to 130 amps (Table 1-6; 65 amps at 24 volts); there are rumors of breakthroughs in the works with outputs to 200 amps or more. In situations where more amperage is needed than can be supplied by a single small-frame alternator, two can be used, or else a single large-frame alternator. Suppliers in the United States include Ample Technology (www.amplepower.com), Balmar (www.balmar.net), Xantrex (www.xantrex.com), and Ferris Power Products (www.hamiltonferris.com); and

in the UK, Ampair (www.ampair.com), Adverc BM (www.adverc.co.uk), and Merlin Equipment (www.merlinequipment.com). (Note: Alternators for use on *gasoline* engines must be *ignition protected* to comply with U.S. Coast Guard and other standards. A *failed ignition-protected alternator should never be replaced with an automotive alternator*, even if the latter is only one-third the price. The alternators supplied by the companies mentioned above all have ignition protection.)

Speed of alternator rotation. Manufacturers have curves or tables that show alternator output (amps) as a function of speed of rotation (rpm)—see Figures 1-24A and 1-24B. Some alternators reach full rated output at much lower speeds than others. The sooner an alternator reaches full output, the more desirable it is in a cruising application because it maximizes effectiveness on those occasions when the engine is idled at anchor solely for battery-charging purposes. For example, for years Balmar has had a 160 amp alternator that has a higher output than its 200 amp alternator; that is, until the alternator speed exceeds 2,400 rpm. In many cruising situations, the 160 amp alternator is not only cheaper but also a better performer. The latest generation Balmar alternators have an even higher low-speed output.

It should be noted that the standard engine pulleys, and the pulleys supplied with high-output alternators, do not enable the alternators to get up to full rated output in some boat installations. This is because the pulleys are geared to automobile engines, which typically "cruise" at 2,500 to 3,500 rpm, whereas many boat engines spend much of their time refrigerating or battery charging at idle speeds between 700 and 1,000 rpm. *Since boat engines and usage vary considerably, alternator pulley size must be geared to individual use.* The following procedure should be used to size alternator pulleys:

1. Determine the alternator speed needed to produce the maximum *required* alternator output as described earlier. Note that this is *not* the maximum *alternator* output, and in general, should not exceed 75% of maximum output to guard against overloading and overheating. (All alternator manufacturers can supply a graph of output versus speed of rotation.)

2. Find the maximum safe operating speed for the alternator (usually 10,000 rpm).

3. Determine the *minimum* engine-running speed in normal use (or normal battery charging and refrigerating speed if this is the predominant use, such as on a cruising boat spending much of its time at anchor).

TABLE 1-6. Typical KKK Alternator Outputs as a Function of Speed of Rotation and Temperature

(A) 140 Amps SAE/105 Amps Hot

Alternator rpm	Alternator amps cold–hot
2,000	43–32
3,000	92–70
4,000	113–88
5,000	124–99
6,000	132–105
6,500	139–108

(B) 160 Amps SAE/130 Amps Hot

Alternator rpm	Alternator amps cold–hot
2,000	40–30
3,000	100–76
4,000	127–98
5,000	148–112
6,000	157–123
6,500	160–131

(C) 190 Amps SAE/165 Amps Hot

Alternator rpm	Alternator amps cold–hot
2,250	87–71
3,000	135–122
4,000	167–150
5,000	180–157
6,000	187–162
6,500	190–165

Cold = 77°F/25°C
Hot = 200°F/93°C

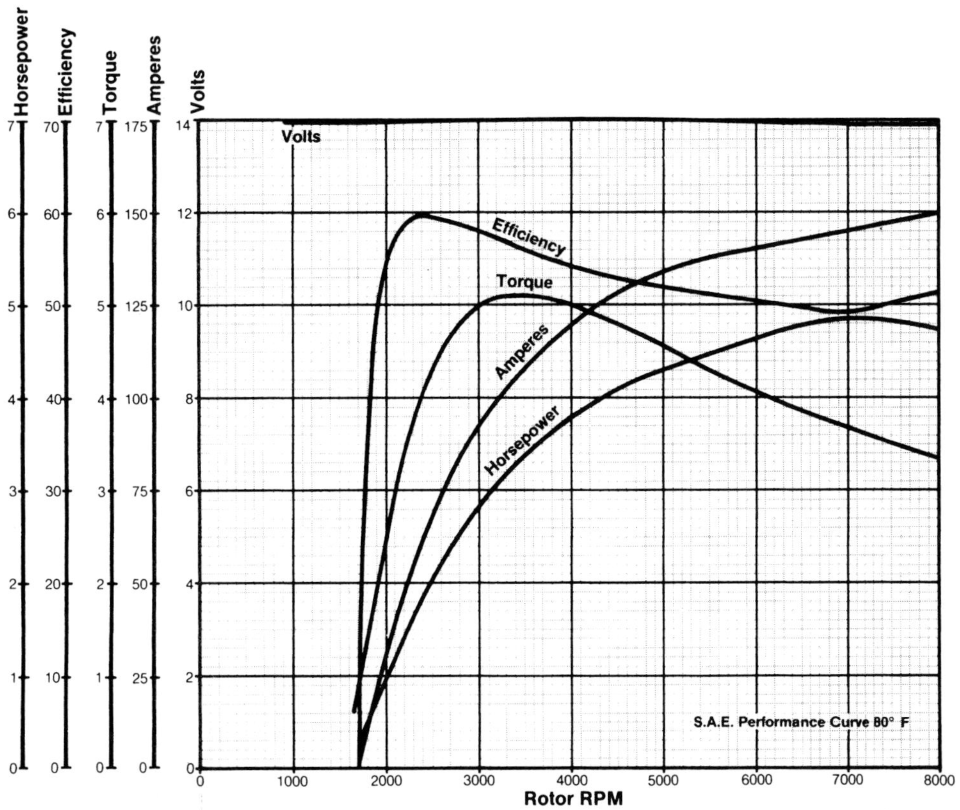

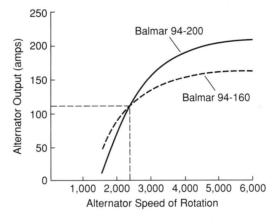

FIGURE 1-24A. An unusually detailed set of performance curves for a 150 amp alternator. *(Energy Control)*

The chart axes (left to right): **Horsepower**, **Efficiency**, **Torque**, **Amperes**, **Volts**, plotted against **Rotor RPM**. Curves labeled: Volts, Efficiency, Torque, Amperes, Horsepower. Label: S.A.E. Performance Curve 80° F.

4. Set up the alternator pulley ratio to achieve the maximum *required* output at this *minimum* engine speed. Then check to make sure that the alternator will not overspeed at maximum engine revolutions. If the alternator will overspeed, power down the pulleys to the point at which the alternator reaches maximum speed only at maximum engine revolutions.

For example:

- We have a 130 amp alternator and a maximum required output of 100 amps (77% of rated output). The alternator reaches 100 amps at 3,000 rpm.
- The maximum safe operating speed is 10,000 rpm.
- The boat spends much of its time at anchor, running its engine at 1,000 rpm to drive the mechanical refrigeration unit.

We need a pulley ratio of 3:1 to achieve an alternator speed of 3,000 rpm. Maximum engine speed is also 3,000 rpm, giving a maximum alternator speed of 9,000 rpm, which is within safe operating limits.

Alternator installation. High-output alternators can create substantial loads (see below) that

FIGURE 1-24B. A comparison of the output curves for a Balmar 160 amp and 200 amp alternator. Note that until alternator speed of rotation reaches almost 2,400 rpm (typically around 1,200 engine rpm), the 160 amp alternator has a higher output.

are sometimes compounded by harmonic vibration. The end result is that what appear to be incredibly rugged mounting brackets will sometimes fracture. If installing a high-output alternator, it is best to get a mounting kit that has been time-tested by the alternator supplier.

In many ways the ideal installation does not replace the existing alternator with a high-output alternator, but instead adds a high-output alternator to the existing alternator (I'll have more to say on this later). However, often the physical space in the engine room cannot accommodate the addition of a second alternator alongside the engine, the traditional location most mounting kits are designed for. But it may be possible to mount the alternator in front of the engine, turned around and facing backward (Figure 1-25). This has the effect of reversing the normal direction of rotation. From an electrical point of view, the alternator doesn't care, but its fan, which is essential to keeping it cool, may be set up for the normal rotational direction. *If an alternator is installed backward, it is essential to fit a bidirectional, or a reverse-direction, fan.* (Some new high-output alternators, including Balmar's, now have dual fans, in which case you can mount the alternator either way.)

Note that if you use a high-output alternator in place of an existing alternator, it often ends up being driven by a single belt that also drives the engine's freshwater pump. In this case, regardless of the desired alternator output, *the limiting factor on alternator output will be the existing belt size:* a single ³⁄₈-inch (10 mm) belt should not be used to handle much more than 75 amps (at 12 volts); a single ¹⁄₂-inch (13 mm) belt not much more than 100 amps (see the Belts and Pulleys sidebar for more detail on belt loading). Over time, the belt tension needed to handle higher loads is likely to damage the bearings in the water pump.

Belt quality varies markedly from manufacturer to manufacturer. When working a belt hard, a certain quality threshold must be met if the belt is to hold up for any length of time. Below this threshold the belt will fail quite rapidly; above it, the belt will last for years. There is no way to tell by looking at a belt whether or not it meets the threshold. I have had excellent results with Gates Green Stripe belts (www.gates.com), and thus always specify those (or relabeled versions of them).

Tachometers. Many engine tachometers operate by sensing the output frequency of the alternator (in which case the tachometer wire will go from the tachometer to a terminal on the alternator). If you use nonstandard pulley ratios to drive the alternator, they will throw off the tachometer calibration. In some cases, you can restore calibration by moving the tachometer wire to a different terminal (called a *tap*); in other cases, adjust the tachometer itself using a separate handheld rpm meter on the end of the engine crankshaft to establish the engine speed. Occasionally, it is simply a matter of living with an under- or over-reading tachometer. With multi-step voltage regulators (see later), the tachometer may also trip out, or flicker on and off, when batteries are nearing a full charge (it is a function of the kind of voltage regulation employed and the reduced output from the alternator). Once again, it is something that just has to be lived with.

Horsepower requirements of alternators.
A nominal 12-volt alternator's output is around 14 volts. At 100 amps, an alternator is therefore producing 14 volts × 100 amps = 1,400 watts. There are 746 watts in 1 horsepower; therefore in theory, this alternator will require 1,400/746 = 1.88 horsepower to drive it.

However, alternators are only 50% to 60% efficient in energy conversion, so this figure needs to be doubled to 3.76 horsepower, and then a further factor must be added for other energy losses such as drive-belt and pulley friction. This results in a power requirement of up to 4 to 5 horsepower at 100 amps. Obviously, at reduced loads the alternator will need less power. (Note that large-frame alternators and large pulleys cause less power loss than small-frame alternators and small pulleys.)

A side loading of this magnitude on an engine's crankshaft pulley may damage the crankshaft oil seal or bearing. Before installing a high-output alternator, check with the engine manufacturer to make sure the motor can handle the load. If it can't, you can eliminate side loading by adding a *stub shaft* to the crankshaft, and either directly driving the alternator with the stub shaft (i.e., eliminating the pulleys and belt) or else adding a separate *pillow-block* bearing to the stub shaft to absorb the side load of the alternator.

Another problem that may occur with small engines and large alternators is that the horsepower absorbed by the alternator at times causes unacceptable propulsive power losses. You can alleviate this situation by fitting a sophisticated voltage regulator with a current-limiting capability that is set to keep the alternator's output below a certain level (see the next section), or else, if the alternator has an external field connection (see Chapter 3), by fitting a switch in the field circuit that enables the alternator to be turned off when the full engine horsepower is needed for propulsion.

FIGURE 1-25. A 200 amp alternator installed backward on our last boat. To ensure adequate cooling, it is essential to either turn the alternator's fan around or else install a bidirectional fan.

ESTABLISHING A BALANCED BATTERY-POWERED ELECTRICAL SYSTEM

Belts and Pulleys

The horsepower requirements of high-output alternators put considerable loads on belts. To gear up alternator speeds at engine idle speeds, smaller than normal pulleys are often used on the alternator, which further increase belt stresses. To determine what size belt is needed in any given application, the following three factors must be taken into account: total hp load, alternator speed, and pulley size.

The specifications in Tables 1-7, 1-8, and 1-9 are adapted from information supplied by the Gates Corporation for its excellent belts:

TABLE 1-7. Horsepower Ratings for 3VX Super HC Molded Notch V-Belts (approx. ⅜ in. belts)

	Alternator Pulley Diameter										
Alternator RPM	2.2"	2.35"	2.5"	2.65"	2.8"	3.0"	3.15"	3.35"	3.65"	4.12"	
1,000	0.87	1.02	1.18	1.34	1.49	1.69	1.85	2.05	2.35	2.82	Rated
2,000	1.52	1.82	2.11	2.40	2.70	3.08	3.37	3.75	4.32	5.19	hp
3,000	2.08	2.50	2.93	3.35	3.76	4.31	4.72	5.26	6.06	7.29	for a
4,000	2.56	3.10	3.65	4.18	4.71	5.41	5.92	6.60	7.60	9.11	single
5,000	2.96	3.62	4.27	4.91	5.53	6.36	6.96	7.75	8.90	10.6	belt

TABLE 1-8. Horsepower Ratings for 5VX Super HC Molded Notch V-Belts (between ½ and ⅝ in.)

	Alternator Pulley Diameter		
Alternator RPM	4.40"	4.65"	4.90"	
1,000	5.22	5.92	6.62	Rated hp
2,000	9.14	10.4	11.7	for a single
3,000	12.3	14.1	15.9	belt

TABLE 1-9. Horsepower Ratings for AX-Section Tri-Power Molded Notch V-Belts (½ in. belts)

	Alternator Pulley Diameter										
Alternator RPM	2.2"	2.4"	2.6"	2.8"	3.0"	3.2"	3.4"	3.6"	3.8"	4.0"	
1,000	1.10	1.32	1.53	1.74	1.95	2.15	2.35	2.56	2.75	2.95	Rated
2,000	1.59	1.96	2.33	2.70	3.06	3.41	3.75	4.09	4.43	4.76	hp
3,000	1.81	2.32	2.81	3.30	3.77	4.24	4.69	5.13	5.56	5.98	for a
4,000	1.83	2.44	3.03	3.61	4.16	4.70	5.21	5.71	6.18	6.63	single
5,000	1.65	2.34	3.00	3.63	4.22	4.78	5.31	5.81	6.27	6.70	belt

As can be seen, the company does not size the 5VX belts for use with pulleys below 4.40 inches, although they are commonly used on smaller pulley sizes. What is clear is that a single 5VX belt will handle any alternator load. To see if the smaller 3VX belt will hold up in a given application:

1. Convert the alternator's rated output to hp on the basis of 100 amps (at 12 volts) = 5 hp (e.g., 80 amps = 4 hp).
2. Consult the alternator's output curve to determine the lowest speed at which the alternator reaches full rated output (generally around 5,000 rpm).
3. Find this speed of rotation in the appropriate table, move across until you find the relevant hp, and then read off the minimum pulley size to meet this load. (For example, using Table 1-7, at a speed of 5,000 rpm, the smallest pulley that will handle 4 hp has a diameter of 2.5 inches.)

4. If the pulley size is larger than previously determined necessary (see pages 24–25), in order to use the smaller pulley size you should use double belts.

In general, once output goes much above 100 amps, a single 3VX belt is not suitable with pulleys under 3 inches in diameter; two belts will be required. The larger the pulleys that can be used, the lower the friction losses and the less the likelihood of slippage.

The pulley grooves must be sized so that the belt does not bottom out in the pulley. *The driving force of the belt must be transmitted via the sides of the belt, not the base of the belt.* Often a high-output alternator comes with a ½-inch pulley in which a 3VX belt will just about bottom out. In this case, the 5VX or AX belt should be used. It should also be noted that the industry standard pulley has a 38-degree taper to the sides of the groove, whereas many alternators come with 34- or 36-degree pulleys, *continued* which will accelerate belt wear. If this is the case, the pulley should be replaced with a 38-degree pulley. Nowadays, some marine engines come with notched serpentine belts, which may be overloaded if the standard alternator is replaced with a high-output alternator. Check with the engine manufacturer.

Regardless of belt and pulley size, belts need tensioning at regular intervals. One way to accurately determine the correct tension is to first measure the distance (in inches) from the center of the crankshaft pulley to the center of the alternator pulley. Then tension a 3VX or AX belt so that it takes 3 to 5 pounds of pressure in the center of the longest span of the belt to depress the belt by $1/64$ inch for every inch measured above. For example, if the pulleys are 16 inches apart, 3 to 5 pounds of pressure should depress the belt by $16/64$, or $1/4$ inch. For the 5VX belts, 8 to 12 pounds of pressure should achieve the same deflection. New belts should be slightly overtensioned and then checked regularly since they will stretch in the first day or two of use.

Establishing Correct Voltage Regulation

So far we have determined the correct type of batteries for a given application (cranking or deep-cycle), sized the batteries to meet the anticipated load, and determined the alternator capability and installation necessary to recharge these batteries. *None of this will be effective in providing a trouble-free DC system unless we correctly tailor the alternator's voltage regulator to the needs of our system. Voltage regulation is one of the most neglected aspects of marine DC systems, and as a result, improper voltage regulation is one of the single greatest causes of DC problems.*

The water tank analogy. The plates within a battery can be compared to a closed water tank that has a series of solid baffles inside it, extending from the top of the tank toward the bottom. The lower sections of these baffles contain semipermeable membranes. A pump (the alternator) pushes in water (current) at one end (Figure 1-26). The first section of the tank fills.

Continuing the tank analogy, the rising water is initially contained by the first baffle and membrane, causing the pressure of the air trapped in this section of the tank to rise until it is high enough to drive water through the first membrane into the second section of the tank. There is now a pressure differential between the first and second tank sections, with the pressure in the second lagging behind the first. As more water is pumped in, the pressure on these two sections will rise until water is driven into the third section, and so on.

Looking now at a battery, the initial charging current is absorbed by the surface areas of the battery plates, causing the voltage to rise. This rising voltage creates a voltage differential between the plate surfaces and the interior areas, driving current into these interior areas.

Pressure (voltage) switch. On the tank, the pump has a pressure switch. Let's say it is set for 14 pounds per square inch (psi). When the first section of the tank gets to this pressure, the pump is switched off. The pressure differential between the different sections of the tank causes water to continue to percolate through the membranes into other sections of the tank. This drops the pressure on the first section until the pump kicks back on and drives the pressure back to the set point. This process continues until the whole tank is up to 14 psi, at which point the pump is turned off until some water is drawn out of the tank, dropping the pressure and causing the pump to kick back on.

With a battery, an alternator (or other charging device) has a voltage regulator. Let's say this is set for 14 volts. When the surface voltage on the plates gets to 14 volts, the alternator is switched off. (Note that when we measure battery voltage at the battery posts, it is, in fact, the voltage on the surface of the plates that is being measured. Therefore, this voltage is sometimes known as *surface voltage*.) After the alternator is switched off, the voltage difference between the surface of the plates and the interior areas will cause charging current to diffuse into inner plate areas. This drops the voltage on the surface of the plates until the voltage regulator turns the

FIGURE 1-26. Battery charge acceptance—the water tank analogy. On charging, the pump first fills the main chamber, compressing the air into the top of the chamber until there is sufficient pressure to drive water through the membrane into the second chamber, and so on. The first chamber will fill rapidly, but thereafter the rate of flow will decrease steadily. On discharging, the air pressure in the main chamber will drive much of the water out of this chamber quite rapidly, but thereafter the rate of flow will decrease as the water has to be driven out of the inner chambers through the membranes.

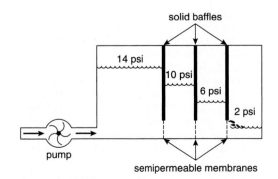

solid baffles

14 psi

10 psi

6 psi

2 psi

pump

semipermeable membranes

alternator back on, driving the voltage on the surface of the plates back up to the set point. Given enough charging time, this process continues until the battery is fully charged (all plate areas are at 14 volts), at which point the voltage regulator switches off the charging device until current is drawn from the battery, dropping the surface voltage on the plates and kicking the charging device back into action.

Charge acceptance rate. When the tank is completely empty, there is no pressure in the interior areas of the tank. When the first section of the tank is filled, the pressure differential between it and the other sections is high, and so the rate of percolation through the membranes is at its highest. As the interior areas of the tank come up to pressure, the pressure differential declines, and the rate of percolation decreases.

With a battery, when it is well discharged, the voltage in the interior areas of the plates is low. When an alternator is turned on, and the surface voltage on the plates rises, the voltage differential through the plate is at its greatest, so the rate of charge acceptance by interior plate areas is at its highest. As these interior areas absorb a charge, the voltage differential decreases, and the rate of current diffusion slows. This is why the charge acceptance rate of a battery declines as it comes up to charge.

As noted, the first segment of the tank is analogous to the surface areas of battery plates—those areas in immediate contact with the electrolyte. The interior sections of the tank are analogous to the interior areas of battery plates. A cranking battery has numerous thin plates, resulting in a large surface area, so this is analogous to the first section of the tank taking up much of the tank's volume. This kind of a battery will accept relatively high charge rates and will come to a full charge quite quickly. A liquid-electrolyte deep-cycle battery has fewer, thicker plates, which is analogous to the first section of the tank being quite small and the other sections being larger. When charged, the first section of the tank gets filled rather quickly (the surface areas of the plates get recharged) after which the charge acceptance rate slows markedly because of the time it takes for the charge to diffuse to the inner areas of the plates. It takes a long time to get a well-discharged, liquid-electrolyte deep-cycle battery back to a state of full charge. To illustrate, if a fully discharged battery is fully recharged, approximately 90% of the charge can be restored in the first 60% of the charging time, with the remaining 10% of the charge taking 40% of the charging time.

Sulfation. If we draw water off our tank, it initially comes out of the first section of the tank. If the tank is refilled immediately after use, the in-

terior areas hardly get discharged and recharge times are short. But if the tank is left in a partially discharged state, its internal pressure will equalize as a result of water from the interior areas flowing to the first section. It will then take some time to refill these interior areas.

If we draw current out of a battery, it initially comes off the surface of the plates. If the battery is recharged immediately (as in a cranking situation), the interior plate areas hardly get discharged and recharge times are short. But if the battery is left in a partially discharged state, its internal voltage will equalize, resulting in interior plate areas becoming discharged. It will now take some time to recharge the battery. If it is not fully recharged, these interior plate areas will be vulnerable to sulfation.

Rate of charge. If a large pump is put on a small tank, it will soon fill the first section of the tank, after which the charge acceptance rate of the tank will decline, causing the output of the pump to taper off. In other words, the pump capacity is largely wasted. At the point when pump output starts to decline, because the first section of the tank was recharged so fast, there will have been little time for the water to filter into interior tank areas, so overall the tank may still be relatively discharged even though the measured pressure is the same as for a full tank. Conversely, if a small pump is put on a large tank, the rate at which the water filters into the interior areas of the tank will more closely keep up with the output from the pump, so that by the time the pressure set point is reached, the tank will be more nearly filled.

So, too, with a battery. If a large alternator is put on a small battery, it will rapidly drive up the surface voltage on the plates, causing the voltage regulator to cut back the alternator's output. The alternator's capacity is largely wasted. At the point when the alternator output is first curtailed, there will have been little time for charging current to diffuse to inner plate areas. Even though the measured voltage is the same as for a fully charged battery, the battery may still be well discharged. Conversely, if a small alternator is charging a large battery bank, the rate of charge diffusion through the plates may keep up with the alternator's output such that the voltage regulator does not curtail alternator output until the battery has reached a high state of charge.

Bulk and absorption charges. Given an empty tank, when the pump is first turned on, the tank will accept the pump's full output—the first section of the tank is being filled. At this time, the limiting factor in the rate of flow is the output from the pump. Once the first area of the tank comes to the set point on the pressure switch, the switch starts to turn the pump on and off to maintain this pressure. The rate of flow is now determined by the rate of percolation into interior areas of the tank. As the interior areas of the tank become filled, and the rate of water percolation through the membranes drops, the pump is turned off for longer and longer periods of time, resulting in a steadily declining output.

Once again, so too with a battery. If the battery is well discharged when an alternator is first turned on, the surface areas of the battery plates, and adjacent areas, will accept the alternator's full output. At this time, the limiting factor in the rate of charge is the output of the alternator. This is known as the *bulk charge phase* of the charging process. Once the surface voltage on the battery plates has reached the voltage regulator's set point (e.g., 14 volts), the regulator starts to turn the alternator on and off to maintain this voltage. The charge rate is now determined by the rate at which the charging current diffuses into interior plate areas. As the interior areas of the battery plates come to charge, and the charge acceptance rate of the battery tapers off, the alternator is turned off for longer and longer periods of time, resulting in a steadily declining alternator output. (This switching on and off takes place hundreds of times a second, and can create considerable electrical interference—see Chapter 8.)

Low versus high regulator settings.
When charging, the rate of current diffusion into the interior areas of battery plates can always be accelerated by raising the voltage regulator set point. This has the effect of increasing the voltage differential throughout the battery plates, considerably reducing recharge times. However, if this set point is raised too high, physical damage will result (the plates will overheat and buckle).

In typical automotive use, we have a thin-plate cranking battery that is rarely discharged by more than a small percentage of its capacity. As noted, the act of cranking draws the charge from the surfaces of the plates, which are then recharged before the battery has time to equalize internally—the inner plate areas retain their charge. In general, the engine and alternator run far longer than is needed to replace this charge. In short, little charge is needed, only the surface areas of the plates need charging, and we have excess charging time. In this undemanding environment, *voltage regulator settings are kept relatively low in order to avoid damaging the battery through overcharging during extended periods of engine-running time.*

In contrast, in many marine applications, a thick-plate deep-cycle battery is deeply discharged over a long period of time, allowing the battery to equalize internally and so draining the charge from the inaccessible inner plate areas.

The engine and alternator are then run for far less time than is needed to restore a full charge. If a typical automotive voltage regulator setting of around 14.0 volts (for a 12-volt system) is used during charging, the rising surface voltage of the battery will cause the regulator to curtail alternator output soon after the battery is 50% charged (Figure 1-27), which is well before battery safety demands that it be cut back. *This unnecessarily prolongs charging times.*

Since a well-designed deep-cycle battery bank will typically be cycling primarily in the region of 50% to 80% of full charge, *an automotive-style voltage regulator cripples charging performance in the region of most interest to boatowners!* As a result, many batteries are perennially undercharged and die prematurely from sulfation. In addition, if battery charging is accomplished by running the boat's main engine at anchor, the engine will be run long hours at low loads to little effect—except to increase wear, tear, and maintenance.

In these circumstances the charge rate needs to be accelerated to the limit the batteries can accept, driving the voltage as high as can be tolerated, so that the inner plate areas will be charged as rapidly as possible. *But if a regulator's voltage setting is raised to produce the maximum safe charge rate in the 50% to 80% state of charge region, the batteries will be overcharged during extended periods of engine running.* This will result in an excessive loss of electrolyte in wet-cells, the drying out and failure of gel-cells and AGMs, and the destruction of the positive plate grids in all batteries, as well as perhaps overheating and buckling of the battery plates.

The dilemma is clear. In many pleasure-boat situations, batteries are periodically discharged deeply (to at least the 50% level), but charging times are restricted. Thus, fast charges are required, which call for higher voltage regulator settings than in automotive applications; otherwise, the batteries will suffer from undercharging, sulfation, and a permanent loss of capacity. But if

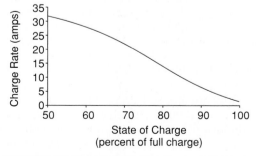

FIGURE 1-27. Output of an alternator controlled by a conventional voltage regulator when charging a 100 Ah battery. Note that the rising surface voltage causes the charging current to be cut back early in the charging process.

ESTABLISHING A BALANCED BATTERY-POWERED ELECTRICAL SYSTEM

voltage regulator settings are raised, extended engine running will likely overcharge the batteries, causing excessive gassing and plate damage.

Voltage regulator solutions. This dilemma is resolved with a sophisticated, computer-controlled, *multistep* ("*smart*") *regulator* (Figures 1-29A, 1-29B, and 1-29C). In the United States, the best-known are those manufactured by Ample Technology, Balmar, and Xantrex; in the UK, Adverc BM, TWC, and Mastervolt (www.mastervolt.com). These regulators maintain a relatively high voltage setting, thus boosting charge rates, until a battery is almost fully charged, and then trip to a lower setting to avoid overcharging. Most have at least three phases:

1. The *bulk* charge.
2. The *absorption* charge.
3. The *float* charge.

The bulk charge. During the bulk charge, maximum alternator output is maintained until the battery comes up to the regulator's absorption voltage (on a 12-volt system, normally in the region of 14.2 to 14.4 volts). Generally (though not always), the bulk charge is more or less a constant-current charge as opposed to the typical automotive constant-voltage charge. To understand the significance of this difference, we'll return to our water tank analogy.

The alternator on a constant-voltage system acts like a *centrifugal* pump (see Chapter 13). As the head pressure the pump is working against increases (as the pressure in the first chamber of the tank rises), the flow rate decreases even though the pump is not yet up to its rated maximum pressure. Pump output steadily tapers down well before the pump approaches its high-pressure limit. In contrast, an alternator on a constant-current system acts like a *constant-volume* pump, which moves the same volume of

Charge Rates as a Function of Voltage and Battery State of Charge

To illustrate the relationship between battery state of charge, charge acceptance rates, and alternator output voltage (as determined by the voltage regulator setting), take a look at Figure 1-28, which provides numbers for a generic, liquid-electrolyte, 100 Ah battery at 80°F/26.7°C. For any given alternator output voltage, find the voltage on the left of the graph, trace across until a curve is met, and then move down to read the charge acceptance rate at that voltage for a battery in that state of charge. For example, if a regulator is holding 13.6 volts, a fully charged 100 Ah battery will accept approximately 1 amp, a three-quarter-charged battery, 7½ amps, and a half-charged battery, 17 amps. If the regulator is holding 14.4 volts, the figures become 2 amps, 14 amps, and 30 amps respectively. (For a 200 Ah battery, these figures can be approximately doubled, as long as the alternator has sufficient output to supply the current.) *An increase of only 0.8 volt on the regulator setting almost doubles the charge acceptance rate throughout the critical 50% of charge to the full-charge range that we are interested in; this cuts charging times in half.*

Turning these figures around reveals another interesting relationship. If a regulator is holding 13.6 volts, a half-charged battery will accept 17 amps, a three-quarter-charged battery, 7½ amps, and a fully charged battery, 1 amp. *The charge rate tapers off rapidly.* To go from three-quarter charge to full charge will take a very long time as the charge rate winds down toward 1 amp. Even if the regulator is holding 14.4 volts, the battery's charge acceptance rate from

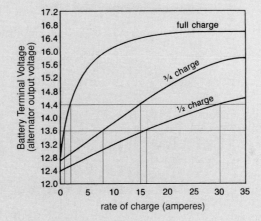

FIGURE 1-28. Charge acceptance rates of a 100 Ah cranking battery as a function of charging voltage and state of charge. Since it is wise to avoid routine discharges of greater than 50% (failure to do so will shorten battery life), this chart covers the charge states of greatest interest. The implications of the chart are discussed in the text. *(Adapted from a table courtesy the Battery Council International)*

three-quarter charged to fully charged winds down from 14 amps to 2 amps. *On a boat where charging is intermittent and engine-running time is restricted, it will be nearly impossible to bring batteries up to full charge even with an elevated voltage regulator setting.*

Now assume a battery is at full charge. A voltage regulator setting of 13.6 volts, producing a charge rate of around 1 amp, will only minimally overcharge a battery. In practice, other losses—both internal and external to the battery—will probably prevent overcharging. But a regulator setting of 14.4 volts, producing a charge rate of 2 amps, will create excessive battery gassing over an extended period, with a consequent loss of electrolyte, potential damage to the battery-plate grids, and the drying out of gel-cells and AGMs.

FIGURES 1-29A AND 1-29B. Balmar and Ample Technology multistep voltage regulators. Note the two potentiometer screws on the right-hand side of the Ample Technology regulator. These are for adjusting the absorption voltage and absorption time. Note also the twelve-terminal connector strip at the bottom; wiring these regulators can get quite involved! *(Balmar and Ample Technology)*

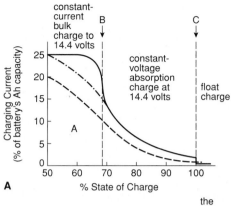

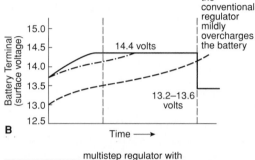

FIGURE 1-29C. Xantrex multistep regulator.

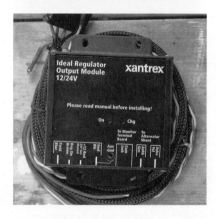

multistep regulator with constant-current bulk charge

multistep regulator with constant-voltage bulk charge

automotive-type constant-voltage regulator

FIGURES 1-30A AND 1-30B. A comparison of the output of a charging device using multistep regulators as opposed to a conventional regulator. Desirable attributes of a marine regulator are a constant-current output of approximately 25% of the Ah rating of the battery being charged in region A of the graphs; tripping to a constant-voltage setting of around 14.4 volts (on a 12-volt system) at point B; holding this voltage until the charge rate falls to 2% of the Ah rating of the battery; and then tripping to a float voltage of 13.2 to 13.6 volts (point C). As temperatures rise above 80°F/26.7°C, the voltage set points should be progressively lowered.

water at each revolution, regardless of the head pressure on the system, until a pressure switch (the voltage regulator) turns it off. Pump output is constant right up to the high-pressure cutout. A constant-current regulator defeats the taper effect inherent in a constant-voltage regulator (Figures 1-30A and 1-30B), producing faster rates of recharge.

As noted earlier, the higher the constant current in relation to a battery's capacity, the faster the battery will be driven to the absorption voltage, but the less the battery will be charged at the point when the absorption voltage is reached, because the alternator will have driven up the surface voltage on the battery plates without allowing time for the inner plate areas to absorb a charge. When fast charging, a higher absorption voltage is needed to drive the battery to the same state of charge as would occur with slower

charging to a lower voltage over a longer period of time. So at lower rates of charge, the voltage at which the bulk charge is terminated can be lower than at high rates of charge (on a 12-volt system, 14.2 volts at a 10% rate of charge rising to 14.4 volts at a 25% rate of charge would be typical).

It is necessary to avoid extremes. *The charging current with a multistep regulator should be equal to the DC load while the engine is running, plus somewhere between 10% (minimum) and 40% (maximum) of the battery's rated amp-hour capacity.* In the previous section on sizing an alternator, I outlined a good middle point to shoot for, which is the DC load plus 25% of rated battery capacity for a liquid-electrolyte deep-cycle battery, and something higher (maybe 33%) for a gel-cell or AGM.

The absorption (acceptance) charge. If the constant-current charge were to be continued too long, it would drive the battery up to potentially damaging voltages. To prevent this, during the *absorption phase, the alternator output is held to the voltage at which the bulk charge is terminated* (14.2 to 14.4 volts on a 12-volt system), allowing the charge rate to be determined by what the battery will accept at this voltage (the rate at which the charge will percolate into inner plate areas at this pressure). This is therefore a constant-voltage charge. It is continued either for a fixed time or until the battery's charge acceptance rate at this voltage declines to 2% of the battery's amp-hour rating. (The specific mechanism that determines the end of this phase is one of the subtle differences between one regulator and another.) The absorption phase gives time for the charge to be absorbed by the inner plate areas. At its termination, a battery will be very nearly fully charged.

The float charge. If the absorption phase were to be continued beyond the fully charged state, the battery would be damaged from overcharging. To avoid this, at the completion of the absorption phase, a multistep regulator trips to a lower constant-voltage float setting (generally between 13.2 and 13.6 volts). This protects the battery from overcharging during periods of extended engine-running time.

Additional features. Various regulators have numerous additional features, in particular:

- A fourth equalization or conditioning phase (Figure 1-31), which is essential for obtaining the maximum life expectancy from wet-cell deep-cycle batteries (see page 12 and Chapter 3).

- Temperature compensation, which lowers the regulator's voltage set point if the battery temperature rises (Tables 1-10, 1-11, and 1-12). When coupled to large alternators, the high currents produced by multistep regulators will cause a battery to warm up, which in turn will increase the battery's charge acceptance rate. (The warmth accelerates the chemical reactions needed for charging.) Unless the voltage regulator setting is lowered, the battery will steadily absorb more current, further raising its temperature, until damage occurs. (Note that the fitting of Hydrocaps to wet-cell batteries exacerbates this problem.) In extreme conditions, a battery can get into a condition known as thermal runaway. In this situation, the battery gets hot enough to absorb just about any level of charging current, which then heats it up more, causing the battery to boil violently, buckle its plates, perhaps melt its case, and maybe even blow up. The maximum acceptable battery temperature is 125°F/52°C. To be safe, anytime a system is

designed to hold sustained charge rates above 10% to 15% of battery capacity, and especially if the target is in the 25% or higher range, *the voltage regulator on high-capacity charging devices must include temperature compensation based on temperature sensing at the batteries* (not in the regulator).

Without temperature-sensing equipment, how can you guard against battery overheating? Anytime a battery case becomes warm to the touch, you should suspect that the internal temperature is potentially becoming dangerously high. (Battery temperature can be determined more accurately by using a digital thermometer on the battery post or withdrawing a sample of electrolyte using a hydrometer with a built-in temperature gauge. See the Testing a Battery section in Chapter 3.)

- A timer during the bulk charge and absorption phases so that if for some reason the battery does not come up to the trip-to-float voltage, or the charge acceptance rate does not drop to the trip-to-float current, the regulator will still trip to float. This safeguards against overcharging as a result of a shorted cell or some other problem.

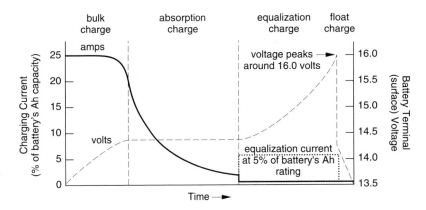

FIGURE 1-31. Equalization (conditioning) cycle on a multistep regulator. At the end of the absorption phase, instead of tripping to float, the charge rate is raised to a constant-current setting of 3% to 5% of the battery's Ah rating and held at this level for several hours (see Chapter 3 for methods of determining when to end an equalization charge).

TABLE 1-10. Gassing Voltages for a 12-Volt Battery as a Function of Electrolyte Temperature

(Absorption voltage on a multistep regulator for wet-cell batteries should be adjusted to approximate these voltages at these *battery* temperatures.)

Electrolyte Temperature (°F/°C)	Gassing Voltage of a 12-Volt Battery	
122/50	13.80	
104/40	13.98	
86/30	14.19	
77/25	**14.34**	(this is the standard rating temperature)
68/20	14.49	
50/10	14.82	
32/0	15.24	
14/–10	15.90	
–4/–20	17.82	

TABLE 1-11. Recommended Temperature-Compensated Charging and Float Voltages for East Penn Gel-Cells

| | Charging Voltage | | Float Voltage | | |
Temperature °F	Optimum (extended charging times)	Maximum (fast charging)	Optimum	Maximum	Temperature °C
above 120	13.00	13.30	12.80	13.00	above 49
110–120	13.20	13.50	12.90	13.20	44–48
100–109	13.30	13.60	13.00	13.30	38–43
90–99	13.40	13.70	13.10	13.40	32–37
80–89	13.50	13.80	13.20	13.50	27–31
70–79	13.70	14.00	13.40	13.70	21–26
60–69	13.85	14.15	13.55	13.85	16–20
50–59	14.00	14.30	13.70	14.00	10–15
40–49	14.20	14.50	13.90	14.20	5–9
below 39	14.50	14.80	14.20	14.50	below 4

Note: Other manufacturers may recommend different voltages for their batteries.   *(Courtesy East Penn)*

TABLE 1-12. Recommended Temperature-Compensated Charging and Float Voltages for East Penn AGMs

| | Charging Voltage | | Float Voltage | | |
Temperature °F	Optimum (extended charging times)	Maximum (fast charging)	Optimum	Maximum	Temperature °C
above 120	13.60	13.90	12.80	13.00	above 49
110–120	13.80	14.10	12.90	13.20	44–48
100–109	13.90	14.20	13.00	13.30	38–43
90–99	14.00	14.30	13.10	13.40	32–37
80–89	14.10	14.40	13.20	13.50	27–31
70–79	14.30	14.60	13.40	13.70	21–26
60–69	14.45	14.75	13.55	13.85	16–20
50–59	14.60	14.90	13.70	14.00	10–15
40–49	14.80	15.10	13.90	14.20	5–9
below 39	15.10	15.40	14.20	14.50	below 4

Note: Other manufacturers may recommend different voltages for their batteries.   *(Courtesy East Penn)*

- A time-delay function so that the alternator is not switched on until a few seconds after an engine cranks. This eliminates cranking difficulties caused by the high loads of a high-output alternator. The alternator output is then sometimes increased gradually (*ramped*) to avoid shock-loading the drive belt.

- A current-limit setting so that the maximum output of a non-hot-rated alternator can be set at a level that will keep the alternator from burning up. The current limit can also be used to hold down the maximum horsepower draw on a small engine.

- A continuous tachometer function. If a tachometer is sensed off the alternator, when a multistep regulator trips from the absorption to the float cycle, alternator output may temporarily cease until the battery's surface voltage has fallen to the float voltage level (the battery equalizes internally). With some multistep regulators, the engine tachometer will stop registering during this period; with others, it will not.

- Sensing of the battery voltage at the batteries as opposed to the alternator, which is important for accurate monitoring and control.

- Spray-proofing of the units to a greater or lesser extent.

The benefits of multistep regulators.
When using a typical automotive voltage regulator, even with a high-output alternator, *it will take up to 7 hours to fully recharge a deeply discharged battery*. Such lengthy charging times are frequently impractical. As a result, many marine batteries are perennially undercharged, DC systems perform well below par, and the batteries fail prematurely from sulfation. (This is probably the number two cause of battery death in the marine environment, with the misapplication of cranking batteries in cycling service being the number one cause.)

With a multistep regulator and a high-output alternator, the charging period can be cut in half. In fact, if charging to 80% of the fully charged level is acceptable, charging times can be consistently reduced to between 1 and 1½ hours a day (or whatever the normal interval between charges is). *This results in a dramatic improvement in DC system performance and also battery life, which translates into far fewer electrical problems and considerable cost savings—more than enough in many instances to pay for the added cost of the alternator, the regulator, and their installation!*

Putting the Pieces Together

Having selected a decent set of batteries, an adequate alternator, and a suitable voltage regulator for a given application, the next task is installing these components in a way that puts them to work most effectively.

One of the key aspects of the installation is to ensure that there is always a battery in reserve with an adequate capacity to crank the engine. It is, in any case, a requirement of industry-wide, standards-setting bodies (the American Boat and Yacht Council—ABYC—in the United States; the International Organization for Standardization—ISO—in Europe) that there be a reserved battery for all but hand-cranked engines. This requirement is normally met by either having a dedicated engine-cranking battery or two house banks that are alternated in use, with the reserve bank kept in a fully charged state (often not the best use of batteries—see below).

In the former case, the reserved battery can be a cranking battery. In the latter case, two banks of deep-cycle batteries will be needed. Many people erroneously believe that deep-cycle batteries are unsuited for cranking applications. They can be used, but because the thicker plates in deep-cycle batteries retard the rate of acid diffusion as compared with thin-plate (cranking) batteries—and therefore retard the rate at which energy can be released—a larger-capacity, deep-cycle battery is required to produce the same cranking capability as a thin-plate battery.

How much larger? If a deep-cycle battery is to be used for engine cranking it is necessary to make sure that it has a CCA rating at least equal to that specified in the engine manual (or at least equal to the CCA rating of the cranking battery it is replacing).

Is It Better to Have One or Two Battery Banks for House Use?

The traditionally popular arrangement of alternating two house banks needs scrutiny before we go any further.

Life cycles. As we have seen, the life expectancy of a battery in cycling service is directly related to the depth to which it is discharged at each cycle—the greater the depth of discharge, the shorter the battery's life (refer back to Figure 1-12 and Table 1-5).

This relationship between depth of discharge and battery life is not linear. As the depth of discharge increases, a battery's life expectancy is disproportionately shortened. Using the Trojan data in Table 1-5, a given battery might cycle through 10% of its capacity 6,200 times, 50% of its capacity 2,900 times, and 80% of its capacity 1,700 times.

Let's say, for argument's sake, that a boat has two 200 Ah battery banks, alternated from day to day, with a daily load of 160 Ah. Each bank will be discharged by 80% of capacity before being recharged. The batteries will fail after 1,700 cycles, which is 3,400 days (since each is used every other day). If the two banks had been wired in parallel to make a single 400 Ah battery bank, this bank would have been discharged by 40% of capacity every day, with a life expectancy of 3,700 days, almost a 10% increase in life expectancy using exactly the same batteries.

There are two immediate conclusions to be drawn from these figures:

1. For a given total battery capacity, wiring the batteries into a single high-capacity bank, rather than having them divided into two alternating banks, will generally result in a longer overall life expectancy for the batteries.
2. All other things being equal, an increase in the overall capacity of a battery bank will generally produce a disproportionate increase in its life expectancy (through reducing the depth of discharge at each cycle).

For battery longevity, a single large bank is preferable to divided banks.

Battery voltage and other considerations. Besides increased battery life, there are other advantages to the single large bank.

Terminal voltage. The efficient functioning of many DC devices is directly related to their input voltage. A small drop in voltage will cause a noticeable reduction in light from an incandescent bulb. Of more significance is the loss of output from electric motors. With declining voltage, a centrifugal bilge pump, for example, will suffer a disproportionate loss of pumping capability, while many other motors tend to overheat, with a distinct risk of burning up. In fact, low voltage is probably one of the primary causes of DC motor failure.

When any battery is discharged, the load on the battery immediately pulls down the voltage and then causes a steady continuing voltage decline until the voltage suddenly falls off, at which point the battery is effectively dead. The extent to which the voltage initially falls, and then the rate at which it continues to decline, is related to the size of the load as a percentage of the battery's overall capacity. The greater the capacity of a battery bank in relation to the load applied to it, the smaller the initial voltage drop and the slower the subsequent rate of voltage decline. Once again, this relationship is not linear. Doubling the size of a battery bank will reduce to less than half the rate at which the battery voltage declines under a given load.

For a given load over a given period of time, a single large battery bank will at all times maintain a higher terminal voltage than a divided bank with each half used alternately.

DC-to-AC inverters. Aside from electric lights and motors, this has particular significance for many inverter-based AC systems. Many DC-to-AC inverters, particularly older inverters, are *line-frequency* inverters in which the peak AC output voltage is directly related to the DC input voltage—as the battery voltage falls off under a load, the peak AC voltage also falls (covered in some detail in Chapter 6). Much of the time this is of no consequence, but some AC loads, notably many microwaves, are quite sensitive to the peak AC voltage, suffering a considerable loss of efficiency as this voltage declines. The sustained higher DC voltage of a single large battery bank, as compared to the voltage of a divided bank, will result in significantly improved performance from these inverter-powered devices. Not only that, but the voltage on a single bank subjected to a heavy inverter load will take more than twice as long as the voltage on a divided bank to fall to the cutoff threshold of the inverter.

Recharge times. When it comes to recharging the batteries, the larger a battery bank the greater the charge it will accept at a given state of charge. If we have a given amount of energy to put back into a battery (the daily load that is withdrawn between charges), and as long as the charging device has an output equal to or greater than the charge acceptance rate of the batteries, then the larger the battery bank, the faster this energy can be replaced, thus limiting charging time. For example, consider a 400 Ah battery

bank in a 50% state of charge, with a charge acceptance rate of 25% of its capacity (i.e., 100 amps) in a system with a daily energy need of 100 Ah. The daily load can be replaced in one hour, at which point the batteries are 75% charged. If the battery bank is increased to 800 Ah, at a 50% state of charge, it will accept 200 amps of charging current, and the load will be replaced in 30 minutes, bringing the batteries to 63% of full charge. The charging time is cut in half. (Note that for the purposes of this example, I have ignored the tapering effect of the charge acceptance rate as a battery comes to charge, which will disproportionately increase the charging time of the 400 Ah battery bank over the 800 Ah bank, and I have ignored all kinds of other issues such as the sulfation that will occur if the batteries are not periodically fully charged.)

At a given state of charge, a given amount of energy withdrawn from a single large battery bank can be replaced faster than the same energy withdrawn from a divided bank with each half charged alternately.

Battery wiring and management. Finally, when it comes to battery installation and management, a single large bank is easier to manage than two smaller banks for a number of reasons. First of all, the bank can be charged directly from an alternator, as opposed to having to use some sort of a switching arrangement (which is always subject to operator error) or battery isolation diodes (which have problems of their own—see below). Second, the voltage regulator can be adjusted for the ideal charging regimen for the single bank, as opposed to the common situation in which, due to batteries of differing sizes, types, or ages in the two banks, none is charged to best advantage. And finally, the single bank is simpler and cheaper to install, requiring less wiring and switches.

A dedicated cranking battery. But none of these advantages would justify a single bank if on just one critical occasion the single bank caused a situation in which the batteries were flat, the engine couldn't be cranked, and as a result, the boat and crew were put in peril. To be viable, the single bank must be combined with a pretty well bulletproof method of ensuring an ability to crank the engine. Since it must be assumed that at some time the house bank will be discharged to the point at which it could not crank the boat's engine, the single house bank must be combined with a separate battery reserved solely for engine cranking and kept in a state of full charge at all times.

This is achieved by wiring all the house loads to the house bank, and *nothing but the starter motor to the cranking battery*, so there is *no possibility of accidentally draining the cranking bat-*

tery in house service. An emergency paralleling switch between the cranking battery and house bank can be added just in case the house bank is needed as a backup for engine cranking, but this function can just as easily be accomplished by keeping a set of jumper cables on board.

The question then is, how to charge the cranking battery and house bank? By far the best arrangement, particularly if the boat has substantial DC needs, is to leave the existing alternator and voltage regulator wired to the engine-cranking battery and to add a second high-output alternator controlled by a multistep regulator and wired to the house bank (Figures 1-32A and 1-32B). This way, the cranking battery and house bank can be charged independently, with the voltage regulation parameters on each alternator adjusted to provide the most efficient charging regimen for the individual battery banks. (In practice, the existing regulator will probably not be adjustable, but in any case, will provide a regimen suitable for a cranking battery. The multistep regulator can be programmed to achieve the maximum state of charge and life expectancy from the house batteries.) If one or the other alternator or voltage regulator fails, the emergency battery paralleling switch, or jumper cables, can be used to charge both battery banks from the remaining alternator.

Charging More Than One Battery Bank from a Common Alternator

Difficulties arise when two battery banks (either two house banks alternated in use or independent cranking and house batteries) must be charged from a single alternator. The various batteries must be paralleled while charging, so that both are charged, but then isolated when the engine is shut down, preventing the cranking battery or reserve bank from becoming discharged in house service. One of two approaches has traditionally been used to accomplish these objectives:

1. A manual battery selector switch is used to parallel the batteries when the engine is running and to isolate the cranking battery or reserve bank when the engine is not running.
2. Battery isolation diodes are used to provide the same service automatically.

In recent years, these approaches have been supplanted by battery paralleling relays, and less commonly, by series voltage regulators. We need to look at all of these.

Battery selector/isolation switch. A four-position switch (OFF, 1, BOTH, and 2) parallels the various batteries when charging and is used

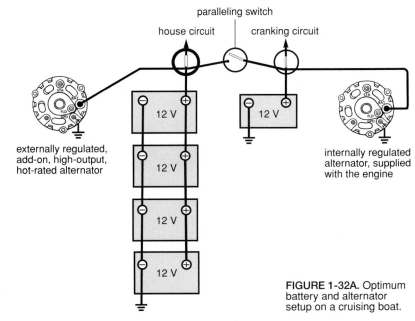

FIGURE 1-32A. Optimum battery and alternator setup on a cruising boat.

FIGURE 1-32B. Twin alternator installation.

to isolate the cranking or reserve house battery when charging is finished. In a conventional two-house-bank installation, the switch is generally wired as in Figure 1-33A. With a dedicated cranking battery and a single house bank, the wiring will be as in Figure 1-33B. Note that in general, there should not be any loads wired to the battery side of a battery selector/isolation switch, since this will void the switch's isolation function. But in practice, there are almost always a few exceptions to this rule: certain pieces of electronic equipment that need to be hooked directly to a battery to operate properly; automatic bilge pumps, so that the boat can be left with the batteries isolated but the pumps operational; the alternator in certain circumstances (see below and Figure 1-33B); battery-charging devices that are to operate when the boat is unattended; and safety or memory devices that need to be permanently energized (e.g., a propane alarm and stereo memory). All of these must have overcurrent protection—fuses or circuit-breakers—as close to the battery as possible (see Chapter 4).

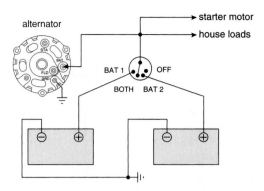

FIGURE 1-33A. Two battery banks alternated in house use with the unused bank kept in reserve for cranking. The battery isolation/changeover switch is paralleled to charge both batteries from a single alternator. Either battery can also be charged independently of the other by switching to the BAT 1 or BAT 2 positions.

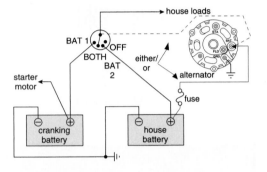

FIGURE 1-33B. Dedicated cranking battery and single house bank. If the alternator is wired to the load side of the switch, either battery can be charged independently, or both together, but there is a risk of open-circuiting the alternator. If the alternator is wired to the house battery, the cranking battery can only be charged by placing the isolation selector switch in the BOTH position, but there is no risk of open-circuiting the alternator.

If the alternator is wired to the load side of a selector/isolation switch (Figure 1-33A—a common installation), either battery can be charged independently, or both together, but the alternator needs special protection. Since its output is fed to the batteries via the switch, if the switch is turned to the OFF position while the engine is running, the alternator will be *open-circuited*, which may destroy its diodes (see Chapter 3).

Some battery switches incorporate a *field disconnect* function, which disables the alternator momentarily before the switch circuit is broken, thus preventing damage. If this is not present, the switch needs to be clearly labeled: "NEVER TURN TO 'OFF' WITH THE ENGINE RUNNING."

Alternator damage can also occur when switching *between* battery banks while the engine is running. Since there must be no interruption of the circuit, the switch needs to be of the *make-before-it-breaks* variety—both batteries are first brought online (the BOTH position) and then one is disconnected. Even so, dirty or corroded points on the switch can occasionally still lead to alternator damage. A *Zap-Stop* or *snubber* (pages 88–89)—a cheap device wired from the alternator output stud to ground, safely shorting out such spikes—will prevent this damage (available from Ample Technology, Xantrex, and others).

If the alternator is wired to the house battery (second option in Figure 1-33B), the cranking battery can only be charged in parallel with the house battery (the BOTH position on the switch).

There is, however, no risk of open-circuiting the alternator.

Charging two battery banks through a battery selector/isolation switch results in a simple and economical installation used by many boatbuilders. However, if two different battery types (for example, a cranking battery and a deep-cycle battery or a wet-cell and a gel-cell) are charged in parallel, one is likely to be chronically overcharged while the other will be chronically undercharged. In addition, this approach is subject to operator error: if the batteries are not paralleled during charging, one will not be charged; if they are left paralleled after charging, they may both be discharged to the point at which it is not possible to crank the engine.

Finally, in many installations the switch, which must be accessible to the user, will be in a panel at some distance from the batteries and the alternator, resulting in long wiring runs. With larger-capacity DC systems, the battery and alternator wiring is going to consist of heavy cables that can prove both expensive and awkward to handle.

There are many cases in which some other approach to battery selection and charging is needed.

Diodes. Split-charging through battery isolation diodes is quite common on larger cruising boats, especially when there are more than two battery banks to be charged (for example, a dedicated engine-start battery in addition to two separate house banks). It is widely used in the charter boat industry. The alternator's output is fed to *diodes*, semiconductors that allow current to flow in one direction but block it in the reverse direction. A diode is assigned to each battery (or battery bank—Figure 1-34). Any number of batteries can then be charged in parallel but are

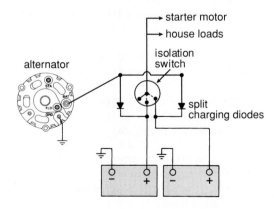

FIGURE 1-34. Split-charging diodes in combination with a battery isolation/changeover switch. Note that even if the isolation/changeover switch is inadvertently turned off while the engine is running, the alternator is not open-circuited.

isolated from one another when in service, so that the cranking battery cannot be accidentally discharged in house service. All batteries will be charged, while there is no way the operator can open-circuit the alternator.

This seems like the ideal setup since there is no user interaction required, and the system is therefore "idiotproof," but there is a severe drawback to diodes that is rarely appreciated. A diode can be compared with a flap valve in a water pipe, closed by a spring. It takes a certain amount of water pressure to open the valve against the spring's pressure. In much the same way, it takes a certain amount of electrical "pressure" (voltage) to open a diode. This is manifested in the form of a voltage drop from one side of the diode to the other. Depending on the type of diode and the current (amperage) flow in relation to the diode's rated current, a diode will typically produce a voltage drop in a charging circuit of from 0.6 to 1.0 volt. I deal with voltage drop in some detail in Chapter 4; all we need to know here is that the difference between a fully charged battery and a flat battery is only 0.8 to 1.0 volt. As a result, differences on the order of a tenth of a volt in voltage regulator settings will have a major effect on charge rates and charge times, *so the 0.6- to 1.0-volt drop of a diode can play havoc with the charging system.*

This is what happens: A typical automotive voltage regulator is mounted inside its alternator. It senses battery voltage for regulation purposes at the output terminal on the alternator, not at the battery. With a diode in the charging circuit, the regulator may be sensing, for example, 14.2 volts, while the voltage at the battery is only 13.6 volts (Figure 1-35). Unless compensated for, such a 0.6-volt drop through a diode will cause the voltage regulator to curtail the alternator's output long before the batteries are fully charged, prolonging charging times unnecessarily and resulting in chronically undercharged batteries that will die prematurely from sulfation—a major cause of battery death in marine use.

Since few builders and installers compensate for diode-induced voltage drop (see Chapter 3 for methods of doing this), as often as not, *fitting an isolator to establish an idiotproof method of ensuring there will always be a charged battery for engine starts unwittingly guarantees that none of the batteries on board will be properly charged!* Almost always, boatowners with diodes will be better off if they throw them away and replace them with a paralleling relay (see next section).

Battery paralleling relays. There is a third approach to charging more than one battery bank from a single charging source that I have always liked. It eliminates both the need for user

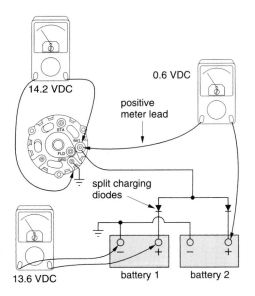

FIGURE 1-35. Measuring voltage drop between an alternator and batteries with split-charging diodes.

0.6 VDC

14.2 VDC

positive meter lead

split charging diodes

13.6 VDC

battery 1   battery 2

interaction and also voltage drop in the charging circuit, thus providing the virtues of isolation diodes (idiotproofing) without the vices (voltage drop). This approach uses a heavy-duty relay or solenoid (an electrically operated switch) wired between the two battery banks.

In early models, the circuit energizing this switch was wired either to the engine ignition switch or to an oil-pressure switch mounted on the engine. With such a switch, anytime the ignition is turned on or the engine is cranked and sufficient oil pressure is built up to close the oil-pressure switch, the battery banks are paralleled for charging. When the engine is shut down, the relay is deenergized, opening the circuit between the battery banks and so isolating them in service. Nowadays, the mechanism for triggering the relay or solenoid is always a voltage-sensing circuit. Whenever this circuit senses a rising voltage on the batteries at either end of the paralleling circuit, it closes.

Whatever the mechanism for triggering the relay or solenoid, as long as the cables between the batteries and the relay are large enough, battery paralleling while charging will be accomplished without significant voltage drop (Figures 1-36A, 1-36B, and 1-36C). The paralleling circuit can be quite short (which keeps down the cable sizes and cost), while a relay with a suitable rating for the task (the maximum rated output of the alternator in most cases) will be cheaper than a battery isolation diode. Note that if one battery bank is heavily discharged and the other is well charged, depending on the relative sizes of the batteries, there may be a high, short-term *inrush* current flow when paralleling first occurs. The paralleling relay and wiring must be rated to handle such a load in order to avoid potentially dangerous overheating.

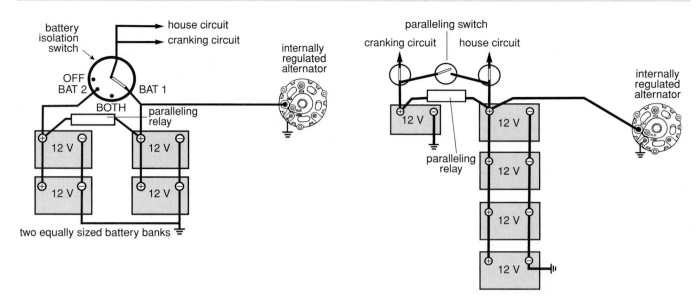

FIGURES 1-36A AND 1-36B. Paralleling relays. All batteries get charged in parallel without voltage drop in the charging circuit, without the need for any user interaction, and without the possibility of accidentally open-circuiting the alternator.

FIGURE 1-36C. Battery paralleling relay. The two cylinders are solenoids (magnetically operated switches) capable of carrying high currents. The circuitry at the top closes the solenoids, paralleling the battery banks, if the voltage rises on either bank. (Courtesy Xantrex)

When relay-based battery paralleling is used on a boat with a dedicated cranking battery and a single house bank, the alternator should be wired to the house batteries, since these will need the most charging (and this keeps the current flow through the paralleling circuit to a minimum). However, if the relay is the type that is triggered by a voltage-sensing circuit, and if the house batteries are well discharged, no charge will go to the cranking battery until the voltage has risen high enough on the house bank to close the relay. If the cranking battery is to be kept charged, it is important to charge the house batteries long enough to reach the trigger point.

Series regulation. In spite of their benefits, all the means described to date for charging battery banks in parallel suffer from a common disadvantage—once battery banks are paralleled, the batteries in both banks will be charged according to the same charging regimen. But different kinds of batteries are commonly used for house service and cranking service (deep-cycle batteries for the house, a cranking battery on the engine). These batteries accept charges in different ways. When charged in parallel, one bank will invariably be somewhat overcharged, while the other will be somewhat undercharged, resulting in a reduced life expectancy for all the batteries. Inequalities are likely to be especially pronounced when a single large house bank is paralleled with a relatively small cranking battery.

The only way to get around this problem is to have a voltage regulator for each battery bank, providing a tailor-made charging regimen for each bank. As mentioned previously, with two alternators this is easy. With one alternator it requires a *series regulator* (available under differ-

ent names from Ample Technology, Balmar, Xantrex, and others). This is a special kind of voltage regulator that is wired between the house bank and the cranking battery (Figures 1-37A and 1-37B). The alternator's output is fed to the house bank, with the voltage regulator set to charge these batteries to maximum advantage, and then anytime the alternator or some other charging source comes online, the series regulator siphons off some of the charge to the cranking battery. The series regulator has its own adjustment points to provide the optimum charging regimen for the cranking battery. Various batteries can be mixed up in house and cranking use without suffering damage, although it should be noted that the cranking battery cannot be charged at a higher voltage than that being applied to the house batteries. This can, in certain circumstances, limit the series regulator's usefulness.

Electronics, windlasses, and bow thrusters. Modern boats are increasingly dependent on electronics not just for peripheral systems, but also for core systems (such as the controls on many engines). Electronic devices are vulnerable to voltage spikes, which can cause electronic failure, and interference (for more on this, see Chapter 8), which can cause false signals and random operation.

In order to partially isolate electronics from spikes and interference on the rest of the boat's circuits, electronic circuits are sometimes powered by their own batteries. This results in at least three battery banks—the cranking battery, house bank, and electronics bank. And a larger boat may have more than one electronics bank. My own (limited) experience suggests that if the single large house bank approach is followed, and this bank and its associated charging devices are properly sized and wired (see Chapter 4), the electronics bank, with its added complexity, is not necessary. If it is used, in most circumstances it is best charged via a voltage-sensitive relay.

A windlass is another device that is often given a dedicated battery up forward. The argument is that because the amperage demands of a windlass (especially a 12-volt windlass) are so high, the cables needed to supply it from a house bank (which is generally well aft) will be too large, cumbersome, and expensive to install (see Chapter 4 for cable sizing procedures), whereas those needed to connect to a nearby battery will be much smaller.

This line of reasoning is flawed since the engine usually will be running when the windlass is in use. As soon as the windlass is turned on, it will start to suck down the voltage on its battery (i.e., take the surface charge off the battery plates). The engine-driven alternator will go to high output, resulting in high charging currents. *The cables to the windlass battery will need to be rated for the maximum output of the alternator*, resulting in cables that are not much smaller than those needed to run the windlass from the house bank in the first place. In spite of these large charging cables, a battery up forward will still see a lower charging voltage than the house batteries because of the long cable runs. (There will be some voltage drop in the cables.) Consequently, the windlass battery will tend to be undercharged, resulting in sulfation and premature death.

There are limits to the argument against a battery up forward. As boats get larger, two things happen: the load imposed by a windlass increases, and the physical distance of the windlass from the house batteries increases. Both factors necessitate larger cables if the windlass is powered from the house bank. Eventually, it does make sense to have a battery up forward, but in such a situation it generally makes more sense to have a 24-volt DC system (see Chapter 2) with a 24-volt windlass powered from the house bank. Doubling the system voltage reduces the required cable sizes to one-quarter (not one-half; more on this later).

Bow thrusters are different from windlasses because of the stupendous loads they can impose (up to 600 amps at both 12 and 24 volts). To run adequate cables to power a bow thruster from the house batteries without power-crippling voltage losses is sometimes impractical. In this case, a battery up forward is needed. It will still need large charging cables, sized for the maximum output of the alternator, and will likely suffer from some measure of chronic undercharging.

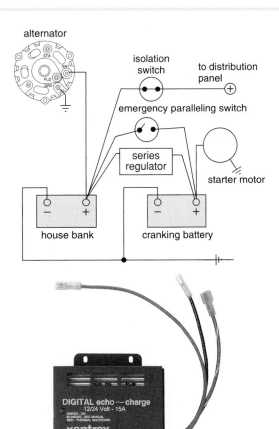

FIGURE 1-37A. Battery charging circuit using a series regulator.

FIGURE 1-37B. A series regulator from Xantrex. *(Courtesy Xantrex)*

Monitoring and Control

To overcome the inherent weaknesses of existing battery technology as applied to many marine applications, we are often forced to drive batteries to their limits, using high rates of charge at elevated voltages to reduce charging times to a minimum.

A variation of just tenths of a volt will make a considerable difference in the charge acceptance rate of a battery. Referring back to the sidebar on page 31 and Figure 1-28, we see that a 0.2 volt increase in the regulated output of an alternator will increase the charge acceptance rate of a battery by close to 20%. At 14.0 volts, a half-charged 100 Ah battery will accept approximately 23 amps of charging current; at 14.2 volts, it will accept approximately 27 amps.

If we are to get the most out of a system without pushing the batteries beyond the limits of their tolerance, we must have very precise monitoring and control of the system. Most off-the-shelf distribution panels fitted to boats incorporate *analog* meters (meters with a swinging arm). These measure voltage and current at various points on the panel, and they are just about adequate for simple circuits and undemanding

Battery Isolation/Selector Switches

FIGURE 1-38. A quality battery switch from Blue Sea Systems. *(Courtesy Blue Sea Systems)*

ABYC and ISO standards require that all battery banks, including cranking batteries (with the exception of those with a capacity of 800 CCA or less), have an isolation switch. The idea is to enable the circuits to be shut down in the event of an emergency, notably a short circuit that is causing an onboard electrical fire. The 800 CCA threshold for cranking batteries (approximately a Group 27 battery, a relatively small battery) has been chosen because the most likely cause of a fire in a cranking circuit is a jammed starter motor, which will discharge up to an 800 CCA battery fast enough for the battery not to have enough residual energy to start a fire. Nevertheless, it is best to include switches in all battery circuits (see Chapter 4). The 800 CCA exclusion is primarily to help manufacturers of smaller boats avoid the cost of a battery switch (Figure 1-38)!

Although the switch is included as an ultimate safety device, almost no switches used as battery selector/isolation switches are designed to be turned on and off under a load. In normal use, they are used to isolate a battery or battery bank only after the loads have been turned off. Such switches are easily damaged if used to make or break high currents—the points become pitted, resistance increases, and in certain instances they can become a fire hazard. *Except in an emergency, a battery isolation/selector switch should not be used to turn off circuits that are powered up. If so used, it may need to be replaced.*

Battery switches are rated for *continuous* use (the switches are tested at the rated current for 1 hour) and *intermittent* use (the switches are tested at the rated current for 5 minutes).

At one time the ABYC required battery isolation switches to have a continuous rating equal to the sum of all the connected loads, which set a standard that was impossible to meet on electrically loaded boats. For example, if an electric windlass is installed, along with a bow thruster and a couple of electric winches,

the sum of the connected loads can easily exceed 1,000 amps at 12 volts.

In practice, the connected loads are not operated all at the same time and, when operated, many are intermittent (e.g., all of the items mentioned above). To accommodate this reality while maintaining system safety, the ABYC standard was rewritten to require a switch to have a continuous rating at least as high as the ampacity of the cable feeding it (for example, if the cable has an ampacity of 300 amps, the switch must have a continuous rating of at least 300 amps). The presumption is that the cable will be overcurrent protected, which will in turn protect the switch (ampacity and overcurrent protection are covered in Chapter 4). If too many loads are turned on, the fuse will blow before the switch melts down. Note that if the continuous rating of the switch is less than the ampacity of the cable, *the overcurrent protection for the cable must be downgraded to protect the switch.*

Another requirement for engine-cranking switches is that the intermittent rating must be at least as high as the maximum cranking current. In recent years, it has been recognized that in many cases this standard is also impossible to meet, since the maximum cranking current on even relatively small diesel engines can be well over 1,000 amps at 12 volts and may be as high as 2,000 amps. However, this current is only sustained for a fraction of a second, and not for the 5 minutes used for intermittent switch ratings.

Blue Sea Systems has developed an Engine Starting Standard based on 10 cranking attempts of 2 seconds each, with a 2-second rest period between them (for a total test time of 2 minutes). The results are cranking ratings that are much higher than intermittent ratings. And it appears that the standard is gaining industry-wide acceptance. If this rating is available to you, use it as a measure of whether any given switch will meet the maximum cranking current specified by an engine manufacturer.

situations. However on heavily loaded boats with complex DC systems (high-output alternators, multistep regulators, wind generators, solar panels, DC-to-AC inverters, etc.), it is more or less mandatory to install a sophisticated *digital* monitoring device (available from Ample Technology, Xantrex, Mastervolt, and others).

At a minimum, we want to measure the amperage flow into and out of the batteries and the battery voltage *at each battery bank* (not the panel, since there may be voltage losses between the battery and panel, resulting in misleading information). In addition, I would recommend a

meter that reads the *gross* alternator output (i.e., before any loads are deducted), especially if you are using a multistep regulator. (You must know the gross alternator output to monitor alternator performance, and in some instances, to avoid overloading and burning out the alternator.)

Ammeters that read up to around 60 amps are wired directly into the relevant circuit, but above this amperage a special *shunt* must be used, with the ammeter wired to the shunt (Figures 1-39A and 1-39B). Where battery amperage measurements are concerned, this shunt is normally wired into the negative cable to the batteries.

With a wired-in shunt, you will need a *continuous* rating of 200 amps even on quite small boats. This is because the entire battery input or output will be flowing through the shunt—in many installations this will include engine-cranking loads and perhaps an electric windlass, bow thruster, and/or electric winches. Boats with larger loads and heavier equipment will need to go to 400 or even 800 amp shunts. Really high-load devices, such as a bow thruster, may still need to be wired to the battery side of the shunt (and thus not measured).

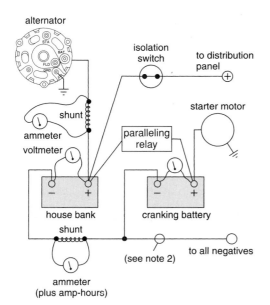

FIGURE 1-39A. Desirable measurement points on a DC system. Notes: 1. One multifunction meter can be used instead of individual meters. 2. With a dedicated cranking battery it is not as important to measure amps in and out, so the ammeter is shown wired to the house batteries. If the batteries are alternated in house use, a second shunt can be placed in the negative cable to the second battery, or else the single shunt can be moved to position 2, where it will measure total current in and out of the batteries.

FIGURE 1-39B. A shunt for measuring high amperages.

Even with accurate amperage and voltage measurements, it still takes a good grasp of the nature of batteries to gain an understanding of the health of the batteries from the readings. An *amp-hour* meter will take the guesswork out of these calculations, providing an instant readout of the state of charge of any battery bank (Figures 1-40A and 1-40B; more in Chapter 3).

Finally, it is worth considering a meter with programmable alarms for such situations as low- or high-battery voltage or low state of charge. These alarms may well warn you of a potentially damaging situation long before it would otherwise be noticed.

In the past, any kind of multifunction monitoring device of the kind being recommended invariably resulted in numerous small-gauge cables being run to the computer and display device (Figures 1-40C and 1-40D). The installation was quite involved and time consuming. At time of writing, Xantrex, Victron, and probably other manufacturers are in the process of greatly simplifying the installation by packaging the computing device with the shunt needed to measure amperage and then using a plug-in data cord to communicate with the display unit (and also various other devices, such as a battery charger and DC-to-AC inverter). The Xantrex unit is called a DC Node; the overall system is a Xanbus. Victron's system is a VENet. The DC Node also accepts battery temperature input and performs a wide range of analytic functions.

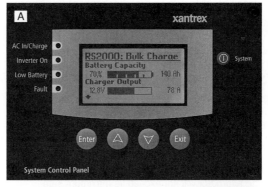

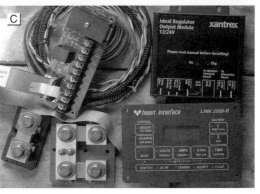

FIGURE 1-40A. A systems monitor with sophisticated networking capable of interfacing with electronic engine control display units and other networked devices on board. *(Courtesy Xantrex)*

FIGURE 1-40B. A basic systems monitor, resembling the fuel gauge in a car.

FIGURE 1-40C. A complete DC monitoring system, including two shunts (one for battery amps, the other for alternator amps), a multistep voltage regulator, and a panel-mounted display and control unit.

FIGURE 1-40D. This is a first-class sophisticated systems monitor from Ample Technology, but it does require quite a bit of wiring. *(Ample Technology)*

TABLE 1-13. Designing Your Boat's DC Electrical System

Question	Answer
1. Do you regularly or even periodically draw power from your battery or batteries, other than to start the engine, when you aren't charging them (i.e., when the engine isn't running)? Note: Do not consider auxiliary charging devices such as solar panels and wind generators in your answer since their output is not wholly predictable, and your system should be able to function adequately without them.	If your answer is No, one or more automotive (cranking) batteries will suffice. Go to Question 8, then Question 10. If your answer is Yes (the great majority of cases), you need deep-cycle batteries. Go to Question 2.
2. Does your boat have an engine?	If No, go to Questions 3 through 6, then study Chapter 6 to ascertain how you can provide sufficient charging capability for your battery bank. If Yes, go to Question 3.
3. How long (in days or in a fraction of a day) between charging intervals? (See page 17. Note that engine or DC generator running time must be long enough during each charging cycle to bring the batteries to a reasonable state of charge. Variables include degree of discharge and voltage regulator setting. See discussion of voltage regulation.)	_____ day(s)
4. What is your boat's total DC electrical demand per day? (See Tables 1-3 and 1-4.)	_____ amp-hours
5. What is the anticipated battery drain between charges? (Multiply Answer 3 by Answer 4.)	_____ amp-hours
6. What is the necessary battery capacity? (Multiply Answer 5 by at least 2½, and preferably by 4.)	_____ amp-hours
7. Will you carry a separate automotive (cranking) battery for engine starts, or will you have two banks of deep-cycle batteries to be alternated for house use and engine starts? Put a checkmark next to your choice.	_____ Option #1 Cranking battery (go to Question 8, then Question 10). _____ Option #2 Second deep-cycle battery bank (proceed with Question 8).
8. How many cold cranking amps does your engine need to start in the coldest weather you can imagine (see page 13)?	_____ amps
9. If you intend to use your deep-cycle banks for engine starting, does their capacity exceed the foreseen demand in Answer 8? Note: If you plan to install two deep-cycle battery banks, each alone should have the necessary capacity for engine starts. In practice, the capacity computed in Answer 6 is almost certain to suffice. Banks can be paralleled for difficult starts.	_____ yes _____ no
10. What is your maximum required alternator output? Note: If your answer to Question 1 was Yes, the output should be one-third the capacity of the house batteries plus the additional load imposed by the boat's operating systems during charging (see Tables 1-3 and 1-4). This may include refrigeration and other large loads that are turned on only when the engine is running. If your answer to Question 1 was No, maximum alternator output should equal the boat's load while the engine is running plus a 33% margin to prevent alternator overheating.	_____ amps
11. What should your alternator pulley ratio be? Note: This is the ratio of the engine output-pulley diameter to the alternator drive-pulley diameter. Adjust the ratio to achieve the output called for in Answer 10 at the minimum projected engine-running speed. Make sure the alternator will not exceed its maximum safe operating speed (usually 10,000 rpm) at maximum engine rpm. See pages 24–25.	_____ : _____
12. What voltage regulator setting should you maintain? If your answer to Question 1 was No, an automotive regulator setting of 13.8 to 14.0 volts will be acceptable. If your answer to Question 1 was Yes, automotive regulators are inappropriate. See the discussion on pages 27–35.	_____ volts
13. Through your answers to the preceding questions you have designed a sensible DC system for your boat. However, you may need to significantly modify this system as you take into account the effects of power inputs from other sources, such as DC-to-AC inverters, wind and water generators, solar panels, and diesel generators. These are the subjects of Chapters 6 and 7.	

1. Differentiate cranking and cycling applications and buy the appropriate batteries.

2. Size a dedicated cranking battery according to the CCA requirement of the engine it is to crank.

3. Size a house battery bank so that its capacity is three to four times the maximum likely amp-hour drain between major recharges. Auxiliary charging devices, such as solar panels and wind generators, are generally best left out of the equation.

4. Combine all the house batteries into a single bank rather than split them into dual banks. Whatever the arrangement, always have a charged battery in reserve for engine cranking.

5. In a single-alternator installation, replace the existing alternator with one that has a hot-rated output in amps that at normal charging speeds of rotation is equal to the DC loads running plus 25% to 30% of the rated capacity of all the batteries being charged.

6. In a dual-alternator installation, use the alternator that comes with the engine to charge the cranking battery and add another alternator as in #5.

7. Ensure that add-on alternators are externally regulated with an adjustable multistep regulator that has temperature compensation based on temperature sensing *at the batteries*.

8. When charging batteries in parallel, use batteries of the same make, type, and age.

9. Locate all batteries in a bank in the same physical space, at the same ambient temperature.

10. Know that the optimum system has twin alternators independently charging an isolated cranking battery and a single large house bank.

11. Use precise instrumentation for effective monitoring and control.

Putting the Pieces Together

To summarize, with the equipment available to boatowners today, it makes sense to wire all the house batteries into a single large bank, with a separate cranking battery reserved solely for engine starts. In the ideal setup, a high-output alternator controlled by a multistep regulator will supplement (rather than replace) the original engine alternator. The high-output alternator will charge the house batteries and the engine alternator the cranking battery, with both alternators regulated to provide the most beneficial charging regime for their respective batteries. An amp-hour meter will continuously monitor the battery state of charge.

Where only a single alternator is available for charging both the house and cranking batteries, use a series regulator if different types of batteries are used for these two functions, or a *paralleling relay* where the same types of batteries are used for both house and cranking service.

Summary: A Balanced System

The description in this chapter of what is needed to establish a balanced DC system on a boat contrasts with the woeful inadequacy of the electrical systems on most boats. Problems start on the production line—boatbuilders are constantly pressured to keep costs down. Good-quality deep-cycle batteries, high-output alternators with multistep voltage regulators, and accurate monitoring devices are expensive and rarely fitted. In addition, much commonly used electrical equipment is regarded as "extra." Builders frequently install batteries, an alternator, and wiring circuits barely adequate to handle the factory-installed items, while additional equipment rapidly overwhelms the system. The net result is a DC system inherently prone to failure.

Analyzing the DC system, and setting the DC house in order, should be one of the first priorities when taking delivery of any boat, whether it has come straight out of the showroom or is a 20-year veteran of several circumnavigations!

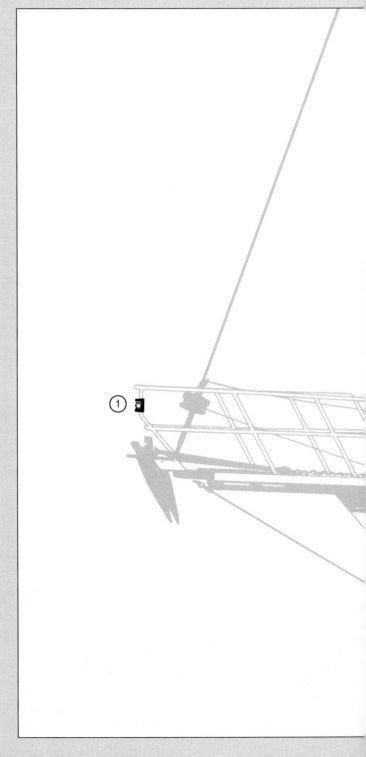

CHAPTER 2

FIGURE 2-1. Just about any modern boat over 30 feet long is loaded down with high-energy consumers. *(Jim Sollers)*

(1) navigation lights
(2) electric windlass
(3) TV in forward stateroom
(4) fluorescent cabin lighting (throughout)
(5) incandescent cabin lighting (throughout)
(6) extension speakers for CD player in all cabins
(7) performance instruments
(8) bow thruster
(9) VCR or DVD player
(10) 110 V outlets (throughout)
(11) CD changer in saloon
(12) TV in saloon
(13) coffeemaker
(14) food processor
(15) microwave
(16) 12 V radio
(17) watermaker
(18) ice maker
(19) cockpit instruments
(20) power tools
(21) washer-dryer
(22) autopilot
(23) nav station
(24) trash compactor
(25) freezer
(26) double refrigerator
(27) radar antenna

Electrical Systems for Energy-Intensive Boats

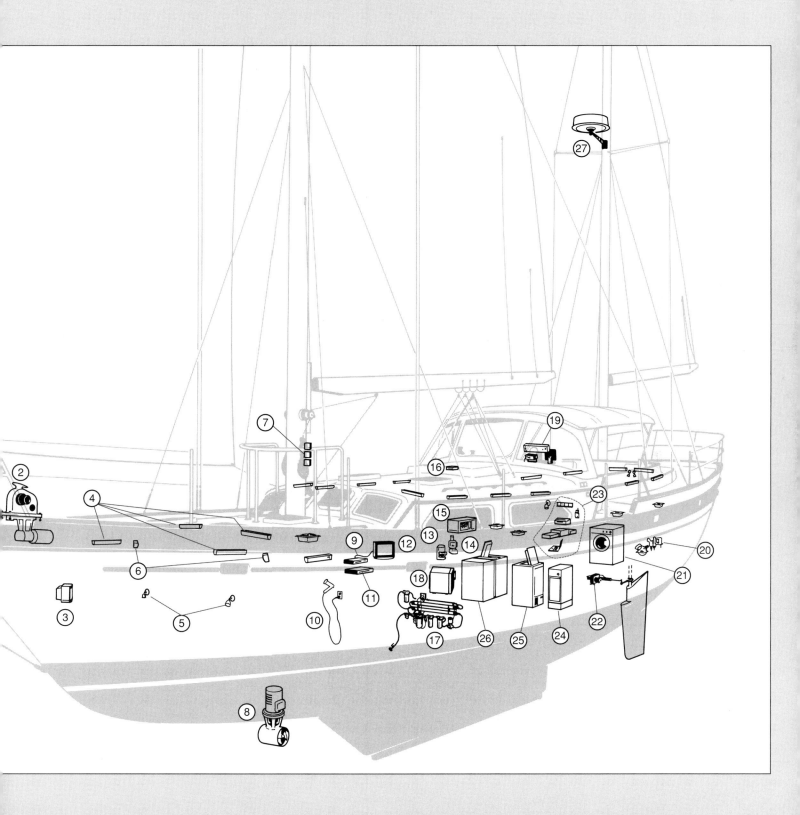

The design processes and parameters laid out in Chapter 1 will enable you to calculate and accommodate the DC needs and energy systems of most cruising boats (power and sail) up to 40 feet long, and many above this length. If this fits your needs, you can skip this chapter. But when your daily energy needs consistently top 200 Ah at 12 volts or 100 Ah at 24 volts (2.5 kilowatt hours [kWh]; refer back to Table 1-4 to see how to calculate energy needs), you will find it difficult to keep up with the load without excessive main engine use for battery charging. Other energy sources (such as an AC or DC generator) and strategies need to be brought into play. In this chapter, I look at a variety of options. Detailed maintenance and troubleshooting information for the specified pieces of equipment are given in later chapters.

Any additional energy sources will impact the way in which a DC system is used and therefore affect its design parameters. This can get quite complicated, but at the end of the day, *the key to it all remains the same—calculating the DC load between charges* (Table 1-4). Once the load is determined, the design approach described in Chapter 1 kicks in.

On boats where the energy demand of one or more individual pieces of equipment is high, higher voltages offer significant benefits. Boats with 24-volt systems are now commonplace in Europe and becoming more common in the United States. The second part of this chapter looks at dual-voltage (12/24-volt) DC systems.

Finally, considerable experimentation has been taking place for many years with much higher DC voltages (120 volts and up), creating a realistic opportunity for electric propulsion of boats to move into the mainstream. I round out the chapter with a look at developments in this field.

Additional Energy Sources

The usual means of augmenting onboard power production has long been an AC generator, run either intermittently or continuously. In recent years, however, several new technologies, showing exciting potential, have supplemented or replaced AC generators. These technologies include DC-to-AC inverters that can be *stacked* to increase their capacity, inverters with a *cogeneration* capability, DC generators, and automatic start/stop functions for AC and DC generators. We'll look at each of these in turn.

AC Generators

Some boatowners run an AC generator much or all of the time, making it possible to meet the boat's full DC load, via a battery charger, on a near-continuous basis. As a result, the demand on the house batteries is minimal.

More frequently, however, boatowners use an AC generator for limited periods of time, such as for cooking if the boat has an electric stove. When the generator is running, it can be used to power a battery charger that is wired to the house batteries, and/or the alternator on the generator engine can provide some charge for the DC system. Note, however, that typically a battery charger powered by a small generator does not work at its rated output (see Chapter 6 for more on battery chargers), and the alternator on a generator engine is relatively small. The net charge is generally less than anticipated.

The alternator is normally wired to the generator's cranking battery. If the boat's house batteries are to see any of the charging current, a paralleling switch or relay will need to be installed between the generator battery and the house bank. It often pays to upgrade the alternator on the generator to a high-output model, but take care not to overload a small generator engine. If you do decide to install a high-output alternator, I recommend wiring the generator's starter motor to the boat's engine-cranking battery (i.e., eliminate the separate battery for the generator) and wiring the high-output alternator directly to the house battery bank (Figures 2-2A and 2-2B).

Regardless of how an AC generator is run, you will have significant problems and inefficiencies. This is because much AC equipment (notably, anything with an electric motor) has a *start-up* or *surge load* (inrush current) that is several times higher than the running load, in many instances as much as six times higher. If an AC generator is not to bog down, it must be rated for the maximum AC surge (start-up) load. This results in a generator that is *grossly* oversized for the running load, and thus is larger, heavier, and costlier than needed most of the time. The other problem with an AC generator is that regardless of the load, it always has to be run at its full rated speed (this is explained in Chapter 7). The net result is that almost all AC generators run underloaded almost all of the time, which is often damaging, is generally inefficient, and always increases maintenance costs and exhaust pollutants, including carbon monoxide (see pages 684–91).

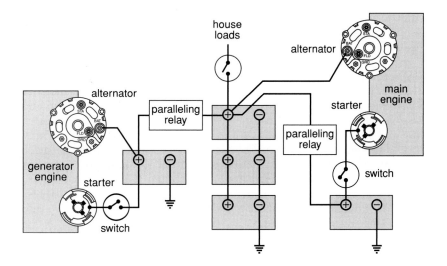

FIGURE 2-2A. A typical generator installation with its own cranking battery, and its alternator wired to this battery. A paralleling relay has been added so that whenever either the generator or the boat's main engine are running, all batteries get charged.

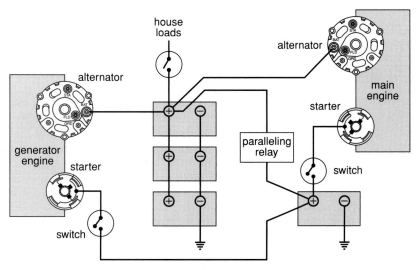

FIGURE 2-2B. A high-output alternator on the generator engine wired to the house batteries. The generator is cranked from the engine-starting battery.

Many boats with an auxiliary AC generator would be better served by a different approach to meeting onboard energy needs.

DC-to-AC Inverters

It is now common practice to install a DC-to-AC inverter either in place of or in combination with an intermittently run AC generator. In the former case, quite astonishing loads may be unwittingly placed on the DC system. These *must* be taken into account when you do your load calculations for the DC system (see Chapter 6 for more on inverters, including additional load calculation tables).

For a boat with heavy electrical demands, it makes more sense to have a hybrid system in which a DC-to-AC inverter powers low-level AC loads for much of the day, while AC generator run time and battery charging occurs in the high-load hours (Figure 2-3; for more on this, see Chapter 6). Still, the cumulative AC load

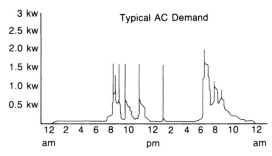

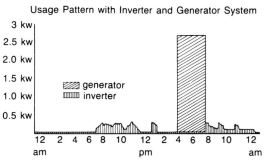

FIGURE 2-3. Patterns of AC use on board. **Top:** Uncontrolled use, requiring the generator to be operated (and under-utilized) 24 hours a day. Note the heavier usage at mealtimes and when AC-powered entertainment equipment is used. **Bottom:** Controlled use, concentrating the use of high-load AC equipment into a limited period of generator operation and running the AC system from a DC-to-AC inverter for the rest of the day. *(Heart Interface)*

transferred to the DC system can be exceedingly high and must be taken into account when you do the load calculation exercise for the DC system.

A hybrid system can partially resolve the primary inefficiency of an AC generator—i.e., the incongruity between its size and running load—by loading the generator as much as possible when it is in use and avoiding its use when AC loads are light. But the generator must still be sized for the surge (start-up) load rather than the running load. To get around this, we need to increase the capacity of the DC-to-AC inverter to handle the maximum AC load on the boat—creating what I call an *inverter-based boat.*

The inverter-based boat. DC-to-AC inverters have a high surge capability and are at their most efficient when run well below their full rated capacity. This fits the AC profile on boats rather well. Many inverters can be *cascaded* to boost output. This is much the same as paralleling batteries to increase their amp-hour capacity. For example, two 2,500-watt inverters can be wired together to create a 5,000-watt (5 kW) inverter. There is no theoretical limit to how far this can be taken, although the practical limit is around 5 kW on a 12-volt system and as high as 10 kW on a 24-volt system. (The limits have to do with such things as cable sizes—see Chapter 4—and the load on the batteries.) However, these values are more than enough to meet the maximum AC needs of most midsize boats, transferring the entire AC load to the DC system.

There is no point in transferring the AC load to the DC system if the DC system is unable to keep up with the load—it will soon crash. To prevent this situation, you will need some kind of generating capability, either AC or DC. But note that because the batteries are now picking up the AC surge loads via the inverter, *this generator can be sized for something closer to an average AC load rather than a surge load, resulting in a generator with as little as one-quarter the rated output of the normal AC generator.* This results in considerable price and weight savings. Additionally, with the generator running at much higher average loadings, it runs more efficiently and is less likely to be damaged. Although you can use either an AC or a DC generator, you will find that for most inverter-based installations, a DC generator is, in fact, preferable (see the DC Generators section beginning on page 55).

Typically, the operator starts and stops the generator, which requires careful monitoring of the DC system to determine when to charge the batteries. In recent years, manufacturers have introduced a number of AC and DC generators with automatic stop and start functions (automatic generator start—AGS; for more on AGS and its possible limitations, see below). This functionality takes the operator out of the charging process and enables boaters to use both DC and AC appliances with little thought given to the impact on the boat's energy systems, much as they would at home or on a boat with an AC generator running 24 hours a day. Two notable proponents of this approach are Fischer Panda (www.fischerpanda.com), with its DC-AC Power System (DAPS), and Glacier Bay (www.glacierbay.com), with its Ossa Powerlite family of products.

The inverter-based boat with an AGS has much to offer, but from the DC design perspective it creates a couple of challenges. The first is to determine how much of a load is put on the DC system between battery charges; the second is to ensure that the batteries can absorb the output of the generator.

How much of a load is put on the batteries? Given that the entire AC load is, at least temporarily, being transferred to the DC system via the inverter, we need to do the same energy-consumption calculation for the AC side as we did for the DC side, convert this calculation to amp-hours at the DC system voltage (12 or 24), and add it to the DC load. Let's say we get a total of 480 amp-hours at 12 volts. The average hourly load is 20 amp-hours (480/24). In theory, we can run the boat with a constantly running AC or DC generator that has a 20 amp output. (If we have an AC generator, the 20 amps are supplied via a battery charger; with a DC generator, the amps are output directly to the batteries.) During those times when the DC load exceeds 20 amps, the batteries are discharged, and when the load is less than 20 amps, the batteries are recharged (Figure 2-4A). Our job, then, is to determine the maximum discharge possible and size the batteries appropriately (i.e., with a capacity three to four times this maximum discharge—see Chapter 1). The resulting battery bank may be quite small.

At the other end of the spectrum, we may wish to keep the running time of the generator to a minimum (e.g., once a day), in which case we will look at the total 24-hour load (480 amp-hours), size a battery bank to meet this (1,400 to 1,900 amp-hours), and then size the generator and other components to charge the batteries as fast as is safely possible (Figure 2-4B).

The actual system design is going to fall somewhere between these two extremes. It will be determined by such things as whether the generator will be operated manually or automatically (if manually, it is likely to be used less frequently, resulting in a greater load on the batteries) and the rated output of available generators. At the end of the day, in addition to determining an appropriate generator size, we need to come up with a number that represents the load on the DC system between charges. This will determine the rest of the DC system design (see Chapter 1).

Ensuring the batteries can absorb the output of the generator. To maximize generator efficiency and keep its running time to a minimum, the battery bank must have a charge acceptance rate high enough to keep the generator operating at close to its full rated output, with the caveat that most small generators should not be run continuously at more than 70% of their rated output. Exceeding this level for extended periods of time runs the risk of burning up the generator.

If you run an AC generator, it will directly feed any AC loads that are online (via a *pass-through* mode in the inverter—see Chapter 6). You will need to use battery chargers and batteries with sufficient capacity to absorb the rest of the generator's rated output (many DC-to-AC inverters incorporate the necessary battery-charging capability). In contrast, the entire output of a DC generator will be fed to the batteries (although some of this will be directly absorbed by the inverter to power whatever AC loads are online at the time).

Whatever generator you choose, subtract the AC and DC loads that will be present when the generator is running from 70% of the generator's rated output, and then size the batteries so they will be able to absorb the remaining output. When making this calculation, if the batteries are to be cycled in the 50% to 80% state-of-charge region, assume that the charge acceptance rate will be no more than 25% (wet-cells) to 30% (gel-cells and AGMs) of the rated capacity of the battery bank. If the batteries are to be cycled at a higher state of charge (for example, between 60% and 90% of full charge), the charge acceptance rate will be lower, and the battery bank will need to be commensurately larger to absorb the output of a given generator.

In practice, it is often easier to reverse engineer a system from a given generator output. For example, let's say we have our eye on a DC generator with a rated output of 250 amps at 12 volts; 70% of this is 175 amps. Our typical DC load (including the AC load transferred to the batteries by the inverter) when the generator is running is 40 amps. This leaves 135 amps of charging capability. We assume a 25% charge acceptance rate for the battery bank. The bank will need a minimum capacity of 540 amp-hours (135 × 4) to absorb the generator's output. If we

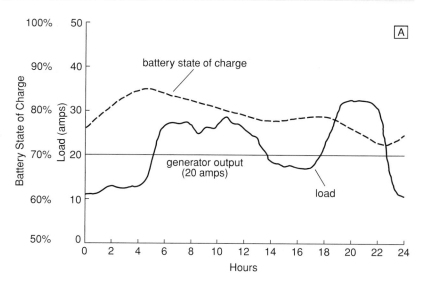

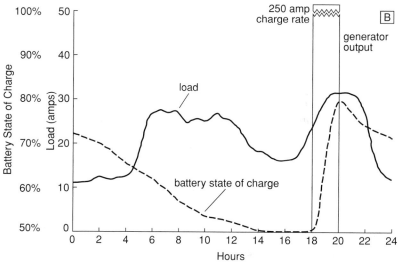

aim to cycle the batteries between 50% and 80% of full charge, this battery bank will be able to handle demands of up to 162 amp-hours (30% of rated capacity) between charges. If the DC load calculation exercise (Chapter 1) calls for a larger battery bank, this is OK; it will absorb more of the generator's output to a higher state of charge, which will increase the average load on the generator and decrease the generator running hours (but may burn up a small generator!). If the DC load calculation calls for a smaller battery bank, and the generator is to run at peak efficiency, the battery bank should not be decreased much below 540 amp-hours. (Of course, you can always use a smaller generator with a smaller battery bank, and then the pieces remain in balance.)

Potential spin-off benefits of an inverter-based boat. You can wire an inverter-based boat so that its shore-power cord is connected to a large

FIGURE 2-4A. A constantly running generator with an output equal to the average load. The batteries will be cycled to some extent.

FIGURE 2-4B. Generator (and battery charging) output concentrated into 2 hours. The batteries will be cycled to a considerable extent.

FIGURE 2-5A. An inverter-based boat plugged into shore power. The shore-power cord only has to keep up with the average load. The inverter (and batteries) will pick up the peak loads.

FIGURE 2-5B. An inverter-based boat with international capability.

FIGURE 2-5C. An inverter-based boat with inverter/charger wired for the primary shore-power region and a battery charger with a lesser charging capability wired for the secondary shore-power region.

bank of battery chargers *and nothing else*. Note, however, that this requires stand-alone battery chargers as opposed to an inverter/charger and may create significant additional expense. The shore-power circuit now terminates at the battery charger(s). The onboard AC circuits create an entirely separate (electrically isolated) AC system that originates at the inverter (and AC generator, if used in place of a DC generator). When plugged into shore power, the boat's AC system will run off the inverters, as at sea, but with the battery chargers recharging the batteries (Figure 2-5A). This has the following benefits:

- The battery chargers only have to keep up with the average load, not the surge load. This

frequently enables the shore-power cord to be downsized over the typical cord, which increases the chances of getting plugged in and finding an adequate shore-power supply (as opposed to being forced to run a generator at dockside because the shore-power supply is inadequate). Note that even when plugged into shore power, the batteries may get cycled (depending on the available shore power, and the output of the battery chargers, in relation to the load on the DC system), and at times a generator with an AGS may kick in to supplement the shore-power cord.

- Marine (but not necessarily shoreside) battery chargers are built around isolation transformers. A shoreside circuit that feeds just a marine battery charger, with the onboard AC circuits isolated from the shoreside circuit, can remove the potential for galvanic corrosion that generally is brought aboard when plugged into shore power (see Chapters 4 and 5). This eliminates the need for, and cost of, a galvanic isolator or isolation transformer. However, to achieve galvanic isolation, the battery charger case must not be grounded to the boat's DC grounding system, which violates ABYC standards. See the important sidebar opposite for more on this subject.

- If the shoreside circuit terminates at the battery charger(s), so do the incoming voltage spikes and surges created by lightning and by problems in the shoreside wiring. Since these spikes and surges do not get onto the boat's circuits, we eliminate a (not unusual) source of damage to electrical and electronic equipment.

- Some modern high-frequency battery chargers will accept input voltages from 90 to 270 volts AC and input frequencies from 45 Hertz (Hz) to 70 Hertz and higher (see Chapter 6). This covers the entire spectrum of AC frequencies used worldwide (see Chapter 4). These battery chargers can be plugged into a 120-volt, 60 Hz supply in the United States or a 240-volt, 50 Hz supply in Europe and still charge the batteries (Figure 2-5B). *All that is needed for a full international shoreside capability is the appropriate shore-power inlets and cords and a selector switch to choose between the inlets* (as opposed to a bulky, heavy, and expensive voltage and frequency converter). This approach to shoreside power is particularly attractive on boats that regularly voyage to international waters. (Note that many European boats use the same shore-power inlet for the standard 16 amp, 250-volt, 50 Hz supply that is used in the United States for a 30 amp, 120-volt, 60 Hz supply, in which case the inlet can serve double duty and no selector switch is needed.)

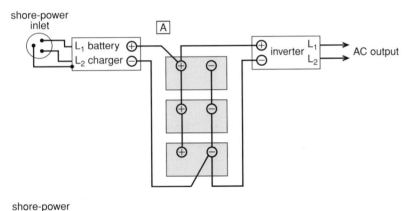

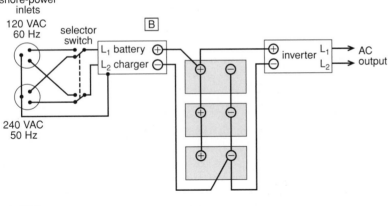

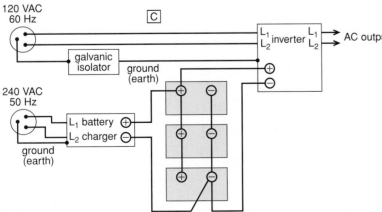

A boat that will spend most of its time in one AC voltage and frequency region (the *primary* region), only occasionally voyaging to a secondary AC voltage and frequency region, can use a modification of this approach to keep down the cost of the necessary battery chargers. This is to wire the shore-power inlet and cord for the primary region to an inverter/charger, thus utilizing the AC pass-through mode of the inverter when plugged into shore power (see Chapter 6) along with the inverter's powerful built-in battery charger (Figure 2-5C). A shore-power inlet for the secondary region is then wired to a smaller battery charger and not connected to the boat's onboard AC circuits. This battery charger will support a limited onboard AC load when connected to shore power overseas. The boat operator will have to manage the AC loads to ensure that the batteries are not wiped out. (If the boat has an AC or DC generator with an AGS, the generator will kick in when necessary to supplement the shore-power cord.) Note that when plugged into shore power in the primary region, such a system will not provide galvanic isolation, which should be installed separately (see Chapter 4).

Cogeneration. Once AC loads get above a certain level, it is not practical to meet them with an inverter-based system, regardless of how it is configured; an AC generator must be run whenever the loads are online. (Note, however, that some of the traditional high-load AC applications that require an AC generator, including air-conditioning, are now being taken over by powerful DC motors, in which case, a DC generator can be used to run the boat—see the section on Fuel Cells, Higher-Voltage DC Boats, and Electric Propulsion later in this chapter.)

In order to maximize efficiencies and minimize maintenance, it is customary on larger yachts to run a relatively small AC generator 24 hours a day to keep up with the long-term light loads. When loads increase, they are either switched to a larger generator or met by paralleling in another generator (i.e., two or more generators are put on the same AC circuits). This

---

Using a Battery Charger as an Isolation Transformer

The ABYC standard for isolation transformers requires a metallic shield between the primary and secondary windings of the transformer (see Chapter 4). The standard specifies that this shield must be capable of carrying the full AC *fault* current in the event of a short circuit. Given this shield, the standard permits the isolation transformer to be wired so that there is no connection between the shoreside AC grounding (green wire) circuit and the boat's DC grounding circuits. This is what blocks galvanic corrosion (covered in detail in Chapter 4).

The problem with using a battery charger as an isolation transformer is that, to my knowledge, none of the isolation transformers inside battery chargers has a shield with the specified short-circuit capability. (Note that it is also the case that the shields on many transformers sold into the marine market as isolation transformers do not have this full fault-current capability.) Consequently, the ABYC's "Battery Chargers" standard requires all battery chargers to be installed with the case connected both to the shoreside AC grounding (green wire) conductor and to the DC grounding circuit. If this connection is made, the battery charger will not function as an isolation transformer. In practice, this connection is often not made. However, I cannot advocate omitting it. All I can do is note the potential application.

One more wrinkle needs to be added to this picture. ISO standards permit the disconnection of the AC grounding wire from the DC grounding circuit (for all the onboard AC circuits) if the incoming AC circuit is protected by a ground fault circuit breaker (GFCB), ground fault circuit interrupter (GFCI), or residual current device (RCD). Chapter 4 explains why disconnecting the two circuits is still not a good idea. However, given the extremely limited AC shore-power circuit that results when only the battery charger is wired to shore power, and given a marine battery charger (i.e., one with an isolation transformer), the inclusion of a GFCB, GFCI, or RCD in the AC supply goes a long way toward mitigating any concerns over breaking the AC-to-DC grounding connection (Figure 2-6) as long as the battery charger is truly a *marine* battery charger (i.e., is built around an isolation transformer). (Once again, for more on this see Chapter 4.)

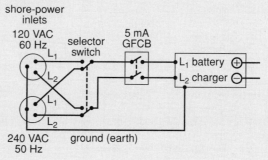

FIGURE 2-6. An international battery charger wired with a GFCB so that the battery charger can also function as an isolation transformer.

paralleling of sources of supply is known as *cogeneration*.

Paralleling two or more AC sources (whether from generators, shore power, or an inverter) requires specialized synchronization equipment to ensure that the AC sources are in phase (a process of aligning the AC output waveforms with one another). Without synchronization, tremendous damage can be done. I once saw the crankshaft on a 2,000 hp engine snapped in half through improper synchronization.

Recent advances in DC-to-AC inverter technology enable some inverters to track the waveform of any other AC power source (either an onboard AC generator or a shore-power cord) and then to switch seamlessly into the same AC circuit, cogenerating in parallel with the existing power source (Figures 2-7A and 2-7B). These inverters are now increasingly used in the home power market.

This form of cogeneration has tremendous potential for an electrically loaded boat that requires an AC generator. In theory, instead of sizing the generator for the surge load, it can once again be sized for something closer to average load. Whenever the load exceeds this level—whether from an ephemeral surge or a sustained high load—the inverter, which has synchronized itself with the generator, kicks in to help. The

AC generator can be sized so that it runs at close to its most efficient output (generally around two-thirds of rated output). Similarly, when plugged into shore power, a DC-to-AC inverter with a cogeneration capability will compensate for low dockside voltage and brownouts caused by the start-up loads of high-load AC equipment on either your boat or someone else's. The key for DC system design is to make some estimate of how much of the AC load will be transferred to the DC system during surge and sustained high-load periods and then design the DC system to handle this load.

Cogeneration raises all kinds of safety issues. In spite of being widespread on large yachts and a well-established technique ashore, it does not comply with current (2005) ABYC standards, which state explicitly that you cannot have two sources of AC power feeding the same circuit. However, these issues are being addressed. It is my belief that cogenerating DC-to-AC inverters will play a major role in future system design on some of the larger boats covered by this book.

Note that because the DC-to-AC inverter in a cogeneration system cannot carry the boat's full AC load (the inverter is meant to buffer an AC generator or the shore-power supply), it is not possible to establish an international capability via suitable battery chargers in the same manner as with the inverter-based boat described above. To get a full international capability, a voltage and frequency converter will be needed on the shore-power connection.

Cogeneration with shore power. As noted, DC-to-AC inverters with a cogeneration capability are becoming increasingly common in the home power market. Although these have tremendous potential on boats, we must address a couple of important safety issues, especially if paralleling with the shore-power cord:

- **Islanding.** A situation in which an inverter synchronizes with the shore-power cord (or a public utility in the case of a home power installation) but then the connection with the public utility is broken. This is potentially lethal. Consider, for example, what happens if the inverter is paralleled with shore power and then someone unplugs the shore-power cord at the dockside receptacle. The inverter will be backfeeding the shore-power cord, causing the protruding pins in the plug on the end of the cord to be live! To deal with this hazard, it is a requirement in the home power market that if islanding occurs, the inverter must break the connection with the public utility within 2 seconds. However, 2 seconds is far too long! The Victron (www.victron.com)

FIGURE 2-7A. An inverter wired to function in the cogeneration mode with an onboard AC generator, but not with the shore-power cord. To also function with the shore-power cord, the inverter needs to be wired into the "downstream" (i.e., boat) side of the selector switch (see Figure 2-7B).

FIGURE 2-7B. An inverter wired to function in the cogeneration mode with both an onboard AC generator and the shore-power cord.

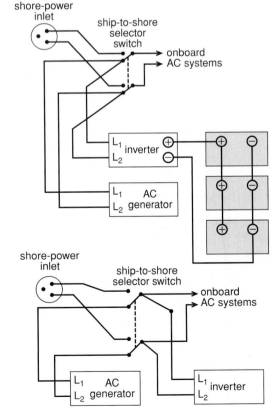

range of cogenerating inverters (Victron was a pioneer in this field) will break the connection within 100 milliseconds.

- **Dealing with the utility company.** In the home power market, cogenerating inverters are used to backfeed the public utility grid when the home power installation has excess solar or wind energy (in effect, the electric meter is run backward). In the United States there are numerous public utility companies. To legally backfeed the grid, a signed agreement is required with the local utility. This, of course, is impractical for a boat that moves from place to place. In other countries, most utility companies would not even dream of letting a private entity backfeed the grid. To deal with this, a somewhat different approach is needed on a boat if the inverter is to be paralleled with a shore-power cord. Victron addresses this issue by monitoring the current flow on the shore-power cord. If this flow drops below 4 amps, the inverter drops out of the cogeneration mode; thus, it can never backfeed the grid.

If you are contemplating cogeneration on a boat, *it is important to only consider inverters built for the marine market.*

Total and peak load analysis. Anytime the DC system is being used to power or buffer the AC system, the load calculations can get quite complicated. It may require a full-boat energy analysis (AC and DC):

1. Calculate the total daily demand (AC + DC) and divide by 24 (hours) to find the average demand. To this number, add a fudge factor for inefficiencies in battery charging, DC-to-AC inverters, etc. Your answer is the minimum continuous shore-power and generator (AC or DC) rating, presuming one or the other will be online 24 hours a day. If generator usage is to be restricted, its minimum continuous rating is the total load + fudge factor divided by the number of hours of generator use.

2. Estimate the maximum drawdown on the DC system that will be created when the combined AC and DC demand exceeds the available supply (generator, battery charger and/or shore power), and/or at times when there is no supply (the generator is shut down or the shore power is disconnected). This is the key number for the continuing DC analysis.

3. Determine the energy usage (AC + DC) during peak hours. Subtract any shore-power or generator (AC or DC) supply from this number to find the maximum (peak) load (AC +

DC) on the DC system. After sizing the DC system, double-check it to ensure it can sustain this load for however long it may last. Note that the amp-hour capacity of the battery bank should be at least four times this peak demand (e.g., if the peak demand is 150 amps, the battery bank should have a minimum capacity of 600 Ah).

In all cases, as far as the DC system is concerned, the intention is to establish *the maximum likely energy consumption between major recharging.* In Chapter 1, 24 hours was selected as the recharge interval on the assumption that battery charging will only take place once a day. If the main engine or a generator that charges the house batteries is run more often, calculate the energy consumption over the heaviest load period (this is often overnight when on passage, especially if the boat has an autopilot, radar, and a high lighting load).

A boat with DC refrigeration (which I recommend for cruising boats—see Chapter 11) requires an additional calculation for the refrigeration load if the boat is left unattended on the hook for a week with no generator run time. Add to this the anchor-light load, which can be greatly reduced by using an LED anchor light with a photoelectric cell to turn it on and off (such as those manufactured by Deep Creek Design— www.firststarled.com, and Orca Green Marine Technology—www.orcagreen.com). Since extended shoreside trips will be infrequent, it is acceptable on these occasions to discharge the batteries down to a 20% state of charge.

From all these numbers, the maximum likely load between charges is used to continue the DC system design as laid out in Chapter 1.

DC Generators

It is frequently more efficient to design the energy systems on a boat around a DC generator than an AC generator. This is because:

- A DC generator is inherently more efficient and can be designed to provide a higher output from a given generator package.

- A DC generator can be run at slower speeds when lightly loaded, which further improves efficiency, lowers maintenance, and extends life expectancy. (A conventional AC generator has to be run at a constant speed regardless of load—see Chapter 7.)

- The batteries will likely require a high rate of charge, which with an AC generator would require a large bank of battery chargers. These are not only expensive but add another layer of inefficiency to the system. (Note, however, that many DC-to-AC inverters incorporate a powerful battery-charging capability that solves this problem.)

DC generators: the small print. All DC generators use some form of an alternator to generate AC power that is then *rectified* to DC. Conventional alternators have brushes on the field circuit (see Chapter 3), but some are brushless. The latter are more or less maintenance free, but the downside is that they make it much harder to achieve the precise voltage regulation required for fast battery charging.

FIGURE 2-8A. A Balmar DC generator using an air-cooled, high-output alternator.

FIGURE 2-8B. A Fischer Panda DC generator using a custom-built, water-cooled alternator.

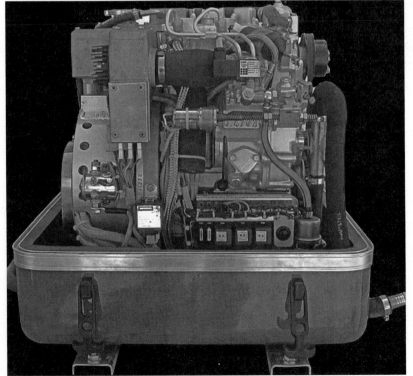

Most DC generators have a manual speed control. When the load is high, the engine should be sped up; when the load is low, the engine should be slowed down. However, some generators have *governors* that adjust the speed automatically according to the load. On the surface, a governor seems a great addition, but in practice it has proved difficult to provide effective governors on the relatively small generators under consideration.

Alternators can be driven via a belt or directly. The latter avoids some maintenance and the energy losses of a belt, but generally it makes the unit less accessible and harder to troubleshoot and repair in the field. Belt-driven units almost always use familiar automotive-style alternators, whereas direct-drive units tend to use custom-built alternators.

Belt-driven alternators are all air cooled, whereas some of the custom-built, direct-drive units are water cooled. Water cooling increases efficiency and output but also significantly increases price and complexity (Figures 2-8A and 2-8B).

Some DC generators (notably those from Fischer Panda and the Ossa Powerlite units from Glacier Bay) come in incredibly compact and well-soundproofed packages. They are easier to fit into a boat and are less intrusive when operating. On the other hand, access is sometimes poor and maintenance becomes a chore. Troubleshooting and repairs are commensurately harder.

In light of these considerations, for DC generators up to about 4 kW of output (250 amps at 12 volts) the best choice for an offshore cruiser is a unit with a traditional alternator. Although this approach is not the most efficient, most compact, lightest, or quietest, it is the most reliable as well as the easiest to work on and repair should a fault develop in an out-of-the-way place. If higher outputs are required (such as for the diesel/electric boat described at the end of this chapter), more sophisticated generators are needed.

Automatic generator start (AGS) devices for DC generators. AGS devices for DC generators vary considerably in their sophistication and capabilities. The simplest are triggered by low battery voltage, have a timed cranking cycle (the starter motor is energized for a set period of time), and shut down the generator either after a timed interval (e.g., 2 hours) or when a preset higher battery voltage is reached. Such an approach has several limitations that do not fit the needs of an inverter-based boat:

- The triggering voltage has to be set low (generally around 11.5 volts on a 12-volt system). If this is not done, the temporary drop in battery voltage that occurs whenever a heavy DC load comes online will cause the generator to start even when the batteries are well charged. But with a low triggering voltage, if the batteries are steadily drained by light loads, they will be pulled down well below 50% state of charge before the generator is cranked, resulting in unnecessary damage to the batteries.

- If the generator is triggered by a high load hitting the DC system and dragging down the voltage on a well-charged battery, it will run for the preset time even though the batteries cannot absorb the full charging output. If, on the other hand, the batteries are drained slowly so that the generator does not kick in until they are almost dead, it will not run long enough to charge them properly.
- If the starter motor is energized for a set time and the engine fires up rapidly, the starter motor will remain engaged and get spun at high speed, which may damage the starter motor (especially if it is the inertia type sometimes found on small generators—see Chapter 7).

The following features are necessary for effective functioning of a DC generator with an AGS on an inverter-based boat:

- The generator should start and stop based on battery state of charge, not voltage.
- The control unit should have additional input sensors that can be used to trigger the stop and start cycles (e.g., when an air-conditioning unit or some other sustained high-load device turns on or off).
- The AGS should measure generator rpm and use this value, not a timer, to terminate the engine cranking cycle. This way, the starter cannot be motored at high speed by the generator.

AGS safety issues. An AGS enables a boat's electrical systems to be used with minimal energy management (as at home), and allows the boat to be left unattended for long periods of time (until the generator fuel runs out) with the fridge and other systems operating. However, there are certain risks, both in terms of safety (e.g., it is essential to disable the start mechanism when anyone is working on the engine) and to the equipment itself (e.g., if a fault develops, it can self-destruct).

What happens, for example, if you close the cooling water intake seacock, forget to disable the generator, and leave the boat? If the generator autostarts, it will melt down the exhaust hose and may start a fire. Or if your boat is unattended, the generator starts, and the exhaust hose comes loose, the generator will pump the boat full of water from its cooling system.

At a minimum, there needs to be an automatic shutdown in the event of low oil pressure or a high temperature. Depending on the control device and the software package, this automatic shutdown may be programmable to include such things as a high exhaust temperature and high bilge water.

Dual-Voltage DC Systems

It is increasingly popular to install high-load, DC-powered devices on boats, such as an electric windlass, a bow thruster, sail reefing devices, and electric winches. Although none of these devices run for more than a few seconds to a minute or so, when they do run, they draw high amperages—up to several hundred amps. Also, they often are located near the ends of the boat, far removed from the batteries. The combination of high amperages over substantial distances tends to produce power-robbing voltage drops in the circuits (see Chapter 4). There are two ways to overcome this: one is to use very large cables; the other is to raise the voltage on the circuit.

When power-hungry circuits are run off a 12-volt system, it is not uncommon to see cables with a diameter the size of your thumb, i.e., 2/0 or 70 mm^2, to as large as 4/0 or 110 mm^2 (cable sizing is covered in Chapter 4). Not only are these cables physically awkward to run, they are also heavy and expensive. Consider a windlass on a 40-foot boat drawing power from a bank of batteries near the aft end of the boat. Altogether there will be up to 100 feet of cable (50 feet in each direction, allowing for detours around lockers and bulkheads). If the cable is 2/0 or 70 mm^2 (not uncommon), it will weigh over 50 pounds and cost (at retail) between \$300 and \$600. Add in a bow thruster, electric winches, sail-handling devices, a DC-to-AC inverter, and a high-output alternator, and you soon have several hundred pounds of weight and a couple of thousand dollars of cable, compounded by the physical difficulties of installing these large cables. Add another 20 to 30 feet of length to your boat, and the weight and cost double. At some point the weight and cost penalties become intolerable—especially if money has been poured into high-tech construction in order to keep the boat's weight down!

Raising the Voltage

Aside from doing without the equipment, the easiest way to reduce the weight and cost associated with its installation is to increase the system voltage. Doubling the voltage to 24 volts results in cables *one-quarter* the size. Given that all the high-current DC electric equipment on boats is readily available in 24 volts, this seems like the obvious thing to do. Unfortunately, there are one or two complications.

First of all, 24-volt equipment typically costs more than the equivalent 12-volt equipment. Automobiles run on 12 volts, and as a result, millions of 12-volt alternators, lightbulbs, fans, and other accessories find their way onto boats each year, holding down the cost. Even when equipment is purpose-built for boats, the fact that most have 12-volt systems leads manufacturers to concentrate on the 12-volt market, frequently making 24-volt equipment a specialty item and therefore more expensive.

Then there is equipment that is just plain hard to find in anything but 12 volts, notably starter motors for engines under 100 hp, glow plugs, and a few electronic items (VHF radios in particular). Even if these were available in 24 volts, should they fail in some out-of-the-way place, they would be almost impossible to replace locally. It is seldom a good idea to fit specialized, hard-to-replace, higher-voltage equipment, especially something as important as a starter motor. That said, 24-volt equipment is more available in Europe than in the United States.

Although much equipment runs cooler and is more reliable at 24 volts (particularly alternators and most electric motors), some items, such as incandescent and halogen lightbulbs, actually benefit from being 12-volt. Because low voltage means relatively high amperages for a given light output, the element in a 12-volt bulb has to be more ruggedly constructed than a lamp with the same light output at a higher voltage. Twelve-volt lamps are therefore better able to tolerate vibration and harsh service conditions.

So, although much DC equipment comes in 24-volt models or, in the case of most electronics, can be run on anything from 11.0 to 30.0 volts or more, and although 24-volt lighting is widely available, it is still difficult to wire an entire boat for 24 volts. Besides, there may be specific reasons for using some 12-volt gear. So you have to make a choice: stick with 12 volts to

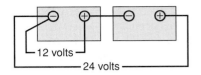

FIGURE 2-9. Tapping a 24-volt battery bank for 12 volts. If done this way, all the batteries will be damaged!

keep things simple, or go to a dual 12/24-volt DC system to take advantage of the lighter cables associated with 24 volts, particularly for high-load equipment. The trade-off is system simplicity against weight. The more critical the weight or the longer the boat, the more likely a dual-voltage system will be the best choice.

Doing things the wrong way. It might seem that all you need to do to get 12/24-volt DC power on a boat is to set up a 24-volt battery bank by wiring two 12-volt batteries in series, then take 24 volts off the ends of the bank and 12 volts off the lower half of the bank. I've heard that in the "old days," when many fishing boats had 32-volt circuits, it was not unusual to count up six cells from the negative battery post and then drive a nail through the top of the battery to establish a 12-volt battery post (Figure 2-9). Maybe this is the origin of the term "tapping" into a battery. In any case, it's a no-no!

If you wire 12-volt equipment to one half of a 24-volt battery bank, the 12-volt equipment will deplete just half the bank whereas 24-volt equipment will deplete the whole bank. The net result is that the half supplying the 12-volt equipment gets run down more than the other half. Recharging the batteries requires a 24-volt alternator or charging device wired across the whole bank, which in turn means that all the charging current flows through both halves of the battery bank. One half is overcharged while the other half is undercharged, shortening the life of both halves. In the process, the half that is being used for 12-volt equipment gets worked harder, which may lead to a rise in its internal temperature. The temperature rise will increase its charge acceptance rate during recharging. In certain circumstances, particularly when heavy loads and deep discharges are combined with fast charging through high-capacity charging devices, this situation can lead to thermal runaway.

Equalizers and Converters

The proper way to set up a 12/24-volt DC system from a 24-volt battery bank is to start with a 24-volt system (including a 24-volt alternator and other charging devices) supplying the high-load equipment—windlass, bow thruster, winches, and sail reefing devices. Then, tap into it for 12 volts for the VHF and any other non-24-volt equipment using either an equalizer or a DC-to-DC converter, sometimes known as a DC power supply (although this term is more commonly associated with devices powered by 120 or 240 volts AC). Either device will ensure that the 12-volt DC load is drawn equally from both halves of the 24-volt battery bank. This way the batteries are kept in an equal state of discharge when in use and recharged equally.

An equalizer and a converter are two variations of the same device, with equalizers being common in the bus market and converters being more usual on boats. Nowadays, both have internal circuitry that utilizes high-frequency switching to convert DC to AC at the input voltage (a nominal 24 volts), a transformer that converts the AC from one voltage to another, and then further circuitry that converts the AC back to DC at the new (output) voltage. In other words, the DC voltage that comes out is different from that which went in. (It's necessary to convert DC to AC and back again because you cannot use a transformer to raise or lower DC voltages; transformers only work with AC. The high-frequency switching uses the same technology found in many DC-to-AC inverters and also in modern battery chargers.) In spite of the similarities between equalizers and converters, there are subtle differences to consider when choosing which to use.

Equalizers.
An equalizer is designed so that it maintains half its input voltage (a nominal 24 volts) at its output voltage (a nominal 12 volts). It is wired both to the 12-volt half of a 24-volt battery bank and also across the full 24 volts (Figure 2-10). The 12-volt loads are wired directly to half of the 24-volt battery bank. Note that the loads are not wired *through* the equalizer. When a 12-volt load is applied, it is initially drawn off the 12-volt half of the battery bank (as outlined above in the Doing Things the Wrong Way section). This drops the voltage on this half of the bank so that it is now below half the total voltage across the 24-volt bank. The equalizer senses the falling voltage and draws off the other half of the battery bank to "recharge" the half under load until the 1:2 voltage ratio between the battery bank as a whole and the half to which the 12-volt loads are wired is restored. This keeps all the batteries in an equal state of discharge/charge. The output voltage of the equalizer fluctuates with its input voltage (the voltage across the 24-volt bank), maintaining the 1:2 ratio. If, for example, the voltage on the 24-volt bank drops to 23 volts, the output voltage will drop to 11.5 volts.

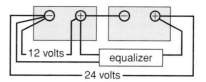

FIGURE 2-10. Basic equalizer installation.

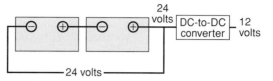

FIGURE 2-11. Basic DC-to-DC converter installation.

Converters.
In contrast to an equalizer, a converter has a fixed output voltage regardless of the input voltage. In the case of a 12/24-volt system, the converter is wired across a 24-volt battery bank and produces a nominal 12 volts at its output (Figure 2-11). The voltage can generally be adjusted from as low as 12.6 volts to as high as 14.5 volts, depending on the application. This output voltage will not change even if the 24-volt battery bank starts to die and its voltage begins to tail off until some cutoff threshold is reached on the input voltage, at which point the converter shuts down. Remember that with an equalizer, the 12-volt loads are wired directly to half of the 24-volt battery bank (not to the equalizer), so the loads do not pass through the equalizer. With a converter, the loads are wired to the output of the converter itself, not to the batteries. That is, the converter is in series with the load; the full-load current passes through the converter.

In addition to stepping down DC voltage, converters can be used to step it up. A boat's 12-volt system, for example, could be stepped up to 24 volts for specific applications. But given that the main purpose of a 24-volt system is to power high-load equipment, it makes little sense to use a converter to power heavy-duty loads, as opposed to using it to power lighter, 12-volt loads as described above.

Equalizer and converter pros and cons.
Equalizers and converters have different benefits and disadvantages, making them suitable for different applications.

The biggest drawback of an equalizer is that, because the 12-volt circuits are tapped directly off the battery bank, they all have to be run back to the batteries. With a converter, a boat can be wired for 24 volts, and then the 24-volt circuits can be tapped at any point to power specific 12-volt loads through the converter. This arrangement can substantially reduce the overall amount of cable in a boat, which is often the primary purpose of installing an equalizer or converter. If the 12-volt loads are light, as they frequently are, a small and relatively inexpensive converter can be used with very short cable runs.

Problems may occur if the 12-volt load is heavy. Because the full 12-volt load normally goes through a converter (see below for possible exceptions), the converter has to be rated large enough to carry the maximum anticipated load, including any surge current when equipment first kicks on—which may be up to several times the running load. For heavy-draw items, the converter will need to be large and expensive. On the other hand, with an equalizer the 12-volt loads are wired directly to the battery, which can supply up to its full output; the battery will handle any surge loads. The equalizer simply "charges" the battery in use from the one not in use at a rate up to the rated output of the equalizer. If the equalizer is unable to keep up with the rate at which the 12-volt battery is being pulled down by the 12-volt load, it catches up after the load is turned off, bringing the two halves of the 24-volt battery bank back into equilibrium. Consequently, it is possible to use an equalizer that is smaller and cheaper than its equivalent converter.

However, aside from the extra cabling, there is a significant downside in using an equalizer in this fashion—the 12-volt half of the battery bank gets cycled more than the 24-volt half, which will shorten the life not only of the 12-volt half but of the bank as a whole. Given the cost of modern batteries, this may impose a significant financial overhead on the system. (Some DC system monitors will track the 12- and 24-volt battery voltages and the battery balance and will warn of faults. Even so, battery life is likely to be shorter than when using a converter.)

Other converter advantages. In addition to increasing battery life expectancy, a converter offers certain other benefits. Because it is in series with the load, it acts as a filter, taking out voltage transients and spikes and producing a clean, pure DC waveform with no "ripple" or electrical interference. This can be particularly beneficial with sensitive electronics (Figure 2-12). (Note, though, that the high-frequency switching in equalizers and converters can itself be a source of radio interference—see Chapter 8 for more on this.) The stable output voltage from a converter has other advantages. To take one example, incandescent and halogen lightbulbs, which are rated at 12.6 volts, are sensitive to any voltage above this rating, such as routinely occurs when the battery is charging. At higher voltages, their life expectancy is dramatically shortened—at 13.6 volts to 30% of rated life; at 14.4 volts to less than 20%. Particularly where halogens are concerned, the higher voltages that occur during battery charging can prove expensive in terms of lamp life. A converter keeps these voltages from reaching the equipment wired to it. On a large yacht, the extension in lamp life can more than pay for the converter (Figure 2-13).

A converter can also be constructed with its own small internal battery so that in the event of a short-term drop in system voltage—say, when cranking a large diesel engine or upon the loss of the principal battery—the internal battery will keep supplying energy to the load. It is essentially an uninterrupted power supply (UPS).

FIGURE 2-12. A DC-to-DC converter supplying a stable, filtered voltage to sensitive equipment. *(Analytic Systems)*

FIGURE 2-13. There are a dozen halogen lights in the main saloon of this Malo 45 and probably as many as thirty in the boat as a whole. (This is a sister ship to our new boat; in ours, we replaced all the halogens with fluorescents—see Chapter 7.)

This is particularly important with key safety-related equipment and is, in fact, a legal requirement for certain pieces of equipment, such as radios, on commercial vessels.

In situations where a higher-capacity UPS is needed or where equipment requires a high start-up current, a converter can be wired to an independent 12-volt battery to act as a trickle charger, with the loads wired directly to the battery, similar to an equalizer installation (Figure 2-14). But in this case, the filtering effect of the converter is lost along with its stable DC voltage. In effect, the converter becomes a 24-to-12-volt battery charger. Ideally, it will have certain internal modifications to prevent battery discharge through the converter, ensure an appropriate charging regimen for the battery, and eliminate the small "standby" drain that most converters incur when not in use. Some manufacturers make these modifications, with the devices marketed as 24-to-12-volt chargers.

Multiple converters provide a degree of redundancy: if one goes down, it will only take out the circuits attached to it. An equalizer, on the other hand, has the ultimate "limp-home" capability in that if it fails, it does not directly affect either the 12- or 24-volt circuits. It simply results

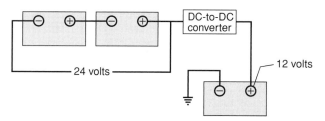

FIGURE 2-14. A DC-to-DC converter used in conjunction with a separate battery to produce an uninterrupted power supply (UPS).

in an increasing imbalance between the two halves of the 24-volt battery bank because the extra drain on the 12-volt half will not get replaced; the negative consequences will worsen the longer the failure is left unaddressed. (We are, in effect, back to Doing Things the Wrong Way.) Unfortunately, the failure may not be detected until the battery bank is ruined, although some equalizer manufacturers do make remote monitoring panels that will warn of an equalizer failure. In contrast, a converter failure will be immediately apparent since the equipment it powers will stop working.

Finally, it's worth noting that converters (but not equalizers) can be built so that the DC output is isolated from the DC input, resulting in galvanic isolation of the 12-volt circuits, just as

Sizing Equalizers and Converters

The general rule of thumb for an equalizer is that it should be no smaller than 120% of the average load, with 150% being a better target. The problem on a boat is defining "average load." The simplest solution is to perform an energy audit: Calculate the total daily 12-volt amp-hour drain on the batteries, divide that number by 24 to get an average hourly drain (in amp-hours), and then size the equalizer so that its amp rating is 150% of that number. For example, take a boat with a 24-hour 12-volt load of 120 amp-hours. The hourly drain is 120/24 = 5 amp-hours. The equalizer should have a minimum rating of 5 x 1.5 = 7.5 amps.

Using this approach, if the daily load is unevenly distributed, the 12-volt half of the 24-volt battery bank to which the 12-volt loads are attached is likely to get unequally discharged during higher-load periods, with balance being restored during lower-load periods. In other words, the 12-volt half of the battery bank will get regularly cycled to some extent, which will shorten the life of all the batteries. A more conservative approach to equalizer sizing would be to determine the average load during higher-load periods and size the equalizer at 150% of this.

What if the 12-volt battery is periodically subjected to sustained higher loads? A good example would be the continuous use of an autopilot and radar on a sailboat on a long passage. These, together with other 12-volt loads such as navigation and cabin lights and refrigeration, can easily put a 250 amp-hour daily drain on some systems. The equalizer should then be sized for 150% of this higher average load: (250/24) x 1.5 = 15.6 amps. More conservatively still, it can be sized for 150% of the average load during the highest-load part of higher-load days or nights. On a sailboat, that would usually be early evening on passage. The total load may be as high as 20 to 30 amps for an hour or so, leading to an equalizer rating of 30 to 45 amps. The more conservative the equalizer sizing, the less the cycling on the 12-volt battery, and the longer the life of all the batteries.

Converter sizing is different. Because the converter supplies the 12-volt DC load, the converter has to be sized to handle the larger of the maximum surge load or the maximum sustained load (adding together all loads that may be on simultaneously) to which it may be subjected. This may well lead to a high current rating, driving up the cost of the equipment.

with an isolation transformer on the AC system. In certain circumstances, this may be a useful corrosion-fighting tool; for example, in radio installations on metal boats, where the radio ground may need to be connected to the hull but kept separate from the ship's ground. The price that has to be paid is a near doubling in the converter cost, although this may look cheap compared to the cost of any corrosion.

Equalizer and converter circuits. Many sailboats have a relatively small auxiliary diesel with a 12-volt starter powered by a dedicated 12-volt cranking battery. There is then a 12/24-volt house battery bank, with an equalizer used to keep the two halves of the 24-volt bank in balance or a converter used to supply the 12-volt loads. The primary charging device is a 24-volt alternator. Two questions arise: how do we charge the cranking battery, and how can we use the 24-volt house battery bank for cranking the engine should the cranking battery fail?

By far the best setup is to incorporate two alternators, generally with a factory-supplied, 12-volt alternator wired to the cranking battery and an add-on 24-volt alternator wired to the house bank. This greatly simplifies wiring and circuitry and builds in an excellent measure of redundancy. If there is only a single alternator it will be a 24-volt alternator wired to the house bank. Depending on whether the boat has an equalizer or converter to supply the house 12-volt loads, this can be wired as follows:

Equalizer circuits. A voltage-sensitive paralleling relay (see Chapter 1) is wired between the positive on the cranking battery and the positive on the 12-volt half of the 24-volt bank. Now, whenever the 24-volt bank is being charged, the equalizer will output half the input voltage from the alternator, raising the voltage on the 12-volt half of the 24-volt bank (Figure 2-15A). This will cause the voltage-sensitive relay to close, paralleling in the cranking battery so that it gets charged. As far as the equalizer is concerned, the cranking battery becomes just another 12-volt load. When the alternator goes off-line, the falling voltage on the circuit will cause the voltage-sensitive relay to open, isolating the cranking battery.

Converter circuits. A converter modified to serve as a battery charger (see above) can be wired between the 24-volt battery bank and the cranking battery to provide a trickle charge to the cranking battery (Figure 2-15B). But in the event the cranking battery is heavily discharged—say, after repeated unsuccessful cranking attempts—it will take a long time to recharge. It might be better to also wire the batteries as above, with a battery combiner and an equalizer, resulting in a hybrid equalizer/converter system (Figure 2-15C).

Emergency cranking. What happens if a 12-volt cranking battery fails and the 24-volt house batteries are needed to crank the engine? With an equalizer, a paralleling circuit with an isolation switch can be wired between the cranking battery and the 12-volt half of the 24-volt battery bank. Some battery paralleling relays include such a paralleling switch, so the additional circuit shown in Figures 2-15A and 2-15C is not required. Closing the switch feeds the starter motor from the 12-volt half of the 24-volt battery bank, with the equalizer balancing out the 24-volt battery bank over time.

With a converter or 24-to-12-volt battery charger (no additional equalizer), the converter/battery charger is unlikely to be rated for cranking current; its output cannot be fed to the starter motor. The same paralleling circuit may be used as with an equalizer (wired directly from the cranking battery to half of the 24-volt battery bank and labeled "emergency cranking circuit"), but in this case the two halves of the 24-volt battery bank will not get properly equalized following cranking and will suffer some measure of damage as a result. Given that emergency cranking from the house bank is likely to be a rare occurrence, however, not much damage will be done. Note that in the absence of a paralleling circuit, a jumper cable can be taken from the cranking battery positive to the 12-volt half of the 24-volt battery bank.

Installation issues. An equalizer has to be installed close to its battery bank; a converter is installed wherever 12 volts are tapped off a 24-volt circuit. Both equalizers and converters are sophisticated electronic devices that need to be mounted in a dry location. Both are between 85% and 95% efficient; the other 5% to 15% of the input energy is dissipated as heat. Be sure to factor this energy loss into your boat's total energy budget, along with the "standby" drain of an equalizer or converter, which can vary from as little as 2.5 mA to as much as 300 mA. The higher the temperature of the unit, the shorter the life of some of its electronic components. To keep down the temperature, you need to mount the unit in a cool environment with a good airflow over it. It is best mounted vertically on a vertical bulkhead to maximize airflow over the cooling fins.

Mostly, the 12-volt requirements on a 24-volt boat are quite modest, but sometimes an equalizer or converter with an unusually high current rating is needed. Units with an output of up to 100 amps are available. Note that if the unit is 90% efficient and is running at full output, it will generate $10 \times 12 = 120$ watts of heat, which is quite a bit of heat. Above 100 amps, higher outputs can be achieved by paralleling two or more units.

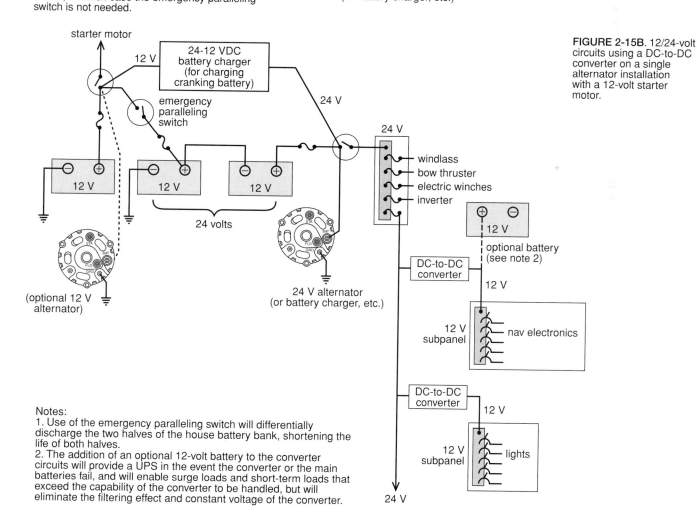

FIGURE 2-15A. 12/24-volt circuits using an equalizer on a single alternator installation with a 12-volt starter motor.

12 V distribution panel

- nav electronics
- lights
- fans
- etc.
- etc.

starter motor

12 V isolation switch

*emergency paralleling switch

cranking switch

paralleling relay

equalizer

24 V isolation switch

24 V

12 V

12 V

12 V

12 V

24 volts

(optional 12 V alternator)

- windlass
- bow thruster
- electric winches
- inverter

24 V alternator (or battery charger, etc.)

*Note: Some paralleling relays have a manual override switch, in which case the emergency paralleling switch is not needed.

FIGURE 2-15B. 12/24-volt circuits using a DC-to-DC converter on a single alternator installation with a 12-volt starter motor.

starter motor

24-12 VDC battery charger (for charging cranking battery)

12 V

emergency paralleling switch

24 V

12 V

12 V

12 V

24 volts

(optional 12 V alternator)

24 V alternator (or battery charger, etc.)

24 V

- windlass
- bow thruster
- electric winches
- inverter

12 V

optional battery (see note 2)

DC-to-DC converter

12 V

12 V subpanel

nav electronics

DC-to-DC converter

12 V

12 V subpanel

lights

24 V

Notes:
1. Use of the emergency paralleling switch will differentially discharge the two halves of the house battery bank, shortening the life of both halves.
2. The addition of an optional 12-volt battery to the converter circuits will provide a UPS in the event the converter or the main batteries fail, and will enable surge loads and short-term loads that exceed the capability of the converter to be handled, but will eliminate the filtering effect and constant voltage of the converter.

FIGURE 2-15C. 12/24-volt circuits using an equalizer and DC-to-DC converters (a hybrid system) on a single alternator installation with a 12-volt starter motor.

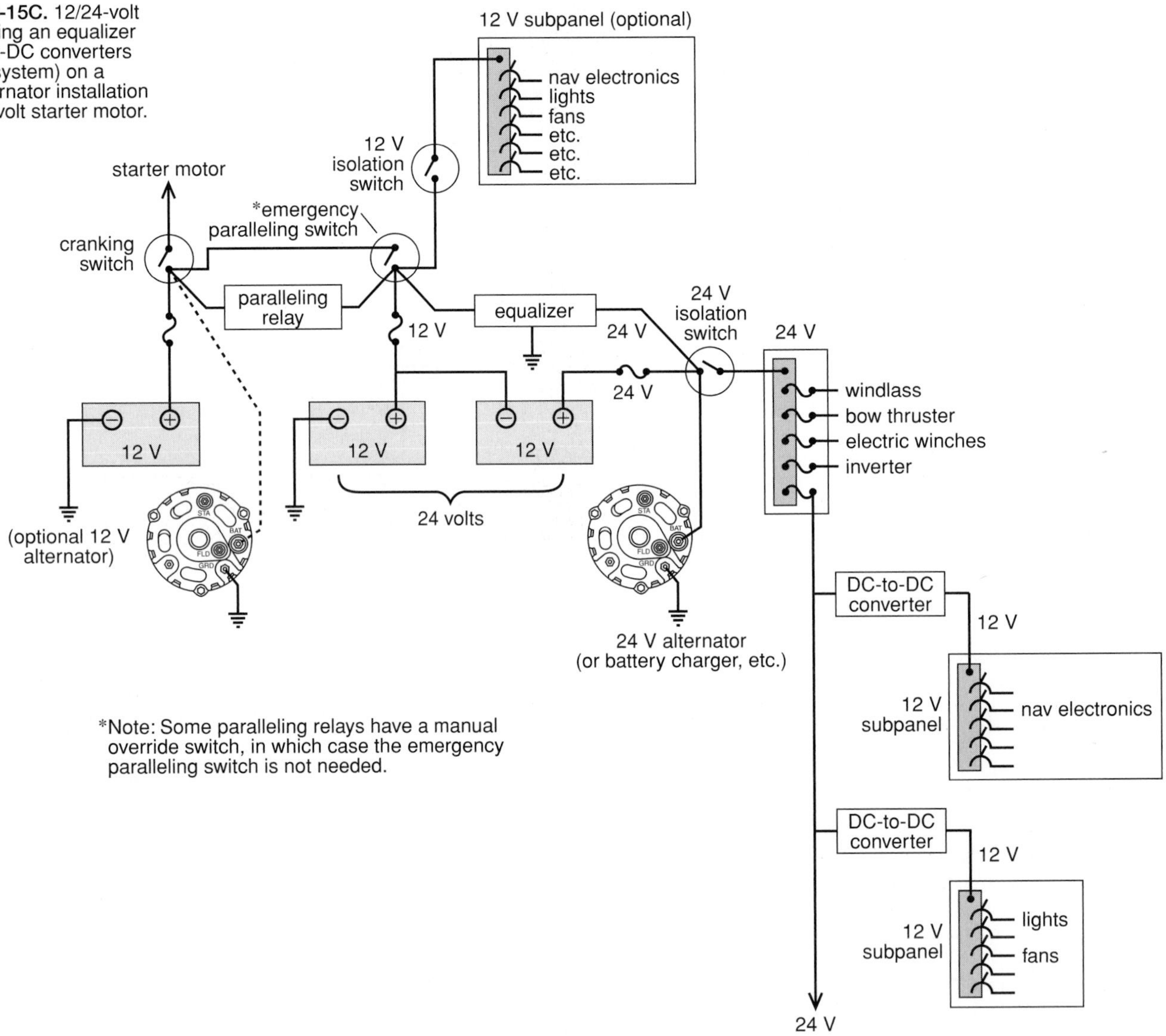

12 V subpanel (optional)

nav electronics
lights
fans
etc.
etc.
etc.

starter motor

12 V isolation switch

*emergency paralleling switch

cranking switch

paralleling relay

equalizer

24 V isolation switch

24 V

12 V

24 V

24 V

(optional 12 V alternator)

12 V

12 V   12 V

24 volts

24 V alternator (or battery charger, etc.)

windlass
bow thruster
electric winches
inverter

DC-to-DC converter

12 V

12 V subpanel

nav electronics

DC-to-DC converter

12 V

12 V subpanel

lights
fans

24 V

*Note: Some paralleling relays have a manual override switch, in which case the emergency paralleling switch is not needed.

Optimum Choices

The primary purpose of using higher DC voltages is to reduce cable weight and expense. But equalizers and converters are not cheap (Figure 2-16). In other words, whatever is saved on cable costs may well be spent on the equalizer and/or converter. We are left with the weight savings—which may be substantial—and certain peripheral benefits associated with converters: easier cable installations due to the reduction in cable size; a UPS if the converter contains its own battery or is wired across a UPS battery; pure DC output with the elimination of voltage spikes, transients, and radio frequency interference; longer life for voltage-sensitive components such as halogen lightbulbs; and perhaps galvanic isolation.

The threshold at which it becomes worthwhile going to a dual 12/24-volt DC system depends more on the sensitivity of a boat to added weight and on the equipment installed on the boat than on boat length. Given the relationship between cable size and cable length, a dual-voltage system is worth considering on sailboats once boat length gets to a ballpark figure of around 60 feet, although it is becoming increasingly common on boats down to 40 feet. On powerboats the threshold will likely be lower. The question, then, is do we use an equalizer, or a converter, or both?

If a boat has a *single 12-volt DC distribution panel*, as many do, from which all the 12-volt loads are taken, we have two choices for feeding this panel. One option is to use an equalizer at the batteries and run a 12-volt feed from one half of the 24-volt house bank to this panel, and from there proceed as with a normal 12-volt boat. The other option is to run a 24-volt feed to the 12-volt panel and install a 24/12-volt converter at this point, supplying the 12-volt panel. The former will likely be necessary if there are high 12-volt surge or intermittent loads; the latter will produce a cleaner 12-volt supply and lengthen battery life. Depending on the kinds of 24-volt loads, we will need either a second (24-volt) distribution panel fed from the full 24-volt battery bank, or else a 24-volt bus bar feeding the various 24-volt circuits through fuses and individual switches. One way or another, the boat will end up with parallel 12- and 24-volt circuits.

If, on the other hand, there are subpanels around the boat, it makes sense to make the primary DC circuits 24-volt and then tap into these at relevant points to add a converter and a 12-volt subpanel for individual pieces of equipment. This setup will substantially reduce both the total cable runs and cable weight on the boat. There may also be additional reasons to use converters for specific loads, such as their capabilities as a UPS.

Perhaps the most useful system is a hybrid, with one equalizer and one or more converters, particularly if the boat's main engine has a 12-volt starter motor and cranking battery. A hybrid system maximizes the flexibility in terms of charging and emergency cranking options, and at the same time maximizes the weight savings in the wiring harness.

Note that all of this may become somewhat academic in a few years. Given the increasing

FIGURE 2-16. A 100 amp equalizer installed on the back of the high-current (battery distribution) DC panel for our new boat (the cabling is not yet in place).

DC loads on cars, the automotive industry has for years been looking at going to a higher voltage in order to reduce the size of wiring harnesses. Just as the industry went from 6 to 12 volts in the 1950s, now it is looking at going from 12 to 36 volts (a nominal 42-volt system). When and if this happens, it will result in an influx of relatively cheap DC equipment at the higher voltage. We can expect the boatbuilding industry to enthusiastically jump on the bandwagon, in which case equalizers and converters will get sidelined except for certain special applications.

Fuel Cells, Higher-Voltage DC Boats, and Electric Propulsion

For years there has been talk of electric propulsion for boats. The principal problem has always been providing adequate battery storage capacity and recharging capability in a package that is more efficient than a traditional diesel engine. Typically, an electric-powered boat requires a large number of heavy and bulky batteries that provide only a limited cruising range, after which you must either plug the boat into shore power to recharge the batteries or else run a fossil-fueled engine to provide battery charging. All too often the net result is no more (and often less) efficient than a traditional installation, is less flexible, weighs more, takes up at least as much space, and costs more! Of course, a boat under electric power is almost noiseless.

Several developments may transform this picture over the next decade. Notable among these are fuel cells, the refinement of high-voltage brushless DC motors and generators, and the application of these motors and generators to diesel/electric boats.

Fuel Cells

A fuel cell combines hydrogen with oxygen (from the atmosphere) to create (fresh) water. In the process, electricity is generated.

What makes this technology so intriguing is that a fuel cell is potentially a very compact device, and a great deal of energy (in the form of hydrogen) can be stored in a small volume. This creates the possibility of providing the necessary energy sources for an electric-powered boat in a lightweight, compact form. However, nowhere in the world is there any infrastructure for the widespread distribution of hydrogen. As a result, the first generation of marine fuel cells (launched in 2004) uses methanol as a fuel. These units are expensive to buy, expensive to refuel, and expensive to maintain, plus they produce a low power output. This technology has a long way to go before it becomes mainstream!

Given that the hydrogen-powered fuel cell is the leading technology for powering electric cars, it is just possible that over the next decade or so we will see the necessary infrastructure developed to make this a viable technology in the marine world, but I'm not holding my breath.

Brushless DC (BLDC) Motors and Generators

BLDC motors have been around for a while. Something very similar to an AC induction motor is created by using permanent magnets in place of the conventional field windings found in a DC motor, and electronic commutation is used in place of the traditional commutator and brushes found in all other DC motors (see Chapter 7 for more on electric motors). In essence, an electronic commutator is a variant of a DC-to-AC inverter that results in AC power being fed to the motor from a DC source (Figure 2-17).

Some electronic commutators produce a square wave (the most common BLDC motor), while others produce a true sine wave (such as that supplied by the utility grid; for more on this see Chapter 6). Electric motors with the latter kind of electric commutation are also known as permanent-magnet (PM) synchronous motors.

Recent developments in BLDC motors, notably from Glacier Bay, incorporate two key pieces. The first—powerful, rare earth, neodymium magnets—results in a high power output from a relatively small and lightweight package.

FIGURE 2-17. An electronic commutator developed by Glacier Bay for its BLDC motors.

The second—the motor controller—is a refinement of electronic commutation into something that is highly tolerant of variable input voltages and versatile and powerful enough for a whole range of motor sizes. These electronic commutators have an "intelligent" part that turns things on and off, controls safety circuits, and monitors various motor performance parameters, and a "power stage" that supplies the commutator current to the motor. On large motors, this current may be hundreds of amps. The intelligent part is more or less the same for all motors; the power stage has to be sized for the motor's horsepower rating. At the time of writing, Glacier Bay has plans to build motors up to 800 hp! (Fischer Panda has a similar range of motors using somewhat different technology.)

BLDC benefits. A number of features make BLDC motors attractive in marine (and many other) applications:

- There need be almost no inrush current; i.e., the inrush current can be more or less the same as the full-load current. This is achieved by including a current limiter in the motor controller.

- Unlike most AC induction motors, which run at speeds fixed by the frequency of the AC power source, these motors can be operated at variable speeds and loads by electronically varying the frequency of the AC output from the motor controller.

- The motors, being DC, do not require a generator that holds a fixed output frequency (as do all AC motors).

- The motor controllers will accept highly variable input voltages. This is particularly beneficial when using smaller generators, which typically have trouble maintaining consistent output parameters.

- The motors are less than half the size and weight of AC induction motors of equivalent output.

- The electrical efficiency is as high as 96%, while conventional AC induction motors generally range from about 78% to 92%.

The relationship between electric motors and generators is thus transformed. A generator no longer has to be sized for the motor start-up load. Furthermore, because the input to a motor is DC, the generator no longer has to be run at a constant speed (as opposed to almost all AC generators, which have to run at nearly full speed regardless of the load on the generator—see Chapter 7). This, in turn, means that when the load is low, the generator can be run at a slow speed, maximizing its efficiency. The variable speed nature of a BLDC motor (as opposed to the fixed speeds of most AC induction motors) also enables the motor's speed to be adjusted to the load, which confers further benefits to the machinery being powered and to generator efficiency.

Air-conditioning. Let's look at this in terms of air-conditioning, which is probably the most common reason for putting an AC generator on a boat. A 16,000 Btu/hour air conditioner has a running load of around 1.4 kW, but a start-up (inrush) load four to six times higher than this. A 4 kW to 6 kW AC generator is needed to start it (depending on how conservatively the generator is rated and its surge capability), with the generator thereafter running at around 15% to 20% of its rated load. In terms of cooling the boat, the air conditioner is typically sized for a worst-case situation, and as a result is oversized for most situations. Because of this, it cycles on and off at regular intervals, resulting in repeated high start-up loads followed by low-load operation. When running, the air conditioner is always running at full output, which tends to be noisy. The air temperature cycles up and down as the thermostat turns the unit on and off.

Now let's put a variable-speed BLDC motor on the air conditioner, powered by a DC generator. Instead of cycling the air conditioner on and off, resulting in fluctuating temperatures and noisy operation, the speed of the air conditioner's compressor can be varied to maintain a constant temperature with less operating noise. This in and of itself is a significant benefit. Because the motor creates no start-up (inrush) load, the generator can be downsized to as little as a quarter the size of a normal AC generator, and then, because the generator's output is DC, the generator can be run at variable speeds to match the variable load from the compressor. The net result is a substantially more-efficient installation that takes up less space, weighs less, requires less maintenance than a traditional AC generator, and results in enhanced air-conditioning performance. For larger air-conditioning demands, multiple independent air-conditioning units can be installed, each with an independent zone controller, with the generator sized to handle the maximum running load and then operated at a speed that is appropriate for however many units are online.

Bigger boats. On bigger boats, a somewhat similar result is often achieved with a conventional AC generator powering chilled-water air-conditioning that has a central unit consisting of several staged compressors and condensers, especially if the compressors are given a "soft" start

FIGURE 2-18. Cascaded battery chargers and DC-to-AC inverters on a superyacht, with multiple chilled-water air-conditioning condensing units beneath them. *(Courtesy Mastervolt)*

(reducing the inrush load—Figure 2-18; Chapter 11 has more on air-conditioning). In effect, as the air-conditioning load cycles up and down, additional compressors and condensers are brought on- and off-line so that the maximum start-up load is that of the total running load plus the start-up load of a single compressor, rather than the start-up load of all the compressors at once. This enables the AC generator to be downsized, but it must still be sized larger than the maximum running load and operated at its full rated speed at all times to maintain the correct output frequency.

As noted earlier, on larger yachts, because of the limitations inherent in operating AC generators, it is customary to employ two or more generators of different sizes. A smaller one takes care of standby and low-level operating loads, while additional generators kick in to handle bigger loads. This requires the output of more than one generator to be supplied to the boat's circuits, which in turn requires sophisticated (and expensive) equipment to synchronize the output waveforms of all generators on the grid. In many cases it necessitates AGS equipment. On some boats, a "dummy" electrical load is also included; at those times when the boat's load is light, the dummy load is switched into the circuit to give the generator some work to do. This avoids maintenance issues associated with low-load operation, but dummy loads are heavy and expensive and require additional switching gear.

All of this complication, additional equipment, and expense can be avoided with a variable-speed DC generator powering BLDC motors! Either a single generator is sized for the maximum running load and then operated at slow speeds when the load is light, or generators

FIGURE 2-19. Kevin Alston of Glacier Bay testing a prototype Ossa Powerlite permanent-magnet DC generator.

are daisy-chained and brought online as needed. Because the generator outputs are DC, there are no synchronization issues.

Permanent-magnet generators. The same technology used in BLDC electric motors can be adapted to produce lightweight, permanent-magnet (PM) generators with a higher power density than anything else on the market (Figure 2-19). Once again, a key component is the use of neodymium magnets.

Over the years, permanent-magnet AC generators have been built by a number of manufacturers, but the results have been mixed. The big advantage is the high power output that can be obtained from a small, lightweight package through the use of powerful rare earth magnets. The core problem is the loss of control over the generator's voltage and frequency as compared with a more conventional generator, in which it is possible to control the output by varying the field current being supplied to the field coils (see Chapter 6). When a permanent-magnet generator is loaded up, the voltage tends to fall. The speed must be increased to compensate, but if this is a conventional AC generator, the frequency then goes up. In other words, the output of these generators tends to be "dirty."

None of this matters if you convert the generator's output to DC and then use it to power BLDC motors that are not sensitive to a fluctuating input voltage. As the load changes, the generator's output can be adjusted by changing the generator's speed. The inevitable time delay between load and speed changes will result in voltage sags and spikes. In a conventional system these fluctuations would cause problems, but BLDC motors take them in stride.

The Higher-Voltage DC Boat

With these two building blocks in place—BLDC motors and permanent-magnet DC generators—some intriguing possibilities open up. As an example, let's take my latest project, a Malo 45 sailboat built in Sweden (www.maloyachts.com). I would have loved to have used this as a test bed for an electric propulsion system, but the pieces were not quite in place. (The boat required an 80 to 100 hp engine, but the largest electric drive for recreational boats being promoted at the time of building (2004) was the Solomon electric drive at 12 hp.)

Given the BLDC motors now in production, I could have driven the propeller with an electric motor powered by a DC generator, creating a diesel/electric propulsion system. The generator would have been much smaller and quieter than the traditional 100 hp Yanmar diesel I installed, and it could have been installed anywhere on the boat, soft-mounted and fully sound-shielded to the point that it would have been barely noticeable when running. I would also have been able to achieve significant weight savings, including eliminating the separate DC generator I installed; it would have been supplanted by the DC generator used for propulsion.

A variable-speed motor provides additional benefits, such as infinite power adjustments when motoring, and a variable-speed generator always runs at close to optimum loadings (as opposed to the typical boat engine, which is mismatched with its propeller at all but one engine speed). Tests of a diesel/electric system performed by Fischer Panda on a 49-foot (15 m) sailboat show no loss of performance with substantial improvements in fuel economy.

Given a DC generator on board, if I powered all my other heavy-duty, motor-driven equipment with BLDC motors (primarily the windlass, bow thruster, and two electric winches), these too could be fed by the generator. The key would be to persuade windlass and other equipment manufacturers to offer the necessary BLDC motors as an option. Glacier Bay and others are working on this. If successful, this approach will not only work for the major power consumers on boats such as mine, but could also supplant the large, heavy, expensive, and complex hydraulic systems (such as Lewmar's Commander system) now used to power high-load devices on large yachts (see Chapter 16).

Higher voltages. Running high-powered DC motors at low voltages (12 or 24) results in large, heavy motors and really large, expensive, and difficult-to-run cable installations. This has led everyone getting into the electric propulsion

The Solomon Technologies Electric Propulsion System

For some years, Solomon Technologies (www.solomontechnologies.com) has been selling permanent-magnet, electronically commutated DC motors for propulsion purposes. The motors operate on 144 volts DC. The largest currently available is rated at 20 hp, although the best tested is 12 hp. The latter produces 74 ft. lbs. of torque and is known as the ST74. It weighs 133 pounds and is 13 inches in diameter and 17 inches long. Solomon Technologies considers the ST74 to be a replacement for a 48 hp diesel engine.

Twelve 12-volt batteries are connected in series for Solomon motors (Figures 2-20 and 2-21). Solomon recommends Group 27 batteries for daysailing, Group 31 for coastal cruising, and 4D for blue-water cruising and catamarans. As the recommended batteries grow in size, the cruising range extends without having to crank a diesel generator, but the volume, weight, and cost of the batteries eat into the benefits of the electric drive. (Twelve 4D batteries weigh 1,620 pounds and occupy 13 cubic feet, as opposed to a typical battery bank on an offshore cruiser of three 8Ds that weigh 490 pounds and occupy 3.8 cubic feet.)

One of the features of a Solomon drive in a sailboat is its regenerative capability. Under sail, if the propeller is allowed to freewheel, the motor will recharge the batteries. However, this charging output is unregulated. If not monitored, it can cook the batteries.

The Solomon system requires an AC generator powering a 144-volt battery charger or a DC generator set up for 144 volts. In the latter case, the inclusion of a DC-to-AC inverter that will convert 144 volts DC to 120 volts AC (or 240 volts AC in Europe) enables the operation of AC equipment. Because of the higher than normal DC input voltage, a much more powerful inverter is practicable than with 12 or 24 volts DC. (Solomon offers a 7 kW inverter that weighs 150 pounds and occupies 1.72 cubic feet.) The final piece of the picture is a separate 12-volt battery bank for remaining 12-volt devices, charged via a DC-to-DC converter (144 volts to 12 volts).

The system works, but the cost is high (an ST74 with generator, inverter, and other pieces will come in at around $30,000 plus installation), and the large battery bank negates the weight and volume gains that accrue from replacing the main engine with a smaller, lighter generator plus an electric motor. In any event, the limited output of the available motors has restricted the application to smaller boats. This is fringe technology, unless the focus shifts from being able to operate the propulsion

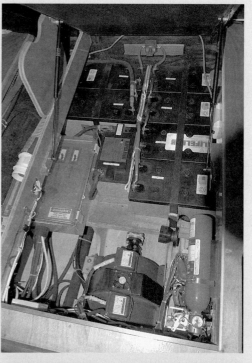

FIGURE 2-20. Diesel/electric installation on a catamaran. The electric motor is in the foreground. This is only half of the battery bank; the other half is in the other hull (which raises certain safety issues).

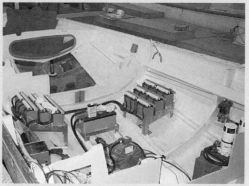

FIGURE 2-21. Solomon Technologies installation in a Hinckley DS42. There are six batteries on either side (which will be under the cockpit seats) powering the electric motor in the center. The two batteries in the center power the sail-handling hydraulic system (just visible at lower right) and have nothing to do with the electric propulsion. *(Courtesy Hinckley)*

motor for extended periods without running the generator—which requires huge battery banks—to a diesel/electric system in which the diesel generator runs whenever motoring—which requires no more batteries than a conventional boat.

A March 2005 filing with the U.S. Securities and Exchange Commission (SEC) revealed that Solomon Technologies was operating at a substantial loss, was facing lawsuits from former executives, and had fallen out with its electric motor supplier. The independent accountants expressed "a substantial doubt about the company's ability to continue as a going concern." Buyer beware!

field to raise system voltages, typically to 120 volts or higher, dramatically reducing motor and cable sizes (the higher-powered Glacier Bay and Fischer Panda motors will run on 400 to 800 volts).

If the operation of a device requires the continuous running of a generator (for example, air-conditioning or an electric stove for cooking), a DC generator can be installed and connected to its BLDC loads with no intermediary batteries in a fashion similar to an AC generator. Extending this DC system to include such things as a windlass, bow thruster, and cockpit winches, however, would require a battery bank to operate the equipment when the generator is not running. To achieve the necessary system voltage, a large number of batteries must be connected in series (e.g., ten 12-volt batteries to produce 120 volts DC).

This raises visions of huge battery banks, but in fact to produce the same kind of energy stor-age capacity as would be found on a more traditional boat with the same equipment (windlass, bow thruster, electric winches, etc.), the physical volume of the batteries and the weight of lead in them need to be about the same. In other words, if an existing 12-volt battery bank (such as mine) has four 8D batteries in parallel, occupying approximately 5 cubic feet and weighing about 650 pounds, its 120-volt replacement might consist of ten Group 27 batteries in series with a similar volume and weight. Instead of thinking in the traditional terms of amp-hours of battery storage capacity, we should think in terms of kilowatt-hours of stored energy—i.e., amp-hours × system voltage. The 8Ds have a rated capacity of around 225 amp-hours at 12 volts = 2.7 kWh each. Four 8Ds thus have a storage capacity of 10.8 kWh. Group 27 batteries have a rated capacity of around 95 amp-hours at 12 volts = 1.14 kWh each. Ten of them will have a storage capacity of 11.4 kWh.

Regulatory and Safety Issues

The introduction of higher-voltage DC systems for boats is revealing weaknesses in existing standards and raising safety issues.

Take, for example, the ABYC standards. The scope of the electrical standards is given as "direct current (DC) electrical systems on boats that operate at potentials of 50 volts or less and . . . alternating current (AC) electrical systems operating at . . . less than 300 volts." This excludes all DC systems operating at potentials above 50 volts. It will take a fair amount of work to revise the standards to accommodate these emerging higher-voltage DC systems.

This work needs to be done in order to provide boatbuilders and installers with clear guidelines for higher-voltage DC systems. Take, for example, the series strings of ten or more batteries that are now being placed on some boats to derive 120 or more volts DC. Some literature being supplied to customers illustrates batteries scattered all over boats in available spaces. This situation is potentially unsafe in at least two ways for which the standards do not currently provide guidance:

1. It results in lengthy connecting straps between batteries. It has always been assumed that battery connecting straps do not require overcurrent protection; the presumption is that the batteries are close together, the straps are short, and the positive terminals are protected as required by the standards, so that as a result short cir-cuits are most unlikely. The longer these connections, the greater the potential for a short circuit to develop. There needs to be overcurrent protection *at both ends* of these cables (see Chapter 4 for more on overcurrent protection).

2. Batteries end up in spaces that may be at different ambient temperatures. This will affect the internal chemistry of the batteries—the rate at which they discharge and recharge—which, in the kind of high-rate discharge and recharge systems being considered, will increase battery temperature differentials, further exacerbating differences in the way the batteries are performing, shortening battery life expectancy, and raising the specter of thermal runaway and battery explosion (see Chapter 1). The standards should require all batteries in a battery bank to be in the same physical space and ambient temperature, with forced-air cooling on larger battery banks.

It is sometimes suggested that 120 volts DC is more dangerous than 120 volts AC, and concern has been expressed at the application of higher DC voltages on boats. However, studies have shown that for a given voltage level it takes four to five times the DC current to have the same physiological effects as a given amount of AC current—i.e., DC is safer. Where DC is potentially more dangerous is in terms of its fire risk in certain switching and fault situations (see Chapter 4).

Aside from powering the boat's systems when the generator is not running, the battery bank will provide a very limited ability to propel the boat without cranking the generator. An attractive proposition is to wire the generator with an AGS that is triggered and shut down by battery state of charge. I would have loved to have had the opportunity to experiment with such a system on my new boat.

The nature of the electronic commutation in BLDC motors is such that as motors get smaller their cost becomes relatively more expensive than conventional motors, unless you get into very high production runs. (Computer fans, for example, are electronically commutated BLDC motors.) It will probably never be cost effective to power 2,000 gph bilge pumps and other such devices with 120-volt BLDC motors.

Also some equipment (notably navigation equipment) is unlikely to be converted to a higher voltage. How can this equipment be operated on a diesel/electric boat operating on 120 or more volts DC? The answer is via a DC-to-DC converter (see earlier in this chapter), which may either power the equipment directly from the 120-volt (or higher) battery bank or via a subsidiary 12-volt battery functioning as a buffer.

The Diesel/Electric Boat

For years the presumption has been that breakthroughs in fuel cell technology would be the seminal innovation that would transform the way energy and propulsion systems are set up on boats. The necessary breakthroughs have been discussed for at least ten years but do not seem to be a whole lot closer! Meanwhile, I believe that a series of incremental improvements and innovations in BLDC motor and DC generator technology have brought us to the point where the diesel/electric boat has moved from the realm of interesting experiment to potential widespread practical application. Although this introduces a whole new set of variables into the equation for DC system design, it still does not alter the fundamental principles outlined in Chapter 1.

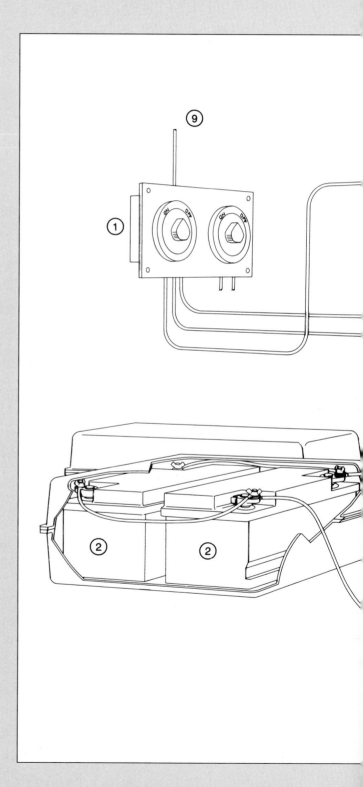

CHAPTER 3

FIGURE 3-1. Keeping your batteries and charging system trouble free should be the first systems maintenance priority of any boater. *(Jim Sollers)*

(1) battery isolation switch
(2) batteries
(3) starter
(4) to starter
(5) alternator
(6) to positive terminal of battery
(7) common ground point
(8) diode (not recommended; see Chapter 1)
(9) to distribution panel

Note: This illustration shows a common installation, but it is not the best approach to wiring batteries and alternators—see the text.

Maintaining and Troubleshooting a Battery-Powered Electrical System

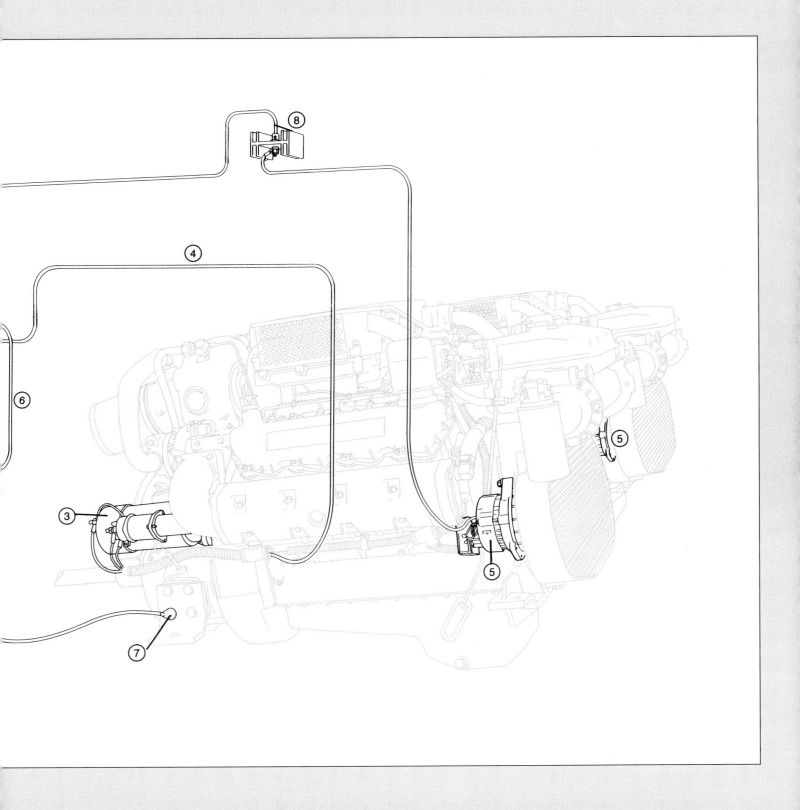

This chapter addresses maintenance and troubleshooting procedures for batteries, alternators, voltage regulators, and associated components and equipment.

Batteries

Safety

Batteries constitute an underestimated danger aboard boats. A fully charged battery contains a tremendous amount of stored energy—more than enough to melt in half a wrench placed carelessly across its terminals. A wet battery's electrolyte, a solution of sulfuric acid, will eat through clothing and cause severe burns. Spilled battery acid, when mixed with seawater, will give off deadly chlorine gas. When working around batteries, always remove jewelry, particularly a wristwatch with a metal band, and be very careful in placing tools. *Take great care with battery acid*; if it gets in your eyes, it can cause blindness. Wear some form of eye protection. Immediately douse any acid splashes with water, then neutralize them with an antacid solution, such as baking powder, baking soda, household ammonia, or antacid medication.

A battery compartment, particularly for a wet-cell battery, needs to be well ventilated. During routine charging, wet-cell batteries emit combustible, lighter-than-air gases—hydrogen and oxygen. Gel-cells and AGMs may do the same if overcharged, and as a result, also require vented compartments. An atmosphere becomes explosive when the concentration of hydrogen exceeds 4% of the air in the space. Never generate sparks around a charging battery (any type). Batteries can explode, with wet-cells spraying acid in all directions.

Wet-cell batteries also emit corrosive fumes. Never install electronic equipment near a wet-cell battery compartment. The equipment will likely suffer irreparable damage.

Batteries should be kept in well-built, acid-proof (plastic, fiberglass, or epoxy-saturated wood) boxes with secure, vented lids (see later in this chapter). Ventilation is important not just to remove explosive gases but also to dissipate the heat generated during rapid discharges and recharges. (This is true for gel-cells and AGMs just as much as for wet-cells.) The degree of ventilation often significantly affects battery life. As long as the batteries don't freeze, the cooler the temperature, the longer the life.

Routine Maintenance

Wet-cell batteries must be periodically topped off with distilled water. A battery's internal plates will be permanently damaged by exposure to air. When you remove the battery caps, you will generally see a short plastic tube going down toward the battery plates, with a slot in each side of the tube. Fluid levels should be maintained at the base of the slots, or if the tubes and slots are not present, at $1/4$ to $1/2$ inch above the plates, but no higher—overfilling will lead to spewing of electrolyte from the filler caps during charging (Figures 3-2A, 3-2B, and 3-2C). *Do not use tap water to maintain the fluid level*, particularly if it comes from a chlorinated source (most city water). Chlorine will shorten the battery's life. Traces of minerals are also damaging, creating internal galvanic currents. In a pinch, clean rainwater is better than nothing at all. Also note that many bottled waters are not suitable because of damagingly high mineral contents.

Record keeping is important with wet-cell batteries. When taking specific-gravity readings, correct for temperature (see below) and keep a record of the readings together with the amounts of water you add. A glance at the record will often give you an advance warning of problem cells or a general deterioration of the battery (more on this in a moment), enabling you to head off an inopportune failure.

Keep the tops of batteries clean. A small amount of dirt, water, or acid will provide a path for electrical leaks that will drain a battery over time. Wiping the battery with a rag dipped in a solution of baking powder, baking soda, or household ammonia will neutralize any acid that may be on it. However, *never sprinkle baking soda directly on a battery case*—if any were to enter a cell through a vent hole, it would cause explosive boiling of the electrolyte and could destroy the cell.

Periodically remove the battery cables (negative first) and clean the terminal posts and clamps. Battery clamps need to be kept free of corrosion (Figure 3-3A). When removing a clamp, do not lever it up with a screwdriver. You are likely to damage the battery plates and also may tear a terminal post loose inside the battery, destroying the battery. Loosen the clamp bolt and ease the clamp jaws open.

FIGURE 3-2A. Topping off wet-cell batteries. In order to maintain wet-cells, it is essential to have good access.

high-water line

low-water line

slot in filler tube

FIGURES 3-2B AND 3-2C. The low-water line is at the top of the plates (3-2B); the high-water line is at the base of the filler tube. Note the slot in the tube (3-2C) so that if the battery is overfilled, venting gases can still escape without driving the electrolyte up the tube.

Then work the clamp gently from side to side and lift it off. A pair of battery-clamp pullers (Figure 3-3B) is a cheap and excellent investment for the toolbox. Why wreck a $400 battery for the lack of a $10 tool? After replacing the cable

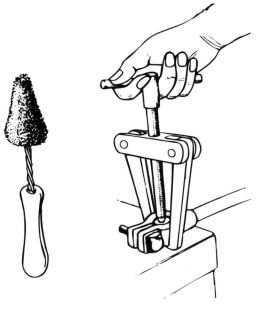

FIGURE 3-3B. A battery-clamp puller and tapered wire brush for cleaning the inside of the clamp. *(Yachting Monthly)*

clamps, coat them and the battery posts with a corrosion inhibitor, grease, or petroleum jelly.

Bring a battery to a full charge anytime it will be left unused for more than a few days. All batteries will discharge slowly when standing idle. The rate of discharge depends to a great extent on temperature and certain features of internal construction. A wet-cell lead/antimony battery will run down faster than a gel-cell or AGM with no antimony in the plate grids. Lead/antimony batteries lose approximately 0.7% of their charge per day at 80°F/26.7°C, rising to 1.75% per day at 100°F/38°C; the higher the temperature, the greater the rate of discharge (Figures 3-4A and 3-4B). The rate of discharge for gel-cells and AGMs at 80°F/26.7°C is as low as 0.1% per day.

If a wet-cell battery is left uncharged for more than a month, especially during the summer, self-discharge will lead to sulfation, the sulfates will harden, and the battery will be damaged permanently. During any extended layup, *be sure to put wet-cell batteries on charge at least once a month* (a small-array solar panel will keep

FIGURE 3-4A. Self-discharge rates for wet-cell batteries. *(Battery Council International)*

FIGURE 3-4B. Self-discharge rates for wet-cells and gel-cells as a function of temperature.

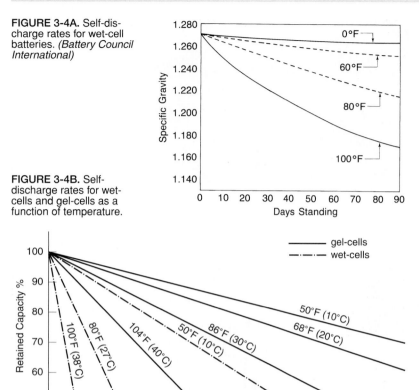

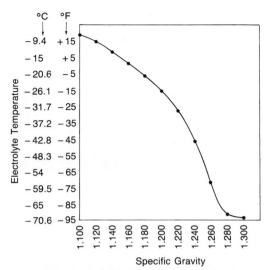

FIGURE 3-5. Battery freezing points at different states of charge. *(Battery Council International)*

TABLE 3-1. Electrolyte Freezing Point as a Function of Battery State of Charge

State of Charge (%)	Freezing Point (°F/°C)
100	−70/−57
75	−45/−43
50	−10/−23
25	5/−15
0	15/−9

a battery topped off and prevent sulfation—see Chapter 6). A fully charged gel-cell or AGM can be left alone for several months.

In cold climates a full charge is also essential to prevent freezing of the electrolyte, which will cause irreparable damage. Figure 3-5 and Table 3-1 show the approximate relationship between a battery's state of charge and the freezing point of its electrolyte. Caution: If a battery freezes, *it may explode if you try to charge it before it has thawed out.*

Battery Installation

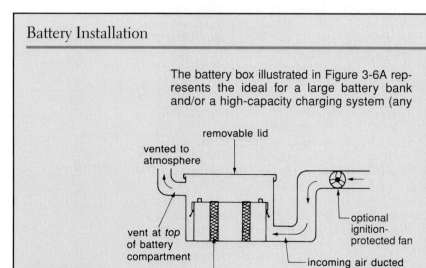

FIGURE 3-6A. An ideal battery box.

The battery box illustrated in Figure 3-6A represents the ideal for a large battery bank and/or a high-capacity charging system (any system approaching 200 amps or more of charging current at 12 volts, 100 amps at 24 volts). The vent (which leads outside and not to interior boat spaces) is at the top of the compartment since the explosive hydrogen gas given off during charging is lighter than air. The removable lid permits ready access for servicing. Well-secured batteries will not break loose even in a capsize. Air enters at the base of the compartment to encourage thorough ventilation. The optional fan further increases ventilation, which also increases the efficiency of battery charging. (If a fan is used, it *must* be ignition protected.) The box is constructed of acid-proof material such as plastic, fiberglass, or epoxy-saturated wood.

In practice, many boats either have no bat-

Battery Installation *(continued)*

tery box at all or something that falls far short of this ideal. The owner of any boat venturing offshore would be well advised to fit a decent box if one is not present. Good-quality batteries weigh around three-quarters of a pound per amp-hour of capacity (at 12 volts); thus a 200 Ah battery weighs about 150 pounds, a 400 Ah battery, 300 pounds. This is a highly concentrated weight, coupled (in wet-cells) with gallons of highly corrosive sulfuric acid (about $1\frac{3}{4}$ gallons per 100 Ah of capacity at 12 volts). Batteries that come loose in a seaway constitute a major safety threat. Containing the batteries and battery acid in an acid-proof container is a matter of common sense.

Building a simple battery box. The following box is adequate for battery banks of up to around 450 amp-hours at 12 volts (two 8D batteries or multiples of smaller batteries to achieve the same capacity). Larger banks may need more sophisticated battery boxes, especially in terms of ventilation.

Begin with a 4-by-8-foot sheet of $\frac{1}{2}$-inch exterior-grade plywood. Mark it out in panels to form a box $\frac{1}{4}$ inch longer and wider on its *inside* than the battery or batteries it is to hold (preferably including a minimum $\frac{1}{2}$-inch air space between the batteries), and a minimum $\frac{1}{2}$ inch higher than the battery depth (including terminal posts) as in Figure 3-6B. If possible, mount the batteries on low stand-offs to encourage air circulation around their bases. Before cutting out the panels, place a layer of fiberglass cloth (just about any weight will do) over the plywood (Figure 3-6C) and thoroughly wet it with catalyzed polyester resin or epoxy resin, the latter being preferable for this purpose. Add resin until the weave of the cloth is filled; the cloth will turn transparent, allowing the pencil marks for the panel cuts to show through.

When the resin has cured, cut out the panels and then saturate all the sawn edges with resin.

Glue and nail the box together with the fiberglass on the inside, making sure all the seams are completely filled with glue. Use an epoxy paste (or epoxy resin with appropriate filler) to seal the seams, even if you used polyester resin for the sheathing. (Polyester resin is brittle and has no gap-filling ability.) Round off the outside corners and bottom edges of the box. Now use masking tape to temporarily affix strips of fiberglass cloth around each corner and edge, overlapping each side of the seam by 2 inches (Figure 3-6D). Wet out the cloth with resin and, progressing from the corner to the edges, work out the wrinkles and air bubbles to achieve a firm bond.

Lay a second strip of cloth over the first,

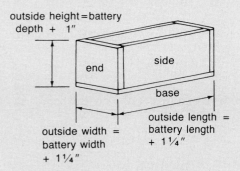

outside height = battery depth + 1"

end · side · base

outside width = battery width + $1\frac{1}{4}$"

outside length = battery length + $1\frac{1}{4}$"

FIGURE 3-6B. Dimensions for a do-it-yourself box of $\frac{1}{2}$-inch plywood.

FIGURE 3-6C. The ingredients: plywood, fiberglass cloth (which will give a smoother, more finished appearance than fiberglass mat or woven roving), epoxy resin and hardener, a roller and brush, acetone for cleaning tools, and a mason jar for saving used acetone.

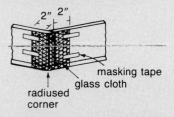

2" 2" · masking tape · glass cloth · radiused corner

FIGURE 3-6D. Sealing and reinforcing the outside corners of the box.

FIGURE 3-6E. The finished box.

overlapping its edges by 1 inch, and repeat. Round off the inside corners with fillets of epoxy paste (Figure 3-6E).

The box will need to be fastened in place, a task that may involve some imagination as well

continued

as an appreciation for the forces that could come to bear in a seaway. Any fasteners through the sides or bottom will need liberal bedding, preferably with a polyurethane adhesive such as 3M 5200 (although the better choice is to not put fasteners through the bottom at all, especially with wet-cell batteries). If the batteries have no handles, place three spacers of ¼-inch plywood in the bottom of the box to separate two lengths of ¼-inch nylon line, the ends of which will emerge above the box sides (Figure 3-6F). With this arrangement the battery can be removed without having to destroy the box!

There remains only the task of fitting a lid. The lid can simply rest on and overlap the box sides, as shown in Figure 3-6G, by setting some short dowels or nails into the box sides and ends to stick out ¼ inch or so. This holds the lid slightly above the box, permitting ventilation. Alternatively, create a vent in the lid (a screened hole will suffice).

Secure the lid with straps sturdy enough to restrain the batteries in the event of a capsize.

Note that the ABYC *Standards and Recommended Practices for Small Craft*, as well as the European ISO standards, require that:

1. Batteries shall be installed in a dry, ventilated location above the anticipated bilge water level.

2. Batteries must be securely fastened against shifting.

3. Positive terminals must be protected against accidental shorting either with some kind of a boot or else by a battery-box lid.

4. There must be no uninsulated metal fuel line or fittings within 12 inches (300 mm) of a battery top or sides.

5. Batteries must not be installed directly (i.e., without an intervening deck, floor, or cabin sole) above or below a fuel tank, fuel filter, or fuel-line fitting.

6. The means of mounting a battery must be impervious to battery electrolyte, while any fasteners must be isolated from areas intended for collecting electrolyte.

7. The tops of wet-type batteries must be readily accessible for topping up with distilled water.

FIGURE 3-6F. Two lengths of ¼-inch line provide a means of lifting the battery out of the box when necessary. Make sure the line is nylon, which is acid resistant.

FIGURE 3-6G. Fitting a lid.

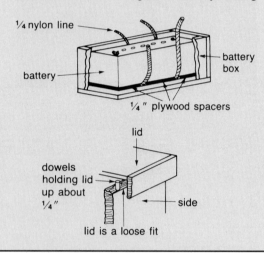

Keep batteries cool. Some capacity loss will occur at elevated temperatures whether the battery is in use or not. *This loss is irreversible* and is part of a battery's aging process (Figure 3-7). The higher the temperature, the greater the loss. Batteries in storage should be kept as cool as possible without freezing.

Testing a Battery

There are five ways to check the state of charge, and/or health, of a battery:

1. Measure the *specific gravity* of its electrolyte.
2. Measure its *open-circuit voltage*.
3. Use a *load tester*.
4. Perform a *capacity test*.
5. Keep track of the amps going in and out with an *amp-hour meter*.

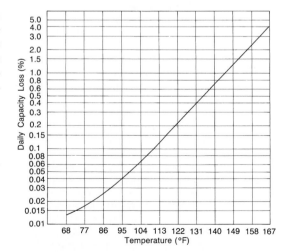

FIGURE 3-7. Permanent loss of battery capacity for gel-cell batteries as a function of temperature. Note: Wet-cell losses will be higher. (*Sonnenschein Battery Co.*)

Specific gravity. The electrolyte in a battery is a solution of sulfuric acid, which is denser than water. As a battery discharges, this acid progressively weakens, becoming less dense. With a wet-cell, you can withdraw samples of the electrolyte from each cell in a battery using a *hydrometer* (Figure 3-8). A hydrometer contains a floating indicator that comes to rest at a certain level in pure water, this level being calibrated for a *specific gravity* of 1.000. The denser the acid solution, the higher the indicator will float, giving a higher specific-gravity reading. To get accurate readings, you have to hold the hydrometer vertically so that the float does not hang up on the side of the tube. As the solution weakens, the indicator will sink. Since specific gravity varies with temperature, better hydrometers incorporate a thermometer that allows any reading to be corrected for nonstandard temperatures. In the United States, the standard temperature is 80°F/26.7°C; in the UK it is 60°F/15.6°C. If the electrolyte is at a nonstandard temperature, use the conversion chart (Figure 3-9) to correct the specific-gravity reading. In theory, the corrected specific gravity can then be correlated accurately with a battery's state of charge.

It should be noted, however, that when a battery is rapidly discharged or recharged, the chemical reactions take place between the active material on the surfaces of the battery plates and the immediately accessible electrolyte, but not in the inner plate areas. Following the discharge or charge, if the battery is left alone, the acid and water diffuse in and out of the plates, the battery equalizes internally, and the electrolyte reaches a homogeneous state. *The only time a specific-gravity reading correlates accurately with a battery's state of charge is when the electrolyte is in this homogeneous state.* At all other times, depending on how recently the battery was used and the magnitude of the current in relation to the battery's capacity, specific-gravity readings will be off by a certain margin, indicating a more discharged state than is in fact the case during discharges, and a less charged state than is the case during recharges. If the battery has been used vigorously, it can take up to 24 hours for the electrolyte to reach a stable state.

There is another phenomenon that affects specific-gravity readings called *stratification*. When recharging, the heavier acid forming in the electrolyte tends to sink to the bottom of the battery, out of reach of the hydrometer. It is not until the battery begins to reach gassing voltages, and the bubbles stir up the electrolyte, that the electrolyte reaches a more homogeneous state. Stratification exaggerates the lag between state of charge and hydrometer readings on recharge (Figure 3-10).

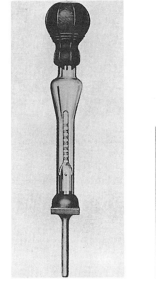

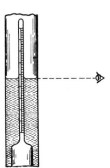

FIGURE 3-8. A battery-testing hydrometer. The correct method of reading it is shown on the right. Keep your eye level with the liquid surface and disregard the curvature of the liquid against the glass parts. *(Battery Council International)*

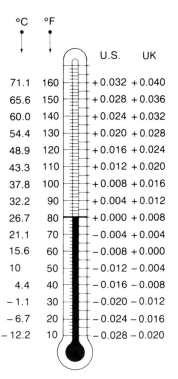

°C	°F	U.S.	UK
71.1	160	+0.032	+0.040
65.6	150	+0.028	+0.036
60.0	140	+0.024	+0.032
54.4	130	+0.020	+0.028
48.9	120	+0.016	+0.024
43.3	110	+0.012	+0.020
37.8	100	+0.008	+0.016
32.2	90	+0.004	+0.012
26.7	80	+0.000	+0.008
21.1	70	−0.004	+0.004
15.6	60	−0.008	+0.000
10	50	−0.012	−0.004
4.4	40	−0.016	−0.008
−1.1	30	−0.020	−0.012
−6.7	20	−0.024	−0.016
−12.2	10	−0.028	−0.020

FIGURE 3-9. Temperature corrections for hydrometer readings in the United States and the UK. Baseline temperature is taken as 80°F/26.7°C in the United States and 60°F/15.6°C in the UK. For example, given a hydrometer reading of 1.250 and an electrolyte temperature of 20°F, in the United States, 0.024 would be subtracted for a corrected specific gravity of 1.226. Looking in Table 3-2, we see that the battery is about 25% discharged. In the UK, the correction factor for an electrolyte temperature of 20°F/−6.7°C is −0.016, yielding a corrected specific gravity of 1.234. Turning again to Table 3-2, we see that the battery is once again about 25% discharged.

Once the electrolyte is in a homogeneous state, and specific-gravity readings have been corrected for temperature, there is a correlation between the specific gravity and the battery's state of charge, which is given in Figure 3-11 and Table 3-2.

The figures in Table 3-2 are for *industry-standard* batteries. In real life, the specific gravity of fully charged batteries varies considerably, from 1.230 to 1.300. The lower figure may be found on some deep-cycle batteries sold in the tropics, where the higher prevailing temperatures promote more efficient battery operation, requiring a less concentrated acid solution. The higher figure may be found on cranking batteries sold in cold climates, where more concentrated acid solutions are needed to boost output (Table 3-3).

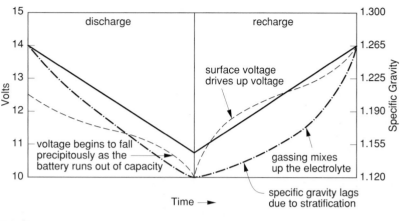

FIGURE 3-10. Voltage and specific gravity during constant-rate discharges and recharges.

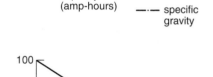

FIGURE 3-11. State of charge as a function of homogeneous specific gravity.

TABLE 3-2. Electrolyte Specific Gravity as a Function of Temperature and Battery State of Charge

Specific Gravity:	80°F/ 26.7°C	60°F/ 15.6°C	State of Charge (%)
	1.265	1.273	100
	1.225	1.233	75
	1.190	1.198	50
	1.155	1.163	25
	1.120	1.128	0

TABLE 3-3. Typical Specific Gravity Variations by Region

Region	Fully Charged Specific Gravity
North of Florida and Northern Europe	1.265–1.280
Florida to San Juan (Puerto Rico)	1.250–1.265
South of San Juan	1.235–1.250

After you install a new battery, be sure to fully charge it and then test it to establish its actual specific gravity (be sure to compensate for the temperature of the electrolyte). *Then log the figures for future reference.* (Note that a battery can be assumed to be fully charged when further charging over a 3-hour period fails to produce any increase in the specific gravity of its electrolyte.)

Every maintenance-conscious boatowner should have a hydrometer if using wet-cell batteries. Be sure to get one specifically designed for battery testing. Some hydrometers are made for antifreeze, others for winemaking! Each is purpose-built to cover an appropriate range of specific gravities.

Open-circuit voltage. A battery is open-circuited when no current is being drawn from it and no charge is being fed to it. The simplest way to open-circuit a battery is to switch off the battery isolation switch. However, never do this with the engine running—you can blow out the diodes in the alternator (see Chapter 1). If you have any equipment, such as a bilge pump, VHF radio, or solar panel, hooked directly to the battery, you must also switch it off or disconnect it to achieve meaningful test results.

Just as with specific-gravity readings, battery voltage readings are affected by the initial strength of the battery acid, the rate of previous discharges and recharges, and the amount of time the battery has been *rested.* Following use, a battery will take a while to equalize internally. If voltage readings are to be a meaningful reflection of the state of charge, the battery must sit for at least 10 minutes; an hour or two is better, and overnight is best. (Gel-cell and AGM batteries may take as long as 48 hours to equalize.) With the battery temperature between 60°F and 100°F (15.6°C and 38°C), the equalized open-circuit voltage can be approximately correlated with state of charge as shown in Table 3-4 and Figure 3-12.

Note that the difference between a fully charged and a half-charged wet-cell battery is only 0.4 volt, and is just a little higher for gel-cells and AGMs! From full charge to full discharge is just 0.8 to 1.15 volts. Most swinging-arm (analog-type) meters are virtually useless in these circumstances, while a meter with an expanded scale (normally covering the region from 8 to 16 volts) is questionable. *Only a good-quality digital meter will give an accurate assessment of the state of charge.* (If an analog meter is used, look for one with an accuracy of ±2% as opposed to the common ±5%; digital meters are typically ±0.2%.)

Since *homogeneous* specific gravity and equal-

TABLE 3-4. Open-Circuit Voltage Versus State of Charge for East Penn Wet-Cell, Gel-Cell, and AGM Batteries

	Open-Circuit Voltage		
% Charged	Wet-cell	Gel-cell	AGM
100	12.70–12.60	12.95–12.85	12.90–12.80
75	12.40	12.65	12.60
50	12.20	12.35	12.30
25	12.00	12.00	12.00
0	11.80	11.80	11.80

Note: These voltages may vary for other manufacturers.

Courtesy East Penn

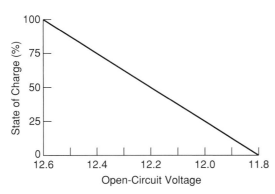

FIGURE 3-12. State of charge as a function of stabilized open-circuit voltage for a wet-cell battery. (A fully charged gel-cell or AGM will have an open-circuit voltage as high as 13.0 volts.)

ized open-circuit voltage are both measuring states of charge, we would expect some sort of a correlation between the two. The relationship is as follows:

At 80°F, the voltage of a single cell = the specific-gravity reading (SG) + 0.84.

The voltage of a 12-volt battery = 6 × (SG + 0.84).

Load testing. *A battery can show a full or nearly full charge on both an open-circuit voltage test and a specific-gravity test, yet still fail to operate correctly due to a severe loss of capacity resulting from sulfation of the plates or shedding of active material.* The voltage and specific gravity are merely reflecting the fact that the *remaining capacity* is fully charged. To check the capacity itself, some form of a *load test* is needed, normally using a *high-load tester (high-rate discharge tester)*.

A traditional high-load tester is a device that is connected either across each cell in turn or across the battery terminals, artificially creating an extremely high load on the battery while measuring voltage. (For testing its gel-cell and AGM batteries, East Penn recommends that the load be set at half the CCA rating or at three times the rated amp-hour capacity, using the 20-hour rat-

ing.) The voltage on a cell or battery in good condition will stabilize above 10 volts (for a 12-volt battery) for 10 or more seconds, while the voltage on a weak cell or battery will begin to fall off rapidly at some point during the test. (The reason is that the reduced cell or battery capacity is soon exhausted so the rate of discharge cannot be sustained.) If a 12-volt battery's voltage falls below 9.5 volts before 15 seconds are up, the battery is in sorry shape.

Modern high-load testers put less of a load on a battery than traditional testers, using sophisticated electronics to deduce the same information as from a high-load tester (Figure 3-13A). Either type of tester is a specialized piece of equipment found in all automotive parts stores (or sometimes borrowed) but rarely found on boats. For professionals (such as marine surveyors), it is an important piece of equipment that should be purchased. For the rest of us, the effect of a high-load tester can be crudely simulated by cranking a diesel engine for 15 seconds. Close the throttle and activate any stop lever to keep the engine from starting. If the engine has an automatic starting advance that is difficult to outfox, shut off the fuel supply. Then crank the motor. While it is cranking, monitor the battery voltage constantly (Figure 3-13B). (On a gasoline engine, close off the fuel supply and disable the ignition before cranking.)

As soon as cranking commences, the voltage will drop but then will more or less stabilize, declining slowly during the rest of the test. (On a 12-volt system, the initial drop normally will be

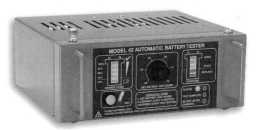

FIGURE 3-13A. Electronic battery tester.

FIGURE 3-13B. Checking battery voltage while cranking.

to around 10.5 volts, depending on the load, cranking cable size and length, battery capacity, and temperature.) If the voltage starts to drop precipitously before 15 seconds are up, the battery is in trouble; it is either seriously discharged or else has lost much of its capacity. Fully recharge the battery and repeat the test. If the battery fails a second time, give it a full capacity test (see below).

To avoid overheating the starter motor when simulating a high-load test, *under no circumstances should you crank the motor for more than 30 seconds*. If you have to test more than one battery bank, you must let the starter motor rest for at least 5 minutes between each bank. The reason is that starter motors do not have the heat dissipation necessary for continuous operation. If they are not given time to cool down between cranking attempts, they will burn up.

High-load testing takes very little out of a battery. As I pointed out in Chapter 1, even if the starter motor is pulling 400 amps, at 15 seconds this amounts to a total of only 400/(4 × 60) = 1.66 amp-hours.

Capacity testing. A capacity test is done by simulating a 20-hour capacity test for a C20 rating (refer back to Chapter 1 for a definition of this rating). First bring the battery to a full charge. Then discharge it at a rate of $\frac{1}{20}$ *of its rated amp-hour capacity* (e.g., at 10 amps on a 200 Ah battery). You can achieve this load by turning on incandescent lights until the required amperage is reached. Be sure to note the time you began the test. Continue the test until battery voltage has fallen to 1.75 volts per cell (10.5 volts on a 12-volt battery). To find the amp-hour capacity of the battery, multiply the load (e.g., 10 amps) by the hours the battery was able to sustain it (e.g., 15 hours): 10 × 15 = 150 Ah. For this example, the battery is down to 75% of its rated capacity. The battery should be immediately recharged to prevent sulfation. (Note that if a battery has a C10 rating, it should be discharged at a rate of $\frac{1}{10}$ of its rated capacity. Also note that as the test progresses and the battery voltage declines, the amperage drawn by the lights will also decline. Therefore, it may be necessary to add another small load to keep the amp draw close to the desired level.)

Any battery below 80% of its rated capacity should be recharged and tested again. If the capacity cannot be brought up to 80% or better, the battery should probably be replaced. Once capacity falls much below this level, batteries tend to fail fairly rapidly. (However, new batteries may test as low as 80% but then gain in capacity over a period of time as the battery is used, especially if the capacity test is repeated

three to five times. See also later in this chapter for some techniques that may help restore lost capacity to older batteries.)

Sailors who venture offshore, or for whom the batteries are vital pieces of equipment, should perform a capacity test on all batteries at the beginning of each boating season or before a long cruise. I also recommend performing a capacity test on new batteries. On several occasions I have found that new batteries are far below rated capacity, generally because they have sat on a shelf for months without being maintained and are already partially sulfated.

Note that some batteries have a "date of manufacture" sticker that has a number and a letter (e.g., 4G). The number is the year of manufacture (2004) and the letter is the month, starting with "A" for January ("G" is July). You should not buy batteries that have been on the shelf for more than two to three months.

Amp-hour meters. An amp-hour meter keeps track of the amps going into and out of a battery, maintaining a running total, which is used to indicate the state of charge of the battery (Figure 3-14). This sounds simple, but is in fact incredibly complicated. The meter must first be calibrated to the specific battery it is metering, and then it must be able to make appropriate adjustments for the inefficiencies inherent in charging and discharging batteries. Unfortunately, no two batteries have the same efficiency ratings, and even the same battery will fluctuate depending on its temperature, state of charge, rate of charge or discharge, age, and so on.

Many amp-hour meters are incapable of accurately reflecting this ever-changing efficiency factor and will need some form of periodic recalibration to bring them back in line with the actual state of charge of the battery. Between calibrations the meter will tend to become less and less in sync with the battery's state of charge. Of the meters on the market, those made by

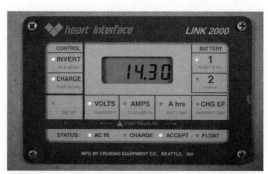

FIGURE 3-14. Sophisticated metering, including amp-hours, built for Heart Interface by Cruising Equipment Company (now part of the Xantrex group). *(Heart Interface)*

(among others) Ample Technology (www.amplepower.com), Xantrex (www. xantrex.com), and Mastervolt (www.mastervolt.com) are excellent.

Problem Batteries

When confronted with batteries that are short on capacity (cannot sustain a load) or are going dead prematurely, the normal reaction is to blame the battery, but often it is not at fault. First, check for some hidden drain such as:

- Dirt and moisture on the top of the battery.

- A piece of equipment left on (especially navigation lights).

- The cumulative load of a number of LEDs (light-emitting diodes) fitted to distribution panels, switches, and meters.

- A carbon monoxide alarm or similar device wired directly to the battery, and/or permanently energized memories on entertainment systems, systems monitors, etc.

- Leaks to ground in the boat's wiring (see the Ground Faults ["Earth" Leaks] section in Chapter 4).

Next, consider the possibility that the battery is not receiving a proper charge (see the relevant discussions under Alternators and Voltage Regulators later in this chapter). All too often a boat sets out on a cruise with fully charged batteries. Every day, due to inadequate charging, a little less is put back into the batteries than is taken out (Figure 3-15). Eventually the batteries will not meet the demands placed on them. The owner assumes that the batteries are at fault, although it is actually the charging system that is

the problem. Batteries repeatedly, and unnecessarily, get replaced—quite a common scenario with cruising boats, particularly those with ferro-resonant battery chargers (Chapter 6) and automotive alternators.

Signs of trouble. Of course, it may be the battery that is defective—all batteries must die sooner or later. Common signs of battery problems are:

A battery that shows nearly full voltage when under no load, but a steadily falling voltage when a load is applied. The battery is short on *usable* capacity. If, on recharging, its voltage comes up rapidly, there is only a limited amount of active material in the plates that is still accepting a charge. This may be due to sulfation or to shedding; in either case the battery will go dead rapidly in use, since only a small fraction of its plate area is still active. In some circumstances, sulfated active material may be brought back to life (see below), but material that has been shed is gone forever.

A wet-cell that never needs topping off with water. The battery is being undercharged. This is certain to lead to sulfation and premature death.

A wet-cell that needs frequent topping off. The battery is being overcharged. Water loss should amount to no more than 2 ounces of water per cell (12 ounces per 12-volt battery) in 30 to 50 hours of battery charging time. If just one cell is using excessive water, it is probably shorted.

Uniformly low specific-gravity readings on all cells. The battery needs recharging. If it cannot be brought up to full charge (as measured by its specific gravity), it is dying. If the difference between the highest and lowest cell readings is more than 0.030, then the low cell is probably

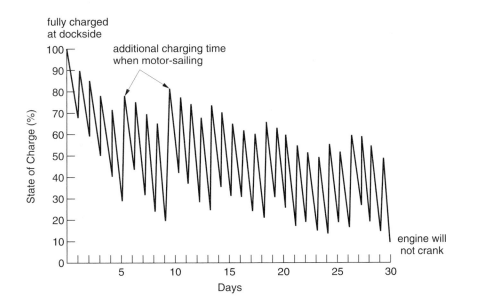

FIGURE 3-15. Daily cycling of a battery with inadequate charging. Despite the fact that the battery is properly sized (three to four times the daily load), eventually the battery fails to meet its tasks. Note that long before the problem becomes apparent, the battery will have been damaged from sulfation through never being fully charged.

dying. And if, after recharging, the difference remains over 0.030, this cell is almost certainly dying (in all probability shorted). If the electrolyte in the hydrometer is murky, the plates are breaking up.

An isolated and unused battery whose voltage shows an appreciable drop (such as from full charge to 75% of charge or less) over two to three weeks. The battery has an internal short. Shed material, or what is known as *dendritic growth*, has bridged the gap between negative and positive plates. It is not salvageable.

A gel-cell or AGM (SVR/VRLA battery) with white powder around its vents. The battery has been overcharged to the point that the valves have opened and vented, drying out the electrolyte and wrecking the battery. In desperate circumstances if the valves are forced open and water is added, the battery may be brought back to life temporarily, but it should be noted that *once the valve seals are damaged the battery will soon be history. So do not do this unless it is certain the battery has dried out.* After the valves have been opened, the battery should be treated as a regular wet-cell (i.e., periodically topped off) until it can be replaced.

A gel-cell or AGM with a black post. The battery probably has a leaking seal around the post, in which case sooner or later it will dry out and fail. To test the seal, remove the cable clamp, brush a soap solution around the post, and then flex the battery case *for that cell*. If the solution bubbles, the seal is definitely gone.

Finally, a battery may simply be old and dying. It may have an accumulation of problems—sulfation, shorts, shedding of active material, etc. Even well-maintained batteries wear out.

Sulfation and equalization—is there life after death? As we saw in Chapter 1, during repeated charges and discharges, lead sulfate builds up throughout battery plates. Initially the sulfate is relatively soft and porous and easily reconverted into active material, but over time it hardens and battery performance steadily declines. Sulfation is a particularly acute problem with deep-cycle batteries that are repeatedly discharged but never brought back to a 100% state of charge—precisely the operating conditions of many boat batteries. Thick-plate wet-cells with antimony-reinforced plate grids are more prone to sulfation than gel-cells and AGMs.

Sulfates need to be dealt with before they harden, so batteries should *never be left in a discharged state* or even a partially discharged state. If sulfates are allowed to harden, they increase the internal resistance of a battery. During charges, the surface voltage of the battery (pages 28–29) rises rapidly, fooling any constant-voltage (automotive-type) regulator into thinking that the battery is fully charged when it is not. The regulator then shuts down the charging output. *Regardless of engine-running time, the sulfated areas remain uncharged.*

To bring sulfated areas back to life, you must equalize the battery (page 12). For equalization, it is necessary to boost charging voltages to a level that will overcome the resistance of the sulfates—sometimes to as high as 16.2 volts on a 12-volt battery. But once the sulfates begin to break down—and at these voltages—an alternator with a standard, automotive-type, constant-voltage regulator would pump out too much amperage and cook the battery, with potentially explosive results. Therefore, you will need some form of current- (amperage) limiting ability to hold the charging amperage to less than 5% of the total amp-hour rating of the battery being equalized (3% to 4% would be better; e.g., 6 to 8 amps for a 200 Ah battery). If the battery voltage rises rapidly, the amperage is too high. Constantly monitor the battery temperature to make sure it does not go above 125°F/52°C. Quite a bit of gassing will occur, so you will have to top off the battery with water when equalization is complete. *This gassing would destroy a gel-cell or AGM (or any other sealed battery), so equalization at these high voltages is strictly limited to heavy-duty wet-cells.* (Lifeline does recommend driving AGM batteries that are used in cycling applications to 15 volts once a year and maintaining that voltage for 3 hours.)

As noted earlier, equalization cannot be carried out with a standard automobile voltage regulator. It requires a purpose-built multistep regulator (page 31) or a purpose-built battery charger (Chapter 6). A large-array solar panel (3 amps or more for every 100 Ah of battery capacity to be equalized) without voltage regulation and hooked directly to the battery will also work, as will an unregulated wind generator (Chapter 6), as long as careful attention is paid to battery voltage and temperature, and the solar panel or wind generator is disconnected when equalization has occurred. Note that some small, unregulated automotive battery chargers can also be used for equalization on an occasional basis, but should not be installed as permanent equipment. (Unlike "proper" marine battery chargers, they do not have isolation transformers; see Chapters 4 and 6).

The only sure way to test for proper equalization is with a hydrometer, checking the cells repeatedly until all cells are up to full charge. Specific gravity will then be around 1.265 for most batteries but will vary from battery to battery (see the Testing a Battery section earlier in this chapter). *You will know the battery will accept no more charge when the specific-gravity readings remain unchanged for 3 hours.* Testing is a tedious business, especially if the battery is hard to reach. However once you have done it a few times, you will be able to identify the weakest (slowest to come to a full charge) cell in the battery, and then you only need to monitor this cell. And experience will teach you at what rate (amperage) the battery can be charged without overheating or excessive gassing.

Important note: some sensitive electronic equipment has a rated input voltage from around 11 volts DC to 16 volts DC. *Equalization at 16 volts may damage such equipment.* Whenever equalizing a battery at voltages above 14.5 volts, always isolate the battery in question. At the very least, be absolutely certain all electronic equipment hooked to the battery is turned off as well as *halogen bulbs* (which are particularly sensitive to high voltages).

Dead gel-cell and AGM batteries. Gel-cell and AGM batteries, particularly if they have been discharged very flat or left in a seriously discharged state for some time, can build up a layer of calcium oxide on the grids, which creates a high resistance and fools most voltage regulators into thinking the battery is charged. The battery will then not accept or hold a charge. Sometimes you can bring a battery back into service with one of the following treatments:

1. Place a moderate load on the battery for just a brief period—its voltage will fall. Immediately put the battery on charge for a couple of minutes, then repeat the process (load followed by charge). Do this three times, and then attempt a full charge. If this fails, try the next suggestion.

2. Kill the battery stone-dead. Place a load on the battery (10 amps is fine) and drag it all the way down until it shows a voltage of 1.0 volt or so. Use equipment that will not burn up as the voltage falls, such as incandescent lights.

   When the battery is completely down, finish it off by shorting out its two terminals with a length of heavy-gauge insulated wire—12 gauge or larger (jumper cables work well). If the wire gets hot, the battery is not down enough; put the load back on. Once it is down, leave it shorted for several more hours.

   Recharge the battery. It will not recover to full capacity, but after several normal discharge/recharge cycles, it may come back to nearly full capacity.

3. Use a high-voltage, low-current charge. A charging source well above 12 volts is needed, ideally with a current-limiting function to hold the current down to a few amps, although this is hard to come by. (You can use one of the multistep regulators with an equalizing function.) In a bind, you may be able to use two good 12-volt batteries wired in series to produce 24 volts, but be sure to disconnect all 12-volt loads from the system. The defective gel-cell battery is hit repeatedly with the high voltage for short periods (a few seconds at a time if using the two batteries; a few minutes if using the equalizing function on a multistep regulator), and then put back onto a normal charge. The high voltage may be sufficient to get the plates accepting a charge once again. Run the battery through several charge/discharge cycles to restore as much capacity as possible.

Alternators

How They Work

A magnet (the *rotor*) is spun inside a series of coils (the *stator*), as shown in Figures 3-16A and 3-16B. As the north and south poles of the rotor pass the coils in the stator, an electrical pulse is generated—positive for the north pole, negative for the south pole. This is *alternating current* (AC), so called because the direction of current flow alternates from positive to negative and back. Two alternations make a *cycle*, which can occur from a few times to thousands of times per second. The number of cycles per second is the *frequency*, expressed as *Hertz* (Hz). Household current (AC) is commonly 60 cycles per second in the United States (50 cycles per second in the UK and Europe); in other words, its frequency is 60 Hz. The voltage and amperage generated in the alternator are determined by the strength of the magnetic field in the rotor, the number of *poles* in the rotor, the number of turns of wire in the stator coils, and the speed of rotation.

Instead of having fixed (permanent) magnets in the rotor, most alternator rotors have a soft-iron core wrapped in a coil of wire (the *field winding*). When *direct current* (DC), which flows in only one direction, passes through the coil, the iron core is magnetized. The stronger the current, the greater the degree of magnetism. Alternator output is controlled *(regulated)* by

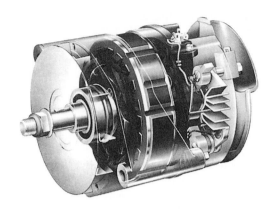

FIGURE 3-16A. An alternator. (Lucas/CAV)

FIGURE 3-16B. Alternator operating principles. The rotor contains the field winding. The voltage regulator varies the direct current passing through the field winding and thus the strength of the resultant magnetic field. Three sets of windings (A, B, and C) are built into the stator, each producing AC output.

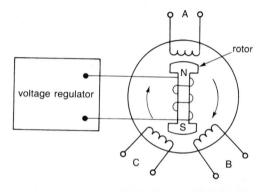

FIGURE 3-17A. Slip rings on a rotor shaft.

FIGURE 3-17B. Alternator construction. (ACDelco)

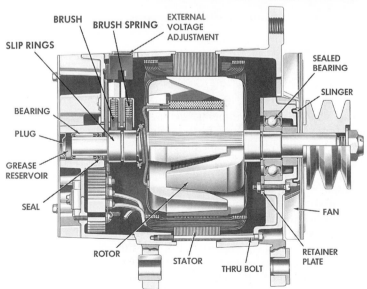

varying the current (the *field current*) fed to the field winding.

The field current is fed to the field winding via two slip rings—smooth, round, insulated discs mounted on the rotor shaft (Figure 3-17A)—each connected to one end of the field winding and each contacted by a spring-loaded carbon brush contained in a brush holder fixed to the alternator housing (Figure 3-17B). The brushes are wired back to the source of the field current.

Some alternators dispense with the brushes and slip rings and instead energize the field windings *inductively*. These are known as brushless alternators. Maintenance is minimized and efficiency often improved, but with a significant jump in cost and, frequently, less precise regulation of the alternator's output.

With both brush-type and brushless alternators, the rotors have multiple interlocking fingers in place of a single magnet. This has the effect of producing multiple north and south magnetic poles when the field winding is energized (Figure 3-18).

As noted, when these north and south poles spin inside the coils of the stator, alternating current is generated in the coils. Regardless of the number of coils or windings (this varies among alternators), they are normally hooked up in such a way as to produce just three effective coils—the resulting power output is known as *three phase* (Figures 3-19A and 3-19B). Some alternators, such as the brushless alternators used in Fischer Panda and Glacier Bay DC generators, are wound for more phases—generally six.

Despite the multiple phases, the current from each phase is still alternating. To be of any use in charging a battery, it must be *rectified* to direct current. This is done with *silicon diodes*. A diode is an electronic switch or check valve that allows electricity to flow in only one direction.

FIGURE 3-18. An alternator rotor constructed to produce multiple north and south magnetic poles.

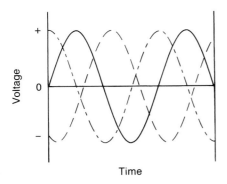

FIGURE 3-19A. Three-phase alternator output.

FIGURE 3-19B. The windings on an alternator stator. Every third winding is connected together.

Imagine first a single-phase alternator. Each end of the stator winding is connected to two diodes. The first diode is placed so it passes only positive impulses and is connected to the battery's positive terminal. The second diode is oriented to pass only negative impulses and provides a return path from the battery's negative terminal to the winding. The complete diode setup is known as a *bridge rectifier* (Figure 3-20). Despite a constantly reversing current flow in the stator, current flows in only one direction to the battery.

In a three-phase alternator, the configuration is a bit more elaborate. Three positive diodes are tied together to form the alternator's positive terminal, which is connected to the positive terminal of the battery. Three more diodes are generally grounded to the alternator frame and connected to the battery via the engine block and the battery ground strap. Another three auxiliary diodes (for an overall total of nine diodes) frequently are installed on the positive side of the three phases, feeding positive current to the voltage regulator and rotor field winding (via the brushes and slip rings) to energize and control the alternator (Figures 3-21A and 3-21B). Sometimes there is only one auxiliary diode (Figure 3-21C); occasionally none. Many Hitachi alternators (common on Yanmar engines) have a slightly different diode arrangement.

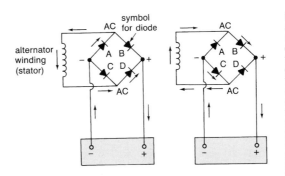

Hot-rated, marine, and isolated-ground alternators. As always, there are cheap ways and expensive ways of making alternators. *If an alternator will be used to recharge heavily discharged, large-capacity battery banks, it is going to be worked many times harder than an automotive alternator, and as a result needs to be more ruggedly built.* Key features are the ability to operate *continuously at full output in high temperatures*, oversized bearings, heavy-duty brushes, and heavy-duty diodes. (These are all features of what, in the United States, are known as *KKK*-rated alternators—Figure 3-22.) In addition, to withstand the marine environment, the alternator should have noncorrosive brush holders (normally brass), plated brush springs and other metal parts (the springs are especially important), and impregnated windings to maintain insulation levels in a damp environment.

Some marine alternators are *ignition protected*, meaning the slip rings and brushes are enclosed in a vapor-tight housing, or the ventilation openings have screens. This will stop internal arcing within the alternator from igniting explosive vapors (e.g., gasoline, butane, or propane) in the engine room. In the United States, ignition protection is legally required with gasoline engines but not with diesel.

Finally, it is desirable for a marine alternator to be constructed with an *isolated ground*. Instead of using the normal practice of grounding the negative side to the alternator case, *the negative is brought out to a separate insulated stud, which must then be wired to the battery's negative terminal.* This eliminates the otherwise high currents that flow through the engine block to ground when the alternator is operating, potentially contributing to stray-current corrosion (see Chapter 5). Isolated-ground alternators are uncommon and expensive, but in certain circumstances, notably on metal boats, may be important. Mastervolt and Balmar (www.balmar.net) are good sources for isolated-ground alternators; many later-generation Hitachi *marine* alternators also have insulated grounds.

FIGURE 3-20. Operation of a single-phase bridge rectifier. In the symbol for a diode, the arrow indicates the direction in which the diode will pass current. In the schematic on the left, current is flowing in one direction from the stator winding through diode D to the battery's positive terminal. Diodes C and B block the flow in the other direction. The return path from the battery's negative terminal to the winding (necessary to complete the circuit) is through diode A. In the schematic on the right, the AC current flow from the stator winding has reversed, passing through diode B to the positive terminal. The return path is through diode C. *The generated current has reversed direction but still flows in the same direction into the battery.*

FIGURE 3-21A.
Schematics of two common three-phase bridge rectifiers. The only difference between the two is the manner in which the stator windings are connected. This is not a distinction we need be concerned with.

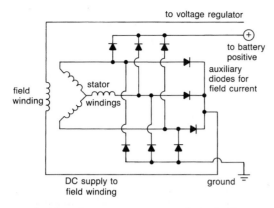

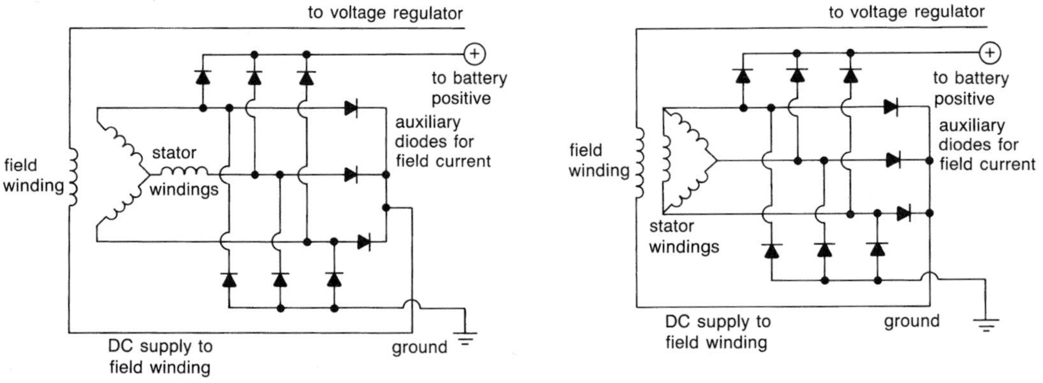

"Star"—connected nine-diode bridge

"Delta"—connected nine-diode bridge

FIGURE 3-21B. What diodes look like in practice. These are large diodes in a high-output alternator. Note that each output wire from a stator winding goes to two diodes mounted on two different heat sinks insulated from one another, one above the other (this is a little hard to see).

FIGURE 3-21C. Another arrangement of the diodes.

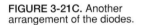

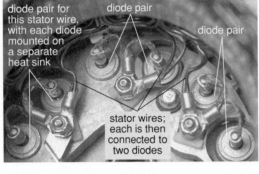

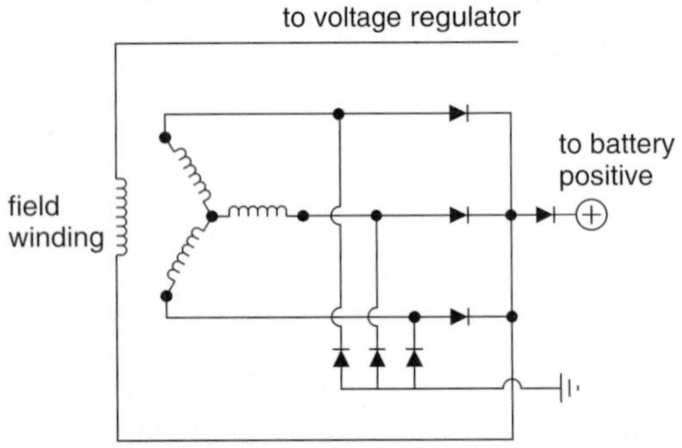

FIGURE 3-22. Automotive alternator versus high-output alternator. Note the difference in the shaft sizes (which translates into different bearing sizes) and slip rings (which translates into electrical load bearing surface). The slip rings on the automotive alternator are badly grooved.

Installation and Maintenance

If installed properly, alternators are virtually maintenance and trouble free. Key aspects of installation are to:

- Use a sufficiently rigid mounting bracket with correct alignment of the drive belt (see Chapter 1).
- Keep the alternator as cool as possible. Every 18°F/10°C rise in temperature approximately halves life expectancy.
- Make sure the alternator is never open-circuited when running (see below).
- Get the correct polarity on the cables (see below).
- Use large enough cables to avoid voltage drop (see Chapter 4).
- Support the cables against vibration.

Maintenance is a matter of keeping the drive belt tensioned and the alternator clean and protected from corrosion.

Open circuits and reverse polarity. Anytime an alternator is electrically disconnected (such as by turning off the battery isolation switch) *while still running*, the residual energy in the stator and the field windings momentarily produces continued output with no place to go. This voltage can easily peak at several hundred volts or more, blowing out all the diodes and the voltage regulator. This can happen in a fraction of a second. *Never disconnect a running alternator!* Snubbers (reverse-avalanche silicon diodes; available from Ample Technology, Xantrex, and others)—otherwise known as *surge-protection devices*—can be connected between an alternator output terminal and ground. These special diodes are set to close well above alternator output voltage but well below the destruction volt-

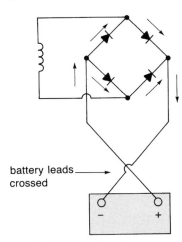

FIGURE 3-23. The effect of reverse polarity on diodes. The result is a direct electrical path from positive to negative terminal—a dead short. Full battery current will flow, burning out the diodes instantly.

age of the alternator diodes. Anytime an alternator is open-circuited, the snubber senses the rising voltage and dumps the alternator output to ground, potentially saving the diodes. However, snubbers have a limited load-carrying capability. Larger alternators would need to have two or more fitted in parallel, and even then, if the alternator is open-circuited when running at high levels of output (as happens when the batteries are well discharged) the snubber(s) are unlikely to save it.

The diodes will be blown out even more certainly by connecting a battery with reverse polarity—connecting the positive lead to the negative terminal and vice versa (Figure 3-23). *When reconnecting batteries be absolutely sure to get the cables the right way around!* Be especially careful when installing new batteries; the position of the terminals may be reversed from one battery to another.

Vibration. A problem that is becoming more common with the increasing use of high-output alternators is the positive cable coming adrift from the alternator's positive stud. Whenever outputs go above 100 amps, large cables are needed, which tend to be stiff and heavy. The positive studs and nuts on many alternators tend to be on the small side. (The assumption is a relatively light cable run to a nearby starter motor solenoid as opposed to a long, heavy cable run to a more distant bus bar or other connection point.) Engine-transmitted vibration can cause the cable-securing nut to work loose. The loose cable then arcs between its lug and the mounting stud until the stud is burned through and the cable drops off the alternator.

Depending on the charging circuit, this cable may be (and frequently is) connected directly to

a battery with no intervening diodes, switches, or fuses. If such a cable should land on the engine block or some other grounded surface, *it will cause a dangerous short circuit across the battery, which may well start a fire or even cause the battery to blow up.* I have recently heard of a couple of cases where the cable arced to the engine pan (sump), burned a hole in it, and caused the engine to self-destruct.

It is essential to ensure that the nut holding the output cable to its stud is locked in some way (e.g., a *Nylok* nut or the addition of a locking nut), and that the cable is properly supported so that it places no strain on the stud. The best way to do this is to add a small strain-relief arm to the alternator, so that the arm is vibrating in sync with the alternator, and to fasten the cable to this arm—Figures 3-24A and 3-24B. It is also essential to ensure that this circuit is properly protected with a fuse (see Chapter 4).

Belt tension and bearings. The load of a high-output alternator can be met only by top-quality belts that are regularly tensioned (as noted in Chapter 1, I always specify Gates Green Stripe belts). If twin belts are fitted, if possible they should be replaced as a *matched set.* To tension a belt, back off the alternator mounting bolts a turn or two, slip a lever between the alternator case and the engine, and lever the alternator out, holding the tension while the bolts are tightened. A short broom handle, hammer handle, or something similar is better for this job than a metal tool since it will not cause shorts or damage the alternator case (Figure 3-24A again). Note: Some modern alternator cases are quite thin, so tensioning must be done with care; special tools are available for belt tightening.

If adding a high-output alternator to an engine, you may be able to incorporate a belt-tensioning device into the alternator brackets (see Figure 3-25 for an example). This is a really handy addition.

Belts are especially prone to slip immediately after engine start-up, when alternator loads are at their highest. A slipping belt will frequently give off a high-pitched, often cyclical, squeal. (Note that the tachometer on many engines works by measuring the frequency of the alternator's AC output—before rectification—which varies directly with engine speed. Anytime a tachometer reading is low or erratic, suspect a slipping alternator drive belt.) If a common belt is used for the water pump and alternator, a slipping belt may also result in an overheated engine.

If a belt is allowed to slip for any length of time, it will heat up the pulley, which will in turn transmit the heat along the shaft to the rotor. This heat can demagnetize the rotor, per-

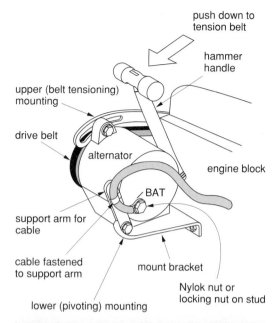

FIGURE 3-24A. Tensioning an alternator. Note the additional cable support bracket to prevent the heavy output cable from vibrating loose from the output stud.

push down to tension belt

hammer handle

upper (belt tensioning) mounting

drive belt

alternator

engine block

BAT

support arm for cable

cable fastened to support arm

mount bracket

Nylok nut or locking nut on stud

lower (pivoting) mounting

FIGURE 3-25. A belt-tensioning device built into an alternator bracket.

FIGURE 3-24B. Note the Nylok nut on the positive output cable and the locking washer under the bolt holding the negative cable.

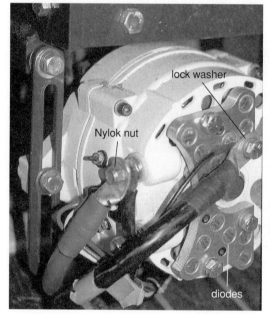

lock washer

Nylok nut

diodes

FIGURE 3-26A. Checking belt tension.

FIGURE 3-26B. Loose belts slip, heat up, harden, and crack.

manently crippling alternator output (the alternator will not recover after it has cooled down). The belt itself will become brittle, most likely with cracks spreading up from its inner edge, and have a glazed appearance on the surfaces that contact the pulleys (Figures 3-26A and 3-26B). Bottom line: Belts must be kept tight! When new, they may need to be retensioned several times during the first 100 hours of service.

Bearings are generally long lived. The pulley-end bearing is the one most likely to fail—it will make a distinctive, medium-pitched rumble. If the bearings are suspect, remove the belt and flex the pulley from side to side and in and out. There should be no sideways movement and only minimal in-and-out movement. Next, turn the pulley by hand; it should turn freely. If you feel a slight roughness as the pulley turns, the bearings may be worn. If the bearings are damaged, carefully check the pulley alignment when installing the new alternator since misalignment may have been the cause of the damage. (Misalignment will also cause accelerated belt wear, creating a heavy black dust that coats neighboring engine surfaces and bulkheads.)

Cleanliness and corrosion. Marine alternators are subjected to prolonged periods of high loading in hot engine compartments, which tends to overheat bearings, diodes, and voltage regulators, causing them to fail. Excess heat also melts the thin, lacquered insulation on coils. This can result in a short circuit or in the coil wire getting burned through like a fuse, breaking the circuit. Burned coils have a distinctive smell—once encountered, easily remembered!

Any dirt will tend to trap heat. The cooling fans on alternators located in dirty, greasy, smoky engine rooms pick up the oily mist and blow it through the alternator. In time a greasy buildup of dirt coats and insulates coils, diodes, etc., causing the alternator to run hot, making burnout more likely. This kind of gook is hard to clean out, and the solution is prevention—keep the engine running cleanly in the first place.

Exposure to salt spray, or just to the marine atmosphere, will lead to corrosion of parts and electrical terminals. Moving parts tend to freeze with intermittent use; brush springs are particularly prone to failure (Figures 3-27A and 3-27B). A periodic shot of WD-40 or electrical cleaner in and around alternator housings goes a long way toward keeping things moving and reducing corrosion on terminals.

FIGURE 3-27A. A failed brush spring has caused this brush to hang up . . .

FIGURE 3-27B. . . . burning the slip ring (and also the brush, which was almost completely burned away).

Finally, if an alternator comes from the factory unpainted, it should not be painted, even to slow corrosion. However nice it looks, that paint is just one more layer of insulation!

Charging Problems

When faced with charging problems, don't be too hasty about tearing into the equipment. One of the following three situations is likely: undercharging, overcharging, or no output at all. First determine which category covers the problem, then work through the relevant procedure below before jumping to any conclusions as to where the problem lies.

Persistent undercharging from an otherwise functioning alternator (Troubleshooting Chart 3-1). If the alternator appears to be working in some fashion (e.g., the ignition light goes out when the engine is running) but the batteries do not appear to be getting properly charged, there is a tendency to suspect the alternator when it may be fine. *First check the batteries.* As discussed earlier in this chapter, dead and dying batteries will not accept a charge. If the batteries are not the problem:

- Check the belt tension. You should not be able to depress the longest stretch of belt with moderate finger pressure more than ⅜ to ½ inch (10 mm to 13 mm). If the output has been fluctuating wildly—especially on initial start-up—perhaps accompanied by belt squeal, the belt is loose.

- Check that the alternator is adequately sized for the demands being made on it and that its speed of rotation is not too slow (see the Sizing an Alternator section in Chapter 1).

- *Check for voltage drop between the output terminal on the alternator and the positive battery post.* (Voltage drop is covered in detail in Chapter 4. At this time it is not necessary to understand the concept, simply how to test for it.) This is a very easy and often revealing test that does not get done nearly often enough.

  With the engine off, turn on some loads (lights, etc.) for a few minutes to discharge the battery. Now start the engine and throttle it up enough to get the alternator up to its full rated output. Keep the alternator at full output (bulk charge) for at least a few minutes to replace the current that has been drained from the battery. Immediately after cranking, and *while the alternator is still at full output* (this is important), use a multimeter set to the DC volts scale to test between the *alternator output terminal* (the largest one, with an insulated

FIGURE 3-28A. Measuring the voltage drop between an alternator and a battery with no split-charging diodes. First, draw down the battery by turning on cabin lights, a freshwater faucet, etc., with the engine off. Then start the engine and immediately hook up the multimeter as shown, being careful to avoid the alternator drive belt. There should be no more than a 0.5-volt drop. Repeat this test from the alternator case to the battery negative post.

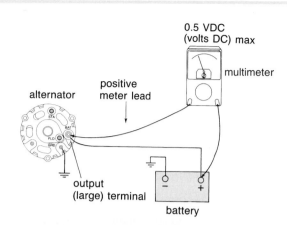

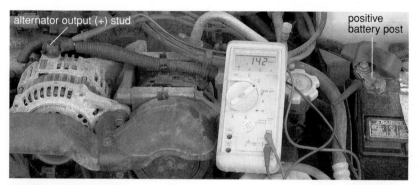

FIGURE 3-28B. Voltage drop is 0.142 volt—well within allowable limits.

FIGURE 3-28C. Measuring the voltage drop between an alternator and a battery with split-charging diodes. There should be no more than a 1.0-volt drop on the positive side of the circuit, and no more than a 0.5-volt drop on the negative side (testing from the alternator case to the battery negative post).

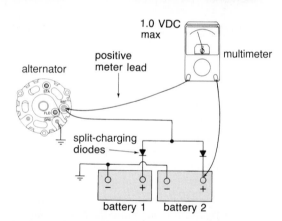

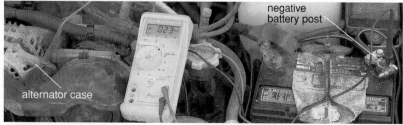

FIGURE 3-29. Testing for voltage drop on the negative side of the charging circuit. It is 0.023 volt—very low.

base and the largest cable coming from it; probably labeled "BAT") and the *battery positive post* (Figures 3-28A and 3-28B). The meter's positive lead goes to the alternator output terminal; the negative to the battery. *Stay clear of the alternator drive belt!* If the meter

has multiple scales (most analog types do), start with the 10-volts DC scale. If this shows no deflection or only a slight deflection, switch to a lower scale (2.5 volts DC). (Multimeter use is covered in Chapter 4.)

In a system with split-charging diodes, the meter should show no more than 1.0 volt at full alternator output; without diodes, no more than 0.5 volt. These figures are the *volt drop* on the circuit (Figures 3-28A and 3-28C). *Any reading above these indicates excessive voltage drop;* the wiring is inadequate, or there is unwanted resistance in the circuit, possibly caused by loose, dirty, or corroded terminals (see the Troubleshooting with a Voltmeter section in Chapter 4). Clean up all connections and try again. If the voltage drop persists, *the wiring is almost certainly undersized for this application and needs to be upgraded* (see Chapter 4 for determining wire sizes). *Undersized wiring is a common problem on boats (including new boats), crippling the effectiveness of many charging systems.*

- Repeat the same voltage drop test with the alternator once again at full output, placing the positive meter lead on the battery's *negative post,* and the negative meter lead on either the *alternator case* or a *ground terminal on the alternator* (Figure 3-29; if the alternator has an insulated ground—desirable, but rare—the ground terminal—probably labeled "GRD"—must be used). *If the volt drop is even as high as 0.5 volt on any system, the circuit has serious resistance that needs to be cleaned up.* Since most alternators are grounded through the case and then through the mounting bracket, engine block, and engine ground strap, clean all the connections in the circuit (mounting brackets and bolts and engine ground-strap terminals). On all but insulated-ground alternators, it is a good idea to install a short ground strap, at least as heavy duty as the alternator's output cable, from the alternator case to the boat's *main negative bus* (see Chapter 5).

- Run the engine for a while with all loads off so that the battery has a chance to come to a full charge. While doing this, monitor the battery voltage with a multimeter placed *across the battery terminals.* The battery voltage will rise steadily and then level off. *This level voltage is the voltage the battery is driven to when the alternator reaches its regulated set point (the absorption voltage) established by its voltage regulator* (Figures 3-30A and 3-30B). *The voltage should be at least 14.0 volts, and as high as 14.4 volts on many marine systems.* If the measured voltage is less than this, the battery is *being undercharged.* The reason for undercharging may be an improperly adjusted voltage regulator, but most likely it is the result of voltage drop in the circuit caused either by inadequate wiring and connections (see above) or else *by installing isolation diodes without compensating for the voltage drop of 0.5 to 1.0 volt caused by the diodes* (see Chapter 1 for an explanation of this; for solutions to the problem, see pages 107–9).

- Check all the connections in any external field circuit (see page 106) to make sure they are clean and tight.

Only suspect the alternator if none of the preceding tests turns up a problem. One or more diodes or stator windings may be open-circuited (pages 99, 104), or the brushes may be worn or not making good contact with their slip rings, in which case output is likely to be erratic (page 100). Such problems are uncommon—an alternator is far more likely to fail outright than it is to partially fail. (Remember, this section is about persistent undercharging *from an otherwise functioning alternator;* for no output, see below).

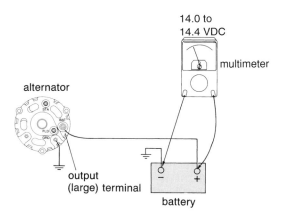

FIGURE 3-30A. Testing for the maximum voltage to which an alternator is driving a battery during charging.

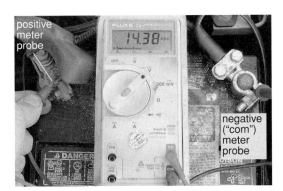

FIGURE 3-30B. Checking the absorption voltage at the battery.

Troubleshooting Chart 3-1.
Battery/Alternator/Regulator Problems: Undercharging

Symptom: Battery never seems to regain full charge.

Is the battery dying or dead? **NO** **TEST:** Check the specific gravity or open-circuit voltage. Charge up and run a load test or capacity test.	**YES** **FIX:** Look for equipment inadvertently left on, dirt or moisture on the battery, or a leak to ground in the boat's wiring. Run an equalization charge on wet-cells; try the dead-battery recovery procedure on gel-cells and AGMs. If battery fails to respond, replace it.
Is belt tension adequate? **NO** **TEST:** Listen for belt squeal. Watch for fluctuating tachometer. Depress the belt—it should not move more than ⅜ to ½ inch under moderate finger pressure.	**YES** **FIX:** Increase tension.
Is the alternator undersized or its speed of rotation too slow? Is charging time inadequate? **NO** **TEST:** Compare demands on alternator with its size and speed of rotation as outlined in Chapter 1. Try charging the battery for at least 3 hours.	**YES** **FIX:** Match alternator with demands (see Chapter 1). Increase routine charging time.
Is there excessive voltage drop in the circuit between the alternator and the battery? **NO** **TEST:** Use a multimeter to test for volt drop *at full alternator output* (during the bulk charge phase) with one meter probe on the alternator positive stud and the other on the battery positive post, and then one probe on the alternator negative and the other on the battery negative post.	**YES** **FIX:** Clean and tighten loose, dirty, and corroded terminals. (Be sure to check the engine ground-strap connections.) Replace faulty or undersized wiring. Remove battery isolation diodes and replace with a battery paralleling relay or adjust the voltage regulator for diode-induced voltage drop.
Is the voltage at the battery too low for effective charging? **NO** **TEST:** As the battery comes to charge (reaches the absorption voltage), monitor the voltage across the battery terminals. Does it stabilize below 14.0 volts?	**YES** **FIX:** Adjust the voltage regulator upward. Compensate for diode-induced voltage drop (see the text). If this is not possible, get rid of battery isolation diodes and/or replace the voltage regulator with a more appropriate model.
Is the voltage regulator wiring defective? **NO** **TEST:** Check external connections and wiring.	**YES** **FIX:** Repair or replace.
If the above tests fail to reveal a problem, check the brushes, diodes, rotor, and stator windings in the alternator (see pages 99–104).	

Troubleshooting Chart 3-2.
Battery/Alternator/Regulator Problems: Overcharging

Symptoms: Battery overheats; wet-cells boil, require frequent topping off with water, and give off an acrid smell; gel-cells and AGMs may blow their vent caps and dry out.

Is the battery dying or dead? If so, it may behave as if overcharged, but will not come to, or hold, a full charge. **NO** **TEST:** Check specific gravity, measure open-circuit voltage, use a load tester, or perform a capacity test (pages 78–82).	**YES** **FIX:** Replace.
Is the battery in a location that is too hot? **NO** **TEST:** Measure temperature of battery compartment. If excessively hot, remedy.	**YES** **FIX:** Increase ventilation to compartment or move battery.
Is the voltage regulator set slightly high for faster charge rates? **NO** **TEST:** Monitor the battery voltage during charging. As the battery comes up to full charge (reaches the absorption voltage), its voltage should not go above 14.4 volts for a wet-cell, 14.2 volts for a gel-cell or AGM.	**YES** **FIX:** It may be wise not to fix this. Occasional mild overcharging is often the price to be paid for realistically fast charge rates. See text.
Is an unregulated wind generator or solar panel overcharging the battery? **NO** **TEST:** See Chapter 6 to estimate probable inputs from these sources. Monitor battery voltage and battery temperature. Voltage should not go above 14.4 volts on a wet-cell and 14.2 volts on a gel-cell or AGM. Battery temperature should not go above 110°F/43.3°C.	**YES** **FIX:** See Chapter 6.
Is the voltage regulator's battery-sensing wire disconnected or broken? Has a diode been installed backward in the sensing wire? Both will lead to violent overcharging, causing vigorous boiling and rapid water loss. **NO** **TEST:** Visual inspection. Corroded sensing-wire terminals will have a similar though less dramatic effect.	**YES** **FIX:** Replace sensing wire. Clean terminals. Put the diode in correctly (see page 109).
Is the voltage regulator short-circuited? This will lead to violent overcharging. **NO** **TEST:** Fit a spare and see whether the problem disappears.	**YES** **FIX:** Replace voltage regulator.

Persistent overcharging (Troubleshooting Chart 3-2). If you have persistent overcharging, there is a problem with the batteries or voltage regulator *but not the alternator*. To check for overcharging, put a voltmeter across the battery terminals and run the engine until the voltage stabilizes (if the batteries are well discharged, this may take several hours). If this absorption voltage is above 14.2 to 14.4 volts, it is too high and the batteries are probably being overcharged (except in cold weather with a temperature-compensated voltage regulator); see page 109 in the Troubleshooting Voltage Regulators section. Note, however, that as batteries, especially wet-cell batteries, reach their last legs, they tend to absorb a higher charging current, gas more than usual, and require frequent topping off. These are also symptoms of overcharging. So before blaming the charging system, check the batteries (high-load and capacity test—see earlier in this chapter).

No output (Troubleshooting Chart 3-3). If an alternator appears not to be charging at all (the ignition warning light stays on, the battery remains discharged, etc.), the first task is to confirm that it is really the alternator that is at fault.

- If you have a multimeter with a clamp-type DC amps capability that can handle the rated output of the alternator, clamp the meter around the output lead from the alternator (make sure it is only around this lead), crank the engine, throttle it up, and check for output (Figure 3-31). Assuming the batteries are somewhat discharged, the alternator output should initially be at least half its rated output, in which case it is working fine.

- If you do not have a suitable clamp-type DC amps meter, *shut down the engine*, turn off or disconnect all auxiliary charging devices (wind generator, solar panels), *switch the battery into the starting circuit* (switch on the relevant battery isolation switch), *switch on the engine ignition* (but do not run the engine),

FIGURE 3-31. A clamp-type DC ammeter—a very useful tool—on a nominal 60 amp alternator.

and check the battery voltage *across the battery terminals*. On a 12-volt system, it should be around 12.5 volts or higher (Figure 3-32A).

- Now check the voltage between the *output* (or positive) *terminal* (the big one) on the alternator and a good *ground* (or negative), such as a clean spot on the engine block. (If the alternator has an insulated ground—see page 87—you must make the ground or negative connection at the negative terminal on the alternator or the battery.)

In a battery installation without isolation diodes, *the voltage at the alternator output should be the same as battery voltage* (Figure 3-32A). If isolation diodes are fitted between the alternator and the batteries, *the voltage at the alternator output* (with the engine shut down) *will read 0* (Figure 3-32B). *If the voltage is neither the battery voltage nor 0, the problem is in the circuit between the alternator and the battery*. (Note that in some circumstances, leakage current through a diode will be high enough to cause a voltage reading at near battery voltage; before condemning the circuit, check with a test lamp—Figure 3-34A—from the alternator output terminal to ground. The lamp should not light. If it does, the isolation diode has failed. For other methods of testing diodes, see pages 97–99.)

- If the circuit seems OK, start the engine, speed it up, and recheck the voltage at the alternator output. *Whatever the system, it should read a volt or more above the original battery voltage*. If it does, the alternator is functioning. If it does not, there is a problem with the alternator or its voltage regulator; the next task is to decide which.

P- and N-type alternators. Some alternators have internal regulators, and in this case, there is little to be done when a problem is traced to the alternator or regulator except fit a new alternator-*cum*-regulator. (The Voltage Regulators section later in this chapter has a few more suggestions.) Many alternators, however, have external regulators controlling the current to the alternator field winding via a terminal on the back of the alternator marked "F," "DF," or "FLD." Most external regulators are connected on the positive side of the field winding (these are P-type alternators—Figures 3-33A and 3-33B), but a few are connected between the negative side of the field winding and ground (N-type alternators—Figure 3-33C). For more on this, see the Voltage Regulators section later in this chapter. For now, the first task is to decide whether the alternator is a P- or N-type.

Shut down the engine, *turn off the ignition and battery isolation switches*, and disconnect the

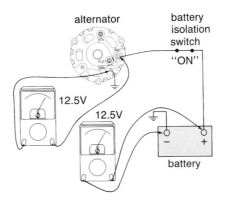

FIGURE 3-32A. Measuring voltage at the battery and at the alternator output terminal with no split-charging diodes. The battery isolation switch and the ignition switch are on, but the engine is *not* running. On a 12-volt system, there should be about a 12.5-volt reading across the battery terminals (with a more or less fully charged battery), with the same reading between the alternator output terminal and ground (its case, unless it has an insulated ground).

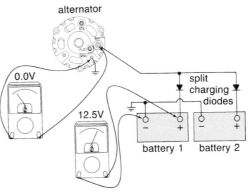

FIGURE 3-32B. Measuring voltage at the battery and at the alternator output terminal with isolation diodes. The battery isolation switch and the ignition switch are on, but the engine is *not* running. On a 12-volt system, the voltage reading across the battery terminals should be around 12.5 volts (with a more or less fully charged battery); the reading between the alternator output terminal and ground should be 0.

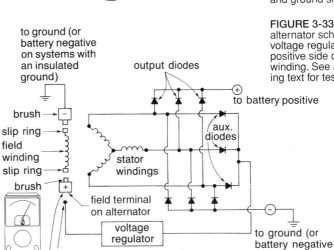

FIGURE 3-33A. P-type alternator schematic—the voltage regulator is on the positive side of the field winding. See accompanying text for test procedure.

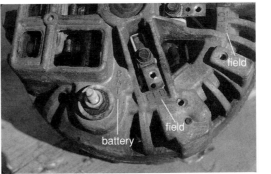

FIGURE 3-33B. Field (FLD) and battery positive (BAT) on an alternator.

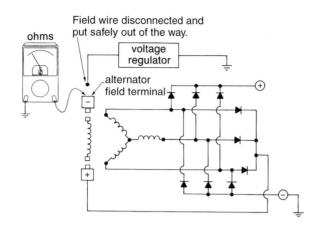

FIGURE 3-33C. N-type alternator schematic—the voltage regulator is on the negative side of the field winding. See accompanying text for test procedure.

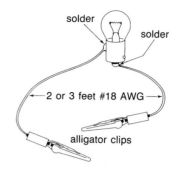

FIGURE 3-34A. A test light.

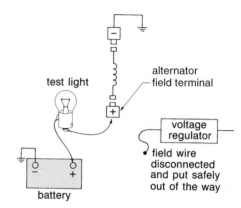

FIGURE 3-34B. Bypassing a P-type voltage regulator. Connect the test light as shown, start the engine, and measure the alternator output voltage as in Figure 3-30A. If it is normal (a volt or more above original battery voltage), the regulator is defective; if it is not, the alternator is defective.

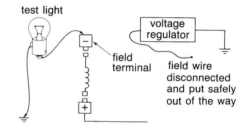

FIGURE 3-34C. Bypassing an N-type voltage regulator.

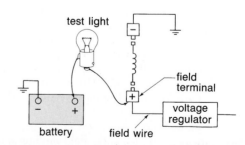

FIGURE 3-34D. *Flashing the field* on a P-type alternator. If the test in Figure 3-34B showed normal output, shut down the engine and reconnect the field wire from the voltage regulator. Start the engine. With the engine running, connect the test light momentarily between the battery and the field terminal. If alternator output is restored (test as in Figure 3-30A), the excitation circuit has failed.

field wire from the alternator. Using the ohms function of a multimeter (on its lowest—R × 1—scale if it is an analog meter), test between the *field terminal* on the alternator and *ground* (Figures 3-33A and 3-33C). A P-type alternator will give a reading close to 0 ohms (generally, somewhere between 2 and 6 ohms); an N-type will give a high reading. It is a good idea when doing this test to rotate the alternator a little to ensure that the brushes are making a good contact with their slip rings.

Voltage regulator or alternator? Once you have established the type of alternator, you need to bypass the voltage regulator so that field current can be supplied *directly to the alternator field winding*. If this causes the alternator to work, *the voltage regulator is bad*. If the alternator still fails to work, *the alternator itself is at fault*. To bypass the voltage regulator, make up a test light as shown (Figure 3-34A), with a minimum 12-watt (1 amp at 12 volts) lightbulb. Disconnect the field wire at the field terminal (F, DF, or FLD) on the alternator and put it *safely out of the way, where it cannot short out*.

If the alternator is a P-type, connect the test light *between the positive terminal on the battery and the field terminal* (Figure 3-34B).

If the alternator is an N-type, connect the test light between *the field terminal and a good ground* (Figure 3-34C).

Start the engine and test the voltage *across the battery terminals*. If the voltage is now indicating a charge (a volt or more above the battery voltage when the alternator is not running), *the alternator is OK, but its voltage regulator is defective* (the current flowing through the test light is energizing the field winding and so bypassing the voltage regulator, which is why there is now alternator output). *If the alternator still does not produce output, the alternator itself is defective.*

If a multimeter is not available or if there is any doubt as to whether the alternator is a P- or N-type, with the engine running, try connecting

MAINTAINING AND TROUBLESHOOTING A BATTERY-POWERED ELECTRICAL SYSTEM the test light from the field terminal first to the battery positive and then to ground. If there is no output on either test, the alternator is bad.

Excitation test: the final test. If the test light from the battery to the field terminal produced output from a P-type alternator, *reconnect the field wire from the voltage regulator* and crank the engine. Connect the test light *momentarily* between the battery and the field terminal *with the engine running*. This is known as *flashing the field* (Figure 3-34D). If the test light restores output *and the alternator continues to work after the light is disconnected*, the problem is nothing more than a failure of the excitation circuit, which is easy to fix (see page 107).

N-type excitation is a little more complicated. If an N-type excitation circuit has failed, none of the tests so far will have produced any output.

N-type alternators with external regulators generally have either an auxiliary output terminal (sometimes marked "AUX"; in any case it will be a second insulated stud on the back of the alternator) or an external excitation wire supplying current to the field winding; sometimes they will have both—see the Voltage Regulators section later in this chapter. Connecting the test light *momentarily* between the *battery positive* and either the *auxiliary* or *excitation terminal* while the alternator is running and with all normal wiring in place will restore lost excitation; if the alternator begins to work and stays working, once again the problem is a failure of the excitation circuit (see page 107).

Last resort. With a really dead battery, many alternators just will not start producing output, and none of the above tests is possible. If the engine has a hand crank and can be started, a 6-volt battery or half a dozen flashlight (torch) batteries can be connected in series to provide enough current to get the alternator going. Connect the negative side of the (flashlight or other) battery to the *alternator case* or a good ground on the engine. Crank the engine and flash the alternator field as described in the previous excitation tests; i.e., touch the flashlight battery's positive wire to the field terminal on a P-type alternator, and to the auxiliary or excitation terminal on an N-type. In the case of an alternator with an insulated ground, connect the flashlight battery's negative to the boat battery's negative terminal or the alternator's negative terminal.

Miscellaneous diode tests. Finally, here are three quick and easy diode tests that should be performed in the case of unexplained battery failures or loss of charge:

1. Connect a voltmeter in the AC-volts mode across the *alternator output stud* and a *good*

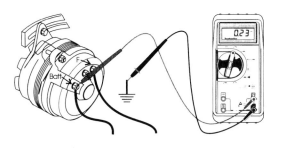

FIGURE 3-35A. Checking ripple voltage. Ripple voltage (AC voltage) can be measured by switching the multimeter to AC volts and connecting the black lead to a good ground and the red lead to the BAT terminal on the back of the alternator (not at the battery). A good alternator should measure less than 0.5 VAC with the engine running. A higher reading indicates damaged alternator diodes. *(Fluke)*

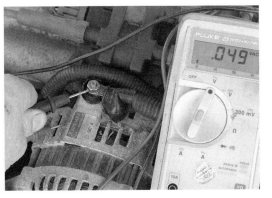

FIGURE 3-35B. Testing for AC ripple voltage from the alternator's positive terminal to negative (the alternator's case). It is very low (0.049 VAC), which is good.

ground (the alternator case, unless it has an insulated ground) *with the alternator running*. The meter will read the *AC ripple* superimposed on the alternator's DC output (Figures 3-35A and 3-35B). To understand this, refer back to Figure 3-19A. After rectification, rather than being a straight line, the DC output of an alternator is composed of the tops of the three curves that form the three phases of the AC output of the alternator and, as such, the output line forms a continuous sequence of shallow waves. When measuring the AC ripple, a meter will be measuring the depth of these waves. *The AC ripple should be no more than 0.5 volt; if it is greater than this, one or more of the diodes is damaged.* Excessive AC ripple is destructive to batteries, especially gelcells and AGMs.

2. *With the engine shut down*, disconnect the alternator positive cable and all other cables (other than a ground cable) and then insert a DC milliammeter *between the positive terminal on the battery and the output stud on the alternator* (Figure 3-36A). The meter will be

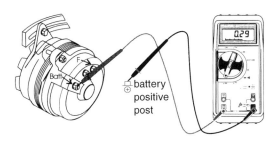

battery positive post

FIGURE 3-36A. Alternator leakage current. To check alternator diode leakage, connect the multimeter between the alternator output terminal and the battery positive post when the engine is not running. Use care when disconnecting the alternator output wire; make sure the battery is disconnected first. Leakage current should be a couple of milliamps at most; more often, it will be on the order of 0.5 milliamp. A leaking diode can discharge the battery when the engine is off. *(Fluke)*

Troubleshooting Chart 3-3.
Battery/Alternator/Regulator Problems: No Alternator Output

Symptoms: Ignition warning light stays on, battery remains discharged.

Is the drive belt loose or broken? **TEST:** The belt should respond to finger pressure with no more than ⅜ to ½ inch of give at its midpoint.	**YES** **FIX:** Tighten or replace.
Is the circuit between the alternator and battery at fault? **TEST:** Either (1) test for output with a clamp-on DC amp meter, or (2) shut down the engine, isolate or shut down auxiliary chargers (solar panels, wind generator, etc.), turn on battery isolation switch, turn on engine ignition switch (but do not start engine), and check voltage (a) across the battery terminals and (b) between alternator output and ground. If voltage at alternator output terminal is neither about the same as the battery voltage (no isolating diodes) or 0 (isolating diodes, dual battery installation), the circuit between alternator and battery is faulty. (Note: Diodes may sometimes show voltage—see text.)	**YES** **FIX:** Check all wiring and connections. Clean and replace as necessary.
Does the alternator have an internal voltage regulator? **NO** **TEST:** Look for absence of alternator field terminal, field wire, and external regulator.	**YES** **FIX:** If a lack-of-output problem has been traced this far and the regulator is internal, you have little choice but to install a new alternator.
If the voltage regulator is external, is it a P-type or an N-type? **TEST:** Shut down engine, turn off ignition and battery isolation switches, and disconnect field wire from alternator. Measure resistance between field terminal and ground: P-type = reading near 0 ohms; N-type = high reading.	**YES** **P-type FIX:** Proceed with Steps 1–3 below. **YES** **N-type FIX:** Proceed with Steps 4–6 below.
(1) Does the alternator fail to work when the P-type voltage regulator is bypassed? **TEST:** Connect a test lamp between alternator field terminal and battery positive terminal. Start engine. Look for rising battery voltage.	**YES** **FIX:** Alternator is broken. Check for damaged brushes and slip rings, or shorted or open-circuited rotor, stator, or diode. See pages 99–104 for possible repair procedure. *continued*

reading any leakage current through the alternator's diodes. This will generally be on the order of 0.5 milliamp, but in any event *should not be higher than 2.0 milliamps.* If it is, one or more of the diodes has a problem.

3. *With the engine shut down, disconnect all cables from the alternator output stud.* Test with an ohmmeter from the alternator output stud to ground, and then reverse the meter leads and test again (Figures 3-36B and 3-36C). In theory, the meter should show an infinite (very high) resistance in one direction and a low resistance (down toward 0 ohms) in the other direction. However, things are not this simple, because it requires a certain "forward voltage" to "open" (*bias*) the diodes in their conductive direction, and this has to be generated by the meter's internal battery. Depending on the meter and the state of its battery, we may get anything from infinity in both directions (most likely), to infinity (or a very high resistance) in one direction and a relatively low resistance in the other direction. If the meter has a specific *diode-testing* capa-

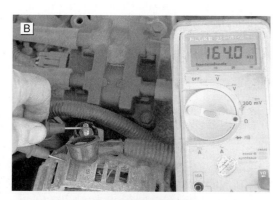

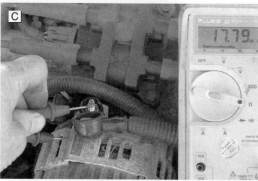

FIGURES 3-36B AND 3-36C. Testing alternator diodes with all leads disconnected from the alternator output (positive) stud. Using the ohms position on the meter, there should be a very high resistance in one direction and a low resistance with the meter leads reversed. But most meters will show a high reading in one direction (in this case 164 kiloohms) and a very high reading in the other direction (in this case 17.79 megaohms).

FIGURES 3-36D AND 3-36E. A more reliable test can be made with a meter that has a diode-testing capability, displaying the voltage drop through the diode. It should be an open circuit (".OL") in one direction and around 0.9 volt in the other direction. The 0.433-volt reading here indicates a shorted diode.

bility (Chapter 4), use it. It may measure either the voltage drop through the diodes or else the resistance (it generally measures the voltage drop). In the former case, it should show *no voltage* in one direction and around *0.9 volt* with the meter leads reversed (Figures 3-36D and 3-36E); in the latter case, it should show a very high resistance (maybe infinity) in one direction and a lower resistance in the other direction. (Some high-end meters will show 0.9 volt in both directions, but will display a diode symbol in the screen with the symbol reversing direction when the meter leads are switched over.) If the test results are different from these, there is a problem with one or more diodes. In particular, *if a low resistance is shown in both directions, the diodes are shorted.*

Repairing Alternators

If the above tests have pinpointed the alternator as the source of a charging problem, the most likely failures are in the diodes and the brushes. Determining what is at fault is generally academic since repair parts are unlikely to be on

Troubleshooting Chart 3-3 *(continued)*

(2) If the alternator worked in Step 1, the voltage regulator is defective. Is it merely a failure of the excitation circuit?	**YES** **FIX:** Repair is comparatively simple (page 107).
NO **TEST:** Shut down engine. Reconnect alternator field wire. Restart engine. Connect test lamp momentarily between field terminal and battery positive terminal. If alternator output is restored and continues after light is disconnected, the excitation circuit is at fault.	
(3) If Step 2 failed to restore continuous output, the regulator needs to be replaced.	
(4) Does the alternator work when the N-type voltage regulator is bypassed?	**YES** **FIX:** Voltage regulator is defective and needs to be replaced.
NO **TEST:** Connect a test lamp between alternator field terminal and a good ground. Start the engine. Look for alternator output in excess of battery voltage.	
(5) Is the voltage regulator's excitation circuit defective?	**YES** **FIX:** Repair is comparatively simple (page 107).
NO **TEST:** Shut down engine. Reconnect alternator field wire. Restart engine. Connect test lamp momentarily between battery positive terminal and alternator auxiliary or excitation terminal. See whether alternator output voltage comes up and stays up.	
(6) If Step 5 failed to restore output, alternator is defective. Check for damaged brushes and/or slip rings, or shorted or open-circuited rotor, stator, or diode. See pages 99–104 for possible repair procedures.	

board. Those adventurous souls wishing to get heavily into alternator repairs should obtain a copy of *The 12 Volt Doctor's Alternator Book* by Edgar J. Beyn (locate a dealer at www.weems-plath.com). The rest of us should always carry a spare alternator and have the deceased rejuvenated by a professional alternator rebuilder; it then becomes the spare.

If you are exploring further, diode testing is covered in more detail at the end of this chapter. An open-circuited diode will simply disable its particular stator winding, leaving the alternator to run at reduced output on the other two windings (and with increased AC ripple). You can remove a short-circuited diode, insulate the end of its stator winding if no replacement diode is available, and continue to operate the alternator at reduced output. Check brushes, rotors, and stators as follows:

Brushes. Since an alternator's brushes carry only the small amount of current needed to energize the field winding in the rotor, they are subject to very little load and wear and rarely require maintenance. In time, however, they wear down, spring pressure decreases, and the brushes fail to seat properly on their slip rings. Corrosion of the brush springs can also cause a loss of spring tension, resulting in poor brush contact with slip rings. This will lead to arcing and pitting of the slip rings. Such problems in turn will lead to improper energizing (excitation) of the field winding and erratic or failed alternator output. Even if no replacement brushes are on board, simply cleaning up the old brushes and the slip rings will sometimes temporarily restore output to a problem alternator.

Brush inspection, cleanup, and replacement is generally straightforward. Unfortunately, however, there are not just dozens but hundreds of different alternators so it is difficult to lay down general rules. Some alternators have external brush holders, some have internal brush holders, and some have the brush holders incorporated in an externally attached voltage regulator housing. If the brush holders are not self-evident but the alternator has an externally attached regulator—often a fairly compact, boxlike unit, normally held on with two screws—unscrew this and the brushes usually will be found inside.

Independently mounted external brush holders generally consist of a small plastic housing held with one or two screws, within which are one or two spade terminals. To free the brushes, remove the housing from the alternator and release the spade terminals by pressing down their retaining tags with a small screwdriver and pushing them inward. Clean the housing before fitting new brushes. When being fitted, some brushes must be held in place in their housings against their spring pressure with a small screwdriver or a toothpick inserted through a hole in the body of the alternator.

Internal brushes are trickier. The whole rear end of the alternator—generally held on with four bolts—must be removed. The alternator case can then be separated on either side of the housing for the stator windings. On some alternators, the brushes are accessible without removing the stator, but on many the stator windings must come out with the rear case, or else various wires will get broken: take care when separating the case, and if necessary make sure it breaks apart in a manner that brings the stator out with the rear housing.

The brush holders will be self-evident; probably the brushes will already have popped out of their holders under their spring pressure. Once again, a toothpick will likely be needed to trap the brushes in their brush holders during reassembly (Figures 3-37A to 3-37K and 3-38A to 3-38F). While the rotor is out, clean its slip rings, polish them with 400- or 600-grit wet-or-dry sandpaper, and test the rotor for shorts or an open circuit (see Figures 3-39A, 3-39B, 3-40A, and 3-40B).

A) points A and B are on either side of the stator windings; when the two halves of the alternator case are pulled apart, they may separate at either point
point A
point B

B) to remove the stator complete with the diode plate, regulator, and brushes, pry it loose at point B
point B

C) voltage regulator
diode plate

D
stator wire to diode connection

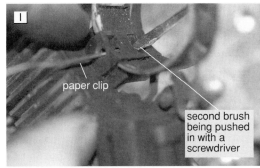

I
paper clip

second brush being pushed in with a screwdriver

E
cutting the stator wire to diode connection

J
the paper clip will now hold both brushes in place during reassembly

F
brush hung up in brush holder

K
paper clip holding the brushes in place

G
burned slip ring

FIGURES 3-37A TO 3-37K. Alternator disassembly. External case removal (3-37A, 3-37B, and 3-37C). In this instance, the case has separated at point A in Figure 3-37A to reveal the voltage regulator (upper half of Figure 3-37C) and diode plate (lower half). On smaller alternators, the stator wires are soldered to the diodes. To test individual diodes these connections must be unsoldered or cut (3-37D and 3-37E). However, if access to the brushes and slip rings is all that is desired, as opposed to individual diode testing, the stator can be pried out of the lower half of the alternator case at point B in Figure 3-37A, complete with the diode plate, regulator, and brushes (see also Figure 3-38B); i.e., there is no need to cut the stator wires as has been done here. Inspection of the brushes shows that one of the brush springs has failed, causing the brush to hang up and burn the slip ring (3-37F and 3-37G). Reassemble by pushing the brushes back in their holders against the springs and holding them in place while the diode plate is put back on the alternator (in this case, the brushes are held with a paper clip; 3-37H to 3-37K.).

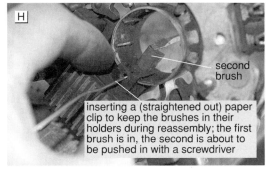

H
second brush

inserting a (straightened out) paper clip to keep the brushes in their holders during reassembly; the first brush is in, the second is about to be pushed in with a screwdriver

FIGURES 3-38A TO 3-38F. Disassembly of a high-output alternator. The rear housing half is being pulled off—complete with the stator windings—to reveal the brushes (which have popped out of their holders under spring pressure), diodes, and stator windings (3-38A and 3-38B). In this case, the stator wires are bolted to the diodes and so are easily disconnected for individual diode testing. A close-up of the brushes and springs (3-38C). Holding the brushes in place with a paper clip during reassembly (3-38D to 3-38F). *(Line drawing by Jim Sollers)*

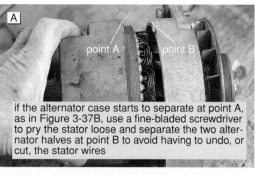

A

if the alternator case starts to separate at point A, as in Figure 3-37B, use a fine-bladed screwdriver to pry the stator loose and separate the two alternator halves at point B to avoid having to undo, or cut, the stator wires

point A   point B

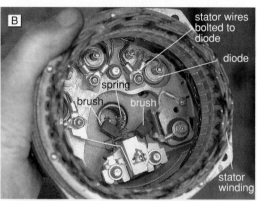

B

stator wires bolted to diode

diode

spring

brush   brush

stator winding

C

brushes

springs

D

paper clip inserted through the back of the housing . . .

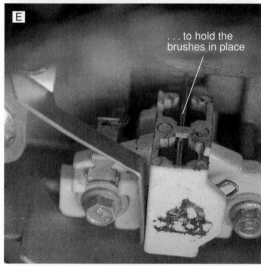

E

. . . to hold the brushes in place

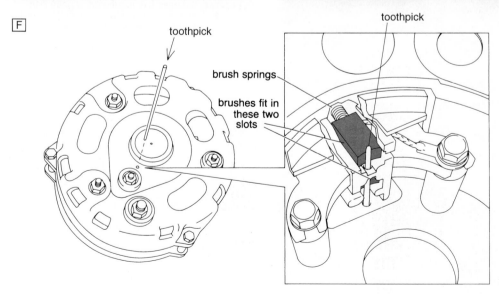

F

toothpick

toothpick

brush springs

brushes fit in these two slots

Rotors. The following test can often be made with the alternator still in place and with minimal disassembly, as shown in Figures 3-39A and 3-40A, although for clarity, I show the test in Figure 3-39B with the rotor removed from its alternator. Note you must *first isolate the alternator electrically*—switch off the battery isolation and ignition switches and disconnect the wiring from the alternator's positive (BAT) terminal. This is essential to avoid damaging the multimeter.

On alternators with external regulators, disconnect the field wire coming from the voltage regulator, disconnect the alternator output lead, set a multimeter to its ohms function (R × 1 scale on an analog meter), and test between the *field terminal* and the *alternator case*. This will test the circuit from the field brush (which is connected to one end of the field winding) to ground.

With P-type alternators, the meter should give a very low reading—probably between 2 and 6 ohms; the higher the alternator's rated output, the lower the reading—since the other end of the field winding should be grounded (through the second brush) to the alternator case (Figure 3-39A, Test 1, and Figure 3-39B). A very high reading indicates an open circuit in the field winding (it is burned out) or that the brushes are

not in contact with their slip rings. Try turning the alternator while conducting the test. If the reading flickers up and down, check the brushes and springs before writing off the rotor. With a very low reading (close to zero), the field winding may be OK, but then again it may be shorted to ground. Many cheap meters are insufficiently sensitive to tell. If you have a cheap meter and are unsure of the test results, you can double-check for a short by connecting a line containing a low-amperage fuse (10 to 15 amps—the fuse is important) from the positive terminal of the battery to the field terminal of the alternator (Figure 3-39A, Test 2). If the fuse blows, the rotor is shorted. (Better yet, buy a decent meter—they are not that expensive!)

With N-type alternators, a multimeter (R × 100 scale if it is an analog meter) connected between the *field terminal* and ground (with the field wire disconnected) should show an open circuit (a very high reading—Figure 3-40A). A low reading indicates a short to ground. The high reading may also be due to an open circuit in the rotor itself, but there is no easy way to check this without further disassembly.

Rotors on alternators with internal or attached regulators (i.e., with no external field terminal) can be tested if you can get access to the brushes or slip rings. Touch the multimeter leads to the two slip rings for the ohms test. Both P- and N-types should give a low reading (2 to 6 ohms, or thereabouts; Figure 3-39B). A high reading

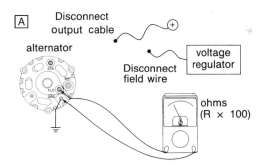

FIGURES 3-39A AND 3-39B. Rotor testing, P-type alternator, external regulator. BAT is the output terminal (leading to the battery positive terminal); FLD is the field terminal.

FIGURES 3-40A AND 3-40B. Rotor testing, N-type alternator, external regulator.

(infinity) indicates an open circuit in the rotor. Perform the fuse test by connecting the wire from the battery positive to the positive brush or slip ring. If in doubt, try both brushes. With P-type alternators, only the negative brush should blow the fuse; with N-types, neither brush should blow the fuse. If both brushes blow the fuse, regardless of alternator type, the rotor is shorted.

Testing from either slip ring to the rotor's shaft should show a very high reading (Figure 3-40B). Anything else indicates a short to ground in the field winding.

Stators. If you can, separate the two alternator halves and disconnect the stator winding wires from their diodes (as noted above, you will probably have to unsolder or cut the wires). You can test the stator windings with a multimeter set to its ohms function (R × 1 scale on an analog meter). There should be *no continuity* (i.e., an open circuit) when testing from any of the three wires to ground (the steel laminations around which the wires are wound—see Figure 3-41A—or the alternator case). There should be continuity, showing only a low resistance (difficult to distinguish from a short, even with a quality meter) when testing across any two wires since this is testing the resistance in the winding. It will vary according to the alternator's rated output, with the resistance being lower on high-output alternators (see Figure 3-41B). Continuity from any wire to ground indicates a shorted winding; no continuity between any two wires

indicates an open-circuited winding. Neither is repairable in the field. With the wires off the diodes, now is a good time to test the diodes (pages 97–99).

FIGURE 3-41A. Testing from a stator winding to ground (the alternator case). There should be an open circuit (O.L—very high resistance).

FIGURE 3-41B. Testing between stator coils. There should be a low resistance (in this case, 0.3 ohm).

Voltage Regulators

How They Work

A voltage regulator controls the output of an alternator by varying the current supplied to the field winding (pages 85–86). This field current is "tapped" off the alternator's output and may be anywhere from 2% to 6% of the output.

A voltage regulator is, in fact, a *current* regulator, both in terms of the field current and also the alternator's output! By varying the field current, it holds the alternator's output current to whatever level a battery will accept at a given charging voltage (page 29), hence the misnomer "voltage regulator." A change of only 1 amp in the field current will alter an alternator's output by up to 50 amps. This gives some sense of how difficult it is to achieve precise voltage control. (The degree to which precise control is achieved is an underappreciated difference between many of the multistep regulators on the market. Those from Ample Technology are especially precise.)

Solid-state voltage regulators. Formerly, voltage regulation was a mechanical affair, but now it is always done with solid-state electronics (Figures 3-42A and 3-42B). These contain transistors that open at a certain voltage, cutting the current to the field winding (rotor) and so disabling the alternator's output, causing the voltage to decline. When the output voltage has fallen to a preset level, the transistors close, restoring the alternator's output. This cycle happens *hundreds of times a second*, making for extremely precise voltage regulation, but at the cost of sometimes severe radio interference (Chapter 8).

Ignition circuits and excitation. The observant reader may have noticed that an alternator's output is used to supply current to the field winding. However, when an alternator is first started, there is no output. Without output there is no field current. Without field current there can be no output! Some initial excitation of the field winding is needed to break this vicious circle. Two approaches are used:

1. The rotor is designed to retain a certain amount of residual magnetism when the alternator is shut down, which is sufficient to produce a low alternator output when the rotor begins to spin. The output feeds back to the field winding, builds up its magnetism, and restores full output. This approach to excitation is uncommon.

2. A separate feed from the battery to the field winding provides initial excitation (Figure 3-43). Since the field winding would drain the battery through this line when the alternator is shut down, a switch is incorporated in the circuit. This is normally an ignition switch, but sometimes an oil pressure or fuel pressure switch (or both) is used. With a pressure

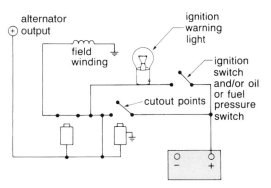

FIGURE 3-43. A voltage regulator (P-type) with excitation circuit. Closing the switch provides initial field current. The battery discharges through the ignition light into the field winding, lighting up the lamp. When the generator output builds, the cutout points close. There is now equal voltage on both sides of the ignition warning light, and the light goes out.

switch, the engine must build up pressure to close the switch before the alternator will kick in. (If problems are experienced with excitation, try jumping out the switches.)

An ignition warning light included in an excitation circuit will glow as long as current flows from the battery through the field winding to ground (i.e., excitation current is being supplied). Once the alternator starts to put out, it supplies current to the field winding. There is now the same, or nearly the same, voltage at both ends of the excitation circuit: alternator output at one end, battery voltage at the other. Without a voltage differential no current will flow (see Chapter 4), and the warning light goes out.

Different Regulators: Internal, External, P, and N

There are hundreds of different regulators in common use. Many are completely internal; others are classified as internal but are attached to the alternator's outside casing, which makes them and their wiring more accessible. Some alternators—especially high-output alternators—have separate, external regulators mounted as an independent unit. These alternators are preferred in boat use as they make troubleshooting and emergency repairs so much easier.

Regulators fall into two broad types: P and N. As we have seen, all regulators function by repeatedly making and breaking the current to the field winding. It is irrelevant whether this is done on the supply side (P, positive) of the winding or the return side (N, negative, or ground); the end result is the same (see Figures 3-33A and 3-33C). Almost all external regulators are P-type; most internal regulators, especially on smaller alternators (up to 55 amps), are N-type.

The Charging Problems section earlier in this chapter outlined a procedure for testing *external* regulators and determining their type (pages 95–96). Some *attached* regulators can be unscrewed and their wires disconnected without

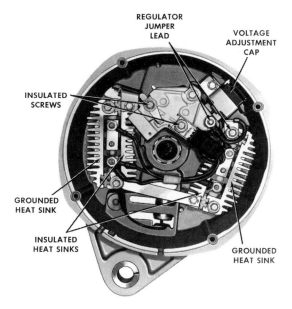

FIGURE 3-42A. A solid-state regulator inside the back of an alternator. *(ACDelco)*

FIGURE 3-42B. Another regulator inside an alternator. This one has no accessible wiring.

removing the brush holders. These can be tested the same way. If the alternator has a wire to only one brush, it is probably a P-type (the other brush is grounded). If wires run to both brushes, it is probably an N-type. In any event, to double-check, *turn off the ignition and battery isolation switches, disconnect the voltage regulator leads from the brushes*, and test in turn *between each brush and ground* with a multimeter set to its ohms function (the lowest scale—R × 1—on an analog meter). P-types will read near 0 ohms on both brushes (generally between 2 and 6 ohms, although one may read 0); N-types will give high readings.

Identifying wiring. Regardless of alternator and regulator type, all will have a field wire and a battery-sensing wire somewhere, and almost all will have an excitation wire.

The field wire. Alternators with external regulators have a terminal on the back to receive the field wire. This terminal will be labeled "F," "DF," or "FLD." Externally attached internal regulators must be unscrewed from the back of the alternator to expose the field wire or wires. Some externally sensed units have two field wires: one connected to the battery excitation line, the other to the voltage regulator. The latter is the main field wire. The field wire normally is connected by a spade terminal (marked "F" or "DF") to one of the two brushes. In the absence of internal identification, or in the case of completely internal regulators, determining the field wire becomes rather involved and is beyond the scope of this book.

The excitation wire. If fitted, the battery excitation wire will come from the alternator (internal regulator) or regulator (externally attached and external regulators) to the ignition switch and/or a pressure switch mounted on the engine block, generally via an ignition warning light.

The battery-sensing (voltage regulation) wire. The battery-sensing wire, which determines voltage regulation, may come from the battery itself (*battery sensed*) but is more likely to be taken from the alternator (*machine sensed*), either from an auxiliary terminal (sometimes labeled "AUX") on the back of the alternator (external and attached regulators) or from inside the alternator itself. Where fitted, an auxiliary terminal will have an *insulated* stud and *no connections to ground*. Normally it will be smaller than the main output terminal.

Common alternators. Many Motorola alternators with attached regulators have the following wiring: A white wire with its own separate spade terminal is the excitation line; the black wire goes to ground; and the red wire goes to an auxiliary terminal post on the back of the alternator. This is the battery-sensing (voltage regu-

FIGURE 3-44. Voltage regulator adjustments on some Delco Remy alternators. In this enlarged view the adjustment cap is in the "low" position. *(ACDelco)*

lation) line. The field wire(s) is (are) under the regulator.

Delco Remy alternators with internal regulators have two spade lugs on the back. The lug numbered "1" is the excitation connection; "2" is the battery-sensing (voltage regulation) terminal.

Powerline alternators with external regulators have two spade lugs on the back. The lug marked "R" is for a tachometer; the one marked "F" is the field connection. These are P-type alternators.

Voltage regulator adjustments. Most solid-state regulators are not adjustable, although some Delco Remys do have a four-position cap that can be rotated for different settings (Figure 3-44); some Lucas/CAVs have high-, medium-, and low-output wires; and some external regulators—notably all multistep regulators—have one or more *potentiometer* (variable resistor) screws, or *dip switches*, to fine-tune the voltage set point(s).

If a regulator is adjustable, only make adjustments while charging into *near fully charged batteries* (at least at the absorption voltage—see Chapter 1) *in good condition*. Make alterations in regulated voltage *a little at a time* (even a 0.2 volt change can have a major impact on charging rates) and then *give the system plenty of time to stabilize at the new level* before considering further adjustments. After making changes, it is a good idea to lock a potentiometer screw against vibration by putting a dab of silicone or polyurethane sealant over the screw head.

Troubleshooting Voltage Regulators

No alternator output at all. Pages 95–97 in the Charging Problems section outlined a procedure for *external* regulators to determine if the alternator or regulator is at fault (Figures 3-34B and 3-34C). Some attached regulators can be removed without disturbing the brushes and treated in a similar fashion.

If these tests indicate that the voltage regulator is malfunctioning, we have an open circuit (no current) to the field winding. This may be the result of a defective switch circuit on battery-excited alternators, a broken or shorted wire, or blown diodes or transistors.

Battery-excited alternators. Always suspect the switches first. The excitation line may run to the ignition switch, to an oil pressure or fuel pressure switch mounted on the engine block, or to both (Figure 3-43). *Rig a jumper wire incorporating a minimum 12-watt test light from the battery positive terminal, crank the engine, and touch the jumper for just a second or two to the battery excitation terminal on the voltage regulator.* If the alternator now works we know this circuit is faulty. The alternator may continue to work after the jumper is disconnected, but when the engine is shut down and then restarted, the alternator field winding will need reexciting to get things going again.

Self-exciting alternators. A self-exciting alternator is designed so that the iron core of the field winding retains sufficient residual magnetism when the unit is shut down to get things moving again when it is put back in operation. Sometimes, however, this residual magnetism will decline to the point at which it will not bring the alternator back to life. Revving up the engine may bring the alternator back into commission. If not, give the field winding its initial excitation with a small positive current to the field or auxiliary terminal on the alternator. The easiest way to do this is to connect a minimum 12-watt test light from the battery positive terminal to the field or auxiliary terminal (Figure 3-34D).

Continuity tests. If the excitation tests fail to restore alternator output, shut off both the ignition and the *battery isolation switch* and use a multimeter set to its ohms function (place an analog meter on its lowest—R × 1—scale) to test the regulator wiring for continuity. You should get a reading of 0 ohms (needle all the way to the right) when the meter probes are touched to both ends of an individual wire. Infinite ohms ("O.L," standing for "overload") indicate a break in the wiring. It may prove necessary to push the probe tip through the insulation at the voltage regulator end of the wires as the connections are inaccessible on many regulators.

If earlier tests showed the regulator is at fault but all its wiring and external circuits are OK, the regulator needs replacing. If no spare is on board, an emergency regulator can sometimes be rigged up as detailed on page 109.

Persistent undercharging of the battery.

The alternator may just be too small for the demands being placed on the system, its speed of rotation may be too slow (wrong pulleys, see pages 24–25), its belt may be slipping, or its charging time may be inadequate. Given a correctly sized alternator and pulleys and sufficient charging time, however, persistent undercharging must be the result of incorrect voltage regu-

lation for the system in question. To see whether this is the case:

- First, it is necessary to bring a battery close to a full charge (at least to the absorption phase) by one means or another. (A full charge is important; test wet-cells with a hydrometer.) Then set the engine to its normal charging speed and check the battery voltage *across the battery terminals.* This test will show the regulated voltage from the alternator that is actually reaching the battery. Depending on the design parameters of the system, the voltage should be anywhere from 13.8 to 14.4 volts. Most boats should be somewhere between 14.0 and 14.4 volts for reasonably rapid battery charging without the risk of excessive overcharging. An exception is a boat fitted with one of the multistep regulators previously mentioned. In this case, if the battery is *fully charged,* the regulator may have tripped to a float setting between 13.2 and 13.6 volts. If so, turn the regulator off and on to put it into its absorption phase.

- *If voltage levels are down, no amount of engine-running time will bring the battery to a full charge.* In this situation, check the voltage *at the output terminal on the alternator.* With the engine running, test between the terminal and a good ground (the alternator case). On alternators with an insulated ground, test between the output terminal and the ground terminal. Voltage may well be a volt or more higher than the battery voltage already measured.

- Voltage drop from the alternator to the batteries can be caused by inadequate wiring and poor connections (see Chapter 4), but it is more likely to occur as a result of battery isolation diodes fitted to allow charging of two or more batteries from the same alternator (see Chapter 1 and Figure 3-45A). *Unless a voltage regulator is compensated for diode-induced voltage drop, the batteries will be permanently undercharged.* If an alternator is undercharging because of diode-induced voltage drop, the best option is to remove the isolation diodes, replacing them with a voltage-sensitive battery-paralleling relay or a series regulator, as described in Chapter 1. Failing this, one of the following procedures will correct the situation:

Adjustable regulators. Raise the voltage setting— see earlier in this chapter. Remember, all adjustments should be made only with a battery that has reached its absorption voltage (i.e., is well charged) and *in small increments, allowing the system to stabilize before making further changes.*

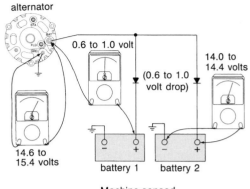

FIGURE 3-45A. Correct voltages on systems with split-charging diodes when the batteries are fully charged. Voltage drop can be measured directly between the alternator output terminal and the battery's positive post as shown.

alternator

0.6 to 1.0 volt

14.0 to 14.4 volts

(0.6 to 1.0 volt drop)

14.6 to 15.4 volts

battery 1   battery 2

FIGURE 3-45B. Machine- (right) and battery-sensed (below) voltage regulators.

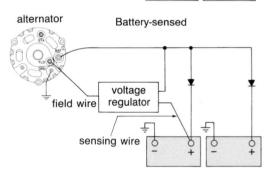

Machine-sensed

alternator

sensing wire

voltage regulator

field wire

Battery-sensed

alternator

field wire

voltage regulator

sensing wire

FIGURE 3-45C. Battery-sensing wire connected to a "house" battery.

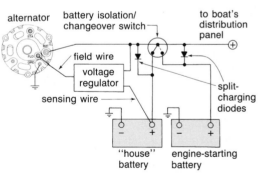

alternator   battery isolation/ changeover switch   to boat's distribution panel

field wire

voltage regulator

sensing wire

split-charging diodes

"house" battery   engine-starting battery

FIGURE 3-45D. A diode installed in a sensing wire to compensate for voltage drop caused by split-charging diodes.

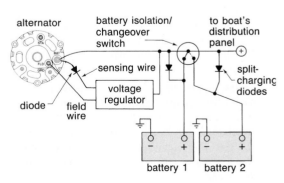

alternator   battery isolation/ changeover switch   to boat's distribution panel

sensing wire

voltage regulator

split-charging diodes

diode   field wire

battery 1   battery 2

Nonadjustable regulators. Either (1) take the regulator sensing wire *directly to the battery positive terminal*, thus bypassing any diodes (Figures 3-45B and 3-45C), or (2) *fit a diode with the same voltage drop as the battery isolation diode into the sensing wire* (Figure 3-45D). Either way the regulator is now sensing more or less the same voltage that the battery is receiving.

1. *Battery-sensing wire connected to house battery.* If the sensing wire is moved to the battery, make sure it does not pass through any switches that may be opened while the engine is running. If this happens *the regulator will sense no voltage and will respond by increasing field current to its maximum.* The same thing will happen if the wire gets broken, so make sure it is well supported and protected. The sensing wire can go to only one battery; otherwise, the batteries would be paralleled via the sensing wire, defeating the purpose of the diodes. *If the sensed battery is fully charged and the other battery is low, the alternator output will shut down and the second battery will be inadequately charged.* Normal practice is to connect the sensing wire to the battery on the boat's house circuit (as opposed to engine cranking), as this battery is generally in the lowest state of charge. Should the engine-starting battery be lower, the batteries should, if possible, be paralleled manually during charging (e.g., by turning a battery isolation/ selector switch to the BOTH position). Remember to isolate the batteries when charging is complete!

   Unfortunately, the sensing line on most internal regulators is inaccessible. Some degree of alternator disassembly is needed to find it, as well as an understanding of the regulator wiring once the alternator is disassembled. Note that the various multistep regulators have external sensing lines that can be run to the battery terminals, bypassing any diodes.

   Anytime a sensing line is wired directly to a battery, it must be fused as close to the battery as possible to prevent the risk of an electrical fire (see Chapter 4).

2. *Diode installed in sensing wire* (Figure 3-45D). The diode will impose approximately the same voltage drop on the sensing wire as is imposed on the output cable by the isolation diodes, thus canceling out the negative effect of the output diodes on the regulating circuit. Once again, finding the sensing line may be a problem. Any diode must be installed with its arrow pointing *toward the voltage regulator.* If it is fitted in reverse, it will block the sensing line altogether; the regulator

will respond with maximum field current at all times and the batteries will be overcharged (if nothing burns up first).

Persistent overcharging of the battery. The battery or batteries overheat, boil or gas, use excess water, and give off an acrid, acid smell. Gel-cell and AGM batteries dry out and fail.

First, check the batteries. Dead and dying batteries will frequently gas and lose electrolyte as if they were overcharged. Note that *excessively hot batteries will automatically overcharge if the voltage regulator is not temperature compensated **at the batteries*** (few are), so there may be no fault in the system itself. Move the batteries to a cooler location and/or add temperature sensing and compensation.

Next, check for excessively high set points on a multistep regulator or overcharging from an unregulated wind generator or solar panel (Chapter 6). Note that since regulators in marine use frequently are set to achieve faster charge rates through higher voltage settings than in automotive use, extended engine running may result in mild overcharging and moderate water loss on wet-cell batteries; this is to be expected. However, these conditions spell death for a gel-cell or AGM!

Regardless of the size of an alternator, serious overcharging cannot occur with correct voltage regulation. If battery voltage is above 14.4 volts, the battery is gassing vigorously, or a wet-cell is experiencing a substantial water loss on all cells, in all probability the voltage regulator's battery-sensing wire is disconnected or broken, or the regulator itself has shorted. If the sensing circuit is broken, the regulator senses no voltage and responds by increasing field current to its maximum. Pay particular attention to *battery-sensed* regulators that have a long wire running to the batteries rather than a short one to the alternator (*machine-sensed*). Any voltage drop *in the sensing wire*, such as would result from corroded terminals,

will have a similar though less dramatic effect.

A short circuit in the voltage regulator will result in permanent maximum output since the regulator supplies maximum field current at all times, a situation similar to the loss of the sensing wire. This, however, is not repairable. Carry a spare regulator.

Emergency Voltage Regulation

The field current for almost all alternators ranges up to a maximum of around 5 amps at full output, although some high-output alternators may go as high as 7 to 8 amps. In an emergency, you can use any external source to supply this current if the voltage regulator is first removed or disconnected. A test wire connected to a 12- or 15-watt DC lamp (Figure 3-34A) will feed approximately 1 amp to the field winding (12-volt system). The lamp acts as a fixed resistance, preventing excessive amperage from reaching the field winding. The higher the lamp wattage, the more amperage it will pass. Divide the wattage by the system voltage to find out how many amps. For example, a 15-watt bulb on a 12-volt system will pass 1.25 amps; a 40-watt bulb, 3.33 amps.

With P-type alternators, connect the lamp between the battery's positive terminal and the alternator's field terminal (Figure 3-34B). With N-type alternators, connect it between the field terminal and ground (Figure 3-34C).

It is important to closely monitor alternator output and battery voltage to guard against overheating and overcharging. If output is too high, decrease the lamp wattage or wire two lamps *in series*; if output is lower than desired, increase the lamp wattage or wire two lamps *in parallel*. When the battery is fully charged, you must switch off or disconnect this field current; likewise when the engine is shut down. If it is left hooked up, it will drain the batteries through the field winding.

Diodes

Frequent reference has been made in the first three chapters to diodes. They will crop up over and over again in other contexts. This is as good a place as any to look at them in a little more detail.

Identification and Rating

Identification. Diodes are imprinted with an arrowhead-like symbol with its tip crossed by a per-

pendicular line (Figure 3-46). The arrow points in the direction of current flow; the perpendicular line symbolizes the resistance to current flow in the opposite direction. Smaller diodes simply have a black band at one end, which corresponds to the perpendicular line; i.e., current flow is from the other end to this end (for those who are interested, I am sticking with the popular conception that current flow is from positive to negative even though technically this is not correct).

FIGURE 3-46. Diode identification. Diodes are rated according to (1) their current-carrying capacity when conducting (e.g., 50 amps), and (2) the voltage they are capable of blocking in the other direction, known as *peak inverse voltage* or PIV (e.g., 50 PIV). The bottommost of the smaller diodes is frequently used in alternators, pressed into a heat sink, in which instance the diode case is electrically in common with the heat sink and usually grounded (or negative).

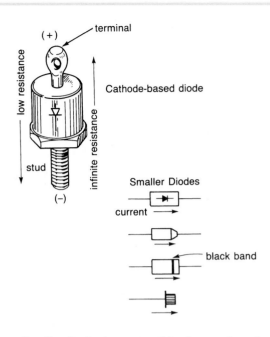

Smaller diodes have pigtail leads at each end. Larger diodes have a terminal on one end and a threaded stud on the other—one connection is made to the terminal on the diode's top, the other is made to the threaded stud on its base. If the arrow points from the terminal to the stud, conduction is from the terminal to the stud. If the arrow points from the stud to the terminal, conduction is from the stud to the terminal.

Rating. Diodes that are conducting are said to be *forward biased*, while those that are not are *reverse biased*. Diodes are rated in terms of their *maximum forward current*, their *peak inverse voltage*, and their *forward voltage drop*:

- The *maximum forward current* specifies the maximum current rating of the diode (the maximum number of amps it can conduct without failure).

- The *peak inverse (reverse) voltage* specifies the maximum voltage the diode will block in the reverse direction. Once voltage goes above this level, the diode will break down and conduct in both directions (a shorted diode).

- The *forward voltage drop* specifies the voltage at which the diode begins to conduct in the forward direction, which is also the voltage drop it will impose on the circuit when carrying its full rated current. In other words, if the forward voltage drop is 0.6 volt (a typical silicon diode), the diode will not begin to conduct until the voltage on the circuit is at least 0.6 volt, and once it is conducting, the voltage "downstream" of the diode will be 0.6 of a volt less than upstream of it. The "lost" voltage represents energy that is dissipated as heat (which

is important—see below). Some diodes have a lower forward voltage drop than others. Conventional silicon diodes run as high as 1.0 to 1.5 volts at full current; Schottky diodes run as high as 0.5 to 0.7 volt at full current.

Diodes come in different sizes to fit different needs. Since the full charging output of an alternator passes through battery isolation diodes, they must be rated to accept this high amperage. If you are upgrading to a high-output alternator, any existing battery isolation diodes will most likely also need upgrading. This can be done by fitting additional diodes in parallel with the original ones. Better yet, get rid of the diodes and replace them with battery paralleling relays (see Chapter 1).

Heat Sinks on Battery Isolation Diodes

Current passing through a diode heats it up. More current produces more heat. The quantity of heat at full current rating may be calculated approximately by taking the diode's forward current rating and multiplying it by the diode's forward voltage drop. For example, if we have an isolation diode with a forward voltage drop of 0.7 volt on a 150 amp alternator, it will generate up to 105 watts (150 amps × 0.7 volt) of heat. If this heat is allowed to build up, it will destroy the diode, so diodes are generally mounted on some kind of a *heat sink*, frequently a finned, aluminum plate. Note: If a heat sink is installed on a vertical service, the fins should be aligned vertically since this will maximize the cooling effect.

Since one side of an isolation diode is connected electrically to its heat sink via the mounting stud, *heat sinks are live*. If the heat sink is connected to the battery positive terminal, shorting out the heat sink to ground is much the same as shorting out the battery terminals. If the heat sink is connected to the alternator, it will be hot (live) whenever the engine is running (Figures 3-47A and 3-47B).

If the heat sink is common with the battery positive terminal, it is not possible to mount two diodes on the same heat sink; this would parallel the batteries through the heat sink and defeat the purpose of the diodes. If the heat sink is common with the alternator output, any number of diodes can be mounted on the same heat sink without affecting the batteries.

Some battery isolation units use three diodes—the alternator feeds one diode, and the other two diodes feed the batteries. Note that the *voltage drop to the batteries is doubled* (Figure 3-47C), which will exacerbate any voltage regulation problems. The diodes are sometimes mounted in an insulated block fitted to the heat sink. In

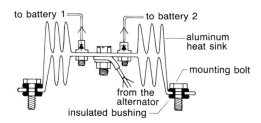

FIGURE 3-47A. Diodes mounted on a shared heat sink for battery isolation. Note that the heat sink is live during alternator operation.

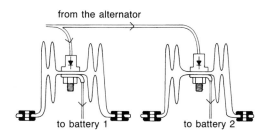

FIGURE 3-47B. In this setup, the heat sinks are connected to the two battery positive terminals via the diode cases, hence the use of independent, electrically isolated heat sinks to avoid paralleling the batteries.

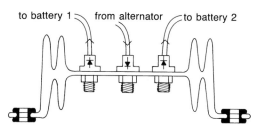

FIGURE 3-47C. Three-diode split-charging setup. Note that the voltage drop is doubled relative to that of a two-diode configuration. The heat sink is still live during alternator operation.

this situation, the heat sink is permanently electrically isolated from its diodes.

Soldering and connections. Excessive heat will damage a diode. Do not solder to the top terminal with the diode mounted on its heat sink; the heat sink will draw the heat down into the diode. Use a large enough soldering iron to get the job done as quickly as possible and so avoid the need to hold the iron to the terminal for prolonged periods. When soldering small diodes with attached wires, clamp a pair of small Vise-Grips or pliers around the wire between the solder joint and the diode. This will act as a heat sink and protect the diode (Figure 3-48). For more information on soldering, see Chapter 4.

Testing Battery Isolation Diodes

All diodes create a voltage drop, normally around 0.6 volt, but sometimes over 1.0 volt.

Schottky diodes are specialized diodes with a voltage drop as low as 0.3 volt. To measure the actual voltage drop, check with a DC voltmeter across the two diode terminals *with the alternator running at full output* (set an analog meter to the 2.5-volt scale). The positive meter lead goes to the alternator side of the circuit (Figure 3-49).

To test an isolation diode's operation, shut down the alternator and turn off the ignition and battery isolation switches. Check with a voltmeter (or test light) from the *battery side* of the diode *to ground*. It will show battery voltage (or light). Now test from the alternator side to a good ground. It should show no or very little voltage. (There may be a small leakage current that will result in a voltage reading. If a meter shows voltage, try with a test light; it should not light.) If there is battery voltage on the alternator side (the test lamp lights), the diode is shorted, another diode in the charging circuit has been installed backward, or some equipment has been incorrectly wired so as to bypass the diodes. If the diode is shorted, the battery will still receive a charge, but will not be isolated from other batteries (although other batteries may still be isolated from this one via their own isolating diodes). If one of the diodes is in backward, the relevant battery will receive no charge when the alternator is running and will soon go dead.

You can also test diodes with an ohmmeter, *but only after disconnecting the batteries;* otherwise, the ohmmeter will be damaged. Set an analog meter to its lowest ohms scale (R × 1). Touch the probes to the two diode terminals, then reverse the probes. If the diode is functional, it will show continuity in one direction (0 or near 0 ohms) and an open circuit in the other (infinite or very high ohms). Where there is continuity, the direction of flow is from the negative probe to the positive probe. A shorted diode will show continuity in both directions. An open-circuited diode will show infinity in both directions.

As noted above (pages 98–99), some meters may not have the necessary forward voltage to show a circuit in either direction, although this is less likely than when doing the alternator tests described earlier. (This is because the nature of alternator construction is such that the alternator tests are, in fact, done on two diodes in series, rather than on a single diode as described here.) Nevertheless, it is best to use a meter with a specific *diode-testing* function. Rather than testing resistance, these meters normally test the voltage drop across the diode. A properly functioning diode will show a voltage, generally around 0.6 volt, in one direction and "infinity" ("O.L") in the other direction; a shorted diode will show 0 volts in both directions; and an open-circuited diode will show "infinity" in both directions.

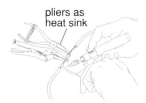

FIGURE 3-48. Soldering small diodes. *(Jim Sollers)*

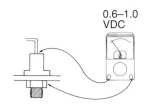

FIGURE 3-49. Testing for voltage drop across a diode. The positive meter lead goes on the alternator side of the circuit.

CHAPTER 4

FIGURE 4-1. Effective troubleshooting of recalcitrant electrical circuits begins and ends with a thorough understanding of the dynamics involved. *(Jim Sollers)*

Understanding and Troubleshooting
Electrical Circuits

This is the longest chapter in this book, which is a reflection of both the complexity of electrical circuits on modern boats and also their importance. It is also the chapter that I have revised the most extensively with each new edition of the book as I grapple with how much information to give the nontechnical boatowner and how to present it.

Once again, I have expanded the depth of the information. If you are a novice, this is tough stuff, but—unfortunately—it's something that you need to master to ensure that your boat is wired for trouble-free operation and that you can troubleshoot any problems that develop.

I've divided the chapter into four sections: Basic Concepts and Measurements, DC Circuits, AC Circuits (which can be ignored for those without AC power on board), and Proper Electrical Installations. If you do nothing else, you should check your boat with respect to this last section and, in particular, check the overcurrent protection (all too many boats come from the factory with inadequate overcurrent protection, resulting in an unnecessary fire risk).

Basic Concepts and Measurements

Electrical circulation is analogous to the circulation of water in a pressurized water system. Since most people have little trouble understanding water flow, there should be, in principle, few obstacles to understanding electrical circuits. But because electricity is invisible, even if we have such an understanding, we still cannot effectively troubleshoot a problem without a tool that will let us "see" inside a circuit. This tool is the multimeter. With these two things—a grasp of basic concepts and a multimeter—it is the rare electrical problem that cannot be solved.

The Water System Analogy

In a pressurized water system, the *rate of flow* through any given pipe is governed by the *pressure of the water* and the *size of the pipe*. The higher the water pressure, the greater the potential flow; the larger the pipe, the greater the flow, up to the capacity of the system's pump.

In an electrical circuit, the rate of flow (*amperage*) through any given wire is governed by the pressure in the wire (*voltage*) and the size of the wire. The higher the pressure (voltage), the greater the potential flow (amperage). The larger the wire, the greater the flow, up to the capacity of the system's generator or battery.

With a pipe of a given diameter, the longer the pipe, the more the cumulative resistance and therefore the less the flow. Moreover, pressure will decline steadily along the length of the pipe, but the *flow rate* will be the same at all points. If 4 gallons per minute comes out at the far end, 4 gallons per minute must go in at the beginning, and 4 gallons per minute will flow through the pipe at all points (Figure 4-2).

With a wire of any given diameter, the longer the wire the more the cumulative resistance (*ohms*) and, therefore, the lower the rate of flow (amps). Moreover, pressure (voltage) will decline steadily along the length of the wire (called *voltage drop*—very significant in boat electrics, as we have already seen), but the rate of flow (amps) will remain constant at all points.

Flow rates and pressure (amps and volts). Consider an open tank of water with a pump on its outlet feeding a pipe with a valve.

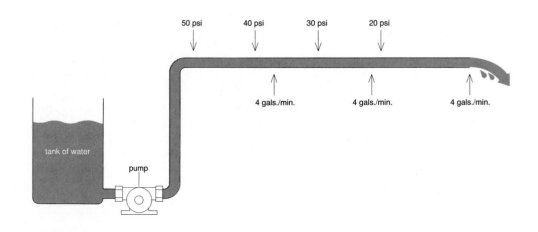

FIGURE 4-2. The movement of electricity through a circuit bears a resemblance to the flow of water in a pressurized water system. Pressure may decline over a long pipe run, but the flow rate remains constant. Similarly, there is a voltage drop through a long wire, but the electrical flow rate (amperage) through the wire is constant. *(Jim Sollers)*

50 psi   40 psi   30 psi   20 psi

4 gals./min.   4 gals./min.   4 gals./min.

tank of water

pump

The outlet from the valve runs through a second pipe onto the ground. The pump is running but the valve is closed, creating, in effect, infinite resistance to flow. In other words, there is no flow through the pipe. The pump will build system pressure upstream of the valve.

An open *switch* is the electrical equivalent of a closed valve; it offers infinite resistance to electrical flow. In other words, it stops all flow through the system. System pressure (voltage) will build upstream of the switch.

Water is used when the valve is opened, and the water is allowed to flow. If the valve is barely cracked (Figure 4-3A), it offers a very high resistance to flow and allows only a small amount of water to pass. The pump is more than capable of maintaining system pressure upstream of the valve while water flows through the valve out onto the ground at no pressure. In other words, the pressure drop from one side of the valve to the other amounts to the pressure on the system.

Electricity is used when a switch is closed and electricity is allowed to flow. Current flowing through a high resistance, such as a lightbulb, is the electrical equivalent of a barely cracked valve; it allows only a small amount of current to flow. Upstream of the resistance, there will be full system voltage. Downstream from the resistance, the circuit runs to ground—either the negative terminal on a battery or *ground potential* on an AC system (see the AC Circuits section later in this chapter). Voltage falls to 0 volts. *The voltage drop from one side of the resistance to the other will amount to the voltage on the system.*

The more the water valve is opened, the lower the resistance to flow, and the more water that will pass through the valve. At some point, if the pipe and valve are large enough and the resistance to flow is low enough, the rate of flow will exceed the ability of the pump to maintain system pressure, and pressure will begin to decline upstream of the valve (Figure 4-3B).

The lower the resistance in a circuit, the more current (amperage) will flow. At some point, if the wire is large enough and the resistance is low enough—a starter motor is a good example—the rate of flow will exceed the ability of the generator or battery to maintain system pressure (voltage). This is why battery voltage falls, generally to around 10.5 volts on a 12-volt battery, when cranking an engine.

As long as the pipes leading to and from the valve are large enough to accommodate the flow without resistance, and as long as the rate of flow

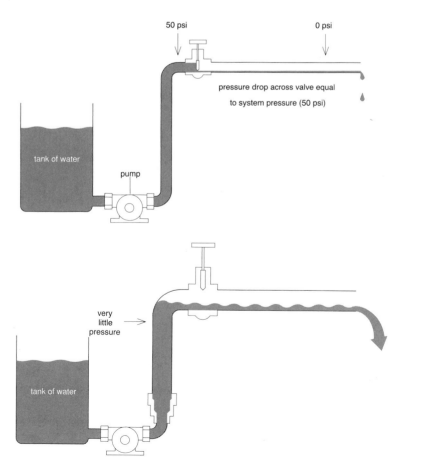

FIGURE 4-3A. A barely cracked valve is analogous to a high-resistance electrical load such as a lightbulb. Each will pass only a small flow, making it easy for the water pump to maintain system pressure upstream of the valve and for the battery to maintain system voltage "upstream" of the resistance. *(Jim Sollers)*

FIGURE 4-3B. The wide-open valve and large pipe in this case permit a flow of water that exceeds the rate at which the pump can maintain system pressure. Similarly, a large, low-resistance wire and low-resistance electrical load (such as a starter motor) will allow current to flow at such a rate that a battery is unable to maintain system voltage. *(Jim Sollers)*

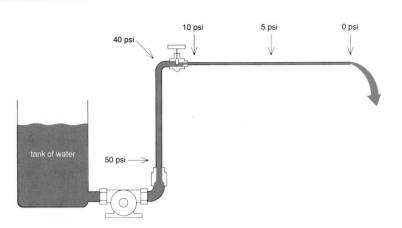

FIGURE 4-3C. At high flow rates a narrow pipe or undersized wire (or faulty connection) will create its own pressure or voltage drop. The pressure (voltage) drop measured across the valve (or electrical load) will now be something less than the pressure (voltage) at the pump (battery). *(Jim Sollers)*

does not exceed the capability of the pump to maintain system pressure, the water pressure will always be at pump pressure above the valve and at no pressure downstream from the valve (Figure 4-3A again). At very high rates of flow, however, the pipes themselves may begin to offer resistance. There will now be a pressure drop along the length of the pipes, followed by a drop of the remaining system pressure across the valve (Figure 4-3C).

As long as the wires leading to and from a resistance *(load)* are large enough to accommodate the flow (amperage) and are free of extra resistance, such as loose or corroded connections, and as long as the rate of flow (amperage) does not exceed the capability of the generator or battery to maintain system pressure (voltage), the pressure (voltage) will always be at system pressure (voltage) above the resistance (load) and drop to 0 volts downstream from the resistance. At very high rates of flow (amperages), the wires and/or their connections may begin to offer their own resistance to flow—they will heat up. The result will be a pressure (voltage) drop along the length of the wires, followed by a drop of the remaining system pressure (voltage) across the resistance (load).

Making Measurements

In a pressurized water system, we can insert gauges at any point to measure the pressure and rate of flow. So too with electrical circuits. We can even go one better and measure resistance to flow (ohms) quite easily; a measurement for resistance must be deduced in a water system.

Measuring pressure (voltage). Water pressure is measured by teeing in a small line and leading it to a pressure gauge. Voltage is measured the same way, with one difference: water pressure gauges are calibrated with reference to atmospheric pressure. Since atmospheric pressure is all around us, this reference point can be

built into the meter quite simply by leaving one side open to the atmosphere: we need only one connection to the water pipe. Essentially, we are measuring the pressure *differential* between the system pressure and atmospheric pressure.

Voltage is measured with reference to *ground* (or *ground potential*). *A voltmeter cannot measure without being connected to this reference point in some way*; a hole in the side of the meter will not work! Therefore *two* connections are needed to measure voltage: one to the pressure point in the circuit, and one to its "ground" ("earth"; Figure 4-4). This ground connection performs the reference function of the open side of the water pressure gauge: we are measuring the pressure *differential* between the system and its ground.

Measuring flow (amperage). In a water system, rate of flow is measured by installing a paddle wheel in the pipe and seeing how fast it spins. Amperage is measured in the same way by installing an *ammeter*—the electrical equivalent of a paddle wheel—in the electrical circuit.

With larger volumes of water, it is impractical to measure the whole flow rate; the paddle wheel would have to be huge. A small restriction is made in the main pipe to cause a slight pressure drop. A smaller pipe bypasses this restriction. The slight pressure drop in the main pipe causes water to flow through the bypass pipe, and a paddle wheel in this pipe measures the rate of flow. This is multiplied by a suitable factor to determine the rate of flow in the main pipe.

High amperage is measured in a similar fashion. A specially calibrated, low-resistance *shunt* is installed in the main wire *(cable)*. A small circuit containing a voltmeter is connected across the terminals of the shunt. The voltmeter measures the voltage drop across the shunt, which is then multiplied by a suitable factor and reconfigured to give the overall rate of flow (amperage).

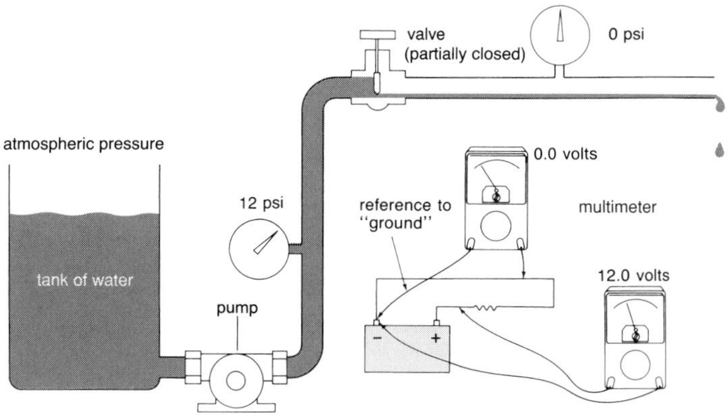

FIGURE 4-4. Pressure and voltage measurements. *(Jim Sollers)*

Measuring resistance (ohms). If water is pumped through a pipe at a carefully regulated pressure and the rate of flow measured, the resistance can be deduced. The greater the flow, the less the resistance.

In electrical work, this is the function of an *ohmmeter*. The meter contains its own power source (a battery), which is the electrical equivalent of a pump and reservoir of water. The meter supplies current (amperage) at a carefully regulated pressure (voltage) to the circuit to be tested—the same as a pump pushing water through a pipe at a carefully regulated pressure. The meter measures the rate of flow (amperage); the less the flow, the greater the resistance (ohms). Instead of displaying this rate of flow (amperage), the meter dial is simply reconfigured to display ohms of resistance.

Ohm's law. As we have seen, pressure (voltage), rate of flow (amperage), and resistance to flow (ohms) are all interrelated. This relationship is summed up in a simple formula known as Ohm's law (named for Georg Simon Ohm [1787–1854], a German physicist):

$I = E/R$, where I = amperage, E = voltage, and R = resistance (ohms).

The formula can be rearranged to find either voltage or resistance:

$E = I \times R$ or $R = E/I$.

With this formula, if we can measure any two of voltage, amperage, or resistance, we can easily calculate the third. The means to measure them is provided by a multimeter.

The Multimeter: An Essential Tool

A multimeter is an essential electrical troubleshooting tool. In fact, given a knowledge of how to use it, I would go so far as to say that it is possibly the *single most important tool on a boat!*

There are two kinds of meters: analog (swinging arm) and digital (Figures 4-5A and 4-5B). In

FIGURE 4-5A. An inexpensive analog meter. *(Professional Mariner)*

FIGURE 4-5B. A more expensive—but more useful—digital multimeter. This meter has numerous functions, including important safety features, not found on cheaper meters. *(Fluke)*

general, the digital meters are easier to use and are more accurate than the analog meters (particularly when dealing with DC systems, where accurate measurements of readings as low as a tenth of a volt are sometimes needed). Since a reasonable digital meter can be bought from discount catalogs relatively cheaply, there really is no excuse not to have one on board.

There are, however, some problems associated with cheaper digital meters. One is a notable quirk known as *capacitive coupling*, where one

AC circuit can at times impose a measurable "ghost voltage" on another circuit even though the two are electrically isolated. This typically occurs with cables that are in a common bundle or around transformers (used principally in battery chargers, inverters, and fluorescent lights). The current generated by this capacitive coupling is minuscule. As a result, as soon as any kind of a load is applied to the circuit, the ghost voltage disappears. But it can be very confusing, for example, if a test is made from a battery charger negative terminal to its case and the meter shows 60 volts! Some more expensive digital meters apply a built-in internal load that enables the meter to distinguish ghost voltages from actual voltage on the circuit.

A second problem with cheaper meters is that they are electrically fragile. It is possible, for example, to generate a high enough voltage from static electricity to blow out a meter by shuffling across a carpet! Finally, cheap meters lack protection circuitry, which is needed to guard against injury to the user and damage to the meter if the meter is accidentally used when switched into the wrong mode or the meter leads are in the wrong sockets (see below).

When buying a meter, boatowners should look for the following refinements:

- A DC amps capability of 10 amps or more and ideally up to 200 amps. The more common *milliamp* scales are useful only for troubleshooting ground leaks and electronics, and the latter are best left alone by the average boatowner.

- Accuracy at the low end of the ohms scale. (Many of the cheaper analog meters are particularly inaccurate when measuring low resistances.)

- The ability to test diodes. As mentioned on page 110, it takes a certain *forward voltage* to make a diode conduct; some meters will not always develop the necessary internal voltage, making diode testing unreliable. It is preferable to buy a meter with a specific *diode-testing* function.

- An *auto-ranging* function, which eliminates the need to switch up and down different voltage, amperage, and ohms scales when using the meter, which in turn eliminates one more potential source of error and damage. (Analog meters are rarely auto-ranging; digital meters usually are.)

- Protection circuitry to guard against injury and meter damage if the meter is used incorrectly, especially if it is used to measure voltage when the test leads are plugged into the current sockets (some meters and meter leads will explode!—see below).

- The ability to read true (as opposed to average) RMS (root mean square) voltage and amperage in the AC mode. This is particularly useful for troubleshooting many DC-to-AC inverters (I explain this in more detail in Chapter 6). However, if a meter has the other desirable attributes listed above but not this one, it will still provide excellent general service.

As with most things, quality costs money. The industry standard in meters is set by Fluke (www.fluke.com), whose top-of-the-line models are fully waterproof and virtually indestructible.

Using a multimeter. AC CIRCUITS CAN KILL! IF YOU ARE IN ANY DOUBT ABOUT WHAT YOU ARE DOING, DON'T GO POKING AROUND AC CIRCUITS!

AC and DC circuits frequently share the same distribution panel. Be sure to disconnect the AC power cord and turn off any DC-to-AC inverter before opening such panels. Merely switching off the incoming breaker will NOT suffice since it will leave hot wires on the supply side in the panel. DISABLE ANY AC GENERATOR THAT HAS AN AUTOMATIC START FUNCTION.

A meter's different functions and scales are accessed by plugging jacks into different holes and/or by turning a multiposition switch (preferable). The meter will have two output leads, one red, and one black. Red is hot (+ or POS); black is ground (– or NEG or COMMON). Switch-type meters sometimes have a different plug-in point for AC and DC measurements; the meter will be clearly marked. Resistance readings are made using the DC terminals.

When taking AC voltage readings, it is immaterial which way the leads are used. However, for reading DC voltages and amperages the red (+) lead should go to the positive side of the circuit and the black (–) to the negative side, or the meter will read backward. On most resistance tests, the leads can be either way around unless the circuit contains a diode.

Any voltage (AC or DC) can blow out an unprotected meter (and possibly injure the operator) when the meter is in the resistance mode. When measuring ohms, *be absolutely certain to electrically isolate the relevant circuit.* When measuring amps, *be careful not to bridge the power leads with the meter probe* (i.e., bypass the resistance created by the equipment in the circuit, as this will create a potentially dangerous short circuit). When changing from one function to another, *be sure to move the meter leads to the appropriate plug-in points (if this is necessary) and/or switch to the appropriate function.*

I once went from testing milliamps with a cheap meter to checking AC voltage. I forgot to reposition the meter leads, with the result that I effectively put a dead short across the AC circuit. The meter had poor internal protection. The two meter leads literally vaporized in a large cloud of smoke, leaving me holding the plastic cases to the probes! I was lucky not to get hurt. *Always double-check the positions of the leads and the switch before taking a reading.*

In order to avoid draining its internal battery, turn a meter off when it is not in use or turn it to the highest AC volts scale if it has no OFF position.

Measuring voltage. You can measure voltage at any point in a circuit by connecting the meter between a *ground* and an *uninsulated terminal or section of wire*—the meter will be *bridging the voltage differential* between the terminal or wire and the ground (Figure 4-6). Most meter probes have sharp points. If necessary you can force the probe into contact with a conductor through a wire's insulation, although you should not do this unless it is absolutely necessary. You can seal the hole in the insulation with a dab of nonsilicone sealant (silicone is slightly moisture-absorbent, and acid-cured, which causes corrosion).

Unless the meter has an auto-ranging function, always begin by selecting the highest potential voltage scale. For example, if the boat has 240- and 120-volt AC circuits, set the meter to the 250 VAC scale initially, even when checking 120-volt circuits. If you inadvertently tap a 240-volt line, the meter will not be damaged. Switch down to a more appropriate scale, such as 150 volts, only after the meter probes are positioned properly. (The meter will be more accurate and easier to read the closer the measured voltage is to the limit of the scale being used. Consequently, 120 volts will be displayed more accurately on a 150-volt scale than on a 250-volt scale.)

Measuring amperage. Note that in general, amperage is far lower in AC circuits than in DC circuits. This is easy to understand. Since watts = volts × amps, amps = watts/volts. Therefore, a 100-watt appliance will draw only 0.83 amp (100/120) on a 120-volt system, whereas the same appliance will draw 8.3 amps (100/12) on a 12-volt system.

Amperage (AC and DC) can be measured by connecting a meter (or a shunt and meter) *in series* with the conductor and the equipment on the circuit (Figure 4-7A). This method requires the circuit to be broken to insert the meter (or shunt) into it. It also means that the *circuit's full current (amperage) will flow through the meter (or shunt)*. Since many meters cannot handle more than 250 mA (milliamps) and very few appliances draw less than half an amp, amperage scales are frequently of little use except for troubleshooting electronics and ground faults (*earth leaks*; see below).

DC stereos, fans, and pumps generally draw from 0.5 amp to a maximum of 6 or 7 amps. For these, a meter with a capability of 10 amps DC is very useful. However, electric winches, wind-lasses, sail-furling systems, and starter motors have power-hungry motors, well beyond this range; therefore, measuring their amps requires a *current clamp*.

A current clamp may be an add-on device or built into the meter itself, a very handy way to go. (Meters that can measure up to 200 amps AC or DC are now widely available—Figure 4-7B.) To use, simply clip the clamp around one of the current-carrying leads in a circuit and take the measurement. The current-carrying cables

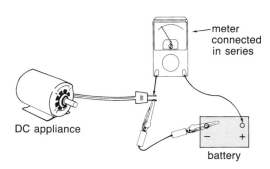

FIGURE 4-7A. Measuring current draw (amps) of a DC appliance.

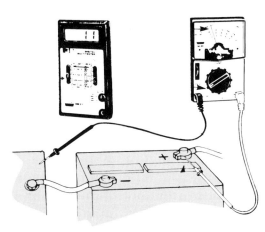

Check batteries   DC voltage

FIGURE 4-6. Using multimeters.

FIGURE 4-7B. A clamp-type meter capable of reading up to 200 amps.

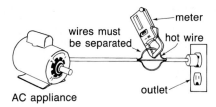

FIGURE 4-7C. Measuring current draw (amps) of an AC appliance. This purpose-built meter (Amprobe is one brand) clips around individual hot wires to measure their induced magnetism, which is directly related to the current they carry. A simple device known as a line splitter can be inserted between the plug and outlet to obviate the need for separating the wires in the cable as shown here.

are the positive or negative cables in a DC circuit; the hot or neutral cables in a 120-volt, U.S.-style AC circuit or a 240-volt, European-style AC circuit; and either one of the hot leads in a 240-volt, U.S.-style AC circuit. You won't have to break the circuit to take a reading, but you must clip the clamp around an individual cable (Figure 4-7C). If the positive and negative cables in a DC circuit are in a common sheath (*duplex cable*), you have to separate them in order to attach the clamp to one of them. You can purchase special "line splitters" to separate AC leads in a common housing without having to cut into the insulating sheath.

Measuring resistance. An ohmmeter is a delicate instrument. If it is hooked into a circuit under pressure, such as a circuit connected to a *power source*, the existing pressure may blow out the meter. (Analog meters are particularly vulnerable to damage; most digital ohmmeters have a greater degree of circuit protection built in.) *An ohmmeter can be used only on disconnected circuits—that is, those that have been isolated from voltage input.* Note that when isolating DC circuits, solar panels are frequently overlooked, but even the limited output of a small solar panel can blow an ohmmeter fuse.

On an analog meter, ohms scales range from small values on the right to large values on the left, in contrast to voltage and amperage scales. That is, 0 ohms reads all the way to the right; infinite ohms reads all the way to the left. Most analog meters have three ohms scales: R × 1, R × 10, and R × 100. For the R × 10 and R × 100 scales, multiply the displayed meter reading by 10 and 100, respectively.

Because the internal power source, and therefore the reference point, for an ohmmeter comes from a battery whose state of charge declines over time, a meter must be recalibrated to the existing state of charge of the battery before every use. With an analog meter, this must be done by the user; most digital meters are self-calibrating. To calibrate an analog meter, touch the meter probes *firmly* together and turn a knob until the meter reads 0 ohms. *You will need to recalibrate an analog meter every time you use it or change the ohms scale (e.g., from R × 1 to R × 100).*

Note that if the needle does not move when

you touch the probes together—i.e., it stays all the way to the left on infinity—you have one of several problems:

- Broken probe wires
- Blown fuse
- Dead or missing meter battery
- Corroded meter battery terminals (so there is no electrical contact)
- Defective meter

When the meter probes are touched to two points in a circuit (e.g., on either side of a switch), the resistance is measured between these points. However, if the circuit has not been properly isolated, the meter may be measuring the resistance around the rest of the circuit rather than between the two probes! *In order to avoid confusion, always disconnect the specific pieces of equipment—wires, switches, and so on—that are being tested* (Figure 4-8A). Don't touch the metal tips of the meter probes when measuring high resistances, or the meter will record the resistance through your body, which may confuse you (Figure 4-8B)!

Testing diodes. A specific diode-testing function is normally required to get meaningful test results from diodes. A meter with such a capability will show the test results in one of two ways: either as voltage drop measured through the diode, or as resistance. As voltage drop, it should be on the order of 0.6 volt with the meter leads applied one way around, and 0.0 volts with the meter leads applied the other way around (Figures 4-9A and 4-9B), although some meters will show +0.6 volt in one direction, and –0.6 volt in

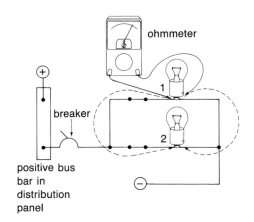

FIGURE 4-8A. Testing a circuit using an ohmmeter. In this example two lights are installed with common supply and ground wires. Because the breaker is open, it might be thought that lightbulb 1 is being tested, whereas it is just as possible that the circuit all the way around through lightbulb 2 is being tested (the dotted lines). To avoid ambiguity, the circuit or piece of equipment being tested should always be isolated.

UNDERSTANDING AND TROUBLESHOOTING ELECTRICAL CIRCUITS

FIGURE 4-9B. The reversal of the meter leads produces an open-circuit reading (".OL"), which is just as it should be (although once again because the diode in question is not disconnected, there is no way of knowing what exactly is being measured).

FIGURE 4-8B. Testing alternator slip rings with an ohmmeter. There should be an open circuit (which would be displayed as ".OL" on this meter) from the slip rings to the rotor shaft, but what is being shown is a high resistance (1.743 megaohms). However, if you look closely, you will see that the operator is touching metal parts in contact with both probes; what is being measured is the resistance through her body!

FIGURES 4-9C AND 4-9D. The same test as in Figures 4-9A and 4-9B, but using the resistance function of the meter (rather than the diode-testing function). There is a high resistance (1.349 megaohms) in one direction and an open circuit ("O.L") with the meter leads reversed, which is typical.

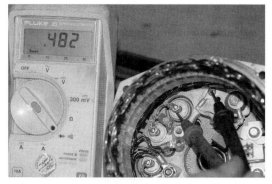

FIGURE 4-9A. A diode test, showing a volt drop of 0.482 volt (which is about right). However, since this diode is wired to another, and then through the attached stator coil to other parts of the alternator circuit, there is no way of knowing what exactly is being measured.

the other. If displayed as resistance, the resistance should be moderately low with the meter leads applied one way around, and very high or an open circuit with the meter leads applied the other way around. Without a specific diode-testing function, many meters will show high

resistance in one direction and very high in the other direction (Figures 4-9C and 4-9D). To test a diode, you must always isolate it from its circuit (which generally requires unsoldering a lead). See Chapter 3 for more on testing diodes.

DC Circuits

Direct current circuits are easy to understand. The flow of electrons—the fundamental unit of electricity—is all in one direction, making a DC system directly analogous to the flow of water in a pressurized water system. Unfortunately, the flow is from *negative to positive* (a fact that was not appreciated until after these terminals were named!), but to avoid confusion I am going to stick to the popular conception of a circuit running from *positive to negative*.

Ground Versus Insulated Return

Ground return. The type of DC circuit that people are most familiar with is the *ground-return* circuit found on automobiles (Figure 4-10). This circuit uses the car's frame as the *ground* (negative) side of the system. *Hot* (positive) wires carry current through switches to all lights, instruments, etc.; these are then *grounded* (earthed) to the car frame. The negative terminal on the

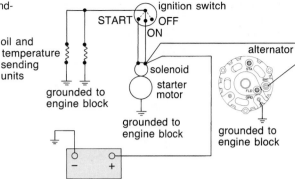

FIGURE 4-10. A ground-return circuit.

oil and temperature sending units

grounded to engine block

START   OFF   ON   ignition switch

solenoid

starter motor

grounded to engine block

alternator

grounded to engine block

battery is connected by a heavy cable to the engine block, which is connected to the car's frame via its mounts or a grounding cable to complete the circuit. The big advantage of such a system is that only one (hot) wire needs to be run to electrical equipment.

Almost all marine engine installations use a ground-return circuit. That is to say, electrical equipment on the engine, such as the starter motor or alternator, is grounded to the engine block, which is connected to the battery's negative terminal with a heavy cable.

Although commonly used, this practice is not the best one for boats. Imagine a poor (resistive) connection between the battery ground cable and the engine block. The battery's negative post will usually be tied into the boat's *common ground point* (Chapter 5), which in turn will likely have the bonding cable connected to it (more on this later). Various through-hull fittings may be connected to the bonding cable. *Rather than take the electrical return path through the resistive battery ground cable, equipment grounded to the engine block may find a path back to the battery via the propeller shaft and propeller, through the water, into a through-hull, up the bonding cable, through the common ground point, and so back to the battery. Stray-current corrosion will follow* (more on this later).

Insulated return. Engine-mounted electrical equipment should ideally be of the *insulated-return* type (Figure 4-11). This requires either

purpose-built alternators and starter motors or equipment mounted in such a way as to electrically isolate it from the engine block. A second ground conductor is then installed to form an insulated return path to the battery. The result is that the engine block is never part of the circuit.

Some purpose-built marine alternators have insulated grounds (e.g., Mastervolt alternators and some from Balmar), but they are uncommon, while isolated-ground starter motors are extremely rare. You can convert existing ground-return alternators to insulated-ground types by drilling out all the mounting holes and installing nylon bushings and washers so as to completely insulate the alternator from the engine block. Then run a separate ground cable from the alternator case to the battery's negative post (or preferably, the boat's common ground point). *This cable must be at least as heavy as the main output cable from the alternator, since it will be a full current-carrying conductor.*

However, it is not easy to electrically isolate a noninsulated alternator and still ensure a sufficiently rigid installation. A good compromise is to connect a *heavy* ground cable *from the alternator case to the boat's common ground point.* This will provide a direct electrical path to the battery that bypasses the engine block, discouraging leakage currents. For additional insurance against corrosion, check the engine ground cable periodically to ensure that its connections are electrically perfect.

Non-isolated-ground starter motors are even harder to isolate than alternators, but since they operate for only a second or two, the duration of any leakage currents will be strictly limited.

The electronic sending units that are mounted on most modern engines to monitor oil pressure and water temperature are generally grounded through the block, as is other electrically operated equipment such as solenoid-type fuel shutdown valves. *Anytime the ignition is on, potentially damaging small currents flow to ground through these units.* The only way to eliminate these currents is to replace the sending units (and other devices) with purpose-built, insulated-ground units. These units will have a separate ground wire carried back to the battery's negative terminal. VDO (www.vdo.com), among others, makes insulated-ground sending devices (see page 111).

The boat's wiring. Whether or not engine installations use a ground-return circuit or have an insulated ground, *the rest of the DC system should never use a ground-return circuit, even if possible* (such as on a steel boat, or on a fiberglass boat with a copper bonding strap running the length of the boat). Using the hull in a metal

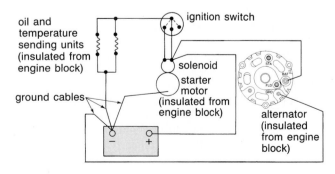

FIGURE 4-11. An insulated-ground return circuit.

oil and temperature sending units (insulated from engine block)

ground cables

ignition switch

solenoid

starter motor (insulated from engine block)

alternator (insulated from engine block)

boat as a ground circuit, or the bonding strap in a fiberglass boat, will result in different parts of the hull and underwater fittings having slightly different voltages. *Corrosion will be rampant.*

All non-engine-mounted DC equipment on boats must have a separate, insulated ground cable that runs back to the ground (negative) side of the distribution panel. The panel ground will, in turn, be connected to the battery's negative terminal. *At no point can the hull or any fittings or fixtures be used as an electrical path. To do so is to invite corrosion.*

Troubleshooting with a Voltmeter

It is very difficult to hurt yourself or do damage when using a meter in its volts mode (as opposed to the amps or ohms mode), especially on 12- and 24-volt DC circuits. I recommend that you run through some of these tests before they are needed just to get some practice with a meter

and also to get comfortable with using it. It can prove to be a surprisingly interesting exercise!

The following tests all refer to a voltmeter and assume a 12-volt circuit. A test lamp (Figure 4-12) could be used to duplicate the tests. Where the meter shows 12 volts, a test lamp will light; no volts, no light; low volts, dim light (or the test lamp barely glows). Remember that to get a voltage reading, or to make the test lamp light up, *a voltage differential must be bridged.*

Basic circuit test. The most basic circuit test is simply to connect the meter between the positive and negative terminals on a battery to read battery voltage directly from *hot* to *ground.*

Load on circuit. Now let us make a circuit from the positive terminal to the negative terminal and put a piece of electrical gear in it (i.e., a resistance). We are placing a load on the circuit (Figure 4-13).

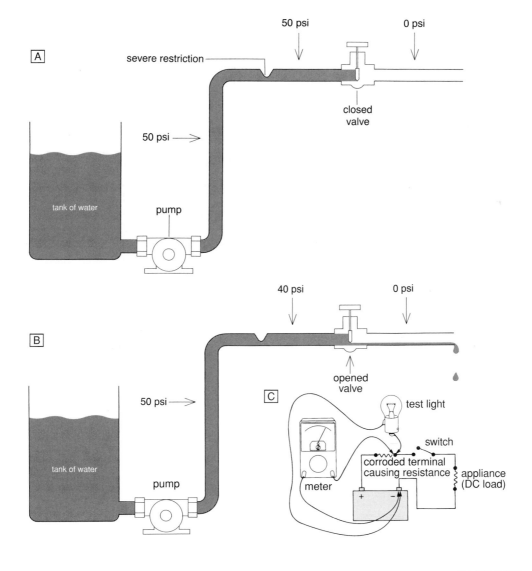

FIGURE 4-12. Troubleshooting DC voltage drops. A corroded terminal, to use one example, is analogous to a severe restriction in a water pipe. If there is an open switch (or a closed valve) on the downstream side of the fault, voltage or pressure will equalize across the fault (A). If the valve is opened, however, water flows and pressure falls across the fault (B). Placing a test light as shown in C is equivalent to cracking the valve, drawing enough current to reveal (by a dim glow rather than intense light) the voltage drop across the faulty terminals. The voltmeter may draw too little current to crack the valve and reveal the fault. *(Jim Sollers)*

FIGURE 4-13. Voltage readings. In a healthy circuit, meter 1 will show no voltage reading, meter 2 will read the system voltage, and meter 3 will again show no voltage.

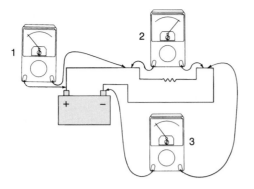

The line all the way to the resistance is *hot*, and all the way back from it is at battery *ground potential*. A meter connected anywhere from the hot side to the ground side, right up to the two terminals on the equipment, will show battery voltage, *but a meter with both probes on one side of the equipment or the other will give no reading* (the meter is not bridging any voltage differential).

Circuit with switch. Now let's put in a battery isolation switch (Figure 4-14). When the switch

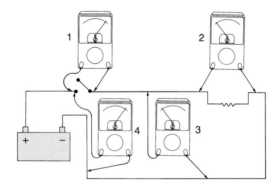

FIGURE 4-14. Voltage readings. Meters 1 and 4 should both show the full system voltage. Meters 2 and 3 should read 0 volts.

is closed, we have exactly the same situation as in the test above and the same procedures apply. A meter placed across the switch will not read anything since it is not bridging any voltage differential. However, when the switch is open (turned off), *only the cable from the battery positive terminal to the switch is hot;* the rest of the circuit will be "bled down" to ground. A *meter placed across the switch will read system voltage, but if placed across the resistance* (the piece of equipment) *will read nothing.*

Consider the analogy with a pressurized water system. If a valve is placed in the line before a restriction (resistance), as long as the valve is open, the pressure (i.e., voltage) will be constant all the way to the restriction (resistance) and will then drop on the other side of the restriction (resistance). But if the valve is closed, the pressure will bleed off the whole system downstream of the valve, and the only pressure differential will be across the valve.

Unwanted resistance. Now let's put some wear and tear on our switch so that the points are dirty and pitted and the switch causes a resistance. When the switch is open (turned off), the situation is the same as when it is open in the test above. When the switch is closed, it is electrically the same as placing a second load (resistance) in the circuit in series with the equipment load. In effect, we have the situation shown in Figure 4-15.

There will be a voltage drop across both resistances. What is more, *the voltage drop across each resistance will be proportional to the amount of its resistance as a percentage of the total resistance in the circuit.* What does this mean in practice?

Test Lights

In the absence of a multimeter, you can perform many useful tests with a test light (see Figure 4-12). On occasion, a test light may give even better results than a multimeter.

For example: The points on a switch are badly corroded, creating resistance. The switch is closed, but there is no load (amperage flow) on the circuit. Because of its high sensitivity and low current draw, the voltmeter may show system voltage downstream of the switch (and hence not reveal the resistance), whereas the test light will impose a small load on the circuit, which will reveal the resistance (the light will only glow dimly).

To understand this, think of a pressurized water pipe with a severe restriction in it and a closed valve farther down the line. (The closed valve is the equivalent of no load, therefore no flow, on the electrical circuit.) Pressure will equalize on both sides of the restriction all the way to the closed valve, and a pressure gauge will not reveal the restriction. However, if we open the valve a little and let some water flow, pressure will drop downstream of the restriction and thus reveal its presence. The drain caused by a test light is the equivalent of opening the valve a little.

We can draw a useful conclusion from this analogy: *When possible, voltage tests should always be made when a circuit is under normal load rather than in a no-load situation. This will reveal weaknesses that otherwise may be hard to find.*

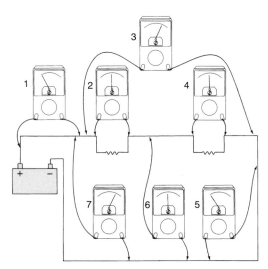

FIGURE 4-15. Voltage readings. There are two resistances in series, each of which (meters 2 and 4) will show a voltage drop of less than the total system voltage. Meter 3 will show the system voltage, as should meter 7. Meter 6 should give the same reading as meter 4, and meters 1 and 5 should read 0 volts. One of the two resistances is unwanted (a faulty switch, for example), and these tests will find it.

On a *closed* circuit, if a voltage test across the input and output terminals of any switch, terminal block, or length of wiring reveals *any* voltage, *there is unwanted resistance in the switch, terminal block, or wire.*

The unwanted resistance is proportional to the voltage shown. For example, a reading of 6 volts on a 12-volt circuit indicates that the resistance is half the total resistance in the circuit. In other words, it is equal to the resistance of the equipment in the circuit. With twice as much resistance as we should have, only half the designed amperage will flow—the equipment will receive only half of its rated amperage. A reading of 3 volts indicates a resistance of 25% of the total resistance in the circuit; the equipment will receive only 75% of its rated amps.

Put another way, if a voltage test across the input and output terminals of a piece of *operating* equipment reveals less than battery voltage, *we have unwanted resistance somewhere else in the circuit due to inadequate wiring or poor connections and switches.* The unwanted resistance is proportional to the extent of the voltage loss at the equipment. It may be on either the hot side or the ground side of the equipment.

Many pieces of equipment (e.g., lights) will run perfectly well with a 10% voltage drop. Assuming a fully charged 12-volt battery with an open-circuit voltage of 12.6 volts, the voltage across the input and output leads to the equipment *when it is switched on* will read 11.3 volts. But other equipment is sensitive to voltage drop, notably battery charging circuits (see Chapter 1),

some electronics, and electric motors (which may suffer a serious loss of power and may also overheat—the number one cause of DC motor failure is low voltage). *Boat circuits should in most cases be designed to limit voltage drop to a maximum of 3% at the equipment* (e.g., given a fully charged battery at 12.6 volts, a voltage reading of 12.2 volts *at the equipment when in use*; for more on this, see the Proper Electrical Installations section later in this chapter).

The major causes of unwanted voltage drop are poor connections and inadequate wiring (see below).

Circuit with multiple switches and a fuse.
Now let us extend our circuit one more time and add a distribution panel with a breaker, another switch for the piece of equipment, and a fuse.

There is really nothing new here, just an elaboration of the previous situation. To make a circuit, all switches must be closed and the fuse operative. Any voltage drop across a *closed* switch or a fuse indicates unwanted resistance; the higher the voltage, the more the resistance. Anything less than system voltage across the terminals of the equipment likewise reveals unwanted resistance in the circuit, on either the hot or the ground side.

If there is no voltage or reduced voltage at the equipment, a comprehensive and logical procedure to test every part of the circuit would be to close all switches, check the fuse, and then test for voltage following the sixteen tests in Figure 4-16. Naturally no one wants to run through such an involved procedure, so what we need are a few simple steps to narrow down the location of a problem.

Generalized troubleshooting procedure with a voltmeter.
If a piece of electrical equipment fails to operate, or operates at below par, *it should be turned on* (if this is not safe or possible, see the Troubleshooting with an Ohmmeter section below) and the voltage checked *across the power leads.* This will yield one of three results (Troubleshooting Chart 4-1):

- The meter shows system voltage. In this case, the equipment itself is at fault—most likely a blown fuse, poor connection, or burnout (for further diagnosis, see the Troubleshooting with an Ohmmeter section).

- The meter shows less than system voltage. There are three possibilities: (1) the battery is flat; (2) there is a short circuit (see below) or partial short in the load, which is dragging down the voltage on the battery; or (3) there is a voltage drop in the circuit. In all three cases, the equipment may be working but below par (e.g., motors run slowly, lights are dim, and

FIGURE 4-16. Trouble-shooting DC voltage drops—a comprehensive test procedure.

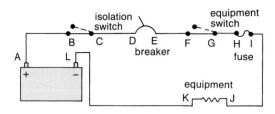

Test sequence (left to right)

Readings	A to L	A to B	B to C	C to L	C to D	D to E	E to L	E to F	F to G	G to L	G to H	H to I	I to L	I to J	J to K	K to L
Battery check; should read about 12.6 volts	•															
Should be no reading. To be certain, switch down progressively to the lowest voltage scale on the meter. Low reading indicates unwanted resistance; 12.6 volts, a break in the line.		•			•			•			•			•		•
Should be no reading. To check, switch down to the meter's lowest scale again. Low reading indicates dirty or corroded switch terminals or points, or too small a switch; 12.6 volts, an open switch or, in H to I, a blown fuse.			•			•			•			•				
Should be 12.6 volts. No reading indicates an open switch; or in I to L, a blown fuse. Less than 12.6 volts in C to L, a voltage drop between A and C. Less than 12.6 volts in J to K indicates unwanted voltage drop somewhere in the circuit.				•			•			•			•		•	

electronic equipment is subject to random errors). To distinguish the three situations, leave the load on and test the voltage across the battery posts.

If the voltage is the *same* at the battery as at the load, the entire system is being dragged down, but without voltage drop—the battery is probably flat. If not, the equipment has a short. (The exception would be very heavy draw DC items, such as a starter motor or electric windlass, which can be expected to pull even a healthy 12-volt DC system down to as low as 10.5 volts [or 24 volts down to as low as 21 volts], at which point the voltage should stabilize for at least 15 seconds before falling any lower.) If, on the other hand, the voltage at the power source remains at or near system voltage while it *falls* at the load, there is a voltage drop on the circuit.

The source of the voltage drop can once again be narrowed down by connecting the meter from the equipment positive lead to a known good ground (J to L in Figure 4-16). *With the load turned on*, if the meter shows *less than system voltage*, there is a voltage loss

on the *positive* side. If the meter shows *system voltage*, the loss is on the *negative* side. *However, there may be losses on both sides!* The voltage loss can be further isolated by using the meter leads to bridge every length of wire and individual component (switches, fuses, and terminal blocks) in the faulty side of the circuit. If at any time the meter gives a reading, this indicates the extent of the voltage drop in this part of the circuit.

Resistive wires need renewing with properly sized, marine-rated cable (see later in this chapter). Resistive connections need to be undone, cleaned, refastened, and coated with a corrosion inhibitor. You can sometimes make resistive switches and breakers serviceable by switching them on and off repeatedly, or if this fails, by cleaning the points with a fine file or wet-and-dry sandpaper (400 to 600 grit); otherwise you will have to replace them.

- The meter shows no voltage. There is a break in the circuit, most likely a switch or breaker is off or a fuse is blown; if not, there is some other discontinuity such as a broken wire. To

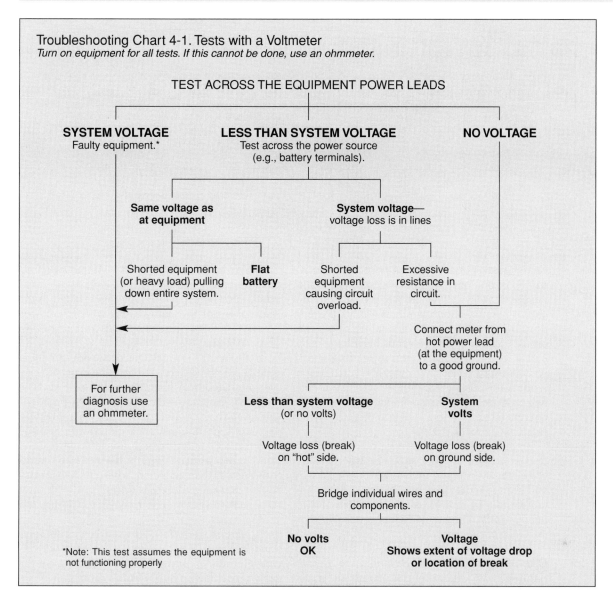

Troubleshooting Chart 4-1. Tests with a Voltmeter
Turn on equipment for all tests. If this cannot be done, use an ohmmeter.

TEST ACROSS THE EQUIPMENT POWER LEADS

SYSTEM VOLTAGE
Faulty equipment.*

LESS THAN SYSTEM VOLTAGE
Test across the power source
(e.g., battery terminals).

NO VOLTAGE

**Same voltage as
at equipment**

System voltage—
voltage loss is in lines

Shorted equipment
(or heavy load) pulling
down entire system.

**Flat
battery**

Shorted
equipment
causing circuit
overload.

Excessive
resistance in
circuit.

Connect meter from
hot power lead
(at the equipment)
to a good ground.

For further
diagnosis use
an ohmmeter.

Less than system voltage
(or no volts)

**System
volts**

Voltage loss (break)
on "hot" side.

Voltage loss (break)
on ground side.

Bridge individual wires and
components.

**No volts
OK**

**Voltage
Shows extent of voltage drop
or location of break**

*Note: This test assumes the equipment is
not functioning properly

---

determine which side of the load (hot side or ground side) the break is on, *turn on all the switches* and connect the meter from the *equipment positive lead to a good ground* (such as the negative battery post, if this can be reached—e.g., J to L in Figure 4-16). If the meter now shows *system voltage*, the break is on the *negative* side; if it still shows *no voltage*, the break is on the *positive* side. To further narrow down the break, use the meter leads to bridge every individual length of wire and component (switches, fuses, and terminal blocks) in the offending side of the circuit. As noted earlier, this should produce readings of 0 volts; when the meter reads system voltage, the break in the circuit is being bridged.

Limitations of a voltmeter. To be effective, many voltage tests, particularly voltage-drop

tests, must be made with a circuit *under load* (see the Test Lights sidebar), but sometimes it is just not possible to turn on the relevant equipment to make the tests (for example, if a short circuit keeps tripping a breaker, or there has been an electrical fire). In this case an ohmmeter is the appropriate troubleshooting tool. In addition it has, as we will see, a specific application in troubleshooting electrical equipment itself.

Troubleshooting with an Ohmmeter

An ohmmeter can be used to duplicate many of the procedures described for a voltmeter. But first remember that *when using an ohmmeter, the circuit or equipment being tested must ALWAYS be electrically isolated from the battery or other power source.*

If a piece of equipment fails to run, place the

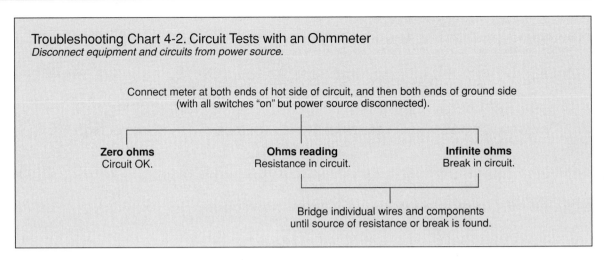

Troubleshooting Chart 4-2. Circuit Tests with an Ohmmeter
Disconnect equipment and circuits from power source.

Connect meter at both ends of hot side of circuit, and then both ends of ground side
(with all switches "on" but power source disconnected).

Zero ohms	**Ohms reading**	**Infinite ohms**
Circuit OK.	Resistance in circuit.	Break in circuit.

Bridge individual wires and components
until source of resistance or break is found.

meter probes at the two ends of the positive supply circuit and then on the two ends of the negative circuit to reveal any problem in the circuit (Troubleshooting Chart 4-2). A *break* in the circuit will produce a reading of *infinite* ohms; *excessive resistance*, causing voltage drop, will show up as a *specific ohms* reading; and a *good, resistance-free circuit* will give a reading of 0 ohms (or very near 0 ohms—sensitive meters will produce a low ohms reading, particularly on circuits rated for a low load and therefore using small-gauge wires).

Breaks and high resistance in a circuit can also be isolated in much the same way as with a voltmeter by bridging individual lengths of wire and components (switches, fuses, and terminal blocks) in turn. *Any break will show up as a reading of infinite ohms; excessive resistance will show as a specific ohms reading.*

Checking equipment. Beyond these uses, an ohmmeter has other useful functions all its own (Troubleshooting Chart 4-3). For example, if preliminary testing indicates a problem with a specific piece of equipment, the internal resistance of the equipment can be checked by testing across its input leads (with any internal fuses

in place, and any *equipment-mounted switch—not* the power switch—turned on). Some resistance is to be expected; how much depends on the nature of the equipment, with low-power items showing a higher resistance than heavy-duty equipment.

In theory, if the amp draw of the equipment is known, the precise resistance to be expected can be calculated by using Ohm's Law (resistance = voltage/amperage—see page 117). In practice, however, many resistances are not what might be expected, particularly incandescent lightbulbs and electric motors, which for different reasons tend to measure low (lightbulbs measure several times lower than expected; when they warm up, their resistance increases dramatically). In any case, most times precise resistance readings are not needed.

A reading of *infinite* ohms indicates an *open circuit* inside the equipment: a lightbulb or heating element is burned out; an electric motor may simply have a blown fuse, a problem with its brushes, or a dirty commutator (Chapter 7), but otherwise it is also burned out. A reading of 0 ohms indicates a *dead short* (except on certain very heavy draw DC motors, such as a starter motor, which have such low internal resistances

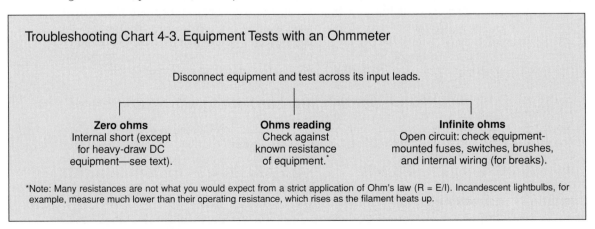

Troubleshooting Chart 4-3. Equipment Tests with an Ohmmeter

Disconnect equipment and test across its input leads.

Zero ohms	**Ohms reading**	**Infinite ohms**
Internal short (except for heavy-draw DC equipment—see text).	Check against known resistance of equipment.*	Open circuit: check equipment-mounted fuses, switches, brushes, and internal wiring (for breaks).

*Note: Many resistances are not what you would expect from a strict application of Ohm's law (R = E/I). Incandescent lightbulbs, for example, measure much lower than their operating resistance, which rises as the filament heats up.

that only a good-quality meter will differentiate between normal resistance and a short).

Short circuits. The matter of shorts deserves more attention. *A short circuit is a direct connection from the hot side of a circuit to the ground side, bypassing the load itself.* It can be a minor current leak or a dead short, in which case very high currents will flow. In the latter case, *if the circuit is not properly protected with a fuse or circuit breaker, it is likely to catch fire. Note that the fire may well NOT be at the source of the short. It may instead be at the most resistive part of the new (short) circuit,* generally the smallest-gauge wire in the circuit or a resistive terminal, since this is where the excessive current flow will generate the most heat. *Replacing the burned wire will not solve the problem.*

An ohmmeter is the perfect tool for tracing shorts (Troubleshooting Chart 4-4): it will show a circuit *(continuity)* where none should exist. Given a short or a suspected current leak (for example, if the batteries die slowly when no equipment is turned on), *disconnect* the circuit to be tested *from its power source,* and disconnect the load from the circuit. Test the equipment as above. If this fails to reveal a problem, *with the circuit still disconnected from the power source and the equipment still disconnected from the circuit,* put all switches and circuit breakers in the ON position and test from any part of the hot side of the circuit to any part of the ground side—the terminals where the equipment was disconnected are generally the most accessible place (Figure 4-17A). The meter should show *infinite* ohms. *Any other reading indicates a short, and the lower the reading, the more serious the short.*

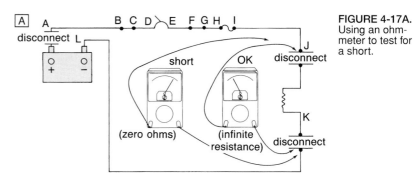

FIGURE 4-17A. Using an ohmmeter to test for a short.

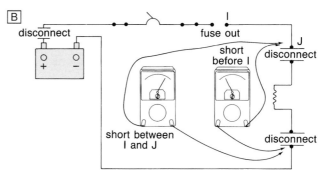

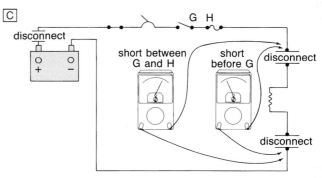

FIGURES 4-17B AND 4-17C. Using an ohmmeter to track down the source of a short (see the text for a full explanation).

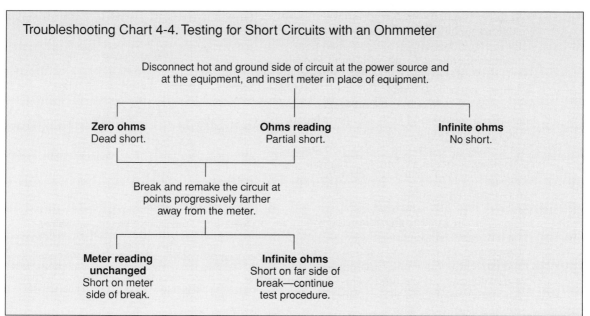

Troubleshooting Chart 4-4. Testing for Short Circuits with an Ohmmeter

Disconnect hot and ground side of circuit at the power source and at the equipment, and insert meter in place of equipment.

Zero ohms
Dead short.

Ohms reading
Partial short.

Infinite ohms
No short.

Break and remake the circuit at points progressively farther away from the meter.

Meter reading unchanged
Short on meter side of break.

Infinite ohms
Short on far side of break—continue test procedure.

The source of a short can be further narrowed down by leaving the meter connected across the wires to the equipment and progressively breaking the circuit (turning off switches, pulling fuses, or undoing terminals) farther and farther back from the meter (Figures 4-17B and 4-17C). If, after a break is made, the meter reading is *unchanged, the short is on the meter side of the break*; if the meter jumps to *infinity*, the short is on the *other* side. In the latter case, the break should be closed and another break made farther from the meter. If the meter reading now remains unchanged, the short is between the two break points; if it jumps to infinity once again, the short is still farther back, and the test procedure needs to be continued.

Ground Faults ("Earth" Leaks)

One of the more insidious problems on board is leakage of very small amounts of current through poor wiring, switches, connections, and equipment insulation to ground. Such leaks slowly drain batteries and can also contribute to devastating stray-current corrosion (more on this later). Leaks to ground are an ever-present possibility in the damp marine environment, especially from bilge pumps and other equipment or wiring located in damp areas of the boat or actually in water.

To locate ground faults, look for current flow to ground that bypasses normal circuits but is not normally great enough to show up as a short circuit. Depending on where in a circuit the leak is, it may occur either only when equipment is switched on or all the time.

Preliminary test. Note: See pages 234–35 for a comprehensive procedure designed to test both the AC and DC circuits for numerous fault conditions, including an alternative approach for tracing ground leaks than that described here.

Switch off absolutely all equipment and *disconnect any solar panels*, but leave on the battery isolation switch. Disconnect the positive cable from the battery and connect a multimeter on an appropriate scale for 12 volts DC (or whatever voltage is appropriate—e.g., 24 volts DC on a 24-volt circuit) between the battery post and the cable (Troubleshooting Chart 4-5). *The voltmeter should give no reading.* If it reads 12 volts, one of two things is happening:

1. One or more circuits are still on, providing a path to ground. Double-check all circuits (including propane and carbon monoxide monitors, which are often "hard-wired" without switches, as are circuits feeding the "memory" function of some stereos, other electronics, and systems monitors).

2. There is a ground leak between the battery and the various switches and breakers that are turned off (depending on the type of meter, this leak may be anywhere from a fraction of a milliamp on up).

The meter shows a leak. If the meter gives a reading, connect it between the *disconnected cable clamp* (NOT the battery post) and the *negative* battery post (Figure 4-18), and then switch it to its most sensitive ohms (resistance) function (R × 1 scale on an analog meter). The meter is now registering any circuit to ground within the boat's wiring.

A reading of less than 10 ohms indicates a piece of equipment left on; 10 to 1,000 ohms, a low-drain piece of equipment left on or a serious leak; 1,000 to 10,000 ohms (the meter may need to be switched to the R × 100 scale), a minor leak; and anything over 10,000 ohms, an insignificant leak.

The magnitude of any leakage current can be found with a meter capable of measuring DC amps. However, many multimeters are limited to a maximum of 250 milliamps, in which case the meter should not be used in this mode if the resistance reading was less than 50 ohms on a 12-volt circuit (100 ohms with 24 volts). A meter with a 10 amps capability can be used with resistance readings as low as 1.25 ohms on a 12-volt circuit (2.5 ohms with 24 volts).

Set the meter to read DC amps, then place it back in line between the *positive* battery post and the disconnected cable clamp. If an analog meter shows no measurable deflection of its needle, progressively switch it down to lower milliamps scales until the leakage current can be measured. Less than 1 mA is insignificant; 1 to 10 mA, a minor leak; 10 mA to 1 amp, a major

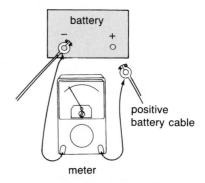

FIGURE 4-18. Pinpointing a ground leak with an ohmmeter. Disconnect the cable clamp from the positive terminal, and connect the meter between the disconnected positive cable clamp and the negative terminal. Readings may be interpreted as follows: less than 10 ohms = equipment left on; 10 to 1,000 ohms = serious ground leak; 1,000 to 10,000 ohms = minor ground leak; greater than 10,000 ohms = little or no leak.

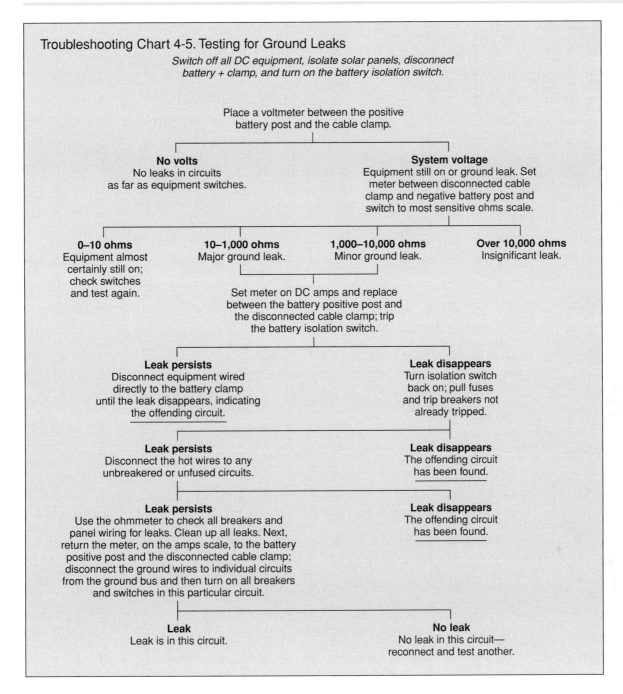

Troubleshooting Chart 4-5. Testing for Ground Leaks

*Switch off all DC equipment, isolate solar panels, disconnect
battery + clamp, and turn on the battery isolation switch.*

Place a voltmeter between the positive
battery post and the cable clamp.

No volts
No leaks in circuits
as far as equipment switches.

System voltage
Equipment still on or ground leak. Set
meter between disconnected cable
clamp and negative battery post and
switch to most sensitive ohms scale.

0–10 ohms
Equipment almost
certainly still on;
check switches
and test again.

10–1,000 ohms
Major ground leak.

1,000–10,000 ohms
Minor ground leak.

Over 10,000 ohms
Insignificant leak.

Set meter on DC amps and replace
between the battery positive post and
the disconnected cable clamp; trip
the battery isolation switch.

Leak persists
Disconnect equipment wired
directly to the battery clamp
until the leak disappears, indicating
the offending circuit.

Leak disappears
Turn isolation switch
back on; pull fuses
and trip breakers not
already tripped.

Leak persists
Disconnect the hot wires to any
unbreakered or unfused circuits.

Leak disappears
The offending circuit
has been found.

Leak persists
Use the ohmmeter to check all breakers and
panel wiring for leaks. Clean up all leaks. Next,
return the meter, on the amps scale, to the battery
positive post and the disconnected cable clamp;
disconnect the ground wires to individual circuits
from the ground bus and then turn on all breakers
and switches in this particular circuit.

Leak disappears
The offending circuit
has been found.

Leak
Leak is in this circuit.

No leak
No leak in this circuit—
reconnect and test another.

leak or some equipment left on; and over 1 amp, equipment left on.

Isolating leaks. To track down a leak, with the amp meter still in place, first trip the battery isolation switch. If the leak persists, it is on *the battery side* of the switch, most likely in some piece of equipment wired directly to the battery. In this case, disconnect the individual wires to the battery clamp one at a time until the leak disappears, indicating which is the offending circuit (Figure 4-19, Test 1).

If, on the other hand, the leak disappears when the battery isolation switch is tripped, the leak is "downstream" of the switch and isolating it becomes rather more involved. First, turn the isolation switch back on. There is likely to be a positive feed from the switch to a distribution panel, at which point most circuits will have either a fuse or a circuit breaker. If any equipment has been turned off at the equipment, but its circuit breaker is still on, now is the time to trip the breaker, or in a fused circuit, to pull the fuse. If at any time the leak disappears, the offending circuit has been found.

If the leak persists, the next step is to discon-

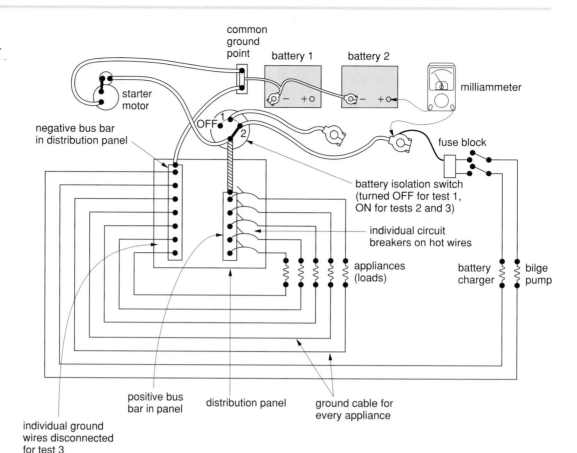

FIGURE 4-19. Testing for ground leaks. At the start of each test, set the meter to the highest amps scale and then progressively switch it down to see if there is a leak. **Test 1:** Battery isolation switch OFF; all circuits connected to the battery clamp (and therefore bypassing the distribution panel) OFF. If there is a leak, disconnect the individual wires from the battery clamp to find the offending circuit. **Test 2:** Battery isolation switch ON; all other switches OFF. If there is a leak, disconnect unfused or unbreakered cables (e.g., the engine cranking cable) at the isolation switch or panel. If the leak disappears, it is in the circuit just disconnected. **Test 3:** Battery isolation switch ON; individual ground cable for a given circuit disconnected at the negative bus bar; all switches and breakers *for the disconnected circuit only* ON. Any leak represents a leak to ground in this circuit.

Labels in figure:
common ground point — battery 1 — battery 2 — milliammeter — starter motor — negative bus bar in distribution panel — OFF 1 2 — battery isolation switch (turned OFF for test 1, ON for tests 2 and 3) — fuse block — individual circuit breakers on hot wires — appliances (loads) — battery charger — bilge pump — positive bus bar in panel — distribution panel — ground cable for every appliance — individual ground wires disconnected for test 3

nect the hot wires to any circuits not on a circuit breaker or fuse (for example, the starter motor and starting circuit—Figure 4-19, Test 2). If disconnecting a cable makes no difference to the meter reading, reconnect this cable before moving to the next. If disconnecting a circuit causes a partial drop in the meter reading, it not only indicates some leakage current in this circuit, but also that there is more than one leak.

If a leak still persists after all circuit breakers have been tripped, fuses pulled, and unbreakered or unfused circuits disconnected, then one of the panel breakers must be leaking, or the panel itself is leaking. Use an ohmmeter (set to the R × 1 scale on an analog meter) to check the breakers and panel wiring. A breaker that is off should produce a reading of infinite ohms across its two terminals, as should any test between the hot side of the panel's wiring and a good ground (for example, the negative bus bar).

Further tests. The tests to date will reveal ground leaks in unbreakered circuits and in other circuits *up to the various equipment switches, breakers, or fuses, but not beyond these points.* If the equipment is switched at the distribution panel (much of it is on modern boats), *this may leave the greater part of the boat's circuits untested.*

To test for ground leaks in the rest of the circuits, you will have to disconnect the ground lead to each circuit in turn at the bus bar in the distribution panel (Figure 4-19, Test 3). If more than one circuit shares the same switch or breaker, disconnect the grounds to all the relevant circuits from the negative bus bar. Replace any fuses that were previously removed from the circuit being tested and turn on all switches and circuit breakers in this circuit. Set the meter to the amps scale, and once again, insert it between the battery positive post and the disconnected cable clamp.

Any current flow indicates a leak to ground in the disconnected circuits(s) that is finding its way back to the battery through other (still connected) circuits. If the path to ground includes underwater hardware (for example, through bilge water to an engine block, the propeller shaft, the propeller, and then a grounded radio ground plate), corrosion is likely. The leak needs to be tracked down and cleared up.

Don't Leave Port Without a Multimeter

There is nothing in these procedures that is terribly complicated. Rather, it is a matter of being logical and methodical. With more complex cir-

Using an Ohmmeter to Test a Masthead Light Circuit

There are some circuits, such as masthead lights, that are inaccessible for much of their length; therefore, isolating faults can be difficult. The ohmmeter will make things much easier. First, disconnect the circuit at the base of the mast and test across the two mast leads. A very low (close to 0 ohms) reading (unusual) indicates a short inside the mast or at the masthead. A low ohms reading (typically 10 to 20 ohms) indicates that both the in-mast wiring and the bulb are good—the problem lies elsewhere. An infinite ohms reading indicates a break in the circuit inside the mast or at the masthead.

If the ohmmeter gives an infinite reading, twist the two wires together, go to the masthead, and remove the bulb. Test the bulb across its two terminals: an infinite reading shows a blown bulb; a low reading tells us that the bulb is working, in which case a test is made across the two wire terminals at the masthead. Since these wires have been shorted together at the base of the mast, this last test should show a low ohms reading. If it is infinite, there is a break in the mast circuit (check for dirty or broken terminals at the light fixture before condemning the in-mast wiring).

Many navigation lights on new boats now use quartz halogen lamps since they provide more light for less amp draw. These bulbs are extremely delicate and must be handled with care (especially at $10 to $15 a lamp!). *Do not touch the bulb;* always grip it with a piece of paper. To remove and install, simply pull the bulbs out of their sockets or push them in—do not twist. Each quartz halogen bulb has two wires that stick straight out; be sure these wires are straight before fitting a new bulb. At the base of the bulb is a small indentation that will mate with a spring clip in the fixture to hold the bulb in place. Once installed, wipe the bulb to ensure that it has no finger grease on it.

Quartz halogen bulbs are sensitive to high voltages, even the elevated voltages common with multistep regulators. *Given a charging device regulated to anything over 14.2 volts, it might be better to stick with incandescent bulbs.* These will also suffer a decline in their life expectancy, but since they are so much cheaper, it is less significant. (For more on the pros and cons of different lighting technologies, see Chapter 7.)

Note: When testing the wiring at the base of an aluminum mast, make an additional test from each wire to the mast itself. Anything other than infinite resistance indicates some sort of a short to the mast, which could cause serious corrosion.

---

cuits and difficult to isolate problems, it often pays to make a sketch on paper of the circuit and all its components, jotting down on the sketch the tests you make. It then becomes a relatively simple matter to draw the correct conclusions from the test results.

It is a rare electrical problem that cannot be cracked in this fashion, using either a voltmeter or an ohmmeter. The more you use a multimeter, the more adept you become in its handling, and the more versatile a tool it turns out to be. This is particularly true of the ohms function, which is frequently poorly understood and therefore rarely used. The multimeter is one of the key components of my toolbox—I would never leave port without one!

AC Circuits

Alternating current circuits in their simplest form also have a *hot* side and a *ground* side as DC circuits do, although the ground wire is known as the *neutral*. Instead of a battery as a power source, there is a generator, either ashore or on board, or sometimes a DC-to-AC inverter (see Chapter 6). The hot wire can be considered the electrical supply side of a load; the neutral wire is the return path to the generator or inverter. But then we have a refinement. *At every shoreside generator, a connection is made from the neutral terminal to a buried metal plate or rod* (Figure 4-20). What this does is hold the neutral side of the circuit at the *earth's potential.* When we measure voltage on an AC system, *we are measuring the differential between the hot side of the system and the earth's potential (ground potential,* sometimes simply referred to as *earth).* The hot side of the circuit is known as the *ungrounded* side; the neutral side as the *grounded* side.

The principal differences between this basic AC circuit and a DC circuit are:

1. The voltage on the AC circuit continuously alternates between positive and negative in

FIGURE 4-20. Basic AC
generator setup.

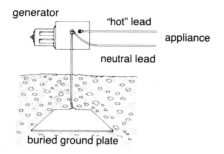

relation to ground potential. To all intents and
purposes, we can ignore this fact as far as this
chapter is concerned (more on this in Chapter 6).

2. The voltage on the AC system is typically
many times higher than that on a DC system—in the United States, a nominal 120
or 240 volts; in Europe, 240 volts. *THESE
VOLTAGES ARE POTENTIALLY LETHAL,*

*SO SAFETY ISSUES ARE A PRIMARY
CONCERN WHEN DEALING WITH AC
CIRCUITS.*

The Importance of Grounding

When a house is wired, the two wires—hot
(ungrounded) and neutral (grounded)—are run
to all fixtures and appliances. The incoming
electrical box is considered to be the *generating
source* for the house, and as such, the neutral circuits are connected to a buried pipe—a *driven
ground rod*—at this point, just as at the power
station.

In the old days that was it. But if a fault developed so that a piece of equipment became hot to
touch, anyone coming into contact with this
equipment completed the circuit to ground and
received a severe shock (Figure 4-21A). What
made the situation particularly dangerous was

FIGURE 4-21A. Two-wire
AC circuit. An appliance
has an internal short that
has made its case "live."
Because there is no direct
path to ground, the circuit
breaker has not tripped. A
person coming into contact
with the appliance
completes the path to
ground and receives a
shock.

FIGURE 4-21B. Household
electrical circuits (U.S.
color code shown). The
neutral and ground circuits
are tied together at the
main panelboard.

FIGURE 4-21C. Three-wire
AC circuit. The short-circuit
current is being safely
conducted to ground by the
grounding cable. If the
short is severe enough, the
high current flow will trip
the circuit breaker. The
person, who forms a less
conductive path to ground,
is protected.

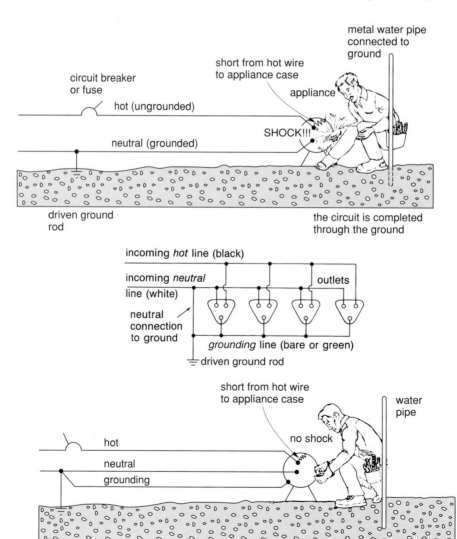

that in many instances the *fault current* could not run to ground *until human or other contact completed the circuit*. In such circumstances, fuses and breakers provide no people protection. Without a path to ground, the kind of currents necessary to blow the fuse or trip the breaker simply do not flow—the fault remains undetected until someone gets shocked or even electrocuted.

To improve system safety, a third grounding wire has now been added to AC circuits (note the term *grounding* is used to distinguish this wire from the *neutral* or *grounded* wire). A grounding wire is connected to the external case of an appliance and also to the neutral wire at the power source (incoming panelboard in a house) and thus to the driven ground rod (Figure 4-21B). In normal circumstances, this grounding wire carries no current, but *should some sort of a fault develop that makes an appliance hot to touch, this wire will conduct the fault current safely to ground* (Figure 4-21C). What is more, *if the leak is a serious one, such as in a short circuit, as soon as it occurs, the grounding wire will allow high levels of current to flow, which will immediately blow any fuse or trip a breaker.*

This grounding circuit is thus a *normally redundant path to ground, paralleling the neutral circuit*. It provides an essential degree of protection against many common electrical faults. Rather like a seat belt or an air bag in a car, it doesn't do any good until a problem develops, but then it might save a life. Any break in the grounding circuit, such as would be caused by cutting the ground pin off an extension cord (a common sight around boatyards!) or by a badly corroded ground connection on a shore-power cord (also common), potentially leaves us with the old-style two-wire circuit that provides fault current with no safe path to ground.

Safety Versus Corrosion

For a boat connected to shoreside power, the dockside receptacle is, in effect, the power source. The neutral and grounding cables will be grounded to a driven metal rod somewhere near the dockside panel that contains the main overcurrent protection device (main circuit breaker). When the boat is plugged into shore power, the neutral circuit on the boat and the grounding circuit are connected to their respective cables, and consequently both are grounded ashore at the point where the cables connect to the driven rod.

Just as in a house, if the case of an appliance becomes hot, the fault current will be conducted safely ashore via the grounding wire. Even in the damp marine environment, we still have excellent protection against shock hazards. There is, however, a snag: the same green (uninsulated) grounding wire that is providing such essential people protection may be contributing to galvanic corrosion. *This corrosion can take place even if the AC circuits are perfectly installed and functioning faultlessly*. It has, in fact, nothing to do with the AC system itself but is simply a parasitic problem that comes aboard with a proper AC installation.

What happens is this: Let's say two boats are lying alongside one another. Both are connected to shore power and are properly wired with the AC grounding circuit connected both ashore and to the onboard DC negative and bonding system (more on this in Chapter 5). The underwater hardware on one boat is protected by zincs, but on the other it is not. In effect what we have is a giant battery: the zincs on one boat form the negative plate; bronze underwater fittings on the other boat form the positive plate; and the water in which the boats are floating is the electrolyte. As soon as both boats plug into shore power, the AC grounding wire completes the circuit between the two "battery terminals" (the underwater hardware on the boats), *causing galvanically generated DC current to flow along the AC grounding wire* (see Figure 4-24). The least noble (galvanically most active) metal will corrode (in this case the zincs—see Chapter 5). When the zincs are depleted, the next least noble metal (e.g., some underwater fitting) will start to go.

As long as a shore-power-based AC system is properly grounded, *if an unmodified AC system is plugged into shore power, it will always invite corrosion. The problem is caused by precisely those steps deemed necessary to safeguard the people on board and swimmers in the water. We end up with an apparent conflict between people safety and boat protection*. The challenge is to find an acceptable response to this situation that sacrifices neither.

Breaking the galvanic circuit. From time to time an ill-conceived recommendation is made to cut the connection between the AC and DC grounding circuits. In theory, this isolates the AC grounding circuit from underwater hardware, breaking the path from shore to water for DC galvanic currents, while still maintaining the shoreside AC grounding connection for people protection. On the surface of things, this is a simple, cost-effective solution to the corrosion problem that does not compromise safety, but in reality *it can result in a highly dangerous situation that has almost certainly caused some deaths*.

As stated in the text, the neutral and grounding wires of an AC circuit are connected to a driven ground rod *at the power source*. In the case of shoreside power, the power source is considered to be the *dockside* (Figure 4-22A); with onboard generators and inverters, it is the *generator or inverter* (Figure 4-22B); and with an isolation transformer, it is the *secondary winding of the transformer* (see page 144). *On a boat, there is never any connection between the neutral and grounding wires at any other point.* This is important for a couple of reasons:

The neutral is a full current-carrying conductor. Were it to be grounded in more than one place, small differences in ground potential, or perhaps undue resistance in the neutral circuit itself, might induce some of the return current to find a path to ground through the grounding circuit, creating a potential shock hazard (Figure 4-23). In the event the neutral circuit failed at the shore-power connections, the full return current would be put on the grounding circuit, creating a potentially lethal situation.

In the case of a shore-power circuit, if the neutral is grounded on board and the boat is then connected with reverse polarity (either through improper wiring ashore or on board, or through inserting a two-pronged shore-power cord the wrong way around), *any neutral-to-ground connection on board the boat will cause the grounding circuit to become hot* (Figure 4-23). *If this circuit is connected to the DC negative* (as it should be—see the text), *the entire DC negative circuit will become hot, creating a hazardous environment both on board and in the surrounding water.* Fuses and circuit breakers will likely provide no protection against potential shocks, since in most cases the resistance of the surrounding water will not allow the passage of sufficient current to blow a fuse or trip a circuit breaker. (If the total resistance of the path through the water is above 10 ohms, for example, this will limit the current flow from a 120-volt circuit to 12 amps, which is not enough to trip a typical 15 amp breaker but is more than enough to kill someone.)

Note that if a boat has two shore-power connections (as many powerboats and large yachts do), the two neutral circuits on board must also be isolated from each other. If the neutrals are connected and one of the shore-power cords is plugged in with reverse polarity, all wires on the other circuit will be live!

It is worth repeating that *shore-power-based AC circuits never have the neutral grounded on board.* Finally, it should be noted that for historical reasons some domestic electric clothes dryers and electric stoves *do* have a neutral-to-ground connection on the appliance frame. *If such an appliance is used on board, this connection must be cut.*

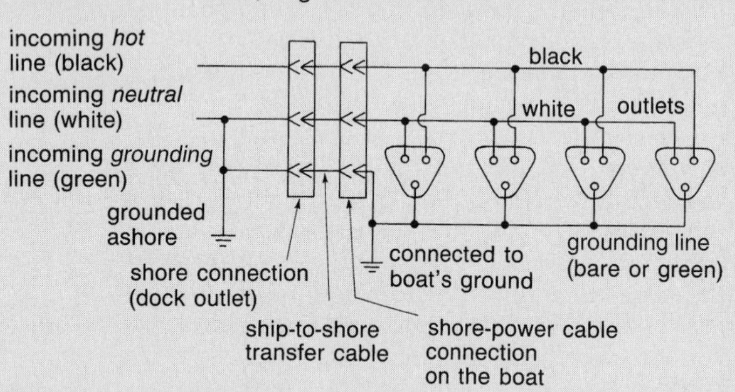

FIGURE 4-22A. Shipboard AC circuits. The neutral and ground circuits are not tied together on the boat—only onshore. The grounding circuit should be connected to the boat's ground as shown.

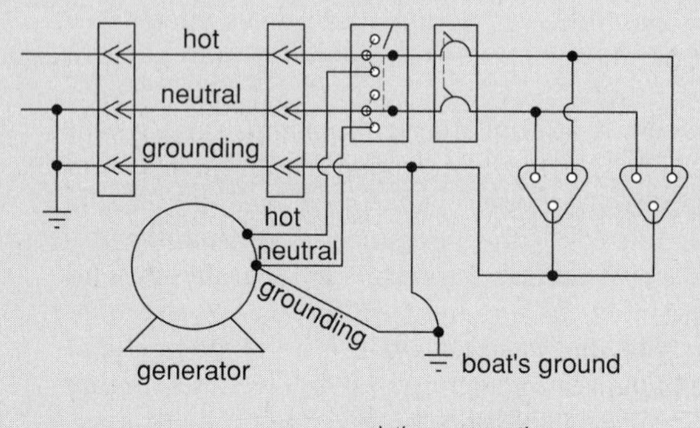

FIGURE 4-22B. An onboard generator has its neutral and grounding wires tied together at the generator case and nowhere else.

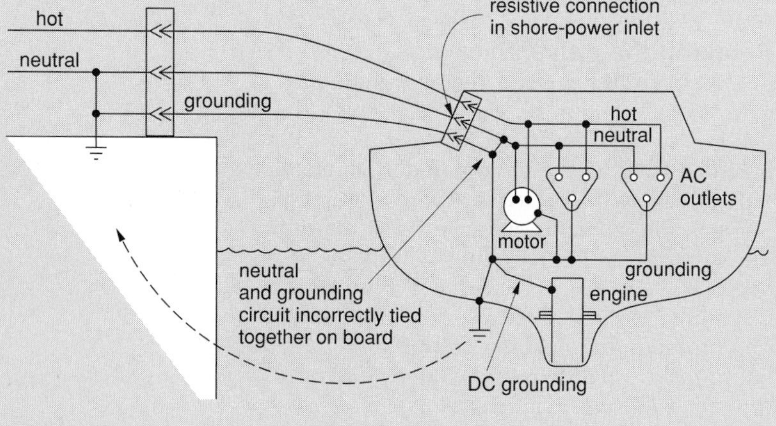

FIGURE 4-23. The neutral and grounding circuits have been improperly wired together on this boat. There is a resistive connection in the neutral circuit. As a result, the return current from the appliances will now find an alternative (lower-resistance) path to ground through the grounding circuit. Since this is (correctly) tied to the DC ground, it can create a shock hazard both on board and for swimmers. If the boat is connected to shore power with reverse polarity, the entire grounding system will be hot.

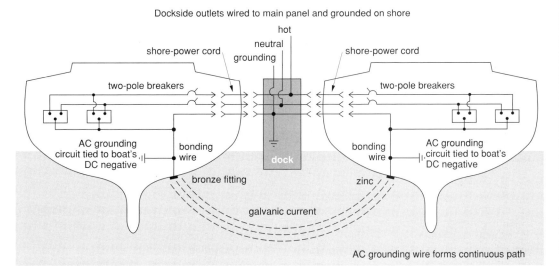

Dockside outlets wired to main panel and grounded on shore

shore-power cord
hot
neutral
grounding

two-pole breakers

shore-power cord

two-pole breakers

AC grounding
circuit tied to boat's
DC negative

bonding
wire

dock

bonding
wire

AC grounding
circuit tied to boat's
DC negative

bronze fitting

zinc

galvanic current

AC grounding wire forms continuous path

FIGURE 4-24. Two vessels connected to shore power both have their grounding circuits properly grounded to the boat's ground. But now the AC grounding wire provides a direct electrical connection between the underwater hardware on both boats. The seawater surrounding the hardware is an electrolyte (an electrically conductive liquid). We have, in effect, a giant battery with two dissimilar metals immersed in an electrolyte and interconnected! Galvanic activity will cause a current to flow along the AC grounding wire; the most easily corroded metal will be steadily eaten away (see Chapter 5). *(Ocean Navigator)*

There are at least three reasons why this is an unacceptable practice:

1. There are times when there may be a serious AC leak into the DC negative circuit, the most likely cause being a defective battery charger or a short between adjacent AC and DC wiring. *Without the AC grounding to DC negative connection, this fault current has no safe path back ashore.* The path through the water is unlikely to pass enough fault current to trip the main AC breaker or the shoreside breaker, in which case the entire negative side of the DC system, and all bonded equipment, will become energized at the full AC voltage, making all grounded equipment potentially lethal to anyone on board and the surrounding water potentially lethal to swimmers.

2. *Proper lightning protection demands that the AC grounding circuit and the DC negative circuit be held to the same voltage potential* in order to minimize the buildup of dangerous voltages in either circuit (Chapter 5). To do this effectively, the two must be electrically interconnected.

3. Quite often, even if the AC grounding to DC negative connection were cut, *there would still be some other unforeseen path to the DC negative.* This might be through a piece of AC equipment that is itself in some way grounded to the DC system (this includes many generators, as well as air conditioners, nonmarine battery chargers, drop-in refrigerators, and some water heaters) or through onboard leaks between the two circuits. *The potential for corrosion would still exist but without the boatowner being aware of it*, with the result that proper preventive measures would not be taken.

The AC grounding to DC negative connection should never be cut (however, see the Ground Fault Circuit Breakers sidebar). The only correct ways to galvanically isolate an AC circuit are with a *galvanic isolator* or an *isolation transformer*.

Galvanic isolators. At the core of a galvanic isolator are two sets of two diodes wired in parallel to conduct in opposite directions (Figure 4-25). It takes a certain voltage (typically around 1.0 volt) to make the diodes conductive. If these diodes are installed in the AC grounding wire, unless there is a leakage current or a stray DC current driven by a voltage in excess of 1.0 volt, the diodes simply will not conduct. In normal circumstances, this effectively breaks the grounding circuit, preventing galvanic corrosion. But in the event of a leakage current with a voltage (AC or DC) above 1.0 volt, the diodes become conductive, ensuring the continuity of the grounding circuit.

Heat dissipation. If a galvanic isolator is used to conduct fault currents, the diodes can get quite hot (depending on the magnitude of the current). To dissipate this heat, they are invariably mounted on a heat sink. Over the years, tens of thousands of galvanic isolators have been sold that consist of nothing more than this—four diodes on a heat sink.

Unfortunately, this kind of a galvanic isolator (you may have one on your boat) may be a fire

FIGURE 4-25. Basic galvanic isolator schematic. It takes a forward voltage of around 0.5 volt to make each diode conduct, and therefore, around 1.0 volt to make a pair of diodes in series conduct. As a result, these diodes will block voltages of up to 1.0 volt, whether they originate ashore or on the boat. Faced with voltages above 1.0 volt, the diodes start to conduct, providing a path for current in either direction.

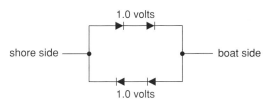

1.0 volts

shore side

boat side

1.0 volts

Swimmers Beware

In recent years, a number of deaths around marinas that were initially classified as drownings have, in fact, been found to have been caused by electric shocks. When improper or faulty grounding of either onboard or dockside wiring is combined with AC leaks to ground, enough current can be fed into the water to paralyze the muscles of a swimmer, resulting in a drowning that leaves no physical evidence of the causative shock.

When a person is in the water, it takes very little current to cause muscle spasms or seizure: currents on the order of 50 milliamps (0.05 amp) sustained for 2 seconds, or 500 milliamps sustained for just 0.2 second, can in certain circumstances cause ventricular fibrillation; currents as low as 5 milliamps can cause muscle seizure. But for any current to be lethal, it has always been assumed that there must be a significant voltage present. I am told there has never been a documented case of electrocution *onshore* with a voltage much below 50 volts.

However, it seems a different criterion is needed to determine dangerous voltage levels when the current is flowing through the water. For the purposes of illustration, let us assume a boat is connected to shoreside power using an extension cord from which the grounding pin has been cut off. A piece of onboard AC equipment, which is in some way or another grounded to the DC negative (as it should be if the boat is properly wired—see the text) develops a short. The fault current, denied a path to ground through the normal ground wire, runs to ground through a bonded underwater fitting.

The fault current will develop a *field* around the boat. At the fitting that is discharging the current into the water, the voltage will be at the full fault voltage (as high as 120 or 240 volts). Resistance within the water will cause the voltage to decrease the farther the distance from the boat until ground potential—i.e., 0 volts—is reached. Depending on the water's resistance and other factors, there will be a *voltage gradient*, creating a declining voltage the farther the distance from the boat. This gradient can be measured in *volts per foot (or meter)*.

A swimmer entering this electrical field will have one part of his or her body at one voltage potential and other parts at another potential. If the voltage differential that is bridged is great enough, current will pass through the body. As a general rule of thumb it appears that *if the voltage gradient is above 2 volts per foot (6 volts per meter), the situation is potentially lethal*. When this figure is looked at in combination with the figures given above for potentially dangerous current levels, it becomes immediately apparent that *quite small leakage currents and voltages can be deadly*.

AC leaks into fresh or brackish water are considered to be more dangerous than leaks into less resistive salt water. Leaks into salt water tend to follow the shortest path to ground, directly to the bottom or to adjacent vessels with well-grounded systems, whereas leaks in fresh water radiate out into the surrounding water from the fitting that is feeding the current into the water. (Note that in salt water, there could still be a severe shock hazard for someone cleaning a boat bottom or checking the propeller or other hardware.)

---

risk if called upon to conduct substantial fault currents, and is also frequently ineffective at blocking galvanic corrosion! The fire risk is easy to understand—it comes from using undersized diodes and inadequate heat sinks. The corrosion issue is a little more complex.

AC leakage voltage. As noted, it takes about 1.0 volt to bias the diodes in a galvanic isolator into conducting. It doesn't matter if the voltage is AC or DC. Given the kinds of metals used on boats and the galvanic voltages they can develop (see Chapter 5), it is just about impossible for 1.0 volt DC to be generated by galvanic interaction, in which case the diodes are not biased, and the galvanic isolator works fine just as long as there is no AC voltage present. However, it is extremely common to find AC leakage voltage on dockside grounding wires that exceeds 1.0 volt AC. Without some mechanism to take care

of this AC voltage, it will bias the diodes into conduction, at which point the galvanic isolator now also conducts low-level DC voltage as well as current, ceasing to function as an isolator.

To take care of AC leakage voltage, a device known as a *capacitor* needs to be wired into the circuit (Figures 4-26A and 4-26B). Capacitors pass AC voltage and current but block DC. If a capacitor is wired around the diodes, anytime low-level AC voltage and current is present, the capacitor allows it to bypass the diodes, thus preventing the diodes from becoming biased into conduction and maintaining the essential function of the galvanic isolator, which is to block low-level DC voltage and current. (Some of you will now be saying, "But what about the AC voltage and current, which is now on the boat's grounding system?" In theory, from a corrosion standpoint, this is OK because AC is not

FIGURE 4-26A. A galvanic isolator—showing the two sets of counterposed diodes—without a capacitor.

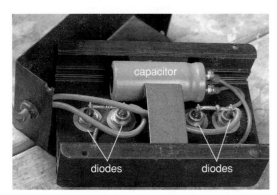

FIGURE 4-26B. A galvanic isolator with a capacitor.

supposed to cause corrosion—more on this in Chapter 5.)

Better-quality galvanic isolators all have capacitors. As of 2004, the ABYC standard requires them. Capacitors come in numerous sizes; the larger the capacitor, the higher the AC voltage and current it will short to ground (the ABYC now requires that capacitors carry up to 3 amps while still blocking DC currents). But regardless of its size, if a capacitor's "carrying capacity" is exceeded, the diodes will once again be biased into conduction, and the isolator will no longer provide protection from galvanic corrosion. Without some kind of a warning device, the boatowner will be unaware of this.

If the diodes are biased into conduction, the boat loses its galvanic isolation, which threatens the underwater hardware but does not create a safety hazard. The same happens if the diodes fail in the shorted position (sometimes as a result of a lightning strike). If, on the other hand, the diodes fail in the open position, the grounding connection between the boat and the dock no longer exists. This is potentially lethal.

Status monitoring. Some years ago the ABYC took an extended look at these issues—the fire risk, the problem created by AC leaks into dockside grounding circuits that bias the diodes into conduction, and the danger that exists if the diodes fail in the open position—and came up with a set of minimum standards that should be met by a galvanic isolator, embodied in a docu-

ment known as A-28 (the ISO has no such standard). A-28 came into force in 2002 and was toughened in 2004. Among other things, it requires any galvanic isolator to have:

- A current rating that is at least equal to the shore-power rating of the AC circuit on the boat (normally 30 or 50 amps in the U.S.; 6 or 16 amps in Europe).
- The capacity to dissipate the heat generated by a short-circuit current that is 135% of the rated capacity of the isolator.
- The ability to conduct up to 3 amps of AC current while still blocking DC current.
- A status-monitoring system that will set off an alarm if the diodes fail in the shorted or open position, if the grounding circuit loses continuity for any reason, if the diodes are biased into conduction, and if the status-monitoring device itself fails.

Galvanic isolators that have a capacitor and comply with ABYC standard A-28 will do an effective job of safely blocking galvanic currents in most circumstances. With status monitoring, in the event the diodes are biased into conduction, or fail open or shorted, the boatowner will be alerted. (Some status-monitoring devices, such as the Boat Brain from KCB Technologies [www.kcbtech.com] conduct additional and very useful tests, such as for reverse polarity.)

The current crop of status monitors will also alarm if the ground connection via the shore-power cord, or onshore, is broken, in which case the shore-power cord needs checking and/or the marina ground circuit needs rewiring. In either case, it is not safe to remain plugged in without fixing the fault.

However, as useful as this function is, it may be discontinued in the future because it leads to numerous alarms resulting from improper dockside wiring and grounding rather than from a problem with the galvanic isolator. The galvanic isolator manufacturers end up having to field a lot of calls, and spend considerable resources troubleshooting problems unrelated to their equipment.

The bottom line. *If buying a galvanic isolator, you should ensure that it complies with the latest version of the ABYC standard, including status monitoring, and check for the presence of a capacitor. If you already have a galvanic isolator on your boat, you should check for a capacitor and compliance with the ABYC standard and probably replace it if it does not comply.*

Galvanic isolator location. Where should a galvanic isolator be placed in the wiring circuit? It might seem that the best place is between the

Ground Fault Circuit Breakers

Notwithstanding what I have written in the text, in certain circumstances the ISO standards for European boatbuilding *do* permit disconnecting the AC grounding to DC negative connection. Under ISO standards, this is allowed if the incoming shore-power cord is protected by a device known as a *ground fault circuit breaker* (GFCB), also called a *residual current device* (RCD), a *ground fault circuit interrupter* (GFCI), or a *residual current circuit breaker* (RCCB). **The ABYC does not allow the same exception.**

A GFCB is a device that senses any imbalance between the current on the hot and neutral wires, such as will occur if there is a leak or short from hot or neutral to ground, and immediately trips a circuit breaker, shutting down the circuit and thus cutting off any potentially hazardous currents that would otherwise end up on the grounding circuits. GFCBs provide a high measure of security against shocks. In theory, a functioning GFCB that is placed next to the shore-power inlet, protecting all the onboard circuits *(whole-boat protection),* eliminates the need for the AC-to-DC ground connection since it cuts off fault currents before they become dangerous.

However, *it is a BAD IDEA to break the AC-to-DC ground connection.* If this is done, protection against ground faults, particularly for swimmers in the water, becomes dependent on the proper operation of the GFCB/RCD/GFCI/RCCB (there are subtle differences among these various devices, which don't concern us here). In a nationwide survey by the National Electrical Manufacturers Association (NEMA) in the United States, *15% to 20% of household GFCIs were found to be inoperative,* the majority put out of action by lightning strikes. Writing about European boats, the lead surveyor for a major U.S. insurance company reports: "Frequently, I find that the trip mechanism in the GFCI has failed." *From a safety perspective, an electronic device is never a substitute for a hardwired connection in the grounding circuit!*

There is another disagreement between the United States and Europe, namely, at what level of leakage current should a GFCB trip? The United States sets the trip limit for people protection (as opposed to machinery) at a low 5 milliamps (0.005 amp); in Europe the limit is 30 milliamps (0.030 amp) for whole-boat protection and 10 milliamps for individual receptacles. The lower U.S. figure was derived decades ago following experiments in which student volunteers were suspended in a swimming pool, and then currents were passed through the water until the volunteers lost muscle control! The United States considers 30 milliamps too high for people protection. There is a secondary issue here concerning how fast a device reacts to a fault. In Europe, 30-milliamp devices are required to trip within 100 milliseconds, which results in a low shock hazard. In the United States, given the low 5-milliamp threshold, there is no trip time requirement.

Any attempt to provide *whole-boat protection* (i.e., installing a GFCB on the incoming shore-power line as opposed to using separate devices at individual AC receptacles) that uses the U.S. trip limit (5 milliamps) is almost certain to result in nuisance tripping as a result of an accumulation of small leakage currents caused by the damp marine environment. Note also that some battery chargers and other pieces of electronic equipment have input *filters* for *noise suppression* (see Chapter 8) that are installed in the power leads, with one leg tied to ground. When the equipment is turned on, it will sometimes trip a GFCB with a low milliamps setting. Until warmed up, the electric heating elements used on electric stoves may do the same thing because of moisture absorption into the insulation material, while the heating elements on electric water heaters commonly leak to ground through the water. All in all, it is impractical to provide whole-boat protection that complies with U.S. people-protection standards. Instead, ABYC standards call for GFCIs to be used to protect individual receptacles in "a head, galley, machinery space, or on a weather deck." Without whole-boat protection, there is now no justification whatsoever for omitting the AC-to-DC ground connection.

Almost all European boats that I see coming into the U.S. market with AC systems already installed have a whole-boat GFCB with a 30-milliamp, 100-millisecond trip limit as the main AC breaker on the boat. (Current ISO standards require either this breaker, or else GFCIs with a 10-milliamp trip in the galley, toilets, machinery spaces, and on deck.) To comply with ABYC standards, the 30-milliamp GFCB must be backed up with 5-milliamp GFCIs, which invariably it is not.

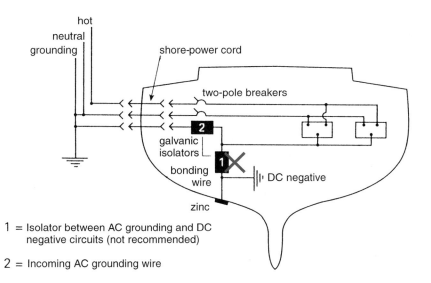

1 = Isolator between AC grounding and DC
    negative circuits (not recommended)

2 = Incoming AC grounding wire

FIGURE 4-27A. Two possible locations for a galvanic isolator. Location 1 might seem best, but may end up with the isolator being bypassed (Figure 4-27B). It can also create a hazardous situation (see the text). Location 2 is required by ABYC standards. However, should the isolator fail in the open-circuited mode, the boat will lose AC grounding protection; should it fail in the close-circuited mode, it will lose galvanic protection. *(Ocean Navigator)*

AC grounding and DC negative circuits (see location 1 in Figure 4-27A). In this position an isolator failure would not in any way compromise the integrity of the ship-to-shore grounding connection. However, as has been noted previously, in reality it is often next to impossible to prevent some circuit or other from bypassing the isolator, rendering it ineffective (Figure 4-27B). The potential for corrosion will once again exist while the boatowner is under the illusion that the problem has been solved. Added to which, if an isolator installed in this position becomes open-circuited and a short develops from an AC

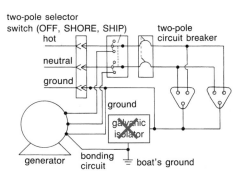

FIGURE 4-27B. A bonding circuit bypassing, and therefore negating, a galvanic isolator placed between the AC grounding circuit and the boat's ground.

The Grounding Connection (Again!)

For safety reasons, the importance of the AC-to-DC grounding connection is stressed at several points in this book. It is also included in the ISO/ABYC standards. However, it needs to be acknowledged that in certain circumstances it can itself become a safety hazard.

Consider the case of a boat with a corroded grounding terminal on its shore-power cord (not uncommon). The AC-to-DC grounding circuits are connected on board, as recommended. A fault develops from the AC hot side to the onboard AC grounding circuit. Because of the corroded connection, this is not conducted back ashore down the grounding circuit but instead is fed to the DC negative circuit by the AC-to-DC grounding connection, then into the water—precisely where we don't want it to be—and back ashore.

The lesson to be drawn from this is not that the AC-to-DC grounding connection should be broken, but that *shore-power cords need regular inspection to ensure that the grounding* *receptacles and prongs are not corroded or damaged.* While we're at it, the hot and neutral receptacles and prongs also need close inspection because *corrosion here can lead to a fire* (and is, in fact, one of the more common causes of electrical fires, especially where higher-amperage shore-power connections are concerned; more on this later).

One other potentially hazardous situation needs to be guarded against. This can occur whenever a boat is out of the water and the onboard AC circuits are energized. If there is a leak to ground and the main circuit breaker fails to trip, the DC negative side will be energized, as will any metal appendages connected to DC negative, such as the propeller shaft and propeller. Touching these appendages could cause electrocution. *If the boat's AC circuits are to be used, a cable should be attached to one of these appendages and fastened to a metal rod driven into the ground.*

Simple Test Procedures for Grounding Circuits on Boats *Without an Isolation Transformer*

Note: See pages 234–35 for a comprehensive procedure designed to test both the AC and DC circuits for numerous fault conditions, including proper grounding.

For people protection, *it is essential to maintain an effective grounding connection between the boat and the dock.* To test, plug the shore-power cord into the boat but not the dock, turn off any onboard generator or DC-to-AC inverter, set a multimeter to its lowest ohms function (R x 1 on an analog meter), and then touch one probe to the grounding blade of the shore end of the cord and the other probe to the boat's AC grounding (green wire) bus bar (Test 1; Figure 4-28A). There should be a low ohms reading. If not, the grounding circuit is faulty and must be fixed. (If you have installed a galvanic isolator, the meter will give a higher ohms reading—see the Testing a Galvanic Isolator sidebar.) Reverse the probes and repeat the test. It should produce the same results in both directions.

If the circuit passed this first test, touch one meter probe to the AC grounding bus and the other to the engine block or main DC negative bus (Test 2; Figures 4-28A and 4-28B). There should be a low ohms reading (with or without a galvanic isolator). If not, the *AC grounding to DC negative connection is faulty and should be fixed.* As noted in the Ground Fault Circuit Breakers sidebar, if this is a European boat with a GFCB, the ground connection may have

been deliberately omitted; if so, I recommend installing it.

These tests will show whether or not there is continuity between the AC grounding circuit and the shore ground terminal on the shore-power cord, and between the onboard AC and DC grounding circuits. Note, however, that if using an ohmmeter, even if there is only one strand of the shore-power cord connected, the test will show continuity. But in the event of a serious ground fault, that strand will still not protect people on the boat or in the water. Unfortunately, you will need a specialized tester to test the ground connection's ability to carry full fault current.

For the last test, with the shore-power cord still *unplugged*, any generator or inverter turned off and *switched out of the AC circuit* (this is important), and *all AC breakers turned on*, touch one meter probe to the AC grounding (green wire) bus bar and the other to the neutral (grounded, white wire) bus bar (Test 3; Figure 4-28A). There should be an infinite ohms reading (an open circuit; boats with an isolation transformer will show a dead short, i.e., 0 ohms). If there is a low reading, the neutral and grounding circuits are incorrectly tied together on board and need to be separated (note that the polarity indicators fitted to some boats will give a high ohms reading—above 25,000 ohms—rather than show an open circuit).

FIGURE 4-28A. Test procedures for grounding circuits. *Unplug the shore end* of the shore-power cord, leaving the *boat end plugged in*, and turn off any onboard generator or DC-to-AC inverter. Bring the cord aboard for easy access to the grounding lug. See the text for the test procedures. *(Ocean Navigator)*

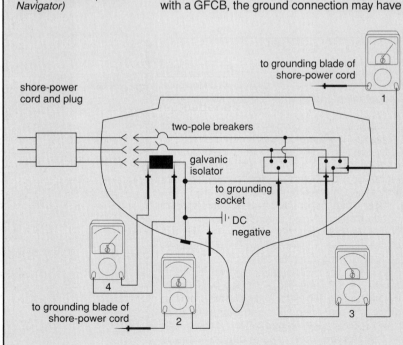

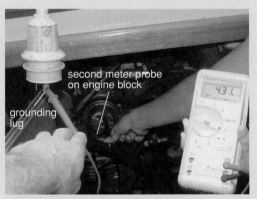

FIGURE 4-28B. Testing from the grounding lug of the shore-power cord (which is plugged into the boat's shore-power inlet at the other end of the cord) to the engine block. There is a high resistance (4.31 megaohms) indicating that the boat's AC grounding circuit is not tied to the boat's DC ground. This situation is potentially dangerous— the connection needs to be made.

Testing a Galvanic Isolator

With the shore-power cord disconnected, use a length of wire to short the two isolator terminals (discharging any capacitor in the isolator) and then place an ohmmeter across these two terminals (Test 4; Figures 4-28A and 4-28C). If the terminals are not accessible, test from the grounding pin of the shore-power inlet to the AC grounding bus in the distribution panel or to any grounding socket on an AC outlet. (You can also discharge any capacitor by shorting these two points.) Wait for the meter reading to stabilize; if the isolator contains a capacitor, this can take anywhere from 1 to 2 minutes up to 10 minutes, depending on the type of meter being used and the rating of the capacitor. Note the reading. Short any capacitor once again, then reverse the meter leads; the meter should show the same ohms reading within 10% to 12% in both directions. A high reading in either direction indicates open-circuited diodes; a 0 ohms reading means shorted diodes. If the meter has a diode-testing capability, you can repeat the same test procedure with the meter in the diode-testing mode. Once the reading stabilizes, it should produce a voltage drop reading of around 0.9 volt in both directions (Figure 4-28D).

With the shore-power cord *plugged into the boat* but *disconnected ashore*, place the leads of a DC ammeter on the *grounding* blade of the shore-power cord and on *any grounded metal ashore (the metal rim of the dockside receptacle should be grounded;* Figure 4-28E). *There may be voltage and current present at the grounding connections* coming from leaks ashore or on other boats, *so don't touch the metal parts of the meter probes when making the connections.* Set the meter to its highest *DC amps* scale and then progressively switch down to lower scales. *The meter should give no reading.* (If the meter's fuse blows, there is a current flow on the grounding wire that exceeds the meter's amperage rating!) If any current flow is present, the isolator is conducting and not blocking galvanic currents. (Sometimes small leakage currents of up to 30 milliamps may be present, which is the allowable threshold in terms of the ABYC standard. On a

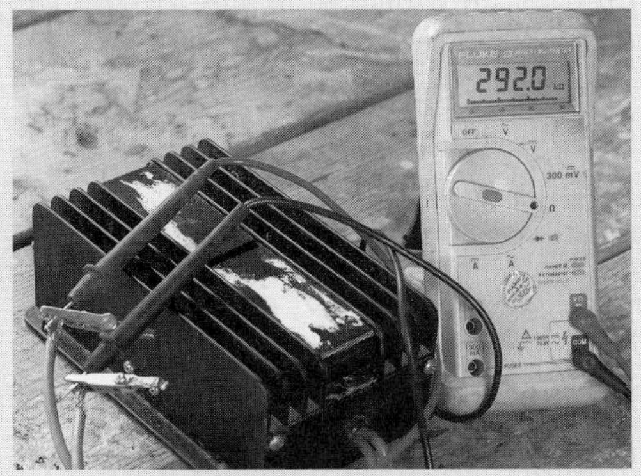

FIGURE 4-28C. Testing a galvanic isolator with a capacitor (meter used in its ohms mode). The capacitor is first discharged (by shorting the leads). The meter will build up to a high reading that should be replicated within 10% to 12% when the meter leads are reversed.

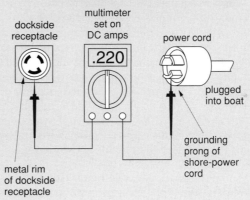

FIGURE 4-28D. Testing a galvanic isolator with a capacitor (meter used in its diode-testing mode). The reading should stabilize at close to 0.9 volt with the meter leads applied in either direction.

FIGURE 4-28E. Testing a galvanic isolator.

dockside receptacle — multimeter set on DC amps — power cord

.220

plugged into boat

metal rim of dockside receptacle

grounding prong of shore-power cord

properly bonded boat with well-maintained zincs, the zincs will corrode so slowly that this current will not be a concern.)

circuit into the DC circuits, the fault current will have no safe path back ashore (we have, in effect, condition 1—see page 137).

ABYC standards require a galvanic isolator to be "connected in series with the AC grounding conductor . . . in a manner that no other ground conductor will bypass the isolator back to the shore-power ground." In practice, this means an isolator must be placed in the *incoming AC grounding wire* immediately downstream of the

shore-power inlet (see location 2 in Figure 4-27A). It is then a simple matter to ensure that nothing bypasses the isolator, as long as *absolutely no wires, except the shore-power grounding wire, are connected to the shore-power side of the isolator. (Note that some TV and phone inlets bypass an isolator, in which case their grounding circuits need to be wired through the isolator, or they need their own isolator.)* If a boat has two shore-power inlets (as many powerboats and larger yachts do), then to be effective, *both grounding circuits must be wired through the isolator (which should then have a current rating equal to the sum of the two circuits), or else there must be a separate isolator on each inlet.*

A final note: The stringent construction requirements of the ABYC standard have considerably increased the cost of galvanic isolators, especially if status monitoring is included; 30 amp units cost over $300, and 50 amp units cost over $500. This has narrowed the cost differential between galvanic isolators and isolation transformers. With the added benefits of an isolation transformer (see below), boatowners should give serious consideration to using an isolation transformer in place of a galvanic isolator.

Isolation transformers.

Galvanic isolators are a relatively low-cost but only partially effective response to the people-versus-boat-protection conundrum. Ultimately the only way to provide full people protection without courting the risk of galvanic corrosion is to install an *isolation transformer* in the incoming shore-power line. Depending on the capability of the transformer, it may also be possible to use it to accept different input voltages (e.g., 240 volts in Europe, 120 volts in the U.S.) and also to boost low dockside voltage.

How it works. The concept of an isolation transformer is straightforward. Shore power is fed into one winding (the *primary*) of a transformer and transferred *magnetically* to another winding (the *secondary*). The primary winding has a *shield*, which is grounded ashore. The secondary winding may or may not be grounded on board. *Either way, there is no direct electrical connection whatsoever between the shoreside supply and the onboard AC circuit*—power is transferred magnetically. We get two desirable consequences:

1. Since the boat's power source is now the secondary side of the transformer, *the only path for onboard leakage currents is back to the transformer, not the dockside supply*; therefore, leaks will not find a path to ground through the water.

2. Since the shoreside grounding wire is not connected to the boat's grounding circuit, there is no ship-to-shore path for galvanic currents.

Although the onboard circuit is sometimes ungrounded (in which case it is said to be *floating*), ABYC standards require *one side of the secondary winding to be grounded on the secondary side of the transformer, with a boat's grounding circuit tied in at this point, and the two then connected to the boat's DC negative* (Figures 4-29 and 4-30). This has the effect of producing a

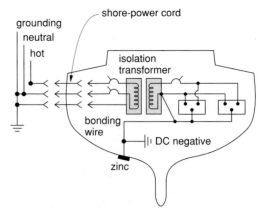

FIGURE 4-29. An ABYC-recommended isolation transformer circuit with the neutral grounded on board. *(Ocean Navigator)*

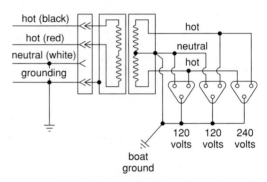

FIGURE 4-30. An isolation transformer circuit for 120/240 volts AC (U.S.). The neutral is not brought on board. The 240-volt appliances are wired to the two hot wires and the safety grounding wire. The 120-volt appliances are wired to one or the other hot wire, the onboard neutral wire, and the safety grounding wire.

polarized circuit on board in which the grounded side of the transformer is the neutral. In the event of either a short in a piece of AC equipment or a leak into the DC circuits, the fault current has a direct path back to the transformer through the grounding circuit.

Because the DC negative will be connected to the engine, and perhaps various pieces of underwater hardware, at first sight the connection to the DC negative appears to bring the earth's ground back into the picture, creating the potential for shock hazards to swimmers. But on reflection it can be seen that regardless of this connection, *the only path for fault current is back to its source, which is the transformer.* Earth ground has no part to play in this circuit. The *fault-current circuit* is completely contained within the boat and its wiring—swimmers will be safe.

Isolation versus polarization. It is important to distinguish an isolation transformer from a *polarization transformer.* The primary and secondary windings in the latter function as in an isolation transformer, creating a *floating* AC circuit on board, one side of which is once again made the

Low Dockside Voltage

Low dockside voltage is a common problem. It generally results from undersized wiring associated with long cable runs, and/or the increasing cumulative load put on dockside circuits by today's electrically loaded boats. Low voltage will often cause equipment to perform poorly, can be damaging, and, in extreme cases, can cause a fire. Any boat with shoreside power should have a voltmeter to enable the voltage to be monitored.

In some U.S. marinas, low voltage is the result of the marina using a three-phase 120/208 distribution system to save money, which results in 120/208 volts (single phase) being supplied to the dockside outlets. In this case, any boat plugging into what should be a 240-volt supply is only getting a nominal 208 volts, which, in practice, may be lower still because of voltage drops in the dockside wiring. On a boat with a U.S.-style, 240-volt system, the nominal 208 volts will now be split between two hot bus bars, each of which will be receiving a nominal 104 volts (in reality, probably below 100 volts). All equipment on the boat, whether rated at

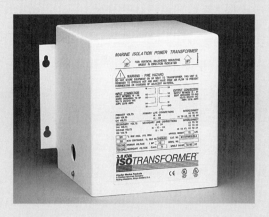

FIGURE 4-31. Charles Industries' Iso-Boost transformer. *(Courtesy Charles Industries)*

120 volts or 240 volts, will be receiving seriously low voltages.

Some isolation transformers (e.g., Charles Industries' Iso-Boost transformers—www.charles industries.com, Figure 4-31) have the capability to boost low voltages by up to 15% (although this is "paid" for with an equivalent loss in available amperage). This capability is really useful.

neutral by tying it to the boat's grounding circuit. This establishes a constant polarity on board, regardless of the polarity at the shoreside receptacle. But on the polarization transformer, *the shoreside grounding connection is fastened to both sides of the transformer and ultimately to the boat's DC negative—the transformer does nothing to provide galvanic isolation.* To get galvanic isolation with such a transformer, it is necessary to once again fit a galvanic isolator in the grounding circuit. It is worth repeating that *as long as the grounding wire is carried on board and connected to the boat's AC grounding and DC negative circuits, there will be no galvanic isolation.*

To date, isolation transformers have been bulky, heavy, and relatively expensive, and therefore not widely used, especially since many of the old-style galvanic isolators provided a cheap substitute that met some of the same needs. However, under development are *high-frequency* (see Chapter 6) isolation transformers that will be radically smaller and lighter (which may reduce the cost) and considerably more versatile (notably their ability to handle different or fluctuating shoreside voltages). Meanwhile, the cost of galvanic isolators has risen significantly. These two developments should make the installation of an isolation transformer on modern AC-loaded boats far more commonplace. *An isolation transformer should, in any event, be standard on all metal boats—NO EXCEPTIONS!—*because of

the inevitable threat of hull corrosion if you plug into shore power without one.

Typical AC Circuits Afloat

Note: In what follows I deal only with what are known as *single-phase circuits*—the kind that are found in every household. Some large yachts with heavy equipment will have industrial-type *three-phase circuits*, but these will never be found on smaller boats.

Color codes. The basic 120-volt AC circuit in the United States consists of a *black* hot wire, a *white* neutral, and a *green* or *bare* ground. The same three-wire circuit in the UK and Europe will carry 240 volts. The old UK color code had a *red* hot, a *black* neutral, and a *green* or *bare* ground (earth); the new European standard code uses *brown* for hot (positive), *light blue* for neutral, and *green and yellow* for ground (earth).

The United States also has a 240-volt circuit, but this is established by supplying a second 120-volt (hot) circuit and wiring 240-volt appliances (typically electric stoves, clothes dryers, and larger air-conditioning units) to both hot circuits (Figure 4-32). This second hot circuit is color-coded *red.* The incoming breaker box will have two hot bus bars, one connected to the black wire and one connected to the red; it will also have the neutral bus bar and ground connection.

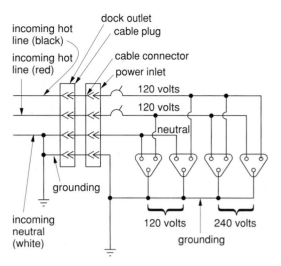

120-volt appliances will be connected to either the black or the red bus bar, together with the normal neutral and ground connections. Usually an attempt is made to spread the load of 120-volt appliances equally between both hot bus bars. The 240-volt appliances will be connected to *both* the black and the red bus bars and the green (or bare) safety wire to ground, with the neutral connection omitted.

In the following text all colors refer to the U.S. color codes:

Red—hot (ungrounded)

Black—hot (ungrounded)

White—neutral (grounded)

Green or bare—ground (grounding)

Ship-to-shore cables. The connection from shore power to a boat is made with a shore-power cord. These cables are often subjected to unfair strain and may be exposed to saltwater and freshwater spray—they clearly need to be assembled from high-quality components according to high-quality standards. The cables themselves must be flexible yet designed for hard service, with oil- and water-resistant insulation. In the United States applicable cable types are labeled "SO," "ST," and "STO" (see Table 4-1 on page 159; the ISO has no such requirements). The terminals at both ends of the cable should have some form of a spray-proof locking cap, although too often all that is available on the shore-power end is a standard household-type outlet, which therefore does not meet ABYC standards. It is particularly important to have the boat end of the cable well secured; if it should come loose and fall in the water it will be potentially lethal. It is best to buy a commercially made shore-power cord with preassembled terminals.

The shore-power *outlet* on a dock must have a *female* receptacle; the *inlet* on the boat must have a *male* receptacle. On boats with isolation transformers or galvanic isolators, the shore-power inlet must be isolated from the hull (it will be anyway in a fiberglass hull, but metal hulls require either a nonmetallic inlet or some form of insulation from the hull). ABYC and ISO standards call for a warning sign on the boat's shore-power inlet (Figure 4-33). Different styles of receptacles and plugs are mandated for different voltage and current ratings (Figure 4-34). None is interchangeable. This is fine until you pull up at a dock with the legally correct shore-power cord and find it won't fit the available receptacle! Once again, shore-power cord manufacturers can supply preassembled adapters, including adapters that will switch from U.S.-style plugs and receptacles to European-style and vice versa, and between different styles in Europe. These are preferable to attempting to jury-rig a connection that may well be unsafe.

Mixing and matching receptacles and plugs. In some U.S. situations, dockside power is available

---

Isolation Transformers: The Fine Print

ABYC standards for isolation transformers require a metallic shield between the primary and secondary windings that is capable of carrying whatever current is necessary to trip the main circuit breaker (approximately 130% of the rated circuit current) in the event that either the primary or secondary winding shorts to the shield (the ISO has no such standard). This shield is grounded back ashore so that there is a direct path back to shore ground for fault current from the primary side of the transformer.

This ABYC requirement is controversial among isolation transformer manufacturers, a number of whom consider it to be unnecessary. *Very few isolation transformers on the market have a shield that can carry full fault current (in fact, most are adapted polarization transformers), and so very few comply with the ABYC standard.* If you are concerned about compliance with the ABYC standard, you need to check this. (To my knowledge, at the time of writing [2005], the only compliant isolation transformers are manufactured by Charles Industries. Their transformers are built specifically to meet the ABYC requirements.)

FIGURE 4-33. An ABYC-recommended notice for a shore-power inlet.

at a U.S. 50 amp, 250-volt receptacle, but the boat has one or two 30 amp, 125-volt inlets. It is common to use a Y-adapter (Figure 4-35) to split the supply in order to feed either one or two inlets. This is an acceptable practice as long as the total amperage drawn with two inlets does not exceed the rating of the components in the single (50 amp) leg.

There is another situation that is the reverse of the above, in which the dockside has two 30 amp, 125-volt receptacles, but the boat has a 50 amp, 250-volt inlet. A standard Y-adapter is often installed in reverse. This practice is dangerous for three reasons:

1. After one 30 amp plug is connected at the dockside, if any 240-volt load is turned on aboard, *the protruding terminals on the second plug will be live.*

2. *If either of the dockside receptacles has reverse polarity, when both are plugged in, they will short-circuit the power supply,* creating a fire hazard.

3. A proper 50 amp, 250-volt, U.S. dockside supply consists of two 125-volt legs that are supposed to be *out of phase.* As I said earlier, I am not going to discuss the subject of phases. It is enough to know that with two out-of-phase legs, *the maximum current that will flow down the neutral wire is the highest current on a single phase.* But if the two 125-volt legs are from the same phase, wired in parallel, *the current flowing through the neutral wire will be the **sum** of the current flowing through both hot wires,* which at full load will be *double the rating of the cable,* meaning that the neutral may *melt down.* To check for proper wiring, test with a voltmeter between the two incoming hot lines—if they are out of phase, the voltmeter will read around 240 volts; if they are in phase, it will read around 0 volts.

If two dockside receptacles are to be used to feed a common inlet on the boat, a special kind of Y-adapter (Figures 4-36A and 4-36B) is needed—

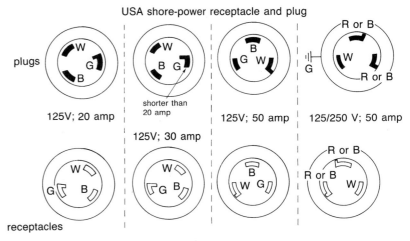

USA household receptacle and plug rated for 125 volts and 20 amps

plug   receptacle

USA shore-power receptacle and plug

plugs

125V; 20 amp   shorter than 20 amp   125V; 50 amp   125/250 V; 50 amp

125V; 30 amp

receptacles

FIGURE 4-34. U.S.-style receptacles and plugs. W = neutral (white); R or B = hot (red or black); G = grounding (green or bare).

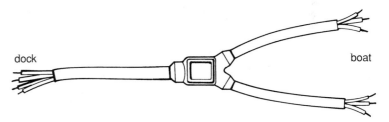

dock   boat

FIGURE 4-35. A blank Y-adapter assembly, which can be used with different end fittings. *(Marinco)*

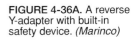

boat

dock

FIGURE 4-36A. A reverse Y-adapter with built-in safety device. *(Marinco)*

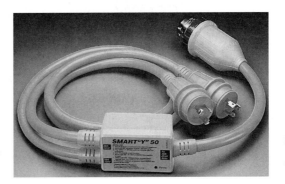

FIGURE 4-36B. Charles Industries' Smart "Y" for 50 amp circuits. *(Courtesy Charles Industries)*

Even if the two incoming 125-volt legs on a U.S. 240- or 250-volt supply are correctly out of phase, there is still a problem that sometimes develops known as a *loose*, or *open*, *neutral*. Let us assume we have a heavy-draw 120-volt appliance on one leg (for example, an air conditioner) that is wired from one of the incoming hot legs to the onboard neutral. And we also have a low-draw 120-volt appliance (for example, a TV) wired from the other leg to the neutral (refer back to Figure 4-32). The air conditioner and TV are both on.

There is a poor connection between the neutral pin on the shore-power cord and the neutral socket in the dockside outlet (this is the loose neutral), which is creating a high resistance at this point. The air conditioner has a low internal resistance. The net result is that instead of the neutral line from the air conditioner being at ground potential (0 volts), it is at something close to line voltage (120 volts) all the way to the resistance (the dockside receptacle) and only at ground potential on the ground side of this resistance (Figure 4-37). The TV, which is wired across the other hot leg and the same neutral, will now effectively be wired across two hot legs; that is, it will be wired into something approaching 240 volts. It is likely to burn up, perhaps setting fire to the boat in the process. (This example is taken from a real-life situation that resulted in the loss of a large motor yacht.)

The situation just described is not confined to the wiring of a single boat with a 240-volt shore-power connection. It can also occur on a boat with a 120-volt shore-power connection if the dockside outlet is wired in such a way that it is one leg of a shoreside 240-volt supply. A loose neutral somewhere on the dock can potentially put up to 240 volts on the circuits of all those boats that are wired for 120 volts and plugged into one or other leg of this 240-volt shore-power circuit.

At one time or another, various utility companies have studied this issue and concluded that loose or open neutrals are responsible for more damage to electrical equipment than lightning strikes. Given the poor wiring in many marinas, it is a fair bet that the problem is even more prevalent in the boat world than it is in homes.

Boats with U.S.-style, 240-volt systems, in which 120-volt appliances are balanced between the two hot legs, must ensure that the neutral connections in the shore-power cord are in good condition. Better yet is to use a polarization or isolation transformer since the shoreside neutral is not brought on board (refer back to Figure 4-30) and the onboard neutral is bolted at the transformer (just as it is bolted at the panelboard in a house), so there is little possibility of a loose neutral developing. Boats with 120-volt shore-power connections can do little to guard against a loose neutral on the dock.

There is a more general problem here; namely, in a house all the incoming connections are bolted, while those at both ends of a shore-power cord are not. Given dirty or corroded pins on a plug, or dirty or corroded sockets in a receptacle, when the cord is plugged in, resistance is likely. The higher the current passing through the circuit, the greater the likelihood of an arcing fault with the potential to start a fire. This is, in fact, a significant cause of fires on boats with higher AC demands (Figures 4-38A and 4-38B).

Circuit breakers and fuses will provide no protection against this kind of a fire because there is no overcurrent condition. *It should be part of your routine maintenance to regularly check the state of the plugs and receptacles in the shore-power circuit and to replace them if you see any sign of corrosion or arcing* (e.g., burn marks, which are quite common). If either the plug or receptacle is damaged, the mating receptacle or plug will almost certainly also be damaged—you should replace both.

FIGURE 4-37. U.S.-style 120/240 VAC system—loose, or open, neutral (grounding circuit omitted for simplicity). If the neutral is broken, there will be 120 volts on the neutral line as far as the break, so that the 120-volt loads are now effectively wired to a 240-volt supply (120 volts on both the hot and neutral legs).

FIGURES 4-38A AND 4-38B. Two fires caused by arcing faults from loose connections in shore-power circuits. Corrosion on the pins and terminals can have the same effect.

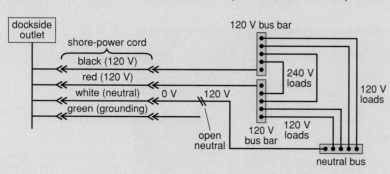

one with internal circuitry that checks the polarity and does not complete the circuit until both plugs are in place.

This kind of Y-adapter will also sense if the two hot lines are in phase, in which case it will not complete the connection to the boat. These adapters are available from Charles Industries, Marinco (www.marinco.com), and Hubbell (www.hubbell.com).

Onboard AC power—specific components. The potentially hazardous marine environment, and the peculiarities of boat AC installations, require one or two components not generally found ashore. These are:

Two-pole circuit breakers. Household circuits use single-pole circuit breakers in the hot lines to appliances, as opposed to two-pole breakers that cut both the hot and neutral lines simultaneously (Figure 4-39). It is an ABYC and ISO requirement that to protect against hazardous reverse polarity situations *the main incoming AC breaker on a boat should be of the two-pole type.* Better yet, two-pole breakers should also be used on all branch circuits, but if the onboard circuits are polarized, the ABYC and ISO permit use of single-pole breakers in the hot side of branch circuits, as in a house. (Note: The ABYC requires the main breaker to be within 10 feet of the boat's shore-power inlet; the ISO within 0.5 meter. If this is not possible, additional fuses or breakers are required within 10 feet or 0.5 meter of the inlet.) If single-pole breakers are used in a polarized system, a reverse polarity warning device must be installed (see below). The exception to this is when a polarization or isolation transformer is fitted.

Never place a breaker, switch, or fuse in the green (or bare) grounding (earth) line. This would defeat its purpose, which is to provide a

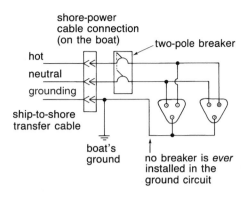

FIGURE 4-39. Two-pole circuit breaker. When a two-pole breaker trips, it stops the current flow to the entire circuit regardless of whether polarity is normal or reversed.

permanent, redundant path to ground to protect against electrical system failures.

Polarity testers. A *polarized* system is one in which the grounded (neutral) and ungrounded (hot) conductors are connected in the same relation to all terminals. Polarization is important to ensure safety on board. The polarity of a household circuit is established by tying the neutral to ground (earth). The polarity of a boat circuit is established in the same way through the shore-side grounding and grounded connections, tied together at a buried rod, or else through tying the neutral and grounding circuits together at an onboard generator frame, an inverter frame, or the secondary side of an isolation transformer (see above).

The wiring for an inverter or generator is all contained within the boat; if it is done correctly, proper polarization will be assured. But even if the boat's AC circuits are properly wired, with a shore-power cord you always have the possibility of plugging into a shoreside receptacle with reverse polarity. If the shore-power cord is feeding into an isolation or polarization transformer on board, the transformer will still ensure the correct polarity (which is why these systems do

---

30 Amp Versus 50 Amp Shore Power

For those U.S. boats with power needs that exceed a 30 amp inlet, and as long as the boat does not have 240-volt equipment, I recommend installing two 30 amp, 120-volt inlets in place of a single 50 amp inlet. The boat will then have two separate hot and neutral bus bars on board, with the AC equipment split between them. In the event you can hook up only one shore-power cord, using suitable switches (built into some AC panels, such as those from Newmar [www.newmarpower.com] and Paneltronics [www.paneltronics.com]), you can parallel these bus bars into a single 30

amp system. However, you will not be able to turn on everything at once, so you will have to use some load management.

There are several advantages to the 30 amp approach:

- It is much more versatile and flexible, offering a greater range of plugging-in possibilities.
- The shore-power cord sets are much lighter and easier to handle.
- Two 30 amp cord sets are considerably cheaper than one 50 amp cord set.

not need a reverse polarity warning device), but *without such a transformer, the neutral side of the boat's circuits will now be hot.* As long as the neutral is not grounded on board (which it should not be—see the Correct Grounding Practices sidebar), the AC circuits will still function just fine. If all branch circuits have two-pole breakers (see above), the breakers will provide some protection for anyone on board. But if (as is more common) all the branch circuits have single-pole breakers, *even with the breakers turned off, the entire AC circuit from the shore-power inlet through the appliances back to the breakers in the AC panel will still be live,* creating a potentially hazardous situation.

To warn of such a situation, the ABYC (but not the ISO) requires onboard circuits with single-pole breakers and no isolation or polarization transformer to have a reverse polarity indicating device. This must be wired in such a way as to be permanently lit or audible in the event of reverse polarity. The normal way is to wire a light or buzzer from the incoming neutral wire to the grounding wire; in the event of reverse polarity, the neutral becomes hot, causing the alarm to activate. In order to keep leakage currents into the grounding circuit to a minimum, the reverse polarity device is required to have a very high resistance of 25,000 ohms or more. (A minimum of 25,000 ohms is used because this results in a 4.8 milliamps drain at 120 volts, which is just below the tripping threshold of U.S.-made GFCIs [5 milliamps], and so in theory, the reverse polarity indicator will not trip a whole-boat GFCI if one is fitted. In practice, additional small leaks elsewhere in the system are likely to cause the GFCI to trip—see the Ground Fault Circuit Breakers sidebar.)

Wired as described, a reverse polarity indicator will sometimes come on even when there is no reverse polarity. This situation is most likely when some high-load AC equipment is operating in a condition where there is undersized wiring or resistance in the neutral connection to the shore. Instead of the neutral wire being held at ground potential by its shoreside connection to ground, it will experience a voltage drop from the load to the ground connection, resulting in the neutral on board being above ground potential. This may cause the reverse polarity indicator to alarm. So although you will not have a reverse polarity situation, you will have a situation that needs attention.

At other times, a reverse polarity indicating device will not sound the alarm even with reverse polarity. This happens when the shoreside connection for the grounding circuit is missing or broken (for example, an extension cord with the grounding prong cut off) *and* the AC

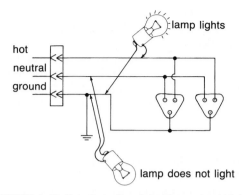

FIGURE 4-40. Polarity testing. A test lamp should light when placed between the hot wire and ground; if it does not light, either the polarity is reversed or the circuit is dead. The lamp should not light when placed between the neutral and ground. If it lights, polarity is reversed. A permanently installed polarity light should have a resistance of at least 25,000 ohms to keep current flow to a minimum.

grounding circuit is not connected to the DC grounding circuit. These two conditions together result in a potentially lethal situation on board; however, with no path to ground through the polarity indicating device, it will not alarm. (Also note that even if the connection between the AC grounding circuit and DC ground is in place, the device will still not alarm in fresh water because of the low conductivity of fresh water.)

Note that older panels with polarity lights may be wired from the hot to ground. If the lamp glows green, polarity is correct; if the lamp fails to light, polarity is reversed.

If you do not have a polarity indicator, you still can easily check polarity. Connect a voltmeter or test light (U.S., 120 volts; Europe, 240 volts) between the *incoming* AC hot wire(s) and a good ground, such as a *grounding* socket on an AC outlet or a through-hull fitting that is below the waterline (Figure 4-40). *REMEMBER, THIS CIRCUIT IS LIVE. IF YOU ARE AT ALL UNSURE OF WHAT YOU ARE DOING, DO NOT DO THIS TEST!* The meter should show system voltage or the light should glow. Next connect the meter or light between the incoming neutral line and ground. The meter should read no volts or the light should remain unlit. If there is voltage or the lamp lights between neutral and ground, but nothing happens between the hot side and ground, polarity is reversed. If there is nothing on either side, the shore power is not hooked up or switched on, or the meter or test light is grounded improperly (or is not working).

Three-prong receptacles. The third prong on 120-volt and 240-volt plugs (both U.S. and European) is the grounding prong (Figure 4-41). Two-prong receptacles and plugs (commonly seen on lamps, small appliances, and electric

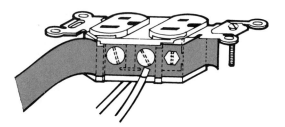

FIGURE 4-41. A three-prong outlet with a grounding socket (U.S.).

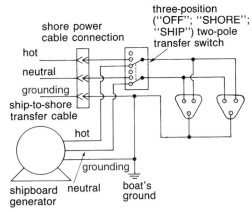

FIGURE 4-42. A ship-to-shore transfer switch. Power must never be admitted to an AC circuit from more than one source at a time.

hand tools) have no grounding connection and so lack this important safety feature. *Two-prong receptacles should never be used on a boat—they are not suitable for the damp marine environment.* In the United States, 120-volt receptacles are wired with the black (hot) lead to the black or brass screw and the white (neutral) lead to the silver screw. Switching these will lead to reverse polarity. (Wiring tip: When wiring a receptacle, give the grounding—green or bare wire—an extra length of wire. If for some reason the outlet gets ripped out, the grounding wire will be the last to come undone.)

For obvious reasons, the ABYC requires that receptacles and matching plugs for AC use *must not be interchangeable* with those for DC use.

Ship-to-shore transfer switch. Boats with a shoreside hookup and an onboard AC generating capability and/or a DC-to-AC inverter use the same AC circuits on board, regardless of the power source. *If two AC power sources are ever switched into an AC circuit at the same time, one or the other power source is likely to suffer extensive damage* (the exception being synchronized power sources—see Chapter 2). *In the absence of synchronization, it must never be possible to switch two AC power sources into the same circuit at the same time.* To prevent this, you need a proper two-pole, ship-to-shore-type transfer switch (or ship-shore-generator switch) that breaks both current-carrying conductors from one power source before making the connection to another power source (Figure 4-42). This transfer switch must at the same time *isolate the shore-power inlet anytime the AC supply is coming from an onboard generator or inverter.* Without this isolation, an onboard AC supply would cause the male prongs in the shore-power inlet to be live, creating a potentially dangerous situation.

Note that many DC-to-AC inverters have a transfer switch built into them, in which case it is possible to wire the shore-power cord through the inverter rather than having both wired to a separate transfer switch. Whenever the inverter senses available shore power, it will automatically switch from the inverting mode to a "pass-through" mode for the shore power.

Volt and frequency meters. Boats venturing abroad will find a variety of different voltages and frequencies. Even "at-home" voltages in many marinas may be low because of voltage drop in inadequate wiring. Appliances with resistive loads, such as lightbulbs, heaters, toasters, or ovens, will tolerate fairly wide variations in voltage and frequency. Most appliances that use induction motors, such as refrigerators, freezers, washing machines, tape decks, and sewing machines, will not. Because we need to know the voltage and frequency of AC power, all AC circuits should have a voltmeter and frequency meter connected at the main breaker.

The most commonly encountered problem is stepping up from 120 to 240 volts (U.S. to Europe), or down from 240 to 120 volts (Europe to U.S.), with a concomitant change in frequency from 60 Hz to 50 Hz (U.S. to Europe) or 50 Hz to 60 Hz (Europe to U.S.). The voltage change is easy enough—it merely requires an appropriate transformer. A frequency change is a little trickier.

A 120-volt motor designed to operate on 60 cycles will overheat and ultimately fail if fed 120 volts at 50 cycles. Changes in frequency also will affect the speed at which motors turn. This is immaterial with most appliances but obviously critical for such things as tape decks.

Without a frequency converter (currently a massive and expensive piece of equipment), the only effective way to compensate for speed changes is by altering internal pulley ratios—an involved procedure. (See the The Inverter-Based Boat section in Chapter 2 for ways to create an international shoreside capability without a frequency converter.)

Testing AC Circuits

Note: See pages 234–35 for a comprehensive procedure designed to test both the AC and DC circuits for numerous fault conditions.

REMEMBER, AC VOLTAGE CAN KILL. IF YOU ARE IN ANY DOUBT ABOUT WHAT YOU ARE DOING, DON'T DO IT! Before working on AC circuits always disconnect the shoreside cable, and turn off any generator or DC-to-AC inverter. *Pay particular attention to inverters:* many have a "sleep" mode that drops the AC output to a low voltage—not measurable with some voltmeters—when there is no load on the circuit, thus reducing the standby drain on the DC system to a minimum. The AC circuit may appear to be dead, but *if a load is accidentally applied, the inverter will almost instantaneously switch to full voltage.* Disable any AC generator that has an automatic start function.

Dockside. AC troubleshooting generally starts at the dockside. Things to look for are correct voltage, correct polarity, and ground faults:

1. **Correct voltage:** Test with a multimeter on the 250 volts AC scale. There will be three sockets in a dockside receptacle. A 120-volt system (U.S.) should give the following results:

   • Hot to ground—120 volts
   • Hot to neutral—120 volts
   • Neutral to ground—less than 5 volts (see note below)

   A 240-volt system (U.S.) should give the following results:

   • Hot 1 to neutral—120 volts
   • Hot 2 to neutral—120 volts
   • Hot 1 to hot 2—240 volts
   • Hot 1 to ground—120 volts
   • Hot 2 to ground—120 volts
   • Neutral to ground—less than 5 volts (see note below)

   A European 240-volt system should give 240 volts for hot-to-ground and hot-to-neutral tests and less than 5 volts for the neutral-to-ground test.

   Note: In theory, the neutral-to-ground voltage will be 0 because the two conductors are tied together at the dockside power source. In practice, the voltage will not be 0 if the circuit being tested is feeding a load. This is because the neutral is a current-carrying conductor, and therefore subject to voltage drop from one end of the conductor to the other. Since the ground carries no current, the voltage between neutral and ground at the load end of

the neutral conductor will equal the voltage drop in the neutral circuit. In marina wiring, if a shoreside outlet is feeding more than one boat, even if there is no load on the receptacle being tested, a load on another circuit wired to that same outlet may also cause a small voltage drop to be registered. If at any time this exceeds 5 volts, the wiring is undersized for the load, or there is some other fault in the circuit (such as a loose neutral—see the sidebar on page 148).

2. **Correct polarity:** The hot and neutral sockets are as shown in Figure 4-34. If the meter shows them to be reversed, the receptacle is wired with reverse polarity. *Unless the boat has an isolation or polarization transformer, do not plug in. To do so may be hazardous to people on board and in the water.*

3. **Ground faults:** *The grounding (green or bare wire) side of an AC circuit is never a current-carrying conductor in normal use.* To test 120-volt receptacles (240 volts in Europe) put one probe of a voltmeter in the *grounding* (green or bare wire) socket of the receptacle *(BE ABSOLUTELY SURE TO GET THE RIGHT SOCKET, DO NOT TOUCH THE METER PROBES, AND DO NOT DO THIS TEST IF YOU ARE AT ALL UNSURE WHICH IS THE GROUNDING SOCKET!)* and dangle the other probe in the water (Figure 4-43). On 240-volt receptacles (U.S.), touch the first probe to the metal shell of the receptacle. Progressively switch down to the lowest AC volts scale. If there is any indication of voltage, there is a serious ground leak. You can measure this leak by switching to the amps and milliamps scales. If the meter shows any leaks to ground whatsoever, do not plug in the shore-power cord (except when the boat has an isolation transformer). If you get a voltage between the grounding circuit and ground, you should inform the marina management or other responsible party to get it fixed. Be sure to keep swimmers out of the water.

Test devices. Marinco and others sell economical, portable ground fault and reverse polarity indicators (Figure 4-44A). In the United States, RadioShack (www.radioshack.com) sells a couple of models at very cheap prices. One of these is an excellent investment—always use it before making a hookup. From time to time, proposals are made suggesting these devices be hard-wired into boats on a permanent basis. However, this is not a good idea because the indicators work by putting a small current down the wire, which is acceptable for testing purposes, but not on a permanent basis.

Switch down to the lowest voltage scale: *any reading indicates a serious leak.*

Be absolutely sure to get the *grounding* socket of the receptacles

multimeter

salt water

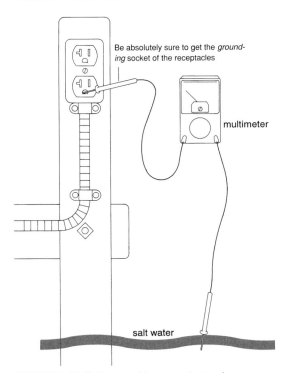

FIGURE 4-43. Using a multimeter to test a shore-power receptacle for leaks. *Remember the receptacle is live—be sure to place the probe in the grounding socket of the receptacle and start with a high AC voltage scale, switching to lower scales as necessary to increase sensitivity. Any reading indicates a leak. DO NOT DO THIS TEST IF YOU HAVE ANY DOUBT ABOUT WHAT YOU ARE DOING. (Jim Sollers)*

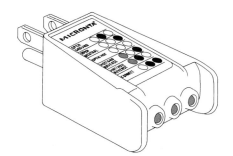

FIGURE 4-44A. Multifunction ground fault tester. *(Jim Sollers)*

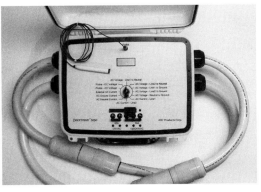

FIGURE 4-44B. A sophisticated, powerful (and expensive) test device for shore-power cords and connections. *(ESC Products Corp.)*

Marine industry professionals may wish to invest in much more robust and versatile test equipment, such as that sold by ESC (www.escproducts.com) at a cost of up to $2,000 (Figure 4-44B).

Onboard circuit testing. As we have seen, a 120-volt circuit (240 volts in Europe) is essentially the same as a 12-volt circuit with one hot wire (black in the U.S.; red or brown in Europe) to the equipment, and the neutral wire (white in the U.S.; black or blue in Europe) back. The third wire (green or bare in both the U.S. and Europe, with green and yellow in newer European installations), although called a grounding wire, is not part of the circuit in normal circumstances. If you are in any doubt about this, read the section on pages 134–35 once again. The same voltage tests can be made between the hot and neutral sides of the circuit (using an appropriate AC scale) as between the hot and ground sides of a DC circuit, KEEPING IN MIND THE LETHAL NATURE OF AC VOLTAGE. SEVERAL OF THE FOLLOWING TESTS ARE DONE ON LIVE CIRCUITS. DO NOT TOUCH THE METER PROBES. DO NOT DO THESE TESTS IF YOU ARE AT ALL UNSURE OF WHAT YOU ARE DOING.

Polarity. With shore power connected, any test from a hot wire to the safety grounding wire should yield 120 volts (240 volts in Europe), and yield 0 volts (or a very low voltage—see the note on page 152) from the neutral wire to the grounding wire. If the hot and neutral wires are reversed, so is polarity. *If the dockside receptacle did not show reverse polarity, the wires are crossed on board and need sorting out.*

A 240-volt circuit (U.S.) is a little different since it has two hot wires and no neutral wire. Again, the third (green or bare) wire is not part of the circuit in normal circumstances. Any test across the two hot wires should yield 240 volts; any test from either wire to the green or bare grounding wire should yield 120 volts.

Open circuits and short circuits. Open-circuit and short-circuit testing is done on all circuits using an ohmmeter, just as with DC circuits, but only *AFTER DISCONNECTING THE SHORE-POWER CABLE, shutting down any generator, disabling an AC generator with an automatic start function, and switching off any DC-to-AC inverter.* The following additional tests can be made for ground leaks and short circuits:

With the AC selector switch turned to the SHORE position, and all equipment unplugged or switched off, but *with the various AC circuit breakers turned on,* use an ohmmeter (R × 1

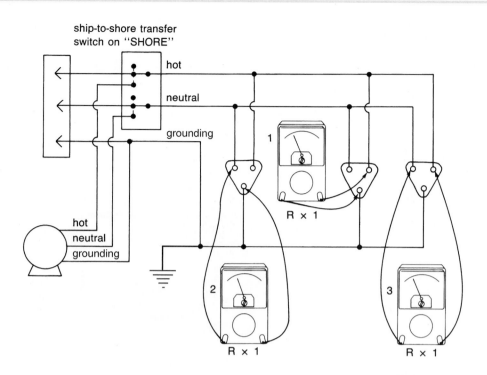

FIGURE 4-45. Testing AC circuits without an isolation transformer. *These resistance tests are carried out with the shore-power cord disconnected, any inverter or generator shut down, and all appliances unplugged or switched off, but with the boat's main breaker turned on. Meters 1 and 2 should show no continuity; a reading of less than infinity indicates a leak to ground (except for some polarity indicating devices and frequency meters that will give a reading above 25,000 ohms). Meter 3 should also show no continuity.*

ship-to-shore transfer switch on "SHORE"

hot

neutral

grounding

hot
neutral
grounding

scale on an analog meter) and test first between the hot wire(s) and the grounding wire (green or bare), and then between the neutral wire and the grounding wire (Figure 4-45). The easiest way is to poke the meter probes into an AC receptacle socket. *There should be no continuity at any time;* i.e., the meter reading should stay on infinity (a polarity indicating device may produce a very high resistance reading—above 25,000 ohms). The sole exception is when a polarized isolation transformer (one leg grounded on the boat) is fitted. In this case, break the grounding leg loose from the transformer case and proceed with the rest of the tests.

Any continuity indicates a leak to ground in the wiring circuits. If the neutral wire is at fault, it may have been incorrectly wired into the boat's ground point. If so, disconnect it. Now, *with the shoreside power still disconnected*, plug in and switch on your appliances, one piece at a time.

Troubleshooting Electric Stoves

Electric stoves commonly have their neutral (grounded) and earth (grounding) wires connected together at the stove frame. *The neutral connection to the frame should always be removed* (see the Correct Grounding Practices sidebar), leaving just the earth (grounding) cable connected to the frame.

If a stove fails to work, first check the fuses, breakers, terminals, and the voltage at the outlet supplying the stove. If these are OK, *and only if it can be done safely* (this procedure exposes live terminals: *REMEMBER, AC VOLTAGE CAN KILL*), turn on the appliance and check for voltage at the heating element terminals. If voltage is present, the element is almost certainly burned up; if voltage is not present, the switches, thermostats, and/or wiring are faulty. You can also perform the following tests:

1. Turn off the power and disconnect the stove. With an ohmmeter (R x 100 scale on an analog meter), check the resistance from each heating element terminal to the stove frame. *Any continuity shows a dangerous short in the element or its wiring.*

2. Now disconnect the heating element: for a stove burner, simply unplug it; other elements, such as electric toasters, can be broken loose at one end. Test with an ohmmeter (R x 1 scale on an analog meter) across both element terminals. Resistances are typically low (around 12 ohms per kW on 120-volt systems; 50 ohms per kW on 240-volt systems). *An open circuit indicates a burned-out element.*

Troubleshooting Electric Water Heaters

If a water heater fails to work, first check the fuses, breakers, terminals, and voltage at the outlet supplying the water heater. If these are OK, *and only if it can be done safely* (this procedure exposes live terminals: *REMEMBER, AC VOLTAGE CAN KILL*), turn on the water heater and check for voltage at the heating element terminals (make sure the water in the heater is cold and the thermostat is turned up high). If voltage is not present, the switches, thermostats, and/or wiring are faulty; if voltage is present, the element is almost certainly burned up.

If voltage is not present at the heating element:

1. Electric water heaters have a high-temperature cutout. Most water heaters installed on boats have a heat exchanger circuit that uses heat from the boat's engine (or generator) to heat the water. On occasion, this will raise the water temperature well above that of typical household water heaters, tripping the high-temperature cutout. So, if the above tests show no voltage at the heating element, look first for the high-temperature cutout (consult the manual) and see if it needs resetting.

2. Next, check for voltage across the power leads into the thermostat (generally at the top; Figure 4-46). If voltage is not present, there is a problem in the circuit to the water heater (recheck the switches, breakers, etc.). If voltage is present, make sure the thermostat is set on "HIGH," double-check

continued

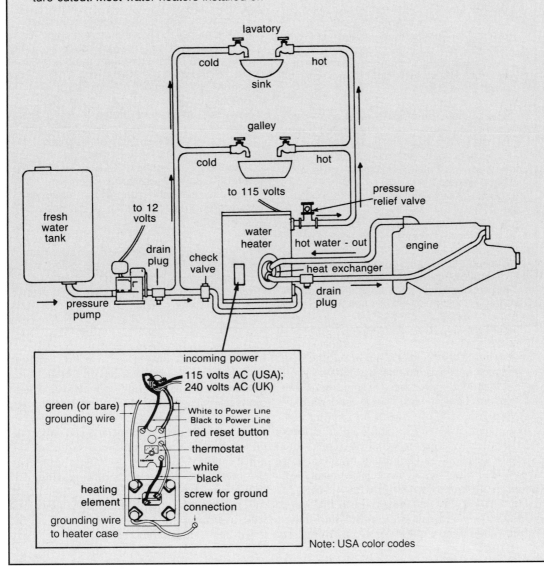

FIGURE 4-46. Typical onboard water heater installation. Water is heated both by the electric water heater and by engine-cooling water via a heat exchanger. *(Allcraft Corporation)*

lavatory

cold   hot

sink

galley

cold   hot

to 115 volts

pressure relief valve

fresh water tank

to 12 volts

water heater

hot water - out

engine

drain plug

check valve

heat exchanger

drain plug

pressure pump

incoming power
115 volts AC (USA);
240 volts AC (UK)

green (or bare) grounding wire

White to Power Line
Black to Power Line

red reset button

thermostat

white
black

heating element

screw for ground connection

grounding wire to heater case

Note: USA color codes

Troubleshooting Electric Water Heaters (*continued*)

any reset button, and check for voltage at the heating element. If there is still none, replace the thermostat.

If voltage is present at the heating element:

1. Turn off the power and disconnect the element. With an ohmmeter (R x 100 scale on an analog meter), check the resistance from each heating element terminal to the water heater frame. *Any continuity shows a dangerous short in the element or its wiring.*

2. Now disconnect the heating element (water heater elements have two wires). Test with an ohmmeter (R x 1 scale on an analog meter) across both element terminals. Resistances are typically low (around 12 ohms per kW on 120-volt systems; 50 ohms per kW on 240-volt systems). *An open circuit indicates a burned-out element.* To replace an element, drain the tank and unscrew the burned-out element. Put in a new gasket and then screw in the new element. Check for leaks before replacing covers.

The number one cause of a burned-out water heater element is turning on the heater when the water tank is empty. The element will burn out in minutes. *Anytime you drain a water heater, you must refill it completely before turning it on.*

Miscellaneous problems:

- The safety valve (relief valve) vents water. Check the thermostat setting—it may be too high. Try reducing it. If the valve still vents, turn off the heater and let it cool. If it still vents after cooling, the valve is defective. If the venting stops after the unit has cooled, the thermostat is probably not cutting off. If

the water heater has a heat exchanger and the relief valve (safety valve) vents only when the engine is running, the operating temperature of the engine may be too high for the water heater.

- Constantly dripping relief valve. There is probably dirt in the valve seat. Take off the valve and clean it.

- On-demand water heater cycles on and off with the water pump. The water system accumulator tank has become waterlogged (Chapter 13). Restore its air charge.

- On-demand heater won't kick on. The flow rate is probably inadequate, or the flow valve on the water heater is clogged. Check for kinked lines and pump problems to correct the flow rate. If the valve is clogged, clean it.

- Rusty water. Glass-lined water heaters are, in fact, made of porcelain-coated steel. All-stainless steel heaters are preferred in marine use because in time the porcelain cracks and then the steel rusts. When this happens, it is time to replace the heater. Before condemning an old water heater, however, make sure that it is really the source of the rust. Break loose a connection on the supply side of the heater; if the water here is rusty, the heater is not the culprit. Also consider whether the boat has been through any unusual turbulence lately; the rust may be nothing more than sediment stirred up from the bottom of the heater's tank.

- Freezing. Freezing destroys any water heater—the tank bursts. Be sure to drain the tank when winterizing. Alternately, add *propylene* glycol antifreeze (which is nontoxic), *not ethylene* glycol (automotive antifreeze, which is toxic).

Any continuity from either a hot or neutral wire to the green or bare grounding wire shows a short or leak to ground in that piece of equipment. *The equipment is dangerous and needs repairing.*

You can use the ohmmeter for another test. Once again, *with the shoreside cable disconnected*, the AC selector switch turned to the SHORE position, all equipment unplugged or switched off, and the AC breakers turned on, test between the hot and neutral wires (U.S., 120 volts; Europe, 240 volts), or the two hot wires (U.S., 240 volts). Boats without isolation transformers should show infinite ohms; anything less

indicates a leak between the wires, or some equipment plugged in and left on. (Note: A frequency meter in the circuit will give a high ohms reading.) Boats with isolation transformers will show a low reading (near 0 ohms), since the meter now in effect is connected across the secondary coil in the transformer. With such circuits, the next step is to trip the main breaker; the meter should jump to infinity, since the transformer has been taken out of the circuit. Any reading other than infinity now indicates a leak, assuming the meter is connected on the downstream side of the breaker.

UNDERSTANDING AND TROUBLESHOOTING ELECTRICAL CIRCUITS

Proper Electrical Installations

Some years ago we were having a problem with our VHF radio. It would receive, but then cut out the minute we keyed the mic to transmit. Since we were in the West Indies far from help, we simply stopped using the radio.

Months later, back at the dock, I prepared to remove the unit and send it in for repairs. When I opened up the fuse holder, I noticed a trace of corrosion on the tip of the fuse. I cleaned the fuse, replaced it, and the radio was back in commission! The corrosion was such that it would allow the passage of the small amounts of current required to receive, but created excessive voltage drop whenever an attempt was made to pass the higher currents needed to transmit. If I had spent a few minutes performing a voltage drop test, I would have found the problem immediately!

With my curiosity aroused, I now peeled back a section of insulation on the coaxial cable to the antenna. The copper braid was severely tarnished and corroded (Figure 4-47). I continued peeling back the insulation, working up the cable. After 7 feet there was still no sign of a reduction in the corrosion. I replaced the entire cable.

The boat was exceptionally dry down below. It had never taken on any appreciable quantities of salt water, and the radio and its associated wiring had not even been subjected to any spray. And yet we had a corrosion problem. This example just goes to show that in the marine environment the electrical circuits on even the driest of boats are still liable to deteriorate simply from salt and moisture in the atmosphere. When wiring electrical circuits, the only sure way to postpone problems for as long as possible is to use the best available materials and to install them to the highest possible standards.

Cables

Cables need strength to resist the vibration and pounding experienced in boats, adequate insulation to prevent ground leaks and to stand up to environmental insults such as oil and ultraviolet degradation, and sufficient size to minimize voltage drop.

Cable construction. Nothing but copper cable is suitable for use in the marine environment. Sometimes aluminum cable is found in household wiring, but this has a lower conductivity than copper and builds up a layer of aluminum oxide on the surface of the cable that creates resistance in connections and terminals; it is not suited to marine use. (In addition, alu-

FIGURE 4-47. Severe corrosion of a coaxial cable caused simply by salt-laden moisture wicking up the wire strands. This section of the cable was 7 feet from the cable termination! The cable had never been subjected to immersion or spray of any kind. Tinned cable would have prevented this corrosion.

minum and unplated steel are not to be used for studs, nuts, washers, and cable terminations.)

With copper cable, an added measure of protection against corrosion can be gained by drawing the individual strands of copper through a tin bath before assembling the cable to form what is known as *tinned cable*. Tinned cable is more expensive than regular cable, but will provide trouble-free service for much longer, and in the long run, is an excellent investment. Its use has become widespread among U.S. boatbuilders, but at the time of writing (2005), is rare in Europe. *If buying a European boat (or any boat, for that matter) that you intend to keep for any length of time, I recommend you insist on tinned cable.*

Stranding. Cables in boat use are subjected to vibration, and at times, considerable shocks. Solid-cored cable of the kind used in household wiring is liable to fracture. Stranded cable is required by both the ABYC and ISO. The ABYC lists three types, based upon the number of strands (column 6 in Table 4-7 on page 167; Figure 4-48). Type 1 cable (solid) is not allowed for marine use; the more flexible Type 2 (nineteen strands) is required for use in general-purpose boat wiring, with Type 3 (many strands—the number varies with cable size) recommended if frequent flexing occurs. (Note: Just to confuse the picture, what the ABYC calls Type 2, the

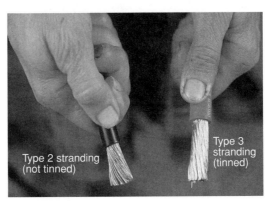

Type 2 stranding (not tinned)

Type 3 stranding (tinned)

FIGURE 4-48. Untinned Type 2 cable (left) versus tinned Type 3 (right). The tinned cable will resist corrosion much better, and the Type 3, with its many more strands, is more flexible, easier to run, and less prone to breakage of the strands.

ISO calls Type 1 or A, while ABYC Type 3 is ISO Type 2 or B!)

Cable insulation. Insulation is the other critical factor in cable construction. It must be able to withstand the ever-present salt-laden atmosphere; contamination by various chemicals, particularly oil, diesel, and dirty bilge water; and exposure to ultraviolet rays from sunlight. Both the ABYC and ISO require the insulation to be fire retardant.

Additionally, the ABYC requires the insulation on all cables to be marked with at least the following information (see the Cable Labeling sidebar for a more detailed explanation of these requirements):

- Type/style
- Voltage
- Wire size
- Dry temperature rating

FIGURE 4-49A. High-quality tinned boat cable, with all kinds of other standards-compliance labeling.

FIGURE 4-49B. Cheap cable; the only information on the insulation is "1 gauge 105°C," which does not comply with ABYC standards.

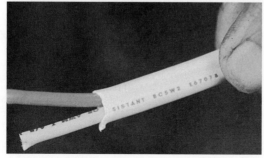

FIGURE 4-49C. Quality cable again—BC5W2—that is also oil resistant (the label is partially cut off). Although it cannot be seen in this black and white photo, the positive cable is red and the negative is yellow.

The ISO has no similar labeling requirements. Much European cable is not labeled, other than the label on the spool on which the cable is supplied to the boatyard. Once the cable is in the boat, you can tell very little about it. In practice, aside from being untinned, it is generally lower-quality cable than that found in comparable American boats (a situation I hope will change over time). Because of the common lack of labeling, currently few of the boats imported into the United States from Europe comply with ABYC standards. *If importing a boat, I recommend you insist on compliance* (to avoid potential problems with sharp-eyed surveyors and insurance companies.)

Labeling. In the United States, Underwriters Laboratories (UL) has a standard for boat cable (BC) called UL 1426. Within this standard are various quality levels for insulation, the highest being 5W2 (see the Cable Labeling sidebar). Most cable used in U.S. boats for both AC and DC circuits now meets or exceeds this standard, in which case the insulation will be marked, among other things, "BC5W2." Such a designation does not necessarily include tinning (although I have never seen BC5W2 cable that was not tinned); therefore, check for tinning separately by physically inspecting the cable (tinned strands are silver-colored, as opposed to copper-colored). Nor does the designation include oil resistance, which will be given in an additional label ("oil resistant") if it is part of the cable construction.

For almost all boat wiring, you will not go far wrong if you use cable that is labeled "BC5W2 Oil Resistant." The cable will most likely have all kinds of other labels, showing compliance with various other UL, Canadian, and European standards, but you can ignore these. (Please note that if the cable is labeled "Marine Grade," this says nothing about its compliance with any standard. "Marine grade" is simply a trademarked phrase of the Ancor company, which does, in fact, sell very good cable!) *The key to good-quality cable is the "BC5W2 Oil Resistant" label.* This cable is available in Europe as well as the United States (Figures 4-49A, 4-49B, and 4-49C).

Welding cable. Welding cable is sometimes used on boats for high-current DC circuits (notably for high-output alternators; DC-to-AC inverters; and electric windlasses, winches, and sail reefing devices). I recommended it for these purposes in the first edition of this book. The reasons for using welding cable are its extreme flexibility (which is particularly useful when running heavy cables in tight quarters) and its tolerance of vibration (for example, when attached to the back of an alternator). The problems with welding cable are that its flexibility

Cable Labeling

The most commonly available cable in the United States that may be suitable for general-purpose marine wiring is classified as THWN (**t**hermoplastic, **h**eat resistant, for **w**et locations, and with a **n**ylon jacket; see Table 4-1), or XHHW (cross-linked [**x**] polyethylene, **h**igh-**h**eat resistant, for **w**et locations). Other grades are MTW (**m**achine **t**ool **w**ire), which is rated for wet locations and is oil, gasoline, and diesel resistant, and AWM (**a**ppliance **w**iring **m**aterial), which is similar to MTW but with a high heat (HH) rating (up to 221°F/105°C), making it suitable for engine rooms. (Note, however, that there are several types of AWM wiring, the most common being designated by the numbers 1015 and 1230; however, *only 1230 or 1015/1230 are suitable for boat use.*)

Wire insulation frequently carries more than one designation, for example, THHN/THWN. In this instance, the insulation has a higher heat (HH) rating in dry locations (up to 194°F/90°C) than it does in wet locations (up to 167°F/75°C).

All cable insulation has this temperature rating. This is its maximum safe operating temperature, which is an important factor in determining the maximum current (amps) rating of the cable (what is known as its *ampacity*—see the text). The temperature rating is generally lower in a wet environment than in a dry environment. Most household wiring is rated at 140°F/60°C dry. Better-quality cable will have a higher temperature rating. In addition to 140°F/60°C, common rating points are 167°F/75°C, 185°F/85°C, 203°F/95°C, and 221°F/105°C. Both the ABYC and ISO require a minimum temperature rating of 140°F/60°C. Much of the cable in European boats is built to this minimum standard, whereas in the United States, 221°F/105°C cable is common.

Looking at Table 4-1, you will see a problem in that the requirements that must be met for these minimum designations are not rigorous enough to determine whether a cable is really suitable for marine use. A good-quality marine-rated cable will exceed all existing UL, Coast Guard, and ABYC/ISO standards. As noted in the text, for general-purpose boat wiring the best approach is to buy cable that is labeled "BC5W2" or "UL 1426." To be on the safe side, cable should always be bought from a recognized marine outlet. Such cable will be more expensive than that bought from a local electrical wholesaler or retailer, but the added cost is insignificant when compared to the cost of troubleshooting and rectifying faulty circuits in the future.

Normal insulation is unsuitable for prolonged immersion in water. Sooner or later current leaks will develop. Even good-quality boat cable should not be run through perpetually damp or wet areas of a boat. For this application, special waterproof, oil-resistant insulation is required, and naturally this is more expensive.

TABLE 4-1. Common Electric Cables Acceptable to the ABYC (U.S.)

Cable	Designation
TW:	**t**hermoplastic insulation (usually PVC), suitable for **w**et locations (140°F/60°C heat-resistant rating)
THW:	**t**hermoplastic insulation (usually PVC), **h**eat-resistant (167°F/75°C rating), suitable for **w**et locations
HWN:	**h**eat-resistant (167°F/75°C rating), suitable for **w**et locations, **n**ylon jacket for abrasion resistance
THWN:	same as HWN, but with **t**hermoplastic insulation
XHHW:	cross-linked (**x**) synthetic polymer insulation, **h**igh-**h**eat resistant (194°F/90°C rating), suitable for **w**et locations (but in this case derated to a 167°F/75°C rating)
MTW:	**m**achine **t**ool **w**ire; usually thermoplastic insulation (PVC) or thermoplastic with a nylon jacket; moisture, heat, and oil resistant; most MTW is rated 140°F/60°C; *the ABYC requires it to be rated 194°F/90°C*
AWM:	**a**ppliance **w**iring **m**aterial; usually thermoplastic insulation (PVC) or thermoplastic with nylon jacket; thermosetting; 221°F/105°C rating
BC5W2 and UL 1426 boat cable:	any cable with this designation is good for general-purpose boat wiring; 5 = the heat rating in a dry environment (1 = 60°C; 2 = 75°C; 3 = 85°C; 4 = 95°C; and 5 = 105°C); 2 = the heat rating in a wet environment (there are two ratings: 1 = 60°C and 2 = 75°C); the insulation on UL 1426 cable is self-extinguishing

For shore-power cords:

Cable	Designation
SO:	hard **s**ervice cord, **o**il-resistant compound
ST:	hard **s**ervice cord, **t**hermoplastic
STO:	hard **s**ervice cord, **t**hermoplastic, **o**il-resistant rating

Note: All are available with several temperature ratings (e.g., 140°F/60°C and 167°F/75°C)

Key: T = thermoplastic, a plastic that can be softened by heating, as opposed to thermosetting, a plastic that is heat-cured into an insoluble and infusible end product

W = wet (moisture resistant)

H = heat resistant (167°F/75°C rating)

HH = high-heat resistant (194°F/90°C rating)

N = nylon jacket

X = cross-linked synthetic polymer, a plastic in which polymers are linked chemically by polymerization

BC = boat cable

comes from its large number of very small strands, and its soft insulation. These strands tend to wick up moisture, encouraging corrosion, and the insulation is not as moisture resistant as other insulation and is easily damaged. Also, some welding cable insulation is dissolved by diesel. For these reasons, *welding cable should not be used on boats*. It does not, in any case, meet the applicable ABYC standards. Stick with BC5W2!

Color coding. A standardized system of DC color coding has been adopted by the ABYC (Tables 4-2 and 4-3). However, in many instances, it is not feasible to follow the system.

The primary consideration (U.S.) is to use red leads on DC positive circuits and black or yellow on DC negative. AC color coding is explained on pages 145–46. (Note that black is also used for the hot leads on AC circuits in the United States, creating the possibility of dangerous confusion. When rewiring a boat, I strongly recommend the use of yellow for the DC negative; it is, in any case, an ISO requirement that if the AC system uses black, the DC system will use yellow for negative.)

Cable sizing. Selecting the proper wire size for a given application is critical, especially where electric motors are concerned. Undersized cables introduce unwanted resistance, resulting in voltage drop at appliances, reduced performance, premature failure, and in extreme cirtcumstances, a fire risk. Since a fire on a boat is potentially so dangerous, let's look at this first.

The potential for fire is the result of a couple of basic electrical facts:

TABLE 4-2. ABYC DC Color Coding

Color	Use
Red	DC positive conductors
Black or yellow	DC negative conductors
Green or green with yellow stripe(s)	DC grounding (bonding) conductors (see Chapter 5)

TABLE 4-3. ABYC Color Codes for Engines and Accessory Wiring

Color	Item	Use
Yellow w/ red stripe (YR)	Starting circuit	Starting switch to solenoid
Brown/yellow stripe (BY) or yellow (Y)—see note	Bilge blowers	Fuse or switch to blowers
Dark gray (Gy)	Navigation lights	Fuse or switch to lights
	Tachometer	Tachometer sender to gauge
Brown (Br)	Generator armature	Generator armature to regulator
	Alternator charge light	Generator terminal/alternator
		Auxiliary terminal to light and regulator
	Pumps	Fuse or switch to pumps
Orange (O)	Accessory feed	Ammeter to alternator or generator output and accessory fuses or switches
	Accessory feeds	Distribution panel to accessory switch
Purple (Pu)	Ignition	Ignition switch to coil and electrical instruments
	Instrument feed	Distribution panel to electrical instruments
Dark blue	Cabin and instrument lights	Fuse or switch to lights
Light blue (Lt Bl)	Oil pressure	Oil pressure sender to gauge
Tan	Water temperature	Water temperature sender to gauge
Pink (Pk)	Fuel gauge	Fuel gauge sender to gauge
Green/stripe (G/x) (except G/Y)	Tilt down and/or trim in	Tilt and/or trim circuits
Blue/stripe (Bl/x)	Tilt up and/or trim out	Tilt and/or trim circuits

Note: *If yellow is used for DC negative, blower must be brown with a yellow stripe.*

(ABYC)

1. All electric cables have a certain internal resistance (generally measured and specified in *ohms per thousand feet*).

2. Anytime a current (amperage) is passed through a resistance, heat is generated; the greater the current in relation to the resistance, the more the heat.

From these two facts it follows that *all cables, when conducting, generate some heat*, with the amount of heat proportional to the resistance of the cable and the magnitude of the current passing through it. At a certain level of current flow, any cable will become hot enough to start a fire. To be safe, in a given environment, cables have to be sized large enough to handle the maximum anticipated amperage on the circuit without becoming dangerously hot.

Cable ampacity. The maximum amperage is normally a function of the amperage rating of the equipment in that circuit. For much equipment the amperage draw is more or less constant, but for some devices (notably many electric motors and DC-to-AC inverters), the amperage is highly variable. A 12-volt windlass, for example, may pull 80 to 100 amps under normal operating conditions, but if it is misused, say, to drag a boat off a sandbar, the current draw may jump to as high as 400 amps. Similarly, an inverter powering a couple of AC lightbulbs will draw just a few amps from a 12-volt DC system, but when powering a microwave, the power draw will jump to well over 100 amps. To deal with these kinds of situations, cables must be sized for the *maximum sustained amperage* on the circuit, and not for some "typical" or "normal" operating load. This maximum sustained amperage is the first key factor in cable sizing calculations.

Ambient temperature. Assume at this point that a particular load results in a specific amperage passing through a cable. Given the internal

---

Temperature Issues

Given the way the bits and pieces that make up the electrical system on a boat come from numerous, different applications, there are all kinds of inherent mismatches that have not been addressed by either the ABYC or ISO. For example:

- The UL standard for testing battery switches allows a 100°C/180°F temperature rise above a 25°C/77°F ambient—i.e., to 125°C/257°F—whereas ABYC and ISO standards permit the use of 60°C/140°F cables. The cables connected to a switch act as a heat sink, conducting heat out of the switch. If a switch is pushed to its limits, the temperature of its terminals may be up to twice the allowable temperature of the cable insulation, which will lead to insulation embrittlement and failure.

- Most circuit breakers are tested on the assumption that a 60°C/140°F cable is attached, using the cable as a heat sink. If a 105°C/221°F cable is attached (the most common type of cable used in U.S. boatbuilding), and the cable is sized such that it is operated at its full-rated ampacity, the cable temperature will rise to 105°C/221°F, overheating the circuit breaker. Testing done along these lines at one boatbuilder resulted in 120°C/248°F temperatures at the circuit breaker terminals. Although a high temperature will not affect the operation of a magnetic circuit breaker (see later), it will cause a thermal breaker to trip prematurely and may be unsafe with either type of breaker.

- Many other electrical system components—such as terminals, terminal blocks, and fuses—are also rated on the assumption that 60°C/140°F cable is being used and that the cable will act as a heat sink. If the cables are allowed to get hotter than 60°C/140°F, problems may occur.

Wiring conservatively. The bottom line here is that it is always best to wire a boat conservatively and to not push the limits of the wiring harness (being conservative also keeps voltage drop to a minimum). The U.S. National Electrical Code (NEC) requires the ampacity (see Tables 4-4A and 4-4B) of cables for continuous-duty circuits (as opposed to intermittent duty) to be 125% of the current on the circuit. (Or put another way, the ampacity of a cable should be downgraded to 80% of its rated ampacity when used for continuous duty; i.e., multiply the ampacity number in the ampacity tables by 0.8. If the cable is in a bundle, do this before applying any bundling factor.) It is especially important not to push cables that have a higher temperature rating (e.g., 105°C/221°F) to their limits, not because the cables will be damaged, but because the heat buildup in components to which the cables are attached may damage those components. Even if using cables with a high temperature rating (e.g., 105°C/221°F), it is a good idea to use the 60°C/140°F columns in the ampacity tables when sizing these cables for continuous currents; this practice will ensure the cable stays cool.

resistance of the cable, a certain amount of heat will be generated. The cable will warm up relative to the ambient temperature of the space through which it is passing, and as a result, will give off heat to this space. As the cable gets warmer, the temperature differential between it and the ambient temperature will increase, which in turn will increase the rate of heat dissipation from the cable into the ambient environment. At a certain temperature differential, an equilibrium will be reached at which the heat is being dissipated from the cable as fast as it is being produced. The temperature of the cable will stabilize.

The key factor in the rate of heat dissipation from a cable is this temperature differential between the cable and the ambient temperature. Regardless of the ambient temperature, this differential will remain more or less constant. As a result, for a given amperage, the higher the ambient temperature, the higher the temperature to which the cable will rise before its temperature stabilizes. Turning this around, we find that *the higher the ambient temperature, the less current a cable can carry before it reaches a given temperature*. In other words, if we are to keep the temperature of a cable at a safe level, *the higher the temperature of the space through which the cable is passing* (the ambient temperature), *the lower the amperage the cable can carry*. Ambient temperature thus becomes the second key factor in cable sizing calculations. If a cable passes through spaces at different ambient temperatures (such as a hot engine room and a cool stateroom), the *highest ambient temperature* is the limiting factor in terms of the cable's safe current-carrying capability.

Cable bundling. There is another variable at work in terms of heat dissipation from a cable. This is the number of cables in a bundle. If two or more are routed together, particularly if inside a common sheath or conduit, the heat generated by the various cables is cumulative. Consequently, the greater the number of cables in a bundle, the lower the safe current-carrying capability of the cables. This is the third key factor in cable sizing calculations. Note, however, that in terms of compliance with ABYC and ISO standards, this derating of cables only applies to circuits carrying over 50 volts, which in practice in

TABLE 4-4A. Allowable Ampacity of Conductors (ABYC)

Conductor Size (AWG)	60°C (140°F)		75°C (167°F)		80°C (176°F)		90°C (194°F)		105°C (221°F)		125°C (257°F)		200°C (392°F)
	Outside engine spaces	Inside engine spaces	Outside engine spaces	Inside engine spaces	Outside engine spaces	Inside engine spaces	Outside engine spaces	Inside engine spaces	Outside engine spaces	Inside engine spaces	Outside engine spaces	Inside engine spaces	Outside or inside engine spaces
18	10	5.8	10	7.5	15	11.7	20	16.4	20	17.0	25	22.3	25
16	15	8.7	15	11.3	20	15.6	25	20.5	25	21.3	30	26.7	35
14	20	11.6	20	15.0	25	19.5	30	24.6	35	29.8	40	35.6	45
12	25	14.5	25	18.8	35	27.3	40	32.8	45	38.3	50	44.5	55
10	40	23.2	40	30.0	50	39.0	55	45.1	60	51.0	70	62.3	70
8	55	31.9	65	48.8	70	54.6	70	57.4	80	68.0	90	80.1	100
6	80	46.4	95	71.3	100	78.0	100	82.0	120	102	125	111	135
4	105	60.9	125	93.8	130	101	135	110	160	136	170	151	180
2	140	81.2	170	127	175	136	180	147	210	178	225	200	240
1	165	95.7	195	146	210	163	210	172	245	208	265	235	280
0	195	113	230	172	245	191	245	200	285	242	305	271	325
00	225	130	265	198	285	222	285	233	330	280	355	316	370
000	260	150	310	232	330	257	330	270	385	327	410	364	430
0000	300	174	360	270	385	300	385	315	445	378	475	422	510

Temperature Rating of Conductor Insulation

Maximum Allowable Amperage

Notes:
1. Engine spaces are assumed to be at 50°C/122°F.
2. For bundling, derate the ampacities given as follows:

Number of cables per bundle	Multiply the ampacity by
3	0.70
4–6	0.60
7–24	0.50
25+	0.40

(ABYC)

boating applications means AC circuits, whereas to be consistent, it should apply to all circuits (the *Code of Practice for Electrical and Electronic Installations in Small Craft* put out by the British Marine Industries Federation applies it to DC as well as AC circuits). The derating also only applies to *current-carrying* cables. In a 120-volt system (U.S.) and 240-volt system (Europe), this means the hot and neutral cables; in a 240-volt system (U.S.), this means both 120-volt cables; and in a 120/240-volt system (U.S.), this means the hot and neutral cables when powering 120-volt loads, and the two 120-volt cables when powering 240-volt loads. In other words, however you slice it or dice it, in a typical AC circuit, there are *two* current-carrying cables. In a DC circuit, the positive and negative cables are both current carrying.

Insulation temperature rating. Finally, the current-carrying capability of a cable is affected by the ability of its insulation to withstand a heat buildup in the conductor, which as we have already seen (Table 4-1), is given in the *temperature rating* of the insulation. The higher the temperature rating of the insulation, the higher the temperature to which the conductor can safely be allowed to rise, and therefore, the greater the current it can safely carry. It is only by putting these four factors together—the maximum sustained load on a circuit, the maximum ambient temperature of the spaces through which the cable will pass, whether or not the cable is bundled with other cables, and the temperature rating of the cable insulation—that a proper choice of a cable can be made for a given application. This is done by reference to an ampacity table such as those shown in Tables 4-4A and 4-4B, in which the ambient temperature is simplified to just two considerations—*outside* and *inside* engine spaces.

Using ampacity tables. Tables 4-4A and 4-4B can be used in a couple of different ways. We can start with a cable of a given size, with an insulation that carries a certain temperature rating, and find out from the table the maximum current the cable can carry inside and outside engine spaces. Or else we can start with a given load (amperage), inside or outside engine spaces, to discover what size cable with what insulation is needed to carry the load. Either way, we end up

TABLE 4-4B. Allowable Ampacity of Conductors (adapted from the ISO standard)

Cross-Sectional Area (mm²)	Temperature Rating of Conductor Insulation											
	60°C (140°F)		70°C (158°F)		85°C to 90°C (185°F to 194°F)		105°C (221°F)		125°C (257°F)		200°C (392°F)	
	Outside engine spaces	Inside engine spaces	Outside engine spaces	Inside engine spaces	Outside engine spaces	Inside engine spaces	Outside engine spaces	Inside engine spaces	Outside engine spaces	Inside engine spaces	Outside engine spaces	Inside engine spaces
0.75	6	not permitted in engine spaces	10	7	12	9	16	13	20	17	25	no derating for engine spaces
1	8		14	10	18	14	20	17	25	22	35	
1.5	12		18	13	21	17	25	21	30	26	40	
2.5	17		25	18	30	24	35	30	40	35	45	
4	22		35	26	40	32	45	38	50	44	55	
6	29		45	33	50	41	60	51	70	62	75	
10	40		65	48	70	57	90	77	100	89	120	
16	54		90	67	100	82	130	111	150	133	170	
25	71		120	90	140	114	170	146	185	164	200	
35	87		160	120	185	151	210	180	225	200	240	
50	105		210	157	230	188	270	232	300	267	325	
70	135		265	198	285	233	330	283	360	320	375	
95	165		310	232	330	270	390	335	410	364	430	
120	190		360	270	400	328	450	387	480	427	520	
150	220		380	285	430	352	475	408	520	462	560	

Maximum Allowable Amperage

Notes:
1. Engine spaces are assumed to be at 60°C/140°F (as opposed to the ABYC's assumption of 50°C/122°F).
2. For bundling, derate the ampacities given as follows:

Number of cables per bundle	Multiply the ampacity by
4–6	0.70
7–24	0.60
25+	0.50

with a cable that has sufficient ampacity for the task at hand. (If the cable is in a bundle, we still need to apply the bundling factor.)

Note 1: Sizing starter motor cables is more complex because the current draw is hard to determine and is intermittent. In practice, the key issue is to keep down the voltage drop (see next section) as opposed to meeting the requirements of the ampacity table. This often results in cables that are undersized in terms of the ampacity tables, but given the short-term duration of cranking loads, the cables do not become hot enough to create a fire hazard.

Note 2: Not only are U.S. cable sizes counterintuitive—the smaller the number, the bigger the cable—but there are also two different cable sizing formulas using the same numbering system! One is American Wire Gauge (AWG); the other has been developed by the Society of Automotive Engineers (SAE). For a given wire size (e.g., 16-gauge), SAE-rated cables have approximately 10%

less copper than AWG-rated cables. SAE sizing is acceptable in DC circuits, *but is not acceptable in AC circuits. To avoid confusion, the best practice is to use AWG-sized cables in all applications.*

Voltage drop. We are not done with cable sizing procedures. The ampacity tables give the *minimum* size of cable, together with the temperature rating of its insulation, that is needed to carry a given amperage inside or outside engine spaces. This calculation is based simply on heat buildup considerations. It says nothing about whether the cable is appropriate for powering the load itself, and frequently it is not! To see why this is so, we need to back up for a moment.

You will recall that all cables have a certain internal resistance, and it is the passage of a current through this resistance that generates heat. The longer a cable, the more its cumulative resistance, and therefore, the more the total heat generated with the passage of a given current. As

TABLE 4-5. Conductor Sizes for 10% Drop in Voltage (ABYC)

Total Current on Circuit (amps)	\	\	\	\	\	\	Length of Conductor from Source of Current to Device and Back to Source (feet/meters)												
	10 (3.0)	15 (4.6)	20 (6.0)	25 (7.6)	30 (9.1)	40 (12.2)	50 (15.2)	60 (18.3)	70 (21.3)	80 (24.0)	90 (27.4)	100 (30.5)	110 (33.5)	120 (36.5)	130 (39.6)	140 (42.6)	150 (45.7)	160 (48.1)	170 (51.8)
12 volts																			
5	18	18	18	18	18	16	16	14	14	14	12	12	12	12	12	10	10	10	10
10	18	18	16	16	14	14	12	12	10	10	10	10	8	8	8	8	8	8	6
15	18	16	14	14	12	12	10	10	8	8	8	8	8	6	6	6	6	6	6
20	16	14	14	12	12	10	10	8	8	8	6	6	6	6	6	6	4	4	4
25	16	14	12	12	10	10	8	8	6	6	6	6	6	4	4	4	4	4	2
30	14	12	12	10	10	8	8	6	6	6	6	4	4	4	4	2	2	2	2
40	14	12	10	10	8	8	6	6	6	4	4	4	2	2	2	2	2	2	2
50	12	10	10	8	8	6	6	4	4	4	2	2	2	2	2	1	1	1	1
60	12	10	8	8	6	6	4	4	2	2	2	2	2	1	1	1	0	0	0
70	10	8	8	6	6	6	4	2	2	2	2	1	1	1	0	0	0	2/0	2/0
80	10	8	8	6	6	4	4	2	2	2	1	1	0	0	0	2/0	2/0	2/0	2/0
90	10	8	6	6	6	4	2	2	2	1	1	0	0	0	2/0	2/0	2/0	3/0	3/0
100	10	8	6	6	4	4	2	2	1	1	0	0	0	2/0	2/0	2/0	3/0	3/0	3/0
24 volts																			
5	18	18	18	18	18	18	18	18	16	16	16	16	14	14	14	14	14	14	12
10	18	18	18	18	18	16	16	14	14	14	12	12	12	12	12	10	10	10	10
15	18	18	18	16	16	14	14	12	12	12	10	10	10	10	10	8	8	8	8
20	18	18	16	16	14	14	12	12	10	10	10	10	8	8	8	8	8	8	6
25	18	16	16	14	14	12	12	10	10	10	8	8	8	8	8	6	6	6	6
30	18	16	14	14	12	12	10	10	8	8	8	8	8	6	6	6	6	6	6
40	16	14	14	12	12	10	10	8	8	8	6	6	6	6	6	4	4	4	4
50	16	14	12	12	10	10	8	8	6	6	6	6	6	4	4	4	4	4	2
60	14	12	12	10	10	8	8	6	6	6	6	4	4	4	4	2	2	2	2
70	14	12	10	10	8	8	6	6	6	6	4	4	4	2	2	2	2	2	2
80	14	12	10	10	8	8	6	6	6	4	4	4	2	2	2	2	2	2	2
90	12	10	10	8	8	6	6	6	4	4	4	2	2	2	2	2	2	1	1
100	12	10	10	8	8	6	6	4	4	4	2	2	2	2	2	1	1	1	1

UNDERSTANDING AND TROUBLESHOOTING ELECTRICAL CIRCUITS

a result, it would seem that the longer the cable, the less its safe current-carrying capability. But this is in fact not the case because the longer the cable, the greater the surface area from which to dissipate this heat, and consequently, the greater the rate of total heat dissipation. The net result is that *when making ampacity calculations, the length of a cable is irrelevant*—it doesn't matter whether a cable is 2 feet long or 2,000 feet long; its current-carrying capability will be the same.

Cable length. When it comes to powering a load, however, the length of a cable is critical, especially for low-voltage circuits. The increasing cumulative resistance with increasing length absorbs power from the circuit, reducing the power available to the appliance or equipment in the circuit, resulting in a loss of performance. The extent of this power loss is what we are measuring when we measure the *voltage drop* from one end of a cable to the other (see earlier in this chapter). The longer a cable in relation to a given current flow, the greater the voltage drop. The only way to reduce this voltage drop is to use a lower-resistance (i.e., larger-diameter) cable.

Voltage drop tables. The relationship between amperage, cable length, and voltage drop has been summarized in various tables, two of which are reproduced in Table 4-5 (for a 10% volt drop at the appliance) and Table 4-6 (for a 3% volt drop at the appliance). These tables are for conventional DC circuits. (On board a boat, voltage drop is not such an issue with AC circuits because of the much higher voltages, although ashore it is often an issue because of the much longer cable runs associated with dockside

TABLE 4-6. Conductor Sizes for 3% Drop in Voltage (ABYC)

Total Current on Circuit (amps)	10 (3.0)	15 (4.6)	20 (6.0)	25 (7.6)	30 (9.1)	40 (12.2)	50 (15.2)	60 (18.3)	70 (21.3)	80 (24.0)	90 (27.4)	100 (30.5)	110 (33.5)	120 (36.5)	130 (39.6)	140 (42.6)	150 (45.7)	160 (48.1)	170 (51.8)
12 volts																			
5	18	16	14	12	12	10	10	10	8	8	8	6	6	6	6	6	6	6	6
10	14	12	10	10	10	8	6	6	6	6	4	4	4	4	2	2	2	2	2
15	12	10	10	8	8	6	6	6	4	4	2	2	2	2	2	1	1	1	1
20	10	10	8	6	6	6	4	4	2	2	2	2	1	1	1	0	0	0	2/0
25	10	8	6	6	6	4	4	2	2	2	1	1	0	0	0	2/0	2/0	2/0	3/0
30	10	8	6	4	4	4	2	2	1	1	0	0	0	2/0	2/0	3/0	3/0	3/0	3/0
40	8	6	6	4	4	2	2	1	0	0	2/0	2/0	3/0	3/0	3/0	4/0	4/0	4/0	4/0
50	6	6	4	2	2	2	1	0	2/0	2/0	3/0	3/0	4/0	4/0	4/0				
60	6	4	4	2	2	1	0	2/0	3/0	3/0	4/0	4/0	4/0						
70	6	4	2	2	1	0	2/0	3/0	3/0	4/0	4/0								
80	6	4	2	2	1	0	3/0	3/0	4/0	4/0									
90	4	2	2	1	0	2/0	3/0	4/0	4/0										
100	4	2	2	1	0	2/0	3/0	4/0											
24 volts																			
5	18	18	18	16	16	14	12	12	12	10	10	10	10	10	8	8	8	8	8
10	18	16	14	12	12	10	10	10	8	8	8	6	6	6	6	6	6	6	6
15	16	14	12	12	10	10	8	8	6	6	6	6	6	4	4	4	4	4	2
20	14	12	10	10	10	8	6	6	6	6	4	4	4	4	2	2	2	2	2
25	12	12	10	10	8	6	6	6	4	4	4	4	2	2	2	2	2	2	1
30	12	10	10	8	8	6	6	4	4	4	2	2	2	2	2	1	1	1	1
40	10	10	8	6	6	6	4	4	2	2	2	2	1	1	1	0	0	0	2/0
50	10	8	6	6	6	4	4	2	2	2	1	1	0	0	0	2/0	2/0	2/0	3/0
60	10	8	6	6	4	4	2	2	1	1	0	0	0	2/0	2/0	3/0	3/0	3/0	3/0
70	8	6	6	4	4	2	2	1	1	0	0	2/0	2/0	3/0	3/0	3/0	3/0	4/0	4/0
80	8	6	6	4	4	2	2	1	0	0	2/0	2/0	3/0	3/0	3/0	4/0	4/0	4/0	4/0
90	8	6	4	4	2	2	1	0	0	2/0	2/0	3/0	3/0	4/0	4/0	4/0	4/0	4/0	
100	6	6	4	4	2	2	1	0	2/0	2/0	3/0	3/0	4/0	4/0	4/0				

Notes: These tables are based on SAE wiring sizes. SAE-rated cables are typically 10% to 20% smaller than AWG-rated cables of the same nominal size (see Table 4-7, columns 2 and 3). Consequently, if a cable is sized by reference to these tables, and then AWG-rated wire of the same nominal size is substituted for SAE, the cable will be somewhat oversized for the application, which is all to the good. Although SAE-rated wiring can be used in DC circuits, *AWG-rated wiring must be used in AC circuits*. (If you find this confusing, blame the ABYC and not me!)

Thermoplastic Versus Thermoset Insulation

Two broad types of cable insulation are available—thermoplastic and thermoset. The principal difference between them is that thermoplastics soften when heated, whereas thermosets undergo a chemical change during the manufacturing process that prevents them from softening. Thermosetting materials have excellent insulating properties. In addition, in a fire they char rather than melt. The charred material becomes brittle and will crumble, but until dislodged, it will still provide some insulation by maintaining a physical separation between the copper conductors. Thermoplastics melt down, with the result that if a short circuit occurs in one cable in a bundle, the heat often melts the insulation on neighboring cables, resulting in additional shorts.

FIGURE 4-50. Short-circuit testing of thermoplastic and thermoset insulation. The thermoplastic melts down faster and burns more vigorously. The thermoset tends to char.

The primary disadvantage of thermosetting materials is cost. Additionally, the insulation tends to be a little stiffer than thermoplastics, making cables that much harder to run in tight quarters. The primary advantage is the significantly greater protection against electrical fires. In the United States, Berkshire Electric Cable Company (becco@javanet.com) is the best-known supplier of thermoset cable to the boat market. Of the thermoplastics, polyvinyl chloride (PVC) is almost universally used for cable insulation.

For both types, the raw materials are mixed in the equivalent of a huge industrial cake mixer, and then the semiliquid compound is *extruded* around its copper conductor to form a finished cable. The properties of the insulation—notably its insulating capabilities; flexibility; heat, oil, moisture, and UV resistance; and fire-retarding capability—are a function of the ingredients that go into the mix. One insulation may look like another, but there are vast differences in quality, which is why it is so important to have the cables built to certain standards and labeled to indicate compliance.

Given that few things are more frightening on a boat than an electrical fire with toxic smoke, fire-retardant insulation is particularly important. Note, however, that *"fire retardant" does not mean the insulation will not burn; it simply means that once a direct heat source is removed, the insulation will stop burning ("self-extinguish") within a set period of time* (Figure 4-50).

Note also that cables insulated and sheathed with PVC should not be installed in direct contact with polystyrene insulation because the polystyrene can cause a breakdown in the cable insulation. Either place a polyethylene sheet between the cable and the polystyrene or place the cable in a conduit.

U.S. Cable-Sizing Formula

The ABYC voltage drop tables have been developed by the application of the formula:

$$cmil = (K \times I \times L)/E \text{ where:}$$

cmil = circular mil area of the conductor (a measure of its cross-sectional area)

K = 10.75 (a constant representing the mil-foot resistance of copper)

I = the maximum current (amps) on the circuit

L = the length in feet of the conductors in the circuit

E = the maximum allowable voltage drop (in volts) at full load

Use the formula to calculate wire sizes for loads and voltage drops not covered by the tables. For example, if voltage drop is to be limited to 3%, what size cables would be required for a 12-volt electric windlass that pulls 200 amps at full load and which will be situated 25 feet from its battery (i.e., with a 50-foot cable run)?

3% of 12 volts is 0.36 volts.

$$cmil = (10.75 \times 200 \times 50)/0.36 = 298611 \text{ circular mils.}$$

Table 4-7 converts circular mils to AWG. In our example a humongous, and totally impractical, 6/0 cable is required. Two 3/0 cables could be run in parallel, but in all probability we would settle for a 10% voltage drop at full load, which can be met with a 2/0 cable (still big!).

Column 2 of Table 4-7 gives minimum SAE cable specifications, which the ABYC considers adequate for DC wiring, and column 3 gives minimum UL cable specifications (AWG), which the ABYC considers necessary for AC wiring. For a given cable size, UL cables (AWG) are larger than SAE (wiring is one of those confusing areas where there are several different standards). Using the UL standards (AWG) for both DC and AC wiring will ensure the best results.

wiring.) Once again, the tables may be used in one of two ways: either to find the maximum amperage a certain size of cable can carry over a specified distance without exceeding the designated voltage drop (10% or 3%), or to find the *minimum* size of cable needed to carry a given amperage over a specified distance without exceeding the designated voltage drop (10% or 3%).

Experience has shown that many loads (notably incandescent lights other than navigation lights) will function satisfactorily with up to a 10% voltage drop in the circuit, but many others (notably electric motors and some electronics) should be wired to keep voltage drop to 3% or less of system voltage (e.g., 0.4 volt in a 12-volt circuit). I recommend always using the 3% table—given the harshness of the marine environment, it just does not pay to start out by trying to cut calculations as fine as possible.

Do the voltage drop calculation first. In almost all instances with conventional DC circuits

TABLE 4-7. Conversion of American Wire Sizes to European Standards

1	2	3	4	5	6		
	Minimum Acceptable Circular Mil[1] (cmil) Area (SAE specs and ABYC for DC Wiring)	Minimum Acceptable Circular Mil[1] (cmil) Area (UL specs [AWG] and ABYC for AC Wiring)			Minimum Number of Strands		
Conductor Size (U.S.)			Conductor Diameter (mm)	Conductor Cross-Sectional Area (mm²)	Type 1 (ABYC)	Type 2 (ABYC), Type 1 or A (ISO)	Type 3 (ABYC), Type 2 or B (ISO)
25			0.455	0.163			
24			0.511	0.205			
23			0.573	0.259			
22			0.644	0.325			
21			0.723	0.412			
20			0.812	0.519			
19			0.992	0.653			
18	1537	1620	1.024	0.823	7	16	
17			1.15	1.04			
16	2336	2580	1.29	1.31	7	19	26
15			1.45	1.65			
14	3702	4110	1.63	2.08	7	19	41
13			1.83	2.63			
12	5833	6530	2.05	3.31	7	19	65
11			2.30	4.15			
10	9343	10380	2.59	5.27	7	19	105
9			2.91	6.62			
8	14810	16510	3.26	8.35	7	19	168
7			3.67	10.6			
6	25910	26240	4.11	13.3		37	266
5			4.62	16.8			
4	37360	41740	5.19	21.2		49	420
3			5.83	26.7			
2	62450	66360	6.54	33.6		127	665
1	77790	83690	7.35	42.4		127	836
0 (1/0)	98980	105600	8.25	53.4		127	1064
00 (2/0)	125100	133100	9.27	67.5		127	1323
000 (3/0)	158600	167800	10.40	85.0		259	1666
0000 (4/0)	205500	211600	11.68	107.2		418	2107
00000 (5/0)	250000		13.12	135.1			
000000 (6/0)	300000		14.73	170.3			

1. 1 circular mil (cmil) = 0.0005067 mm², and 1 kcmil = 1,000 cmil = 0.5067 mm².

Notes:
1. Type 1 (ABYC) is no longer accepted in boat wiring by ABYC.
2. The lesser ABYC requirements for DC circuits reflect the fact that some of the industry is using SAE-rated cable. Using the UL specs for both DC and AC is preferable.

In Europe a slightly more involved procedure is often used to determine cable sizes. The allowable volt-drop-per-amp-per-meter must be calculated. Taking the windlass example, a 3% volt drop on a 12-volt circuit is 0.36 volt. At a maximum current of 200 amps, this gives an allowable volt-drop-per-amp of:

0.36/200 = 0.0018 volt (1.8 millivolts [mV, thousandths of a volt]).

Now we have a hitch. Some European volt drop tables are based on the *total length of the circuit* (as in the ABYC tables), but other tables are based on the *meter run* of the circuit, which means it is necessary to measure only the distance *in one direction* in order to enter the table. Table 4-8 is a *meter-run* table. The circuit is 7.5 meters (25 feet) in one direction, so the allowable volt-drop-per-amp-per-*meter run* is:

0.0018/7.5 = 0.00024 volt (0.24 mV).

Enter Table 4-8 in the DC millivolt (mV) column. Reading down we find 0.25 mV, which is very close to the 0.24 mV we are looking for. Reading across to the left-hand side, we find we need a cable with a cross-sectional area of 185 mm^2 (which is pretty close to AWG 6/0—see Table 4-7). If we decide to accept a 10% volt drop on the circuit, the allowable volt-drop-per-amp-per-meter run is now:

1.2/(200 x 7.5) = 0.0008 volt (0.8 mV).

Reentering Table 4-8, we find the nearest mV readings are 0.67 and 0.96. When we cannot find an exact correlation, we always use the *larger* cable, which in this case is 70 mm^2. This is pretty close to AWG 2/0; the formula worked again! (Unless precise electrical engineering is needed, European readers can use the ABYC tables to determine an American Wire Gauge size for a cable and then use Table 4-7 to convert this to squared millimeters. But remember that the American tables require measurements in *feet*, both *to and from* the load.)

(i.e., below 50 volts), the cable sizes required to keep voltage drop within acceptable limits (particularly if the 3% volt drop table is used) are larger than those needed to meet ampacity requirements. Consequently *the voltage drop calculations are almost always the limiting factor in cable sizing procedures.* As a practical matter, *if you use the 3% voltage drop table for sizing cables, and you use cables with a 221°F/105°C temperature rating, you will not need to use the ampacity tables at all.* Problems arise when using a higher voltage drop (e.g., 10%) and/or cables with a lower temperature rating, especially for short cable runs in a hot ambient environment (for example, the DC power leads to an engine room–mounted DC-to-AC inverter). In this case, the ampacity tables often produce a larger cable size than the voltage drop tables. *If voltage drop is above 3%, or the cable temperature rating is below 221°F/105°C, on short cable runs you should always double-check the cable size by referring to the ampacity tables.* If there is a conflict between the tables, *always use the larger cable size.*

If more than one appliance will be operated from common cables, the cables must be rated for the total load of all appliances. The ground cables (neutral on AC circuits) to all fixtures must be sized the same as the hot cables since they carry an equal load.

Connections and Terminals

Poor connections are the bane of many an otherwise excellent electrical installation. The keys to success are using the proper terminals, installing them with the proper tools, and keeping moisture out of them.

TABLE 4-8. European-Style Volt Drop Table

Conductor Nominal Cross-Sectional Area (mm^2)	Volt-Drop-per-Ampere-per-Meter DC (mV)	Volt-Drop-per-Ampere-per-Meter AC (mV)
1.0	53	53
1.5	34	34
2.5	18	18
4	12	12
6	7.6	7.6
10	4.5	4.5
16	2.7	2.7
25	1.7	1.7
35	1.2	1.2
50	0.96	0.98
70	0.67	0.69
95	0.48	0.52
120	0.38	0.42
150	0.31	0.36
185	0.25	0.32
240	0.19	0.27
300	0.15	0.24
400	0.12	0.23
500	0.093	0.22
630	0.071	0.21

Note: This table is based upon distances measured in meter-runs—i.e., it is necessary to measure the circuit in only one direction. See the text for an explanation of how to use it.

Proper terminals. Crimp-on connectors and terminals have gained almost universal acceptance in marine wiring. However, it should be noted that every one is a potential source of trouble. Let me explain. The exposed end of the cable core, protruding from the terminal, provides an entry path for moisture to wick up into the wiring, causing corrosion and resistance; the terminal forms a hard spot in the wiring so that any vibration will tend to cause the wire to fracture where it enters the terminal; and the terminal itself will be fastened to a terminal block or piece of equipment that may use a screw of a dissimilar metal, opening up the possibility of galvanic corrosion.

Terminal construction. It makes sense to use the very best terminals available, and as usual, there is more to this than meets the eye. A quality terminal will include the following features (none of which are likely to be found on the cheap terminals available at auto parts stores!—Figures 4-51A, 4-51B, and 4-51C):

- An *annealed, tin-plated*, copper terminal end. The annealing softens the copper so that the retaining screw will bite into it for maximum conductivity. The tin plating enhances corrosion resistance.

- A *seamless* tin-plated brass or bronze sleeve to crimp onto the cable, preferably with a serrated inside surface to enhance its mechanical grip. A seamless sleeve can be crimped from any angle and will hold the wire better than a seamed sleeve.

- A *long, nylon* insulating sleeve, extending up over the wire insulation. Nylon will not crack or punch through when crimping, and it is UV, diesel, and oil resistant (unlike the PVC found on cheap terminals). If the long sleeve contains an extra brass sleeve, a double crimp can be made—once on the terminal barrel and once on the sleeve around the wire insulation—to provide maximum strain relief (Figure 4-51D).

On wire sizes larger than 4 AWG (20 mm²), uninsulated *lugs* are used to terminate cables. Key features to look for in such lugs are once again an annealed terminal end, tin plating, and a seamless construction. In addition, *the lower end of the barrel should be closed to prevent water entry* (Figure 4-52). A long barrel will enable a double crimp to be made.

Matching terminals to cables. A terminal must be matched to both its cable and its retaining screw or stud. Terminals are given a simple color code: red for 22- to 18-gauge wire (0.5 to 1.0 mm²); blue for 16- to 14-gauge (1.5 to 2.5 mm²);

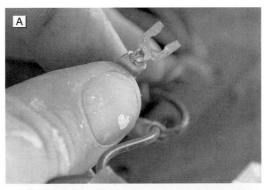

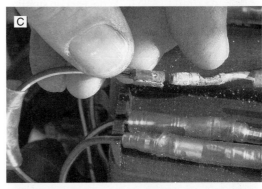

FIGURES 4-51A, 4-51B, AND 4-51C. A multitude of sins! Poor-quality terminals that corrode easily; improper crimping that cut through insulation; inadequate sealing of terminals; and in all cases, untinned cables that are also corroding.

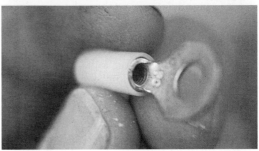

FIGURE 4-51D. A quality terminal—tinned, annealed copper; serrated, seamless sleeve; quality insulation.

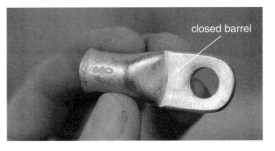

closed barrel

FIGURE 4-52. Note the closed barrel, which will prevent moisture wicking up into the cable.

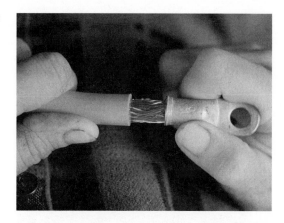

FIGURE 4-53. Larger sizes of Type 3 cable (multi-stranded) are often a tight fit in their terminals and sometimes hard to get in without clipping a few strands.

and yellow for 12- to 10-gauge (3.0 to 6.0 mm^2).

Each cable size (e.g., 10 AWG/6.0 mm^2) has a given amount of copper. This copper is divided into a specific number of strands; the greater the number of strands, the larger the circumference of the resulting conductor (because of the additional air spaces between strands). Consequently, multistranded (ABYC Type 3/ISO Type 2) cables have larger conductors than those with fewer strands (ABYC Type 2/ISO Type 1) or a single strand (ABYC Type 1). For smaller cable sizes, terminals tend to be a moderately loose fit, so all three cable types will fit in the same terminal. But on larger cable sizes, a terminal that makes a close fit on an ABYC Type 1 cable will not fit a Type 3 cable. To get a good fit, especially with Type 3 cables, it helps to get the cable and terminals from the same supplier (Figure 4-53).

Terminal types. Ring-type terminals are preferred to spade because they cannot pull off a loose screw. Locking spades are preferred to straight spades (Figure 4-54). Both the ABYC and ISO prohibit wrapping the end of a conductor around a screw head and tightening the screw because stranded conductors tend to splay out, compromising the connection. For similar reasons, it is not acceptable to have a screw in a terminal block bear directly on stranded conductors; a pressure plate must be placed between the screw and the conductor.

Wire nuts are frequently used to make connections in household circuits in the United States, although not in Europe. They are not suitable for marine use since the threaded metal insert is made of steel and will rust; what is more, the lower end of the nut is open to the atmosphere. When used on stranded conductors, the threads on the insert can cut through the conductors, causing the nut to come loose and the connection to fail. If you do use wire nuts, always install them with the open end down so that the nut does not become a water trap. It is also a good practice to seal the nut with polyurethane

sealant. However, it is a much better practice to "just say no" to wire nuts as they are specifically disallowed by the ABYC and ISO.

Proper tools. *It is simply not possible to turn out successful crimps without the right tools.* This means a *properly sized insulation stripper* (not a pocketknife; see Figures 4-55A to 4-55G) and a *properly sized crimper.*

There are two types of crimp: an indented crimp, in which a deep slot is made in the terminal, and an elliptical crimp, in which the terminal is compressed around its circumference. To avoid the risk of cutting through any insulation, *an indented crimp is normally made only on an uninsulated terminal* (although it is permissible to use it on *nylon-sleeved terminals,* since the nylon resists cracking); for insulated terminals, it is important to use an *elliptical* crimp (most cheap crimping tools will do both—it is simply a matter of choosing the right slot; Figure 4-56).

But rather than use a cheap crimping tool, every maintenance-conscious boatowner should have a ratcheting-type crimper in the toolbox (Figure 4-57). This type of crimper should assure a perfect crimp every time. After completing a crimp, *tug on it to see if it will come off.* If the crimp is poorly done, you want to know now and not later! Note that the standard test for a 16 AWG (1.0 mm^2) connection is a 15-pound (60 Newtons) pull. And by the time you get to 10 AWG (6.0 mm^2), the pull is up to 40 pounds (200 Newtons), so don't be shy about giving the connection a good tug with a pair of needle-nose pliers (Figure 4-58).

Special crimping tools are needed for larger cable sizes (Figures 4-59A, 4-59B, and 4-59C), but these need not be expensive. (The Ancor catalog is an excellent source for wiring products and installation tools—www.ancorproducts.com.) These large cables will be carrying heavy loads, which require perfect electrical connections if problems are to be avoided (Figure 4-60). (Ohm's law tells us that voltage = amperage × resistance. On a 100 amp circuit, a resistance of just 1/100 of an ohm (0.01 ohm) will cause a 1-volt drop, which is close to 10% on a 12-volt circuit. Since watts = volts × amps, this will generate 100 watts of heat.)

While on the subject of tools, let me also mention *split-shank screwdrivers.* These have a blade divided into two sections that can be squeezed apart in the slot of a screw, gripping the screw. This is an invaluable tool when trying to do up terminal screws in cramped quarters.

Soldering. Soldering is a controversial subject. A properly soldered connection creates the best

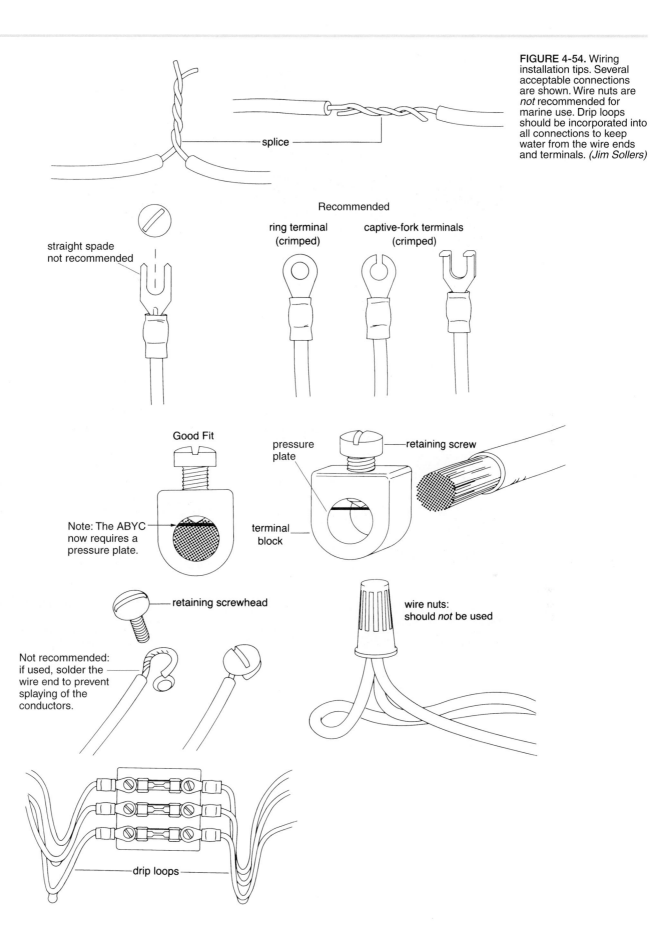

FIGURE 4-54. Wiring installation tips. Several acceptable connections are shown. Wire nuts are *not* recommended for marine use. Drip loops should be incorporated into all connections to keep water from the wire ends and terminals. *(Jim Sollers)*

splice

straight spade
not recommended

Recommended

ring terminal
(crimped)

captive-fork terminals
(crimped)

Good Fit

Note: The ABYC now requires a pressure plate.

pressure plate

retaining screw

terminal block

retaining screwhead

Not recommended: if used, solder the wire end to prevent splaying of the conductors.

wire nuts: should *not* be used

drip loops

FIGURE 4-55A. A cheap wire stripping and crimping tool. Note the stripping section is labeled "STR" (for stranded cables) on one side and "SOL" (for solid cored cables) on the other side. The STR side should be used with boat cables.

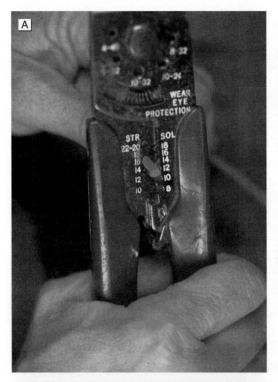

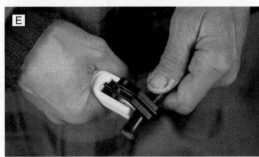

FIGURE 4-55B. A useful tool for stripping smaller cable sizes. The plastic stop can be set to ensure just the right amount of insulation is taken off.

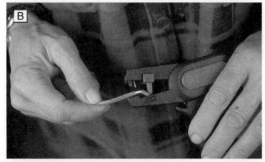

FIGURE 4-55C. Another excellent tool for stripping smaller-sized cables.

FIGURES 4-55D TO 4-55G. An insulation stripper for large cables. A small spring-loaded blade cuts through the insulation. It is run around in a circle and then dragged sideways to cut a slit in the insulation, which is then peeled off.

electrical connection, but all too often the soldering is not done properly. In any case, ABYC regulations require every joint to have a *mechanical* means of connection other than solder. The reason for this is that if the joint gets hot (through excessive resistance or a high current flow), the solder may melt and the joint will fall apart. So soldering frequently becomes just an adjunct to a crimped connection, but when crimped connections are also soldered, the solder wicks up the

cable and creates a hard spot, which is then liable to fail from vibration. *The consensus among professionals is that a properly made crimp, done with the proper tools, is frequently a more reliable termination than soldering.*

Some terminals come pre-tinned with low-temperature solder in a heat-shrink sleeve. A conductor is simply slipped into the terminal and a heat-gun applied (Figure 4-61). The solder melts into the wire at the same time as the sleeve

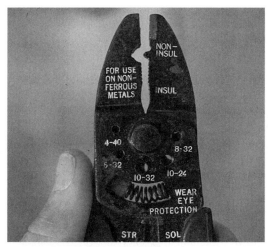

FIGURE 4-56. The crimping end of a cheap tool. Note the different sections for NON-INSUL (noninsulated) and INSUL (insulated) terminals.

FIGURE 4-57. A ratcheting crimper is an excellent tool that makes it difficult to mess up!

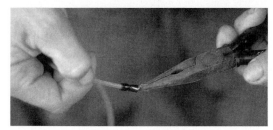

FIGURE 4-58. Tugging on a terminal to make sure it is well attached.

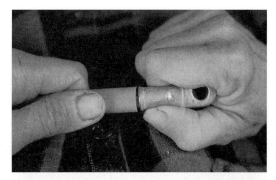

FIGURE 4-59A. Putting a terminal on a large (2/0, 70 mm²) cable.

FIGURE 4-59B. A cheap but effective crimping tool for large cables.

FIGURE 4-59C. The finished crimp. A little too much insulation was cut off this cable; it would be better if the insulation butted up to the terminal.

FIGURE 4-60. The crimp in Figure 4-59C cut in half, demonstrating the high degree of compaction of the cable strands (it looks like solid copper).

FIGURE 4-61. A low-temperature solder connection with built-in heat-shrink tubing. The solder sleeve is just beginning to melt into the lay of the two cables. At the same time the heat-shrink sleeve is starting to clamp down around the cables.

shrinks down. It seems like a neat idea, but unless the wire is spotlessly clean, the solder may not tin properly; the solder penetration may be poor; and the solder melting point is so low that if the joint heats up it may well fail. Additionally, as mentioned, the ABYC does not allow solder to be the sole means of mechanical support in a connection. Although the heat shrink provides a degree of mechanical connection, it is not the same as a crimp. For these reasons, these terminals are not recommended.

Sealing terminals. Heat-shrink tubing is widely available and consists of a plastic tube that is slipped over a terminal and then heated. It is preferable to heat the tube with a proper heat gun, but a small propane torch or even a

Soldering On Board

Most soldering aboard can be done with a 50- to 100-watt soldering iron; a few large jobs are best done with a propane torch. Soldering irons may be bought to use with 12- and 24-volt systems. Although a soldering iron is electrically greedy (a 50-watt iron will draw close to 5 amps at 12 volts), you will only be using it intermittently and for short periods, so it shouldn't present a great problem. Also available are small, pocket-sized, temperature-controllable butane soldering torches.

Solder is always used with *flux*, an agent that helps keep the metal surfaces clean while being soldered. Fluxes are either acid based or rosin based. Only rosin-based fluxes can be used in electrical work; acid fluxes will corrode copper wire.

There are numerous grades of solder, rated by their percentages of tin, lead, or silver. The best all-around solder for electrical work is 60-40 (60% tin, 40% lead). Avoid cheap solders with higher percentages of lead. Solder comes in rolls of either solid or rosin-cored wire. Rosin-cored wire has a hollow center with flux already in it, whereas solid solder requires an external application of flux. Rosin-cored solder is suitable for most marine uses and is much more convenient.

The keys to successful soldering are having a well-tinned soldering iron and tinning the individual pieces to be bonded *before* the joint is made. To tin the iron, clean its tip down to bare metal with a file, heat it up, and then touch rosin-cored solder to it. The solder should flow over the whole tip to form a clean, shiny surface. If it will not adhere to areas of the tip, there are impurities. Sometimes scratching around with a knife and the solder (to lay on more rosin) will clean these areas, but it may be necessary to go back and start again with the file. During soldering, the tip of the hot iron should be wiped periodically with a damp rag to remove burnt flux and old solder.

To tin wire ends and terminals, clean them down to bare, shiny metal and then hold the iron to the part to heat it. Touch the solder *to the part*, not to the iron (Figure 4-62). When the part is hot enough, the solder will flow over and into it, at which point the iron may be withdrawn—the tinning is complete. Once again, if the solder will not adhere to certain areas, those areas are not clean enough. To speed the heating of the part, place a drop of solder on the iron itself where it is in contact with the part. The actual tinning should always be done by applying the solder as described above.

To make a joint, bring two tinned surfaces together and add heat until the solder from the two parts melts and flows together. At that point, remove the heat. Most times, you should not need to add more solder. *Keep the two parts secured while the solder sets up. Do not allow them to move.* If they do move, the joint will crack, making it weak and electrically resistive.

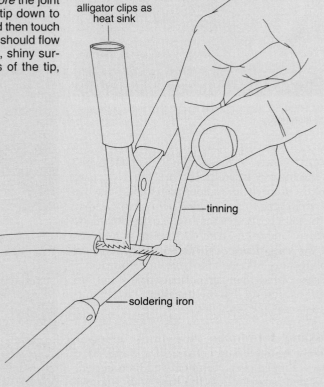

FIGURE 4-62. Soldering practices. Note that an alligator clip or a strip of aluminum used as a heat sink will protect the insulation from melting. When tinning (applying solder to the wire—not necessary on tinned wire), touch the solder to the wire, not to the iron. As a preparatory step, sandpaper or file the tip of the iron to a pyramid-shaped point of bright metal, then heat the iron, file it bright again, and working fast, run on a little solder. Try to achieve a good coating of solder over the entire point and ½ inch or so down the tip. Before making a joint, scrape the wire clean and bright. Place the parts to be soldered in firm contact. Use enough heat, but don't overheat. Keep the joint and wire immobile while the solder cools. *(Jim Sollers)*

alligator clips as heat sink

tinning

soldering iron

cigarette lighter will do. The tubing contracts to form a tight fit around the terminal barrel and wire (Figures 4-63A to 4-63D).

There are three types of heat shrink: *thin wall*, *dual wall* (thin wall lined with an adhesive), and *heavy wall with sealant*. The thin wall (commonly found at RadioShack in the U.S.) provides insulation, *but not weatherproofing*. The adhesive in the dual wall and heavy wall is squeezed out of both ends of the tubing as it contracts, *forming an extremely effective barrier to moisture penetration*. The heavy wall provides an added margin of abrasion resistance over the dual wall (Figure 4-64). One or two companies have a line of "waterproof" terminals that have a length of heat-shrink tubing already built onto the terminal sleeve.

Some joints that need insulating are an awkward shape with protruding corners and screws. In these instances, electricians' putty comes in handy. It is a pliable substance, similar to plasticine, which can be molded around the connection to fair it so that it can be wrapped smoothly with heat-shrink tape. (Heat-shrink tape may be bought in rolls and is known as *self-amalgamating tape* in the UK.) The putty itself has a high insulating value but is too soft to be left uncovered.

Installing Cables

ABYC and ISO standards require individual cables to be at least 16 AWG (1.0 mm^2). This size provides a minimum of physical strength. In both AC and DC systems, exceptions are made for cables completely inside an equipment housing (these can be 18 AWG/0.75 mm^2). The ABYC (but not the ISO) also makes exceptions for cables included with other cables in a common sheath (these can be 18 AWG) and for circuits below 50 volts that have a current flow of less than 1 amp (mostly monitoring and electronic circuits, but also many AC control circuits for heating and air-conditioning; the cables can be any size).

Separation of DC from AC. For obvious safety reasons, both the ABYC and ISO would like to see DC and AC wiring harnesses separated—"a DC circuit shall not be contained in the same wiring system as an AC circuit"—but in practice both standards qualify this to the point where it is almost meaningless. They do this by allowing a "sheath" as a means of separation, and then define a sheath so loosely that it includes a layer of insulation tape wrapped around either the DC or AC cables. The outer layer of insulation on duplex and triplex cables also counts as a sheath. Regardless of the definition of a sheath, maintaining DC and AC cable

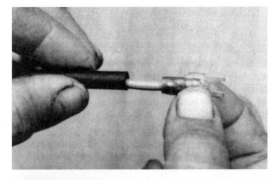

FIGURE 4-63A. Sliding a length of heat-shrink tubing over a terminal.

FIGURE 4-63B. Heating the heat shrink with a heat gun.

FIGURE 4-63C. The completed terminal. Note the glue squeezed out of the heat-shrink tubing. The heat-shrink sleeve will not only provide waterproofing, but also a fair measure of strain relief at the hard spot where the cable exits the terminal.

FIGURE 4-63D. Heat shrink being applied to a large cable. The purpose-built heat gun shown in this photo (and Figure 4-61) is a really handy tool.

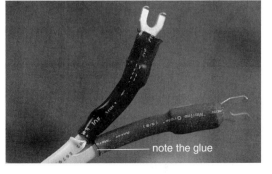

FIGURE 4-64. Cheap, thin-walled, nonadhesive heat shrink (left) versus quality, heavy-walled, adhesive heat shrink (right). The two started out the same size. The cheap stuff will not pull down to make a tight fit, and in any case, provides no waterproofing; it is largely a waste of time and money.

note the glue

separation is a good idea, not just for safety reasons but also to minimize induced electrical interference. However, it is often difficult to apply in practice.

Interference. Induced interference occurs because current (amperage) passing through a conductor sets up a magnetic field around that conductor. This induces voltage in neighboring conductors and also in the original conductor; the latter is known as *self-inductance*. Self-induced voltage is proportional to the size of any loop formed by the wire. The two power leads on a circuit (hot and neutral in most AC circuits; positive and negative in a DC circuit) are part of a single circuit, so if they are physically separated, it has the effect of making a loop and increasing self-inductance.

In AC circuits, the power leads are invariably run together, minimizing induction, but in DC circuits, separate positive and negative cables are often used. When separated, in extreme cases (rapid switching of high currents combined with high *inductance*), voltage *spikes* of hundreds of volts can be created with severe impacts on electronic equipment. To minimize self-inductance, *power leads should always be run together.* Better yet is to twist power leads together, in which case the magnetic fields cancel out.

Whenever possible, twisted conductors should especially be used (preferably within a Mylar or braided shield) where cable runs come close to sensitive electronic equipment and compasses. Note that you can rapidly twist long cable runs by securing one end of the cables and then clamping the other end in an electric drill chuck and running the drill slowly. Keep the wires taut to avoid a terrible tangle! To be effective, the pitch of the twist—i.e., the distance between each twist in the cables—has to be short relative to the distance to sensitive equipment (such as compasses).

Twisting is not possible with heavier cable runs, but in most applications *duplex* cable (the positive and negative conductors are run together in a common sheath) can be used. When it comes to high-current DC circuits, however, individual positive and negative cables are invariably used. To minimize magnetic and induced voltage impacts, the positives and negatives should be taped together every 4 to 6 inches (10 to 15 cm). However, this will not fully eliminate magnetic impacts, with the result that some high-current circuits with frequent switching (such as DC-to-AC inverters) can be problematic. In this case, if the equipment is wired with two negative and positive cables (or hot and neutral) in parallel in a quad formation as shown in Figures 4-65A and 4-65B, with the positive and negative cables diagonally across from one another, magnetic impacts will be eliminated. (I am grateful to Wayne Kelsoe of Blue Sea Systems for this information, derived from wiring minesweepers.)

Note that Chapter 8 raises some additional cable installation issues related to minimizing unwanted radio frequency interference (RFI).

Making and supporting cable runs. As you run each cable, label both ends. This is most easily done using self-adhesive wire markers, which come in a book or dispenser containing all the letters of the alphabet, a collection of numbers, and "+" and "−" symbols, although there are a number of different approaches (Figures 4-66A, 4-66B, and 4-66C). You can obtain wire markers from any electrical wholesaler. Alternatively, you can handwrite a label and cover it with clear heat-shrink tubing (the heat shrink is also a good idea over wire markers since they tend to come unglued over time).

When renewing cables inside masts and other inaccessible locations, attach the new wires to the ends of the old and pull the new into place as you withdraw the old. It is a good idea to pull a piece of string through along with the new wires and to leave the string in place in case of future additions. With tall masts, fasten the cables along their length to a cord or stainless steel wire; otherwise, they are likely to break under their own weight and movement.

Chafe protection. Anytime a cable is run through an area where it may chafe (e.g., passing through a bulkhead) or suffer other damage (e.g., from loose objects rattling around in a

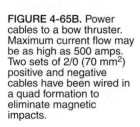

FIGURE 4-65A. Paralleled positive and negative (or hot and neutral cables on an AC circuit) in a quad formation that will minimize any magnetic and interference influences created by the current flowing through the cables. *(Jim Sollers)*

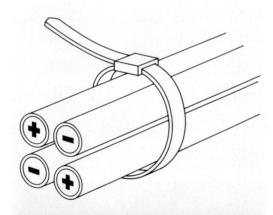

FIGURE 4-65B. Power cables to a bow thruster. Maximum current flow may be as high as 500 amps. Two sets of 2/0 (70 mm²) positive and negative cables have been wired in a quad formation to eliminate magnetic impacts.

UNDERSTANDING AND TROUBLESHOOTING ELECTRICAL CIRCUITS

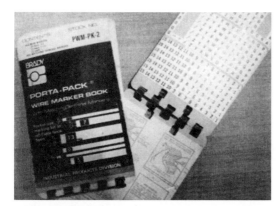

FIGURE 4-66A. A book of wire markers.

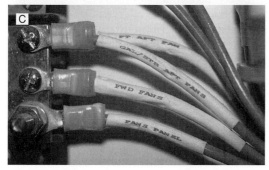

FIGURES 4-66B AND 4-66C. Using labeled heat shrink to identify circuits.

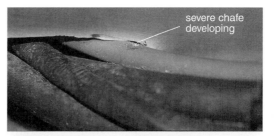

FIGURE 4-67A. A chafe point. If hot and positive cables chafe through, there is the potential for a dead short to develop, which is likely to start a fire (see the section on Overcurrent Protection).

FIGURE 4-67B. Excellent chafe protection (using hoses) on our old Pacific Seacraft 40.

FIGURE 4-67C. A neat panel installation with flexible conduit providing chafe protection for cables.

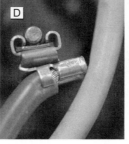

FIGURES 4-67D AND 4-67E. This cable pressing on the terminal resulted in a short circuit. The solution was a hard plastic chafe protector.

locker), it must be fully protected (Figures 4-67A to 4-67E). You can do this by lining the holes through bulkheads with rubber grommets or grommet material (which can be bought in rolls), except in the case of watertight bulkheads in metal hulls. In this situation, the usual method is to weld a pipe stub through the bulkhead, with the cable passing through it, thread the end of the stub, and screw on an appropriate watertight cable seal.

Where cables in a bundle make a tight bend around a hard edge, you run the risk of a condition known as *cold flow*, i.e., the insulation is slowly displaced, leading to bare conductors and short circuits. To prevent cold flow, it is essential that you ensure the cables on the inside of the bend (against the hard surface) are not under pressure. (Cold flow has been cited as the cause of a number of boat fires.)

Inside lockers, and anywhere else cables need protection, PVC pipe can be used as a conduit. The pipe is cheap, widely available (at any hardware store), and easy to work with (all you need is a hacksaw and PVC cement). Any pipe must have a good-sized drain hole (at least ¼ inch) drilled at all low spots (at all angles of heel) to prevent water entrapment. Electrical wholesalers also carry a whole range of cable conduits; I prefer plastic because it will not corrode. The advantage of conduit over pipe is that the top comes off for adding and removing cables. Pipe and conduit should always be oversized because sooner or later you are bound to add extra cables.

Supporting cables. The ABYC and ISO require that cables not run in conduit be bundled together and supported against vibration at least every 18 inches (450 mm). A broad variety of plastic cable ties and clips are readily available for your use. You can do a very neat job of bundling with plastic spiral wrap, which comes in diameters from ¼ inch and up (Figures 4-68A, 4-68B, and 4-68C). Note that black plastic has a greater resistance to UV degradation than white. Black plastic should be used on all external wiring and also is preferable on internal wiring unless aesthetic reasons dictate otherwise.

Current-carrying cables should be at least 2 inches (25 mm) above the level at which the automatic bilge pump switch operates *with no connections whatsoever below the foreseeable water level* (connections that get submerged almost always result in stray-current corrosion—see the next chapter). Do not run any cable closer than 2 inches (50 mm) to a wet exhaust and 9 inches (250 mm) to a dry exhaust. "Nonmetallic straps or clamps shall not be used over engines, moving shafts, other machinery or passageways, if failure would result in a hazardous situation." (ABYC; the National Marine Electronics Association [NMEA] requires stainless steel clamps insulated with a nonmetallic material in these areas.)

Cables should, if possible, always enter junction boxes from the base. To avoid trapping moisture, a "drip loop" should be formed in the wire before making a terminal fast. Note that under ABYC/ISO standards no more than four terminals can be stacked on a single stud (Figure 4-69).

Safety concerns. The ABYC requires ungrounded (positive) battery cables that do not have overcurrent protection (they should have—see below) to be routed in such a way as to avoid contact with any part of the engine or power train. This is an obvious safety precaution that is frequently violated. If an unprotected cable shorts to an engine block, it creates an uncontrolled arc welder, burning through metal and setting fire to things in its path. (While writing this, I had a phone call from a distressed owner in just this situation; not only did the short start an expensive fire, but it also burned through the engine pan, causing the loss of the engine oil and the destruction of the engine!)

For AC circuits, the ABYC and ISO require

FIGURES 4-68A AND 4-68B. Plastic spiral wrap lends itself to being put on and taken off multiple times, and will expand or contract to accommodate changing wire bundle sizes.

FIGURE 4-68C. Tywrap used to hold a cable bundle in place. This type of Tywrap can be undone and reused in the event it's necessary to add cables to the bundle.

FIGURE 4-69. No more than four cables should be stacked at a single terminal, and in general, stacking of cables should be avoided at battery posts. This installation is asking for trouble. If stacking cables, place the higher-current circuits closer to the bus bar or battery terminal.

UNDERSTANDING AND TROUBLESHOOTING ELECTRICAL CIRCUITS

that all current-carrying connections (i.e., hot and neutral) be made inside some form of an enclosure. An additional requirement is that tools must be necessary to access the connections; this is to prevent children and others from accidentally touching the connections.

Distribution Panels

A distribution panel, as its name implies, takes battery or AC current and distributes it to the individual circuits on a boat. Several factors need to be taken into account when choosing a location for a distribution panel:

- The back of the panel must be readily accessible to simplify wiring and troubleshooting tasks. The best situation is a permanent mount in a bulkhead with a clear approach to the other side. Far too many panels have very poor access to the wiring terminals, which makes simple wiring tasks difficult.

- If the back of the panel is not readily accessible, the panel must be set in a hinged frame with the cables run in such a manner that the panel can be opened wide without stressing any connections (i.e., the cables need to exit the panel along the hinge line, with some kind of a stress-relief loop).

- Although the panel must be kept dry, it is normally most usefully located in the navigation area, which is generally close to the companionway hatch. If spray is ever likely to be a problem, the front of the panel should be protected with a clear plastic screen. (As an added security measure, I do not have opening hatches and portlights in the navigation area.)

- If at all possible, the panel should be close to the boat's batteries to keep heavy cable runs to a minimum.

On larger boats with more complex systems, it generally reduces the amount of cable on the boat and simplifies the wiring harness if there are several panels. Typically, these will include:

- A high-current DC panel, which contains the battery switches and any circuits that bypass the switches (see below), and which is close to the house battery bank (this keeps heavy cable runs to a minimum).
- The main distribution panel in the navigation station.
- Subsidiary panels in the cockpit and engine room, and maybe elsewhere (e.g., the galley).

Panel size and layout. For obvious reasons, it is an ABYC and ISO requirement to maintain some separation between AC and DC panels and wiring. Ideally the panels should be separate, but in practice this is rarely the case, resulting in the requirement that "in the case of systems with combined AC and DC panelboards, the panel shall be designed so that when the panel is open there is no access to energized AC parts without the use of tools" (ABYC). This requirement is generally met by adding a screwed-on cover to the back of the AC section of the panel.

The face of all panels must be marked with the system voltage and its type (AC or DC; Figures 4-70A and 4-70B). A combined panel needs a clear delineation of the two sections of the panel. If a boat has dual DC voltages (12 and 24), these also need to be delineated. On boats with AC motors, a generator, and/or a DC-to-AC inverter, both the ABYC and ISO require AC panels to include an AC voltmeter.

Panel size is a function of available space, budget, and the number of circuits in a boat. In some respects. the ideal (seldom realized) is to have an individual breaker for every circuit on

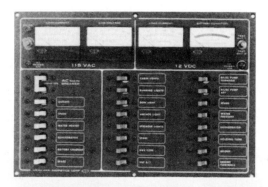

FIGURE 4-70A. Combined AC and DC panel. Note, however, the clear separation of AC and DC breakers, with different colors used for the two sets of breakers. *(Marinetics)*

FIGURE 4-70B. The panel on our new boat, with 12 VDC, 24 VDC, and 120 VAC clearly delineated.

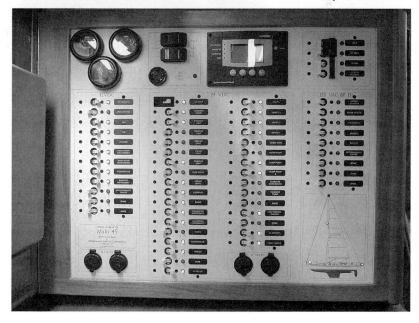

the boat, although this can result in enormous panels, both in terms of size and expense. (The largest panel I ever saw was 6 feet by 3 feet with upward of 200 breakers, each with its own LED light! Note that recent developments in touch-screen controls allow multiple panel functions on small screens—see the end of this chapter.)

Panel organization. With a conventional panel there is almost always a need to develop some logical groupings to cut down on the overall number of breakers. When doing this, it is only natural to think of placing similar fixtures (e.g., lights) on a common breaker, but this is not the best approach. Should the light circuit fail, all the lights will go out at once. It is best to break things up a little and build in some redundancy: for example, have the port-side lights on one breaker and the starboard-side lights on another; the GPS on one breaker and the radar on another; and so on. If you have more than one bilge pump, put them on separate breakers (unless they bypass the distribution panel alto-gether—see below).

Finally, you should have a logical sequence for the breakers in the panel, especially if the panel is a large one; for example, place all the naviga-tion-related breakers in one block, the pumps in another, and so on. If the panel has a switch for backlighting, I like to place it at one corner so that if I'm fumbling around in the dark, it is easy to find and identify.

Panel wiring and breakers. On the DC side of a panel, typically, the positive side of the bat-teries is connected via a battery isolation switch through a *single-pole* main breaker (i.e., it only breaks this one conductor) to a copper or brass bar, known as a *bus bar*, to which a series of circuit breakers are connected. These breakers feed the individual circuits on the boat (Figure 4-71). The ground side of the circuits returns to a second (negative) bus bar, which does not have to be in the panel. (In fact, wiring the panel is simpler if it is not—Figures 4-72A and 4-72B; however, note that the farther the negative bus bar is physically removed from the positive bus

FIGURE 4-72A. Negative bus bars adjacent to a distribution panel.

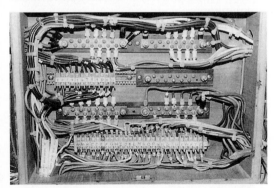

FIGURE 4-72B. Neatly installed bus bars and terminal strips. Note that everything is labeled, which will help in future troubleshooting. The four terminals stacked on one stud at the top left are acceptable under ABYC recommendations but would have been better spread out over a couple of studs. In the lower left the cable sheath reads "Boat Cable"—this is tinned, multi-stranded UL 1426 cable. A spare bus bar (middle right) has been fitted for future needs.

FIGURE 4-71. Beautifully installed circuits.

bar, the greater the potential for the development of magnetic fields and interference—see above.) A single heavy connection is made from the DC negative bus to the boat's *common ground point* and then back to the negative side of the batteries (this ground cable needs to be the same size as the positive cable feeding the DC panel).

AC panels. On the AC side, the shore-power inlet (or onboard AC generator) is wired to the main AC breaker in the panel (sometimes via a polarization or isolation transformer). The breaker *must* be a *two-pole* breaker—i.e., it simultaneously breaks both current-carrying conductors in the circuit—see page 149. From the breaker, the two current-carrying conductors (typically, a hot and a neutral, although in a U.S. 240-volt circuit, it will be two hots) are connected to individual copper bus bars. Breakers connected to the hot bus bar(s) supply the loads. In both a U.S. 120-volt circuit and a European 240-volt circuit, if the boat has polarized AC circuits (almost all do), a series of single-pole breakers feed the individual AC circuits. The neutral side of these circuits is tied to the neutral bus bar. A U.S. 240-volt circuit has no neutral; instead, the load is tied to two 120-volt hot bus bars through a two-pole breaker, which simultaneously breaks both conductors. In all cases, the third green or bare grounding wire in an AC circuit is run from the loads to another (grounding) bus bar.

As with the DC side of a panel, neutral and grounding bus bars do not need to be in the panel; they can be adjacent, but should be close. This considerably reduces the amount of wiring in the panel, simplifying installation and troubleshooting. An AC neutral bus will need a cover to comply with the ABYC/ISO requirement that all exposed current-carrying connections be made within some sort of an enclosure. At no time should more than four connections be stacked up on any terminal on a bus bar or breaker (Figure 4-73). If a breaker serves more than four circuits, a feed can be taken to a bus bar and the individual circuits taken off this bus bar.

Ampere interrupting capacity (AIC). In certain circumstances, the main circuit breakers (AC and DC) may have to break very high amperages. In such a situation, the *points* inside the breaker tend to arc over. The ability of a circuit breaker (or fuse) to safely handle such a situation is described in terms of its *ampere interrrupting capacity* (AIC). On the AC side, the AIC is a function of the rated voltage and current on the circuit, as shown in Table 4-9.

Given that the potential short-circuit current on a DC circuit is related to the size of the battery bank, the AIC on the DC side is a function

FIGURE 4-73. A block of breakers. Note the hot bus bar on the left of the breakers with the individual circuits to the loads on the right. The bus bar shows some signs of corrosion. It is not a good idea to make multiple connections to a breaker as at the upper right (see the text).

of battery capacity (for both 12- and 24-volt circuits) as shown in Table 4-10.

Note that if a battery bank is expanded, the main circuit breaker may need a higher AIC rating. If the circuit breaker does not have the required AIC rating, a fuse with the necessary rating can be installed "upstream"—i.e., closer to the batteries (it may, in any case, already be installed—see below).

Given that the capacity of house battery banks is almost always specified in terms of amp-hours rather than cold cranking amps, it

TABLE 4-9. AIC Ratings for AC Circuit Breakers

Shore-Power Rating (volts)/ AC Generator Rating (amps)	Minimum Ampere Interrupting Capacity (AIC)	
	Main circuit breaker (amps)	Branch circuit breakers (amps)
120/30	3,000	3,000
120/50	3,000	3,000
120, 240/50	5,000	3,000
240/50	5,000	3,000

TABLE 4-10. AIC Ratings for DC Circuit Breakers

Total Connected Battery Capacity (cold cranking amps)	Minimum Ampere Interrupting Capacity (AIC)	
	Main circuit breaker (amps)	Branch circuit breakers (amps)
650 or less	1,500	750
651–1100	3,000	1,500
over 1100	5,000	2,500

will be necessary to check the battery specifications from the manufacturer to translate amp-hours to CCA. You can calculate a crude approximation for deep-cycle wet-type batteries by multiplying the amp-hour rating by 4, and for gel-cells and AGMs by multiplying the amp-hour rating by 5.

Strain relief. The final step in a panel installation is to form all the cables into neat bundles and to fasten them properly against vibration. It is essential to make sure that any battery cables are under no strain since, with their weight, they can occasionally vibrate loose. If a hot cable makes contact with a grounded terminal, there will be an uncontrolled arc welder at work in the back of the panel!

Overcurrent Protection

Once in a while I teach a seminar in Marine Electrics. I have one or two stunts and gimmicks designed to hold the attention of my students. The most exciting moment comes when I create a dead short across a 12-volt battery using a length of 12-gauge (3 mm^2) cable. The moment I throw the switch on the circuit, the cable vaporizes, filling the entire room with a cloud of noxious smoke and forcing us to hastily evacuate the premises (Figures 4-74 and 4-75A to 4-75F)!

I am not suggesting that you should try this experiment, but I bet a fair number of people reading this have already unintentionally set up the same test apparatus on their own boats, or had it set up by someone else. It is done by wiring one or more pieces of equipment directly to the boat's batteries without installing a fuse or circuit breaker at the battery positive connection. *Every single one of these connections without a fuse or a circuit breaker is a cable meltdown waiting to happen.* All it takes to set things in motion is a short to ground (earth), such as may occur if the insulation gets damaged or a terminal comes adrift and contacts a grounded object.

Unfortunately, the plethora of electric circuits

FIGURE 4-74. How a short circuit occurs.

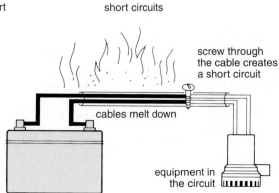

short circuits

screw through the cable creates a short circuit

cables melt down

equipment in the circuit

FIGURES 4-75A TO 4-75F. The effect of a dead short. This sequence of photos was taken over a couple of seconds demonstrating the catastrophic speed with which short circuits can cause major fires and render a boat uninhabitable. The cables had high-quality fire-retardant insulation, which nevertheless burned freely as long as the heat source (the short circuit) was maintained, but ceased burning once the circuit was broken.

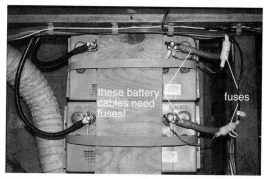

FIGURE 4-76. A neat battery installation with only one heavy cable to each battery post and one light (fused) cable to the positive posts for the monitoring circuits. Hopefully the main positive cables are fused close by!

on modern boats, as compared to boats of even a few years ago, has greatly increased the likelihood of unprotected circuits (Figure 4-76). Worse yet are older boats that have been upgraded by tacking on additional circuits, rather than by rewiring the boat. And worst of all are generally boats on which the owners themselves have done the wiring!

The net result is that nowadays *electrical shorts are without question the number one cause of fires on boats.* Insurance statistics from BoatU.S. show that 55% of boat fires are electrical in origin, of which more than half are caused by short circuits, *most of them in the DC circuits,* with the next biggest electrical category being voltage regulators. By comparison, engine overheating causes 22% of fires, and fuel leaks (almost all on gasoline-engine boats) cause another 8%. So be warned: If you, or anyone else, adds any circuits to your boat, make sure they are properly protected! Better yet, make a complete wiring diagram for your boat and ensure that all existing circuits are properly protected. It is amazing how many boats come from

boatbuilders with one or more unprotected or inadequately protected circuits. (Note that circuits used solely for data transfer between electronic devices are the only ones that do not require overcurrent protection.)

All of which leaves us with three questions:

1. What size fuse or circuit breaker should be used on a given circuit?
2. What is the best practical method for ensuring that all circuits are properly protected?
3. Where in a circuit should overcurrent protection be located?

What size fuse or circuit breaker? There is a popular misconception that fuses and circuit breakers (*overcurrent protection devices*—OPD) should be sized according to the current rating (amperage) of the equipment on a circuit. This line of thinking misunderstands the purpose of the overcurrent device, which is *to prevent the wiring in the circuit from melting down in the event of a short circuit.* Since the most heat in any circuit will be developed by the section of wiring with the highest resistance (the smallest wire), for any given circuit, *an overcurrent device is sized to protect the smallest wire in the circuit.*

For example, if a GPS, which draws minimal current, is hooked into a circuit wired with 12-gauge (3 mm²) cable, the overcurrent device should be rated to protect the wire from melting down, not the GPS. Something on the order of a 20 amp fuse or breaker will do fine. Separate protection (generally a fuse, probably as low as 1 amp) will be needed for the GPS or any other equipment on the circuit.

Having said this, if a circuit breaker in a distribution panel protects a circuit to a single load, and the protection required by the load is less than that required by the cables, the breaker can

---

Simplified Selection Procedure for Overcurrent Protection Devices

1. Determine whether a fuse or a circuit breaker is most appropriate.

2. Determine the ampacity of the smallest cable to be protected by the overcurrent device.

3. Determine the maximum continuous current that will flow on the circuit.

4. Check the AIC ratings tables (Tables 4-9 and 4-10) to find the minimum acceptable AIC for the circuit.

5. Select a fuse or circuit breaker that meets

the AIC rating and that has an amp rating no higher than the cable ampacity and at least as high as the continuous load (as long as this load does not exceed the ampacity of the cable).

6. If this is a circuit to an electric motor, check that the fuse or circuit breaker will respond slowly enough to an overload condition to handle the start-up (inrush) current without nuisance blowing or tripping.

(Adapted from a procedure courtesy Blue Sea Systems)

always be sized to protect the load, down to about 5 amps, which is typically the smallest breaker available. If, on the other hand, the same approach is used for a breaker that protects several circuits, the sizing is a little more complex. Two factors must be considered: (1) the total load of all the electrical equipment to be served by the breaker, and (2) the current-carrying capability of the *smallest* wire being protected (Figure 4-77A). The breaker must be sized according to the *lower* of the total load or current-carrying capability of the smallest conductor.

Subsidiary panels. It should be noted that if a breaker feeds another subsidiary panel or fuse block, and if all the conductors from the panel or fuse block to individual appliances are protected by their own breakers or fuses, the only conductor that the first breaker has to protect is the feeder cable to the subsidiary panel. In this case, the breaker will be rated according to the lower of the total load on the subsidiary panel, or the current-carrying capability of the conductor to the feeder panel (Figure 4-77B). The same design approach governs the sizing of fuses for battery cables. The fuse generally protects the circuit up to the main breaker in the panel, in which case it is sized to protect the smallest cable up to the panel.

Determining ampacity. The current-carrying capability (*ampacity*) of cables is given in Tables 4-4A and 4-4B. These are used to determine the *maximum* circuit breaker or fuse rating (you can always go lower). As with sizing cables, the tem-

perature rating of the cable and the ambient temperature must be taken into account, with the ampacity of any given cable being derated for bundling. If there is not an exact match between cable ampacity and available breaker ratings, ABYC (but not ISO) standards permit the next highest rated breaker to be used on all but main distribution panel breakers (these cannot exceed 100% of the circuit rating), as long as the breaker's rating does not exceed 150% of the ampacity of the cable it is protecting. (For example, if a cable is rated at 17 amps in a given environment, but the only breakers available are rated at 15 and 20 amps, the 20 amp breaker, at 117% of the cable rating, is acceptable.) In practice, given that fuses and breakers can generally handle overload conditions of up to 130% for extended periods (see the Circuit-Breaker Performance sidebar), there should be no need to oversize overcurrent devices.

Electric motors. Electric motors commonly have their own overcurrent protection. If this is not the case, the overcurrent protection on circuits with motors should be rated at 100% of the load, assuming the cable has at least this ampacity. Circuit breakers for motor loads have to be designed to handle the start-up, or inrush, current, which may be up to six times the running load. This requires a circuit breaker with a slow response to overload conditions—generally a thermally operated breaker (see the Circuit-Breaker Performance sidebar).

One situation needs particular attention. If a motor gets into what is known as a *locked-rotor* state (which means the motor is jammed—for example, a bilge pump with a piece of trash in the impeller), its current draw rises sharply, potentially overloading the circuit and/or melting down the pump housing. If the rise in current is high enough and the circuit or motor is properly breakered or fused, the breaker or fuse will trip or blow.

But sometimes, particularly with bilge pumps, there is a long run of marginally sized wiring to the motor. If a locked-rotor condition develops, the *total resistance in the circuit may be sufficient to limit the current flow to a level that will not trip the breaker or blow the fuse but which nevertheless is high enough over time to start a fire.* Using a lower-rated fuse or breaker is not the answer since it may lead to nuisance tripping with normal inrush currents. *The wire size needs to be increased so that the voltage drop on the circuit is lowered to a level at which sufficient current to trip the breaker or blow the fuse can flow.* In any event, the ABYC requires that *all motors and motor circuits be designed and protected in such a way that they can withstand a locked-rotor condition for 7 hours without creating a fire hazard.*

FIGURE 4-77A. The smallest cable in a circuit determines the level of overcurrent protection.

FIGURE 4-77B. Overcurrent protection of feeder cables and subsidiary circuits.

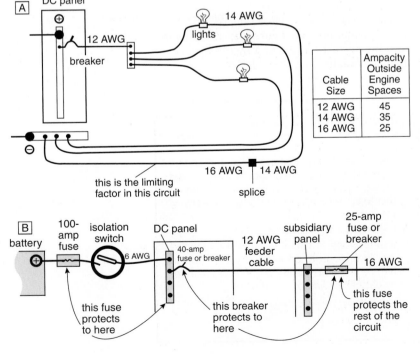

Cable Size	Ampacity Outside Engine Spaces
12 AWG	45
14 AWG	35
16 AWG	25

(Typically, if the motor may melt down it is given an internal heat-sensitive trip device; some of these devices reset themselves once the motor has cooled off, and some need manual resetting.)

High-current circuits. Historically, high-current DC circuits (100 amps and up) have been the hardest to protect simply because of the lack of affordable overcurrent protection devices. This is no longer the case. Relatively cheap (and compact) breakers rated at up to 150 amps are widely available, together with cheap (and compact) fuses up to 800 amps (Ample Technology, Xantrex, Blue Sea Systems [www.bluesea.com], and others). There is simply no excuse for not protecting all high-current circuits, including the cranking circuit.

However, these circuits have large cables that are awkward to handle. The neatest way to deal with them, and provide the necessary protection, is to run a single heavy cable, normally 2/0 gauge (70 mm^2), from the positive post on the house batteries to a battery isolation switch. This cable is fused as close to the battery as possible, with an appropriately sized fuse. (For example, UL 1426 BC5W2 [i.e., 105°C] 2/0 AWG [70 mm^2] cable has a current-carrying capability—ampacity—of 330 amps outside engine rooms, and 280 amps inside engine rooms.)

Another cable (the same size as the first) is run from the isolation switch to a high-current bus bar, which is nothing more than a heavy metal plate drilled and tapped to take a series of bolts. The cable from the isolation switch is bolted to the bus bar. The bus bar is mounted on a phenolic, or plastic, base plate, with another series of bolts set up parallel to the bolts in the bus bar. Fuses are bolted in place between the bus bar and these (electrically isolated) bolts. Now we can attach the boat's various high-current circuits (typically a windlass, a high-output alternator, the DC panel, and maybe sail reefing

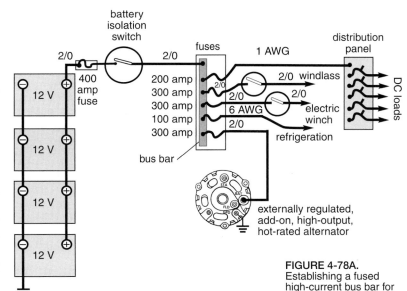

FIGURE 4-78A. Establishing a fused high-current bus bar for the high-load circuits on a boat.

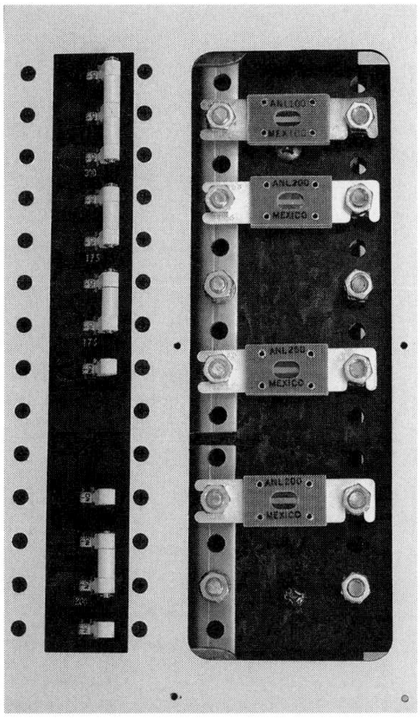

FIGURE 4-78B. A fused bus bar in the high-current panel for our latest boat. There is room for additional circuits. Note the break in the bus bar about one third of the way up—some of the circuits are on the battery side of the battery isolation switch, and some are on the load (downstream) side.

Cables in Parallel

On DC-loaded boats, particularly those that are using 12 volts and have not gone to 24 volts, I increasingly see high-load requirements met by running two smaller cables in parallel rather than one very large cable (e.g., two 2/0 AWG [70 mm^2] cables, as opposed to a single 4/0 AWG [110 mm^2] cable). The primary reason is because the smaller cables are easier to run.

This practice is acceptable as long as the parallel cables are properly overcurrent protected. You can either tie the end terminals together and protect both cables with a single fuse or breaker that is sized on the basis of just *one* of the cables, or else provide separate protection for each cable.

What is *not* acceptable is to provide a single fuse or breaker sized on the aggregate ampacity of the paralleled cables. The reason is that if one of the cables is accidentally disconnected, the amp rating of the overcurrent protection device will now considerably exceed the ampacity of the remaining cable(s), creating a fire risk if there is a short circuit.

Copper is the standard material used for electric cables, terminals, and bus bars. However, brass (and sometimes bronze) is often also used for bus bars. It is a little known fact that brass has only 28% of the electrical conductivity of copper, while some bronzes are as low as 7%. In other words, to safely carry the same current as a copper bus bar, a brass bus bar needs to have four times the cross-sectional area, and a bronze bar needs up to twelve times. Consequently large bus bars are needed to carry high currents. The use of undersized brass bus bars is quite common; faced with continuous high currents, they can get hot enough to start a fire.

Stainless steel has only 3% of the electrical conductivity of copper; in other words, it is a poor conductor. The use of stainless steel bolts and washers is common in high-current circuits. *Any cable terminal bolted down with a stainless steel bolt must be in direct contact with the bus bar it is bolted to.* If a stainless steel washer is allowed to come between a cable terminal and the bus bar (which is not that uncommon), the washer will put a resistance in the circuit. This resistance will not only impair the performance of the equipment in the circuit, but can also create a great deal of heat—sometimes enough to start a fire. Because there is no short circuit, and therefore no excessively high current flows, a fuse or circuit breaker will not protect against this kind of a fire. I have seen several fires that began this way.

Note that if a terminal is only loosely attached to a bus bar (or anything else, for that matter), it will tend to arc whenever current flows (whenever the equipment is turned on). The higher the current flow, the more powerful the arc, and the greater the risk of starting a fire

(Figures 4-79A and 4-79B). Once again, a fuse will do nothing to protect against this kind of a fault because it is not an overcurrent situation. *It is imperative that every connection in a high-current circuit be well bolted down, preferably with a Nylok nut or a similar fastener that will not vibrate loose.* As noted in Chapter 1, high-output alternators need special attention given the inherent vibration in the installation.

Very often high-current devices are mounted on some kind of a plastic base (e.g., many bus bars and fuse holders; I am using "plastic" in a very broad sense) or else incorporate a plastic housing (e.g., battery switches). *It is essential that no part of the plastic is ever compressed between the fasteners or metal surfaces that hold cable terminals in place.* This is because the plastic may deform over time, or may soften if the connection gets hot, loosening the contact with the cable terminal, and creating a risk of arcing leading to a fire (I have seen this a number of times).

This is particularly important with many battery switches. The terminal posts often come out through the (plastic) battery housing. There is then a nut on each terminal post that holds it in place in the housing, with another nut to hold the cable terminal on the post. In spite of the fact that the terminal posts come through the plastic housing, the cable terminal is trapped between two nuts, and thus there is solid metal-to-metal contact on both sides of the cable terminal. However, if you remove the inner nut (the one that holds the terminal post in the battery housing), and then add a cable terminal and tighten the outer nut, the cable terminal is now trapped between the plastic housing and the outer nut, creating a fire risk. All too often I see battery switches on which the inner nut has been removed in order to stack additional cable terminals on the terminal post. *This must never be done!* If the terminal post is not long enough to take the connections you wish to stack on it (remember, there should not be more than four), you need to run a cable from the switch to a separate bus bar and then connect the other cable terminals at the bus bar.

Finally, here's a neat idea from a reader for covering positive bus bars to prevent short circuits with nearby grounded circuits or components (it also works for weatherproofing in damp locations): Place the bus bar in a Tupperware or similar container and drill tight-fitting holes for the cables. The lid will come off easily for access and make a watertight seal when in place.

FIGURE 4-79A. A terminal with an oversized hole in a windlass installation resulted in a poor connection that generated enough heat to char the surrounding insulation. The first time this boat runs aground and the skipper tries to kedge off, subjecting the windlass circuit to a sustained high load, the boat is likely to catch fire!

FIGURE 4-79B. A loose nut in this shoreside inlet caused an expensive fire.

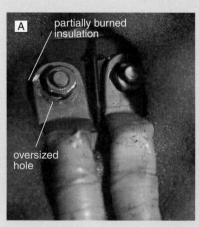

A
partially burned insulation
oversized hole

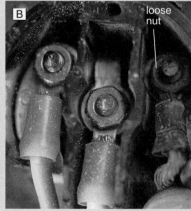

B
loose nut

devices) to these isolated bolts (Figures 4-78A and 4-78B). The various fuses are sized according to the current-carrying capability of the cables bolted to them. For example, a windlass may well need a 2/0 cable with a 300 amp fuse, while a distribution panel will normally have cables on the order of 4-gauge, protected with a fuse of around 150 amps.

Cranking batteries. If the boat has an isolated cranking battery (as recommended in Chapter 1), there should be an in-line fuse close to the battery in the cable to the starter motor. To prevent this fuse blowing under a heavy cranking load (such as occurs in cold weather), it should be a *slow blow fuse* (see the Fuse Performance sidebar) and rated at 150% or more of the ampacity of the cranking cables (even overrated like this, the fuse will still protect against a meltdown if the starter motor or its cables short out—see page 190). If the boat has two battery banks, alternated in use, with the cranking circuit coming off whatever bank is in service, the two banks will be wired to a "1, 2, BOTH, OFF" switch, with fuses at the batteries in the two feeder cables. The output of the switch will go to the high-current bus bar, as above, and the cranking circuit will simply be another of the fused circuits coming off the bus bar, with its fuse rated as described.

Circuits that bypass the isolation switch.

Some circuits will still need to bypass the isolation switch so they may be left on when the rest of the boat is shut down. These circuits typically include a bilge pump and any charging devices (e.g., solar panels, maybe a wind generator, and the inverter if it also doubles as a battery charger) that need to be left on when the boat is not in use (other examples are a carbon monoxide or propane alarm, DC systems monitoring devices, power supplies to electronics with a memory function, and sometimes a fridge and freezer). All but the inverter are wired to a separate auxiliary bus bar that is fed by a fused cable tied into the *battery* side of the isolation switch. Each circuit is, in turn, fused at the bus bar (Figure 4-80). Given the heavy cable likely to be associated with the inverter, it is best to wire the inverter directly to the terminal on the switch and provide it with its own fuse as close to the switch as possible.

The net result of such an approach is that *every single circuit on the boat will be fully overcurrent protected at its source.* However, if you wire as suggested, the circuits that bypass the battery switch are fused but not switched; in other words, they can never be turned off. I like it this way since it prevents the bilge pump and other key circuits from being accidentally turned off,

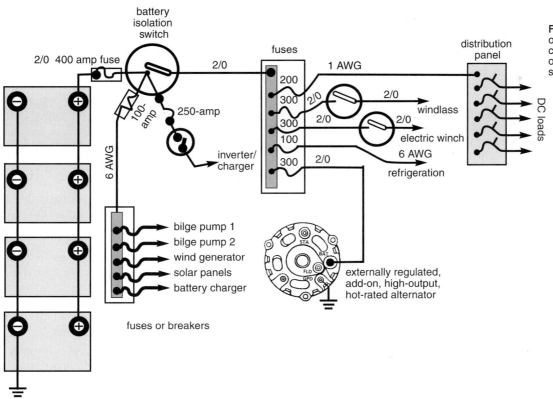

FIGURE 4-80. Providing overcurrent protection for circuits on the battery side of the battery isolation switch.

FIGURES 4-81A AND 4-81B. The high-current panel I designed for our latest boat (front and back). It combines battery isolation switches and overcurrent protection for all the high-current circuits on the boat and those on the battery side of the isolation switches, in a single neat, standards-compliant package (manufactured by MMES—www.wewire boats.com).

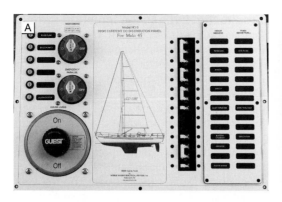

but others prefer a switch or circuit breaker in this circuit (Figures 4-81A and 4-81B).

Overcurrent protection location. The goal of overcurrent protection is to provide protection at the *source of power* for each circuit. With DC circuits, the overcurrent protection is always placed in the positive side of DC circuits, never in the negative side. (Apart from anything else, an unbroken connection to DC negative needs to be maintained at all times to protect against stray current corrosion. Note that some European boatbuilders install a battery switch in the DC negative side as well as on the positive side, but this is not recommended.)

Power source. The ultimate source of power for any DC circuit is the battery, but the practical source of power is the connection point of the circuit to the DC system. This point may be at the battery, the battery switch, the distribution panel or a subsidiary panel, some distribution bus bar, or other connecting point.

If the cables in the new circuit are no smaller than the cable that feeds the new circuit's point of connection, then the overcurrent protection for the feeder cable will protect the new circuit—no additional protection is needed. The same will apply even if the feeder cable is larger than the cables in the new circuit—if the feeder cable's overcurrent protection has been downsized to the point at which it effectively protects the new circuit. But if the new circuit is not adequately protected by overcurrent devices already in place, additional protection is required *at its point of connection*, i.e., at its source of power.

7-, 40-, and 72-inch rules. Sometimes there are physical limitations as to how close an overcurrent protection device can be placed to the source of power (and in any case, fuses, circuit breakers, and switches should not be installed in battery compartments because of the risk of corrosion coupled with the potential presence of explosive gases). The question then arises, how close is close enough? The generic answer for

the ISO is within 200 mm of the source of power; for the ABYC it is within 7 inches (pretty much the same thing).

Both organizations allow certain exceptions, with the ISO being more liberal. If the 200 mm is "impractical," "each conductor shall be contained within a protective covering, such as sheathing, conduit or cable trunking, for its entire length from the source of power to the circuit breaker or fuse." How far you can go without overcurrent protection is limited only by your interpretation of "impractical."

The ISO specifically exempts altogether a couple of circuits from the overcurrent requirement. These are "the main power feed circuit from the battery to the engine-cranking motor, if sheathed or supported to protect against abrasion and contact with conductive surfaces" and "the main power feed from the battery to the panelboard (switchboard), distribution panel or fuse block, if sheathed or supported to protect against abrasion and contact with conductive surfaces."

The ABYC has similar, but more restrictive language, driven in part by U.S. Coast Guard requirements for boats with gasoline engines (either main engines or generator engines). The exceptions to the "7-inch rule" are as follows (Figure 4-82):

• A cable connected *directly to a battery* that is also "contained throughout its entire distance in a sheath or enclosure such as a conduit, junction box, control box or enclosed panel" must have its overcurrent protection "as close as practicable to the battery, but not to exceed 72 inches (1.83 m)." Note the "as close as practicable" phrase, which is relatively new language. There is no longer the blanket 72-inch allowance that there used to be.

• A cable connected to a *source of power other than the battery* (i.e., connected to the battery switch, the distribution panel, or some other point in the DC circuits) that is similarly contained in a sheath, etc., must have its overcur-

Fuse Performance

The performance of fuses is defined by a number of factors, including:

- The *rated voltage.* Typical ratings are 32, 60, 125, 300, 500, 600, and 750 volts. The rated voltage specifies the maximum circuit voltage for which a fuse can be used without affecting its *interrupting (breaking) capacity* (AIC—see below). If the circuit voltage is lower than the rated voltage, that is OK. Note that for a given fuse, the rated voltage may be less in DC applications than it is in AC.

- The *minimum fusing current* is the current (amperage) at which a fuse just reaches the temperature at which it will melt, after which small increases in current or temperature will cause it to melt (blow). The minimum fusing current is always significantly higher than the actual rated amperage of a fuse. The relationship between the two is described by the *fusing factor,* which typically varies between 1.25 and 2.00 (i.e., the minimum fusing current is 1.25 to 2.00 times higher than the rated amperage).

- The *rated amperage* is the nominal amperage of the fuse (the amperage printed on its body). It is commonly and incorrectly assumed to be the maximum current the fuse or circuit breaker can carry before it blows or trips, when in actuality the rated amperage is considerably less, depending on the fusing factor. In other words, all fuses can indefinitely carry more than their rated current.

- The *melting time* (also called the *pre-arcing time*) is the time interval between the moment when a current above the minimum fusing current starts to flow to the time when the fuse blows. The higher the current above the minimum fusing current, the shorter the melting time. The melting time is shown in graphs that display the current against the melting time (the *time-current characteristic*).

- A *fast blow* fuse is one in which the melting time reduces rapidly with small increases in current above the minimum fusing current (i.e., the fuse blows rapidly—it has little *thermal delay*); a *slow blow* fuse is one in which the melting time reduces slowly as the current rises above the minimum fusing current (i.e., the fuse blows slowly—it has substantial *thermal delay*).

- The *ampere interrupting (breaking) capacity* (AIC) is the maximum current (amperage) a fuse can safely interrupt at its rated voltage. For a given fuse, it is usually considerably less in DC applications than it is in AC. If the AIC is exceeded, the fuse may arc over and fail to break its circuit.

- *Ignition protection* is required in many applications on boats that have gasoline engines (either the main engine or a generator engine).

Given that the minimum fusing current is always higher than the rated current, in normal circumstances it always takes more than the rated current to make a fuse blow. How much more is a function of the fusing factor. This varies according to fuse type and manufacturer and even nationality (European standards tend to use a higher fusing factor—i.e., it takes more current to blow a fuse with the same rating as a U.S. fuse).

Given that a fuse is a thermal device (it is activated by a change in temperature), its performance is affected by the ambient temperature: the higher the ambient temperature, the warmer the fuse will be before any current flows, and the less current will be needed to blow the fuse. Fuses in hot engine rooms may well be effectively derated by up to 20%, bringing the minimum fusing current down to something close to the rated current. Any kind of resistance in a fuse holder, such as that caused by corrosion on fuse contacts, will also cause localized heating, effectively derating the fuse. Faced with nuisance blowing, you should always check the ambient temperature and look for corroded or resistive connections.

Fast blow fuses are used to protect sensitive electronics that cannot tolerate extended overcurrent and overvoltage situations. Slow blow fuses are used to minimize the chances of nuisance blowing on circuits that have high inrush currents (e.g., electric motors, which typically and momentarily draw four to six times more current on start-up than when running). For general circuit protection, a slow blow fuse is normally preferable to a fast blow fuse because it will still provide ultimate short-circuit protection while minimizing the chances of nuisance blowing.

---

rent protection "as close as practicable to the point of connection to the source of power, but not to exceed 40 inches (1.02 m)." Once again, the "as close as practicable" phrase is relatively new language in contrast to the former blanket acceptance of 40 inches.

- "Overcurrent protection is not required in conductors from self-limiting alternators with integral regulators if the conductor is less than 40 inches (1.02 m), is connected to a source of power other than the battery, and is contained throughout its entire distance in a

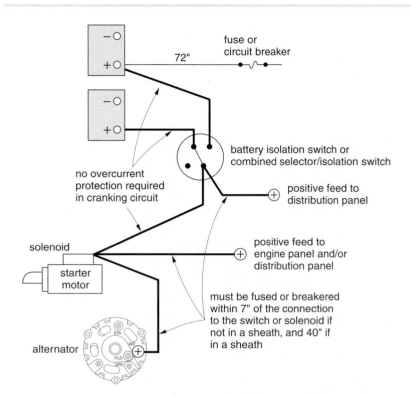

fuse or
circuit breaker

72"

battery isolation switch or
combined selector/isolation switch

no overcurrent
protection required
in cranking circuit

positive feed to
distribution panel

solenoid

positive feed to
engine panel and/or
distribution panel

starter
motor

must be fused or breakered
within 7" of the connection
to the switch or solenoid if
not in a sheath, and 40" if
in a sheath

alternator

STA
BAT
FLD
GRD

FIGURE 4-82. Maximum unfused or unbreakered cable lengths under ABYC standards. Note that although the ABYC accepts unprotected cables up to the lengths shown, it is preferable to provide full overcurrent protection *at the batteries for all cables* (see the text).

sheath or enclosure." This exception covers the standard alternator that comes with a marine engine or generator, and that is wired to the starter motor solenoid, and from there to the batteries, and which is almost never overcurrent protected. Note that if the alternator is replaced by a high-output alternator with an external regulator, or even an alternator with an internal regulator but which is wired back to the batteries, or if a second alternator is fitted with an external regulator or wired back to the batteries, the new alternator needs overcurrent protection at its connection to the source of power—i.e., wherever it ties into the DC system (for more on this, see below).

- As with the ISO, cranking motor circuits are not required to have overcurrent protection. This exception originates in the automotive field where starter motor cables are short and well secured. In the marine field where cranking circuits may be long, a hazard may be created. If a car catches fire, the occupants can pull over and jump out; if a boat catches fire, it is not so simple. *It makes no sense to have any unprotected circuits on a boat.* Protecting cranking circuits, however, is problematic. In cold weather, the inrush current on a 12-volt starter motor may be as high as 1,500 amps; the cranking current may be as much as 200 amps. Typically, cranking cables are undersized even for the cranking current, let alone the inrush

current. This situation does not pose a safety problem because these currents are only sustained for a few seconds, so the cables do not have time to get hot enough to create a fire hazard. But if overcurrent protection is based on the ampacity of the cables (as required by ISO and ABYC standards for all other circuits), any fuse will blow whenever the engine is cranked. My response is to oversize the fuse to avoid nuisance blowing, knowing that in the event of a dead short, the very high current flows will cause it to blow (for the typical auxiliary diesel with a 12-volt starter motor, I use a 300 amp slow blow fuse). Given that the standards require no fusing in the cranking circuit, I am not concerned by the fact that this fuse does not comply with the general prescription for sizing overcurrent devices.

Charging devices. We now have to consider an issue that is routinely overlooked and misunderstood. All alternators, battery chargers, DC generators, wind generators, and solar panels are technically a "source of power." To comply with the standards, the cables connected to them need to be overcurrent protected within 200 mm/7 inches of their connection to the charging device, except that the ABYC (but not the ISO) exempts "self-limiting devices." This exception covers solar panels, internally regulated alternators (and possibly all alternators, including externally regulated alternators—it's arguable), and wind generators that are based on alternators (as opposed to those built around electric motors—see Chapter 5). It does not cover most battery chargers, which, as a result, either need internal overcurrent protection (a built-in fuse or breaker) or additional external protection within 200 mm/7 inches of the output terminals. Also it may not cover externally regulated alternators, in which case a fuse is required within 7 inches of the output terminal (this fuse is almost never fitted).

Check your own boat. As the electrical load on boats increases, so too does the complexity of electrical circuits, and the potential for short circuits and electrical fires. It is more important than ever to wire all circuits with proper overcurrent protection, and yet so often this protection is omitted. I urge you to take a close look at all the cables attached to your battery positive posts, and if you find any that are unfused, take immediate steps to correct the situation. It will be time and money well spent. A fire at sea can be a terrifying experience. Smoke billowing out of the companionway hatch is not the way to find out that your boat is improperly wired!

Circuit-Breaker Performance

The performance of circuit breakers is defined by similar factors as for fuses, including:

- The *rated voltage*. Note that some circuit breakers are specified for AC only, others for both DC and AC. In the latter case, the DC voltage is generally much less than the AC. When using circuit breakers on DC circuits, it is important to ensure that the breaker really is suitable for the circuit in question.

- The *rated amperage* is the circuit breaker's nominal current-carrying capability, but in fact is significantly less than the current it takes to make the breaker trip.

- The *tripping amperage*. Generally the tripping amperage is at least 130% of the rated amperage at ambient temperature. (Many thermal circuit breakers will carry 140% of their rated amperage for up to an hour before tripping.)

- The *trip time* is the time it takes the breaker to trip at a given level of overcurrent (the equivalent of the melting time with a fuse). It is given in a graph that shows current against time (Figure 4-83). Just as with a fuse, a breaker can be fast acting or slower acting—the latter are needed primarily on electric-motor circuits where the inrush current to the motor may be several times its operating current.

- The *ampere interrupting capacity* (AIC) is the maximum current (amperage) the breaker can safely interrupt at its rated voltage. It is usually considerably less in DC applications than in AC applications. If the AIC is exceeded, the breaker may arc over and fail to break its circuit. Circuit breakers fall into two AIC categories: (1) those that will meet the AIC target but will not be operable afterward (in the U.S. they are tested to a standard known as UL 1077; in Europe to PC1), and (2) those that will meet the AIC target and still remain operable (they are tested to UL 489 or PC2). UL 489/PC2 is a much tougher standard (the breaker has to remain operable), so circuit breakers with this label are higher quality than those tested to UL 1077/PC1. Sometimes a breaker is tested to both standards, in which case the AIC rating is likely to be higher when tested to UL 1077/PC1 than for UL 489/PC2.

- *Ignition protection is* required in many applications on boats that have gasoline engines (either the main engine or a generator engine).

continued

Magnetic Circuit Breaker Trip Time Versus Current
Typical time/current characteristices at +23°C/+73.4°F
(trip time at rated current)

Curve F1 (instantaneous) for DC

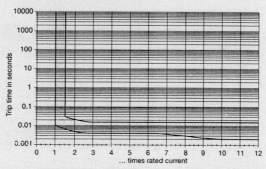

Curve K1 (short delay) for DC

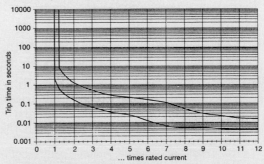

Curve M1 (medium delay) for DC

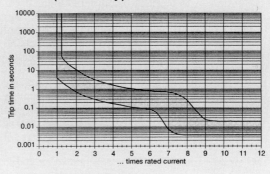

Curve T1 (long delay) for DC

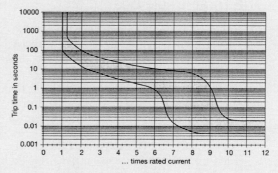

FIGURE 4-83. Trip time curves for a high-quality (UL 489/PC2) circuit breaker from ETA (www.e-t-a.com), ranging from instantaneous to long delay. *(Courtesy E-T-A)*

There are two broad categories of breakers: thermal and magnetic. Thermal breakers heat up as current passes through them; once a certain temperature is exceeded, the breaker trips. In high ambient temperatures, they may be subject to nuisance tripping (for every 10°F/5°C rise in temperature above 80°F/ 26.7°C, they are derated by approximately 10%). On the other hand, they tend to respond more slowly than magnetic breakers to over-current situations, and as such, are suited to circuits with high start-up or inrush currents (e.g., motor circuits). They are also very tolerant of shock and vibration. However, given the wide range of ambient temperatures in which boats operate, they are not always well suited to this environment; they work better in homes and similar environments where the temperature is more or less constant.

Magnetic breakers sense the magnitude of the current magnetically and are unaffected by temperature, making them the breaker of choice in many marine applications. They tend to respond faster than thermal breakers to overcurrent situations, which makes them appropriate for circuits that are not tolerant of high surge currents, but they can be a liability in motor circuits.

Magnetic and thermal features can be combined, with additional "hydraulic" elements thrown in, to produce different response characteristics such as a high tolerance for inrush currents but a very rapid response in the event of a short circuit. If you need specialized circuit protection, you should consult circuit breaker manufacturers.

Some breakers can be overridden manually (i.e., held "on" even though the fault condition still exists). These breakers are not acceptable to the ABYC and ISO. *Trip-free* breakers are needed, which cannot be overridden or reset until the overcurrent condition has been eliminated. The ABYC and ISO also do not accept circuit breakers that automatically reset themselves (known in Europe as "J-type" breakers); the exception is some thermal breakers on equipment that has additional overcurrent protection in the feeder circuit.

The degree to which a circuit breaker is designed to also function as a switch (i.e., routinely make and break circuits under load) varies considerably. Some will be damaged by repeated use in this fashion, while others will not. In Europe, the "M-type" breaker is designed for occasional manual disconnection but is not intended for regular use as a switch, while the "S-type" breaker is designed for regular use as a switch. Handles may be the toggle or rocker type. The marine industry seems to have standardized on the toggle type that can be easily knocked off or on by accident, even though the rocker type is far less prone to such accidents.

Electronic (solid-state) circuit breakers are becoming more common. They are compact and economical, can be precisely regulated, and can incorporate all kinds of other features such as current-monitoring capabilities (see The Three-Cable Boat section). However, many automatically reset themselves (and thus violate the trip-free requirement); few meet the AIC requirements of the ABYC standards; and, if they fail, most fail in the closed (shorted) position, as opposed to circuit breakers that tend to fail in the open position. In most applications, they do not comply with current ABYC standards (which are based on traditional circuit-breaker technology). However, they are widely used in DC circuits on aircraft, for which there are rigorous safety standards. There is ongoing discussion as to whether or not the ABYC standards should be revised.

The Three-Cable Boat

Modern electrically loaded boats have substantial wiring harnesses that are complex, heavy, and expensive both in terms of cable costs and installation time. The primary reason for this is the centralization of switching functions at the main distribution panel and at subsidiary distribution panels, using switches (normally circuit breakers) placed in the power feeds to all the devices on the boat. This requires the power feeds to almost all devices to be led from the panel switches (circuit breakers) to the devices themselves, resulting in a large bundle of cables coming off the back of even modest-sized panels, with the majority of these cables being run in parallel with other cables for much of their length. We end up with a huge amount of cabling—thousands of feet on even a midsize boat, weighing hundreds of pounds.

Remotely operated switches. Let's imagine a different approach to switching loads, in which two heavy cables—one positive and one negative—are run down the center of the boat: a "two-wire bus." Wherever we want to install a piece of equipment, we tap into this two-wire bus at the closest point to our equipment. For each piece of equipment, we add a switch at the point of the positive connection to the two-wire

Heat Issues Again

As noted previously, most circuit breakers and fuses are tested on the assumption that they will be installed in circuits using 60°C/140°F cables. In other words, the temperature of the attached cables will not go above 60°C/140°F. On boats (particularly in the United States), cables with a 105°C/221°F temperature rating are commonly used. If the cables in a circuit are sized so that they will be operated at or near their maximum ampacity for extended periods of time, the heat generated by 105°C/221°F cables will effectively derate fuses and thermal circuit breakers.

In practice, if cables are sized to minimize voltage drop, they will almost never be operated at their rated ampacity, which will keep the temperature down. The cables most likely to be pushed to their limits for extended periods of time are the DC cables feeding a DC-to-AC inverter on a boat that works the inverter hard (see The Inverter-Based Boat section in Chapter 2). Because of the large cables required, they are often sized close to rated ampacity. Every effort should be made to install larger cables.

bus. This switch performs the function of the switch in the distribution panel or subpanel.

If you think about it for a moment, you will see that such an approach eliminates every piece of paralleled cabling on the boat. *This removes more than half the cabling from most boats, and almost completely eliminates those large bundles of cables found on most contemporary boats.* There are major potential savings to be had in terms of installation time, wiring harness weight, and cost. Wiring complexity is massively reduced, as is the likelihood of any problems, and troubleshooting wiring problems that do occur is greatly simplified. The downside, of course, is that the circuit (load) switches end up in all kinds of inconvenient and inaccessible places.

But now let's imagine for a moment that we can operate our switches remotely, and that all that is required to do this is a single data cable (a *data bus*) run through the boat in parallel with the two-wire bus, with each of the remotely operated switches wired to this data cable, and the data cable hooked into one or more touch-pad control panels that can be placed anywhere on the boat. We have removed the principal difficulty that stands in the way of scattering the load switches all over the boat. *The single data cable now replaces every section of paralleled load cabling on a contemporary boat.* We have what is known as a *distributed power* system.

We can use this data cable for something else. On most modern boats there is a mass of data cables, also run in parallel, which includes cables from the depth and speed transducers, wind instruments, and various navigational electronics. Then there's the data coming from what may be literally dozens of sensing devices scattered throughout the boat, measuring such things as battery voltage and temperature, alternator temperature, amperage at different points, engine water and oil temperature, oil pressure,

engine speed, exhaust temperature, and so on. All of this data can, in principal, go down the same data cable. The engine harness is reduced to a positive and negative power cable and a data cable; the eleven cables to the systems monitor are reduced to multiple connection points to the boat's data cable; all other networking cables are replaced by this data cable; and so on.

We have, in effect, a three-cable boat—two power cables and a data cable!

The technology for such a boat already exists, and in fact is widely used in the automotive field and in industrial controls, and is being applied in marine engine controls and integrated navigation systems. The potential for applying this technology to power distribution on boats is becoming increasingly recognized, with more and more companies entering the field. The competition is underway to see which specific approach, or approaches, will become dominant.

The overcurrent protection challenge. It is possible to take a conventional circuit breaker or switch that complies with UL and ABYC standards and add components and circuitry to make it remotely operable (a remotely operated circuit breaker—ROCB), and in fact this is presently done in a number of applications, notably remotely operated battery switches with overcurrent protection. However, there are issues related to response time, cycle life, and the power consumption required to do this. As a result, the focus for remote switching has been almost entirely on using solid-state devices, notably what are known as metal oxide semiconductor field effect transistors (MOSFETs) because these can be configured to turn on and off just about any current level (amperage) at an economical cost, while being relatively easy to control via very low power, remotely operated circuits.

In the kind of system envisaged, with direct connection of branch circuits to a two-wire bus via remotely operated switches, the switches must provide branch circuit protection as defined in UL, ABYC, and other standards (the principal relevant standards are UL 1077, UL 489, and ABYC E-11). As noted above, there is ongoing discussion within the ABYC and other standards-writing organizations as to what these requirements mean in the context of solid-state switching (as opposed to conventional switching, which operates by making and closing an air gap between two points). In any event, it seems that in and of themselves most of the existing (2005) MOSFET-based electronic circuit breakers (ECBs) do not meet these requirements (in particular, when they fail, they tend to fail shorted and not open), and as such do not qualify as branch circuit breakers: additional circuit protection is needed for standards compliance.

As a result, in order to ensure compliance with branch circuit breaker requirements, most solid-state circuit breaker manufacturers are currently moving down a similar path, which is to cluster a number of ECBs in a power distribution module. In these modules, each ECB circuit is protected by a conventional circuit breaker and/or a fuse that meets the AIC and other requirements, with the ECB serving as a switching relay and overload protector. This represents a halfway technology on the road to economical, standards-compliant, remotely operated, stand-alone electronic circuit breakers.

Power distribution modules (PDMs).

Although power distribution modules as currently manufactured are conceptually similar to a conventional subpanel on a boat, there are some important differences. Because the individual electronic circuit breakers in such a box can be remotely operated from any appropriate panel wired into the data circuit (and even with wireless devices, or through a cell phone or the Internet, given the appropriate bridges or gateways), unlike a subpanel these boxes do not need to be readily accessible: they can be placed at any convenient location close to the loads they are controlling, with significant potential savings in cabling and installation time.

When it comes to the circuit breakers within these boxes, a manufacturer typically uses a single electronic circuit breaker design that has a maximum amperage rating (determined by the ampacity of the MOSFETs within it) high enough to handle the highest load it is intended to protect and/or switch (i.e., it is designed for the worst-case amps load). The breaker circuitry includes a device that measures current flow through the circuit. The breaker control circuit is such that it can be programmed to trip at any amperage up to the breaker's maximum amp rating. This enables the exact same breaker to be used for multiple amp ratings, with the rating determined through the software program, not through the breaker's physical construction.

Most of these breakers can be reprogrammed to a different trip value or a different set of trip characteristics (e.g., time delay) in situ, either via the data bus control panel or by plugging the appropriate device into the data circuit. A boatbuilder can build a boat with all the same breakers, and then program them individually to appropriate trip characteristics once the boat is finished—and change the trip characteristics if the equipment on the circuit is modified. The nature of the control circuits is such that much more precise trip characteristics are possible than with conventional magnetic or thermal circuit breakers.

The current (amperage) measuring device and small microprocessor found in electronic circuit breakers result in the opportunity for some really interesting and creative uses for these breakers. For example, a bilge pump breaker might be programmed to:

- Intermittently turn on the bilge pump and monitor the current (amp) draw. If it is above a certain level, it signifies water in the bilge, so the pump stays on until the current draw drops to a dry bilge level. This gets rid of those troublesome float switches.

- Shut down the pump and trigger an alarm if the current draw goes too high, signifying a locked rotor or some other problem. This eliminates the primary cause of motor burnout.

- Trigger an alarm if the pump stays on for more than a certain length of time, indicating excess water in the bilge.

- Log whenever the pump comes on, and for how long, and store this data to be displayed later at the boat's control panel, sounding an alarm if the pump comes on more often than usual (signifying water ingress of some sort).

In other words, unlike traditional circuit breakers, electronic breakers have the potential to operate as "smart" devices, with powerful circuit control and diagnostic features. At the most basic level, anytime the current flow on a circuit goes above normal, the operator can be alerted. The greater the number of sensing devices wired into the data bus shared by the circuit breaker, and the more information there is on the bus, the greater the potential for creative engineering in terms of what remotely operated electronic circuit breakers and switches can be programmed to do. There is a whole world opening up here, the surface of which has been barely scratched.

Hurdles. There are certain hurdles that still have to be overcome. In order for any device to communicate on a data bus and to be remotely controlled via the bus, all devices on the bus must "speak" a common "language." This requires a transceiver (a mini microprocessor, often simply called a chip) at each device that will serve as the interface between the device and the bus. There are numerous chips that have come out of the automotive and industrial controls fields that are currently being investigated for use in boat systems. Key issues include:

- Cost.
- Ensuring that "mission critical" messages get through.
- Protecting the data bus and other components of the physical layer against voltage spikes, radio frequency interference, and the marine atmosphere.
- Keeping the "parasitic" power requirements (the energy required to run the chips and the microprocessors in the keypads, and to put data on the bus) down to an acceptable level (once you start to remotely operate a large number of devices, this load can climb to several amps at 12 volts, which is a major energy overhead on an energy-conscious boat).
- Making the data transfer fast enough for specific applications (for example, when you switch a light on and off, you expect a near-instantaneous response, but depth information only needs to be transmitted every second); in general, the higher the data transmission speed, the greater the energy used.
- Having sufficient bandwidth on the bus to handle all the data likely to be put on it (including future additions); distributed power systems require relatively low bandwidth whereas radar, electronic charting, and video require high bandwidth, so we are, in fact, likely to end up with two or more data buses on a boat (resulting in a four- or even a five-cable boat).
- Devising an *open system*, which allows access to any manufacturer (as opposed to a proprietary system controlled by one manufacturer).
- Ensuring that the system is adaptable to future changes without requiring a specialist to reprogram existing installations every time a new device is introduced.
- Providing a "limp-home" capability for essential circuits in the event the boat's electronics are wiped out.

These kinds of issues are close to being resolved. It is my sense that by the time I write the next edition of this book, distributed power systems will have fully come of age and the wave of complexity in boat electrical systems that engulfed the boating industry in the latter part of the twentieth century will have crested and will be receding. I have high hopes that over the next decade the three-cable (or four- or five-cable) boat will greatly simplify wiring harnesses and significantly improve the reliability of onboard electrical circuits. It will not, however, change any of the basic prescriptions in this chapter concerning cable sizing, overcurrent protection, and AC and DC systems installation.

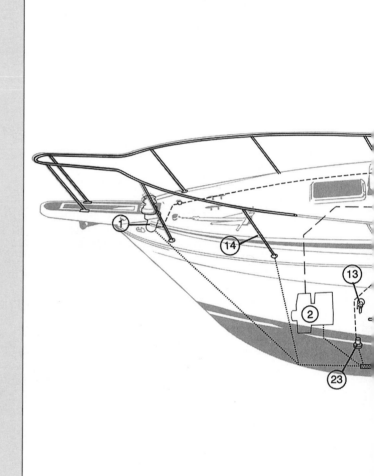

CHAPTER 5

FIGURE 5-1. Effective bonding and grounding techniques will head off problems with corrosion and electrical interference, not to mention minimize damage from lightning strikes. *(Jim Sollers)*

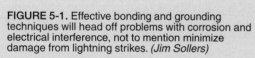

------------------ 12 V ground
(return)

— · — · — · — 120 VAC
grounding

······················ bonding
strap jumper

engine
ground

immersed
ground

(1) windlass
(2) air conditioner
(3) bonding strap
(4) freezer
(5) air conditioner compressor
(6) refrigerator
(7) water heater
(8) radio and instruments
(9) steering and engine controls
(10) batteries
(11) battery isolation switch
(12) fuel tanks
(13) through-hull
(14) stanchions
(15) metal keel
(16) chainplates
(17) deck fills
(18) stem fitting
(19) metal rudder
(20) distribution panel
(21) generator
(22) struts
(23) pump
(24) blower
(25) lights
(26) lightning rod

The theme that binds the subjects in this chapter together is the connecting, or grounding, of one conductive material to another, and the potential impact this has in terms of promoting or inhibiting corrosion, damage from lightning, and electrical safety.

Corrosion and grounding are two of the hardest issues to get a handle on in the boating world, not the least because the science is often incomplete, disagreement sometimes arises among the experts, and all kinds of self-anointed "experts" are pushing their own theories.

In this chapter, I am essentially relying on positions developed by the ABYC over many years for two reasons:

1. I believe these positions are well grounded in the available evidence and represent a consensus position.
2. The nature of the standards development process within the ABYC is such that it responds in a measured (although sometimes rather slow) manner to emerging science, and as such, at any given time ABYC standards form a sound basis for installation decisions on boats.

Corrosion

Corrosion is an ever-present fact of life with boats. The mixing of salt water and different metals is, in itself, enough to cause *galvanic corrosion*; the addition of electricity can be a potent catalyst leading to highly destructive *stray-current corrosion*.

Galvanic Corrosion

It is a "fact of nature" that when immersed in an electrically conductive fluid (an *electrolyte*), all metals have a specific *electrical potential* that is measurable as a voltage. It is another "fact of nature" that no two metals have the same electrical potential. As a result, if two different met-als are placed in the same electrolyte, their differing electrical potentials will produce a voltage difference, measurable simply by placing the probes of a sensitive voltmeter on the two pieces of metal.

The galvanic series. If we take one piece of metal and put it in an electrolyte, and then one at a time, place a whole series of different metals in the same electrolyte, measuring the voltage difference between the first metal and each of the others, we will be able to construct a table that ranks all the metals in terms of their voltage difference with the first (*reference*) metal (Figures 5-2A to 5-2E). It doesn't matter what metal

FIGURE 5-2A. The natural voltage of a galvanized anchor swivel with respect to a reference metal (in this case a silver/silver chloride half cell) is here around 960 millivolts (the voltage of the zinc coating).

FIGURE 5-2B. When the same meter is connected to a shackle that has lost its galvanizing, the voltage reading drops to 440 millivolts.

FIGURE 5-2C. When connected to a bronze through-hull, the reading drops to 240 millivolts.

FIGURE 5-2D. When connected to a stainless steel rigging toggle, the reading drops to 175 millivolts.

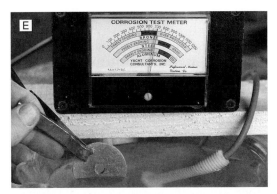

FIGURE 5-2E. When connected to a piece of (marine-grade) aluminum, the reading jumps to 700 millivolts (a little lower than expected, perhaps because of mild oxidation of the surface of the aluminum).

is used as the reference metal—the order of the metals in the table will come out pretty much the same (there may be some minor variations), although the voltages measured at each test will vary according to which metal is used as the reference.

In the marine world, the most commonly used *reference electrode* is a *silver/silver chloride half cell*, and the situation of most interest to boatowners is that of metals immersed in *moving seawater* (the movement resulting from a boat's being underway or from tidal flow at a mooring or anchorage). Taking these as the benchmarks, and further defining moving seawater as being between 50°F/10°C and 80°F/26.7°C and flowing at a rate of 8 to 13 feet per second (approximately 5 to 8 knots), we end up with Table 5-1, the galvanic series table.

Galvanic cells. Voltage is akin to pressure in a water system. If we have two tanks of water at differing pressures and we make a connection between the two tanks, water will flow from the higher-pressure tank to the lower-pressure tank until equilibrium is reached. In much the same way, if we immerse two different metals in an electrolyte, resulting in a voltage difference between them, *anytime a connection is made between these two metals*, an electrical current, measurable with a sensitive ammeter, will flow through the connection (Figure 5-3).

There is a difference, however, between the metals and the water tanks, for no matter how much current flows, the natural potential of the two metals will never equalize (remember, this voltage difference is a characteristic of the metals). It is rather as if the lower-pressure water tank has a hole in it, and so the flow of water will not cease until the higher-pressure tank runs out of water. The problem, when it comes to metals, is that this "running out of water" is arrived at *through the dissolution of one of the metals involved in the flow of current.*

TABLE 5-1. Galvanic Series of Metals in Seawater

Metals and Alloys	Range of Corrosion Potential (relative to silver/silver chloride half cell; volts)
Magnesium and Magnesium Alloys	−1.60 to −1.63
Zinc	−0.98 to −1.03
Aluminum Alloys	−0.76 to −1.00
Cadmium	−0.70 to −0.73
Mild Steel	−0.60 to −0.71
Wrought Iron	−0.60 to −0.71
Cast Iron	−0.60 to −0.71
13% Chromium Stainless Steel, Type 410 (active in still water)	−0.46 to −0.58
18-8 Stainless Steel, Type 304 (active in still water)	−0.46 to −0.58
Ni-Resist	−0.46 to −0.58
18-8, 3% Mo Stainless Steel, Type 316 (active in still water)	−0.43 to −0.54
78% Ni/13.5% Cr/6% Fe (Inconel) (active in still water)	−0.35 to −0.46
Aluminum Bronze (92% Cu/8% Al)	−0.31 to −0.42
Naval Brass (60% Cu/39% Zn)	−0.30 to −0.40
Yellow Brass (65% Cu/35% Zn)	−0.30 to −0.40
Red Brass (85% Cu/15% Zn)	−0.30 to −0.40
Muntz Metal (60% Cu/40% Zn)	−0.30 to −0.40
Tin	−0.31 to −0.33
Copper	−0.30 to −0.57
50-50 Lead/Tin Solder	−0.28 to −0.37
Admiralty Brass (71% Cu/28% Zn/1% Sn)	−0.28 to −0.36
Aluminum Brass (76% Cu/22% Zn/2% Al)	−0.28 to −0.36
Manganese Bronze (58.5% Cu/39% Zn/1% Sn/1% Fe/0.3% Mn)	−0.27 to −0.34
Silicon Bronze (96% Cu max./0.8% Fe/1.50% Zn/2.0% Si/0.75% Mn/1.60% Sn)	−0.26 to −0.29
Bronze Composition G (88% Cu/2% Zn/10% Sn)	−0.24 to −0.31
Bronze Composition M (88% Cu/3% Zn/6.5% Sn/1.5% Pb)	−0.24 to −0.31
13% Chromium Stainless Steel, Type 410 (passive)	−0.26 to −0.35
90% Cu/10% Ni	−0.21 to −0.28
75% Cu/20% Ni/5% Zn	−0.19 to −0.25
Lead	−0.19 to −0.25
70% Cu/30% Ni	−0.18 to −0.23
78% Ni/13.5% Cr/6% Fe (Inconel) (passive)	−0.14 to −0.17
Nickel 200	−0.10 to −0.20
18-8 Stainless Steel, Type 304 (passive)	−0.05 to −0.10
70% Ni/30% Cu Monel 400, K-500	−0.04 to −0.14
18-8, 3% Mo Stainless Steel, Type 316 (passive)	0.00 to −0.10
Titanium	−0.05 to +0.06
Hastelloy C	−0.03 to +0.08
Platinum	+0.19 to +0.25
Graphite	+0.20 to +0.30

Anodic or Least Noble (Active) ↑

Cathodic or Most Noble (Passive) ↓

(Based on a table courtesy ABYC)

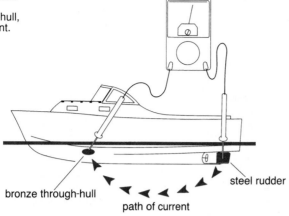

FIGURE 5-3. If an ammeter is placed between the rudder and the through-hull, it will read a small current. *(Jim Sollers)*

bronze through-hull

steel rudder

path of current

What happens can crudely be described as follows: Given any two metals immersed in an electrolyte, when an electrical connection is made between them, the current flows through the connection from the higher-voltage metal to the lower-voltage metal. The effect of this is to raise the voltage of the lower-voltage metal above its natural potential. In an effort to reestablish equilibrium, the lower-voltage metal discharges a current into the electrolyte. This current flows through the electrolyte to the higher-voltage metal, completing the electrical circuit between the two pieces of metal. Unfortunately *the current flowing through the electrolyte is generated by an electrochemical reaction that steadily consumes the lower-voltage metal*—a process known as *galvanic corrosion* (Figure 5-4).

As long as the external circuit remains in place between the two metals, the current from the higher-voltage metal will prevent the lower-voltage metal from reestablishing equilibrium at its natural potential, causing the reaction to continue. We have what is known as a *galvanic*

cell or *couple*. Eventually the lower-voltage metal will be entirely consumed, while the higher-voltage metal will remain intact. The metal that is feeding the current into the electrolyte is known as the *anode*; the metal that is receiving the current from the electrolyte and discharging it into the external circuit is known as the *cathode*.

The most commonly known galvanic cell is the lowly flashlight battery, which contains two dissimilar metals and an electrolyte, with the cathode forming the positive terminal and the anode forming the negative terminal. When an external circuit is made (for example, through a flashlight bulb), the anode is steadily consumed until it is destroyed, at which point the battery is dead.

Since the cathode in a galvanic cell does not dissolve, it is also referred to as the *most noble*, or *passive*, metal in this relationship, while the anode is referred to as the *least noble*, or *active*, metal. It should be noted that this relationship is entirely relative; depending on its position in the galvanic series table, a metal will be cathodic with respect to metals that have a lower electrical potential but anodic with respect to those with a higher potential.

Galvanic corrosion via the green wire.

For a galvanic cell to be formed, it is necessary only to have two different metals immersed in the same electrolyte (body of water) and electrically connected in some way. Corrosion will occur, even if the metals are on different boats. This fact has become abundantly clear in recent decades with the rapid expansion of shore-power-based electrical systems. Many of these pass galvanic currents from one boat to another or to the dockside down the grounding (green or bare) wire of the AC shore-power cord (refer back to Chapter 4).

As we saw in Chapter 4, this kind of galvanic couple is easily broken with a galvanic isolator or an isolation transformer, although all too often one of these devices is not fitted and corrosion occurs, sometimes at a devastating rate. *All boats, particularly metal boats, should break the galvanic connection between the boat and the AC grounding wire with either a galvanic isolator or an isolation transformer, with the latter being by far the preferable option.*

Dezincification, and pitting and crevice corrosion.

So far we have considered galvanic cells containing two dissimilar metal objects. But most metallic materials in marine use are *alloys*—mixtures of more than one metal. And even "pure" metals contain impurities. Add a little salt water, and many can generate internal

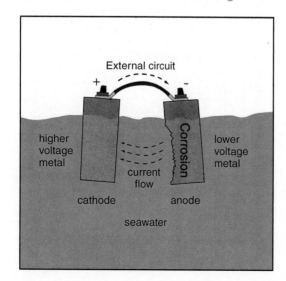

FIGURE 5-4. A simple galvanic cell. *(Professional Boatbuilder)*

External circuit

+

−

higher voltage metal

Corrosion

lower voltage metal

current flow

cathode

anode

seawater

galvanic corrosion; a notorious example is screws made of brass, which is an alloy of copper and zinc. In the presence of an electrolyte these two metals, being widely separated on the galvanic scale, become highly interactive, eating up the zinc in the alloy and leaving a soft, porous, and worthless fastener (identifiable by a change in color from yellow brass to red copper).

Steel. To a certain extent, the prerequisites for the establishment of these internal galvanic cells vary from alloy to alloy. Steel, for example, requires not only an electrolyte but also oxygen. However, since oxygen is readily available both in the atmosphere and in dissolved form in seawater, galvanic corrosion (evidenced by rust) is an ever-present possibility. The waterline area on a steel boat is especially vulnerable, for here the hull is constantly wetted in a highly oxygenated atmosphere.

Untreated steel is particularly susceptible to corrosion. It often comes from the foundry with a coating of *mill scale*, which has a potential about 0.3 volt above that of regular steel. In the presence of an electrolyte and oxygen, a galvanic cell is established between the underlying plate and the scale; the plate is the anode, and pitting will occur until the scale loosens and falls off. Once the mill scale is gone, impurities in the steel itself will ensure that the process of galvanic interaction (rusting) continues.

The manner in which aluminum and stainless steel establish internal galvanic cells is somewhat different from steel. First of all, whereas very little difference exists in the rate of rusting of one grade of steel as compared to another, marked differences exist in the susceptibility to corrosion of different grades of both aluminum and stainless steel. Consequently, *it is absolutely essential to use marine-grade alloys in boat construction and also for fasteners and hardware.* Second, in contrast to steel, the presence of oxygen *slows* the corrosion process of both aluminum and stainless steel whereby they develop an inert oxide film. When oxygen is removed, this oxide skin breaks down. If an electrolyte is then added, corrosion is likely to be rampant.

Aluminum. Corrosion is a serious problem with aluminum alloys because of their active position in the galvanic series—they are anodic with respect to almost all other metals used in boatbuilding. In the presence of moisture, galvanic corrosion can also occur between the base metal and the weld metal in welded tanks.

Pitting corrosion on aluminum alloys is a localized phenomenon that occurs when the passive oxide film breaks down in small areas, allowing the areas to become active. Crevice corrosion occurs when there is contact between the aluminum and some other material (e.g., the support structure for a tank) such that water can enter the space between the two but not circulate freely. The oxygen within the crevice area is consumed, the passive oxide film on the aluminum breaks down, and corrosion commences. With both pitting and crevice corrosion, the corrosion will continue as long as moisture is present.

Stainless steel. Oxidized stainless steel is called *passivated* and is one of the more corrosion-resistant alloys available for marine use (refer back to Table 5-1). However without the oxide layer, stainless steel becomes *active*, making it vulnerable to localized attack. Active areas of stainless steel frequently evidence themselves by rust stains on surrounding surfaces.

Since oxygen is readily available in the atmosphere and in seawater, there is little risk of corrosion in most circumstances, but *if stainless steel is used in an area where stagnant water can collect, sooner or later its passivity will break down, and it will become active* (normally in isolated pinholes and crevices) and will begin to "feed" on itself (Figure 5-5), just as the copper in a brass screw feeds on the zinc. The active area is the anode; the passive area is the cathode.

FIGURE 5-5. Crevice corrosion on a stainless steel propeller shaft caused by stagnant water with low oxygen content in the stern tube.

When first discovered in 1913, stainless steel was heralded as a wonder metal, and in many ways it was. However, after almost a century and hundreds of millions of dollars of research, it is clear that it has very definite limitations, particularly in the marine environment.

There are more than 500 different grades of stainless steel, all of which get their stainless quality by alloying chromium with iron (steel). In the presence of oxygen, the chromium forms a relatively inert skin that is highly resistant to corrosion—stainless steel; this oxidized skin is said to be *passivated*. The minimum percentage of chromium required in the alloy to create this condition is around 12%, with higher levels providing greater corrosion resistance. Typically, up to 20% chromium is used for better grades of stainless steel.

In addition to chromium, nickel is sometimes added to the mix, which further enhances corrosion resistance. Stainless steels without nickel or with very low levels of nickel fall into two broad categories known as *ferritic* and *martensitic;* those with higher levels of nickel fall into a category known as *austenitic* (Figure 5-6A). *Duplex* stainless steels are a combination of austenitic and ferritic.

Ferritic and martensitic stainless steels are not suitable for marine use. Rather conveniently, they are easily identifiable since they are magnetic (Figure 5-6B), whereas austenitic stainless steels are nonmagnetic or have very low levels of magnetism. All too often ferritic or martensitic fasteners are found on boats—notably the screws on many "all-stainless" hose clamps—steadily rusting away. If the screw is undone a turn or two, the band will be seriously corroded where it has been in contact with the screw (Figure 5-6C). For marine use, boat-owners should use hose clamps stamped "all

FIGURE 5-6A. Common grades of stainless steel found in the marine world.

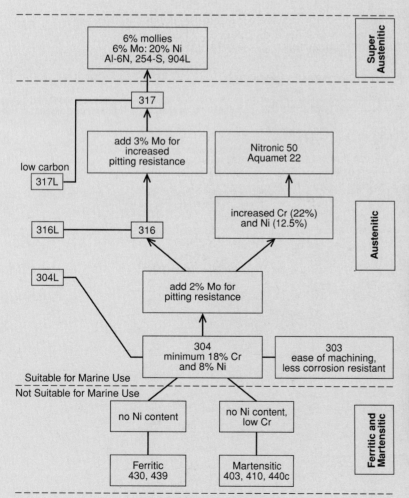

- 6% mollies
  6% Mo: 20% Ni
  Al-6N, 254-S, 904L — **Super Austenitic**

- 317
- low carbon 317L
- add 3% Mo for increased pitting resistance
- Nitronic 50 Aquamet 22
- 316L — 316
- increased Cr (22%) and Ni (12.5%) — **Austenitic**
- 304L
- add 2% Mo for pitting resistance
- 304 minimum 18% Cr and 8% Ni
- 303 ease of machining, less corrosion resistant

Suitable for Marine Use
Not Suitable for Marine Use

- no Ni content
- no Ni content, low Cr
- Ferritic 430, 439
- Martensitic 403, 410, 440c — **Ferritic and Martensitic**

FIGURE 5-6B. An "all-stainless" hose clamp with a screw of an inferior (magnetic) corrosion-prone grade of stainless.

FIGURE 5-6C. A perfectly good-looking "all-stainless" hose clamp, which, when the screw was backed off a turn or two, revealed considerable corrosion inside the screw housing, caused by using an inferior grade of stainless steel for the screw.

Is Stainless Steel Really Stainless? (*continued*)

FIGURE 5-6D. A good-quality all-stainless hose clamp using a 300-grade corrosion-resistant screw.

300 stainless steel"—see below—or clamps that come from a manufacturer who uses nothing but austenitic stainless steel (Figure 5-6D), such as AWAB clamps made by ABA Group (www.abagroup.com).

Different alloys of stainless steel are given an identification number. The ferritic and martensitic steels fall in the 400 series (with individual numbers between 400 and 450); the austenitic steels are mostly 300 series, although a few are 200 series. Of the austenitic stainless steels, 304 is widely used in the marine field for fasteners, stainless steel fittings, propeller shafts, rigging, and so on. It is sometimes also known as 18-8 since it has 18% chromium and 8% nickel in its mix.

Despite its widespread use, 304 is not the best of the austenitic stainless steels. Higher corrosion resistance is found (in ascending order of resistance) with:

- 316, which has a slightly higher nickel content than 304, and 2% added molybdenum that further enhances its corrosion resistance.
- 317 (1% more molybdenum than 316, with even better corrosion resistance).

- More specialized alloys, such as Nitronic 50, also called Aquamet 22, which has 21% chromium, 12% nickel, 4% manganese, and 2% molybdenum.
- The recently developed "super austenitic" alloys containing 6% molybdenum (nicknamed the "6% mollies").

In the old days of metal alloying, the processes could not be controlled as precisely as they can be today. As a result, manufacturers tended to err toward the high end of the chromium, nickel, and molybdenum percentages that were needed to ensure compliance with a given alloy. It is ironic that with today's more precisely controlled processes, metals can be accurately alloyed to the lower end of the prescribed limits, with the result that today's 317 may be no more corrosion resistant than yesterday's 316.

Finally, it should be noted that when many stainless steels are welded, the differential heating of the metal in the area of the weld causes the chromium to combine with carbon in the steel, removing the chromium from its passivating film-forming role. These areas become anodic with respect to the rest of the stainless steel, leading to galvanic corrosion called *weld decay* or *intergranular corrosion*, which is particularly noticeable around welds on many stainless steel fuel and water tanks, and leaks soon develop. On small welded pieces, intergranular corrosion can be avoided by heating the entire piece after welding to around 2,000°F/600°C and then rapidly cooling it. For larger structures where this is not practical, a *low-carbon-content stainless steel should be used for all welded structures*, identified by the letter "L" after its number (e.g., 304L or preferably 316L). **This is particularly important for all-stainless steel tanks** (for more on tanks, see Chapter 12).

In such localized instances of corrosion, the surrounding passive stainless steel forms a large cathodic area in relation to the small anodic pinhole or crevice, resulting in rapid corrosion of up to ¼ inch (6 mm) per year (see the Is Stainless Steel Really Stainless? sidebar).

It is important to note that the stainless steel alloys that are more corrosion resistant are only more resistant to the *initiation* of corrosion. If the protective (passivated) layer breaks down and the alloy becomes active, corrosion will

continue at a similar rate to alloys that are less corrosion resistant.

Preventing galvanic corrosion. What we have seen so far is that for galvanic corrosion to occur, three preconditions must be met:

1. There must either be two dissimilar metals or dissimilarities within one piece of metal.
2. The dissimilar metals must be in contact with an *electrolyte* (an electrically conductive fluid).

Common Locations for Stainless Steel Corrosion

As noted in the text, the corrosion resistance of stainless steels is dependent upon the integrity of the oxide layer formed by the chromium. There are several ways the integrity of this layer can be breached:

1. Microscopic, water-retaining cracks or scratches on the surface of the metal can lead to crevice corrosion.

2. In the presence of an electrolyte, microscopic impurities on the surface of the metal will likely result in the formation of a galvanic cell, causing pitting.

3. Anytime an oxygen deficiency at the surface of the metal leads to the oxide layer breaking down, and an electrolyte is present, corrosion is pretty well guaranteed. Locations in which this situation commonly occurs are:

   • Any area with stagnant water, such as between a propeller shaft and a propeller, in the threads under the propeller nut, around the keyway, where the rubber sleeve of a Cutless bearing is in contact with the shaft, under barnacles, and under monofilament fishing line if it gets wrapped around a propeller shaft. In all instances, problems are reduced by frequent boat use since this provides a regular supply of freshly oxygenated water.

   • Any damp areas where stainless steel fasteners are deprived of oxygen, such as wooden-boat plank fastenings that are below the waterline (therefore, bronze or galvanized steel screws should always be used). Note that if a boat is moored in a protected harbor or in a canal where there is little or no current, it is a good idea to move the boat at least once a week to ensure that a fresh supply of oxygen-laden water comes in contact with any underwater stainless steel hardware.

   • Under the nylon insert in Nylok nuts.

Sailboats are vulnerable in a number of additional locations:

• Inside the lower terminals of swaged-on rigging fittings, which tend to collect water, and inside barrel-type turnbuckles. In both instances, corrosion is invisible, and the first sign of trouble is likely to be a rigging failure.

• Inside centerboard trunks—particularly around hinge pins and the attachment points of lifting cables—where water is stagnant and oxygen levels are depleted.

• Wherever stainless steel fasteners pass through the hull, deck, or spreaders. If any moisture becomes trapped in the hole, the moisture will eventually become deoxygenated, causing the stainless to turn active, often with no external evidence. (Through-deck chainplates are particularly vulnerable since the flexing of the rig almost always breaks down any caulking seal, allowing moisture to penetrate—see Figure 5-7.)

Besides using 316 stainless steel or some other specialized alloy, you can enhance corrosion resistance by polishing the surface of the metal (either electrochemically or mechanically) and by ensuring that if a fastener must be used in an area where moisture may penetrate, the fastener is properly bedded in a completely waterproof sealant (3M 5200, for example, but not silicone, which is minutely porous). Even so, stainless steel, despite its popularity, is not the best choice in many instances for the applications in which it is commonly used.

Note that even where pitting and crevice corrosion are not a problem, austenitic stainless steels in certain environments are subject to *stress corrosion cracking* and *corrosion fatigue*, both of which occur at the microscopic level, making problems almost impossible to detect until a sudden failure occurs.

active corrosion

FIGURE 5-7. A chainplate bolt that showed no external evidence of corrosion. The shiny parts are especially active.

3. There must be an electrical connection between the metals (other than the path provided by the electrolyte; Figures 5-8A and 5-8B).

If these three preconditions are met, a galvanic cell will form in which one metal (the anode) will corrode while the other (the cathode) will be unharmed.

The rate of current flow in a galvanic cell, and therefore the rate at which the anodic metal dissolves, depends on a number of factors, the most important of which are:

1. The voltage difference between the two metals; in principle, the greater the difference, the more the potential for corrosion. Anytime the voltage difference, as shown in Table 5-1, exceeds 0.25 volt (250 mV), corrosion is pretty well certain.
2. The relative exposed surface areas of the two metals—the *area effect*. A large cathodic area (a bronze rudder, for example) connected to a small anodic area (a steel heel bearing) will soon destroy the anode, whereas a large anode (a steel rudder) in relation to a small cathode (a bronze heel bearing) will corrode slowly.
3. A process known as *polarization*. When two metals form a galvanic cell, they are initially quite reactive, but soon some of the by-products of that reaction (various salts and oxides of the metals) insulate the surface of one or the other metal, reducing the rate of reaction and thus of corrosion. The effect of polarization varies markedly from one metal to another and according to such factors as whether the water is moving or not (moving water tends to flush the salts and oxides away, keeping the reaction going) and how much oxygen the water contains.
4. The conductivity of the electrolyte. Salt water is relatively conductive, whereas fresh water sometimes is not (it depends on the level of dissolved salts and minerals, which is highly variable from one lake or river to another).

Knowing these facts, many times it is possible to build a boat and install equipment in such a way that *one or more of the three preconditions for galvanic corrosion is not present, in which case such corrosion simply will not occur*. If prevention is not entirely possible, a grasp of the factors determining the rate of corrosion can be used to implement measures that slow corrosion to "acceptable" levels. Either way, key considerations are:

Use the right metals. Use *marine-grade alloys* and be sure to use them in the appropriate

FIGURES 5-8A AND 5-8B. A steel shackle once again. Note that as long as it is immersed, it develops a voltage potential, but the second it is taken out of the water, the circuit is broken and with it the corrosion potential.

applications. For example, use only austenitic stainless steels, and if stress corrosion cracking or corrosion fatigue is possible, substitute bronze, Monel, or titanium.

Don't mix underwater metals. By not mixing underwater metals, you minimize the differences between the voltages of the various metals in the boat, thus minimizing the potential for corrosion.

In metal boatbuilding, whatever grade of steel or aluminum is used for the hull plating also should be used in the hull reinforcement, as well as for deck stringers, pipe stubs, and any other metal fixtures in physical contact with the hull. On all other boats, anytime two pieces of metal are likely to be in contact with the same body of water (even if this is nothing more than a few drops of salt water caught in the head or threads of a fastener), the same metals should be used.

If the mixing of metals is necessary, use Table 5-1 to ensure that the metals are galvanically close to one another. However, this table is not in itself an infallible guide, since it does not take polarization effects into account. For example, if we need to fasten an aluminum cleat with something stronger than an aluminum fastener, looking at the table we see that all the bronzes and brasses are galvanically closer to aluminum than passivated stainless steel, and so we might be tempted to select a bronze fastener. However,

Cleaning Up Cosmetic Corrosion

Corroding stainless steel fasteners and hardware will frequently create unsightly rust spots on the hardware and leave stains on neighboring surfaces. These should not be ignored as they may be symptomatic of pitting or crevice corrosion that may be doing structural damage. You can clean the stains by treating them with diluted oxalic or phosphoric acid. Depending on the strength of the solution, phosphoric acid seems to work faster. (One brand widely available at paint, hardware, and auto stores that is quite powerful is Jasco Metal Etch—www.jasco-help.com; read the manufacturer's instructions before using it.)

Apply the acid solution with a stiff bristle brush (for small areas, I use a toothbrush), or in the case of severe staining, with a stainless steel brush or bronze wool, as long as it will not scratch the surface being cleaned. (Never use steel wool because it will leave tiny flecks of steel that subsequently rust.) Brush until the stain disappears and then flush thoroughly with fresh water. Polishing the stainless now will slow future corrosion.

You can treat aluminum corrosion with the same acid etch. First, however, you should scrape, brush, and sand down to clear metal. The acid will clean the exposed metal surface. Then rinse off the acid with water. If you plan to paint the surface, it is important that the water run off in an even sheet and not bead up. Beading indicates surface contamination with grease, which means you will need to do additional cleaning and etching. As soon as the surface has fully dried, prime it with a two-part epoxy primer such as Awlgrip 545, finishing off with either a topcoat of two-part linear polyurethane (such as Awlgrip—www.awlgrip.com); a two-part epoxy paint (noting, however, that these tend to lose their gloss over time); or a good-quality one-part polyurethane or exterior enamel.

---

both aluminum and stainless steel develop inert oxide films that, in the absence of other disturbing influences, reduce galvanic interaction to a minimum, whereas in the presence of moisture, any copper-based fastener (bronze and brass) will continually break down the protective film on the aluminum, causing extensive corrosion. (The copper "plates out" on the aluminum, creating very active galvanic cells with greatly accelerated corrosion. A variation of this can occur if a raw-water strainer with a brass screen is used on an aluminum engine, allowing copper from the screen to plate out in the engine.)

Consequently, *copper alloys should never be used in combination with aluminum;* passivated stainless steel or Monel is normally the appropriate choice for fasteners.

Minimize any area effects. You can minimize area effects by ensuring that all fasteners and all metals used for welding are *at least as noble as, and perhaps a little more noble than, the metals they are fastening.* This will create a small cathodic area in relation to a large anodic mass, protecting the fastener or weld from corrosion while generating very little corrosion in the anode.

Keep electrolytes away from metal surfaces. Avoid structural elements that will form pockets of trapped dirt and moisture, and use proper coatings and sealants. Without an electrolyte in contact with metal, galvanic corrosion cannot occur.

In order to keep moisture away from metal surfaces, take care in the placement of frames, stringers, and floors in metal boats and provide limber holes for drainage. Discontinuous welding, particularly on box-section frames, is an invitation to trouble. Ventilation to eliminate condensation is especially important. Beyond these measures, there are numerous modern coatings that create a surface impervious to moisture. In all cases such coatings have to be planned for *at the design stage,* both to ensure adequate surface preparation of the underlying metal, particularly in inaccessible areas on the interior of the hull, and also to eliminate sharp or rough edges that will result in thin coats of paint being easily breached.

Steel can be given a substantial amount of extra protection with a coating of zinc—*galvanizing*—prior to painting. Since zinc is more anodic than steel, anytime the paint layer is damaged, allowing moisture access to the metal and so establishing a localized galvanic cell, the zinc will corrode, protecting the steel and in fact plating out on the steel to "heal" the scratch. Proper coatings are not so important with aluminum (which will develop its own relatively inert oxide skin) or many bronze fittings (which are naturally resistant to corrosion; however, note that *manganese bronze,* unlike other bronzes, has a high percentage of zinc and as a result is susceptible to *dezincification*—it should more properly be called a *brass*). Stainless steel should *not* be painted since the exclusion of oxygen from the surface of the metal may cause its protective oxide film to break down.

A word of caution must be given at this point: Painting a *cathodic* metal to isolate it from galvanic activity will *always* help to slow or stop corrosion at an interconnected anodic metal since the paint reduces the exposed cathodic area, which in turn reduces the level of galvanic current generated at the anode. But when an *anodic* metal is painted, if there is a galvanic connection to any unprotected cathodic surface, the galvanic current will be concentrated at any flaws in the paint job on the anode (scratches or pinholes, for example). We now have a very unfavorable area effect—a relatively large cathodic area drawing current from a very small anodic area—which may well cause *severe localized pitting* of the anode. The resulting damage is frequently more harmful than would have been the case with modest corrosion over the entire surface of the anode. Thus it is sometimes better to leave an anodic surface unpainted, allowing it to suffer mild generalized corrosion, rather than to risk this concentrated corrosion.

Electrically isolate individual pieces of metal. Electrical isolation will break any potential galvanic circuits between individual pieces of metal. Besides isolation from an electrolyte, in many cases a surface coating will also provide a fair measure of electrical insulation (depending on the type of paint). However, when two metal objects are fastened together, minor projections on one or the other surface are likely to cut through the paint job to make a connection, so it's best to use additional insulating materials. These may include some form of grease, thread compound, or caulking around a fastener (zinc pastes, proprietary products such as Lubriplate—www.lubriplate.com, Tef-Gel—www.tefgel.com, and Duralac—www.llewellyn-ryland.co.uk, or compounds such as 3M 5200—www.3M.com); a gasket of neoprene or PVC with an insulating sleeve around any bolt and an insulating washer under its nut; or a rugged, nonconductive insert fitted to the hull of a metal boat to which a through-hull is mounted (Figures 5-9A and 5-9B). It is an ABYC requirement that *any galvanically incompatible below-the-waterline fitting be insulated from a metal hull.*

Note that carbon, which is increasingly used in hulls, decks, and masts, is a very noble material that is cathodic with respect to almost all metals found on boats. It is important to electrically isolate all metallic hardware from any carbon structures.

Above and beyond these various measures, further corrosion protection can be provided *cathodically,* either via a *bonding system* or with an *impressed current system* (see the Bonding and Cathodic Protection section below).

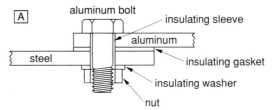

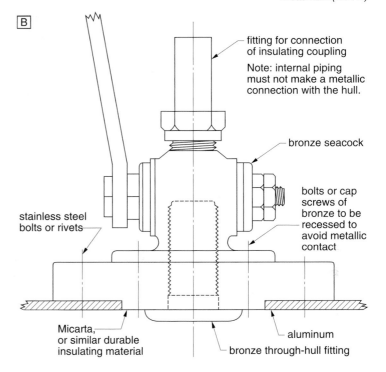

FIGURE 5-9A. The use of insulating washers and sleeves to electrically isolate dissimilar metals that are fastened together.

FIGURE 5-9B. The use of a rugged, electrically non-conductive insert to isolate a bronze seacock from a metal hull. *(ABYC)*

Stray-Current Corrosion

Galvanic corrosion can set up currents between fittings that are measured in milliamps (mA) and millivolts (mV)—a *thousandth* of an amp or volt. However, faulty electrical circuits can establish currents *hundreds* and even *thousands* of times stronger. Such *stray currents* can originate from within a boat, from shoreside fittings and ship-to-shore cables, or from neighboring boats. In all cases, a leak from a hot wire allows current to find a path to ground through bilge water, damp areas of the boat, or the seawater, rather than through proper channels.

Any metal fitting that feeds a current into water may be corroded, *regardless of the composition of the metal and regardless of its position in the galvanic series table relative to other metals.* If, for example, a current is fed from a bronze through-hull to a zinc anode (see the Cathodic Protection section below), it is the bronze through-hull that will corrode. It is the direction of the current flow that determines which metal will corrode. *Zinc anodes do nothing to protect*

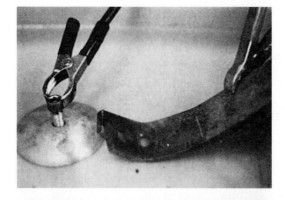

FIGURE 5-10A. A test rig to simulate stray-current corrosion. Here 5 amps of DC current are being passed from the stainless steel flat bar to the zinc anode via the electrolyte (salt water).

FIGURE 5-10B. After less than 3 hours, the stainless steel is severely corroded, whereas the zinc is unharmed.

some experiments suggest that in certain circumstances they can. In any event, in many instances the point is academic. Because DC leaks are frequently superimposed on AC circuits, we must pay careful attention to eliminating sources of stray currents from both.

Real-life examples. In normal circumstances, electric currents are confined to the cables and the equipment in their circuits. For a stray current to develop, there must first of all be a mechanism for the current to escape from a circuit—a short circuit, or some other fault that feeds the current to hardware in contact with water—and second there must be some reason for the current to run to ground through water rather than through other cables. Anytime these two preconditions are met, corrosion is pretty well certain. The following examples are drawn from real life:

against stray-current corrosion. Galvanic corrosion is by its nature a relatively slow process (the metals themselves have to generate the current), but stray-current corrosion, with its potential for far higher levels of current flow, can be devastating. In worst-case scenarios, *stray currents can wipe out hardware in a matter of hours* (Figures 5-10A and 5-10B).

DC stray currents are particularly destructive, whereas there is considerable debate as to whether AC leaks lead to any corrosion at all. In theory, they do not, but experience as well as

1. A bilge pump float switch has a leaking seal that allows bilge water to penetrate the float until the water reaches the level of the two switch terminals. Current now tracks through the water from one switch terminal to the other, bypassing the switch. The pump does not kick on, because the resistance of the water keeps the current flow below that needed to run the pump. Nevertheless, the terminal feeding the current into the water corrodes until its cable falls off, at which point the switch is no longer operative, and the bilge pump is out of action (Figures 5-11A and 5-11B). *This happens almost anytime the seals on a submerged switch fail.* The more general point here is that if (1) any kind of a cable connection or terminal is submerged, (2) water penetrates the connection

FIGURE 5-11A. A leaking seal on a float switch will result in stray-current corrosion at the positive switch terminal. This will eat the positive cable off the terminal, disabling the switch and pump. *(Jim Sollers)*

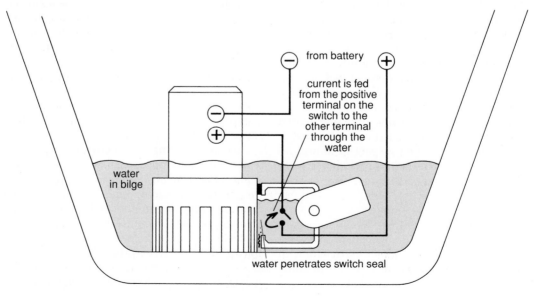

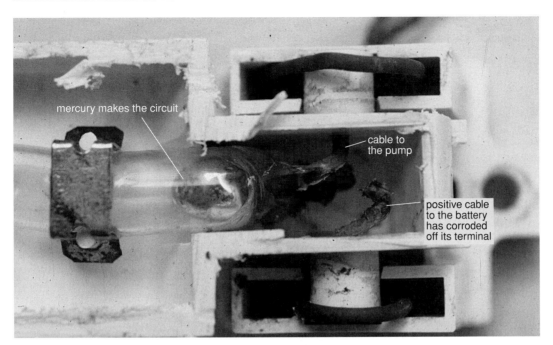

mercury makes the circuit

cable to
the pump

positive cable
to the battery
has corroded
off its terminal

FIGURE 5-11B. A bilge pump switch with a leaking seal. Salt water penetrated and rose to the level of the switch terminals, at which point the power supply cable began feeding current directly into the water to the other terminal. The supply cable was eaten through until it fell off its terminal.

or terminal, and (3) there is any path to the boat's negative system through the water, then whenever voltage is present (which it will be all the time on the positive side of many circuits), stray-current corrosion is probable. This scenario is why ABYC and ISO standards prohibit connections below the foreseeable level of bilge water.

2. A 12-volt bilge pump is wired with undersized wiring that creates a 10% voltage drop (1.2 volts) on the ground side of the circuit (not at all unusual). The motor has some path to ground through the bilge water. (The most likely path is carbon dust from worn brushes that enable current to "track" to some metal part of the pump—such as the motor housing or impeller shaft—that is in contact with the bilge water.) Under normal circumstances, this would not create a problem. But because of the voltage drop on the circuit, when the pump is running, the negative side of the pump is 1.2 volts positive with respect to battery negative. That difference is enough to cause some of the current passing through the circuit to find an alternate path to the battery negative: via the pump housing, to the bilge water, to an unbonded through-hull, to the surrounding seawater, to the propeller and propeller shaft, to the engine block, and finally to the engine ground strap back to the battery negative. The pump housing and through-hull, which are both feeding the current into water, will corrode.

3. A bilge pump is wired with cables that are not color-coded. In the course of making the con-nections, the positive and negative cables get crossed over. The pump doesn't care—it will work fine. However, now the entire circuit through the pump back to its float switch is hot at all times, while the switch creates an infinite resistance in the ground circuit when-ever the pump is not running. Regardless of the quality of the wiring and connections on the ground circuit, if there is any kind of an electrical leak from the pump (e.g., via carbon dust from the brushes), it will have no path back to ground except through the water and various fittings in contact with the water—corrosion will be rampant.

4. A compass light is wired with the switch in the negative side of the circuit (as with the bilge pump above). An accidental connec-tion from what should have been the ground side of the light (but which is now the hot side) to the binnacle allows current to find a path to ground: through the compass hous-ing, to the binnacle, to the steering cable, to an unbonded rudderpost, to the propeller, and then back to the engine and battery nega-tive. The rudderpost, being the part that feeds the current into the water, corrodes until the rudder drops off (this happened!). This exam-ple illustrates why *you should never put switches or fuses in the ground side of a circuit*: this can break the path to ground, exacerbat-ing the risk of stray-current corrosion.

Sources of stray currents. Given the fact that all electrical currents, whether AC or DC, seek the path of least resistance back to their

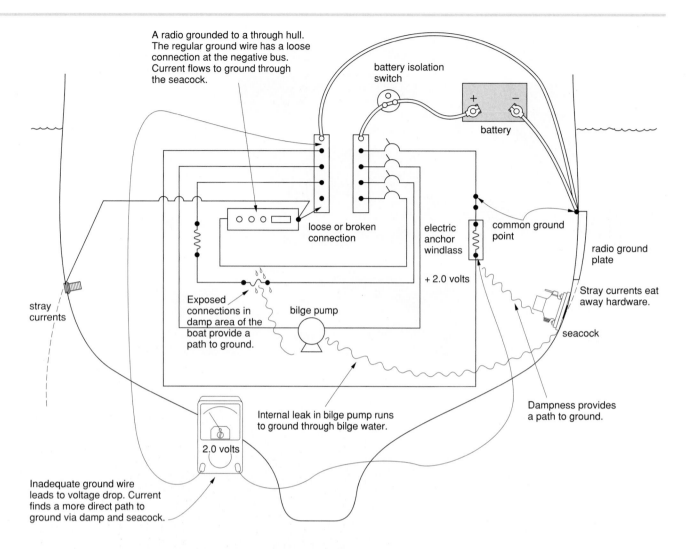

A radio grounded to a through hull. The regular ground wire has a loose connection at the negative bus. Current flows to ground through the seacock.

battery isolation switch

battery

loose or broken connection

electric anchor windlass

+ 2.0 volts

common ground point

radio ground plate

Stray currents eat away hardware.

seacock

stray currents

Exposed connections in damp area of the boat provide a path to ground.

bilge pump

Internal leak in bilge pump runs to ground through bilge water.

Dampness provides a path to ground.

2.0 volts

Inadequate ground wire leads to voltage drop. Current finds a more direct path to ground via damp and seacock.

FIGURE 5-12. Stray-current sources.

source, stray currents almost always arise as a result of (1) some defect in wiring or a piece of equipment that allows an electrical leak into damp areas of the boat, bilge water, or the surrounding water; combined with (2) *a resistance in the proper path to ground so that the path through the boat and the water now has less resistance than the path through the ground circuit.* Some of the more common sources of stray currents are shown in Figure 5-12. In particular, watch for the following:

- Any connections or terminal blocks in damp or wet areas.

- Any damage to conductors, especially positive conductors, in damp or wet areas.

- Screws, staples, or other fasteners that go through wiring.

- Corrosive salts on terminal blocks or connections that form a "bridge" to neighboring circuits; the salt acts as an electrolyte so that any current following this path will corrode the terminal that is discharging the current.

- Undersized wiring or resistive connections that result in voltage drop, especially on the negative side of circuits, making it more likely that other, less resistive, paths to ground will be found.

- Any grounding system that haphazardly grounds different circuits and pieces of equipment to through-hulls, bonding conductors, and lightning conductors (see the Lightning Protection section below), resulting in voltage differences from one part of the ground circuit to another. *All equipment should have an insulated ground that leads back to a central ground bus bar in the main distribution panel,* which in turn leads to a *common ground point or bus* (see the Grounding section at the end of this chapter), and from there back to the battery negative terminal. From the negative side of any piece of equipment, *there should only be a single path back to battery negative.*

- Voltage drop in radios with external (immersed) ground plates. When transmitting, the voltage on the plate will differ from the negative battery terminal voltage, generating currents between the plate and any underwater metal grounded to the battery, such as the engine and the propeller shaft.

- Any traditional (brush-type) DC motor in a damp or wet area (primarily because of the potential for carbon dust from the brushes to permit current to track to the motor case).

- Some navigation lights, which have the negative side connected to the metal housing. If there is any resistance in the negative circuit, the operating current will be encouraged to run to ground through the housing and some other path.

- Shore-power circuits that do not have an isolation transformer or a functioning galvanic isolator (see Chapter 4), thus providing a path for stray currents, as well as galvanic currents, onto the boat's grounding circuits. In particular, look for:

  1. Equipment on the boat that may tie the neutral side of a shore-power AC system to the boat's grounding system, bypassing any galvanic isolator. Note that many nonmarine battery chargers make this neutral-to-grounding connection.

  2. Some reverse polarity lamps that function by making a low-resistance connection between the hot or neutral wire and the grounding circuit, providing a path for galvanic or stray currents to bypass any galvanic isolator. To prevent this, many older reverse polarity lamps have a spring-loaded switch (normally off) that is held on momentarily to check polarity, then remains off the rest of the time, thus isolating the polarity indicator. For situations of reverse polarity such as just described, recent ABYC regulations require a permanent light or alarm that has a resistance of at least 25,000 ohms (which will pretty much eliminate stray currents).

  3. Cable TV, since the TV will likely be grounded on board, while the grounded sheath of the incoming cable will likely bypass any isolator or isolation transformer.

  4. Any conductive connection from a metal hull to the shore, such as an aluminum ladder from the deck to a dock, since this will once again bypass any galvanic isolator or isolation transformer.

Preventing stray-current corrosion. As stated earlier, stray currents can only arise when faulty electrical equipment or wiring allows a current to escape from a piece of equipment or its circuit *and* also creates a situation in which a lower-resistance path back to the energy source is found outside of the boat's wiring. Once this point is grasped, a number of key measures for preventing stray-current corrosion become clear:

- Only use electrical equipment on your boat that is rated for marine use. This is a must because there are frequently subtle differences in marine design and materials that reduce the chances of leaks from electrical equipment. For example, as noted, many automotive battery chargers have a direct connection between the incoming AC side and the DC side, whereas all marine chargers isolate the two sides of the transformer from each other.

- Use multistranded, tinned wire with marine-quality terminals for all wiring. In the long run, this wire is the only way to ensure corrosion free, and therefore resistance free, circuits.

- Keep all electrical cabling out of damp areas of a boat. If this is not possible, at the very least do not make any connections in damp locations.

- Be sure that marine electrical systems always use a grounded negative, with no switches, fuses, or breakers in the ground side. In the event a leak develops from a piece of DC equipment, as long as the equipment is grounded and the ground circuit is unbroken with a low-resistance path back to the battery, the leak will be conducted back to the battery without causing corrosion.

- Only use marine wiring that is the *insulated-return type*; i.e., a separate ground wire is run back from every piece of equipment to the ground bus, as opposed to using the hull in a metal boat or the bonding system or some other circuit in a nonconductive boat. Once again, this is to ensure an unbroken, low-resistance path back to the battery.

- Be sure ground cables are sized at least as large as positive cables to avoid voltage drop on the ground side of the circuit (any voltage drop will encourage current to seek a lower-resistance path back to the battery). In general, although a 10% voltage drop is often considered acceptable, in marine wiring 3% is a far better figure to shoot for.

- Avoid using a single ground cable to ground more than one appliance, for two reasons. First of all, using one ground cable requires added connections in the grounding circuit, every one of which is a potential source of corrosion, resistance, and voltage drop. Second, unless the cable is carefully sized, if more than one load is turned on at the same time, excessive voltage drop is likely.

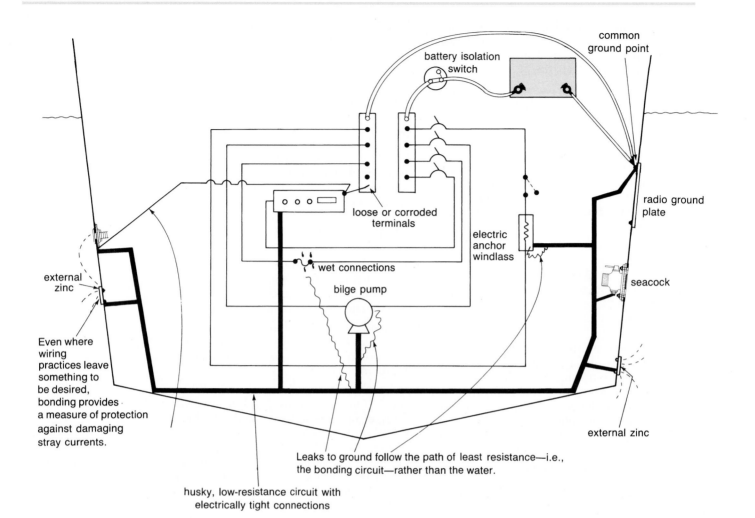

common
ground point

battery isolation
switch

loose or corroded
terminals

electric
anchor
windlass

wet connections

bilge pump

radio ground
plate

seacock

external
zinc

**Even where
wiring
practices leave
something to
be desired,
bonding provides
a measure of protection
against damaging
stray currents.**

external zinc

Leaks to ground follow the path of least resistance—i.e.,
the bonding circuit—rather than the water.

**husky, low-resistance circuit with
electrically tight connections**

FIGURE 5-13. Bonding
and ground leaks.

• Terminate all DC negative circuits, AC grounding circuits, bonding, and lightning-protection circuits at a single common ground point or bus (see the Grounding section at the end of this chapter). This will hold these circuits to a common voltage, discouraging stray currents from circulating around the different circuits.

• Ensure the engine on a metal boat has insulated-ground sending units and a heavy ground strap from the alternator ground to the boat's common ground point (or even better, use an insulated-ground alternator and starter motor—see pages 122–23).

The key thing to remember is that even if a stray current should develop, as long as it has a low-resistance path back to the battery (or to the AC source in the case of AC circuits), and as long as this path does not include discharging the current into an electrolyte, it will not cause stray-current corrosion (Figure 5-13). An added measure of security against stray-current corrosion can be provided by bonding.

Bonding and Cathodic Protection

Bonding is the practice of electrically tying together major metal objects on a boat (e.g., rigging and chainplates, engine and propeller shaft, stove, metal fuel and water tanks, fuel deck-fill fittings, metal cases on electrical equipment, etc.) and connecting them to the boat's ground.

The purpose of a bonding system is to provide a low-resistance electrical path between otherwise isolated metal objects, *preventing the buildup of voltage differences between these objects* (Figure 5-14). The bonding circuit is then connected to the boat's ground, which in

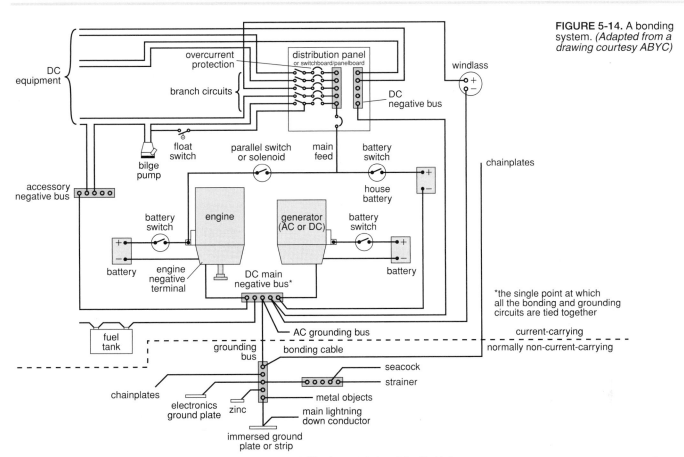

FIGURE 5-14. A bonding system. *(Adapted from a drawing courtesy ABYC)*

DC equipment

overcurrent protection

distribution panel
or switchboard/panelboard

branch circuits

DC negative bus

windlass

chainplates

float switch

bilge pump

parallel switch or solenoid

main feed

battery switch

house battery

accessory negative bus

battery switch

engine

generator (AC or DC)

battery switch

battery

battery

engine negative terminal

DC main negative bus*

*the single point at which all the bonding and grounding circuits are tied together

fuel tank

AC grounding bus

current-carrying

grounding bus

bonding cable

normally non-current-carrying

chainplates

electronics ground plate

zinc

seacock

strainer

metal objects

main lightning down conductor

immersed ground plate or strip

turn is connected through underwater hardware to the earth's ground, thus holding the entire system at ground potential. To be effective, a bonding circuit needs electrically perfect connections with conductors that ensure no voltage differences between bonded fittings.

Because of this need for electrically perfect connections, the connection between a propeller shaft coupling and its engine is not adequate for bonding the propeller shaft (especially with flexible couplings). Instead, connect a jumper wire across the coupling and set up a spring-loaded bronze brush against the shaft and tie into the bonding strap (Figure 5-15). Bond rudderstocks with a similar brush arrangement or else attach a flexible strap to the stock.

Bonding Functions

A bonding circuit can serve multiple purposes at once. It can:

- Serve as the AC grounding circuit on the AC side.
- Provide a path to ground for the high voltages and currents associated with a lightning strike (see the Lightning Protection section below).

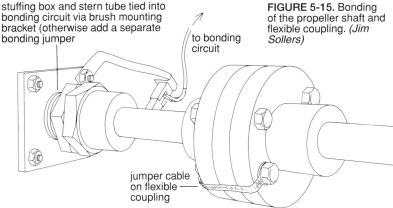

stuffing box and stern tube tied into bonding circuit via brush mounting bracket (otherwise add a separate bonding jumper

to bonding circuit

FIGURE 5-15. Bonding of the propeller shaft and flexible coupling. *(Jim Sollers)*

jumper cable on flexible coupling

- Help to minimize radio frequency or electromagnetic interference (RFI/EMI; Chapter 8).
- Prevent damage to underwater hardware from stray currents originating within the boat by providing stray currents with a direct path to battery negative that precludes their passing through any underwater hardware.
- Be tied to a zinc anode to control galvanic corrosion.

Note that if a bonding system is installed solely for corrosion control, it only needs to include hardware in contact with water, either external or internal (primarily bilge water or the raw-water circuit on the engine). Other items are included for safety and RFI/EMI-suppression reasons, with the comprehensiveness of the bonding circuit varying markedly from boat to boat. The U.S. Coast Guard and the ISO *require* metal fuel tanks and fuel-fill fittings to be bonded when gasoline engines are installed, but this is optional with diesel engines.

The different possible functions of a bonding system require cables of different sizes. Some general rules are listed below:

- For cathodic protection, no cable should be smaller than 8 AWG (8 mm^2).
- For lightning protection, no cable should be smaller than 6 AWG (13 mm^2).
- No bonding cable connected to a piece of electrical equipment (AC or DC) should be smaller than the current-carrying cables in the circuit. The reason is that in the event of a short to the equipment case, the bonding cable may end up carrying full fault current; if it is undersized, it may start a fire.

The last requirement means that in the case of any connections to or between engines, *the bonding cable must be rated to handle the full engine-cranking current*; i.e., it will need to be a heavy cable. So if the bonding cable is to be used for multiple functions (as opposed to running individual cables for these functions), *it must be sized to meet the most demanding function* (in most cases, other than connections to engines, this is the 6 AWG/13 mm^2 cable needed for lightning protection).

Bonding cables should not be run from one piece of *electrical* equipment to another and then back to battery negative (i.e., do not wire the equipment in series). Instead each piece of electrical equipment should have a separate bonding cable wired back to the boat's common bonding bus, and from there back to the boat's common ground point (i.e., wire the equipment in parallel). This principle is the same as not using a common ground wire for more than one appliance, and instead giving each appliance its own ground wire back to the source of power. *Nonelectrical* hardware, such as a bonded through-hull, can be, and often is, wired in series.

Cathodic Protection

So far so good. But when two dissimilar pieces of metal with different voltage potentials, such as a stainless steel propeller shaft and a copper radio ground plate, are immersed in seawater,

bonding the two will make precisely the circuit needed to promote galvanic corrosion! Bonding may be a case of jumping from the frying pan into the fire. However, *if the bonding system is in turn connected to a piece of zinc immersed in seawater, the zinc, being less noble than any boatbuilding metal, will be the object to corrode, providing protection to all the more noble metals on the galvanic table* (Figures 5-16A and 5-16B). When the zinc is gone, the next least noble metal that is connected in the bonding circuit will start to corrode (the hull on a steel or aluminum boat!).

Sacrificial zinc anodes. This explanation is the logic behind sacrificial zinc anodes. All the boat's underwater metal fittings are bonded, and the bonding system is connected to one or more well-placed zincs in reasonable proximity to the metal fittings they are protecting (or attached to them, in the case of metal hulls and rudders). The zincs are eaten up and thus protect the hardware. In technical parlance, the zincs drive the rest of the hardware cathodic. As long as the zincs supply enough current, corrosion will be held at bay. Clearly it is vital to renew the zincs

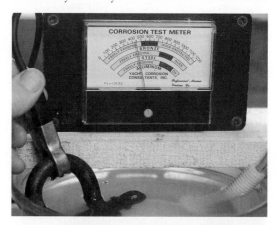

FIGURES 5-16A AND 5-16B. A steel shackle, once again, at its natural voltage of around 440 millivolts. When wired to an immersed galvanized shackle, the voltage potential jumps to that of the zinc coating on the galvanized shackle (810 mV). The zinc is now being sacrificed to protect the steel shackle.

from time to time to provide fresh sacrificial material.

For a zinc to work, it has to have a near electrically perfect connection with the bonding circuit (Figure 5-17). For example, when connecting remotely placed zincs to wood and fiberglass hulls, *do not put* a stainless steel bolt through a zinc and connect a bonding wire to the bolt. The zinc will soon corrode at the point where it contacts the stainless steel, and the connection will deteriorate. Zincs should have *cast-in plates and fasteners* to maintain a good electrical contact throughout the life of the zinc. On wooden hulls, insulate the zinc and its fastenings from the hull to reduce the possibility of alkali attack (see pages 217, 219).

Never paint zincs and be sure to replace them *before* they wear out (see the Sizing Zincs sidebar).

Protection voltages. To protect most metals against corrosion, their voltage must be reduced approximately 200 millivolts (0.20 volt) below the voltage given in Table 5-1. A steel hull, for example, which Table 5-1 shows as being −0.60 to −0.70 volt relative to a silver/silver chloride half cell, should be reduced to −0.80 to −0.90 volt (the ABYC currently recommends −0.84 volt). Aluminum is something of a special case. According to Table 5-1, an aluminum hull should be reduced to somewhere between −0.96 and −1.20 volts (depending on the alloy), but because aluminum is sensitive to overprotection (see below) it should not be reduced much below −1.00 volt. Since the voltage of a zinc with respect to a silver/silver chloride half cell is around −1.00 volt (Table 5-1), if enough zincs are provided, the voltage potential of any steel or aluminum hull can be reduced to −1.00 volt, providing more than enough protection for steel hulls and just about enough for aluminum. When determining the protection voltage on immersed stainless steel, it should be based on a 200-millivolt shift over *passivated* stainless steel, not active stainless steel.

Protection current. The amount of current required to achieve the 200-millivolt negative shift needed for cathodic protection will depend primarily on the area of metal to be protected and the insulating effect of any paint layer (or oxide film in the case of bare aluminum); the greater the exposed area, the higher the current needed for protection. The hardware on a fiberglass hull requires very little current, whereas a steel hull with a defective paint job requires quite a bit. Current requirements also rise in moving water.

The current that a zinc produces depends on its exposed surface area; its overall capacity (its ability to maintain this current over time)

FIGURE 5-17. A zinc on a feathering propeller. Galvanic interaction between the zinc and the stainless steel fasteners holding it on the propeller has eaten away the zinc to the point where it is no longer making a firm contact with the propeller. Its galvanic protection role is seriously compromised. This is not uncommon with propeller and shaft zincs. The better ones have a cast-in frame that ensures the fasteners, and the electrical connection, remain tight.

depends on its weight. Therefore zinc surface area and weight have to be matched to the amount of metal to be protected, the rate at which the zinc(s) customarily corrode, and the frequency of haulouts. A certain amount of trial and error may be needed to get the balance right (see the Sizing Zincs sidebar).

Direct fastening—for example, to a metal hull or rudder—makes an excellent electrical connection. But in general, the best *current distribution*—that is, the most effective distribution of the galvanic current generated by zincs—is obtained by remotely mounting the zincs more or less equidistant from the metals to be protected. Depending on the amount of metal to be protected and its distribution, more than one zinc may be required. The use of several anodes, rather than one large anode, provides better current distribution.

Finally, it should be noted that a zinc will protect only those metals that *are both wired to it and immersed in the same body of electrolyte.* From the standpoint of galvanic corrosion, the bodies of raw water inside a heat exchanger, refrigeration condenser, engine block, or bilge all constitute independent electrolytes. For cathodic protection, any metal components in contact with these bodies of water *require their own zincs;* this is particularly important for heat exchangers and condensers since here we find high temperatures and high water velocities, both of which tend to accelerate corrosion.

Impressed currents. Zinc anodes work by generating a small galvanic current that makes the boat's underwater fixtures cathodic with

Sizing Zincs

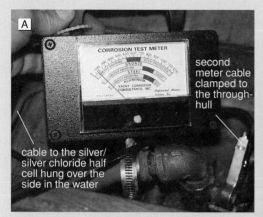

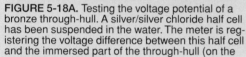

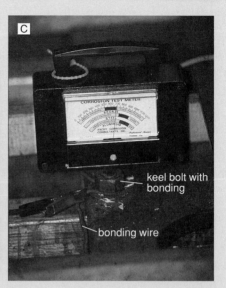

FIGURE 5-18A. Testing the voltage potential of a bronze through-hull. A silver/silver chloride half cell has been suspended in the water. The meter is registering the voltage difference between this half cell and the immersed part of the through-hull (on the outside of the hull). The millivolt reading is very low (below 100 mV), indicating there is no galvanic protection. Since this is a bronze through-hull, it does not need galvanic protection, although there is evidence of corrosion on the valve stem, which may well be from stray currents (the through-hull is in the bilge and is often under bilge water; bonding would be a good idea).

FIGURE 5-18B. A millivolt reading from a keel bolt wired to a lightning grounding system but not connected to a zinc. Note that the reading of –300 mV is close to that given for lead in Table 5-1.

FIGURE 5-18C. The millivolt reading from the same keel bolt after wiring to a bonding system, which in turn is connected to a zinc. The 400 mV shift in the voltage reading indicates that the zinc is providing more than enough cathodic protection.

cable to the silver/silver chloride half cell hung over the side in the water

second meter cable clamped to the through-hull

keel bolt without bonding

keel bolt with bonding

bonding wire

The ABYC outlines the following general procedure for determining zinc area, using a millivolt meter with a silver/silver chloride half cell (a half cell can be readily obtained through many marine chandlers or catalogs and will plug into just about any digital multimeter):

1. Isolate the underwater metal (it has to be in contact with the seawater) to be protected by disconnecting any bonding wire. Suspend the half cell in the nearby water and then measure between the metal and the half cell with the millivolt meter (Figures 5-18A and 5-18B). The meter should give a reading that corresponds to those given in Table 5-1 (for example, –50 to –100 mV for *passivated* 304 stainless steel; –460 to –580 mV for *active*). Note that it may take a while for the reading to stabilize.

2. Now place the zinc anode in the water, connect it to the bonding circuit, reconnect the bonding wire to the metal, and measure the voltage again (Figure 5-18C). Once again, it may take a while for the reading to stabilize. The sacrificial zinc is working and has a large enough surface area if there is at least a 200 mV shift in the reading (e.g., to between –250 and –350 mV for passivated 304 stainless steel or –660 to –780 mV for active 304). Note that many "corrosion" meters have the dial arranged to read these millivolt figures as positives rather than negatives, but the numbers will be the same. If the metal in the bonding circuit has been without protection for some time, it will take a while to polarize and for the voltage reading to stabilize. The stabilization time will vary according to the elapsed time since protection was removed, the area of the zinc, the area of the metal, the motion of the water, and other factors.

Over time a zinc is consumed. As surface area diminishes and corrosive residues build up, protection declines. A zinc needs upgrading or replacing anytime the voltage produced by it drops below the level required for the protection of the type of metal in the circuit. If this occurs sooner than the next planned haulout, the weight of the zinc (not its surface area) should be increased (Table 5-2).

TABLE 5-2. Weight of Zinc for Cathodic Protection of Boats

Hull Material	Boat Length				
	22 ft. cruiser	30 ft. cruiser	32 ft. sailboat	40 ft. cruiser	48 ft. cruiser
Wood or fiberglass	1.5 lbs.	1.6 lbs.	3.6 lbs.	3.5 lbs.	4.4 lbs.
Steel	31 lbs.	81 lbs.	53 lbs.	128 lbs.	185 lbs.
Aluminum	23 lbs.	38 lbs.	44 lbs.	64 lbs.	100 lbs.

Notes:
1. Source unknown. These are conservative figures designed to provide protection for at least one year and with a substantial allowance for faster-than-anticipated zinc consumption.
2. The following formula can also be used for determining zinc weight: $W = kL(B + 2d)/15.6$ where: W = weight of zinc in pounds; k= 0.165 for fiberglass hulls, 1.000 for steel boats, and 0.625 for aluminum hulls; L = waterline length in feet; B = beam in feet; and d = draft in feet.

(Courtesy Wood Marine Ltd.)

respect to the zinc. The same effect can be produced by feeding controlled amounts of DC current through the water to fittings (and the hull, if metallic). This is the basis for *impressed-current* cathodic protection systems.

A *reference electrode* senses the voltage of the metal to be protected. A control unit then uses the boat's batteries to send an appropriate current to one or more anodes projecting through the hull. This current flows to the underwater metals, driving them cathodic (just as the current generated by a zinc anode does).

Power requirements. The amount of power required to operate such a system varies enormously. Looking at a steel hull as an example, and depending on the quality of the paint job, we find that to provide cathodic protection, we will need anywhere from 0.1 mA to 10 mA of protective current for every square foot of submerged hull area. On a 30-foot boat, this translates to between 4.5 and 450 amp-hours per week, with a "fair average" probably being around 100 amp-hours a week. With a poor paint job, or a hull bottom scraped clean of paint in a grounding, this figure could easily climb to more than 250 amp-hours—a substantial energy requirement. As a result, impressed-current systems tend to be confined to larger vessels with a 24-hour-a-day generating capability. (The notable exception is the impressed-current systems widely available for MerCruiser inboard/outboard installations, in which the battery drain is kept down by meticulous attention during manufacture to the paint job on the outboard unit, the addition of separate zincs on the lower unit, and a current limit of 200 mA on the controller.)

Preventing damage. Some impressed-current systems adjust the protective current automatically, but others have to be set manually (the MerCruiser system is automatic). Either way, it is important to avoid overprotection. A side effect of any cathodic protection system is that it makes the electrolyte alkaline in the vicinity of the cathode. Anytime steel or aluminum is reduced much below –1.00 volt, this alkalinity will reach levels that are corrosive to aluminum. (The threshold for damage is around –1.20 volts; because of the risk of severe hull damage, the ABYC does not recommend the use of impressed-current systems on aluminum hulls.) At the same time, hydrogen bubbles will begin to evolve at the cathode; these are liable to lift off paint (known as *cathodic disbondment*— blistering paint with clean metal beneath it is a pretty good indication of overprotection). Since the greatest current density, creating the greatest likelihood of damage, will be found at the areas of the cathode that are closest to the

anodes, the anodes on impressed-current systems must be mounted in metal hulls with an insulating shield that extends over the surrounding area of the hull (the width of the shield is determined by the maximum current output of the anode).

Overprotection and wooden boats. Wood hulls, and the wooden backing blocks often found with bronze through-hulls fitted to fiberglass boats, are even more sensitive to overprotection than steel or aluminum. Once protection voltages go below –0.500 volt or less, the wood surrounding a cathode will come under increasingly severe alkali attack. In some cases the wood can be, to all intents and purposes, destroyed in just a year or two (Figure 5-19). Since these kinds of voltages are just as easily achieved with zincs as with impressed currents, *cathodic protection on wooden boats has to be applied with a great deal of care.* Isolated bronze through-hulls should probably not be protected at all (the ABYC states: "Protection . . . for metal appendages on nonmetallic boats may not be justified if the metals are galvanically compatible."); other fixtures should be given the minimum necessary protection current, well below the capability of a zinc. To make this possible a "corrosion controller"—a

FIGURE 5-19. Destruction of wood due to overprotection of underwater metal fittings. Because of alkali attack, the entire bow area of this wooden boat has had to be heavily patched with epoxy filler.

Note: See the end of this chapter for a comprehensive procedure designed to test both AC and DC circuits and bonding circuits for numerous fault conditions.

The integrity of a bonding circuit is critical to both cathodic protection and the elimination of stray-current corrosion. It should be checked from time to time. With a boat on dry land, testing is simple. But before conducting the following test, make sure that either the boat is unplugged from AC shore power, or else there is a temporary ground connection from some bonded hardware—normally the propeller shaft—to the earth's ground. (This is an essential safety measure to guard against being shocked by a defective AC system—see the sidebar on page 141—and has nothing to do with testing the bonding system.)

Now place the two probes of a good-quality digital ohmmeter on any two pieces of hardware tied into the bonding system. The reading should not exceed 1 ohm (Figures 5-20A and 5-20B); ideally, the reading will be as low as 0.01 ohm, indicating a near-perfect circuit). Similarly, you should not get a reading in excess of 1 ohm from a zinc anode to any hardware it is protecting.

Once a boat is in the water, the current produced by the zinc and other underwater metal makes resistance (ohms) readings impossible. The easiest way to test the bonding system under these circumstances is to obtain a millivolt meter and a silver/silver chloride half cell. Unplug the shore-power cord and disconnect the battery from the DC circuits. Lower the half cell over the side into the water on the end of a long cable, which is plugged into one socket of the meter, while you touch the other meter probe to the various pieces of underwater hardware.

Take a voltage reading from each piece of metal and note it. *The voltage on all underwater hardware connected into the bonding system should be the same; if it is not, there are problems in the wiring or connections.* If the bonding system is working, and the zincs are in good condition, the voltage will be at least 200 mV below the voltage given in Table 5-1 for the most negative metal protected by the bonding system. If the voltage shift produced by the zinc is less than this, the bonding circuit is not properly protecting the lower-voltage fittings, and the fittings will likely corrode.

Next, reconnect the battery to the DC system and turn on one circuit after another, checking the millivolt reading at any fitting each time. *If at any time the voltage reading changes, there is a leak into the bonding circuit from the DC circuit that has just been turned on.* This may simply be the result of poor connections or wiring, or it may be the result of a partial short somewhere. To check the wiring, run a jumper wire from the battery positive to the piece of equipment on the circuit and check the millivolt reading; repeat this from the ground side of the equipment to the battery. If either test corrects the millivolt reading, the problem lies in the wiring on the side of the circuit being jumped out; if neither test corrects the problem, the equipment is at fault.

Finally, plug in the shore-power cord. This may result in a change in the millivolt reading. A change indicates that the bonding system is tied into the AC grounding system (as it should be), and the AC grounding system has no galvanic isolation. In this case, galvanic corrosion through the shore-power cord is likely, and a galvanic isolator or isolation transformer should be installed. Now turn on the AC circuits one at a time, checking once again for any permanent change in the voltage readings as each circuit is turned on. *Any leaks, either AC or DC, must be tracked down and cleaned up.*

FIGURE 5-20A. The resistance between a bronze propeller and the shaft zinc protecting it and its stainless steel propeller shaft is 0.1 ohm, indicating a good connection.

FIGURE 5-20B. Very high resistance (28.25 megaohms) between two through-hulls indicates that they are not tied together with a bonding circuit.

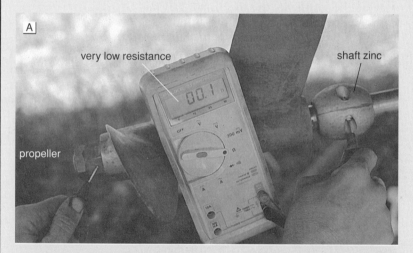

very low resistance

shaft zinc

propeller

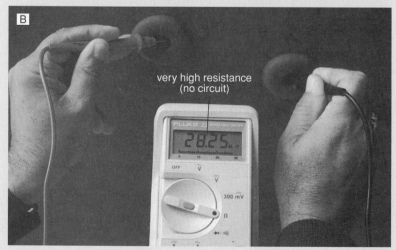

very high resistance (no circuit)

variable resistance coupled to a millivolt meter—is sometimes installed between the zinc and the hardware, and the resistance adjusted to produce the desired voltage at the hardware. Otherwise the zinc surface area must be kept low enough to keep the protection voltage in the desired range.

Unbond and Isolate

An opposite approach to bonding and cathodic protection, which is more prevalent in Europe than the United States, is to unbond all underwater fittings, isolate them electrically, and allow them to reach equilibrium at their own voltage. For this to work, it is necessary to have *all top-quality underwater fittings (e.g., bronze) of a similar metal and insulated from all electrical circuits*. In practice, since most through-hulls on fiberglass boats are connected to rubber or plastic hoses, the through-hulls are already electrically isolated unless connected by a bonding circuit. On metal boats, through-hulls should in any case be mounted on insulated blocks to reduce galvanic interaction between the hull and fittings. (Note that manganese bronze, which is frequently used for propellers and has been used for propeller shafts and through-hulls, contains a high percentage of zinc; *it will dezincify if used without cathodic protection*.)

An unbonded hull will need electrical systems of the insulated-return type (which should be mandatory in boats in any case, with the possible exception of engine circuits). In addition, *the AC system should have an isolation transformer*. Failing that, the AC grounding circuit will need a galvanic isolator (Chapter 4).

We had an unbonded boat in warm tropical and semitropical waters for 12 years with no signs of corrosion except for minor pitting around the bronze housing to the knotmeter impeller and a trace of corrosion between the bronze propeller and its stainless steel shaft. Part of our success with an unbonded hull was undoubtedly due to the fact that our internal circuits were wired to high standards throughout with very heavy wire, and we had no external radio grounds or other potential sources of stray current.

Unbonded boats will still need sacrificial zinc anodes at specific spots, such as a zinc collar where a stainless steel propeller shaft interacts with a bronze propeller (we had a variable-pitch propeller on which it was not possible to mount a shaft collar, hence our corrosion), and manufacturer-recommended zincs in the raw-water engine-cooling circuit and any refrigeration and other condensers. Steel hulls and rudders will need their own zincs.

Unbonded boats are likely to have problems providing adequate lightning protection (see below) and adequate grounding systems for SSB (single-sideband) radio (see Chapter 8).

Lightning Protection

In some parts of the world lightning is a rarity, but in others it can be quite common; worldwide, in any given hour, there are 2,000 thunderstorms in progress, for a total of more than 16 million a year! Parts of the eastern seaboard of the United States are notorious for electrical storms (Figure 5-21). Since lightning tends to strike the highest object in its vicinity, a boat out on the water is peculiarly vulnerable—a sailboat, with its tall mast, is an obvious target (Figure 5-22). The traditional response to this situation has been to use the mast as a lightning rod, conducting a strike "safely" to ground, and so providing a degree of protection for the boat and its occupants; more recently there have been claims that it is possible to prevent strikes altogether through the use of lightning dissipators (more on this below).

Both the ABYC and ISO have standards governing the installation of lightning protection systems. Another organization in the United States—the National Fire Protection Association (NFPA)—has a similar standard. It is instructive that the NFPA at one point (2000) decided to withdraw its standard on the grounds that there was insufficient science to support it, but was pressured into restoring it by academics, the insurance industry, and some government officials. There has also been a raging debate in academic circles, which has spilled over into some strongly worded papers on the Internet, about the efficacy or otherwise of lightning dissipators (with many academics being quite clear that they don't work as advertised). These controversies highlight some of the uncertainties underlying current concepts of lightning protection on boats. Nevertheless, broad agreement does exist on certain principles. The information that follows is based on these principles, with the primary goal being to protect people from injury, and the secondary goal to protect the boat and its equipment.

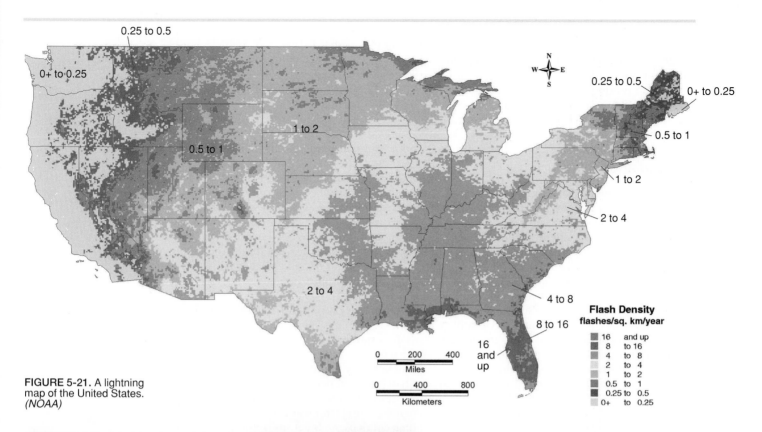

FIGURE 5-21. A lightning map of the United States. (NOAA)

0.25 to 0.5

0+ to 0.25

1 to 2

0.5 to 1

0.25 to 0.5

0+ to 0.25

0.5 to 1

1 to 2

2 to 4

2 to 4

2 to 4

4 to 8

8 to 16

16 and up

Flash Density
flashes/sq. km/year

16	and up
8	to 16
4	to 8
2	to 4
1	to 2
0.5	to 1
0.25	to 0.5
0+	to 0.25

0   200   400
Miles

0   400   800
Kilometers

FIGURE 5-22. A lightning storm in the Gulf of Maine.

The Importance of Grounding

Lightning from thunderclouds is generated from collisions between ice particles. The particles are generally of two types: small raindrops that freeze while being carried up in strong updrafts, and hail that consists of agglomerations of falling ice particles. In typical rebounding collisions between the two types, the small ice particles come away positively charged, leaving an equal and opposite charge on the hail. The small particles continue upward in the updraft, causing the upper regions of the cloud to be positively charged. The hail particles produce a negatively charged lower region.

The voltage difference between the cloud and the surface of the earth or water becomes huge, and the pressure to regain an equilibrium enormous. However, air is normally a good insulator, so a charge has to build up to a tremendous intensity before it becomes sufficient to jump the gap between the earth or sea and the cloud above. But once the energy reaches this level, the resultant giant spark (actually, a series of increasingly long sparks, known as *stepped leaders*, that ultimately connect with an *attachment spark* from the ground) *ionizes* the path through the air (Figure 5-23). Ionized air *is* a good conductor, so now the whole system balances out in a fraction of a microsecond with an enormous current flow (i.e., the main lightning strike, which goes from the ground to the cloud and not the other way around).

The properties of lightning have been known for quite a long time, but the mystery of the charge transfer in collisions is being pieced together only now. The microphysics calls on a fair bit of surface and chemical physics, well into the PhD realm; my thanks to three PhDs—Ewen Thomson, Richard Cohen, and

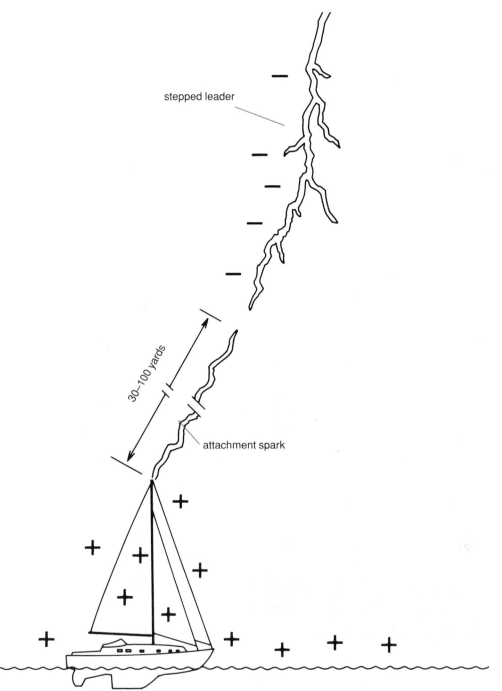

FIGURE 5-23. Stepped leaders and an attachment spark. *(Jim Sollers)*

stepped leader

30–100 yards

attachment spark

Gregory Dash—for helping me with these concepts.

Lightning rods. Lightning protection systems work by setting up an air terminal (a lightning rod) that has a low-resistance connection to earth ground. This air terminal provides a path for the charge on the surface of the earth to launch the upward-going attachment spark that connects with the stepped leaders emanating from the clouds, resulting in an ionized path for the lightning strike. The low-resistance path through the boat is designed to contain the strike in a manner that protects the crew and boat, and hopefully, the electrical and electronics systems as well (although this is much more difficult—see below).

Traditionally, this type of lightning protection has involved raising a pointed conductor as high as practicable and connecting it electrically to the earth or the ocean (Figure 5-24A). Electrons from the surface of the ocean are attracted to the cloud above, accumulating on the point of the lightning rod. The theory has been that the

FIGURE 5-24A. Conventional lightning protection onshore. *(Jim Sollers)*

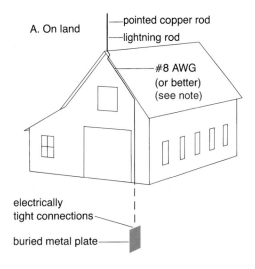

A. On land
- pointed copper rod
- lightning rod
- #8 AWG (or better) (see note)

electrically tight connections

buried metal plate

physical constraints caused by the geometry of the point greatly increase the electron density. Since the electrons are all of the same charge, and like charges repel one another, there is a pressure to "push" electrons off into the surrounding atmosphere where they neutralize the oppositely charged electrons above. However, recent research suggests that blunt (rounded) rods are more effective at launching the attachment spark. Either way, a simple ⅜- to ¾-inch-diameter (10 to 28 mm) copper rod (pointed or rounded) is all that is needed as the air terminal; the optimum diameter is probably around ⅝ inch.

FIGURES 5-24B AND 5-24C. Lightning protection. Note that on powerboats it may prove impossible to include all deck areas in the theoretical zone of protection (which, in any case, may not be completely effective—see the text). A grounded metal spike higher than any mast-mounted antenna will provide additional protection on both power- and sailboats. *(Jim Sollers)*

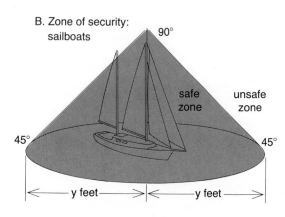

B. Zone of security: sailboats

90°

safe zone   unsafe zone

45°   45°

← y feet → ← y feet →

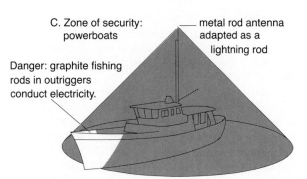

C. Zone of security: powerboats

metal rod antenna adapted as a lightning rod

Danger: graphite fishing rods in outriggers conduct electricity.

One school of thought holds that the process of attracting charged particles to the lightning rod actually increases the possibility of a strike, and therefore a lightning rod should *not* be fitted to a boat. The consensus of expert opinion is that this position is not supported by the evidence. When the charge density begins to approach the level needed for a lightning strike, electrons will accumulate on the surface of any object in the vicinity, including a mast (regardless of whether or not the mast is grounded or that it is a poor conductor). Any lightning strike will then follow the path of least resistance to equalize the points of maximum charge density. *The top of the mast, with or without a lightning conductor, is likely to be one of these points.* The poorly grounded mast simply increases the likelihood of damage because of the lack of a low-resistance path for the current.

Failure to provide an adequate path to ground will cause a lightning strike to find its own route, with damaging results. If the route is through people (for example, crewmembers standing close to or holding a stay or shroud), the lightning may kill them. If the lightning is tracking down a wet wooden mast—a resistive path—it will generate a tremendous amount of heat, explosively boiling the moisture in the mast and perhaps blowing its seams wide open. If it is running to ground through an internal chainplate and then jumping to the ocean outside the boat, it may blow a hole in the boat. If it is running to a through-hull with an inadequate surface area to dissipate the heat caused by the strike, it will likely blow the through-hull out of the boat or melt the surrounding resin in a fiberglass hull. And so on; the examples are many. A well-grounded lightning rod will not stop a lightning strike, but it will lessen the extent of the damage should a strike occur.

The zone (cone) of protection. The *zone (cone) of protection* is a concept that serves as a guideline for designing lightning protection systems. The idea is that a well-grounded lightning rod provides a zone of protection for an area around its base with a radius equal to the height of the rod (Figures 5-24B and 5-24C)—i.e., extending out at a 45-degree angle from the tip of the rod. This is, in fact, not something that is defined by lightning physics—there are plenty of examples of strikes to the sides of grounded metal towers—but it is nevertheless a useful design concept resulting in a fair measure of protection (see The Rolling Ball Concept section below for a refinement of the zone of protection). Given the height of a sailboat mast, if it is used as a lightning conductor, the whole boat will fall within its zone of protection, whereas powerboats need some form of elevated lightning rod to establish such a zone (see below), and even then the whole boat may still not be included (particularly the bow). Occupants will need to stay clear of unprotected areas during lightning storms.

Parallel (alternate) paths. As noted, this zone of protection is by no means absolute. What is more, the main conductor from a mast-mounted lightning rod to ground inevitably has some internal resistance (more properly, *impedance*, which is a measure of resistance in an AC circuit, and which is, technically, the correct term in relation to lightning). Given a lightning strike, this impedance will encourage part of the strike to follow other paths to ground—what are often called *parallel (or alternate) paths*, although this terminology is opposed by some. (Even if the term is not technically justified, the concept is a useful one for visualizing what is going on.) In the case of a sailboat, the rigging is one likely parallel path.

The extent to which a lightning strike will follow these parallel paths is proportional to the impedance of these paths as compared to the impedance offered by the main lightning conductor. Even if the impedance of the parallel paths is relatively high, given the enormity of the voltages and amperages involved in a lightning strike, the parallel paths will still be highly charged—perhaps to tens of thousands of volts. If these parallel paths themselves do not have a low-impedance path to ground, the behavior of the strike will become quite unpredictable; it may, for example, pass through any people bridging the gap between a charged piece of rigging and a grounded fitting on the boat (such as the steering wheel) or generate dangerous side flashes. To avoid this, all likely parallel paths also need to be tied into the lightning-grounding system (see below).

People protection. Because the protection afforded by a zone of protection is not absolute, and because of the risk of side flashes, the best people protection is achieved by staying out of the water and remaining inside a closed boat, as far as possible, during thunderstorms. If forced to remain on deck, do not dangle arms and legs overboard, and unless necessary for safe boat handling, avoid contact with any metal objects. *It is especially important not to bridge two metal items (e.g., the steering wheel and the backstay), since in the event of a strike they may be at very different voltage potentials, encouraging the current to run to ground through the bridging body.*

The rolling ball concept. In recent years a modified concept of the zone of protection, known as the *rolling ball concept*, has gained currency. It is derived in part from studies that

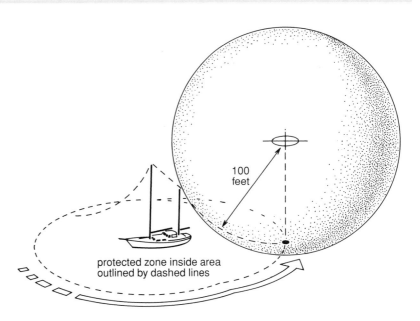

FIGURE 5-25. The rolling ball concept of the zone of protection, based on an attachment spark of 100 feet (30 m). *(Jim Sollers)*

suggest that during the development of a lightning strike, the stepped leaders have to work their way to within 100 feet (30 m) or so of the surface of the earth before an attachment spark completes the circuit. In this case, any mast with a height greater than 100 feet will not necessarily provide a zone of protection with a radius equal to the mast height—the zone of protection may be less than that.

Using the rolling ball concept, we can imagine a large ball with a radius of 100 feet that we roll across the surface of the water into the boat from all directions. Whenever the edge of the ball hits the mast (or any other part of the boat), the circumference of the ball from the point of contact to the water defines the limit of the zone of protection (Figure 5-25). For masts that are up to 100 feet high, this zone will be broadly the same as the traditional zone of protection, but for masts over 100 feet, the ball will contact the mast at 100 feet, and this will define the limit of the protected zone.

The Path to Ground

Whatever is used as a lightning rod, its tip should be at least 6 inches (150 mm) above anything else on the boat. So even an aluminum sailboat mast should be capped by some form of a masthead rod (Figure 5-26). This rod must then be connected as directly as possible to a good ground. The key to success is to keep the lightning moving in a straight line and to conduct it to as large an immersed ground plate as possible.

Cables. Previous ABYC and other standards required that any lightning conductor be 8 AWG (8 mm²) copper wire or larger, but these

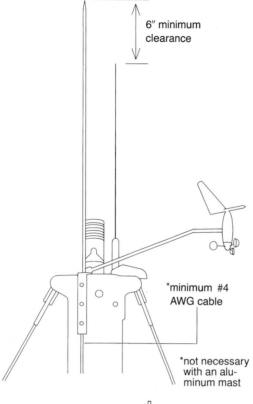

6" minimum clearance

*minimum #4 AWG cable

*not necessary with an aluminum mast

FIGURE 5-27. All the pieces in an ABYC-compliant lightning protection system on a sailboat with an aluminum mast. *(Jim Sollers, adapted from a drawing courtesy Chestnut Hill Industries)*

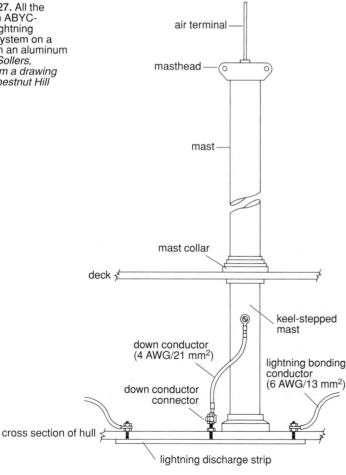

air terminal

masthead

mast

mast collar

deck

keel-stepped mast

down conductor (4 AWG/21 mm²)

down conductor connector

lightning bonding conductor (6 AWG/13 mm²)

cross section of hull

lightning discharge strip

standards have been revised to require the main (primary) down conductor from the lightning rod to the external ground plate (see next paragraph) to be 4 AWG cable (21 mm²), and all other conductors in the lightning grounding system to be at least 6 AWG (13 mm²). An aluminum mast is sufficiently conductive to serve as the main down conductor (Figure 5-27); a wooden mast needs a 4 AWG (21 mm²) cable run down the mast.

Cable types. The ABYC standard calls for cables with Type 2 stranding (ISO Type 1 or A) for use in lightning protection systems and not Type 3 (ISO Type 2 or B); braided copper, which is sometimes found on boats, is not allowed. Apparently, a flat copper bar of adequate ampacity or flattened copper tubing is better than any cable. I'm told the reason has something to do with the physics of how the massive voltage and current spikes of a lightning strike are conducted on the surface of the cable strands or copper. (This stuff is all a bit beyond me; what interests me are trustworthy prescriptions on what to do about it.)

Ground plates.
The direct path to ground should be maintained from the base of a mast or other lightning conductor all the way to an external ground plate. On a metal-hulled boat, the ground plate can be the hull itself. On wood and fiberglass boats, an external keel or metal centerboard plate will do well. Otherwise a ground plate will need to be fitted that should be made of corrosion-resistant materials (e.g., copper, Monel, or bronze) with a *minimum* area of 1 square foot (930 cm²; the current ISO requirement is for 0.25 square meter [approximately 2.5 sq. ft.]), and placed so that it remains immersed at all times. Fresh water is less conductive than salt water—as much as ten times the contact area may be needed to safely dissipate a strike.

Edge effects. Research suggests that a lightning strike is dissipated primarily from the edges and corners of a ground plate, so that a long metal grounding strip (say, 1 inch by 12 feet [25 cm by 3.6 m]) may be more effective in dissipating a strike (some estimates say twice as effective) as a square metal plate with the same surface area. The edges and corners of the strip must be kept clean and clearly defined, rather than faired into the hull.

A recent variation on the long copper strip concept is a copper plate with several longitudinal slots machined into it (Figure 5-28). This has the effect of greatly increasing the total linear length of the edges within the framework of a relatively compact grounding plate, making installation a great deal easier. However, some researchers

FIGURE 5-28 (left). A lightning ground plate with machined slots to maximize the edge length. There is some disagreement as to whether this has any practicable effect when the edges are relatively close together. *(Courtesy Chestnut Hill Industries)*

FIGURE 5-29 (right). Tin-plated copper split-shank bolt and tinned cable end making an electrically tight and corrosion-resistant connection in a lightning protection system. *(Courtesy Chestnut Hill Industries)*

question the efficacy of the added edge because of the proximity of the edges to one another.

Note that although the *sintered* ground plates (composed of numerous bronze spheres bonded loosely together) frequently used for radio grounds have an effective surface area many times that of their actual surface area (i.e., the surface area in contact with the water consists of all the exposed surfaces of the spheres), and as a result, have been promoted at times as lightning grounding plates, the area of the water just microinches from the plate is no more than that of the outside dimensions of the plate. This water area seems to be the limiting factor in dealing with the incredibly high current flows of a lightning strike, in which case the effective grounding area is no more than the plate's actual surface area, making most of these plates too small to serve as a lightning grounding plate. What is more, there are numerous reports of sintered ground plates disintegrating when confronted with a lightning strike; it is presumed that the water in the pores of the plate (between the spheres) boils explosively.

Electrical connections. Regardless of the approach to the grounding plate, all electrical connections must be made with heavy-duty connectors to first-class standards (Figure 5-29) and properly protected against corrosion (such as with heat-shrink tubing and various anticorrosion sprays or greases). Solder should not be used as the primary means of connection because the heat generated by a strike may melt it, causing the connection to fail (in practice, if a 4 AWG cable [21 mm^2] is used, it is highly unlikely that enough heat will be generated to melt solder).

Parallel paths.

In addition to the main down conductor, any potential parallel paths for lightning must be effectively grounded. To do this, connect a minimum 6 AWG (13 mm^2) cable from the base of the rigging (the chainplates) and any other parallel paths to the ground plate (Figures 5-30A and 5-30B). Lightning does not like to turn corners, so to the extent possible when making these connections, run a cable directly from the base of each chainplate and fixture down to the ground plate. In other words, wire the conductors in parallel as opposed to a series connection (i.e., running a grounding cable horizontally around the boat from one fixture to another, with a single connection down to the ground plate).

Grounding the parallel paths in this fashion has the added advantage that most of the grounding cables will be running more or less vertically, whereas most of the boat's electrical wiring will be more or less horizontal. The two sets of cables will intersect more or less at right angles, and in the event of a lightning strike, will minimize the extent to which the boat's wiring becomes electrically charged, which, in turn, will minimize electrical and electronic damage (see the Protecting Electrical Circuits and Electronics section below).

To minimize the chances of side flashes, if a bend is needed in a grounding cable, the bend must not form an arc of less than 90 degrees, and the minimum radius of the bend must be 8 inches (203 mm) or more. For added security from side flashes, any substantial metal object within 6 feet (1.8 m) of any of the paths to ground needs to be tied into the grounding system with 6 AWG (13 mm^2) cables (as with cathodic bonding, silicon bronze through-hulls are probably better excluded).

Grounding strip approaches. In recent years concern has been expressed that any grounding cables or copper strap inside the boat near the waterline running to a connection with the external grounding plate or strip may encourage

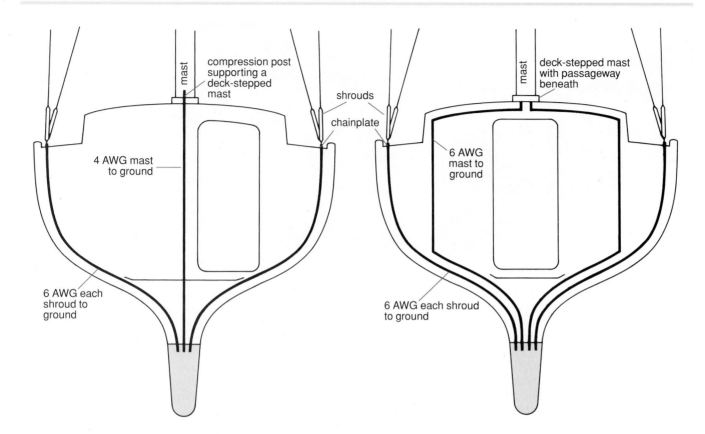

mast

compression post
supporting a
deck-stepped
mast

shrouds

chainplate

4 AWG mast
to ground

6 AWG each
shroud to
ground

mast

deck-stepped mast
with passageway
beneath

6 AWG
mast to
ground

6 AWG each shroud
to ground

FIGURES 5-30A AND 5-30B. Lightning protection cabling with a deck-stepped mast. The mast at left is supported by a compression post that offers a straight run to ground for a 4 AWG lightning conductor. If, however, there is a passageway in a bulkhead beneath the mast step (right), NFPA 302 requires 6 AWG conductor to be run from the mast down both sides of the hull to ground. *(Jim Sollers, adapted from drawings courtesy Professional Boatbuilder)*

side flashes through the hull to the water, blowing a hole in the boat. A couple of different approaches have been suggested to deal with this, both based on the idea of using an external grounding strip running lengthwise below the waterline, in place of a conventional grounding plate:

1. Run a grounding strip (bus) inside the boat to match the external strip with the two through-fastened. The various grounding cables can then be connected to this grounding bus. This arrangement is particularly attractive for many fiberglass sailboats since the stemhead fitting can be tied into the internal bus at the forward end, the backstay and the engine at the aft end, and the various chainplate and other grounding cables along the length of the bus. However, *it is essential that the two grounding strips (inside and outside the boat) be electrically connected at both ends, and ideally, also at intermediate points*. If not, lightning currents flowing through the internal bus may jump through the hull to the external bus, blowing a hole in the boat (for this reason, the internal grounding strip is likely to be removed from the ABYC standard).

2. Use the external grounding strip in place of the internal grounding bus as the grounding point for all the grounding cables by running

bolts through the strip into the boat at a number of points, and then connecting the various grounding cables directly to the external grounding strip via these bolts. This eliminates the internal bus and its risk of associated side flashes, and also leads the grounding cables more directly to ground.

In practice, few people want to go to the trouble of fitting an external grounding strip so this discussion is somewhat moot. The alternative, though, is the very real possibility of side flashes from the various grounding cables that are running to the central ground point, and from there to the external ground plate (or keel, if used). There is an ongoing discussion as to how best to deal with this situation.

Carbon fiber masts. Carbon is a conductor, so in theory, carbon fiber masts are conductive and can be used as a down conductor just like an aluminum mast. However, the epoxy resin used with the carbon is not a conductor, and so a low-impedance path to ground is not assured. In the event of a strike, any impedance will cause heat that will melt the resin. Consequently, carbon fiber masts should be treated the same as wooden masts—i.e., given a lightning rod and a 4 AWG ($21 mm^2$) down conductor connected to an external ground plate (the owner who has just paid tens of thousands of dollars to get weight off aloft is going to cringe at adding this heavy cable!).

Protecting engines. Engines, being such large hunks of metal, should be tied into the grounding system regardless of whether they are within 6 feet (1.8 m) of a grounding conductor or not. Most already have a connection to ground via the propeller shaft and propeller, but oil coating the various bearings can make this resistive. If high currents pass this way, the resistance can create enough heat to damage the bearings. What is more, the last thing you want to do is to route lightning currents the length of the boat to the propeller, with the consequent risk of side flashes damaging people and/or the boat. So although in most instances a propeller in salt water has enough surface area to dissipate a lightning strike, and has occasionally been recommended as a candidate for a ground plate, lightning currents should be *discouraged* from following this path to ground. This is best done by directly connecting the engine to the ground plate, grounding strip, or grounding bus. On metal boats, a minimum 6 AWG (13 mm²) connection also must be made from the engine block to the hull (a stringer or frame in a dry area) to reduce the chances of side flashes.

Powerboats. As noted earlier, with a powerboat, you may have a problem setting up a lightning rod that is high enough to include the whole boat in its zone of protection. An outrigger with conductivity better than or equal to 4 AWG (21 mm²) copper cable can sometimes be raised up sufficiently to create the necessary zone; otherwise, a lightning rod will have to be mounted on a short mast. In all cases, as on a sailboat, a minimum 4 AWG (21 mm²) cable with excellent electrical connections must lead as directly as possible to an adequate ground plate.

The use of an antenna is sometimes recommended as a lightning rod, but many have various *impedance-matching circuits* that will reduce their effectiveness. However, if you choose to use an antenna, to be effective it must be a *metal* one (most are fiberglass), it must be properly grounded via a *lightning arrestor*, and if it has a loading coil (a cylinder at the base of the antenna), the coil will need a *lightning bypass* (Figure 5-31).

A *lightning arrestor* is a device that is inserted in the line between the coax cable and the antenna at the base of the antenna. It has another connection (minimum 6 AWG/13 mm² copper wire) to the boat's lightning ground plate. In normal circumstances, the lightning

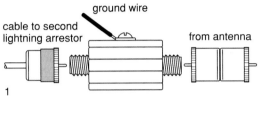

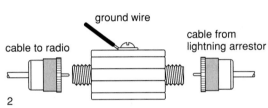

FIGURE 5-31. The use of lightning arrestors and metal oxide varistors (MOVs—see the text) to protect electronics and other equipment from the effects of a lightning strike. The various devices create a path to ground for the high voltages and currents associated with a strike. However, the efficacy of the lightning arrestors is disputed by some authorities. *(Ocean Navigator)*

arrestor is nonconductive to ground. But when hit by very high voltages, it shorts to ground, in theory causing a lightning strike to bypass the coax—although the effectiveness of such devices is a matter of some dispute. Lightning arrestors are available through various marine catalogues.

A *lightning bypass* is a simple device that is fitted in parallel with a loading coil. It contains a small gap that will not conduct in normal circumstances, but which lightning can easily bridge, bypassing the loading coil and providing a direct path to ground (once again, with debatable effectiveness).

Protecting Electrical Circuits and Electronics

So far the emphasis has been on protecting people and the boat. Electrical systems and electronics are another matter. A lightning strike may have a potential of up to 100 million volts, resulting in multiple current surges of up to 175,000 amps, with temperatures running as high as 60,000°F. The near-instantaneous buildup and then cessation of these massive currents creates an intense magnetic field. Any conductor within the expanding and contracting magnetic field will have a current induced along its length (this is the same principle—passing a wire through a magnetic field—that is employed to generate electricity in alternators and generators). The effects can be felt hundreds and sometimes thousands of feet away. So aside from the massive voltages and currents produced by the strike (whether direct or nearby), there may be substantial voltages and currents induced in any part of the boat's wiring. Given the low voltages on which modern electronics operate, even a relatively small voltage surge can do considerable damage.

Electronic equipment. While there is nothing that can provide sure protection from a direct hit, or from these induced voltages and currents, certain measures can improve the chances that the electrical and electronic gear on board will come through in one piece. When installing such equipment, keep all leads (power, ground, and antenna) as short as possible, without any loops, and as far as practicable, run them at right angles to lightning grounding cables (certainly not in the same bundle!). During electrical storms, if possible, disconnect these leads (with the exception of grounding cables to metal equipment cases or chassis).

In practice the equipment is rarely disconnected. The relevant leads are frequently inaccessible, and in any case, the equipment may be needed during the storm. So the next best option is to build protection into the circuits. *A circuit breaker or fuse does not constitute protection*—the response time to current surges is too slow, and even if a breaker is already tripped or a fuse is blown, lightning can bridge the terminals.

What we need are surge protection devices (SPD), commonly known as transient voltage surge suppressors (TVSS) or lightning arrestors, that also include surge capacitors.

Transient voltage surge suppressors (TVSS). Over the past 30 years or so, with the widespread use of electronics in everything from computers to traditional household appliances, TVSS devices have become increasingly sophisticated, available, and affordable. In normal circumstances, they do nothing, but in the event of a voltage spike that exceeds a specific *clamping voltage* (the voltage at which the device now shorts this spike to ground), they divert the spike to ground.

In the literature, reference is also sometimes made to the maximum continuous operating voltage (MCOV), which is often confused with the clamping voltage. The MCOV applies to devices for AC circuits. It is the maximum voltage the device can carry on a *continuous* basis without being damaged. In a lightning strike, this voltage is rapidly exceeded. On a 120-volt circuit,

the MCOV might be as low as 130 volts, with the clamping voltage nominally at 330 to 400 volts.

Clamping voltage is actually variable. It depends on the amount of current to be conducted, the speed with which the device responds, and the point in time during the surge event that the voltage is measured. For example, consider a lightning transient that rises to 50,000 volts in 5 nanoseconds, but which is then shorted to ground by a device that starts to conduct at 5 nanoseconds and clamps the surge to 500 volts in 100 nanoseconds. Even though the clamping voltage may be described as 500 volts, at any point in time before the 100 nanoseconds, the voltage will be much higher than this. As such, for detailed comparisons between devices, the clamping voltage specification should also include the clamping time and the amount of current that can be clamped, as in Table 5-3. For a given current spike, the faster the clamping time and the lower the clamping voltage, the better the protection provided.

TVSS devices sold in the United States should comply with Underwriters Laboratories' UL 1449 standard (the second edition, which is much tougher than the first), while European equipment should be marked "CE" ("Conformité Européene," signifying compliance with relevant European Union standards). (Note that the European standard is tougher than UL 1449, particularly in terms of handling the heating effect that comes from the repeated high currents associated with many lightning strikes or overvoltage conditions arising from other sources.) A device should have a clamping voltage of 400 volts or less for 120-volt AC systems, 800 volts or less for 240-volt systems, and ideally something around 6 volts above nominal system voltage on DC systems (e.g., 18 volts on a nominal 12-volt system). It should stop functioning if its circuits are damaged (i.e., create an open circuit, rather than allow equipment on the circuit to continue to be energized).

TVSS fine print. A recommendation is sometimes made that TVSS devices should be able to absorb at least 600 *joules* (a measure of the amount of energy that can be absorbed without damage—i.e., the severity of lightning strike that can be handled). Unfortunately, the way the standards are written and compliance is measured, this is almost meaningless. Joule ratings have very little to do with the quality of a product.

In Chapter 4 I pointed out that many times, voltage surges or overvoltage conditions originating from events other than lightning are a more likely cause of electrical and electronic failures than lightning (see the Loose [Open] Neutrals and Arcing Faults sidebar on page 148). Most TVSS devices are not designed to handle surges

CORROSION, BONDING, LIGHTNING PROTECTION, AND GROUNDING

that have a duration much beyond the very rapid *transients* associated with lightning. The metal oxide varistors (MOVs) that are the key component heat up until something gives; some simply fail, but others may explode.

In the event the MOVs fail, many units provide no warning, while still leaving the load connected to the circuit, so now there is no circuit protection. Better-quality TVSS devices include a thermal fuse that prevents MOV failure or explosion. On some, the fuse simply protects the MOVs, so fuse failure disables the TVSS but leaves the load connected, but on others the fuse is on the power feed to the load so that if the fuse blows, the circuit to the load is broken. Most times you can't tell what you are buying by reading the information on the box in which a device comes. UL is considering requiring a warning label if a device does not break the circuit to the load when it fails.

A considerable step up in quality comes with TVSS devices that disconnect the load in an overvoltage situation (rather than blowing a fuse), and the best will automatically reconnect the load when the overvoltage condition clears (see, for example, Panamax products—www.panamax.com). It is important to read the small print on the packaging!

Whole-boat protection versus equipment protection. TVSS devices can be installed at the origination of circuits (e.g., at the AC and DC panels) or at the equipment. The former provides whole-boat protection of some kind, but leaves extensive cable runs that may pick up induced voltage spikes. The latter requires more devices but will provide better protection to particularly sensitive equipment. The two approaches are best combined, although it is difficult to find over-the-counter surge protection devices for installation on the power leads to DC equipment. (Surge protection devices for AC equipment and phones, in the form of protected outlet strips, can be bought from any hardware store. Some options for DC protection are the SCL/8 from Panamax, the YachtGard [www.yachtgard.

com], and the ZoneDefender [www.atlanticscientific.com]).

Given the importance of a GPS to modern navigation, and given the low cost of many handheld models, as an added insurance measure, I recommend that all boats voyaging offshore carry at least one spare unit in a tin box. In the event of a lightning strike that destroys the rest of the electronics, the GPS in the tin should come through unscathed. (Wrapping a GPS and other handheld devices in aluminum foil should also work.)

Surge capacitors. As noted, a TVSS is wired between the power leads to equipment and ground. In normal circumstances, it is not a current-carrying conductor. When the circuit is hit with a transient voltage, it takes the TVSS a certain amount of time to respond, during which time the voltage and current on the circuit itself are rising rapidly. A surge capacitor is a device that is installed in the circuit itself (AC only), and as such, is normally current carrying. It absorbs surges and/or reduces the rate at which the voltage and current rises. Because it is installed in the circuit, there is no time delay in terms of its response. However, the amount of surge current a capacitor can absorb is generally limited to a few amps. For this reason, in terms of lightning protection a surge capacitor should only be used in conjunction with a TVSS. Used like this, it can provide an added measure of protection to AC circuits, handling fast, low-energy surges that may get past a TVSS (Figures 5-32A, 5-32B, and 5-32C).

Discharge current	5,000 amps	10,000 amps	20,000 amps	40,000 amps	60,000 amps
Clamping voltage	240	480	840	1,300	2,000
Clamping time (nanoseconds)	—	10	—	—	30

TABLE 5-3. Clamping Voltage and Time as a Function of Surge Current for a Sample TVSS Device

Note: The higher the surge current, the longer it takes for the device to "clamp" it, and the higher the clamping voltage. In the nanoseconds prior to clamping, the voltage will be even higher.

FIGURES 5-32A, 5-32B, AND 5-32C. The effect of adding a TVSS and a surge capacitor to an AC circuit hit by a voltage spike (transient).

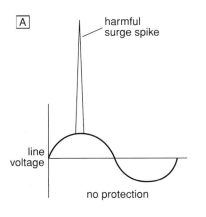

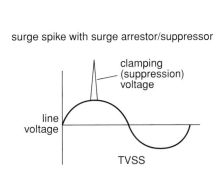

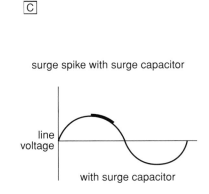

Antennas. There are many stories of vaporized antennas. Antennas are almost impossible to protect in the event of a direct strike to the antenna, even with the use of lightning arrestors and bypass devices (one source for quality antenna protectors is Polyphasor—www.polyphasor.com). The best form of lightning protection for all antennas and the equipment to which they are attached is to disconnect them completely from associated equipment and to ground the antenna cable—both the inner conductor and the outer braided shield—by clipping on a heavy jumper cable and running this to a good ground (but who does this?).

On a ketch, placing antennas on the mizzen rather than the mainmast will increase their chances of not being hit directly. On vessels with single masts, it is worth considering some place other than the masthead, particularly when the transmission and reception range of the equipment is unrelated to the height of the antenna (for example, a satnav or GPS). If the antenna can be placed within the zone of protection provided by the mast, its chances of surviving will be greatly enhanced.

Lightning Prevention

All the foregoing has been predicated upon the impossibility of preventing a lightning strike, and has therefore focused on means to dissipate the strike with as little damage as possible. In recent years, there have been a number of claims that it may be possible to prevent a strike in the first place. The theory once again rests upon the concept that charged electrons from the surface of the earth can be made to congregate on a metal point, where the physical constraints caused by the geometry of the point will result in electrons being pushed off into the surrounding atmosphere.

Lightning dissipators. What is done is to build a lightning dissipator that has not just one point, but many points (Figure 5-33), some of which look like an old-fashioned bottle brush. The initial claim was that *with proper connection to the earth's surface*, the static electrical charge can be bled off as it builds up, with the result that the voltage differential between the earth and any charged clouds in the vicinity of the boat is kept down to a level at which the boat is "invisible" to lightning and so will not get struck. This concept met with a storm of derision from many leading academics and there was plenty of evidence that structures protected with lightning dissipators still got struck. Opponents argued that the magnitude of the charge that can be dissipated is insignificant

bottle brush–type lightning dissipator

FIGURE 5-33. A bottle brush–type lightning dissipator.

compared to that of both a cloud and individual lightning strikes, and in any case, the emitted ions will not reach the clouds to achieve the charge neutralization.

Recent claims based on the lightning dissipator concept—now called a *streamer-delaying air terminal*—are more modest and based on the concept that a terminal will discharge the static charge in the immediate vicinity of the terminal. This, it is argued, will reduce the likelihood of the connection of an upward-moving attachment spark (called a "streamer") with a downward-moving stepped leader. Without this connection, there is no lightning strike to this particular location (some other upward-moving attachment spark in the vicinity will make the connection). "We only have to influence the behavior of the ground charge a very small percentage to affect streamer formation a fraction of a second from that specific point, so a competing streamer will be . . . the first to complete the strike" (Lightning Master, "The White Papers: Structural Lightning Protection," www.lightningmaster.com). In the event there is still a strike, a conventional grounding system is also installed that conducts the strike to ground.

Almost all the support for these concepts from within the scientific community comes from people either directly involved with the manufacture and marketing of these devices or with links to the manufacturers. This support is countered by very strong opposition from much of the rest of the independent research community, who are mainly academics or in government (especially aerospace) research laboratories.

Even if lightning dissipators are partially effective, it is clear that they are not fully effective, in which case a boat can still get struck. Given that the key to successful installation of a dissipator (or streamer-delaying terminal) is proper grounding, which is necessary in any attempt to bleed off the earth's surface charge, even if the device does not work as predicted, it will still function as a conventional lightning rod and grounding system. In this case, the boat is protected by conventional means, and the added cost of the dissipator is hard to justify.

A lightning-protected boat. At the end of the day, it must be recognized that there is no such thing as a lightning-proof boat, only a lightning-protected boat. In a major strike, the forces involved are so colossal that no practical measures can be guaranteed to protect sensitive electronic equipment (especially microprocessors). However, the structural integrity of the boat and the safety of its occupants can be considerably protected, and in the process, the boat's electrical circuits and electronics may also be saved. The measures needed to attain this degree of protection are neither complex nor particularly expensive—it makes sense to carry them out.

Notes:

1. After a strike or nearby strike of any size, the compass (even a fluxgate) should be swung to check for deviation.

2. In 1992, Ewen Thomson and Robert Rothschild made a video for the Florida Sea Grant program called *Lightning Protection of Sailboats* (Florida Sea Grant No. NA89AA-D-SG053, Project No. R/MI-10, 1992). Although Ewen describes it as getting a "little dated," it still contains much useful information. A VHS copy is available for $15 from Florida Sea Grant, University of Florida, P.O. Box 110409, Gainesville, FL 32611.

Grounding

Proper grounding practices have formed a major part of both Chapter 4 and this chapter, specifically in relation to AC grounding, bonding for corrosion prevention (both galvanic and stray current), and lightning protection. When you also include the two grounded circuits found on most boats (the AC neutral and the DC negative), it can all get a little confusing. So let's tie the pieces together.

Grounded Versus Grounding

The first thing to keep in mind is that the *grounded* circuits (AC neutral and DC negative) are full current-carrying circuits, whereas the *grounding* circuits are not current carrying in normal circumstances (with the exception of the small currents generated by a cathodic protection system). The second thing to remember is that *the AC neutral is never grounded on board* (except with isolation transformers, inverters, and onboard generators—see Chapter 4) and can be ignored for the purposes of this discussion.

Grounded. The *DC negative conductors* are wired to one or more *DC negative buses*. There is normally an *(accessory)* bus close to the DC distribution panel, which in turn is connected to a heavy-duty *(main negative)* bus to which are fastened the battery negative, the engine ground strap, and any other heavy-duty DC negative cables (for example, a direct connection to an alternator case or the negative from an anchor windlass—Figure 5-34). Note that although it is a common practice to select a substantial bolt on the engine block as the DC main negative bus, this is not the best choice. It is preferable to set up a separate bus bar.

Grounding. Bonding and lightning conductors are separate from the DC negative conductors but are wired in a similar, parallel fashion (i.e., to bonding/lightning bus bars). The bonding/lightning circuits must be kept *electrically separate* from the DC negative circuits with the exception of a *single common connection* to the boat's *common ground point* or bus bar (see below). This separation is maintained because the DC negative conductors are subject to a certain amount of voltage drop when conducting, so different parts of the DC negative circuit will at different times be at different voltages (not quite at ground potential). If the DC negative circuits were to be tied to the bonding/lightning circuits at more than one spot, this would encourage small circulating currents within these circuits that could cause stray-current corrosion.

The purpose of the various, normally non-current-carrying (bonding/lightning) grounding systems is to provide a path to ground *within the*

boat's wiring for AC fault currents, stray currents, and lightning. In order to do this, it is *not* necessary to have separate AC grounding, bonding, and lightning conductors fastened to all major metal objects—in theory the same cable can serve all three purposes, *as long as it is rated for the job.* However, in practice the AC grounding cable is always run as a separate circuit to all AC appliances and outlets, terminating at the AC grounding bus, from where a connection is made to the common ground point or bus bar.

In most circumstances, the 6 AWG (13 mm^2) cable required for lightning grounding is then more than adequate for combined lightning and bonding purposes, the exception being heavy-draw DC equipment, notably starter motors, on which any bonding cable must be at least as large as the DC negative cable (see page 214). When the situation requires a heavier cable for bonding purposes than for lightning protection, the bonding cable can serve also for lightning protection.

The cables on those items that require bonding (for cathodic protection) but do not need to be tied into the lightning grounding system (for example, some bilge pumps) can be smaller than 6 AWG (13 mm^2), but they must be at least as large as the DC negative cable to the equipment in question and should not be smaller than 8 AWG (8 mm^2). Note that on any DC equipment in which the DC negative connection is also tied to a metallic housing (case grounded), as long as the negative conductor is at least 8 AWG (for corrosion bonding) or 6 AWG (for lightning bonding), no additional bonding conductor is required. If the DC-negative-to-case connection is not present (insulated-ground equipment), bonding will require the addition of a third wire to the equipment case.

The Common Ground Point

A grounding point or bus should be established as the boat's *common ground point.* All the *non-current-carrying grounding circuits* are fastened to this bus, including:

- A connection to the main DC negative bus (this will not be current carrying since it is not part of the circuit to the batteries).
- The grounding wire (green or bare) from the AC distribution panel (*never* the neutral wire).
- The lightning/bonding circuits.
- Ground connections to radio ground plates.
- The external ground plate or strip (for lightning dissipation).
- Any zincs for cathodic protection.

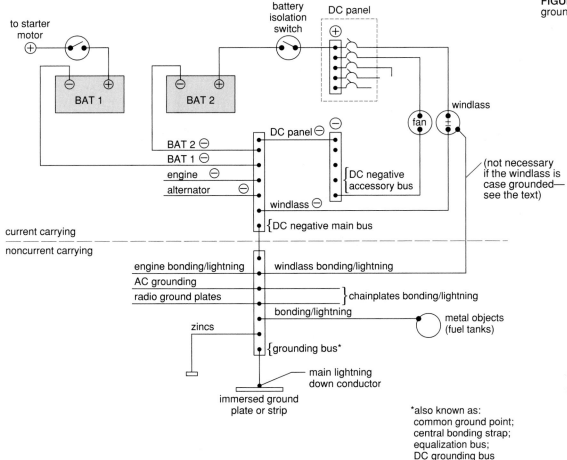

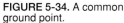
FIGURE 5-34. A common ground point.

battery isolation switch

DC panel

to starter motor

BAT 1

BAT 2

windlass

fan

BAT 2 ⊖
BAT 1 ⊖
engine ⊖
alternator ⊖

DC panel ⊖

{ DC negative accessory bus

windlass ⊖

(not necessary if the windlass is case grounded—see the text)

current carrying

noncurrent carrying

{ DC negative main bus

engine bonding/lightning
AC grounding
radio ground plates
zincs

windlass bonding/lightning

} chainplates bonding/lightning

bonding/lightning

metal objects (fuel tanks)

{ grounding bus*

main lightning down conductor

immersed ground plate or strip

*also known as:
common ground point;
central bonding strap;
equalization bus;
DC grounding bus

The function of this common ground point or bus bar is to hold the DC negative circuit and the various grounding circuits to a common (earth) potential.

This common grounding point or bus bar used to be referred to as a boat's *central bonding strap* and is now sometimes called an *equalization bus* or *DC grounding bus*. It is the same thing as any internal *grounding strip* for lightning grounding purposes (pages 224–26). As with the DC negative, it need not be more than a single substantial bolt (bearing in mind that the ABYC and ISO limit the number of connections to a single terminal to four), which is normally connected directly to the immersed lightning ground plate, but it is best made of a substantial copper bus bar (the ABYC requires a minimum width of ½ inch/13 mm and a minimum thickness of ¹⁄₃₂ inch/1 mm). If possible, a grounding bus bar should be mounted directly over the external ground plate or strip (to maintain a straight path to ground for lightning). If this is not possible, *the main down conductor from the lightning rod or dissipator should go directly to the ground plate*, with the grounding bus tied in via a separate conductor.

Notes:

1. In practice one large bus can serve as both the main DC negative bus and the common ground point. Conceptually, however, it helps to separate them, and it is also not a bad idea in practice since it is often advantageous to have the main DC negative bus and the common ground point in separate physical locations. If they are physically separated, it is important to maintain the current-carrying and non-current-carrying distinction between the two bus bars.

2. Sometimes grounding is done to improve the performance of radios. In this case, ordinary electric cables do not work well for the grounding circuit. What is needed is flat copper foil tape (for more on this, see Chapter 8). However this copper tape may not have the ampacity, or may not be suitable in other ways, to serve for bonding or lightning grounding, in which case it will have to be run in parallel to the other grounding circuit(s).

Comprehensive Grounding and Corrosion Test Procedure

In both this chapter and Chapter 4, I outlined a number of tests for the AC, DC, and grounding/bonding/cathodic protection systems. Once in a while, you will encounter a ground fault or corrosion problem that is difficult to track down and fix. The following is a comprehensive test procedure that uses all the previous tests, and adds a couple more, in a manner that should enable you to pinpoint and resolve the problem. It requires a digital multimeter, a silver/silver chloride half cell that can be plugged into one side of the meter, and a fair degree of organized persistence. (Be sure to take notes of what you have done and log the readings at every step; at some point you will be glad you did this.)

Phase 1: Dockside Tests (conducted at the dockside outlet with the boat *not* plugged in).

These tests are made around live AC outlets. *MAKE SURE YOU GET THE CORRECT SOCKETS AND DON'T TOUCH THE METAL PARTS OF THE METER PROBES.*

Test 1: Test from the dockside neutral to dockside ground, with the meter in the AC volts mode. The reading should be close to 0 volts, but may be up to 5 volts because of voltage drop on the neutral wires (see page 152).

- Above 5 volts but below system voltage—there are dockside wiring problems that need to be rectified.

- System voltage (e.g., 120 or 240 volts)—either the meter leads are in the wrong socket, or there is reverse polarity at dockside that needs to be rectified.

Test 2: Test from the dockside ground to the seawater, with the meter in the AC volts mode (see page 152). The reading should be 0 volts. If not, there is a dockside leak to ground that needs to be rectified (its magnitude can be measured by switching to the AC amps mode).

DO NOT PLUG THE BOAT INTO SHORE POWER IF THE DOCKSIDE OUTLET FAILS ANY OF THESE TESTS.

Phase 2: Boat Ground Tests (boat *not* plugged in ashore, and any AC generator and/or DC-to-AC inverter turned off).

Test 3: Test from the grounding (green wire) terminal on the boat's shore-power inlet to the AC grounding (green wire) bus bar on board, with the meter set to its lowest ohms reading (see page 142). (Note: It may be easier to plug the shore-power cord into the boat's shore-power inlet and then bring the shore end belowdecks to bring the grounding pin into proximity with the grounding bus bar.) The reading should be close to 0 ohms (below 1 ohm).

- Open circuit (e.g., infinite ohms)—check for an isolation transformer. If none is present, the grounding circuit is dangerously defective (broken somewhere).

- High or fluctuating ohms reading—check for a galvanic isolator. If present, put the meter in the diode-testing mode and then reverse the meter leads and test again. The reading should be around 0.9 volt in both directions; if not, the galvanic isolator and/or grounding circuit is defective. (Note: If the galvanic isolator has a capacitor, the readings may take a while to stabilize—see page 143.)

- Lower ohms reading (but above 1 ohm)—there is potentially lethal resistance on the grounding circuit.

Test 4: Test from the grounding (green wire) terminal on the boat's shore-power inlet, or the grounding pin on the shore-power cord (as in Test 3), to grounded metal ashore (shore-power cord *not* plugged in ashore), with the meter in the *DC* amps mode, switching down to milliamps. Any reading indicates galvanic current. If a galvanic isolator is installed, it is not blocking these currents (note that currents up to 30 mA are acceptable). If no galvanic isolator (or isolation transformer) is installed, one is needed.

Test 5: Test from the boat's AC grounding (green wire) bus bar to the engine block or DC main negative bus bar, with the meter set to its lowest ohms reading (see page 142). The reading should be close to 0 ohms (below 1 ohm).

- Open circuit (e.g., infinite ohms)—no AC to DC grounding connection, which is potentially lethal. The connection needs to be made (note that some European boats with a whole-boat GFCB omit this connection; even with a GFCB, it should still be installed—see page 140).

- Resistance between 1 ohm and infinity—there are poor connections that need cleaning up in the AC to DC grounding circuit.

Test 6A: Test from the boat's AC grounding (green wire) bus bar to the AC neutral (grounded, white wire in the U.S.) bus bar, with the meter set to its lowest ohms reading (see page 142). Isolate any AC generator and DC-to-AC inverter and turn off all AC breakers. There should be an open circuit (e.g., infinite ohms), unless there is a reverse polarity indicating device. Then depending on where the device is installed in the circuit, there may be a reading of 25,000+ ohms.

- Lower ohms reading—there is a connection, or fault path, between the neutral and grounding circuits that needs to be removed.

Test 6B: Test from the boat's AC grounding (green wire) bus bar to the AC neutral (grounded, white wire in the U.S.) bus bar, with the meter set to its lowest ohms reading (as above). With the boat still disconnected from shore power, turn on the main AC breaker. There should be no change in the meter reading.

- Below 1 ohm—there is either an isolation transformer on board, or else an AC generator or DC-to-AC inverter has now been brought into the circuit. If none of these apply, there is an illegitimate neutral-to-ground connection that needs removing. Remove any neutral-to-ground connection and reopen the breaker.
- 25,000+ ohms reading—a reverse polarity indicating device has been brought into the circuit. This is OK. Reopen the breaker.

Test 6C: Test from the boat's AC grounding (green wire) bus bar to the AC neutral (grounded, white wire in the U.S.) bus bar, with the meter set to its lowest ohms reading (as above). With the boat still disconnected from shore power, turn on all the branch AC breakers one at a time. There should be no change in the meter reading.

- Low ohms reading at any time—there is an incorrect neutral-to-ground connection on the circuit that has just been energized. The connection needs to be broken.

Test 7 (for boats with two shore-power inlets): Test from one AC neutral (grounded, white wire in the U.S.) bus bar to the other, with the meter set to its lowest ohms reading. There should be an open circuit (e.g., infinite resistance). Anything lower than this indicates an illegitimate cross-connection or some other fault. (Note that some AC panels have an AC selector switch that parallels these circuits; given such a panel, make sure that the switch is not in this position.)

Phase 3: Galvanic and Stray-Current (Ground Leak) Tests (boat *not* plugged in ashore, and any AC generator and/or DC-to-AC inverter turned off)

Test 8: Place a silver/silver chloride half cell in the water, plugged into the meter's negative socket, and place the positive probe on the engine block or DC main negative bus bar, with the meter set to measure *DC* millivolts. Disconnect the bonding wires from any zincs. Note the millivolt reading (it may take quite a while to stabilize).

Test 9: Place a silver/silver chloride half cell in the water, plugged into the meter's negative socket, and place the positive probe on the engine block or DC main negative bus bar, with the meter set to measure *DC* millivolts (as above). Reconnect any bonding wires to zincs. Note the millivolt reading (it may take quite a while to stabilize). There should be at least a 200 mV negative shift from Test 8 (see page 216).

- Less than a 200 mV negative shift—there is inadequate galvanic protection (zincs worn out or not enough surface area).
- Substantially more than a 200 mV negative shift—there is overprotection (too much active zinc surface area).

Test 10: Leave the half cell in the water and move the meter's positive probe to each piece of bonded underwater hardware in turn, noting the millivolt reading. Any change of more than 10 mV or so from one fitting to another indicates poor connections in the bonding circuit, which need cleaning up before proceeding to the final tests.

Test 11: Place a silver/silver chloride half cell in the water, plugged into the meter's negative socket, and place the positive probe on the engine block or DC main negative bus bar, with the meter set to measure *DC* millivolts (as in Tests 8 and 9). Turn off all AC and DC breakers and plug in the shore-power cord. There should be little or no change in the millivolt reading. A substantial change indicates no galvanic isolator (or isolation transformer) or an ineffective galvanic isolator.

Test 12: Turn on all AC and DC breakers one at a time, noting the millivolt reading each time. Any change in the reading of more than about 10 mV indicates a ground leak in this circuit that needs to be traced and rectified.

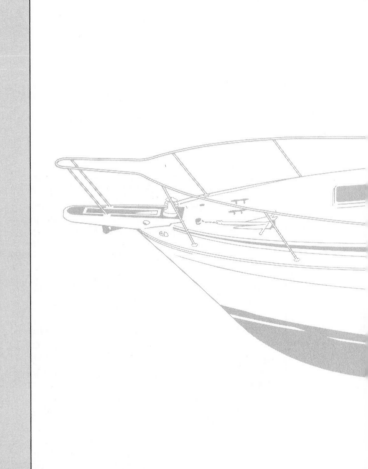

CHAPTER 6

FIGURE 6-1. Alternative sources of electrical power can go a long way toward easing life aboard. Become your own power company. *(Jim Sollers)*

_____ 12 VDC

_ _ _ _ _ _ _ _ _ 120 VAC

(1) wind generator
(2) batteries
(3) 110 VAC shoreside receptacle
(4) shunt regulator
(5) 110 VAC load center
(6) to AC appliances
(7) generator set
(8) distribution panel
(9) DC-to-AC inverter
(10) battery charger
(11) solar panel
(12) isolation transformer

Battery Chargers, Inverters, Wind and Water Generators, and Solar Panels

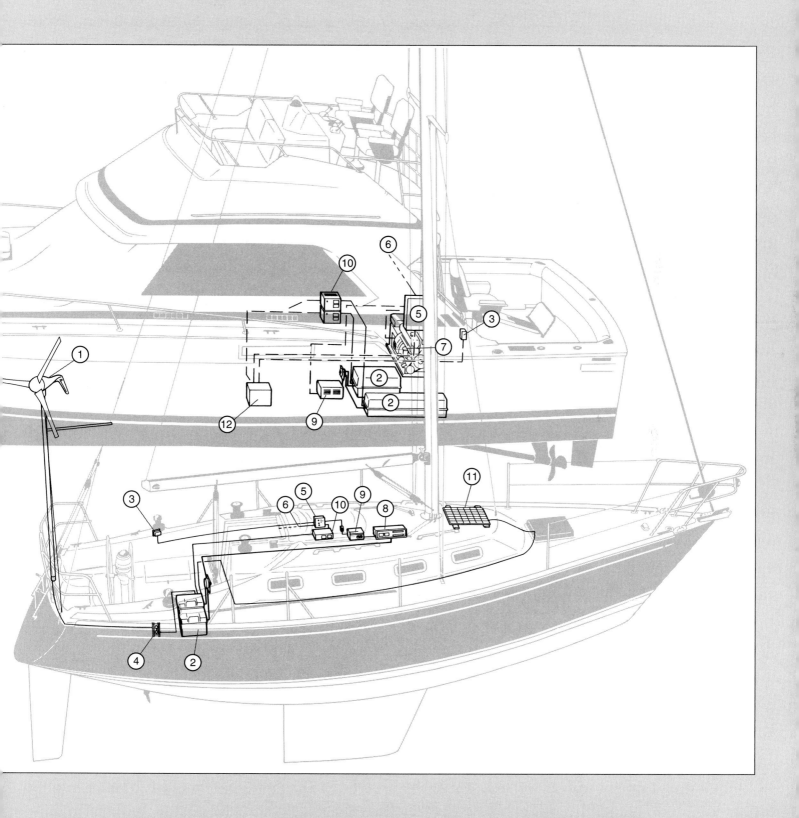

This chapter deals with various auxiliary power sources, both AC and DC. Battery chargers and DC-to-AC inverters are opposite sides of the same coin; one converts AC power into DC power for battery charging, the other transforms a battery's DC power into AC power. Wind and water generators and solar panels produce direct current for battery charging.

Battery Chargers

How They Work

To understand both battery chargers and inverters, some understanding of the nature of alternating current (AC) is needed. Alternating current is generated by spinning a magnet inside a set of coils (an alternator—see Chapter 3) or by spinning a set of coils inside a magnet. As the positive and negative poles of the magnet pass a coil, positive and negative pulses are generated in the coil, causing the electrical output to oscillate continuously from positive to negative and back again, rather than flowing in one direction as in a DC circuit. From a positive voltage peak to a negative voltage peak and back to a positive voltage peak is one cycle. A graph of voltage against time forms a series of sine waves (Figure 6-2). The number of cycles in 1 second is the *frequency* (*Hertz*, or *Hz*) of the current. In the United States, AC generators are held to a speed of rotation that produces 60 cycles a second (60 Hz). In the UK and Europe, frequency is held to 50 Hz.

In a battery charger, AC power is fed into a *transformer*—a device for changing voltages. The incoming AC voltage (generally 120 volts in the U.S.; 240 volts in Europe) is stepped down to near battery voltage—12, 24, or 32 volts, depending on the system. But this is still alternating current. To use it for battery charging, it must be *rectified* to direct current using electronic check valves or switches of one kind or another.

Types of chargers. The two basic components of a battery charger—a transformer and rectifiers—can be put together in numerous different ways. For decades, the most common in the marine field was the *ferro-resonant charger*, which has a transformer wound so that given the

rated input voltage and frequency (for example, 120 VAC at 60 cycles a second), the desired output *(finishing)* voltage (for example, 13.8 VAC) results. All that remains to be done is to rectify the output to DC, something that can be readily accomplished with diodes (Figure 6-3). There are numerous ferro-resonant chargers still found on boats, but for reasons that will soon become apparent few are produced or sold anymore.

Other types of chargers use a *linear transformer*. The transformer is wound to produce a higher finishing voltage than that of a ferro-resonant transformer. The output is then *regulated* by some electronic circuitry (Figures 6-4A and 6-4B) using *SCRs* (silicon-controlled rectifiers), *triacs*, or *MOSFETs* (metal oxide semiconductor field effect transistors)—all are devices for switching circuits on and off in response to a control signal.

Although SCRs, which operate on the secondary (battery) side of the transformer, and triacs, which operate on the primary (incoming or *line-voltage*) side of the transformer, have also been more or less phased out in modern battery charger production, many are still found on boats.

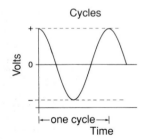

FIGURE 6-2. Characteristics of AC power. The current cycles back and forth from positive to negative polarity. The number of cycles in 1 second is its frequency (Hertz or Hz).

FIGURE 6-3. A basic battery charger circuit. The transformer steps down the incoming 120- or 240-volt AC power to around 14.0 volts (12-volt charger). The rectifying diodes convert this to DC, which is then fed to the battery. If more than one battery is to be charged, the output is channeled through distribution diodes.

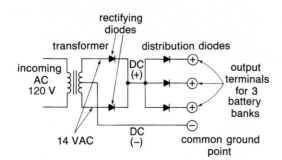

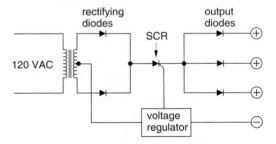

FIGURE 6-4A. A simple SCR-controlled battery charger schematic.

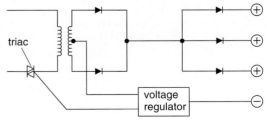

FIGURE 6-4B. A simple triac-controlled battery charger schematic.

MOSFET technology, used in *high-frequency (switch mode)* battery chargers, has become the dominant technology. This is an outgrowth of power supplies in the computer market. In this type of battery charger, sophisticated electronics are used to pump up the incoming AC line frequency from 50 or 60 cycles a second to 50,000 or even 100,000 cycles before it enters the transformer. *The higher the frequency, the greater the efficiency of the transformer and the smaller and lighter most of the components.* The high-frequency output of the transformer is rectified with MOSFETs, which also regulate the charger's output by using more or less of the available *pulse (pulse width modulation)*. The end result is a charger that is smaller, lighter, more sophisticated, and more powerful than anything else on the market, but also considerably more complex.

Ferro-Resonant as a Yardstick

Given the past market dominance of ferro-resonant chargers, and the large number still to be found on older boats, a good way to open up a discussion on the subject of battery chargers is to look at the pros and cons of this type.

The most obvious advantage is the extreme simplicity of the design. It is relatively economical to produce and has proved incredibly reliable over the years. But price and reliability are one thing; performance is another. The simplicity of design that produces this excellent track record is also the ferro-resonant's chief stumbling block. Since there are no regulating circuits, the only way to avoid overcharging a battery with a ferro-resonant charger is to wind the transformer in such a way as to keep its finishing voltage below 14.0 volts (for a nominal 12-volt system—in practice most manufacturers set a target of between 13.6 and 13.8 volts). Once a battery's voltage has been driven up to this level, the transformer's construction must ensure that its output is down to no more than milliamps.

The nature of the transformer is such that the current tapers off as the finishing voltage is approached (Figure 6-5). As a result, once a battery is 50% charged, many ferro-resonant chargers are already below 50% of rated output. *By the time the battery is 75% charged, the output of even a large charger will be down to a trickle of amps.* To bring a deeply discharged battery back to a state of full charge is likely to take the better part of 24 hours.

If a boat is used only for weekends and then left in a slip with shore power for the following week, the necessary extended charging times will not be a problem. But in any kind of a situation where there is pressure on charging times, the batteries will not be properly charged and

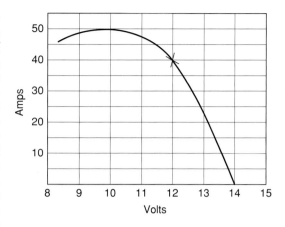

FIGURE 6-5. A charging curve for a nominal 40 amp ferro-resonant charger. Note how rapidly the charging current declines as the battery voltage rises.

sooner or later will succumb to progressive sulfation (see Chapter 1).

Despite this weak charging performance, *once batteries are fully charged, the continuing trickle charge from many ferro-resonant chargers is high enough to slowly boil away the water or dry out the electrolyte in any unused battery that is left permanently connected* (which is precisely the operating condition of many boat batteries when a boat is left in its slip connected to shore power). Ferro-resonant chargers should *never* be used on gel-cell and AGM batteries. Numerous boatyards, marinas, and battery dealers have horror stories relating to ferro-resonant chargers.

There is another problem. Since the output voltage and current are determined by the input voltage and frequency, fluctuations in the line voltage or frequency (quite common with inadequate dockside wiring and onboard generators) will cause uncontrolled fluctuations in the output, resulting in under- or overcharging. The frequency in particular must be accurate to within ±2 cycles.

Overall, this is not a rosy picture. Over the decades, ferro-resonant chargers have been a major factor in premature battery death on boats. The bottom line is that *if high performance is wanted, a different design is needed.*

Performance Implies Regulation

To achieve fast charge rates, *a transformer must be wound to give a finishing voltage well above the voltage on the DC system.* The charger will then have the ability to maintain a high voltage differential over the batteries it is charging. The higher the differential, the more current that can potentially be pumped in, depending on the overall capability of the charger and the battery's ability to absorb the charging current.

However, the other side to this picture is that *any charger that has the capability to pump in high amperages at high voltages also has the capability to destroy the battery.* Some kind of a

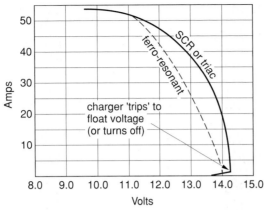

FIGURE 6-6. Basic SCR or triac charger output as compared to a ferro-resonant. Although the two curves look similar, at 13.0 volts the SCR or triac is producing 34 amps as compared to 25; at 13.5 volts the SCR or triac is producing 25 amps as compared to 13; and at 13.8 volts the SCR or triac is producing 15 amps while the ferro-resonant is below 1 amp.

regulation circuit is essential to control the output of the charger as the battery comes up to full charge.

Constant voltage regulation.

A basic SCR or triac charger is likely to have a *constant-voltage regulation circuit* similar to that found on an automotive alternator (Chapter 1). The charging curve (Figure 6-6) is not too dissimilar to that of a ferro-resonant charger, with the significant exception that *the rate of charge is considerably higher during the important later stages of charging.* Once the battery reaches the regulator's voltage set point, the charger either switches off or trips to a lower *float* setting to avoid overcharging. In addition to a better output curve, the higher potential finishing voltage on the transformer, which is then regulated down, provides some leeway to compensate for changes in line voltage and frequency. The net result is a significant gain in performance but with an increase in complexity.

Multistep regulation.

For decades, this was pretty much the state of the art until the introduction of *multistep chargers* in the late 1980s and their refinement in the 1990s. These have a transformer that is wound with the capability of giving *continuous full output at high charging voltages.* The regulator, which may be of the SCR, triac, or MOSFET type, is then controlled by a microprocessor or microcomputer. *The sophistication of the charging regimen is now limited solely by the ingenuity of the programmer.* In theory, a customized program can be tailor-made for any battery in any application. In practice, most multistep chargers have a similar program consisting of a *bulk charge*, perhaps an *absorption charge*, a *float charge*, and maybe an *equalization cycle* (Figure 6-7). A few have *sulfation recovery programs* that can, in certain circumstances, bring completely flat and badly sulfated batteries back to life.

Bulk, absorption, and float charges are described in detail in Chapter 1. Note that *effective battery charging requires the absorption charge.* So-called *two-step chargers* do not have this function; they simply trip to float once a battery has been driven to the bulk-charge termination voltage. *These batteries are likely to be persistently undercharged.*

While some multistep charger programs are almost entirely factory preset, others allow the user to determine the various voltage trip points, current- and time-limiting parameters, and the equalization program. The best are now preprogrammed for several different battery types (wet-cell, gel-cell, and AGM)—the user simply selects a switch position for the type of battery being charged. A charger may have a single output, but

FIGURE 6-7. Output curves of a multistep charger. One plane represents amps; the other, volts. The transformer is wound so that the charger is capable of producing continuous full output to high charging voltages. The output is regulated to provide a bulk charge at a constant current to a relatively high voltage, an absorption charge at this voltage, and then a float charge at a much lower voltage. *(Xantrex)*

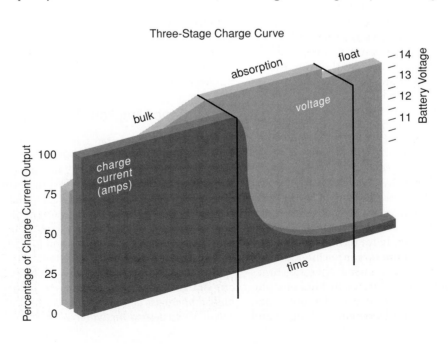

Three-Stage Charge Curve

most have at least dual outputs, and many have three.

Line frequency versus high frequency.
Such multistep programs can be used with both standard-frequency *(line-frequency)* transformers and also with high-frequency transformers. In the last edition (1996) of this book, I wrote: "There is an ongoing debate about the merits of the two approaches. On the one hand we have the 'conservatives' who see high-frequency switchers as notoriously unreliable—the electronics are very complex and difficult to regulate. On the other hand are those who point out that in the computer world everybody went away from ferro-resonant to high-frequency switchers about five or six years ago, and that problems have long since been solved." Since that time, the performance and reliability of high-frequency battery chargers has dramatically improved, and they now completely dominate the marketplace.

High frequency. There is no question that high-frequency switchers have significant advantages over conventional battery chargers, and not just in terms of size and weight. The very nature of the high-frequency process makes many of these chargers both *insensitive to input frequency*, whether it be the fluctuating frequency of a poorly governed AC generator or the difference between European and American frequencies, and also *tolerant of high variations in input voltage.* Some contemporary battery chargers will now accept input frequencies from 45 to 70 Hertz and input voltages from 90 to 270 volts. This makes them truly universal—they can be plugged into any shore-power source around the world. As noted in Chapter 2, this creates the potential to provide a universal shoreside capability for a cruising boat at a very modest cost. The output of a high-frequency charger is also close to *pure* DC, in contrast to many conventional chargers that have a superimposed AC *ripple*, which can be destructive to batteries, particularly gel-cells and AGMs.

On the other side of the coin, there is still the question of complexity (Figure 6-8) and its potential impact on reliability, and the fact that high-frequency technology, in its "raw" state, is very dirty electrically; switching high currents on and off rapidly has a tendency to generate large amounts of radio frequency interference (RFI—see Chapter 8). Manufacturers of high-frequency switchers have invested and are continuing to invest considerable sums of money to overcome (filter out) RFI—with varying degrees of success—but there are still some pretty awful products on the market with respect to RFI.

Microprocessor-controlled chargers represent not simply a linear development of older charger

FIGURE 6-8. A modern high-performance, high-frequency battery charger. *(Analytic Systems)*

technology, but a radical advance. Not only will batteries be kept more fully charged in less time than was previously possible, but their life expectancy will also be extended, sometimes several times over. The larger and more expensive the batteries, the greater the potential benefit; a good-sized bank of deep-cycle batteries may well repay the cost of a quality high-frequency charger through extended battery life alone.

Recommended features.
So where does this leave us? In addition to a multistep charging program, a performance-oriented battery charger (Figure 6-9) should have as many of the following features as possible:

- Some kind of a limit to the bulk-charge phase so that if the charger is not tripped into the absorption and float stages, it still will not "cook" the batteries.

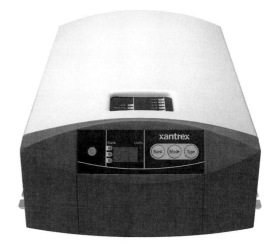

FIGURE 6-9. A latest-generation battery charger. *(Xantrex)*

Small AC Generators and Battery Chargers

Most AC generators are rated using a resistive load (such as a heater) rather than inductive loads (such as an electric motor) because the resistive load results in the highest possible output rating. This rating is expressed as watts, volt-amps, kilowatts (kW), or kilovolt-amps (kVA) (where the "kilo" stands for 1,000; e.g., 2 kW = 2,000 watts; 2 kVA = 2,000 volt-amps).

In DC circuits, watts = volts x amps, but this is not so with many AC appliances. Here watts = volts x amps x power factor (PF). Resistive loads have a power factor of 1.0, so watts *really do* = volts x amps. But induction motors and fluorescent lights, to name two common items, have a PF of less than 1.0, sometimes as low as 0.5. What this means in practice is that the rated wattage of an appliance gives a false idea of its power consumption. Consider a 60-watt, 120-volt fluorescent light with a PF of 0.6. At first we might think it would draw 60/120 = 0.50 amp. But watts = volts x amps x PF. Therefore, amps = watts/(volts x PF). So amps = 60/(120 x 0.6) = 0.83 amp. The amp draw is two-thirds higher than expected. *When calculating wattage for induction motors and fluorescent lights, in the absence of specific information on power factors, it is best to take the rated watts and allow half again as much.* In other words, *count a 60-watt fluorescent light as a 90-watt load.* The corollary to this is that most AC generators will not be able to power inductive loads with a wattage rating that is anywhere near the rated output of the generator.

In particular, many battery chargers, especially those in some inverters, create a large inductive load with a relatively low power factor (often around 0.7). The situation is often compounded by the fact that the charger needs a high and stable peak voltage (the top of the sine wave) to perform properly, whereas when many small AC generators are loaded up, the peak voltage falls. The net result is that to get the full rated output from many battery chargers, an AC generator will need an output rating (kW or kVA) that is approximately double the input rating (in watts) of the battery charger. The closer the battery charger's power factor to 1.0, the more charging output that can be expected from a given AC generator. Some chargers and inverter/chargers (e.g., those from Victron Energy, www.victronenergy.com) can be programmed to "ignore" the poor output from a small generator, resulting in near full rated output from the charger (Figure 6-10).

FIGURE 6-10. Typical battery charger specifications sheet (Xantrex MS2000 inverter/charger). Additional information would be useful. *(Xantrex)*

Electrical Specifications—Charger

Output current	100 amp DC
Battery voltage (nominal)	12 VDC
Battery voltage range	10.3–15.5 VDC
Charge control	Three-stage with manual equalizer
Charge temperature compensation	Remote battery sensor (included)
Efficiency	85% typical
AC input power factor	0.95
Input current (for 100 amp charging)	15 amp RMS nominal
AC input voltage	120 VAC nominal
AC input voltage range	90–135 VAC
Compatible battery types	Wet-cell/gel-cell/AGM
Echo-charge output current	Single, 10 amp

- Temperature compensation for the voltage regulation program, based on temperature measurement *at the batteries* (see Chapter 1 for more on why this is important). Note that most chargers with multiple outlets (generally two or three) sense battery temperature at a single bank. If the sensed battery bank is running cooler than the other battery bank(s), the other bank(s) are likely to get overcharged. Some newer-generation chargers, however, sense the battery temperature at all banks and adjust each output accordingly.

- Independent voltage sensing for each charger output, preferably at the batteries (and not at the charger). Note that most chargers with multiple outputs only sense battery voltage at one bank, which then determines the voltage regulation parameters for all banks. Some newer-generation chargers, however, sense the voltage at all banks, and adjust the voltage regulation parameters for each bank accordingly.

- Load sharing between all outlets. Many battery chargers with multiple outlets divide the available charging current equally among the banks, which are current-limited at that charge rate, even if the batteries connected to one or more outlets are not drawing the allowable current. Other chargers have the ability to transfer unused output on any outlet to the remaining outlets, up to the full rated charger

ABYC-Required Features

The ABYC standard for battery chargers includes the following requirements:

- There must be an ammeter to measure the battery-charging current either at the battery charger or mounted remotely.

- The high-voltage (incoming AC) and low-voltage (secondary side of the transformer) circuits must be isolated from one another (i.e., there needs to be an isolation transformer—see the Testing an Isolation Transformer sidebar).

- The AC input must have an integral (i.e., built into the charger) circuit breaker or fuse (except on self-limiting battery chargers, which effectively means most ferro-resonants).

- The DC positive output(s) must have overcurrent protection (a fuse or some kind of a breaker) within the charger, or clear instructions in the installation manual to include protection within 7 inches of the connection to the charger at the time of installation. (Overcurrent protection is covered in more detail in Chapter 4.)

- The DC positive output(s) require additional overcurrent protection at their point of connection to the boat's DC circuits (i.e., the bat-teries or wherever the battery charger is tied into the DC circuits; Figure 6-11).

- The DC negative side of the battery charger and the negative conductors to the boat's DC circuits are not to be connected to the battery charger case (i.e., the case is isolated from the charger's DC negative output, although it will be electrically tied to it elsewhere—see the next item).

- The battery charger case is to be connected to both the AC and DC grounding systems (and will therefore be electrically connected to the DC negative output at the boat's common ground point, which is where the DC negative circuits and bonding/grounding circuits are tied together). Note that the DC bonding/grounding connection is in addition to the DC negative connection. It is commonly omitted either by accident (the charger will still function just fine but could, in certain circumstances, be hazardous) or deliberately (for galvanic isolation; see also Chapter 2, page 53). If installed, the DC bonding/grounding cable needs to be the same size as, or maybe one size smaller than, the DC negative cable. This is because in certain fault circumstances it could carry the full DC output of the charger.

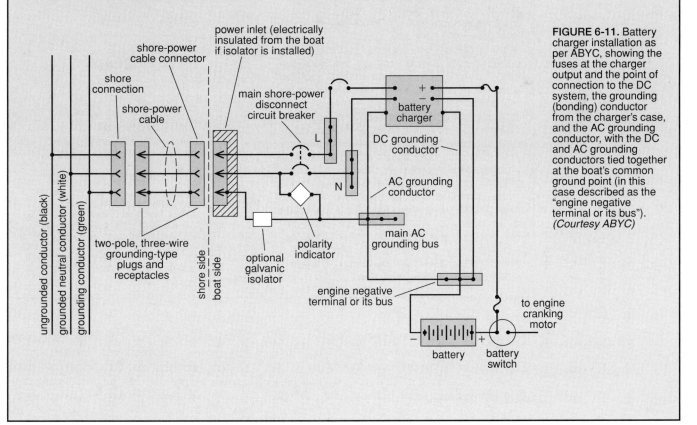

FIGURE 6-11. Battery charger installation as per ABYC, showing the fuses at the charger output and the point of connection to the DC system, the grounding (bonding) conductor from the charger's case, and the AC grounding conductor, with the DC and AC grounding conductors tied together at the boat's common ground point (in this case described as the "engine negative terminal or its bus"). *(Courtesy ABYC)*

Comparing Battery Charger Outputs

There are no industry standards for rating battery chargers, which makes comparisons difficult. Some chargers will produce or even exceed their rated output at all states of battery charge; others are far below their rated output at any likely state of battery charge, making their nameplate rating borderline fraudulent.

Take ferro-resonants, for example. The general practice is to rate these chargers at 2.0 volts per cell (i.e., 12.0 volts if intended for a 12-volt system). That is to say, a charger rated at 80 amps can be expected to produce this level of output at 12.0 volts. At higher voltages, due to the nature of ferro-resonant design, the output falls dramatically.

The only time a charger will be charging into a battery at 12.0 volts is when the battery is stone dead! In a properly designed DC system, the batteries will not fall below 50% of charge, giving an open-circuit voltage of around 12.2 to 12.4 volts on a 12-volt system. To put a charge in the battery, the charger must drive the voltage to 13.0 volts or higher. *At these voltages, the output of a ferro-resonant charger will already be less than half its rated output, and as the batteries more nearly approach a full charge, the output will continue to fall off rapidly* (Figure 6-12). It follows that a 12-volt yardstick for rating output is meaningless for judging real-life charging performance!

For a comparison of the effective charging capabilities of different battery chargers, the output at a higher charging voltage must be used. The problem is in determining how much higher. Fast-charging a battery requires a higher voltage than trickle-charging. Fast chargers need to be compared on the basis of their output at 14.0 volts or more, but at these voltages the output of a ferro-resonant charger will be, *by design,* down to milliamps.

Comparison, as a result, becomes a relatively complicated process. The required charger output (amperage) will be a function of the available charging time, the total number of amp-hours to be put back into the batteries, and the DC load to be sustained while charging (see the What Size Battery Charger? sidebar). The voltage level at which this output must be sustained will be a function of the rate of charge needed as a percentage of battery amp-hour capacity. (For example, a 25 amp charge into a 400 amp-hour battery bank is a 6.25% rate of return. This can be accomplished at a lower charging voltage than a 25 amp charge into a 200 amp-hour battery bank, which is a 12.5% rate of return. In the latter case, a higher charging voltage is needed to drive up the batteries' charge acceptance rate; refer to Chapter 1).

The choice of a voltage at which to compare charger outputs thus becomes a somewhat arbitrary affair. The important points to remember are (1) to choose a voltage related to the desired rate of charge—say 13.6 volts for float charging with continuously available AC power, 14.0 volts when there is not a great deal of pressure on charging times, and 14.4 volts for a fast charger; and (2) to then use charger output *at this voltage* as a basis for comparison of performance (all charger manufacturers have output curves containing this information, though some are reluctant to give them up). It is also worth noting how rapidly the charger output rises or falls (if at all) on either side of the chosen voltage; this will give you some idea of performance in the early and late stages of charging.

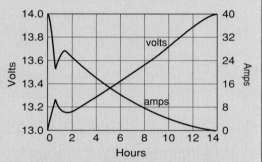

FIGURE 6-12. The output curves of a nominal 80 amp ferro-resonant charger on a well-discharged 200 Ah battery. Note that within a few minutes battery voltage is above 13.0 volts, and charger output is below 26 amps, although in practice the battery is still almost completely discharged. It takes 14 hours to bring the battery to anything near a full charge. *(Adapted from a graph courtesy Ample Technology)*

output for any individual outlet (Xantrex calls this feature *current foldback*). In practice, the house bank is the only one that is likely to accept a high rate of charge in normal circumstances and, as such, should get most of the charger's total rated output. Note that in many installations, there will, in any event, be some kind of paralleling relay between battery banks (independent of the battery charger), in which case the charger only needs a single output wired to the house bank; every time the voltage on the house bank comes up, the other banks will get paralleled and charged.

What Size Battery Charger?

There are several factors to consider when sizing a battery charger for a given application. The most important are (1) whether the charger is intended for continuous use or intermittent use (the time available for recharging); (2) the amp-hours that must be put back into the battery; and (3) the typical DC load (if any) on the battery while charging is taking place.

To determine a minimum battery charger capability, or in a situation where a continuous source of AC power is available (for example, at the dockside or with a 24-hour-a-day AC generator), the charger should be sized to keep up with the average DC load, with sufficient extra output to maintain the batteries on a float charge. To do this, *at a float voltage of somewhere between 13.2 and 13.6 volts*, the charger needs to have a rated output equal to the continuous DC load, *plus 5% to 10% of the amp-hour capacity of the batteries it is charging*. (When a multistep charger is being used, some industry sources feel 10% should be the lower limit; if output is much less than this, the charger may have trouble driving the batteries to the bulk-charge termination voltage, creating the potential for damage through overcharging. All smart chargers should have some sort of a *time-limiting circuit* to terminate the bulk-charge phase in order to avoid these kinds of problems.)

When AC power is only intermittently available, the charger must be able not only to keep up with the DC load but also to recharge the batteries in the available time. The *average charge rate* can be established by taking the total charge that must be put into the batteries (in amp-hours), dividing this by the number of charging hours available, and adding in the DC load while charging. Regardless of charger type, such a charging current will still not fully recharge the batteries due to the tapering charge acceptance rate as a battery comes to charge; an initial charge rate of *up to double* the figure arrived at will be needed to compensate for this.

It sometimes seems that it is impossible to have too much charger capability, but this is not necessarily the case. In a well-designed DC system, boat batteries are rarely discharged by more than 50%. Due to internal resistance in a battery, at a 50% level of discharge, and at a charger output regulated to 14.2 volts, a liquid electrolyte battery will not accept a rate of charge much above 25% of its overall amp-hour capacity. As its state of charge rises, this charge acceptance rate declines below 25%.

Gel-cells and AGMs will accept a higher rate of charge (with AGMs higher than gels). Even so *there is generally little practical advantage to having a charger capability, at charging voltages, much in excess of 30% of the battery's overall amp-hour capacity, although a system designed to push AGMs hard might go as high as 40%.* To this must be added the boat's DC load while the charger is in operation. This will determine the maximum, practical battery charger output in most situations. If the calculation of the charge rate required to charge the batteries in the available charging time produces a figure higher than this, the chances are that *no amount of charging capability will bring the batteries to a full charge in the available time.*

For any given charger (or alternator) output, even with a multistep regulator, David Smead of Ample Technology (www.amplepower.com) points out that the length of time required for a full charge can more or less be found by taking the current available for battery charging (i.e., first subtracting any DC loads coming off the charger), multiplying this figure by 0.8 (to take account of inefficiencies in the charging process), dividing the result into the number of amp-hours that must be put back into the battery, and then adding 30 to 45 minutes for a gel-cell or AGM, or 60 to 90 minutes for a wet-cell (to allow for the battery's declining charge acceptance rate as it comes to charge). If this figure exceeds the available charging time, once again the chances are the battery will not be fully charged.

- A power factor as close as possible to 1. The power factor is, in practice, a measure of the efficiency of the charger (see the sidebar on page 242), especially when connected to a small AC generator. Some chargers may have a power factor as low as 0.7 (i.e., for a given generator output, you will not get more than 70% of the battery-charging capability you might expect); others are close to 1.0 (i.e., you get the nameplate output in most circumstances).

- The best radio frequency interference (RFI) and electromagnetic interference (EMI) suppression that is available. RFI/EMI suppression is quite costly, but cheap chargers can be electrically noisy. The Europeans tend to have tougher standards in this regard, so the CE mark is a desirable feature. In the United States, compliance with the FCC Rule 15, Part B regulations is an indication of a quality product.

- A very low ripple voltage on the output (battery) side. The ripple voltage should be a max-

Testing an Isolation Transformer

A battery charger intended for marine use must have an isolation transformer in which the incoming AC power flows through one coil and transfers power magnetically to a totally separate coil. This second coil, which is electrically isolated from the incoming AC side, supplies power to the DC side. All marine battery chargers use isolation transformers, but some automotive chargers do not—*the neutral AC wire may be common to both sides of the transformer* (Figure 6-13A). In this case, should the incoming neutral and hot leads get crossed, the common line will be hot! This can happen quite easily with improper wiring, or by inserting a two-prong plug the wrong way around, resulting in a reverse polarity situation in which *the entire negative side of the boat's DC system can sometimes be charged at full AC voltage, creating a severe shock hazard for those aboard and for swimmers* (see Chapter 4). Even without reverse polarity, *an automotive-type common neutral connection will bypass any galvanic isolator and encourage stray-current corrosion.* Only marine battery chargers should be used on boats.

To test that an isolation transformer is functioning properly, first completely disconnect the battery charger both from shore power and the boat's DC circuits. Then, using a multimeter *with a diode-testing capability*, test between all output terminals and all incoming AC terminals, *reversing the meter leads* at each test (Figure 6-13B). An isolation transformer should read an open circuit (infinite ohms) between any input terminal and any output terminal.

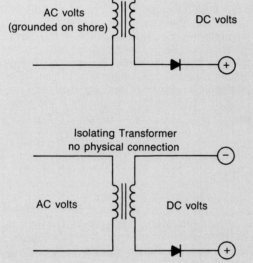

FIGURE 6-13A. Marine battery chargers use an isolation transformer to eliminate any direct electrical connection between the incoming shore power and the boat's AC system.

FIGURE 6-13B. Testing from an AC inlet prong on the AC cord of a battery charger to the DC output cable. There should be no continuity (displayed on this meter as "1.").

imum of 5% of the output voltage. For a 12-volt system, this is 0.70 volt; for 24-volts, 1.4 volts. Better-quality chargers will be less than half of this. The ripple voltage is measured by putting an AC voltmeter across the output leads, preferably when the charger is at full output (this is when the ripple voltage is likely to be highest).

- Short-circuit and reverse polarity protection, so that if the output leads are accidentally shorted or reversed, the charger is not destroyed.

- A remote control, especially if the charger is in a somewhat inaccessible location.

- The ability to integrate the inverter, or inverter/ charger, with an onboard information bus that is tied to a wide range of equipment, such as multistep regulators, an automatic generator start (AGS), a battery monitoring system, and load-management devices. This feature is undoubtedly the direction more-complex systems on boats are evolving in (e.g., Xantrex's Xanbus, and Victron's VENet).

Troubleshooting

Safety. Before attempting to open any battery charger, unplug it from its power source and disconnect all its batteries. AC POWER CAN

KILL. Accidentally shorted DC circuits can blow out diodes and expensive electronics.

Warning: Most chargers now incorporate at least some solid-state circuitry. Shorting out the battery leads to test for output (to see if the leads will spark) or connecting batteries in reverse may blow out expensive electronic circuits. Some chargers may be damaged by turning them on when they are not connected to a battery. Good chargers, however, are protected against all these eventualities, and this kind of protection is well worth paying for.

No output. Before blaming the charger for no output:

1. Check the incoming AC shore-power connection or onboard generator.
2. Check all relevant circuit breakers.
3. Check the charger's incoming AC fuses— often there are two. If the fuses blow repeatedly, see below.
4. Check the charger's AC switch.
5. Double-check the hot and neutral AC terminals at the charger with a voltmeter or test light to make sure the charger really is receiving power (see the Testing AC Circuits section in Chapter 4).
6. Check the AC load on an inverter/charger that is plugged into shore power or an AC generator, and which is operating in its pass-through mode (see the Inverters section below). If the unit has a power-sharing capability, and the AC load is absorbing all the available AC power, the battery charger will get shut down. Turn off AC loads and check the charger again.
7. Note that the battery charger side of an inverter/charger (see below) may have a time delay before coming online—up to 10 seconds after plugging into shore power. If this is the case, a transfer switch will engage after the delay, probably with an audible click. If the transfer switch is faulty, the battery charger will not come online (to check the transfer switch, see the Inverters section below).

Where present, a remote control for a charger is wired in series with the AC on/off switch, but will be in the circuit *after* the "on" light (if fitted). If the remote control is off, the "on" light will glow, *but the charger will be off.* Check that the remote switch is on and double-check for AC power across its two terminals on the charger. If in doubt, fit a jumper wire across its terminals. *Unplug the charger to do this!*

AC side OK but no output to the batteries (ammeter does not register).

1. Check that the battery selector switch is in the correct position.
2. Check the leads from the charger to the batteries and any fuses or switches in the line; make sure the battery leads are connected with the correct polarity.
3. Turn off the charger and test the battery voltage. It should be around 12.0 to 12.5 volts (on a 12-volt system). Turn on the charger and test across its positive and negative terminals; *if the voltage is now higher than the previously measured battery voltage, the charger is working.* (If the battery is already fully charged, an automatic charger may simply have turned itself off. If it has a manual switch, turn it to manual. If not, put a load on the battery for a few minutes to drop its voltage below the regulator kick-in voltage. Note that a *completely dead battery* will sometimes not accept any charge; in this case, try another battery.)
4. If the charger is hot, let it cool down. It may simply be tripping on its *thermal-overload protection.* In this case, it will cycle on and off almost inaudibly at intervals of several minutes (this is most likely with simple SCR chargers).

Troubleshooting Chart 6-1.
Battery Charger Problems: No Output

Checking the AC Side

Warning: AC power can kill. Before opening any battery charger, unplug it from the power source and disconnect all its batteries. Accidentally shorted DC circuits can blow out diodes and expensive circuits.

Is AC voltage reaching the charger? (Use a voltmeter or test light on the incoming AC terminals to check for incoming voltage.) **YES**	**NO**	Check the AC supply—the incoming shore power or onboard generator; fuses, breakers, and switches (including remote control switch if present); and wiring.
Are the charger's AC fuses blowing every time it's plugged in? **YES**	**NO**	Go to Checking the DC Side next page.
If a capacitor is fitted across the incoming AC lines, remove it and try again. Do the fuses still blow? **YES**	**NO**	Fit a new capacitor.
Repeat the test above with any thermistor or varistor, and the rectifying diodes. Do the fuses still blow? **YES**	**NO**	Fit a new thermistor, varistor, or rectifying diodes.
Replace the transformer.		*continued*

5. If the charger has an ignition-protection circuit, disconnect the wires leading to it and test again. When the engine is shut down these wires should be sensing no voltage; if they are sensing voltage, the charger will not come online. If the charger works with the circuit disconnected, it can be used in this fashion but *must be switched off before cranking the engine or it may be damaged.*

6. An overloaded charger with a DC overload circuit breaker will cycle on and off with an audible click (once again, this is most likely with simple SCR chargers). Reduce the load and check for shorts in the boat's wiring or DC equipment. If the circuit breaker trips

with the AC power off, the charger has a shorted distribution (output) diode.

7. Still no output? If the charger has an internal DC circuit breaker and/or an ammeter, bridge across it/them with jumper wires.

AC fuses blow immediately upon plugging in. High-frequency and multistep chargers contain a fair amount of sophisticated electronics, which are well beyond the scope of this book. Low-tech chargers, particularly ferro-resonants, have very simple circuitry (Figure 6-14A), which will include a transformer and diodes, and perhaps:

1. A circuit to compensate for variations in incoming AC voltage. This is known as *line compensation.*

2. A thermistor and/or a varistor connected across the low-voltage side of the AC transformer to adjust output for changes in temperature and to protect against voltage spikes.

3. A capacitor connected across the high-voltage (incoming AC) side of the transformer.

4. Current-limiting and voltage-regulating circuits.

5. Automatic "off" and "on" circuits.

6. An ignition-protection circuit that shuts down the charger during engine cranking and running. This prevents overload from the starter motor and conflict between alternator and battery charger voltage regulators.

7. Various filters to reduce radio interference.

If you can identify the components, the following tests may isolate a problem.

Look for a shorted transformer, capacitor (if fitted), rectifying diode, or either a thermistor or varistor (if fitted). The transformer is a bulky unit

Troubleshooting Chart 6-1 *(continued)*	
Checking the DC Side	
With the charger connected to a charged battery, check the output voltage at the charger—first with it off and then with it on. Is there a voltage increase? **NO**	**YES** The charger is OK. Perform the same test at the battery. If there is no voltage rise, the circuit between the charger and the battery is defective—check all terminals, breakers, switches, and wiring. If there is a voltage increase, the charger is working but may be suffering from voltage drop (see pages 124–25).
Does the charger have an automatic shutdown circuit? **NO**	**YES** Override it with a manual switch (if fitted) or discharge the battery for a few minutes and try again.
Does the charger have an ignition-protection circuit? **NO**	**YES** Disconnect it and try again. If the charger now works it can be used without this circuit, taking care to switch off the charger before firing up the engine.
Is the charger hot? **NO**	**YES** It may have tripped on its thermal-overload protection. Reduce the DC load, allow it to cool, and try again.
Did the charger show maximum amperage before tripping off (probably with an audible click)? **NO**	**YES** It is tripping on overload. Disconnect all DC loads from the battery and try again. Check for shorts in the boat's DC equipment and wiring, or overloading of the charger. Maybe the battery itself is shorted.
Open the charger (see the warning previous page) and put a jumper wire across the two terminals to any internal breaker and the ammeter. Does the charger now work? **NO**	**YES** Replace the breaker or ammeter.
If all tests to this point fail to isolate the problem, call a specialist.	

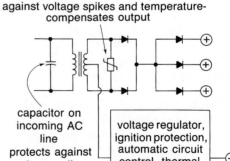

thermistor and/or varistor protects against voltage spikes and temperature-compensates output

capacitor on incoming AC line protects against voltage spikes

voltage regulator, ignition protection, automatic circuit control, thermal overload, noise suppression filters

FIGURE 6-14A. A basic battery charger schematic with voltage regulator.

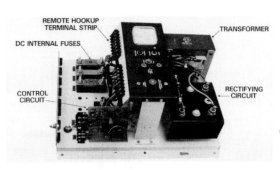

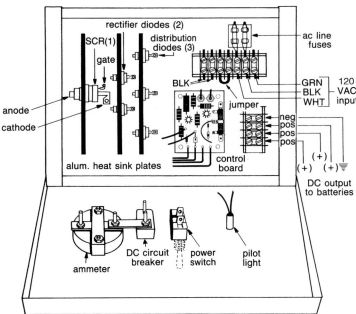

with two AC supply wires running into it and two or more wires running out to the rectifying diodes (Figure 6-14B). A capacitor (if fitted) is a cylindrical object wired *across* the incoming AC wires; a thermistor or varistor is a much smaller electronic component, which will be wired across the output wires to the rectifier diodes.

1. Disconnect any capacitor and try the charger again. Note that long after a battery charger is shut down, a capacitor can hold a lethal charge. Before handling a capacitor, use a length of INSULATED wire to short out its two terminals, which will discharge any residual charge. If the charger works without the capacitor, install a new one with the same rating (see the symbols on its side; for capacitor testing, see pages 298–99).

2. Disconnect the thermistor or varistor and try again; if the charger works, install a new thermistor or varistor.

3. Disconnect the two wires to each rectifying diode (they may need to be unsoldered). If the fuses still blow, the transformer is shorted; if not, the diodes are shorted.

4. After unsoldering the diode connecting wires, test the diodes with an ohmmeter that has a diode-testing capability; they should show continuity in only one direction (see the Diodes section in Chapter 3).

Battery will not come to charge.

1. Check for some load that may inadvertently have been left on the battery or for a leak to ground (see Chapter 4 and the comprehensive test procedure at the end of Chapter 5).

2. Many battery chargers with multiple-battery-charging capabilities have only one battery-voltage sensing line. If this line senses a fully charged battery, *no matter how dead the other batteries are, the charger will stay off until the voltage on the sensed battery falls below the charger's kick-in point.* In this case, the *most-used battery* should be connected to the charger output terminal that has the battery-

sensing capability. Alternatively, during battery charging, connect all batteries in parallel via the battery selector switch.

3. If problems with undercharging persist, load up the batteries and turn on the charger so that it is putting out at its full rate. Check the output voltage on the charger and at the batteries. If there is a significant difference (more than 0.3 volt), there is an unacceptable voltage drop in the wiring and switches (Figure 6-15), or else there are battery isolation diodes in the circuit that are crippling the charger's performance (see Chapter 1). The battery charger will sense a higher voltage than the battery actually receives and will shut down

FIGURE 6-14B. Component layout of a simple charger. This is a ferro-resonant charger, but with an automatic shutdown circuit to avoid overcharging batteries. *(Marine Development Corporation)*

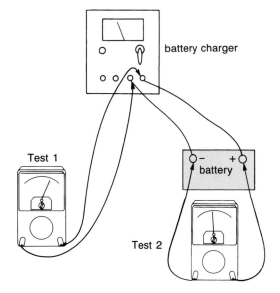

FIGURE 6-15. Checking battery charger output. Load up the battery so that the charger goes to full output, then test the voltage between the charger's output terminals (Test 1) and between the battery's terminals (Test 2). There should be no difference between Test 1 and 2. If 2 is lower, there is a voltage drop in the wiring and/or connections between the charger and the battery. This should not exceed 3% of system voltage (i.e., 0.36 volt on a 12-volt system).

too soon. Measure voltage both at the battery posts and the battery terminal clamps; any difference here indicates a poor clamp connection that needs cleaning.

Voltage drop caused by inadequate wiring is a major cause of undercharging. Situate a charger as close to its batteries as possible and no more than 10 feet away. However, do not place a battery charger in or over a battery compartment with wet-cell batteries. Gases emitted during charging will corrode sensitive electronic parts. Use Table 4-6 to determine wire size based on maximum charger output and maximum 3% voltage drop—the larger the wire, the better.

4. Now bring the batteries to a near full charge (the *absorption phase*, at which point the regulated voltage from the battery charger has stabilized) by one means or another, then check the charger's output voltage. If it equals the rated output voltage (anywhere from 13.8 volts with some ferro-resonants up to 14.4 volts with multistep chargers), the charger is OK. In this case, if the previous test showed no voltage drop to the batteries, the charger may have too low a charging voltage to effectively charge the batteries, it may be undersized for its job, or the batteries may be failing.

5. If the charger output voltage is low, before trying to adjust it (if it is adjustable), be certain the batteries are near fully charged. In the case of chargers with a float cycle, make sure the charger has not tripped to the float setting. Also, check the incoming AC power *at the charger.* Low input voltage will produce low output voltage if the charger does not have *line compensation.*

Persistent overcharging. The batteries boil and lose water; gel-cells and AGMs dry out and fail. Many ferro-resonants left permanently connected to shore power will produce a low-level overcharge. The charger should be switched off once the batteries are charged, or else a small DC load (for example, a cabin light) can be left on to absorb the excess output (these chargers should not, in any case, be used on gel-cells and AGMs). On other chargers, overcharging may be the result of improper regulation, or once again the batteries may be at fault, most likely from one or more shorted cells. Batteries will often overcharge when housed in hot locations, unless the charger has temperature compensation based on temperature sensing *at the batteries.* (This feature used to be rare but is becoming increasingly common, and it is essential when trying to fast-charge large battery banks, especially gel-cells and AGMs.)

If the output voltage on constant-potential chargers is higher than rated, check the incoming AC voltage; high input will produce high output unless the charger has line compensation. Continuously high output to good, cool batteries will be the result of an internal short in the voltage regulation circuit (where fitted—i.e., non-ferro-resonant battery chargers); this requires a specialist's attention.

Inverters

DC-to-AC inverters, which convert battery power to AC power, present the enticing prospect of being able to use all kinds of useful household gadgets on board without the noise, weight, space requirements, exhaust fumes, and expense of a generator. Blenders, toasters, coffeemakers, even microwaves are seemingly no problem! Few recent innovations have had such a far-reaching impact on shipboard living standards. But is there a downside? That depends on whether the right choice is made between competing inverters, and on whether the boat's power systems are properly set up to handle the chosen inverter.

How They Work

To understand inverters, it is necessary to delve a little deeper into the nature of AC power. As noted above, AC voltage cycles continuously from positive to negative and back. A graph of voltage against time forms a series of sine waves (refer back to Figure 6-2).

The nominal system voltage—120 volts, 240 volts, etc.—is in fact more or less an average known as *root mean square* (RMS) voltage. The voltage at the peak of the sine waves—both positive and negative—is considerably higher than the nominal (RMS) voltage of the system (Figure 6-16). Peak voltage is found by multiplying the RMS voltage by 1.414 or dividing by 0.707. A 120-volt (RMS) circuit has a peak voltage of 169.7 volts, and a 240-volt (RMS) circuit has a peak voltage of 339.36 volts.

Why use such an odd divisor as 0.707? Because from any given peak voltage, this number gives us an RMS voltage that will do the equivalent amount of work as the same DC volt-

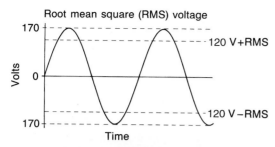

FIGURE 6-16. Peak voltage and RMS voltage in AC circuits (nominal 120-volt AC).

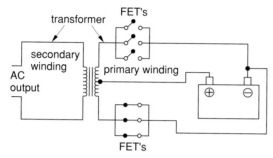

FIGURE 6-17. Circuitry of a basic line-frequency modified-sine-wave inverter. Current from the negative side of the battery is fed through banks of field effect transistors (FETs) to the primary winding in the transformer. Cycling the switches on and off produces alternating current that is stepped up by the transformer to the appropriate voltage.

age: 169.7 peak volts of AC will do the same work as 120 volts of DC—120/0.707 = 169.7.

The earth—meaning the planet, globe, world—is the common reference point for AC electrical circuits. The earth has its own ground potential or voltage, which is given a value of 0 (just as the negative side of a DC circuit is given a value of 0). Alternating current of 120 volts surges first to 169.7 volts positive and then to 169.7 volts negative with respect to this common reference point, for an RMS value of 120 volts.

Types of inverters. A DC-to-AC inverter essentially reverses the mechanism of a battery charger, producing line voltage (120- or 240-volt AC) from DC battery voltage. In essence, two steps are required: the first to convert DC to AC, and the second to step the AC up to the required voltage.

Inverters fall into two broad categories: those that produce a *true-sine-wave output* equivalent to that produced by a generator or an electricity company, and those that produce a *stepped-square-wave output* (generally referred to as a *modified-sine-wave output*). There are two technologies for producing either waveform, one based on *line-frequency switching*, the other based on *high-frequency switching*. This gives us four possible base combinations: line-frequency stepped square

wave, line-frequency sine wave (generally known as *hybrid*), high-frequency stepped square wave, and high-frequency sine wave.

Line-frequency inverters. Crudely speaking, inside a line-frequency inverter there is a transformer with a primary (low-voltage) winding and a secondary (high-voltage) winding. The positive and negative sides of a battery are fed through banks of high-current switches (*field-effect transistors*—FETs) to the primary winding (Figure 6-17). The switches are turned on and off alternately at a rate determined by a high-frequency *crystal oscillator* (a device that holds a very stable frequency) in a manner that feeds battery current through the transformer first in one direction and then in the other; i.e., alternating the direction of current flow at a frequency that is regulated by the oscillator. This alternating current is stepped up by the transformer to produce alternating current in the secondary winding at the desired output voltage.

The rate at which the FETs switch on and off determines the frequency of the AC output, and is set to produce 60 cycles a second in the United States and 50 cycles a second in Europe (the same as a power company, hence the designation *line frequency* for these inverters). Since the FETs are either on or off, the waveform produced by such an inverter is a stepped square wave (Figure 6-18A). However, because the industry has settled on the term "modified sine wave," I will use it from this point on.

The transformers are wound in such a way that with normal battery voltages, the peak of the modified sine wave is lower than that of a true sine wave. The length of the wave is then regulated to maintain an RMS voltage of 120 volts. As the load on such an inverter increases, so too does the load on the battery that is powering it. The heavier the load, the lower the battery's voltage will be. Since this type of inverter's output voltage is *directly proportional* to its input volt-

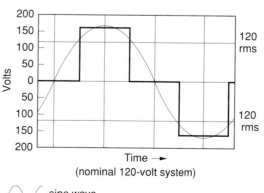

FIGURE 6-18A. A stepped square wave (modified sine wave). The peak voltage is lower than with a true sine wave, but the RMS voltage is the same.

FIGURE 6-18B. Pulse width modulation on a modified-sine-wave inverter maintains a constant RMS voltage at differing battery input voltages.

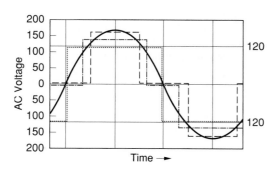

FIGURE 6-19. A hybrid inverter. *(Xantrex)*

FIGURES 6-18C AND 6-18D. A modified-sine-wave inverter subjected to varying loads at varying battery voltages. Note the wide variation in output voltage (from 126.3 to 99.5) as measured by an *averaging* meter (as opposed to an RMS meter—see the text), and the changing waveform, but the stable frequency (60.02 Hz).

FIGURE 6-18E. The sine-wave output from an inverter also maintains a very stable voltage and frequency.

age, the output voltage will also fall. To compensate for the falling voltage, the wavelength has to be increased so that the inverter maintains its RMS voltage but with a resultant increasing loss of any resemblance to a sine wave (Figure 6-18B). This process of changing the length of the modified sine wave to maintain a constant RMS voltage is known as *pulse width modulation* (Figures 6-18C and 6-18D).

High-frequency inverters. High-frequency inverters utilize similar switching to feed battery current through a transformer, first in one direction and then the other, but now the FETs switch on and off *thousands* of times a second (anywhere from 16,000 on up), resulting in high-frequency alternating current at battery voltages in the primary winding of the transformer. This low-voltage, high-frequency AC is stepped up by the transformer to the desired AC output voltage, rectified to high-voltage DC, and then switched from positive to negative once again at line frequency to produce AC at the correct frequency. Because the cross-sectional area of a transformer is indirectly proportional to the frequency of the alternating current applied to it, *the higher the frequency of the initial switching operation, the smaller and lighter it is possible to build the transformer and thus the inverter.*

In the final switching stage:

1. A modified-sine-wave high-frequency inverter utilizes the same single positive and negative pulse in each AC cycle as a modified-sine-wave line-frequency inverter. As a result, on some inverters, the voltage and pulse width also vary with battery input voltage, just as with the line-frequency pulse-width-modulated inverters, but on others an additional regulation circuit produces a constant voltage and pulse width. As far as I know, no high-frequency inverters sold into the marine market currently produce a modified-sine-wave output (although some have in the past).

2. A sine-wave high-frequency inverter uses multiple pulse-width-modulated steps in each

cycle to create a sinusoidal output waveform that is indistinguishable, as far as AC equipment is concerned, from a true sine wave. What is more, the peak voltage and waveform are unaffected by changes in battery voltage—in fact, the output is frequently cleaner than that from a power company! As far as I know, all high-frequency inverters sold into the marine market currently meet this description (Figure 6-18E).

Hybrid inverters. Hybrid inverters (Figure 6-19) do the initial switching of the battery current at high frequency (as with a high-frequency inverter). The difference is that this switching has the line frequency embedded in it. Perhaps it is best think of it in this way: instead of the switching producing high-frequency AC (i.e., the direction of battery current flowing through the primary side of the transformer is switched back and forth at high frequency), high-frequency switching occurs first on the positive side only (i.e., the battery current is pulsed through the transformer multiple times in the same direction) and then on the negative side only (i.e., the battery current is pulsed through the transformer multiple times in the other direction), with the timing of the move from pulsing in one direction to the other based on line frequency.

The net result is that although there is high-frequency switching of the battery current, the transformer is seeing a reversal of the direction of the current flow at line frequency, and as such, a line-frequency transformer—a large, heavy inverter—is needed. The output of the transformer is line-frequency AC, with the high-frequency pulsing embedded in it. This output is first regulated through pulse width modulation of the high-frequency switching that produces the pulses, and then it is run through a *low-pass filter* to produce a low-distortion sine wave from a line-frequency transformer. (I am told that the primary reason for the initial high-frequency switching is that it substantially reduces the low-pass filter requirements over what is needed to try and get a sine wave out of line-frequency switching.)

This seems like an unnecessarily complicated process, but it has certain advantages for the end user that will be explored below, with the result that at the time of writing Xantrex (www.xantrex.com), by far the largest builder of inverters for the U.S. market, with both line-frequency and high-frequency models, is switching most of its product line into hybrid inverters, while both Mastervolt (www.mastervolt.com) and Victron Energy (www.victronenergy.com), its primary competitors, have a number of well-established hybrid inverters.

Pros and cons of different technologies. What are the pros and cons of the different technologies? The first point that is immediately apparent is the physical difference between line-frequency, hybrid, and high-frequency inverters. A 2,000-watt line-frequency or hybrid model (either modified sine wave or sine wave) will weigh in at 40 pounds (18 kg) on up and will occupy approximately 1 cubic foot of space; its high-frequency counterpart (once again, either modified square wave or sine wave) will weigh half as much (and often much less) and occupy as little as one-third the space (Figure 6-20).

However, the high-frequency inverter is more likely to create radio frequency interference (Chapter 8), and it has a higher component count, which historically has translated into a higher failure rate, although this is no longer the case. The high-frequency process is not easily "reversible" for battery charging, whereas it is simple to run line-frequency inverters "back-

FIGURE 6-20. Line-frequency versus high-frequency inverter construction. The line-frequency inverter (occupying most of the picture) is rated at 1,000 watts, while the high-frequency inverter (the small unit in the foreground) is rated at 1,500 watts! Each of the three small transformers in the center of the high-frequency inverter (the square units) is capable of producing 500 watts of output, as compared to the 1,000 watts from the heavy bulky transformer that dominates the line-frequency inverter.

ward" when another source of AC power comes online. As a result, most line-frequency inverters incorporate powerful battery-charging capabilities, while a number of the high-frequency models do not.

Within the general class of high-frequency inverters, sine-wave inverters are frequently less efficient than other inverters in converting DC to AC (typically, around 85% efficient as opposed to 90% for a modified-sine-wave inverter), and they have a higher *standby drain* (the amount of current consumed when the inverter is on but not powering a load). The standby drain is particularly important for cruising sailors; if DC resources are limited, but an inverter is to be left on for long hours, the standby drain can become a significant part of the boat's overall DC load.

If an inverter will be powering electric motors (for example, an air-conditioning or refrigeration system or a washing machine), it is likely to be confronted with high surge (*start-up* or *inrush*) loads (up to six times the running load of the motor). As a general rule, line-frequency and hybrid inverters (i.e., those built with line-frequency transformers) have a significantly greater ability to handle surge loads than high-frequency inverters. This is an important consideration in many installations, and one of the reasons why manufacturers such as Xantrex and Mastervolt have in recent years put more emphasis on their hybrid inverters and less on high-frequency inverters.

Finally, all sine-wave inverters (hybrid and high frequency) are more expensive than modified-sine-wave inverters in terms of dollars per watt of output, although this differential has been declining. Is there any reason to pay the extra money for a sine wave?

How important is the waveform? Many AC loads, such as incandescent lights, toasters, hair dryers, and coffeemakers, are *resistive*. They are not in the least bit sensitive to waveform. In fact, they will run as well on DC as on AC as long as the voltage is correct. At the other end of the spectrum are certain loads, mostly high-tech electronics (such as laser printers and SCR- or triac-based electronic controllers, as well as odd-ball things such as some electric clocks in bread-makers and other appliances), which will not function on a modified sine wave and may also self-destruct. In between, we have a gray area.

With a modified sine wave, you are likely to experience some picture degradation on a TV, hum on the stereo, and probably some loss of efficiency on induction motors (often resulting in the motor running hotter than normal, which may lead to premature failure). Microwaves, popular

FIGURE 6-21A. A sample inverter performance sheet (Xantrex RS2000 inverter/charger). Note that the surge rating is at a substantially lower temperature than the continuous power rating; in a hot ambient environment, the surge capability will be lower than that given. *(Xantrex)*

Inverter Specifications	
Output wave form	Sine wave
Total harmonic voltage distortion	<3%
Output power continuous	2,000 W/2,000 VA continuous at –4°F to 122°F (–20°C to 50°C)
Surge rating	5,000 W/5,000 VA for 5 seconds at 32°F to 77°F (0°C to 25°C)
AC output voltage	120 VAC ±5%
Input DC voltage rating	12 VDC nominal, 10 to 16 VDC
AC output voltage load regulation	104–127 VAC
AC output voltage DC line regulation	108–125 VAC
AC output frequency	60.0 ±0.05 Hz
Power factor (lag or lead)	0 to 1.0
Peak efficiency	>89%
Efficiency at 2,000 W	>85%
Idle power consumption	<5 W
AC overvoltage shutdown level	128 VAC
AC undervoltage shutdown level	108 VAC
DC low voltage shutdown	10 volts
DC overvoltage shutdown	16 volts

appliances to run off inverters, are an interesting case. They appear to be sensitive to both peak voltage and waveform. When powered by a pulse-width-modulated modified-sine-wave inverter, many microwaves become increasingly inefficient the lower the battery input voltage—and therefore the lower the output voltage and the wider the output pulse.

Most battery chargers for cordless tools work fine on a modified sine wave, but some do not. If the charger starts to get warmer than it does when using shore power, do not use it with a modified-sine-wave inverter.

In the final analysis, unless you have specific pieces of equipment that demand a true sine wave, the point at which a loss of performance in other equipment tips the balance in favor of the extra cost of a sine-wave inverter (and its likely lower efficiency) is a matter of personal choice. But it should be noted that as the reliability of the complex electronics in true-sine-wave inverters goes up, the relative price differential with modified-sine-wave inverters comes down, and the screening for RFI and EMI emissions improves, there will be less and less justification for buying a modified-sine-wave inverter.

Recommended inverter features. With the above in mind, the following features should be considered when selecting an inverter for a particular application:

- A true sine wave, if possible, as long as the inverter comes with the other features necessary for the installation.
- Adequate output, in watts, to meet the maximum continuous load. Note that there are various ways of rating inverters, all producing different results, and that output tends to decline as temperature goes up. Given that inverters often operate in relatively high ambient temperatures, and in any case get hot at full power, the point of interest is the *continuous rated output at 105°F/40°C or higher* (some manufacturers will rate at 122°F/50°C, which is even better). What you may also see is a "P30" rate, which is the rated output for 30 minutes in a less-demanding environment. If used to size an inverter, this rating may result in an undersized unit. It is important to compare apples to apples (Figure 6-21A).
- A high-enough surge rating. On some (high-frequency) inverters, the surge rating may be as little as 150% of the continuous rating, whereas for line-frequency inverters, it may be as high as 300% of this rating.
- High efficiency at converting DC to AC. Note, however, that the peak, or maximum, efficiency is invariably given, which is generally only achieved under a relatively low load. To make an effective comparison of inverters over the full range of their output, you must look at the efficiency curve (all manufacturers will have one; Figure 6-21B).
- A low standby drain when the inverter is turned on but not supplying an AC load. Depending on how important it is to minimize the DC load on a boat, and whether or not an inverter will be left on for many hours

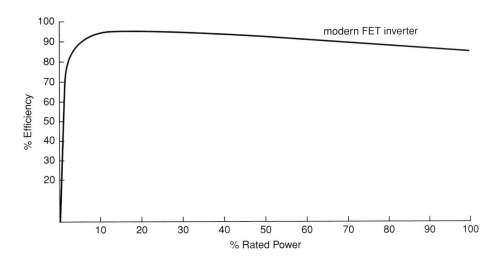

FIGURE 6-21B. Power versus efficiency curve for a typical line-frequency inverter (the high-frequency and hybrid inverters do not do quite as well).

(as opposed to turning it on for specific uses), this can be a significant issue.

- A remote controller. This goes back to the point above. If the inverter will only be used intermittently (as most are), and the standby drain is an issue (as it commonly is), and the inverter is somewhat inaccessible (as is generally the case), then it is important to be able to turn it on and off from a remote panel.

- A built-in transfer switch. This switch enables the inverter to be hard-wired (i.e., directly connected) to an AC input (shore power and/or an AC generator). Anytime a source of AC power is available, the inverter automatically switches from its invert mode to a pass-through mode, so that the AC loads are now supplied by the AC source and not from the DC system.

- Dual AC inputs. This feature allows two AC sources (e.g., shore power and an AC generator) to be hard-wired to the inverter. If either of them comes online, the inverter will switch to its pass-through mode. However, in most cases it will not be able to bring both online at once (i.e., parallel two sources of supply) because of issues with synchronization and islanding (see Chapter 2).

- A powerful multistep battery-charging capability, with less than 5% ripple (see the Battery Chargers section above) and *temperature-compensated voltage regulation based on temperature sensing at the batteries*. If the charger has more than one output, there should be independent temperature sensing for all high-current outputs (some outputs may be current-limited to relatively low levels—see below—in which case temperature sensing on these outlets is not as important). The battery-charging capability that comes with many inverters is at least as great as that of many stand-alone battery chargers that cost about the same (i.e., the

battery-charging capability is, in a sense, free). Note that this capability will not be needed with the inverter-based international boat described in Chapter 2 because it requires stand-alone battery chargers.

- In some instances (but not many—see later in this paragraph), it is useful to have two or more independent battery-charging outputs, preferably with independent multistep voltage regulators for each output. In the case of some inverter/chargers, the primary output is rated for the charger's full output and controlled by a multistep regulator, and then there are up to two more outputs, current-limited to 10 amps each, or 20 amps for one, regulated by a series voltage regulator (see Chapter 1; Xantrex calls their series regulator an Echo Charge). As desirable as this may look, if the boat's DC installation includes some kind of an electronic paralleling relay (see Chapter 1) between the house battery bank and other battery banks (a common practice nowadays, especially on electrically loaded boats), whenever the house bank is being charged by the inverter, the other banks will be paralleled with it. At this time, the paralleling relay will bypass any independent outlet(s) from the inverter, rendering the outlet(s) irrelevant. In this case, a single charger outlet wired to the house bank is all you need.

- A power-sharing capability so that when the inverter is in the pass-through mode, if the external AC source cannot handle both the onboard AC load and the demands of the inverter's battery charger (which may be quite substantial), the battery charger's output is reduced to the point that it does not overload the external supply.

- The best RFI/EMI suppression available. RFI/EMI suppression is quite costly; cheap inverters and inverter/chargers can be electrically noisy. The Europeans tend to have tougher standards in this regard, so the CE mark is a desirable feature. In the United States, compliance with the FCC Rule 15, Part B regulations is an indication of a quality product.

- The ability to integrate the inverter, or inverter/charger, with an onboard information bus that is tied to a wide range of equipment, such as multistep regulators, an automatic generator start (AGS), a battery monitoring system, and load-management devices. This feature is undoubtedly the direction more-complex systems on boats are evolving in (e.g., Xantrex's Xanbus and Victron's VENet).

- High- and low-voltage alarms and shutdowns; high-temperature shutdown.

- The ability to *stack* or *cascade* the output from two or more inverters (i.e., wire the outputs in parallel to increase the power available to the boat's onboard AC circuits). This ability will be a necessity with many inverter-based systems as described in Chapter 2.

- A cogeneration capability. In some systems applications, this capability may be the key to considerably downsizing an AC generator and greatly improving the overall efficiency of the AC system (Figure 6-21C; see Chapter 2).

- Weatherproofing and "ruggedizing," including such things as a drip-proof design, an aluminum chassis and case (as opposed to galva-

nized or painted steel), coated circuit boards, and testing to stringent vibration standards (such as UL 458 Marine Supplement).

- Ease of installation, which is largely a function of the accessibility of the various cable terminals (AC and DC) and the ease with which a remote control and monitoring panel can be fitted.

- Reliability. This is a tough one, since manufacturers are not going to broadcast their failures. However, anecdotally it can often be determined that some brands and models seem to give less trouble than others.

- A minimum 24-month warranty (guarantee).

Batteries: The Limiting Factor

Regardless of inverter choice, keeping up the battery voltage is, as often as not, the single biggest problem faced by any inverter user. It is not hard to see why.

Take a 1,200-watt, 120-volt microwave. Since watts = volts × amps, amps = watts/volts (I am ignoring power factor issues). When in use, the current absorbed by a microwave will be 1,200/120 = 10.0 amps.

But if we take that same microwave and power it with an inverter connected to a 12-volt battery, the current drain on the battery will nominally be 1,200/12 = 100 amps. In reality an inverter is not 100% efficient in converting battery power to AC power. The current drain will be 5% to 15% higher than the 100 amps—i.e., between 105 and 115 amps—more than ten times as much as on the 120-volt system. This drain will impose a tremendous strain on any battery bank.

There are two factors at work here:

1. The high rate of discharge that some AC loads impose on a battery.
2. The overall drain on the battery if even relatively light AC loads are sustained for any length of time.

High-rate discharges. Battery amp-hour ratings are based on a slow rate of discharge (over a period of 20 hours in the U.S.; 10 in the UK). As the rate of discharge increases, the battery's amp-hour capacity declines sharply (refer back to Figure 1-13A). Even a small 300-watt DC-to-AC inverter will impose a load of up to 27.5 amps on a 12-volt system (300/12 = 25 + 10% for inefficiency = 27.5 amps). A 1,500-watt inverter can impose a staggering load as high as 137.5 amps—close to that of a small starter motor. Imagine what cranking an engine continuously for half an hour would do to the batteries!

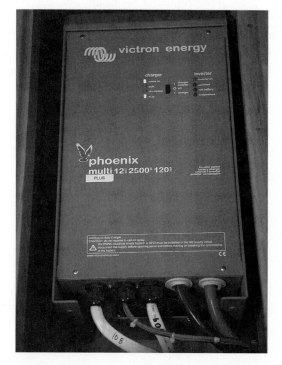

FIGURE 6-21C. An inverter with cogeneration capability.

At these kinds of loads, usable battery capacity (i.e., what can be withdrawn before the battery voltage drops below a threshold level) will be only a fraction of rated capacity. Output voltage will fall off sharply after only a short period of time, and the inverter will trip off due to low battery voltage (Figure 6-22). The battery will recover and tolerate another short burst of energy, but not as long as the first. Sooner or later, repeated high-load discharging of batteries for prolonged periods will cause internal damage.

It should be noted that in terms of deep-cycle batteries, gel-cells can deliver their stored current faster than wet-cells, and AGMs deliver faster than gel-cells. Given equal-capacity batteries subjected to equal loads, the terminal voltage will hold up better on a gel-cell than a wet-cell and on an AGM better than a gel-cell. This has particular significance when using a line-frequency modified-sine-wave inverter on loads that are sensitive to peak AC voltage, notably many microwaves. As the battery terminal voltage declines, the peak AC voltage will decline, and microwave efficiency will decline (Figure 6-23); the gel-cell will, because of its higher terminal voltage, do a better job maintaining microwave efficiency than the wet-cell, and the AGM will do better than the gel-cell. All batteries will do even better if the battery voltage is boosted by the output from an engine-driven alternator. At no time should the sustained rate of discharge of a battery bank exceed 25% of its rated amp-hour capacity.

Overall drain on the batteries. The intensity of a load is just one aspect of the impact of inverters on batteries; the duration of the load is the other. A microwave used for 15 minutes a day will pull fewer amp-hours (around 30 Ah in a 12-volt system) out of a battery than a typical DC lighting load. But sustained use of just about any AC item will put a heavy drain on the batteries. *A single 100-watt lightbulb run off an inverter powered by a 12-volt battery for 24 hours will drain the battery by 220 amp-hours!*

To avoid excessive discharges, *battery capacity should total at least two and a half and preferably four times the anticipated need between charges* (Chapter 1). An inverter load is obviously a cyclic load—the batteries are discharged and then recharged. *Only good-quality deep-cycle batteries will withstand this kind of treatment for any length of time* (Chapter 1). So although it is a relatively easy matter to find an inverter that meets typical AC needs (see the AC section in the Calculating Loads sidebar), it is nowhere near as easy to supply the batteries and battery-recharging capabilities needed to support the

inverter. Unless a boat has enormous battery banks, or the inverter is integrated into an inverter-based boat as described in Chapter 2 (including an AC or DC generator, preferably with an AGS), large-capacity inverters should be used at their full rated output only on rare occasions and for brief periods of time. Where inverters really shine is with light (300 watts or less), moderate-duration AC loads, or on heavier, short-term loads.

Battery protection. Repeated discharging below 50% of full charge will eventually kill even the best deep-cycle batteries. Because inverters can discharge batteries rapidly, they invariably incorporate a low-battery-voltage shutdown circuit. If an inverter is connected to a relatively small battery bank (as is typical), under a heavy load the battery voltage will fall disproportionately fast compared to the decline in the battery's state of charge. To prevent the inverter from kicking off prematurely under these kinds of heavy, short-duration loads, most times the low-voltage trip point is set somewhere between 10.0 and 11.0 volts (for a 12-volt inverter). But under a light load, any battery that is pulled down to 10.0 volts will be *stone dead* and will suffer significant

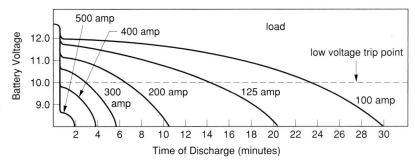

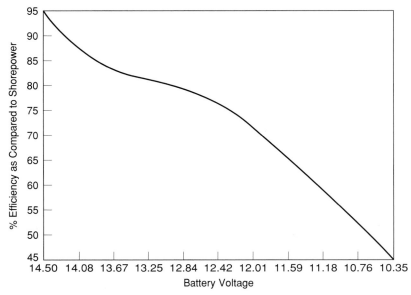

FIGURE 6-22 (top). Battery voltage as a function of load. The greater the load put on a battery, the steeper and more rapid the drop in battery voltage. The graph assumes a fully charged 100 Ah battery. Simultaneous use of three typical morning appliances, such as a hair dryer, coffee-maker, and toaster, will pull the battery below 10 volts in less than 4 minutes!

FIGURE 6-23 (bottom). Microwave efficiency as a function of battery voltage, when powered by a modified-sine-wave inverter. *(Adapted from a graph courtesy Ample Technology)*

internal damage. In other words, *the low-voltage trip protects the inverter, not the battery*. It is useless to rely on an inverter's low-voltage cutout to protect batteries; some other means of monitoring them is needed (Chapter 1).

Recharging the batteries. Whatever is pulled out of the batteries must be replaced (plus up to 20% more to allow for inefficiencies in the charging process). Given the ability of even a moderate-size inverter to rapidly deplete a battery bank, unless inverter use is sandwiched between extended periods of battery charging, some form of high-capacity fast charging is essential for the survival of the DC system. For example, on a boat with an anticipated daily demand of around 120 Ah, a battery bank of up to 480 Ah will be needed, while the boat will need a recharging capability of around 145 Ah per day (120 × 1.2).

Many line-frequency inverters and some high-frequency inverters can be used "backward" to charge a battery. Two-thousand-watt inverters have a 100+ amp charging capability at 12 volts, controlled by sophisticated multistage regulation programs designed to recharge batteries at the fastest safe rate (Figure 6-24). Without such a battery-charging option, a high-capacity (and relatively expensive) battery charger may well be required to support the inverter.

This is all very well if there is a regular independent source of AC power with which to charge the batteries, but what happens when this is not the case? At such times the principal means of recharging batteries will be the boat's main engine and alternator or perhaps an AC or DC generator. However, there is little point in transferring the AC load to the DC system if the engine has to be run long hours to recharge the batteries! If battery-charging hours are to be kept to a minimum, the engine-driven alternator must be upgraded to a high-output model with a multistep regulator, or the generator must be sized to meet the need.

In the above instance, *to support the inverter alone*, an alternator output of 120 to 150 amps will likely be needed (25% to 30% of the amp-hour rating of the batteries). If an AC generator is to be used for battery charging, and generator time minimized, it will need to be connected to a similar battery-charging capability (i.e., 100+ amps), and may need a rated output as high as 3 kW to support just the battery charger (this depends on the power factor rating of the charger—see above—and how the generator is rated).

Matching the Demand to the System

Light AC demands. If AC demands are occasional and light, and if, as is so often the case, a boat is used on weekends only and then kept in a slip with shore power throughout the week, an inverter can readily be wired into existing circuits. It will be important to fit deep-cycle batteries appropriately sized for the weekend load, but beyond this, little need be done.

Inverter size can be calculated as described in the Calculating Loads sidebar. The type will depend on whether there will be any waveform-sensitive equipment on board, and on questions such as size, weight, RFI suppression, historical reliability, standby drain, and cost. If a reversible inverter is used, the inverter's battery-charging capability will recharge the batteries during the nonuse period. With all other inverters, if the boat does not currently have a battery charger, it will almost certainly need one.

Moderate AC demands. The picture becomes a little more complex with heavier AC demands. A more substantial battery bank is required. The inverter's battery charger, or an independent battery charger, may well need to be backed up by a high-output engine-driven alternator coupled to a multistep regulator. Many sailboats, which typically use their engines less than powerboats, will still have limited battery-replenishment capabilities, but may be able to make up the deficit with solar panels and/or a wind generator. One way or another, most owners of powerboats up to 30 feet long and cruising sailboats up to around 40 feet would find that an inverter offers considerable improvement in creature comforts with very few drawbacks.

Heavier AC demands. As the anticipated AC load increases, there comes a point at which the DC system will be overwhelmed even if the inverter is not. In such circumstances, it is time

FIGURE 6-24. A battery charger program for a modified-sine-wave inverter. *(Trace Engineering)*

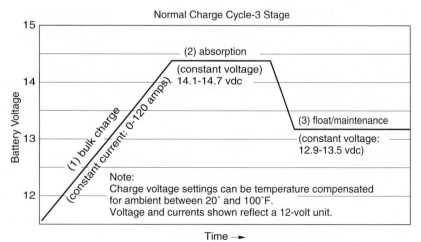

Normal Charge Cycle-3 Stage

(2) absorption
(constant voltage) 14.1-14.7 vdc

(1) bulk charge (constant current: 0-120 amps)

(3) float/maintenance
(constant voltage: 12.9-13.5 vdc)

Note:
Charge voltage settings can be temperature compensated for ambient between 20° and 100°F.
Voltage and currents shown reflect a 12-volt unit.

Battery Voltage

15 — 14 — 13 — 12

Time →

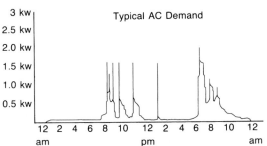

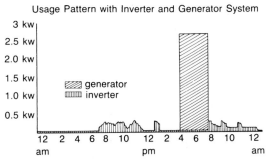

FIGURE 6-25. Combined inverter/generator use—patterns of AC use on board. **Left:** Uncontrolled use, requiring the generator to be operated (and underutilized) 24 hours a day. Note the heavier usage at mealtimes and when AC-powered entertainment equipment is used. **Right:** Controlled use, concentrating the use of high-load AC equipment into a limited period of generator operation and running the AC system from a DC-to-AC inverter for the rest of the day. *(Heart Interface)*

to think of a dual inverter/generator (AC or DC) setup. *The key to a successful inverter/generator system is to concentrate all the high-load AC items into 1 or 2 hours a day, during which time the generator is run, and to then power the light AC loads from the inverter alone throughout the rest of the 24 hours* (Figure 6-25). During the generating hours, the generator will not only meet the AC needs but also provide the power either for a battery charger or for the inverter to switch into its battery-charging mode (a DC generator will charge the batteries directly). The battery-charging amps can be supplemented by attaching a high-output alternator with a multi-step regulator to the generator engine. The inverter, battery charger, or DC generator, together with the alternator, will provide a formidable overall battery-charging capability that is able to compensate for the demands on the DC system during the rest of the day.

Since the strengths and weaknesses of generators and inverters tend to be mirror images, this arrangement can be ideal. For example, generators like to be run at close to full load, but without an inverter it is not unusual to have a boatowner run the generator just to watch the TV or VCR. This is a waste of fuel and hard on the generator, whereas inverters are efficient at this kind of light load. Or there might be a heavy load but of short duration, such as when warming something in the microwave for 3 minutes. With an inverter, there is no need to crank the generator and then shut it down again. Finally, when the main engine is running, the inverter can be used for AC power rather than the generator with no drain on the batteries (the alternator will be supplying the current).

With this kind of system, a considerable step up in capability, sophistication, and versatility comes with the inverter-based boat described in Chapter 2 coupled to a DC or AC generator with an AGS.

Eventually, of course, the AC load becomes so great that only a 24-hour-a-day AC generator can meet it. Air-conditioning, in particular, is such a power hog that once it gets above 16,000 Btu, there is rarely a way around an AC genera-

tor. But the level of AC consumption at which a 24-hour-a-day generator becomes necessary is far higher than many people realize, and even here an inverter with a cogeneration capability (see Chapter 2) will enable an AC generator to be considerably downsized and used far more efficiently than in the past.

The comforts of home. So the enticing prospect of constantly available AC power on board without the need for a generator is a real one, but only in a limited sense, and even then not one that can be met by simply wiring an inverter to the ship's batteries. First, you must choose an appropriate inverter for the task at hand, and then as with any additional DC load, particularly such a potentially heavy load, you must look at the boat's overall power equation and take whatever steps are necessary to keep this in balance.

Without such a holistic approach, the inverter is likely to become a cancer that destroys key components of the DC system; with such an approach, you truly can enjoy many of the comforts of home, although the cost of upgrading the DC system to handle the inverter may be more than the cost of the inverter itself!

Inverter Installation

Inverter installation is generally straightforward, bearing in mind the following points:

Location. An inverter is a complex electronic device, incorporating different metals. With the addition of moisture, all the ingredients for galvanic and stray-current corrosion—water, electricity, and dissimilar metals—are present. An inverter must be kept dry and protected from spray or condensation. Additionally, performance is related to temperature. Particularly at high levels of output, an unrestricted flow of cool air is needed to carry off the heat of operation (some inverters that don't already include a fan have a temperature-activated fan as an option—this is highly recommended in boat use).

(continued on page 262)

Calculating AC Loads

An inverter must be sized to handle the peak AC load it will be subjected to. Make a list of all the AC appliances to be run from the inverter, together with the power draw (in watts) of each item (Table 6-1). Determine which appliances you are likely to use simultaneously. Add the wattages to find the maximum likely demand at any given point in time, then choose an inverter with a continuous rating equal to this demand. On the surface of things, this appears to be quite simple, but note:

- Induction-type AC motors (AC refrigerators and air-conditioning systems, pumps, washing machines) can pull three to six times their rated power on initial start-up (Table 6-2). A 400-watt refrigeration compressor motor may draw up to 2,400 watts momentarily. When making load calculations, you must make a separate accounting of these *surge* loads. No individual surge load may be greater than the inverter's surge rating, and two or more appliances with high surge ratings must never be switched on simultaneously if their combined rating exceeds the inverter's surge rating. In practice, if a line-frequency inverter (including a hybrid) is

sized for the continuous load, most times it will have the capacity to handle the surge load; on the other hand, some of the high-frequency inverters will not do as well.

- Resistive loads (incandescent lights, heaters, toasters, electric stoves) can pull several times their rated load while heating up. A 100-watt lightbulb can momentarily draw 700 watts when it is first switched on!

- Power factors. As noted in the sidebar on page 242, many AC loads have a power factor of less than 1.0, which means more power is required in the real world than is reflected on the nameplate wattage. *When calculating wattage for induction motors and fluorescent lights, in the absence of specific information on power factors, it is best to take the rated watts and allow half again as much. In other words, count a 60-watt fluorescent light as a 90-watt load.*

In the example, the greatest likely AC load is combined use of the microwave and the coffeemaker. An inverter with a continuous rating of 2,500 watts will be more than large enough (in fact, given the short time a coffeemaker is at full power, a 2,000-watt inverter will likely be more than adequate). With separate use of the microwave and the coffeemaker, a 1,500-watt inverter will suffice.

Calculating DC Loads

List the wattage of all the AC appliances to be run off the inverter, making allowances for power factors. Estimate each item's hours of daily use. Multiply the wattage by the hours to get a total daily load for each appliance. Add the loads and then divide by the DC system voltage (12 on a 12-volt system) to find the total daily amp-hour drain. Multiply this by 1.1 to allow for inefficiencies in the inverter (Table 6-3). If the inverter is to be run off the house batteries, add in the load of any DC appliances that will be run concurrently (Chapter 1) to give the total load on the batteries between battery charges.

TABLE 6-1.

Typical AC Appliance Loads

Appliance/Tool	Watts
13 in. television	80
19 in. television	100
VCR deck	50
Stereo	50
Curling iron	50
Lamp	100
Blender	300
⅜ in. power drill	500
Small hand sander	500
Ice maker	200
Small coffeemaker	1,000
3 cu. ft. refrigerator	150
Compact microwave	750
20 cu. ft. refrigerator	750
Medium-size microwave	1,200
Hand vacuum cleaner	800
Hair dryer	1,250
Toaster	1,200

TABLE 6-2. Typical Loads for Induction Motors

Motor Requirements (hp)	¼	⅓	½	¾	1	2	3
Starting watts (inrush)	750+	1,000+	1,500+	2,000+	3,300+	4,000+	5,000+
Running watts	350	400	600	750	1,100	2,000	3,000

TABLE 6-3. Sample Load Calculations

Appliance	Watts	Hours of Use	Watt-Hours
TV	100	2	200
VCR	50	2	100
Stereo	50	2	100
Coffeemaker	1,000	0.2 (12 min.)	200
Toaster	1,200	0.1 (6 min.)	120
Microwave	1,200	0.3 (18 min.)	360
Blender	300	0.2 (12 min.)	60
Vacuum cleaner	800	0.1 (6 min.)	80
Hair dryer	1,250	0.1 (6 min.)	125

Total watt-hours = 1,345.
Total amp-hours = 1,345 ÷ 12 = 112 (12-volt system).
Adding a 10% conversion inefficiency = 112 x 1.1 = 123 amp-hours.

TABLE 6-4. Sizing DC-to-AC Inverters

STEP	ANSWER
1. Do you know the AC load in watts for each appliance on your boat? Note: Where a power factor is appropriate, such as with induction motors or fluorescent lights, multiply the load rating by the power factor to obtain a true rating. See Table 6-1 for typical loads for AC appliances. If you have no specific power factor, add half again as many watts to the rating (e.g., a 60-watt fluorescent light counts as a 90-watt load).	If your answer is No, list all onboard AC appliances and find out their rating in watts. If the surge or start-up load rating is greater than the operating load rating, list it in a separate column. Then go to Step 2. If your answer is Yes, go directly to Step 2.
2. How many hours a day is each appliance drawing power?	List hours of use in a column by each appliance's load rating.
3. Multiply the (power-factor-adjusted) rating by the daily use of each appliance (answers to Question 1 x answers to Question 2). Add all appliance sums together to get the total 24-hour AC load in watt-hours.	_____ total watt-hours/day
4. How often do you fully charge your battery? Give answer in days—two times a day, once every 2 days, etc.	_____ day(s)
5. If charging more than once a day, divide Answer 3 by Answer 4 to find the maximum AC demand between charges (e.g., divide by 2 if charging two times a day). If charging less than once a day, multiply Answer 3 by Answer 4 (e.g., multiply by 2 if charging once every 2 days).	_____ watt-hours

Answer 5 is your total AC load between battery charges.

STEP	ANSWER
6. Divide Answer 5 by 12 on a 12-volt system (24 or 32 on 24- or 32-volt systems) to get an approximate amp-hour demand on your DC system. Note: Multiply by 1.1 to account for inverter inefficiencies and add in the standby drain of the inverter between battery charges (e.g., a 200-milliamp drain [0.2 amp] for 24 hours = 0.2 x 24 = 4.8 amp-hours).	$\dfrac{\text{watt-hours demand of AC appliances}}{\text{system voltage}}$ x 1.1 = _____ amp-hours demand
7. Add to Answer 6 the amp-hour demand placed directly on the battery bank by DC appliances, as calculated from Chapter 1, to get total amp-hour demand.	_____ total amp-hour demand
8. Multiply Answer 7 by a minimum of 2½, and preferably 4, to get the Ah capacity of the battery bank that will be needed to power the inverter and other DC loads. Note: Use only top-quality deep-cycle batteries.	_____ Ah capacity

Answer 8 is your needed battery capacity.

STEP	ANSWER
9. Is Answer 8 totally impractical for your boat or budget?	If your answer is No, go to Step 11. If your answer is Yes, go to Step 10.
10. You will have to limit your AC load based on your boat's battery bank, or recharge the batteries more often to reduce the load between charges. Determine your maximum battery bank Ah size; divide this by a minimum of 2½, preferably 4; subtract the amp-hour demand you anticipate from those DC appliances you wish to use; divide the quotient by 1.1 to determine a maximum amp-hour draw; and multiply the resulting figure by 12 for 12-volt systems (24 for 24-volt systems) to give a maximum AC demand in watt-hours. Go back to Steps 1, 2, and 3 to find ways of bringing the total AC load down to the maximum allowable level. Take high-demand AC items and arrange to use them when other sources of power are available so that their load is not thrown onto the batteries.	_____ watt-hours based on _____ Ah capacity of the battery bank
11. Calculate the maximum foreseeable continuous AC load—or peak load—by adding the power factor–adjusted ratings of all the AC appliances listed in Step 1 that might be used at the same time.	_____ watts peak load
12. Now calculate the maximum foreseeable AC surge rating by adding the surge ratings of all AC appliances that might come online simultaneously.	_____ watts surge load

The inverter must be large enough to handle the larger of Answers 11 and 12.

STEP	ANSWER
13. Take Answer 7 and multiply it by 1.1 to find the amp-hours that must be put back in the battery bank.	_____ amp-hours
14. Take Answer 8 and divide it by 4 to get a desired rate of charge from a battery charger or alternator. Add any residual DC loads when charging. Multiply the sum by 1.3 to find the continuous rating of an alternator at normal battery-charging speeds of rotation.	_____ rate of charge (amps) + _____ residual DC load (amps) x 1.3 = _____ continuous alternator rating (amps)

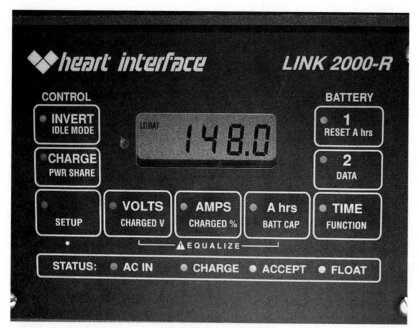

FIGURE 6-26. An inverter remote control as part of a DC systems monitor. Note the heavy current draw (148.0 amps) and the "LOBAT" (low battery) warning.

(continued from page 259)

The ABYC requires an inverter to have a label at the main electrical panel warning that the electrical system includes an inverter, plus a "visible means" of determining that the inverter is online or in standby (idle) mode. The latter requirement pretty much necessitates some kind of a remote panel to be installed at the main electrical panel (Figure 6-26).

The DC side. It is critical to avoid voltage drop in the supply cables from the battery. Very heavy cables are needed—larger inverters on 12-volt systems have peak currents up to 1,000 amps, requiring 4/0 cables (110 mm²) on even 5- to 10-foot cable runs (or two 2/0 [70 mm²] cables in parallel—see the Cables in Parallel sidebar on page 185). To minimize voltage drop, the inverter should be as close to its batteries as possible without actually being in the battery compartment, since batteries give off corrosive and explosive fumes.

Large cables are awkward and hard to handle (Figure 6-27). As likely as not there will be others

FIGURE 6-27. DC cable installation on an inverter. Note the heavy cables and bolted connections, which will now be covered by protective boots.

Alternative installation with independent battery isolation switch if:
1. Inverter load exceeds battery selector switch rating
2. Panel mounted battery selector switch involves excessively long cable runs
3. Only one battery bank is to be used with the inverter

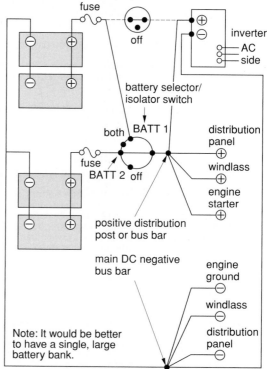

Note: It would be better to have a single, large battery bank.

FIGURE 6-28A. Wiring diagrams for an inverter, showing the DC side and one or two battery banks.

—connecting to the starter motor, the boat's distribution panel, a high-output alternator, and perhaps an electric windlass. *Do not attempt to attach all these cables at the battery posts.* Instead, establish substantial negative and positive distribution posts or bus bars at a suitable location (Figures 6-28A and 6-28B) with a single, very heavy cable leading back to each battery terminal (see Chapter 4).

Any short circuit in the supply cables will create a potentially dangerous dead short across the batteries. Install a high-capacity circuit breaker (expensive) or slow blow fuse (up to 250 amp rating on a 2,000-watt, 12-volt inverter) as close to the batteries as possible (Chapter 4 again).

Note that in order to minimize the standby power drain, *most inverters are not protected against reverse polarity* (protection would require power-consuming diodes). *If the battery cables are connected in reverse, instant and catastrophic damage will occur that is not covered under the warranty.* (Some inverters have an internal "tattletale" diode that blows in the event of reverse polarity; this way the manufacturer can tell that

BATTERY CHARGERS, INVERTERS, WIND AND WATER GENERATORS, AND SOLAR PANELS

FIGURE 6-28B. A heavy copper bus bar serving as the boat's main negative bus bar. There is severe discoloration on the connections as a result of corrosion in the marine atmosphere. Tin plating would greatly enhance the corrosion resistance.

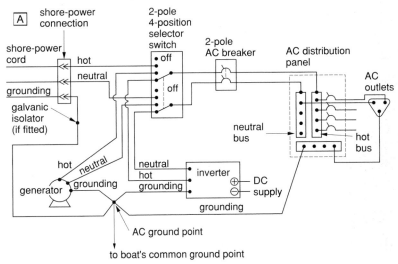

Notes:
1. This is for a typical AC installation *without an automatic transfer switch.*
2. If there is no onboard generator, a 2-pole, 3-position selector switch is needed ('off', 'shore-power', 'inverter').
3. If a separate battery charger is fitted, see Figure 6-29C.

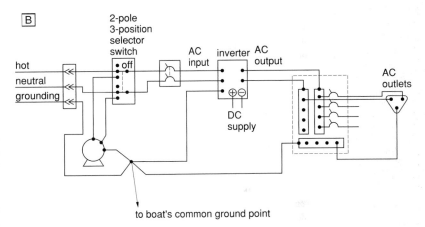

Note: If any loads exceed the capacity of the inverter, or a separate battery charger is fitted, see Figure 6-29C.

the inverter was connected incorrectly and will not pay any warranty claims!)

The AC side. *AC power can be lethal. When in the standby mode, many inverters will not give a voltage reading with a typical multimeter, but the instant a load is applied (such as when a person touches the AC output terminals), the inverter may go to full output. Whenever wiring or troubleshooting an inverter or working on the AC circuits on an inverter-equipped boat, make sure the inverter is isolated from its batteries.*

If another AC source is connected to an inverter's AC output, instant and catastrophic damage is likely. This is so even if the inverter has an AC-sensing and transfer function. In this case, there will be provision for a separate AC input to the inverter. *Under no circumstances should it be possible to bring the inverter and another AC source online on the same circuit at the same time* (the exception is an inverter with a cogeneration capability—see Chapter 2). Figures 6-29A, 6-29B, and 6-29C illustrate several different wiring options that will prevent such an occurrence. Note that in installations where the inverter is not wired to all the onboard AC circuits (Figure 6-29C), the AC output of the inverter is wired to its own hot and neutral bus bars. *These must not be connected to the hot and neutral bus bars for the non-inverter AC loads.*

As noted earlier, many inverters have an *automatic transfer switch.* In this case, other sources of AC power (shore power and/or a generator) can be routed through the inverter (Figures 6-29B and 6-29D). Anytime the inverter senses

another AC source online, it automatically switches to the pass-through mode and into the battery-charging mode (if the unit includes a battery charger). When the other source of AC power drops out, the inverter switches back to its AC mode.

If the inverter does not have the capability to handle some onboard loads (notably air-conditioning), these loads must be supplied from an AC panel that is independent of the inverter (Figure 6-29C). Note also that *if an independent battery charger is fitted, it must be on this independent AC panel to avoid a situation in which the inverter is trying to run the charger that is charging the inverter's battery. This kind of loop will waste battery energy at best, and at worst may damage the inverter and charger.*

FIGURE 6-29A. An AC wiring diagram for an inverter without an automatic transfer function.

FIGURE 6-29B. An AC wiring diagram for an inverter with an automatic transfer switch.

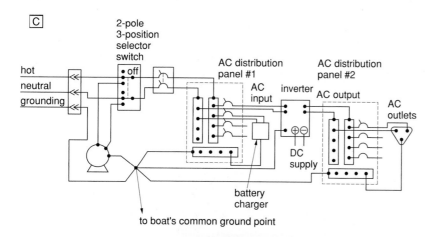

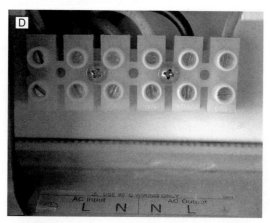

FIGURE 6-29C. An AC wiring diagram for an inverter with an automatic transfer function, and with two AC panels wired to isolate the inverter both from heavy loads that it cannot handle and also from an independent battery charger. AC distribution panel #1 handles loads that are not to be supplied by the inverter, such as a water heater, an electric stove, and the battery charger. These appliances can be used only when shore power is available or the generator is online.

FIGURE 6-29D. A typical AC wiring box on an inverter with an automatic transfer switch.

All inverters in marine use must connect the inverter's neutral to its grounding circuit when in invert mode (this complies with the need to ground the neutral at the power source—see Chapter 4), but must break this connection when another AC source is online (so as not to ground the neutral at any place other than the power source). All marine models do this automatically, but shore-based inverters do not; *it is important to buy only an inverter built specifically for marine use.*

Troubleshooting

No AC output when in invert mode. If the unit has just been installed, double-check the installation for correct polarity on the DC side. Reverse polarity may have caused irreparable damage. Check all wiring, fuses, and switches (make sure the inverter is turned on!). Make sure that any breakers on the AC output side have not tripped. Check for DC input (read the voltage at the input terminals on the inverter) and AC output (once again, read the voltage at the inverter; this will necessitate removing the cover from the AC connection box and exposing potentially live AC circuits, so exercise appropriate caution).

If there is no DC input, there is a problem in the DC circuit. This should be easy to trace.

If there is DC input but no AC output:

1. Feel the inverter to see if it is hot; it may simply have tripped on its high-temperature shutdown.

2. If it is not hot, disconnect any remote control panel, double-check that the inverter is turned on, and test for AC output again; if it is now present, there is a problem with the remote control panel.

3. Still no AC output? Ensure there is an AC load turned on; maybe the inverter is in its standby or sleep mode.

4. Still no AC output? Turn off the inverter and the DC supply. Disconnect the AC output wires from the inverter and connect an AC lightbulb, or some other AC load, directly to the inverter, and then turn everything back on again (if the inverter has an AC outlet, plug the lightbulb into this). If the lightbulb does not light (or the load does not run), there is a problem with the inverter.

Note that unless the inverter produces a true sine wave, *most voltmeters will read 10 to 20 volts low when measuring the AC output.* Only true RMS voltmeters will be accurate. When the inverter is in standby mode, with no load online, you may get only a very low voltage reading (Figures 6-29E and 6-29F). Depending on the nature of the load-sensing circuit, small AC loads may not trigger the inverter into action; before concluding there is a problem, try a heavier load.

Inverter is hot. Most likely the high-temperature cutoff has tripped. Allow the unit to cool and try again. If the inverter has an internal fan, check its operation. The unit may be in an area without adequate ventilation, such as an engine room.

Overload tripped. Switch off all appliances and reset (if manual trip). Bring appliances back online one at a time and see if any load trips the inverter. If a load trips the inverter, this may be a result of excessive start-up (inrush) current, too much AC equipment turned on at the same time, or a short in an individual piece of equipment or its wiring. Also check for undersized DC cables (they will be warm) or voltage drop across loose or corroded connections (Chapter 4).

Low voltage tripped. Most likely the battery capacity or charging capability is inadequate for the loads being placed on the system. Check battery state of charge and condition. Check also for undersized cables and loose or corroded terminals.

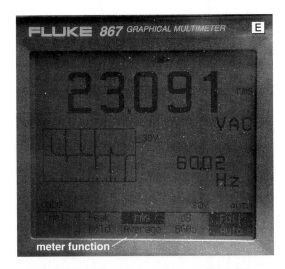

meter function

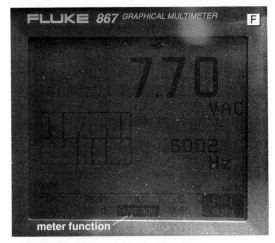

meter function

FIGURES 6-29E AND 6-29F. An inverter in idle mode. Note that when using a true RMS meter we get 23 volts, but when the meter is switched to the averaging function the voltage drops to 7.7.

Note that some trips reset automatically and others must be set manually. There may also be manual circuit breakers inside some units. Check the instruction book.

No AC output when in pass-through mode. The AC supply from a shore-power cord and/or an AC generator can be wired directly to the input side of many inverters. In this case, whenever an external AC source is detected, the inverter switches from the invert mode to a pass-through mode. This switching is carried out by a transfer switch. There is generally a time delay of 7 to 12 seconds associated with the operation of the switch. When the switch engages, you will often hear an audible click.

The transfer switch will not operate if there is excessively low voltage on the shore-power cord or AC generator, so if the pass-through mode is inoperative, the first thing to check is the voltage across the incoming AC line(s). Remember, *these lines are potentially lethal*, so exercise appropriate caution—see Chapter 4—and *if you are at all unsure about what you are doing, don't do it!* The transfer switch will also not operate if the frequency is incorrect, but to check this requires a specialized meter that is unlikely to be on board.

If AC input is present at the correct voltage (and frequency) but the transfer switch is still not working, it may have a blown fuse inside the unit, most likely caused by an overvoltage condition (voltage spike) on the AC input. (If the fuse is blown, the inverter will still work in the invert mode, but not the pass-through mode.) To test the fuse, *turn off all AC sources*, turn off the inverter, turn off the DC supply, and disconnect the AC input wires. Test with an ohmmeter across the AC hot and neutral input terminals—there should be a resistance, probably on the order of 150 to 170 ohms (this is the resistance in the transfer switch circuit). If there is an open circuit, the fuse has blown. To get to it, the case will need to be removed and a search made of the circuit boards.

Shore-power breaker trips when the boat is plugged in. If the shore power trips off when the boat is plugged in, check for:

1. A ground fault circuit interrupter (GFCI) (or ground fault circuit breaker [GFCB], residual current device [RCD], or residual current circuit breaker [RCCB]) at the shore-power outlet (ashore) and/or whole-boat ground fault protection on the boat (common on European boats, but almost never found on U.S. boats; see Chapter 4 for more on these devices).

2. An inverter with a pass-through mode and its associated transfer switch.

3. AC circuits that are not powered by the inverter, resulting in a separate inverter neutral bus bar and main neutral bus bar (see Figure 6-29C).

If these three conditions exist, then the inverter neutral bus bar has probably been incorrectly wired to the main neutral bus bar. What is happening is this: When the inverter is in its invert mode, it ties its neutral to ground (see above). Because the inverter neutral bus bar is incorrectly tied to the main neutral bus bar, the main neutral bus bar is now also tied to ground. When the boat is plugged in, before the inverter's transfer switch has time to operate (with its 7- to 12-second time delay), the GFCI detects the neutral-to-ground condition and trips out. To test for this condition, check with an ohmmeter between the two neutral bus bars. There should be an open circuit (infinite resistance).

Any connection between the inverter neutral bus bar and the main neutral bus bar needs to be broken. If there are not two separate bus bars, as is sometimes the case, a second bus bar will need to be installed (or the existing one physically cut in half).

Note that GFCBs and GFCIs have a test button that simulates a ground fault condition to see if the unit will trip. If your boat has a DC-to-AC inverter with an idle mode, only test a GFCB/GFCI when shore power is present or the inverter is in full invert mode; if you test it in idle mode, the GFCB/GFCI will appear to fail, and may be damaged.

Erratic operation. The inverter trips continually on low voltage when appliances are turned on. Check for a starting overload (high inrush current), undersized cables, and loose or corroded connections. Check the voltage drop from one end of the DC cable to the other *when under full load*. Feel the cables to see if they are warm. Check the condition of the battery.

Equipment problems. Appliance motors run slow and hot, transformers hum, the microwave is slow, the TV has lines on it, etc. The inverter output is probably closer to a square wave than a modified sine wave! Moreover, the greater the load and the lower the battery voltage, the "squarer" it may get (check the batteries). To reduce these problems, you may need to use sensitive equipment only at the batteries' peak state of charge and with no other AC equipment online or with an engine-driven alternator running to keep the battery voltage up. If this doesn't work, you need a true-sine-wave inverter.

Wind and Water Generators

In the trade wind belts and other areas with relatively sustained winds above 10 knots, no other device on the market can come close to generating as much power as a wind generator without having to run an engine. In some cases, a wind generator can almost completely free a sailboat from any need to run its engine, with major savings on fuel and maintenance bills, not to mention the reduction in noise and elimination of exhaust fumes.

Wind generators in particular have made a tremendous impact on the cruising scene (Figures 6-30A and 6-30B). The rest of this section focuses on them, although almost all the information is equally applicable to towed water generators (wind generators and water generators are essentially the same units fitted with different propellers/impellers/turbines/vanes).

FIGURES 6-30A AND 6-30B. Air Marine (left) and Fourwinds (right) wind generators, two popular models. Note the line attached to the tail of the Fourwinds in order to turn it out of the wind and stop it, and the loop around the support pipe, which is then used to tie off the blades. The Air Marine is braked and shut down electronically (via a stop switch).

How They Work

A wind generator is a simple device that uses a propeller or turbine to convert wind energy to a rotating force that is used to spin a generating device. A formula for calculating the electrical power that can be extracted from the wind is:

$P = E \times D^2 \times V^3 \times K$, where P = power in watts, E = the efficiency at converting the available wind energy to electricity (theoretically, this can be as high as 59%, but in practice is around 30% to 40%; the smaller a wind generator, the harder it is to attain high efficiency numbers), D = the blade diameter (in feet, inches, or meters), V = the wind speed (in knots, mph, or meters per second), and K = a constant (which will be different according to what units have been used for D and V).

Regardless of (1) the units that are used for D and V, (2) the efficiency of the wind generator,

---

Prop-Shaft Generators

When under sail, some boats with fixed-pitch propellers (not feathering or folding) can use a freewheeling propeller to spin an alternator and generate power. Note, however, that freewheeling the propeller will damage some transmissions (see Chapter 10); in general, this should only be done with two-shaft transmissions. When freewheeling, there is likely to be an annoying rumble, and wear of the transmission bearings and Cutless bearing will be accelerated. Under power, the alternator will be driven by the engine, also producing power.

A regular automotive alternator will not work in such an application because of the relatively low speed of shaft rotation when freewheeling. We need an alternator that is purpose-built to maximize its output at a low speed of rotation; ideally, it should begin to generate power below 500 rpm and reach full rated output by 2,500 rpm.

The approximate shaft speed (rpm) that will be available to drive an alternator can be calculated with the formula: shaft speed = (100 x BS x P)/9.6, where BS = boat speed (knots) and P = propeller pitch (inches).

For example, at a boat speed of 5 knots with a propeller that has a 12-inch pitch, we get shaft speed = (100 x 5 x 12)/9.6 = 625.

This formula presupposes 20% propeller slip. The slip may well be higher than this, in which case the shaft speed will go down. In practice, many times you can get a good sense of shaft speed by painting a dot on the shaft or coupling and counting how many times it turns in, say, 5 seconds and multiplying this by the appropriate number (in this case, 20) to get to revolutions per minute.

The formula only gives the freewheeling shaft speed and not the amount of energy available to drive an alternator. That component is a function of the propeller size, which should be at least 14 inches in diameter for a three-bladed propeller and 16 inches for a two-bladed propeller. Note that propellers with a pitch below 12 inches are unlikely to be effec-

tive; the higher the pitch, the better. Folding and feathering propellers will not work at all.

Let's say the chosen alternator reaches its full rated output of 20 amps at 2,500 rpm and has a maximum rated speed of 10,000 rpm. The engine is a typical small marine diesel with a maximum speed of 3,500 rpm and a transmission ratio of 2:1, resulting in a maximum shaft speed of 1,750 rpm. In this case, we could fit pulleys to the shaft and alternator with a ratio of up to 5.7:1 (10,000/1,750 = 5.7). The alternator will likely have a pulley of approximately 2 inches in diameter, so to achieve a 5.7:1 ratio the pulley on the shaft will need to be 11.4 inches in diameter. In practice, it is unlikely there will be room to fit such a large pulley.

Let's assume an 8-inch pulley, giving a 4:1 pulley ratio. In this case, at a freewheeling shaft speed of 625 rpm, the alternator will be turning at 2,500 rpm—enough to achieve full rated output at this sailing speed. If the boat speed drops to 4 knots, the shaft speed will decline to 500 rpm, and the alternator speed to 2,000 rpm. (The assumption here is that the propeller will provide enough energy to keep the shaft turning at the freewheeling speed, even with the alternator loaded up. This may well not be true—it will be a function of propeller pitch and size—in which case the shaft speed and alternator output will decrease.)

To fit the pulley to the propeller shaft, either the shaft will need to be removed from the propeller coupling to allow the pulley to be slid on, or a split pulley, which clamps around the shaft, will be needed. The alternator is generally mounted on a bracket fastened to the engine transmission (gearbox). A shaft alternator installation should include an electrically operated solenoid clutch on one or another pulley so that the unit can be disengaged when not needed, and/or a switch to disable the field circuit (which will put the alternator into freewheel mode at those times when it is not needed or when full engine power is required).

or (3) the value of K, there are a couple of interesting relationships that hold in this wind-energy conversion formula:

1. Because the blade diameter is squared, a doubling of the diameter produces a theoretical fourfold increase in generator output ($2 \times 2 = 4$).
2. Because the wind speed is cubed, a doubling of the wind speed produces a theoretical eightfold increase in output ($2 \times 2 \times 2 = 8$).

In other words, theoretical output increases rapidly with increasing blade diameter and wind speed.

In practical terms, at wind speeds less than 5 knots, *the wind has insufficient energy to produce output from any wind generator*. At 5 knots, the more-efficient generators will begin to trickle-charge a battery, whereas less-efficient designs may not kick in until the wind speed has picked up to as high as 7 knots. Once the kick-in speed is reached, the output of the various devices on the market picks up slowly at first and then rises with ever-increasing rapidity as the wind speed rises. Above 10 knots or so, for any given wind speed, *output is broadly determined by blade diameter*. Given a propeller with a large-enough diameter, the wind now contains sufficient energy to meet the electrical needs of most cruising sailors.

Given that (1) cruising sailors spend most of their time at anchor, and (2) anchorages tend to be sheltered (and even in the trade wind belt, wind speeds in anchorages rarely exceed 15 knots and are generally less than this), then it follows that *the primary interest of most cruisers should be the output of a wind generator at wind speeds between 5 and 15 knots*, rather than the maximum output at higher wind speeds. When checking output figures, it is best to focus on the lowest wind speed at which the generator will start to generate, and the low end output from there to 15 knots. You can pretty much forget about the rest of the power curve.

On those models that can be converted to a water generator, the propeller is removed so that a towed impeller can be used to spin the generator. Typically a boat moving at near hull speed will generate more than enough electricity to keep up with the entire DC demand—a very useful capability, especially on transoceanic downwind runs when apparent wind speeds tend to be light and wind generators are, as a result, ineffective. (At a boat speed of 5 knots, output for a 12-volt water generator is normally around 5 amps, rising disproportionately with any additional increase in speed.)

Wind and water generators can be built around either a brushless alternator or a DC electric motor. The differences need not concern us here except to note that although both types produce alternating current in the output windings, in the alternator type this output is *rectified* to DC with *diodes* (see the Alternators section in Chapter 3), while in the DC-motor type the output is rectified to DC using a *commutator* and *brushes* (see Chapter 7).

Pros and Cons

The alternator types need no brushes to generate electricity, and so in this sense are maintenance free, whereas the DC-motor types need brushes to pick up the current from the commutator. The commutator and brushes require periodic maintenance. In addition, a poor contact between the brushes and commutator can create annoying RFI (see below). If mounted on a pole (as opposed to hung in the rigging), almost all wind generators (alternator and DC-motor type) require brushes and what are known as *slip rings* between the generator and its wiring to the batteries (Figure 6-31A). Slip rings are necessary to allow the generator to rotate around its mounting pole (see below).

One or two wind generators dispense with these slip rings and brushes by allowing the output cable to twist up. On some, it is assumed the law of averages will prevent the cable twisting too much. On others—e.g., the Kiss, www.svhotwire.com—a tether on the tail limits the number of turns that can be made to three, after which the unit can be unwound by hand if necessary (Figure 6-31B). The Kiss also has an internal spring

FIGURE 6-31A. A cutaway of an AirX wind generator showing the stator windings at left, the slip rings in the center, and the voltage regulator and rectification circuits at right. *(Southwest Windpower)*

stator windings

voltage regulation and rectification

slip rings

that, after it has been wound three turns, has sufficient force to unwind the unit one turn if the wind dies. The Kiss is offered with optional slip rings, in which case the contact is made with mercury, as opposed to brushes, eliminating a maintenance point.

The lower-output (small blade diameter) wind generators are almost silent. Of more significance is the fact that they can be used in any wind speed without damage, which means that they can be left operating when a boat is unattended. Their biggest drawback is that, except in sustained strong winds, they simply do not have the capacity to keep up with the demands of an electrically loaded boat, particularly one with DC refrigeration.

In the past some (but not all) of the higher-output wind generators, which do have the capacity to keep up with the demands of an electrically loaded boat, have been quite noisy (for a given speed of rotation, the larger the diameter of the blades, the faster the tip speed, and the greater the likelihood of noise generation). In addition, in strong winds, the centrifugal forces developed by the large propellers (from 54 to 60 inches in diameter [1.4 to 1.8 m]) have also caused some units to self-destruct! Improvements in blade design, materials, and manufacturing tolerances, combined with methods to regulate the top speed of generators, have reduced these problems. But even where there are no limits on the wind speed that can be tolerated, high output can be a problem; when a boat is left unattended with little or no load to absorb the generator output, the batteries can be seriously overcharged (particularly gel-cells and AGMs) unless some means is used to regulate the generator. These two issues of speed control (*governing*) and voltage regulation need a closer look.

Speed control. Six different approaches are commonly used to keep the speed of large wind generators under control:

1. Tie off the blades when the wind pipes up; in strong winds and rough seas this can be a nerve-racking operation!

2. Install a centrifugally activated friction brake inside the generator housing. This brake, however, may not be powerful enough to handle sustained wind speeds much above 35 to 40 knots. In these conditions, the generator once again has to be tied off. Once activated, the brake may need to be reset by hand, requiring some disassembly.

3. Add a centrifugally operated air brake to the blades themselves. It is possible, from a mechanical point of view (though perhaps not from an electrical one—see below), to leave a generator with an air brake in operation on an unattended boat for extended periods (Figure 6-31C). Note that when deployed, these air brakes can be noisy.

FIGURE 6-31B. A Kiss wind generator, which has no slip rings. The cord hanging from the tail limits the number of times it can turn in order to protect the output cables from damage.

FIGURE 6-31C. An air brake on a Fourwinds generator. At high speed, the centrifugal force causes the stainless steel plates to open out, creating substantial wind resistance.

air brake

4. Design the generator with a furling or tilt-back mechanism that progressively turns the machine out of the wind as the wind speed picks up. This approach is more popular on the large wind generators found in the home power market than it is on boats, but periodically it finds an application in the marine market.

5. Build the blades so that they flutter and stall at higher wind speeds. This is effective but can be exceedingly noisy (some of the early wind generators using this approach sound like a howling banshee once the wind speed gets much above 20 knots).

6. Control the speed electronically by shorting out the windings in the generator. This has the effect of putting enough of a load on the generator to stall it out in all but the highest wind speeds and to keep it turning slowly in very high winds. If the windings are shorted, the wind generator has to be specially built with this in mind to keep it from burning up because of the heat generated in its windings.

From the user's perspective, electronic braking (#6 above) is without question the most attractive, especially since it can be combined with a remote stop switch and also with sophisticated voltage regulation (see below). Note that if the generator can be converted to a water generator, any attempt to brake it electronically may burn it out (this is because the much higher density of water over air creates much greater resistance to being stopped).

An electronic stop switch operates by first disconnecting the wind generator from the batteries (open-circuiting the wind generator) and then immediately afterward shorting the generator's windings. This requires a "break-before-it-makes, single pole, double throw" switch (SPDT) in the positive feed from the wind generator to the batteries. Switched one way, it connects the generator to the batteries; switched the other way, it first breaks the battery connection and then connects the generator's positive output cable to its negative cable (Figure 6-32). If installing such a switch, make absolutely certain it is the wind generator that is being shorted and not the batteries!

Voltage regulation. With an effective governor, any wind generator can be kept going in just about any wind condition (the Fourwinds folks—www.fourwinds-ii.com—had several that survived 100+-knot winds in Hurricane Andrew). However, the boat's DC system may not be able to handle the output! To take an extreme example, one of the high-output generators in a sustained wind of 25 knots or more will produce up to 400 amp-hours a day at 12 volts. Without a heavy load on the DC system, this will eventually cook even the largest battery bank. There are times when some form of regulation is needed.

A conventional alternator is regulated by varying the field current to the field coil, altering its magnetism (Chapter 3). *All* wind generators, however, have *permanent magnets with a fixed level of magnetism*, so this option is not available for controlling output.

Four methods are used to regulate a wind generator's output:

1. Manual control. The battery voltage is monitored and the generator is shut down when the battery is charged. This approach is entirely dependent on the operator and *should not be used on larger generators without an overspeed device, nor should the wind generator be left unattended for more than a few hours.* Years ago we had a WindBugger that was caught in a 50-knot squall while we were ashore; the resulting high output melted the brush holders, but not before the generator had the batteries gassing vigorously (Figures 6-33A and 6-33B).

2. Open-circuit the generator. A device senses battery voltage and open-circuits the generator (i.e., disconnects it from the battery) when the battery voltage reaches a certain level. However, without a governor, *releasing the load*

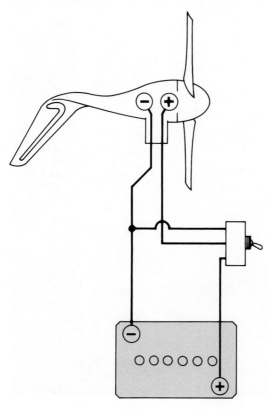

FIGURE 6-32. A stop switch circuit. The wind generator positive cable is fed to the center of the switch. From there it can either be shorted back to the negative side (to stop the generator) or fed to the battery (for battery charging). *(Jim Sollers)*

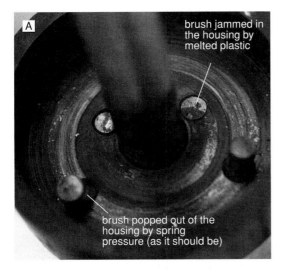

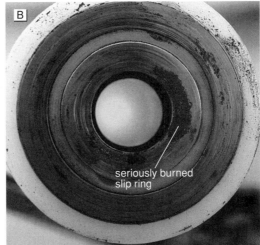

brush jammed in the housing by melted plastic

brush popped out of the housing by spring pressure (as it should be)

seriously burned slip ring

FIGURES 6-33A AND 6-33B. Brush and slip ring damage from overspeeding. The plastic housing melted around the two rear brushes, seizing them in the housing, and the slip ring is seriously burned.

can allow the generator to speed up uncontrollably and dangerously. As a general rule, wind generators should never be left in an open-circuited state. Note that many voltage regulators for solar panels (photovoltaic [PV] regulators) operate by open-circuiting the panels when the batteries are charged. *This type of solar panel regulator* (known as a series relay regulator) *is not suitable for a wind generator.*

3. Dissipate the wind generator's excess output as heat. This can be done through transistors mounted on a heat sink (a *shunt* regulator—Figures 6-34A and 6-34B) or by diverting the generator's output to another load (a *dummy* load) as the battery comes up to charge (a *charge-divert* regulator; the output is normally fed to a fixed resistor, but it could be switched into a hot water tank and put to useful work;

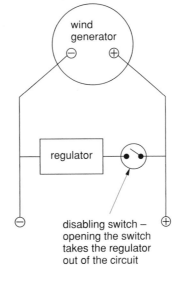

FIGURE 6-34A. A shunt regulation circuit.

wind generator

regulator

disabling switch – opening the switch takes the regulator out of the circuit

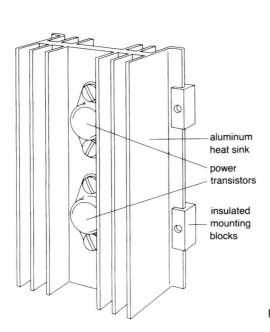

aluminum heat sink

power transistors

insulated mounting blocks

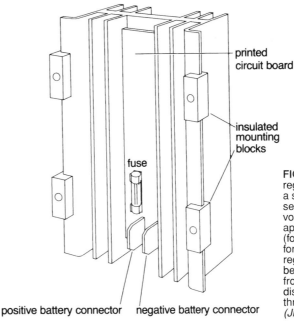

printed circuit board

insulated mounting blocks

fuse

positive battery connector   negative battery connector

FIGURE 6-34B. A shunt regulator. The regulator is a solid-state device sensitive to battery voltage. As the voltage approaches a preset limit (for example, 14.0 volts for a 12-volt battery), the regulator allows current to be diverted increasingly from the battery to be dissipated as heat through the heat sink. *(Jim Sollers)*

FIGURE 6-34C. A circuit for a charge-divert regulator.

FIGURE 6-34D. A set of resistors for installation as part of a charge-divert regulator. *(Everfair Enterprises)*

wind generator is used with the regulator disabled, the battery voltage must be monitored since it is quite possible to do some serious and permanent damage through overcharging. Once the regulator gets to its voltage set point, it switches the generator's output from the batteries to the transistors and dissipates it as heat.

Higher-performing shunt regulators employ pulse width modulation. As a battery comes to charge, the charging current to the batteries is switched on and off rapidly, allowing fine control of the charge rate. Depending on the level of sophistication in the electronics, it is possible to achieve a full multistep charging regimen, as described in Chapter 1, together with an equalization function (although many cheaper regulators are not nearly this sophisticated—it is important to read the specifications carefully). As with high-end multistep regulators for alternators, the regulator may have temperature compensation based on temperature measurement at the batteries and also voltage sensing at the batteries.

When a shunt regulator dissipates excess charging current, it creates heat—sometimes quite a bit of heat. The regulator must be in a cool place with good airflow (see Figure 6-34B). Shunt regulators generally have a fairly low amperage rating, sufficient only to handle the loads of the wind generator in question. If the wind generator output is teed into the ship's battery-charging circuits, the engine-driven alternator can feed back through the shunt regulator, burning it up and creating a fire risk. If not already installed in the regulator, a protective diode sized to handle the wind generator's full output must therefore be installed between the shunt regulator and the ship's battery-charging circuit (Figure 6-35A).

Figures 6-34C and 6-34D). Shunt regulators are generally wired in parallel to the output cable to the generator, progressively siphoning off more of the generator's output as a battery comes to charge; charge-divert regulators are generally wired in series with the output cable, switching the output from the batteries to the dummy load at a certain voltage set point (e.g., 14.2 volts) and then switching the output back to the batteries after the battery voltage has dropped a fixed amount (e.g., 1.0 volt).

4. Short-circuit the generator's output. The effect of putting a short across the windings is to increase the load on the generator, slowing it down and reducing its output.

Some sophisticated regulators (such as the C Series from Xantrex/Trace—www.traceengineering.com) can be configured to operate in two or more different modes.

Shunt regulation. Crude shunt regulation is the constant-voltage type—the wind generator output is cut back progressively as battery voltage rises. Regulators are set to around 14.4 volts, which means generator output may start to taper off at as low as 13 volts, which is too low for effective fast charging or equalizing of deep-cycle batteries. This type of shunt regulator should have a disabling switch (see Figure 6-34A) so that at specific times the full generator output can be maintained until the batteries come up to 14.0 volts or higher. Note, however, that anytime a

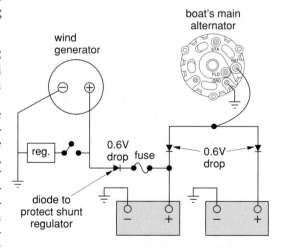

FIGURE 6-35A. A wiring schematic for a wind generator charging a single battery and using a shunt regulator.

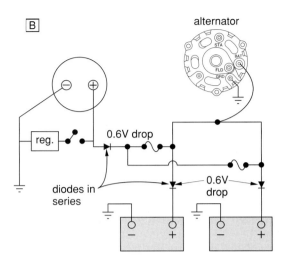

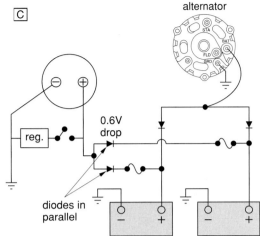

FIGURE 6-35B. Charging two batteries—incorrect installation. This approach produces excessive voltage drop.

FIGURE 6-35C. Charging two batteries—correct installation.

If this diode is already built into the regulator, the regulator's set point will be compensated for the diode-induced voltage drop on the charging circuit (Chapters 1 and 3), but if a diode has to be added, it will cause a voltage drop of around 0.6 volt. With a crude regulator, the regulator may now start to cut in when the battery voltage is as low as 12.4 volts and limit output at the battery to 13.8 volts. If the regular charging circuit also incorporates battery isolation diodes for split-charging, there will be an *additional* 0.6-volt drop (Figure 6-35B), producing a cut-in voltage at the battery of 11.8 and a final voltage of 13.2—much too low to be of any use. In other words, the wind generator must be hooked in *downstream* from any battery isolation diodes (it would be much better to get rid of these diodes—see Chapter 1), and if the wind generator regulator is adjustable, its setting must be raised to compensate for the total voltage drop on the charging circuit. To charge two batteries independently, a wind generator will need its own pair of battery isolation diodes to avoid paralleling the batteries through its charging line (Figure 6-35C).

Charge-divert regulation. The principle is the same for charge-divert regulation as that for shunt regulation, except that generally the full output of the generator is either going to the batteries or to the dummy load—there is not much sophistication here! With a larger wind generator, when the output is going to the dummy load, a lot of heat can be created. The resistor must be placed in a location with good airflow, particularly if the generator is to be left in operation when the boat is unattended. The resistor can be a specially designed heating element in the hot water tank, in which case excess wind generator output will heat the water. The Fourwinds people have quite a bit of experience with this approach.

Note that, in principle, you can feed 12 or 24 volts DC to a standard AC heating element in a water heater, but because of the much lower output voltage from the wind generator than the normal AC voltage, little current (amps) will flow, and little water heating will occur. To calculate an appropriate resistor, take the wind generator's rated output in watts (e.g., 300 watts), divide this by the system voltage (e.g., 12 volts) to derive maximum amps (300/12 = 25). Ohms law tells us that resistance = amps/volts, so an appropriate resistance is 25/12 = 2.1 ohms.

Short-circuit regulation. Southwest Windpower, manufacturer of the Air Marine and AirX wind generators (www.windenergy.com), has been perfecting the short-circuit type of regulator for a number of years. In its most recent incarnation, the regulator has an adjustable voltage set point (with a factory default setting of 14.1 volts for a 12-volt system). When battery voltage reaches the set point, the regulator disconnects the wind generator from the batteries and then shorts the output windings, braking the generator (see above). When battery voltage falls to a preset level (12.75 volts for a 12-volt system), the regulator reconnects the generator to the batteries. The voltage differential between the "on" (12.75 volts) and "off" (14.1 volts) set points ensures that the generator does not *short cycle* once the batteries are fully charged.

This kind of regulation can be combined with electronic braking and stopping. It lends itself to a sophisticated, multistep charging regimen and can also incorporate maximum power point tracking features—MPPT (see the section on solar panel voltage regulation later in this chapter). At the time of writing, it represents the most advanced and effective regulation technology for wind generators (Figure 6-36).

Note, however, that voltage sensing for regulation purposes is taking place at the wind gen-

FIGURE 6-36. A maximum power point tracking (MPPT) voltage regulator, plus rectification circuits and electronic braking, in an AirX wind generator—these devices are getting pretty sophisticated! *(Southwest Windpower)*

claimed output:
"typical performance (cold windings),"
or "voltage limiter inoperative"

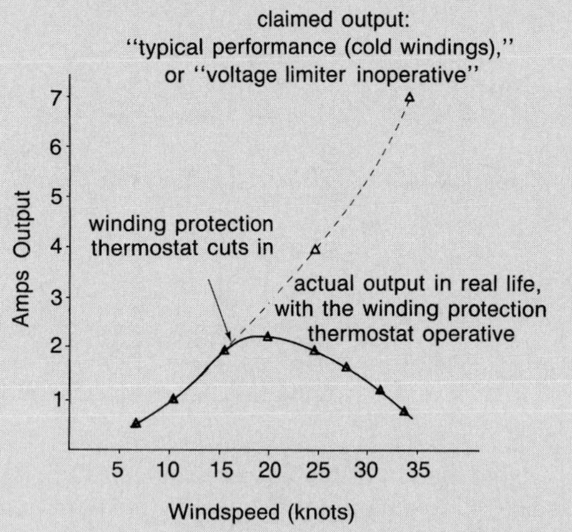

FIGURE 6-37A. Performance curve of a wind generator with a winding protection thermostat.

winding protection thermostat cuts in

actual output in real life, with the winding protection thermostat operative

Amps Output

Windspeed (knots)

Air-X Power Curve

Power Output (watts)

Instantaneous Wind Speed (knots)

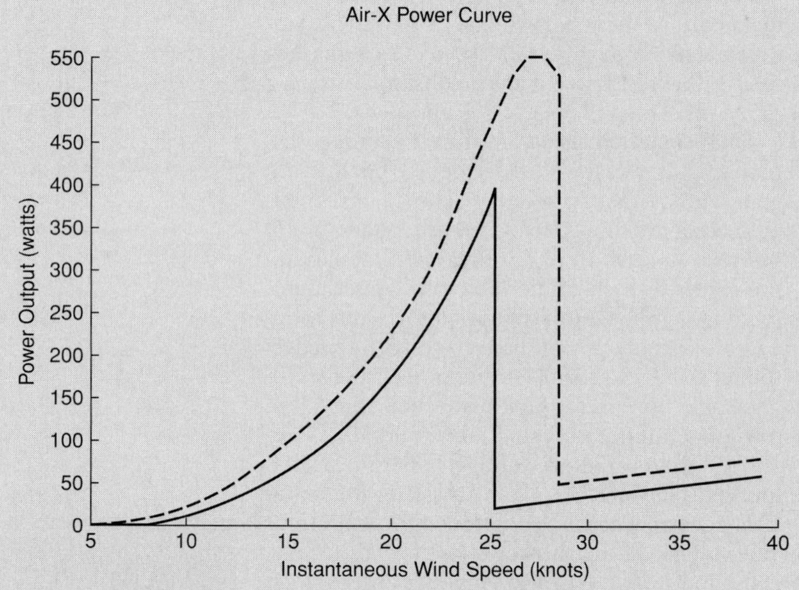

FIGURE 6-37B. Performance curve for the AirX. Note the two curves, with the upper (higher output) curve representing output in a steady wind state, and the lower curve representing output with some degree of turbulence (not specified). *(Southwest Windpower)*

There are no industry-wide standards for comparing wind generator outputs. Some specifications are borderline fraudulent, others are just hopelessly optimistic.

Certain alternator types have stator coils that will overheat at higher levels of output. To protect the coils from burning up, a temperature-sensitive switch is added (a *winding protection thermostat*). As the wind pipes up, or in a particularly hot environment, the switch may be off more than it is on, crippling output. Beware a product description in which the small print reads "typical performance, cold windings," or "voltage limiter inoperative" or something similar (Figure 6-37A)!

Figure 6-37B is the output curve for Southwest Windpower's AirX, currently the most popular wind generator on the market. It is unusual since it gives two output curves—one for a steady wind state, and a lower one for turbulent conditions. As with all wind generator output curves, the battery voltage at which these curves are derived is not given.

However, the battery voltage is important. Most companies use the output of a wind generator at 12.0 volts for rating purposes, although this is too low for battery charging! For any given wind speed, a much better basis for comparison would be the output (amps) at 14.0 volts (for a 12-volt system). In any event, when making comparisons, try to pry this information out of the manufacturer and use the same voltage.

What is less obvious is that *the kick-in speed is also affected by battery voltage*—the higher the voltage, the higher the kick-in speed. When making comparisons between generators, be sure the kick-in speed is at 12.0 volts or higher (and not an open circuit). At this voltage some wind generators will get going in 5 knots of wind, while others will need 7 or 8 knots, *severely affecting their utility in most popular cruising grounds*. It is also important to remember that even in the trade wind belt (e.g., the Caribbean), most boats spend most of the time anchored in relatively protected anchorages where wind speeds much above 10 knots are uncommon. As a result, *as far as output is concerned the two key indices are the kick-in speed at 12.0 volts and the output at 14.0 volts given a wind speed of 10 knots.*

erator and not at the batteries. If the wind generator is installed with undersized cables, voltage drop (see Chapter 4) in the cables will cause the voltage regulator to sense the shutdown voltage well before the batteries are at this voltage, resulting in undercharged batteries (see Chapter 1). Ironically, the higher the wind speed and

thus the output of the wind generator, the greater the volt drop, and the less the batteries get charged! For effective wind generator operation, the cables must be properly sized.

Making choices. Because of these many factors, making an informed choice between wind generators is not easy. First you must assess the boat's power needs, the type of cruising the boat will do, and the available winds in the cruising grounds. For example, someone intending to do transoceanic passages would probably benefit from a water generation option, while another person intending to cruise the Gulf of Maine in the summertime, where winds are characteristically below 10 knots much of the time, might consider solar panels a better investment!

In making a choice, the tendency is to go for the higher-output wind generators on the assumption that more must be better. Although this is often so, it is not necessarily the case. If a boat is used on weekends and for an annual vacation but is kept on a mooring for the rest of the year, the primary function of a wind generator is likely to be to keep up with the loads on the mooring—the bilge pump, perhaps a 12-volt refrigeration unit (although this may be more than a small generator can handle), and a float charge on the batteries—rather than the load when cruising. A lower-output wind generator that will safely run continuously may prove to be a better investment than one of the high-output units. The low-output unit will be essentially maintenance free, quiet, and unobtrusive. It will continue to produce electricity in storm conditions on ocean passages after many of the higher-output types have been shut down. It's true that over a weekend's cruising it will not keep up with the load and the batteries will slowly be discharged, but then they can be replenished during the week. On longer vacations, the engine-driven alternator will be needed to supplement the wind generator.

At the other end of the scale from a boat used only infrequently is a boat used for extended cruising in, for example, the Caribbean. Fan and refrigeration loads will be high and one of the higher-output wind generators will be a far more valuable investment than a small generator. As mentioned previously, the critical output is that in winds from 5 to 15 knots, not the maximum rated output.

Then there are things that are really hard to judge other than by experience. For example, as a boat pounds and rolls at sea, the differing weights and balance points of different wind generators will cause them to yaw from side to side to a differing extent. This yawing causes a substantial loss of output, so under conditions found at sea, generator output will differ significantly from the output on land in the same wind conditions. (Some generators are unbalanced to the point that on a heeled boat, a pole-mounted unit will not stay aligned with the wind; this is the kind of thing that does not show up on land.)

Factors determining which generator to choose will likely include the following:

- The reputation of the manufacturer.
- The physical space available for the propeller; generally speaking, the bigger the better.
- The output at low wind speeds (5 to 15 knots).
- The ability to leave the generator operating in any wind speed.
- The ease with which a generator can be shut down in high winds (e.g., with a switch versus tying it off).
- The availability of a voltage regulator if the unit is to be left operating unattended and the sophistication of the voltage regulation program (multistep and MPPT versus constant voltage or charge divert).
- The noise at higher speeds (this is an important issue that often does not become apparent until after a unit has been put into operation).
- Whether or not the wind generator can be converted to a water generator for passage-making.
- The ease of installation (some wind generators are far more complex than others).
- The length of the warranty (some are only 90 days; others, 3 years).
- And of course, the price.

Installation and Maintenance

To be effective, all wind generators must have a wind-seeking capability, produced by hanging the generator in the rigging or by placing it on a pole-mounted bearing assembly into which brushes and slip rings are normally built (Figures 6-38A and 6-38B). The brushes, rotating with the generator, receive its output, feeding this output to the fixed slip rings (or vice versa), which transmit the output to the batteries.

Clearly any generator must be mounted high enough, or in a sufficiently out-of-the-way location, to avoid being a hazard to people moving around on deck. The higher the unit, the greater the wind strength, and therefore the more the output. But on the other hand, unless the generator can be completely braked with a switch (e.g., Air Marine and AirX), or it has a remotely operated brake (as some models of the Fourwinds II do), the generator has to be accessible enough for the operator to shut it down (by turning it out of the wind) and tie off the blades, sometimes in rough conditions when the unit will be swinging wildly from side to side. These contradictory requirements are not easy to bal-

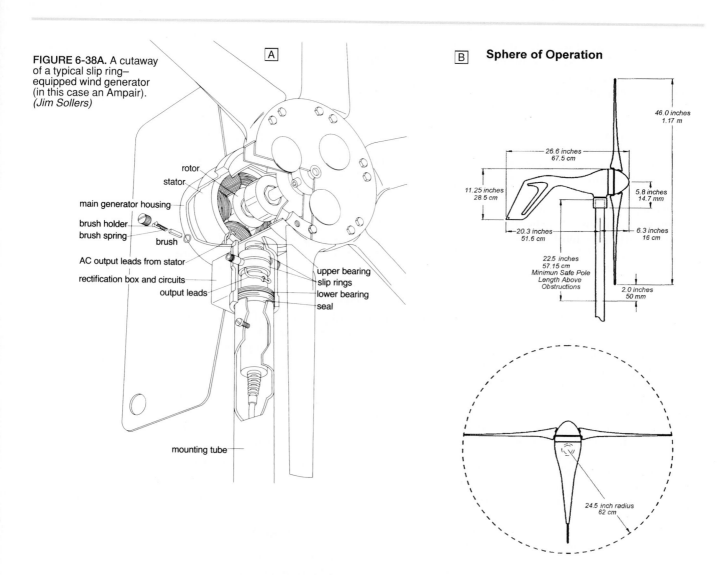

FIGURE 6-38A. A cutaway of a typical slip ring–equipped wind generator (in this case an Ampair). *(Jim Sollers)*

A

rotor
stator
main generator housing
brush holder
brush spring
brush
AC output leads from stator
rectification box and circuits
output leads
upper bearing
slip rings
lower bearing
seal
mounting tube

B **Sphere of Operation**

46.0 inches
1.17 m

26.6 inches
67.5 cm

11.25 inches
28.5 cm

5.8 inches
14.7 mm

20.3 inches
51.6 cm

6.3 inches
16 cm

22.5 inches
57.15 cm
Minimun Safe Pole
Length Above
Obstructions

2.0 inches
50 mm

24.5 inch radius
62 cm

FIGURE 6-38B (top right and right). An exploded drawing of the AirX wind generator. *(Southwest Windpower)*

B **Exploded View of *AIR-X marine***

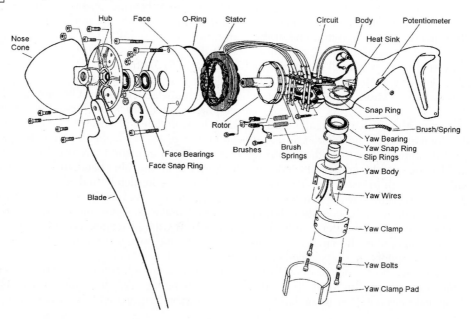

Nose Cone
Hub
Face
O-Ring
Stator
Circuit
Body
Potentiometer
Heat Sink
Snap Ring
Brush/Spring
Yaw Bearing
Yaw Snap Ring
Slip Rings
Yaw Body
Yaw Wires
Yaw Clamp
Yaw Bolts
Yaw Clamp Pad
Rotor
Brushes
Brush Springs
Face Bearings
Face Snap Ring
Blade

ance. Inevitably there are times, particularly with some of the larger generators, when shutting down a machine can be quite hazardous.

Wiring a generator is simplicity itself. Almost all are attached directly to a battery so that when the boat is unattended, and the battery isolation switch is turned off, the generator can still be left online (see Chapter 1 for circuit diagrams). Wire should be sized for a maximum 3% voltage drop at full rated output (Chapter 4). Note that if most alternator types are connected to a battery with reverse polarity (i.e., the positive and negative leads crossed) instantaneous damage will occur that is not covered by any warranty!

The DC-motor types require a diode in the positive cable to prevent a reverse drain from the batteries when the generator is not running (this diode may already be present with some regulators); the alternator types already have this diode in the rectification circuit. All models must have a fuse in the positive cable close to the batteries. *This fuse is an essential safety device: it prevents a short in the generator circuit from putting a dead short across the batteries and thus melting down the wind generator wiring.*

The problem with such a fuse is that if it blows, it open-circuits the generator, which in high winds may then self-destruct. To avoid this situation, the fuse rating must be at least as high as the *maximum possible output from the generator*, which in the case of the larger generators may be 25 amps or more. A 40 to 50 amp fuse will, in most instances, serve the purpose of ultimate wiring protection without threatening the generator. If using cables with a 105°C/221°F temperature rating (commonly available in the United States from marine outlets) a 40 amp fuse will require a minimum cable size of 12 AWG (3.0 mm²); a 50 amp fuse will require 10 AWG (5.0 mm²) cables (see the ampacity table in Chapter 4). However, if using 60°C/140°F cables (common in Europe), the cable sizes must be increased to 10 AWG (5.0 mm²) and 8 AWG (8.0 mm²) respectively.

It is desirable, but by no means necessary, to install an ammeter to monitor performance. Battery voltage can be measured with existing meters.

Maintenance. Given the wide variety of wind generators available, it is possible to make only a few general points on maintenance. Brushes and brush springs are the most obvious point of failure (Figures 6-39A, 6-39B, and 6-39C). Alterna-

FIGURES 6-39A, 6-39B, AND 6-39C. Wind generator components—alternator type. This rotor has two permanent magnets; each has a set of stator coils (6-39A). One set of coils can be seen on the right in the generator housing; the other set is in the other half of the housing, which has been removed. Looking into the base of the same generator (6-39B), we can see the output shaft and slip rings (see above) have been removed to expose the brushes. A complete wind generator kit (6-39C).

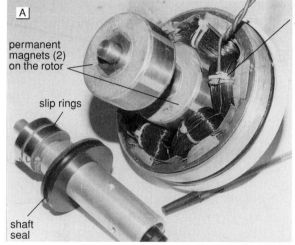

A

permanent magnets (2) on the rotor

slip rings

shaft seal

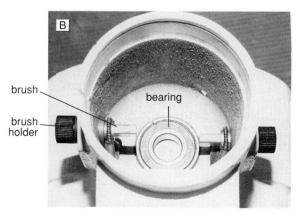

B

brush

brush holder

bearing

one set of stator coils (another set in the other half of the generator housing goes with the second permanent magnet)

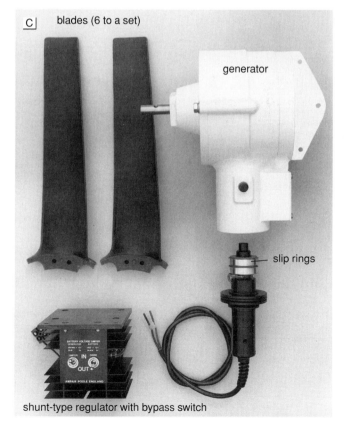

C   blades (6 to a set)

generator

slip rings

shunt-type regulator with bypass switch

tor types will have brushes only on the slip rings, and none at all if no slip rings are present. DC-motor-type generators will have brushes to collect the output from the commutator, as well as slip ring brushes if they are fitted. Some larger generators have four brushes on the commutator.

Check brushes and brush springs periodically for wear, corrosion, and loss of tension. If brushes or springs are defective, inspect the commutator or slip rings for burning or pitting (see pages 311, 314).

Check the shaft bearing occasionally by gripping the blades and attempting to move the shaft up and down and side to side. Any play indicates the need for bearing replacement, which will require generator disassembly. See below for one or two precautions to observe when taking the unit apart.

Check all external fasteners periodically. Most wind generators are subject to a certain amount of vibration, and fasteners will sometimes work loose. Add a drop of Loctite thread-sealing compound when replacing them.

To cure excessive vibration, detach the turbine blades individually (if this is possible) in *opposite pairs* (assuming they come in pairs), weigh them on a postal scale, and correct any differences. Be sure to mark them so that you can replace them as matched pairs. After reinstallation, check the alignment as shown in Figure 6-40.

Fiber-reinforced plastic blades are UV-degradable in sunlight. If the surface becomes crazed and powdery, sand them lightly and paint with a two-part polyurethane paint.

The leading edge of unprotected spruce blades will wear down just from the impact of bugs, rain, etc. The blades must be kept smooth for maximum efficiency and noise reduction, so recoat the blades with epoxy or two-part polyurethane.

Many generators have aluminum housings with stainless steel fasteners, shafts, and bearings. Add salt spray and this is a recipe for corrosion. Rinse the housings from time to time with fresh water. Watch closely for any signs of galvanic interaction. If present, remove the relevant fastener or part, apply a corrosion inhibitor (such as Tef-Gel, Duralac, or a Teflon-based grease), and replace. Pay particular attention to the pivot points on any air-brake, furling, or tilt-back mechanism, making sure that they are free and lubricated.

Troubleshooting and Repair

Radio frequency interference (RFI). A poor contact between a brush and a slip ring or commutator can create arcing that generates RFI. The frequency will vary with the wind generator speed, but is most likely to interfere with ham radio operations, sometimes on boats a good distance away. The DC-motor type of wind generator is the worst offender. Solutions are to keep brushes in good condition and commutators and slip rings clean. If problems persist, wire in capacitors across the output leads of the wind generator as close to the brush holders as possible. Bill Owra, manufacturer of the Fourwinds, suggests three in parallel, rated at 7.5 microfarads, 0.01 microfarad, and 0.001 microfarad (available from electronics stores; some are polarity sensitive and must be installed the right way around, while others are not).

Erratic output. If the generator has brushes (DC-motor type or any wind-seeking generator with slip rings), check the brushes for adequate spring tension and the slip rings and/or commutator for a clean mating surface. Otherwise look for loose or corroded connections (see the following voltage and resistance tests).

No output from the generator:

1. Check all fuses and switches (there may be a fuse inside any voltage regulator).
2. With the generator spinning in a wind that would normally be high enough to produce output, check the voltage across the output

FIGURE 6-40. To check wind generator blade alignment, place the generator, blades up, on a flat surface with one blade tip just touching a wall. Draw a pencil mark on the wall at the blade tip and slowly rotate the blades, checking the alignment of each as it passes the mark. If blades are out of alignment, adjust them by putting pieces of tape or some other shim material under the blade clamp.

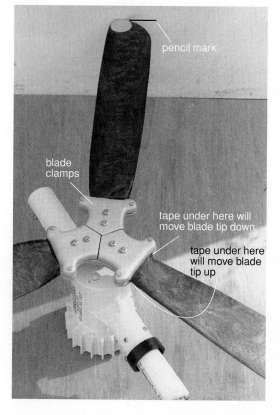

pencil mark

blade clamps

tape under here will move blade tip down

tape under here will move blade tip up

leads *as close to the generator as possible*. It should be a little above battery voltage (normally around 0.5 volt higher—you need a good digital multimeter), in which case the wind generator is working. If it is high (it may run to 40 volts or more), the charging circuit is open at some point; check the fuses and switches once again. Open-circuited wind generators can give quite a shock at high speeds: *Be careful.*

3. Check the continuity of all wiring with an ohmmeter (see Chapter 4). Be sure to disconnect the generator from the batteries first and immobilize its blades; any output is likely to damage the ohmmeter.

4. With the generator still disconnected from the battery, let the blades spin and check the open-circuit voltage. It should be well above battery voltage.

5. If there is no output, disconnect any voltage regulator and try again.

6. If there is still no output, check all brushes and brush springs for possible sticking.

7. If there is still no output, if a rectifier is fitted (alternator types), test the diodes as outlined on page 111; on DC-motor types inspect the commutator (see pages 311, 314).

8. Finally, as a crude test, disconnect the generator's output leads from the batteries, short the leads together, and try spinning the propeller blades by hand. If everything is working, the blades should be noticeably more difficult to turn than normal. If not, there is likely some internal fault in the generator: check the stator (alternator types) or armature (DC-motor types).

Generator hard to turn. The output leads may be shorted (see above), but otherwise there is a mechanical problem. Most likely are (1) corroded bearings from the failure of a shaft seal—both bearings and seals need replacing; (2) friction from a bent shaft—it may be possible to remove it and straighten it; or (3) magnets coming loose and binding (the generator will probably be "squeaking").

Many magnets are simply glued in place, and moisture in the marine environment can cause corrosion under the glue bond, causing the bond to give way. If no other damage has been done, after you've cleaned the seating surfaces, you can glue the magnets back in place with an epoxy glue (MarineTex, often found on boats, will do), *making sure that each magnet goes back in the same place from which it came and the same way around* (don't let them get mixed up or turned around!). Handle magnets with care (they will shatter if dropped) and clamp them

Troubleshooting Chart 6-2. Wind Generator Output Problems	
Symptom: Generator provides no battery charging when battery voltage is below the preset cutoff level of the voltage regulator (if one is fitted).	
Note: Many of the following tests involve checking the voltage on an open-circuited generator. An open-circuited (i.e., disconnected from its battery) wind generator can produce up to 100 volts and give a severe shock. Be careful!	
Disconnect the generator leads at the battery and check for voltage with the generator spinning. Is voltage present? **NO**	**YES** Generator is OK.
Disconnect the output leads at the generator and check for voltage at the generator output terminals with the generator spinning. Is voltage present? **NO**	**YES** Generator is OK. The fault is in its circuit. Check all fuses, switches, breakers, and terminals. Bypass any diode or voltage regulator to see if this is the problem.
Inspect all brushes and brush springs for wear, corrosion, loss of tension, or sticking. Replace as necessary and spin again. Is voltage present? **NO**	**YES** Generator is OK.
DC-motor-type generators: Inspect the commutator for burning and pitting (pages 311, 314). *Alternator-type generators:* Test the rectifying diodes (page 111); repair as necessary and spin again. Is voltage present? **NO**	**YES** Generator is OK.
The generator is probably defective. Check its stator or armature (see Chapters 3 and 7).	

gently while the glue sets (they are brittle and easily cracked).

If there is evidence of moisture inside a wind generator, it is a good idea to flush the various coils with mineral spirits, blow them dry (with an air compressor if available, but otherwise with the exhaust from a vacuum cleaner or even a bicycle pump), and then bake the unit in an oven at no more than 200°F/93°C for several hours.

Disassembly. It is impossible to be specific, but these are a few points to watch for (Figures 6-41A to 6-41E):

1. It is frequently crucial to align housing halves to within ±1 degree. Before separating any housings, mark the two halves for an exact realignment. A line scribed across the joint works best.

2. The permanent magnets used in wind generators are powerful and may hold housings

A

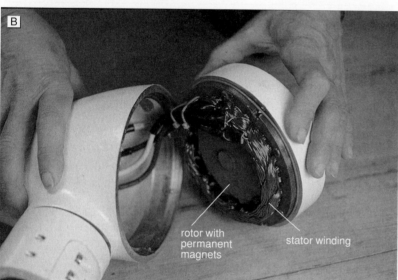

B

rotor with permanent magnets

stator winding

C

slip rings

voltage regulator and rectifier

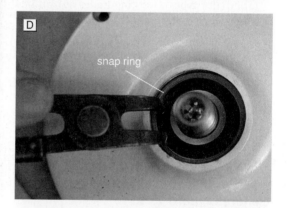

D

snap ring

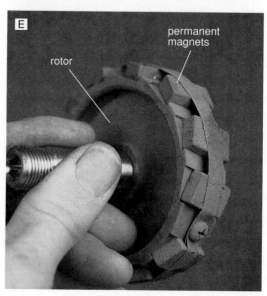

E

rotor

permanent magnets

FIGURES 6-41A TO 6-41E. Disassembly of an Air Marine. Undo the front housing screws after the blade assembly has been removed (6-41A). Separate the two housing halves (6-41B). A view of the slip rings and voltage regulator (6-41C). Remove a bearing-retaining circlip to knock out the bearing (6-41D). The rotor assembly with magnets glued in place and held with a band (6-41E).

together with a strong magnetic force. Some housings have threads for the addition of jacking screws to aid in separation; others must be levered apart carefully with screwdrivers. When replacing them, keep fingers well out of the way—the magnets may grab the housings and pull them together uncontrollably.

3. The magnets will attract any metal particles or flakes lying around. *Work in a scrupulously clean environment and check the magnets before reassembling.* It is particularly important to keep the air gap between the magnets and the stator (armature) clean.

4. Whenever a unit is opened, pay special attention to any shaft seals where the drive shaft exits the housing. Some units rely solely on "sealed" bearings and have no additional shaft seals. These bearings do not always keep out salt water for long and may need replacing.

5. Various armature and stator tests can be carried out as outlined in the sections on universal motors (Chapter 7) and alternators (Chapter 3).

6. Any glued-in-place magnets should be given a tug to make sure they are still firmly bonded in place.

Solar Panels

The promise of solar panels is great—"free energy from the sun"—but the reality can be disappointing if an installation is not sized and mounted correctly, and if the panels themselves cannot withstand the marine environment—and many can't. This is not to say that solar panels do not have a place on boats, particularly for maintaining batteries at full charge when a boat is left unattended; it is just a matter of getting things in perspective.

Basic Terminology

Solar panels are silicon-based semiconductors that convert sunlight directly into electrical energy. There are three types:

1. *Single crystal* (monocrystalline) *units,* in which each cell is cut from a single silicon crystal. Typically, these convert around 12% of the received light into electricity, although some newer units from British Petroleum (BP) have gotten this up to 16% to 18% (using what is known as laser-grooved buried-grid [LGBG] technology).

2. *Polycrystalline units,* in which the individual cells are composed of multiple, smaller crystals, are a little less efficient (around 10%), but easier and cheaper to manufacture.

3. *Amorphous silicon units,* in which vaporized silicon is deposited on some substrate, with a conversion efficiency of 6% to 8%. These are the cheapest to produce and can be made flexible.

A number of different technologies have been used in the laboratory to create solar panels with an efficiency of up to 30%. There are persistent rumors that these new technologies are becoming affordable and will revolutionize the solar power market. However, it must be said that these rumors have been going around for 30 years now, and while there have been incremental improvements in efficiency and reliability over time, we have yet to see any dramatic changes in the solar panel market.

With conventional silicon-based technology, where single cells are visible in a panel, each cell has an open-circuit voltage in direct sunlight of around 0.5 volt *regardless of its size;* the open-circuit voltage of the panel can be roughly determined by adding the number of cells (e.g., 30 cells = 15.0 volts). The output (amperage) of a cell, on the other hand, is *directly proportional to its surface area.* Since amorphous silicon panels are not much more than half as efficient as the others, almost twice the surface area is required for a given level of output (the amorphous silicon panels also suffer an additional loss of output of 10% or more in the first year or two after manufacture, but then stabilize).

Output specifications The *open-circuit voltage* (V_{oc}) for a panel is generally what is given in the literature. It is measured by disconnecting a panel from its battery and placing a voltmeter across its leads. Specification sheets also include *short-circuit current* (I_{sc}), which is the maximum current a panel can produce with its output terminals shorted, at which point its voltage will drop to zero. *Neither describes real-life performance.* For this we need to measure the output (amperage) at *battery-charging voltages,* and this number will not be in the specifications!

What will be in the specifications is the *load current* (I_{mp}, or *current at maximum [peak] power*) and the *load voltage* (V_{mp}, or *voltage at maximum [peak] power*). These two multiplied together give a panel's *rated wattage* (P_{max}, or *maximum [peak] power;* Figures 6-42A and 6-42B). Sometimes only the wattage (maximum

FIGURES 6-42A AND 6-42B. Typical solar panel specification sheets.

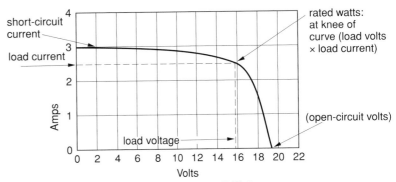

Rated Power	40 Watts
Current (typical at load)	2.55 amps
Voltage (typical at load)	15.7 volts
Short-circuit current (typical)	3.0 amps
Open-circuit voltage (typical)	19.5 volts

or peak power) and the voltage (load voltage, V_{mp}, or voltage at peak power) are given, in which case the current (load current, I_{mp}, or current at peak power) can be found by dividing the voltage into the wattage. Even this will not tell us how many amps a battery is receiving.

Key Factors in System Design

How many amps? Solar panels are rated in a certain set of standard test conditions (STC), the two most important of which (from a boatowner's perspective) are the assumption of *direct overhead sunlight* and a *panel temperature of 25°C/77°F* given an ambient temperature of 20°C/68°F (the panel temperature is higher than the ambient temperature because the dark color of the silicon absorbs heat). The output is frequently displayed in the form of an I-V (current and voltage) curve (see Figures 6-43A, 6-43B, and 6-43C). There may be curves for several different temperatures. The peak power—

the solar panel's rated output—occurs at the "knee" of the 25°C curve.

The voltage at peak power will vary from panel to panel, principally as a function of the number of cells in the panel. Whatever this voltage may be, it is always higher than battery-charging voltages; i.e., when connected to a battery, the voltage will drop. Because of this, *even in standard test conditions*, the output (in watts) at battery-charging voltages is always less than the rated output, often by as much as 20% to 25%.

To find out how much less, it is necessary to look at the charging current that will be available at battery-charging voltages. For example, consider a 50-watt panel that is rated at 17 volts, and which is therefore putting out 2.94 amps at this voltage (watts/volts = amps). We find from the 25°C I-V curve that at 13.0 volts (a typical battery-charging voltage if the battery is somewhat discharged, or if the charging voltage is being held down by a concurrent load) its output is 3.0 amps. Although the amperage has risen marginally, because of the lower voltage the output (in watts) is reduced to 13.0 × 3.0 = 39 watts—22% less than the rated output (I'll return to this issue below—see the Maximum Power Point Tracking section). Note, however, that if you want to know how many amps (as opposed to watts) are being put into the battery, the I-V curves are pretty flat from zero to load voltage, so the amperage will be pretty close to the rated load current.

There are other losses that must be accounted for. On land, solar panels are set up on angled mounts that are designed to intercept as many of the sun's rays as possible. But if this is done on a boat, every time the boat turns, the panel will lose the sun. As a result, a solar panel on a boat is almost always mounted more or less horizontally in a fixed location. (Hotwire Enterprises—www.svhotwire.com—is one source of well-designed folding and angled solar panel mounts for boats.)

Even in the tropics, the sun is directly overhead (known as *solar noon*) for only a brief period each day. For the rest of the day the sun's rays intersect the panel at ever shallower angles and with decreasing intensity. Figure 6-43D indicates the decline in panel output on either side of solar noon.

Should a cloud obscure the sun or a shadow be cast over the panel (e.g., from rigging, sails, or a boom), there will be a further, dramatic fall in panel output. Even partial shading of a single cell in a string of cells connected in series can dramatically reduce the output of all the cells. To minimize this, some panels have small blocking diodes built into the panel itself in a manner that minimizes losses from shading.

FIGURES 6-43A, 6-43B, AND 6-43C. The relationship between temperature and output for three popular panels. These curves represent maximum output in bright sunlight, rather than realistic output in normal operating conditions. At 122°F/50°C, output on a 36-cell panel begins to taper off at 15 volts; on the 30-cell panel, it tapers at 11 volts, which is much too low for effective battery charging in hot climates. *(Siemens Solar)*

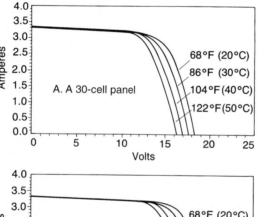

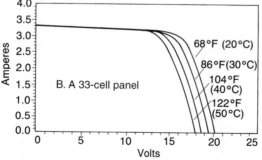

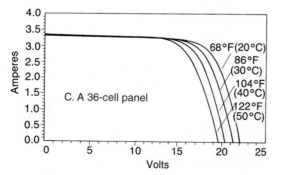

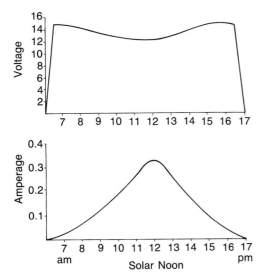

FIGURE 6-43D. Output voltage and amperage in relation to solar noon. Note the drop in voltage as the temperature rises at solar noon and on into the early afternoon, and the relatively narrow band of time during which a panel puts out at anywhere near its rated output. Panel output can be considerably increased by adjusting the angle of the panel during the course of the day to maintain as near to a right angle to the sun as possible.

The net result is that even in sunny climates, daily panel output will rarely exceed more than the equivalent of the panel's rated output sustained for 4 to 5 hours a day, perhaps 6 hours in some locations in the summer, and it may be considerably less than this; it is best to base calculations on the assumption of 4 hours a day. A 6-watt panel in a 12-volt system can be expected to produce only 24 watt-hours = 2 amp-hours a day; a 30-watt panel, 120 watt-hours = 10 amp-hours a day (i.e., amp-hours per day at 12.0 volts = rated wattage/3). In many instances a panel will not do even this well. Given a desired daily output (for example, 60 amp-hours at 12 volts), the necessary panel wattage for a 12-volt system can be determined by multiplying by 3: 60 × 3 = 180 watts.

At what voltage? As with any charging device, to put a charge into a battery a solar panel must be able to maintain a healthy voltage differential over the battery's rising voltage, perhaps as high as 14.0 volts *at the battery.*

A 12-volt solar panel will have anywhere from 30 to 36 cells in series, giving a nominal open-circuit voltage of from 15.0 to 18.0 volts. This would seem to be more than adequate for battery charging, but in fact this is not always the case.

As solar noon approaches, the black silicon in a solar panel heats up. In the tropics the panel temperature is certain to exceed the 25°C/77°F temperature used for rating purposes, producing a decline in the panel voltage of approximately 1.0 volt for every 12°C/22°F to 15°C/27°F temperature rise (refer back to Figures 6-43A, 6-43B, and 6-43C). At 50°C/122°F (not uncommon in the tropics) the nominal voltage of a 30-cell panel will be reduced to 13.3 volts or less; that of a 33-cell panel to 14.8 volts or less; and that of a 36-cell panel to 16.3 volts or less. The 30-cell panel is below effective battery-charging levels and will suffer a steady decline in its output as a battery comes up to charge.

At the time of installation, a blocking diode is also frequently added to the wiring to the battery (see below—such diodes are in addition to the bypass diodes found in some panel junction boxes and are not to be confused with them). Diodes cause an additional voltage drop of around 0.6 volt. A 30-*cell panel with a blocking diode, particularly in a hot climate, will be almost completely ineffective for battery charging;* even a 33-cell panel will start to suffer a decline in its output as a battery comes up to charge.

In the tropics, any 30-cell panel is likely to prove a marginal battery-charging source. A 33-cell panel will develop effective battery-charging voltages, but with little margin for other losses (e.g., voltage drop through diodes and in transmission lines, resistive connections, and poor sunlight). A 36-cell panel will develop effective battery-charging voltages in just about any application. In *temperate climates* a 33-cell panel will develop adequate battery-charging voltages on all but the hottest days.

In general terms, for effective battery charging in hot climates a panel needs a *minimum load voltage* (at standard test conditions) *after deducting the voltage drop of any diode* of 16.0 to 17.0 volts; in temperate climates a minimum load voltage after deducting the voltage drop of any diode of 15.0 to 16.0 volts is adequate.

Blocking diodes. The reason for installing blocking diodes is that while a solar panel puts out in sunlight, without the diode it takes back after dark (although the reverse current flow is much less). But *the voltage drop through a diode will often reduce the output of a panel by more than the nighttime drain back into a panel without the diode!* So although such diodes are fitted routinely, *they would often be better left out.*

The key factor here, once again, is the number of cells in series in a panel. A 36-cell panel generally has a high-enough voltage to be able to handle a diode in all circumstances with no appreciable loss in performance; a 33-cell panel will suffer some loss of performance, especially in high-temperature applications; and a 30-cell panel will suffer a serious loss of performance in almost all applications.

The one time a blocking diode is more or less mandatory is when it is intended to cover the panel for any length of time (e.g., when you are not using the boat) while leaving the panel connected to the battery—it will steadily drain the battery (unless it has a voltage regulator that prevents this—see below). However, panels are rarely covered (unless a boat has a covered slip), and such a situation would in any case best be handled by putting a switch in the circuit, rather than a diode, so that the panel can simply be disconnected from the battery.

Voltage regulation. Figure 6-43A typifies the output of a so-called *self-regulated* solar panel. Actually, this panel is constructed with just 30 silicon cells, keeping down the output voltage. As battery voltage rises and more nearly equalizes with panel voltage, panel output declines. As we have seen, if we add temperature projections for warmer climates (especially the tropics), a diode, and perhaps minimal voltage drop in a circuit, *a self-regulating solar panel will frequently fail to charge a battery adequately,* regardless of the rated output. For effective charging, more cells are needed.

But a panel that will maintain an effective battery-charging voltage may have enough capacity to slowly overcharge a battery when a boat is not in use. The critical point comes if the *panel's rated output at 14.0 volts is above 0.5% of the amp-hour rating of the batteries to which it is connected* (e.g., above 1 amp when connected to a 200 amp-hour battery bank). If the panel's capacity exceeds this level, it should be turned off when leaving the boat, or else fitted with a voltage regulator (Figure 6-44).

Cheaper regulators are generally built around a simple voltage-sensing circuit and a series relay. When the voltage reaches a set point, the relay opens and disconnects the solar array from the batteries (solar panels suffer no harm when open-circuited in this fashion). Other regulators switch the solar panel's output to some kind of a resistor (a shunt regulator) or a load such as a heating element in a water heater (a divert regulator; see the Shunt Regulation and Charge-Divert Regulation sections on pages 272–73).

More-sophisticated solar panel regulators have come a long way in the last few years with some now including multistep charging programs. Other desirable features are a *nighttime dropout* function, which disconnects the panel from the battery anytime the regulator senses a negative current flow and thus eliminates the need for a blocking diode. Also desirable is some form of an *equalizing* function, or disabling switch, so that at times the regulator can be taken out of the circuit, concentrating the panel's full output on the battery.

Maximum power point tracking (MPPT). Maximum power point tracking (MPPT) is the latest wave in voltage regulation for solar panels. It is finding its way into other applications (such as the AirX wind generator from Southwest Windpower). It is an extension of the higher-end pulse-width-modulated regulators referred to in the Shunt Regulation section on pages 272–73. In essence, an MPPT regulator is a DC-to-DC converter (see Chapter 2). It includes (1) a DC-to-AC inverter that takes the incoming DC power from a solar panel and converts it to high-frequency AC, (2) a transformer that changes the voltage, (3) a rectifier to convert the output of the transformer back to DC, and (4) electronic control circuits. Why such a complicated device?

As noted above, the output voltage of a solar panel is normally determined by the voltage of the battery that it is charging. This is regardless of what the panel's nominal voltage may be. The peak power, however, is developed at a higher voltage (the "knee" of the power curve). The difference between the two voltages can reduce the real-life output as compared to the rated output by as much as 25%. With MPPT technology, the panel's output voltage is freed from control by the battery's voltage. The more-sophisticated devices incorporate a microcomputer that monitors battery voltage, state of charge, and solar panel output, then calculates the solar panel voltage that will maximize its output in this specific set of conditions. The control circuit in the DC-to-DC converter is used to achieve the desired result, bringing the panel output back up to something closer to its rated output—an increase of as much as 25% in output.

There are some drawbacks:

- While top-of-the-line MPPT regulators are up to 99% efficient, they are expensive. Cheaper models may be as low as 85% efficient, dissi-

FIGURE 6-44. Regulated solar panels with diodes in the regulators. Note that some regulators with a nighttime dropout function do not require a diode.

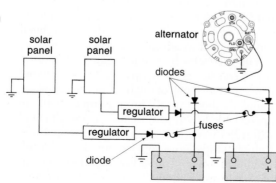

BATTERY CHARGERS, INVERTERS, WIND AND WATER GENERATORS, AND SOLAR PANELS

pating 15% of the solar panel's output as heat. This immediately negates much, if not all, of the gain in charging efficiency. Most models are now around 95% efficient.

- The sophistication of the electronic control circuits varies markedly from one product to another, and with it the optimization of the charging capability of the solar panel.

- MPPT devices include a lot of complex electronics that switch currents at very high rates; clearly, there is the potential for failure and for significant RFI emissions, which in the better units, is effectively suppressed.

In spite of its drawbacks, MPPT is a technology that seems certain to find an increasing number of applications. It is bringing another improvement in the efficiency of boat DC systems.

Float charging. To combat sulfation, many boatowners leave their batteries hooked to a battery charger when in the slip. But this practice can cause overcharging, and in any case, the shore-power cord may bring with it the risk of galvanic corrosion and stray currents (Chapter 5) that will consume zincs and then attack underwater hardware.

An alternative is to unplug the shore-power cord and wire a small solar panel to each battery bank (Figures 6-45A and 6-45B). All you need is a rated panel capacity at 14.0 volts of around 0.3% of the amp-hour capacity of the battery bank to be floated (e.g., a 1.2 amp—15 watt—panel on a 400 amp-hour battery bank). *As long as there is no drain on the battery bank*, and the batteries are in good condition, this setup will indefinitely maintain the batteries in a state of full charge with only minimal water consumption (but note that even such things as an LED

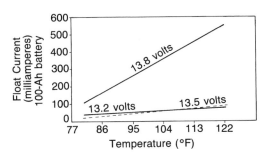

FIGURE 6-45A. Float current versus temperature and battery float voltage. Using 13.2 to 13.5 volts as a desirable float voltage, a constant float current of 50 milliamps would be sufficient for a 100 Ah battery at 86°F/30°C. 50 mA x 24 hours = 1.2 amp-hours. 1.2 x 3 (the factor for converting amp-hours to watts at 12 volts—see pages 282–83) = 3.6. A panel output of 3.6 watts is needed for every 100 Ah of battery capacity to be floated.

FIGURE 6-45B. Solar panel for keeping the batteries topped off on our old Pacific Seacraft 40. Not an ideal location (because of potential shading) but well protected from physical damage.

on a bilge pump circuit with a couple of other similar low-drain circuits—such as a carbon monoxide monitor—can eventually run down the batteries). With good-quality deep-cycle batteries, the panels will pay for themselves in extended battery life alone.

Installation

Given the fact that solar panel output is so sensitive to even small voltage drops, marine-quality wiring and terminals must be used when making an installation. The terminals at the panel are particularly vulnerable to corrosion and need to be completely sealed. *There should be no other connections in this circuit above deck*—a continuous length of cable should be run directly to a deck seal. Any connections, if necessary, should be made *inside* the boat.

A good rule of thumb for determining a cable size is to take the maximum short-circuit current (see the panel specifications sheet) of all the panels in a particular circuit, multiply this figure by 1.25, and treat this result as the required current-carrying capacity of the panel wiring. Then refer to the 3% voltage drop table in Chapter 4 to select an appropriate cable size.

If the panel is to be hooked directly to a battery (which it will have to be for float charging—see the preceding circuit diagrams), *there must be a fuse in the wiring as close to the battery as possible. Without such a fuse, any short in the wiring will cause a dead short across the battery and likely start a fire.*

Multibattery systems. Many split-charging systems use isolation diodes (Chapters 1 and 3), which introduce a voltage drop of around 0.6 volt. If a solar panel is to be used in a split-charging system with isolation diodes, *it will not need*

FIGURE 6-46A. An unregulated solar panel. If the panel is installed upstream of the main blocking diodes, it will not need its own diode.

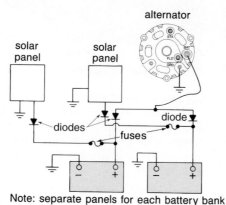

FIGURE 6-46B. Unregulated solar panels with diodes. The diodes may be better omitted (see the text).

Note: separate panels for each battery bank

nected *downstream* of any split-charging diodes. But in this case the panel's output can be fed to only one battery—if fed to two it would parallel the batteries via its wiring. Where two batteries need to be charged independently, two separate panels should be used (Figure 6-46B).

If a panel uses a voltage regulator, the regulator will quite likely include a diode of its own. In this case additional diodes are not needed and the installation should be as in Figure 6-44.

Location. Published specifications apply only to solar panels in direct sunlight angled to intercept the sun's rays at approximately 90 degrees. This is virtually impossible to achieve on a boat! If the panels are set up on angled mounts, as is normally the case on land, they will lose the sun every time the boat turns (Figure 6-47A). As a result, panels are almost always flat-mounted (Figure 6-47B), which is generally the best compromise. (In this case they should be mounted on blocks to keep them off the deck and to maintain an air space that will help cool them.) In the tropics, with the sun nearly overhead, the panels will perform quite well; the farther north you go, the poorer the angle becomes.

Although a solar panel does not require direct sunlight to reach its maximum output voltage, anything that restricts the impact of the sun (including poor angles) has a marked effect on the amperage produced. Even small shadows that partially shade the panels can cause a significant drop (the loss of output varies markedly from one make and type of panel to another, which is of some significance when making

its own blocking diode, which would only introduce an extra unwanted voltage drop. The panel should be installed upstream from existing diodes (Figure 6-46A).

If, on the other hand, a panel has a built-in diode, the wiring to the battery should be con-

FIGURES 6-47A, 6-47B, AND 6-47C. Typical solar panel placements. *(Line drawings by Jim Sollers)*

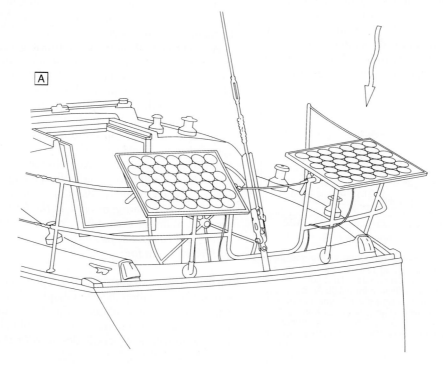

A

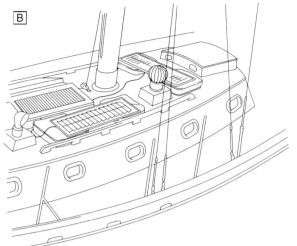

choices in many applications). On sailboats, the mast, boom, sail cover, and even rigging shadows can ruin output completely. An outboard mount aft is probably the best location for output, but may be vulnerable to pooping waves or docking damage (Figure 6-47C). Another good spot is on top of a bimini or pilothouse.

Troubleshooting

Panel construction is the principal factor limiting solar panel life in marine use, with water ingress through delamination, poorly sealed cable boxes, and cracking of cases and covers being the main problems. If a solar panel has a warranty in marine use of less than 10 years (some are as long as 25 years), I would consider its construction suspect and would look for another product.

If a panel is physically sound but appears not to be working, disconnect it and check its open-circuit voltage in sunlight (Troubleshooting Chart 6-3). If it is between 16 and 20 volts, the panel itself is functioning, although it may have a reduced output due to internal shorts from moisture ingress. The output can be checked by placing an ammeter in series with the output cable. The blocking diode (if fitted), wiring, and connections should be checked for undue resistance (Chapters 3 and 4). Before using an ohmmeter, be sure to disconnect the solar panel as its output is capable of damaging the meter.

Troubleshooting Chart 6-3. Solar Panel Problem: No Apparent Output	
Disconnect the panel's leads *at the battery* and check for voltage *in bright sunlight*. Is there voltage? **NO**	**YES** If the voltage is 16 to 20 volts, the panel is probably OK. If the voltage is less than 16 volts, check fuses, connections, wiring, and any blocking diodes for discontinuities and voltage drop (see Chapter 3). Note: Before making any tests with an ohmmeter, *block out the panel* to avoid damaging the meter.
Disconnect the panel's leads *at the panel* and check for voltage across the panel's output terminals *in bright sunlight*. Is there voltage? **NO**	**YES** If the voltage is 16 to 20 volts, the panel is probably OK, but its wiring is defective. Check as above. If the voltage is less than 16 volts, there are problems with the panel and its internal wiring.
The panel is defective; if it has a built-in diode, jump it out and test again.	

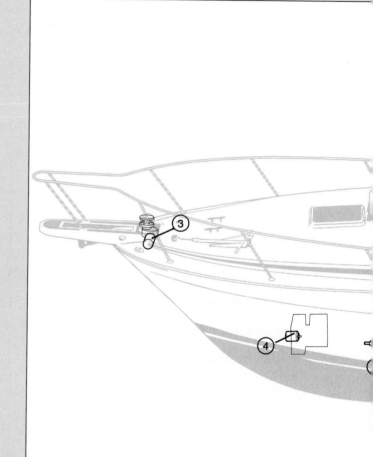

CHAPTER 7

FIGURE 7-1. Electric motors and generators are found throughout modern pleasure boats. Although initially mysterious, they are readily maintained and repaired. *(Jim Sollers)*

(1) starter motor
(2) pump
(3) anchor windlass
(4) air conditioner fan motor
(5) freezer compressor
(6) air conditioner compressor
(7) blower
(8) refrigerator compressor
(9) bilge pump
(10) freshwater pump
(11) macerator pump

AC Generators, DC Generators, Electric Motors (DC and AC), and Electric Lights

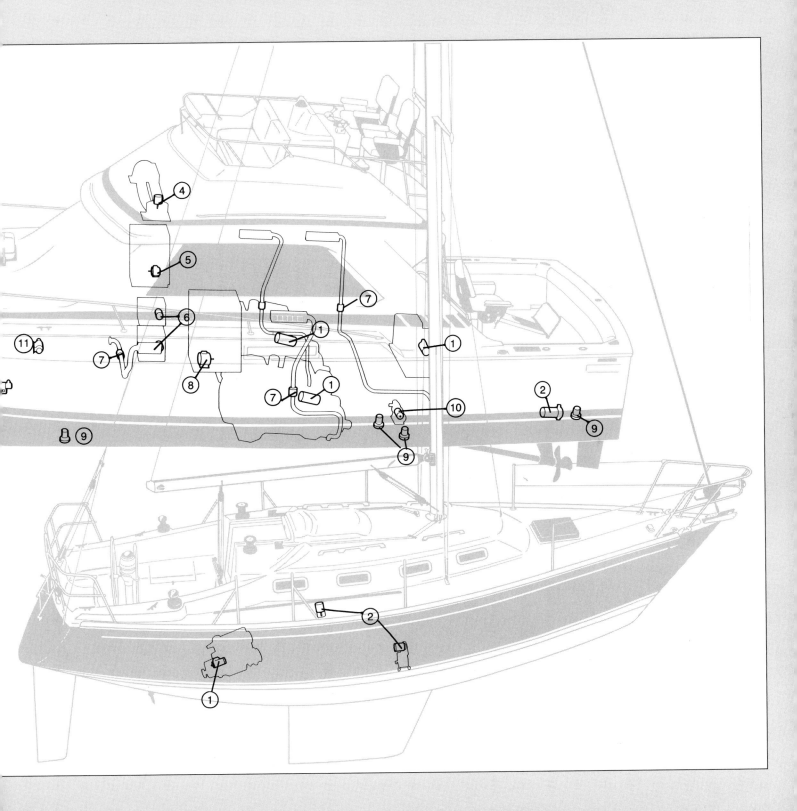

This chapter focuses on the electrical side of generators and on electric motors (including starter motors) and lights. Integrating a generator into the overall systems design is covered in previous chapters; the power (engine) side is covered in Chapter 9.

AC Generators

When surveys are conducted among cruising sailors regarding the reliability of different pieces of equipment, AC generators often rank high on the failure list. Many of these failures can be attributed to poor installation decisions, especially regarding the location of a generator.

Most generators are air cooled at the generator end of things. Inside a generator are a number of insulated copper windings. Inevitably, this insulation has small defects and voids. In the humid marine atmosphere, moisture from the cooling air can collect in these voids and defects. Fresh water is an insulator, but salt water is a conductor. In any case, add a few impurities to fresh water, and it also becomes a conductor. On boats, generators are all too often installed where the cooling airflow will also pick up dust and other contaminants, adding these impurities. The combination of moisture and dirt degrades the insulation.

These problems are compounded by the fact that generators are often installed in restricted compartments where high ambient temperatures build up, lowering the ampacity of the insulation on the various windings and conductors (see Chapter 4) and stressing electronic components in control circuits. Now add the fact that generators on boats are often somewhat undersized for some of the surge (inrush) currents they face, especially if the boat has air-conditioning. The peak currents stress insulation that already has a lowered capability. Localized short circuits develop in the windings, further degrading the insulation. It's not long before there is a failure beyond the ability of the boatowner to repair (Figures 7-2A and 7-2B). Meantime, the engine itself frequently runs below par because of a combination of the high ambient inlet air temperature, and not infrequently, a restricted air supply for combustion purposes (diesel engines require lots of fresh air—see Chapter 9).

Probably the single most important installation issue in terms of heading off unnecessary trouble is to install a generator in a location where it will receive the coolest, driest, cleanest cooling (and combustion) air possible on that particular boat. As an aside, it is worth mentioning that when considering location and installation, one critical safety issue that is often not given nearly enough attention is minimizing the potential for carbon monoxide poisoning (which is currently one of the leading causes of deaths on boats). See Chapter 15 for more on this.

How They Work

AC power requires a stable frequency of 60 Hz (U.S.) or 50 Hz (Europe). In the past, the frequency has always been determined by the speed with which a magnet is rotated within a coil of wire or vice versa (see Chapter 6). The desired frequency (60 Hz or 50 Hz) has been maintained by running an engine, and thus the electric generator driven by it, at a constant speed regardless of the load placed on it. This is the underlying basis for all conventional generators.

Take, for example, a 60 Hz generator. The output cycles from negative to positive 60 times a second, which is 3,600 times a minute. If the generator is driven by an engine running at 3,600 rpm (a small, high-speed engine), it will have two magnetic poles (negative and positive) to create 60 Hz output; but if driven by an

FIGURES 7-2A AND 7-2B. Stator winding failures as a result of high ambient temperatures, contamination, and voltage spikes. *(Reprinted with permission. © 1985–2004. Electrical Apparatus Service Association, Inc.)*

engine running at 1,800 rpm (a larger, slower-turning engine), it will have four poles; and at 1,200 rpm (uncommon on small generators), it will have six poles. For 50 Hz output the respective engine speeds are 3,000 rpm, 1,500 rpm, and 1,000 rpm (which explains why the AC output from a given engine powering a 50 Hz generator is always lower than when powering a 60 Hz generator—the engine has to be run slower, and therefore develops less power).

With the advent of modern solid-state electronics, using the same kind of technology used in inverters, this relationship between speed of rotation, the number of magnetic poles, and the generator's output frequency can be broken. It is now possible to produce a stable output frequency from a fluctuating generator frequency, allowing stable AC power to be produced from a variable-speed power source.

This results in a number of different approaches to generating AC power on board:

1. The traditional generator (genset), in which the engine is regulated (governed) to a constant speed and coupled directly to a generator. This is still by far the predominant method of generating AC power on board.
2. A variable-speed clutch, belt driven off the boat's main engine, which mechanically compensates for changes in engine speed, imparting a constant speed of rotation to a generator. Such devices are uncommon, not least of all because they tend to be inefficient at energy

conversion and have been supplanted by modern electronics.
3. A hydraulic pump, belt driven off the main engine, which powers a constant-speed hydraulic motor coupled to a generator. Once again, this type is inefficient and has been largely supplanted by modern electronics.
4. Solid-state variable-speed technology (VST), which takes the fluctuating output of a variable-speed engine-driven alternator and feeds it through a modified DC-to-AC inverter to produce stable AC power. This technology is becoming more widespread.

All four approaches have physical similarities at the generator end of things. For our purposes they can be separated into two broad categories: *alternator* types, which produce AC by spinning a magnet *(rotor)* inside a set of coils (the *stator*—see pages 85–86); and *armature* types, which spin the coils inside magnets (Figure 7-3).

Alternator types. Just as with an automotive alternator, a DC current is passed through a set of *field windings* on the rotor, creating a magnetic field that induces output in the stator windings (the exception to this is generators that have permanent magnets on the rotor—see below). But unlike an alternator, when a generator is shut down the rotor retains a degree of *residual magnetism*. This is sufficient to induce a low-level output in the stator when the generator is restarted. This stator output is then used to sup-

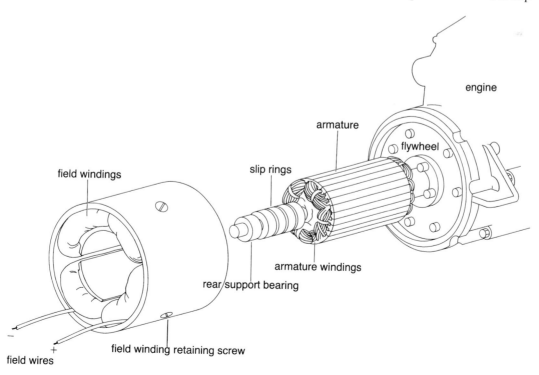

FIGURE 7-3. An armature-type AC generator, with frame and field windings removed. *(Jim Sollers)*

ply the field current necessary to produce full generator output. The generator is said to be *self-exciting*.

In operation, some alternator-type generators tap one of the stator windings for the field current, using a *bridge rectifier* (Chapter 3) to convert part of the AC output of the stator to the DC current required by the field windings. This current is then fed to the rotor via brushes and slip rings. Just as with an alternator, a voltage regulator is used to control the field current and thus the generator's output.

Brushless alternator types. Most alternator-type generators, however, are *brushless*. On start-up the residual magnetism in the rotor stimulates a separate *exciter winding* in the stator, which in turn induces AC output in a winding on the rotor. Diodes built into the rotor rectify this output to DC, which is used to power the field windings. No brushes or slip rings are needed to supply the field current to the rotor (Figure 7-4A; a few expensive automotive alternators are built the same way, but these rarely turn up in the marine field).

In addition to the exciter windings and the main stator windings, many brushless generators include another auxiliary winding in the stator. The output from this winding is rectified to DC and controlled by a voltage regulator (commonly called an automatic voltage regulator or AVR; Figure 7-4B). On larger generators (8.0 kW and up), this output is normally used to power and control the exciter windings (Figure 7-4C). On smaller generators, it will charge the generator engine's starting battery (Figure 7-4A again). In the former case, failure of the auxiliary winding, its rectifier, or the regulation circuit will disable the output of the generator. In the latter case, a failure of the auxiliary winding circuit will have no effect on the main AC output; it can safely be ignored when troubleshooting the generator's AC output.

Although brushless generators now dominate the marine generator marketplace, in general they do not have as good an electric-motor start-

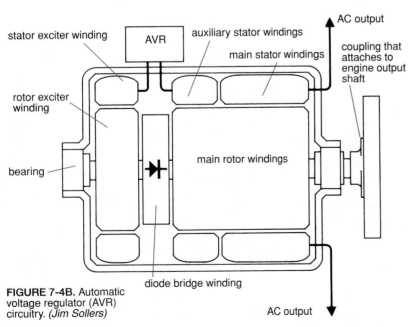

A = field windings
B = main stator windings
C = exciter windings
D = auxiliary windings

FIGURE 7-4A. A simplified wiring schematic for a brushless AC generator in which the auxiliary windings are used for battery charging. Note that: The windings for the main stator (B), exciter (C), and battery-charging circuits (D) are all built into the stator. The battery-charging circuit (D) is independent of the generator's AC output. The rotating field, or rotor (A), has no slip rings or brushes and its diodes are built in. This generator is self-regulating—there is no voltage regulation circuit. Output voltage is determined principally by the speed of rotation, but it is also affected by generator load. No-load voltage can be altered by plugging a different numbered lead (1, 2, or 3) into the capacitors in the exciter circuit (C). Frequency can be changed from 60 Hz to 50 Hz by changing the engine rpm. Because this will alter voltage as well, it will be necessary to tap different capacitor and output terminals (on the terminal block) to get the desired voltage (e.g., in the UK, 240 volts at 50 Hz).

FIGURE 7-4B. Automatic voltage regulator (AVR) circuitry. *(Jim Sollers)*

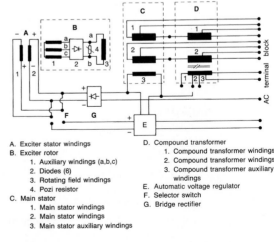

A. Exciter stator windings
B. Exciter rotor
  1. Auxiliary windings (a,b,c)
  2. Diodes (6)
  3. Rotating field windings
  4. Pozi resistor
C. Main stator
  1. Main stator windings
  2. Main stator windings
  3. Main stator auxiliary windings

D. Compound transformer
  1. Compound transformer windings
  2. Compound transformer windings
  3. Compound transformer auxiliary windings
E. Automatic voltage regulator
F. Selector switch
G. Bridge rectifier

FIGURE 7-4C. A simplified wiring schematic for a brushless AC generator in which the auxiliary windings are used to power the generator voltage regulation circuit. Voltage regulation is found only on larger generators. Most smaller generators will be of the type illustrated in Figure 7-4A. *(Westerbeke)*

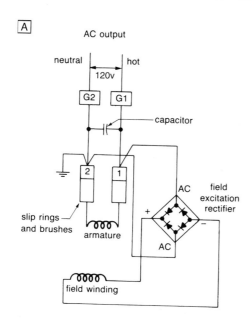

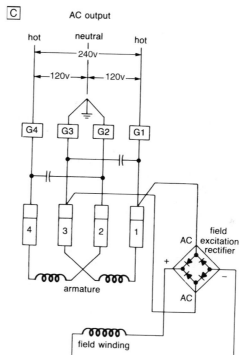

FIGURES 7-5A, 7-5B, AND 7-5C. Wiring schematics for armature-type AC generators. Two brushes, 120 volts (7-5A). Three brushes, 120/240 volts (7-5B). Four brushes, 120/240 volts (7-5C). *(Westerbeke)*

ing (i.e., surge or inrush) capability as the brush-type generators, and they do not have such a tight regulation of the generator's output voltage and frequency. The reason is that it is harder to establish precise control of the field current created in the rotor through the indirect (induced) mechanism of the exciter windings than it is through the direct mechanism of a voltage regulator wired into the field circuit via brushes.

Armature types. Multiple coils are wound around the rotor or *armature*, and two or more electromagnets are mounted in a fixed position inside the generator case. The armature is spun inside these magnets, producing alternating current in the armature coils. This AC output is fed to slip rings on the end of the armature shaft, where it is picked up by spring-loaded brushes and conveyed to the boat's AC distribution panel.

The generator field windings are once again designed to retain a degree of magnetism when the generator is at rest, which is sufficient to produce a low level of output in the armature when the armature is first spun. This output is tapped for field current. Since generator output is AC, and field windings require DC, the field current must first be rectified via a bridge rectifier. (A few generators supply current to the field windings by a direct feed from the boat's batteries, thus eliminating the need for a rectifier.)

This type of generator may have two, three, or four slip rings and brushes, depending on internal configuration and power output. The simplest (small 120-volt AC generators in the U.S.; 240 volts in Europe) have two slip rings

and brushes: one is hot; the other is neutral, and is grounded to the generator frame, thus preserving the requirement to ground the neutral at the power source, as discussed in Chapter 4—Figure 7-5A. Small 120/240-volt AC generators (U.S.) have three slip rings and brushes: two are hot (120 volts each); one is neutral, and is once again grounded to the generator frame—Figure 7-5B.

Larger generators (120-volt, 240-volt, and 120/240-volt) have four slip rings and brushes (Figure 7-5C): two are hot; two are neutral, and are tied together and grounded to the generator frame at some point.

The field windings are bolted to the inside of the generator case. The simplest generators have two field windings (a two-pole generator) to produce one magnetic field (north and south), but most have two sets of windings (a four-pole generator), and some have three sets (a six-pole generator).

General Maintenance

Note: The engine side is covered in Chapter 9.

Most generators have bearings that are sealed for life. A few have grease fittings, which need one shot once or twice a year, but *no more*. The only other things that need attention are any brushes. Those on armature-type generators carry the full output current of the generator. If

---

AC Generators: Recommended Features

There are all kinds of trade-offs when purchasing AC generators. When making your choice, the following are desirable features:

- Lower, rather than higher, operating speeds (e.g., 1,800 rpm versus 3,600 for 60 Hz, or 1,500 versus 3,000 for 50 Hz). This reduces noise and extends engine life, but increases size, weight, and cost.

- Three- or six-cylinder engines, which result in smoother and quieter operation, with less vibration, than two- and four-cylinder engines.

- An engine that produces its maximum torque at or a little below the operating speed of the generator (the torque will be shown on a power curve produced by the engine manufacturer).

- Clustering all the service points (filters, etc.) on one side of the engine in order to improve access (generators tend to get stuffed into tight quarters, so access for servicing should always be factored in).

- The ability to water-cool the generator end of things, so the generator won't need outside air to cool it (Figure 7-6).

FIGURE 7-6. A Fischer Panda generator with a water-cooled stator. These generators have a high output relative to their weight.

- Sizing of the generator so that it will not operate for any length of time below 25% of its rated output and spends most of its time between 35% and 70% of rated output. When comparing generator outputs, make sure the same things are being compared (e.g., continuous rating to continuous rating, not some other rating such as an intermittent, or 30-minute, rating).

- A surge rating that is high enough to handle the surge, or start-up, loads on the boat. Due to differences in the way generators are built, two generators with the same output rating may have significantly different surge capabilities.

- Voltage and speed regulation that hold the voltage and frequency to within a maximum variation of ±5% of the rated voltage and frequency, all the way from no load to full load, and preferably to within ±1.5%. Many of the smaller, internally regulated brushless generators have notoriously unstable regulation, especially when hit with rapidly changing loads. In general, externally regulated units are more stable than internally regulated, and alternator types with brushes are more stable than the brushless.

- A low temperature rise above the ambient temperature *at full continuous output*. The temperature rise describes the extent to which the generator will heat up in operation relative to the ambient temperature. In general, the more copper in the windings, and the higher the quality of the generator, the lower this temperature rise will be. It should not exceed 95°C/203°F to 105°C/221°F.

- Safety shutdowns for at least the following (all of which are required by the ABYC): low oil pressure, high coolant temperature, and high exhaust temperature (the latter is often missing). Some generators also monitor the winding temperatures.

- Ease of maintenance and repair at sea, with worldwide availability of parts and service.

---

they are allowed to wear down or stick in their brush holders so they make an imperfect contact with their slip rings, arcing will occur and expensive damage will be done to the slip rings.

These brushes need to be checked regularly (Westerbeke, a popular marine generator manufacturer, recommends every 200 hours) and replaced once they are worn to half their original length. They must move freely in their brush holders and have reasonable spring tension. If in doubt, replace them. *Brushes must always be put back in the same holders and the same way around.* To avoid confusion, remove and replace them one at a time. New brushes are bedded in as described on page 314.

Any brushes on alternator-type generators carry low-level rotor excitation current, not generator output current, and so are far less subject to wear. They need checking only every 500 hours.

Occasionally, vibration will cause a field winding to work loose on armature-type generators. The windings are mounted with bolts through the outside of the generator case. These bolts will be evenly spaced on either side of the case with two-pole generators, spaced every 90 degrees with four-pole generators, and every 60 degrees with six-pole generators. Check them for tightness from time to time.

Troubleshooting Operating Problems

WARNING: THE OUTPUT FROM A GENERATOR CAN KILL! Some of the following tests involve working around an operating generator. At all times keep hands, clothing, and hair away from moving parts, and IF YOU ARE IN ANY DOUBT ABOUT WHAT YOU ARE DOING, DON'T DO IT!

If a generator has a circuit for remote or automatic starting, make sure it is disabled before working on the unit.

Frequency wrong. A frequency meter is a necessity, not a luxury, for effective monitoring, control, adjustment, and troubleshooting of any onboard generator. In the absence of a meter, frequency can be checked using an electric clock with a second hand, and another *accurate* timepiece, such as the time beeps from station WWV on the 2.5, 5, 10, 15, and 20 MHz single-sideband frequency. If the electric clock runs slowly, frequency is low. If it runs fast, frequency is high.

Given a correctly functioning generator, frequency is directly related to speed of rotation (ignoring, for the time being, VST generators). Depending on internal construction, with some

TABLE 7-1. Typical Generator Speeds, Frequencies, and Voltages[1]

Load	Speed	Hz	Voltage (120)	Voltage (240)
No load	1,830	61	129	258
Half load	1,800	60	120	240
Full load	1,755	58.5	115	230

1. Generator governed to a nominal 1,800 rpm.
Note that variations outside this range indicate improper governing or, when frequency drops off and an *engine bogs down*, an overloaded generator or a malfunctioning engine. If the load is not reduced rapidly, expensive electrical damage is possible.

older style (analog) frequency meters, a generator may appear to come to its designed frequency at several different speeds (e.g., 1,200, 1,800, and 3,600 rpm). As the generator comes up to its designed speed, the frequency meter may come up to the correct frequency, go past it and off the scale, and then come up again. It may do this as many as three times, which is normal.

Once the generator speed has stabilized, frequency should be as designed (60 Hz in the U.S.; 50 Hz in Europe). However, most boat-generator *governors* (speed-regulating devices) are not sensitive enough to hold a constant speed from no load to full load. The governors are set to permit mild overspeeding (maximum 63.5 Hz in the U.S.) on no load, to be about right at half load, and to permit mild underspeeding on full load. As a result frequencies will normally vary (usually ±5%) from a couple of cycles over to a couple of cycles under (Table 7-1). Belt-driven variable-speed-clutch generators are likely to show a wider variation with changes in engine speed.

Frequency low. Switch off the load and check again. If the frequency returns to normal, the generator is probably overloaded (or its propulsion unit is losing power due to mechanical problems). Beware the starting loads of many electric motors, which can be *several times* the motor rating and can bog down a generator. If frequency is still low after shutting down the loads, check the speed of the propulsion unit before blaming the generator. Many engines have mechanical governors that are adjusted by loosening a locknut and turning a screw—check the engine manual. With belt-driven generators, check belt tension and constant-speed clutches; on hydraulic units, check the oil level.

Frequency too high. The propulsion unit is overspeeding. Adjust the governor accordingly.

Frequency varies erratically. Check the AC circuit for high, fluctuating loads, such as the cycling on and off of an air-conditioning or refrigeration compressor, or a microwave on anything less than full power. (Most microwaves on Defrost cycle or lower-power Cook settings are *not* actually operating on less than full power. The microwave simply cycles on and off at timed intervals, sometimes only a second or two apart. A full-size, 1,500-watt microwave will give a small 3 kW generator's governor a very hard time.)

If the frequency continues to wander with all AC loads off, the governor on the propulsion unit is defective. Governors sometimes will *hunt*, a condition in which they constantly and rhythmically cycle the engine speed up and down. Refer to the engine manual.

Voltage wrong. Voltage is generally a function of generator speed and load—the faster the generator spins and the less the load, the higher the voltage. Unless the generator reaches its designed minimum speed, it cannot reach its designed output voltage. This is particularly true of belt-driven variable-clutch units. If the driving pulleys are sized wrongly, or the boat's engine turns over too slowly, the generator cannot reach its designed voltage.

A generator is rated at a certain maximum output (in kilowatts, kilovolt-amps, or amps) at a particular voltage (e.g., 5 kW, 5kVA, or 42 amps at 120 volts). At anything less than full output, as the load is decreased, the voltage will tend to rise. Externally excited generators prevent voltage from going too high by using a voltage regulator to reduce the current to the field windings, just as with an alternator. Internally excited generators tend to be less tightly controlled.

Since voltage is related to speed, if voltage is off, first check the speed by checking the frequency. Since generator speed is likely to vary somewhat with load, some variations in voltage are to be expected (refer back to Table 7-1). Typical ranges from no load to full load may be as much as 130 volts down to 108 volts (on a 120-volt genset) or 260 volts down to 225 (on a 240-volt genset). Voltages above and below these levels may damage onboard equipment and must be corrected. Some external voltage regulators incorporate a *potentiometer* (a variable resistor) with a small screwdriver slot in the end for fine-tuning generator voltage.

Voltage low. Always check the voltage *at the generator*; low voltage may simply be the result of voltage drop through inadequate wiring. Before making any adjustments (where they are possible), perform all the tests outlined for low frequency. Next, feel the voltage regulator (if external) or generator to see if it is hot ("hot" means too hot to touch). Overheating will play havoc with some of the solid-state components and can lead to erratic regulation or a slow tapering off of output voltage—to as low as half voltage. If it is hot, allow the unit to cool down and hope that no damage has been done.

Check the condition of any brushes and brush springs and ensure that they are making good contact with their slip rings (see below).

With *external regulation*, if the voltage is still low, adjust the potentiometer. If voltage cannot be brought up enough, *do not force the potentiometer.* Check generator speed yet again. Perhaps it really is in the wrong speed range. Otherwise, the voltage regulator is probably defective.

With *internally excited* generators, check the diodes and the field windings as detailed below.

If the generator has capacitors, check the capacitors (see below—*please note the cautions as capacitors can pack a lethal punch*).

Voltage high. Check engine speed and frequency. If correct, adjust the voltage regulator potentiometer on units with external regulation. If the voltage cannot be brought down, the voltage regulator probably has an internal short.

Erratic output. This may be due to a fault in the voltage regulator, or it may be the result of worn, badly seated, and arcing brushes on those generators that have brushes. If the slip rings have also been burned, pitted, or worn out of round, you will have to send the armature to a machine shop to be *turned down*. A step in a slip ring is acceptable. For more on this, see the section on commutator cleaning on pages 311, 314.

No Output—Armature Type

WARNING: THE OUTPUT FROM A GENERATOR CAN KILL! Some of the following tests involve working around an operating generator. At all times keep hands, clothing, and hair away from moving parts, and IF YOU ARE IN ANY DOUBT ABOUT WHAT YOU ARE DOING, DON'T DO IT!

If a generator has a circuit for remote or automatic starting, make sure it is disabled before working on the unit.

Preliminary test. First remove all the loads from the generator. With the unit running, check for voltage at the generator's AC terminals. The generator may be working, but there may be an open switch or broken wire to the boat's circuits (there will be system voltage at the generator). Next check the engine tachometer to see that the generator is spinning at or close to its rated speed. Still no output?

Externally excited generator. If the generator is externally excited by the boat's 12-volt battery (not common), there will be an external field (F or FLD) terminal on the back of the generator. With the generator circuit switched on (but not necessarily running), test between this and a good ground. It should read at least several volts

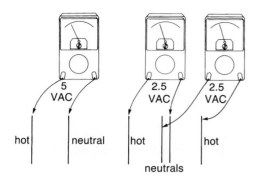

FIGURE 7-7. Checking for residual voltage.

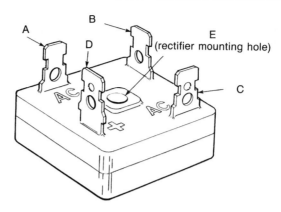

FIGURE 7-8. Testing a bridge rectifier. (Resistance values given are for Westerbeke BC generators, commonly found on boats.) 1. Set multimeter to R x 1 scale on an analog meter. Zero the meter. 2. Connect the (+) lead from the meter to D. With the (–) meter lead, momentarily contact A, B, C, and E. No deflection of the meter needle should occur, showing infinite resistance. 3. Remove the (+) lead from D and connect the (–) lead to it. With the (+) lead, momentarily touch A, B, and C. Points A and C should show an 8-ohm resistance, ± 2 ohms; B should show a 40-ohm resistance, ± 5 ohms. 4. Touch E with the (+) lead. No deflection of the needle should occur. 5. Place the (+) lead of the meter on A and the (–) on C. No deflection of the needle should occur (infinite resistance). Reverse the connections and the same should occur. *If the rectifier fails any of the above tests, it is defective and should be replaced.* (Westerbeke)

DC. If it does not, there is a fault in the external excitation wiring or voltage regulator. If voltage is present, there is a fault in the field windings, armature, brushes, or capacitors (see relevant sections below).

Internally excited generator. If the generator is internally excited (which it most likely will be) remove whatever covers are necessary to expose the bridge rectifier and disconnect the field leads from the positive (+ or red) and negative (– or black) terminals. Label the leads so that they can be reconnected correctly and then place them safely out of the way. (If the negative terminal is not marked, it is the one *opposite* the positive terminal.) Operate the generator with no load and measure for voltage between the hot and neutral output leads. There should be a low voltage generated by the residual magnetism in the field windings (Figure 7-7; on Westerbeke two-brush units, it is around 5 volts AC; on three- and four-brush units, 2.5 volts AC). If residual voltage is present, the armature, brushes, and capacitors (if fitted, they will bridge the output leads) are almost certainly OK and the problem lies in the rectifier, field windings, or regulation circuit (see next section). If residual voltage is *not* present, the unit may simply have lost its residual magnetism. Otherwise the problem is in the armature, brushes, or capacitors (see below).

Residual voltage present. Connect a 12-volt battery to the field leads that were disconnected from the bridge rectifier—positive to positive, negative to negative. Run the generator without a load and measure the voltage at the output leads. If voltage is now present (50 to 70 volts on Westerbekes), the generator itself is OK, but there is a fault in the bridge rectifier. If voltage does not rise, the field windings (or their wiring) are defective.

Testing a bridge rectifier. First make sure the generator is fully isolated. Leave the positive and negative leads disconnected from the bridge rectifier and disconnect the two AC leads (the other two leads, sometimes color-coded yellow).

Using an ohmmeter (R × 1 scale on an analog meter), connect the positive meter lead to the positive terminal and touch the negative meter lead to the other terminals in turn (Figure 7-8). All should show infinite resistance (no needle deflection). Reverse the leads and repeat. They all should show a circuit with a small resistance (between 5 and 50 ohms on Westerbekes). Check across the two AC terminals, then reverse the leads and recheck. Both tests should show infinite resistance. If the rectifier fails *any* of these tests, one or more diodes are defective.

Testing field windings. First make a close visual inspection of the wires running into and out of each field winding, looking for broken, burned, or chafed spots. If the wiring seems intact, connect an ohmmeter (R × 1 scale on an analog meter) between the positive and negative field wires (previously disconnected from the bridge rectifier), or in the case of externally excited generators, between the field terminal and a good ground, such as the generator case (scratch a spot bare to make a good contact). A zero reading indicates a shorted winding; most field windings will show a resistance varying between 12 and 40 ohms; the lower the output of the generator, the higher the resistance. A very high reading (R × 100 scale on an analog meter) indicates an open circuit in the field windings or their attendant wiring. Finally, on internally excited generators test between each of the field wires going to the bridge rectifier (the ones previously disconnected) and the generator case (R × 1 scale on an analog meter). Any continuity (0 ohms or low reading) shows a short to ground.

Residual voltage not present. The unit has lost its residual magnetism or there is a fault in the armature, brushes, or capacitors (if fitted). Residual magnetism is easily restored by *flashing the field.* Reconnect any leads to the rectifier. *With the generator shut down,* simply connect a 12-volt battery (or even a 6-volt flashlight battery) across the positive and negative field winding ter-

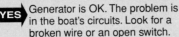

Troubleshooting Chart 7-1. Armature-Type AC Generators: No Output	
Is there output voltage at the generator's AC terminals? **NO** **TEST:** Check for AC volts at the terminals after disconnecting all electrical loads from the generator.	**YES** Generator is OK. The problem is in the boat's circuits. Look for a broken wire or an open switch.
If the generator is *externally* excited, is there DC voltage at the field terminal? **NO** **TEST:** Locate the field terminal on the back of the generator. With the generator switched on but not necessarily running, attach a DC voltmeter between the terminal and a good ground. It should register several volts.	**YES** **FIX:** Check the capacitors, brushes, and armature. Check the field windings. Replace any defective parts.
Check the excitation circuit and voltage regulator.	
If the generator is *internally excited*, is there residual voltage? **NO** **TEST:** Expose the bridge rectifier and label and disconnect the positive and negative field wires, placing them out of the way. Operate the generator with no load and measure the voltage between the hot and neutral output leads. Presence of a low voltage indicates that there is residual magnetism in the field windings.	**YES** **FIX:** Connect 12 volts to the disconnected field wires, run the generator, and test for AC voltage at the output terminals. If there is voltage, check the rectifier. It likely needs repair or replacement. If there is no voltage, check the field windings and replace as necessary.
Is there voltage when you flash the field? **NO** **TEST:** Reconnect all leads. With the generator shut down, connect a battery across the field winding terminals and hold for 10 seconds. Try the generator again.	**YES** The generator is OK.
Check the capacitors, brushes, and armature (see text).	

capacitor terminals

FIGURES 7-9A, 7-9B, AND 7-9C. Capacitors store electricity. Their capacity to do so is measured in microfarads (µF, or sometimes mfd or MFD). Because there often is sufficient electricity stored to administer a shock, discharge capacitors with a lightbulb (see text) or a screwdriver (as shown) before working with them.

minals at the rectifier—positive to positive, negative to negative—and hold for 10 seconds.

Be sure to connect the leads from the battery to the rectifier the correct way around. Reverse polarity will blow out the diodes. Make the connections at the rectifier before making those at the battery to avoid waving around hot leads that might accidentally blow something out. After flashing the field, disconnect the battery and operate the generator. If output is not restored, it is time to check the armature, brushes, and capacitors (if fitted).

Testing a capacitor. Capacitors (round or nearly round cylinders with one or two spade terminals—Figure 7-9A) must be discharged before testing (Figures 7-9B and 7-9C), as they store electricity and can pack a *POTENTIALLY LETHAL PUNCH, EVEN WHEN DISCONNECTED FROM A POWER SOURCE.* Discharging is often done by bridging the capacitor terminals with a screwdriver (as in the photographs!), but this can be hard on the capacitor. It is better to rig a 120-volt lightbulb (240 volts in Europe) with two test leads and touch the leads to the capacitor terminals. Now connect an ohmmeter (R × 100 scale on an analog meter) to the capacitor terminals. The meter should go to 0 ohms and slowly return to high (Figures 7-10A and 7-10B). Reverse the meter leads and repeat; the same results should be obtained. If the meter fails to go down, the capacitor is open-circuited; if the meter goes down and stays down (0 ohms), the capacitor is shorted. Check between each capacitor terminal and its case. There should be an open circuit. If not, there is a short. Capacitors are rated in *microfarads*, and additionally are rated for continuous and intermittent duty. Replace with the same size and type.

Testing an armature and brushes. Armature winding resistances are very low (typically around 1 ohm) and so can only be measured with a very accurate meter. With most meters it will be difficult to distinguish between a low resistance and a short. Nevertheless, I have included the test procedure for those with sufficiently sensitive meters.

Isolate the generator. Discharge and disconnect any capacitors (see above). Connect an ohmmeter between each brush in turn and the generator case (a good ground). The neutral (grounded) brushes should show a short (i.e., 0 ohms), and in fact should be wired to the generator case at some point. If they do not show a short, the wiring to the brush is defective.

On a two-brush generator, one brush is hot and one is neutral. On a three-brush generator, the two end brushes are hot and the middle one is neutral. On a four-brush generator, the two end brushes are hot and the middle two are neutral.

The hot brushes will show a low resistance (around 1 ohm). If they show no resistance (R × 1 scale on an analog meter), the armature is shorted. If they show high resistance (R × 100 scale on an analog meter), the armature is open-circuited. In either case it needs rewinding. Note: An open circuit may also be the result of a brush that fails to make electrical contact with its slip ring, and *it may not necessarily be the brush being tested* since the circuit from a hot brush to the generator case is completed through a neutral brush. Be sure the brushes are seating properly.

Before condemning an armature, remove and inspect all the brushes and their springs. Connect the ohmmeter between the slip rings. On generators with two slip rings, there should be a low reading (around 1 ohm). With three slip rings, there are three possible measurements: between 1 and 2, 1 and 3, and 2 and 3. Measurements of 1 to 2 and 2 to 3 should give a low reading (R × 1 scale on an analog meter), and one of 1 to 3 should give a higher reading—approximately double.

With four slip rings, there are six possible combinations! Between 1 and 2, 3, or 4; 2 and 3 or 4; and 3 and 4. Measurements of 1 to 3 and 2 to 4 should give approximately the same low reading (R × 1 scale on an analog meter); all the others should give no reading (open circuit). If any continuity is found between 1 to 2, 2 to 3, 3 to 4, and 1 to 4, there is a short in the armature.

Finally, test between each slip ring and the armature shaft (R × 100 scale on an analog meter). There should be no continuity between any slip ring and the shaft. A zero reading at any time indicates a short in the armature.

No Output—Alternator Type with Brushes

WARNING: THE OUTPUT FROM A GENERATOR CAN KILL! Some of the following tests involve working around an operating generator. At all times keep hands, clothing, and hair away from moving parts, and IF YOU ARE IN ANY DOUBT ABOUT WHAT YOU ARE DOING, DON'T DO IT!

If a generator has a circuit for remote or automatic starting, make sure it is disabled before working on the unit.

FIGURES 7-10A AND 7-10B. Testing capacitors. Discharge first (see Figures 7-9B and 7-9C). Test across the capacitor terminals with an ohmmeter (R x 100 scale on an analog meter). The meter should jump to 0 ohms and slowly return to high. If it fails to go down, the capacitor is open-circuited. If it goes down and stays down (0 ohms), the capacitor is shorted. Testing from any terminal (or lead) to the case (R x 100 scale on an analog meter) must show infinity. If not, the capacitor is shorted.

FIGURE 7-11A. Externally exciting a brush-type AC alternator. *(Kohler)*

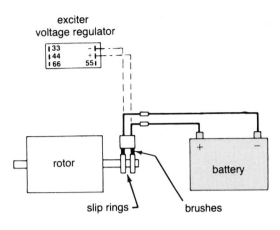

exciter
voltage regulator

rotor

battery

slip rings

brushes

Preliminary test. With the unit running, check for AC voltage *at the generator*. If this is OK, the boat's AC circuit is at fault. If there is no voltage at the generator, *shut it down*, locate the voltage regulator, and check its fuse (if fitted). If OK, check the brushes and brush springs to ensure they are making contact with the slip rings. If OK, disconnect the positive and negative field leads from the voltage regulator to the brushes, first labeling them so that you can replace them properly. Connect a 12-volt battery to the field leads—positive to positive, negative to negative—and run up the generator (Figure 7-11A). It is now being externally excited by the battery. Check for AC output. If present (it may range anywhere from 20 to 100 volts), the voltage regulator or its stator winding is probably defective. If there is no AC output, the rotor or the stator is probably defective.

Testing the rotor. Make a visual inspection for damaged insulation, windings, or slip rings. Pitted or burned slip rings will have to be turned down in a lathe. Spin the rotor by hand and flex its shaft to check the bearings. Check between the slip rings with an ohmmeter (R × 1 scale on an analog meter). Resistances are typically from 3 to 5 ohms. Check for continuity between each slip ring and the rotor shaft (R × 100 scale on an analog meter). Any continuity indicates a short.

Testing the stator. Label and disconnect all leads from the terminal block. Test between the leads on each set of stator windings (R × 1 scale on an analog meter). Resistances are very low (typically from 0.06 to 0.34 ohm; Figure 7-11B) and indistinguishable from a dead short on most meters. The windings that supply the voltage regulator will have a slightly higher resistance (typically from 1 to 4 ohms). Test between each lead of a winding and the leads on *other* windings (R × 100 scale on an analog meter). There should be no continuity.

No Output—Brushless Alternator Type

WARNING: THE OUTPUT FROM A GENERATOR CAN KILL! Some of the following tests involve working around an operating generator. At all times keep hands, clothing, and hair away from moving parts, and IF YOU ARE IN ANY DOUBT ABOUT WHAT YOU ARE DOING, DON'T DO IT!

If a generator has a circuit for remote or auto-

FIGURE 7-11B. Right: Stator leads on Kohler generators. **Below:** Stator winding resistance readings, when cold, in ohms. *(Kohler)*

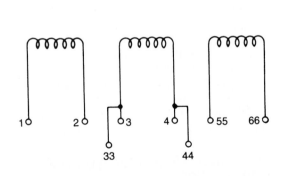

1   2   3   4   55   66

33   44

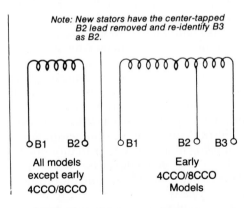

Note: New stators have the center-tapped B2 lead removed and re-identify B3 as B2.

B1   B2

All models except early 4CCO/8CCO

B1   B2   B3

Early 4CCO/8CCO Models

Leads	4CCO	4CCFO	7CCFO	8CCO	10.5CCFO	12.5CCO	12.5CCFO	16CCO	16.5CCFO	20CCO
1-2, 3-4, 33-44	.25	.34	.18	.14	.07	.07	.07	.07	.07	.07
55-66	2.8	4.2	1.26	1.1	1.1	1.1	1.1	1.4	1.4	1.4
B1-B2 (w/o center-tapped winding)	.15	.20	.10	.08	.06	.06	.06	.06	.06	.06
B1-B2 (with center-tapped winding)	.10	—	—	.06	—	—	—	—	—	—
B1-B3 (with center-tapped winding)	.15	—	—	.08	—	—	—	—	—	—

matic starting, make sure it is disabled before working on the unit.

Preliminary test. With the unit running, check for AC voltage *at the generator*. If this is OK, then the problem is in the boat's AC circuit.

Winding and diode tests. If no voltage is present at the generator, shut it down and remove its covers. Test all the windings as explained below: stator, rotor, exciter, and for larger generators only, the auxiliary winding if it powers the exciter windings.

Stator windings. Stator windings terminate in the main output terminal block. Disconnect all leads, grounds, and interconnections from the terminal block, first labeling everything and noting positions so you can put it all back correctly.

Each set of stator windings will have at least two leads—three if the generator can be used on both 50 Hz and 60 Hz. (On these units, the outermost leads on a winding are for 50 Hz; the lead tapped closer to the center of the winding is for 60 Hz.) Test the resistance between the two outermost leads on each winding (R × 1 scale on an analog meter). These readings will be very low—on the order of 0.2 to 0.8 ohm (smaller generators will show higher resistance). All but the most sensitive meters will show a dead short. Infinity indicates an open-circuited coil.

Now test from every stator lead to ground (R × 100 scale on an analog meter) and from the leads on one stator coil to another. Any continuity indicates a short to ground or between windings.

Rotor windings. The rotor may have up to three sets of windings, and as many as six diodes, located on or around the rotor. Turn the rotor over to identify the diode(s):

1. *Diodes screwed into the end of the rotor* (smaller generators; Figure 7-12A). To test the winding(s) quickly, check (R × 1 scale on an analog meter) between the top connection and the base of the diode. It should read about 1 to 4 ohms (the smaller the generator, the lower the reading). Again, less-sensitive meters will show this as a short. If resistances are out of line, to test the windings more thoroughly, unsolder the wires from the top(s) of the diode(s), using the lowest heat possible. Make sure no solder splashes onto the windings since it will melt the thin, lacquered insulation. Remove the diode(s) and test between the wire(s) that have been unsoldered and the wires that were attached to the base of the diode(s). A 1- to 4-ohm resistance should be present. Check for continuity between each lead and the rotor shaft (R × 100 scale on an

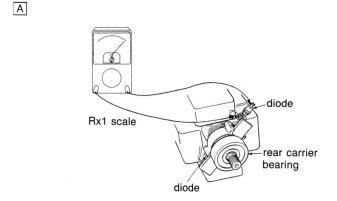

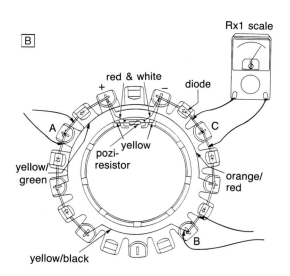

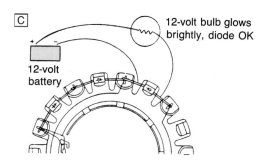

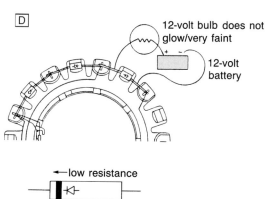

FIGURES 7-12A TO 7-12D. Diode placement on brushless generators. For small generators (one or two diodes), test field winding resistance at leads shown (7-12A). For larger generators (six diodes), check resistance of field windings A, B, and C at the points shown (7-12B). When testing a diode in place, use a 12-volt battery and a lamp equipped with jumper leads (7-12C and 7-12D). *(Westerbeke)*

analog meter). Any continuity indicates a short in a winding.

2. *Diodes spread around the rotor* (larger generators). The individual winding resistances can be measured with the diodes in place by measuring between each diode on each side of a winding. Do not include the diode (Figure 7-12B).

3. *Diode testing.* Diodes cannot be checked in place with an ohmmeter. However, a test can be made using a 12-volt battery and a lamp with attached jumper leads (Figures 7-12C and 7-12D). The lamp should light brightly one way and glow faintly with the leads reversed. If the lamp lights in both directions, the diode is shorted; if it doesn't light at all, the diode is open-circuited.

Should you have to remove diodes for any reason, you can test them using a multimeter with a diode-testing capability (Chapter 4). If the meter measures the resistance, with the leads applied in one direction, it will show infinity (open circuit); in the other, a circuit. Typical resistances may range from below 10 ohms to several hundred ohms. If the meter measures voltage drop, with the leads applied in one direction, the meter will show a low voltage (typically around 0.6 volt); in the other, an open circuit. Readings other than this indicate a failed diode.

Exciter windings. Exciter windings will be the only set of connections left untested, excluding any battery-charging circuit. If the terminals are bridged by one or more capacitors (Figure 7-13), then the excitation windings are not powered by an auxiliary circuit (smaller generators). On the other hand, if there are no capacitors, we have an auxiliary circuit to deal with (larger generators).

Capacitor-type circuits: Discharge the capacitor or capacitors as described earlier in this chapter, label all connections, and unplug.

As with the stator windings, the exciter windings will probably be tapped for both 60 Hz and 50 Hz. Measure resistance (R × 1 scale on an analog meter) between the two leads farthest apart. It should be anywhere from 0.5 to 3 ohms (a short on most meters). The smaller the generator, the higher the resistance. Measure from each lead to ground (R × 100 scale on an analog meter) and to all stator leads. Any continuity indicates a short.

Test capacitors as before. Note that where a brushless generator with capacitor-type excitation windings (small generators) suffers from low voltage, *the capacitor may be at fault even if it checks out OK with the tests outlined.* Try changing the capacitor.

Auxiliary winding–type circuits: Small brushless generators do not use the auxiliary winding in the stator to feed the exciter windings. Thus the auxiliary winding and its bridge rectifier and regulation circuit can be ignored when troubleshooting generator output. In larger generators that use the auxiliary winding (no capacitors on the excitation windings), the resistance of the excitation windings can be read from the positive and negative terminals of the bridge rectifier. Resistances may be considerably higher than in capacitor circuits. Measurements from either of these points to ground (R × 100 scale on an analog meter) should read infinity. If not, a winding is shorted.

Disconnect and test the bridge rectifier as outlined earlier in the chapter.

After disconnecting its leads, test the auxiliary winding in the stator across its two output leads, at least one of which will run to one of the AC terminals on the bridge rectifier. Once again resistances should be low (1 to 2 ohms). You should find no continuity (R × 100 scale on an analog meter) between either auxiliary winding lead and ground or any other winding lead (stator windings and excitation windings). If continuity is present, there is a short.

If you have found no problem at this stage, then the voltage regulation circuit needs testing, which unfortunately is too complex for this book.

Flashing the field: On rare occasions exciter windings may lose their residual magnetism.

FIGURE 7-13. Exciter winding capacitor connections on brushless generators. The frequency of the generator is changed from 60 Hz to 50 Hz by changing the engine speed. Voltage is then adjusted by connecting the relevant lead to the capacitor and leaving the other one loose. The no-load voltage of the generator can be raised or lowered by switching leads 7, 8, and 9. The higher the number on the lead connected, the higher the no-load voltage. *(Westerbeke)*

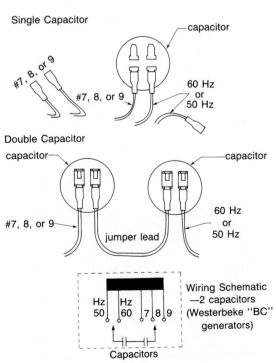

This can be restored by flashing the field with a 12-volt battery. *With the engine running and all wiring in place*, momentarily touch the leads from the battery to the two capacitor terminals (small generators) or the positive and negative terminals (be sure to get the correct polarity!) on the bridge rectifier (large generators). If two capacitors are fitted, touch the two capacitor terminals that have the leads, not the two terminals that are bridged. (Note: It may be possible to flash the field by following these steps: *shut down the generator*, switch it into the boat's circuits—i.e., the AC selector switch is in the "Generator" position—TURN OFF ALL AC LOADS, wire a couple of leads to a 9-volt battery, and then push these leads into the hot and neutral sockets of any onboard AC receptacle for a couple of seconds. This applies the battery voltage to the stator windings. *BEFORE POKING ANYTHING INTO AN AC RECEPTACLE, MAKE SURE THERE IS NO POSSIBLE SOURCE OF AC POWER!*)

No output on battery-charging circuit (if fitted). Identify the bridge rectifier. The auxiliary stator winding will have two leads running to the two AC terminals on the bridge rectifier. Disconnect these terminals and measure the winding resistance across the two leads (R × 1 scale on an analog meter). It should be very low (0.5 to 0.2 ohm) and indistinguishable from a dead short on most meters. Check from each lead to ground (R × 100 scale on an analog meter). Any continuity indicates a short. Check to all other stator leads. Once again, any continuity indicates a short.

Remove the DC connections from the bridge rectifier (label as necessary) and test it as described earlier in the chapter.

The output from the rectifier will be regulated by a solid-state voltage regulator. About all that can be done with this is to check all wiring and terminals. It will be subject to all the same problems regarding voltage drop, undercharging, etc., outlined in the Troubleshooting Voltage Regulators section in Chapter 3.

Disassembly and Bearing Replacement

Worn bearings make a distinctive rumble and should be replaced as soon as detected. If these are left unattended, armature or rotor vibration will lead to accelerated wear, and ultimately to damage to any brushes and slip rings, while various wires are likely to work loose or chafe through. The field windings on armature-type generators may come loose and start rubbing on the armature.

Generators have few parts, and disassembly is straightforward. If the generator is belt driven, begin by removing the pulley. Remove any brushes, taking care to note the position of all wires, which way around the brushes go, and in which brush holders they go. Unbolt and remove the end bearing retaining plate; the bearing will be pressed into the plate or will be held with a small retaining plate. To get at the bearing in the other end, you must withdraw the armature/rotor, taking care not to drag it against the field windings/stator coils.

This procedure leaves the field windings/stator coils and any rectification and voltage regulation circuits still attached to the generator case. To reassemble the unit, reverse the process.

Variable-Speed Technology (VST)

There are two principal limitations with a traditional genset:

1. To achieve the desired output frequency, a generator must be run at a fixed speed, which is typically 1,800 or 3,600 rpm (U.S.; 1,500 or 3,000 rpm in Europe). Unfortunately, these speeds do not coincide with the peak power ratings of most engines! As a result, engines normally have to be oversized, and even at full generator load are run at less than 100% of their rated output.
2. Regardless of the load on the generator, the engine must be run at this required generating speed. Even on standby, a 12 kW generator will still be running at full speed. Aside from being inefficient and unnecessarily noisy, low-load operation, particularly with diesels, is damaging to the engine and will run up maintenance bills while shortening engine life.

Variable-speed technology (VST) solves both these problems. Typically, an engine is used to drive a specially wound alternator that, even at low engine speeds, produces three-phase AC (as with an automotive alternator—Chapter 3), or even six-phase (there are efficiencies to be gained by increasing the number of phases) at an AC voltage that is higher than the desired output voltage (e.g., 120 or 240 volts), and at a frequency that will vary with engine speed. This variable output is rectified to high-voltage DC and then fed through a DC-to-AC inverter to produce AC at the desired frequency and voltage (Chapter 6). As with other DC-to-AC inverters, this output may be in the form of a modified sine wave (a stepped square wave) or a true sine wave.

For a given output, VST generators tend to be smaller and lighter than traditional generators. What is more, the output voltage and frequency are tightly regulated, as opposed to the fluctuating voltage and frequency on many traditional generators. Because the voltage and frequency are determined electronically, it is much easier to synchronize (parallel) the outputs from two or more generators, which creates some interesting design possibilities not explored in this book.

VST generators consist of two principal components—the engine-driven alternator and the electronics box (DC-to-AC inverter)—plus, in most instances, a remotely mounted monitoring and control panel. These generators can be belt driven off an existing propulsion engine (usually the boat's main engine) or directly coupled to a separate engine to form a stand-alone genset.

Belt-driven VST generators. At the time of writing, belt-driven VST generators are available in the United States with outputs of 2.5 kW and 5 kW, with the ability to mount two 5 kW units on one engine to produce 10 kW. European ratings tend to be lower. Early models had a stepped-square-wave output (modified sine wave), which suffers from the same limitations as a modified-sine-wave DC-to-AC inverter, but newer models have a true-sine-wave output.

Pros and cons. Unless a boat has some particularly high-load AC appliance that exceeds the capability of a DC-to-AC inverter, and which is to be used only intermittently, it is difficult to see the benefits of a belt-driven VST generator over those of a DC-to-AC inverter. (The one clear exception is for a powerboat that spends a good bit of time underway with the air conditioner running. A belt-driven VST generator attached to the main engine will run the air conditioner without having to run an auxiliary generator.)

In most circumstances, a VST generator is more expensive than a DC-to-AC inverter; is more complicated to install (requiring special mounting brackets and perhaps idler pulleys); requires more maintenance (belt loadings are high so the belts require regular attention); and produces AC power only when the engine is running, whereas the DC-to-AC inverter is available 24 hours a day. Many DC-to-AC inverters have the added advantage that they can be used as a battery charger when connected to shore power. (This capability has been added to the inverter part of some VST generators. It should be noted that the early generation of stepped-square-wave VST inverters would not run a number of stand-alone battery chargers and, in fact, damaged some.)

Belt-driven VST generators are less efficient than most other generators because of the horsepower absorbed by the drive belt and the small losses in the inverter. Overall, it takes close to 2 hp to produce 1 kW of output (as opposed to 1.3 to 1.5 hp with a traditional generator). The power absorbed by the generator can also be a problem if the unit is mounted to a relatively small auxiliary sailboat engine. A 2.5 kW unit requires 4.25 hp at full load, and a 5 kW unit needs 8.5 hp, so there may be times when a belt-driven VST generator simply can't be used. For a given level of output they are, however, considerably cheaper than a traditional genset (because there is no need to pay for the engine).

Stand-alone VST generators. Typically, a specially wound stator is bolted up to the rear end of an engine, with a brushless, superconducting permanent magnet (the rotor) coupled directly to the end of the crankshaft. There are no belts, pulleys, brushes, adjustments, or maintenance requirements of any kind.

The alternator is incredibly compact—a 6 kW generator is typically half the size and weight of a traditional generator—and more efficient than a traditional generator. The inverter box produces a true-sine-wave output that is not only cleaner and more stable than that of any traditional generator, but also cleaner and more stable than that produced by most electricity companies! The package can be designed so that much of the time the generator engine runs at the most efficient point on its power curve. The principal drawbacks are the difficulty of designing an engine control circuit that will respond fast enough to high surge (inrush) loads, the complexity of the electronics, and the price (which is generally about 30% more than a comparably rated traditional genset).

Troubleshooting VST generators. The inverter end of things is liable to have various over-temperature and overload protection devices—see the Inverters section in Chapter 6.

Low voltage (generator bogs down). The engine speed on belt-driven VST generators is set manually; on stand-alone generators it may be either manually or electronically controlled. If a generator is unable to handle a load, there are two options: reduce the load, or increase the engine speed.

Sometimes the surge or start-up load of a large AC motor may overwhelm a generator. The solution is to turn off the load, increase the engine speed, and try again. If the engine bogs down from full speed, the load is simply too great for the generator. Where more than one high-surge-load motor may come online simultaneously (e.g., a dive compressor and an air conditioner), a *load-sequencing* device can be installed that will automatically delay the start-up of one motor until the other is up to speed (this applies to any AC system with a limited capacity, including systems using a DC-to-AC inverter or a traditional AC generator).

Belt-driven generators. Just as with a regular alternator, belt alignment and tension are critical to long life. If output is erratic and accompanied by belt squeal when a heavy load is applied, the belt is loose. If output is erratic but the belt is OK, the brushes are probably not making proper contact with the slip rings (see page 100). In the case of no output, perform the various tests outlined on pages 94–97 to determine if it is the alternator's voltage regulator circuit that is at fault or the alternator itself, remembering that *any output from the alternator is potentially lethal high-voltage AC and must be treated with appropriate respect. IF YOU ARE IN DOUBT ABOUT ANY TEST, DON'T DO IT!*

DC Generators

DC generators were not mentioned in previous editions of this book because they represented a minuscule, fringe application on boats. This is changing, primarily because of the increasing marketplace penetration of DC-to-AC inverters, the increasing efficiency and reliability of these inverters, the ability to stack or cascade inverters to the point that they can handle the boat's entire AC load (the inverter-based boat described in Chapter 2), and the increasing availability of AGS packages that can maximize the efficiency of generator operation while making operation more or less automatic. Within such a framework, a DC generator can have significant advantages over an AC generator (see Chapter 2 for a discussion of these issues).

Traditional Alternators Versus VST

The initial output of all modern DC generators is AC, from an alternator of some kind. This AC output is at a frequency that varies with the speed at which the alternator is being driven and is rectified to DC for battery-charging purposes.

Typically, rectification circuits are internal to an alternator, but they can also be in the form of an external diode pack. The latter has the advantage of getting the diodes, which are heat sensitive, away from the heat generated by the alternator (which can be quite considerable when an alternator is running at full output). Either way, the voltage on the AC side of the diode pack will be determined by battery voltage (as with any other automotive-style alternator). See Chapter 3 for a detailed description of this type of alternator, including troubleshooting procedures.

Modern electronics offers the possibility of a different approach, modeled on the VST concepts described above. In this case, the output of the alternator is not tied to battery voltage, but is allowed to rise to a much higher voltage (typically 240 volts, but it may be as high as 400 volts) at a variable frequency (which is a function of the speed of rotation of the alternator and the number of its phases—i.e., how the stator is wound). Just as with the VST AC generator, this high-voltage AC is fed to an external electronic device, but instead of being converted to AC at a standard voltage and frequency, it is transformed to battery-charging voltages and rectified to DC for battery-charging purposes. The control circuit provides a sophisticated, multistep battery-charging regimen.

There are several distinct advantages to this approach:

1. It once again gets the sensitive electronics away from the heat of the generator.

2. If the generator is any distance from the batteries being charged, instead of the heavy cables required in DC circuits, much smaller cables can be used for the much higher voltage (e.g., 240 volts) in the circuit to the electronics.

3. It lends itself to using brushless, permanent-magnet alternators.

4. The regulation circuit in the electronics can be used to control the speed of the engine driving the generator, maximizing overall efficiency.

The obvious disadvantage is the significant increase in the complexity of the electronics, together with its associated cost.

The best-known generators of this type are the Fischer Panda AGT Indirect DC (IDC) generators (www.fischerpanda.com), which have sophisticated, highly efficient, brushless, water-cooled alternators producing a considerable output from a relatively small and lightweight package. For pros and cons of this approach versus using a more traditional belt- or direct-driven alternator, see Chapter 2. The Glacier Bay Ossa Powerlite generators (www.glacierbay.com) are another (powerful) example of this technology (Figure 7-14).

FIGURE 7-14. Stator (right) and rotor (left) from an Ossa Powerlite generator. It is unusual since the superconducting, permanent-magnet rotor spins *outside* the stator (on all other generators, the rotor spins *inside* the stator). This has the effect of increasing the rotor speed for a given engine speed, which in turn increases the power that can be obtained at that engine speed. *(Glacier Bay)*

Electric Motors

How They Work

All electric motors, regardless of type, operate on the same general principles. A magnetic field is established inside the motor case, either with fixed permanent magnets or by using electromagnets (coils of wire [field windings] wrapped around iron shoes that become magnetized when a current is passed through the windings).

An armature or rotor is mounted on bearings inside this magnetic field. An armature contains another series of windings on an iron frame that also becomes magnetized when a current is passed through the windings. A rotor usually contains a set of fixed metal bars (although some have windings similar to an armature). In either case, like or opposing magnetic fields between the motor case and the armature or rotor drive the armature or rotor around in its bearings—we have an electric motor. Depending on methods of construction and details of operation, electric motors fall into four broad categories: series wound, shunt wound, permanent-magnet, and induction.

Series- and shunt-wound motors. The magnetic field inside the motor case is created by a couple of field windings. This type of motor uses a wound armature with anywhere from four windings on up (depending on motor construction). Each armature winding terminates in a copper bar. These bars are separated by insulation and arranged in a circle on the end of the armature shaft to become a *commutator*. Electricity is conducted to both the field windings and the armature windings (via spring-loaded brushes; Figure 7-15). The individual armature winding connected to the commutator bars in contact with the brushes is magnetized, and this magnetic attraction or repulsion (depending on the direction of rotation) interacts with the magnetic field produced by the field windings, causing the armature to turn.

As the armature turns, the brushes connect with another segment of the commutator, deenergizing the first winding on the armature and energizing the next. It in turn is attracted or

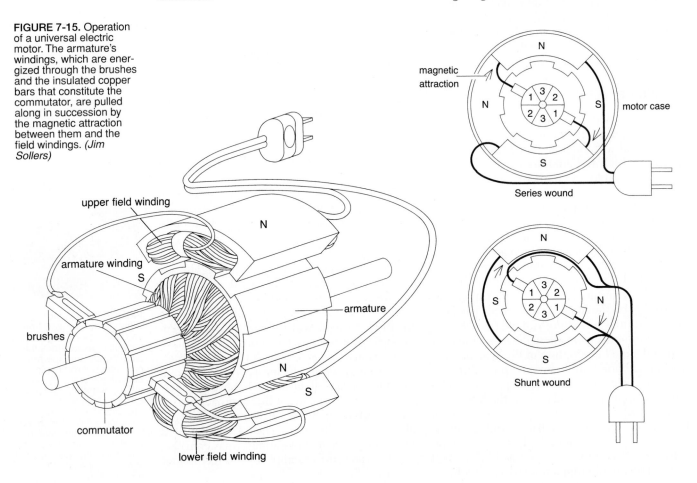

FIGURE 7-15. Operation of a universal electric motor. The armature's windings, which are energized through the brushes and the insulated copper bars that constitute the commutator, are pulled along in succession by the magnetic attraction between them and the field windings. *(Jim Sollers)*

repelled by the field windings and keeps the armature turning.

The brushes and armature windings are offset slightly from the field windings so that when the energized armature winding is attracted or repelled by the field magnet, the armature is pulled (or pushed) around. Without this offset, the motor would remain locked in one position.

Series-wound motors. These have the field and armature windings connected in series: the current flows first through a field winding, into a brush, through an armature winding, out the other brush, through the second field winding, and then back to the power source. The entire current flows through the field windings.

Shunt-wound motors. These have the field and armature windings in parallel. The current flows from a common terminal through both the field and armature windings, then back to another common terminal. The field current can be varied independently of the current passing through the armature.

Speed. The speed of a series-wound motor is governed by its load; the higher the load, the slower the speed. If this type of motor is run without a load, it will run faster and faster until it ultimately self-destructs. These motors are generally used inside a sealed, composite unit with the load permanently attached to the shaft. Shunt-wound motors maintain a near-constant speed over a wide range of loads.

Universal motors. A unique feature of some series-wound motors is that they can operate on both DC and AC power at about the same speed as long as the voltage is about the same and the AC frequency is not above 60 Hz. Motors with this kind of capability are known as *universal* motors, and are commonly found in such things as vacuum cleaners, hair dryers, and power tools.

Permanent-magnet motors. In conventional permanent-magnet motors, permanent magnets replace the field windings, so there is no field winding circuit. These motors resemble shunt-wound motors in all other respects (brushes, commutators, wound armatures). Brushless permanent-magnet motors (see Chapter 2) dispense with the brushes and commutator and instead use electronic circuitry to achieve the same effect.

Induction motors. Induction motors work on AC power only. The motor case contains a series of coils (field windings) known as the stator. These are energized by an AC power source. Because of the pulsating nature of AC power, alternating from positive to negative and back, a pulsating magnetic force is set up in the stator windings. This pulsating magnetic force creates (*induces*) a magnetic force in a series of windings or copper bars arranged around a rotor (which takes the place of the armature in a series-wound, shunt-wound, or conventional permanent-magnet motor). This happens without any connection to the AC source. Opposing magnetic forces cause the rotor to turn.

Once an induction motor starts spinning, it will keep spinning as long as current flows. The problem is to get it moving in the first place. A number of different methods are used to start induction motors; the principal ones found in boat motors are:

Split-phase (resistance) starting. A separate set of *phase* or *start* windings is added to the field windings, offset from the *run* windings, and

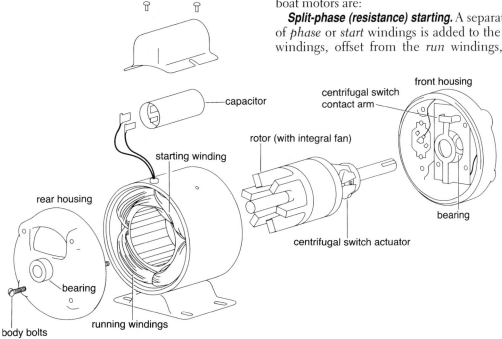

capacitor

centrifugal switch contact arm

front housing

starting winding

rotor (with integral fan)

rear housing

bearing

centrifugal switch actuator

body bolts

running windings

bearing

FIGURE 7-16A. A split-phase capacitor-start induction motor. *(Jim Sollers)*

FIGURE 7-16B. Operation of the centrifugal switch on a split-phase motor.

FIGURE 7-16C. A shaded-pole induction motor.

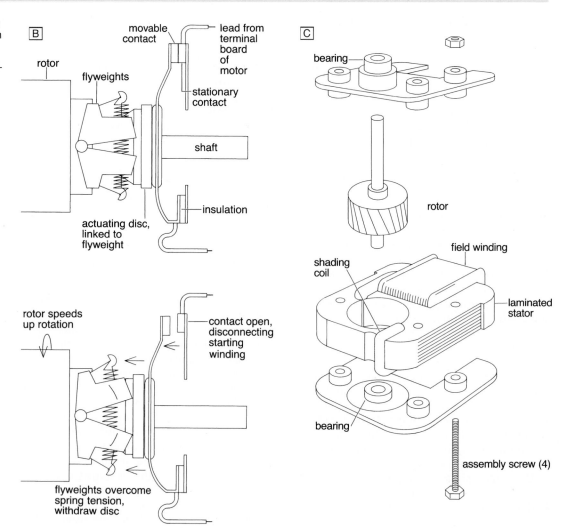

designed to generate an offset magnetic force to get the motor moving (Figure 7-16A). As the motor comes up to speed, a centrifugal switch or a current-sensing switch generally cuts off the start windings, often with an audible click (Figure 7-16B).

Capacitor starting. *Capacitor-start* motors further refine the starting process by the addition of one or two capacitors—round or oval cylinders with two spade terminals on one end, usually fitted under a cover on top of the motor. They store an electric charge and have the same effect as an offset magnetic force. Some capacitor-start motors have no switch on the start windings, which remain energized at all times; others have a switch. Where two capacitors are fitted, the second maintains partial current to the start windings even after the main start circuit is switched off. This makes for smoother running and reduces hum.

Shaded-pole starting. Shaded-pole motors have a copper strap around a section of the field magnet. This creates a magnetic asymmetry that gets the motor moving (Figure 7-16C). Shaded-pole motors are simple, inexpensive, and reliable, but since the magnetic asymmetry is a permanent feature, even when they are running at full speed, they are also inefficient.

Speed Regulation

Series- and shunt-wound motors. Series- and shunt-wound motors are commonly controlled by varying the current to the field windings. This is done either by a multiposition switch or with a rheostat and knob, which permits continuous adjustment of the field current. Newer devices may have solid-state regulators similar to the voltage regulators found on alternators, but with an added manual controller to adjust output. On such devices, a short circuit will result in maximum speed at all times; an open circuit will disable the motor. Motors designed to run at a single, constant speed are likely to have a governor.

Tapped-field speed control. The field winding has three to six connections at different points along its length. The closer a connection is to the end of the winding, the shorter the length of winding energized when current is applied, and therefore the less the resistance (since resistance is a function of wire length). Changing the resistance changes the amount of current that flows and thus the magnetic field, which in turn changes the speed of the motor. So by connecting (tapping into) the field winding at different points, we vary motor speed. The different points are accessed by a multiposition selector switch (Figure 7-17A).

Rheostats. A rheostat generally consists of a circular coil with a spring-loaded contact that can be rotated to any point on the coil. Current is fed into the coil at one end and flows along it until reaching the contactor, which then becomes the exit path for the current. As more coil is included in the circuit the resistance increases, causing less current to flow. The rheostat is inserted into the supply line to the field windings, controlling the current fed to the windings and therefore motor speed (Figure 7-17B).

Governors. A governor is mounted on the end of an armature shaft (Figure 7-17C). As the armature spins, the governor's flyweights are thrown outward by centrifugal force against spring pressure. As a result the various levers move the actuator pin out, and this in turn opens the points, cutting off the current to the armature windings. The motor slows, centrifugal force declines, the weights are pulled back in by the springs, the points close, power is restored to the armature windings, and the motor speeds up once again. Motor speed is set by adjusting the spring pressure on the flyweights; the more pressure, the greater the centrifugal force needed to open the points, and therefore the faster the motor will spin before the points are opened. Things to look for when troubleshooting governors are burned or corroded points, a dirty or rusty shaft (interfering with the movement of the actuator pin), and any dirt or corrosion on the rest of the linkage or the springs.

Induction motors. Since induction motors work by using the pulsating nature of AC power, their speed is tied directly to the frequency in the AC system (i.e., 60 Hz or 50 Hz). As such, speed is not normally variable. The motors may have anywhere from two to six or more field windings (*poles*). Speed then becomes a function of the frequency and number of poles. At 60 Hz, two poles will yield approximately 3,500 rpm, four poles 1,750 rpm, and six poles 1,160 rpm (note that this is somewhat below the 3,600, 1,800 and 1,200 rpm that might be expected—for reasons that are not relevant to this book). Speed

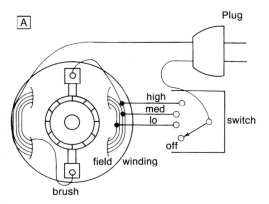

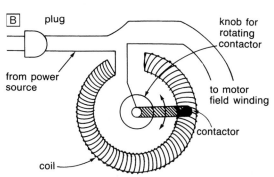

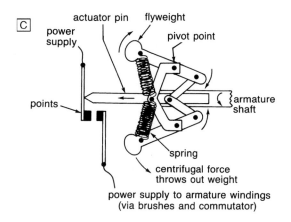

FIGURES 7-17A, 7-17B, AND 7-17C. Regulating the speed of universal motors. Multiposition switch (7-17A). Rheostat (variable resistor; 7-17B). Mechanical governor (7-17C).

regulation of induction motors is generally available only by switching poles into or out of the circuit.

Troubleshooting

Preliminary testing—all motors. First, feel the motor to see if it is hot. If it is, check for a potential overload condition (e.g., hairs wrapped around the impeller on a bilge pump). Note that a locked rotor (the motor cannot turn at all) for all intents and purposes puts something close to a dead short on the circuit. If a breaker doesn't trip or a fuse doesn't blow, any electric motor will overheat, and most will melt down. Unless the

FIGURE 7-18. A clip-on ammeter.

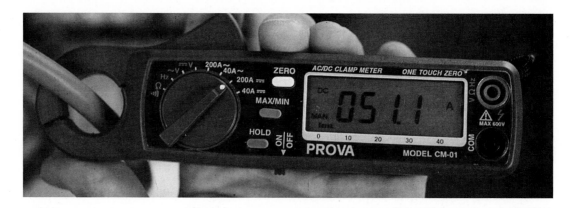

FIGURES 7-19A, 7-19B, AND 7-19C. Testing amperage on DC motors. Place the meter in series with an open switch (7-19A). Place the meter in series with the plug (7-19B). Break a connection loose and place the meter in the circuit (7-19C).

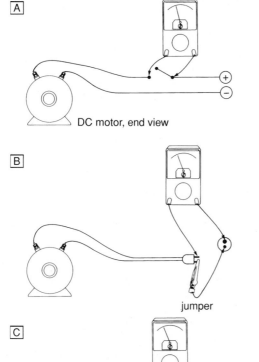

A

DC motor, end view

B

jumper

C

some automatically reset while others are manually reset). Severe voltage drop results from defective wiring and switches, a shorted motor (either because of electrical problems or because of a locked rotor), or a dead battery in a DC circuit.

Amperage test. In recent years, clip-on ammeters (Figure 7-18) have become widely available. They will read up to 200 amps AC or DC and are built into a digital multimeter; having one on a boat is a great asset. Fluke (www.fluke.com) and other companies also make stand-alone clip-on ammeters, which are plugged into a regular multimeter and clamped around a cable. These are capable of measuring up to 1,000 amps DC or 750 amps AC. Note that in all cases the meter must be clipped around a single cable (positive or negative, hot or neutral) and not around both power leads. On 240-volt AC motors (U.S.), test both power leads one at a time; they each should be pulling approximately the same number of amps. Once again, note that in order to work, the meter must be clipped around a single power lead. If the hot and neutral leads are in a common sheath, you will have to find some means to separate them to take an amps measurement.

In the absence of a clip-on ammeter, many meters have up to a 10 amp DC capability. To use this capability, the meter is connected *in series* with the hot lead to the appliance (Figures 7-19A, 7-19B, and 7-19C). This can be done either by turning off the switch and jumping it out with the meter leads, or by unsoldering or otherwise breaking loose a connection.

If a motor is pulling more amps than rated, it has a short (check for a locked or jammed rotor); if it is pulling no amps, it is open-circuited. An open circuit can result from a blown fuse, a tripped breaker, a turned-off switch, a broken or disconnected wire, brushes not contacting the commutator, or a burned winding in the motor itself.

Induction motors are notoriously inefficient—the smaller the motor, the greater the inefficiency. If the motor is rated in watts, you can cal-

motor is specifically designed for variable voltage, low voltage can result in a similar situation, since many motors will slow down, once again resulting in a partial short circuit.

Voltage test. Check the voltage at the motor, preferably across its input terminals. If these are inaccessible, check at the nearest power outlet or terminal block. Switch the motor on and off. If there is no voltage at the motor, check all fuses and circuit breakers; also look for an over-temperature shutdown device (commonly built into larger AC motors and also some DC motors;

culate its *rated* amperage by dividing the watts by system voltage. *Actual amperage may be more than twice this*, and on initial start-up, as much as six times higher! This can make it difficult to distinguish partial shorts from normal operation. Dead shorts will draw heavy amperage continuously; open circuits, no amps.

Resistance tests. *Disconnect the motor from its power source* and connect an ohmmeter (R × 1 scale on an analog meter) between the hot and ground leads (12-volt motors), the hot and neutral leads (120-volt, U.S; 240-volt, Europe), or the two hot leads (240-volt, U.S.). The meter should show a small resistance, depending on the type and size of the motor. In general, the more powerful the motor, the lower the resistance. Note, however, that the resistance is likely to be less than that calculated by an application of Ohm's law to the motor's rated voltage and amperage (or wattage). This is because an operating motor develops a higher resistance than a static motor, and motors are rated at their operating characteristics.

If the meter shows 0 ohms, the motor has an internal short (DC motors that have a heavy current draw, such as starter motors, may show so little resistance that only the most-sensitive meters can distinguish between normal internal resistance and a short). If the meter shows infinite resistance (R × 100 scale on an analog meter), the motor is open-circuited at some point. Likely causes are an open switch or high-temperature trip device, a broken wire, burned brushes or brush springs, or a burned winding.

Leave the meter connected (R × 1 scale on an analog meter) and turn the motor by hand. On motors with brushes, the reading may flicker up and down uniformly, but any sudden or erratic difference probably indicates problems with the brushes or the commutator.

If the motor has variable speeds, such as on a food processor, switch through the range (or turn the speed-adjusting knob) and observe the ohms reading. It should increase or decrease gradually. Any sudden deviations indicate a problem. An exception is when the switch is turned off—the reading should jump to infinity; if it does not, the switch is defective.

If the preceding tests indicate a problem in the motor, you will need to dismantle it. Generally this is a simple and obvious procedure. Take care not to break any wires when removing end covers and housings, especially on universal motors, where brush and field winding wires may be attached to two different parts of the casing. Motor casings and covers often must be reassembled exactly as they came apart. It is always a good idea to make a couple of punch marks or scratches in the paint across a joint so that they

TABLE 7-2. Typical Running Amperages for 120-Volt Induction Motors[1]

Horsepower	120-Volt Motor (amps)	240-Volt Motor (amps)
1/6	4.4	2.2
1/4	5.8	2.9
1/3	7.2	3.6
1/2	9.8	4.9
3/4	13.8	6.9
1	16	8
1 1/2	20	10
2	24	12

1. Starting currents for split-phase motors are five to seven times higher, and two to four times higher for capacitor-start motors.

can be realigned exactly. Universal and permanent-magnet motors with spring-loaded brushes are likely to launch brushes into space during incautious disassembly. Extra care is needed.

Electrical problems.

Series- and shunt-wound motors (including universal motors). The most likely problem areas are the brushes and the commutator (Figures 7-20A to 7-20D). The brushes must be free-moving in their holders, have sufficient spring tension to contact the commutator firmly, and as a general rule, should be at least as long as they are wide (Figures 7-20E to 7-20M). When worn beyond this point, they need replacing. The commutator must be clean, relatively shiny (a light film or surface mottling is OK), and smooth (a step worn by the brushes is OK; Figure 7-21A). Any pitted or darkened segments indicate a short or open circuit in one of the armature windings (Figure 7-21B); the armature needs replacing or rewinding.

Commutator testing: Test the armature and commutator with an ohmmeter. Touch one probe to one commutator segment and the other probe to the adjacent segment. The ohms reading should be low, but not zero. Test adjacent segments all around the commutator; all should read about the same. No ohms (needle all the way to the right on an analog meter) indicates a short between windings (except with some cheap meters insufficiently sensitive to distinguish normal readings from a short). High ohms (needle all the way to the left on an analog meter) indicates an open circuit (a burned winding). Finally, test between the armature shaft and each commutator segment (R × 100 scale on an analog meter). A zero reading at any time indicates a short to ground (Figure 7-21C).

Commutator cleaning: A dirty commutator that checks out OK and is in reasonable shape (not pitted, out of round, or excessively worn)

(continued on page 314)

FIGURES 7-20A TO 7-20D. Motor disassembly and troubleshooting. In most cases, removing a couple of bolts provides access to the brushes and commutator (7-20A and 7-20B). In this case, salt water (from a leak in the boat) wicking down the power cable has corroded one of the brushes into its holder (7-20C), causing it to arc to the commutator and burn the commutator (7-20D).

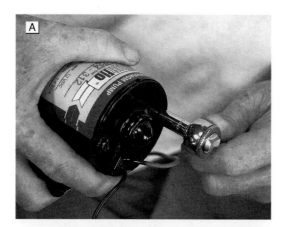

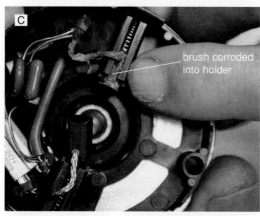

brush corroded into holder

burned commutator

FIGURES 7-20E TO 7-20M. Disassembly and testing of another motor. Mark the cover joint so the cover can be replaced (7-20E). Undo the retaining bolts (7-20F) and pry off the cover (7-20G). The brushes have good spring tension and plenty of length; they are OK (7-20H). A close look at the commutator; it is OK (7-20I). The permanent magnets are glued into the motor housing. Sometimes rusting of the case—like this (7-20J)—will cause the glue bond to fail, but these are OK. Test with an ohmmeter from one commutator bar to another (7-20K); expect a low reading. This commutator tests out OK. Test from each commutator bar to the rotor shaft. It should read infinity (no circuit), which on this meter is displayed as shown (7-20L). The commutator tests out OK. Clean out the grooves between the commutator segments (7-20M). In spite of this motor's external corrosion and poor appearance, it is fine . . . and did not need to be disassembled!

brushes

AC GENERATORS, DC GENERATORS, ELECTRIC MOTORS (DC AND AC), AND ELECTRIC LIGHTS

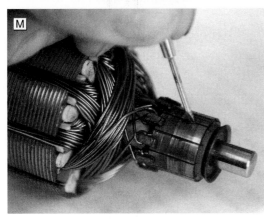

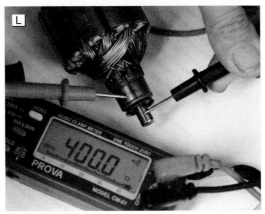

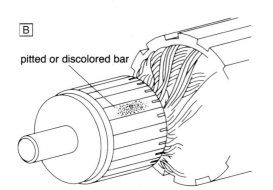

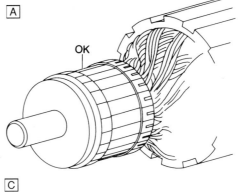

Ohms Rx1

commutator bars

Ohms Rx100

A

OK

B

pitted or discolored bar

C

FIGURE 7-21A. Maintenance procedures for universal motors. A worn and grooved commutator is OK as long as the ring is shiny. *(Jim Sollers)*

FIGURE 7-21B. A pitted or dark bar results from an open or short circuit in the armature winding (see also 7-20D). *(Jim Sollers)*

FIGURE 7-21C. Testing an armature. Testing between adjacent bars on the commutator should give a low ohms reading (see also 7-20K); all readings should be about the same. Testing from each commutator bar to the shaft should show infinity, indicating an open circuit (see also 7-20L). *(Jim Sollers)*

(continued from page 311)
can be cleaned by pulling a strip of fine sand-paper (600- or 400-grit wet-or-dry) lightly back and forth until all the segments are uniformly shiny (Figure 7-21D). Cut back the insulation between each segment of the commutator to just below the level of the copper segments by drawing a knife or sharp screwdriver across each strip

FIGURE 7-21D. Polishing a commutator. *(Jim Sollers)*

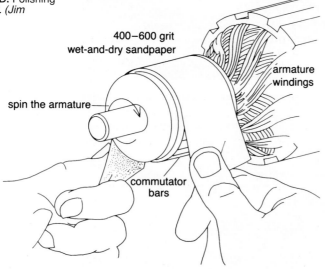

400–600 grit wet-and-dry sandpaper

spin the armature

armature windings

commutator bars

of insulation. Take care not to scratch the copper or burr its edges (Figure 7-21E). Use a triangular file to bevel the edges of the copper bars. Always renew the brushes at this time.

Brush renewal: Pull out the old brushes and thoroughly clean away all traces of carbon from the commutator and motor housing with a proprietary cleaner, such as CRC 2018 Lectra Clean or WD-40. Dry thoroughly afterward. Slip in the new brushes, *which must slide in and out of their holders without binding.* The commutator ends of the new brushes will need *bedding in:* wrap some sandpaper around the commutator under the brushes (Figure 7-21F), with the sanding surface facing out. Use coarse sandpaper first, to get a rough fit, and then very fine sandpaper, such as 600- or 400-grit wet-or-dry, to get a good finish; *do not use emery cloth.* Then spin the armature, or work the sandpaper backward and forward, until the brushes are bedded to the commutator; they should be almost shiny over their whole surface. Remove the sandpaper and blow out the carbon dust, taking care to blow it away from the armature and not into its windings!

Field winding testing: The field windings will have a wire running into one winding, around to the other(s), and out. One end may or may not be grounded to the motor case. Test with an ohmmeter (R × 1 scale on an analog meter) between the ungrounded end of the field winding wire and the other wire or the motor case (scratch around to get a good ground). If the meter reads 0 ohms, the field windings or wires are shorted to ground (except on large motors being tested with a cheap meter not sensitive enough to read field winding resistances). A high reading (analog meter on R × 100 scale) indicates the field windings or their wiring are open-circuited (burned through like a fuse, or a broken

FIGURE 7-21E. To cut back the insulation on a commutator, modify a hacksaw blade as shown. At 1, the mica insulation is flush with the commutator bars. Cut back as in 2 (good) or 3 (better). Avoid cutting back as in 4 or 5. *(Jim Sollers)*

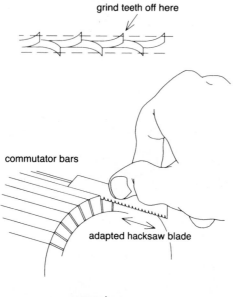

grind teeth off here

commutator bars

adapted hacksaw blade

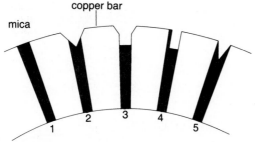

mica

copper bar

1   2   3   4   5

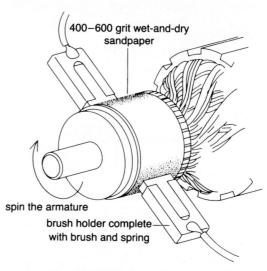

400–600 grit wet-and-dry sandpaper

spin the armature

brush holder complete with brush and spring

FIGURE 7-21F. Bedding in new brushes. *(Jim Sollers)*

wire). On those motors with governor-type speed controls, check the governor for free movement, the springs for reasonable tension, and the points for any signs of pitting and corrosion.

Permanent-magnet motors. Test and repair permanent-magnet motors in exactly the same way as universal motors, except you have no field windings to worry about.

Induction motors. Induction motors generally have no brushes, commutator, or armature windings to concern us (some do have armature windings). Field windings are tested as for universal motors. Shaded-pole motors have little else to go wrong electrically. Split-phase motors have one or two special problem areas:

Thermal overload trip: If the motor is very hot (too hot to touch), let it cool down. Some thermal overload trips reset themselves; others have to be reset by pushing a button on the motor housing.

Motor hums but does not start: Probably the start windings are not energizing. Spin the motor by hand (with the switch turned on). If it gets going, the start circuit is bad. Check for a centrifugal switch in the open position or one that has dirty or corroded points. If present, the switch will be on the end of the rotor shaft. Clean and lubricate it, and ensure free movement of all its parts. If the motor has capacitors, test these (refer back to Figures 7-10A and 7-10B).

Motor starts and kicks off: The start windings are not switching off when the motor comes up to speed. Check the centrifugal switch, if fitted.

Mechanical problems. Motors are mechanically very simple. A bearing supports the armature (rotor) at both ends. Sometimes a fan is added to the shaft.

Small motors have bushings for bearings (brass or bronze sleeves), which require a very little amount of light machine oil periodically. Do not overdo it as excess oil will carry dirt into the motor windings.

Larger motors have ball bearings. Most are sealed for life, but a few older ones have external grease nipples (which need one shot of grease occasionally). Worn bearings produce distinctive rattles and rumbles. With the power off, armatures (rotors) should turn freely by hand with no catches or rough spots. There should be no up-and-down or sideways movement, and almost no in-and-out movement (end play).

The clearance between an armature (rotor) and its field winding shoes (or magnets) is quite small. Any misalignment or serious bearing wear will cause the armature to rub on the shoes (magnets). This will produce a shiny spot on both the armature and shoe and must be fixed. If the armature and its bearings appear to be in

good shape, check any fastenings to the field windings. On some motors, the windings are bolted through the motor case and can work loose with vibration.

Starter Motors

Given that the engine cranking circuit is one of the more troublesome electric motor circuits on boats, it deserves special attention.

Starter motor circuits. The heavy amperage draw of a starter motor requires heavy supply cables. Ignition switches are frequently located some distance from the battery and starter motor. To avoid running the heavy cables to the ignition switch, a special kind of switch—a *solenoid*—is installed in the cranking circuit and used to turn the starter motor on and off (Figures 7-22A, 7-22B, and 7-22C). The solenoid is triggered by the (remotely mounted) ignition switch. The wiring between the solenoid and the ignition switch carries little current, and as a result can be relatively light weight.

A solenoid contains a plunger and an electromagnet. When the ignition switch is turned on, it energizes the magnet, which pulls down the plunger, which closes a couple of heavy-duty contacts, thus completing the circuit to the starter motor (Figures 7-22D and 7-22E).

Some starting circuits include a *neutral start* switch, which prevents the engine from being

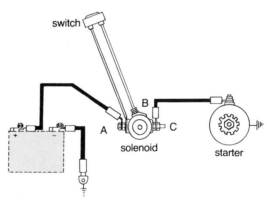

FIGURE 7-22A. A starting circuit with an inertia starter. To bypass the switch, connect a jumper from A to B. To bypass the switch and the solenoid, connect a heavy-duty jumper (e.g., a screwdriver) from A to C.

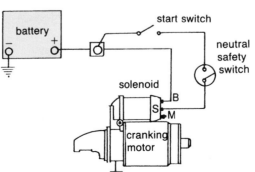

FIGURE 7-22B. A starting circuit with a preengaged starter. To bypass the switch, connect a jumper from terminal B to terminal S on the solenoid. To bypass the solenoid and switch, connect a heavy-duty jumper (e.g., a screwdriver) from terminal B to terminal M. See also Figure 7-24A. *(PCM)*

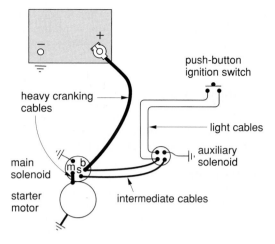

FIGURE 7-22C. A starting circuit with main and auxiliary solenoids. To bypass the switch circuit, connect a jumper from B to S on the main solenoid. To bypass the solenoid and switch, connect a heavy-duty jumper from B to M.

push-button ignition switch

heavy cranking cables

light cables

main solenoid

auxiliary solenoid

starter motor

intermediate cables

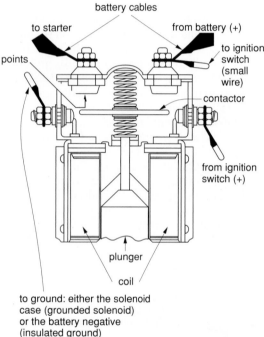

FIGURE 7-22D. Solenoid operation. Upon closing the ignition switch, a small current passing through the solenoid's electromagnet pushes the contactor up against spring tension, completing the circuit from the battery to the starter motor.

battery cables

to starter

from battery (+)

points

to ignition switch (small wire)

contactor

from ignition switch (+)

plunger

coil

to ground: either the solenoid case (grounded solenoid) or the battery negative (insulated ground)

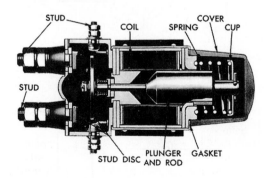

FIGURE 7-22E. A cutaway of a typical solenoid. (Detroit Diesel)

STUD   COIL   SPRING   COVER   CUP

STUD

STUD   DISC   PLUNGER   GASKET
              AND ROD

cranked when it is in gear. Some heavy-duty circuits have two solenoids. The first is energized by the ignition switch to close the circuit to the second, which then operates the starter motor. (This is done because the main solenoid itself draws a moderately heavy current, requiring

fairly heavy cables. Adding a second light-duty solenoid enables lighter wires to be run to the ignition switch.)

The ground side of a starter motor circuit almost always runs through the starter motor case and engine block to a ground strap, which is connected directly to the battery's negative terminal post. However, on rare occasions an insulated ground is used, in which case the starter motor is isolated electrically from the engine block; a separate cable grounds it to the battery.

Inertia and preengaged starters. Most starter motors are series-wound motors although some newer ones have permanent magnets. Regardless of motor type, there are two basic kinds of starters: inertia and preengaged. Inertia starters are mostly found on older engines; as far as I know, all modern engines have preengaged starters. Some newer starter motors have a reduction gear (generally between 2:1 and 3.5:1) between the electric motor and the drive gear (the *pinion* gear) that engages the engine flywheel. This enables a smaller, lighter, faster-spinning motor to do the work of a larger motor.

Inertia starters. The solenoid for an inertia motor is mounted independently, at a convenient location. The pinion gear is keyed into a helical groove on the motor shaft. When the solenoid is energized, the motor spins. Inertia in the gear causes it to spin out along the helical groove and into contact with the engine flywheel, which is then turned over (Figure 7-23A).

Sometimes an inertia starter's pinion will stick to its shaft and not be thrown into engagement with the flywheel. In this case, the motor will whir loudly without turning the engine over. A smart tap on its case while it is spinning may free it up. However, don't do this too often, as it's hard on the gear teeth. Also, don't do this to a permanent-magnet motor—it may crack the magnets or break them loose from the motor case (as far as I know, there are no inertia starters with permanent-magnet motors).

At other times the pinion may jam in the flywheel and not disengage. In this case you can often gain access to the end of the armature shaft via a cover, normally located in the center of the rear housing of the starter motor. *With the engine shut down,* turn the squared-off end of the shaft back and forth with a wrench to free the pinion.

Preengaged starters. The solenoid of a preengaged starter is *always* mounted on the starter itself (a surefire indicator). When the solenoid is energized, the electromagnet pulls a lever, which pushes the starter motor pinion into engagement with the engine flywheel; the main solenoid points now close, allowing current to

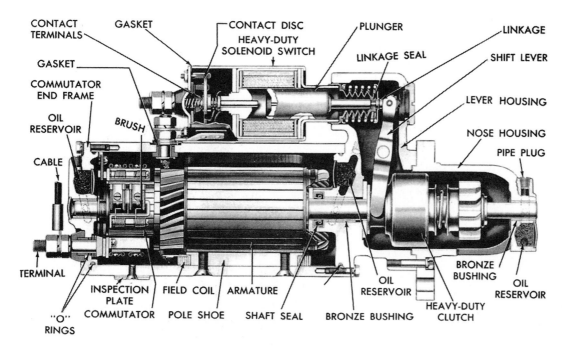

FIGURE 7-23A. An inertia-type starter motor. *(Detroit Diesel)*

Figure 7-23A labels: TERMINAL · FIELD COIL · TERMINAL · CENTER BEARING · BUSHING · BUSHING · COVER BAND · POLE SHOE (LAMINATED) · BRUSH · COMMUTATOR END FRAME · COMMUTATOR · ARMATURE · BENDIX DRIVE (FRICTION-CLUTCH TYPE) · DRIVE HOUSING

FIGURE 7-23B. A preengaged starter motor with a solenoid mounted on it. *(Detroit Diesel)*

Figure 7-23B labels: CONTACT TERMINALS · GASKET · CONTACT DISC HEAVY-DUTY SOLENOID SWITCH · PLUNGER · LINKAGE · GASKET · COMMUTATOR END FRAME · OIL RESERVOIR · BRUSH · LINKAGE SEAL · SHIFT LEVER · LEVER HOUSING · NOSE HOUSING · PIPE PLUG · CABLE · TERMINAL · INSPECTION PLATE · "O" RINGS · COMMUTATOR · FIELD COIL · ARMATURE · POLE SHOE · SHAFT SEAL · BRONZE BUSHING · OIL RESERVOIR · HEAVY-DUTY CLUTCH · BRONZE BUSHING · OIL RESERVOIR

flow to the motor, turning it over. Preengaged starters mesh the drive gear with the flywheel *before* the motor spins, greatly reducing overall wear (Figure 7-23B). Unlike an inertia starter, once the engine fires up, the pinion gear does not get thrown out of engagement with the flywheel. As the engine speeds up, it has the potential to spin the gear at a very high speed. To prevent damage to the starter, the gear is mounted on a clutch arrangement that allows it to freewheel until it is disengaged by deenergizing the solenoid.

Troubleshooting. Never crank a starter motor continuously for more than 15 seconds when performing any of the following tests. Because starter motors are designed for only brief and infrequent use, they generally have no fans or cooling devices. *Continuous cranking will burn them up. Note: Some of these tests will create sparks. Be sure to vent the engine room properly, especially with gasoline engines.*

Remember: A battery that is almost dead may show nearly full voltage on an open-circuit voltage test. If a starter motor fails to work, turn on a couple of lights (wired to the cranking battery) and try to crank the engine. The lights should dim but still stay lit. If the lights remain unchanged, no current is flowing to the starter; if the lights go out, the battery is dead or the starter is shorted. Check the battery first (see the Testing a Battery section in Chapter 3).

Note that burned coils in a solenoid or starter motor have a distinctive smell; once encountered,

Troubleshooting Chart 7-2.
Starting Circuit Problems: Engine Fails to Crank

Note: Before jumping out solenoid terminals, completely vent the engine compartment, especially with gasoline engines, since sparks will be created.

Turn on some lights powered by the cranking battery and try to crank the engine. Do the lights *go out?*	If the solenoid makes a rapid "clicking," the battery is probably dead; replace it. If the solenoid makes one loud click, the starter motor is probably jammed or shorted; free it up or replace it as necessary. Before taking the starter out, try turning the engine over by placing a wrench on the crankshaft pulley nut. If the engine won't turn this is the problem; there may be water in the cylinders (page 382) or the engine may be seized up.
When cranking, do the lights *dim?*	Check for voltage drop from poor connections or undersized cables. Try cranking for a few seconds, then feel all connections and cables in the circuit— battery and solenoid terminals, and battery ground attachment on the engine block. If any are warm to the touch, they need cleaning. If this fails to show a problem, use a voltmeter as shown in Figure 7-25, then try to crank the engine. If there is no evidence of voltage drop, check for a jammed or shorted starter.
Is the ignition switch faulty? **TEST:** With a jumper wire or screwdriver blade, bridge the battery and ignition switch terminals on the solenoid. If the starter motor now cranks, the ignition circuit is defective.	**YES** Replace ignition switch or its wiring as needed.
Is the solenoid defective? **TEST:** Use a screwdriver blade to jump out the two heavy-duty terminals on the solenoid. (This procedure is tricky: Observe all precautions outlined in the accompanying text.) If the starter now spins, the solenoid is defective.	**YES** Replace the solenoid.
Is there full battery voltage at the starter motor when cranking? **TEST:** Check with a multimeter between the starter positive terminal and the engine block when cranking.	**YES** The starter is open-circuited and needs replacing. First check its brushes for excessive wear or sticking in their brush holders.
No voltage: The battery isolation switch is probably turned off!	

you will never forget it. It is not a bad idea to sniff them before starting any other detective work— this may rapidly narrow the field of investigation.

Preliminary tests. A couple of quick steps will isolate problems in the starting circuit. The solenoid will have two heavy-duty terminals: one is attached to the battery's positive cable; the other is attached with a second cable (or short strap in the case of preengaged starters) to the starter itself. There will also be one or two small terminals. If only one of the small terminals has a wire attached to it, this is the one we need. If both small terminals have wires attached, one is a ground wire; we need the *other one* (it goes to the ignition switch). If in doubt, turn off the ignition and battery switches and test from both solenoid terminals to ground with an ohmmeter (R × 1 scale on an analog meter). The ignition switch wire should give a small reading; the ground wire will read 0 ohms.

Turn the battery isolation switch back on. Now bypass the ignition switch circuit (and neutral start switch if fitted) by connecting a jumper wire or screwdriver blade from the *battery terminal* on the solenoid to the *ignition switch* terminal (Figures 7-24A, 7-24B, and 7-24C). If the motor cranks, the ignition switch or its circuit is faulty. If the solenoid clicks but nothing else happens, the battery may really be dead (check it again), or the starter is probably bad. (But note that the solenoid on a preengaged starter will sometimes throw the pinion into engagement with the flywheel but then fail to energize the motor due to faulty main points, so *always check*

FIGURE 7-24A. A typical preengaged starter motor and solenoid. Jumping across 1 and 2 bypasses the ignition switch; 1 and 3 bypasses both the ignition switch and the solenoid. The starter should spin but will not engage the engine's flywheel.

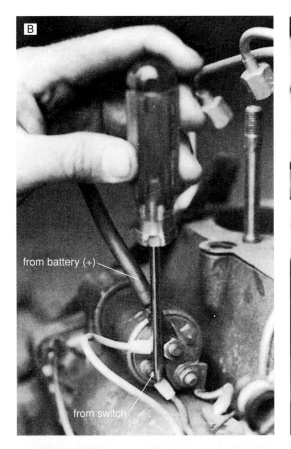

FIGURES 7-24B AND 7-24C. Bypassing the ignition switch by jumping out the two smaller wires.

from battery (+)

from switch

from battery (+)

from switch

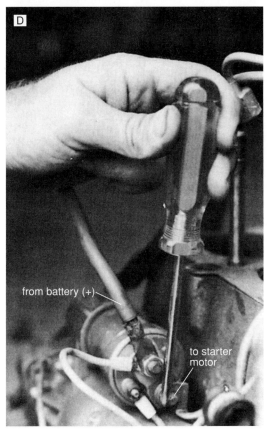

FIGURES 7-24D AND 7-24E. Bypassing the solenoid altogether by jumping out the two main cable terminals.

from battery (+)

to starter motor

from battery (+)

to starter motor

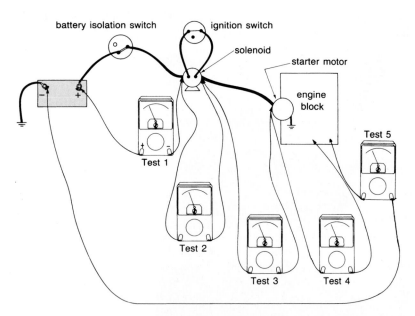

battery isolation switch ignition switch
solenoid
starter motor
engine block
Test 1
Test 2
Test 3
Test 4
Test 5

FIGURE 7-25. Testing for voltage drop in starter motor circuits. Test while the engine is being cranked (see the text).

the solenoid before condemning the motor.) If nothing at all happens, there is either no juice to the solenoid (check the battery isolation switch) or the solenoid is defective.

If the starter failed to work, use a screwdriver to jump out the *two heavy-duty terminals* on the solenoid (Figures 7-24A, 7-24D, and 7-24E). Warning: *The full battery current may be flowing through the screwdriver blade*; considerable arcing is likely, and a big chunk may be melted out of the screwdriver blade! Do not touch the solenoid or starter case with the screwdriver: This will create a dead short. Hold the screwdriver *firmly* to the terminals. If the starter now spins, the solenoid is defective. If the motor does not spin, *it* is probably faulty. If no arcing occurred, there is no juice to the solenoid.

A motor with an inertia starter can be cranked by jumping a defective solenoid as described. A preengaged starter, however, will merely spin without engaging the engine flywheel since the solenoid is needed to push the starter pinion into engagement with the flywheel. In this case, have someone hold the start switch on while you jump the main solenoid terminals. If the cranking problem is a failure of the solenoid *points* (most likely), this will crank the engine; if the problem is a failure of the solenoid *coil*, the pinion will still fail to engage the flywheel. In the latter case, you can remove the solenoid to access the pinion fork, allowing you to manually engage the gear while you jump out the main solenoid points. This should get the engine going in an emergency, but may leave the pinion rattling up against the flywheel when the engine is running.

Voltage drop tests. The above tests will quickly and crudely determine whether there is juice to the starter motor and whether or not it is func-

tional. More insidious is the effect of poor connections and undersized cables; these create voltage drop in the circuits, rob the starter motor of power, and result in sluggish cranking or failure to crank at all, especially when the engine is cold. A potential result is a burned-out starter motor. (If you have to replace the starter motor, always do a volt drop test after fitting the new one to ensure it doesn't burn out also.)

A quick test for voltage drop can be made by cranking (or trying to crank) for a few seconds and then feeling all the connections and cables in the circuit—both battery terminals, both isolation switch terminals, the solenoid terminals, and the battery ground attachment point on the engine block. If any of these are warm, there is resistance and voltage drop and the connection needs cleaning.

You can make more accurate tests with a voltmeter. Run the positive meter probe to the battery positive post (not the cable clamp), and the other probe to the solenoid positive terminal, and *crank the engine* (Figure 7-25, Test 1; volt drop tests can only be made when the circuit is under a cranking load). Switch down the voltage scales on an analog meter. *Any voltage reading shows voltage drop in this part of the circuit.* Clean all connections and repeat the test. Switch back up the voltage scales and perform the same test (cranking the engine) across the two main solenoid terminals (Test 2). Switch down the scales. Any voltage indicates resistance in the solenoid (see below for cleaning dirty and pitted points). Repeat the same test from the solenoid outlet terminal to the starter motor hot terminal (Test 3). The cumulative voltage drop revealed by these tests should not exceed 0.7 volt on a 12-volt system (1.4 volts on a 24-volt system). It is not unusual to find 2.0 volts!

Now test from the starter motor case to the engine block (Test 4); then test from the engine block back to the battery negative post (not the cable clamp—Test 5). The latter test frequently reveals poor ground connections. The cumulative voltage drop revealed by these tests should not exceed 0.3 volt on a 12-volt system (0.6 volt on a 24-volt system). It is not unusual to find 1 volt or more.

The total voltage drop on both the positive and negative sides of the circuit should not exceed 1.0 volt on a 12-volt system (2.0 volts on a 24-volt system). All too often, it is much higher than this. If the voltage drop is still too high after cleaning and tightening all the connections in the circuit, and after correcting any problems revealed with the solenoid (Test 2; the volt drop across the solenoid terminals should be below 0.3 volt), then the cranking cables and engine ground cable need to be replaced with larger cables.

Amperage tests. Many modern multimeters incorporate a clip-on ammeter that can measure up to 200 amps DC. Although the inrush current of even a small diesel engine starter motor will be on the order of several hundred amps, the sustained cranking current is below 200 amps. One of these meters can be used to measure it, providing a rapid indication of whether or not the starter motor is receiving the kind of current it needs to operate. The test will prove far more useful if you have already tested the engine when it is cranking properly and made a note of the current draw to provide a benchmark. Note that the draw will vary according to the ambient temperature and the engine temperature, so testing in different conditions is recommended.

Motor disassembly, inspection, and repair.

Before removing a starter motor from an engine, isolate its hot lead, or better still, disconnect it from the battery. The starter will be held to the engine by two or three nuts or bolts. If it sticks in the flywheel housing, a smart tap will jar it loose (but check first to see that you didn't miss any of the mounting bolts, and don't whack a permanent-magnet motor!).

Inertia starters. Remove the metal band from the rear of the motor case. Undo the locknut from the terminal stud in the rear housing. Do not let the stud turn; if necessary, grip it carefully with Vise-Grips (mole wrenches). Note the order of all washers; they insulate the stud, and it is essential that they go back the same way.

Undo the two (or four) retaining screws in the rear housing. If tight, grip with a pair of Vise-Grips from the side to break them loose. Lift off the rear housing with care; it will be attached to the motor case by two brush wires. Lift the springs off the relevant brushes and slide the brushes out of their holders to free the housing.

Preengaged starters. To check the solenoid points on a preengaged starter (Figures 7-26A to 7-26K and 7-27J to 7-27M), remove the battery cable, the screw or nut retaining the hot strap to the motor, and all other nuts on the stud(s) for the ignition circuit wiring. Undo the two retaining screws at the very back of the solenoid. The end housing (plastic) will pull off to expose the *contactor* and the *points*. (Note: A spring will probably fall out; it goes on the center of the contactor.) Check the points and contactor for pitting and burning and clean or replace as necessary. A badly damaged contactor can sometimes be reversed to provide a fresh contact surface. In a similar way, the main points can sometimes be reversed in the solenoid end housing, but take care when removing them because the Bakelite housing is brittle.

To remove the solenoid *coil* (electromagnet),

undo the two screws at the flywheel end of the solenoid and turn the coil housing through 90 degrees. The coil will now pull straight off the piston. The piston and fork assembly generally can be removed only by separating the starter motor case from its front housing (see below).

If it is necessary to undo the pivot pin bolt on the solenoid fork, mark its head so that it can be put back in the same position. Sometimes, turning this pin adjusts how far the pinion is *thrown* when it engages the flywheel.

Remove the two starter motor retaining screws from the rear housing and lift off the rear cover; it comes straight off and contains no brushes. This will expose the brushes and commutator.

All starters. The motor case, complete with field windings, can now be pulled off to expose the armature. If the end cover was held with four short screws as opposed to two long ones, there will be four more screws holding the motor case at the other end (Figures 7-26L to 7-26O and 7-27A to 7-27I). Note that both end housings will probably have small lugs so that they can be refitted to the motor case in only one position.

Inspect the commutator and brushes for wear as previously detailed in the section on series- and shunt-wound motors. Without a very sensitive ohmmeter, it will be impossible to distinguish between normal resistances and a short when doing the various winding and resistance tests. Any high resistance indicates an open circuit.

There will be four brushes instead of two to handle the high loads. Some brush leads are soldered in place; other brushes are retained with screws. If replacing soldered brushes, cut the old leads, *leaving a tail long enough to solder to.* Tin this tail and the end of the new brush wire and solder them together (see Chapter 4 for more on soldering).

The brushes attached to the field windings are insulated; those to the end housing or motor case are uninsulated. When replacing the end housing of an inertia starter, hold the brushes back in their holders and jam them in this position by lodging the brush springs against the *side* of the brushes. Once the plate is on, slip the springs into position with a small screwdriver, and then put the metal band back on the motor case.

The pinion. Given the intermittent use of boat engines and the hostile marine environment, the pinion (or drive gear, often known as a *bendix*) can be especially troublesome. Pinions are particularly prone to rusting, especially where salt water in the bilges has contacted the flywheel and been thrown all around the flywheel housing.

Inertia starters are more prone to trouble than preengaged starters. Dirt or rust in the helical grooves on the armature shaft will prevent the

(continued on page 325)

FIGURE 7-26A. Disassembling a preengaged starter. First, identify the main components.

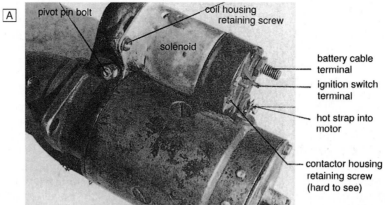

pivot pin bolt
coil housing retaining screw
solenoid
battery cable terminal
ignition switch terminal
hot strap into motor
contactor housing retaining screw (hard to see)

FIGURES 7-26B TO 7-26O. Step-by-step solenoid disassembly of a typical preengaged starter motor. Remove the battery cable (7-26B). Disconnect the solenoid from the starter motor (7-26C). Disconnect the cable to the ignition switch (7-26D). Take the cover bolts off the solenoid (7-26E and 7-26F). Bend the starter motor strap out of the way so the solenoid cover can be pulled off (7-26G). Remove the solenoid cover (7-26H); there is a spring in here that may fall out. A view of the contactor plate, showing the burned contactor (7-26I). Note the severe pitting on the surfaces of the contactor (the circular disc) and the points (7-26J). Sometimes the contactor can be flipped over to reveal an unused surface, and as in this case, the points can be rotated in their housing to bring a new surface into action (7-26K). Otherwise, they can be filed and sanded smooth. Removal of the rear plate to expose the brushes (7-26L and 7-26M). These brushes are worn almost completely down (7-26N and 7-26O). This starter motor is pretty well worn out!

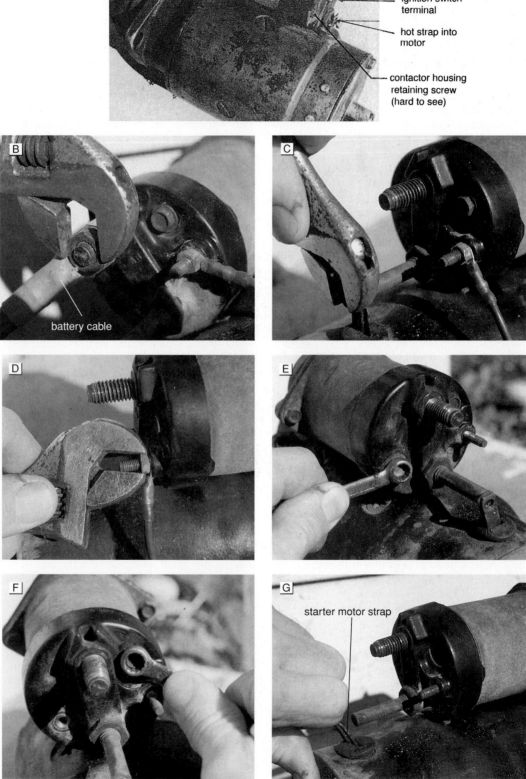

battery cable

starter motor strap

contactor

burned point that makes
contact with contactor

burned point

unused portion
of point

brushes almost
completely worn away

worn-out brush

commutator

FIGURES 7-27A TO 7-27E. Removing and disassembling another recalcitrant reconditioned starter motor. Note how poorly the brushes are seating on the commutator; whoever rebuilt this did a lousy job.

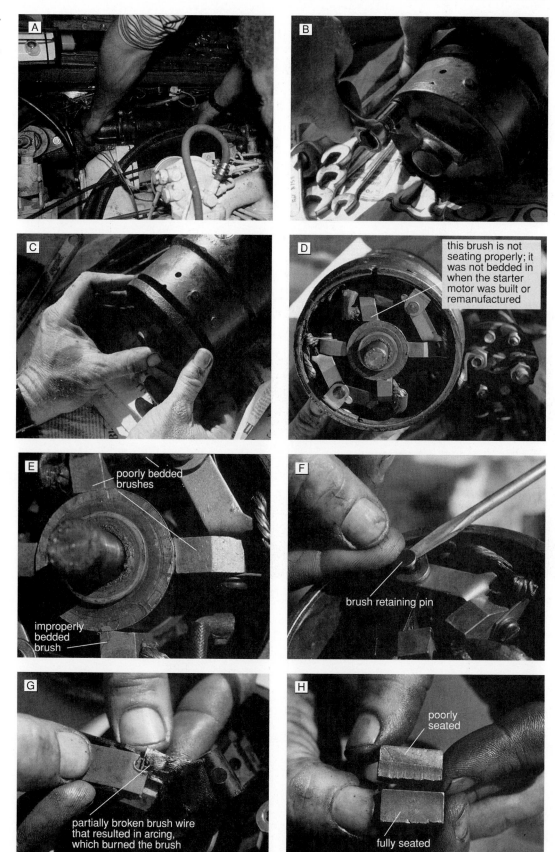

A

B

C

D
this brush is not seating properly; it was not bedded in when the starter motor was built or remanufactured

E
poorly bedded brushes

improperly bedded brush

F
brush retaining pin

FIGURES 7-27F AND 7-27G. We found a brush wire that was damaged and arcing to its brush.

G
partially broken brush wire that resulted in arcing, which burned the brush

H
poorly seated

fully seated

FIGURE 7-27H. A comparison of a properly seating brush with one that was never bedded in.

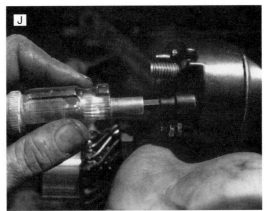

FIGURE 7-27I. Cleaning the commutator. There is a fair amount of pitting in evidence as a result of arcing from the poorly seated brushes.

FIGURES 7-27J TO 7-27L. Disassembly of the solenoid. More burning of electrical contact surfaces!

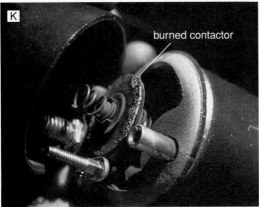

burned contactor

burned contactor and point

unused half of point that can be rotated into service

FIGURE 7-27M. Cleaning up a contact surface on a piece of emery cloth.

cleaning the point

emery cloth on a flat surface

(continued from page 321)
pinion from moving freely in and out of engagement with the flywheel.

A small resistance spring in the unit keeps the pinion away from the flywheel when the engine is running. If this spring rusts and breaks, the gear will keep vibrating up against the flywheel with a distinctive rattle.

In automotive use, the shaft and helical grooves are not oiled or greased since the lubricant picks up dust from any clutch plates and causes the pinion to stick. In marine use, however, there are no clutch plates in the flywheel housing and the shaft should be greased lightly to prevent rusting.

The pinion assembly is usually retained by a spring clip (a snap ring or circlip) on the end of the armature shaft, occasionally by a *reverse-threaded* nut and cotter pin (split pin). An inertia starter has a powerful *buffer* spring that must be compressed before the clip can be removed. Special tools are available for this, but a couple of small C-clamps or two pairs of adroitly handled Vise-Grips usually will do the trick.

Check the clutch unit on a preengaged starter by ensuring that it locks the pinion gear to the motor in one direction of rotation and freewheels in the other.

Electric Lights

Although individual electric lights on a boat draw relatively little current, the cumulative lighting load on many modern boats is one of the highest electrical loads—especially when halogen lights are sprinkled liberally all over the cabin overhead, as they tend to be on larger yachts (Figure 7-28). The interaction between these lights and the electrical system powering them is a complex one that raises not just the obvious issue—energy consumption—but also a number of other concerns, including lamp life expectancy, the quality of the light emitted, and the heat produced. These need to be looked at within the framework of significant technological developments in the lighting field that have occurred in recent years.

Today, in terms of lighting boats, there are a number of different technologies from which to choose:

- *Incandescent:* conventional lamps in which a resistive element heats up and emits light.
- *Halogen:* a variation on a conventional lamp that creates light somewhat more efficiently.
- *Xenon:* a modern replacement for many halogens.

- *Fluorescent:* these can be subdivided into traditional fluorescent lights (hot cathode fluorescents) and cold cathode fluorescents (CCF).
- *Light-emitting diodes (LEDs):* these produce light from semiconductors.

Following is a list of the key issues to consider with respect to any lighting technology:

- The efficacy at converting electricity to light, as measured in lumens per watt. A *lumen* is a measure of the all-around light output of a device. *Lumens per watt* is thus a measure of how much light is produced for a given level of energy consumption.
- The manner in which light output varies with fluctuations in the supply voltage, sometimes called *light variation percentage*. Voltage may range from as low as 11.0 volts on a 12-volt system to as high as 14.4 volts, with the light variation percentage being as high as 90%.
- The lamp's rated life expectancy, and the degree to which this is affected by fluctuations in voltage.
- The color of the light, which can vary from a

FIGURE 7-28. Multiple halogen lights in a modern boat (a Beneteau 57). *(Beneteau)*

reddish yellow to a cold white. Light color is expressed in terms of *color temperature*, in degrees Kelvin (K). Visible (red) light starts at around 1,000°K; lamps work their way up through reddish yellow (around 1,800°K) to a warm white (around 2,800°K), to a medium white (around 3,200°K), to a cool white (around 5,500°K).

- The impact of ambient temperature on the functioning of the light. Some fluorescents, for example, have difficulty starting in cold conditions.
- The external temperature of the lamp itself, which can vary from low (fluorescent) to extremely high (halogen).
- Whether or not a light can be dimmed.
- The lamp's ultraviolet (UV) output, which can fade fabrics, photographs, etc.
- The extent to which the light causes RFI (radio frequency interference). This primarily applies to fluorescents.
- Whether or not the lamp requires any special handling or installation requirements. Most halogens, for example, will be damaged by finger grease. And because of their high operating temperature, most halogens require protective lenses in order to prevent people and objects from getting burned.
- The ease of lamp replacement and maintenance. Fluorescents, in particular, use ballasts that require quite a bit of work to replace in the event they fail.
- Physical size and shape—surface or flush-mount, etc.
- Price.

Let's use these parameters to review the competing technologies.

Incandescent Lights

An incandescent lamp has a tungsten filament in a glass envelope filled with an inert gas such as nitrogen or argon. The filament has a resistance that causes it to heat up when a current is passed through it. When the temperature gets above 1,000°K, visible light is produced, but the heat causes some of the filament to evaporate. The more power applied (that is, the higher the voltage):

- The higher the temperature.
- The more light produced.
- The more the wavelength of the light shifts toward blue (i.e., bright white).
- The faster the tungsten filament evaporates

and fails. The tungsten ends up on the inside of the lamp glass as a black deposit.

Incandescents are extremely inefficient at converting electrical energy into light, often producing less than 10 lumens per watt, with a maximum efficacy of 17.5 lumens per watt. (The latter is not found on boats, where the lamps tend to be toward the lower end of the efficiency spectrum.) Fluctuations in voltage have a major impact on light output, which can vary by up to 90% with the kind of voltage fluctuations found on boats. Bulb life is generally under 1,000 hours and is dramatically shortened at higher voltages, such as those typically found with fast-charging systems. At 14.4 volts, the life expectancy of a nominal 12-volt bulb may be reduced to as little as 20% of its rated life.

Incandescent lamps are commonly found inside dome lights and in reading lamps. Their chief benefits are that they are inexpensive and widely available, produce an attractive light color, create no RFI, are not sensitive to ambient temperature, and require no special handling. UV light is not an issue. They can be dimmed by lowering the supply current, which will lower the temperature of the filament and shift the color of the light more toward red. In spite of these benefits, they have little place on a boat whose owners are conscious of energy and maintenance issues.

Halogen Lights

Halogen lights (sometimes known as "quartz halogen") and xenon lights are refinements of a regular incandescent bulb, generally at a higher cost. As with other incandescents, halogen lamps have a tungsten filament that is heated to give off light. In the halogen lamp, the filament is mounted inside a crystal ("quartz") case filled with an inert gas (nitrogen, argon, krypton, xenon) to which is added halogen. Xenon lamps have xenon as the primary inert gas.

When the lamp is lit, particles of tungsten evaporate from the filament. In a conventional incandescent lamp, this evaporation eventually leads to lamp burnout. In a halogen lamp, the evaporated tungsten combines with the halogen vapor and gets redeposited on the filament, although not necessarily in the same place it came from. Consequently, the filament eventually thins out and fails.

The filament in a halogen lamp can be raised to a higher temperature than that in a conventional incandescent, creating a whiter light that:

- Renders most objects in their natural colors.
- Results in a higher light output for the same power consumption.

- Gives a longer lamp life than regular incandescent lamps.
- Produces no blackening of the bulb over the life of the lamp, resulting in very little light loss as the lamp ages.

The nature of the bulbs and filaments is such that the light can be highly focused, making halogen lamps excellent reading lamps, in which case they are fitted with a parabolic aluminized reflector (PAR).

The extent to which halogen lamps are more efficient than regular incandescents is quite variable, however, and is often not as significant as many boatowners believe. Typically, halogens put out around 15 lumens per watt, although some give less, while a few may go as high as 20 lumens per watt. Lamp life is around 2,000 hours at rated voltage (12.6 volts on a 12-volt system), although it is dramatically shortened at higher voltages. At 13.8 volts (the lowest likely voltage regulator setting on an alternator or battery charger on a 12-volt system), life expectancy of a nominal 12-volt halogen bulb is reduced to just 30% of rated life; at 14.4 volts, life expectancy is below 20% of rated life (Figure 7-29).

Note also that 24-volt incandescent and halogen lamps tend not to have as long a service life as 12-volt versions. This is because the filaments in the 24-volt models are finer and more prone to damage from vibration and the shocks that occur when a boat is pounding to windward. Given the cost of replacing halogen bulbs, on 24-volt boats with a large number of halogen lights, it's worth considering using 12-volt units powered by a DC-to-DC converter that steps down 24 volts to a stable 12 volts. Even on a 12-volt boat, many larger yachts use a DC-to-DC converter (12 volts to 12 volts) to ensure a stable, relatively low voltage for halogen lighting circuits.

Halogen lamps must run hot if the tungsten evaporating from the filament is to react with the halogen and get redeposited on the filament. Hot spots on the bulbs can go as high as 1,230°F/670°C. That's why halogen bulbs call for special handling: finger grease will get etched into the glass, causing damage; the lamps need a covering lens to prevent people from getting burned and to prevent the lamp from starting a fire if something comes in contact with it; and the installation must ensure adequate airflow to dissipate the heat from the fixture. The lamps also emit UV rays that can damage fabrics and artwork, though many halogen lenses block these rays.

Halogens can be dimmed, but then the internal temperature drops to the point at which the tungsten vapor does not combine with the halogen, substantially reducing lamp life. If the lamp is subsequently run hot, however, tungsten deposits on the glass will be vaporized and redeposited on the filament, limiting the loss of bulb life. As with incandescents, dimming shifts the light output toward the red end of the spectrum. Halogens create no RFI and are not sensitive to ambient temperature.

Note that although it's possible to buy adapters that convert standard incandescent lamp fittings to halogen fittings, *this should only be done if the light fixture has been designed to handle the additional heat of the bulbs.*

Xenon Lights

Xenon lights are similar to halogens, but xenon is the primary inert gas. Of all the gases commonly used to fill lamps, xenon is the most effective at lowering the rate of evaporation of the filament and therefore extending lamp life. A xenon lamp's life varies from a rated 5,000 hours up to 20,000 hours. Xenon lamps put out a white light (generally around 2,800°K) but operate much cooler than halogens, and as a result, require no special handling or covering lenses. Xenon bulbs are less sensitive to fluctuations in voltage and can be dimmed with no loss of life (life expectancy actually goes up when the bulb is dimmed). They emit no UV rays. But the xenon reduces the efficacy of a lamp to between 8 and 13 lumens per watt, placing xenon lamps somewhere between incandescents and halogens.

Xenon gas is expensive, so the lamps vary in the percentage of xenon gas in the mix filling the bulb. As a general rule, the more xenon, the longer the life but the lower the efficiency. XH bulbs are a hybrid xenon/halogen with a brighter, whiter light and shorter life expectancy; X bulbs have more xenon. In all cases, lamp quality

FIGURE 7-29. Lamp life versus voltage for halogen lamps.

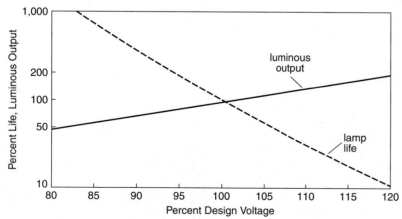

Note the radical change in lamp life from over 1,000% of rated life at 80% of design voltage to 10% of rated life at 120% of design voltage.

varies from one manufacturer to another, with a significant impact on service life. THHC (www.thhclighting.com) is recognized by many as a market leader; the company calls its popular XH bulb a Xelogen.

In most applications, xenon lamps are a better choice than halogens because of their longer service life, tolerance of voltage fluctuations, and ease of handling. Even so, on an energy-conscious boat, fluorescent lights are almost always a better choice than xenons.

Note that the xenon lamps referred to in this section should not be confused with the high-intensity discharge (HID) xenon technology found in modern automotive headlights. This technology has not yet found its way onto boats, other than in some spotlights.

Fluorescent Lights

Fluorescent lights use a light-producing technology that's completely different from all lamps with resistive filaments. Fluorescents have a glass tube filled with an inert gas (generally argon) and a small amount of mercury. The inside of the tube is coated with phosphor powder, and there is an *electrode* (cathode) at each end (Figure 7-30). A high AC voltage is applied to the electrodes, causing electrons to flow from one to the other. The electrons interact with the mercury, causing it to release photons of UV light that react with the phosphor to emit visible light. The key result from a boatowner's perspective is that very little of the available energy is turned to heat as opposed to light, resulting in a light output of anywhere from 50 lumens per watt to over 100 lumens per watt. This is three to six times more efficient than incandescents, halogens, and xenons (and also most current LED technology—see below).

Put another way, an entire cabin can be lit with a 26-watt fluorescent light that puts out around 1,700 lumens. For the same power consumption, only around 400 lumens of light output will be produced by an incandescent dome or reading light, and perhaps 500 lumens from a xenon or halogen light.

Fluorescents also have a high rated life expectancy—anywhere from 3,000 hours up to 20,000 hours—although in practice the extent to which this life span is realized varies widely. It depends on such factors as the type of fluorescent, the quality of construction, and the operating environment.

Fluorescent lights operate on high-voltage AC power, which can be supplied at line frequency (60 Hz or 50 Hz), resulting in the flickering seen with many fluorescents, or at high frequency (typically, 20,000 Hz or higher), in which case there is no flickering.

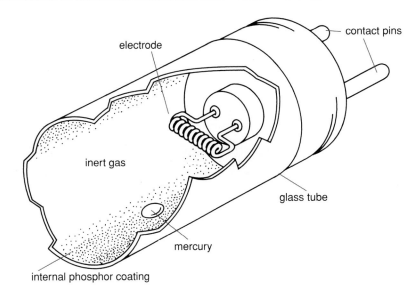

FIGURE 7-30. Fluorescent lamp construction. *(Jim Sollers)*

Fluorescents that run off a DC power supply (12 volts or 24 volts) have a built-in DC-to-AC inverter to create the necessary AC supply, which is invariably output from the inverter at a high frequency. Compact fluorescents also operate at a high frequency. Unfortunately, high-frequency switching often generates RFI. Fluorescents must be built in a manner that suppresses RFI, especially if the light unit is close to a navigation station or anywhere else where there may be sensitive electronics.

Regardless of whether the power source is AC or DC, there will be a transformer to step up the voltage. The device that does the voltage and frequency conversion, and which includes any inverter, is called a *ballast* (Figure 7-31).

The degree to which different fluorescent lights are sensitive to fluctuations in the supply voltage, both in terms of the variation in the light output and also life expectancy, is largely a function of the sophistication of the electronics. Some brands are quite sensitive, and some show little sensitivity. The electronics in the ballast can be manipulated to produce different color temperatures, resulting in anything from a very cool white light to a relatively warm light.

There is no difference between DC and AC fluorescent tubes. Any tube of the correct

FIGURE 7-31. A ballast unit in a Thin-Lite fluorescent light.

transformer

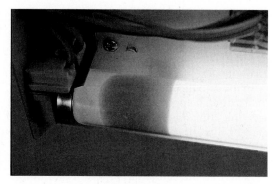

wattage and size, with the right connecting pins, will work. There are, however, significant differences in manufacturing quality, so it's best to buy name-brand lamps.

Once a fluorescent light starts to act up (e.g., it's slow to come on, it flickers, or there is a purple flash at the end of the tube when coming on), or once the ends of the tube are substantially blackened (Figures 7-32A and 7-32B), the tube should be replaced right away, rather than waiting for total failure. This will help protect the much more expensive—and harder to replace—ballast unit that powers the tube. In a dual-tube unit, both tubes should be replaced at the same time. Note that although 13-watt (single tube) and 26-watt (dual tube) units are the most common fluorescent lights on boats, 15- or 30-watt units, which use a larger-diameter 15-watt tube, are more efficient and less prone to failure.

Since the marine environment is humid, all fluorescent lights on boats should have special humidity protection, often designated by the letters "HH" for "high humidity."

Hot cathode fluorescent lights. Conventional hot cathode fluorescent lights have tungsten electrodes (cathodes) that are similar to the filament in an incandescent, halogen, or xenon lamp. The electrodes get hot, resulting in a slow loss of tungsten, manifested by a blackening of the ends of the tubes. The electrodes are relatively fragile and can be destroyed by shocks and vibration. Failure of an electrode puts the lamp out of service.

The electrodes are most stressed when the lamp is turned on, especially in cold weather. For this reason, life expectancy is at least partially a function of the number of starts. It's generally not a good idea to install fluorescent lights where they will be repeatedly turned on and off for short lengths of time—for example, in a head compartment—and conventional fluorescents are inappropriate on boats that will spend extended periods in cold climates.

Rated life expectancy is based on a stable voltage (12.6 volts for a 12-volt system) and temperature (70°F/21°C), with the light left on all the time. However on a boat, voltages may fall below 11.0 volts when the batteries are down or if there is significant voltage drop in the wiring, they may rise above 14.4 volts when charging with a multistep regulator, and the light may get turned on and off frequently. As a result, life expectancy can be a fraction of rated life.

Many fluorescent lights marketed for boats have come out of the recreational vehicle market. The best known of these are manufactured by Thin-Lite (www.thinlite.com), whose products are economical and generally work well. But they may not be RFI suppressed or humidity protected, and they are significantly and adversely affected by fluctuating voltages and temperatures. At the present time, the Cadillacs of the marine fluorescent light market are manufactured by Resolux (a German company distributed in the United States by Imtra—www.imtra.com) and Alpenglow (www.alpenglowlights.com; Figure 7-33).

The Resolux lights in particular:

- Have high efficacy (80 to 100 lumens per watt).
- Are tolerant of substantial voltage fluctuations (depending on the model, the light output

FIGURE 7-33. Alpenglow fluorescent lights on our old Pacific Seacraft 40—excellent, reliable lights.

Troubleshooting Fluorescent Lights

Most fluorescent lights incorporate a transformer (also known as a ballast) and a starter, which is a cylinder that plugs into a fixture inside the lamp base. Fluorescents running on 12 volts or 24 volts do not have starters. If a fluorescent lamp flickers on and off or will not come on:

- Check the power supply and voltage drop at the light (Figures 7-34A and 7-34B).
- Switch off the unit, remove the tubes, clean all contacts and pins on the light fixture and tubes with a clean rag or 400- to 600-grit wet-or-dry sandpaper, replace the tubes, and try again. (Most tubes are removed by twisting 90 degrees and pulling down gently.)
- Still no light? Try a new tube. If the unit has two tubes, replace both.
- Still no light? Try a new starter, if the unit incorporates one.
- Still no light? Replace the ballast. The new one will have a wiring diagram with it, or a diagram will be glued to the lamp base.

switch is turned off; as a result the meter shows system voltage across the switch

FIGURES 7-34A AND 7-34B. Checking the power supply (voltage) at a lamp and its amp draw.

---

only varies by 8% to 15% over a range of voltage fluctuations from 10 volts to 15 volts on a 12-volt system).

- Are protected against low voltage, which can burn up the ballast on some other units.
- Have a high rated life expectancy (8,000 hours).
- Are well shielded for RFI suppression.
- Are protected against high humidity.
- Will operate in temperatures down to 5°F/ –15°C.

Cold cathode fluorescent lights. Conventional fluorescents heat thin-filament cathodes to a high temperature. The cathodes degrade every time the lamp is lit and slowly burn out—the most common mechanism for tube failure. As the cathodes age, the tube gets harder to light up, which stresses the ballast unit and leads to ballast failure. The thin filaments are also susceptible to damage from shocks and vibration.

In the last few years, Taylorbrite (www.taylorbrite.com) has introduced a new technology—cold cathode fluorescents (CCF)—to the marine marketplace. These lights have a far more substantial cathode than a conventional fluorescent. The cathode is activated by an electronic process rather than by heating (Figure 7-35). The net result is improved efficacy (80 lumens per watt) over many traditional fluorescents, but with less sensitivity to voltage fluctuations, shocks, and vibration. The Taylorbrite units are "Marine UL Listed," which means they

FIGURE 7-35. Preliminary testing of CCF lights.

have been tested for (among other things) shock, vibration, moisture resistance, and RFI suppression.

These lights have a warm white output (3,000°K). The nature of the electronic ballast means the units can be dimmed, which isn't possible with most conventional fluorescents because they need to run at full power to keep the filaments hot. The life expectancy of cold cathode fluorescents is not affected by being frequently switched on for short periods of time. They have a significantly longer predicted life span than a traditional fluorescent—rated at 5,000 to 25,000 hours.

This is a great set of characteristics. We will have to see how the lights work out in service in the marine environment. One issue that will be of concern to long-distance cruisers is the fact that currently cold cathode fluorescents have no replaceable parts—if a lamp fails, the entire unit has to be replaced (Figure 7-36). If this lighting is installed on a cruising boat, it would be prudent to stock up on a few spares.

LED Lights

LED lights hold great promise for energy conservation, but fully realizing the benefits—especially in a marine environment—requires a reasonable understanding of the technology.

LEDs are commonly red and green, although they can be found in any pure color (blue, green, yellow, red). As with fluorescent lights, any visible color can be created by activating phosphors with UV or blue light or by combining pure colors. White light, for example, can be created by combining red, green, and blue, which are its constituent parts; these are known as RGB lights.

For years, getting white light out of an LED was the holy grail of the LED industry. In 1993,

Shuji Nakamura, working for the Nichia Corporation, discovered how to create a strong blue source from gallium nitride semiconductors, and based on this discovery, he created white light by exciting phosphors (Nakamura is now a folk hero in Japan). Since then, other technologies have been developed that have substantially reduced the price of white LEDs and produced a much warmer white light—now as low as 3,200°K as opposed to the 5,500°K cool white of other white LEDs. There has been a quantum leap in the light output of these devices, with the newer ones putting out the equivalent light of hundreds of LEDs from just a few years ago, making white LEDs increasingly cost effective and popular.

As a source of light, LEDs have always had a low efficacy, generally ranging from around 10 lumens per watt up to a high of 20 lumens per watt (more on quantifying LED output below). However, this is rapidly changing. At present (2005), the best widely available white LEDs (for example, Luxeon LEDs from Lumiled—www.lumiled.com) deliver more than 20 lumens per watt, with efficacy predicted to rise to more than 50 lumens per watt in the near future. Efficacies of over 60 lumens per watt have already been achieved in the laboratory, with forecasts of theoretical efficacies as high as 200 lumens per watt. As an example of how fast this technology is developing, between 2002 and 2003, the efficacy of Luxeon white LEDs rose by 20% and the brightness by 250%, while the per-lumen cost dropped 50%. In 1993 it took 200 red LEDs to create enough light for a traffic light, in 1996 it was down to 100, in 1998 below 20, and today it can be done in the laboratory with 1 LED.

Beam width. The manner in which LEDs are constructed limits the light output to a fixed beam, as opposed to the all-around output from most other light sources. In the past, LED beam widths have typically been narrow, but at the time of this writing have been widened to 140 degrees.

To get significant light output over a significant area from narrow-beam LEDs with a low light output, a number of them must be clustered together and angled in different directions, which is still a common approach. The result is not much more efficient—and sometimes less efficient—than incandescent and halogen lights; currently, the *best* output is about 15 to 20 lumens per watt of energy consumed, as opposed to 50 to 100 lumens for fluorescents. This simple statement provides a misleading picture, however, because it does not take into account a benefit of the directional nature of LED lights.

The typical incandescent, halogen, xenon, or

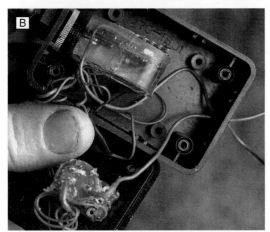

FIGURES 7-37A AND 7-37B. Deep Creek Design prototype for LED area lighting with just four high-intensity LEDs (left). Note it is being powered by a 9-volt battery! The same light also has a red LED (right).

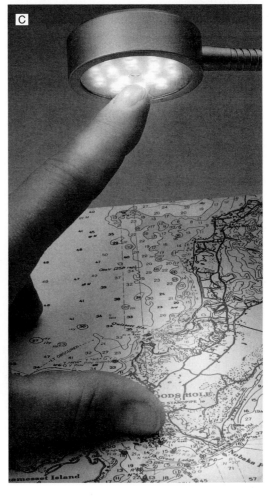

FIGURE 7-38C. Chart lighting that is activated, and changed from white to red, by touching the lamp surface! *(Courtesy Frensch)*

FIGURES 7-38A AND 7-38B. Deep Creek Design prototype for chart lighting (7-38A). There's a sophisticated electronics package in here (7-38B), including a pulse-width-modulated DC-to-DC inverter.

fluorescent light has some kind of a lens or reflector to channel light emitted in nonuseful directions into a useful direction. This redirection typically has high associated light losses. An LED light, on the other hand, can be designed so that the entire output is directed where it is wanted, so that substantially fewer lumens of light output are needed to provide the same level of illumination in the desired area. Put another way, an LED light with an efficacy of 20 lumens per watt can compete with a fluorescent with an efficacy of, say, 40 lumens per watt. Once LED efficacy starts to creep up toward 40 lumens per watt, even for general lighting purposes, they will be able to compete with the efficacy of most fluorescents (Figures 7-37A and 7-37B).

In the meantime, LEDs already have clear advantages for courtesy lighting and where low-level, highly-focused task lighting is required—for example, some reading lights and lighting of instrument panels (Figures 7-38A, 7-38B, and 7-38C).

Candelas Versus Lumens

LED output is generally given in *millicandela* (mcd), a measure of the intensity of a light in a given direction as measured at its source, rather than lumens. (1,000 millicandela = 1 candela, also known as 1 candlepower.) When comparing one LED light to another, the mcd rating needs to be considered in conjunction with the viewing angle; for any given mcd rating, the greater the viewing angle, the more the light output.

However, defining light output in terms of candelas gives little sense of illuminating capability. A light source could be emitting with an intensity of 1 candela in all directions or just in a narrow beam. Its intensity is still 1 candela, but its ability to illuminate an area will be very different.

A lumen, on the other hand, is a function of both candelas and area. It is a measure of the total light output of a device, which is why it provides a much better general basis for comparing output and efficacy.

However, as noted in the text, unless all-around lighting is wanted, light output measured in lumens still does not necessarily reflect the real-life efficacy of a particular light source because much of the light may be emitted in a direction that is not useful. In terms of *area illumination*, the key criterion is *lumen output over the area that needs to be lit*. Since this depends on the specific lighting situation, there is unfortunately no single published parameter that allows a definitive comparison of one light to another. The context must always be taken into consideration.

In some other applications, the key criterion is *intensity* (candela) *over a defined arc*, rather than the ability to illuminate an area. This is particularly the case for navigation and anchor lights.

The benefits of LEDs are especially noticeable for red and green navigation lights (Figures 7-39A and 7-39B). Red and green LEDs utilize the full lumens-per-watt output of the light and concentrate it solely on the necessary arc. By contrast, putting a colored lens in front of an incandescent bulb radiating light in all directions reduces the light output to between 1 to 5 lumens per watt. The lens absorbs all the color wavelengths other than red or green, allowing only the red and green through, which effectively reduces the efficacy of the light to a

FIGURE 7-39A. Red and green LEDs in a masthead tricolor light. *(Deep Creek Design)*

FIGURE 7-39B. An LED navigation light from Orca Green Marine Technology (OGM).

fraction of its rated efficacy. (The same considerations apply to red nighttime lighting inside a boat, and also, incidentally, to traffic lights, in which a 12-watt LED cluster can replace a 150-watt lightbulb.)

Other considerations. LEDs, including their drivers, are solid-state devices with no moving parts, no filaments, no mercury, and no fragile glass. As a result, they have high resistance to shocks and an extremely long life. This long life expectancy makes it reasonable to consider placing LEDs in totally sealed—and therefore waterproof—housings. Essentially, the entire fixture will be replaced if the light fails.

AC GENERATORS, DC GENERATORS, ELECTRIC MOTORS (DC AND AC), AND ELECTRIC LIGHTS

LED Drivers

An LED is a semiconductor device that is very sensitive to changes in current (amperage). A small change in applied voltage can push enough current through an LED to destroy it. For this reason, LEDs must be used with some variant of a current-regulating device known as a *driver*. The driver may be nothing more than a simple resistor, but is more likely to be a *linear regulator* or a full-fledged, multifunction DC-to-DC converter.

Resistors are inefficient and dissipate much of the current on the circuit as heat, which negates the primary purpose of the LED in the first place—efficacy—and contributes to premature failure since LEDs, like most electronic devices, are sensitive to heat. The output voltage varies with the input voltage, and higher voltages will reduce LED life. Resistors are being supplanted by other technologies.

Linear regulators are still resistive-type devices—meaning that any power at a voltage level above that used by the LED is wasted as heat—but they do produce a more stable power supply than a simple resistor. The output voltage typically varies with input voltage, negatively impacting LED life, but not to the same extent as with a resistor. Linear regulators are widely used in the current crop of LED lights available for boats. Over time, they are likely to be supplanted by DC-to-DC converters.

DC-to-DC converters are the wave of the future for driving LED lights. These converters are 90% efficient and as a result waste very little energy in the form of heat, which in turn is important in prolonging the life of the newer, high-power LEDs. As with other DC-to-DC converters, these devices:

- Maintain a tightly controlled output voltage.
- Accept a wide range of input voltages (some will take anything from 6 volts to 40 volts DC).

- Can employ pulse width modulation to dim lights electronically so that no energy is wasted in the dimming process (as opposed to resistive-type dimming that wastes energy as heat).
- Can include a thermal management algorithm to reduce the light output if the LEDs start to get dangerously warm (for example, if a light unit is mounted in a cabin overhead with restricted ventilation and a tropical sun beating down on the deck above).
- Given the necessary existence of a microprocessor within the unit, they can be designed to include other benefits that innovative and imaginative engineers will undoubtedly devise, such as changing the color temperature of the light.

An interesting feature of dimming by pulse width modulation is that whereas the color temperature of incandescent, halogen, and xenon bulbs shifts toward red as a light is dimmed, an LED can be dimmed with no change in color temperature. Essentially, the driver is turning the LED on and off hundreds of times a second; to dim it, the LED is turned on fewer and fewer times. Whereas red symbols on a chart become hard to see under a red light, with a dimmed white light none of the chart colors "fade."

Note that as with other solid-state devices that switch currents at high frequencies, drivers based on DC-to-DC converters can create significant amounts of RFI, so it's important that they be RFI suppressed.

It's important to note, however, that life expectancy numbers are derived in laboratory conditions. White LEDs have a life expectancy of 50,000 hours, as opposed to 100,000 hours for other colors. Well before LEDs reach the end of life, there is a significant loss of light output, such that Taylorbrite only rates its white LED units for 10,000 hours, and some units from other manufacturers are rated as low as 3,000 hours. The new Luxeons are reputed to retain 70% of their original output after 50,000 hours of operation. Numbers I have seen from other companies indicate a fairly linear loss of approximately 2% of light output per 1,000 hours of use. Unlike other light sources, end of life for an LED is defined as the point at which its light output has declined to 50% of its initial output, rather than in terms of complete failure.

This rated life expectancy is the rated life of the LEDs themselves. The drivers will have their own life expectancy, which may turn out to be the limiting factor in the life of the light. There are a number of unknowns here that cannot be completely resolved in the laboratory.

Looking ahead. In short, LED lights are still expensive, have decidedly limited light outputs—although that's constantly and rapidly improving—and to a considerable extent, have an unknown life expectancy in the marine envi-

FIGURES 7-40A AND 7-40B. First-generation (left) and second-generation (right) LED anchor lights. The second generation has considerably more sophisticated electronics, more rugged construction, and greater visibility. *(Deep Creek Design)*

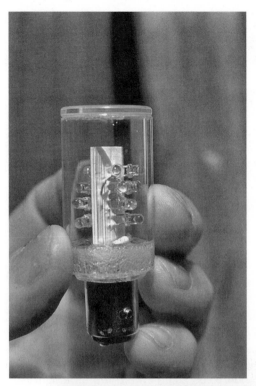

FIGURE 7-41. The OGM light shown in Figure 7-39B also includes white LEDs so that when it's used as a masthead tricolor light, it can do double duty as an anchor light.

ronment. Nevertheless, the technology is exciting and definitely worth watching.

At present, the premium LED lighting in the marine market are those units produced by Deep Creek Design (www.firststarled.com). The company has consistently been on the cutting edge of this technology, and its products have a number of features not offered by the competition. For several years, we have had one of their FirstStar anchor lights (Figure 7-40A). A built-in photoelectric cell turns the light off in the daytime. It fits a standard bulb socket, puts out an excellent light, and draws well under half an amp (at 12 volts), but costs over $100. The latest generation (MKIII) bulb produces more light for less current draw (Figure 7-40B). As I write, I have on my desk samples of LED task lighting and area lighting. Another innovative company is OGM (www.orcagreen.com; Figure 7-41).

2004 saw the release of the first generation of LED dome lights powerful enough to compete with a 30- to 40-watt incandescent light or a 15-watt fluorescent fixture, while only using around 5 watts of power (0.4 amp at 12 volts). It doesn't seem unreasonable to think that within a few years LED lighting will almost completely supplant all other forms of DC lighting on an energy-efficient boat since it will be both more cost effective and efficient.

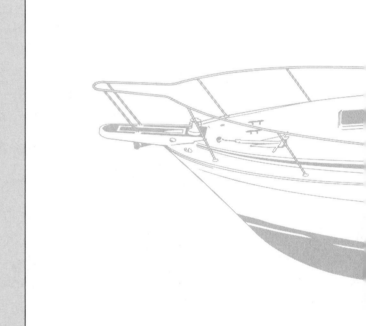

CHAPTER 8

FIGURE 8-1. Trouble-free marine electronics depend to a large extent on proper installation. *(Jim Sollers)*

————————— 12 VDC

- - - - - - - - - 12 V ground
(return)

— · — · — · — 120 VAC

▨▨▨▨▨ ground

(1) GPS antenna
(2) insulated backstay SSB antenna
(3) copper mesh ground plane
(4) radar
(5) VHF antenna
(6) wind indicator
(7) weatherfax
(8) radios
(9) antenna tuner
(10) copper foil ground plane
(11) depth sounder/speed/log transducers
(12) instruments
(13) battery isolation switch
(14) batteries

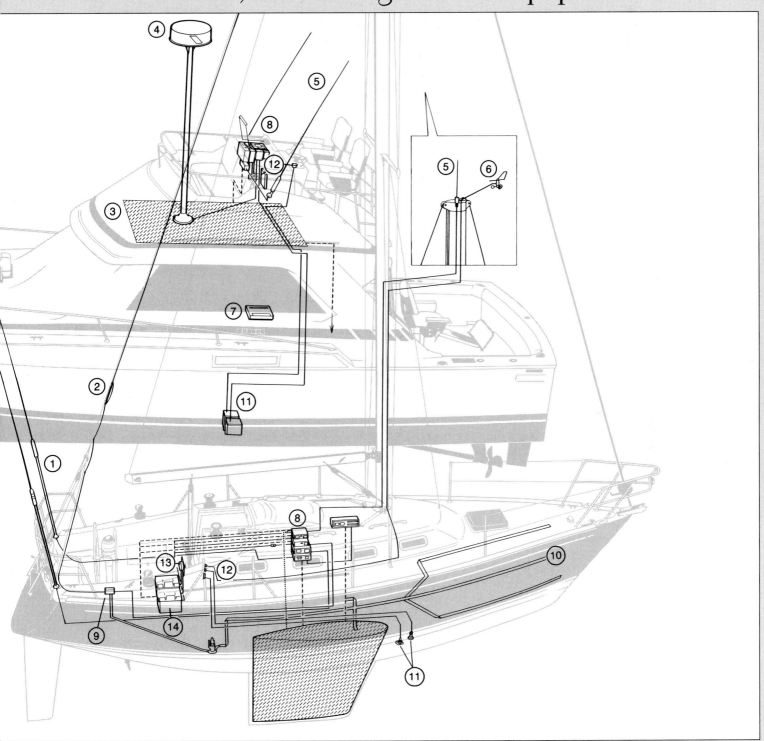

With the growing use of chip-based technology in everything from washing machines to sophisticated navigation systems, modern boats have an ever-increasing variety of electronic components and devices on board, all in a humid and salt-laden atmosphere that is a naturally harsh environment for all electronics. Added to this is the fact that a boat is also a highly compact environment, so devices end up in close proximity to one another, with cable and antenna runs for numerous pieces of equipment frequently bundled together, creating a fertile breeding ground for *electromagnetic interference* (EMI) and *radio frequency interference* (RFI). (Making a distinction between the two is important to some technical folks, but is not important in terms of the concerns of this chapter.)

Ensuring *electromagnetic compatibility* (EMC) between devices has long been a concern of organizations that write standards for ships, and it has been taken up by the ISO, resulting in a number of directives. In this respect, the ISO is ahead of the ABYC, with the result that the CE mark on electrical and electronic equipment is a useful indication that it meets fairly rigorous EMC standards. Faced with a choice between a piece of equipment that is CE-marked and one that is not, and in the absence of other determining factors, I would choose the marked equipment. (In the United States, look for compliance with FCC Rule 15, Part B, also known as FCC 15B.)

Given well-built devices, most electronic equipment is highly reliable *as long as it is kept cool and dry*. Equipment that is placed in well-protected and ventilated areas, with unobstructed cooling vents, should give years of trouble-free use. Difficulties that do arise, including EMI/RFI, are usually a result of problems that are *external* to the equipment. We can often do something about these problems, which is the focus of this chapter.

Marine Electronics

Preliminary Troubleshooting

Unit will not come online or operates intermittently. As with all other electrical equipment, the primary suspect is always the power supply. Check all switches, breakers, and fuses. Check the equipment manual to see if there are any internal fuses that might have blown. Some units—most notably radar—may have more than one fuse.

Check the voltage across the power leads as close to the equipment as possible. Check for voltage drop *with the unit switched on*. Check radios in the *transmit* mode, since this draws the most current (see Chapter 4 for more on voltage drop tests).

An SSB draws a particularly high amperage in the transmit mode (up to 30 amps at 12 volts). It is normally rated for operation at 13.8 volts (on the assumption that an engine-driven alternator is in operation). Even with a good, low-resistance circuit, when transmitting without a DC generating source online, if the battery is at all low, undersized, or starting to fail, the voltage is likely to fall well below the rated operating voltage, lowering performance. It may be necessary to run the engine.

If a voltage test at the equipment reveals low voltage, check the voltage across the battery, with the equipment in its maximum-current-draw mode. If the voltage falls at the battery, the battery is the problem (Chapter 3). If the battery voltage holds up, the problem is in the circuit—check all connections, terminal blocks, fuse holders, and switches for voltage drop (Chapter 4).

Unit comes online but gives no data (or obviously incorrect data). If the device has power, and a voltage drop test has shown no unacceptable losses in the line, the problem lies elsewhere:

Operator error. The number one suspect is the operator, especially with a more-sophisticated device like a GPS. Failure to study owner's manuals and memory lapses from infrequent use both contribute to such problems. But perhaps the most difficult errors to spot are those that arise from a firm but faulty memory of how to operate a piece of equipment, since we are convinced we are doing things right!

Difficulties also arise from entering incorrect data. For example, common errors include confusion between local time, daylight savings time, and GMT; entering latitudes as south instead of north; entering longitudes as east instead of west; and punching in the wrong coordinates on waypoints.

Voltage fluctuations. A number of problems are associated with low- or high-voltage conditions. Engine cranking will sometimes pull system voltage below the critical minimum needed to maintain internal memories, which become

Troubleshooting Chart 8-1.
Electronic Equipment Problems: Unit Will Not Come Online

Symptom: No lights, no beeps, etc.

Is there a problem with the voltage supply? **NO** **TEST:** Check the voltage at the equipment when it is turned on.	**YES** **FIX:** If no volts or low volts, check the battery, switches, fuses, connections, etc., for voltage drop as outlined in Chapter 4.
Are there blown fuses or tripped circuit breakers within the unit? **NO**	**YES** **FIX:** Replace or reset as necessary.
If unit still will not come online, call a specialist.	

Troubleshooting Chart 8-2.
Electronic Equipment Problems: Unit Comes On but Gives No Data or Incorrect Data

Is the data entered inaccurately? **NO** **TEST:** Check procedural execution against instructions in owner's manual.	**YES** **FIX:** Study owner's manuals and reprogram unit, carefully entering data. See text for common GPS errors.
Is the data itself incorrect? **NO** **TEST:** Check the programming—GMT, latitude and longitude, waypoints, etc.	**YES** **FIX:** Reprogram the unit as necessary. Note: If the unit operates properly after reprogramming, but the symptoms recur after the unit has been turned off, the internal memory battery is probably dead; replace it.
Are voltage fluctuations affecting the unit? **NO** **TEST:** Check for voltage fluctuations at the unit, particularly low voltage during use of high-load items (e.g., engine cranking, electric windlass).	**YES** **FIX:** If there is low voltage or voltage spikes, review the boat's DC systems installation; if necessary, connect the unit to a separate battery.
Is interference affecting the unit? **NO** **TEST:** Check for interference—noise on radios, low signal-to-noise ratio (SNR) readings on lorans and ham radio, lines on TV and other screens, and random readings on depth sounders.	**YES** **FIX:** If interference is present, isolate the source by progressively turning off electrical equipment until the interference stops. Correct the problem. Alternatively, tune a portable radio to the operating frequency of the malfunctioning unit and move the radio around using it as a "noise sniffer."
Are the unit's ground connections dirty? **NO** **TEST:** Check all ground connections.	**YES** **FIX:** Disconnect and clean all ground connections—even if they appear sound. If unit gives correct data after this fix, the equipment is OK. If problem persists, go to next step. *continued*

Is the antenna sited incorrectly? **NO** **TEST:** Follow hints given in text.	**YES** **FIX:** Move antenna and observe whether improved performance results.
Is the coaxial cable or its connectors faulty? **NO** **TEST:** Remove the coax connection from the back of the equipment and inspect closely for corrosion; repeat for any other in-line connectors. Just behind the coax connection to the equipment (or any other in-line connectors) carefully peel back a small piece of the outer coax insulation and inspect the braid for tarnishing and corrosion. If both ends of the coaxial cable can be disconnected, test with an ohmmeter (R x 100 scale) from the center pin of one connector to its case. Any reading less than infinity indicates an internal short (probably in one of the connectors). Now short the center pin on the connector to its case and test between the pin and the case on the other connector (R x 1 scale). Any reading of more than 2 or 3 ohms indicates excessive resistance.	**YES** **FIX:** Clean connections. Replace shorted or defective cable and connectors. If the braid is corroded, replace the coax and its connection. If the braid is clean and shiny, replace the insulation and seal with 3M 5200 or some other sealant.

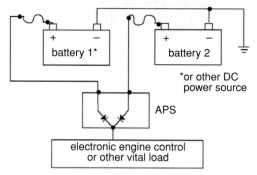

FIGURE 8-2. The wiring diagram for Newmar's Automatic Power Selector. *(Newmar)*

corrupted and must be reset and reprogrammed. Some large electric winches may affect memory-based equipment the same way. The solution is to:

- Provide a large-enough battery bank to handle these peak loads.

- Connect electronic equipment to a separate battery that is not subjected to these loads. (However, in general I do not recommend separate electronics batteries—see Chapter 1 and below.)

- Turn off electronics during periods of high battery demand (but this is, in effect, an admission that the DC system has not been adequately designed and set up—the DC system needs attention).

- Provide some kind of an uninterrupted power supply (UPS), generally a DC-to-DC converter with its own internal battery and battery charger (see Chapter 2). Another approach is to install an Automatic Power Selector (available from Newmar—www.newmarpower.com—and others), a device wired between two battery banks that automatically selects the one with the highest voltage (Figure 8-2). (Note that the APS is little more than a couple of isolation diodes. As such, it introduces a volt drop between 0.6 and 0.9 volt on

the circuit to the electronics, and thus, in some circumstances, may be self-defeating.)

Voltage *transients* (spikes) and surges can have an effect similar to, or more damaging than, low voltage. When a heavy electric motor, such as a starter motor, an anchor windlass, or an electric winch, is turned off, the collapsing magnetic field in the motor windings causes a sudden voltage rise. In normal circumstances, the boat's batteries act as a giant filter to absorb such transient voltages, but not always.

Often a recommendation is made to connect electronic equipment to a separate battery (I did this in the last edition of this book!), but in practice any electronic battery will share a common ground circuit with the battery powering the motor, so the transients are just as likely to be on the common ground. Once again, the best response is to size the house battery bank properly (see Chapter 1) and to wire everything to first-class standards with minimal voltage drop (see Chapter 4), in which case the batteries will act as an adequate filter. The electronics should be able to handle any remaining transients, especially if equipment is CE-marked or manufactured to FCC Rule 15, Part B. If not, the installation of a DC-to-DC converter, with or without a built-in UPS, will provide a filtered source of power to electronics—but at a significant price.

Whatever the battery configuration, it should be noted that while most electronic equipment will digest a wide range of input voltages—from 10 volts to as much as 40 volts—some equipment (notably some depth sounders) cannot tolerate voltages even as high as 16 volts. To be on the safe side, *whenever equalizing batteries at high voltage levels be sure to isolate electronic circuits.* (Halogen lightbulbs are also particularly sensitive to overvoltage, while the operating life of any incandescent lightbulb will be dramatically reduced by elevated voltages—see Chapter 7.)

Some electronic gear depends on internal memories powered by small nicad (nickel cadmium) batteries that maintain the equipment in a user-ready state when turned off. These batteries have a life expectancy of from 2 to 3 years and up (we have one still functioning after 7 years). As they begin to die, memory lapses occur, especially when units are switched off for longer periods of time. Normally the equipment will still be usable but only by reprogramming at every use. If dead batteries are left in place, they may begin to weep and corrode expensive circuit boards. They may do this even before giving signs of failure. To be on the safe side, memory batteries should be checked every couple of years for any signs of external corrosion and replaced immediately if such signs are present.

Then there are the problems associated with antennas, ground planes, and interference (noise)—the subjects of the next sections.

Antennas and Radio Grounds

Antennas

Antennas come in a bewildering array of shapes and sizes. To be effective, each must be matched to the operating frequency of the equipment to which it is attached. This is a simple matter when the equipment operates on a single frequency (loran, satnav, and GPS) or on a narrow band of frequencies (VHF radio), but it becomes quite complex when a wide band of frequencies is covered (high-frequency radio, specifically ham and SSB).

Since most off-the-shelf antennas for a particular piece of equipment (VHF, SSB, etc.) look pretty much alike externally, it is hard to judge one brand against another. However, internal construction varies markedly in quality. Such features as all-soldered connections, high-quality brass sleeves, and rugged mounting brackets serve to differentiate antennas for the long haul from antennas that will probably have to be replaced in a few years. *Always buy a quality antenna from a reputable manufacturer.* Radio equipment is only as good as the antenna to which it is fitted (Figure 8-3; Shakespeare is one major manufacturer—www.shakespeare-marine.com).

Gain. The principal yardstick for measuring relative antenna performance is *gain*, expressed in decibels (dB). A 3 dB gain antenna doubles the power of outgoing and incoming signals, 6 dB quadruples it, and 9 dB magnifies it eight times.

Increased performance (decibel rating) is achieved by concentrating the signal into a narrower beam width; the signal is the same strength, but its energy is focused into a narrower and consequently more powerful beam. A 0 dB antenna radiates uniformly in all directions, including straight up. A 3 dB antenna concentrates horizontal radiation into a band ±80 degrees wide at the expense of the vertical, but still radiates in a 360-degree arc around the antenna. This horizontal concentration is carried even further in 6 dB (±35-degree beam width) and 9 dB antennas (±20-degree beam width). See Figure 8-4A.

Signal concentration can be taken only so far. If a boat is rolling heavily, a highly concentrated signal may well undershoot or overshoot another station; the signal will fade in and out. The higher the gain of an antenna, the more sensitive it is to heeling—at a 40-degree angle of heel, the useful signal strength of a 9 dB antenna will be no more than that of a 0 dB antenna. For this reason, and to avoid overly long antennas (the higher the gain, the longer the antenna), sailboats rarely use antennas with a higher gain than 6 dB, with 3 dB being the norm (Figure 8-4B).

With VHF radios, radio transmission is *line of*

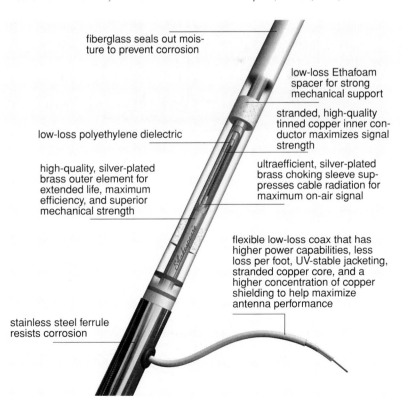

FIGURE 8-3. Features of quality equipment. *(Shakespeare)*

fiberglass seals out moisture to prevent corrosion

low-loss Ethafoam spacer for strong mechanical support

low-loss polyethylene dielectric

stranded, high-quality tinned copper inner conductor maximizes signal strength

high-quality, silver-plated brass outer element for extended life, maximum efficiency, and superior mechanical strength

ultraefficient, silver-plated brass choking sleeve suppresses cable radiation for maximum on-air signal

flexible low-loss coax that has higher power capabilities, less loss per foot, UV-stable jacketing, stranded copper core, and a higher concentration of copper shielding to help maximize antenna performance

stainless steel ferrule resists corrosion

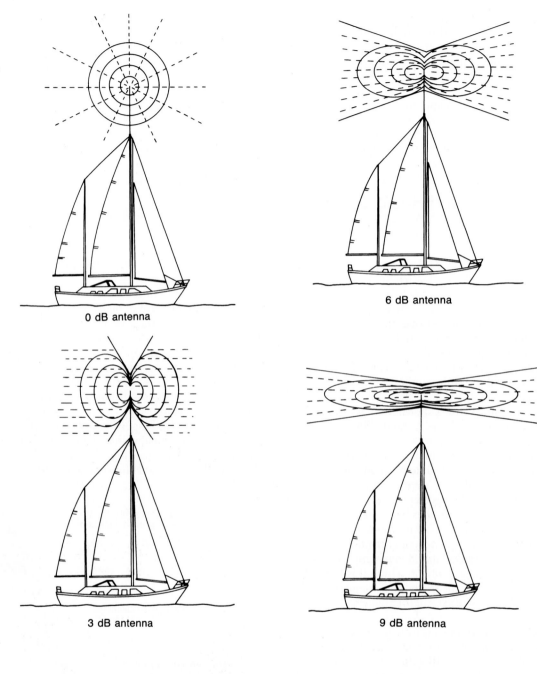

FIGURE 8-4A. VHF antenna gain and signal radiation patterns; the higher the antenna gain, the more concentrated and far-reaching the signal.

0 dB antenna

6 dB antenna

3 dB antenna

9 dB antenna

FIGURE 8-4B. Antenna gain versus boat stability. A very high gain antenna is not suited for a small boat; the narrow signal pattern can overshoot or undershoot distant stations when the boat rolls. *(NMEA)*

antenna

TABLE 8-1. VHF Antenna Range in Nautical Miles

Receiver Antenna Height (feet)	Transmitter Antenna Height (feet)							
	8	12	24	40	60	120	200	400
8	7	8	9	11	13	17	21	28
12	8	9	10	12	14	18	22	29
24	9	10	12	14	15	19	23	30
40	11	12	14	15	17	21	25	32
60	13	14	15	17	19	23	27	34

Note: The formula for calculating the geographic range of an antenna is: ($\sqrt{\text{height above water in feet}}$) x 1.22 = range in nautical miles. If the height is in meters, multiply by 2.21. The calculation is performed for both the receiving and transmitting antennas, and then the two numbers are added.

sight, making antenna height a more important factor than gain in determining antenna performance. Since high-gain antennas are generally longer and more expensive than low-gain antennas, a small, 3 dB masthead antenna often will outperform a deck-level, 17½-foot, 9 dB gain or an 8+-foot, 6 dB gain antenna—and at considerable savings (Table 8-1). Of course if the mast ever goes over the side, the antenna goes with it.

SSB antennas. Whip antennas for SSB are long—from 17 feet (5 m) to 35 feet (10 m), with 23 feet (7 m) being common. They need to be supported in a couple of different places and mounted where they are not likely to be used as a grab bar.

Knowledgeable radio operators frequently make their own antennas, tuning the antenna length to the specific frequency being used (Figure 8-5). Dipole antennas (in which a *transmission line* from the radio feeds two equal-length antenna arms) are particularly useful since there are not the same grounding problems (see below) as with the typical *vertical* antenna (either an *untuned whip* antenna or an *insulated backstay*).

There are plenty of books that discuss antenna construction in great detail. For the rest of us, except in special circumstances, it is best to follow the equipment manufacturer's recommendations concerning an antenna, which normally results in buying a whip antenna or using a backstay. For high-frequency transmissions the antenna is then coupled to an *antenna tuner* (either manual or automatic) that electronically manipulates the fixed-length antenna to produce the correct effective length for the frequency on which the radio is transmitting.

An insulated backstay needs an insulator that is at least 2 feet from the masthead (to ensure the antenna does not in any way short to the mast), as well as one at the lower end that is high enough to be out of reach (when transmitting, a SSB antenna can create a painful burn). The connecting cable from the antenna to the antenna tuner requires a special kind of

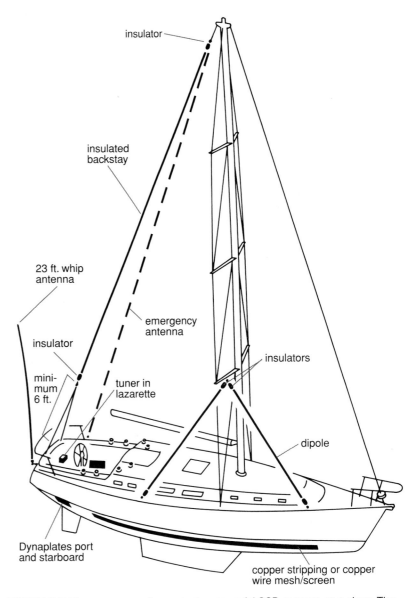

FIGURE 8-5. There are several ways to rig a powerful SSB antenna on a sloop. The long-wire insulated backstay is the most popular. A 23-foot whip on the transom is the simplest way to retrofit a boat with SSB capability. Many voyaging boats carry a spare long-wire antenna that can be rigged on a halyard or topping lift if the main antenna fails. A dipole antenna temporarily rigged to a lower spreader while at anchor provides the best reception and transmission. *(Jim Sollers, adapted from a drawing courtesy Ocean Navigator)*

cable called GTO-15. When transmitting, this cable becomes part of the radiating system, and in doing so, dissipates part of the signal strength into the boat, the water, and any wiring that is close by. To reduce these losses, the GTO cable should be as short and direct as possible (i.e., mount the antenna tuner as close to the backstay or a whip antenna as possible). Note that corrosion in the connection between the GTO cable and the backstay or antenna tuner is a frequent source of degraded performance—check these connections at least once a year.

Note also that some ham experts maintain that on fiberglass boats the lower backstay insulator can be omitted. They argue that the fiberglass hull provides sufficient insulation at high frequencies, thus allowing the antenna tuner to be wired directly to one of the chainplate bolts, with a short connection from the tuner to ground. In this case, you would need a jumper cable from the stay to the chainplate to bypass any resistive connections between the wire terminal and the chainplate. However, this setup will put the radiating part of the antenna within easy reach, which may be hazardous. For this reason, the National Marine Electronics Association (NMEA) specifies that any backstay antenna should have an insulator "a minimum of 6 feet from any horizontal deck where a person could reach the backstay."

Antenna Installation

The signals collected by antennas are measured in *millionths* of a volt. Only antennas sited correctly with perfect electrical connections will work properly. Poor performance on newly installed equipment is nearly always a result of inadequate antenna or ground installations, particularly with SSBs, ham radios, and lorans. Deteriorating performance on older units is likely to result from corrosion in coax cables and connectors.

Siting an antenna. For line-of-sight antennas, height is a key issue (e.g., VHF and cell phones; Figure 8-6), but for any equipment receiving satellite signals, height is irrelevant (e.g., GPS and satellite phones). In the latter case, the important factor is a clear view of the sky.

Radar antennas need to be free from reflected onboard signals, with a minimum spacing of 3 feet (1 m) from the tip of the antenna to the nearest object (this is not possible with a mast mount). The antenna needs to be sited so that people do not come within its radiating path at eye level; this means a minimum height above deck of 8 feet (2.5 m). To avoid missing close-in targets, the antenna should not be above 30 feet (9 m) high.

Some pieces of equipment will interfere with others, while some will not. SSB in the transmit mode can be a particular problem for loran and differential GPS beacons—the SSB antenna should be sited as far as possible from the other antennas—while cell phones can mess up GPS signals. Table 8-2 outlines recommended minimum horizontal spacing of antennas and is adapted from the NMEA's *Installation Standards for Marine Electronic Equipment Used on Moderate-Sized Vessels* (version 1.1).

Coax cable. The connection from most antennas to the equipment is made with coaxial (coax) cable (with SSB, the coax runs between the transceiver and the antenna tuner). Coaxial cable consists of an inner core of copper wire surrounded by a substantial insulating sleeve (the *dielectric*), which is further enclosed in metal braid and topped with another insulating sheath (Figure 8-7). The signal received by an antenna is trapped between the wire core and the braid and conducted to the receiver. The braid also excludes unwanted signals radiating from other sources, such as rigging, wiring circuits in the boat, etc.

Coax cable comes in different resistance ratings, sizes, and qualities.

Resistance. Almost all marine antennas require 50-ohm coax, but TV antennas use 75-ohm coax. *TV antenna cable, regardless of its quality, is not suitable for marine antennas.*

Size. The most commonly found 50-ohm coax cables in marine use, ranging in size from the smallest to the largest, are called RG-58, RG-8X (RG-8 mini or RG-8M), RG-8/U, and RG-213; 75-ohm cable comes as RG-59, RG-6, and RG-11.

FIGURE 8-6. Correct antenna mount and placement. *(Ocean Navigator)*

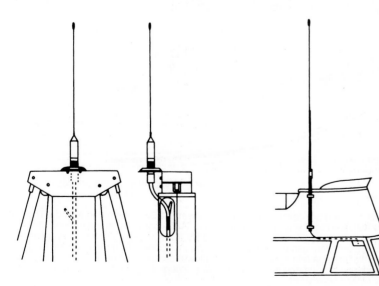

TABLE 8-2. Minimum Horizontal Spacing (in feet) Between Antennas for Different Types of Radio-Based Equipment

	VHF	GPS	DGPS	SSB	Radar	Sat com	Loran	Cell phone	Satellite TV
VHF	4 ft.	3 ft.	1 ft.	3 ft.	2 ft.	6 ft.	1 ft.	2 ft.	3 ft.
GPS	3	0.5	1	4	1[1]	6[5]	2	5[3]	2–3
DGPS	1	1	0.5	4	2–3	10	2	1	1
SSB	3	4	4	10	2–3	6	3	2	4
Radar	2	1[1]	2–3	2–3	2[2]	6	3	1[1]	4[4]
Sat com	6	6[5]	10	6	6	6	6	6	6
Loran	1	2	2	3	3	6	0.5	2	4
Cell phone	2	5[3]	1	2	1[1]	6	2	3	4
Satellite TV	3	2–3	1	4	4[4]	6	4	4	4

1. GPS, satellite TV, and cell phone antennas must not be installed in the beam of a radar antenna.
2. One radar antenna must not be installed at the same height as another; there must be a minimum vertical separation of 18 inches.
3. Cell phones can interfere with GPS.
4. The spacing between satellite TV antennas and radar antennas must be increased for higher-output radars (6 kW, 10 kW, and 25 kW).
5. GPS antennas should be mounted below the transmitted beam of sat com (satellite communications) antennas.
Note: To convert feet to centimeters, multiply by 30.

(Courtesy National Marine Electronics Association)

The larger the cable, the lower the losses in transmitting and receiving a signal, but since these losses are also related to the frequency of the signal, it is not possible to give absolute figures. Losses are specified as so many *decibels per 100 feet* at a particular *frequency*—the higher the frequency, the higher the aggregate loss. See Tables 8-3 and 8-4, which are based on data from Ancor (www.ancorproducts.com), and Belden (www.belden.com). Figure 8-8 gives the frequencies of radio-based equipment found on boats. Note that a cable with a given specification—e.g., RG-58—may be available with differently sized wire gauges for the core, with larger wire sizes resulting in lower transmission losses. The actual loss numbers should always be checked with the manufacturer.

The large RG-8/U and the even larger RG-213 cost more than other cables, are more obtrusive, and are stiff and awkward to run. As a result, RG-8X (RG-8 mini or RG-8M) cable is used for most marine applications. When used with equipment that operates at lower frequencies (up to 100 MHz), such cable is generally good for runs up to 100 feet; for higher-frequency

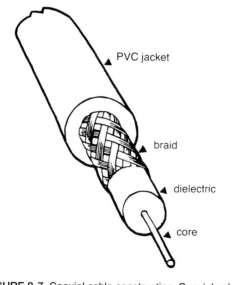

FIGURE 8-7. Coaxial cable construction. Coaxial cable consists of an inner core of copper wire surrounded by a substantial insulating sleeve (the dielectric), which is enclosed in a metal braid and topped with another insulating sheath.

TABLE 8-3. Representative Loss (Attenuation) in dB per 100 Feet of 50-Ohm Coaxial Cable[1]

Frequency (MHz)	Cable Size			
	RG-58	RG-8X	RG-8/U	RG-213
50	3.1 dB	2.1 dB	1.3 dB	1.3 dB
100	4.5	3.1	1.9	1.9
200	6.6	4.5	2.8	2.8
400	10.0	6.6	4.2	4.2
700	14.2	9.1	5.9	5.9
900	16.6	10.7	6.9	6.9
1,000	18.1	11.2	7.4	7.4
Nominal OD	3/16 in.	1/4	13/32	13/32
Conductor (AWG)	20	16	13	13
Impedance	50	50	52	50
Minimum bend radius (when installing)	2 in.	2.5	4.5	5

1. Note that actual losses differ from one cable manufacturer to another.

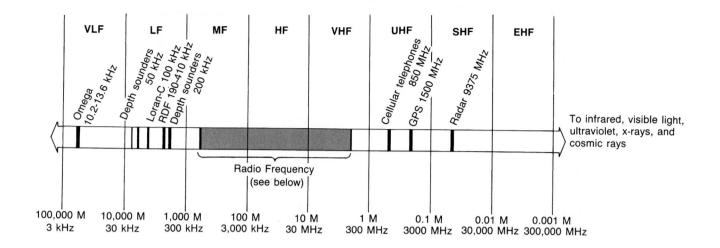

(Frequency: 1,000 Hz = 1 kHz; 1,000 kHz = 1 MHz)

$$\text{Wavelength in meters} = \frac{300}{\text{frequency in MHz}}$$

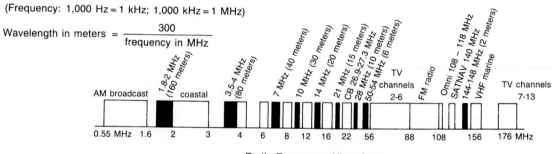

Radio Frequency Allocations.
Ham radio bands are black.

FIGURE 8-8. The frequency spectrum, including the radio frequencies commonly used by boats.

equipment, the maximum allowable run should be reduced, and if the run needs to be longer, the lower-loss RG-8/U cable should be substituted.

Table 8-5 provides maximum acceptable signal losses for different types of equipment. *Note that this table includes losses from cable junctions, each of which should be counted at 0.5 dB (i.e., two junctions = 0.5 × 2 = 1.0 dB).* In order to calculate acceptable cable losses, subtract the cable junction losses from the number extracted from Table 8-5. Then size the cable to keep its losses below the resulting number.

If the maximum cable-plus-junction loss in any proposed installation exceeds the number in Table 8-5, you will need to do one of the following:

- Eliminate junctions in the cable.
- Modify the cable route to reduce its length.
- Change the cable type to a lower-loss cable.

As an example, consider a VHF masthead antenna on a 56-foot (17 m) mast, with a coax junction (connector) at the base of the mast, and

TABLE 8-4. Representative Loss (Attenuation) in dB per 100 Feet of 75-Ohm Coaxial Cable[1]

Frequency (MHz)	Cable Size		
	RG-59	RG-6	RG-11
50	2.4 dB	1.5 dB	0.9 dB
100	3.4	2.1	1.2
200	5.0	3.2	1.7
400	7.4	4.5	2.4
700	10.0	5.9	3.3
900	11.3	6.8	3.7
1,000	12.0	7.3	3.9

1. Note that actual losses differ from one cable manufacturer to another.

TABLE 8-5. Maximum Acceptable Signal Losses

Equipment	Maximum Loss (dB)	Operating Frequency
VHF	3	162 MHz
SSB	3	2–30 MHz
Cell phone	3	850 MHz or 1.9 GHz
TV	6	54–806 MHz
Satellite TV	6	1.6 GHz
GPS	3	1.5 GHz
DGPS	3	150–500 kHz

1,000 kHz = 1 MHz; 1,000 MHz = 1 GHz.

(Courtesy National Marine Electronics Association)

TABLE 8-6. Calculating Signal Losses for a VHF Radio Antenna Cable

Frequency of Equipment (MHz; from Table 8-3)	Cable Type	Total Length (feet)	Divide Length by 100	Approximate Loss per 100 Feet at Frequency (160 MHz)	Cable Loss (dB)	Junction Loss	Total Loss
162	RG-58	89	0.89	5.0	4.45	0.5	4.95
162	RG-8/U	89	0.89	2.6	2.31	0.5	2.81

a 33-foot (10 m) cable run from the mast to the radio (see Table 8-6). The total cable length is 89 feet (27 m). The operating frequency is around 160 MHz.

The loss with the RG-58 is well above the maximum allowable signal loss of 3 dB (see Table 8-5) but is acceptable with the RG-8/U.

When it comes to higher-frequency equipment, especially that in the GHz range, and given the higher cable losses at higher frequencies, it is very hard to keep the total loss within the limits given in Table 8-5. About the best we can do is to keep the cable runs as short as possible and avoid junctions.

Quality. Insulation is important. Many coax cables have a *foam-core* dielectric, which reduces power losses in the line as compared to a solid polyethylene dialectric. However, some foam is open cell and acts as a wick, allowing any moisture that finds its way through improperly sealed connections to corrode the core conductor and the braid. Other foam is closed cell and does not suffer from a wicking problem. In marine applications, use only cable with a *closed-cell* foam or *solid polyethylene* dielectric.

The external insulation on cables varies tremendously in its thickness, quality, and resistance to ultraviolet (UV) degradation. Better-quality cables are *noncontaminating*, a designation meaning that when it is subjected to UV, the outer insulation does not shrink to the point at which the braid below *prints through*. Given a choice, noncontaminating cable is the best buy, although some other cables (such as those manufactured by Ancor) do have UV-resistant insulation, even though they do not meet the specific provisions of the noncontaminating standard.

The braid is equally important. Some coax uses aluminum braid, which is out of the question for marine use. *It must be copper*, preferably *tinned* copper (with the inner core also tinned). There are further differences in the *tightness of the weave*. Cheap coax has loosely woven braid, which is electrically "leaky," leading to signal loss, distortion, and interference. Braid is described by percentage; 98% is the best.

To summarize, coax for marine use should be tinned (both the braid and the core), with a stranded (not solid) core, and at least a 96%

braid, plus a noncontaminating jacket if possible. RG-8X will serve for most purposes, except where long cable runs are needed for a VHF or other equipment with higher operating frequencies, in which case, RG-8/U should be used. At the top of the line is RG-213, the same size as RG-8/U but with a completely waterproof and UV-resistant insulation. It has twice the quality but is twice the price and a little hard to work with—even professionals have to struggle with connectors on RG-213—and is not worth fooling with except on some special radar systems.

(Note: The cable supplied with some antennas and many depth sounders *cannot be cut or shortened*. Read the instructions carefully before modifying prewired equipment.)

Coax connections. Faulty antenna connections rank right up there with power supply deficiencies and operator error as principal causes of electronic malfunctions. Anytime equipment performance is unsatisfactory, check all connections, particularly those exposed to the weather.

Although noncontaminating cable is waterproof, it can still wick up considerable amounts of water through its ends just from humidity in the air—never mind rainwater and salt spray. The water is sucked along the copper braid by capillary action, corroding the braid and ruining line efficiency (this is where tinned wire once again more than pays for itself in the long run). Coax connections must be made with proper connectors and then sealed to keep out all moisture. The connectors themselves must be high quality—the regular connectors found at Radio-Shack (U.S.) do not stand up to the marine environment. Better choices would be RadioShack's premium fittings or those manufactured by Amphenol (www.amphenolrf.com, available through one or two marine catalogs and various marine electronics suppliers) and Shakespeare. The best connectors are gold-plated brass, rather than nickel plated.

Regardless of the terminal, bear in mind the following points when making all connections (Figures 8-9A and 8-9B):

- *Connectors have a restricted operating range in terms of the frequencies with which they can be used.* This is given in Table 8-7. Make sure to select an appropriate connector.

- Cables should not be spliced together—always use the proper terminals.

- The connector must match the cable. The standard terminal is a PL-259, which fits RG-8/U and RG-213 cable. This mates with an SO-239 socket. RG-8X (RG-8M) uses a UG-176U adapter to neck the PL-259 down to cable size, while RG-58 uses a UG-175U adapter. Two cables are connected by screwing their respective PL-259s into a barrel connector, sometimes numbered PL-258. BNC connectors are also relatively common; the others listed in Table 8-7 are not so common. Any good electronics store should have all these connectors.

- It is permissible to join cables of different sizes (e.g., RG-58 and RG-8/U) as long as their impedance matches to within 2 ohms (in this case, they are both 50-ohm cables), and as long as you use the proper terminals.

- Coax connectors should always be soldered. Because of installation errors with soldered connections, many manufacturers now include pressure-crimped terminals with their equipment. These are not recommended for marine use. Sooner or later (generally sooner), corrosion will develop in the terminal, creating resistance and interfering with the signal. What is more, you will need special tools to install them properly.

- Installation procedures are illustrated in Figures 8-9A and 8-9B. If you need to fit a waterproof jacket (available quite cheaply from RadioShack and other electronics stores), slide it up the cable before doing anything else. Before fitting a connector, tin the core cable and the braid (if not already tinned) and make absolutely certain that no stray wires from the braid can short the core cable. (This would make the antenna inoperative and

might do expensive damage to the equipment.) The braid must make a clean fit inside the connector, all the way around. When soldering the braid, avoid excessive heat, which may melt the dielectric. If you are inexperienced in soldering, get help.

- Unless a custom-made waterproof boot has been fitted, coat the connector with a waterproof sealant or with an electrician's putty, such as Coax-Seal; then seal the whole joint with heat-shrink or self-amalgamating tape. (Allow the sealant, if used, to partially set before adding the tape.) Install drip loops (Figure 8-9C) even on well-insulated connections. When checking a connector, look for corrosion around the center pin and tarnish on the braid.

Testing coax and connections. *Never short the center pin and connector housing on a cable connected to an antenna or electronic equipment. Expensive damage may result.*

If the coax can be disconnected at both ends, test with an ohmmeter (R × 100 scale on an analog meter) from the case of one of the connectors to its center pin. Anything less than infinite resistance shows a short (probably in the connector installation or at a sharp bend). Now clip a jumper wire between the pin and the case on one connector and test at the other end (R × 1 scale on an analog meter). Resistance should be close to zero (depending on the length of the cable). Higher readings show unwanted resistance, such as corroded wire or poor connections.

Emergency VHF antenna. A serviceable temporary antenna can be made from any 19-inch (480 mm) length of wire (a coat hanger, for example) stuck in the antenna socket in the back of a radio. The range will be limited because of the antenna's minimal height above sea level. Take care not to short this antenna to the outside

TABLE 8-7. Connector Types and Their Suitability for Different Equipment

Connector Type	Maximum Operating Frequency	Impedance (ohms)	Permitted Uses
UHF (PL-259)	300 MHz	50	VHF, SSB, DGPS, stereo
BNC	4.0 GHz	50	VHF, SSB, DGPS, GPS, cell phone
TNC	2.5 GHz	50	VHF, SSB, DGPS, GPS, cell phone, Mini-M
N	11.0 GHz	50	VHF, SSB, DGPS, GPS, cell phone
F	2.0 GHz	75	TV, GPS
Mini UHF	2.5 GHz	50	cell phone
SMA	12.0 GHz	50	satellite phone
SMB	4.0 GHz	50	
FME	200 MHz	50	VHF, SSB

(Courtesy National Marine Electronics Association)

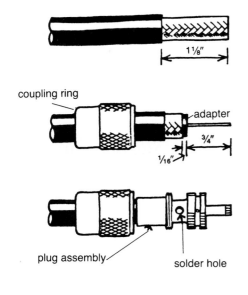

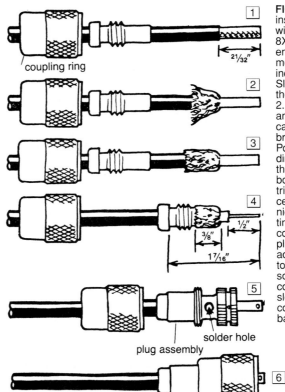

FIGURE 8-9B. Method of installing coax connectors with adapters (RG-58, RG-8X [RG-8 mini]). 1. Cut the end of the cable even. Remove the vinyl jacket ²¹⁄₃₂ inch; do not nick the braid. Slide the coupling ring and the adapter onto the cable. 2. Fan the braid slightly and fold back over the cable. 3. Compress the braid around the cable. 4. Position the adapter to the dimension shown. Press the braid down over the body of the adapter and trim. Bare ½ inch of the center conductor; do not nick the conductor. Pretin the exposed center conductor. 5. Screw the plug assembly onto the adapter. Solder the braid to the shell through the solder holes. Solder the conductor to the contact sleeve. 6. Screw the coupling ring onto the back of the shell.

FIGURE 8-9A. Method of installing coax connectors without adapters (RG-8/U, RG-213). 1. Cut the end of the cable even. Remove the vinyl jacket 1⅛ inches; do not nick the braid. Make sure the braid is evenly distributed. 2. Bare ¾ inch of center conductor; do not nick the conductor. Trim the braided shield ¹⁄₁₆ inch back from the end of the dielectric and tin the braid. Slide the coupling ring onto the cable. 3. Screw the plug assembly onto the cable. Solder the plug assembly to the braid through the solder holes. Solder the conductor to the contact sleeve. Make sure no loose strands of braid can short out the core.

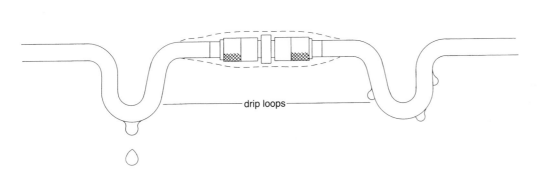

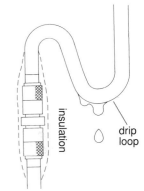

FIGURE 8-9C. Install drip loops, even on well-insulated connections. (*Jim Sollers*)

of the terminal socket, as you might damage the radio. The radio should be used only on low power and as little as possible since lengthy transmissions could eventually do damage.

Radio Grounds

Although not critical with VHFs, and not necessary with GPS, a good ground is essential for effective SSB transmissions (particularly when using a vertical antenna) and for loran performance. On these types of equipment, the ground system complements the antenna, and one will not function with full efficiency without the other. This relationship, known as a *counterpoise*, is somewhat analogous to a diver (the radio

signal) on a springboard (the ground). A better spring makes for a better dive; a better ground makes for a better transmit signal.

Metal boats have a wonderful ground in the hull, but what constitutes a good ground in wood and fiberglass boats is debatable. Most experts call for anywhere from 10 to 100 square feet (1.0 to 10 sq. m) of flat metal surface (copper mesh, metal foil tape, aluminum plate, etc.), but see below for a contrary view. For high-frequency radio transmission, the Coast Guard requires an underwater ground that is at least the equivalent of 12 square feet of copper. Anything made of metal that is flat and *fractions of an inch* (this is important—the farther the distance, the less the effect) from the water has proven effective.

Creating a ground. A tremendous ground can be bonded directly into the hull or placed under internal ballast of boats under construction. If copper mesh is used, open edges (loose strands) should first be soldered together. If a boat has a solid ballast casting—internal or external—the casting can be used as a ground either by tapping directly into it or by connecting it to a keel bolt.

Ground areas can be distributed throughout the boat and need not be in actual contact with the seawater. On bonded boats, a ground is sometimes established by running copper foil tape—available in 3- and 6-inch (8 and 15 cm) rolls from good marine electronics stores and from Newmar—in parallel with the bonding wires and connecting this to all through-hulls, the engine, etc. (2 in./5 cm is the minimum foil width that should be used; the longer the tape, the wider it should be).

Note that copper foil offers the least resistance to radio-wave AC currents, and as such it should always be used in place of electric cables to make ground connections for radios, including the connection from an automatic antenna tuner to ground. The tape itself should be folded rather than rolled around corners (Figure 8-10). To connect to a single terminal on the back of a piece of equipment, fold the tape into an arrowhead shape and drill it to fit over the terminal.

In certain circumstances, grounding straps may create a risk of galvanic corrosion. This can be eliminated by placing capacitors in the ground system between the ground strap and underwater hardware. One way to do this is to fasten the copper tape to an insulating piece of plastic, cut a gap across the tape approximately 1/10 inch wide (2.5 mm), and solder several 0.15 µF (microfarad) ceramic capacitors (available from electronics stores) across the gap. At times, these capacitors may carry significant levels of current, so they need to be good quality—look for something rated from 50 MHz to 500 MHz, with a current rating of 375 watts or higher. The capacitors will block stray DC currents but allow radio frequency ground currents to flow.

For boats with an inadequate ground plane, *sintered* bronze ground plates are available. These are made of a porous bronze that allows seawater to permeate the whole plate, increasing its actual surface area many times over its external dimensions. A relatively small plate (12 by 3 in./300 by 75 mm) theoretically has a total surface area of several square feet. There is some debate as to the efficacy of these plates in real use, and some question as to their ability to dissipate a lightning strike (Chapter 5), so it is always best to get the largest practical size. It is not possible to have too much ground plane.

A contrary viewpoint. Gordon West, the well-known ham radio expert, conducted a series of SSB tests in Long Beach, California, on a 40-foot (12 m) sailboat using a variety of grounds. These included a 100-square-foot internal ground plane, an isolated immersed through-

FIGURE 8-10. Radio grounds. Any boat with a solid ballast casting—internal or external—can use it as a ground either by connecting to a keel bolt as shown here or by tapping directly into the casting. Boats with an inadequate ground plane can use a sintered bronze ground plate—always get the largest practical size. You can't have too much ground plane.

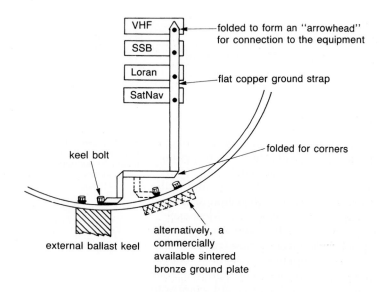

VHF
SSB
Loran
SatNav

folded to form an "arrowhead" for connection to the equipment

flat copper ground strap

folded for corners

keel bolt

external ballast keel

alternatively, a commercially available sintered bronze ground plate

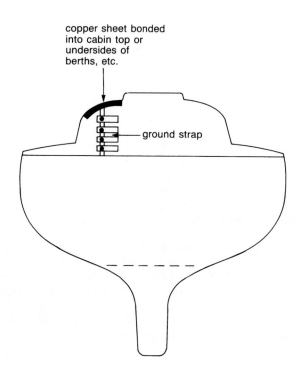

copper sheet bonded into cabin top or undersides of berths, etc.

ground strap

hull, and a couple of differently sized copper foil ground planes hung over the side. In all cases, he concluded that the immersed ground planes, down to the smallest, did better than the internal ground plane, in spite of the latter's much larger surface area.

His conclusion was that with modern automatic antenna tuners, it was perfectly adequate to ground to a single bronze through-hull or an external ground plate as long as it was close to the antenna tuner (no more than 15 feet/5 m away), immersed at all times, and had a connec-tion made with copper foil. He also doubted that sintered bronze ground plates provided any improvement over a copper or bronze plate with the same physical dimensions.

He concluded, "When it comes to your high-frequency radio, your best ground is the element you're floating in, plain old seawater. If you aren't taking advantage of it, you may be losing valuable antenna current. Run a low-reactive copper-foil ground to seawater, and your transmit and receive signals will dramatically intensify over long and short signal paths." (*SAIL*, October 2001.)

Electromagnetic and Radio Frequency Interference

The abundance of radio-based equipment on modern pleasure boats and the plethora of cir-cuits in close proximity to one another (antenna cables, power cables, engine-charging circuits, AC circuits, etc.) make interference problems (electrical *noise*) increasingly commonplace.

Interference is caused by unwanted radio fre-quency energy, much of it generated on board, although a small proportion can be traced to external origins. This energy is picked up by antenna systems and wiring circuits and fed to receivers, which may not be able to distinguish between noise and signals if they share similar frequencies. Hissing, buzzing, crackling, pop-ping, and other undesirable noises on radios will compete with the true signal, perhaps making it unintelligible. Depth sounders and radio direc-tion finders (RDF) may give false readings, and lines and ripples are likely on TV screens. The SNR (signal-to-noise ratio) meter on a loran will show a loss of signal when equipment generates interference on its wavelength. GPSs and other devices may output incorrect data.

Interference is transmitted principally by con-duction and radiation. Conducted interference flows from its source through circuits directly to receivers; radiated interference is picked up by wiring circuits acting as antennas and then con-ducted to receivers. Wires conducting interfer-ence can themselves act as antennas, reradiating the signal and creating a complex of radiated and conducted signals (Figure 8-11).

Good Installation Practices

Interference can be minimized or eliminated by using good installation practices (see, for exam-ple, NMEA's *Installation Standards for Marine Electronic Equipment Used on Moderate-Sized Vessels*, version 1.1). Cables should be properly sized with quality terminations (see Chapter 4). In the second edition of its *Code of Practice for Electrical and Electronics Installations in Boats* (not to be confused with the NMEA publication cited above), the British Marine Electronics Association (BMEA) places the supply cables to electrical and electronic equipment in five groups, notably:

A. AC cabling, including onboard AC circuits, shore-power circuits, AC generators, micro-waves, and AC refrigerators and freezers.
B. Depth sounders, SSB *transceivers* (i.e., with a transmit capability), and telex.
C. General DC circuits (including navigation lights) and engine instrumentation.
D. Low-power radio-based devices, including VHF, SSB *receivers*, cell phones, weatherfax and Navtex receivers, fax receivers, and enter-tainment radio.
E. Data-signal cabling from information sensors to central processing units (CPUs) and from CPUs to visual display units (VDUs).

The BMEA recommends that while the cables for the devices in each group can be run together, so far as is possible, the different groups should be physically separated, and in particular, the "three main cable ducts for Groups 'C,' 'D,' and 'E' should have their own routes separated at all times by 100 mm (4 in.)."

Additionally, "due to the high level of RF out-put power present in SSB installations, all SSB cables and earthing (grounding) arrangements are to be treated as a special case. In general all SSB cables should be as far as practically possible away from all of the boat's other wiring. On a boat this can be difficult to implement . . . The most satis-factory route is low down adjacent to the bilges."

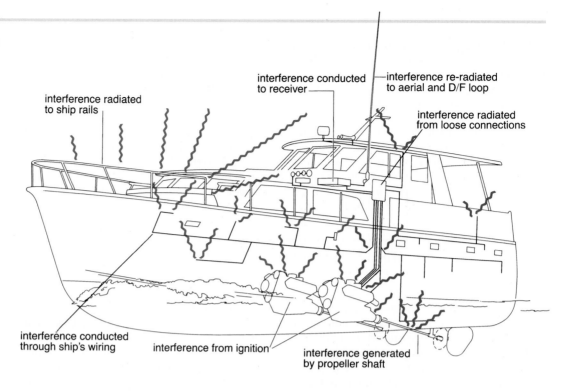

interference conducted
to receiver

interference re-radiated
to aerial and D/F loop

interference radiated
to ship rails

interference radiated
from loose connections

interference conducted
through ship's wiring

interference from ignition

interference generated
by propeller shaft

Radio receiving equipment should *not* be mounted in the following areas:

- Next to, or closely facing, VDUs or equipment such as radar and SSB that generate high-frequency radio transmissions.
- In the main arc of a transmitting or receiving antenna, or next to an antenna cable junction box.

Compasses, especially fluxgate compasses, are very sensitive to interference and deviation generated by electrical equipment. All power leads should be kept 3 feet (1 m) away from compasses. If this is not possible, the leads should be run in twisted pairs and/or shielded (see below).

As noted in Chapter 4, the hot and ground (negative or neutral) cables (both DC and AC) to loads should be run as pairs and should not be physically separated (the more they are separated, the greater the probability they will create magnetic fields that will induce transient voltages in other cables). If you have to separate them (e.g., to set up a separate negative bus bar adjacent to a DC distribution panel), keep them as close together as is practicably possible. The higher the currents flowing in these cables, and the more the current fluctuates (e.g., feeder cables to a DC-to-AC inverter, which are subject to very high current flows, switched on and off at a very rapid rate), the more important it is to keep the cables physically strapped together. In some instances, it is best to run paralleled hot and ground cables to loads with the resulting four cables strapped together such that the two hot cables and two ground cables are diagonally across from one another in the bundle (see Chapter 4).

Sources of Interference

The principal sources of onboard interference are anything that creates radio frequency signals or abruptly varies or switches a current, including:

- Communications and navigation equipment, including radar.
- Computers, microprocessors, and VDUs.
- Electronic sensors, such as depth transducers and fluxgate compasses.
- Any other electronic device with capacitive or inductive parts, such as fluorescent lights.
- Equipment with high-frequency switching, such as DC-to-AC inverters, DC-to-DC converters, and many battery chargers.
- Alternators and voltage regulators.
- Hermetic compressors on DC refrigeration systems.
- Electric motors, especially those with commutators and brushes (all DC motors [except for brushless DC and permanent-magnet synchronous motors] and some AC motors).
- Ignition systems on gasoline engines.
- Electric tachometers.
- Sparks at switch contacts.
- Static electricity from rotating propeller shafts.

Anything that generates sparks or voltage pulses—even loose rigging—can create interference. The closer the frequency of a potential interference signal is to the frequency of other radio equipment, and the greater the power of the radiated signal, the more likely it is to create interference. (Figure 8-8 summarizes the operating frequencies of common electronic equipment.)

Tracking Down Interference

To track down interference in a radio or some other electronic gear, leave it switched on (or tune a handheld RDF to the interference frequency) and shut off all the boat's circuits one at a time—fluorescent lights, the engine, AC circuits, etc. If the interference ceases at any point, the offending circuit has been pinpointed. If it continues when all circuits are shut down, the interference is probably coming from adjacent boats or the shoreside. But note that radio interference, particularly as it affects low-, medium-, and high-frequency units such as loran, SSB, and ham radio, may be generated by sources about which we can do nothing, including sunspots, solar flares, the aurora borealis, and distant thunderstorms.

Another way to narrow down the source of interference is to disconnect the antenna from an affected receiving device. If the noise ceases, it is radiated noise that is being picked up by the antenna; if it persists, it is being conducted through the power leads (in which case filtering may be required—see below).

A cheap transistor radio tuned to the AM band can become an effective noise sniffer. Adding a small coil of wire as a loop antenna will improve its effectiveness. Tune it between stations so that it picks up only interference and move around the boat holding it close to suspect items. The radio will crackle and hiss louder where interference is generated.

Engines have a number of potential noise-makers (especially gasoline engines). When tracking down a culprit, start with the alternator. If it has an external field lead, disconnect this to disable the alternator; otherwise remove its belt. Crank the engine. If the interference has ceased, it is in the charging circuit. If it persists, it is either in the ignition circuit (gasoline engines) or the result of static electricity generated by the rotating propeller shaft. The latter generally produces intermittent *crackles* as the static discharges, rather than the rhythmic interference keyed to engine rpm associated with alternators and ignition circuits.

You can eliminate propeller shaft interference by fitting a bronze brush to the propeller shaft and wiring it to ground or to the boat's bonding system (these brushes are available in the U.S. from ProMariner—www.pmariner.com). This practice is also a good idea for reducing the risk of galvanic corrosion. Bridge flexible couplings with a jumper wire (refer back to Figure 5-15) in order to maintain a good ground circuit between the engine and propeller shaft.

Charging circuits. If disabling the alternator indicated that the problem is in the charging circuit, and if the alternator has an external regulator, to determine whether it is the alternator or its voltage regulator that is at fault, disconnect the field wire *from the regulator* and run the field wire *temporarily* to the battery *positive* (P-type alternator—see Chapter 3) or to a good ground (N-type alternator). Then restart the engine. This will drive the alternator to full output. If the noise reoccurs, the alternator is at fault; if it does not, the regulator is the problem (in either case, see below for fixes).

Preventing (Suppressing) Interference

Since receivers cannot distinguish between a useful signal and noise at the same frequency, interference needs to be suppressed at its source rather than in the receiver. As mentioned previously, the first line of defense against interference is suppressed equipment constructed to CE and/or FCC 15B standards, wired with properly sized and installed cables that have resistance-free connections. After this, the best noise filter you can have (on a DC system) is a properly sized and charged battery in good condition. Suppression measures then fall into four broad categories: isolation, shielding, filtering, and bonding.

Isolation. Before installing new electronic gear, it is a good idea to place it in its intended location and to wire it using the intended cable runs, but with some slack. Use the equipment, including its transmit mode if it has one, with all equipment on the boat turned on to see if it will be subject to interference. Sometimes simply moving a piece of equipment a few inches or running its cables via a different path will solve problems. You'll save yourself a lot of trouble if you can determine this before making cutouts in bulkheads and fascia panels!

Isolation can also take the form of an isolated electronics battery. But as mentioned previously, this frequently unnecessarily complicates the DC system installation and may still not solve the problem. You should avoid this option if possible.

FIGURE 8-12. Shielded
cable. Note the cable
retaining clamps are
grounded to a copper
strap, which is itself
connected to the boat's
ground. *(Lucas Marine)*

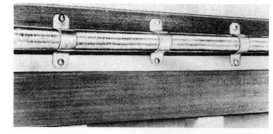

FIGURE 8-13A. A shielded
alternator.

FIGURE 8-13B. Screening
or shielding techniques.
Since voltage regulators
are a major contributor
to interference, some
are shielded with a metal
box (right). The bottom
photo shows the large
threaded fitting (A) where
a screened cable screws
onto the box. This cable
carries all the wiring to
the alternator. Any wiring
coming into the box acts as
an antenna both inside and
outside the box, unless
effectively filtered where it
enters the box. The round
protrusions (B) are built-in
filters for all unscreened
incoming wires, such as
the battery positive wire.
The nut (C) is the grounding connection for the
screening box itself.
(Lucas Marine)

Shielding. Shielding consists of putting a grounded metal jacket around cables or equipment. This prevents interference from entering or leaving the equipment (Figure 8-12).

The equipment cases on many pieces of equipment (such as some battery chargers and inverters) are designed to act as shields. The cases are grounded to complete the shielding. Shielded cables are used for many electronic circuits and are readily available from marine chandleries. Where shielded cables leave and enter equipment, the braid must make a good electrical contact with the equipment case to avoid leaks. If individual wires need shielding, it is sometimes possible to slide a piece of soft copper tubing over the wire.

Since alternators and voltage regulators are major contributors to interference, a few expensive alternator installations are shielded (Figures 8-13A and 8-13B). The alternator's metal case grounds out radiated noise produced within, the various leads to and from the regulator are run through a shielded cable, and the regulator itself is placed in a metal box. A special ferrule ensures adequate grounding where the braided cable enters the alternator and regulator housings. The cable run is kept as short as possible (no loops!) and grounded at points along its length if necessary. The engine, alternator, regulator box, and screened wiring harness are all grounded. These measures should, however, rarely be needed.

Filtering. Shielding will take care of radiated noise, but conducted noise is another matter. For that, you will need special *filters*, which are a combination of coils (*inductors*) and capacitors.

Radio frequency energy is alternating current; it forms waves of different lengths. An inductor provides a high-resistance path to alternating current (the higher the frequency, the more the resistance) but little resistance to direct current (the degree of resistance to DC depends on the size and length of the wire used to wind the coil). An inductor installed in series in a DC line will tend to block radio frequency energy while passing direct current.

A capacitor, on the other hand, conducts alternating current but blocks direct current. The higher the frequency, the lower the resistance of the capacitor to AC currents. So if we combine an inductor with a capacitor we can "hold up" radio frequencies with the inductor and then short them safely to ground with the capacitor without causing a short in the DC circuit. This is the principle behind filters. Since the wiring of the inductor will be carrying the full current of the circuit that is being filtered, it must clearly be

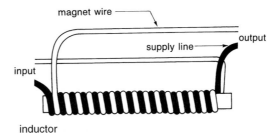

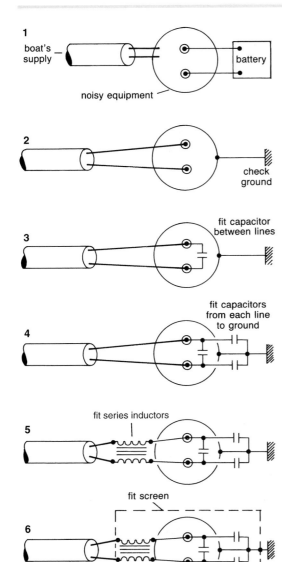

FIGURE 8-14B. Making an inductor. 1. Use insulated magnet wire (copper) obtainable at radio supply stores. The size depends on the current drawn by the appliance as indicated in the table below. 2. Take a length of ⅜-inch ferrite rod (used for portable radio antennas, also obtainable at radio supply stores) as indicated below. The rod can be cut to length by filing a groove in it and breaking it over a sharp edge. 3. Make 20 turns around the rod with the equipment supply line and magnet wire as shown in the illustration. 4. Slip a piece of PVC tubing over the inductor and dip it in varnish to seal it. 5. Connect both ends of the magnet wire to ground.

Equipment Current Rating (amps)	Wire Size (AWG)	Ferrite Rod Length (in.)	(mm)
1	23	1.5	40
2	20	2	50
5	17	3	75
10	14	4	100
15	12	5	130
20	11	6	150
25	10	6	150

FIGURE 8-14A. Specific ways to reduce interference. 1. If possible, disconnect the piece of equipment experiencing interference from its power supply and provide power via a separate battery with short leads. If this reduces interference, supply-line filters will be effective. 2. Next, if the equipment has a metal case, make sure it is effectively grounded. 3. Try a 1 μF capacitor between the supply leads (positive and negative). 4. Connect a 1 μF capacitor from each terminal to ground. 5. Make up inductors as outlined in Figure 8-14B and fit these in the supply lines. 6. Place the equipment in a screening box and use feed-through filters on all lines. 7. If all else fails, try moving the equipment and/or its leads. *(John French, Electrics and Electronics for Small Craft, Beekman Publishers)*

rated to carry the load (which may be more than 100 amps in some alternator installations).

Filters are fitted in hot (positive) leads as close to offending equipment as possible to reduce the potential area for conducting and radiating unwanted frequencies (Figures 8-14A and 8-14B). The filters are then connected to a ground. (In severe cases of interference, filters are sometimes added to both hot and ground cables.)

Different filters suppress different kinds of interference. Many have specific voltage and current ratings, so it is important to match them to the application. Filter manufacturers for the marine marketplace include Newmar, Pro-Mariner, and Gold Line (www.gold-line.com).

Many DC-to-DC converters function as excellent filters, producing a very clean power supply. Some, however, are electrically noisy (they all incorporate high-frequency switching that is inherently noisy but then differ in the extent to which this noise is suppressed).

For an SSB, many installers recommend placing a *line isolator*, a special filter (a *choke*) available from The Radio Works (www.radioworks.com) and others, between the transceiver and the antenna tuner, and as close to the tuner as possible. Another kind of specialized choke, known as a *ferrite bead* or *toroid*, is placed around both ends of the cable to the tuner. Toroids clip around the cable and as such must be matched to its size. (They come in many shapes and sizes and are available from The Radio Works, Digi-Key Corporation [www.digikey.com],

Palomar [www.palomar-engineers. com], and others.)

Bonding. Both shielding and filtering take unwanted frequencies and *short them to ground*. Bonding all equipment cases and metal objects to a common ground helps reduce interference by holding everything at the same potential (voltage). If there are no voltage differences and a good ground with seawater, there will be no arcing or buildup of static electricity (hence a brush on the propeller shaft), and voltage transients and other sources of interference will be shorted out. Proper bonding is an important part of any electrical installation.

Bonding cables terminate at the boat's common ground point, which is also the termination point for DC negative cables, so the two are electrically interconnected. Knowing this, some installers take a short cut by connecting the green bonding wire for a given piece of equipment to a DC negative point somewhere nearby, rather than running the bonding wire all the way to the common ground point. This does little good in terms of preventing interference and may actually promote it. The only point at which the two cables should be joined is the common ground point.

Specific measures for noise suppression. Effective RFI suppression involves good design and good discipline in the manufacture and installation of equipment, especially charging equipment. A fully screened, isolated-ground marine alternator properly fitted as original equipment will be far more effective in reducing electrical noise than any number of filters and other devices tacked onto the system at a later date. Even without such screening, you will go a long way toward eliminating interference by using properly sized cables with sound connections, including a ground cable from the alternator to the common ground point (regardless of whether or not the alternator is grounded through its mount bracket). In fact, an alternator ground cable will often solve persistent interference problems.

Your motto should be "Do it right in the first place." It may seem to cost more, but in the long run, it will not only be cheaper but will perform better than patched up electrical circuits. This becomes even more true with the explosive growth of onboard electronic equipment and microprocessors.

The following measures may help bring residual problems under control. (Note: Frequent use is made of pigtail capacitors, which have one hot lead and a mounting plate that serves as a ground connection; or coaxial capacitors, which have two leads, one of which goes to ground. Mounting plates must be firmly fastened to ground. Connections are made as indicated below. Keep leads as short as possible—*cut them down if possible*; it will improve the operating characteristics of the capacitor.)

Gasoline engines. Ignition systems produce a distinct popping synchronized with engine speed. Specific measures to reduce interference are:

- Fit resistor-type spark plugs (from an auto parts store).

- If copper-cored (wire-cored) high-tension (HT) leads are used between the distributor and spark plugs, fit *suppressed* plug caps and a suppressed distributor cap, or else change to suppression/resistance HT leads.

- If using suppression/resistance (resistive) HT leads, fit *screened* plug caps and a screened distributor cap (auto parts store). In a marine environment, replace the HT leads every 2 years.

- Install a suppressor resistor (auto parts store) in the HT cable from the coil to the distributor cap. Mount the coil on the engine to keep the lead to the distributor as short as possible. Keep the low-tension (LT) and high-tension (HT) leads as far apart as possible.

- Install a 1.0 μF, 200-volt capacitor (electronics store) between the ignition coil's hot terminal (the one from the ignition switch, *not* the one going to the distributor) and ground (the engine block), or

- Fit a filter at the coil *in series* with the wire from the ignition switch. A suitable filter is a low-pass PI-type LC filter rated at 5 amps (auto parts store). Mount it to the engine or coil bracket as close as possible to the coil and ground it well.

- Make sure the coil case is well grounded to the engine block.

- If the engine has a tachometer that takes its pulses from the alternator, make sure the tachometer wire is shielded and the shield grounded at both ends.

Alternators and voltage regulators. Alternators and voltage regulators produce whining, whistling, and howling noises; the intensity varies with alternator output rather than engine speed. Radiated noise decreases by the square of the distance from the source to the receiver, so you can greatly reduce its impact by keeping sensitive electronics away from charging

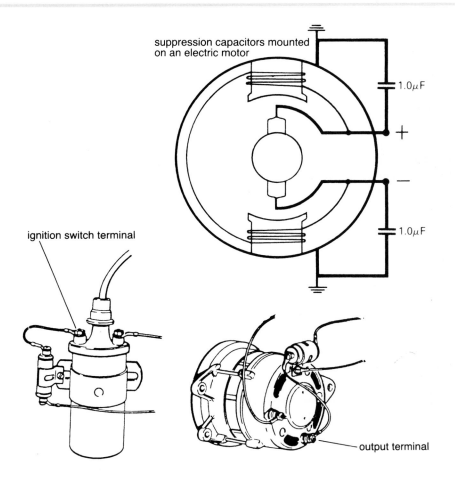

suppression capacitors mounted on an electric motor

1.0μF

+

1.0μF

ignition switch terminal

output terminal

FIGURE 8-15. Noise suppression on electric motors, alternators, and coils. Note that radio interference from ignition systems produces a distinct popping that is synchronized with the engine speed. Alternator interference produces whining, whistling, and howling noises that are tied to the alternator output rather than the engine speed.

devices. Minimize conducted noise in the regulation circuit by keeping a voltage regulator close to its alternator. Beyond this, try the following (Figure 8-15):

- If the alternator is grounded through its mount to the engine block (most are), fit a separate ground strap from the alternator to the engine block, or better yet, to the boat's common ground point (see Chapter 5).

- Connect a 1.0 μF, 200-volt capacitor between the output terminal on the alternator and ground, or

- Fit a filter rated at the full alternator output in series with the output line.

- Connect a 1.0 μF, 200-volt capacitor from the voltage regulator's battery connection to ground.

- Alternator *ripple* (a superimposed AC waveform carried over from the alternator's AC side to the DC side) requires heavy medicine: wire a 10,000 μF to 20,000 μF capacitor (readily available for computers) in parallel with the previous capacitor to eliminate interference at the loran frequency.

Electric motors (brush type).

- Clean the commutator and brushes.

- Connect a 1.0 μF, 200-volt capacitor across the input and output leads as close to the motor as possible (inside the case if possible).

- If this fails, connect a 1.0 μF, 200-volt capacitor from each brush lead to the motor case (Figure 8-15).

TVs and fluorescent lights. Turn off the offending equipment. Newer fluorescent lights have built-in noise-suppression circuits. With 12- and 24-volt fluorescent lights, interference tends to increase with higher battery voltages, so it may be more pronounced when the battery is charging. Two fluorescent lights mounted within 10 feet of each other can set up *harmonics*, which magnify problems. A screening material can be put inside the light cover to block interference radiated from the tubes (see the Video Displays section below).

Battery chargers. Some chargers (particularly half-wave-rectified ferro-resonant chargers and some high-frequency switchers; see Chapter 6) can be noisy. While experimenting with various chokes and filters will sometimes help, a better approach is to check the battery charger installation itself; in particular, make sure the charger is close to the batteries—no more than 10 feet away—and wired to the batteries with adequately sized cables for minimal voltage drop. Check all terminals, switches, and connections to ensure they are clean and tight. If the noise problem persists, return the charger to the manufacturer!

Video displays. CRT (cathode ray tube) display tubes (video depth sounders, raster-scan radars) radiate interference *through the face of the tube*. This affects loran reception in particular. If you suspect this as a source of trouble, cover the display tube temporarily with aluminum foil. If the tube is at fault, the interference will cease. CRT-produced interference can be eliminated by installing a transparent conductive shield in front of the tube (available from Ecom— www.glareshield.com and others). Made of plastic and coated with a very thin metal film, this shield will reduce light transmissions from the tube by about 5%—hardly noticeable—and impart a slight tint.

Radio installations. Antennas, antenna cables, and power leads to equipment should be routed as far as possible from likely sources of interference, especially engine-charging circuits, fluorescent lights, and TVs. In particular, keep the power leads supplying electric motors 3 feet from antenna cables. Ideally, you should run power leads at right angles to antenna leads, although this may not be feasible. At the very least, do not bundle them with antenna leads. Keep power leads short and large enough to prevent significant voltage drop. Thoroughly ground equipment cases to the bonding system. Finally, an antenna matched correctly to its equipment and tuned efficiently will give the best possible signal-to-noise ratio (SNR) and enable the equipment itself to filter out much unwanted noise.

Loose rigging. Tighten turnbuckles. If necessary, connect jumper cables across turnbuckles (rigging screws) and shackles; connect chainplates to the bonding system (if installed—in any case rigging should be grounded for lightning protection).

Saving Soaked Equipment

Anytime electronic equipment takes a bath, if it was not already off, turn it off immediately to prevent internal shorts from damaging sensitive circuits. Salt is then the big problem. Salt is *hygroscopic*, meaning it attracts moisture. Salt dissolved in moisture forms an electrolyte that promotes galvanic reactions between dissimilar metals, such as a piece of wire and its soldered terminal.

In the humid marine environment, any electrical equipment into which salt has insinuated itself is more or less doomed—sooner rather than later. For instance, after a particularly wet and wild beat from Venezuela to Grenada, our autopilot went haywire, making all kinds of random responses. A day later it seemed to be working fine, but then it developed a random tendency to go nuts. Although I'm generally reluctant to tear into electronic units, circumstances forced me to take it apart. Eventually I found one tiny grain of salt, no bigger than a pinhead, which had been left behind by an evaporating drop of water. Every time the humidity rose, this speck of salt absorbed moisture and shorted out a sensitive circuit board. I was able to rinse it out with a cotton swab dipped in fresh water and put the autopilot back in business. It was still functioning when we sold the boat 12 years later!

Electrical equipment that has suffered saltwater intrusion will need to be opened and flushed thoroughly with clean fresh water (first remove any internal battery). If the equipment can't be worked on immediately, it is better to store it in fresh water than let the salt go to work. *As long as the unit is dried completely before being reconnected to a power source*, the fresh water may do no harm—certainly less harm than the salt! Mineral spirits and stove alcohol may also be used for flushing; alcohol, in particular, is itself hygroscopic and so will tend to draw water out of components. WD-40 or some other penetrant/dispersant will have much the same effect.

When flushing, pay particular attention to terminal blocks: remove the wires, rinse the cable ends, and use a syringe to flush the block. Remove fuses from their holders and wash both the fuse and holder. A coaxial cable connector, unless fully waterproofed, will hold salt and moisture that will likely short the terminal: open the connector, flush it thoroughly, and dry; if there is sufficient cable, cut and replace.

After flushing, the real difficulty lies in drying out some of the labyrinthine passages in electronic equipment and in drawing water from encased components such as capacitors. A good airflow will drive water from many inaccessible areas. An air compressor is best; failing that, use a fan or a vacuum cleaner's exhaust. A prolonged period of low heat—bright sunshine or perhaps an oven set no higher than 150°F/66°C—may be needed to draw out all the water from individual components. The part *must be dry* before reentering service. Any moisture is likely to create internal shorts and cause rapid and irreparable damage. Before placing the unit online, test for normal resistances if known (R × 1 scale on an analog meter); then test between the power leads and equipment case for any signs of shorts.

Even if a rescue attempt is successful, the equipment should thereafter be treated as suspect; at the first opportunity return it to the manufacturer or an authorized dealer for thorough testing and servicing.

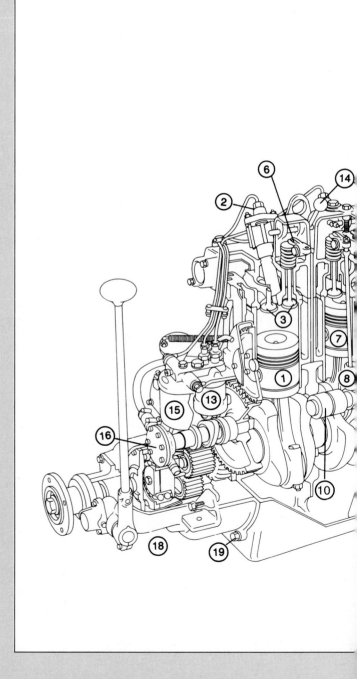

CHAPTER 9

FIGURE 9-1. Diesel engines can deliver years of trouble-free service—given proper preventive maintenance procedures. *(Jim Sollers)*

(1) piston
(2) injector
(3) valve
(4) turbocharger
(5) oil filter
(6) valve rocker
(7) pushrod
(8) cam follower
(9) air intake
(10) camshaft
(11) starter
(12) lube oil pump
(13) fuel injection pump
(14) compression release
(15) fuel filter
(16) water pump
(17) crankshaft
(18) cone clutch
(19) oil drain

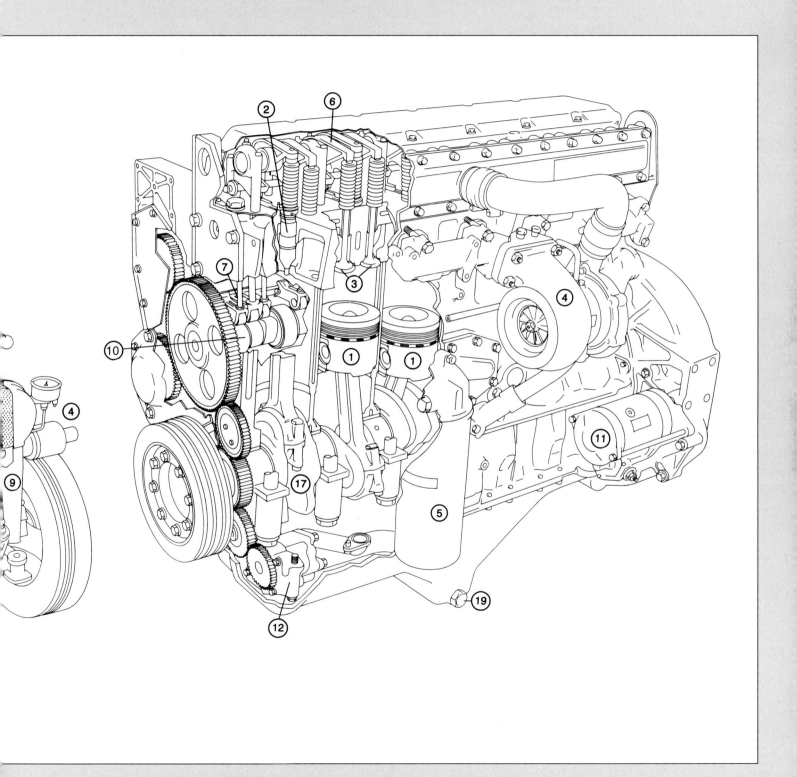

Diesel engines are remarkably simple in principle and require little in the way of routine maintenance, although what little is required is essential to a long life.

How They Work

A piston compresses air in a cylinder. Compression is measured in terms of the *compression ratio*, the cylinder volume with the piston at the bottom of the cylinder compared with the volume when the piston is at the top of its stroke. Compressing air heats it up—the more it is compressed, the hotter it becomes. At compression ratios between 16:1 and 23:1, air temperature rises to over 1,000°F/580°C, well above diesel fuel's ignition temperature of 750°F/ 400°C.

When the piston is near the top of its stroke, diesel is sprayed (injected) into the cylinder of compressed, superheated air and ignites immediately, raising temperatures and pressures even higher, which drives the piston forcefully back down the cylinder—a *power stroke*. (Diesels are frequently called compression-ignition [CI] engines since they do not have a true ignition system. *The diesel fuel is ignited solely by the high temperatures attained by compressing air.*)

Four-cycle engines have two more piston strokes in the cycle (Figure 9-2). On its next upward stroke, the piston expels the gases resulting from combustion through an *exhaust valve*; on its next downward stroke, it sucks clean air into the cylinder via an *inlet valve*. The cylinder is now filled with clean air, and the piston is at the bottom of its stroke, ready to start over.

Some diesel engines operate on *two cycles*, reducing the four cycles described into two strokes of the piston, once up and once down the cylinder. The best known are Detroit Diesels, widely used in powerboats.

Detroit Diesels have a mechanically driven supercharger mounted in the air inlet, which compresses the incoming air (Figures 9-3A and 9-3B). As the piston nears the bottom of its power stroke, exhaust valves are opened and most of the exhaust gases exit the cylinder. A moment later the descending piston uncovers a series of *ports* in the cylinder wall, and the pressurized inlet air rushes in, driving the remaining exhaust gases out the exhaust valves and refilling the cylinder with fresh air. The piston now has reached the bottom of its stroke and is on its way back up the cylinder. The exhaust valves close and the ascending piston blocks off the inlet ports in the cylinder wall. The cylinder is full of clean air and a new compression stroke is underway.

The air system. Diesel engines require large amounts of air for combustion. Every hour, a small diesel is likely to draw in as much air as is needed to fill a medium-sized room. On many boats, engines are crammed into tight spaces and then walled in with soundproofing insulation, with little thought to the air supply. If the air supply is restricted, it will lower efficiency—particularly at higher engine speeds and loads—and shorten engine life.

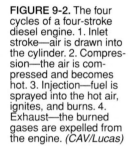

FIGURE 9-2. The four cycles of a four-stroke diesel engine. 1. Inlet stroke—air is drawn into the cylinder. 2. Compression—the air is compressed and becomes hot. 3. Injection—fuel is sprayed into the hot air, ignites, and burns. 4. Exhaust—the burned gases are expelled from the engine. *(CAV/Lucas)*

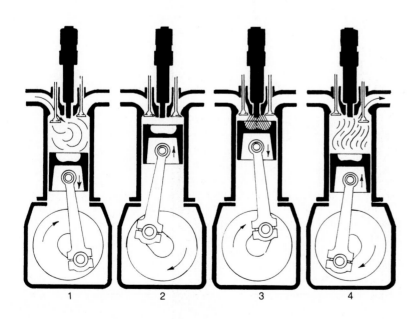

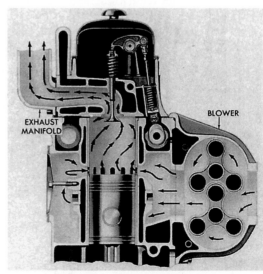

FIGURE 9-3A. Operation of a two-cycle Detroit Diesel—the principal components. *(Detroit Diesel)*

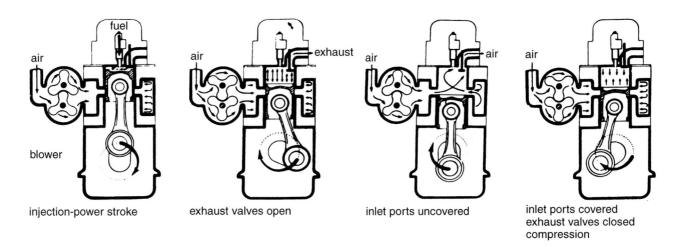

| injection-power stroke | exhaust valves open | inlet ports uncovered | inlet ports covered exhaust valves closed compression |

FIGURE 9-3B. Operation of a two-cycle Detroit Diesel; refer to the text for an explanation. *(Detroit Diesel)*

One way to see if the supply is adequate is to close up the engine room and run the engine at full speed and full load for a couple of minutes (including any other engines that are in the same space, such as an AC generator). Then with the engine(s) still running, open an engine door or hatch and see if there is any pressure compensation (i.e., does the door get sucked in, or is it difficult to open out?). If so, there is a problem that needs correcting. More precise pressure measurements can be made with a manometer (see page 404).

The inlet air must be clean. The efficient running of a diesel depends on the engine maintaining compression. *Even small amounts of fine dust passing through a ruptured air filter or a leaking air-inlet manifold can lead to rapid piston-ring wear and cylinder scoring*, which pave the way for expensive repairs. What is more, *once dirt gets into an engine, cleaning it out properly is impossible*. Small particles become embedded in the relatively soft surfaces of pistons and bearings, and no amount of oil changing and flushing will break them loose. This dirt accelerates wear.

Over time, air filters get slowly plugged up, progressively restricting airflow to the engine (which is independent of any restriction of the airflow into the engine room). This reduces the amount of oxygen reaching the cylinders, and combustion suffers, especially at higher loads. The engine begins to lose power, and the exhaust shows black smoke from improperly burned fuel. Pistons, valves, turbochargers, and exhaust passages carbon up, further reducing efficiency and leading to other problems. The engine is likely to overheat, and in extreme cases, to seize.

Consequently, air filters must be kept clean! The interval for changing filters depends on the operating conditions. In general, the marine environment is relatively free of airborne pollutants, making filter changes an infrequent occurrence (except when pets are kept on board—it is surprising how fast hairs can clog a filter). Long filter-change intervals, however, can lead to complacency and a forgotten air filter. *Changing a filter at set intervals, even if it appears to be clean, is far better than forgetting it.*

The fuel system. A fuel injection pump is an incredibly precise piece of equipment that can be disabled by even *microscopic* pieces of dirt or traces of water. It is also the *single most expensive component of an engine*, and about the only one that is strictly off-limits to the amateur mechanic. Attempts to solve problems invariably make matters worse. It is therefore of vital importance to be *absolutely fanatical about keeping the fuel clean.* Yet so many boatowners treat their fuel systems with indifference. According to CAV, one of the world's largest manufacturers of fuel injection equipment, *90% of diesel engine problems result from contaminated fuel.*

The diesel fuel flowing through a fuel injection system acts as a lubricant, with the degree of *lubricity* varying according to grade and quality. There is no way that quality can be checked outside of a laboratory. However, it is worth noting that in the United States and other parts of the world, two grades are commonly available—No. 1 and No. 2. No. 1 has a lower viscosity, and is commonly used in the wintertime in cold climates. It has less lubricity than No. 2, reducing the life of moving parts such as injection pumps and injectors. In general, if you have a choice, use No. 2. If obliged to use No. 1, some experienced cruisers recommend adding up to a quart of outboard motor oil to every 100 gallons of diesel in order to improve its lubricity. Added in these low quantities, it will certainly do no harm (more is not recommended because it may lead to excess carbon deposits in the engine).

Contaminated fuel. Fuel can be contaminated by dirt, water, and bacteria. Even minute particles of dirt can lead to the seizing of injection-pump plungers or to scoring of cylinders and plungers. If the dirt finds its way to the injectors, it can cause a variety of equally damaging problems, such as plugged or worn injector nozzles.

Water in the fuel opens another can of worms. It leads to a loss of lubrication of injection equipment, resulting in engine seizure. In the combustion chamber, water causes misfiring and generally lowers performance. In addition, water droplets in an injector can turn to steam in the high temperatures of a cylinder under compression. This happens with explosive force, which can blow the tip clean off an injector! Raw fuel is then dumped into the cylinder, washing out the film of lubricating oil, while the injector tip rattles around, beating up the piston and valves. During extended periods of shutdown, which are quite common with most boat engines, water in the fuel system will also cause rust to form on critical parts. Note that two of the more common sources of water in the fuel are fuel tank vents located where they can get submerged when a boat is well heeled or in large following seas and/or a poor seal on a deck-fill fitting (all too often deck fills are placed close to the low point on side decks where standing water can accumulate). If you're having a new boat built, it is worth ensuring that any vents and deck fills will not be underwater on any point of sail.

Bacteria can grow in even apparently clean diesel fuel, creating a slimy, smelly film that plugs filters, pumps, and injectors. The microbes mostly live in the fuel-water interface, requiring both liquids to survive (anaerobic bacteria), and less commonly at the surface (aerobic bacteria). They find excellent growth conditions in the dark, quiet, nonturbulent environment found in many fuel tanks. The best protection is a fuel tank designed so that any water can be removed (see pages 526–27). As a backup, two types of biocide are available to kill these bacteria. The first is water soluble; the second is diesel soluble, which is preferable. Follow the instructions on the can if adding these chemicals to a tank. Various other diesel fuel treatments on the market are not generally recommended by fuel injection specialists. For example, some treatments contain alcohol to absorb water, but alcohol attacks O-rings and other nonmetallic parts in some fuel system equipment.

The lubrication system. Lubricating oil in a diesel engine works much harder than in a gasoline engine, owing to the higher temperatures and greater loads encountered. This is especially the case with today's lightweight, high-speed, turbocharged diesels. Diesel engine oil also has additional problems to contend with, notably acid and soot formation.

Diesel fuels contain traces of sulfur (the sulfur content of fuels in much of the developed world is much lower than it used to be—in the U.S., it is required to be below 0.3%—but high-sulfur fuels are still found elsewhere). Although it is a thoroughly destructive practice, which should be avoided in every way possible, many cruising boat engines, particularly those in auxiliary sailboats, are operated for short periods without properly warming up (e.g., when pulling out of a slip) and/or for long hours at light loads when charging batteries or refrigerating at anchor. The engine runs cool, which causes moisture to condense in the engine. These condensates combine with the sulfur to make sulfuric acid, which attacks sensitive engine surfaces. Low-load and cool running also generate far more carbon (soot) than normal. This soot gums up piston rings, and coats valves and valve stems, leading to a loss of compression and numerous other problems (Figure 9-4).

Diesel engine oils are specially formulated to hold soot in suspension and deal with acids and other harmful by-products of the combustion process. Other additives reduce engine wear, raise the oxidation temperature of the oil, prevent foaming, help the oil adhere to metal surfaces when the engine is shut down, raise the oil's viscosity when hot, and lower its viscosity when cold. There is some pretty sophisticated chemistry in a good engine oil!

The API designation. Using the correct oil in a diesel engine is vitally important. Many perfectly good oils designed for gasoline engines are not suitable for use in a diesel engine. The American Petroleum Institute (API) uses the letter C

FIGURE 9-4. This engine only has 700 hours on it, but has been completely wrecked by repeated low-load, low-temperature operation.

piston rings gummed into their grooves

major carbon buildup

(for Compression ignition) to designate oils rated for use in diesel engines, and the letter S (for Spark ignition) to designate oils rated for use in gasoline engines. The C or S is then followed by another letter to indicate the complexity of the additive package in the oil, with the better packages having letters later in the alphabet. Thus any oil rated CC, CD, CE, CF-4, or CG-4 is suitable for use in diesel engines, with the CG-4 oil being the best at the time of writing (Detroit Diesels use CD-II). Cruisers going to less-developed countries should carry a good stock of the best-grade oil money can buy.

Oil changes. As the oil does its work, the additives and detergents are steadily used up. The oil wears out and must be replaced at frequent intervals, far more frequently than in gasoline engines. In particular, if you use high-sulfur-content fuels, such as those likely to be found in many less-developed countries and much of the Caribbean, or the soot content increases because of extended periods of low-load running, shorten your oil-change intervals to as little as every 50 hours. When you change the oil, install a new filter to rid the engine of its contaminants (some engine manufacturers extend the filter-change interval to every other oil change).

If regular oil changes are not carried out, sooner or later the acids formed will start to attack sensitive engine surfaces, and the carbon will overwhelm the detergents in the oil, forming a thick black sludge in the crankcase and in the oil cooler (if fitted). The sludge will begin to plug narrow oil passages and areas through which the oil moves slowly, eventually causing a loss of supply to some part of the engine. A major mechanical breakdown is underway, and all for the sake of a gallon or so of oil, a filter, and less than an hour's work. One major bearing manufacturer estimates that 58% of all bearing failures are the result of dirty oil or a lack of oil.

Synthetic oil. Synthetic oils are less volatile than mineral oils, which gives them a greater high-temperature stability, reducing sludge formation, and offering better protection in high-heat situations. They have a higher *film strength*, so they tend to adhere better to bearing surfaces, improving their antiwear characteristics; they flow better at cold temperatures; they resist oxidation; and they may improve fuel efficiency. However, they get a mixed reception in the marine world, largely because there is little real-life test data, and therefore some uncertainty as to how they will perform in the marine environment.

Synthetic oils are expensive but they are reputed to last much longer than mineral oil, allowing oil-change intervals to be extended and thus recouping some of the additional cost. However, given the contaminants generated by marine diesels, I would not extend oil-change intervals without specific recommendations from an engine manufacturer. In the absence of such a recommendation, the added expense of synthetics is hard to justify at this time.

Centrifuges and bypass filters. A typical *full-flow* engine oil filter has a mesh size of around 30 microns (1 micron is one-millionth of a meter or approximately 0.00004 inch), which is relatively large (a finer mesh would plug faster and need changing more often). Particles of dirt smaller than 30 microns pass through the filter and circulate continuously with the oil. Various studies have shown that of the microscopic particles that pass through the filter, *the most destructive in terms of engine wear are those in the 10- to 20-micron range.*

Two devices have been developed to catch these particles—centrifuges and bypass filters. Both of these devices are tapped into the pressurized oil gallery that leads to the engine bearings, bleeding off a certain percentage of this oil (normally around 10%) and draining it back to the crankcase (the amount of oil bled off must be kept low so as not to cause a damaging drop in engine oil pressure).

In the case of a *centrifuge*, oil is fed through a bowl mounted on bearings and then out of two small nozzles at the base of the bowl. The oil is driven through these nozzles under pressure from the engine oil pump, causing the assembly to spin at a high speed. The size of the nozzles, coupled with the engine oil pressure and the oil's viscosity, determines the rate of flow through the filter. The centrifugal force generated by the spinning bowl causes entrained particles of dirt to be thrown out of the oil onto the centrifuge's outer housing (Figure 9-5). Here the dirt accumulates as a dense, rubbery mat. Periodically the outer housing is removed and the dirt cake is dug out.

Centrifuges will remove particles down to 1 or 2 microns in size. Their principal drawback is that to date none has been manufactured to operate on the relatively low oil-flow rates of an auxiliary engine. Centrifuges are big-engine devices (100 to 200 hp on up—see TF Hudgins at www.tfhudgins.com).

A *bypass filter*, on the other hand, can be bought for any size engine. These contain a fine-mesh filter element that can filter particles down to 1 micron in size (depending on the manufacturer and the element). A restriction built into the filter at some point keeps the flow rate down to a level that will not cause a drop in the engine oil pressure (Figure 9-6). One brand of bypass filter (manufactured by Puradyn, www.puradyn.com) also includes a heating element that vaporizes any water or fuel in the oil.

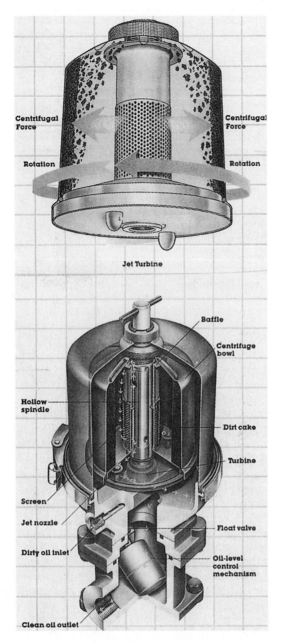

FIGURE 9-5. The innards of the Spinner II oil centrifuge. Oil entering through the central axis is driven by the engine's oil pump out of the jets at the bottom, causing the drum to spin. Since dirt is heavier than oil, it is thrown outward to accumulate on the outer walls of the unit. *(TF Hudgins)*

Labels: Centrifugal Force · Centrifugal Force · Rotation · Rotation · Jet Turbine · Baffle · Centrifuge bowl · Hollow spindle · Dirt cake · Turbine · Screen · Jet nozzle · Float valve · Dirty oil inlet · Oil-level control mechanism · Clean oil outlet

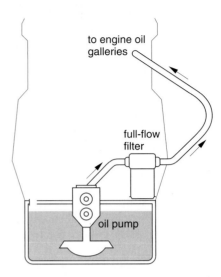

Labels: to engine oil galleries · full-flow filter · oil pump

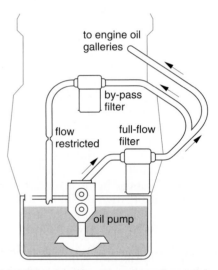

Labels: to engine oil galleries · by-pass filter · flow restricted · full-flow filter · oil pump

FIGURE 9-6. A bypass filter removes smaller particles from the oil than a full-flow filter does. The bypass loop has a restriction that limits the oil flow through the circuit to around 10% of the total oil flow through the engine. After 10 to 20 minutes of operation, all the oil in the engine will have passed through the bypass filter. *(Ocean Navigator)*

The net result of either a centrifuge or a bypass filter will be cleaner oil with reduced engine wear and extended engine life. The cost, relative to the return, is low. Many larger engines come fitted with one or the other as standard equipment, but few smaller engines have either; they are worth considering as add-on equipment.

Preventive Maintenance

The first priority for preventive maintenance is to have an engine-hour meter, so you know how long the engine has been run, and so you can keep a log of all the maintenance that is performed.

If properly installed and adequately loaded, most diesels will run trouble free for thousands of hours with little more than regular fuel-, oil-, and air-filter changes; the procedures are detailed below. However, as previously mentioned, all too many diesels in sailboats are run repeatedly for short periods of time, during which they do not warm up properly, or they are run for long hours at light loads (generally for battery charging and/or refrigeration at anchor). Both of these are liable to dramatically shorten life expectancy and increase maintenance. So a key prerequisite to successful preventive maintenance is to set up the boat's systems so that the diesel does not have to be operated in this manner.

In terms of routine maintenance, Table 9-1 can serve as a general guide. One or two grease points may need periodic attention (the engine manual

TABLE 9-1. Basic Preventive Maintenance for Marine Diesel Engines

Immediately after start-up	Daily (when in regular use)	Weekly (when in regular use)	Semiannually (or more often)	Annually (or more often)
Check oil pressure. Check raw-water flow from the exhaust (unless the engine has dry exhaust).	Check engine oil level. Check freshwater coolant level in the header tank. (Do not open when hot!)	Check transmission oil level. Check pulley belt tensions. Clean raw-water strainer if necessary. When in dusty environments, check air filter and replace if necessary. **Change the engine oil and filters** every 100 to 150 operating hours (including any turbocharger oil filter).	Take a sample of fuel from the base of the fuel tank. Check for water and/or sediment. Check cooling system zinc anodes and replace as needed. When in clean environments, check air filter and replace as necessary. **Change the fuel filters** every 300 operating hours or more frequently as needed.	Check all coolant hoses for softening, cracking, and bulging. Check all hose clamps for tightness. Check the raw-water injection elbow on the exhaust for signs of corrosion. Replace as needed.

will indicate where; many modern engines have no grease points), and belts to auxiliary equipment must be kept tight (no more than ½ inch/13 mm of deflection under moderate finger pressure in the center of the longest belt run).

Clean fuel. Keeping the fuel clean is arguably the single most important maintenance task. Biocides will help ameliorate some fuel problems after they develop, but by far the best measures are preventive—those that avoid taking on contaminated fuel in the first place, and which detect and remove any contaminants taken on board rather than neutralize them. To do this:

- Ensure that all cans used for carrying fuel are spotlessly clean.
- If taking on fuel from a barrel (which happens from time to time in less-developed countries), first insert a length of clear plastic tubing to the bottom of the barrel, plug the outer end with a finger, and then withdraw the tube. It will bring up a sample of fuel from all levels of the barrel, enabling you to see serious contamination.
- *Filter all fuel* using a funnel with a fine mesh, or preferably, one of the multistage filter funnels (commonly known as Baja filters) now available through various marine catalogs and at some marine chandlers. Just as good, at a fraction of the price, are the Teflon-coated aircraft filters sold by West Marine and others. If there are *any* signs of contamination, *stop refueling at once.*
- Take regular samples from the bottom of the fuel tank to check for contamination. If there is no accessible drain valve, find some means of pumping out a fuel sample (Figures 9-7A and 9-7B). At the first sign of contamination,

FIGURE 9-7A. Pumping a fuel sample from the base of a tank.

FIGURE 9-7B. The sample. This tank needs to be cleaned!

water

water and sediment

FIGURE 9-7C. Built-in fuel tank sampling pump on our old Pacific Seacraft 40.

drain the tank or pump out the fuel until no trace of contamination remains. Any especially dirty batch of fuel should be completely discarded—it's not worth risking the engine for the sake of a tankful of fuel. (On our own boats, and all others with which I am involved in the design process, I always include a fuel-sampling pump that is permanently plumbed to the lowest point in the main fuel tank—Figure 9-7C. This allows me to withdraw a fuel sample at any time and pump it into a see-through container, such as an old plastic milk jug or jam jar; all I need is 1 cup of fuel, and serious contamination is immediately apparent. *This inexpensive measure will do more to protect your fuel system than anything else you can do.* We have twice found contamination that we were able to remove before it did any damage.)

- When leaving the boat unused for long periods (e.g., when it is laid up over the winter), fill the fuel tank to the top. This eliminates the air space and cuts down on condensation in the tank. Also add a biocide. When returning the boat to service and before you crank the engine, pump a fuel sample from the base of the tank to remove any condensates.

- Periodically flush the fuel tank(s) to remove accumulated sediment.

Fuel filters. Most people regard fuel filters as the first line of defense against contaminated fuel. As should be clear by now, I regard them as the *last line of defense,* whose function is to deal with any *minor* contamination that escapes the preventive measures designed to keep the fuel tank clean.

Without exception, every marine diesel engine should have both a primary and a secondary fuel filter. All engines come from the manufacturer with an engine-mounted secondary filter located somewhere just before the fuel injection pump. *If this is the only filter, a primary filter MUST be installed* (Figures 9-8A and 9-8B). It needs to be mounted *between* the fuel tank and the lift pump, not *after* the lift pump, because any water in the fuel supply that passes through a lift pump gets broken up into small droplets that are hard to filter out.

Primary and secondary filters do not have the same function. A primary filter is the main defense against water and larger particles in the fuel supply, but it does not guard against microscopic particles of dirt and water. These are filtered out by the secondary filter.

A primary filter needs to be a *sedimenter* type that is specifically designed to separate water from fuel. Sedimenters are extremely simple, generally consisting of little more than a bowl and deflector plate. The incoming fuel hits the deflector plate, then flows around and under it to the filter outlet. Water droplets and large particles of dirt settle out. The better-quality filters then pass the fuel through a relatively coarse filter element (10 to 30 microns).

A primary filter should have a see-through bowl with a drain plug or valve so that water can be rapidly detected and removed. The ABYC

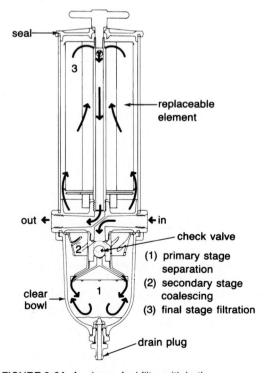

FIGURE 9-8A. A primary fuel filter with both a sedimenter function and a replaceable filter element. *(Racor)*

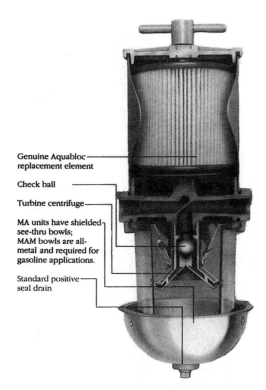

Genuine Aquabloc replacement element

Check ball

Turbine centrifuge

MA units have shielded see-thru bowls; MAM bowls are all-metal and required for gasoline applications.

Standard positive seal drain

FIGURE 9-8B. A cutaway of a good-quality primary filter. *(Racor)*

FIGURE 9-8C. A set of valved primary filters, which allows any one to be changed while the engine is running. *(Racor)*

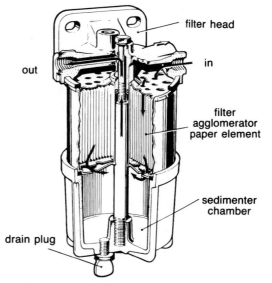

filter head

out

in

filter agglomerator paper element

sedimenter chamber

drain plug

FIGURE 9-8D. A secondary filter. This one has a separate water-collecting bowl; many don't. *(Lucas/CAV)*

requires valves "to be of the type that cannot be opened inadvertently, or shall be installed in a manner to guard against inadvertent opening"—this generally means putting a plug in the valve outlet—and specifies that "tapered plug valves with an external spring shall not be used." Beyond this, the filter may have an electronic sensing device that sounds an alarm if water reaches a certain level, a float device that shuts off the flow of fuel to the engine if the water reaches a certain level, or both.

Powerboats should have two or more primary filters mounted on a valved manifold that allows either filter to be closed off and changed without shutting down the engine (Figure 9-8C). That way, if there is a problem with dirty fuel, the filters can be changed with the engine running. Such an arrangement would also be a good idea on many motorsailers. A vacuum gauge mounted between the primary filters and the lift pump is an excellent troubleshooting investment. (A rising vacuum indicates that the filters are starting to plug.)

A *secondary filter* is designed to remove very small particles of dirt and water droplets (Figure 9-8D). It cannot handle major contamination because its fine mesh will soon plug. Secondary filters are normally the spin-on type and contain a specially impregnated paper element that catches dirt. Water droplets are also too large to pass through the paper and therefore adhere to

it. As more water is caught, the droplets increase in size (*coalesce* or *agglomerate*) until they are large enough to settle to the bottom of the filter, from where they can be periodically drained. The filter mesh should be in the range of 7 to 12 microns. In certain special applications, it may be as small as 2 microns.

Note that problems with plugged filters are most common in rough weather because any sediment in a tank gets stirred up. Frequently multiple filter changes are required. This is the worst possible time to be changing a filter once, let alone multiple times! You can completely avoid these problems by using the measures recommended above to keep the tank and fuel clean in the first place. (In over 25 years of cruising, I have never had even a moderately contaminated fuel filter.)

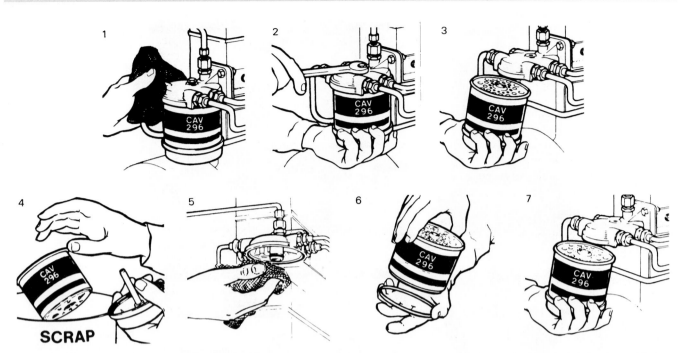

FIGURE 9-9. Changing a filter element with a replaceable element. 1. Clean all external dirt from the unit before attempting to service. Unscrew the thumbscrew in the base and drain the accumulated water and sludge. 2. Unscrew the center bolt and at the same time hold the base of the unit to prevent it from rotating. 3. Release the filter element complete with the base by pulling the element downward while at the same time turning it slightly so that it comes free from the internal O-ring. 4. Detach and discard the element. Detach and inspect the lower sealing ring for damage. Renew the ring if defective. 5. Clean out the sedimenter base. Complete cleaning by rinsing with clean fuel oil. Clean the unit head and inspect both the upper sealing ring and the O-ring for damage. Renew any imperfect sealing ring. 6. Replacement sealing rings may be obtained from the supplier of the filter element. 7. Check that the upper sealing ring and O-ring are positioned correctly in the head and fit a new filter element to the head. Rotate the element slightly when fitting it to slide easily over the O-ring. Ensure that the lower sealing ring is positioned correctly in the base and offer up the base to the assembled head and element. Guide the center stud through the center tube of the element and engage it with the center bolt. Make sure that the rims of the element and base are seating correctly before tightening the center bolt. Do not overtighten. *(Lucas/CAV)*

"Magic box" devices. Every once in a while, a new device comes on the market that claims to have highly beneficial properties for preventing fuel contamination or cleaning up contaminated fuel. Some of them (such as the De-Bug device and Algae-X, which are based on passing the fuel through a magnetic field) come with impressive testimonials. I am often asked whether or not they do what they claim. The answer is, "I don't know!" What I do know is that if you keep the tank clean, filter all fuel taken on board, sample the fuel tank after refueling, keep the tank topped off when not in use, and maybe periodically use a biocide (however, if you keep water out of the tank, even this will probably be unnecessary), you should not have fuel problems. If you want to add additional devices, it will do no harm.

Changing fuel and oil filters. Changing fuel and oil filters is straightforward enough, but note that many diesel fuel systems need *bleeding* after a filter change (pages 388–93). Note also that some turbochargers have their own oil filter,

which *must be replaced whenever the engine oil filter is changed.* To change a filter:

1. Scrupulously clean off any dirt from around the old filter or filter housing (Figure 9-9).

2. Provide some means to catch any spilled fuel or oil. (I find disposable diapers—especially the ones with elasticized sides since they can be formed into a bowl shape—to be ideal!)

3. Most primary fuel filters have a central bolt or wing nut that is loosened to drop the filter bowl. Screw-on filters (both fuel and oil) are undone with the appropriate filter wrench. This tool should be a part of the boat's tool kit (note that more than one size of filter wrench may be needed for fuel and oil filters). In the absence of a filter wrench, wrap a V-belt around the filter, grip it tightly, and unscrew the filter. Failing this, hammer a large screwdriver through the filter; it may be messy, but at least you'll be able to remove the filter.

4. If a fuel filter has a replaceable element, take a close look at the old one. If it isn't more or less spotless—as it should be in a well-main-

tained fuel system—find out where the contamination is coming from and stop it before it stops the engine!

5. Fuel filters are often filled with clean diesel before installation. This reduces the amount of priming and bleeding that has to be done, but this practice carries with it the possibility of introducing contaminants directly into the injection system. For this reason, *never fill the secondary filter before installing it.* Normally the priming can be done by operating the lift pump manually (pages 389–90) or with a built-in electric lift pump. Sometimes on larger installations, it pays to install an additional electrically operated lift pump on a separate bypass manifold. This pump is placed before any filters and is used to push fuel through the filters, priming the system. Just as effective, with nothing to go wrong, is the installation of an outboard motor–style fuel priming bulb (the rubber kind you squeeze to prime an outboard). Install it in the fuel line between the fuel tank and the primary filter. (If you choose this option, be sure it is designed for use with diesel. West Marine carries suitable priming bulbs.)

6. If the new filter has its own sealing ring, *ensure that the old one doesn't remain stuck to the filter housing.* If the new filter has no sealing ring, you will have to reuse the old one. In order to prevent this, buy a stock of rings and fit one at each filter change. Note that some sealing rings have a square cross section—they *must* go in without twisting.

7. The sealing rings of screw-on filters should be lightly lubricated before installation. These filters are done up hand-tight, and then given an additional three-quarter turn with the filter wrench. If a fuel filter is done up with a wing nut, check closely for leaks around the nut when finished. This is a likely source of air in a fuel system and one of the first places to look if an operating problem develops immediately after a filter change.

After changing an oil filter, if the engine has a manually operated stop device, activate this device and then crank the engine for 15 seconds or so (but not much more, because the starter motor may overheat). This will pump oil into the new filter and prelubricate the engine. Then go ahead and crank the engine. If this is not done, the engine will run without oil pressure until the filter is filled. Once the engine is running and the oil is up to pressure, inspect the oil filter to make sure there are no leaks.

Routine oil and filter changes take little time and are relatively inexpensive but are too often neglected. *Nothing will do more to prolong the life of an engine than this simple routine maintenance.*

Oil analysis. The other tool that can greatly help to extend engine life is regular oil analysis. If an oil sample is taken at each oil change, or at least once a year, and sent to a laboratory for analysis, all kinds of trouble in the making can be detected at an early stage and headed off before serious damage is done (Figure 9-10). The cost of

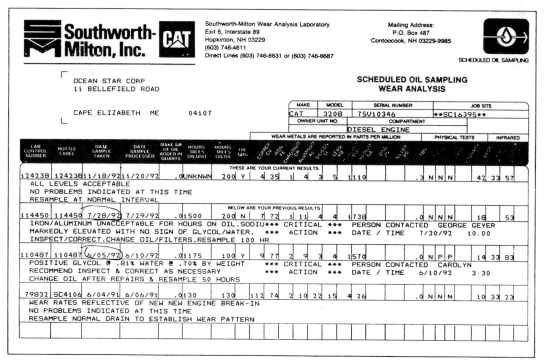

FIGURE 9-10. An oil analysis reporting the results of a series of tests performed on the oil of the *Ocean Navigator*'s *Ocean Star*. The earliest analysis is at the bottom; the latest is at the top. The second analysis revealed problems with the freshwater cooling system (glycol in the oil); the third revealed problems with saltwater intrusion into the engine from a faulty exhaust installation (indicated by the high sodium levels). *(Ocean Navigator)*

analysis is between $10 and $15; the time and trouble involved in taking a sample is minimal.

To be of maximum benefit, oil samples must be taken on a regular basis so that a typical wear pattern can be established for an engine, enabling detection of abnormalities when they occur. Oil samples have to be taken when the oil is hot and from approximately the mid-sump level so that the sample is representative of the oil in the engine. Clearly *the sampling pump and bottle must be spotlessly clean* to avoid misleading contamination. The laboratory will need to know what type and grade of oil is in the engine, how many hours the oil has been in service, and how much oil has been added since the last oil change. The more information that is provided, the more useful the results of the analysis are likely to be.

Many marinas, marine surveyors, boatyards, or mechanics can provide the address of a local laboratory. The lab will be able to provide sample bottles, labels, and sampling pumps. Better labs will also provide some literature to help in understanding the results of the analysis (www. oilanalysis.com is an excellent Web site for more than you ever wanted to know on this subject).

Air filters. Some engines have no air filters, but most small diesels have a replaceable paper element–type filter (Figure 9-11A). Less common is an oil bath–type filter (Figure 9-11B). The latter forces the air to make a rapid change of direction over a reservoir of oil. Particles of dirt are thrown out by centrifugal force and trapped in the oil. The air then passes through a fine screen that depends on an oil mist drawn up from the reservoir to keep it lubricated and effective.

In time, although the oil may still look clean, the reservoir fills with dirt, the oil becomes more viscous, less oil mist is drawn up, and the filter's efficiency declines. To prevent this, you must periodically empty the oil from the reservoir and thoroughly clean the pan with diesel or kerosene. At this time, also flush the screen with diesel or kerosene and blow it dry. When refilling the reservoir with oil, *be careful not to overfill it*—excess oil can be sucked into an engine, causing damaging *runaway* (pages 405–6).

The cooling system. Cooling systems, especially raw-water cooling systems, are one of the more common sources of trouble, usually as a result of some kind of a blockage and/or problems with the raw-water pump. The raw-water filter and raw-water pump impeller are regular maintenance items. Unfortunately, on too many engines the raw-water pump impeller is very hard to get at. If access is difficult, the following are worth doing:

1. Replace the impeller with a Globe long-life impeller (www.globerubberworks.com), which will have a longer service life and can tolerate more abuse than a standard impeller. (However, note that not all the impellers cross-referenced in the Globe catalog are exact replacements.)
2. Replace the pump cover with a Speedseal cover (www.speedseal.com), which will make pump cover removal and replacement much easier (Figures 9-12A and 9-12B).

FIGURE 9-11A. A replaceable paper element for an air filter. *(Caterpillar Tractor Company)*

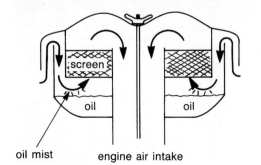

FIGURE 9-11B. An oil-bath air cleaner.

FIGURE 9-12A. A Speedseal kit with two different cover plates for different water pumps. *(Speedseal)*

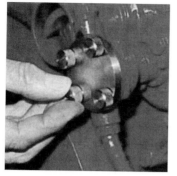

FIGURE 9-12B. Speedseal cover being removed.

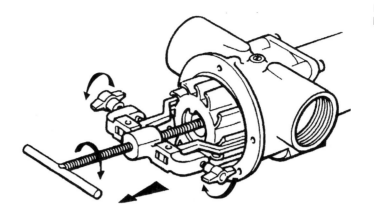

FIGURE 9-13. An impeller puller. (ITT/Jabsco)

An impeller puller (approximately $50 from West Marine and chandleries) will greatly simplify impeller removal (Figure 9-13).

Zinc anodes. *Any zinc anodes in the cooling system (the raw-water side) need replacing well before they are consumed* (Figures 9-14A and 9-14B). If this turns out to be more than once a season, you must solve a corrosion problem before a heat exchanger is eaten through or some other expensive damage is done (zincs are frequently neglected at great cost—Figures 9-14C and 9-14D). (Note

that an increasing number of modern engines do not have zincs. The manufacturers have succeeded in getting tight-enough control over the metals in the engine to ensure galvanic compatibility. However, make absolutely sure an engine really has no zincs before assuming this!)

External corrosion on a heat exchanger will be obvious (it will leak water!) but internal corrosion is harder to detect. If you suspect the tubes are leaking between the raw-water and freshwater sides, drain the raw water and remove the end

anode

pencil anode about half consumed—it should be replaced

zinc pencil anodes

FIGURE 9-14A. A zinc anode in the cooling system of a Yamaha diesel engine.

FIGURE 9-14B. Many heat exchangers have zinc pencil anodes. These should be replaced when they are no more than half consumed.

zinc totally gone; heat exchanger will be corroding

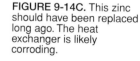
zinc totally gone; heat exchanger will be corroding

FIGURE 9-14C. This zinc should have been replaced long ago. The heat exchanger is likely corroding.

FIGURE 9-14D. Persistent neglect of the zinc on this heat exchanger caused it to corrode through several times. It would have been easier to replace the zinc than repeatedly patch up the heat exchanger!

Seizure	Excessive oil consumption	Rising oil level	Low oil pressure	High exhaust back pressure	Loss of power	Overheating	Poor idle	Hunting	Misfiring	White smoke	Blue smoke	Black smoke	Knocks	Low cranking speed	Lack of fuel	Low compression	Poor starting	Problem
															●		●	Throttle closed/fuel shut-off solenoid faulty/tank empty
					●										●		●	Lift pump diaphragm holed
					●		●		●						●		●	Plugged fuel filters
					●		●		●	●			●		●		●	Air in fuel lines
					●		●		●	●		●	●				●	Dirty fuel
					●		●		●	●		●	●				●	Defective injectors/poor quality fuel
					●		●								●		●	Injection pump leaking
					●	●	●					●	●				●	Injection timing advanced or delayed
						●						●						Too much fuel injected
	●				●				●	●	●					●	●	Piston blow-by
					●				●	●						●	●	Dry cylinder walls
					●	●	●			●	●					●	●	Valve blow-by
											●							Worn valve stems
					●		●			●	●					●	●	Decompressor levers on/valve clearances wrong/valves sticking
									●	●							●	Pre-heat device inoperative
									●			●					●	Plugged air filter
				●	●							●					●	Plugged exhaust/turbocharger/kink in exhaust hose
●			●			●												Oil level low
●	●		●											●				Wrong viscosity oil
●			●	●														Diesel dilution of oil
			●															Dirt in oil pressure relief valve/defective pressure gauge
							●	●										Governor sticking/loose linkage
							●											Governor idle spring too slack
●						●												Defective water pump/defective pump valves/air bound water lines
●						●												Closed sea cock/plugged raw-water filter or screen/plugged cooling system
●		●				●				●	●					●	●	Blown head gasket/cracked head/water in cylinders
●						●												Uneven load on cylinders
					●								●			●	●	Worn bearings
						●												Seized piston
					●									●			●	Auxiliary equipment engaged
														●			●	Battery low/loose connections/undersized battery cables
●					●	●						●						Engine overload/rope in propeller
		●									●							Leaking turbocharger oil seals
	●														●		●	Water in the cylinders

caps. If water is dribbling out of any of the tubes, you know they have failed. You can use the heat exchanger temporarily, although with some loss of capacity, by plugging both ends of the offending tube(s) with a piece of softwood doweling.

Antifreeze. On the freshwater side, the antifreeze will need renewing at least every 2 years. Antifreeze does not lose its antifreezing properties, but various corrosion-prevention and anti-foaming inhibitors get used up and need replacing.

In recent years, long-life antifreeze (e.g., General Motors' Dex-Cool) has been introduced to the automotive market, and is being used in some marine engines. For years there also have been persistent rumors of problems with it, and now there are a number of class-action lawsuits against General Motors. To avoid antifreeze problems, adhere to the engine manufacturer's recommendations. If these include the use of long-life antifreeze, I would still change it *at least every 2 years* (and not the 5 years it is reputed to last).

Injection elbow. Typically, exhausts are water cooled. The cooling water is injected into an elbow coming out of the exhaust manifold. In most installations, this injection line should have a vented loop (see below) that will have a valve that needs cleaning from time to time. Sooner or later, the nipple or elbow will corrode through, so inspect them periodically (galvanized nipples threaded into a bronze elbow, which you see from time to time, will corrode especially fast). Carry a spare nipple and elbow. A temporary elbow repair can be made by wrapping a strip of rubber cut from an inner tube tightly around the elbow and clamping with two hose clamps or Jubilee clips (Figures 9-15A and 9-15B).

Electrical systems. The starting and other electrical circuits must be kept free of corrosion and from vibration or contact with hot or moving parts; keep the wires neatly bundled and properly fastened. On boats with wet bilges (mostly older, wooden boats), starter motors can be a source of trouble due to water getting thrown up into the pinion gear and causing rust. If this is a possibility, periodically remove the starter and lubricate the pinion gear.

Scheduled overhauls. Beyond this, engine manufacturers lay down specific schedules for overhaul procedures of such things as injectors and valve clearances. However, since the marine environment and engine use vary so much, one engine may need work much sooner than another, especially if it's subjected to a poor operating regimen, while for other engines some

of the maintenance intervals may be safely extended (such as injector overhauls). For this reason, I tend to subscribe to the philosophy "If it ain't broke, don't fix it!" At the first sign of trouble, however—difficult starting, changes in oil pressure or water temperature, a smoky exhaust, vibration, or a new noise—the problem must be resolved right away; delay may cause expensive repair bills (see the Troubleshooting sections).

Given that the timing of overhauls of such things as injectors and valve clearances is not critical, and that such maintenance sometimes has unintended consequences (e.g., a gasket is not properly replaced and an oil leak develops), I particularly recommend that maintenance be done when the boat will remain in the neighborhood of the mechanic for some time afterward. This way, if an issue develops it can be resolved with as little inconvenience as is possible. The corollary to this is to *avoid maintenance that is not especially time sensitive immediately prior to an ocean passage* or a voyage where it will be difficult to deal with secondary problems if they arise.

FIGURE 9-15A. A corroded galvanized exhaust elbow. The hot gases and water from the engine exhaust have eaten right through it.

FIGURE 9-15B. The same corroded exhaust elbow patched with rubber inner tube and hose clamps. This repair held for 200 hours of engine-running time.

Troubleshooting Part 1: Failure to Start

When troubleshooting an engine, study the symptoms before dismantling anything. All too often, engines are taken apart without good cause, in the process often destroying the evidence needed to figure out the problem!

It is necessary to distinguish two differing situations when dealing with an engine that will not start. The first is a failure to crank—the engine will not turn over at all. The second is a failure to fire—the engine turns over but does not run (see below).

Failure to Crank

When an engine will not crank at all, the problem is almost always electrical (see the Starter Motor Circuits section in Chapter 7), but occasionally it is the result of water in the cylinders or a complete seizure of the engine or transmission. Before checking the electrical system, see if the engine can be turned over by hand with the hand crank (if fitted) or by placing a suitably sized wrench on the crankshaft-pulley nut (turn

(continued on page 382)

Every year I get a number of e-mails from people with flooded engines and/or generators. More often than not, the engine has functioned fine for years, but then a long-dreamed-of cruise was undertaken and at some point the engine flooded. The common thread is that on an offshore passage, the boat got into rougher conditions or bigger seas than it had seen before. The large waves rushing past the boat set up hydrostatic pressures that caused water to siphon into the engine. Even on new boats, way too many engines and generators are still installed in a manner that makes this scenario possible.

A less common cause of engine flooding is the installation of a scoop-type water inlet facing forward on the outside of the hull. Anytime the boat is moving at more than a few knots, this generates pressure in the raw-water system. In normal circumstances, the vanes in the rubber impeller raw-water pump (see page 397) will hold this pressure at bay when the engine is not running. But should the vanes get damaged, water will be driven up through the heat exchanger and into the exhaust, where it will build up and flood the engine. Scoops, if used, should be fitted backward (i.e., with the opening facing aft).

On any engine that is below the waterline (most sailboat engines) both the water-injection line into the exhaust and the exhaust pipe itself create the potential for water to siphon back into the exhaust, fill it, and flow into the engine via open exhaust valves (Figures 9-16A, 9-16B, and 9-16C). The injection line must be looped at least 6 inches (15 cm) above the *loaded* waterline *at all angles of heel*, and preferably 12 inches (30 cm), with a siphon break at the top of the loop (Figures 9-16D and 9-16E).

Siphon breaks. Traditional rubber-flap siphon breaks (Figure 9-16F) tend to plug with salt. Once plugged, they are inoperative and may also spray salt water all over the running engine and its electrical systems (Figure 9-16G), adding insult to injury. The spring-loaded types (e.g., Scot Pump—www.scotpump.com—Figure 9-16H) are far less prone to plugging than the traditional rubber-flap type. My preference, however, is to remove the valve element altogether, add a hose to the top of the vented

continued

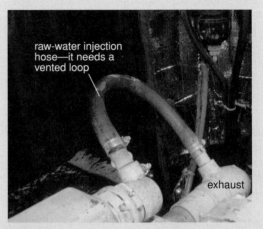

FIGURE 9-16B. Another installation without a vented loop.

FIGURE 9-16C. Yet another installation without a vented loop!

FIGURE 9-16A. An improper raw-water installation. The water injection line goes directly from the heat exchanger to the exhaust without a vented loop.

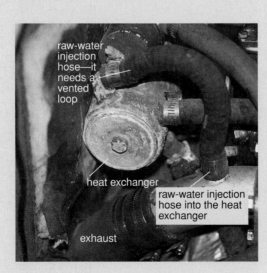

Siphon Breaks (continued)

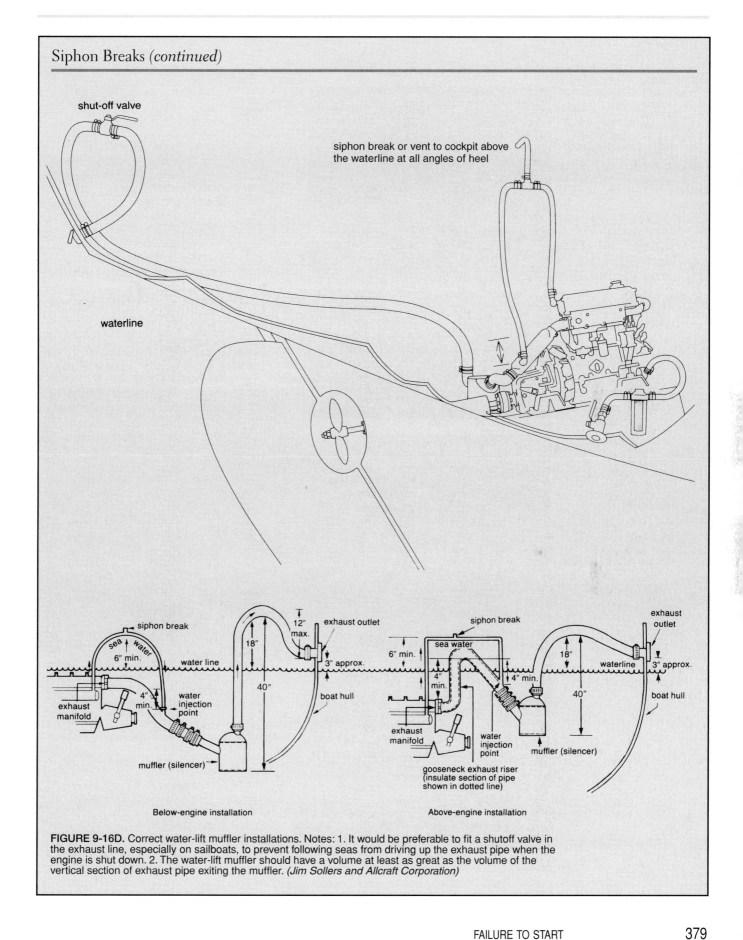

shut-off valve

siphon break or vent to cockpit above the waterline at all angles of heel

waterline

Below-engine installation

siphon break

sea water

6" min.

water line

exhaust manifold

4" min.

water injection point

12" max.

exhaust outlet

18"

40"

3" approx.

boat hull

muffler (silencer)

Above-engine installation

siphon break

sea water

6" min.

4" min.

4" min.

exhaust manifold

water injection point

gooseneck exhaust riser (insulate section of pipe shown in dotted line)

muffler (silencer)

18"

40"

waterline

exhaust outlet

3" approx.

boat hull

FIGURE 9-16D. Correct water-lift muffler installations. Notes: 1. It would be preferable to fit a shutoff valve in the exhaust line, especially on sailboats, to prevent following seas from driving up the exhaust pipe when the engine is shut down. 2. The water-lift muffler should have a volume at least as great as the volume of the vertical section of exhaust pipe exiting the muffler. *(Jim Sollers and Allcraft Corporation)*

FIGURE 9-16E. The same engine as in Figure 9-16A after installation of a vented loop in the raw-water circuit, well above the waterline.

vented loop above the waterline at all angles of heel

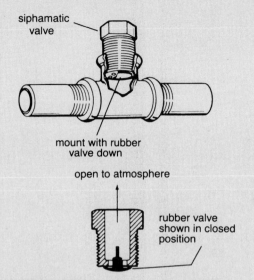

siphamatic valve

mount with rubber valve down

open to atmosphere

rubber valve shown in closed position

FIGURE 9-16F. A Kohler siphon break. *(Kohler)*

FIGURE 9-16G. This boat has a vented loop that was spraying water into the engine room, so the owner capped the loop and rendered it inoperative!

the vented loop had been leaking so the owner capped it; it is now useless

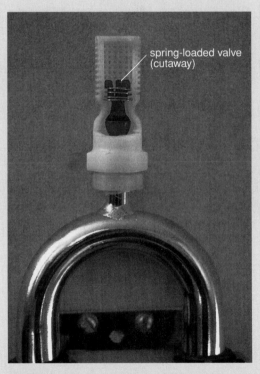

spring-loaded valve (cutaway)

FIGURE 9-16H. A spring-loaded siphon break.

loop, and discharge this well above the water-line (into the cockpit works well; Figure 9-16I). If you plan to do this, you must discharge above the highest point in the exhaust hose to prevent water weeping out of the discharge fitting when the engine is running. Installed like this, the vent hose will never plug and cannot put salt water in the engine.

Exhaust hose. The exhaust and injection water end up in a water-lift-type muffler (silencer). From here, loop the exhaust hose well above the *loaded* waterline (at least 12 inches/

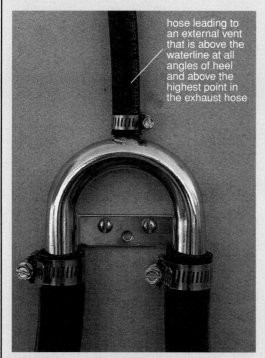

hose leading to an external vent that is above the waterline at all angles of heel and above the highest point in the exhaust hose

FIGURE 9-16I. A siphon break on an engine-cooling circuit that has been adapted by removing the valve and adding a length of hose, which is vented into the cockpit.

30 cm) and then maintain a slope of at least ½ inch per foot down to the through-hull. If the exhaust hose is long, place the loop close to the engine to minimize the volume of water that can flow back into the muffler when the engine is shut down. Also make sure there are no low spots where water can be trapped to flow back into the engine when the boat pounds and rolls. In sailboats, it is a good idea to install an *accessible* positive shutoff valve at the through-hull in case following seas threaten to drive up the back of the boat when the engine is not in use.

On many modern boats, a water separator is installed at the top of the exhaust loop (see, for example, Halyard, the originators of this device—www.halyard.eu.com—or Centek Industries—www.centekindustries.com). This separates the cooling water from the exhaust gases, allowing them to be discharged separately. It also, in effect, functions as a giant siphon break, adding another layer of protection against engine flooding. Another way to minimize the chance of backflooding through the exhaust is to install a plenum, or gooseneck, at the high point in the hose. This is nothing more than a chamber in which the exhaust hose from the engine comes in at the top, and the hose to the through-hull exits from the bottom. If a wave drives a slug of water up the exhaust, the sudden increase in exhaust cross section and volume in the plenum acts as a temporary reservoir that drains as soon as the hydrostatic pressure eases.

The higher an exhaust, water separator, or plenum/gooseneck is looped above the waterline, the greater the security from siphonic action, but the greater the back pressure (see page 403) since the cooling water has to be lifted to this high point. (Note also that when the engine is shut down, the water in the vertical section of the exhaust pipe will run back into the water-lift muffler; therefore, the muffler must have a volume at least as great as that of this vertical section of pipe.) To keep back pressure within acceptable limits, the vertical lift of the cooling water should not exceed 40 inches (1 m) on naturally aspirated engines (i.e., without turbochargers). This corresponds to a back pressure at full load of somewhere around 1.5 psi. On turbocharged engines, the water lift should be kept down to 20 inches (½ m) to give a full-load back pressure of around 0.75 psi.

In situations where a standard water-lift exhaust will create excessive back pressure, a *standpipe* exhaust may be used in which the muffler is raised as in Figure 9-16J. In general, the less the back pressure, the less the silencing effect, so an additional in-line muffler (silencer) may be required. The dry section of exhaust from the exhaust manifold to the standpipe needs effective insulation.

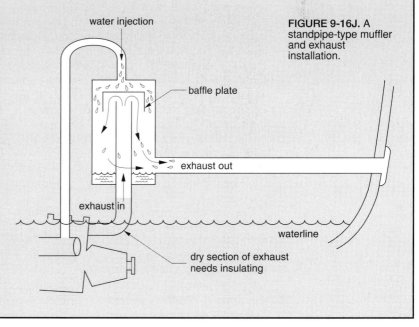

water injection

baffle plate

exhaust out

exhaust in

waterline

dry section of exhaust needs insulating

FIGURE 9-16J. A standpipe-type muffler and exhaust installation.

(continued from page 377)
the engine in its normal direction of rotation to prevent accidentally undoing the nut). If the engine has a manual transmission, put it in gear and turn it with a pipe wrench on the propeller shaft, but only after wrapping a rag around the shaft to avoid scarring it.

If the engine is locked up solidly, it has probably seized and will need professional attention. If it turns over a little and then locks up, or turns with extreme difficulty, water may have siphoned into the cylinders through a water-cooled exhaust (see the Siphon Breaks sidebar). The other way water may have got in is from excessive cranking, since anytime an engine is cranked the raw-water pump will push water into the exhaust, but until the engine fires there will not be the necessary exhaust gases to lift the water out. Eventually enough water can accumulate to flood the engine. (If an engine requires extensive cranking, either periodically drain the water-lift muffler or temporarily close the raw-water inlet—but be sure to remember to open it once the engine starts.)

Water in the engine. Water, especially salt water, that remains in the engine for any length of time will do expensive damage to bearing and cylinder surfaces, requiring a complete engine overhaul. If the water is discovered in time, it can be eased out of the exhaust and the engine will continue to operate.

Water is not compressible, so any attempt to rapidly crank an engine with water in a cylinder that is on its compression stroke is likely to do damage (piston rings get broken and connecting rods bent). If the engine has decompression levers and a hand crank, simply turn it over several times. If it does not have decompression levers, a professional will often remove injectors and blow the water out of the injector holes. However, all too often injectors are difficult to remove, and when amateurs try to remove them, damage is done. On the other hand, if the engine can be turned over in small increments, then on the compression stroke the water in those cylinders can be forced a little at a time past the piston rings without breaking them. This is especially the case on engines with some wear on them. The key thing is not to force the process.

So, to remove water, either *close the throttle so the engine will not start, or disable the engine in some other way* (this is really important!). Flick the starter motor on and off, or use a wrench on the crankshaft-pulley nut (this gives more control) to turn the engine over bit by bit, turning in the normal direction of rotation and pausing between each movement. Don't rush things!

Another way to do this involves more work but minimizes the risk of doing damage. Remove the valve cover and push a coin (such as a U.S. quarter or a UK 5 pence piece) in between the tops of the valve stems and the rocker arms. This will crack the valves open. Now turn the motor over a little at a time, and the water will be forced out the valves. Note that on some engines the clearance between the tops of the pistons and the valve faces is quite small. If the engine locks up again when doing this, the coins may be holding the valves open too far. Take the coins out before something gets bent!

Once the engine has turned through two complete revolutions, it should be free of water. Spin it a couple of times *without starting it*. Now check the crankcase for water in the oil. If any is present, change the oil and filter. Start the engine and run it for a few minutes to warm it, then shut it down and *change the oil and filter again*. Now give the engine a good run to drive out any remaining moisture. After 25 hours of normal operation, or at the first sign of any more water in the oil, *change the oil and filter for a third time*.

Put appropriate siphon breaks in the cooling and exhaust system (see the Siphon Breaks sidebar). (For more on water in the engine, see pages 406–7.)

Engine Cranks but Won't Fire

If an engine will not start as usual, it is important to stop cranking and start thinking! Those extra couple of cranks in the hope that some miracle will happen very often flatten the battery to the point at which the engine cannot be started at all. Most starting problems are simple ones that can be solved with a little thought—and frequently in a whole lot less time than it will take to recharge a dead battery!

A diesel engine is a thoroughly logical piece of equipment. If the airflow is unobstructed, the air is being compressed to ignition temperatures, and the fuel injection is correctly metered and timed, the engine more or less has to fire. Troubleshooting an engine that won't start boils down to finding the simplest possible procedure to establish which of these three preconditions for ignition is missing.

Checking the airflow. A failure to reach ignition temperatures or problems with the fuel supply are the most likely causes for starting failures. The airflow is the easiest to check, however, so investigate it first.

Does the engine have air? This may seem like a stupid question, but certain engines (notably Detroit Diesels) have an emergency shutdown device—a flap that completely closes off the air inlet to the engine and guarantees that no ignition will take place. Once the flap is activated, even if the remote operating lever is returned to its normal position, the flap will remain closed until manually reset *at the engine*. (*Note that stopping an engine by closing the air flap will soon damage the supercharger's air seals and should be done only in an emergency, such as engine runaway—more on this later.*)

If the engine doesn't have an air flap, what about the air filter? It may be plugged, especially if the engine has been operated in a dusty environment. It may have a plastic bag stuck in it or even a dead bird (which I found on one occasion). If the boat has been laid up all winter, a bird's nest may be in there. Or maybe someone placed a plastic bag over the air inlet when winterizing the engine.

Does the engine have a turbocharger? Poor oil change procedures or operating behavior (particularly racing the engine on start-up and just before shutdown—more on this later) may have caused the shaft to seize in its bearings. Remove the inlet ducting and use a finger to see if the compressor wheel spins freely.

The other side of the airflow equation is the ability to vent the exhaust overboard. Starting problems, particularly on Detroit Diesels, may sometimes be the result of excessive back pressure in the exhaust. *The most obvious cause would be a closed seacock.* Other possibilities are excessive carbon buildup in the exhaust piping or in the turbocharger. In cold weather, there could be frozen water in a water lift–type muffler, which has the same effect as a closed seacock.

Achieving ignition temperatures. If there is no obstruction in the airflow, perhaps the air charge is not being adequately compressed to achieve ignition temperatures. Although numerous variables may be at work here, an attempt must be made to isolate them in order to identify problems.

Cold-start devices. The colder the ambient air, the lower its temperature when compressed, and the harder it is to get it up to ignition temperatures. As if this were not enough, cold thickens engine oil, which makes the engine crank sluggishly. Slower cranking gives the air in the cylinders more time to dissipate heat to cold engine surfaces and more time to escape past poorly seated valves and piston rings. In addition, a battery that puts out 100% of its rated capacity at 80°F/27°C will put out 65% at 32°F/0°C, and only 40% at 0°F/–18°C.

Cold is a major obstacle to reliable engine starting (refer back to Figure 1-11A). As a result,

Troubleshooting Chart 9-2. Diesel Engine Problems: Engine Cranks but Won't Fire	
Note: See Chart 7-2 if engine won't crank.	
Is the engine cranking slowly? Note: Stop cranking and save the battery! **NO**	**YES** FIX: If slow cranking is due to cold, see below. Try the methods for boosting speed listed in the text under Cranking Speed. If these fail, recharge the batteries.
Is the engine too cold? **NO** TEST: Check cold-start devices. If glow plugs and manifold heaters are working, the cylinder head will be noticeably warmer. See text under Achieving Ignition Temperatures for testing glow plugs.	**YES** FIX: Replace faulty glow plugs or manifold heaters; warm the engine, inlet manifold, fuel lines, and battery using a hair dryer, lightbulb, or kerosene lantern. Raise temperature slowly and evenly—concentrated heat can crack the engine castings.
Is the air supply obstructed? **NO** TEST: Check any air flaps, air filter, and exhaust seacock for blockage or closure.	**YES** FIX: Open air flap; replace air filter element; open exhaust seacock.
Is the fuel level too low? **NO** TEST: Check the fuel level in the tank.	**YES** FIX: Add fuel. It may also be necessary to bleed the fuel system (see pages 388–93).
Is the fuel delivery to the engine obstructed? **NO** TEST: Check to see that no kill devices are in operation; all fuel valves are open; no fuel filters are plugged; the remote throttle is actually advancing the throttle lever on the engine; and any fuel solenoid valve is functioning.	**YES** FIX: If the Stop or Kill control has been pulled out, push it in. Check power supply to and operation of fuel solenoid valve by connecting it directly to the battery with a jumper wire. If see-through fuel filters are plugged, change filters. Open the throttle wide.
Is the fuel delivery to the injectors obstructed? **NO** TEST: Open throttle wide, loosen an injector nut, and crank the engine. Note: If fluid spurts out when conducting this test, make sure the fluid is fuel, not water.	**YES** FIX: If no fuel spurts out, check primary, secondary, and lift-pump filters, and bleed the system. Check fuel lift pump for diaphragm failure. If fuel still does not flow, go back and check system for fuel level, blockages, and air leaks. Only after all else has been eliminated, suspect injection pump failure.
Is the compression adequate to achieve ignition temperature? **NO** TEST: (1) Suspect inadequate cylinder lubrication or piston blowby.... (2) Suspect valve blowby....	**YES** FIX: (1) On engines with custom-fitted oil cups on the inlet manifold, fill cups with oil and then crank engine. On others, remove air filter and squirt oil into the inlet manifold as close to the cylinders as possible while cranking. See Compression in text. (2) If valves are poorly seated, a top-end overhaul is needed.
Suspect incorrect timing, a worn fuel injection pump, or worn or damaged injectors.	FIX: Replace pump or injectors. Timing problems indicate a serious mechanical failure; correction requires a specialist.

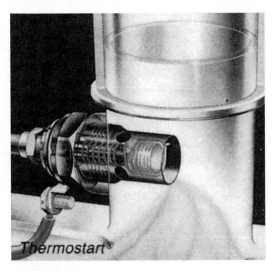

FIGURE 9-17. A Thermostart flame primer. *(Lucas/CAV)*

process (some Detroit Diesels). Note that starting fluid *should not be used in most instances* (see the Starting Fluid and WD-40 sidebar).

If glow plugs and manifold heaters are working, the cylinder head or manifold will be noticeably warmer near the individual heating devices. If they are not working, first check the wiring in the circuit. There is frequently a solenoid activated by the ignition switch, or a preheat switch, in the same way that a starter motor solenoid is activated by the ignition switch. You can perform the same kinds of circuit tests to this circuit as to a starting circuit (see the Starter Motor Circuits section in Chapter 7, but substitute "glow plugs" for "starter motor").

Check glow plugs with an ammeter (they should draw about 5 to 6 amps per plug on a 12-volt system) or an ohmmeter (around 1.5 ohms per plug). To test the amp draw in the absence of a suitable clamp-on DC ammeter, place a DC ammeter in the power supply line between the main hot wire and each glow plug *in turn* (not in the main harness itself, since this may carry up to 40 amps on a six-cylinder engine). Test resistances by disconnecting the hot wire from each glow plug and checking from the hot terminal on the plug to a ground, using the most sensitive ohms scale on the meter (Figure 9-18). Only a good ohmmeter will be accurate enough to distinguish between a functioning glow plug and a shorted plug.

many engines incorporate some form of a cold-start device to boost the temperature of the air charge during initial cranking. The most common device is a glow plug—a small heater installed in a precombustion chamber. Glow plugs are run off the engine-cranking battery, becoming red hot when activated.

Other devices include a heater in the air inlet manifold—perhaps a heating element, or a *flame primer* (a device that ignites a diesel spray in the inlet manifold, thus warming the entering air; Figure 9-17), or a carefully metered shot of starting fluid to trigger the initial combustion

FIGURE 9-18. Using a multimeter to test a glow plug. *(Jim Sollers)*

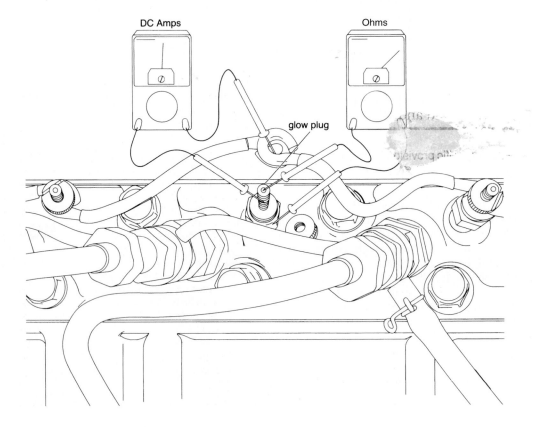

You can unscrew a glow plug, hold it against a good ground (the engine block), and turn it on. It should glow red hot (Figure 9-19; be careful not to burn yourself). However, if the plug is seized in the cylinder head, soak it in penetrating fluid and leave it for a while before trying to get it out; it is not uncommon for heavy-handed mechanics to break them off!

If a flame primer is not working, check its electrical connections and fuel supply. If the unit has been removed, test the heating coil by jumping it from the battery. Also check the fuel discharge and atomization, but *not at the same time since this may result in an uncontrolled flare-up.*

Any safe means used to boost the temperature of the engine, battery, and inlet air will help with difficult starting. This includes using a hair dryer, lightbulb, or kerosene lantern to warm fuel lines, filters, manifolds, and incoming air; removing oil and water, warming them on the galley stove, and returning them; heating battery compartments with a lightbulb; or removing the battery, putting it in a heated crew compartment, and returning it once it is warm.

A propane torch flame can also be used to boost temperatures. Gently play the flame over the inlet manifold and fuel lines, and across the air inlet when the engine is cranked so that it heats the incoming air. *Never use a torch in the presence of gasoline or propane vapors.* Do not play the torch flame over electrical harnesses, plastic fuel lines and fittings, or other combustibles!

Raise temperatures slowly and evenly, playing the heat source over a broad area. Concentrated heat may crack an engine's castings. Boiling water or very hot oil may do the same.

red-hot glow plug

battery negative

Compression. When an engine is operating, the lubrication system maintains a fine film of oil on the cylinder walls and the sides of the pistons. This oil plays an important part in maintaining the seal of the piston rings on the cylinder walls. After an engine is shut down, the oil slowly drains back to the crankcase. An engine that has been shut down for a long period of time may suffer a considerable amount of *blowby* when an attempt is made to restart it because the lack of oil on the cylinder walls and piston rings reduces the seal, and therefore the compression.

An engine that grows harder to start over time is probably also losing compression, but this time because of poorly seated valves and piston-ring wear. *(Note that a Detroit Diesel exhibits the same symptoms if the blower is defective.)* The air in the cylinders is not compressed enough to produce ignition temperatures.

FIGURE 9-19. Testing a glow plug by wiring it directly across a battery. The plug can be held at the top, but the probe should not be touched!

Starting Fluid and WD-40

Unless sp........n for the use of starting fluid is m........ngine (e.g., some Detroit Diesels ....illars), do not use it at all. It is suck........ the air charge and, being extrem........e, will often ignite before the piston ....the top of its compression stroke. This can result in serious damage to pistons and connecting rods. For some reason, Detroit Diesels seem to tolerate starting fluid better than four-cycle diesels.

If starting fluid must be used, do not spray it directly into the air inlet manifold. Rather, spray it onto a rag and hold this to the air intake. This will control the amount being drawn in. Adding a little diesel to the inlet manifold will also help the engine to pick up once the starting fluid fires.

Diesels will run on WD-40 at far less risk of premature detonation than that possible with starting fluid. In fact, if the battery is low but it is necessary to do some extended cranking—such as when you are having problems purging a fuel system—you can open the throttle wide and spray a continuous stream of WD-40 into the air inlet while cranking. The engine will fire and continue to run as long as the spray is maintained. The engine speed can be controlled by varying the rate of spray until the fuel system is bled and the engine takes over. This is also an effective way to get a drowned engine running again, after the water has been driven out of the cylinders and the oil and filter changed. Note, however, that WD-40 should not be used in conjunction with manifold heating devices since it may ignite in the manifold and blow back, causing a fire.

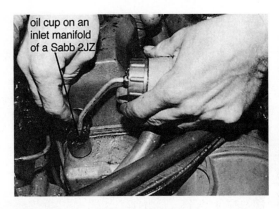

oil cup on an
inlet manifold
of a Sabb 2JZ

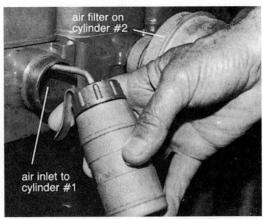

air filter on
cylinder #2

air inlet to
cylinder #1

Short of a *top-end* overhaul, there is not a lot that can be done about valve blowby. Piston blowby and a loss of cylinder lubrication, however, can be cured temporarily by adding a little oil to the cylinders. The oil dribbles down and settles on the piston rings, sealing them against the cylinder walls.

If you have plenty of battery reserve, set the throttle wide open and crank for a few seconds. Then let the engine rest for a minute. This allows three things to happen: (1) the injected diesel will dribble down onto the piston rings; (2) the initial heat of compression will take the chill off the cylinders; and (3) the battery will catch its breath. Then try cranking again.

If the engine still won't start, or if little battery reserve remains, introduce a small amount of oil directly into the engine cylinders.

On engines with custom-fitted oil cups on the inlet manifold (for example, many older Sabbs—Figure 9-20), fill the cups with oil, then crank the engine. On others, remove the air filter and squirt oil into the inlet manifold as close to the cylinders as possible, while cranking the engine. The oil will be sucked in when the engine cranks. Let the engine sit for a minute or two to allow the oil to settle on the piston rings. After starting, the engine will smoke abominably for a few seconds as it burns off the oil—this is OK. Put the air filter back in place as soon as the engine fires.

When applying oil to the cylinders, use only a couple of squirts in each cylinder. Oil is noncompressible so too much will damage the piston rings and connecting rods. Also, keep the oil can clear of turbocharger blades—a touch of the can will result in expensive damage.

Oil used in this fashion is often a magic—albeit a temporary—cure for poor starting, but the engine needs attention to *solve* the compression problem.

Cranking speed. No diesel will start without a brisk cranking speed (at least 60 to 80 rpm; most small diesels will crank at 200 to 300 rpm). The engine, especially when it is cold, just will not attain sufficient compression temperature to ignite the injected diesel. If a motor turns over sluggishly, stop cranking and save the battery.

Check the battery's state of charge. If it is fully charged, check for voltage drop (which may be robbing the starter motor of power) between the battery and the starter motor (Chapter 7). Assuming a good battery and a properly functioning starting circuit, the techniques in the sections on Cold-Start Devices and Compression (see above) will help generate that first vital power stroke. Sometimes the following tricks will also boost cranking speeds:

- If fitted with decompression levers and a hand crank, turn the engine over a few times by hand to break the grip of the cold oil on the bearings. Assist the starter motor by hand-cranking until the engine gains momentum, then knock down the decompression levers.

- Disconnect all belt-driven auxiliary equipment (refrigeration compressor, pumps, etc.) to reduce the starting load.

- Place a hand over the air inlet and then crank. Restricting the airflow will reduce compression and help the engine build up speed. Once the engine is cranking smartly, remove your hand—the motor should fire. *Never block the air inlet on an operating engine—the high suction pressures generated may damage the engine and cause injury.*

- An additional trick for *sailboats with a manual transmission and a fixed-blade propeller* is to sail the boat hard in neutral with the propeller freewheeling, then start cranking and throw the transmission into forward. The additional momentum of the propeller may bump-start the engine.

Solving fuel problems. If an engine is cranking smartly, with sufficient compression to produce ignition temperatures, but still won't start, the culprit is almost certainly the fuel system. Unfortunately, the fuel system has the potential for causing a considerable number of problems! Some are easy to check, but others can only be guessed at.

Check the obvious. Diesel engines are shut down by closing off the fuel supply. On some engines, this occurs when the throttle is closed; others continue to idle at minimum throttle settings and have a separate Stop control to shut off the remaining fuel supply. Has the Stop control inadvertently been left pulled out? Has an emergency shutdown device, such as the air flap on a Detroit Diesel, been inadvertently tripped? Is the throttle open to the position specified for starting by the engine manufacturer? *A diesel will never start with the throttle closed.* Trace the throttle cable from the throttle lever in the cockpit to the engine and make sure that it is actually advancing the throttle lever on the engine.

Is there plenty of fuel in the tank? The fuel suction line is probably set an inch or two off the bottom of the tank; if the boat is heeling, air can be sucked in even when the fuel level appears to be adequate. Is the fuel valve (if fitted) open? If there is fuel and the valve is open, but no fuel is reaching the engine, is there a small filter screen inside the tank on the suction line? If so, it may have become plugged. If such a screen is fitted, *throw it away*—this is not the place to be filtering fuel. (Sometimes it is extremely difficult to get at this filter screen, but you may be able to force it off the end of the pickup line, or punch big holes in it, by poking a piece of doweling or a sturdy piece of wire down the suction line into the tank.)

Most engines have mechanical lift pumps, but a few have electrical pumps. With the latter there should be a quiet clicking when the ignition is first turned on. If you are in doubt about an electric pump's operation, loosen the discharge line and see if fuel flows.

Solenoid valve. Many newer engines have a solenoid-operated fuel shutdown valve that is held in the closed position by a spring when the ignition is turned off. When the ignition is turned on, it energizes an electromagnet that opens the valve. Anytime the electrical supply to the solenoid is interrupted, the magnet is deenergized and the spring closes the valve. Any failure in the electrical circuit to the valve will automatically shut off the fuel supply to the engine.

Some solenoid fuel valves are built into the back of the fuel injection pump—they are identified by a couple of wires coming off the pump close to the fuel inlet line. Others are mounted separately but close to the pump (Figure 9-21). A rod coming from the back of the valve actuates a lever on the pump. You can check the opera-

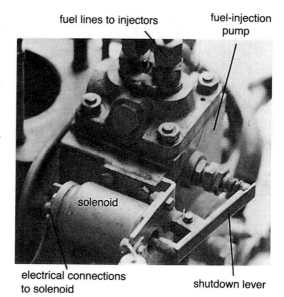

fuel lines to injectors
fuel-injection pump
solenoid
electrical connections to solenoid
shutdown lever

FIGURE 9-21. A solenoid-operated fuel shutdown valve.

tion of a solenoid valve by connecting it directly to a battery with a jumper wire. Take care to get the positive and negative leads the right way around. If the valve has only one wire, this is the positive lead; if two, one will run to ground, and you want the other one.

Fuel filters. The primary fuel filter should have a see-through bowl that should be checked for water and sediment (Figure 9-22A). If the bowl is opaque, open the drain on its base and take a sample. On many fuel systems, this will let air into the system, so you will also need to bleed the system (see below). It is not uncommon for a primary fuel filter element to be completely plugged. If this is the case, don't take chances;

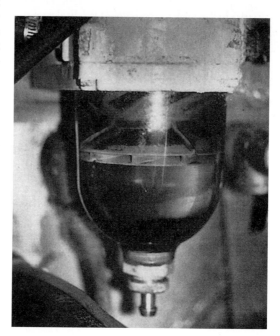

FIGURE 9-22A. A primary fuel filter with a see-through bowl. The sediment is a sure sign that the tank needs flushing. (This filter does not meet current Coast Guard regulations because it has no protective metal deflector plate around its base.)

FIGURE 9-22B. The fuel filter inside the top of a lift pump.

FIGURE 9-22C. To clean a lift-pump filter, undo the central retaining bolt, lift off the cover, remove the filter screen, flush it in clean diesel, and replace it. Make sure the cover gasket is undamaged and that you make a good seal when replacing the cover—any leakage here will let air into the fuel system. (Perkins Engines Ltd.)

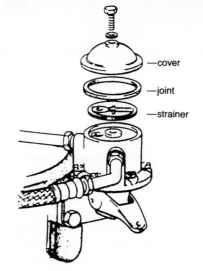

—cover

—joint

—strainer

replace it along with the secondary filter element and drain the tank or pump it down until all traces of contamination are removed. If filters clog repeatedly, it is likely that sediment has built up inside the tank to the level of the fuel pickup. The tank needs opening and flushing.

If there is no primary filter, or if there is any sign of contamination making its way past the primary filter, *check the filter screen in the lift pump*, which can normally be found by undoing the center bolt and removing the cover (Figures 9-22B and 9-22C).

Assuming the tank has fuel and the filters are clean, the next step is to find out if the fuel lines have air in them.

Bleeding (purging) a fuel system. Air trapped in the fuel system can bring many diesels to a halt, although the extent to which this is true varies markedly from one engine to another. Detroit Diesels and modern common rail diesels (e.g., the latest models from Volvo Penta—www.volvopenta.com) can be purged simply by opening the throttle and cranking, whereas many older diesels can be completely disabled with even tiny amounts of air. When air has to be purged from a fuel system, the process is known as *bleeding*.

Traditional diesels. With the exception of Detroit Diesels and other common rail systems (see below), typical fuel systems for small diesel engines are shown in Figures 9-23A and 9-23B. Fuel is drawn from the tank by a lift pump (sometimes called a feed pump) and passes through the primary filter. The lift pump pushes the fuel on at low pressure through the secondary filter to the injection pump. (On some engines, the lift pump is incorporated into the back of the fuel injection pump rather than being a separate item.) The injection pump meters the fuel and pumps exact amounts at precise times and at very high pressures down the injection (*delivery*) lines to the injectors, then into the cylinders. Any surplus fuel at the injectors returns to the secondary filter or tank via *leak-off*, or return, pipes.

The more cylinders an engine has, the greater the number of fuel lines. The various filters and lines can sometimes become a little confusing. Just remember that the secondary fuel filter is generally mounted on the engine close to the fuel injection pump, whereas the primary filter is generally mounted off the engine, or on the engine bed, closer to the fuel tank. The filters should have an arrow on them to indicate the direction of fuel flow; sometimes the ports will be marked "IN" and "OUT."

FIGURES 9-23A AND 9-23B. Fuel system schematics. Note the two different types of fuel injection pumps in common use on four-cycle engines—distributor type and jerk type. They are easily distinguished since the fuel lines are arranged in a circle on the former and in a straight line on the latter. (Lucas/CAV)

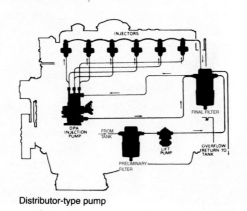

Distributor-type pump

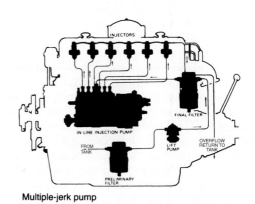

Multiple-jerk pump

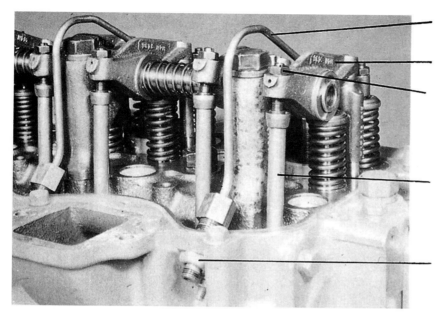

FIGURE 9-24. Internal fuel lines. Shown here are the fuel lines inside a valve cover and their point of entry into the engine. (*Caterpillar Tractor Company*)

fuel line to injector

rocker arm

valve clearance adjusting screw

push rod

fuel line adaptor (external fuel line has been removed)

There will be an injection line (delivery pipe) from the injection pump to every injector, but the leak-off pipes go from one injector to the next, then down a common pipe to the secondary filter or fuel tank. This makes it easy to distinguish delivery pipes and leak-off pipes on most engines. A few engines, however (notably many Caterpillars), have *internal* fuel lines and injectors that are hidden by the valve cover. In this case, each delivery pipe runs from the fuel injection pump to a fitting on the side of the cylinder head, and from there all is hidden (Figure 9-24).

At various points in the system are bleed nipples—normally on the filters and the injection pump (Figure 9-25); there should be one on the top of the secondary filter. On the base of a mechanical lift pump is usually a small handle, enabling it to be operated manually (Figures 9-26A and 9-26B). Pump this handle up and down. If it has little or no stroke, spin the engine a half turn or so to free the manual action. (See the Lift Pump Failure section below for an explanation of this.) Electric pumps are activated by turning on the ignition.

Engines that have neither an external lift pump nor an electric pump generally have a manual pump attached to the injection pump, to one of the filters, or at some other convenient point in the system (Figure 9-27). Bleeding follows the same procedure as that used on a mechanical lift pump.

Open the bleed nipple on the secondary filter and operate the lift pump (Figure 9-28A). If the filter has no bleed nipple, loosen the connection on the fuel line coming out of the filter. Fuel should flow out of the bleed nipple or loosened connection *free of air bubbles*. If bubbles are present, operate the lift pump until they clear, then

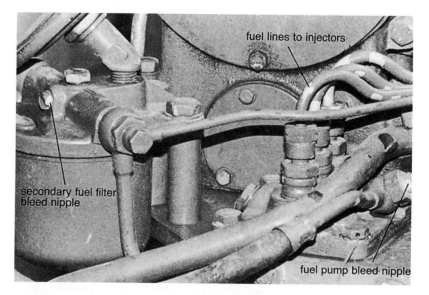

FIGURE 9-25. The bleed points on a Volvo MD 17C.

fuel lines to injectors

secondary fuel filter bleed nipple

fuel pump bleed nipple

close the nipple or tighten the connection. This should have purged the air from the suction lines all the way back to the tank, including both filters. If any of the fuel lines have a high spot, however, a bubble of air may remain at this point and be extremely hard to dislodge.

Take the trouble to catch or mop up all vented fuel. Diesel will soften, and eventually destroy, much electric cable insulation and also the rubber feet on flexibly mounted engines.

The next step is to bleed the fuel injection pump. Somewhere on the pump body, there will be one or perhaps two bleed nipples. (Some modern pumps are self-bleeding and have no nipples.) If the pump has more than one nipple, open the low one first and operate the lift pump until the fuel that flows out is free of air bubbles (Figures 9-28B, 9-28C, and 9-28D). Close the

FIGURE 9-26A. Operating a manual fuel lift (feed) pump. *(Perkins Engines Ltd.)*

lever for manual operation of a fuel lift pump

FIGURE 9-26B. Manual operation of a lift pump on a Yanmar.

FIGURE 9-27. A manual fuel pump mounted on a fuel filter.

electronic water-sensing device

manual pump

filter drain

FIGURE 9-28A. Bleeding a secondary fuel filter. *(Perkins Engines Ltd.)*

nipple and repeat the procedure with the higher one. The injection pump is now bled.

Bleeding the fuel lines from the injection pump to the injectors is the final step. To do this, set the governor control (throttle) *wide open* (this is essential) and crank the engine so that the injection pump can move the fuel up to the injectors. This should take no more than 30 sec-

onds. In any event, do not crank the starter motor for longer than 30 seconds at any one time because serious damage can result from internal overheating. If the engine has decompression levers and a hand crank, turn it over by hand to avoid running down the battery.

If the engine has no hand crank, the injection pump must be properly bled before attempting

FIGURE 9-28B. Bleeding the fuel inlet pipe to a distributor-type fuel injection pump. *(Perkins Engines Ltd.)*

FIGURE 9-28D. Bleeding the upper nipple on a distributor-type fuel injection pump. *(Perkins Engines Ltd.)*

FIGURE 9-28C. Bleeding the lower nipple on a distributor-type fuel injection pump. *(Perkins Engines Ltd.)*

leak-off pipe

injector hold-down bolts   injector nut

FIGURE 9-29A. The location of the injector nut.

this last step. Frequently the battery is already low because of earlier cranking attempts; therefore, pumping up the injectors one time, let alone having to come back to try again if rebleeding is necessary, will be touch and go.

When the fuel eventually reaches the injectors, provided the engine is not running, a distinct *creak* will be heard at the moment of injection. It's a useful noise to be familiar with. If it is present when any attempt is made to crank an engine, there is no need to bleed the fuel system (unless water is being injected!).

If the engine will still not fire, loosen one of the injector nuts (these hold the delivery lines to the injectors—Figures 9-29A and 9-29B) and crank again. A tiny dribble of fuel, free of air,

FIGURE 9-29B. Injectors on a Volvo.

Valve cover

Injector hold-down nut

Injector leak-off pipe

Decompression lever (in decompressed position)

Injector nut

should spurt out of this connection at every injection stroke for this cylinder (every second engine revolution on a four-cycle engine). If there is no fuel, or there is air in the fuel, the bleeding process has not been done adequately and needs repeating. On engines with internal fuel lines, loosen the nuts on the delivery pipes where they enter the cylinder head, *not the nuts on the injectors,* so that none of the vented diesel gets into the engine oil.

Do not overtighten injector nuts because you may collapse the fitting that seals the delivery pipe to the injector (tighten the nuts to 15 foot-pounds if you don't know the manufacturer's recommended setting). *Anytime you loosen an injector nut, you must check for leaks once the engine is running. Fuel leaks on engines with internal fuel lines will drain into the crankcase, diluting the engine oil and possibly leading to engine seizure.*

Common rail systems. A common rail system has a high-pressure pump that continuously circulates diesel at very high pressure (as much as 20,000 psi) to a *common rail* that supplies all the injectors, with the surplus returning to the fuel tank. The injectors are opened either mechanically or electronically at the appropriate moment for injection, allowing fuel into the cylinders and metering its quantity. A Detroit Diesel system is shown in Figures 9-30A and 9-30B.

An electronic common rail system allows the injection process to be fine-tuned to the operating conditions. It can respond instantaneously to changes in load and can be fine-tuned to give multiple pulses of diesel that provide a "softer" combustion process, more even power generation, less stress on the engine, and less noise. In the process, harmful emissions are greatly reduced. If for no other reason, we will see many more common rail systems in the future as emissions regulations are toughened (in the U.S. in 2006, 2007, and 2009).

Common rail fuel systems are self-purging. As long as the tank has fuel in it, the suction line is free of breaks, and the fuel pump works, the diesel flowing through the system will drive out any air. To check the fuel flow, undo the return line from the cylinder head to the tank, then crank the engine; a steady flow should come out (not the little dribbles that come from other injection pumps).

Persistent air in the fuel supply and/or fuel starvation. One of the more aggravating problems on many traditional four-cycle diesels can be persistent air in the fuel system. Air can come from poor connections, improperly seated filter housings (especially if the problem occurs after a filter change), and pinholes in fuel lines caused by corrosion and vibration against bulkheads or the engine block. If the boat has more than one fuel tank and a selector valve, the valve itself may be admitting air. Since the only part of the fuel system under suction pressure is that from the tank to the lift pump, this is the most likely problem area.

If the primary filter has a see-through bowl, loosen the bleed nipple on the secondary filter, operate the hand pump on the lift pump, and watch the bowl. Air bubbles indicate a leak between the fuel tank and the primary filter or in the filter gasket itself. No air means the leak is probably between the filter and the pump.

In the absence of a see-through bowl, locate the fuel line that runs from the lift pump to the secondary filter. Disconnect it *at the filter.* Place it in a jar of clean diesel fuel and pump. If there is a leak on the suction side, bubbles will appear in the jar.

Any air source on the lift pump's discharge side should reveal itself as a fuel leak when the engine is running. When the engine is shut down, the fuel may suck in air as it siphons back to the tank. Next time the engine is cranked, it will probably start and then die.

FIGURE 9-30A. A typical two-cycle diesel engine fuel system. *(Detroit Diesel)*

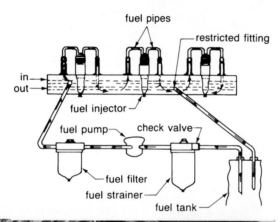

fuel pipes

restricted fitting

in
out

fuel injector

fuel pump

check valve

fuel filter

fuel strainer

fuel tank

FIGURE 9-30B. A Detroit Diesel (common rail) fuel system. *(Detroit Diesel)*

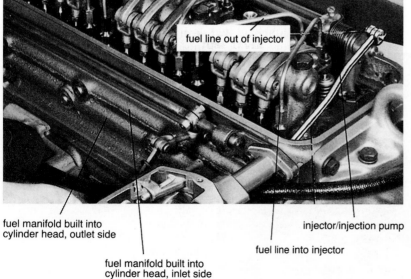

fuel line out of injector

fuel manifold built into cylinder head, outlet side

fuel manifold built into cylinder head, inlet side

fuel line into injector

injector/injection pump

FIGURE 9-31A. The diaphragm on a fuel lift (feed) pump.

A similar problem can arise when the leak-off pipe from the injectors is teed into a fitting on the secondary fuel filter with another (overflow) line running from here back to the tank (this is a common arrangement). When the engine is shut down, fuel will sometimes siphon down the overflow line and cause air to be sucked into the system. In this situation, there is no external evidence of the air source, making for frustrating detective work! To cure the problem, either move the leak-off pipe so that it runs directly to the fuel tank (in which case, if there is more than one fuel tank, the fuel must be directed to the one in use) or add a length of flexible fuel line between the injectors and the secondary filter. Loop this above the level of the filter and injectors and drill a small ($\frac{1}{16}$ inch) hole in it at its highest point. This hole will act as a siphon break.

Sometimes fuel tanks are deeper than the lifting capability of the pump so the pump may fail to raise the fuel when the tank is almost empty, or it may fail to raise enough fuel (*fuel starvation*) at higher engine loadings. If the fuel pickup line has a filter on it inside the tank, and this becomes plugged, it will have the same effect; as previously mentioned, this is no place to filter the fuel. *If the tank vent is plugged, over time the tank will develop a vacuum and once again starve the engine of fuel.* When troubleshooting, the tank vent invariably gets forgotten, but if your engine starts and runs fine for some time, then begins to lose power, suspect the vent.

Lift pump (feed pump) failure. Many small four-cycle diesels found in boats use a diaphragm-type lift pump (Figures 9-31A and 9-31B). Newer engines tend to use electric pumps. Larger engines, and Detroit Diesels and other common rail systems, use a gear-driven pump (Figures 9-32A and 9-32B).

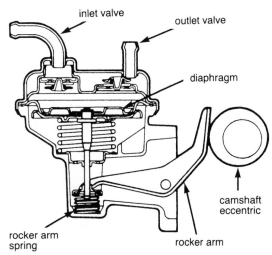

FIGURE 9-31B. A typical mechanical fuel pump. (*AC Spark Plug Division, General Motors Corp.*)

A diaphragm pump has a housing that contains a suction and a discharge valve, plus the diaphragm. A lever, which is moved up and down by a cam on the engine's camshaft or crankshaft, pushes the diaphragm in and out. This lever can also be operated manually, but if the engine is stopped in a position that leaves the diaphragm lever fully depressed, the manual lever will be ineffective until the engine is turned over far enough to move the cam out of contact with the lever.

Diaphragm pumps are nearly foolproof, but eventually the diaphragm will fail. When this happens, little or no fuel will be pumped out of the fuel system's bleed nipples when the lift pump is operated manually. Older pumps often have a drain hole in the base from which fuel will drip if the diaphragm has failed, but Coast Guard regulations have banned this for newer pumps.

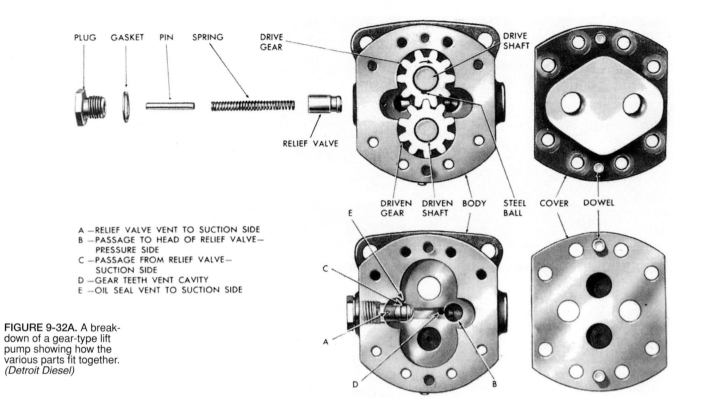

PLUG GASKET PIN SPRING DRIVE GEAR DRIVE SHAFT

DRIVEN GEAR DRIVEN SHAFT BODY STEEL BALL COVER DOWEL

RELIEF VALVE

A —RELIEF VALVE VENT TO SUCTION SIDE
B —PASSAGE TO HEAD OF RELIEF VALVE—
      PRESSURE SIDE
C —PASSAGE FROM RELIEF VALVE—
      SUCTION SIDE
D —GEAR TEETH VENT CAVITY
E —OIL SEAL VENT TO SUCTION SIDE

FIGURE 9-32A. A breakdown of a gear-type lift pump showing how the various parts fit together. *(Detroit Diesel)*

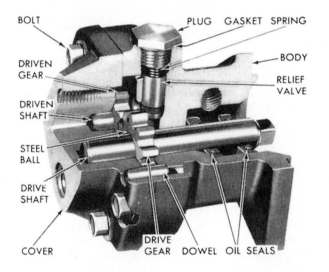

BOLT PLUG GASKET SPRING

DRIVEN GEAR

DRIVEN SHAFT

STEEL BALL

DRIVE SHAFT

BODY

RELIEF VALVE

COVER DRIVE GEAR DOWEL OIL SEALS

FIGURE 9-32B. A cutaway of a gear-type lift pump. *(Caterpillar Tractor Company)*

FIGURE 9-33. Diaphragm replacement on a lift pump. *(Volvo Penta)*

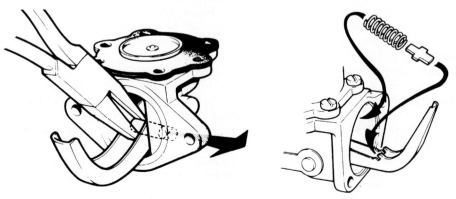

A spare diaphragm, or better yet a complete pump unit, should be part of the spare-parts kit on boats that cruise offshore. Diaphragms are accessible by undoing a number of screws (generally six) around the body of the pump and lifting off the top half. The method of attaching the diaphragm to its operating lever varies; it may be necessary to remove the whole pump from the engine (two nuts or bolts) and play with, or remove, the operating lever (Figure 9-33). When replacing the top of the pump, to get the diaphragm properly situated, keep the lever halfway down until the screws for the lid have been tightened.

If the lift pump fails and there is no spare on board, it is still possible to keep an engine running by rigging up a fuel supply above the level of the engine and gravity-feeding it through the secondary filter to the injection pump.

If the air inlet and exhaust are unobstructed, compression is good, the tank has fuel, and the system is properly bled, it is time to feel nervous, check the bank balance, and call a mechanic!

Troubleshooting Part 2: Operating Problems

Overheating

Engines are either *air cooled* (rare in marine use); *raw-water* cooled (Figure 9-34; the seawater is circulated directly through the engine—also rare); or *heat-exchanger* cooled. Engines with heat exchangers have an enclosed *(freshwater)* cooling circuit with a header tank. The cooling water passes through a heat exchanger, which has seawater on its other side, carrying off the engine heat.

Heat exchangers are either inside the boat (Figures 9-35A and 9-35B), complete with their own raw-water circuit and pump, or they are fit-

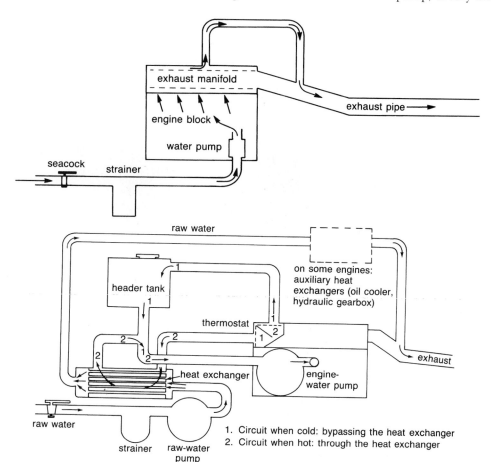

FIGURE 9-34. Raw-water cooling.

FIGURE 9-35A. A heat-exchanger schematic.

1. Circuit when cold: bypassing the heat exchanger
2. Circuit when hot: through the heat exchanger

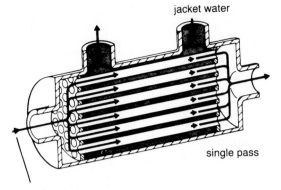

FIGURE 9-35B. Single- and double-pass heat exchangers. *(Caterpillar Tractor Company)*

jacket water

single pass

cooling water

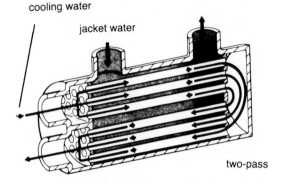

jacket water

two-pass

cuit specifically to cool the engine oil and exhaust.

Overheating can be the result of a number of things, but the primary suspect is always a loss of flow in the raw-water circuit. For this reason, as well as to prevent following waves from driving up the exhaust pipe, a water-cooled exhaust should ideally exit high enough in the stern for you to see or hear if water is coming out of it. It will then be possible for you to tell at a glance whether the raw-water side of the cooling system is functioning in some fashion, although you will not be able to tell if the flow is up to normal. (This can be done by holding a gallon container under the exhaust, timing how long it takes to fill, calculating the flow rate, and comparing this to the engine specifications or what is normal. It is an excellent idea to measure and log the flow rate before problems arise so as to establish a benchmark for future reference. Since raw-water flow rate is directly related to engine speed, the data must be collected at one particular speed—say, 1,000 rpm.)

It should be an iron habit to check the exhaust for proper water flow every time the engine is started.

Overheating on start-up. Check the raw-water side first.

Raw-water side. The seacock on the raw-water circuit is probably closed! If not, check the raw-water filter (Figures 9-36A and 9-36B). If this is clear, close the seacock, disconnect the raw-water hose, and reopen the seacock to make sure water floods into the boat. If not, there's something stuck in or over the inlet. If water comes

ted to the outside of the boat in direct contact with the seawater (a *keel cooler*) and so require no raw-water pump.

Most engines with a raw-water pump and circuit pass the raw water through any oil coolers (for the engine and hydraulic transmission) and then discharge it into the exhaust, although some include an engine oil cooler and transmission oil cooler in the freshwater circuit. Some keel-cooled engines have an extra raw-water cir-

FIGURE 9-36A. A raw-water filter.

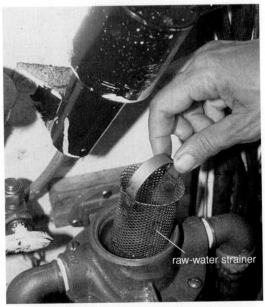

raw-water strainer

FIGURE 9-36B. Removing the raw-water strainer for cleaning.

396   DIESEL ENGINES

in, the next thing to check is the raw-water pump. Almost all raw-water pumps are the rubber impeller type (Figure 9-37A). If the pump runs dry, the impeller will tear.

If the pump is belt driven, check the belt. If this is OK, remove the pump cover (usually four or six screws) and check the impeller (Figures 9-37B and 9-37C). Make sure that when the pump turns, the impeller is not slipping on its shaft. If the impeller is damaged, pull it out with pliers (Figure 9-37D) or pry it out with two screwdrivers (Figure 9-37E), unless you happen to have an impeller puller (refer back to Figure 9-13). Note that impeller manufacturers cringe at the suggestion to use screwdrivers (see Figure 9-37F from ITT/Jabsco)! A few impellers have a locking screw (Figure 9-37G) or a retaining circlip (e.g., the Atomic 3 diesel; if the shaft comes out with the impeller, the pump will have to be unbolted from the engine in order to replace an adapter in the back of the pump).

FIGURE 9-37C. Cracked vanes on a raw-water pump impeller.

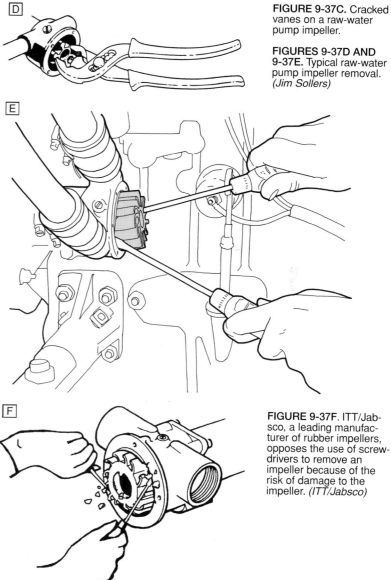

FIGURES 9-37D AND 9-37E. Typical raw-water pump impeller removal. *(Jim Sollers)*

FIGURE 9-37F. ITT/Jabsco, a leading manufacturer of rubber impellers, opposes the use of screwdrivers to remove an impeller because of the risk of damage to the impeller. *(ITT/Jabsco)*

FIGURE 9-37A. A typical raw-water pump.

FIGURE 9-37B. A raw-water pump with its cover removed. Three out of six vanes on the impeller are missing!

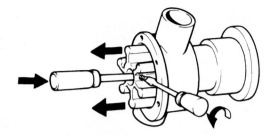

FIGURE 9-37G. Most flexible water pump impellers can be pried or pulled out . . . but some are secured to the shaft with a circlip (not shown) or setscrew (illustrated). The latter can be removed by prying out the shaft far enough to access the setscrew. *(Volvo Penta)*

permanent "set"

FIGURE 9-37H. Even though the impeller tips are still curved, if the vanes retain a "set" after removal, the impeller needs replacing.

Before pulling an impeller all the way out, make a note of the way the vanes are bent down in the pump housing. If the vanes have taken a permanent "set" (i.e., do not straighten out once the impeller is removed—Figures 9-37H and 9-37I); are worn flat (the tips should be curved); or are in any other way damaged, cracked, or brittle, the impeller needs replacing. Any pieces missing from an impeller need tracking down—they will most likely be found in the heat exchanger (if fitted; Figures 9-37J and 9-37K) and sometimes at the raw-water injection elbow (Figure 9-37L). When installing a new impeller, as you push it in, rotate it so that its vanes bend down the same way as on the old one (I hope you wrote that down!). For rebuilding a pump, see Chapter 13.

If the raw-water pump is irreparably damaged

and no spare parts are on board, you have a couple of options for limping home:

1. If the boat has a saltwater washdown pump, plumb this to the raw-water cooling system and use it in place of the raw-water pump. In a bind, you can also use the freshwater pump.

FIGURE 9-37I. Vanes with a permanent set. This impeller is ready for replacement. *(ITT/Jabsco)*

FIGURE 9-37J. Tracking down the missing vanes from the impeller shown in Figure 9-37B. The first one was found in the pump discharge elbow; the second in the tubing; and the third . . .

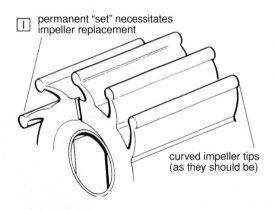

I — permanent "set" necessitates impeller replacement

curved impeller tips (as they should be)

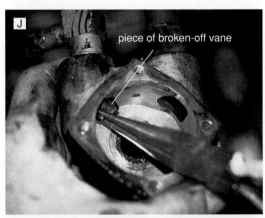

J

piece of broken-off vane

FIGURE 9-37K. . . . in the heat exchanger (the most likely place to find missing vanes). Note the smaller pieces of rubber lodged in two of the heat exchanger tubes.

FIGURE 9-37L. Checking a raw-water injection nozzle for obstructions; this is a likely spot for debris to build up.

K

pieces of broken-off vanes

L

raw-water injection nipple

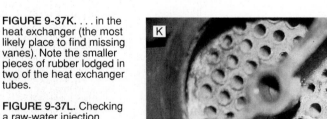

Either pump will probably have a sufficient flow rate to enable the engine to be run at cruising speed, but you will need to keep a close eye on the temperature.

2. Rig a funnel well above the engine and plumb a hose from it to the heat exchanger. Fill it from a bucket. The flow rate will be slow because this is gravity fed, but that's OK because it's going to be hard work keeping the funnel filled! You can adjust the flow rate by moving the funnel up and down. Maintain the engine speed at whatever speed keeps the temperature from going much above normal. I know a couple of people who got themselves out of a tight spot in this manner.

Freshwater side. If the raw-water circuit is functioning as normal and the engine is freshwater cooled, check the level in the coolant recovery bottle (if fitted) or expansion tank. *Warning: Never remove the cap when it's hot. Serious burns may result.* If the level is low, find out where the water is going (adding red food dye may help in tracing leaks). Possibilities are leaking hose connections, heat exchanger or oil cooler cooling tubes that have corroded through (see the Water in the Crankcase section later in this chapter), or a blown head gasket. A blown head gasket will likely cause air bubbles in the cooling system when the engine is running, and these will be visible in the header tank; the header tank may also smell of exhaust fumes. Finally, note that a pressure cap on the header tank with too low a pressure rating, or a pressure cap that has failed, will allow the coolant to boil away over time (the pressure rating will be stamped on the cap; the required pressure is given in the engine specifications).

Overheating during normal operation.
Check the oil level. If a low oil level is causing the engine to overheat, expensive damage may be in the making.

Raw-water side. If the raw-water intake is not set low enough in the hull, a well-heeled sailboat can suck in air. The heeling will have to be kept down until the through-hull can be moved.

The raw-water inlet screen (if fitted) on the outside of the hull may be blocked with a piece of plastic. Throttle down, put the boat in reverse, throttle up, and then shut down the engine once the boat has reverse way on it. With a little luck, the reverse propeller thrust and water flow will wash the plastic clear. To confirm this, loosen a hose below the waterline and see if water flows into the boat. If the flow is restricted, check for barnacles on the inlet screen or in the water intake.

Check the raw-water filter. If it contains a lot of silt, the heat exchanger (or the engine itself on

Troubleshooting Chart 9-3. Overheating on Start-Up	
Is water coming from the raw-water discharge? **NO**	**YES** Check the coolant level in the freshwater circuit (if fitted). Caution: Do not remove header-tank pressure cap when hot. If the level is low, refill and find the leak.
Is the raw-water seacock closed? **NO**	**YES** Open and then check the raw-water overboard discharge. The raw-water pump may have failed from running dry.
Is the raw-water strainer plugged? **NO**	**YES** Clean and then check the raw-water discharge as above.
Has the raw-water pump failed? Inspect the drive belt and tension or replace as necessary. Make sure any clutch is operative. If the belt and clutch (if fitted) are OK, remove the pump cover and inspect the impeller vanes. Make sure the impeller turns when the engine turns. **NO**	**YES** Tighten or replace the drive belt as necessary. Replace a damaged impeller. Track down any missing vanes.
Check for collapsed or kinked raw-water hoses, an obstruction over the raw-water inlet on the outside of the hull (break a below-the-waterline hose loose as close to the raw-water seacock as possible and see if there is a good flow into the boat), or a plugged raw-water injection nozzle into the exhaust. Is the water-lift silencer frozen?	

raw-water-cooled boats) may be silted up. Feel the freshwater inlet and outlet pipes to the heat exchanger; if it is doing its job, there should be a noticeable fall in the temperature of the water leaving the heat exchanger. Many heat exchangers have removable end caps and can be rodded out with a suitable wooden dowel. With severe cases of scaling, you will need to obtain special solvents from an engine rebuilding facility and pump these through the heat exchanger; you should get professional advice. Note that if any other heat exchanger or a refrigeration condenser is fitted in series with the engine-cooling circuit, an obstruction in any of these will reduce the raw-water flow through all of them.

Raw-water-cooled engines (without a freshwater circuit) are likely to develop scale around the cylinders over time (Figure 9-38), especially if run above 160°F/71°C. As with heat exchangers, descaling requires professional advice.

Check for collapsed cooling hoses, a loose raw-water pump drive belt, or poor pump performance. This is another reason that a high-set overboard discharge is useful—you can readily measure the pump flow.

Troubleshooting Chart 9-4.
Overheating in Operation

Check the raw-water overboard discharge. Is the flow less than normal? **NO**	**YES** Check for obstructions in the raw-water circuit (see Troubleshooting Chart 9-3). In addition, check the raw-water circuit for silting, scale, and other partial obstructions (see the text).
Check the oil level. Is it low? **NO**	**YES** Refill with the correct grade and viscosity of oil.
Is the boat overloaded? (Check for a rope around the propeller, a heavily fouled bottom, adverse conditions, excessive auxiliary equipment, or an oversized propeller.) **NO**	**YES** Reduce the loading.
Check the coolant level in the freshwater circuit (if fitted). Caution: Do not remove the header-tank pressure cap when hot. Is the level low? **NO**	**YES** Refill and find the leak.
Is the freshwater circuit air-locked? **NO**	**YES** Break the hoses loose at the freshwater pump and water heater (if fitted) and bleed off any air.
Is the thermostat operating incorrectly? (Remove and test as outlined in text.) **NO**	**YES** Replace.

There is probably a mechanical problem (e.g., faulty fuel injection; a partial seizure)—see the text.

FIGURE 9-38. Corrosion in a raw-water-cooled cylinder head. Note the scale partially plugging the water passage on the right-hand side of the photograph.

Where the raw water is injected into the exhaust (on both raw-water- and heat-exchanger-cooled engines), a relatively small nozzle is sometimes used to direct the water down the exhaust pipe and away from the exhaust manifold. If scale forms in the raw-water circuit, this nozzle is likely to plug, restricting the water flow (refer back to Figure 9-37L).

Freshwater side. If the raw-water flow is normal, check any header tank as above, but *only after allowing the engine to cool.*

A broken alternator belt will put the freshwater pump out of commission. If you have no spare belt on board, jury-rig the pump by forming a belt out of nylon twine. Put a loop in one end, run the other end through the loop, and pull it up tight (nylon has quite a bit of stretch,

so use this to tension the "belt"). If the line is small gauge, run it around several times. If no suitable line is on board, unlay a piece of three-strand anchor or mooring line to get line of a suitable size and use that. Tape the ends of the line to the belt so they don't catch on anything.

A water pump does not create much of a load, so this belt should hold for some time. However, if it starts to slip, it will heat up and melt, so you need to inspect it regularly. You are unlikely to be able to run the alternator with it because of the higher load imposed by the alternator (especially if the batteries are down and the alternator is loaded up). If you really need the alternator, you can give it a try, but you will need to keep the engine speed down in order to keep the alternator output low enough for the belt to survive.

If the belt is OK, perhaps the engine is overloaded (a rope around the propeller, an oversized propeller, a badly fouled bottom, or too much auxiliary equipment), causing it to generate more heat than normal. Maybe the ambient water temperature is higher than normal. For example, a boat moving into the tropics may experience a 40°F/22°C rise in the ambient water temperature. This temperature increase will lower the temperature differential between the raw water and fresh water in the heat exchanger, causing the engine temperature to

temperature-sensing pickup

thermostat housing bolts

FIGURE 9-39A. The thermostat housing on a Volvo MD 17C.

FIGURE 9-39B. The thermostat removed from a Volvo MD 17C.

thermostat

FIGURE 9-39C. Checking the operation of a thermostat. *(Volvo Penta)*

rise a little (in which case the raw-water flow rate is probably lower than it should be and/or the raw-water side of the heat exchanger needs cleaning).

An overheated engine can generate hot spots that cause pockets of steam to build up in the cylinder or head. These can sometimes air-lock cooling passages, the cooling pump, the heat exchanger, or the expansion tank, especially if the piping runs have high spots where steam or air can gather. *Note that when a domestic water heater is plumbed into the engine-cooling circuit, as most are, there is frequently a high spot in the tubing that can cause an air lock.*

The thermostat may be malfunctioning. You will find the thermostat under a bell housing near the top and front of the engine (Figures 9-39A and 9-39B). Take it out and try operating without it. This will make most engines run cool, but will cause a few—for example, some Caterpillars—to run hot, in which case, it should not be done. To test the thermostat, put it in a pan of water and heat it (Figure 9-39C). It should open between 165°F/74°C and 185°F/ 82°C, except on some Caterpillars, which open as high as 192°F/89°C, and some raw-water-cooled engines, which open between 140°F/ 60°C and 160°F/71°C.

Finally, problems with temperature gauges

are rare. If suspected, consult the Problems with Engine Instrumentation section.

Smoke

The exhaust of a diesel should normally be perfectly clear. The presence of smoke can often point to a problem in the making, and the color of the smoke can be an even more useful guide.

Black smoke. When unburned particles of carbon from the fuel blow out of the exhaust, black smoke results. On many older engines, any attempt to accelerate suddenly will generate a cloud of black smoke as the fuel rack opens and the engine slowly responds. Once the engine reaches the new speed setting, the governor eases off the fuel rack and the smoke ceases immediately. This smoke is indicative of a general engine deterioration: the compression is most likely falling, the injectors need cleaning, and the air filter should be changed. If the engine is otherwise performing well, there is no immediate cause for concern but the engine is serving notice that a thorough service is overdue.

If black smoke persists once an engine is up to speed, the engine is crying out for immediate attention. The following are likely causes for the smoke:

- Obstruction of the airflow through the engine. Likely causes are a dirty air filter, restrictions in the air inlet ducting, or a high exhaust back pressure (see below; fouled exhausts are not uncommon on sailboats, so don't ignore this). Turbocharged engines in particular are sensitive to high back pressure. Many engines on auxiliary sailboats are tucked away in little boxes. As often as not, these boxes are fairly well sealed to cut down on noise levels. Unless such a box is adequately vented, *this setup can strangle the engine*, particularly at higher engine loadings and in hot climates where the air is less dense.

- Overloading of the engine (e.g., by wrapping a rope around the propeller). The governor reacts by opening the fuel control lever until more fuel is being injected than can be burned with the oxygen that's available. This improperly burned fuel is emitted as black smoke. Black smoke on new boats should raise the suspicion of an overloaded engine caused by the wrong propeller or too much auxiliary equipment.

- Defective fuel injection. If an engine is not overloaded and the airflow is unobstructed, poor injection is the number one suspect for black smoke.

- Excessively high ambient air temperatures (e.g., in a hot engine room on a boat operating in the tropics). The density, thus the weight, of the air entering the engine will be reduced, leading to an insufficient air supply, especially at high engine loadings.

Blue smoke. Blue smoke comes from burning oil. Oil can find its way into the combustion chambers only by making it up past piston rings; down valve guides and stems; or in through the air inlet from leaking supercharger or turbocharger seals, an overfilled oil-bath air filter, or a crankcase breather.

Engines that are repeatedly operated for short periods, or are idled or run at low loads for long periods, do not become hot enough to expand the pistons and piston rings fully. They then fail to seat properly, and oil from the crankcase finds its way into the combustion chamber. In time, the cylinders become *glazed* (very smooth), while the piston rings get gummed into their grooves, allowing more oil through. Oil consumption rises and compression declines. Blowby down the sides of the pistons raises the pressure in the crankcase and blows an oil mist out of the crankcase breather. Carbon builds up on the valves and valve stems and plugs the exhaust system. Valves may jam in their guides and hit pistons. *Repeated short-term operation and prolonged idling and low-load running will substantially increase maintenance costs, including major overhauls, and shorten engine life.*

White smoke. White smoke is caused by water vapor in the exhaust or by totally unburned, but atomized, fuel. Given that almost all exhausts are water cooled, there is the potential to create steam, but in practice, the cooling water flow should be such that this situation does not happen in normal circumstances. (Note, however, that in cold weather, vaporized water in the exhaust gases is likely to condense into steam.) To determine whether white smoke is water or fuel,

Troubleshooting Chart 9-5. Smoke in Exhaust	
Smoke	
Black	**Blue**
Obstruction in airflow: Dirty air filter Defective turbo/supercharger High exhaust back pressure	Worn or stuck piston rings
	Worn valve guides
Excessively high ambient air temperature	Turbo/supercharger problems: Worn oil seals Plugged oil drain
Overload: Rope around propeller Oversized propeller Heavily fouled bottom Excessive auxiliary equipment	Overfilled oil bath–type air filter
	High crankcase oil level/pressure
Defective fuel injection	
White Lack of compression Water in the fuel Air in the fuel Defective injector Cracked cylinder head/leaking head gasket	

Note: When an exhaust is water cooled, it is difficult to distinguish white smoke from the normal exhaust.

hold your hand under the exhaust for a few seconds and then sniff it to see if it smells of diesel. If it does, one or more cylinders are not firing. If the weather is cold and the engine has just been started, the most likely cause is poor compression, especially if the smoke clears as the engine warms up. If the smoke persists, there may be a defective injector.

Loss of Performance

High back pressure. The exhaust is an integral part of the airflow through an engine. Any restriction will generate *back pressure* (see the Measuring Exhaust Back Pressure sidebar). This will cause an engine to lose power, overheat, and probably smoke (black). The most likely causes of high exhaust back pressure are:

- A closed or partially closed sea valve on the exhaust exit pipe.
- Too small an exhaust pipe, too many bends and elbows, too great a lift from a water-lift muffler to the exhaust exit (refer back to Figure 9-16D), or a kink in an exhaust hose.
- Excessive carbon formation in the exhaust system caused by long hours of operation at light loads (such as when battery charging or refrigerating at anchor).
- In wintertime, frozen water in a water lift–type muffler at initial start-up. This may produce a hissing immediately after cranking, or bubbles in the raw-water strainer, as the trapped exhaust looks for an escape path.

Generally, the easiest way to check for a fouled exhaust is to remove the exhaust hose from the water-lift muffler, then wipe your finger inside the muffler and use a flashlight to look up the hose. There should be nothing more than a light carbon film. What you may find is a heavy carbon crust. In this case, the entire exhaust system, including the exhaust valves, is likely to be fouled (probably because you have only been running the engine for short periods and/or for long hours at low loads). A significant overhaul is needed.

An exhaust should be broken loose and inspected annually until you know for sure that it is not fouling, and maybe every other year after that.

Knocks. Diesel engines make a variety of interesting noises. Each of the principal components creates its own sound, and a good mechanic can often isolate a problem simply by detecting a specific *knock* coming out of the engine.

The symphony, however, is frequently garbled by a variety of fuel and ignition knocks. Differences in the rate of combustion can cause noises that are almost indistinguishable from mechanical knocks, especially on two-cycle diesels. But if you run the engine at full speed and then shut down the governor control lever (the throttle), a fuel knock will cease at once, whereas a mechanical knock will probably still be audible, although not as loud as before because the engine is now merely coasting to a stop. Knocks that gradually get louder over the life of an engine (especially if accompanied by slowly declining oil pressure when the engine is hot) are almost certainly mechanical knocks.

Some fuel knocks are quite normal, especially on initial start-up. Diesels are much noisier than gasoline engines and have a characteristic *clatter* at idle, especially when cold. (Note that electronically controlled common rail injection systems eliminate this clatter.) The owner of a diesel will have to become accustomed to these noises in order to detect and differentiate out-of-the-ordinary fuel knocks. These can have several causes, such as poor-quality fuel (low cetane rating, dirt or water in the fuel), faulty fuel injection, injection timing too early, and oil in the inlet manifold from leaking turbocharger or supercharger seals (oil is sucked into the cylinders causing premature ignition).

A sudden loud knocking, especially on start-up, is likely to be a stuck injector that is now dumping nonatomized diesel into the cylinder. Combustion is delayed and then there is a sudden flare-up. Damage to the piston and cylinder as well as the fuel injection pump is possible. To determine which injector is knocking, loosen the injector lines at the injectors one at a time until fuel spurts out (don't do this with a two-cycle Detroit Diesel or any engine with a common rail fuel injection system—fuel will flood out!). If the engine has internal fuel lines, loosen the delivery pipes *at the external fittings on the cylinder head* so that fuel doesn't run down into the crankcase.

If the knocking ceases, you have found the offending cylinder; if not, tighten the fuel line and loosen the next. If you find the offending injector but have no replacement injector on board, you can run the engine with the injector line loose. However, you will need to collect the diesel that continually dribbles out the injector line (and you will, of course, suffer a significant loss of power). If the knocking is not stopped by loosening the injection lines, it is almost certainly a mechanical problem.

The more common mechanical knocks arise from worn piston pin or connecting rod bearings, worn pistons, and worn main bearings. All these mechanical problems require professional help. *Do not ignore new noises!*

Exhaust back pressure can be checked with a sensitive pressure gauge designed to measure in *inches of mercury* or *inches of water* rather than in pounds per square inch (psi). (See Table 9-2 for conversion of one to the other.) It can also be checked with a homemade manometer. This need be nothing more than a piece of clear plastic tubing of any diameter greater than ¼ inch, fixed in a U-shaped loop to a board about 4 feet long. The board is marked off in inches (Figure 9-40).

Set the board on end and half fill the tubing with water. Connect one side of the tubing to a fitting on the exhaust as close to the exhaust manifold as possible (but 6 to 12 inches *after* a turbocharger). Leave the other end of the tubing open. If the manifold has no suitable outlet to make the connection, drill an ¹¹⁄₃₂-inch hole, tap this for a ⅛-inch pipe fitting (standard pipe thread), and screw in an appropriate fitting. When finished, remove the fitting and fit a ⅛-inch pipe plug.

Note the level of the water in the tube with the engine at rest. Then crank the engine and *fully load* it. *This is important; if necessary, tie the boat off securely to a dock, put it in gear, and open the throttle.* The exhaust back pressure will push the water down one side of the tubing and up the other. The difference between the two levels, measured in inches, is the back pressure in *inches of water column*. On naturally aspirated engines and Detroit Diesels, it should not exceed 40 inches of water (3 inches Hg; approximately 1.5 psi); on turbocharged engines, including turbocharged Detroit Diesels, it should not exceed 20 inches of water (1.5 inches Hg; 0.75 psi).

All too often an engine is found to be well outside these limits, especially where long exhaust runs with numerous bends are involved. Anything that can be done to shorten the hose run, reduce bends, and *enlarge the hose size* will help reduce back pressure.

TABLE 9-2. Pressure Conversion Factors

To convert	Into	Multiply by
Psi	Hg″	2.036
Hg″	Psi	0.4912
Psi	H₂O″	27.6776
H₂O″	Psi	0.03613
H₂O″	Hg″	0.07355
Hg″	H₂O″	13.5962

FIGURE 9-40. A simple homemade manometer to check exhaust back pressure.

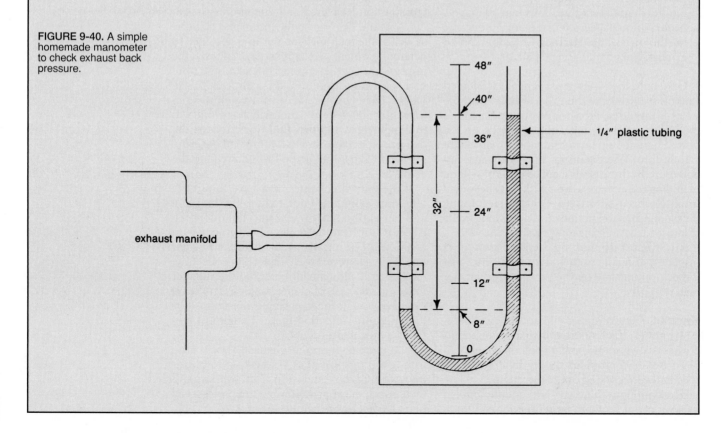

exhaust manifold

48″
40″
36″
32″
24″
12″
8″
0

¼″ plastic tubing

Misfiring. Many diesels idle unevenly due to the difficulty of accurately metering the minute quantities of fuel required at slow speeds. This is not to be mistaken for misfiring, which will be felt and heard as rough running at all speeds.

Misfiring may be rhythmic or erratic. The former indicates that the same cylinder(s) are misfiring all the time; the latter means that cylinders are misfiring randomly. Rhythmic misfiring is caused by a specific problem with one or more cylinders, such as low compression or faulty fuel injection. If it occurs on start-up and then clears up once the engine warms, it is almost certainly due to low compression; initially the air in the cylinder is not reaching ignition temperature, but as the engine warms, the air gets hotter until the cylinder fires.

Once again, you can track down the guilty cylinder(s) of a rhythmic misfire by loosening the injector nut on each injector in turn (with the engine running) until fuel spurts out (don't do this on a common rail system). If the engine changes its note or slows down, the cylinder was firing as it should; retighten the nut. If no change occurs, the cylinder is misfiring, and you need to investigate further (of course, if no fuel spurts out, you know why it's not firing!).

Erratic misfiring on all cylinders is the result of a general engine problem, frequently contaminated fuel. If the misfiring is more pronounced at higher speeds and loads, in all probability the fuel filter is plugged. If it is accompanied by black smoke, the air filter is probably plugged, or there is some other problem with the airflow (carbon in the exhaust, defective turbocharger, etc.).

Poor pickup. Poor pickup, or a failure to come to speed, is most likely a result of one or more of the following:

- Insufficient fuel caused by a plugged filter (don't forget the filter screen in the top of the lift pump), a nearly empty tank, a plugged filter screen on the pickup tube in the tank, or a blocked tank vent causing a vacuum in the tank.
- A clogged air filter, in which case the engine is likely to be emitting black smoke.
- Supercharger or turbocharger malfunction—black smoke is likely.
- Overloading due to an improperly matched propeller, a heavily fouled bottom, too much auxiliary equipment, or perhaps a rope around the propeller.
- Excessive back pressure in the exhaust.
- Low compression, perhaps resulting in misfiring.

- Improper fuel injection.
- Too much friction—a partial seizure is underway.

Seizure. Seizure of the pistons in their cylinders is an ever-present possibility anytime serious overheating occurs or the lubrication breaks down. Overheated pistons expand excessively and jam in their cylinders. An engine experiencing a seizure *bogs down*—that is to say, fails to carry the load, slows down progressively, probably emits black smoke, and becomes extremely hot. If immediate steps are not taken to deal with the situation, total seizure—when the engine grinds to a halt and locks up solidly—is not far off.

If the beginning of a partial engine seizure is detected, the correct response is not necessarily to shut down the engine immediately because as it cools, the cylinders are likely to lock up on the pistons. The load should be instantly thrown off and the engine idled down as far as possible for a minute or two to give it a chance to cool off. (This action assumes that the seizure is not due to the loss of the lubricating oil or cooling water. In either of those situations, there is no choice but to shut down as fast as possible.)

Engine Runaway or Failure to Shut Down

Diesel engines will run on oil as well as diesel. If oil finds its way into the combustion chambers, an engine can run away uncontrollably. Sources of such oil are:

- Leaking turbocharger oil seals.
- Too much oil (almost always from overfilling after an oil change) in the crankcase on those engines that connect the crankcase breather to the engine air inlet (most engines do this).
- Diesel dilution of the engine oil on engines with internal fuel lines.
- Seriously worn valve guides, allowing oil to work its way into the cylinders.

In extreme cases, enough oil can be drawn into the engine to cause it to speed up out of control and not shut down when the fuel rack is closed. Runaway is more prevalent on two-cycle diesels than four-cycles, and that's why some Detroit Diesels have an emergency air flap that cuts off all air to the engine and strangles it. In the absence of an emergency air flap, the only way to stop runaway is to cut off the oxygen supply to the engine with a CO_2 (carbon dioxide) fire extinguisher or by jamming a boat cushion or something similar into the air inlet. Make sure you don't get your hand in the way! And ensure that whatever you use is strong enough to not break up under the sudden vacuum, because the pieces may foul the engine, necessitating an expensive overhaul.

Then there are engines that are stopped by pressing a button in the engine panel (most Yanmars). This closes the electrically operated fuel solenoid, shutting off the fuel supply to the engine. Sometimes the engine fails to stop when the button is pushed. The engine can always be stopped by finding the solenoid, identifying the rod it moves, and then pushing this rod in or out by hand. But before doing this, check the ignition switch—if it has been inadvertently turned off, it has probably disabled the Stop button. (I can tell you from personal experience that after you've been climbing around in the engine room looking for the solenoid, and then spent some time trying to troubleshoot it, you feel a little silly when you find this out!)

Water in the Crankcase

Although it should get burned off in normal operation (especially on modern diesels), a certain amount of water can find its way into the crankcase from condensation of steam formed during combustion, but appreciable quantities can come only from the cooling system. The sources are strictly limited:

- Water siphoning in through exhaust valves from a faulty water-cooled exhaust installation (see the Siphon Breaks sidebar).
- A leak from a gear-driven (as opposed to belt-driven) raw-water pump.
- Corrosion in an oil cooler.
- A leaking head gasket.
- Leaks around injector sleeves (where fitted).
- A cracked cylinder liner (or one with a pinhole caused by corrosion from the water-jacket side).
- A leaking O-ring seal at the base of a wet liner.

Leaking head gaskets, injector sleeves, cylinder liners, and cylinders are beyond the scope of this book. Water backing up the exhaust has already been dealt with (see the Siphon Breaks sidebar). A gear-driven water pump should have a weep hole in its base. If you find water in the crankcase and suspect the pump, make sure this weep hole is not plugged. If water is coming out of it, rebuild the pump.

The cooling tubes on oil coolers with raw water circulating on the water side (as opposed to water from the engine's freshwater cooling circuit) are especially prone to damage. The combination of heat, salt water, and dissimilar metals is a potent one for galvanic corrosion. All too many oil coolers are made of materials unsuited to the marine environment (e.g., brass). Oil coolers are expensive and often hard to find. Before starting on a long cruise, make sure your cooler is marine grade (bronze and cupronickel), and if necessary, *adequately protected with sacrificial zinc pencil anodes. These zincs should be checked every month or so until the consumption rate is known, and replaced when only partially eaten away* (no more than 50%). (Note that an increasing number of modern engines do not have zincs.)

When an oil cooler tube fails during engine operation, oil is likely to be pumped into the cooling system. On a raw-water-cooled oil cooler, the oil will show itself as an overboard slick. On a freshwater-cooled oil cooler, the oil will appear in the header tank. When the engine is at rest, water from the cooling system may find its way into the oil side of the cooler and siphon into the crankcase.

If you can identify the offending tube in the oil cooler, you may be able to plug it at both ends with a piece of doweling. However, only do this if the oil cooler can be opened to expose the tube stack and you can see from which tube oil is dribbling; in reality, the necessary access to the tubes often is not available. Failing this, you can find fittings to bypass the oil and water sides of a leaking oil cooler. And while you can still run the engine until a replacement is found, do so only at low power loadings and only after changing the engine oil and filter. Keep a close eye on the oil pressure and engine-temperature gauges.

Leaks from the freshwater side into the engine can be more damaging than saltwater leaks if the fresh water includes antifreeze. The antifreeze will cook out on bearings and other surfaces, proving just about impossible to remove. If you suspect a freshwater leak into the engine, do not run the engine until the leak has been tracked down and fixed, and the engine oil has been changed.

One condition may be encountered that is sometimes mistaken for a water leak into the engine but in fact may not be—condensation in the valve cover, leading to emulsification of the oil in the valve cover (it goes gooey and turns a creamy color—Figure 9-41) and rusting of the valve springs and other parts in the valve train. This situation happens from time to time when an owner periodically runs the engine for relatively short periods of time to charge a battery or just to make sure it is still working. The engine never warms up properly, but it generates enough heat to create condensation in the valve cover.

FIGURE 9-41. Emulsified oil inside a valve cover (the cover has been removed from the engine). In this instance, the problem was caused by a blown head gasket.

If you start the engine, run it long enough and hard enough to thoroughly warm it up. If necessary, tie off the boat firmly, put the engine in gear, and open the throttle a little.

Low Oil Pressure

Low oil pressure is a serious problem, but occurs infrequently. When confronted with low oil pressure many people assume that the gauge or warning light is malfunctioning and ignore the warning. Given the massive amount of damage that can be caused by running an engine with inadequate oil pressure, this is the height of foolishness. *Anytime low oil pressure is indicated, immediately shut down the engine, find the cause, and fix it.*

The problem is likely to be one of the following:

- Lack of oil, the most common cause of low oil pressure and the least forgivable.
- The wrong grade of oil in the engine—with a viscosity that is too low.
- Lowering of the oil viscosity by overheating, even though the correct grade is in the engine.
- Diesel dilution of the oil from leaking internal fuel lines. (Once enough diesel has found its way into the oil to lower the pressure to a noticeable extent, it will be possible to smell the fuel in the oil if a sample is taken from the dipstick.)
- Worn bearings (these do not, as a rule, develop overnight—a very gradual decline in oil pressure occurs, especially at low engine speeds when the engine is hot). Any rapid loss of oil pressure accompanied by a new engine knock indicates a specific bearing failure that needs immediate attention.
- Oil pressure relief valves sometimes malfunction, venting oil directly back to the sump,

with a consequent loss in pressure. Problems with pressure relief valves are rare, but simple to check. Almost invariably, the pressure relief valve is screwed into the side of the block somewhere and can easily be removed, disassembled, cleaned, and put back. The spring is liable to be under some tension, so take care when taking the valve apart. After cleaning, reset the spring's tension to maintain the manufacturer's specified oil pressure. Run the engine until it is warm and check the oil pressure. If it is low, shut down the engine and tighten the relief valve spring a little (if it is adjustable). If no amount of screwing down on the spring brings the oil pressure up to the manufacturer's specifications, the problem lies elsewhere.

- A well-heeled sailboat will sometimes cause the oil pump suction line to come clear of the oil in the pan (sump), allowing the pump to suck in a slug of air. The oil pressure will drop momentarily, generally with a sudden, alarming clatter from the engine. This is especially likely to happen if the oil level is a little low. Check the level, top off as necessary, and put the boat on a more even keel.
- The failure of an external oil line or gasket (e.g., to an oil cooler) will cause a sudden, potentially catastrophic loss of oil and pressure. The engine is likely to suddenly clatter loudly. You must shut it down immediately. There will be oil all over the engine room! Less easy to spot is the loss of oil that accompanies a corroded cooling tube in an oil cooler. The oil will be pumped out of the exhaust (or into the header tank), and sometimes water will enter the crankcase (see above).
- Oil pumps rarely, if ever, give out as long as you keep the oil topped off and clean and regularly change the filter. Over a long period of time, wear in an oil pump may produce a decline in pressure, but not before wear in the rest of the engine creates the need for a major rebuild. At this time, always check the oil pump.
- The oil pressure gauge is unlikely to malfunction (see below for troubleshooting engine instruments). However, note that some oil pressure sending units (the piece that screws into the engine and sends a signal to the gauge) have a surge suppressor built into them (such as many Yanmars). On occasion (notably, when the engine is warmed up and throttled back, causing the oil pressure to fall a little), this device will result in the gauge showing a sudden complete loss of oil pressure, which will not recover until the engine is speeded up. It can be a little unnerving, but

there is no problem with the oil pressure. To stop this, remove the surge suppressor from the base of the sending unit.

Inadequate Turbocharger Performance

Poor turbocharger performance will cause symptoms similar to those caused by a plugged air filter—reduced power, overheating, and black smoke. Be sure to check the airflow through the engine before turning your attention to the turbocharger. This includes looking for obstructions in the exhaust, air leaks between the turbocharger and the inlet manifold, exhaust leaks between the exhaust manifold and the turbocharger, and dirt plugging the fins on any intercooler or aftercooler.

Turbochargers spin at up to 200,000 rpm; the speed of the blade tips can exceed the speed of sound, and temperatures are as high as 1,200°F/650°C—hot enough to melt glass. The degree of precision needed to make this possible means that *repairing turbochargers is strictly for specialists.*

A turbocharged engine *should never be raced on initial start-up*—the oil needs time to be pumped up to the bearings. Similarly, *never race the engine before shutting it down;* the turbine and compressor wheel will continue to spin for some time but without any oil supply to the bearings, and the residual heat will turn any oil in the bearings into abrasive carbon.

Clean oil is critical to turbocharger life—the bearings will be one of the first things to suffer from poor oil change procedures. Many engines have a bypass valve fitted to the oil filter so that if the filter becomes plugged, *unfiltered* oil will circulate through the engine—if the filter is neglected for long, the turbocharger will soon be damaged. Note that some turbochargers also have their own oil filter, which must be changed at the same time as the engine oil filter.

Any loss of engine oil pressure, such as from a low oil level or the use of the wrong grade of oil in the engine, will also threaten the turbocharger. When a turbocharger is under load, insufficient oil for as little as 5 seconds can cause damage. Damage to bearings will allow motion in the shaft, permitting the turbines to rub against their housings.

A dirty or damaged air filter or leaks in the air inlet ducting will allow dirt particles into the turbocharger that will erode the compressor wheel and turbine. The resulting imbalance and loss of performance will lead to other problems.

Before condemning a turbocharger, conduct the following tests:

1. Start the engine and listen to it. If a turbocharger is cycling up and down in pitch, there is probably a restriction in the air inlet (most likely a plugged filter). A whistling sound is quite likely produced by a leak in the inlet or exhaust piping.

2. Stop the engine, *let the turbocharger cool,* and remove the inlet and exhaust pipes from the turbine and compressor housings (these are the pipes going into the *center* of the housings; Figures 9-42A and 9-42B). This will give you a view of the turbine and compressor wheels. With a flashlight, check for bent or chipped blades, erosion of the blades, rub marks on the wheels or housings, excessive dirt on the wheels, and oil in the housings. The latter may indicate oil seal failure, but first check for other possible sources, such as oil coming up a crankcase breather into the air inlet, oil from an overfilled oil bath–type air cleaner, or a plugged oil drain in the turbocharger that is causing oil to leak into the turbine or compressor housings.

3. Push in the wheels and turn them to feel for any rubbing or binding. Do this from both sides.

If these tests reveal no problems, the turbocharger is probably OK. If it failed on any count (except dirty turbine or compressor wheels), remove it as a unit and send it in for repair.

Cleaning turbocharger wheels. Mark both housings and the center unit with scribed lines so you can put them back together in the same relationship to each other. Allow the unit to cool before removing any fasteners or the housings may warp. If the housings are held on with large snap rings (circlips), leave them alone—they will come apart easily enough but will require a hydraulic press to put back together! Housings held with bolts and large clamps may be taken apart (Figure 9-43).

If the housings are difficult to break loose, tap them with a soft hammer or mallet. Pull them off squarely to avoid bending any turbine blades. Only use noncaustic solutions to clean turbines (degreasers work well; I am told that various carburetor cleaners also do a good job) using soft-bristle brushes and plastic scrapers. Do not use abrasives; the resulting damage to the blades will upset the critical balance of the turbines. Make no attempt to straighten bent blades—the turbocharger demands a specialist's help.

After reassembly, spin the turbines by hand to make sure they are turning freely. Before starting the engine, crank it for a while to get oil up to the turbocharger bearings.

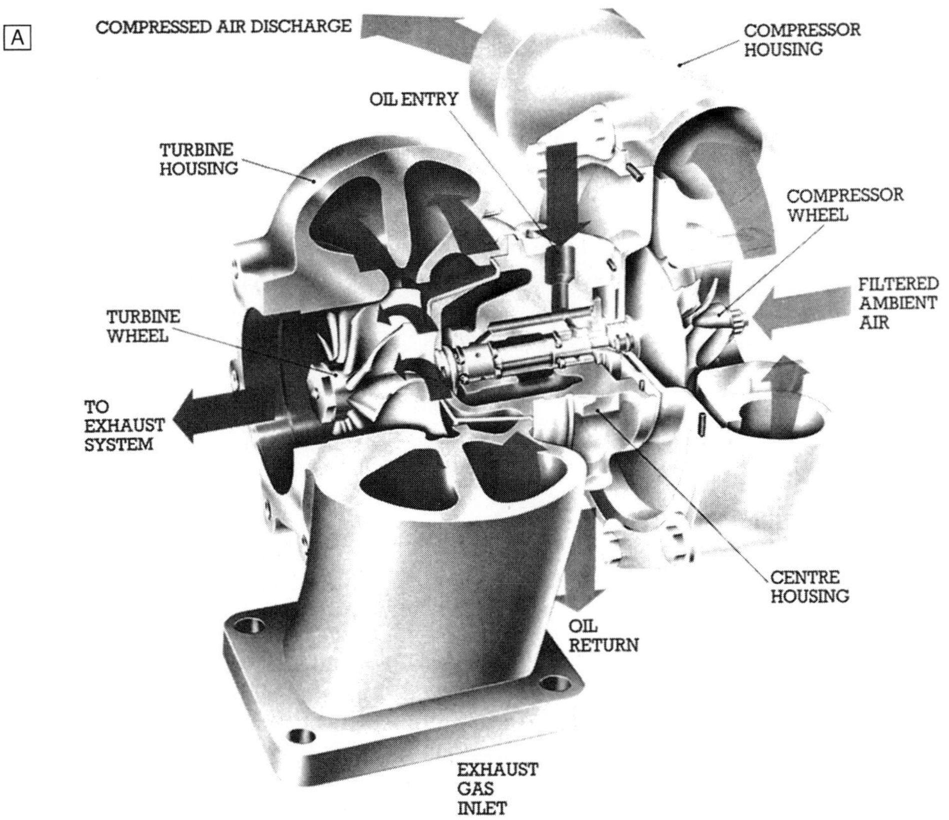

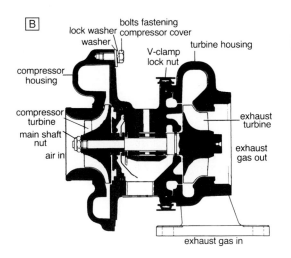

A — COMPRESSED AIR DISCHARGE

COMPRESSOR HOUSING

OIL ENTRY

TURBINE HOUSING

COMPRESSOR WHEEL

FILTERED AMBIENT AIR

TURBINE WHEEL

TO EXHAUST SYSTEM

CENTRE HOUSING

OIL RETURN

EXHAUST GAS INLET

FIGURE 9-42A. A cutaway view of a turbocharger. (Garrett Automotive Products Co.)

B — bolts fastening compressor cover
lock washer
washer
V-clamp lock nut
turbine housing
compressor housing
compressor turbine
main shaft nut
air in
exhaust turbine
exhaust gas out
exhaust gas in

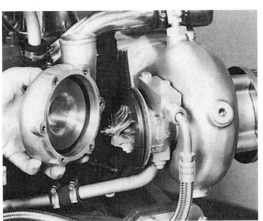

FIGURE 9-42B (left). A typical turbocharger. (Holset Engineering Co. Ltd.)

FIGURE 9-43. Removing a turbocharger housing. (Perkins Engines Ltd.)

Problems with Engine Instrumentation

Some old engines are still found with thermometer-type temperature gauges and mechanical pressure gauges and tachometers. All will have some kind of a metal tube from the engine block to the back of the gauge. Gauge failure is normally self-evident—the gauge sticks in one position. Temperature gauges and their sensing bulbs have to be replaced as a complete unit, oil pressure gauges may just have a kinked sensing line, and tachometers may perhaps have a broken inner cable.

All new engines use electronic instruments comprising a sending unit on the engine block connected to a gauge, warning light, or alarm (Figure 9-44). Detecting problems is not quite so straightforward, but the tests below should work.

Over the next decade, all marine engine manufacturers are likely to move toward using sophisticated electronic control and data man-

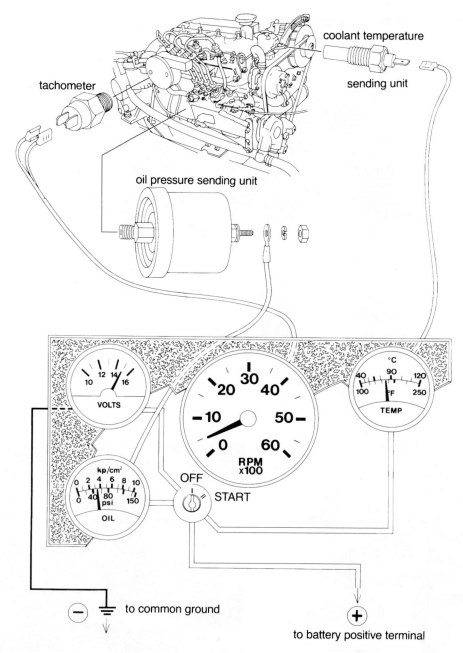

coolant temperature

tachometer

sending unit

oil pressure sending unit

VOLTS

RPM x100

OFF

START

°C
TEMP

kp/cm²
psi
OIL

⊖ to common ground

⊕ to battery positive terminal

agement systems based on the CAN (controller area network) technology now dominant in the automotive field. This technology is extremely robust and trouble free, but when problems do occur, identifying and troubleshooting them generally requires a technician to plug in a purpose-built computer. There will be less and less room for the boatowner in a bind to troubleshoot and jury-rig a system as described below.

Ignition warning lights. Most alternators require an external DC power source to *excite* the alternator before it will start generating power (Chapter 3). An ignition warning light is installed in the *excitation line* to the alternator.

When the ignition is turned on, current runs from the battery down this line to the alternator, causing the light to glow. When the engine fires up, and the alternator begins to put out, the light is extinguished. If the light fails to come on when the ignition is switched on, check the bulb first (on older units; newer units have an LED, in which case test for voltage). If it is OK, the most likely problem is a break in the wire to the light or in the excitation line running to the alternator, or an electrically poor connection. If the light comes on and stays on after the engine is running, the alternator is almost certainly not putting out (Chapter 3).

All other warning lights and alarms.

These use a simple switch. Positive current from the battery is fed via the ignition switch to the alarm or warning light and from there down to a switch on the engine block. If the engine reaches a preset temperature, or oil pressure drops below a preset level, the switch closes and completes the circuit.

Most switches (sending units) are the earth-return type; that is, grounded through the engine block (Figures 9-45A and 9-45B). However, some are for use in insulated circuits, in which case they have a separate ground wire. Many sending units incorporate both an alarm and a variable resistor that connects to a gauge. In this case, there will be two wires on an earth-return unit, and three on an insulated unit (Figure 9-45C).

If you suspect problems with an *alarm* or *warning light* (for *gauges*, see below), turn on the ignition switch and:

1. Test for 12 volts between the alarm or light positive terminal and a good ground (Figure 9-46, Test 1). No volts—the ignition circuit is faulty; 12 volts—proceed to the next step.

2. To test the alarm or light itself, disconnect the wire from the sending unit and short it to a good ground (Figure 9-46, Test 2). The alarm or light should come on. If not, conduct the same test from the second terminal on the back of the alarm or light (the one with the wire going to the sending unit) to a good ground. No response—the alarm or light is faulty; response—the wire to the sending unit is faulty.

3. If the alarm or light and its wiring are in order, the sending unit itself may be shorted (the alarm or light stays on all the time) or open-circuited (it never comes on, even when it should). Switch off the ignition, disconnect all wires from the sending unit, and test with an ohmmeter (R × 1 scale on an analog meter) from the sending unit terminal to a good ground (Figure 9-46, Test 3). A temperature warning unit should read infinite ohms—unless the engine is overheated, in which case it will read 0 ohms. An oil warning unit reads 0 ohms with the engine shut down and infinite ohms at normal operating pressures.

Temperature and pressure gauges.

Most gauges have three terminals, although there may be as many as five. We are interested in those marked "I" or "Ign" (the power feed from the ignition switch), "G" or "Gnd" (a ground connection for the lighting circuit), and "S" or "Snd" (the connection to the sending unit on the

W = warning light or alarm wire
G = gauge wire

Sending Units

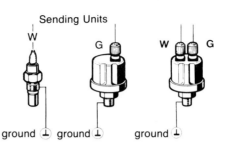

FIGURE 9-45A. Sending units for alarms and gauges. **Left:** Simple sensor with a warning contact (W), as used, for example, with an oil pressure warning light. **Middle:** Sensor for use with a gauge. **Right:** Sensor with contacts for both a gauge and a warning device. *(VDO)*

Warning light or alarm

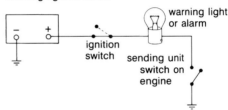

FIGURE 9-45B. Warning light, alarm, and gauge circuits.

Gauge

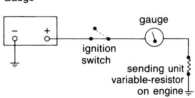

Combined alarm and gauge

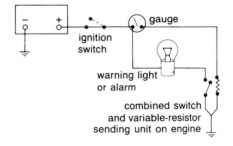

Combined alarm and gauge (another approach)

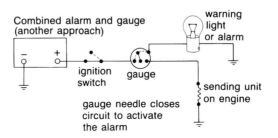

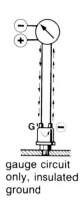

gauge circuit
only, insulated
ground

engine block). Positive current is fed from the battery via the ignition switch to the gauge (I or Ign) and from there down to the sending unit (S or Snd) and then to ground (Figure 9-47).

To test a gauge:

1. Test for 12 volts from the gauge positive terminal to a good ground (Figure 9-47, Test 1). No volts—the ignition switch circuit is faulty; 12 volts—proceed to the next step.

2. Disconnect the sensing line (which goes to the sending unit) *from the back of the gauge* (Figure 9-47, Test 2). A temperature gauge should go to its lowest reading; an oil pressure gauge should go to its highest reading, although just to confuse things, a few behave the same as a temperature gauge!

3. Connect a jumper (a screwdriver will do) from the sensing line terminal on the gauge to the negative terminal on the gauge (or a good ground on the engine block if there is no negative terminal; Figure 9-47, Test 3). A temperature gauge should go to its highest reading; an oil pressure gauge should go to its lowest reading (except as noted above).

4. If the gauge passed these tests, it is OK. Reconnect the sensing line and disconnect it at the

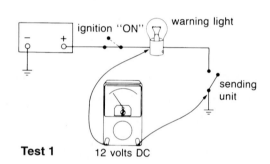

Test 1

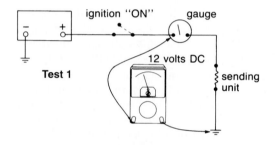

Test 1

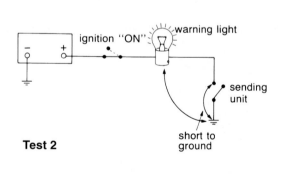

Test 2

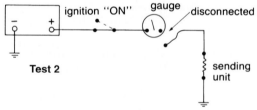

Test 2

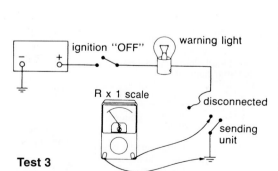

Test 3

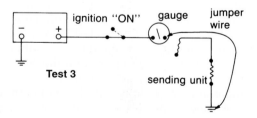

Test 3

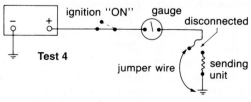

Test 4

sending unit on the engine (Figure 9-47, Test 4). A temperature gauge should go to its lowest reading; an oil pressure gauge should go to its highest reading (except as noted above). Short the sensing line to the engine block. A temperature gauge should go to its highest reading; an oil pressure gauge should go to its lowest reading (except as noted above). If not, the sensing line is faulty (shorted or open-circuited). The most likely trouble spot is in the plug connector for the main engine wiring harness (generally found toward the back of the engine). Undo the plug and check all the sockets and pins for damage or corrosion and correct as necessary. Most times, this will cure wiring problems. If not, make sure the ignition switch is turned off, then use an ohmmeter (R × 1 scale on an analog meter) to test the sending line first from the gauge to the relevant terminal on the plug, then from the other half of the plug to the sending unit. You should get a very low resistance both times. Infinity, or a high resistance, indicates resistance, or a break, in the circuit.

5. To test a sending unit, switch off the ignition, disconnect all wires, and test with an ohmmeter (R × 1 scale on an analog meter) from the sending unit to a good ground (Figure 9-48). Most temperature senders vary from around 700 ohms at low temperatures, to 200 to 300 ohms at around 100°F/40°C, down to almost 0 ohms at 250°F/120°C, while most oil pressure senders vary from around 0 ohms at no pressure to around 200 ohms at high pressure. However, there are differences from one manufacturer to another, and some gauges may work in the opposite direction; the important thing is to get a clear change in resistance with a change in temperature or pressure.

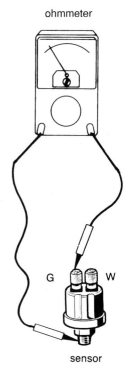

ohmmeter

G W

sensor

FIGURE 9-48. Testing a sending unit. (VDO)

Tank-level gauges. Old-style tank-level gauges have been electronic, but in recent years pneumatic gauges have become increasingly popular.

Electronic gauges. A float is put in the tank either in a tube or on a hinged arm (Figure 9-49). As the level comes up, the float or arm rises, moving a contact arm on a variable resistance (a kind of rheostat). Positive current is fed from the battery via the ignition switch to the gauge, down to the resistor, and from there to ground. The gauge registers the changing resistance.

The same tests apply to the gauge, the sensing

FIGURE 9-49. **Left:** Electronic fuel tank sensor. Because of its construction, the immersion pipe sensor is suitable only for use with fuel tanks. The float unit is mounted on the guide bar, making contact with the two resistance wires via the contact springs. Resistance varies according to the height of the float, varying the gauge reading. The protective tube and the flooder provide excellent damping. **Middle and right:** Typical differences between a swinging arm–type water tank sensor (middle) and a fuel tank sensor (right). For electrically conductive media, the electrical resistance element must be positioned in the assembly flange, with the level of the liquid transmitted mechanically up to the element. (VDO)

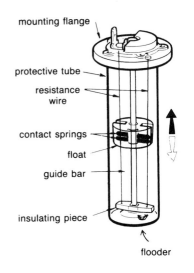

mounting flange
protective tube
resistance wire
contact springs
float
guide bar
insulating piece
flooder

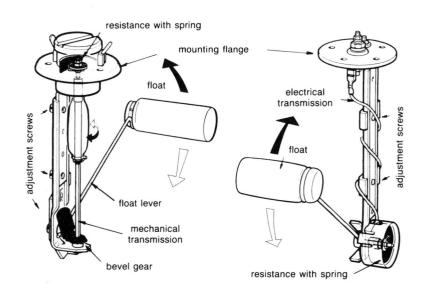

resistance with spring
mounting flange
float
adjustment screws
float lever
mechanical transmission
bevel gear

electrical transmission
float
adjustment screws
resistance with spring

FIGURE 9-50. A pneumatic tank-level gauge. The gauge has been calibrated to the various tanks in the boat, with the relationship between the gauge reading and the tank volumes codified in the tables beneath the meter.

line, and the sending unit as to the oil pressure gauge. Sending-unit resistances are similar—near 0 ohms on an empty tank, up to around 200 ohms on a full tank.

If everything checks out OK, but the unit always reads empty, the float on the sending unit is probably saturated or there is a mechanical failure—for instance, a broken or jammed arm. A saturated swinging arm–type float can be made temporarily serviceable by strapping a piece of closed-cell foam to it.

Pneumatic sensors. Pneumatic sensors are becoming increasingly popular due to their versatility and simplicity. A tube is inserted to the bottom of the tank and connected to a small hand pump mounted on the tank gauge panel. The gauge itself is teed into the tube just below the pump (Figure 9-50).

When the pump is operated, air is forced down the tube and bubbles out into the tank. Depending on the level in the tank (and hence in the tube) more or less pressure is needed to drive all the fluid out of the tube. The gauge registers this pressure in *inches of water* (in the tank) or *inches of diesel*. The owner draws up a table converting the gauge readings to gallons—the conversion will vary from tank to tank depending on the tank size and shape. The gauges come with instructions on how to draw up this table. If the instructions are missing, or your tank is an odd shape, the best bet is simply to empty the tank, then add known quantities of fluid (e.g., 5 gallons at a time), stroking the hand pump and noting the gauge reading after each addition.

Pneumatic level gauges are more accurate than electronic gauges. What is more, apart from leaking connections or kinked tubes, there is nothing to go wrong. As many as ten tanks can be measured with one gauge simply by switching the gauge and pump into the individual tank tubes. Since there is no fluid in the tubes beyond the level of the tanks themselves, there is no possibility of cross-contamination from one tank to another. This means diesel, water, and holding tanks can all be measured with the same unit (note, however, that when inserted into a holding tank, the small air tubes have a tendency to get plugged with effluent, which then results in a false full-tank reading).

Wide, shallow tanks. The one problem with all pneumatic gauges is the fact that they do not work well with wide, shallow tanks because there is very little change in the fluid level with significant changes in volume. What is more, even a little heeling will create substantial changes in fluid levels from one side of the tank to the other, resulting in false readings. An increasing number of modern boats have relatively flat bottoms and shallow bilges. No gauge will give accurate readings on tanks fitted to these spaces.

Winter Layup and Recommissioning

Winter Layup

The following is a reasonably comprehensive winterizing checklist (Figure 9-51). One or two of these items will not need to be performed every year (such as breaking loose the exhaust to check for carbon buildup or removing the inner wires of engine control cables to lubricate them), but most should be:

1. Change the oil and oil filter at the beginning of the winter, not the end. The used oil will contain harmful acids and contaminants that should not be allowed to go to work on the engine all winter long. Change the transmission oil at the same time.

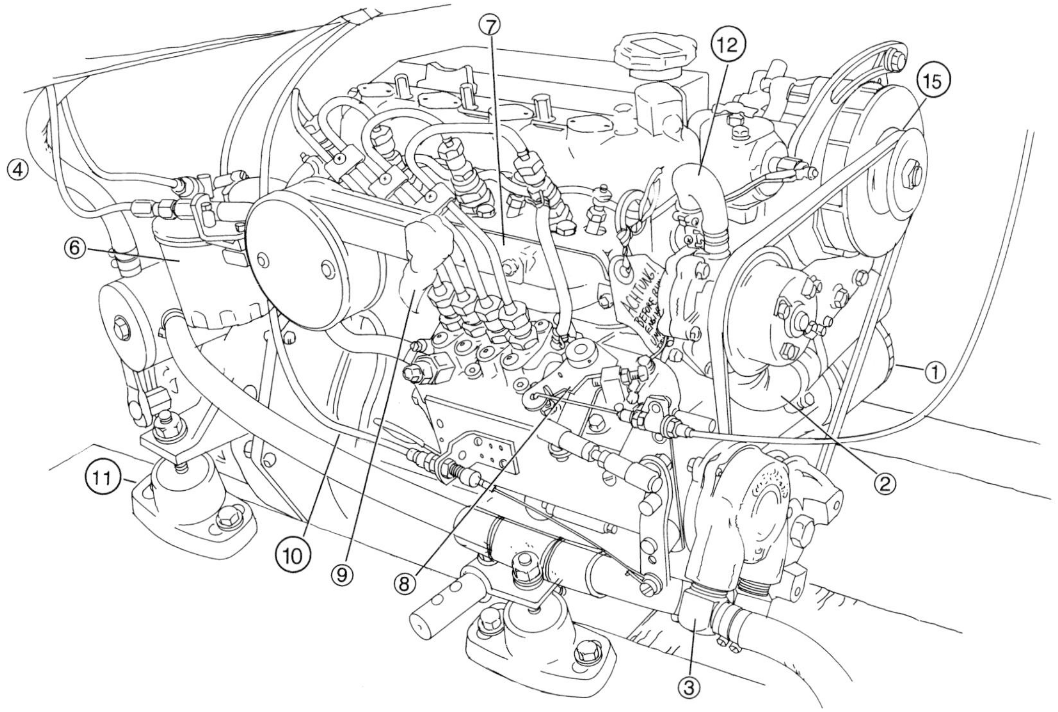

FIGURE 9-51. Winter layup maintenance points (see the text for an explanation). *(Jim Sollers)*

2. Change the antifreeze on freshwater-cooled engines. The antifreeze itself does not wear out, but it has various corrosion-fighting additives that do. Always mix the water and antifreeze before putting it in the engine. A 50-50 water-antifreeze solution provides the best protection. (Note: Some antifreezes now come premixed, in which case they should not be diluted.)

3. Do one of the following: Drain the raw-water system, taking particular care to empty all low spots. Clean the strainer. Remove the rubber pump impeller, grease it lightly with petroleum jelly, and replace. Leave the pump cover screws loose; otherwise the impeller has a tendency to stick in the pump housing. Leave a prominent note as a reminder of what has been done! Run the engine for a few seconds to drive any remaining water out of the exhaust. Drain the base of a water-lift muffler.

Or: Close the raw-water seacock and make a routine inspection (as above) of the strainer and raw-water pump impeller. Disconnect the engine suction hose from the seacock, dip it in a 50-50 solution of antifreeze and water, and run the engine until the solution emerges from the exhaust. (Note: Ethylene glycol—commonly found in antifreeze—is harmful to the environment, so use propylene glycol instead, which is commonly used for winterizing drinking water systems. Propylene glycol is often sold already diluted

to a 50% solution, in which case do not dilute it further.)

4. Wash the valves on any vented loops in warm water to clean out salt crystals.

5. Break the exhaust loose from the exhaust manifold or water-lift muffler (not visible in illustration) and check for carbon buildup; inspect the raw-water injection elbow for corrosion. Remove the raw-water hose from the injection nipple and check for any obstruction (this is a likely spot for scale and debris to get trapped).

6. Check the fuel filters and fuel tank for water and sediment; clean as necessary. Fill the tank to minimize condensation.

7. Squirt some oil into the inlet manifold and turn the engine over a few times (without starting) to spread the oil around the cylinder walls.

8. Grease any grease points.

9. Seal all openings into the engine (air inlet, breathers, exhaust) and the fuel tank vent. Put a conspicuous notice somewhere as a reminder to unseal everything at the start of the next season.

10. Remove the inner wires of all engine control cables from their outer sheaths. Clean, inspect, grease, and replace. Check the sheathing as outlined on pages 431–33.

11. Inspect all flexible feet and couplings for signs of softening (generally from oil and diesel leaks) and replace as necessary.

12. Inspect all hoses for signs of softening, cracking, or bulging, especially those on the hot side of the cooling and exhaust systems. Check hose clamps for tightness and corrosion, especially where the band goes inside the worm gear. (Undo the clamps a turn or two to inspect the band. When undoing clamps, push in relatively hard on the screwdriver so that the screw does not come out of its housing, leaving the band stuck to the hose!)

13. Remove the inlet and exhaust ducting (not visible in illustration) from any turbocharger and inspect the compressor wheel and turbine for excessive deposits or damage. Clean as necessary.

14. Make sure that batteries (not visible in illustration) are fully charged, and in the case of wet-cells, that they are topped off and recharged monthly.

15. Lightly spray the alternator and starter motor with WD-40 or some other moisture dispersant/lubricant.

If there is any likelihood of salt water having contacted the starter motor pinion, remove the starter and lubricate the pinion.

Recommissioning

When you're ready to start boating again, perform the following tasks before you set sail:

1. Unseal engine openings and tighten the raw-water pump cover if loose. If the paper gasket is rubbed with grease or petroleum jelly, it will not stick to the cover or pump body next time the cover is removed.

2. Replace all zincs.

3. Capacity-test the batteries.

4. Tighten alternator and other belts.

5. Prime the cooling system.

6. Crank the engine without starting it until oil pressure is established.

7. Once running, check the oil pressure, the raw-water discharge, and the engine for oil and water leaks.

8. After the boat has been in the water for a few days, check the engine alignment (see Chapter 10).

Do-It-Yourself Engine Survey

With older engines, or if buying a second-hand boat, it is sometimes useful to do an engine survey. The following is a nonintrusive set of procedures that can be undertaken by just about anyone without using specialized tools, and which has no disassembly beyond loosening a hose clamp or two and undoing a few screws. Most times, it will give you a pretty good sense of impending problems. For a more detailed survey, you will need to hire a professional.

1. Check for an engine hour meter and a maintenance logbook showing regular oil and filter changes and other periodic maintenance (Figures 9-52A and 9-52B). Without this, you have no way of knowing if the engine has been reasonably cared for.

2. The fuel system is the single most expensive system on the engine:

   a. Make sure there is a primary (off the engine) as well as a secondary (on the engine) fuel filter.

   b. Inspect the primary filter for contamination. If contaminated, inspect the secondary filter.

A

fill port.

2. Fresh water engine driven pump pulls coolant from heat exchanger through engine block and thermostat back thr exhaust manifold and into heat exchanger to be cooled.

07-01-82 Changed lub oil & filters TJD
20.1 HRS
08-24-82 Changed lub oil & filters TJI
91.0 HRS
10-16-82 Changed lub oil & filters TJI
119.5 HRS
08-02-83 Changed lub oil & filters TJD
187.7 HRS
10-22-83 Changed lub oil & filters TJI
215.3 HRS
08-06-84 Changed lub. oil & filter TJI
280.8 HRS
10-21-84 Changed lub oil & filters TJI
313.1 HRS 46 HRS CHANGED BELT
01-14-85
01-23-85 Changed lub oil & filter TJD
59.6 HRS Changed antifreeze
10-21-85 Changed lube oil & filters (ALL) TJD
97.5 HRS
7-30-86 Changed lube oil & filter JD
156.6 HRS
0-18-86 Changed lube oil & filters TJD
175.1 HRS
7-10-87 Changed lube oil & filter JD
221.4 HRS
0-31-87 Changed lub oil & filters JD
306 HRS

---

416   DIESEL ENGINES

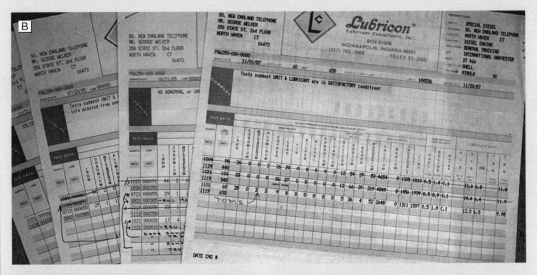

water

FIGURES 9-52A TO 9-52O. A do-it-yourself diesel engine survey. Any kind of an engine log (in this case, written in the back of the engine manual) is important (9-52A). Regular oil sampling is an excellent indication of attention to maintenance issues (9-52B). Fuel tank sample showing significant water contamination. If any of this has made its way through to the injectors, there may be serious damage (9-52C). An oil sample after 50 hours on a new engine; note that it is almost translucent (9-52D). The same engine after 150 hours—the oil is black from carbon in suspension (9-52E). This is normal, but any kind of sludge is a sign of trouble. Checking for sludge and emulsified oil inside the oil fill opening (9-52F). Note the oil immediately beneath this water pump, from a leaking oil seal where the pump bolts up to the engine (this is a gear-driven pump rather than belt driven), and the salt crystals lower down from a leaking water seal (9-52G). A rebuild is needed. Cracked raw-water pump impeller vanes (9-52H). Raw-water injection hose removed from the raw-water injection nipple (9-52I). Checking the injection elbow for corrosion (9-52J). The galvanized pipe and fittings used in this installation are especially prone to corrosion. Checking for carbon deposits in the exhaust system (9-52K). Quality hose clamps, but they're not much use with this kinked hose (9-52L)! Checking hose clamps for corrosion (9-52M). Inspecting the engine feet for softened or perished rubber (9-52N). Inspecting the shaft seal for corroded hose clamps, a defective hose, or seal leaks (9-52O).

    c. If the secondary filter is contaminated, you have reason to feel a little nervous. In any event, check any filter in the lift pump.

    d. In all cases, draw a sample of fuel from the low spot of the fuel tank. If contaminated, pump down until clean (Figure 9-52C).

3. Pull out the oil dipstick and wipe the oil onto your fingertips (Figures 9-52D and 9-52E). If the oil has not been changed recently, it will be black. Up to 50 hours or more after an oil change, it should still have an element of translucency. If it is really heavily sooted, there may be blowby past the piston rings, lowering the engine compression.

4. For a more serious oil analysis, send a sample to a laboratory.

5. Remove the oil filler cap, and also any oil filler cap on top of the valve cover, and look at the underside of the cap(s). Run your finger around inside the opening (Figure 9-52F). If there are sludgy black *continued*

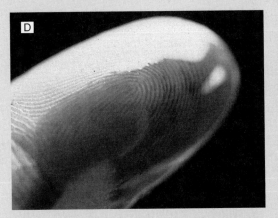

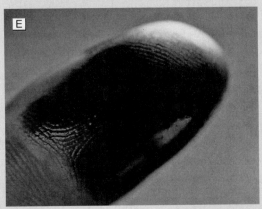

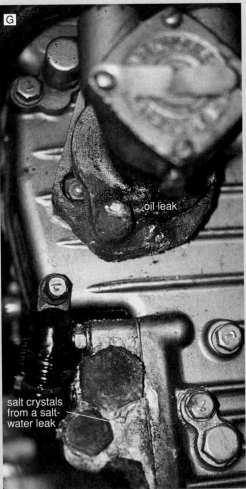

oil leak

salt crystals from a salt-water leak

oil filler opening

deposits, oil change procedures have almost certainly been seriously neglected. If there is emulsified oil (creamy in color and texture), there is water in the oil. Bad news in both cases!

6. Take a sample of oil from the transmission. If this is at all black, it is indicative of a slipping/burning clutch.

7. Check the raw-water circuit:

   a. Check the pump's exterior for signs of water and/or oil leaks (Figure 9-52G). Remove the raw-water pump cover and check the impeller for missing vanes, cracks, or excessive wear (the impeller tips will be worn flat; Figure 9-52H).

   b. Remove any zincs from the heat exchanger. If corroded to the point of nonexistence or near nonexistence, they have been neglected and expensive corrosion problems are possible.

   c. Remove the end caps from the heat exchanger and inspect the tube stack for scaling, blockage, or corrosion.

   d. Check for the existence of a vented loop. If not present, the engine may have flooded with salt water at some point.

damaged impeller

e. Remove the valve from any vented loop and flush in fresh water.

f. Remove the water injection hose from the exhaust elbow and check for debris blocking the injection point (Figure 9-52I).

g. Inspect the elbow for corrosion (Figure 9-52J).

8. Remove the exhaust hose from the water-lift muffler and check for anything more than a light film of carbon (Figure 9-52K). If heavier carbon deposits are present, the valves and engine may be seriously carboned up. After cleaning the exhaust, run

continued

exhaust hose removed from water-lift silencer

look in here for carbon buildup

kinked hose seriously interfering with cooling

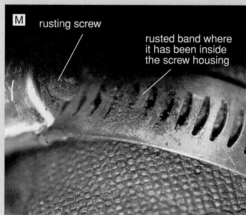

rusting screw

rusted band where it has been inside the screw housing

a back-pressure test and reduce the back pressure if it is excessive.

9. While working around the cooling and exhaust systems, inspect the hoses and squeeze them, looking for soft spots, cracking, or other problems (Figure 9-52L).

10. When undoing any hose clamps for the previous items, inspect the screws for rusting, as well as the bands (where they are in contact with the screws; Figure 9-52M). If rust is present, inferior hose clamps have been used (see Chapter 5), in which case the screws are not 300 series stainless steel. You should consider replacing the hose clamps (and any others like them, especially those on the exhaust system).

11. Inspect the rubber engine feet for signs of oil and diesel spills and for softening of the rubber (which will be caused by these spills; Figure 9-52N).

12. Check the propeller shaft seal (stuffing box or other type of shaft seal) for signs of leaks (Figure 9-52O), particularly for rusting of any components that may have been subjected to salt water thrown out by the propeller shaft (many engine control brackets and cables are vulnerable). Make sure there is adequate access to maintain the shaft seal (some require the engine to be removed!; more on this in the next chapter).

13. Operate the engine controls to make sure they are smooth and free from undue resistance and that the gearshift clicks into neutral at the appropriate point.

14. Notice that the engine has not yet been started! Make sure it is cold before trying to crank it, then activate any cold-start devices and crank. It should fire pretty well immediately. If it does not, and there is no problem with the fuel supply, it is probably suffering a loss of compression, which may necessitate a major rebuild (it may be a good idea to have a mechanic run a compression test). It's best to run this test on a colder day (the colder, the better; the warmer the weather, the less likely it is that compression problems will be revealed).

15. Immediately after cranking, check the exhaust for smoke. An initial thin blue haze is OK, but if it persists, the engine is burning oil. White vapor may be unburned fuel, in which case the engine will almost certainly be misfiring and quite likely has a compression problem (especially if it was slow to start).

16. Shut down the engine, close the throttle, and pull out any stop lever or close the fuel rack so the engine will not start. Place a DC voltmeter across the hot terminal on the starter motor and the battery positive terminal and crank. You will be measuring the volt drop on the starting circuit (see the Starter Motors section in Chapter 7). If the volt drop is more than 1 volt, the starting circuit needs attention (see Chapter 7). Repeat this test from the engine block to battery negative.

17. Now move the meter leads to the battery posts (positive and negative) and crank for 15 seconds. The voltage will stabilize and then slowly decline. If it starts to drop rapidly, the cranking battery is either not charged or is reaching the end of its life (see the Testing a Battery section in Chapter 3).

18. By now the battery will be somewhat discharged. Start the engine, and immediately (while the alternator is at full output) test with a DC voltmeter from the alternator's positive (output) terminal to the battery's positive terminal. You will be measuring the volt drop in the charging circuit (see Chapter 4). If it is more than 0.5 volt on a 12-volt system or 1.0 volt on a 24-volt system, the cables are undersized, there is other unwanted resistance, or the circuit has isolation diodes. For more on this, see the Charging More Than One Battery Bank from a Common Alternator section in Chapter 1.

19. Load up the engine and make sure it will come to full rated rpm. If not, the propeller may be incorrectly sized. The engine may emit some black smoke as you come up to speed. If this continues when at speed, there may be an obstruction in the inlet air or the exhaust, or a fuel injection problem.

20. While the engine is at full load, find the crankcase breather (generally from the crankcase to the air inlet) and see if you can get your finger over the end of it. If it is blowing out a steady stream of gas, there is serious blowby and a major overhaul is in the cards.

21. Run the engine for a while, monitoring the voltage across the battery posts until it stabilizes (this may take some time). This stabilized voltage is the absorption voltage for the charging system (see Chapter 1). If it is below 14.2 volts on a 12-volt system (28.4 for 24 volts), the batteries are probably being perennially undercharged (see Chapter 1).

For more on diesel engines, see my *Marine Diesel Engines,* second edition, published by International Marine.

CHAPTER 10

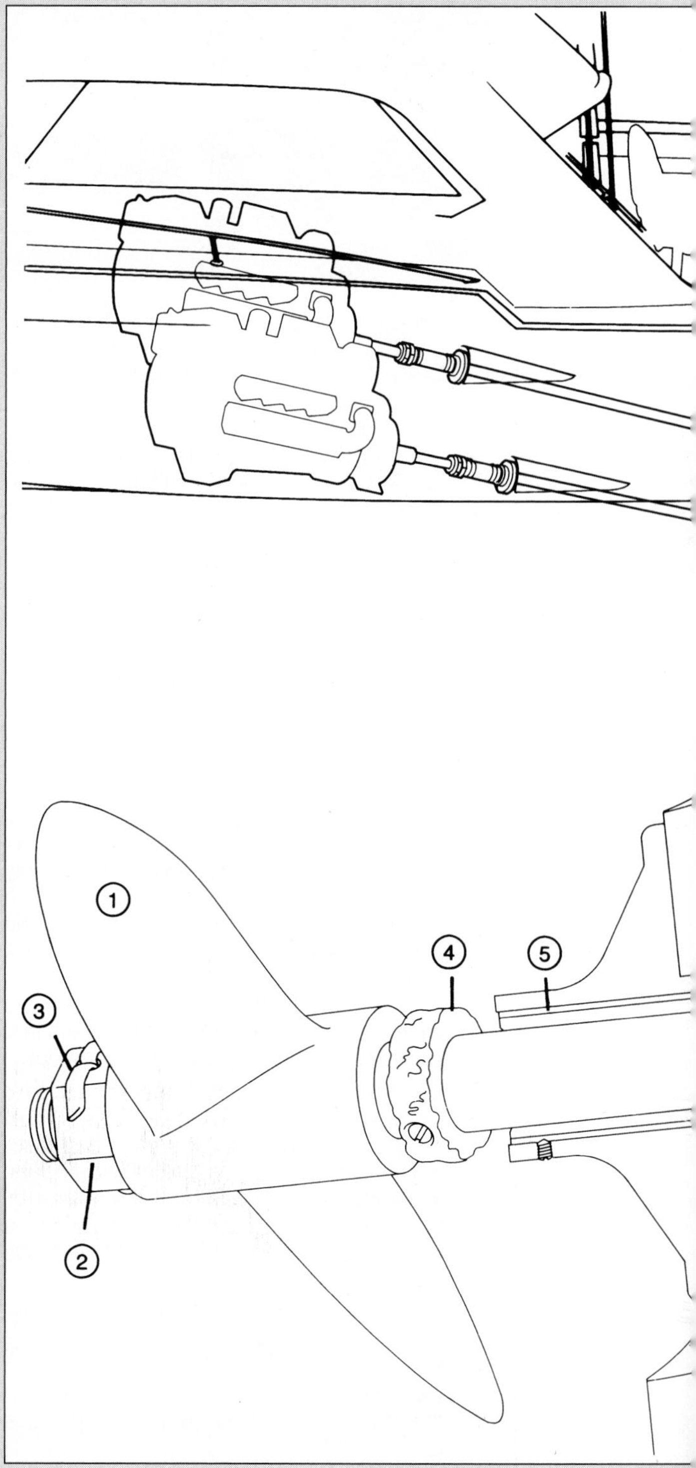

FIGURE 10-1. The space between engine and propeller is easily maintained, yet is all too often neglected. *(Jim Sollers)*

(1) propeller
(2) retaining nut
(3) cotter pin
(4) zinc
(5) rubber sleeve (Cutless) bearing
(6) bearing
(7) stern tube
(8) propeller shaft
(9) flexible stuffing box
(10) packing rings
(11) locking nut
(12) compression spacer
(13) adjusting nut
(14) shaft coupling
(15) output shaft
(16) transmission
(17) input shaft
(18) clutch discs

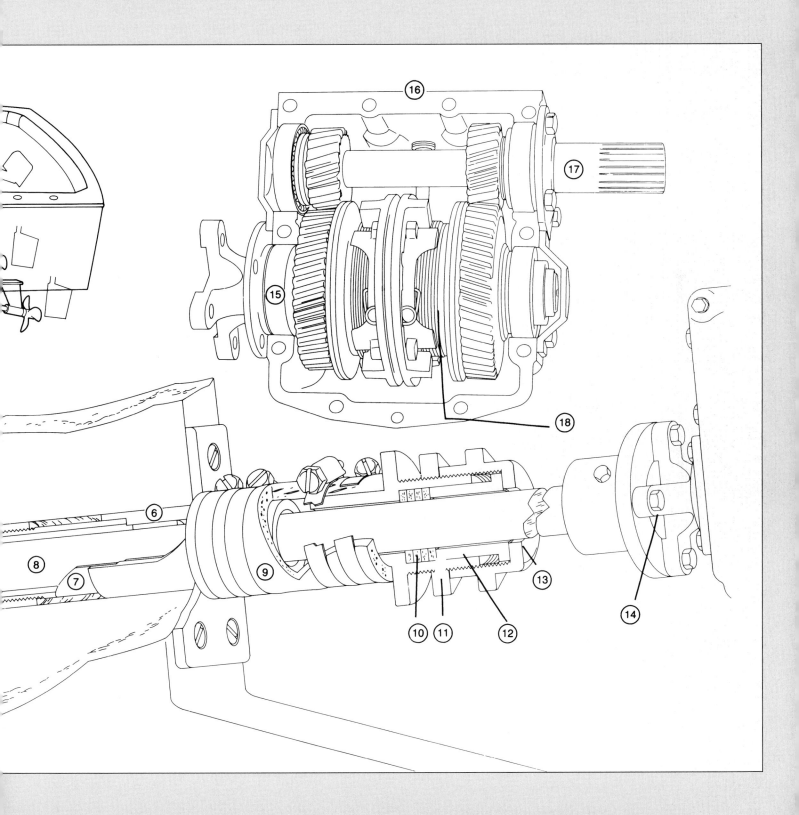

Most inboard engines have an attached transmission, or gearbox, coupled to a propeller shaft that is sealed in the boat with some kind of a shaft seal (a *stuffing box—packing gland—*or one of the newer mechanical or lip-type seals). An increasing number, however, use some kind of *inboard/outboard* arrangement, or *saildrive,* to dispense with the propeller shaft and its associated seal. When used, a propeller shaft is supported just in front of the propeller with a rubber sleeve bearing (commonly known as a *Cutless* bearing, although Cutless is a registered trademark) that is inserted in the deadwood or in an I (P) or V (A) bracket (strut).

These components are all relatively trouble free and as a result tend to get ignored. They do, however, require periodic inspection and some maintenance.

Transmissions and Shaft Brakes

Transmissions: How They Work

Manual transmissions (gearboxes) are still found in some boats. These are generally of the planetary, or epicyclic, type. Far more common are hydraulic planetary transmissions (Figure 10-2) and two-shaft transmissions, with the latter dominating the marketplace in the past decade (in other words, as time goes by, we will see fewer and fewer planetary transmissions, either hydraulic or manual).

Planetary transmissions. The engine turns a drive shaft that rotates constantly in the same direction as the engine (Figure 10-3). Deployed around and meshed with a gear on this shaft are two or three gears (the *first intermediate* gears) on a carrier assembly. These mesh with more gears (the *second intermediate* gears), also mounted on the carrier assembly. The second intermediate gears engage a large geared outer hub. The carrier assembly, with its collection of first and second intermediate gears, is keyed to the output shaft of the transmission.

On one end of the drive shaft is the forward clutch. Engaging forward locks the entire drive shaft and carrier assembly together—the whole unit rotates as one, imparting engine rotation to the output shaft of the transmission via the carrier assembly (Figure 10-4A). This is very efficient because no gears are involved in imparting drive to the output shaft.

Reverse is a little more complicated. The forward clutch is released and a second clutch engaged. This locks the outer geared hub in a stationary position. Meanwhile the drive gear is still rotating the intermediate gears. Unable to spin the outer hub, the intermediate gears rotate around the inside of the hub in the *opposite* direction to the drive gear. The carrier assembly imparts this reverse motion to the output shaft (Figure 10-4B). There are some energy losses in the gearing.

Manual and hydraulic versions of a planetary box are very similar. The principal difference is that the reverse clutch of a manual box consists of a brake band that is clamped around the hub, whereas in a hydraulic box, a second clutch, similar to the forward clutch, is used.

A manual box uses pressure from the gearshift lever to engage and disengage the clutches. A hydraulic box incorporates an oil pump; the gearshift lever merely directs oil flow to one or the other clutch, with the oil pressure doing the actual work. While quite a bit of pressure on the gear lever is needed to operate a manual transmission, shifting gear with a hydraulic transmission is a fingertip affair.

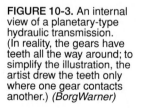

FIGURE 10-2. A typical hydraulic transmission. (BorgWarner)

FIGURE 10-3. An internal view of a planetary-type hydraulic transmission. (In reality, the gears have teeth all the way around; to simplify the illustration, the artist drew the teeth only where one gear contacts another.) (BorgWarner)

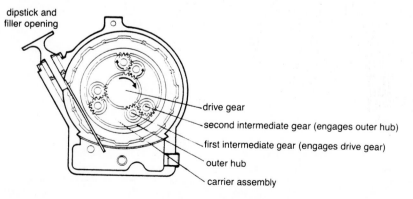

selector lever

neutral switch
dipstick and
filler opening

breather

regulator
valve plug

output
coupling

dipstick and
filler opening

drive gear

second intermediate gear (engages outer hub)

first intermediate gear (engages drive gear)

outer hub

carrier assembly

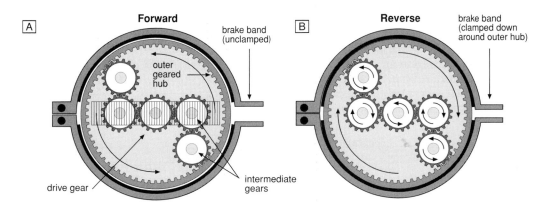

A Forward

outer geared hub

brake band (unclamped)

drive gear

intermediate gears

B Reverse

brake band (clamped down around outer hub)

FIGURE 10-4A. In forward gear in a manual planetary (epicyclic) transmission, the brake band is unclamped while the forward clutch locks the drive gear, carrier assembly, and geared hub together so that they rotate as one (schematically represented by the band across the center of the illustration, locking all the gears). Engine rotation is imparted to the output shaft. *(Michael D. Ryus)*

FIGURE 10-4B. When in reverse in a manual planetary (epicyclic) transmission, the forward clutch is released, leaving the carrier assembly free to rotate around the drive gear, while the brake band is clamped down, locking the geared hub. The carrier assembly is driven around the hub in the opposite direction to the drive gear, imparting reverse rotation to the output shaft. *(Michael D. Ryus)*

Two-shaft transmissions. The engine is coupled to the transmission's input shaft, to which two gears are keyed, one at either end. A second shaft, the output shaft, has two more gears riding on it; one of these engages one of the input gears directly, and the other engages the second input gear via an intermediate gear (Figure 10-5A). These two output gears are mounted on bearings and rotate freely around the output shaft.

The drive gears impart continuous forward and reverse rotation to the output gears. Each output gear has its own clutch, and between the two clutches is an engaging mechanism. Moving the engaging mechanism one way locks one gear to the output shaft, giving forward rotation; moving the mechanism the other way locks the other gear to the shaft, giving reverse rotation (Figure 10-5B).

In a *manual* two-shaft transmission, when the clutch-engaging mechanism is first moved to either forward or reverse, it gently presses on the relevant clutch. This initial friction spins a *disc carrier*, which holds some steel balls in tapered

FIGURE 10-5A. A two-shaft Hurth transmission with the cover removed. *(Hurth)*

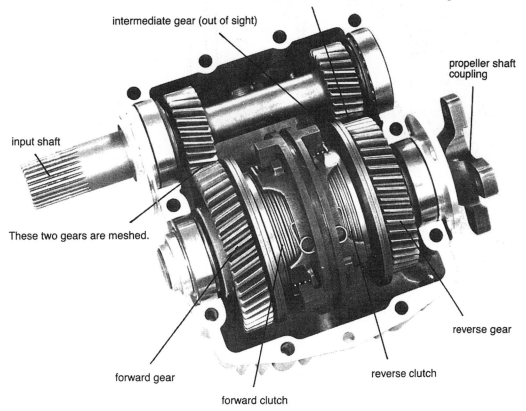

These two gears are *not* meshed—engagement is provided by the intermediate gear, which reverses the direction of rotation of the reverse gear.

intermediate gear (out of sight)

input shaft

These two gears are meshed.

propeller shaft coupling

reverse gear

forward gear

forward clutch

reverse clutch

grooves. The rotation drives the balls up the grooves. Because of the taper in the grooves, the balls exert an increasing pressure on the clutch, completing the engagement (Figure 10-5C). Only minimal pressure is needed to set things in motion, and thereafter, a clever design supplies the requisite pressure to make the clutch work, but without the necessity for oil pumps or oil circuits. Shifting gear is once again a fingertip affair. In a *hydraulic* two-shaft transmission, an oil pump provides the pressure for operating the clutches, just as in a hydraulic planetary transmission.

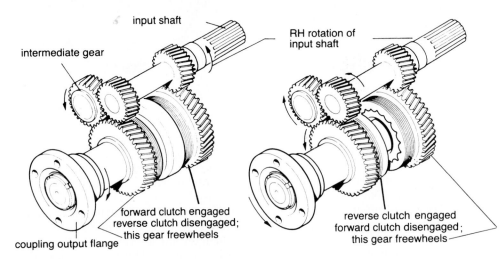

FIGURE 10-5B. Forward and reverse in a two-shaft transmission. When the forward clutch is engaged (left), the output shaft rotates in the opposite direction to the input shaft; when the reverse clutch is engaged (right), the output shaft is rotated in the same direction as the input shaft, via the intermediate gear. *(Hurth)*

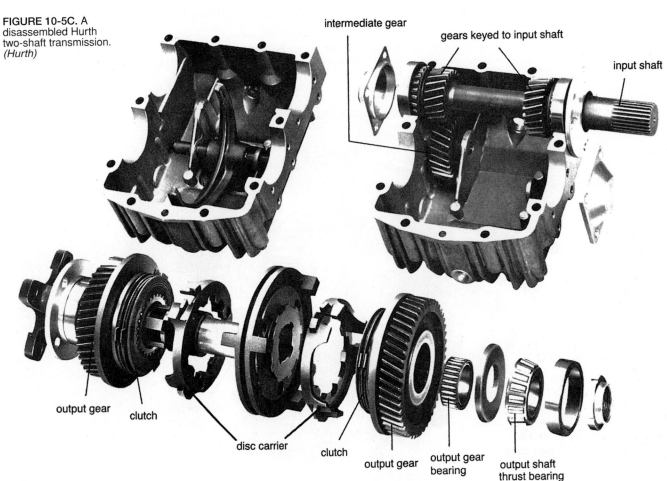

FIGURE 10-5C. A disassembled Hurth two-shaft transmission. *(Hurth)*

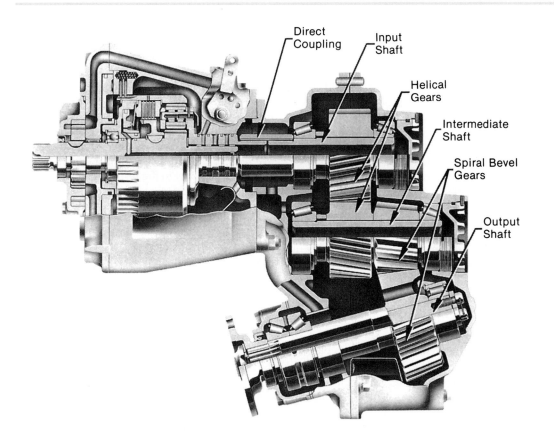

FIGURE 10-6. A V-drive transmission. *(BorgWarner)*

Labels on figure: Direct Coupling, Input Shaft, Helical Gears, Intermediate Shaft, Spiral Bevel Gears, Output Shaft

V-drives. A V-drive is simply an arrangement of gears that allows the engine to be installed *backward*, placing it directly over the output shaft (Figure 10-6). This enables far more compact engine installations to be made, and in particular, enables sportfishing boats and other planing-type hulls to have the engine installed right in the stern of the boat, which is the best spot from the point of view of weight distribution. All transmission types can be used with V-drives.

Inboard/outboards. Inboard/outboards are exactly what their name implies—an inboard engine coupled to an outboard motor–type drive assembly and propeller arrangement (Figure 10-7). These units have definite advantages in planing craft, notably:

- Inboard/outboards allow an engine to be mounted in the stern of the boat, which is the best place in terms of weight distribution on many planing hulls.

- The outboard unit can be pivoted up and down hydraulically. This enables these boats to take full advantage of their shallow draft to run up onto beaches. It also permits infinite propeller-drive angle–hull attitude adjustments for changes in boat trim, and it makes trailering easy.

- The whole outboard unit turns for steering, greatly increasing maneuverability and removing the need for a separate rudder.

- There is no propeller shaft, stern tube, or stuffing box to leak into the boat.

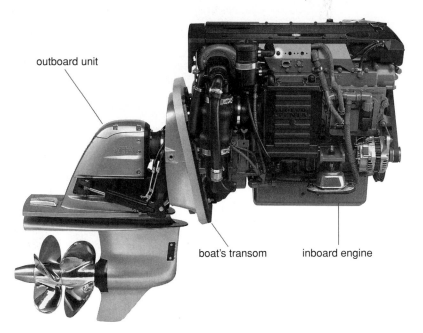

FIGURE 10-7. A Volvo inboard/outboard. *(Volvo Penta)*

Labels on figure: outboard unit, boat's transom, inboard engine

Naturally, there are drawbacks. The extra gearing and sharp changes in drive angle absorb a little more power than a conventional transmission; the U-drives in the transmission tend to have a relatively high failure rate if driven hard; and above all, most outboard units are built of relatively corrosion-susceptible materials. If the boat is kept dry-docked between use or the outboard unit is raised out of the water, this latter point is not a great problem; if the unit is left in the water, it can be.

Observing all maintenance schedules is important, particularly oil changes, greasing of U-joints, and replacing those all-important zincs.

Saildrives. Saildrives are an adaptation of an inboard/outboard in which the drive leg is permanently immersed and cannot be tilted up and down (Figure 10-8). Many boatbuilders, especially in Europe, like them because they are much easier to install than a traditional engine and take up less room. Essentially, you cut a big hole in the bottom of the boat, then bond in an adapter plate. The engine and its leg bolt to this adapter plate. There is no stern tube, shaft seal, and stern (Cutless) bearing; no engine alignment is required. The total cost of an installation (engine, transmission, and installation) is significantly less than that of a traditional installation.

From the boatowner's perspective, a saildrive eliminates the hassles associated with the shaft seal. Saildrives are also soft mounted, eliminating much vibration and making for a quieter installation. They are reputed to offer less drag under sail (I can't confirm this, except to note that many racing boats use them). They may have higher mechanical losses than a transmission and shaft seal because of the two right-angle changes of drive direction. But because the propeller is put in the water in the horizontal plane (as opposed to the propeller shaft being angled downward as it is in most conventional installations), the propeller is more efficient at moving the boat (saildrive manufacturers claim 10% to 12% improved efficiency). This is a substantial list of potential benefits.

The single biggest drawback is corrosion. The drive leg is aluminum and, if not properly installed, it can rapidly become a giant galvanic anode with respect to the rest of the boat's underwater metal (and that of other boats when plugged into shore power without some form of galvanic isolation—see Chapter 4). Thus the drive leg should be electrically isolated and adequately protected with sacrificial zincs.

Saildrives come with attached zincs, which need regular attention and replacing before 50% of the anode has been consumed; if neglected, loss of the zinc can result in expensive damage. Note that there have been a number of reports regarding Volvo saildrives and total zinc loss as a result of galvanic corrosion between the zinc and its fasteners (causing the zincs to fall off). A much better way to manufacture zincs and prevent their loss is to cast them around a steel plate that the fasteners go through. Keep an eye on those zincs! In terms of other maintenance, Volvo recommends replacing the diaphragm that seals the saildrive in the bottom of the boat every 7 years, but few owners do this. Many saildrives over 20 years old are still operating with the original diaphragms.

Other than corrosion, the most likely source of saildrive problems is getting monofilament fishing line up the back of the propeller and winding this into the shaft seal, damaging it. The boat will have to be hauled to replace the seal.

Maintenance

Transmission maintenance is minimal (Figures 10-9A and 10-9B). It generally boils down to keeping the exterior clean (important for detecting oil leaks); periodically checking the oil level (unless there is a leak, it should never need topping off); checking for signs of water contamination (water emulsified in engine oil gives it a creamy texture and color; in automatic transmission fluid, it looks more like a strawberry frappe!); and changing the oil annually. If there is an oil screen or a magnetic plug (or both) in the base of the transmission, inspect them for any signs of metal particles or other internal damage when changing the oil. If the transmission has a raw-water-cooled oil cooler with a sacrificial zinc anode, you *must check the zinc anode regularly and change it when only partly eaten away.*

FIGURE 10-8. A Volvo saildrive unit with a folding propeller. *(Volvo Penta)*

inboard engine

seal that goes in the base of the hull

permanently immersed drive leg and propeller

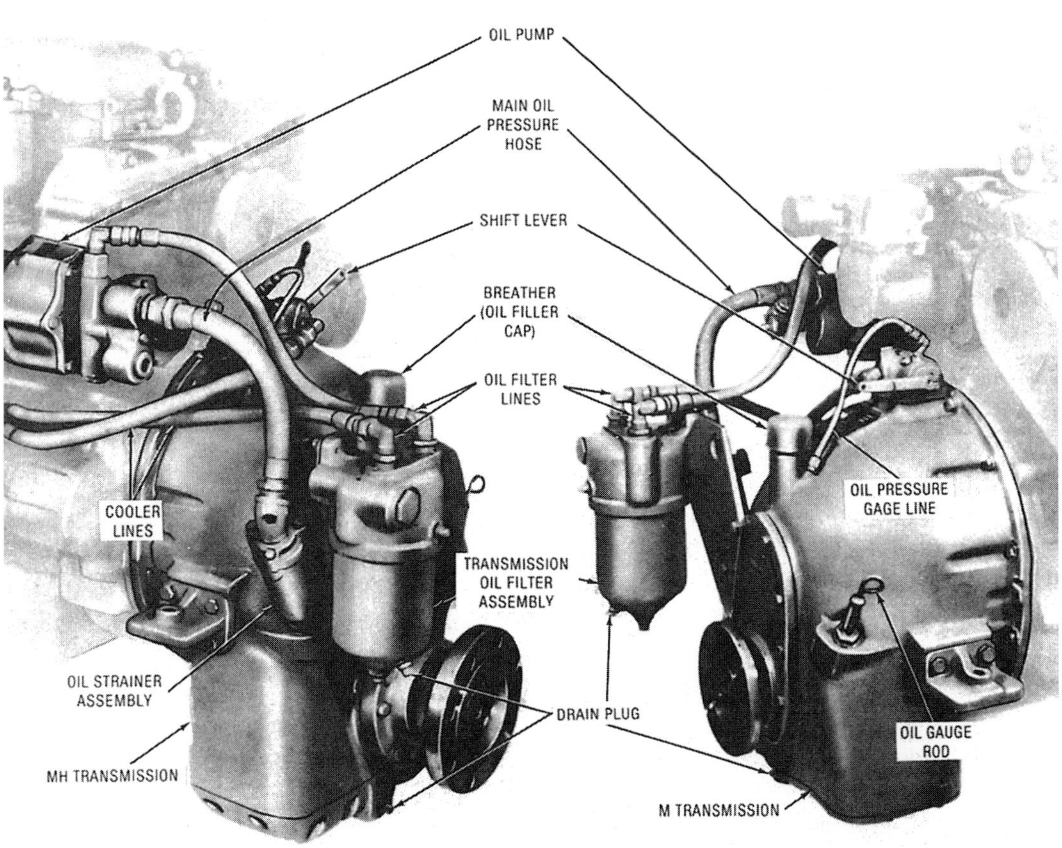

FIGURE 10-9A. Principal external components on a relatively large hydraulic transmission. *(Detroit Diesel)*

Labels in figure 10-9A:
- OIL PUMP
- MAIN OIL PRESSURE HOSE
- SHIFT LEVER
- BREATHER (OIL FILLER CAP)
- OIL FILTER LINES
- OIL PRESSURE GAGE LINE
- COOLER LINES
- TRANSMISSION OIL FILTER ASSEMBLY
- OIL STRAINER ASSEMBLY
- MH TRANSMISSION
- DRAIN PLUG
- OIL GAUGE ROD
- M TRANSMISSION

Most transmissions operate on 30-weight engine oil or automatic transmission fluid (ATF type A—normally Dextron II or Dextron III; the latter is an improved formulation of the former and is interchangeable with it). Check the engine manual and be sure to use the specified oil. When checking the oil level, run a hydraulic transmission for a couple of minutes, then shut it down to make the check. On some transmissions, the dipstick is screwed all the way in to check the level; on others the threaded portion is kept on top of the housing—check the manual.

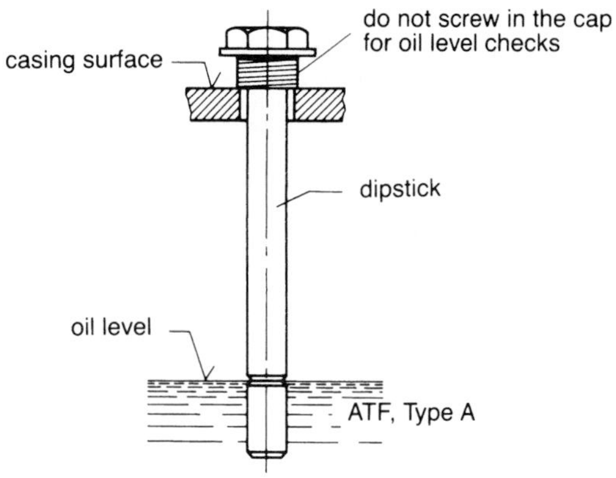

FIGURE 10-9B. Checking the oil level on a Hurth transmission. *(Hurth)*

Labels in figure 10-9B:
- do not screw in the cap for oil level checks
- casing surface
- dipstick
- oil level
- ATF, Type A

Troubleshooting

The majority of transmission difficulties arise as a result of improper clutch adjustments (manual transmissions) or problems with the control cables (hydraulic transmissions), rather than from problems with the transmission itself (see below; Hurth clutches, in particular, are sensitive to improper cable adjustments). However, before discussing these issues, there are a couple of problems peculiar to hydraulic boxes that I want to note.

A buzzing sound indicates air in the hydraulic circuit, generally as a result of a low oil level. This will lead to a loss of pressure and slipping clutches. Most hydraulic transmissions also have an oil pressure regulating valve that passes oil back to the suction side of the oil pump if excess pressure develops. If the valve sticks in the open position, the clutches may slip or not engage at all. On the other hand, if the valve sticks closed, the clutches will engage roughly (as they also will do if gears are shifted at too high an engine speed). The valve is generally a spring-loaded ball or piston screwed into the side of the transmission—removing it for inspection and cleaning is easy (Figure 10-10).

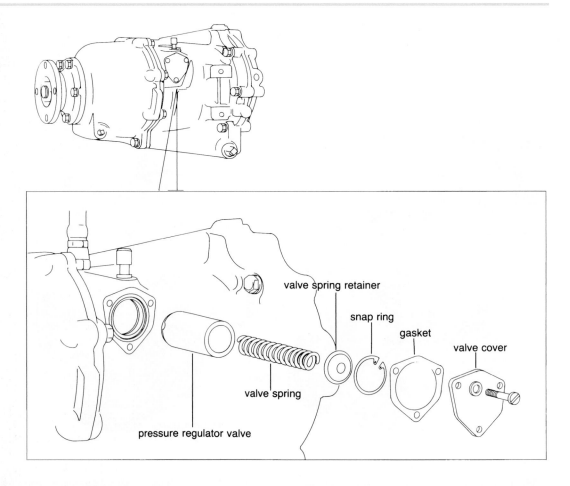

FIGURE 10-10. An oil pressure regulating valve. *(Jim Sollers)*

valve spring retainer

snap ring

gasket

valve cover

valve spring

pressure regulator valve

FIGURE 10-11. Operating principles of a Paragon transmission, a manual planetary gearbox. For forward, the lever (1) is pushed toward the engine; the shift yoke (2) moves back the other way (toward the coupling), sliding the shift cone (3) along the output shaft (3a), thus moving out the cam levers (4). The cam levers bear on the pressure plate (5), compressing the friction discs (6) in the clutch. The friction discs press against the gear carrier (7), causing the motion of the input shaft (8) to be transmitted to the output shaft (3a). The pressure plate is adjusted by backing out the lock bolt (5a), screwing up the castellated nut (10), and retightening the lock bolt. For reverse, the gear lever (1) is moved the other way, compressing the reverse band (9), which locks around the gear carrier like a huge hose clamp. *(Jim Sollers)*

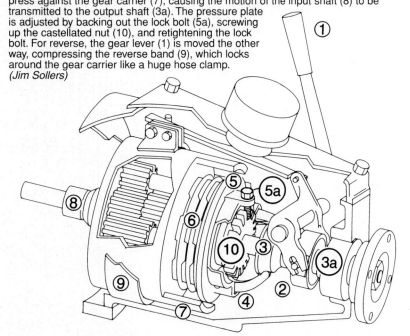

Manual planetary transmission clutch adjustments. The top of most manual transmissions unbolts and lifts off. Inside are adjustments for forward and reverse gears. On those models with a brake band for reverse (the majority in small boats), reverse is easier.

Move the gear lever into and out of reverse—the brake band will be clearly visible as it clamps down on the hub and unclamps (Figure 10-11). On one side of the band will be an adjusting bolt. If the transmission is slipping in reverse, tighten the bolt a little at a time, engaging reverse between each adjustment. Adjustment is correct when the gear lever requires firm pressure to go into gear, and clicks in with a nice, clean feel.

It is important not to overdo things. Put the box in neutral and spin the propeller shaft by hand. *If the brake band is dragging on the hub, it is too tight—the box is going to heat up and wear will be seriously accelerated.* If no amount of adjustment produces a clean, crisp engagement, the brake band is worn out and needs replacing—or at least relining.

To adjust the forward clutch, first put the transmission into and out of gear a few times to see what is going on. The main plate on the back

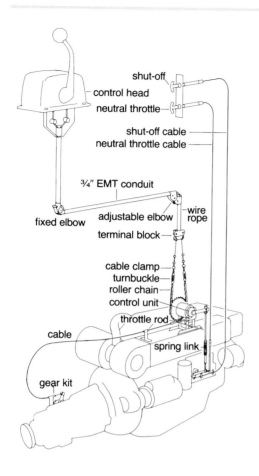

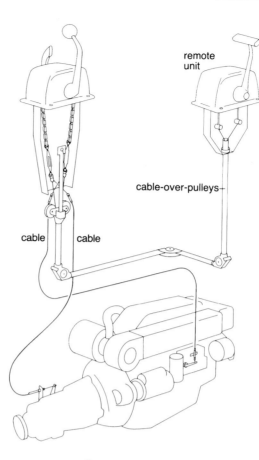

FIGURE 10-12. Typical remote engine and transmission controls comprising three sections: the cockpit or pilothouse control, the cable system, and the engine control unit. **Left:** An enclosed cable-over-pulley system. **Right:** A dual-station installation, with the main station using push-pull cables, and the remote station using a cable-over-pulley system. **Below:** A dual-station installation using remote bellcrank units and single-lever controls. On many modern boats, the cockpit control unit incorporates an electronic device that sends a signal to an operating unit at the engine and transmission. The only physical connection between the cockpit and engine is the data cable. *(Morse Controls, adapted by Jim Sollers)*

of the clutch unit (it pushes everything together) will have either one central adjusting nut or between three and six adjusting nuts spaced around it. Tighten the central nut by one flat. For multiple adjusting nuts, put the box into neutral and turn it over by hand. As each adjustment nut becomes accessible, tighten it by one-sixth of a turn. After going all the way around, try engaging the gear again. Repeat until the gear lever goes in firmly and cleanly. Lock the adjusting nuts. Do not tighten to the point at which the clutch drags in neutral (the propeller shaft will turn slowly when the engine is running); if overtightening seems necessary, the friction pads on the clutch plates are probably worn out and need replacing.

Hydraulic and two-shaft transmission control cables. With the exception of manual boxes that have a gearshift handle, most two-shaft transmissions today use a push-pull cable to move the shift lever on the box (Figure 10-12), although an increasing number in the future will "fly by wire"—i.e., be controlled electronically. A push-pull cable is one that pushes the lever in one direction and pulls it in the other. *More transmission problems are caused by cable mal-*

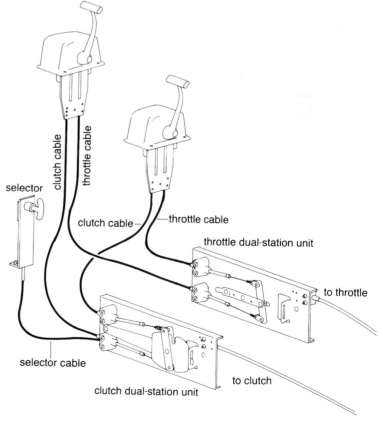

functions than anything else. Faced with diffi-culties, always suspect the cable before blaming the box.

If the transmission operates stiffly, fails to go into either or both gears, stays in one gear, or slowly turns the propeller when in neutral (*clutch drag*), make the following checks (Troubleshooting Chart 10-1):

- See that the transmission actuating lever (on the side of the transmission) is in the neutral position when the remote control lever (in the cockpit or wheelhouse) is in neutral.

- Ensure that the actuating lever is moving fully forward and backward when the remote control is put into forward and reverse. This is particularly important on Hurth boxes.

- Disconnect the cable at the transmission and double-check that the actuating lever on the box is *clicking* into forward, neutral, and reverse. Note: Hurth boxes do not have a distinct click when a clutch is engaged. However, the lever must move through a minimum arc of 30 degrees in either direction. Less movement will cause the clutches to slip.

More is OK. As *the clutches wear, the lever must be free to travel farther.* If the transmission actuating lever is stiff, or not traveling far enough in either direction, make sure that it is not rubbing on the transmission housing or snagging any bolt heads.

- While the cable is loose, operate the remote control to see if the cable is stiff. If so, replace the cable. Note that forcing cables through too tight a radius when routing them from the control console to the engine is a frequent cause of problems.

- Inspect the whole cable annually, checking for the following (Figure 10-13A): seizure of the swivel at the transmission end of the cable conduit; bending of actuating rods; corrosion of the end fittings at either end; cracks or cuts in the conduit jacket; burned or melted spots; excessively tight curves or kinks (the minimum radius of any bend should be 8 inches); separation of the conduit jacket from its end fittings; or corrosion under the jacket (it will swell up; Figure 10-13B). If at all possible, remove the inner cable and grease it with a Teflon-based waterproof grease before replac-

FIGURE 10-13A. Checking transmission control cables. *(Morse Controls, adapted by Jim Sollers)*

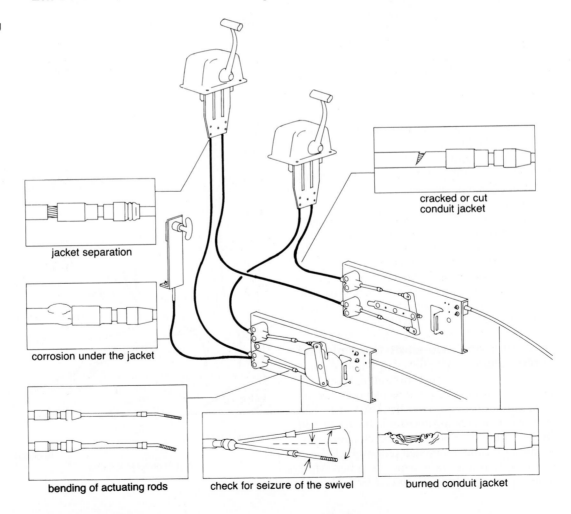

jacket separation

corrosion under the jacket

cracked or cut conduit jacket

bending of actuating rods

check for seizure of the swivel

burned conduit jacket

FIGURE 10-13B. A corroded engine control jacket. The inner cable is stainless steel and is just fine, but the spiral-wound outer case is steel that has rusted right through.

ing. Replace cables at least every 5 years and keep an old one as a spare.

Miscellaneous operating problems. If the oil is kept clean and topped off and the clutch or cables are properly adjusted, problems tend to be few and far between.

Overheating. Heavily loaded transmissions, especially hydraulic transmissions, tend to get hot (too hot to touch). In fact, many that do not have an oil cooler would benefit from the addition of one. Excessively high temperatures, however, are likely to arise only if the oil level is low (a smaller quantity of oil has to dissipate the heat generated); the clutches are slipping (creating excessive friction); or an oil cooler is not operating properly.

A slipping clutch should be evident from a loss of performance. The intense heat generated will soon warp clutch plates and burn out clutch discs. *The oil in the transmission will take on a characteristic black hue and may well smell burned.*

Oil cooler problems may arise on the water and oil sides. Transmission oil generally remains pretty clean, but a slipping clutch and other problems occasionally create a sludge that can plug up the oil side of a cooler. And if the clutch is slipping, the oil will be darkened in color. If the cooler is raw-water cooled, a more likely scenario is that silt, corrosion, and scale are interfering with the heat transference on the water side.

Water in the transmission. If the transmission has an oil cooler, the cooler is the most likely source of water, especially if it is a raw-water type. Pinholes form in cooler tubes just as in engine oil coolers. *Regular inspection and changing of any sacrificial zinc anodes is essential.* The only other likely source of water ingress is through the transmission output seal. For this to happen, the seal must be seriously defective and the bilges must have large amounts of water slopping around, both of which were far more

---

Troubleshooting Chart 10-1.
Transmission Problems

Symptoms: Failure to engage forward or reverse; clutch drag in neutral; or tendency to stick in one gear.

Move the remote control lever through its full range a couple of times. Does it move the operating lever on the transmission itself through its full range? **YES**	**NO** Check for a broken, disconnected, slipping, or kinked cable.
Is the remote control lever free-moving? **YES**	**NO** Break the cable loose at the transmission and try again. If still stiff, remove the cable from its conduit, and clean, grease, and replace. If the cable moves freely when disconnected from the transmission, move the transmission lever itself through its full range. If binding, the transmission needs professional attention.
When the remote control is placed in neutral, is the transmission lever in neutral? **YES**	**NO** Adjust the cable length.
Is the transmission oil level correct? (Most transmissions have a dipstick; hydraulic transmissions frequently make a buzzing noise when low on oil.) **YES**	**NO** Add oil and run the engine in neutral to clear out any air.
Does the transmission output coupling turn when the transmission is placed in gear? **YES**	**NO** The transmission needs professional attention.
Does the propeller shaft turn when the transmission coupling turns? **YES**	**NO** The coupling bolts are sheared or the coupling is slipping on the propeller shaft. Tighten or replace setscrews, keys, pins, and coupling bolts as necessary.

There must be a fault with the propeller:
1. It may be missing or damaged.
2. A folding propeller may be jammed shut.
3. A controllable-pitch propeller may be in the "no pitch" position.
4. If this is the first trial of the propeller, it may simply be too small and/or have insufficient pitch.

common years ago when leather seals and wooden boats were the norm.

If you discover the water in a reasonable time and remove it, eliminate the source, and change the transmission oil a couple of times to flush the transmission, you stand a good chance of preventing any lasting damage.

Loss of the transmission oil. The rupture of an external oil line will produce a sudden, major, and catastrophic loss of oil, which will be immediately obvious. Less obvious will be the loss of oil through a corroded oil cooler. If it is raw-water cooled, the oil will go overboard to form a slick; if freshwater cooled, it will rise to the top of the header tank.

Although the seal around the clutch actuating lever or the seal on a hydraulically operated shaft brake (see below) occasionally leaks small quantities of oil, the most likely candidate for this kind of leak is the output-shaft oil seal. This is true particularly if the engine and propeller shaft are poorly aligned (which leads to excessive vibration), or if the propeller shaft has been allowed to freewheel when the boat is under sail. Alignment checks and seal replacement are dealt with below. On rare occasions, the oil gets pumped through some ruptured seal into the flywheel housing.

Slow engagement. With a two-shaft transmission, a delay in engagement when shifting into gear normally indicates wear in the thrust washers. The transmission should be professionally serviced before too long.

Replacing an output-shaft seal.

1. Unbolt and separate the two halves of the propeller coupling (Figure 10-14A). Mark both

halves so you can bolt them back together in the same relationship to each other.

On some boats with vertical rudderposts, the propeller shaft cannot be pushed far enough aft to provide the necessary room to slide the transmission coupling off its shaft! The propeller hits the rudderstock and will go no farther. In this situation, remove the rudder or lift the engine off its mounts to provide the necessary space (this is an awful lot of work to change an oil seal).

2. Remove the coupling half attached to the transmission output shaft. This coupling is held in place with a central nut, which is done up tightly on most modern boxes; on some older boxes, it is just pinched up and then locked in place with a cotter pin (split pin).

The coupling rides on either a splined shaft (one with lengthwise ridges all the way around) or a keyed shaft. (In the latter case, do not lose the key down in the bilges when removing the coupling!) The key will most likely stick in the shaft. If there is no risk of its falling out and getting lost, leave it there (tape it to the shaft for the time being); otherwise hold a screwdriver against one end and tap gently until you can pry up the end and remove the key.

Some couplings are friction-fit on their shafts and should be removed with a proper puller (Figure 10-14B). This is nothing more than a flat metal bar bolted to the coupling and tapped to take a bolt in its center. The bolt screws down against the transmission output shaft, forcing off the coupling.

FIGURE 10-14A. A transmission oil seal and output coupling arrangement. The recesses machined into the faces of the two coupling halves assist in shaft alignment. *(Jim Sollers)*

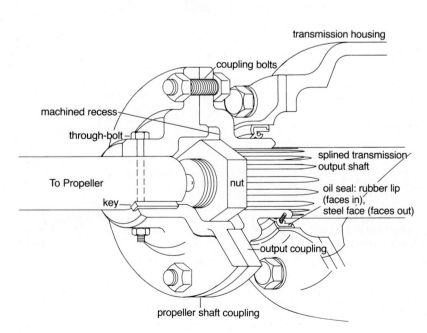

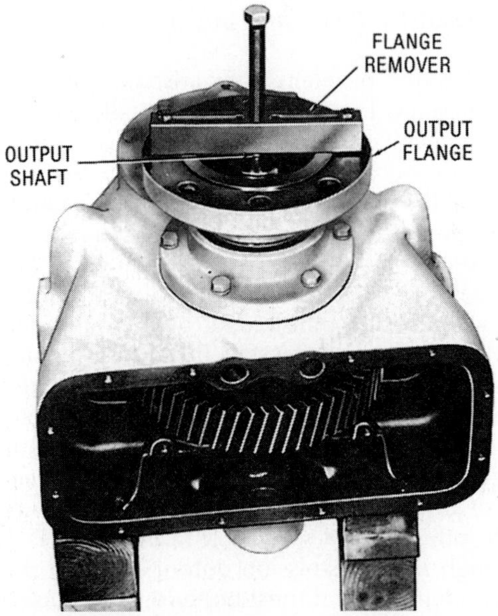

transmission housing

coupling bolts

machined recess

through-bolt

To Propeller

key

nut

splined transmission output shaft

oil seal: rubber lip (faces in), steel face (faces out)

output coupling

propeller shaft coupling

FLANGE REMOVER

OUTPUT SHAFT

OUTPUT FLANGE

FIGURE 10-14B. Removing an output shaft coupling with a simple coupling puller. *(Allison Transmission)*

3. Transmission oil seals are press-fit into either a separate housing or the rear transmission housing. Most seals consist of a rubber-coated steel case with a flat face on the rear end and a rubber lip on the front end (the end inside the transmission). A spring inside the seal holds this lip against the coupling face to be sealed.

Removing a seal from its housing is not always easy. If at all possible, unbolt the housing from the transmission and take it to a convenient workbench. This is often fairly simple on older boxes and boxes with reduction gears, but may not be feasible on many modern hydraulic boxes. You may be able to dig out the seal with chisels, screwdrivers, steel hooks, or any other implement that comes to hand; it doesn't matter if the seal gets chewed up, *as long as the housing and shaft (if still in place) are unscratched.*

4. New seals go into the housing with the rubber lip facing into the gearbox and the flat face outside. Place the seal squarely in its housing and then tap it in evenly using a block of wood and a hammer. *If you force the seal in cockeyed, it will be damaged.* The block of wood is necessary to maintain an even pressure over the whole seal face—*hitting a seal directly will distort it.* Push in the seal until its rear end is flush with the face of the transmission housing. Once in place, some seals require greasing (there will be a grease fitting on the back of the gearbox), but most need no further attention.

5. Reassemble the coupling and propeller shaft by reversing the disassembly steps. Check the alignment of the propeller shaft (see below) anytime the coupling halves are broken loose and reassembled.

Many transmissions have *preloaded* thrust bearings. The transmission output shaft, on which the coupling is mounted, turns in two sets of tapered roller bearings—one facing in each direction (Figure 10-15). Between the two sets is a steel sleeve. When the coupling nut is pulled up, this sleeve is compressed, maintaining tension on the bearings and eliminating any play. Anytime the coupling nut is undone, use a torque wrench and note the pressure that is needed to break the nut loose. When reinstalling the nut, tighten it to the same torque *plus 2 to 5 foot-pounds.* In any event, the torque should be at least 160 foot-pounds on most BorgWarner boxes, but the couplings should still turn freely by hand in neutral with only minimal drag. If the transmission needs a new spacer between the thrust bearings, a special jig and procedure are necessary, and the whole transmission reduction gear will have to go to a professional.

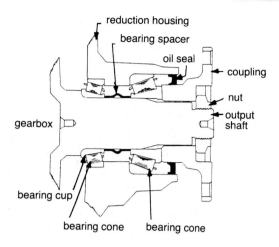

FIGURE 10-15. Preloaded thrust bearings. (*BorgWarner*)

On an older transmission in which the coupling nut is done up less tightly and restrained with a cotter pin, it is essential that you replace the nut properly. The best approach is to moderately tighten the nut, making sure everything is properly seated, then back it off an eighth of a turn or so before inserting the cotter pin. Put the transmission in neutral and turn the coupling by hand to ensure there is no binding. This type of coupling sometimes leaks oil between the shaft and the coupling; to prevent this, smear a little gasket sealer around the inside of the coupling before fitting it to the shaft.

Shaft Brakes

When a boat is being towed or is under sail with the motor shut down, the flow of water over a fixed-blade propeller will spin the propeller unless the propeller shaft is locked in some way. This is of little concern with manual and two-shaft transmissions, except that it creates unnecessary wear on bearings, oil seals, and the shaft seal. But *on some hydraulic transmissions (e.g., some Detroit Diesels), it will lead to a complete failure of the transmission* since no oil is pumped to the bearings when the engine isn't running. Some output-shaft oil seals (particularly rawhide seals) will also fail. Freewheeling propellers can also make quite a racket.

The propeller shaft on a manual transmission can be locked simply by putting the transmission in gear. The same holds for two-shaft transmissions. Note that you must always lock the transmission in the opposite direction to that in which the boat is moving (i.e., if sailing or being towed forward, put the transmission in reverse). If you don't, the clutch may slip and burn up (the critical speed at which this happens on Hurth transmissions seems to be around 6 knots).

A hydraulic transmission cannot be locked by putting it in gear. Without the engine running, the oil pump will not be working, and there will be no oil pressure to operate the clutches. You need a shaft brake (except with folding and feathering propellers), and you have essentially two choices.

Hydraulic units. Hydraulically operated shaft brakes all have a spring-loaded piston riding in a cylinder that has an oil line plumbed to the transmission oil circuit. When the engine is at rest, the spring forces the piston down the cylinder to operate the brake. When the engine is started, oil pressure from the transmission oil pump forces the piston back up the cylinder against the spring pressure, releasing the brake. These units are thus automatic in operation, overcoming the main objection to older manual units, which was the probability of leaving the brake on, putting the transmission in gear, and burning up the brake.

Four variations on the hydraulic theme are widely available:

1. *Caliper disc.* These operate as on a car. A disc is bolted between the two propeller shaft coupling halves. A hydraulically operated caliper grips the disc to stop rotation (Figure 10-16).
2. *Cam disc.* Similar to the above except that the disc has several cams. A hydraulically operated arm locks into the cams.

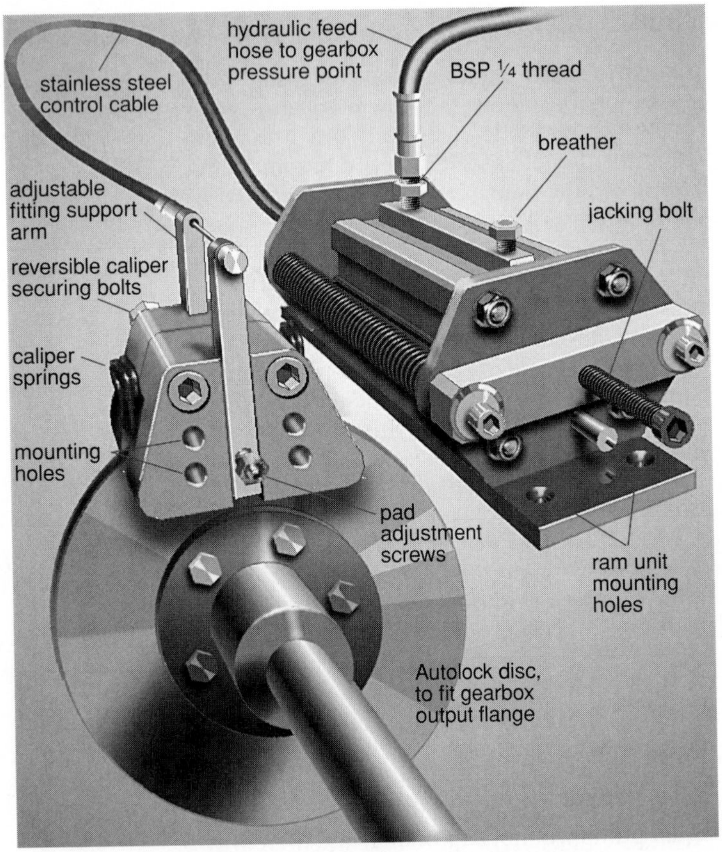

FIGURE 10-16. A hydraulic shaft lock. *(Brunton's Propellers)*

- stainless steel control cable
- hydraulic feed hose to gearbox pressure point
- BSP ¼ thread
- breather
- adjustable fitting support arm
- jacking bolt
- reversible caliper securing bolts
- caliper springs
- mounting holes
- pad adjustment screws
- ram unit mounting holes
- Autolock disc, to fit gearbox output flange

3. *Brake band.* A hydraulically operated brake band clamps around the propeller shaft coupling.
4. *Plunger type.* A slotted sleeve is clamped around the shaft, and a hydraulically operated plunger locks into one of the slots.

Manual units. On older manual units, a brake pad clamps around a block on the shaft or coupling. There is the obvious inherent risk that an owner will forget the brake when the engine is next started and, as a result, burn up the brake. Newer manual units, however, have a notched disc clamped to the propeller shaft, with a plunger engaging the notch. If the brake is left engaged when the engine is started and put in gear, the plunger is simply forced out of the notch and held back by another spring-loaded pin until it is set manually once again (Figures 10-17A and 10-17B).

Problem areas.

- On hydraulic units, any oil leaks through faulty piston seals, connections, or hoses will cause the loss of the transmission oil and ultimately transmission failure. Adding a hydraulic shaft lock may, in fact, void a transmission warranty.

- The manual plunger types have a tendency to jump out during hard sailing. Spring tension on the latching pin can be increased to hold the plunger in place, but then it becomes more difficult to disengage the plunger.

- The cam disc, hydraulic plunger, and manual notched-disc plunger-style units can be set only at low propeller speeds. Ignoring this is likely to result in damage to the former unit; in the latter two cases, the plunger will jump out. It may be necessary to slow the boat and reduce propeller freewheeling before engaging the device; in other words, these devices are shaft locks rather than shaft brakes.

Maintenance.
Hydraulic units. Pay close attention to the hydraulic lines and inspect them regularly for any signs of leaks around the piston seals. Check the brake linings on caliper and brake band units for wear. *Don't allow them to slip*—a lot of heat will be generated. Check any sleeve mounting bolts from time to time.

Manual units. The control cable is a Morse type. Figure 10-13A shows a number of points to watch for with Morse cables. The plunger unit is mounted on a bearing within which the propeller shaft rotates. The bearing is sealed for life. Check for undue play once in a while, and while you're at it, also check the setscrews that lock the central sleeve to the propeller shaft. If water is being thrown around this area (generally from a leaking shaft seal), the bearing will rust out over time.

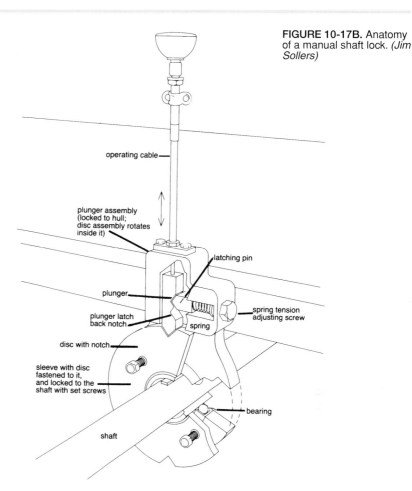

FIGURE 10-17B. Anatomy of a manual shaft lock. (Jim Sollers)

operating cable

plunger assembly (locked to hull; disc assembly rotates inside it)

latching pin

plunger

plunger latch back notch

spring tension adjusting screw

spring

disc with notch

sleeve with disc fastened to it, and locked to the shaft with set screws

bearing

shaft

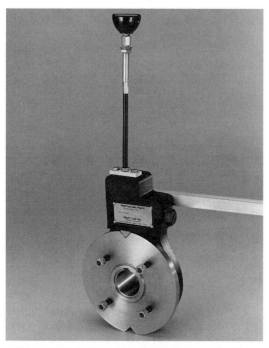

FIGURE 10-17A. A manual propeller shaft lock. (Shaft Lok)

Connecting a Transmission to a Propeller Shaft

Couplings

Couplings should always be keyed to their shafts and then pinned or through-bolted so that they cannot slip off (Figure 10-18A). The practice of locking a coupling with setscrews is not very seaworthy (Figures 10-18B and 10-18C). If a coupling is held this way, be sure the setscrews seat in good-sized dimples in the shaft, and preferably are tapped into the shaft a thread or two so that there is no risk of slipping. *Should they slip, the propeller and shaft are liable to pull straight out of the boat in reverse, leaving the ocean pouring in through the open shaft hole!* (I hear of one or two instances of this every year.) Just for insurance, it is a good idea to place a stainless steel hose clamp (Jubilee clip) around the shaft in front of the shaft seal; if the coupling should ever work loose, the hose clamp will stop the shaft from leaving the boat. (With high-speed shafts, use either two hose clamps with the screws on opposite sides of the shaft to provide some bal-

ance, a specially made collar bolted around the shaft, or a propeller shaft zinc).

Of course, if you have to remove a coupling (e.g., for shaft removal), you'll probably find that it's frozen immovably in place. You can remove a stubborn coupling by making a coupling puller as in Figure 10-14B or by: (1) separating the coupling halves, (2) inserting a length of pipe on the end of the shaft (it must have a diameter less than the size of the hole in the coupling), and (3) pulling the coupling halves together again with elongated bolts (Figures 10-19A, 10-19B, and 10-19C). Make sure to pull up the bolts evenly to avoid distorting the coupling halves. Heating the coupling with a blowtorch may help loosen it, but given the awkward access to many couplings, you must be careful not to wave the blowtorch around and accidentally scorch surrounding surfaces. If the coupling won't come off, you'll have to cut the propeller

FIGURE 10-18A. Shaft couplings should be keyed (as shown here), although many are not, and preferably through-bolted, as opposed to being held by a setscrew, as in this case. At least this setscrew is lock-wired in place so it cannot vibrate loose.

FIGURES 10-18B AND 10-18C. This setscrew is not locked in place. If it comes loose, the propeller shaft will pull out the back of the boat in reverse. It was removed and the shaft was drilled for a through-bolt. Note the flexible coupling in Figure 10-18B, which helps damp engine vibration.

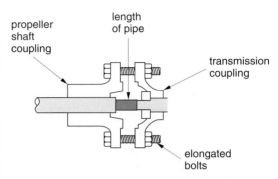

FIGURE 10-19A. Using a short length of pipe to remove a coupling from its propeller shaft.

FIGURES 10-19B AND 10-19C. In this case, an appropriately sized socket is being used as a spacer to remove a stubborn coupling.

shaft and replace both the shaft and coupling (you may be able to salvage the coupling by using a bench press to drive out the shaft).

Engine Alignment

Most engines use conventional couplings, either solid or flexible, between the transmission and the propeller shaft. Accurate alignment is critical to smooth, vibration-free running and a long life for the transmission bearings, transmission oil seals, and the stern (Cutless) bearing. Engine alignment should be checked periodically (it is traditional to recommend once a year, but in practice modern hulls are stable enough that in most cases this can be extended to every couple of years). When checking the alignment, the boat must always be in the water (the hull may well have a different shape there than on land; it is preferable to wait a few days to a week after launching a boat to give the hull time to settle, especially a wooden hull). However, alignment cannot be checked unless

the propeller shaft is straight and the two coupling halves are exactly centered on and square to their shafts. Therefore, *a coupling should be fitted to its shaft and, if necessary, machined to a true fit in a lathe before putting the shaft in the boat.* The flanges on the coupling halves should also be exactly the same diameter.

Flexible feet and couplings. Almost all engines today are mounted with flexible feet and couplings. *They are not substitutes for accurate engine alignment.* Modern, lightweight hulls tend to flex in a seaway, whereas engines are necessarily extremely rigid. The principal reason for flexible feet is to absorb hull movements and lessen hull-transmitted engine vibrations, not to compensate for inadequate alignment. Flexible feet slowly compress over time, while the rubber is subject to softening, especially if it becomes soaked with oil or diesel fuel. Inspect the feet annually and replace them if deteriorated (Yanmar recommends every 2 years, although I know no one who does this—the feet are expensive!). Always check the feet and replace them if necessary before checking the alignment.

Checking and adjusting engine alignment. To check alignment, undo the coupling bolts and separate the coupling halves (first mark the two halves so you can put them back in the same relationship). If there is a flexible insert, remove it. In cases where a long run of propeller shaft is unsupported by a bearing, the shaft will sag down under its own weight and the weight of its coupling half. In this case, the correct procedure is to calculate half the weight of the protruding shaft, add to it the weight of the coupling, and then pull up on the shaft by this amount with a spring scale (like those used for weighing fish; Figure 10-20). In practice, smaller shafts can generally be flexed up and down by hand to get a pretty good idea of the center point, then supported with an appropriately sized block of wood. A notch in the wood will hold the shaft and allow it to be rotated.

Preliminary check. There should be a machined step on one coupling half that fits closely into a recess on the other. Bring the two halves together—the step should slip into the recess cleanly and without snagging at any point. If it does not, the shafts are seriously misaligned, and the engine must be moved around until the two halves come together (Figures 10-21A and 10-21B). When the halves come together, the circumferences of the couplings should be flush with one another (Figure 10-21C); if one has a larger diameter than the other, this eliminates a couple of useful checks (see below), but is not insuperable.

Assuming the couplings come together cleanly, bring the faces into contact and then try to insert a feeler (thickness) gauge into the gap between the coupling faces. Start with a very thin feeler gauge. If it slides in, work up to thicker gauges until some resistance is felt when pushing the gauge in. Be careful not to push the faces apart or you will completely mess up the readings. Note the width of the gap. Repeat this procedure at the bottom of the faces and on both sides (Figure 10-21D). The difference in the gap from any one point to another should not exceed 0.001 inch (one thousandth of an inch) per inch of coupling diameter, or 0.01 mm (one hundredth of a mm) per cm of diameter (e.g., 0.003 in. on a 3 in. diameter coupling, or 0.06 mm on a 6 cm diameter coupling). Note

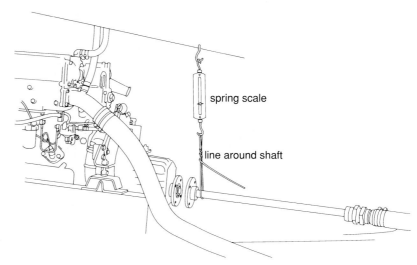

FIGURE 10-20. Using a spring scale to eliminate shaft droop during engine alignment. The scale is tensioned until it reads one-half the free-hanging weight of the shaft plus the weight of the coupling. *(Jim Sollers)*

that if alignment is spot on, you will be unable to get a feeler gauge in anywhere, but almost always the faces will only make contact at one point, and the feeler gauge will slide in at all other points.

If the gap at any point exceeds tolerable limits, turn the propeller shaft coupling through 180 degrees while holding the transmission coupling stationary, then measure the clearances again. If the widest gap is still in the same place, the engine alignment needs correcting. If the widest gap has also rotated 180 degrees, either the propeller shaft is bent, or its coupling is not squarely on the shaft, or both. For accurate alignment, the shaft and the coupling should be removed from the boat and *trued up* by a machine shop.

To adjust alignment, the engine must be moved up and down and from side to side until the clearances all around the coupling are in tolerance. Some engines have adjustable feet (Figure 10-21E), which greatly simplifies things; others need thin strips of metal (shims) placed under the feet until acceptable measurements are reached. Make sure that all feet take an equal load, otherwise when the mounting bolts are tightened you risk distorting the engine block and causing serious damage.

Initial adjustment. If the gap between the coupling faces is wider at the top of the couplings than at the bottom (Figure 10-21F), raise the front feet until the gaps at the top and bottom are equal. This has the effect of pivoting the engine around the rear feet and dropping the height of the output coupling on the transmission with respect to the propeller shaft coupling. Now, even if the top and bottom gaps between the coupling faces are the same, the transmission coupling may well be lower than the propeller shaft coupling. All four engine feet will need to be raised an equal amount until the couplings

FIGURES 10-21A TO 10-21H. The shaft and coupling problems shown here (10-21A) will make accurate engine alignment impossible. For effective alignment, both shafts must be square to their couplings; the coupling faces must be square; and the coupling diameters must be exactly the same. Bore alignment (10-21B). The machined step on one coupling half must slip easily into the recess on the other. Serious misalignment (10-21C). The step on one coupling half will not slip cleanly into the other half, and the flanges are clearly not lined up. The engine must be moved around until the two halves come together cleanly. Once the coupling flanges match and the machined step fits into its recess, use a feeler gauge at four points around the circumference of the coupling to measure misalignment (10-21D). If needed, raise an engine foot to adjust alignment (10-21E). In Figure 10-21F, the widest gap is a little to one side of the top of the coupling. The engine front will need to come up and also move across to the left. After getting the top and bottom flange gaps equal, the flange halves are likely to be at different heights (10-21G); in this case, the entire engine will have to be lowered. To shift the engine sideways, knock the slotted end of the foot with a mallet (10-21H). *(Caterpillar Tractor Company and Jim Sollers)*

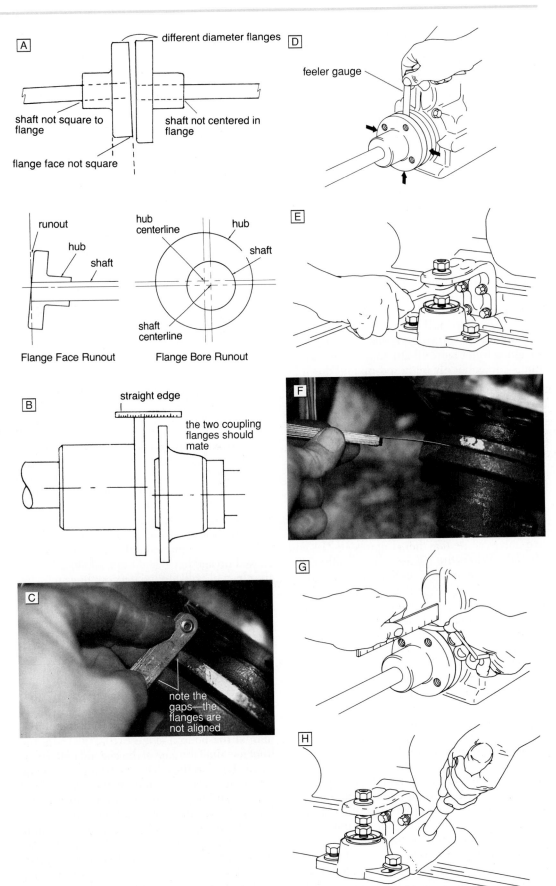

A — different diameter flanges

shaft not square to flange

flange face not square

shaft not centered in flange

runout

hub

shaft

Flange Face Runout

hub centerline

hub

shaft

shaft centerline

Flange Bore Runout

B — straight edge

the two coupling flanges should mate

C — note the gaps—the flanges are not aligned

D — feeler gauge

E

F

G

H

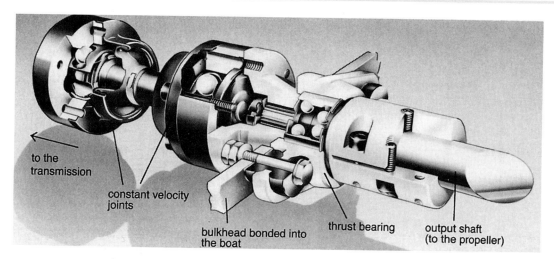

FIGURE 10-22. **Left:** Constant-velocity joints, such as this Aquadrive unit, compensate for shaft misalignment. **Below:** How constant-velocity joints handle different types of misalignment. *(Aquadrive)*

to the transmission

constant velocity joints

bulkhead bonded into the boat

thrust bearing

output shaft (to the propeller)

are level with one another. Check the level by laying a straightedge across the top and bottom of the couplings. (If the couplings have different diameters, this cannot be done.)

If, on the other hand, the gap between the coupling faces is wider at the bottom than the top, you will have to lower the front feet and then probably the whole engine as well (Figure 10-21G).

Side-to-side alignment. Once the gaps between the top and bottom coupling faces are equal, and the couplings are the same height, check the side gaps. If one is greater than the other, move the front of the engine toward the side that has the greater gap until the gaps are the same. Then place a straightedge across the sides of the couplings to make sure they are in alignment. If they are not, you will have to move the entire engine sideways. This is always the most difficult part of engine alignment because there are almost never any jacking screws for sideways movement. So the engine has to be levered across in a crude, and somewhat uncontrolled, fashion—all too often suddenly moving too far!

With a bit of luck, the engine feet will have two hold-down bolts on each foot: one through a close-fitting hole, and the other through a slot. To shift the engine sideways, loosen the bolts and knock the slotted end of the foot using a mallet, or lever it, so that the foot pivots around the other bolt (Figure 10-21H).

Now it's time to go back and run the feeler gauges all the way around the coupling faces once again. If the clearance is within tolerance, and a straightedge across the couplings at top and bottom and both sides shows the coupling sides to be aligned, bolt down the engine and check the alignment once again. Unfortunately, tightening the bolts often throws out the alignment, in which case more adjustments will be needed. If this happens, loosen the mounting nuts one at a time and check the alignment after

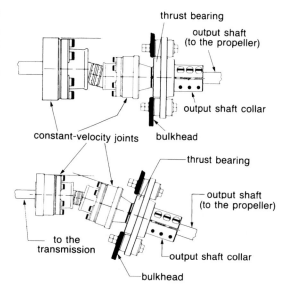

thrust bearing

output shaft (to the propeller)

output shaft collar

constant-velocity joints

bulkhead

thrust bearing

output shaft (to the propeller)

to the transmission

output shaft collar

bulkhead

each is loosened; you may find it is just one nut that is causing the problem.

Engine alignment can be a time-consuming and frustrating business. Patience is the order of the day.

Constant-Velocity Joints

Back in the 1950s, constant-velocity joints (CVJs) were developed for front-wheel-drive cars. They were a special refinement of a universal joint, allowing a limited amount of shaft play in all directions. CVJs have since been adapted for marine installations, notably by Aquadrive (Figure 10-22—www.aquadrive.net; see also the Python-Drive from PYI Inc.).

CVJs are used in pairs; one joint has a short, splined shaft that slides into a splined collar on the other joint. The entire unit is bolted between the transmission and propeller shaft, and according to manufacturers, will permit misalignment of up to ½ inch or 13 mm! Since reverse thrust of the propeller would pull the two sliding shafts apart, the unit is combined with a *thrust bearing*. The propeller shaft is locked into this bearing, which in turn is fastened to a *hull-bonded bulkhead* that absorbs all forward and reverse thrust from the propeller, leaving the CVJs to cope solely with misalignment. The engine can now be soft mounted, eliminating much hull-transmitted vibration. Thus CVJs not only eliminate alignment issues, but also provide a quieter and smoother installation.

CVJs require no maintenance; the various bearings are packed in grease and sealed in rubber boots. However, because all the main components are steel, watch carefully for corrosion, especially on boats with wet bilges. Should the rubber bearing boots ever get damaged, they will need immediate replacement. Despite the tolerance of CVJs for extreme misalignment, their life expectancy will be increased if alignment is kept fairly accurate. Ironically, however, perfect alignment can lead to accelerated wear, so a very small amount of misalignment is desirable (my understanding is that with perfect alignment the whole assembly is likely to "chatter").

Shaft Seals

The few pages on shaft seals in earlier editions of this book provoked more reader response than any other topic. Clearly this subject is of concern to many boatowners. Although most boats still have a traditional stuffing box, or packing gland, *mechanical* seals and *lip-type* seals increasingly are being used.

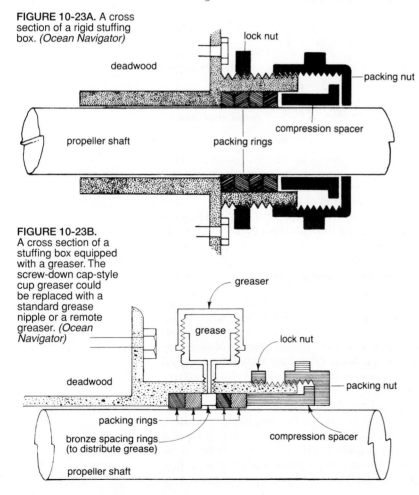

FIGURE 10-23A. A cross section of a rigid stuffing box. *(Ocean Navigator)*

FIGURE 10-23B. A cross section of a stuffing box equipped with a greaser. The screw-down cap-style cup greaser could be replaced with a standard grease nipple or a remote greaser. *(Ocean Navigator)*

Stuffing Boxes (Packing Glands)

In all forms of a stuffing box, a chamber is formed around a shaft. Rings of greased flax or something similar *(packing)* are pushed in, and some form of a cap is tightened down to compress this material around the shaft, creating a close fit that excludes almost all water from the shaft/packing interface (Figure 10-23A). Some stuffing boxes have grease fittings, and in this case, a bronze spacer ring is generally incorporated between the second and third rings of packing and directly below the grease fitting, allowing the grease to be distributed around the stuffing box (Figure 10-23B). A shot of grease (or one turn on the grease cup) should be put in about every 8 hours of engine-running time.

At one time most stuffing boxes were bolted to the deadwood on a boat (rigidly mounted, often incorporating a stern bearing—Figure 10-24A), but today the majority are flexibly mounted in a length of hose that in turn is fastened to the inner end of the shaft log (stern tube; Figures 10-24B and 10-24C). *If this hose fails, water may pour into the boat at an alarming rate.* Note that the ABYC standards require shaft seals "to be constructed so that, if a failure occurs, no more than two gallons of water per minute can enter the hull with the shaft continuing to operate at low speed." This requirement can most easily be met by minimizing the gap between the shaft log and the propeller shaft.

The hose on a flexible shaft seal must have two *all-stainless-steel* hose clamps at each end, with *300-grade* stainless steel screws. Many "all-stainless" clamps have inferior screws that soon rust. Quality clamps have "300 SS" or "AWAB" stamped on them; the screws are *nonmagnetic* (see Chapter 5). Inspect the hose annually for any signs of cracking or bulging, and undo the

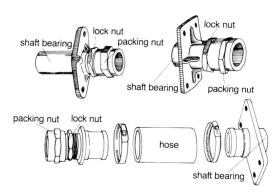

FIGURE 10-24A. Rigid stuffing boxes (top) and a flexible stuffing box (bottom). *(Wilcox Crittenden, adapted by Jim Sollers)*

FIGURE 10-25. There is not enough room in this installation to back off the packing nut; as a result, the packing has not been changed in 10 years! The stuffing box has been leaking profusely, corroding the coupling and everything else in range of the saltwater spray produced when the shaft is turning. The transmission controls were close to failing, and an electric water heater was almost corroded through. The leak was such that a dead battery, or a failed bilge pump, could have resulted in the loss of the boat in just a few days.

FIGURE 10-24B. A flexible stuffing box. Note the use of double hose clamps, with all 300 stainless steel construction—a quality installation.

FIGURE 10-24C. A stuffing box with single hose clamps in which the screws are 400 series stainless steel that is corroding. Meantime, the packing nut has corroded to the shaft. One way or another, when the engine is next put in gear something is likely to tear loose, allowing large amounts of water to enter the boat!

clamps a turn or two *to make sure that galvanic corrosion is not eating away the band where it contacts the worm screw.* If it is necessary to replace the hose, the propeller shaft coupling will have to be broken loose and the coupling removed from the shaft (see above).

Stuffing box blues. The concept of a stuffing box is simple enough. Done right, *on a properly installed and aligned engine,* the packing will not leak when a shaft is at rest, but when the shaft is in motion, it will allow the occasional drip. Done wrong, the stuffing box will leak continuously, or else the shaft will be permanently damaged.

Note the emphasis on the *engine installation and alignment.* It is an unfortunate fact of life that many engines are not properly aligned, or else they suffer from other installation problems such as a misaligned strut or stern (Cutless) bearing. In these cases, the shaft whips around inside the stuffing box, beating the packing back against the sides of the box and allowing more and more water into the boat, both with the shaft turning and with it at rest. Regardless of the skill of the mechanic who fitted the packing, the stuffing box will need constant attention and will still never give satisfactory service.

Even on a properly installed engine, a stuffing box needs some maintenance, including adjustment, greasing, and periodic replacement of the packing, which otherwise hardens over time and may then damage the shaft. Access to many stuffing boxes is poor, to say the least, making such maintenance an onerous chore—it is not uncommon to have to hang upside down in a cockpit locker with insufficient room to swing the necessary wrenches. In extreme cases, notably some V-drives and boats with very short propeller shafts, the packing cannot be reached or replaced without removing either the propeller shaft coupling or the engine (Figure 10-25; this is in clear violation of ABYC standards, which call for sufficient clearance "along the shaft line to permit replacement of the packing without uncoupling the shaft or moving the engine").

Poor access and difficulties in packing adjustment and replacement often lead to neglect. Add a little engine misalignment and vibration, and the stuffing box is soon dripping when the engine is at rest as well as when the shaft is turning. In time this drip becomes a trickle. When the engine is running, salt water is sprayed all over the back of the engine room; when the boat is left unattended, the automatic bilge pump and its battery become the sole line of defense against sinking—the loss of the pump can result in the loss of the vessel. Small wonder then that many owners regard their stuffing box with hostility, little realizing that in most instances the engine installation is the source of their problems rather than the stuffing box. It's the old story of shooting the messenger rather than heeding the message!

Packing adjustment and replacement. A stuffing box is meant to leak. When the shaft is turning, two or three drops a minute are needed to keep the shaft lubricated. If the leak is worse than this, tighten down the nut or clamp plate to compress the packing a little more. If a greaser is fitted, pump in a little grease first. Tighten down the nuts no more than a quarter turn at a time. With a clamp plate, tighten the two nuts evenly.

Start the engine and put the transmission in gear for a minute or two. *Shut down the engine.* Feel the stuffing box and adjacent shaft; *if they are hot, the packing is too tight.* A little warmth is acceptable for a short while as the packing beds in, but any real heat is unacceptable. It is quite possible (and common) to score grooves in shafts by overtightening the packing, in which case the shaft will never seal and will have to be replaced. (Sometimes it can be turned end for end to place a different section in the stuffing box.)

If the shaft cannot be sealed without heating, replace the packing. You should, in any case, renew the packing every few years, since old packing hardens and will score a shaft when tightened. The hardest part of the job generally is getting the old packing out. *It is essential to remove all traces of the old packing or the new wraps will never seat properly.* With a deep, awkwardly placed stuffing box, it is next to impossible to pick out the inner wraps of packing with screwdrivers and ice picks; you need a special tool consisting of a corkscrew on a flexible shaft (Figure 10-26; available from West Marine and other chandleries—www.westmarine.com). Unless this tool is on hand, it is not advisable to

start digging into the packing, especially if the boat is in the water. Appreciable quantities of seawater may start to come into the boat as the packing is removed, in which case speed is of the essence.

Packing itself comes as a square-sided rope in different sizes: $\frac{3}{16}$ inch (5 mm), $\frac{1}{4}$ inch (6 mm), $\frac{3}{8}$ inch (10 mm), etc. It is important to match the packing to the gap between the shaft and cylinder wall. You can buy packing as preformed rings to match the stuffing box (the best option for most people) or by the roll. When cutting rings off a roll, make about five tight wraps around the propeller shaft at some convenient point and then cut *diagonally* across the wraps with a very sharp knife.

To fit new rings of packing, grease each with a Teflon-based waterproof grease before installation, and tamp down each ring before putting in the next. I use some short pieces of pipe slit lengthwise, slipped around the shaft and pulled down with the packing nut or clamp plate to *gently* pinch up the inner wraps (not too tight, or the shaft will burn). Stagger the joints from one wrap to another by about 120 degrees. Don't forget the greasing spacer (if one is fitted) between the second and third wraps.

Dripless packing. Although many of the problems with traditional stuffing boxes result from poor engine installations, some can be attributed to the nature of the packing itself. Greased flax has done sterling service over the years, but it is an ancient product. It is not unreasonable to expect that twenty-first-century technology might produce more effective packing compounds and this is, in fact, the case.

In the first edition of this book, I mentioned graphite packing tape, which we used for 10 years, but I also mentioned potential problems with galvanic corrosion (graphite is at the noble end of the galvanic series table—see Chapter 5). Since then, the ABYC has specifically prohibited the use of graphite packing tape ("graphite impregnated packing material shall not be used because of the possibility of galvanic incompatibility with the shaft material"). But this is of no concern because for some years there has been a better product, commonly known as drip-free or dripless packing.

The original drip-free packing consisted of shredded Teflon (PTFE; Figure 10-27). Similar products are now available from West Marine and others (dripless packing; for all I know, it's the same stuff), which have a slightly crumbly, clay-like consistency that can be rolled between your palms until it is an appropriately sized diameter to go in the stuffing box. (It tends to break up as you push it in, but that's OK.)

Dripless packing is sandwiched between outer

FIGURE 10-26. A packing removal tool. *(Jim Sollers)*

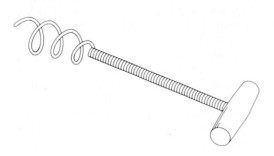

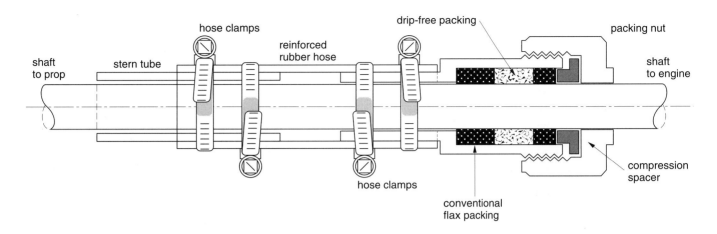

FIGURE 10-27. Teflon-impregnated grease (drip-free packing) installed between inner and outer rings of flax. *(Ocean Navigator)*

and inner rings of conventional packing, which keeps it from working its way out of the ends of a stuffing box. After the first ring of packing is in, massage the dripless material into an appropriate shape, daub it in a special (PTFE-based) grease, then push it into place. Add the outer ring of packing, and tighten the packing nut just enough to stop all drips. That's it! Since it's moldable, dripless packing will conform to even corroded and grooved shafts. It will not eliminate drips in cases of severe engine misalignment or shaft vibration, but it does work exceptionally well in most situations. Once installed, it almost never needs renewing and very rarely needs adjustment. Typically, problems arise from improper installation (not reading the instructions!) and from overtightening the packing nut, causing the stuffing box to run hot. In this case, simply undoing the packing nut may not relieve enough pressure to stop the heating, and it may be necessary to pick out the packing and put it back in.

Mechanical Seals

Mechanical seals are not an adaptation of the traditional stuffing box, but instead are a complete replacement. A mechanical seal has two components: a boot or bellows, which is attached to the inner end of a shaft log; and a sealing ring *(rotor)*, which is attached to the shaft and rotates with it (Figures 10-28A, 10-28B, and 10-28C). The face of the boot has a hard machined surface (a *stationary flange*); the sealing ring sometimes consists of a stainless steel unit, but other times consists of a second machined surface embedded in another boot. One or the other of the two components either contains a spring or is constructed so that it resists compression. On installation the two components are pushed together against the spring or boot resistance, and then the sealing ring is clamped to the shaft so the pressure is maintained. As the shaft rotates, the machined

faces of the stationary flange and the sealing ring form a close-enough fit to keep water out of the boat.

On a properly installed and aligned engine, such a seal will eliminate all leaks. Once installed there is no adjustment or maintenance beyond a routine inspection of the hoses, clamps, and sealing faces. Since no part of the seal is bearing on the propeller shaft, there is no risk of overheating or scoring the shaft. What is more, the seal will be effective regardless of the surface condition of the shaft (i.e., the seal will work even if the shaft is corroded or otherwise damaged). This is an impressive list of attributes.

Problem areas. Many face seals work perfectly—after 5 or 10 years, the owner hasn't seen a drip and is ecstatic. But then there are the ones with problems. Generally the problems have not stemmed from an outright failure of the seal itself, but have resulted from unforeseen operating conditions or improper engine installation and alignment. For example, a one-cylinder diesel engine placed on flexible mounts will jiggle all over the place. When the throttle is pushed forward, the force of the prop may push the engine forward as much as $\frac{3}{8}$ inch, which may allow the seal faces to open up and spray water everywhere. In addition, there is the movement that occurs when a boat is under sail. As the boat comes about, the heavy mass of the engine may cause it to sway from one side to the other, moving one half of the seal sideways, potentially resulting in a severe leak until the boat rights itself.

As a result, some installations require a greater initial compression than others. As far as sideways movement is concerned, some seals have a broad seating surface that allows the seal to oscillate without loss of contact, while others have either a lip or a chamfer built into the face of the stationary seal and sealing ring so that the two are held in a positive mechanical alignment.

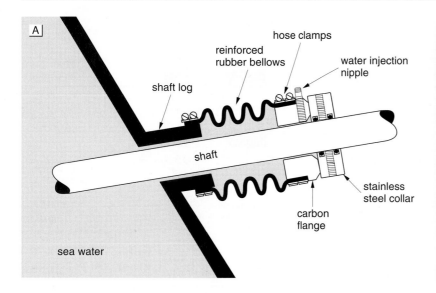

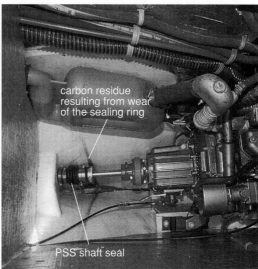

FIGURE 10-28C. A PSS shaft seal installed in our old Pacific Seacraft 40. Note the black line on the hull sides caused by the slow wearing away of the carbon sealing flange.

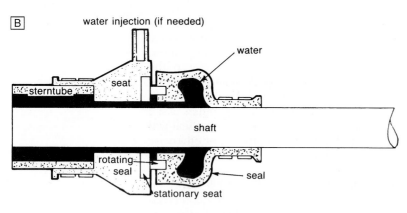

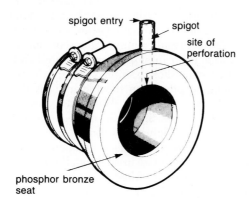

FIGURES 10-28A AND 10-28B. Two types of mechanical seals. Mechanical seals all work on the same principle—two sealing surfaces are held in contact by some sort of "spring" pressure. A PSS shaft seal (10-28A). A Crane shaft seal (10-28B). *(Ocean Navigator and Halyard Marine)*

The nature of the boots or bellows has come under close scrutiny over the years. Some early bellows were susceptible to softening caused by diesel, oil, and gas, reducing their operating life. These were weak in compressive force and got weaker over time. Some seals containing a spring had failures when the spring came through the bellows. Any kind of a bellows failure is, of course, potentially catastrophic. Nowadays, newer, more chemically resistant and re-

silient materials and expensive high-tech construction methods are mostly used.

Regardless of the engineering that has gone into a mechanical seal, its success and life expectancy in any given application will depend to a considerable extent upon the conscientiousness of the seal installer. Shafts must be deburred before installation, and sealing rings must be properly secured to the propeller shaft, with the fasteners locked against vibration. If a bellows is attached cockeyed to a shaft log, or the seal is inserted crookedly into the other end of the bellows, the seal faces will be subjected to uneven pressure; even if the seal does not leak, it will wear rapidly. And finally, if provision is not made to lubricate a seal, it will eventually burn up.

Two situations can typically cause a loss of lubrication. The first is high boat speed, which creates a vacuum that sucks the water out of the stern tube. The second is a haulout, which allows the water to drain out of the shaft log. To combat both situations, most rotating seals include an option for water injection using water from the engine's raw-water circuit. If water injection is not used, there may be an air-vent valve that will release trapped air after a haulout, allowing the stern tube to refill with water. If not, *it is essential*, once a boat is back in the water, *to pull back and hold the boot until water spurts out of the seal face.*

Failures. With two decades of engineering and experience behind them, properly installed mechanical seals will perform as advertised, even under adverse conditions. But don't forget that mechanical seals are *two-part* seals (the boot and sealing ring) in which the two parts are not, and cannot be, fastened together. If the two halves become separated, or the seal between them is damaged, the seal is likely to leak far more rapidly than a traditional stuffing box. This will happen if the sealing ring fastened to the propeller shaft works loose. For this reason, some owners like to put a hose clamp or propeller shaft zinc around the shaft behind the sealing ring as a security precaution.

If a seal fails, at the very least the propeller shaft coupling must come off in order to replace it. On some boats, the propeller also has to come off to create sufficient longitudinal shaft movement to get off the coupling, and occasionally the engine has to be moved off its mounts. In the meantime, if the boat is in the water, the flow rate from the failed seal into the boat is determined by the clearance between the shaft log and the propeller shaft. On those boats in which a rubber sleeve bearing is inserted in the shaft log (mostly boats with a propeller in an aperture in the rudder), the flow rate is almost always relatively low, such that a bilge pump can keep up with it. But on those boats in which the rubber sleeve bearing is installed in a separate strut (the majority of modern boats), the flow rate may be quite high (see below for more on rubber sleeve bearings). In the latter case, it is worth ensuring that the shaft log makes a close-enough fit around the propeller shaft to keep the maximum flow rate down to a level that the bilge pump can handle.

In the midst of revising this section of the book, I found the bilge pump on my boat constantly kicking on. An investigation revealed that the sealing ring on my shaft seal had worked loose, and the two halves of the seal had separated. Water had been flowing into the boat since the last time I used it, two weeks previously! The boat had not sunk because the shaft log on our boat is a moderately close fit around the shaft, which kept the flow rate relatively low, and we have a large battery bank, which was able to support the bilge pump for two weeks. Further investigation revealed that the locking screws had been left out of the sealing ring when it was installed. The ring is now properly locked and a propeller shaft zinc is behind it as a backup!

Lip-Type Seals

It is this nagging fear of a major leak as much as any other factor that causes many boatowners to remain wary of mechanical seals. The various lip-type seals on the market attempt to address these concerns by seeking to eliminate the leaks of a stuffing box without in any way increasing the risk of a catastrophic failure. This is done, essentially, by replacing the packing in a conventional stuffing box with a nitrile lip seal of the type universally used to seal crankshafts and output shafts in engines and transmissions.

Lubrication. As with mechanical seals, the concept of lubrication is straightforward, but the engineering can get quite complex. The simplest units are *water lubricated* and closely resemble a flexible stuffing box. One end of the seal body is fastened to the shaft log with a length of hose; the other end has a recess into which the seal is slipped. In order to keep the seal lubricated, provision is made to maintain a water supply from the engine's raw-water circuit. Experience has shown that unless corrected for, shaft vibration will cause such a seal to leak, so a rubber sleeve–type bearing is built into the inside of the seal body, forming a close fit around the propeller shaft. This keeps the seal in constant alignment with the shaft, regardless of engine misalignment and other problems (Figure 10-29).

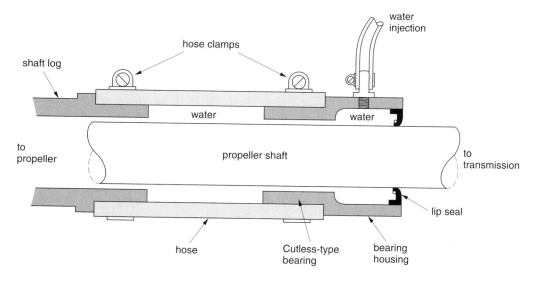

FIGURE 10-29. A water-lubricated lip seal.

FIGURE 10-30. An oil-
lubricated lip seal.

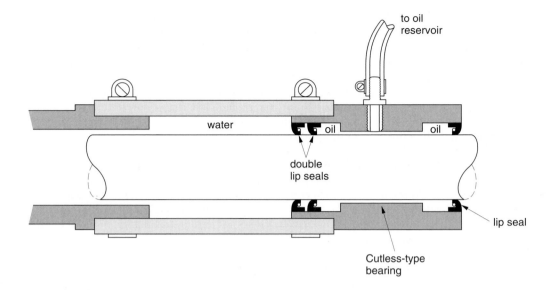

to oil
reservoir

water   oil   oil

double
lip seals

lip seal

Cutless-type
bearing

Other seals are *oil lubricated.* These are physically similar in appearance, but instead of a single seal at the inboard end, they have seals at both ends of a tube (Figure 10-30). Lubrication is provided by a gravity-feed tank of oil set above the seal. There seems little doubt that the oil-lubricated seals last longer than the water lubricated, but on the other hand, the oil reservoir must be checked regularly, and if it is allowed to run dry, the seal will heat up and fail. Unlike the water-lubricated seals, these shaft seals require a minimal level of operator attention and maintenance.

Failures. In practice, operator error has been a nuisance but not a big issue. As with mechanical seals, *the number one reason for lip-seal failures is improper installation.* The seals are generally installed over the inboard end of the propeller shaft and then slid into place toward the outboard end. The lip on the seal is facing aft. *If the end of the shaft is not adequately chamfered during installation, there is a good possibility that the lip will be rolled under (Figure 10-31). If the seal is put in at all cockeyed, it will probably leak.* Nei-

ther of these situations is easily detected until the boat is in the water, at which point you have to haul the boat back out and remove the propeller shaft coupling to repair the seal—an expensive and time-consuming business.

Even if properly installed, *a lip-type shaft seal, which has the seal bearing directly on the propeller shaft, will leak if the shaft is not in an unblemished condition and polished.* One way to get around this is to give the seal a machined inner sleeve, which is rigidly fastened and sealed to the propeller shaft, and then enclose this in an oil-filled outer sleeve containing a bearing surface and lip seals. The outer sleeve is fastened with a bellows to the stern tube. The inner sleeve now becomes the seal-seating surface, so the condition of the propeller shaft is not critical.

Lip-type seals have been around long enough for us to know that they work. The oil-filled lip seals (not the water-lubricated ones) do require a minimal level of maintenance. With a lip seal, if neglect or some other failure causes a complete seal failure, the rate of leakage is not likely to exceed that of a badly leaking stuffing box—the potential for a major failure is less than that of a mechanical seal. Replacement once again requires removal of the propeller shaft coupling, which on some boats may also require removing the propeller as well as moving the engine.

A Dripless Future?

Properly installed, with a proper engine installation, just about any shaft seal will work well. Even a traditional stuffing box can be almost drip-free; with dripless packing it can be dripless.

Unfortunately many engines are not properly installed, or they subsequently develop alignment or shaft problems. In such instances the

FIGURE 10-31. A rolled-
over lip seal resulting from
improper installation (the
end of the shaft was not
properly chamfered).

traditional stuffing box begins to leak, requiring more and more attention, and dripless packing will be unable to do more than perhaps reduce the rate of leakage. In contrast, mechanical and lip seals will clearly tolerate a wider range of deficiencies while still maintaining a dripless seal. Which is the better seal in a given application is to some extent a question of the type of deficiency being dealt with (e.g., a mechanical seal will handle a damaged shaft that would destroy most lip seals), and to some extent is a subjective judgment based upon your perception of the potential for a major leak.

Eventually, installation deficiencies are such that NO seal will work properly. The failure to recognize this is at the root of many of the complaints concerning stuffing box replacements. The owner sees a mechanical seal or a lip-type seal as the solution to a *stuffing box* problem instead of recognizing that the boat has an *engine alignment* or *propeller shaft* problem. When the stern tube continues to leak, the disgruntled owner blames the seal and the seal installer.

Note: Rudder shaft seals are similar to propeller shaft seals, including traditional stuffing box seals, and also lip seals. The same maintenance and adjustment issues arise. For more on rudder shaft seals, see Chapter 14.

Struts, Bearings, and Propellers

Struts

In the old days, the propeller shaft invariably emerged out the back of a hull through a shaft log mounted in the deadwood, with the propeller mounted immediately aft of the deadwood. With today's flatter-bottomed hulls, the propeller shaft must extend some way beyond the shaft log before there is adequate hull clearance to mount the propeller. This run of exposed shaft needs a strut to support it. Some are in the shape of an I, and some a V. The V-shaped strut is inherently stronger. On sailboats, an I-shaped strut is almost always used because it minimizes drag.

All too often these struts are inadequately mounted. The stresses from a fouled propeller or bent shaft will work them loose. If the strut is through-bolted, with accessible nuts on the inside of the hull, check the fasteners annually and tighten as necessary. If the bolts are a loose fit in the hull due to elongated holes, a good dollop of bedding compound combined with a good-sized, well-bedded backing block will tighten things up. Many struts, however, are glassed in place. If the strut develops any play, some extensive repair work will be necessary (in a bind, it may be possible to drill through the strut and hull and add a backing block and bolts).

Rubber Sleeve (Cutless) Bearings

Most stern bearings consist of a metal or fiberglass pipe with a ribbed rubber insert in which the shaft rides (Figures 10-32A and 10-32B). Water circulates up the grooves to lubricate the bearing. Externally mounted bearings in a strut (Figure 10-33A) need no additional lubrication, but some bearings installed in shaft logs and deadwoods (Figure 10-33B) have an additional

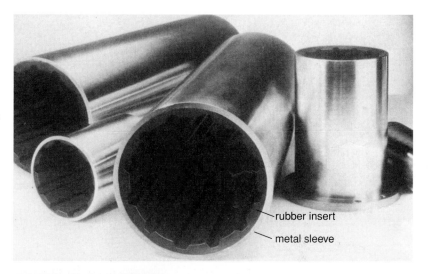

rubber insert

metal sleeve

FIGURE 10-32A. Cutless bearings. *(BF Goodrich)*

FIGURE 10-32B. A rubber sleeve bearing with curved grooves, which is reputed to help the water flow through the bearing. *(PYI)*

lubrication channel into the stern tube. In place of the ribbed rubber, various plastics are sometimes used.

With a properly aligned engine, most rubber sleeve bearings will last for years (unless operated in silty water, which accelerates wear), as long as they are lubricated adequately. They require no maintenance. At the annual haulout, flex the propeller shaft at the propeller; if there is more

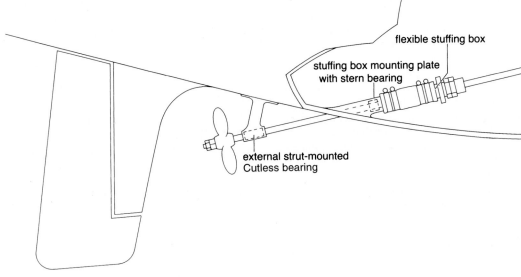

FIGURE 10-33A. A propeller shaft supported by an external strut. *(Jim Sollers)*

flexible stuffing box

stuffing box mounting plate with stern bearing

external strut-mounted Cutless bearing

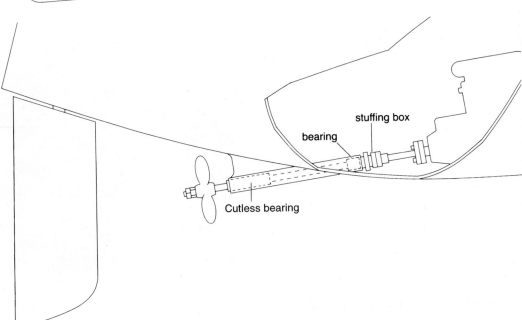

FIGURE 10-33B. A propeller shaft supported in a stern tube. *(Jim Sollers)*

stuffing box

bearing

Cutless bearing

than minimal movement (¹⁄₁₆ inch of clearance between the shaft and bearing per inch of shaft diameter, or 2 mm per cm of shaft diameter), the bearing needs replacing. If not renewed, a worn rubber sleeve bearing will allow excessive shaft vibration, which will rapidly wear stuffing box and transmission bearings and oil seals. A rubber sleeve bearing worn on only one side is a sure sign of engine misalignment.

Replacement. Most bearings are a simple sliding fit in the deadwood or strut; some are then locked in place with setscrews but others are not (the ABYC says they should be, with at least two setscrews). Once any setscrews are loosened, a strut-mounted bearing can sometimes be replaced with the propeller shaft still in place. The

problem is that there generally is not enough room between the hull and strut to maneuver the tools needed to knock the bearing aft. However, by sliding a piece of pipe (with an outside diameter a little less than that of the bearing) up the propeller shaft, you can knock the bearing up the shaft into the space between the strut and hull (Figure 10-34A). Then file or grind down the bearing's outer case until it breaks apart or slides back easily through the strut and off the shaft.

If the bearing won't budge, you can bring greater pressure to bear in a more controlled fashion by making a homemade bearing puller as shown in Figure 10-34B. Cut a slot in a metal plate allowing it to slide over the propeller shaft with sufficient clearance for the bearing to pass

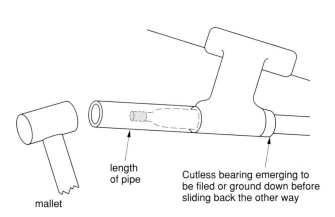

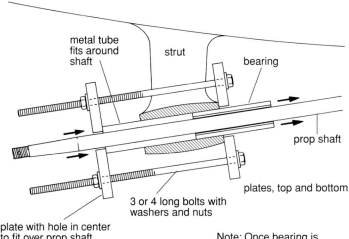

FIGURE 10-34A. Removing a rubber sleeve (Cutless) bearing from a strut, with the propeller shaft still in place.

metal tube fits around shaft

strut

bearing

prop shaft

plates, top and bottom

plate with hole in center to fit over prop shaft and allow bearing to pass through

3 or 4 long bolts with washers and nuts

Note: Once bearing is clear of strut, grind in half to remove from shaft.

length of pipe

Cutless bearing emerging to be filed or ground down before sliding back the other way

mallet

FIGURE 10-34B. If the bearing cannot be removed as in Figure 10-34A, greater pressure can be brought to bear by making a tool as shown. *(Jim Sollers)*

through it. Take a second plate and drill a hole just large enough to clear the propeller shaft. Find a piece of pipe that fits around the shaft but which has an outside diameter less than that of the bearing. Fasten the two plates together with two long bolts and tighten the bolts to drive the bearing out of the strut. Once out of the strut, file or grind down the bearing case as above until it breaks apart or slides back through the strut.

In almost all other cases, the propeller shaft must come out to renew a rubber sleeve bearing. A strut-mounted bearing can generally be knocked out from the inner side of the strut, but care must be taken not to damage the strut or its mounting. To drive out a hull-mounted bearing (i.e., in the deadwood), the stuffing box has to be removed from the inner end of the stern tube.

Not infrequently, the bearing refuses to budge. In this case, given a strut, a simple puller can be made as shown in Figure 10-34C. In the case of a hull-mounted bearing, or in the absence of a puller, make two longitudinal slits in the bearing with a hacksaw blade so you can pry out a section, allowing the rest to flex inward. Take care not to cut through the bearing into the surrounding strut or stern tube. Then lightly grease a new bearing and push it in using a block of wood and *gentle* hammer taps. You don't want the bearing to be a tight (interference) fit because it may distort. If a metal-shelled bearing is packed in ice before installation, it will shrink a few thousandths of an inch—enough to ease the installation.

Any retaining setscrews *must tighten into dimples in the bearing case* and should be locked in place with Loctite or something similar. Setscrews must not press on the bearing case since this could distort it, causing friction between the rubber bearing and the propeller

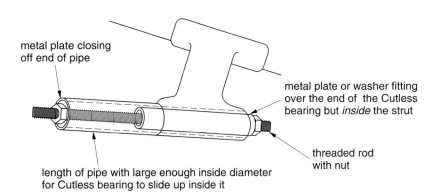

metal plate closing off end of pipe

metal plate or washer fitting over the end of the Cutless bearing but *inside* the strut

threaded rod with nut

length of pipe with large enough inside diameter for Cutless bearing to slide up inside it

FIGURE 10-34C. A homemade tool for rubber sleeve (Cutless) bearing removal. The bearing is drawn out by tightening the nuts.

shaft. The shaft itself should *not* be a tight fit in the bearing sleeve.

Most bearing cases are made of naval brass or stainless steel. Fiberglass-epoxy (FE) cases are becoming more common, however. This material works just as well as the metals and is especially recommended for steel and aluminum hulls, where it will eliminate the risk of galvanic corrosion. Its only disadvantage is that if the bearing is a tight fit, there is a greater risk of damaging the bearing when knocking it in or out.

Propellers

The number one problem with propellers is fouled lines, generally your own! These can be a devil of a job to clear. Before resorting to snorkeling gear and a knife, shut down the engine, put the transmission in neutral, and have some-

FIGURE 10-35. A Spurs line cutter.

one pull on the fouled line while a second person rotates the propeller shaft by hand in the opposite direction from which it was turning when the line was caught. Often the line will simply unwind.

Effective line cutters (Figure 10-35) can be installed on a propeller shaft that will cut right through trailing lines, but I must say I have mixed feelings about these. First because I would rather salvage than destroy our lines, but second, and more importantly, because if we foul a fishing or lobster-pot line, I feel we have some obligation to protect it rather than undermine someone else's livelihood.

Another common problem is bent propeller blades. These can cause quite a bit of vibration. It is advisable to check the blades at the annual haulout. Set up a pointer (a piece of wood or a pencil) on the hull side or strut so that it nearly touches the tip of one propeller blade (Figure 10-36). Rotate the propeller by hand. Any differences in the blade clearances will become apparent immediately.

Some propellers are made of little more than high-tensile brass (for example, manganese bronze is approximately 60% copper, 40% zinc). Without adequate cathodic protection, such propellers will suffer from dezincification (Chapter 5) and crumble in time (dezincified manganese bronze takes on a pinkish hue). The best propellers are made of a nickel-bronze-aluminum (nibral) alloy.

There is galvanic interaction between many propellers and their propeller shafts. The normal means of providing galvanic protection is to fit a zinc collar to the propeller shaft, but many of these come loose after they have been partially

eaten away. The better ones have an internal nonzinc band that remains firmly clamped to the shaft at all times.

Fixed pitch versus controllable pitch. A propeller blade is manufactured with a certain *pitch*—the theoretical advance (in inches or cm) of the propeller in one revolution, which is crudely a function of the angle at which it cuts the water. If the propeller blade is held at the same angle in relation to its hub whenever the propeller is in use, it is known as a *fixed-pitch propeller*.

When a propeller is matched to an engine, it is designed to develop its maximum thrust (i.e., be at its most efficient) more or less at the maximum rated engine speed. With a fixed-pitch propeller, at any speed other than full engine speed, the power absorbed by the propeller will be less than what the engine can develop at that speed of rotation. The only way to get the propeller to absorb all the available power is to increase the propeller's pitch, which is done by rotating the propeller blades in relation to its hub—such a propeller is known as a *controllable-pitch propeller* (see below).

Standard propellers. Standard propellers have a fixed pitch. As noted, the blade shape will usually be optimized to produce maximum thrust in forward at full engine speed (resulting in a cambered-blade surface as opposed to a flat-blade surface). At all other speeds, the propeller is increasingly inefficient. Sometimes the propeller is deliberately optimized for a lower engine speed, which is logical on many sailboats as most cruising is by preference done at about three-quarters of the maximum engine speed. The trade-off here is that if an attempt is made to drive the engine to its maximum speed, it may overheat, will likely emit black smoke, and may get damaged; the engine warranty may also be voided. Finally, for all cambered-blade props, given that the blades are optimized for forward thrust, the shape is especially inefficient in reverse.

Propellers are mounted on keyed and tapered shafts and retained by a propeller nut with either a second locking nut or a cotter pin (split pin). There may or may not be a *fairing piece* over the top of the nut to smooth out the water flow (Figure 10-37).

Removing and refitting standard propellers. To remove a standard propeller, always use a propeller puller. If one is not available, in a bind you can back off the retaining nut on the propeller (but not all the way) and use a piece of hardwood and a hammer to hit the propeller smartly behind its boss and jar it loose from the taper on the shaft. Note, however, that this is to be avoided if at all possible (it may damage the

FIGURE 10-36. Using a pointer to check for propeller blade misalignment. *(Jim Sollers)*

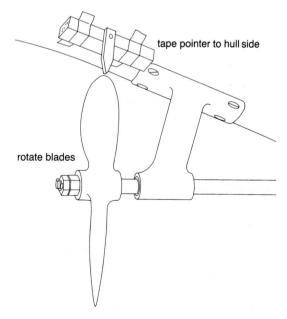

tape pointer to hull side

rotate blades

transmission), and a propeller puller should always be found or made (see Figure 10-38). (I have had complaints from professionals about even suggesting the use of a hammer, because all too often there is limited room to swing a hammer, and people end up hitting the shaft, strut, or propeller blade. If you can get a good swing at the propeller and it still won't come off, concentrate on the spot with the keyway—this is the most likely point of binding. If the propeller won't move, try heating its hub with a propane torch. Move the torch around the hub in a circular fashion to avoid excessive localized heating. If the propeller *still* won't move, don't just hit it harder—as noted, you may end up doing damage to the thrust bearings and clutch plates in the transmission, which are at the other end of the propeller shaft. This is especially likely with smaller transmissions.)

When refitting a standard propeller, fit it first without its keyway and place a *nongraphite* (i.e., non-pencil) mark on the shaft at the inboard end of the propeller hub (putting a piece of tape around the shaft, with its edge flush with the propeller hub, works well). Then remove the propeller and refit the propeller with its key, checking to see that the hub comes back up to the mark. This will ensure that the key is not oversized or improperly seated. Lock the retaining nut securely. In earlier editions of this book, I recommended greasing the shaft to help in future propeller removal, but this has been challenged by some experts on the basis that the grease may dissipate over time, leaving the hub loose on the shaft. And in any case, friction between the tapered shaft and the propeller hub is important in minimizing the stresses imposed on the propeller key and nut.

Removing feathering and folding propellers.
NEVER remove folding and feathering propellers with heat or hammering! There is a high probability you will damage the hub and internal gearing and/or fry the lubricant inside. Instead, consult the manufacturer—the best ones offer special prop pullers that will remove the propeller quickly, safely, and easily. Consider carrying one aboard.

Folding propellers.
Folding propellers have two significant benefits over other propeller types. They have the least amount of drag when under sail, and the least likelihood of any propeller type on the market of snagging seaweed, fishing lines, lobster-pot warps, and other debris.

The *old style* has two hinged blades. When sailing, the blades are held in the closed position by the flow of water over the propeller. When the engine is cranked and put in forward, the cen-

trifugal force opens the blades partway, and then the developed thrust drives them all the way open, sometimes with considerable force. The net result is a fixed-pitch propeller. In reverse, any thrust developed tends to close the blades. This tendency is counteracted by centrifugal force, but efficiency is often minimal.

The most common problem with this type of propeller is a failure to open at all because of weeds or barnacles in the hinge. Partial opening of one or another blade will result in severe vibration. These propellers must be kept clean. Thrust in reverse is minimal, and even in forward, the propellers are typically very inefficient (often converting less than 50% of the available shaft horsepower into thrust).

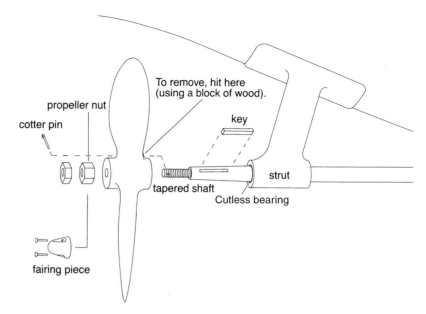

FIGURE 10-37. Propeller installation. The half nut, which would be between the blades and the locking nut, can be dispensed with when a fairing nut is used. *(Jim Sollers)*

FIGURE 10-38. A propeller puller. *(Jim Sollers)*

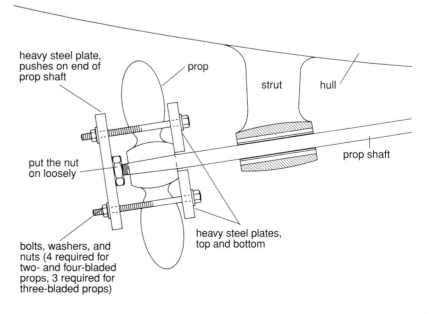

FIGURE 10-39A. A Varifold folding propeller. *(Brunton's Propellers)*

1. propeller hub nut
2. nut locking screw
3. blade pins
4. blade pin locking screws
5. anode retainer
6. anode retainer screws
7. anode
8. shaft
9. shaft key

The *new style* of folding propellers—e.g., Flex-O-Fold (www.flexofold.com), Gori (www.gori-propeller.com), Brunton's Varifold (www.bruntons-propellers.com or www.varipropusa.com), and Volvo (www.volvopenta.com)—have a gear on the base of each propeller blade that is engaged with the other blade(s). This ensures that the blades open and close in tandem (Figures 10-39A to 10-39F). The design is such that these propellers open better and are far more efficient in both forward and reverse than traditional folding propellers. In fact they are as efficient as any other propeller on the market and more efficient than many. (In tests conducted at the University of Berlin in Germany, the Flex-O-Fold was as efficient in forward gear as the best

FIGURE 10-39B. A Varifold propeller in the folded position.

FIGURE 10-39C. The geared hub of a contemporary folding propeller.

gearing on the base of folding blades; this ensures the blades all fold and open together

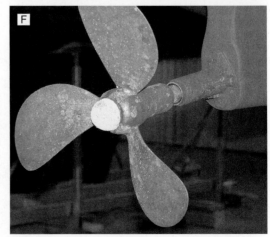

FIGURES 10-39D, 10-39E, AND 10-39F. Flex-O-Fold propellers.

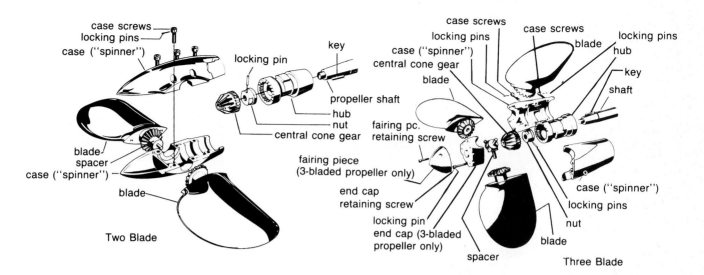

case screws
locking pins
case ("spinner")

locking pin

key

propeller shaft

hub
nut
central cone gear

blade
spacer
case ("spinner")

blade

Two Blade

case screws
locking pins
case ("spinner")
central cone gear
blade

case screws
blade

locking pins
hub

key

shaft

fairing pc.
retaining screw

fairing piece
(3-bladed propeller only)

end cap
retaining screw

locking pin
end cap (3-bladed
propeller only)

spacer

case ("spinner")

locking pins

nut

blade

Three Blade

fixed-blade propellers and substantially more efficient than many feathering propellers.) The blades open to a preset position and as such have a fixed pitch. They are especially suitable for high-speed multihulls. Some manufacturers offer these props in three- and four-blade versions and very large diameters for big boats and high-horsepower engines.

Feathering propellers. As with the new-style folding propellers, a feathering propeller has a gear on the base of each propeller blade, but in this case it engages a central gear mounted on the propeller shaft. The whole unit is enclosed in a case (Figure 10-40; see, for example, www.pyiinc.com, www.martec-props.com, www.bomon.com, www.varipropusa.com, and www.peluke.com).

When the engine is cranked and put in gear, the propeller shaft and the gear mounted on it turn while the case and blades tend to lag due to inertia. The blades are in a feathered position. The rotating gear on the propeller shaft turns the propeller blades inside the case. The blades have a preset stop, so that they cannot rotate beyond a certain point. This preset stop determines the pitch of the blades. Once it is reached, the propeller shaft spins the whole unit including the case. When the engine is shut down, water pressure on the blades forces them back to the feathered position.

When put in reverse, the propeller shaft once again drives the blades to their full pitch before spinning the whole unit. And unlike a standard fixed-pitch propeller, a feathering propeller has the same efficiency in reverse as in forward. This is because the blade faces are reversed; as a result, considerably more thrust is developed than by a standard propeller (note, however, that some feathering propellers have flat blades with

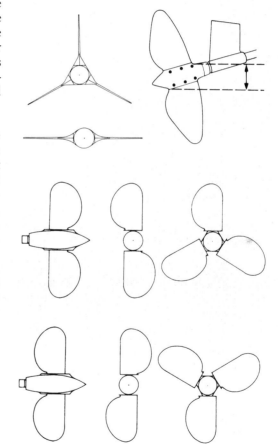

FIGURE 10-40.
Top: Fully feathering propellers. **Left:** The operation of Max-Prop propellers. Under sail, the Max-Prop feathers to a low drag shape. In forward, the torque of the prop shaft acts to force the blades open to a preset pitch at any throttle setting. In reverse, as in forward, the torque of the shaft will rotate the blades 180 degrees, presenting the same leading edge and pitch in reverse. *(Max-Prop)*

little camber; these are significantly less efficient in forward than most standard propellers and new-style folding propellers).

On many older models, the blade pitch can be adjusted by altering the stops, but to do this, the case must be disassembled and on some propellers (notably Luke—Figure 10-41—and Prowell) the stops have to be machined down or

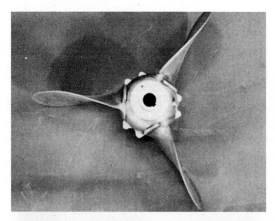

FIGURE 10-42. This zinc is past its replacement date! Note that galvanic interaction between the stainless steel fasteners and the zinc has caused the zinc to become loose. This will interfere with the electrical connection (metal to metal) between the zinc and the propeller, rendering the zinc ineffective regardless of how much of it is left.

built up by welding in additional material. On others, the stops are adjustable mechanically. Newer feathering propellers tend to have an external pitch-adjustment mechanism (the pitch can be changed with no disassembly). A couple of brands offer independently adjustable forward and reverse pitches, which is very useful because prop walk (the "paddlewheel effect") in reverse can be greatly reduced or even eliminated by flattening the reverse pitch without compromising the forward pitch. Note that in all cases these pitch-adjustment capabilities do not in any sense equate with a controllable-pitch propeller (see below). It is simply a method for fine-tuning the pitch(es) in the event the propeller was not properly matched to the boat and engine in the first place—or as the boat gains weight and the engine loses power over the years!

Maintenance is a matter of checking sacrificial zinc anodes regularly (Figure 10-42) and renewing the grease every 1 or 2 years. To renew the grease some units must be taken apart (e.g., older Max-Props) whereas on others a grease fitting is simply screwed into the case (e.g., Luke, Variprop). In the former case, make a careful note of where everything goes and put it all back the same way. A waterproof bearing grease such as Lubriplate Marine-Lube "A" works well (lighter Teflon greases will be washed away). Some man-

ufacturers insist that you use their own proprietary grease; take heed and use it—there is a good reason.

If the propeller blades are stiff to rotate by hand, or have *hard* spots, it may simply be the result of too much grease, so take a little out. If that doesn't work, check for small burrs on the gears or minor damage on any of the bearing surfaces (the propeller blade bases, bearing surfaces in the case, and the hub). Remove the cone gear and reassemble the unit. Now check each individual blade for stiffness and test the rotation of the case around the hub; you should be able to isolate problem areas. *Dressing up* with emery cloth or a fine file will solve most problems. Be sure to replace the zinc anode tailcones when they are about two-thirds gone—you are protecting a lot of very expensive machinery inside these props!

Gori three-bladed folding propeller. The Gori three-bladed folding propeller is unique in a couple of ways. It combines the blade-rotation characteristics of a feathering propeller, which maximizes thrust in reverse as well as forward, with a folding propeller, which minimizes drag and the likelihood of fouling objects. Its other unique feature is that if the engine is put in reverse (so the blades rotate to the reverse position), and this continues until the boat is moving backward, and then the engine is put in forward, the blades will spin in forward but in the reverse position. (Note that the boat must be going backward before shifting into forward—the reverse water flow over the blades is needed to hold them in the reverse position.) This has the effect of increasing the blade pitch in forward—what Gori calls its *overdrive* position.

As I noted earlier, pitch is normally maximized at something close to full engine speed, with the result that at any speed under full speed, the engine has "excess" power. By increasing the pitch in the overdrive position, the power demands of the propeller at lower engine speeds, or when motorsailing, can be better matched to the available engine power, lowering the engine speed for a given boat speed. The Gori propeller, in other words, has a partial controllable-pitch function.

As always, there are downsides. The first is that if using the overdrive when motorsailing, the boat must be moving in reverse before shifting back into forward, which may require temporarily spilling the wind from the sails in order to get the boat going backward. The second is that when maneuvering at a dock, the propeller may go into overdrive when you don't want it to! It is also questionable to what extent, if at all, it results in any fuel savings.

Controllable-pitch propellers. A traditional controllable-pitch propeller has the propeller hub bolted to the boat with a mechanism to move the propeller shaft forward and aft. Moving the shaft rotates the propeller blades in the hub, changing their pitch. Propeller pitch can be matched to engine speed to maximize the thrust and efficiency over the full speed range as opposed to at a single point on the engine's speed/power curve. Depending on the model, it is sometimes possible to align the propeller blades with the water flow—i.e., fully feather the blades—when sailing. This kind of propeller is rarely found on recreational boats. A new variant has recently (2004) been introduced by the Norwegian firm West Mekan (www.westmekan.no; it is sold under license in the UK by Darglow Engineering, www.props4yachts.com).

Brunton Autoprop. The Brunton Autoprop is a feathering propeller that uses some very clever engineering to perform these pitch-adjusting functions automatically (Figures 10-43A and 10-43B). The blades are designed and weighted so they increase the pitch at lower engine speeds, resulting in increased speed for a given engine speed and lower fuel consumption. The blades also reverse when the engine is put in

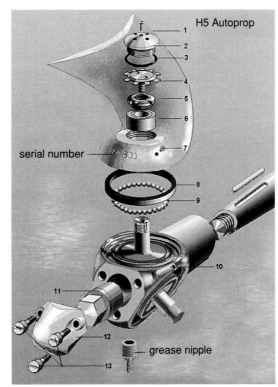

H5 Autoprop

serial number

grease nipple

reverse, providing the same thrust in reverse as in forward. Vibration can be a more common problem than with the best modern feathering or folding propellers. Under sail, the water flow past the boat causes the blades to feather. It should be noted that the manner in which the blades are weighted results in the lower one hanging down somewhat, causing more drag than with a fully folding or feathering propeller (Figure 10-43C).

The Autoprop is probably best suited for motorsailer applications or for boats that make long and frequent passages under power. Although it does work as advertised, it also takes a little getting used to, especially when going into reverse. Initially, nothing seems to happen, then suddenly, the propeller kicks in with considerably more thrust than you get from a typical propeller.

FIGURE 10-43B. What an Autoprop looks like in practice. *(Brunton's Propellers)*

FIGURE 10-43C. The way the blades are weighted causes one to hang down when under sail, creating a little more resistance than a feathering propeller. *(Brunton's Propellers)*

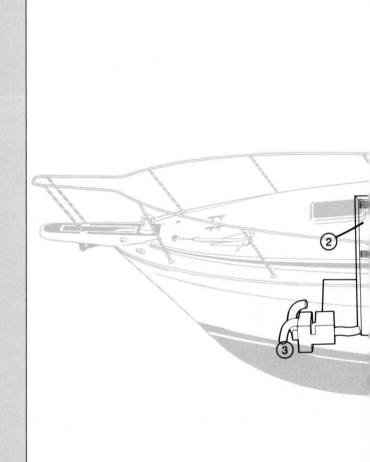

CHAPTER 11

FIGURE 11-1. Problems aboard can crop up almost anywhere, but most can be ignored as long as the beverages and the mahimahi are kept cold. *(Jim Sollers)*

(1) compressor
(2) plenum
(3) air conditioner
(4) freezer
(5) refrigerator
(6) pump
(7) strainer
(8) air conditioner raw-water intake
(9) holding plate in icebox
(10) belt-driven compressor
(11) condenser (in engine raw-water intake line)

Refrigeration and Air-Conditioning

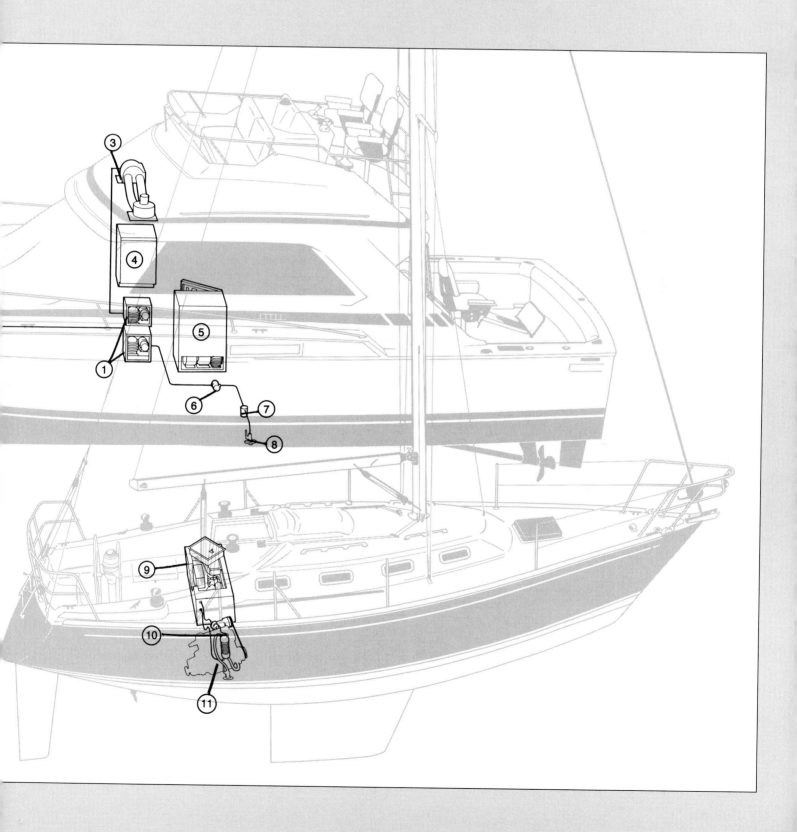

CFCs and the Ozone Hole

Since the first edition of this book was published in 1990, the refrigeration world has been turned upside down. Chlorofluorocarbons (CFCs), which include R-12 (Freon-12), the substance used as the refrigerant in all marine and household refrigeration units built prior to 1991, and hydrochlorofluorocarbons (HCFCs), which include R-22 (Freon-22), the substance formerly used in almost all air-conditioning, were fingered as two of the main culprits in the destruction of the earth's ozone layer.

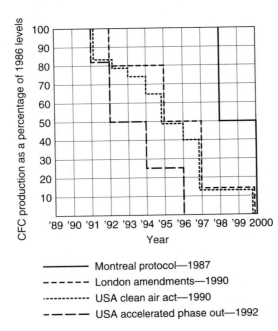

FIGURE 11-2A. This graph shows the accelerated phaseout of CFCs. Their production was completely banned in the industrialized world by 1995.

— Montreal protocol—1987
- - - - - London amendments—1990
······· USA clean air act—1990
— — — USA accelerated phase out—1992

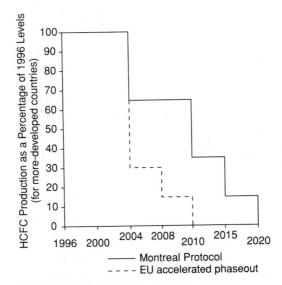

FIGURE 11-2B. HCFC phaseout schedule (for more-developed countries).

— Montreal Protocol
- - - - EU accelerated phaseout

Worldwide, governments moved with unaccustomed alacrity to deal with the problem. The Montreal Protocol of 1987 laid down a schedule to phase out the production of CFCs by the year 2000 and HCFCs by the year 2030. Subsequently this schedule was accelerated on several occasions (Figure 11-2A; see, for example, the United Nations Environment Programme Web site at www.unep.org/ozone; another excellent Web site is that of the International Institute of Refrigeration at www.iifiir.org—click on the Regulations/Standardization link).

A complete ban on the production of CFCs was in place by December 31, 1995. Environmentally, this has been a huge achievement, but in the space of a few short years, every existing marine refrigeration unit was made obsolete! HCFCs (used in most air-conditioning) are now scheduled for complete phaseout by the year 2020 (Figure 11-2B), with partial phaseout well before this (e.g., a 35% reduction from 1996 levels in 2004, 65% by 2010, and 90% by 2015). Now that CFCs are history, the European Union (EU) is further accelerating the phaseout of HCFCs with a 70% reduction from 1989 levels in 2004, 85% by 2008, and full phaseout by 2010.

When the production bans were first discussed, it was commonly assumed that the major chemical companies would find a *drop-in* replacement for R-12—that is to say, a non-ozone-depleting substance that could simply be exchanged for R-12 within the confines of an existing system.

Although drop-in replacements for R-12 were developed (such as R-409A and various "blends," including MP-39 and MP-66), the automotive air-conditioning and household appliance refrigeration industries converted to a substance known as HFC (hydrofluorocarbon)-134a as the substitute for R-12. HFC-134a has zero ozone depletion potential (ODP) and performs in a similar fashion to R-12, but unfortunately it requires special oils and is incompatible with the mineral oils that have always been used to lubricate R-12 systems. In addition, its use necessitates some modifications to compressor seals and other rubber components (primarily hoses) as well as a minor tweaking of system-operating parameters.

Marine Refrigeration

For various reasons, the industry-wide switch to HFC-134a left much of the marine refrigeration industry out on a limb. In the 1990s, a number of different refrigerants (including R-409A and several blends) were tried before the marine industry also standardized on HFC-134a (also called R-134a). As a result, today we have a declining number of R-12 systems in service, some systems with R-409A, a fair number with various blends, and an increasing number with HFC-134a (Figure 11-3). *Therefore, the first rule when servicing a marine refrigeration unit is to find out what is in the system and make sure to use compatible products!*

The legal framework in the United States.

Concurrent with the phaseout of CFCs has been a remarkable rise in the price of these substances. In 5 years, R-12 went from around $1 a pound to $10 a pound; in another 8 years, it was up to $30 a pound! Not only have traditional refrigerants become more costly, but their use and that of the replacement refrigerants have also been regulated by stringent new laws. For example, in the United States, under Section 608 of the Clean Air Act of 1990 and its subsequent amendments:

- Since July 1, 1992, *it has been illegal to vent controlled refrigerants* (CFCs and HCFCs, including the blends) *to the atmosphere. De minimus* releases are permitted, which basically covers the unavoidable venting that occurs when connecting and disconnecting refrigeration gauge sets to perform service work.

- Since November 15, 1992, *it has been illegal to sell cans of controlled refrigerants* weighing less than 20 pounds *to the general public* (this measure removed the popular 12-ounce cans from automotive and hardware stores). This ban on sales of controlled refrigerants to the general public was extended on November 15, 1994, to include *all* can sizes.

- Since July 13, 1993, anyone servicing or opening CFC- or HCFC-based refrigeration or air-conditioning equipment (including that using blends) has had to possess at least one EPA (Environmental Protection Agency)-certified piece of recovery and recycling equipment capable of removing and saving just about all the refrigerant from the system that is to be worked on.

- Since August 12, 1993, *it has been illegal for all but EPA-certified technicians to service refrigeration and air-conditioning equipment containing CFCs and HCFCs* (including the blends).

- On November 15, 1995, the prohibition on knowingly venting refrigerants was extended to substitutes for CFCs and HCFCs (including HFC-134a). However, *the regulations laying out the manner in which this prohibition is to be enforced have never been adopted.* A draft regulation was published in June 1998 with a

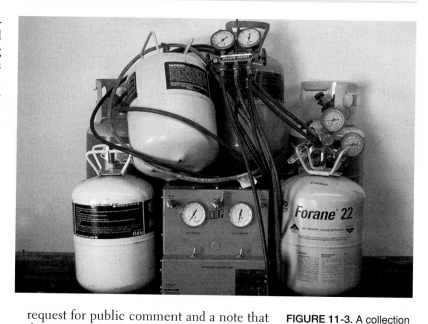

request for public comment and a note that the EPA would then "address comments and issue the final rule." The final rule has not been issued; therefore, as of 2004 the word from the EPA is: "The proposed regulations concerning the use and sale of HFC-134a have not been finalized. It remains legal to purchase and use the refrigerant without certification. It also remains legal to knowingly vent HFC-134a into the atmosphere." (This statement was in an e-mail to me from the EPA Recycling Program Manager.) Currently, you can walk into any Wal-Mart or automotive store in the United States and buy an unlimited number of 12-ounce cans of HFC-134a plus the hose and adapter needed to put it in a refrigeration system, and you can do so legally. *This will change overnight if the proposed regulations are ever adopted.* For a copy of the proposal, see www.epa.gov/ozone/title6/608/regulations/63fr32044.pdf (Proposed Rules, *Federal Register* 63, no. 112, Thursday, June 11, 1998); for a general over-view of Section 608, see www.epa.gov/ozone/title6/608/608fact.html.

The legal framework in Europe.

Europe has been more aggressive in the phaseout of ozone-depleting refrigerants. Regulations introduced in October 2000 (European Regulation Number 2037/2000) made it illegal to sell CFCs or use them in maintaining and servicing existing units after January 2001, although existing systems may be kept in service until they fail. It has been compulsory to recover and destroy CFCs from systems being taken out of service since January 2002. It is also compulsory to have all systems that contain more than 3 kg (6.6 pounds) of controlled substances (CFCs or HCFCs) tested for

FIGURE 11-3. A collection of different refrigerants used in marine systems over the past decade, plus an EPA-certified evacuation and recovery pump.

refrigerant leakage annually. (Most boat systems will not reach the 3 kg threshold, but some air-conditioning systems on larger yachts will.)

As noted above, HCFCs are being phased out well ahead of even the amended Montreal timetable, with dramatic production cutbacks in 2003 and 2004. Since January 2004, it has been illegal to use HCFCs in new equipment. Virgin HCFCs will be banned in servicing existing equipment in 2010 (only recycled refrigerant will be allowed), and recycled refrigerant will be banned in 2015.

In recent years, the focus in Europe has shifted from the ozone layer to global warming and the Kyoto Protocol, an international agreement designed to reduce the emission of greenhouse gases. The European Climate Change Programme (ECCP) has been established to see that Europe meets the commitments made in the Kyoto Protocol. HFCs (including HFC-134a) have been identified as one of the substances with a global warming potential (GWP).

In 2003, through the ECCP, a proposal to reduce emissions of fluorinated greenhouse gases controlled by the Kyoto Protocol (this includes HFC-134a) was adopted.

Currently (2005), it is proposed to phase out the use of CFCs in automobile air-conditioning and other mobile uses (this includes boats) by 2015. The withdrawal of the United States from the Kyoto agreement threatened the treaty, but it was revived in late 2004 when Russia signed it, thus bringing it into effect for the signatory countries in February 2005. This will likely accelerate the moves to phase out HFCs.

It seems quite possible that within a few years, at least in Europe, HFC-134a will be gone with, as yet, no clear replacement (possibilities include carbon dioxide and HFC-152a, both of which have a lower GWP than HFC-134a; in the U.S., Glacier Bay is already using HFC-404A in place of HFC-134a). We are almost certain to witness another major upheaval in the marine refrigeration and air-conditioning world (an excellent Web site to keep abreast of the situation in Europe is http://europa.eu.int/comm/environ ment/climat/home_en.htm).

The cruising sailor. So where does this leave the cruising sailor? The situation of an *uncertified* sailor who has been accustomed to carrying a can of refrigerant on board and topping off a refrigeration system from time to time (the procedures are described later in this chapter) is an interesting one. In Europe, cruisers had better leave their refrigeration systems alone, but in the United States, until the regulations concerning HFCs are adopted, sailors with refrigeration systems containing HFC-134a can (legally) do

pretty much what they want (of course, there are also environmental and moral issues . . .). For those with CFCs, HCFCs, and the blends, it is not illegal to carry such cans on board (note that CFCs are completely illegal in Europe), but when it comes to connecting the can to the system we enter a gray area.

In the United States, the primary concern of the EPA is to prevent unnecessary releases of refrigerant. As long as care is taken to minimize releases when purging the hoses, simply connecting a can to top off a unit *probably* does not constitute an offense. Although one part of the regulations implies that since August 12, 1993, such topping off can be done only by a certified technician with access to recovery and recycling equipment, the wording is ambiguous. *The EPA has told me quite explicitly that the relevant section was not intended to cover topping off and that "you can go ahead and charge your own systems. You don't need, and will not need, to be certified or to have recovery equipment."* However, if hose connections and disconnections cause "unnecessary" releases, such as would occur, for example, if a high-pressure hose were to be disconnected while filled with liquid, this would violate the de minimus rule on releases.

On one thing there is no discussion. *Since August 12, 1993, only certified technicians are allowed to open a refrigeration system containing CFCs, HCFCs, or a blend. Any procedure beyond a simple topping off clearly constitutes "servicing" or "opening" an appliance and as such falls under the provisions of the regulations.*

When it comes to enforcement, *the Coast Guard has the legal authority to enforce all applicable U.S. laws on U.S.-registered vessels (whether Coast Guard–documented or simply state-registered) in all international waters, and also within the waters of other nations if granted permission to do so by that nation.* In other words, U.S. citizens shouldn't think they can avoid these regulations when overseas. Whether or not the Coast Guard will actually play a role in enforcement is another question (as far as I know, it has not). It has been suggested to me that their policy may be that violations detected in the process of a routine vessel inspection would be reported to the EPA for further action.

U.S. penalties for lawbreakers are severe—fines up to $25,000, with rewards up to $10,000 for those turning in violators.

Steering a prudent course. R-12 is history. An existing, well-built R-12 system, particularly a hermetic system (one without an external drive belt), should run for many years without needing further attention. It cannot be serviced in Europe, but can be in the United States and the less-developed countries. If problems arise, and R-12 is unavailable or prohibitively expensive, and you are outside of Europe, you can keep your system going with R-409A or one of the blends if they are available (although in some instances, the change in refrigerant may result in problems). If these refrigerants are not available, it is time to think of starting again. Aside from HFC-404A, the only practical choice in new refrigeration systems at the present time is HFC-134a, even though it, too, may be banned in Europe in a few years.

With all systems, the greatest risk for the foreseeable future is the accidental use of the wrong refrigerant and oil when carrying out service work. It is always a good idea to check that your technician is aware of what to use (the refrigerant and oil should be clearly identified by labels on the unit and also in the literature that came with it), is familiar with the system in question, and in the case of an HFC-134a system, *only uses gauge sets and equipment dedicated to HFC-134a and nothing else.* (This is to prevent the possibility of cross-contamination from another system.) Cruisers going overseas with a system charged with HFC-134a, R-404A, R-409A, or a blend would be well advised to carry both oil and refrigerant if only to have it available for use by a local technician.

Balancing Refrigeration Needs with Boat Use

So much for the general picture. Let's get into specifics. The keys to a successful refrigeration system are first, matching the unit to the boat's energy resources and patterns of use, and second, ensuring a proper installation. If these two things are done right, the unit will gives years of satisfactory use. If either is wrong, it is likely to become a millstone around the boatowner's neck. Over the years I have learned the hard way, and wasted thousands of dollars tailoring our own systems to our specific needs. This is not uncommon for tropical cruisers. In fact, we have met numerous cruisers who have invested thousands and still don't have a satisfactory system.

Problems are especially likely with boats going from temperate climates, such as northern Europe or the northern United States, to hotter climates, such as the Mediterranean, the Caribbean, or Baja California. The higher ambient air and water temperatures of these areas increase the power demands of the refrigerator and/or freezer while at the same time decreasing the efficiency of the refrigeration unit—all the variables are moving in the wrong direction. It is not unusual to find boats that have perfectly adequate refrigeration at home having to run engines 3 or 4 hours a day to keep up with refrigeration demands in the tropics, or the battery charging necessitated by the refrigeration unit, sometimes still with poor results. As often as not, if the refrigeration unit is DC powered, the boat will also suffer repeated battery failures.

Iceboxes: The Key to Sizing a Refrigeration Unit

At the heart of many refrigeration failures is the icebox. The function of a refrigeration unit is to remove heat from an icebox and its contents and also to combat heat gain over time, thus keeping the contents of the icebox cold. Once the box and its contents are initially cooled down, the rate of heat influx into the icebox is the key component in determining the necessary size of a refrigeration unit. In terms of heat gain, there are four principal factors at work:

1. The nature and thickness of the insulation.
2. The quality of icebox construction.
3. The overall dimensions of the icebox—the larger it is, the greater its surface area, and therefore its heat absorption.
4. The temperature differential from the inside to the outside of the icebox; a given icebox in "freezer" mode will always require considerably more refrigeration capability than when in "refrigerator" mode.

Insulation issues. Heat is transferred from the outside of an icebox to the inside by *conduction, convection,* and *radiation.*

Conduction. In the context of iceboxes and refrigeration, conduction is the primary mechanism by which heat passes through insulation.

All substances have a measurable thermal conductivity, which is expressed in terms of a *K-factor,* which tells us the rate at which heat will travel through the substance. Using American units, K is a function of the number of British thermal units (Btu) of heat that will pass through 1 square foot of a 1-inch-thick material over a period of 1 hour, if the temperature differential from one side to the other is 1°F. (1 Btu is the amount of heat needed to raise 1 pound of water by 1°F. The metric equivalent is a calorie [small "c"] or Calorie [large "C"], which is the amount of heat needed to raise 1 gram [calorie] or 1 kilogram [Calorie] of water by 1°C. 4 Calories = 1 Btu.)

Copper, which is highly conductive, has a

If your boat will be used in cooler climates for anything other than extended cruising, think long and hard before adding refrigeration to an existing icebox! Given the cheap cost of ice, and its ready availability in most places, the benefit relative to the cost is hard to see.

If your boat is moving from a cooler climate to a warmer one, or is already in a warm climate, onboard refrigeration becomes much more attractive, but I would still think long and hard before adding it. The issue here is a little different: the benefit is much more obvious, and the cost is no higher, but if the icebox insulation is at all questionable, the energy requirements will become a major drain on the boat's energy systems. Before installing refrigeration, it is important to make a *realistic* assessment of the quality and effectiveness of the icebox insulation as described in the text.

If an icebox is substandard (as almost all older and many new iceboxes are), *adding refrigeration will create a permanent onboard energy crisis.* You may be able to salvage an existing icebox by such measures as improving the door and/or hatch seals, plugging a drain, and adding insulation either inside the box or to its exterior, but in almost all cases the recommended course of action is to rip out the box and build a new one, using the construction approaches described in the text. But this is not what most people want to hear!

If the icebox is up to snuff, by far the easiest way to retrofit a refrigeration unit is to use one of the constant-cycling DC units (see the text) as opposed to an engine-driven or holding-plate system. There will be an evaporator plate or box that must be screwed to the icebox wall as high in the box as possible, so make sure the wall is rugged enough to take the weight; and before buying the unit, make sure the evaporator plate will fit through the icebox hatch/door! A hole will need to be drilled through the icebox (once again, as high as possible) for the refrigerant lines coming off the evaporator plate. There will also be a thermostat of some sort, with a wire that can be run through the same hole as the refrigerant lines. After the lines are installed, the opening around them must be sealed (sprayed-in foam, available at any hardware store, works well).

The compressor/condensing unit to which the refrigerant lines attach can be mounted in any convenient locker close by the icebox, and wired to a suitable DC source. If the unit is air cooled, it will need a good supply of fresh air (the manual will tell you how to achieve this). If it is water cooled, the airflow is not an issue, but a through-hull of some sort will be needed (once again, the manual will tell you what to do).

On most modern units, all the relevant components come precharged with refrigerant and are simply plugged together—there is no vacuuming and charging. In this case, installation is relatively straightforward and well within the abilities of amateurs.

K-factor of 2,712; air, which is not very conductive, has a K-factor of 0.16. The lower the K-factor, the greater the insulating property, often expressed as an R-value. The *R-value*—the resistance to the passage of heat—is expressed as the reciprocal of the K-factor. In the case of copper, with a K-factor of 2,712, the R-value is $1/2712 = 0.00037$; for air it is $1/0.16 = 6.25$.

Convection. As we have just seen, air has low conductivity and therefore a high insulation value in terms of slowing the movement of conducted heat. So why not just put a big air gap around an icebox? Because the air molecules up against the hot surface (the outside of the insulation gap) will warm up, become lighter, and rise, while those against the cold surface (the inside of the insulation gap) will cool off, become heavier, and sink. This will set up a *convective* air current that will transport heat from the outside surface to the inside, at which point the heat will warm the inner surface (the icebox wall) and be conducted into the icebox; the insulating value of the air is substantially negated by this convective process.

Most insulation seeks to use the low conductivity of air while simultaneously eliminating the convective path. It does this by breaking up the air into numerous small, sealed cells, generally through the use of *closed-cell* foam. Each air pocket forms a tiny convective cell. So now, instead of the heat being moved directly from one side of the insulation barrier to the other by convection, it has to move from cell to cell by a process of conduction through the cell walls and then convection inside the cells. This greatly slows the rate of heat transfer.

Radiation. Radiated heat is caused by the transmission of electromagnetic energy through space. This energy excites molecules on the surface of objects it strikes, generating heat that is then transmitted through the object and to adjacent objects by conduction and convection.

Most radiated heat can be eliminated by reflecting it back toward its source. For example, a highly polished aluminum surface such as aluminum foil will reflect back 90% to 95% of radiated heat. If radiation is the primary source of heat gain, *radiant barriers* are a highly effective means of blocking its further transmission.

To be effective, a radiant barrier has to reflect the radiant heat back into an open space from which the heat can be dissipated. If this is not the case (for example, a radiant barrier embedded between two pieces of foam), the reflected heat will be trapped, raising the temperature of both the surrounding material and also the radiant barrier itself, at which point the radiant barrier forms a conductive surface, so little has been gained.

Testing insulation. The effectiveness of insulation is specified in terms of its R-value per inch (or cm) of thickness; the higher the number, the better it is. R-values are cumulative—insulation that is 3 inches thick will have three times the R-value of the same material that is 1 inch thick.

Given the different ways heat can be transmitted, there are numerous tests for measuring R-values, each one giving different results. The same material tested, for example, as a radiant barrier may well come up with a radically different R-value if tested as a conductive barrier. For this reason, the published insulation numbers for various insulation materials are only useful for comparing these materials in icebox use if:

1. The same testing procedure has been used.
2. The insulation values are derived using a test methodology that reflects icebox use in boats.

Of the numerous tests recognized in the United States, the ASTM C-518 test is one that is useful. The material to be tested is placed between two plates, one of which is held at 100°F/37.8°C and the other at 0°F/–17.8°C, and the rate of heat transfer is measured. These temperatures are indicative of the temperature differential between the ambient temperature of a closed-up boat in the tropics and the internal temperature of an icebox in a freezer application. Note that ASTM C-518 is primarily a test of conduction and convection, not of radiation. But given that few iceboxes in boats are subjected to direct sunlight (the main source of radiant heat in this environment), the test should more or less approximate the onboard environment of a freezer operating in the tropics, which is the worst-case scenario for a boat refrigeration system.

I know of no independent ASTM C-518 side-by-side testing of insulation materials commonly used in boat refrigeration, but I do have the following results (see Table 11-1) from Glacier Bay of tests run at their facility (reprinted with their permission and available on their Web site—www.glacierbay.com). In looking at these, it must be recognized that Glacier Bay is the manufacturer of a competing superinsulation product—see below.

TABLE 11-1. Properties of Popular Icebox Insulation Materials

Product	R-Value per Inch	Moisture Penetration
Various radiant barriers	3 to 4[1]	Very low
White beaded polystyrene	3.84	Medium
Blueboard polystyrene	4.92	Very low
Urethane board	6.0	Medium
Foil-covered polyiso-cyanurate foam	6.35	High
Two-part poured-in foam	4 to 6[2]	High

1. When tested as a radiant barrier, these products have much higher R-values, commonly exceeding R-20 per inch, but it is questionable how useful this is in terms of icebox insulation.
2. Poured-in foams produce very uneven results, often leaving voids. *(Adapted from tables courtesy Glacier Bay)*

The Glacier Bay tests were run on dry samples. Given the temperature differential from one side of icebox insulation to the other and the high humidity of the marine environment, if the insulation is at all porous, which allows moist air to penetrate it, this moisture is likely to condense out in the insulation. Since moisture is highly conductive, those materials that allow moisture penetration will see a significant drop in their R-values over time while those materials that do not, will not.

The three insulation materials commonly used to construct iceboxes are poured-in foam, urethane board, and Blueboard. Because of the moisture permeability of the urethane board and poured-in foams, Blueboard is probably the best material over the long term. It is also the cheapest. (For more on icebox construction details, see below.)

Superinsulation. Some quite astonishing gains in insulation values can be made using vacuum-based superinsulation panels (vacuum insulation panels—VIP), although at a high cost (the cost will fall dramatically if a mass market is developed for this technology).

The underlying concept is the same as for a thermos bottle (vacuum flask). If all the air can be evacuated from an insulation space, there will be no molecules available to transfer heat from one side to the other. The problem is that when you create a vacuum on the flat surfaces found in iceboxes, you literally generate tons of surface pressure that will collapse any panel. Consequently, some kind of a support structure (the *core* material) is required inside a vacuum panel. When subjected to a vacuum, most materials suitable to provide this core *outgas* to some extent, lessening the vacuum and providing the molecules necessary to transfer heat. Outgassing can be counteracted by including *getter* substances, which absorb the gases. Desiccants, which soak up moisture, are also frequently

FIGURES 11-4A TO 11-4G. Vacuum panel construction. The carbon-silica aerogel core material (11-4A and 11-4B). Putting the core material in a Mylar bag with three sides heat sealed (11-4C). Heat-sealed seams (11-4D). One section of the seam is left unsealed. The vacuum is pulled through this section (11-4E). The vacuum chamber (11-4F). Once the panel is vacuumed down, the remaining section of edge is heat-sealed inside the vacuum chamber. A finished panel (11-4G). The Mylar skin is relatively fragile and easily damaged. The panel is encased in fiberglass to protect it.

added to the mix. This leaves the problem of finding an impermeable material to seal the outside of the panel.

Experiments have been made with a variety of core materials, getters, desiccants, and external membranes. The net result has been panels with an initial R-value per inch of anywhere from 20 to 70, but with a variable service life. Some are warranted for 25 years; others are reputed to have a high failure rate within a few months.

The marine refrigeration company with the most experience in this field is Glacier Bay. At the time of writing, their latest generation Barrier Ultra-R panels use a carbon-silica *aerogel* core material that also acts as a getter and desiccant, and which is sealed in a metalized flexible membrane (Figures 11-4A to 11-4G). These panels have an R-value per inch of 50 (using the ASTM C-518 test), and are warranted for 25 years (this R-value is in the center of a panel; there will be higher heat losses at the ends and corners). The aerogel core is less sensitive to a loss of vacuum than most other core materials. As a result, if the vacuum fails altogether, according to Glacier Bay the panels will have a residual R-value per inch of 9, which is higher than any traditional icebox insulation material.

Vacuum panels are a great addition to an icebox, but I recommend that they either be buried in conventional poured foam or added to conventional foam (Blueboard) insulation. That way, if the vacuum fails for any reason, the icebox will still have adequate conventional insulation to avoid an expensive retrofit (Figure 11-5). In any event, without additional insulation, the ends and corners of vacuum panels may sweat.

VIP versus traditional insulation. Note that once the total insulation thickness (vacuum panel plus conventional insulation) gets to be 4 to 6 inches (10 to 15 cm) thick, the additional benefits of vacuum-based insulation become increasingly marginal. (For more on the declining benefits of additional insulation, see the Heat Loss Calculations section below.) Kevin Alston of Glacier Bay has written me: "Many of our potential customers ask us if they are really going to be better off with our insulation than with 6 inches of foam. From a thermal standpoint the answer is, not much. What they're paying for is space. If they have the room to put in 6 inches of foam and still have the size of box they need, then that's certainly what they should do. If they are crunched for space, that's where we come in. If you're going to be cruising, you need a properly insulated box—period. That means a minimum of 4 inches and preferably 6 inches with conventional foams. All you're getting from us is the ability to do it in much less space."

In other words, if there is space enough to add 3 or more inches (7.5 cm) of insulation to the vacuum insulation, it is largely a waste of money to buy the vacuum panels in the first place! A balance has to be struck between taking full advantage of the space-saving potential of vacuum insulation and adding some traditional insulation as insurance against a failure of the vacuum. Where this balance is struck will depend on the need to maximize the volume of the icebox against your individual level of paranoia about the life expectancy and reliability of the vacuum panels.

FIGURE 11-5. The icebox for our new boat is formed entirely from fiberglass-encapsulated Barrier Ultra-R vacuum panels, which were then wrapped in 2 inches of Blueboard as insurance against any panel failures.

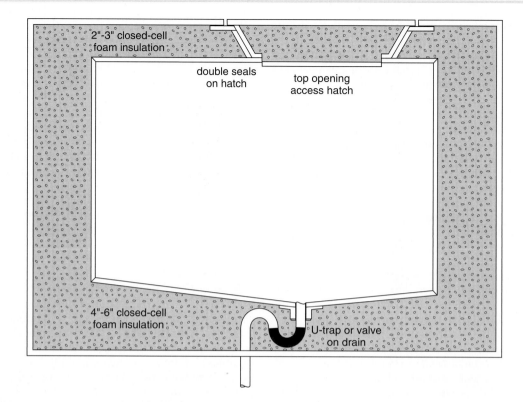

FIGURE 11-6. A "proper" icebox. The better insulated the box, the less the refrigeration unit will have to run to keep it cold. Note that omitting the drain will improve its performance (see text). *(Ocean Navigator)*

Labels in figure: 2"–3" closed-cell foam insulation; double seals on hatch; top opening access hatch; 4"–6" closed-cell foam insulation; U-trap or valve on drain

All vacuum-based panels must be installed with care and in a manner that ensures they will never be punctured. A fastener carelessly driven through the case will instantly destroy your investment. If vacuum panels are used in conjunction with other insulation, they are best embedded in the middle of the insulation. This will not only provide a physical gap between the vacuum insulation and any fasteners accidentally put through the icebox wall or surrounding cabinets, but it will also prevent sweating at edges and corners.

Construction issues. Unfortunately, many iceboxes installed in even expensive boats are unnecessarily large and poorly built. Very often a substantial improvement in performance can be gained by converting some of the interior volume to additional insulation (Figure 11-6).

In terms of a well-constructed icebox, the following are some key features to look for (Figures 11-7A to 11-7E):

- Multiple layers of board-type insulation are more likely to achieve a void-free construction than poured foam (Figure 11-7A).
- Seams should be sealed with some kind of bedding compound or with sprayed-in foam. (It is essential that there be no air paths that bypass layers of insulation—Figure 11-7B—because any such air path renders the insulation ineffective, regardless of its thickness or R-value.)

- As noted, after superinsulation, Blueboard or board urethane are the best insulation choices.
- In general, a vapor barrier should NOT be installed on the outside of the insulation because it will be almost impossible to make it vapor tight. Consequently it is more likely to end up trapping moisture than keeping it out.
- If at all possible, there should be a ventilated air gap between the outside of the insulation and the surrounding cabinetry or hull. This gap will enable the insulation to breathe and help prevent moisture contamination.
- A radiant barrier (highly reflective aluminum or a proprietary product such as Heat Shield; www.heatshieldmarine.com) on the outside of the insulation, coupled to an air space, will minimize radiant heat input (Figure 11-7C).
- All access hatches should have double seals (Figures 11-7D and 11-7E).
- Drains, where fitted, must have a U-trap or valve to stop cold air from sinking out the bottom of the icebox. (Drains are a holdover from the days when iceboxes really were "ice boxes," with constantly melting ice. There is really no need to put a drain in a modern icebox, and they would be better omitted or plugged.)

Top-opening versus front-opening hatches/ doors. In previous editions of this book, I recommended only top-opening iceboxes, because

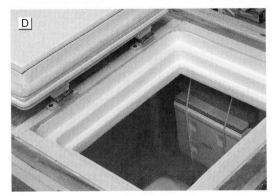

FIGURES 11-7A TO 11-7E. A void in poured-in foam. Voids such as this are common (11-7A). Sealing edges with sprayed-in foam (11-7B). Aluminum foil glued (with sprayed-on contact adhesive) to the exterior of the insulation to create a cost-effective, and easily applied, radiant barrier (11-7C). A double-sealed, top-opening hatch on a freezer. The hatch itself (built by Glacier Bay) contains a vacuum panel (11-7D). Testing the seal on an icebox hatch (11-7E). If there is no resistance to pulling out the $5 bill, the seal is not effective, in which case no amount of money spent on insulation will make the icebox efficient. If the hatch has a double seal (as it should), it should be possible to feel the bill pull past the first seal (there will be a slight lessening of resistance to its withdrawal) and then the second seal (there will be no resistance once past it).

they minimize heat influx when the door is open. However, I have subsequently realized that the energy cost of a front-opening door is quite small. If the entire volume of air in an 8-cubic-foot box spills out at 35°F/1.7°C and gets replaced with air at 100°F/37.8°C, it will add a heat load of 20 Btu. On a 12-volt DC system, this will take about 0.5 Ah out of the batteries. The convenience of a (well-sealed) front-opening door, especially on a refrigerator, outweighs this heat load (Figures 11-8A and 11-8B).

In actuality the downside of the front-opening door is not the heat loss but rather the humid air that enters every time the air in the icebox gets exchanged (by opening the door). It results in ice buildup on the evaporator plate or holding plate, which rapidly diminishes the rate of heat transfer. (Household refrigerators solve this problem with automatic deicing circuits, which are not available with marine refrigeration.) Most likely to cause trouble is an icebox with both a top-opening lid and a front-opening door—the slightest leak around both seals will lead to a constant flow of humid air into the icebox, resulting in a major frosting problem. Excellent lid and door seals are essential.

FIGURES 11-8A AND 11-8B. The convenience of a front-opening icebox (11-8A) versus digging through the contents to find something (11-8B).

With all hatches and doors, the edges of the opening and door or hatch must (of necessity) be sealed with some hard material (generally fiberglass or wood), which then connects interior surfaces to exterior surfaces. The thermal conductivity of this edging material is inevitably many times above that of most insulations. For example, some studies show that E-glass has forty-five times the conductivity of poured foam. These edges form a path for heat entry into the icebox. To minimize the heat gain in the icebox, edge materials should be as thin as is commensurate with the necessary physical strength (Figure 11-9).

Heat loss calculations. Given a well-constructed icebox with a properly sealed hatch and/or door and using closed-cell foam for insulation, it is reasonable to assume an R-value of around 5 per inch of insulation (e.g., 4 inches [10 cm] of insulation = R-20).

If the insulation thickness is doubled, the rate of heat loss is halved; if the insulation thickness is quadrupled, the rate of heat loss is cut to a quarter. To see how this works, consider the following sample icebox:

- 2 inches of insulation (R-10) = 1,000 Btu heat loss.
- 4 inches (R-20) = 500 Btu heat loss (one-half).
- 6 inches (R-30) = 333 Btu heat loss (one-third).
- 8 inches (R-40) = 250 Btu heat loss (one-quarter).
- 10 inches (R-50) = 200 Btu heat loss (one-fifth).

Note that adding 2 inches of insulation (from R-10 to R-20) cuts the heat loss by 500 Btu, 2 more inches cuts it by 166 Btu, 2 more inches by 83 Btu, and 2 more inches by 50 Btu. From R-30 to R-50, the heat-loss reduction is only 133 Btu.

This clearly illustrates the diminishing returns from increasing insulation thickness, as well as increasing R-value. The last R-20 of the Barrier Ultra-R insulation mentioned above (rated at R-50) does not contribute that much.

Icebox calculations. One way to calculate the daily (24-hour) heat load of an icebox is to measure its interior surface area (in square feet), estimate as best you can the insulation thickness, use Table 11-2 to find the heat loss per square foot, and multiply this number by the surface area. If different sides have different insulation thicknesses, do the calculations separately, then add them to get a total heat load. Note that this table is based on the scenario of an icebox in typical use on a boat in the tropics, and as such, is reasonably conservative; in temperate climates, the heat load will be less.

Table 11-2 will enable you to calculate the daily heat load in Btu. Sometimes it is useful to have the heat load specified in watt-hours (see below). To convert Btu to watt-hours, divide by 3.413. For example, if the daily heat load is 3,700 Btu, 3,700/3.413 = 1,084 watt-hours per 24 hours, which is 1,084/24 = 45 watts per hour.

TABLE 11-2. Heat Influx per 24 Hours per Square Foot of Interior Icebox Surface Area

Insulation Thickness (in.)	Total R-Value	Refrigerator (Btu)	Freezer (Btu)
2	10	150	280
3	15	120	225
4	20	100	185
5	25	90	170
6	30	80	150
8	40	66	120
10	50	60	110

Notes:

1. A doubling of the insulation thickness does not cut the heat load in half but reduces it by a third.
2. As noted in the text, there is a rapidly diminishing return in terms of increasing insulation thickness: with a refrigerator, going from 2 inches to 4 inches reduces the heat load from 150 Btu to 100 Btu per square foot (a reduction of 50 Btu), but the addition of another 2 inches of insulation (from 4 inches to 6 inches) only drops the heat load by 20 Btu. In other words, there is a trade-off between the loss of available icebox volume and insulation thickness and icebox effectiveness. For a refrigerator, the crossover point is generally considered to be around 4 inches; for a freezer, around 6 inches.
3. The heat load imposed by a freezer is dramatically higher than that imposed by a refrigerator (this is because of the considerably higher temperature differential between the inside and the outside of the icebox). Keeping down the volume of freezer boxes will go a long way toward lightening the load on a refrigeration system.
4. If superinsulation is used, ignore the Insulation Thickness column and instead use the appropriate row in the Total R-Value column (e.g., if using superinsulation with an R-value of 40, use the next to the last row [for refrigerators] to extract the heat load numbers; bear in mind that the overall R-value of the superinsulation will be lower than expected because of the higher rate of heat transfer at the ends and corners).

(Adapted from tables courtesy Glacier Bay)

Testing an Existing Icebox for Its Heat Loss

Crude Calculations

To approximate summer and tropical conditions, close up the boat and heat its interior to at least 90°F/32°C, preferably 100°F/37.8°C, making sure that the boat is uniformly hot all around the icebox area. Stock the box with a typical sampling of food and drink and then suspend a block of ice of known weight (10 to 20 pounds/4.5 to 9 kg) as high in the box as possible. Simulate normal use by opening and closing the box, removing items, adding fresh produce, etc. After a measured period of time—at least 6 hours—remove the remains of the block of ice and reweigh it. (Terminate the test and reweigh the ice once it has been reduced to much below 50% of its original weight.)

To calculate the heat gain (in Btu) of the box during this period, multiply the reduction in the weight of the block of ice (in pounds) by 144. Divide this answer by the number of hours of the test (6, in our example) and multiply by 24. This number will approximate the daily (24-hour) heat gain of the box in refrigerator use when in the tropics. For freezer use, multiply this figure by 1.85. If the figures are much above those derived from Table 11-2, there is a problem with the icebox.

Depending on how far short of the recommended standards an icebox falls, it may be possible to improve its performance by modifying hatches, removing drains, and adding insulation. In particular, iceboxes frequently have large voids between existing insulation and adjacent bulkheads and cabinetry. You can fill these voids by drilling holes in surrounding countertops and pouring in a two-part urethane foam mixture. If an icebox is unnecessarily large, adding superinsulation to its interior will result in a dramatic improvement in efficiency but at a high cost. If an icebox is seriously delinquent, it may prove necessary to bite the bullet, rip it out, and start from scratch.

More Precise Calculations

The methodology described above is very crude. It fails to account for all kinds of variables that will skew the results. With just a little more effort and precision, you can make much more accurate calculations of an icebox's heat loss and insulation R-value (see the examples in the Comparative Testing of Insulation sidebar). The approach here is the same as above, but with the following refinements:

- When you weigh the block of ice, also measure its temperature. For these tests, it's worthwhile acquiring a meter that reads temperatures (such as a Fluke 51 meter [www.fluke.com] or a millivolt meter with a temperature probe) and several thermocouples that plug into the meter. A K-type thermocouple with a beaded end works well. The ice is likely to be below 32°F/0°C. Find its weight in pounds, multiply the weight by however many °F it is below 32°F, and multiply this result by 0.5. The answer is the number of Btu the ice will absorb before it begins to melt. For example, a 10-pound block of ice at 17°F is 15°F below 32°F. It will absorb 10 x 15 x 0.5 = 75 Btu before it starts to melt. Add this number to the heat gain calculated above (i.e., the weight reduction of the ice x 144) to get the total heat gain.

- Measure the internal temperature of the icebox at regular intervals—say, every half hour. I do this by placing a thermocouple in the icebox (away from the walls) and bringing its lead out through the lid, making sure the lid still seals. When you measure the internal temperature, do the same for the external (ambient) temperature. Subtract the internal temperature from the external temperature to get the temperature differential. At the start of the test, the internal temperature will fall for an hour or two, then stabilize. When it shows a steady rise over an hour or two, it's time to stop the test. At the end of the test, add all the differentials and then divide by the number of readings to get an average temperature differential.

- Calculate both the surface area of the interior of the icebox and the external surface area of the insulation (in square feet). You may have to make an educated guess. Add them, then divide by 2 to get an average surface area.

Now you're ready to do some calculations. Take the total heat gain and divide it by the number of hours of the test to get the Btu gain per hour. Divide this result by the average temperature differential to find the Btu/hour/°F temperature differential. Divide this by the average box area (in square feet) to find the Btu/hour/°F temperature differential per square foot. Divide this by the thickness of the insulation in inches (average thickness if it varies) to find the icebox's K-factor. Divide this into 1 to find the R-value per inch of insulation. If the result is below 5 for conventional foam insulation, there may be a problem with the lid seals or drains or with the insulation—water saturation and/or voids.

Vacuum Panels

You can take a similar approach to gauge the overall performance of an icebox constructed

continued

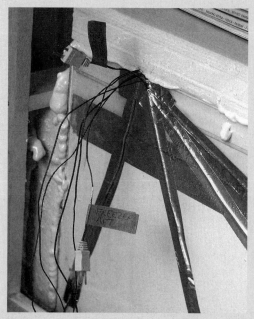

FIGURE 11-10. Thermocouples taped to all the Barrier Ultra-R vacuum insulation panels from which my new icebox is built.

from vacuum panels. Note that once insulation values start to go above R-20 to R-30, the heat gained by an icebox tends to come through drains, door seals, and voids in the insulation rather than through the insulation itself. Consequently, when calculating the R-value of superinsulated iceboxes, you will never get as high an R-value as the rating of the insulation. With this in mind, if the R-value is well below its expected level and the panels themselves are suspect, it may be possible to narrow down underperforming vacuum panels by taping thermocouples to the outside of the panels and then dropping the temperature well below freezing by either running a freezer or adding dry ice. The outside temperature of the vacuum panels may be pulled down a few degrees, but if it drops substantially, or one panel is well below the others, this indicates the insulation is performing poorly and the vacuum has probably failed. On our latest project (a Malo 45 sailboat built in Sweden), I built the icebox with thermocouples attached to every vacuum panel, with the leads coming out into a locker so I can monitor the performance of the panels over time (Figure 11-10).

Refrigeration Options

Once you've determined the overall energy demand of an icebox, you must decide what kind of refrigeration unit to use to meet this demand.

Refrigeration is not something that can just be tacked onto a boat. It is a major power consumer, particularly in warm climates where DC refrigeration (the most common) can account for between 50% and 75% of a boat's total DC demand. A refrigeration unit has to be carefully integrated into a boat's available power supplies, which in turn are going to be a function of how the boat will be used. A boat used for weekend cruising, for example, will have shore power available in its slip all week, whereas one used for long-term offshore cruising will not. It may well be the case that two identical production-line boats with similar refrigeration demands are best served by radically different types of refrigeration units.

A boat with a 24-hour-a-day AC generator can obviously use household-style AC refrigeration units; less common is holding-plate AC refrigeration. In the absence of a constant source of AC power, there are three popular refrigeration choices: engine-driven (with holding plates), constant-cycling DC, and holding-plate DC.

AC refrigeration. Constant-cycling AC refrigeration requires a constant source of AC power. If this is available, constant-cycling AC using household appliances is the cheapest and simplest option. This situation, however, should not be confused with the AC power now increasingly made available by a DC-to-AC inverter. Any attempt to run AC refrigeration from an inverter will result in substantially greater energy losses than in most other systems—it would be better to install a DC system.

Holding-plate AC refrigeration (Figure 11-12) requires intermittent operation of a generator. It employs one or more tanks filled with a solution that has a freezing point below that of water. The tanks are fitted to the icebox. When the refrigeration unit is running, it freezes the solution in the tanks, then the unit shuts down. The tanks slowly thaw out, absorbing the heat that leaks into the icebox, keeping the box cold. When the tanks have almost defrosted, the unit is turned back on to refreeze them. In a well-designed system, even in the tropics, the tanks will hold down the temperature in the icebox for 24 hours, requiring no more than 1 to 2 hours of refrigeration running time to be refrozen.

However, running an engine in order to spin a generator that is used to power an electric motor that spins a refrigeration compressor that could

(continued on page 475)

Comparative Testing of Insulation

From time to time, some pretty wild claims are made for various types of insulation. I have been particularly interested in comparing the performance of Barrier Ultra-R vacuum panels and Heat Shield to that of Blueboard foam insulation. I know of no testing that specifically measures performance in boat icebox applications, so I set up my own test as follows (Figures 11-11A to 11-11E):

1. I built six iceboxes out of Melamine-faced Masonite, each with an interior volume of 1 cubic foot. They were insulated as follows:
   - Box 1: 1 inch of Blueboard on all 6 sides.
   - Box 2: 1 inch of Blueboard + 1 inch of Heat Shield.
   - Box 3: 2 inches of Blueboard.
   - Box 4: 2 inches of Blueboard + 1 inch of Heat Shield.
   - Box 5: 3 inches of Blueboard.
   - Box 6: 1 inch of Barrier Ultra-R (Figure 11-11A).

2. I gave each box a double closed-cell rubber gasket for the lid.

3. I placed the boxes on two parallel 2-by-4-inch studs to minimize the surface area that was in contact with other surfaces and also to create an air space beneath the boxes. I ran a fan at a slow speed to maintain air circulation in the room and to achieve an even ambient temperature. Most of the tests were conducted in a room with the shades drawn to prevent direct sunlight striking any box, since most boat iceboxes are not subjected to direct sunlight. I did, however, conduct one test using two 500-watt halogen lamps shining on the boxes as a heat source, to simulate high-radiant-heat input.

4. In each box, I suspended a tray punctured with drain holes over a bowl. (The tray was made of plastic for its low thermal mass and conductivity.) I added 32 ounces (2 pounds) of ice to the tray (Figures 11-11B, 11-11C, and 11-11D). I estimated the ice temperature to calculate its heat gain before it reached its melting point.

5. I closed up and sealed the boxes to prevent air leaks.

6. I recorded the ambient air temperature and internal temperature of the boxes at hourly intervals (Figure 11-11E) with a Fluke 51 meter and K-type beaded thermocouples, determined the differential, and calculated the average differential at the end of the test.

7. At the end of the test, I weighed the remaining ice and determined the Btu heat influx on the basis of 144 Btu per pound of ice

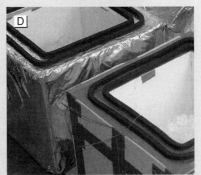

FIGURES 11-11A TO 11-11E. A 1-cubic-foot Barrier Ultra-R icebox undergoing tests (11-11A). Weighing the ice for the test (11-11B). The ice suspended over a bowl (to catch the melt water; 11-11C). Note the double seals on the icebox lids. The icebox in the background (11-11D) has an outer layer of Heat Shield. Five iceboxes in a test (11-11E). Note the thermocouple wires coming out of each box to measure the internal temperature and calculate the temperature differential with the ambient temperature.

melted, plus the heat gain prior to melting.

8. I calculated the K-factor for each box as described in the Testing an Existing Icebox for its Heat Loss sidebar, and from this I derived the R-value of the insulation (the reciprocal of the K-factor).

There are numerous potential sources of error in the methodology I've described, but within reasonable tolerances. For example, the Fluke meter and thermocouples have a basic accuracy in this context of ±0.2°F, which may affect the R-value calculations by up to 0.2—not particularly significant when dealing with materials having an R-value of around 5 or

continued

higher. Similarly I weighed the ice using a kitchen scale with an accuracy of ±0.5 ounce, which could skew the R-values by another 0.15. My estimate of the heat gain of the ice before reaching its melting point (20 Btu for all tests) is particularly crude, but even if it is off by 5 Btu, the calculated R-values will be affected by no more than 0.2. My Masonite icebox liner provided some additional, and unknown, insulation value that skewed all results in favor of the insulation, such that the thinner the insulation, the greater the benefit.

The results I got from one test to another were surprisingly consistent (see Table 11-3 and the subsequent calculations for a sample set of results and calculations; the Barrier Ultra-R box was not in this test), which enabled me to draw some clear conclusions:

• The Blueboard consistently achieved better than R-5 per inch.

• The temperature differential from the inside to the outside of the boxes tracked the ambient temperature in a remarkably consistent fashion, with the better insulation resulting in

a greater temperature differential. That is, the interiors of these boxes were kept cooler than the interiors of the boxes with inferior insulation.

• On the two boxes where 1 inch of Heat Shield was substituted for 1 inch of Blueboard, the temperature differential was lower with the Heat Shield (i.e., the box interiors were warmer) and the heat gain was higher (i.e., the Heat Shield had a lower R-value). In other words, the Heat Shield performed worse than an equivalent thickness of Blueboard. Much to my surprise, although the Heat Shield performed better in the radiant heat test than it did in the conducted and convective heat tests, it still did not outperform the Blueboard. Given the higher cost of Heat Shield and the greater difficulty in installing it, on the basis of these tests, I cannot recommend it.

• The icebox insulated with Barrier Ultra-R had an R-value around R-16—well below the R-50 given by Glacier Bay for its vacuum panels. This was not unexpected, since the

TABLE 11-3. Sample Test Results and Calculations

Time	Ambient Temperature	Box 1		Box 2		Box 3		Box 4		Box 5	
		Internal temperature	Difference with ambient temperature	Internal temperature	Difference with ambient temperature	Internal temperature	Difference with ambient temperature	Internal temperature	Difference with ambient temperature	Internal temperature	Difference with ambient temperature
Initial ice weight		32 ounces		32 ounces		32 ounces		32 ounces		32 ounces	
0730	60.0										
0830	69.0	50.0	19.0	48.2	20.8	48.4	20.6	42.4	26.6	43.8	25.2
1030	72.0	50.6	21.4	47.4	24.6	47.2	24.8	42.2	29.8	42.2	29.8
1130	73.2	51.6	21.6	48.2	25.0	48.0	25.2	42.8	30.4	42.4	30.8
1230	74.8	52.4	22.4	48.8	26.0	48.6	26.2	43.4	31.4	43.0	31.8
1330	75.8	53.4	22.4	49.4	26.4	49.4	26.4	44.2	31.6	43.6	32.2
1430	77.9	55.2	22.7	50.6	27.3	50.2	27.7	45.0	32.9	44.2	33.7
1530	78.0	56.4	21.6	51.6	26.4	50.8	27.2	45.8	32.2	44.6	33.4
1630	77.2	57.8	19.4	52.6	24.6	51.8	25.4	46.8	30.4	45.4	31.8
1730	75.2	58.6	16.6	53.2	22.0	52.2	23.0	47.6	27.6	45.8	29.4
1830	73.2	58.0	15.2	53.0	20.2	51.8	21.4	48.0	25.2	45.8	27.4
1930	72.0	58.0	14.0	52.8	19.2	51.6	20.4	48.0	24.0	45.8	26.2
2030	70.6	57.8	12.8	52.8	17.8	51.6	19.0	48.0	22.6	45.6	25.0
2130	69.2	57.2	12.0	52.6	16.6	51.4	17.8	48.0	21.2	45.6	23.6
2230	68.2	56.8	11.4	52.2	16.0	51.0	17.2	48.0	20.2	45.4	22.8
Ending ice weight		4.75 ounces		8 ounces		10.5 ounces		11.75 ounces		13 ounces	
Ice melted		27.25 ounces		24 ounces		21.5 ounces		20.25 ounces		19 ounces	
Average temperature difference		16.833333°F		20.86°F		21.486666°F		25.74°F		26.873333°F	
Average surface area		7.08 sq. feet		8.33 sq. feet		8.33 sq. feet		9.75 sq. feet		9.75 sq. feet	
Total test time		15 hours		15 hours		15 hours		15 hours		15 hours	

Comparative Testing of Insulation *(continued)*

test procedure, with its exaggerated hatch seal and edge effects relative to the small icebox volume, was especially unfair to Barrier Ultra-R. This is because Barrier Ultra-R is susceptible to heat losses via the edges of the panels (the metalized Mylar skin on the Barrier panels conducts heat out to, and through, the edges), whereas with proper sealing such losses are negligible with Blueboard and Heat Shield. The smaller the Barrier Ultra-R panels, the greater the proportional heat loss through the edges; and the smaller the icebox, the greater the length of the edges relative to the volume of the box (e.g., a box of 1 cubic foot has 12 feet of edges—a 1:12 ratio; a box of 4 cubic feet has 24 feet of edges—a 1:6 ratio; and a box of 9 cubic feet has 36 feet of edges—a 1:4 ratio). Nevertheless, the tests showed that Barrier Ultra-R meets its intended purpose of providing effective icebox insulation with just 1 inch of material as long as the vacuum in the panels is never compromised. Larger panels and boxes will undoubtedly achieve a higher R-value.

R-value calculations:

- Box 1: [(27.25 x 144)/16 [ounces] + 20 [Btu to freezing point—32°F] = 265.25/7.08 [surface area] = 37.464689/16.833333 [temperature difference] = 2.2256251/15 [time] = 0.148375. Reciprocal = R-6.74/1 [insulation thickness] = 6.74 per inch.

- Box 2: [(24 x 144)/16] + 20 = 236/8.33 = 28.331332/20.86 = 1.3581654/15 = 0.0905443. Reciprocal = R-11.04/2 = 5.52 per inch.

- Box 3: [(21.5 x 144)/16] + 20 = 213.5/8.33 = 25.630252/21.486666 = 1.1928445/15 = 0.0795229. Reciprocal = R-12.57/2 = 6.29 per inch.

- Box 4: [(20.25 x 144)/16] + 20 = 202.25/9.75 = 20.743589/25.74 = 0.8058892/15 = 0.0537259. Reciprocal = R-18.61/3 = 6.20 per inch.

- Box 5: [(19 x 144)/16] + 20 = 191/9.75 = 19.589743/26.873333 = 0.7289658/15 = 0.0485977. Reciprocal = R-20.58/3 = 6.86 per inch.

(continued from page 472)
have been driven directly off the engine in the first place involves a lot of unnecessary energy losses! What is more, the directly engine-driven compressor will, in most instances, have a higher output than the AC unit and therefore a potentially reduced holding-plate pull-down time (depending on the ability of the holding plates to absorb additional compressor output—see the Engine-Driven Refrigeration section below).

In other words, it is rarely worthwhile to run a generator simply for refrigeration purposes, but if the generator is to be run for other loads (e.g., water making, water heating, or cooking) regularly enough and long enough to support the refrigeration system, and has surplus capacity that can usefully be diverted to AC refrigeration, then holding-plate AC refrigeration is attractive. The AC unit will, of course, be operable with shore power. In addition, it will use a hermetic

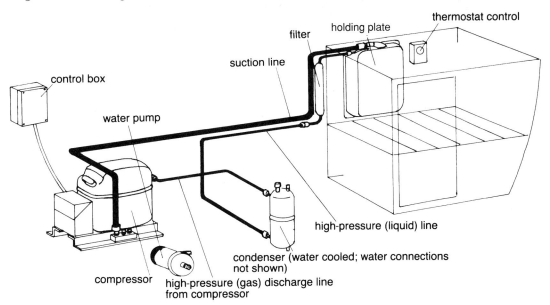

FIGURE 11-12. A hermetically sealed AC compressor with holding plates. *(Frigoboat)*

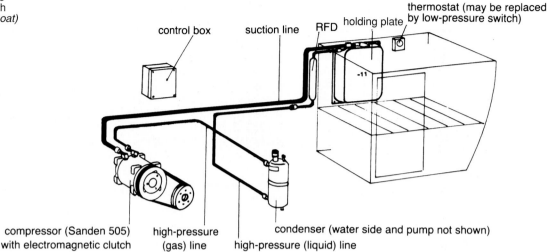

FIGURE 11-13. Engine-driven refrigeration with holding plates. *(Frigoboat)*

control box · suction line · RFD · holding plate · thermostat (may be replaced by low-pressure switch)

-11

compressor (Sanden 505) with electromagnetic clutch · high-pressure (gas) line · high-pressure (liquid) line · condenser (water side and pump not shown)

compressor, enabling a system to be built that will not suffer from the small leaks that sometimes plague the belt-driven compressors used in engine-driven and most high-capacity DC refrigeration systems.

The AC system will take a substantial potential load off the DC system, which on some boats will enable the battery banks and other equipment to be downsized with significant savings in weight and volume.

Engine-driven refrigeration. Holding plates are used once again, but this time the refrigeration compressor is directly belt driven from an engine instead of being driven by an electric motor, eliminating the intermediary energy losses (Figure 11-13; see, for example, Sea Frost—www.seafrost.com). Automotive air-conditioning compressors are invariably used, resulting in extremely high nominal refrigerating and freezing capabilities.

On the surface of things, the beauty of such a system is that given the horsepower available with most engines, a large and powerful refrigeration compressor can be used, minimizing the holding-plate freeze-down time and the engine-running time. Given that the compressor is directly driven by the engine, engine-driven refrigeration also appears to be the most efficient.

Holding plates: the limiting factor. Unfortunately for refrigeration systems of the size commonly found on pleasure boats, neither of these propositions—power and efficiency—is necessarily true! The reason is related to the rate at which heat can be withdrawn from a holding plate—i.e., the rate at which the plate can be frozen. This rate is largely a function of the surface area of the evaporator tubing in the holding plate, the spacing of these tubes (the closer together, the

faster the rate of heat removal), and the temperature differential between the refrigerant in the evaporator coil and the solution in the holding plate.

Except in large systems with multiple holding plates, the rate of heat removal is always well below the nominal refrigerating capability of the compressor on the system—in other words, no matter what size refrigeration compressor you put on the engine, only a certain amount of its capacity can be used, and the holding-plate freeze time cannot be accelerated beyond a certain point. This, in turn, means that regardless of compressor capacity, for most systems the engine will have to be run at least 1 hour a day and almost always longer than this (in the tropics, 2 or more hours are common).

If a high-output alternator is put on the same engine and wired to a large-enough battery bank to absorb the alternator's output, even with the added inefficiencies in DC refrigeration (the alternator charges batteries that supply an electric motor that spins a compressor that could have been turned by the engine in the first place), sufficient energy can be put into a battery bank to meet the daily refrigeration load in less engine-running time than needed for engine-driven refrigeration. In other words, if minimizing engine-running time is a goal, the DC approach often does a better job of capturing the available power from the engine than the engine-driven approach does. The net result is that although from a refrigeration perspective DC refrigeration is less efficient, from a whole-boat energy analysis, it will be more efficient on those boats where the goal is to minimize engine-running time.

Consider also the fact that the "typical" cost of buying even a small marine diesel engine and having it professionally installed is anywhere from $12,000 on up, and the life expectancy of such an engine is 5,000 hours of running time on up. As a result, the capital cost—excluding maintenance and fuel bills—of running the engine is almost always at least $1 per hour, and all too often it can be $3 or more per hour. That's a significant overhead if the engine is being run solely for refrigeration purposes.

Other considerations. As noted, this argument breaks down if the engine will be regularly run for other reasons (as it is, for example, on many charter boats), in which case engine-driven refrigeration can be tacked on as just another load. The argument also does not hold in the case of large iceboxes with multiple holding plates that have the capacity to absorb a high compressor output (note that the holding plates made by Glacier Bay have the highest heat absorption capability of any on the market; Figures 11-14A, 11-14B, and 11-14C illustrate three different holding plates). In this case, engine-driven refrigeration may be the best choice. However, it does suffer from one other major drawback—you must run the engine to refrigerate, even at dockside.

Another issue is the nature of the solution in the holding plate. Some plates use an antifreeze solution, which freezes progressively as the temperature is lowered (and as a result does not hold uniform temperatures in an icebox), while others use a *eutectic* solution, which freezes and melts at a constant temperature (Figure 11-15).

Sometimes an engine-driven system is combined with a DC or AC system (for use when the engine is not running or at dockside) by adding

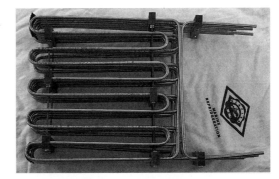

FIGURE 11-14A. The evaporator coil from a Glacier Bay holding plate, with six coils in parallel.

FIGURE 11-14B. A Dole Refrigerating Company holding plate. It also has a relatively closely spaced coil but in a single loop (as opposed to multiple loops in parallel). *(Dole Refrigerating Company)*

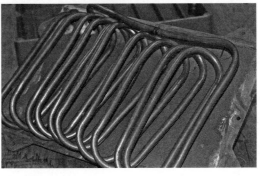

FIGURE 11-14C. An evaporator coil from a Sea Frost holding plate.

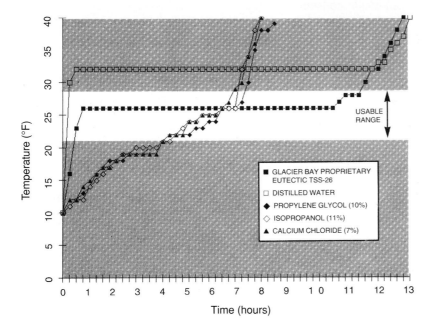

FIGURE 11-15. Thaw temperatures for holding-plate solutions. *(Glacier Bay)*

Legend:
- ■ GLACIER BAY PROPRIETARY EUTECTIC TSS-26
- □ DISTILLED WATER
- ◆ PROPYLENE GLYCOL (10%)
- ◇ ISOPROPANOL (11%)
- ▲ CALCIUM CHLORIDE (7%)

USABLE RANGE

Temperature (°F) vs. Time (hours)

FIGURE 11-16. Constant-cycling DC refrigeration. Note the substantial air duct to the air-cooled condenser. If this becomes obstructed, or there is not an equally sized duct to disperse the hot air from the other side of the condenser, performance will suffer drastically. *(Adler Barbour)*

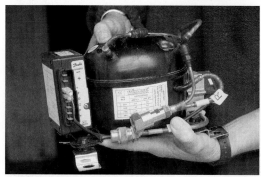

FIGURE 11-17. The popular Danfoss BD50 compressor.

a second evaporator coil to the holding plates. The trade-off here is the volume of the holding plate occupied by the second evaporator coil (reducing the plate's overall capacity, and sometimes the length and the rate of heat removal of the primary, engine-driven evaporator coil) as

well as the added complexity and cost versus the ability to run the unit at dockside without cranking the engine.

Although expensive, an engine-driven unit will compare very favorably in terms of cost with high-capacity DC systems and even small DC systems if the boat's batteries and charging systems have to be upgraded to support DC refrigeration. (In this case, given the weight and bulk of the added batteries, the engine-driven system will also compare very favorably on these grounds.)

Constant-cycling DC refrigeration. A small refrigeration unit (Figure 11-16) is permanently connected to the ship's batteries and controlled by a thermostat in the icebox. Every time the temperature rises beyond a set point, the unit kicks on until the icebox is cooled down, then the unit switches off; it constantly cycles on and off (just as a household refrigerator does).

Aside from household appliances, constant-cycling DC refrigeration is the cheapest initial option. Norcold (www.norcold.com) and others build drop-in units similar to household refrigeration units (many of which can also be run off AC power when available), or a refrigeration unit can be added to a purpose-built icebox. Either way, most units currently available use Danfoss BD35 and BD50 variable-speed compressors with HFC-134a refrigerant (Figure 11-17; http://compressors.danfoss.com).

Constant-Cycling Capacity Calculations

For many of the latest generation constant-cycling DC units, the limiting factor in the system is not the compressor's capacity, but the rate at which the evaporator plate can pull heat out of the icebox. For the typical aluminum evaporator plate (similar to what is in a household refrigerator), this rate is somewhere between 1 and 7 Btu per square foot, per °F temperature differential between the plate and the icebox per hour. (This huge range—1 to 7 Btu—reflects a lack of good data, differences in evaporator construction techniques, and the insulating effect of ice buildup on the plates; assuming 3.5 Btu is conservative in most applications.)

Let's assume an evaporator plate with a total surface area of 3 square feet, with a temperature differential of 25°F between the plate surface and the icebox interior (this is a reasonable assumption for a refrigerator; on a freezer, a 15°F temperature differential would be a better number). This will remove around 260 Btu per hour (3 x 25 x 3.5 = 262.5). If the

refrigeration unit is running for 45 minutes an hour, the total amount of heat removed in 24 hours will be (262.5 x 24 x 45)/60 = 4,725 Btu.

We can work this backward. Let's say we have an estimated heat load of 5,000 Btu on a refrigerator (the maximum I currently recommend for constant-cycling DC refrigeration), and we want to limit refrigeration run time to 45 minutes an hour. Every hour we must remove 5,000/24 = 208 Btu of heat. To keep the running time to 45 minutes an hour, the rate of heat removal must be (208 x 60)/45 = 278 Btu per hour (in terms of watts per hour, this is 278/3.413 = 81.4 watts per hour). If the temperature differential between the icebox interior and evaporator plate is 25°F, we need an evaporator plate with a surface area of 278/(25 x 3.5) = 3.18 square feet. This is a moderately large evaporator plate (although maybe not as big as it seems, because in many situations both surfaces will be absorbing heat, doubling the effective surface area), demonstrating that

Constant-Cycling Capacity Calculations (*continued*)

we are approaching the practical limits of the system. If the evaporator plate is smaller, the refrigeration unit will run longer.

If we run the same numbers for a freezer that has a heat load of 3,500 Btu (once again, the maximum I currently recommend), and a temperature differential of 15°F, with a 75% duty cycle, we end up with an evaporator plate area of 3.7 square feet if only one surface is absorbing heat. The plate will almost certainly be mounted on stand-offs, so both sides will be absorbing heat, in which case the plate needs to be approximately 2 square feet.

Let's assume we are using one of the largest plates commonly available (from Frigoboat—www.frigoboat.com—Figure 11-18), which is 40 by 16 inches (101 by 40 cm)—i.e., 4.4 square feet on each side (0.44 sq. m). If mounted on stand-offs, its heat absorption rate in a freezer is 4.4 x 2 x 15 x 3.5 = 462 Btu per hour, which is (462 x 45)/60 = 346.5 Btu on a 75% duty cycle (i.e., the refrigeration unit runs 45 minutes in the hour). This results in a potential heat absorption of 346.5 x 24 = 8,316 Btu per day. Note that Isotherm (www.isotherm.com) manufactures even larger evaporator plates (up to 59 by 17 inches [150 by 43 cm]).

In practice, at the kind of temperatures found in freezer applications, the refrigeration compressor will not have anywhere near the capacity to pull down the plate at a rate of 462 Btu per hour (the lower the evaporator temperature, the lower the capacity of a compressor; see Table 11-4). In this case, the compressor has now become the limiting factor in the system—the refrigeration run time will be commensurately longer. (Note: The new Danfoss BD80 compressor, which has 50% more capacity than the BD50 used in the following tables, will change this relationship.)

For example, let's take a Danfoss BD50 in a freezer application. We want to hold the box temperature at 10°F. We assume a 15°F temperature differential between the box and the evaporator plate, which means the plate is at –5°F. Using the –10°F column in Table 11-4

FIGURE 11-18. Frigoboat's largest evaporator plate. It can be bent to wrap around the inside of an icebox.

(because there is no –5°F column), we find the maximum rated output of the compressor at this evaporator temperature is 245 Btu per hour. For a 3,500 Btu capacity, the unit will run for 3,500/245 = 14.3 hours. To handle this compressor output, we need an evaporator plate with a minimum surface area of 245/(15 x 3.5) = 4.7 square feet (or 2.4 square feet if mounted on stand-offs).

Please note that these are pretty crude numbers based upon arguable assumptions! However, in the absence of anything better, the methodology outlined provides some kind of a mechanism for calculating evaporator plate sizes and approximate refrigeration unit running times, from which the approximate load on the DC system can be calculated.

TABLE 11-4. Danfoss BD50 Vital Statistics: Capacity in Btu per Hour (watts in parentheses)

Compressor RPM	Evaporator Temperature					
	–20°F/–29°C	–10°F/–23°C	0°F/–18°C	10°F/–12°C	20°F/–7°C	30°F/–1°C
2,000	95 (28)	142 (42)	201 (59)	273 (80)	359 (105)	458 (134)
2,500	119 (35)	176 (52)	247 (72)	335 (139)	442 (130)	570 (167)
3,000	142 (42)	211 (62)	296 (87)	401 (117)	529 (155)	682 (200)
3,500	167 (49)	245 (72)	342 (100)	464 (136)	612 (179)	790 (231)

Note: This assumes a condensing temperature of 130°F/55°C, an ambient and suction gas temperature of 90°F/32°C, and a liquid temperature of 90°F/32°C (the U.S.'s ASHRAE standard). For refrigeration applications, the 0°F or 10°F columns are reasonable capacity guides; for freezer applications, the –10°F column is reasonable.

(Courtesy Danfoss)

These systems have a limited refrigerating capability. I would consider the upper limit to be 5,000 Btu per day in a refrigerator and 3,500 Btu per day in a freezer. This refrigerator number (5,000 Btu per day) is much higher than I have previously recommended, while I have previously flat-out recommended against constant-cycling DC freezers. My change in positions reflects a considerable increase in the capacity of Danfoss compressors over the past 10 years, coupled with an equivalent improvement in efficiency. The newly introduced (2005) Danfoss BD80 compressor will raise these Btu limits for both refrigerators and freezers (my guess is to around 8,000 Btu per day for a refrigerator and 5,000 Btu per day for a freezer).

Power drain. In terms of power consumption, a good general rule is that in refrigeration use, with an air-cooled system, assume 5.0 Btu of heat removal for 1 watt-hour of energy consumed—i.e., 5,000 Btu = 5,000/5.0 = 1,000 watt-hours, which is 1,000/12 = 83.3 Ah at 12 volts, and 1,000/24 = 41.6 Ah at 24 volts. (The rate of heat removal per watt of energy consumed by the compressor will be somewhat higher with water cooling, but will be offset by the energy absorbed by a water pump, if one is fitted; see below.) Remember to add at least 10% for inefficiencies in the charging process.

In freezer use, assume 4.0 Btu of heat removal for 1 watt-hour of energy consumed—i.e., 3,500 Btu = 3,500/4.0 = 875 watt-hours.

Table 11-5 gives more precise numbers for air-cooled systems based on reasonably conservative performance numbers (once again, with water cooling the heat removal will be somewhat higher but will be offset by the energy

absorbed by a water pump, if one is fitted).

Compressor speed. Note that the slower the compressor's operating speed, the more efficient it is (i.e., more Btu of heat are removed from an icebox per watt-hour of energy consumed). There are significant benefits to be had from running a compressor longer hours at slower speeds, rather than shorter hours at higher speeds (as long as the energy saved at the compressor is not used up by running a water pump for longer hours; for more on this, see below). Whatever the load, unless there is some kind of a continuous battery-charging device that keeps up with the demands of the refrigeration unit, this kind of a battery drain will cycle the ship's batteries on a daily basis. Table 11-6 gives the current consumption of a BD50 compressor running on 12 volts (for 24 volts, halve these numbers):

The DC system. The batteries on a boat used for weekend cruising can be recharged at dockside during the week. But on those boats that engage in more extended cruising, if there is no constant battery-charging source (either from running the boat's main engine on a powerboat or from a battery charger powered by an AC generator), a high-capacity DC system is needed to support the refrigeration load. The DC system will include such things as deep-cycle batteries, a high-output alternator, a multistep regulator, and maybe a wind generator with backup solar panels. If not already installed, such a DC system will cost several times more than the constant-cycling DC refrigeration unit!

Appropriate choices. Constant-cycling DC refrigeration is therefore an appropriate choice for a boat that has relatively modest refrigeration needs, is used for weekend cruising, has contin-

---

TABLE 11-5. Danfoss BD50 Vital Statistics: Btu of Heat Removed per Watt-Hour of Energy Consumed

Compressor RPM	Evaporator Temperature					
	−20°F/−29°C	−10°F/−23°C	0°F/−18°C	10°F/−12°C	20°F/−7°C	30°F/−1°C
2,000	3.49	4.09	4.81	5.57	6.31	7.00
2,500	3.47	3.97	4.58	5.28	6.05	6.88
3,000	3.43	3.93	4.55	5.26	6.05	6.89
3,500	3.37	3.91	4.54	5.23	5.94	6.66

Note: This assumes a condensing temperature of 130°F/55°C, an ambient and suction gas temperature of 90°F/32°C, and a liquid temperature of 90°F/32°C (the U.S.'s ASHRAE standard). For refrigeration applications, the 0°F or 10°F columns are reasonable guides; for freezer applications, the −10°F column is reasonable.

(Courtesy Danfoss)

TABLE 11-6. Danfoss BD50 Vital Statistics: Current (amp) Consumption at 12 Volts

Compressor RPM	Evaporator Temperature					
	−20°F/−29°C	−10°F/−23°C	0°F/−18°C	10°F/−12°C	20°F/−7°C	30°F/−1°C
2,000	2.28	2.87	3.50	4.18	4.90	5.65
2,500	2.86	3.65	4.45	5.26	6.10	6.94
3,000	3.52	4.43	5.37	6.33	7.31	8.32
3,500	4.20	5.18	6.24	7.39	8.61	9.91

(Courtesy Danfoss)

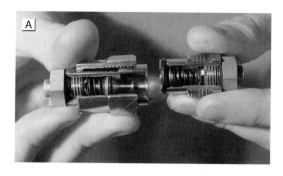

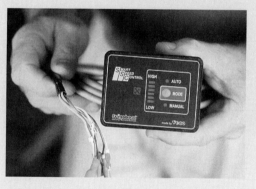

FIGURES 11-19A, 11-19B, AND 11-19C. Frigoboat's quick-connect couplings and precharged tubing. Isotherm and others have similar fittings.

uously operating battery-charging devices, or already has a high-capacity DC system. Given a powerful-enough DC system, large refrigeration needs can be met through multiple units and iceboxes. If the heat load of a large icebox exceeds the capacity of a single constant-cycling refrigeration unit, install two or more units.

In terms of installation issues and complexities, an increasing number of units come precharged with refrigerant, with the various subcomponents precharged, and a variety of quick-connect fittings that allow you to assemble the unit more or less without the use of tools and without having to evacuate and charge anything (Figures 11-19A, 11-19B, and 11-19C). This is

"Smart" Speed Devices

The slower Danfoss BD50 and BD35 compressors are run, the more efficiently they operate (see Table 11-5). Whereas in the past, much refrigeration design work was premised on running compressors at full speed for a 50% duty cycle (e.g., the compressor runs for 30 minutes in the hour), the focus nowadays tends to be on running the compressor at lower speeds (and outputs) closer to 100% of the time. To do this, Frigoboat has developed its Smart Speed Control (SSC; Figure 11-20), Danfoss has a similar Adaptive Energy Optimizer (AEO), and Isotherm has its Automatic Start Up (ASU).

The AEO is illustrative. It starts a compressor at around its mid-speed (2,600 rpm) and then ramps up the speed 12.5 rpm every minute (i.e., the speed increases by 12.5 x 10 = 125 rpm every 10 minutes; Figure 11-21). If the icebox has not been pulled down to the thermostat's shutdown temperature within 60 minutes, the compressor is switched to full speed (3,500 rpm).

When the shutdown temperature is reached and the unit is restarted, it does so at the shutdown speed minus 400 (i.e., in this case 3,500 – 400 = 3,100 rpm) and then ramps up again at 12.5 rpm every minute. After the initial pull-down

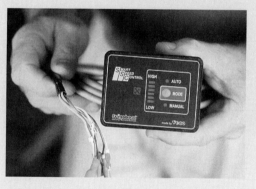

FIGURE 11-20. Frigoboat's Smart Speed Control.

from a warm box, the icebox should be cold, so the unit will not run long enough to increase the speed by 400 rpm before it shuts down again. Let's say it stops at 3,300 rpm. Next time it starts, it will do so at 3,300 – 400 = 2,900 rpm.

The compressor is now starting from a slower speed, resulting in a lower refrigeration output, so it will take longer than the last time to pull the icebox down to the shutdown temperature. However it will still probably not run long enough to increase the speed by 400 rpm, so the next time it restarts, it will be even slower, and the pull-down time will be even

continued

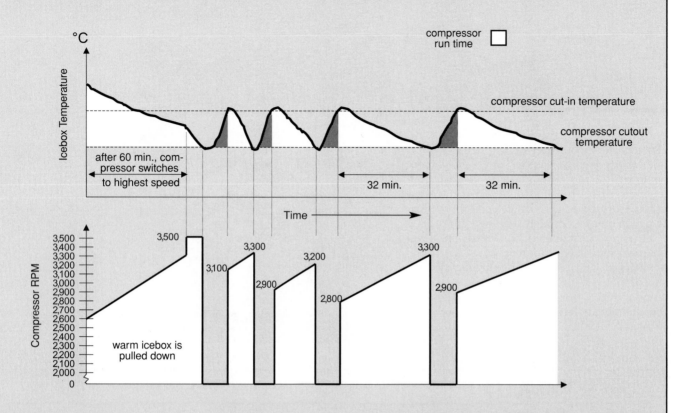

FIGURE 11-21. The Danfoss Adaptive Energy Optimizer (AEO), showing the relationship between icebox temperature, compressor run time, and compressor speed. (Danfoss)

longer. It keeps this up until the pull-down time is 32 minutes, at which point it reaches equilibrium. (Over 32 minutes, if the speed increases at 12.5 rpm per minute, the total increase is 12.5 x 32 = 400 rpm; this then drops 400 rpm at the next start.)

This process extends compressor running times, but at reduced speeds, significantly boosting overall efficiency. It has the added benefit in warm climates, when the *head* pressure on a compressor is high at start-up, of keeping down the initial load on the compressor. This greatly reduces the risk of burning out the compressor electronics (which is one of the more common causes of failure on older systems).

Anytime the power to the unit is shut down (as opposed to the thermostat shutting it off), the controller starts the process again (i.e., at 2,600 rpm). If you load the icebox with warm produce, some controllers have a manual override that enables the refrigeration unit to be switched to continuous full output until (manually) reset to automatic—a useful feature.

The Frigoboat SSC is similar to the Danfoss AEO in that it ramps up the compressor speed from a relatively slow start. It measures the time it takes to pull an icebox down and compares this to an ideal operating profile, adjust-

ing the compressor speed accordingly. The aim is to keep the compressor running for approximately 50 minutes in the hour. In point of fact, Rob Warren of Frigoboat says the ideal would be to keep the compressor running continuously and then vary the speed to match the load, but customers would be disconcerted by the lack of any shutdown time.

The Isotherm ASU monitors battery voltage and icebox temperature. Anytime voltage is above 13.2 volts (on a 12-volt system), indicating some charging device is online, the ASU ramps up the compressor to full speed. In the case of holding-plate systems, when the voltage is above 13.2, the plate is frozen. With voltages below 12.8 (i.e., no charging device online), it shuts down the compressor until the holding plate is defrosted, and then runs the compressor at the slowest speed commensurate with maintaining the desired box temperature (i.e., no attempt is made to refreeze the holding plate). Given a low-output charging device (such as a solar panel), anytime battery voltage starts to creep above 12.8, the ASU will ramp up the compressor (until the holding plate is frozen) to the extent that the charging device will support the added load without the battery voltage falling below 12.8 volts.

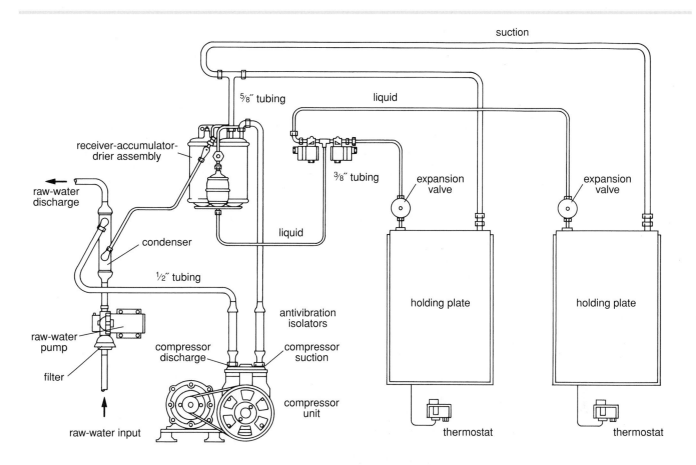

FIGURE 11-22A. A ½ hp DC holding-plate refrigeration unit. *(Jim Sollers, adapted from a drawing courtesy Glacier Bay)*

an excellent innovation. If the connections can also be undone without losing the refrigerant charge (some can), it enables you to change out subsystems in the boonies without special equipment, which is really handy.

Holding-plate DC refrigeration. Holding plates for refrigeration systems with relatively light loads can be pulled down over time by the small Danfoss compressors found in constant-cycling units (see, for example, Isotherm and Technautics—www.technauticsinc.com), with some potential efficiency gains.

However, the addition of holding plates increases cost, weight, and complexity in most systems (the holding plates require expansion valves, which must be "tuned" to the system, as opposed to the capillary tubes used in other small DC systems, which require no user interaction; Isotherm, however, uses capillary tubes), and the plates take up otherwise usable space in the icebox. Also, holding plates do not hold as consistent a temperature in the icebox as evaporator plates. In the end, the benefits of holding plates over an evaporator plate in small DC systems are arguable.

High-capacity DC systems. To take full advantage of a holding-plate system, a larger compressor is needed, commonly driven by a ½ hp DC motor (Figures 11-22A and 11-22B; see, for example, Glacier Bay and Sea Frost). A suitable bank of good-quality deep-cycle batteries can sustain a refrigeration load of up to ½ hp for

FIGURE 11-22B. Holding plates in the icebox on our old Pacific Seacraft 40, driven by a Glacier Bay ½ hp DC unit.

Most constant-cycling DC refrigeration units come with an air-cooled condenser—the vital component that dissipates the heat taken out of an icebox. In warmer climates, the air temperature in a closed-up boat can rapidly climb to 100°F/37.8°C or more, rendering an air-cooled condenser increasingly ineffective just when the refrigeration demands of the icebox are greatest. Unless the condenser is built with a large-enough surface area to handle the high ambient temperature (many are not), the unit will start to run almost continuously, draining the batteries. It may still not refrigerate properly, and there is a distinct risk of burning up the compressor. If you are likely to venture into warmer climates using air-cooled refrigeration on your boat, pay particular attention to the surface area and the thickness of the condenser when choosing one unit over another.

FIGURES 11-23A AND 11-23B. Frigoboat's keel cooler. Note the zincs for protection against galvanic corrosion (which may not be necessary given that this is bronze; see Chapter 5) and the grounding tab, which must be connected to the boat's grounding system to protect against stray-current corrosion.

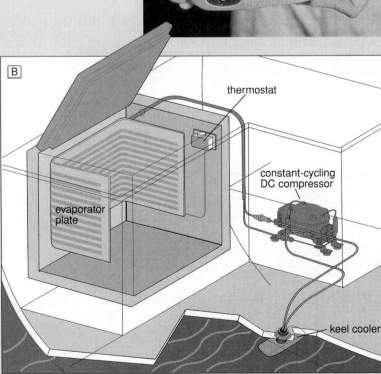

thermostat

constant-cycling DC compressor

evaporator plate

keel cooler

Considerable improvements in the efficiency of any air-cooled condenser will be achieved if the temperature of the cooling air is lowered and/or the speed of the airflow over the condenser is accelerated. If you are planning to cruise your boat in warmer climates, at the least consider ducting in air from the coolest part of the boat to achieve the greatest possible airflow over the condenser. WAECO Adler Barbour (www.waecousa.com), Sea Frost, and others have add-on kits to achieve this (WAECO calls its kit a Booster Power Duct Kit; Isotherm has an Air Hose Ventilation Kit).

Your other option, if your existing condenser is undersized, is to fit a water-cooled condenser. Water is a far more efficient cooling medium than air, and even in the tropics, the water temperature rarely exceeds 85°F/30°C.

If the water-cooling circuit requires a water pump (not all do; see below), the critical ambient air temperature at which water cooling becomes more energy efficient than air cooling (in spite of the added energy consumption of the water pump attached to the water-cooled condenser) is generally around 95°F/35°C. Note that this temperature is the temperature of either the space occupied by the air-cooled condenser or of the air used to cool the condenser if the air is ducted in from elsewhere; it is not the temperature in the boat (which may be considerably cooler).

Below 95°F/35°C ambient air temperature, a pump-driven water-cooled condenser is frequently less efficient in terms of overall power consumption than an air-cooled condenser, especially a well-designed air-cooled condenser, because of the added power drain of the water pump. As the temperature rises above 95°F, water cooling becomes progressively more efficient. By 110°F/43°C, it is significantly more efficient.

The question then becomes, at what point does the increasing efficiency of water cooling justify the added expense, installation requirements, complexity, maintenance (including winterizing), and likelihood of problems developing? In practice, water cooling, especially with a water pump, is difficult to justify, particularly if you can duct in cooler air from elsewhere in the boat to achieve a similar result with less complexity and fewer maintenance issues.

Through-Hull Condensers and Keel Coolers

In recent years, Isotherm and Frigoboat have introduced a couple of interesting variations on water cooling for constant-cycling DC refrigeration units. Both dispense with a water pump.

Isotherm installs a condensing coil in a through-hull; Frigoboat adds a small keel cooler to the outside of the hull and the refrigerant is circulated through that. In other words, in both cases the refrigerant is taken to the water rather than bringing the water to the refrigerant with a pump.

At anchor, Isotherm's through-hull version (called "SP" for "self-pumping") requires the boat to have some minimal rocking motion in order to constantly change the water in the through-hull. If this does not occur, the water steadily heats up, rendering the refrigeration unit increasingly ineffective. The through-hull must be offset as far as possible from the boat's centerline (this maximizes the rocking action in a calm anchorage). The hose attached to the through-hull must have a minimum inside diameter (ID) of 1½ inches (38 mm); generally, a galley sink drain is used.

Frigoboat's keel cooler (Figures 11-23A and 11-23B) does not suffer from this lack of boat motion problem to the same extent, but nevertheless will benefit from being offset from the centerline. In some waters it may require scrubbing to remove biofouling. (The extent to which fouling interferes with its heat-exchange properties is under investigation; it may not be as great as many assume.)

Keel coolers have to be sized for a broad range of water temperatures and optimized for typical temperatures. As a result, they have limitations in extreme conditions. In very cold water (like that in Maine or the Baltic at the beginning of the boating season), there is a tendency for the refrigerant in the system to puddle out in the keel cooler, making it difficult to establish refrigerant flow at the start of the refrigeration cycle.

In most situations, either approach represents an excellent innovation, providing efficiency benefits over traditional water cooling by eliminating the energy drain of the water pump, as well as simplifying the installation and removing the maintenance (including winterizing) associated with a water pump.

Through-hull condensers and keel coolers must be grounded to the boat's common ground point. If this is not done, any kind of a DC electrical short (e.g., from a thermostat) to any of the copper tubing in the refrigeration system can put stray current into the water via the through-hull or keel cooler. The current will find its way back to battery negative via the propeller and propeller shaft or a grounded through-hull. In the process, it will destroy the through-hull or keel cooler in short order (see Chapter 5).

---

extended periods (1 to 2 hours at a time). The current draw of the unit will be around 40 amps at 12 volts (half this at 24 volts) on a fully defrosted holding plate, tapering down to as little as 20 amps at the end of the freeze cycle. Such a system will handle substantial refrigeration and freezer loads (up to ten times the small, constant-cycling units). However, it will only function if backed with a continuous DC charging source or a high-capacity DC system (Sea Frost recommends a minimum battery bank of 660 Ah at 12 volts). The refrigeration control circuitry should include the ability to turn the unit on and top it off whenever the engine is cranked. This will optimize engine-running time and minimize the load on the batteries.

A large-capacity DC holding-plate system is expensive, even ignoring the cost of upgrading the DC system should that be necessary, but it has a considerably greater refrigerating capability. It may also be more efficient than a constant-cycling system or a small DC compressor coupled to holding plates, which means that although it consumes far more power when running, it will provide an equivalent refrigeration capability for less overall power consumption, or else a greater capability for the same overall power consumption. (Although data is available that quantifies the efficiency gains of larger compressors over smaller compressors, I know of no data that compares the likely lower efficiency of a holding plate to an evaporator plate. As a result I have not seen any data to quantify the overall efficiency differences between the systems.) If the DC system includes a large wind generator and/or a large-enough array of solar panels, the needs of substantial iceboxes can be met when cruising without having to crank the engine.

Constant-cycling DC refrigeration versus holding-plate refrigeration. For a decade or more I have been an advocate of high-capacity holding-plate DC refrigeration rather than constant-cycling refrigeration because the holding-plate system has had considerably greater capacity and efficiency. I have recommended such a system to numerous people, designed one for a number of boats, and put it on my own boats. However in recent years, technology and legal changes have altered the cost-benefit analysis on which this recommendation was based. In particular:

- The relative efficiency of the small compressors used in constant-cycling units versus the larger versions used in holding-plate systems has improved.

- The efficiency of the small compressors can be further boosted by a variable-speed device such as the Smart Speed Control (SSC) from Frigoboat, the Adaptive Energy Optimizer (AEO) from Danfoss, or the Automatic Start Up (ASU) from Isotherm (see the "Smart" Speed Devices sidebar). Note that these efficiency gains are made by running compressors for longer hours at lower loads and thus can only be realized on air-cooled units or those with a water-cooled circuit without a water pump (i.e., a keel cooler or through-hull condenser—see the Air Cooling Versus Water Cooling sidebar). The reason is that if a water pump is run for longer hours, its added power drain cancels out the efficiency gains of the compressor.

- The refrigeration capability of the constant-cycling compressors has increased by over 50% in recent years (and with the introduction of the new Danfoss BD80, it has just gone up another 50%). In the past, in warm climates, the available constant-cycling refrigeration units were often marginal in terms of their capacity to handle even midsized refrigerators and freezers and reliably maintain the necessary temperatures for a dependable freezer. This is no longer the case.

- Then we have the changes in the insulation world. Improved insulation around an icebox considerably reduces the refrigeration load, enabling it to be met by a lower-capacity refrigeration unit. If you are on a limited budget but want to improve the efficiency of your refrigeration unit, upgrade the insulation. You will achieve the same increase in efficiency as you would by investing in an expensive high-capacity holding-plate system and at less cost.

When you put these things together and look at them in light of the fact that the high-capacity holding-plate DC refrigeration systems are commonly four times as expensive as a constant-cycling unit, it is difficult to justify the added cost for many boats. However, it must be recognized that:

- If superinsulation is part of the equation, it can rapidly eat up a large part of the cost savings.
- Although they are better than they used to be, the constant-cycling units still have a limited ability to handle refrigeration loads; for tropical cruising, the upper limit on a well-insulated icebox is somewhere around 15 cubic feet for a refrigerator and 5 cubic feet for a freezer. Larger iceboxes will need either some

kind of a holding-plate system or more than one constant-cycling unit in the icebox. Another approach is to break up the refrigeration load into multiple smaller iceboxes using individual constant-cycling units.

Spin-off benefits. There are spin-off benefits associated with constant-cycling refrigeration that need to be factored into the equation:

- First and foremost is the maintenance issue. Constant-cycling refrigeration utilizes what are known as *hermetic* compressors. They are sealed inside the refrigeration unit, as opposed to the externally driven compressors that have predominated in high-capacity holding-plate systems, including engine-driven systems. The latter have seals that often leak refrigerant over time; the former do not. The elimination of the leaks with hermetic compressors becomes ever more important as the legal framework within which refrigeration units are operated is tightened (this is especially the case in Europe), increasing the cost and difficulty of servicing units. (Note that all AC systems—constant cycling and holding plate—also have hermetic compressors, as does the Glacier Bay Micro HPS system; see below.)

- Most of the constant-cycling units employ a *capillary tube* to dispense the refrigerant. A capillary tube has no moving parts, in contrast to the expansion valves used in most holding-plate systems that not only have a number of moving parts but also require considerable expertise to set up and adjust properly. In general, as long as it is properly installed, you can pretty much fit and forget a constant-cycling unit (much as with a household refrigerator), whereas the high-capacity holding-plate units require some maintenance and are more prone to trouble. In the event the system fails and needs replacing, the constant-cycling unit will be cheaper and easier to replace. (Note that capillary tubes are less efficient than expansion valves, but on the low-capacity constant-cycling units, the difference is not that significant.)

- Constant-cycling refrigeration eliminates holding plates and replaces them with a thin evaporator plate or box, the same as the evaporator plate or box in a household refrigerator. This frees up a fair amount of volume in the icebox. Between the weight savings on the refrigeration unit itself and on the holding plates, you will remove a considerable amount of weight from the system (generally at least 100 pounds). When a unit is first turned on, an evaporator plate pulls down much faster than a holding plate, and it holds a much more consistent icebox temperature than most holding plates.

- Because constant-cycling units have a relatively low-capacity compressor, the demands on the cooling system (the condenser, an essential component in the refrigeration process) are considerably less than the demands of the high-capacity DC systems. As noted above, this lower demand can be met by an adequately sized air-cooled condenser, a small keel cooler installed on the outside of the hull, or a through-hull condenser, removing the need for a water-cooling circuit along with its pump and associated energy drain and maintenance.

Hybrids. If this were the end of the story, it would make a pretty strong argument for constant-cycling DC units in many applications where previously holding-plate refrigeration was recommended. But the simple lines I have drawn are blurred by recently introduced hybrid systems such as Glacier Bay's Micro HPS (Hybrid Plate System; Figures 11-24A and 11-24B).

The Micro HPS. The Micro HPS is a high-capacity holding-plate system that uses a powerful new hermetic DC compressor (Figure 11-25). It eliminates the maintenance issues associated with externally driven compressors. The electrical windings in hermetic compressors are generally cooled by the refrigerant gases on the suction side, adding the heat of the windings to the work the compressor has to do. The Masterflux compressor in the Micro HPS uses the discharge gas from the compressor to cool the windings, adding this heat to the condenser's load rather than the compressor's load. The net effect is an improvement in efficiency over a conventional hermetic compressor.

The Micro HPS system comes in a compact, precharged, skid-mounted configuration that simply needs the refrigerant and cooling lines to be connected—in other words, the installation is no more complicated than that for many constant-cycling units (although it still needs to be vacuumed down, as opposed to a number of constant-cycling units that do not need vacuuming). It uses downsized holding plates that are somewhere between an evaporator plate and a traditional holding plate, thus reducing the volume and weight of the holding plates. The net result is something midway between a constant-cycling unit and a traditional holding-plate unit; it is reported to have a higher efficiency than a constant-cycling unit, up to ten times the refrigerating capability (as long as the holding plates have the capacity to absorb this capability), and less potential for leaks than a traditional holding-

FIGURES 11-24A AND 11-24B. Two views of a Glacier Bay Micro HPS system.

FIGURE 11-25. A Masterflux 2 hp hermetically sealed refrigeration compressor.

plate system using an externally driven compressor. If the emphasis is on capacity and efficiency, the refrigeration load may best be met with a hybrid system, although it will take a few years to assess the cost-effectiveness of this approach and its precise position in the marketplace.

The Blast Chiller. Another interesting concept from Glacier Bay, which has been around for a while without gaining much traction in the marketplace, is the Micro Blast Chiller. The latest variant has a refrigeration unit that uses a Masterflux compressor with propane as the refrigerant. It comes as a complete unit in which the evaporator is part of the unit instead of being installed in the refrigerator. A fan blows air over the evaporator, dropping the air temperature to well below freezing. This air is then ducted into the icebox to refrigerate the contents.

Making Choices

Where refrigeration loads are relatively light, and in situations where a boat is used primarily on weekends and plugged into shoreside power during the week (enabling batteries that are discharged over the weekend to be recharged, and the DC refrigeration system to be run off the battery charger at dockside), constant-cycling DC refrigeration is by far the most economical, trouble free, and easy to install for most boats.

If greater capacity is required in a situation where (1) engines are run regularly, (2) the DC system is somewhat weak, and (3) refrigeration is not required at dockside, then engine-driven refrigeration makes sense. These are the conditions found on many charter boats.

If an AC generator is constantly running, household constant-cycling equipment will be the most economical. If an AC generator is intermittently but regularly operated, AC holding-plate refrigeration makes sense.

In most other situations, some variant of DC refrigeration is the best choice because it can:

- Minimize engine-running hours.
- Be operated from shore power via a battery charger (whereas an engine-driven system requires the engine to be run at dockside).
- Be left to run at anchor until the batteries go dead (one of the design parameters I set myself is a battery and refrigeration balance that will allow the boat to be left unattended for up to a week without the fridge and freezer melting down). In contrast, engine-driven refrigeration requires someone to be on the boat to run the refrigeration unit every day.

With respect to the DC options, I believe the balance of the argument has shifted in favor of constant-cycling DC refrigeration, even on a hard-core cruising boat (although the jury is still out on the hybrid systems). Better yet is to have two (or more) units—separate fridge and freezer installations—to provide built-in redundancy. You will still have cost savings over a high-capacity holding-plate DC system, some of which you can put into improved insulation. The end result will be a virtually maintenance-free refrigeration system that is compact, quiet, and reliable; optimizes the icebox volume and keeps down weight; and has built-in redundancy—all at a cost that is less than a high-capacity holding-plate system.

Air-Conditioning

With ever more powerful electrical systems on boats, air-conditioning is becoming more widespread; however, it is an enormous power consumer (far more than refrigeration) that has to be carefully considered. Except for liveaboards in hot climates, air-conditioning is largely unnecessary on a cruising boat. If you have any kind of a breeze you can substitute awnings, wind scoops, and ventilation for it, especially if you anchor the boat out, lying head to wind and funneling the breeze down the fore hatch.

Nowadays, most air-conditioning units come with a reverse-cycle option that can be used to heat instead of cool, with the heat being extracted from the water. For water temperatures as low as 40°F/5°C, reverse-cycle heating is up to three times more efficient than electric heating. Below 40°F/5°C you will need supplementary heat (it need be no more than a freestanding electric heater).

Air-Conditioning Options

If you plan to install air-conditioning, you have several options:

- A portable unit, similar to a household window unit, installed in a hatch and removed when the boat goes to sea. This approach is economical and requires no modifications to the boat. It is the only approach that does not require a cooling-water circuit and is popular with liveaboard cruisers.

- Self-contained units installed in one or more cabins in the boat (similar to a household window unit, except for being water cooled). Power is generally provided from shore power at dockside and an AC generator at sea. Although an inverter-based boat (see Chapter 2) with 5 kW or more of inverter capacity can run a 16,000 Btu air-conditioning unit, it does so at a tremendous load on the DC system (over 150 amps at 12 volts), which almost always makes it impractical. A self-contained air conditioner is relatively simple and economical to install. It comes as a drop-in, premanufactured unit, minimizing the chances of installation problems.

- Central air-conditioning, in which a central condensing unit provides air-conditioning at a number of outlets. This is achieved in three different ways:

1. The use of a single evaporator unit (the radiator-like device that produces the cold air) at the condensing unit, from which cold air is ducted as needed to different outlets on the boat (similar to most household air-conditioning). The condenser/evaporator comes as a premanufactured unit to which the wiring, cooling-water circuit, and ducting are added. The refrigerant circuit is a sealed unit, eliminating installation problems on the refrigerant side. The system requires space-consuming air ducts, and does not lend itself well to individual zone controls. It is a relatively low-cost option.

2. Liquid refrigerant is piped from the condensing unit to individual evaporators around the boat, each with its own thermostatically controlled fan. The refrigerant tubes are easy to run and take up almost no space. Once again, the system does not lend itself particularly well to individual zone controls. There is one master control, usually in the larger cabin, with only a fan speed control on the slave outlets (consequently, if the thermostat in the main cabin does not call for cooling, there will be no cooling in the other cabins). Given that the installer has to run the refrigerant tubing and evacuate and charge the system, *this system has the greatest potential for installation problems and subsequent refrigerant leaks*. In addition the relationship between the master and slave evaporators makes these systems difficult to charge and balance.

3. A central condensing unit is used to chill water (a *tempered water* or *hydronic* system). This chilled water is piped around the boat and run through individual radiators, each with its own thermostatically controlled fan. The condenser/water chiller comes as a premanufactured unit, minimizing the chances of installation problems on the refrigeration side. Water plumbing, which is easy to install and troubleshoot, is then run through the boat, taking up little space, with radiator/fan units at each outlet. The system lends itself well to individual zone controls. When used for reverse-cycle heating, a diesel-fired heater or some other heat source can be added to the water loop to boost temperatures if the outside water temperature gets too low for effective heating. Tempered-water air-conditioning is currently by far the most popular approach on large yachts and is finding an application on ever-smaller boats. It is, however, relatively expensive. Multiple condensing/chilling units can be installed in parallel to meet just about any demand.

- Glacier Bay has small evaporator units (Arctic Air) that will run off their holding-plate DC refrigeration systems at those times when the refrigeration need has been met and there is surplus refrigeration capability (e.g., when motorsailing or plugged into shore power). If the Glacier Bay refrigeration system is already on the boat, or is to be installed, this is a relatively economical way to get a modest air-conditioning capability.

Sizing an Air-Conditioning Unit

The amount of air-conditioning that is required in a given space is a function of the volume of the space, the temperature differential that is to be maintained between the outside temperature and the inside temperature, and the rate of heat influx into the space. Given that most boat cabins have similar amounts of headroom, the volume calculation is generally reduced to square footage or square meters. The heat load is then expressed by the formula: heat load = $A \times (T_1 - T_2) \times K$, where A = the area of the space to be air conditioned, $(T_1 - T_2)$ = the temperature differential from outside the boat to inside, and K = a constant that approximates the rate of heat influx. K will vary according to the type of space being heated, such as a cabin with few portlights and hatches, a saloon with more glass, or a wheelhouse with a great deal of glass.

To determine the heat load in Btu per hour (which is how most air conditioners are specified), use the following values:

- A = area in square feet.
- $(T_1 - T_2)$ = 20°F in Mediterranean-type climates, 30°F in the tropics.
- K = 3.5 for below-deck cabins with minimal portlights or hatches; 5.0 for mid-deck areas, such as cabins or saloons with moderate amounts of glass; 7.0 for deck saloons and pilothouses with a lot of glass.

To determine the heat load in watt-hours, use these values:

- A = area in square meters.
- $(T_1 - T_2)$ = 10°C in Mediterranean-type climates, 15°C in the tropics.
- K = 20 for below-deck cabins; 30 for mid-deck saloons; 40 for deck saloons and pilothouses with a lot of glass.

Note that these numbers (adapted from Climma Marine Air Conditioning—www.veco.net) are conservative (i.e., if an air conditioner is matched to the calculated load, it is likely to have surplus capacity; see also Figure 11-26).

For example, let's say we have a boat to be used in the tropics with a 10-by-12-foot mid-deck saloon: A = 10 × 12 ft = 120 sq. ft; $(T_1 - T_2)$ = 30°F; and K = 5.0.

The heat load (Btu per hour) = 120 x 30 x 5.0 = 18,000 Btu (a 16,000 Btu air conditioner will do the job).

An alternative approach. Cruisair (a major manufacturer of air-conditioning equipment for boats—www.cruisair.com) has a less conservative approach to sizing air-conditioning units. It is based on U.S. design conditions, which equate more or less to a Mediterranean-type climate, rather than tropical cruising, and it uses the following numbers:

A. Below-deck cabins: 60 Btu/sq. ft/hr (650 Btu/sq. m/hr).

B. Mid-deck areas: 90 Btu/sq. ft/hr (970 Btu/sq. m/hr).

C. Deck saloons with a lot of glass, 120 Btu/sq. ft/hr (1,300 Btu/sq. m/hr).

Using the mid-deck number, the heat load for a 120-square-foot cabin comes to 10,800 Btu per hour.

For a whole-boat calculation, consider each space. Note, however, that it is not necessary to total all the spaces to determine the total air-conditioning load. Instead make an assessment of the pattern of usage. For example, most likely you will not be using sleeping cabins in the daytime, so you do not need to add them to the daytime load (which will consist primarily of communal areas).

Installation Issues

Until recently, all air conditioners were charged with HCFC-22. As noted at the beginning of the chapter, this is one of the refrigerants being phased out in the United States and has, to a large extent, already been phased out in Europe. So far, no single replacement for it has emerged. In Europe, 407C is commonplace; in the United States, 410A. Another refrigerant, 417A, has been developed as a drop-in replacement. For many years to come, it will be essential when servicing an air-conditioning unit to check the label to see what is in the system and to make sure that the same, or compatible, substances are used.

Cooling circuits. Except for the hatch units, all air-conditioning systems on boats use water cooling. Almost all use centrifugal pumps (see Chapter 13). To retain its prime, a centrifugal pump *must be installed below the waterline with all components leading uphill at all angles of heel from the through-hull to the pump.* It is also preferable for the pump to have its own seacock rather than share a raw-water supply with other equipment. This is because if the raw-water supply gets obstructed, the other equipment may suck air back through the centrifugal pump, causing problems for both the air conditioner and the other equipment. The seacock should have an external scoop strainer *facing forward* (this is important) to ensure that the pump is always primed (if it faces aft, when underway it will suck the water out of the pump causing a loss of prime). Note that this

FIGURE 11-26. A quick and easy way to estimate air-conditioning needs.

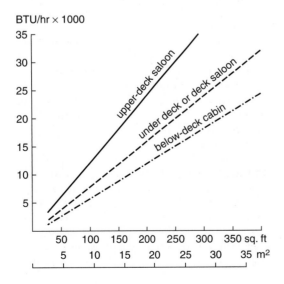

BTU/hr × 1000

REFRIGERATION AND AIR-CONDITIONING

is the opposite way around for any scoop strainer on an engine raw-water intake. The seacock will need a strainer on its inboard side.

When installing an air conditioner, especially a chilled-water unit, it is worth giving some thought to winterizing procedures, in particular ensuring that all cooling circuits are easy to drain. Generally, it is preferable to put antifreeze in the chilled-water circuit. The raw-water circuit will still need winterizing.

Bonding. It is important to electrically ground the metal skids the condensing and evaporating units are mounted on. This is done by making a bonding connection from the skid to the boat's common ground point (see Chapter 5). If this is not done, and there are any stray DC currents (such as might arise if DC wiring abrades against copper tubing in the refrigeration system and shorts to the tubing), severe stray-current corrosion is possible.

Condensates. On those units that run refrigerant or chilled-water lines through the boat, the return refrigerant lines from the evaporator units or the cold-water lines to the units will sweat profusely if not properly insulated. The insulation needs to fit tightly, with all seams fully sealed.

In the humid marine environment, the evaporator unit(s) on an air conditioner generate a fair amount of condensation. Consquently the unit needs a condensate collection pan and drains that are effective at all angles of heel. The condensate can be drained to the bilge or else to a separate sump with its own bilge pump. On some units, the condensate is plumbed to a spe-cial valve in the raw-water circuit to the cooling pump. This valve operates on the venturi principle (when flow is accelerated through a narrowed aperture, it creates suction), sucking the condensate into the raw-water line and discharging it overboard through the raw-water discharge through-hull. Note that if the venturi fails, the boat may get flooded! A separate condensate drain to the bilge is safer.

Condensate drains for air-conditioning or evaporator units in accommodation spaces should *never* drain to compartments that contain diesel or gasoline engines. This is to avoid the possibility of carbon monoxide fumes working their way back up the drain. Similarly, if the system has air ducting, and a duct passes through an engine space, it must make a continuous run so that any carbon monoxide cannot be picked up and fed to accommodation spaces (for more on carbon monoxide, see Chapter 15).

Start-up loads. The start-up loads on air conditioners are high. If the AC system is at all marginal, you may need either an air conditioner with a *soft-start* program or else some kind of a load-management device that will prevent the air conditioner from being started simultaneously with other loads (e.g., Charles Industries' automatic transfer switch—www.charlesindustries.com—and similar products from other companies; note that the rotary compressors found on many newer air conditioners are easier to start than reciprocal compressors). If you are using 120-volt AC air-conditioning on a U.S.-style, 240-volt AC boat with two 120-volt bus bars, it is important to try to balance the loads between the bus bars.

Refrigeration and Air-Conditioning: Maintenance, Troubleshooting, and Repair

Given a properly chosen and installed refrigeration or air-conditioning unit, the key to being able to troubleshoot any problems that might arise is an understanding of how the unit works and what its normal operating parameters are.

How Refrigeration Works

Water boils at 212°F/100°C. Or does it? In a pressure cooker, water boils at more than 240°F/116°C, which is why food cooks so much faster (Figure 11-27). The reason for this is that anytime pressure is increased, the boiling temperature goes up; conversely, when pressure is decreased, the boiling temperature goes down. Water boils at 212°F *only at sea-level atmospheric* *pressure.* At any other pressure, the boiling temperature is higher or lower.

There is a corollary to this. If the temperature of a vessel of steam, which is at atmospheric pressure, falls below 212°F/100°C, the steam will condense into water. At higher pressures, this condensation will take place at higher temperatures.

Changes of state. When water turns into steam at atmospheric pressure, the water is at 212°F/100°C and so too is the steam. But *quite a bit of energy is needed to bring about this change of state from water to steam, even though no change of temperature occurs* (Figure 11-28). This is seen easily. Put a thermometer in a pot of

FIGURE 11-27 (left). The relationship between pressure and the boiling point of water. At position 1 (24 inches Hg vacuum) water boils at 142°F/61°C. At position 2 (atmospheric pressure) water boils at 212°F/100°C. At position 3 (30 psi) water boils at 272°F/133°C.

FIGURE 11-28 (right). Latent heat graph for water. This graph shows the amount of heat required to turn 1 pound of ice at 0°F/–17.8°C into steam at 212°F/ 100°C.

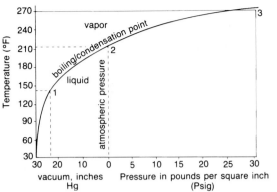

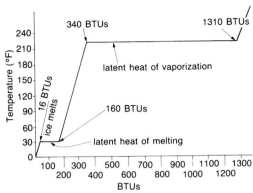

water, bring the water to a boil, and then boil it all away. The water will start to boil quite quickly, but will take some time to boil away even though there will be no further rise in temperature. The converse also applies—in the process of condensing, steam gives up a large amount of heat even though the steam and water are both at 212°F/100°C.

Because heat absorbed and lost during changes of state does not result in a change in temperature (and cannot be measured with a thermometer), it is called *latent heat.* For a vapor (or gas) to condense into a liquid, it must give up *latent heat of condensation;* for a liquid to boil into a vapor or gas, it must absorb *latent heat of vaporization.*

These two concepts—the changing of boiling or condensation temperatures with changes in pressure, and the latent heat of vaporization and condensation—are at the heart of almost all re-

frigeration and air-conditioning systems. Let's see how it works, using HFC-134a as a refrigerant.

The refrigeration cycle. At atmospheric pressure, liquid HFC-134a vaporizes, or boils, into a gas at –15°F/–26°C, just as water boils at 212°F/ 100°C (see Table 11-7). When HFC-134a is pressurized, its boiling temperature rises (Figure 11-29). At 100 psi (pounds per square inch), HFC-134a boils at 87°F/30°C; or put another way, if it is already in gaseous (vapor) form at 100 psi and if its temperature falls below 87°F/30°C, it will condense into a liquid. At 170 psi its boiling/condensation temperature is 120°F/48°C. At 220 psi the boiling/condensation temperature is 137°F/58°C.

In a refrigeration system, HFC-134a gas is pulled into a compressor and compressed (Figures 11-30A and 11-30B), generally to between 125 and 175 psi. At 125 psi the gas will condense if its temperature falls below 100°F/38°C;

FIGURE 11-29. The temperature-pressure curve for HFC-134a.

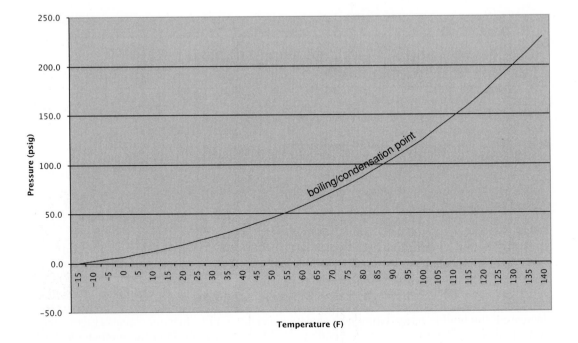

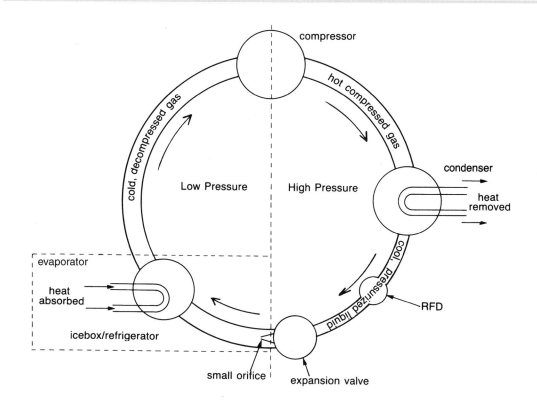

FIGURE 11-30A. The refrigeration cycle.

compressor

hot compressed gas

cold, decompressed gas

Low Pressure

High Pressure

condenser

heat removed

evaporator

heat absorbed

cool, pressurized liquid

RFD

icebox/refrigerator

small orifice

expansion valve

at 175 psi, below 121°F/49°C. The hot gas is cooled in a *condenser*; its temperature falls below its condensation point at this pressure, and it turns into a liquid. In liquefying, it gives up a large amount of latent heat of condensation to the condenser. (Note: Air conditioners use different refrigerants; these have similar properties to HFC-134a but with different boiling/condensation temperatures.)

The pressurized liquid enters a receiver-filter-drier (RFD—Figure 11-31); the receiver and the filter-drier are often two separate units. An RFD is nothing more than a tank with a fine screen and some desiccant (water-absorbing substance). The RFD filters out dirt or trash, absorbs moisture, and acts as a reservoir of liquid HFC-134a. Most RFDs have a sight glass on top (more on this later) or located nearby.

From the RFD, the pressurized liquid HFC-134a goes to the refrigerator or freezer. There it is sprayed through a very small orifice into a length of finned tubing known as an *evaporator*, much like the radiator of a car. The orifice may consist of nothing more than a very small piece of capillary tubing, or it may be incorporated in a special valve that regulates the size of the orifice according to the needs of the system—a *thermostatic expansion valve* (TXV).

The evaporator tubing is connected directly to the suction side of the compressor so that its pressure is held well down—typically anything

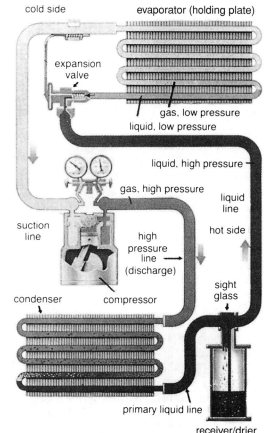

cold side

evaporator (holding plate)

expansion valve

gas, low pressure

liquid, low pressure

liquid, high pressure

gas, high pressure

liquid line

suction line

hot side

high pressure line (discharge)

sight glass

condenser

compressor

primary liquid line

receiver/drier

FIGURE 11-30B. A typical refrigeration system. Follow the arrows from the compressor through the condenser to the receiver-drier, expansion valve, and evaporator, then back to the compressor. (This is an air-cooled condenser—fan not shown.) *(Four Seasons)*

TABLE 11-7. Pressure-Temperature Chart for HFC-134a

Pressure (psig ["Hg])[1]	Temperature (°F)	Pressure (psig)	Temperature (°F)	Pressure (psig)	Temperature (°F)
[22]	−62.38	37	42.00	145	109.4
[20]	−55.02	38	43.00	150	111.5
[18]	−48.85	39	43.98	155	113.6
[16]	−43.50	40	44.95	160	115.6
[14]	−38.76	41	45.91	165	117.6
[12]	−34.49	42	46.85	170	119.6
[10]	−30.60	43	47.78	175	121.5
[8]	−27.02	44	48.70	180	123.3
[6]	−23.70	45	49.61	185	125.2
[4]	−20.59	46	50.51	190	126.9
[2]	−17.67	47	51.39	195	128.7
0	−14.92	48	52.26	200	130.4
1	−12.31	49	53.13	205	132.1
2	−9.84	50	53.98	210	133.8
3	−7.47	51	54.82	215	135.5
4	−5.21	52	55.65	220	137.1
5	−3.04	53	56.48	225	138.7
6	−0.95	54	57.29	230	140.2
7	1.05	55	58.10	235	141.8
8	2.99	56	58.89	240	143.3
9	4.86	57	59.68	245	144.8
10	6.67	58	60.46	250	146.3
11	8.42	59	61.23	255	147.7
12	10.12	60	62.00	260	149.2
13	11.77	61	62.75	265	150.6
14	13.38	62	63.50	270	152.0
15	14.94	63	64.24	275	153.4
16	16.46	64	64.98	280	154.7
17	17.95	65	65.71	285	156.1
18	19.40	66	66.43	290	157.4
19	20.81	67	67.14	295	158.7
20	22.19	68	67.85	300	160.0
21	23.55	69	68.55	305	161.3
22	24.87	70	69.24	310	162.5
23	26.16	75	72.62	315	163.8
24	27.43	80	75.86	320	165.0
25	28.68	85	78.98	325	166.2
26	29.90	90	81.97	330	167.4
27	31.10	95	84.87	335	168.6
28	32.27	100	86.66	340	169.8
29	33.43	105	90.37	345	171.0
30	34.56	110	92.99	350	172.1
31	35.68	115	95.53	355	173.3
32	36.77	120	98.00	360	174.4
33	37.85	125	100.4	365	175.4
34	38.91	130	102.7	370	176.3
35	39.96	135	105.0	375	177.3
36	40.99	140	107.2	380	178.2

1. Psig = pounds per square inch gauge (as opposed to psia, pounds per square inch absolute). Gauge is measured with respect to atmospheric pressure, and absolute is measured from an absolute vacuum; i.e., psig = (psia − atmospheric pressure). "Hg = inches of mercury, a common way of measuring a vacuum; i.e., pressure below atmospheric pressure.

(Glacier Bay)

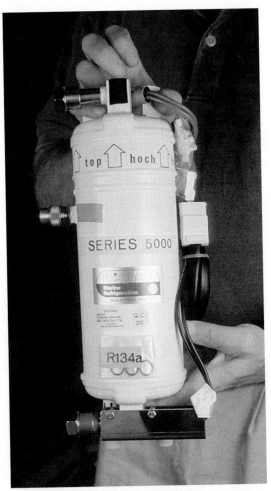

FIGURE 11-31. Receiver-filter-drier unit for an engine-driven (high-capacity) refrigeration system.

from 30 psi down to a substantial vacuum, maybe as low as −10 inches of mercury. At 30 psi, liquid HFC-134a evaporates (vaporizes) at any temperature above 35°F/2°C; at −10 inches of mercury, it evaporates (vaporizes) at any temperature above −31°F/−35°C.

When the pressurized liquid HFC-134a sprays into the low-pressure zone of the evaporator, the sudden drop in pressure causes it to vaporize—it boils off into a gas. In doing so, it absorbs large amounts of latent heat, pulling this heat out of the refrigerator or freezer and thereby cooling it down. The gas returns to the compressor, is recompressed, and goes back to the condenser where it is converted back into a liquid, giving up latent heat of condensation in the process. The latent heat of condensation given up in the condenser is the same latent heat of vaporization that was absorbed in the evaporator; the heat has been taken from the food compartment of the refrigerator or freezer and transferred to the condenser.

The condenser dissipates the heat it has gained in one of three ways: (1) a fan blows air over a radiator, and the air carries off the heat (just as with a car radiator or household refrigerator); (2) seawater is pumped through the condenser, carrying the heat overboard (just as with a heat exchanger on an engine's cooling circuit); or (3) the condenser is placed in the seawater (a keel cooler or through-hull condenser). Water-cooled condensers are up to twenty-five times more effective than air-cooled.

An air conditioner works in exactly the same fashion, except that it uses refrigerants that are more efficient at the higher temperatures used in air-conditioning.

All refrigeration and air-conditioning units are lubricated by oil, which circulates with the refrigerant. Refrigerant oils are specially blended for extremely low temperatures and specific refrigerants; no other type can be used. As noted, the new refrigerants require new oils, and in many instances different oils and refrigerants are *totally incompatible*—it is essential to get the correct oil and refrigerant for your system!

Routine Maintenance

Properly installed refrigeration and air-conditioning units require little maintenance. If the condenser is water cooled, it will probably have a sacrificial zinc anode that will need inspecting on a regular basis and replacing well before it is corroded away. If corrosion is rapid (the zinc needs replacing more than once a season), *you have a galvanic or stray-current problem that needs resolving before the condenser fails,* an event that can result in the total destruction of a refrigeration or air-conditioning system.

During a winter layup, make sure to drain the condenser or it is likely to freeze and burst. The drain must be at the lowest point and effectively remove all water. Alternatively, mix up an antifreeze solution, break the pump suction loose, and pump this through the water circuit (see the Winter Layup section in Chapter 9 for more on this).

Drive belts. The belt on a belt-driven compressor must be correctly aligned (Figure 11-32A). With the belt off, a length of ½-inch (13 mm) doweling should drop cleanly into the grooves on the two pulleys. Make a belt moderately tight—tighter than alternator belts (Figure 11-32B). The compressor must be mounted extremely rigidly. Without a solid mount, correct alignment, and adequate tension, it will chew up its belt at regular intervals. If the belt vibrates excessively, particularly when a long belt run is involved, you need an idler pulley to bear against the center stretch of the belt.

At certain speeds, compressors will sometimes

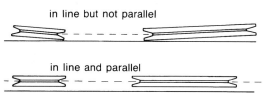

FIGURE 11-32A. Pulley alignment.

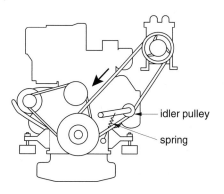
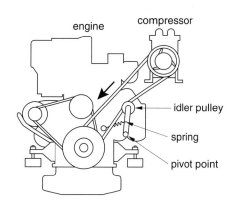

FIGURE 11-32B. Idler pulley arrangements. An idler pulley goes on the slack side of a belt.

set up harmonic vibrations, which are amplified through the compressor mounts, bulkheads, etc. The belt may well dance or jump. There is nothing wrong with the compressor. Try tightening the drive belt a little; perhaps add an idler pulley on the slack side of the belt. Check the alignment of the pulley and stiffen the compressor mount.

DC motors. Inspect the brushes and commutator in DC motors every year or two, depending on the amount of use (Chapter 7). If brushes are allowed to wear down to the point at which they make a poor contact on their commutator, arcing will occur. Before the motor stops altogether, alerting you to the problem, expensive damage will probably have been done. Periodic brush inspection is important!

Topping off. Externally driven compressors tend to leak minute amounts of refrigerant from around the shaft seal (see the next sidebar). Just as with an automotive air conditioner, top off the system every year or so (see the Charging and Topping-Off Procedures section later in this chapter).

Externally driven compressors have a seal where the drive shaft emerges from the compressor (Figure 11-33). Almost all use a face seal, which is pretty much the same as a mechanical shaft seal on a propeller shaft—it consists of two finely machined surfaces held against one another by spring pressure. In most cases, one half is carbon and the other

FIGURE 11-33. A compressor seal on a belt-driven reciprocal compressor. *(Jim Sollers and R-Parts)*

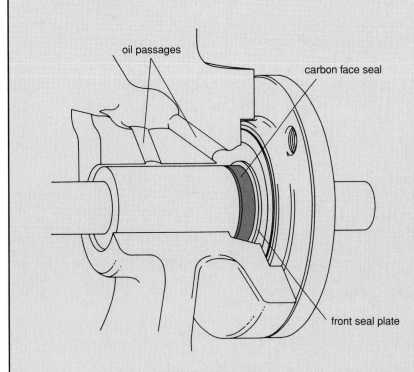

oil passages

carbon face seal

front seal plate

polished steel. The seal is completed by a fine film of oil between the two faces.

It is normal for such a seal to leak minute quantities of refrigerant, necessitating an occasional topping off. The probability of a leak is increased the longer a unit is left idle (the oil film does not get renewed). *Anytime an externally driven compressor is left unused for more than a couple of months, the shutoff valves should be closed on either side of the compressor to isolate it from the rest of the refrigerant charge in the system.* Be sure to place a conspicuous note on the main refrigeration breaker reminding you that this has been done so that the unit does not get restarted with the valves closed. An alternative to closing the valves is to find someone to periodically run the unit. (The same goes for a car; even in the wintertime, the air-conditioning should be run briefly every month or so.)

These seals rarely fail. If the system is left idle and loses its refrigerant charge, no harm will come to it. The charge can generally be replaced and the unit run as normal.

Note that if the seal faces are held together by spring pressure, *pressing in on the drive shaft may open the seal faces and release refrigerant and oil.* This is particularly relevant when directly coupling a compressor to an electric motor (as opposed to driving the compressor via a pulley and belt). *If the compressor and motor are mounted too close together, it may result in the loss of the refrigerant and oil.* Once again, the refrigerant and oil can generally be replaced without damage being done.

Troubleshooting and Repair

Troubleshooting starts long before a problem develops. Identify all the components and get a feel for normal operating temperatures at different points. Feel the lines from time to time, particularly those going into and out of the compressor, the condenser (both refrigerant and water lines), the expansion valve or capillary tube, and the evaporator. Find the sight glass (if fitted) and observe it during a number of starts—from a warm unit and from an already cold unit. See how quickly the stream of bubbles appears and then disappears as the condenser produces liquid. The sight glass will not necessarily be completely full of liquid (in which case it goes completely clear), but it should show a solid stream of bubble-free liquid. Check the sight glass at least monthly; if the bubbles begin to take longer to clear or refuse to clear at all, the unit is losing refriger-

ant and the compressor may be in danger of burning up.

If a pump-supplied water-cooled condenser (i.e., not a keel cooler or through-hull condenser) has its own overboard discharge (which I would recommend for troubleshooting reasons), measure the cooling-water flow. Get a thermometer and measure the temperature of the seawater and then the temperature of the overboard discharge. Do this at different points of the cycle for a holding-plate refrigeration unit to gain some idea of typical in-and-out cooling-water differentials. These figures can be used to crudely calculate the efficiency of the system as follows:

1. Take the cooling-water flow rate in gallons or liters per minute and multiply this by 8.3 (gallons) or 2.2 (liters) to convert it into pounds.
2. Find the temperature differential between the cooling water coming out of the condenser and that going into it in °F.

3. Multiply your result from step 1 by your result from step 2, then multiply that figure by 60. This will give you the approximate rate of heat removal in Btu per hour (it can be converted to watts per hour by dividing by 3.413). The figure will overstate performance; to improve accuracy multiply by 0.9 if the cooling water is salt water, then by 0.75 to take account of various extraneous heat sources. This will give you a fairly conservative approximation of system performance. The unit will probably be well short of its advertised capabilities—this is quite normal!

Pressures. Before problems develop, the adventurous may want to hook up a set of gauges (see below) and get an idea of normal operating pressures under different conditions.

Initial pressures. Suction and discharge (head) pressures are affected by a dozen different factors. Nevertheless, a few broad generalizations can be made. Let's look first at refrigerators and freezers using HFC-134a. If an icebox and evaporator are warm to start with, initial suction pressures will probably run around 30 psi, discharge pressures around 175 psi. The pressures in a small, constant-cycling water-cooled unit will come down gradually, perhaps to about 10 psi and 140 psi (air-cooled units in hot climates may have discharge pressures as high as 180 psi). Large-capacity units with holding plates will keep coming down steadily. Suction pressures at the cold part of the cycle may range anywhere from 10 psi down to –10 inches of mercury (a considerable vacuum); discharge pressures range from 125 psi to as low as 100 psi.

These numbers can be more precisely quantified by referring to Table 11-7. With air cooling, the high-side temperature should be somewhere between 20°F/11°C and 30°F/17°C above that of the temperature of the cooling air. Let's say the cooling air is 90°F/33°C. The high-side temperature will be 110°F/43°C to 120°F/ 49°F. Referring now to the pressure-temperature chart for HFC-134a, we see the pressure should be between 145 psi and 175 psi. With water cooling, the high-side temperature should be around 15°F/8°C more than the water temperature. Let's say the water is 84°F/29°C (the Caribbean). The high-side temperature will be around 99°F/37°. The pressure should be around 125 psi.

If pressures are higher than expected, an air-cooled condenser may be clogged or the flow of cooling air otherwise restricted, or the fan may be defective; a water-cooled condenser may have a restricted water flow or poor heat transfer due to scaling or fouling (for more on this, see the Condenser Problems section later in the chapter).

Troubleshooting Chart 11-1.
Refrigeration and Air-Conditioning Problems: A Brief Overview

Unit fails to run. Is there a fault in the AC or DC circuit to the compressor or compressor clutch? **NO** **TEST:** Check the voltage *at the compressor or clutch.*	**YES** **FIX:** Check all fuses and shutdown devices. Reset or bypass any over-temperature or over-current shutdown device mounted on the compressor itself. Jump out the compressor or clutch directly to check its operation. If OK, jump out individual shutdowns to find the problem in the circuit.
Unit still fails to run—the compressor or clutch is faulty. Test motors as outlined in Chapter 7, or replace the clutch unit (pages 501–4) A hermetically sealed compressor will need replacing.	
Unit cycles on and off. Is the condenser hot? **NO** **TEST:** Feel the condenser (water cooled) or inspect the fan and fins (air cooled). Check water flow or air ducting.	**YES** Check the flow of cooling water and its temperature. If the condenser is air cooled, check its fans and fins. If the boat has recently moved into warmer ambient conditions, the condenser may be undersized.
Unit cycles on and off. Is it undercharged? **NO** **TEST:** Check the sight glass— a mass of bubbles indicates a low refrigerant charge. If the sight glass is clear, switch off the unit, wait 15 minutes, and turn it back on. Watch closely; if the sight glass remains clear, the unit is out of refrigerant.	**YES** Recharge as necessary.
The unit runs but fails to cool the icebox or boat properly. Is the condenser hot? **NO** **TEST:** See above.	**YES** See above.
The unit runs but fails to cool the icebox or boat properly. Is it undercharged? **NO** **TEST:** See above.	**YES** See above.
The unit runs but fails to cool the icebox or boat properly. Is the compressor vibrating or excessively noisy? **NO** **TEST:** Listen to the compressor.	**YES** Run the compressor tests outlined on pages 505–6.
The unit runs but fails to cool the icebox or boat properly. Is there a temperature differential across the RFD or at any point in the lines? **NO** **TEST:** Feel with your hand.	**YES** The RFD or line is blocked. It will need replacing.
An expansion valve or capillary tube may be plugged or frozen, or its superheat setting may be too high (see the text). The unit may simply be undersized for the demands being placed on it.	

FIGURE 11-34. Typical
operating pressures for
an air-conditioning unit
using HCFC-22 with a
water-cooled condenser.
For a given seawater
temperature and ambient
air temperature, read off
the anticipated compressor
suction and discharge
pressures. For example,
with a 70°F/21°C seawater
temperature and an
80°F/27°C ambient (in
the cabin) air temperature,
on this unit expect a
suction pressure of 70 psi
and a discharge pressure
of 200 psi. When charging
(see text) add refrigerant
a little at a time until these
pressures are approxi-
mated. If at any time the
suction begins to frost,
the unit is overcharged.
(Lunaire Marine)

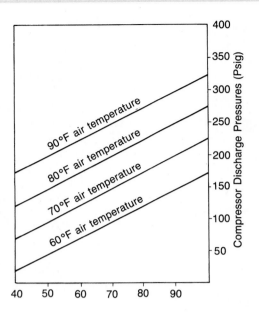

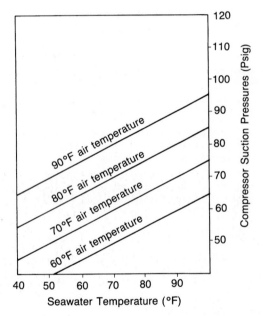

Leak detection. Refrigerant leaks are the number one problem in boat refrigeration and air-conditioning. There are three ways to detect leaks:

Electronic leak detectors. These are ultrasensitive, in fact too much so around belt-driven compressor seals, where a small leak is both normal and permissible. Note that a special detector is needed with HFC-134a.

Halide leak detectors (will not work with HFC-134a). With these, a fitting screws onto a standard propane torch. The flame heats a catalyst, and a hose is used to *sniff* around the refrigeration unit. If refrigerant is present, the flame will change color: no leak, pale blue; slight leak, pale green; medium leak, brilliant green; and a serious leak, brilliant peacock blue. Halide leak detectors are simple to use and reasonably cheap, but unfortunately when many refrigerants (e.g., CFCs and HCFCs) are heated using a halide detector they decompose to nasty things like phosgene (a toxic gas). For this reason, other leak-detection methods are preferable. If *any* leak is detected, it needs fixing.

Soap solutions (50% dishwashing liquid). Sponge or brush the solution onto the part in question. If the solution bubbles, there is a bad leak. On brass fittings, never use soap solutions that contain ammonia, since over time the ammonia may cause the brass to fail.

Note that leaks often leave a telltale trace of refrigeration oil.

If a unit slowly loses efficiency over a month or two and you can find no leak, suspect the hoses. Neoprene and hydraulic hoses are sometimes used in place of proper refrigeration hose, and they have been found to leak several ounces per foot per year through pores in the hose itself. But because the leak is not concentrated at any one point, leak-detection equipment very often will not pick it up. (Note that HFC-134a requires special nylon-lined hoses.)

Air conditioners. Air conditioners with HCFC-22 and its substitutes run at higher pressures and temperatures (Figure 11-34). They should stabilize fairly rapidly (after a few minutes) with suction pressures of 60 to 80 psi and discharge (head) pressures anywhere from 150 to 250 psi. The warmer the ambient air temperature and the cooling water, the higher the pressures. (If a pressure-temperature chart for the refrigerant is available, head pressures can be checked in much the same way as above.) In extremely hot conditions, the pressure may go as high as 90 psi on the suction side and 300 psi on the discharge side. If the unit is started on a freezing day, the ranges will be lower.

Failure to run. On AC and DC units, check the voltage *at the compressor* as described in Chapter 4. Remember, *AC VOLTAGES CAN KILL.* Many electrically powered compressors have overload (high-temperature) and low-voltage cutouts. If tripped, these may require manual resetting, or the unit may have to cool down before it will reset automatically. If you can get the unit to run, *check for voltage drop at the compressor during operation.*

If you find an electrical problem with any system, trace it back through the circuit. Primary suspects, as always, are fuses, circuit breakers, and connections (Figures 11-35A, 11-35B, and 11-35C). Additionally, there are likely to be one or more high- and low-pressure or temperature cutout switches or solenoids on the system itself (as opposed to the compressor) and maybe a relay or two. Bypass each in turn to see if it is causing a problem. If it is, before condemning it make sure it is not performing its proper function (for example, cutting out because of genuinely low pressure due to a loss of refrigerant).

Large AC systems. Larger AC compressors have starting capacitors. If the motor hums but won't

start, the capacitor may be faulty. Test as outlined in Chapter 7 or replace with a good one.

Constant-cycling DC systems. If a constant-cycling DC, hermetically sealed compressor will not work despite adequate voltage, first turn it off and give it a smart *knock* with a soft-faced mallet and try it again—it may simply be stuck! If there is voltage at the battery input to the control unit (the + and − terminals—Figure 11-36) but no

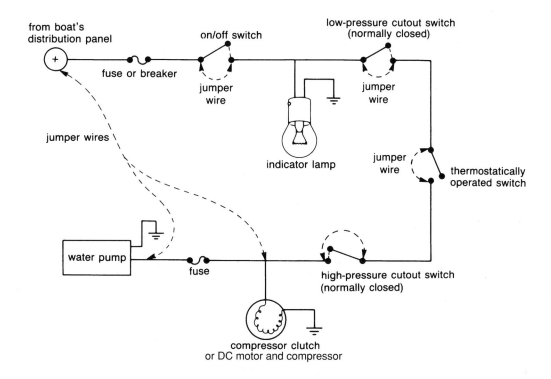

FIGURE 11-35A.
Schematic of a simple engine-driven or DC refrigeration system. To operate, all switches and breakers must be closed and any fuses intact. To troubleshoot the clutch or water pump, first check the ground connection, then connect a jumper wire from the positive terminal, as shown. If the unit now works, there is a problem in the circuit. Jump out individual switches to isolate the problem as shown, starting from the positive supply end of the circuit.

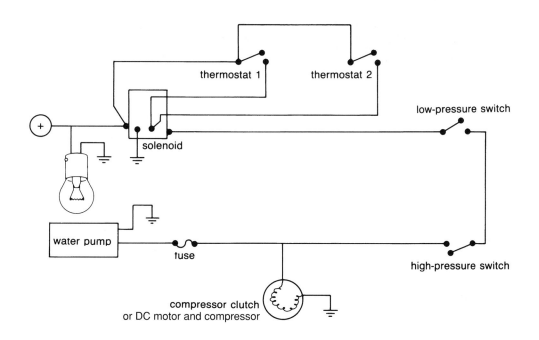

FIGURE 11-35B.
Schematic for a unit with dual holding plates and thermostats. The thermostats supply power to close a solenoid, which then supplies power to the clutch, or a DC motor and compressor, and water pump circuit. With either thermostatic switch closed, power is supplied to close the solenoid; when both are open the circuit is broken.

FIGURE 11-35C.
Schematic of a more complex system, with dual holding plates and thermostats, and individual shutdown solenoids on each holding plate to close off the flow of refrigerant to that plate. The thermostats supply power to close the main solenoid and also open individual solenoid valves on the liquid lines to each expansion valve. When a thermostat opens (i.e., breaks the circuit), its liquid line solenoid closes and shuts down its holding plate. The diodes prevent power from one thermostat feeding back via the common connection on the main solenoid to the other thermostat's liquid line solenoid valve, which would keep the solenoid valve open when it should be closed. When both thermostatic switches open, the circuit is broken and the unit shuts down.

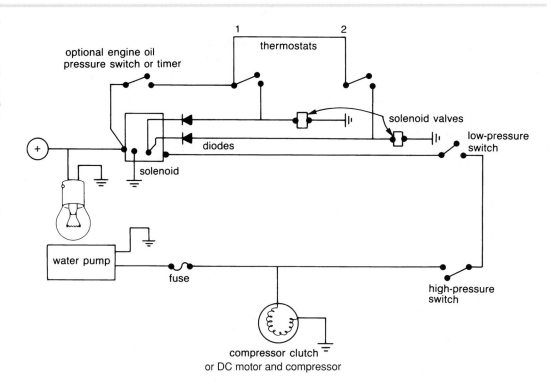

output voltage to the compressor, the failure may be in the control unit. To test, remove the control unit from its mounting bracket, disconnect the cable plug from the lead-in pins on the compressor case, and test for AC voltage across the plug terminals with the meter in the AC volts mode and the refrigeration circuit powered up.

FIGURE 11-36. Typical Danfoss BD compressor connections. *(Danfoss)*

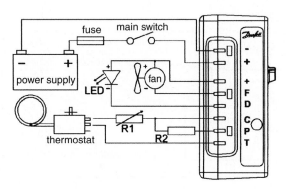

FIGURE 11-37. An exploded view of a Sanden clutch. *(Sanden International)*

(The control unit contains a DC-to-AC inverter that outputs AC power to the compressor, thus the need to test its output in the AC volts mode.)

Failure (no AC volts) is especially likely if the unit is an older one that has been repeatedly started in a hot ambient temperature with a warm icebox. This situation results in a considerable start-up load that overheats the electronics and causes them to fail. In recent years, a variety of soft-start techniques have been incorporated into the controllers to deal with this problem (see the "Smart" Speed Devices sidebar).

Danfoss has stopped making the controllers for its older models, but Frigoboat and Adler Barbour controllers will work (the Frigoboat ones are considerably cheaper). Disconnect the old controller and check if it has three or four connecting pins, then specify accordingly.

If there is voltage from the output of the controller to the compressor motor, with the con-

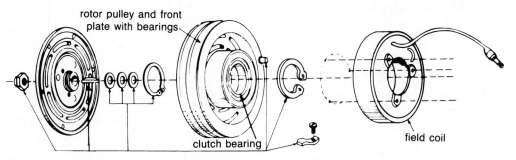

accessory kit: nut, key, shims, snap rings, coil, lead wire clamp with screw, retainer screws

troller still disconnected, test with an ohmmeter (R × 1 scale on an analog meter) between the three or four input pins on the compressor; if the motor windings are intact, the reading should be 2 to 3 ohms between any two pins. An open circuit indicates a burned-out winding; a very low reading indicates a shorted winding.

Engine-driven systems. Engine-driven compressors employ an electromagnetic clutch using 12 or 24 volts from the boat's battery. The drive pulley freewheels around the clutch unit, which is keyed to the drive shaft. Energizing the clutch locks the unit and drives the compressor. When the engine is running with the clutch disengaged, the pulley turns but its center hub remains stationary. When the clutch is energized, the center hub turns with the pulley (Figure 11-37).

If the compressor fails to operate, energize the clutch and *make sure the center hub is turning.* If it is not, check the voltage at the clutch and its ground wire. If there is no voltage, or a severe voltage drop, test the clutch by jumping it out directly from the positive terminal on the battery. If the clutch still fails to work, it needs replacing. This is reasonably easy with Blissfield and Climate Control compressors, but Sankyo/Sanden compressors require two special tools, which long-distance cruising sailors might want to buy: a clutch front-plate wrench (spanner) and a front-plate puller (Figures 11-38 and 11-39A to

clutch front-plate wrench (spanner)

front plate puller

rotor puller set

clutch rotor installer set

clutch plate installer

dipstick

11-39R). A couple of other tools—a rotor puller and installer set, and a clutch plate installer—are useful but not necessary. (Blissfield, Climate *(continued on page 504)*

FIGURE 11-38. Special tools used in servicing Sanden compressors. *(Sanden International)*

FIGURES 11-39A TO 11-39R. Replacing a clutch on a Sanden compressor. *(Sanden International)*

FIGURE 11-39A. 1. Insert the two pins of the front-plate wrench into any two threaded holes of the clutch front plate. Hold clutch plate stationary. Remove hex nut with ¾-inch (19 mm) socket.

FIGURE 11-39B. 2. Remove clutch front plate using puller. Align puller center bolt to compressor shaft. Thumb-tighten the three puller bolts into the threaded holes. Turn center bolt clockwise with ¾-inch (19 mm) socket until front plate is loosened. Note: Steps 1 and 2 must be performed before servicing either the shaft seal or clutch assembly.

FIGURE 11-39C. For HD-series compressors, remove bearing dust cover as shown.

FIGURE 11-39D. 3. Remove shaft key by lightly tapping it loose with a screwdriver and hammer.

FIGURE 11-39E. 4. On older models, remove the internal bearing snap ring by using snap ring pliers (pinch type).

FIGURE 11-39F. Note: On newer models, the snap ring is below the bearing, and step 4 will not be necessary.

FIGURE 11-39G. 5. Remove the external front housing snap ring by using snap ring pliers (spread type).

FIGURE 11-39I. Align thumb-head bolts with puller jaws and finger-tighten.

FIGURE 11-39H. 6. Remove rotor pulley assembly. First insert the lip of the jaws into the snap ring groove (snap ring removed in step 4). Then place rotor puller shaft protector (puller set) over the exposed shaft.

FIGURES 11-39J AND 11-39K. Turn puller center bolt clockwise using ³⁄₄-inch socket until rotor pulley is free.

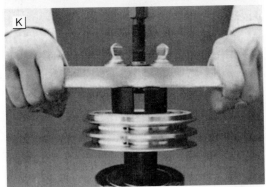

FIGURE 11-39L. 7. Remove field winding; if necessary, loosen winding lead wire from its clip on top of compressor front housing.

FIGURE 11-39M. Use spread-type snap ring pliers to remove snap ring and field coil.

FIGURE 11-39O. Using the rotor installer set, place the ring part of the set into the bearing cavity. Make certain the outer edge rests firmly on the outer race of the rotor bearing. Now place the tool set driver into the ring as shown.

FIGURE 11-39N. Clutch installation: (1) Install the field coil. Reverse the procedure outlined in step 7, "Remove field winding." Coil flange protrusion must match the hole in the front housing to prevent coil movement and correctly locate the lead wire. (2) Replace the rotor pulley: Support the compressor on the four mounting ears at the compressor rear. If using a vise, clamp only on the mounting ears—never on the compressor body. Then align the rotor assembly squarely on the front housing hub.

FIGURE 11-39P. Tap the end of the driver with a hammer while guiding the rotor to prevent binding. Tap until the rotor bottoms against the compressor's front housing hub (there will be a distinct change of sound during the tapping process). (3) Reinstall the internal bearing snap ring with pinch-type pliers. (4) Reinstall the external front housing snap ring with spread-type pliers. (5) Replace the front-plate assembly. Check that the original clutch shims are in place on the compressor shaft. Next replace the compressor shaft key, then align the front-plate keyway with the compressor shaft key.

FIGURE 11-39Q. Using the shaft protector, tap the front plate onto the shaft until it bottoms on the clutch shims (there will be a distinct sound change). (6) Replace the shaft hex nut. Torque to 25 to 30 footpounds. Note: SD-505 torque is 156 ± 26 inches/pounds (180 ± 30 kg/cm).

FIGURE 11-39R. (7) Check the air gap with the feeler gauge to 0.016 to 0.031 inch. If the air gap is not consistent around the circumference, lightly pry up at the minimum variations; lightly tap down at points of maximum variation. Note: The air gap is determined by the spacer shims. When reinstalling or installing a new clutch assembly, try the original shims first. When installing a new clutch onto a compressor that previously did not have a clutch, use 0.040, 0.020, and 0.005 shims from the clutch accessory kit. If the air gap does not meet the specification in step 7, add or subtract shims by repeating steps 5 and 6.

(*continued from page 501*)
Control, and Sanden compressors account for the majority in engine-driven applications.)

To remove a Climate Control or Blissfield clutch assembly, a special tool is normally used to lock the pulley hub so that the pulley retaining nut can be undone. Without this tool, you will have to devise some means of holding the hub. A universal deck plate key works well (Figures 11-40A to 11-40D). Place a wrench on the bolt and hit the wrench smartly to jar the bolt loose. Take out the bolt.

Do not hit the pulley rim to break it loose from its tapered shaft. Find a ⅝-inch NC (coarse thread) bolt to fit the threads in the center of the pulley and wind in the bolt to back off the pulley. Unbolt the clutch retaining plate from the compressor block (four bolts). Replace the whole clutch and pulley assembly as one.

Unit cuts on and off. One of the temperature or pressure switches is cutting in and out. The switch is probably working correctly, indicating a fault in the system. If the unit is cutting out on high pressures, check the condenser (see below). If it is cutting out on low pressures, check the refrigerant charge (see below).

If high pressures are combined with heavy frosting on the suction line back to the compressor and a clear sight glass after adding refrigerant, the unit is probably dangerously overcharged, and the compressor is at risk of serious damage.

Unit fails to cool down or cools too slowly. Likely causes are a loss of refrigerant, condenser problems, or compressor problems; less likely are capillary tube or expansion valve problems.

FIGURES 11-40A TO 11-40D. Clutch replacement on a Climate Control compressor (Blissfield is the same). Use a universal deck plate key to hold the pulley stationary while undoing its retaining bolt (11-40A). Screw off the pulley with a ⅝-inch NC (coarse-thread) bolt (11-40B). The pulley has been removed to reveal the clutch coil (11-40C). Undo the four bolts—one in each corner of the base plate. The clutch has been removed to reveal the shaft seal assembly (11-40D).

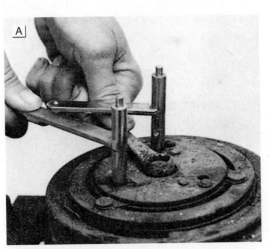

clutch coil retaining bolt

Loss of refrigerant—units with a sight glass.
Check the sight glass. A steady stream of fast-moving bubbles indicates the unit is probably low on refrigerant. However, run the system until cold, periodically checking the sight glass. If the stream of bubbles remains when the unit is cold, the unit is almost certainly low on refrigerant. If the sight glass is completely clear, the unit is filled either with vapor (almost completely out of refrigerant) or with liquid (functioning OK). Faced with a clear sight glass, shut the unit down and give it 15 minutes to allow pressures to equalize internally. Restart it while watching the sight glass. If no bubbles appear, there is no refrigerant. Watch closely—the bubbles may appear for just a few seconds, and then only as a large, slow-moving bubble hovering in the top of the sight glass; if this happens the refrigerant charge is OK.

Hook up the gauge set (see below). When not running, a *warm* unit low on refrigerant will show pressures of 50 psi or less on both gauges. (Note: A fully charged cold unit will also show low pressures, so make sure the unit is warm.) When running, a unit low on refrigerant will have generally low pressures on both the suction and discharge sides, and the compressor discharge temperature will be lower than normal.

Loss of refrigerant—units without a sight glass.
After running for a while, the evaporator plate on a constant-cycling unit should have a slight coating of frost over the entire plate, but little or no condensation or frost on the suction line where it approaches the compressor or on the compressor itself (larger-capacity systems, especially in freezer use, may show frosting). In an undercharged system, the frosting will only cover part of the plate, while the rest of the plate may be cold and sweaty but not frosted. If seriously undercharged, there may be no frosting at all—just a cold, sweating plate. (Note that a seriously overcharged system may exhibit the same symptoms, except that there is likely to be frosting on the suction line toward the compressor and maybe on the compressor itself.)

Condenser problems. If the condenser is operating inefficiently, the compressor discharge and suction temperatures and pressures will be abnormally high.

Air-cooled condensers are totally dependent on a good flow of cool air over the condenser fins. If the condenser is in an enclosed space or an engine room, ambient air temperatures will climb and condenser efficiency will fall dramatically. Likewise, if the cooling fins are plugged with dust, efficiency will fall. Make sure any air-cooled condenser has an adequate flow of cool air. If necessary, duct air into the bottom of the condenser compartment (minimum 4 in./100 mm duct) and vent the top of the compartment (minimum 4 in. diameter vent). Never obstruct the ducts. Fan motors require no maintenance except an occasional light oiling of shafts and bearings. Note that DC fans, if connected with reverse polarity, will run in reverse, greatly reducing efficiency. If the motor fails to operate, make all the usual voltage tests at the motor before condemning it.

The efficiency of a *water-cooled* condenser is directly related to the rate of water flow through it and the temperature of the cooling water. Any decrease in flow or rise in water temperature will have a marked effect on performance. Many condensers that work fine in cooler climates prove inadequate in the tropics. If the condenser has a separate overboard discharge, measure the flow rate and compare it against the previously measured rate. If it has fallen, inspect the intake strainer for plugging and all the hoses for kinking or collapsing. Next check the pump impeller (Chapter 13). Finally, some condensers have a removable cover, which allows the water tubes to be *rodded out* (use a wooden dowel with care), but most do not.

If a condenser is proving inadequate due to higher ambient water temperatures, before condemning it, try increasing the water flow. If it is using the engine's water pump, the flow rate may be only 1 to 2 gallons a minute, especially at engine idle. Installing a separate pump could easily increase this to 4 to 6 gallons a minute.

Compressor problems. If noise levels are above normal, check discharge temperatures (this is when it is handy to have a sense of normal operating temperatures). If these are high, check the condenser.

If the compressor's valves are leaking (Figures 11-41A and 11-41B), or the head gasket is blown between the high and low sides, the compressor will also run hot. A failed valve will often make a *clacking* noise at idle speeds. If the compressor has stem-type service valves (as opposed to Schrader valves—see the Charging and Topping-Off Procedures section below), hook up a gauge set and make the following tests:

- Run the compressor, closing the suction-side service valve *to the system* (all the way in, clockwise). The compressor should rapidly pull a complete vacuum (–28 to –30 inches of mercury). Shut down the compressor.
- If a vacuum of –28 inches of mercury cannot be pulled, the suction valve or head gasket is bad (or the stem valve is not properly closed).
- If a vacuum of –28 inches of mercury can be pulled, but it rises fairly rapidly to atmospheric pressure (0 psi) after the compressor is shut down, the shaft seal is leaking.

FIGURE 11-41A. A cutaway of a reciprocal compressor.

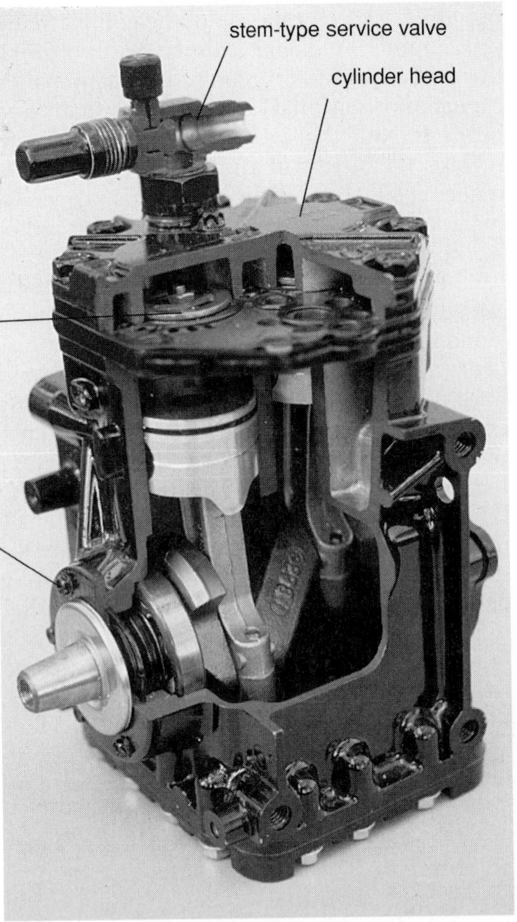

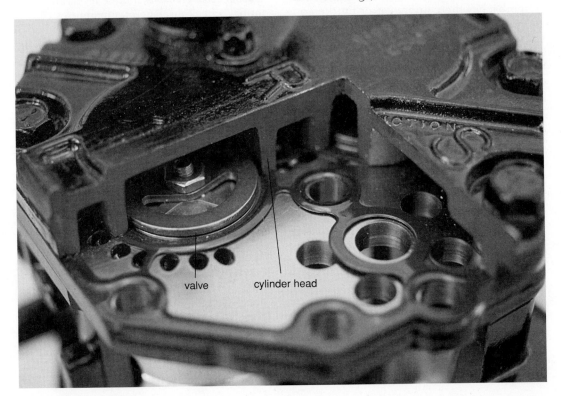

- If a vacuum of –28 inches of mercury can be pulled, but it rises fairly rapidly to a positive pressure after the compressor is shut down, the discharge valve or head gasket is leaking.

If the compressor has Schrader-type service valves, run it normally for 5 minutes, then shut it down. If the suction and discharge pressures equalize in less than 2 minutes, the head gasket or valves are almost certainly bad.

Capillary tube or expansion valve problems. Capillary tubes either work or they don't; there is no adjustment. The tube should be warm where the liquid refrigerant goes in and cold where it sprays out. If the temperature changes sharply at any other point, there is a partial blockage at this point.

Expansion valves have a remote sensing bulb, which controls expansion valve operation. It is strapped to the exit pipe from the evaporator or holding plate and connected to the top of the expansion valve with a length of capillary tubing. *If the capillary tube is broken or kinked, the whole valve needs replacing.*

An expansion valve should be warm where the liquid refrigerant enters it and cold where the evaporator tubing exits. There will generally be a filter screen on the inlet side. If the valve is frosted all the way up the body and close to the inlet, the filter is probably plugged. Gauges will show an abnormally low suction pressure and the unit will not cool down properly—the filter needs cleaning (call a technician).

FIGURE 11-41B. The valves, which are accessed by removing the cylinder head.

REFRIGERATION AND AIR-CONDITIONING

Any moisture in the system will freeze in the expansion valve orifice and plug it. Gauges will show an abnormally low suction pressure and the unit will not cool down. The compressor discharge line will run cooler than normal, and the evaporator side of the expansion valve will be warmer than normal. These symptoms are similar to those accompanying a plugged filter. To distinguish between the two, allow the whole system to warm up, then restart it. With a plugged filter, the suction gauge will immediately show abnormally low pressures; if moisture is the problem, it will take a minute or two to produce abnormally low pressures. To combat frozen moisture, repeatedly shut down the unit and allow the expansion valve to warm up. Start the unit again. With any luck the ice will thaw out, and the moisture will be picked up by the drier. If the expansion valve still freezes, the unit will have to be bled down and the drier replaced—a certified technician with recovery equipment will once again be needed.

To test the operation of an expansion valve, hook up a set of gauges and run the unit until it is cold. Then, with the unit still running, warm the remote sensing bulb (wrap a hand around it). After a few seconds, the suction pressure gauge should show a slight rise (a pound or two) as the expansion valve opens and admits more refrigerant. The suction line to the compressor will probably start frosting up. *Let the bulb cool back down* or else excess liquid refrigerant may pass through

the evaporator and cause *liquid slugging* at the compressor (which may damage the compressor's valves). The suction pressure should drop again. If the valve appears to be working, its *superheat* may simply need adjusting (see below).

Air conditioners. Check the filter on the air inlet to the evaporator at regular intervals. A plugged filter will result in rising temperatures and pressures, with a general loss of performance. Check the fan, making all the usual voltage tests. *Remember, this is AC voltage. IT CAN KILL!*

Superheat. Superheat adjustments are only made on systems with thermostatic expansion valves (TXVs—i.e., not on capillary tube systems). The concept is not an easy one to grasp.

The suction side of a compressor lowers the pressure in an evaporator. At any given evaporator pressure, there is a specific temperature above which liquid refrigerant allowed into the evaporator will boil (see Table 11-7). As long as the outlet to the evaporator remains above this temperature, any liquid refrigerant entering will vaporize before it reaches the outlet. But if the evaporator is cooled to this temperature, liquid will pass through the evaporator with a risk of liquid slugging at the compressor.

The purpose of a TXV is to supply as much liquid refrigerant as can be vaporized in the evaporator without allowing a surplus that would pass through the evaporator in liquid form (Figures 11-42A and 11-42B). It does this by respond-

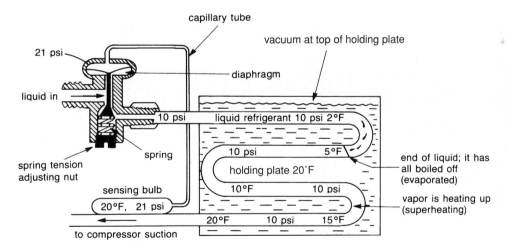

FIGURE 11-42A. Expansion valve operation on an R-12 system (HFC-134a is very similar). The compressor is holding the pressure in the evaporator coil to 10 psi. At this pressure, the liquid R-12 emerging from the expansion valve will boil at any temperature above 2°F/–16.7°C. Since the holding plate is at 20°F/ –6.7°C, the refrigerant rapidly boils off, pulling heat from the holding plate. Once the refrigerant has boiled off, the vapor continues down the evaporator, slowly equalizing (more or less) with the holding-plate temperature of 20°F/–6.7°C. The difference between the refrigerant's boiling temperature at this pressure (2°F/–16.7°C) and the temperature at which the refrigerant emerges from the evaporator (20°F/–6.7°C) is its superheat (18°F/10°C), which in this case is excessively high. The expansion valve bulb contains a sealed charge of R-12. This too will equalize at the temperature of the evaporator coil at the outlet to the holding plate (20°F/–6.7°C). At this temperature, R-12 in a sealed chamber has a pressure of 21 psi. There is thus an 11 psi (21 – 10 = 11) pressure difference between the evaporator coil and the pressure transmitted by the bulb to the diaphragm in the expansion valve. This pressure differential is counteracted by the spring in the expansion valve. Adjusting the spring determines the extent to which the valve will open, and thus regulates the refrigerant flow and the superheat.

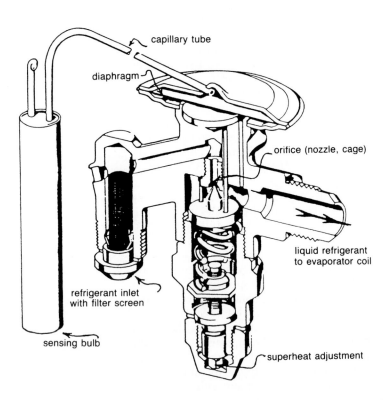

capillary tube

diaphragm

orifice (nozzle, cage)

liquid refrigerant
to evaporator coil

refrigerant inlet
with filter screen

sensing bulb

superheat adjustment

FIGURE 11-42B. A cutaway view of an expansion valve. *(ALCO Controls)*

ing to the outlet temperature of the evaporator in a manner that maintains it at 6°F to 10°F (3.3°C to 5.5°C) above that temperature at which liquid slugging will occur. Superheat is this difference between the vaporization temperature of the refrigerant at the given evaporator pressure (as shown in Table 11-7) and the actual temperature of the evaporator's outlet.

A properly set valve reduces the supply of refrigerant if the superheat falls below the set point. This lowers the pressure in the evaporator (because the compressor is sucking against an increased restriction), which lowers the vaporization temperature of the refrigerant, restoring the superheat differential. As iceboxes cool down, the rate of heat removal slows, and a TXV responds by decreasing the refrigerant flow, which results in a steady drop in the pressure in the evaporator and thus in the suction pressure at the compressor.

Checking superheat. To check superheat settings, use a gauge set to determine the compressor's suction pressure, then read across the gauge needle to the various temperature scales in the center of the gauge. Select the appropriate scale for the refrigerant in use (HFC-134a, R-22, etc.) and read off the temperature given (or else look up the corresponding temperature in a pressure-temperature chart). *This is the minimum vaporization temperature of this refrigerant at this pressure.* Next, *precisely measure the temperature of the compressor suction line where it exits the evap-*

orator (this is generally where the sensing bulb is strapped on). This temperature measurement requires a sensitive electronic thermometer. *The amount by which this temperature exceeds the temperature read off the suction pressure gauge is, in theory, the degree of superheat in the system.*

A problem arises at this point. Frequently the compressor may have a long suction line containing bends and restrictions. The pressure measured at the compressor will be lower than that at the evaporator outlet, and *it is this latter pressure that is needed to determine the superheat.*

Some idea of the pressure drop in the suction line can be gained by watching the suction gauge while the unit runs and then cutting off the compressor. The pressure will jump and then slowly climb until it equalizes with the high side. This initial jump is fairly indicative of the pressure drop to the evaporator (if this jump is more than a pound or two, the suction lines are undersized—a relatively common problem—and need upgrading for optimum performance). The pressure registered immediately after the jump is the pressure to be used when reading off the minimum vaporization temperature of the refrigerant.

All this is rather academic, since equipment sensitive enough to measure evaporator temperatures accurately is unlikely to be available. In practice, cruder methods for setting up the superheat generally have to be used.

Superheat adjustments. Most expansion valves have a screw or squared-off stem in the body of the valve, covered with a ¾-inch (19 mm) cap nut. Remove the nut. Moving the screw beneath it in and out alters the amount of fluid passing through the expansion valve. (If there is no external superheat adjusting screw, the screw will be inside the discharge port of the expansion valve, and the valve must be taken out of the system to get at it! Avoid these valves like the plague.)

A system must be properly charged before making superheat adjustments.

Superheat adjustments are made while the unit is running, but only on a cold unit. To do otherwise is to invite liquid slugging at the compressor when the unit cools.

When making superheat adjustments, *never move the screw more than a half turn at a time and wait several minutes for the system to stabilize* (up to 20 minutes on a large-capacity holding-plate unit).

If the flow of refrigerant is increased, the suction pressure will rise slightly, and the suction line at the evaporator outlet will cool. If the flow of refrigerant is decreased, the opposite happens. If at any time the suction line frosts heavily all the way back to the compressor and down the compressor side, excessive refrigerant may be passing through the system, putting the compressor in danger of liquid slugging. (This situation also arises with overcharging of refrigerant; note also that some large-capacity systems with high refrigerant flows, especially in freezer service, may frost back to the compressor in normal service.) Restrict the flow or shut down the unit before damage occurs.

When a refrigeration or freezer system is cold, superheat can be adjusted to permit frosting of the suction line where it exits the evaporator. No damage to the compressor will occur as long as this frosting does not reach the compressor. (Even if it does, there is generally a degree of safety built in.)

Holding-plate units with multiple plates *in series* (one after the other) should be adjusted to permit frosting of the suction line where it exits *the last plate*. If the plates are *in parallel*, each will have its own expansion valve, which should be adjusted to permit mild frosting of the suction line where it exits the holding plate.

Air-conditioning units operate at higher pressures and temperatures, and the suction line should be cool at the compressor. If it is not, the expansion valve should be opened farther. *The suction line should never frost*; if it does, there is danger of liquid slugging at the compressor.

Holding plates fail to hold over. If this has always been the case, the icebox may have inadequate insulation or the unit and holding plate may just be too small. If the failure is a new problem, check the items covered under the Unit Fails to Cool Down or Cools Too Slowly section. In addition:

1. Consider whether a recent change in operating conditions (such as a move to warmer waters) is exposing a basic weakness for the first time.

2. Check the seal on the icebox lid or door.

3. Ask yourself if icebox usage has changed. For example, are some recently arrived heavy beer drinkers continually putting fresh cans of warm beer into the fridge? This is the WB (warm beer) factor!

4. See if the holding plates are heavily iced. This will insulate them and reduce the rate of heat removal from the icebox.

5. Over time, some icebox insulation will become permeated with water, resulting in a steady loss of efficiency. If icebox performance declines over time for no obvious reason, drill into the insulation low down on the icebox and check for moisture. If present, the icebox needs rebuilding.

Overcharge/undercharge symptoms. If a water-cooled unit with a TXV acts as if it is overcharged after a move into warmer waters (or undercharged after a move into colder waters), the RFD may be too small. This is especially likely on an engine-driven system using a small, automotive RFD. It should never be necessary to adjust the refrigerant charge for a change in water temperature or climate.

Charging and Topping-Off Procedures

In what follows it is essential to remember that at least in the United States and on U.S.-registered vessels, *it is illegal for an uncertified boatowner to do more than top off a system, and even when topping off, there must be no more than minimal releases of refrigerant to the atmosphere.* In Europe, it is illegal for uncertified boatowners to do *any* work on their refrigeration and air-conditioning systems.

Handling Refrigerant

Refrigerants are reasonably safe and inert gases, but a few precautions must be observed:

1. Refrigerant gases are heavier than air, and in large quantities will displace the oxygen needed to breathe (which makes them asphyxiants). In the small enclosed space of a boat, gases from leaks will sink into the bilges and gradually replace the air in the cabin, making the air progressively unbreathable. Serious leaks MUST be dispersed with a good airflow through the cabin.

2. Do NOT solder or braze on a system with refrigerant in it. It is unsafe. At high temperatures, R-12 will produce a gas similar to phosgene, which was used in the trenches in World War I (i.e., it is extremely toxic, and inhalation may cause death).

3. Never add any refrigerant to the high-pressure side of a unit when it is running. The high pressures may burst the can of refrigerant.

4. Do not leave refrigerant containers in direct sunlight or allow them to heat up beyond 125°F/52°C. (At higher temperatures, the resulting higher pressures may cause the can to burst.)

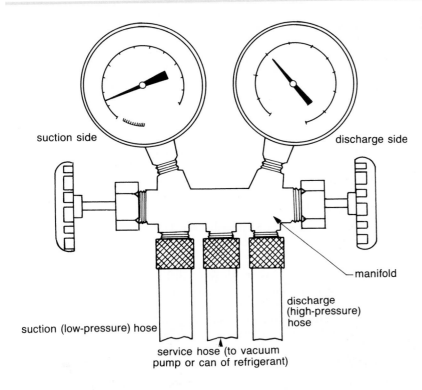

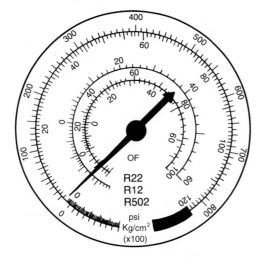

FIGURE 11-43. **Top:** A refrigerant gauge set, which is an essential tool for self-sufficient, refrigeration-equipped boats. **Right:** A suction-side gauge. The outer band indicates pressure; the inner bands indicate the evaporation/condensation temperature (°F) of R-22, R-12, and R-502 refrigerants at any given pressure.

FIGURE 11-44. Engine-driven compressor gauge connections.

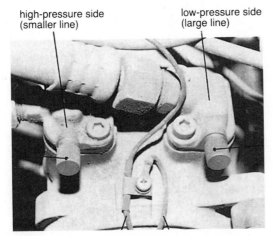

5. Cans of refrigerant contain liquid in the bottom and gas in the top. If the can is inverted when charging a system, liquid will come out. Professionals sometimes invert cans, but amateurs should always play it safe—charge with the gas, and never invert the can (the exception is the blends, which need to be charged as a liquid—consult a technician).

6. Evaporating refrigerant is extremely cold. It can cause frostbite and permanent eye damage. Wear safety glasses.

7. Different refrigerants and oils are incompatible—*be absolutely sure to use the correct one for a given unit.*

Charging Without a Gauge Set

Charging hoses can be bought from any automotive store or from Wal-Mart and similar stores. One end will fit a 12-ounce (or similar) can of refrigerant. The other will need whatever fitting or adapter is necessary to make a connection to the valve on the suction side of the compressor (unfortunately, there are a number of different valves in use).

First, install the hose on the can of refrigerant. To do this, back the valve on the end of the hose all the way out, and screw the hose onto the can. The valve is now screwed in. It will pierce the top of the can (you will hear refrigerant hissing out of the other end of the hose). Continue to screw in the valve until it closes off the refrigerant flow. Remove the cap from the suction valve on the compressor and loosely connect the other end of the hose to the valve. (On no account should you make a connection to the compressor discharge side; if you cannot positively identify the suction side, consult a technician.) Open the valve on the can of refrigerant so that refrigerant blows out of the loose connection at the compressor, and then snug up the connection. Now close the valve on the can of refrigerant. Making the connection in this fashion ensures that the hose is fully purged of all air.

The suction valve may be a Schrader type, a stem type (see the Making Connections section below), or one of several types of quick-connect fittings. With it *open to the system*, start the unit. (For larger systems with sight glasses, see the Charging a System section below.) For small, hermetic, constant-cycling systems without a sight glass, open the valve on the can of refrigerant for 5 seconds or so, then close it and let the system settle down for 10 minutes. What you want to see is the entire evaporator plate frosting as described above, but without frosting or sweating of the suction line at the compressor. If the evaporator plate is only partially frosting, open the refrigerant valve for another 5 seconds or so, and then let the system settle down once again. Continue to do this until the whole plate frosts. Then close the valve on the compressor and on the can of refrigerant, remove the hose, and cap the suction valve on the compressor.

Smaller systems take only a few ounces of refrigerant and are vulnerable to overcharging, so take things slowly. Larger systems that are low on refrigerant may take quite a bit of refrigerant. If the frost line is only advancing very slowly on the evaporator plate, leave the valve on the can open longer. As the can discharges, it may well get heavily frosted. This is normal.

Gauge Sets

A refrigeration gauge set is not expensive ($20 to $50—shop around), and it is an *essential* troubleshooting tool. Newer gauge sets have what are called *low-loss* fittings; these minimize refrigerant releases and are recommended. If using more than one refrigerant (in different systems), *use a dedicated gauge set for each system to avoid the possibility of cross-contamination*. Note that most gauge sets purchased for HFC-134a have connections that are designed for automotive air-conditioning systems. These are different from most marine refrigeration connections (the majority of which use ¼-inch SAE flare connections). You will need adapters to make a hookup.

A gauge set includes one red and one blue gauge screwed into a *manifold*; below each gauge is a hose (Figure 11-43). On either side of the manifold is a valve. A third hose, the service hose, is located between the two gauge hoses. When the gauge valves are closed, the gauges will register the pressure in their respective hoses. When either valve is opened, its hose is connected with the service hose. When both valves are opened at the same time, all three hoses equalize with one another. The blue side of a gauge set always connects to the suction (low-pressure) side of a compressor, the red side to the discharge (high-pressure) side. Suction and discharge connections will be found on the suction and discharge fittings on the compressor. Belt-driven compressors generally have the cylinder head stamped "SUCT" and "DISCH"; hermetically sealed compressors may not be labeled, but it doesn't matter. *The suction line is always larger than the discharge line* (Figure 11-44). There may also be other hose connections around the system, but the two closest to the compressor are the ones to use.

Making connections. *It is vitally important that no dirt enters a system. Before making any connections make sure that everything is spotlessly clean. Tighten the hose fittings by hand only.*

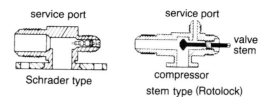

FIGURE 11-45A. Schrader valve and stem-type (Rotolock) valve—the two most commonly found types of service valves.

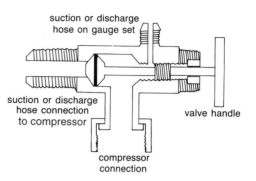

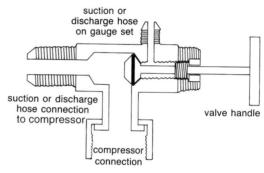

FIGURE 11-45B. Stem-type (Rotolock) valve operation. **Top:** Valve is closed to system but open to gauge set (for compressor removal, etc.). **Middle:** Valve is closed to gauge set but open to system (for normal operation). **Bottom:** Valve is open to both system and gauge set (for monitoring performance, etc.).

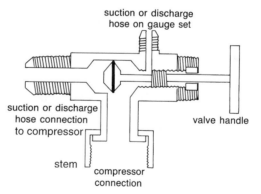

The hose connections on the compressor will be fitted with service valves. These will be Schrader valves, *stem-type (Rotolock)* valves (Figure 11-45A), or some kind of quick-connect fitting. Schrader valves are the same as valves on bicycle and car tires, with a spring-loaded pin. One end of each hose on the gauge set has a metal piece for depressing the pin in a Schrader valve—this end must always go on the valve.

Stem-type valves have a squared-off shaft, which is screwed in and out to open and close the valve (Figure 11-45B). There are three possible positions: all the way out (counterclockwise

FIGURE 11-46A. Purging a gauge set using refrigerant already in the system. Preliminary step: If the system has stem-type valves, fully backseat the valves. 1. Close both gauge valves. 2. Loosen the suction and discharge hose connections at the gauge set; tighten the service hose connection. 3. Tighten the suction and discharge hose connections at the compressor one at a time. 4. Schrader valves: Allow refrigerant to blow out of the loosened connections at the gauge set and then snug up. Stem-type valves: Turn the valves clockwise a half turn to one turn, allowing refrigerant to blow out of the loosened connections at the gauge set, then snug up. 5. Connect the service hose loosely to a can of refrigerant, crack open either gauge valve, allow refrigerant to blow out of the loosened connection at the can of refrigerant, and snug up. Purging is complete.

FIGURE 11-46B. Purging a gauge set using a can of refrigerant. Preliminary step: If the system has stem-type valves, fully backseat the valves. 1. Close the valve on the can of refrigerant. 2. Tighten the service hose at the can of refrigerant. 3. Close the gauge valves. 4. Tighten all three hose connections at the gauge manifold. 5. Fit the hoses loosely at the compressor. 6. Open the valve on the can of refrigerant. 7. Crack each gauge valve in turn, allowing refrigerant to blow out of the loosened connection at the compressor, then snug up. Now close the gauge valve if the compressor has Schrader valves (to avoid adding refrigerant to the system). Purging is complete.

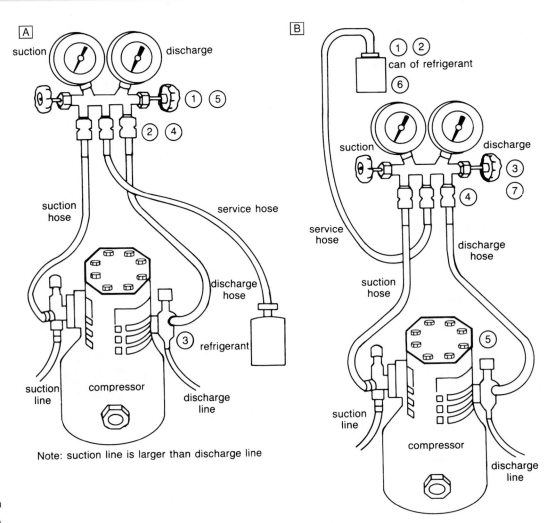

Note: suction line is larger than discharge line

or anticlockwise) closes off the gauge hose to the system but leaves the compressor hooked in; the middle position (a turn or so clockwise) opens the gauge hose to the system while still leaving the compressor hooked in; and all the way in (clockwise) closes off the compressor to the system but leaves the gauge hose connected to the compressor. A proper ¼-inch square ratchet wrench—obtainable from refrigeration supply houses—is highly recommended for stem-type valves. The use of adjustable wrenches or pliers soon messes up valve stems.

Purging a gauge set. Once a refrigeration or air-conditioning unit is charged, *it is essential that no air be allowed to enter the system.* What this means in practice is that anytime you hook up a gauge set for charging, you must purge the air from the gauge set hoses and replace it with refrigerant before making the final connections. When doing this, *refrigerant releases must be kept to an absolute minimum.* To purge a gauge set, first shut down the unit (if it is running). There are

then two methods (Figures 11-46A and 11-46B):

Using refrigerant already in the system (presupposing it has at least a partial charge). Close both gauge valves, loosen the hoses below the gauges, and prepare to screw the hoses onto their compressor connections.

If the compressor has Schrader valves or a quick-connect fitting, as each hose is done up (or attached), it will open the valve, and refrigerant gas will blow out of the loosened connection at the gauge manifold. Snug up the connection. This hose is purged.

If the compressor has stem-type valves, turn the valves fully counterclockwise before making any connections. Attach the hoses at the compressor and snug up, but leave the hoses loose at the gauge manifold. Turn the valve stems clockwise a half turn to one turn. Refrigerant will blow out of the loosened connections at the gauge manifold. Snug up these connections. The hoses are purged.

For both types of valves, connect a can of refrigerant to the service hose, leaving the hose loose at the can. Crack open either one of the gauge valves—refrigerant will blow out of the loose connection at the can. Snug up the connection. Purging is complete. (Note that if the can has a Schrader valve, the pin on the service hose must go on the can.)

Using a can of refrigerant. Close the valve on the can, then connect the can to the gauge manifold with the service hose and tighten both connections. Tighten the other two hoses at the manifold and connect them *loosely* at the compressor (we do not want to open a Schrader valve at this stage). Close both gauge valves and open the valve on the can of refrigerant. Crack each gauge valve in turn, blowing refrigerant out of the loose hose connection at the compressor before tightening the connection. If the compressor has Schrader valves or quick-connect fittings, close the gauge valves to avoid adding refrigerant to the system. Purging is complete.

On a unit with Schrader valves or quick-connect fittings, once the hoses are attached, the gauges are always open to the system; where stem-type valves are fitted, the valves must be opened a half turn to one turn clockwise.

Charging a system. Purge the hoses. Check to see that *both gauge valves are closed* and the stem-type valves on the compressor (if fitted) are open one turn. *Make sure the can of refrigerant is upright.* For an initial charge, without starting the system open the valve on the can of refrigerant. Open the suction-side gauge valve. Refrigerant will enter the unit. Wait until the suction pressure stabilizes (probably around 60 to 70 psi on an HFC-134a system, but this depends on the ambient temperature; the pressure should be approximately the same as the pressure corresponding to this ambient temperature according to the pressure-temperature chart). Now close the suction valve on the gauge set.

Charging with a sight glass. Locate the sight glass on the system. It will probably be on top of or next to the RFD. (Some air-conditioning units do not have a sight glass—see below.) Take a look in it; it will be clear. Start the unit and watch the sight glass. Fairly soon, foamy, fast-moving bubbles will appear as the first liquid refrigerant comes out of the condenser mixed with gas bubbles. The bubbles should steadily decrease. In a fully charged, fully cold system, they will disappear altogether, leaving a sight glass that is once again either completely clear but filled with liquid or else with a steady stream of bubble-free liquid pouring through it.

If a unit is very low on refrigerant, the initial charge of refrigerant is not going to be enough to produce a steady stream or clear the sight glass.

The problem is to determine how much more to put in—too much will damage the compressor. The final charge can be determined only with the unit cold. In the case of air conditioners and refrigeration units without holding plates, this will take only 5 minutes or so, but where holding plates are fitted, if the plates are warm it may take from 20 minutes to 2 hours, and perhaps even longer.

Monitor the sight glass continually. If the stream of bubbles is still pretty steady once the unit has cooled down a bit, with the unit running open the suction-side gauge valve to let in more refrigerant. The bubbles will start to decrease. After a while there should be a steady stream or maybe just one big bubble hovering in the top of the sight glass. Close the gauge valve and let the unit stabilize. If more bubbles appear, add more refrigerant. Let the unit get really cold—don't rush things—before doing the final topping off. Eventually the sight glass will have a solid stream of refrigerant or be completely clear (all liquid). Don't add any more refrigerant.

Using the pressure-temperature chart for the refrigerant in the system, if the unit has an air-cooled condenser, check to see what high-side pressure is expected if the discharge temperature is 20°F to 30°F (11°C to 17°C) above the ambient air temperature; with water cooling, assume a discharge temperature 15°F/8°C above the ambient water temperature. If the high-side pressure is well below the expected pressure, more refrigerant is probably required. If it is high (typically, much over 200 psi on an air-cooled refrigeration unit, 125 psi on a water-cooled unit, or 250 psi on an air conditioner), and/or the suction line on a refrigeration unit starts to frost heavily all the way back to the compressor, the system may well be overcharged. There should be no frosting of the suction line with an air conditioner.

Charging without a sight glass. Most air-conditioning manuals specify a set of operating pressures at certain ambient air and cooling water temperatures (refer back to Figure 11-34). Measure the air and water temperatures, refer to the graphs provided, and read off the suction and discharge pressures. Continue adding refrigerant until these pressures, or something close to them, are reached. When charged and in operation, the compressor suction line will be cool and probably sweating. If it is warm, the charge is inadequate; if it is frosting, the charge is excessive. (This applies to air conditioners only; many refrigeration and freezer units run colder, and some frosting of the suction line is acceptable.)

Removing a gauge set. *Shut down the unit.* Close off any can of refrigerant, but leave its hose connections tight. Open both gauge valves until the system equalizes, with both gauges reading the same pressure. Close both gauge valves. Loosen the hose connection at the can of refrigerant, allow the hose pressure to bleed off, and remove the hose from the can of refrigerant.

Schrader and quick-connect valves. Remove each hose in turn at the compressor as fast as possible. Refrigerant will vent from a Schrader valve as long as the valve stem is depressed, which is why the hoses must be undone quickly.

Stem-type valves. Backseat the valves counterclockwise. Crack one of the gauge valves and bleed off its hose through the service hose. Close the gauge valve and observe the pressure—if it climbs back up, the stem valve is not properly seated (the high-pressure side may show a slight pressure rise initially but then should stabilize). When the stem valve is holding, bleed off the hose and remove it. Repeat this process for the other hose.

Cap all valves and hose ends to make sure that no dirt can enter the system.

For an in-depth look at marine refrigeration, see my *Refrigeration for Pleasureboats*, published by International Marine.

Vacuuming (evacuating) a unit. If a unit loses all its charge, or gets opened up to the atmosphere in any way, it is likely to be contaminated by air and moisture. Moisture is a particular problem. Water droplets freeze instantly as they emerge from a capillary tube or expansion valve, plugging up the orifice. Water will also react with the refrigerant to form corrosive acids. A filter-drier will eliminate some contaminants, but a unit must be basically clean before charging. All air must be removed since the gases in air do not liquefy at the temperatures and pressures found in a refrigeration system; they end up in the condenser, occupying space that would otherwise be taken by the refrigerant, and as a result cutting condenser efficiency.

A unit is cleaned out with a *vacuum pump*, a specialized piece of equipment that only a refrigeration specialist is likely to have and/or be licensed to use.

A gauge set is connected to the service fittings on a compressor and the vacuum pump is hooked up to the service hose on the gauge set. Both the gauge valves, and any stem-type valves, are opened on the compressor and the pump is turned on. The pump sucks all the air out of the system and should suck it down to an almost complete vacuum (–29.2 inches of mercury).

As the pressure falls (the vacuum increases) so too does the evaporation temperature of water (refer back to Figure 11-27). At a vacuum of 29 inches of mercury, water boils at below 70°F.

Thus if a unit is vacuumed down on any day that the temperature is above 70°F, any moisture in the system will boil off and be drawn out by the pump. Note that *a cold system must be allowed to warm up to the ambient temperature before vacuuming.* Once the pump is pulling a complete vacuum it should be left on for *at least 30 minutes*, and preferably for an hour or two.

At some point the gauge valves should be closed while a unit is at a full vacuum and the vacuum pump is turned off. If the pressure (vacuum) is observed for 5 minutes or so, it will soon be clear if the system has any leaks—if the vacuum declines there is a leak. In this case the unit will have to be pressured up, and tested for leaks (see the Charging Procedures and Leak Detection sections above).

Vacuuming with a compressor. In the absence of a vacuum pump it is possible to evacuate a system using the compressor, but this procedure should be carried out only if there is no other choice. It is not as effective as a vacuum pump, risks damaging the compressor (especially a hermetic or swash-plate compressor), and may be illegal (depending on where it is done and the refrigerant in use; remember also that opening a unit to service it is illegal in all developed countries—except in the case of HFC-134a in the U.S., and this may change). The procedure is as follows:

1. Connect the gauge set to the compressor. Close the gauge valves. Loosen the discharge hose at the gauge set. Open stem-type valves (if fitted) one turn. Connect a can of refrigerant to the service hose. Open the can's valve wide and then the suction gauge valve wide. Refrigerant will blow around the system and out through the discharge hose at the loose connection on the gauge manifold. Let it blow for a few seconds, then close the valve on the can of refrigerant, tighten the discharge hose while it is still venting, and close the suction-side gauge valve (both valves will now be closed). Disconnect the service hose at the can of refrigerant. At this point most of the moisture and air will have been blown out of the system.

2. Put an inch or two of clean *refrigeration oil* in a jam jar. Start the unit and turn on the compressor. Keep down the compressor speed if at all possible (for example, idle the engine on an engine-driven unit; use the lowest speed on a unit with a manually operated speed controller). Open the discharge-side gauge valve; the compressor will pump down the system through the open service hose. When the gas flow from the service hose slows (this won't take long), dip the hose into the jar of refrig-

eration oil so that no air can be sucked back in. Watch the suction gauge.

3. The service hose in the oil will stop bubbling and the suction gauge will go into a vacuum quite quickly (within a minute or two). If it doesn't, there is a bad leak on the system (the service hose will continue to bubble) or the compressor is defective. Engine-driven and other powerful compressors should pull a vacuum of up to –28 inches of mercury; smaller units will pull a little less. Once the system is at its deepest vacuum, close the discharge gauge valve, and *shut down the compressor.* The unit is now evacuated.

4. Reconnect the can of refrigerant. Loosen the service hose at the gauge manifold. Open the valve on the can of refrigerant and purge the service hose (blow off a little refrigerant at the loosened connection on the manifold and then snug up the hose connection). Open the suction-side valve and fill the unit with refrigerant. Loosen the discharge hose at the gauge manifold and blow off refrigerant again; we are back at step 1: Close the valve on the can of refrigerant, tighten the discharge hose while it is still venting, and close the suction-side gauge valve (both valves will now be closed). Disconnect the can of refrigerant.

5. Repeat steps 2 and 3.

6. Reconnect the can of refrigerant, purge the service hose as in step 4, and charge the unit (see above). *Do not, on any account, remove the gauge set until enough refrigerant has been put in the system to give a positive pressure, or you will have wasted your efforts!*

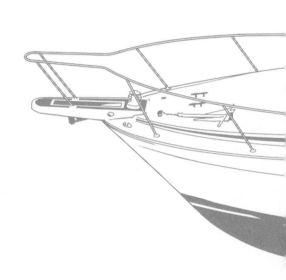

FIGURE 12-1. Problems with onboard plumbing can ruin a cruise faster than anything else. A familiarity with the system—and where everything is located—is highly recommended. *(Jim Sollers)*

_____ cold water

---------- hot water

(1) Y-valve
(2) macerator pump
(3) toilet pump
(4) shower sump
(5) lavatory basin
(6) vented loop
(7) galley sink
(8) ice maker
(9) shower
(10) freshwater fill
(11) head overboard discharge
(12) head raw-water intake
(13) holding tank
(14) lavatory basin drain
(15) galley sink drain
(16) water heater
(17) air conditioner raw-water intake
(18) engine cooling water intake
(19) auxiliary raw-water intake
(20) freshwater tank
(21) freshwater pump
(22) washdown system
(23) holding tank pumpout
(24) bilge pump
(25) bilge pump strainer
(26) collection box
(27) foot pump

Tanks, Plumbing, Toilets, and Through-Hull Fittings

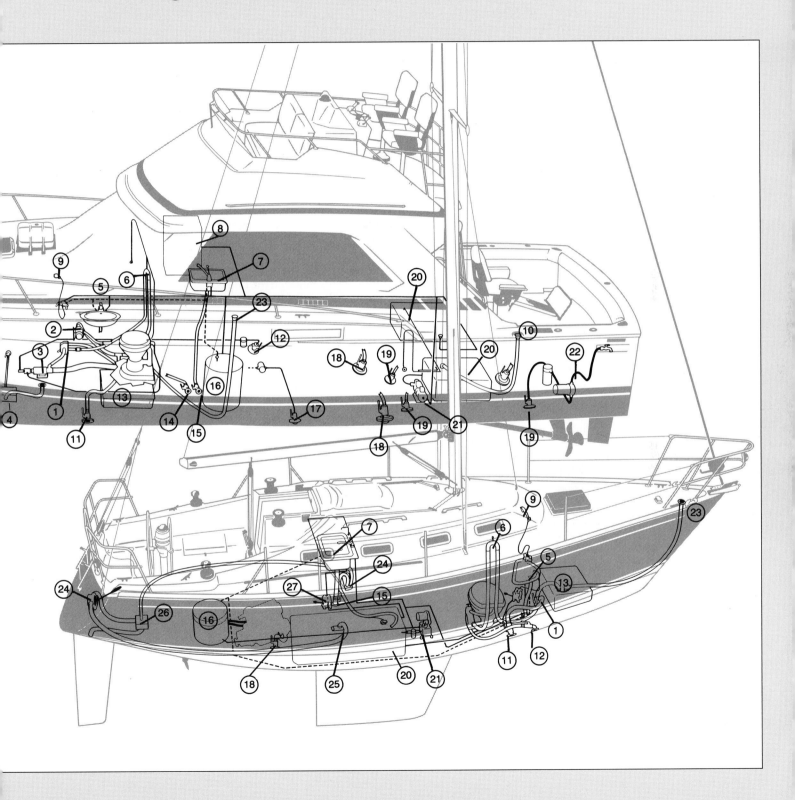

Tanks and Fittings

When we built our first cruising boat some 25 years ago, I gave a lot of thought to the question of fuel- and water-tank materials and construction. My primary concern was to ensure the integrity of the tanks for the life of the boat.

We built fiberglass tanks into the boat, and they were a great success. However, it should be noted that *built-in gasoline fuel tanks are illegal*—in the United States, the relevant regulations are found in the Code of Federal Regulations (CFR), Title 33; in Europe, in ISO 10088—whereas built-in diesel and water tanks are not. However, ISO standards require that if used as diesel tanks, built-in tanks must be pressure tested and labeled the same as any other fuel tank.

At the time of writing, I am in the process of fitting out our new boat, a Malo 45. We are faced with the exact same issue. We may have this boat well into my retirement years, and as I don't want to be faced with the prospect of ripping out the tanks and replacing them when I am getting old and feeble, it is essential that the tanks have the ability to outlast me! This is a pretty tall order to fill.

Choices for tanks include built-in tanks (which, depending on hull material, might be wood, fiberglass, aluminum, or steel) and independent fiberglass, stainless steel, steel, aluminum, and plastic tanks. All are in use today.

Built-In Tanks

It has always seemed to me a missed opportunity that more builders of fiberglass and composite boats do not use integral tanks. I have tried (unsuccessfully) to persuade the builders of my last two boats to go this way.

The benefits of built-in tanks are:

- They exploit every possible cubic inch of available space.
- They eliminate the small air spaces between tanks and the hull in which debris and objects can get lodged.
- If built into the bottom of the boat, they effectively form a double bottom so that if the hull gets breached in the area of the tank, the boat will still not take on water.
- The ability to fully utilize all the available volume in the bilges often removes the necessity to place additional tanks under settee berths and sleeping berths. This lowers the center of gravity on the boat and frees up prime storage space.

This is a substantial list of positive benefits. The principal concerns are:

- If a tank fails, the boat must be ripped apart to fix it. Since every tank is a custom fabrication, quality control is difficult, which increases the chances that one small mistake in construction or layup could cost a builder dearly. This issue can only be addressed by proper quality control.
- There is a fear of the fluid in the tank permeating the hull layup on fiberglass and composite boats, especially boats with balsa or foam cores. This concern can be addressed in one of two ways: (1) by careful layup of the laminate, with additional protection against the hull; or (2) by building a tank up against the hull but on a sheet of plastic so that it does not bond, then removing the tank and plastic sheet and testing the tank before bonding it in place. There are now two independent "skins"—the tank wall and the inner hull skin—between the fluid in the tank and the hull core. (Note that if integral diesel tanks are used in a cored area of the hull, the ABYC requires that the core be constructed so that it will not deteriorate from contact with diesel fuel or permit fuel to migrate through it.)
- The tops of centerline tanks form a flat surface, thus eliminating any defined bilge at this point. If the boat takes on water when heeled, the water will tend to run up the sides of the boat. However, as long as there is a decent bilge sump between the tanks, even when heeled, water entering the boat will run along the "gutter" formed where the tank edge meets the hull, finding its way into the sump.
- Integral tank construction is relatively labor intensive and expensive.

Desirable features. Certain types of hulls lend themselves to integral tanks (especially centerline tanks, which get the weight in the best possible place and are the most likely to protect against a breach in the hull). They are:

- Hulls with internal ballast. There are no keel bolts needing access.
- Hulls with traditional "wineglass" sections. The hull shape mitigates against any flexing that might damage tank bonds, as opposed to hulls with flat sections that are more prone to flexing. The deep hull sections ensure that, whatever the angle of heel, pickup lines will not suck dry before the tank is empty.

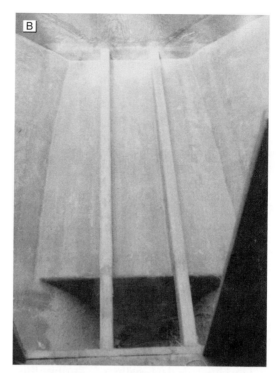

FIGURE 12-2A. Integral freshwater tank construction. The wineglass sections especially lend themselves to integral tanks. The hullside has been lined with a layer of resin-rich mat to seal it (the hull is, in any case, not cored). The half pipe on the centerline is a limber pipe for draining the bilges up forward. Note the spaces below the baffles and the cutout at the top of each to allow for water and air circulation. The baffles (and tank top) are constructed from fiberglass flat stock so they won't be vulnerable to water damage (with an added epoxy-sealed stringer at the top of each baffle to provide a bonding surface for the tank top). The tank has been painted with water tank paint to seal it. This was a mistake (see the text). The area in front of the forward baffle is the boat's sump; forward of this is a diesel tank. Placing the sump between the two maintains total separation of the drinking water tank from the diesel tank.

FIGURES 12-2B AND 12-2C. The tank top and cabin sole in place. There is not a cubic inch of wasted space!

Certain other features of the tank construction on our first boat are worth noting (Figures 12-2A, 12-2B, and 12-2C). To maintain total separation of the diesel and water tanks, we placed the boat's bilge sump between the diesel and water tanks. If the fuel tank had leaked, we would have picked it up in the bilge before it got into a water tank. We had three water tanks, so if one failed we still had a water supply. We had heard that fiberglass tanks imparted an unpleasant taste to water, so we painted the insides of the water tanks with water-tank paint before installing the tops. This was a mistake, since over time the paint slowly peeled off. (We never did detect any taste.) Instead of using paint for water tanks, lay up the innermost laminate with a resin (preferably epoxy) approved for use in potable water systems (in the United States, use one approved by the Food and Drug Administration [FDA]).

Other materials. Over the years, some builders of laminated-wood (strip-planked or cold-molded) vessels have experimented with built-in plywood and epoxy tanks. I don't know what kind of success or problems they have had, but I imagine similar considerations apply as with glassed-in tanks. However, I would be very concerned about adequately sealing a plywood tank. The slightest damage to the surface of the tank, or improper sealing of access holes, will eventually lead to delamination of the plywood, resulting in expensive repairs.

In metal boats, built-in tanks can be constructed with less labor, fewer quality control problems, and less likelihood of suffering damage as a result of the working of the hull than is the case with fiberglass, composite, or laminated-wood hulls. Nevertheless, such tanks are a potential time bomb. Sooner or later, all metal tanks are likely to corrode, once again raising the specter of expensive repairs or replacement. I would think long and hard before putting integral metal tanks in a boat. I would not use metal tanks (integral or stand-alone) for holding tanks (effluent is too corrosive).

Aluminum Tanks

Let's look a little closer at this corrosion problem with metal tanks (built-in or stand-alone), starting with aluminum.

Aluminum has been widely used as a tank material in the marine world for many years. In particular, it is used for foamed-in-place gasoline tanks in many smaller powerboats and for diesel tanks on larger boats. In spite of its popularity, there are numerous instances of failures in aluminum tanks. Some years ago, these failures prompted Underwriters Laboratories (UL) to initiate "A Study On Problems with Aluminum Fuel Tanks in Recreational Boats" (1994). This report was summarized in a Coast Guard *Boating Safety Circular* (#79, April 1997). The opening paragraph of the report reads:

"The limited data gathered during this research showed that aluminum fuel tanks failed in many different types, makes, and models of recreational boats owned by the general public. Boats from 3 to 27 years old, 17 to 57 feet in length, inexpensive to very expensive, and used in both salt and fresh waters . . . were reported to have experienced significant problems associated with the aluminum fuel tanks installed as manufacturers' standard equipment."

Corrosion. The primary reason these tanks fail is corrosion, regardless of whether or not marine-grade aluminum alloys are used in construction (the applicable ABYC standards [H-24 and H-33] recommend the use of 5052, 5083, or 5086 magnesium-bearing alloys; the ISO standard specifies "no more than 0.1% copper"). This corrosion occurs "on the bottom of tanks,

under hold-down straps, at voids under flotation foam" and where "surfaces of the fuel tanks have prolonged contact with water in the bilge."

The report notes that "aluminum is one of the more reactive metals in the galvanic series table" (see Chapter 5), making it subject to three types of corrosion: pitting, crevice, and galvanic (Figure 12-3). In all three cases, although the causes of corrosion may differ, the mechanism is the same—an electrochemical reaction that results in the dissolution of the aluminum.

All it takes to set this corrosion in motion is moisture. Bilge water, in particular, contains all kinds of impurities that have been washed off the decks or flushed out of the boat, and as a result, forms "a high-conductivity electrolyte very rich in impurities" creating "a very harsh corrosive environment."

Coating aluminum tanks with anticorrosion paints and surface treatments will help prevent corrosion, but they can be a double-edged sword. If the coating is breached and moisture is added, any tendency toward galvanic corrosion is likely to be concentrated at this point, accelerating the rate of localized corrosion. In general, aluminum tanks should be left bare.

Bonding. Because of their position in the galvanic series table, aluminum alloys are likely to suffer corrosion anytime they are in electrical contact with a less anodic metal (just about any other boatbuilding metal) at the same time as both are in contact with an electrolyte. This electrical contact includes that between the base metal and weld metal in welded tanks, the contact that occurs when fittings are screwed into a tank, and the connection that may be created by a *bonding* circuit (the wiring of the tank to the boat's grounding system).

Bonding is an ABYC, USCG, and ISO requirement for gasoline tanks, and an ABYC recommendation for all metal fuel tanks; the ABYC also recommends that water and other tanks be bonded for lightning protection. But once bonded, the bonding wire forms an electrical connection between the tank and any other bonded metal, with bilge water forming a potential electrolyte. In such a situation, if both metals are submerged in bilge water (or any other water, for that matter), the other metal is almost always higher in the galvanic series table, and as such, is less reactive than aluminum, in which case the aluminum corrodes (see Chapter 5). In other words, widespread galvanic corrosion is probable anytime a bonded tank is in contact with bilge water in which another bonded metal object is also submerged, such as an engine pan. (This is one reason why ISO 15083 ["Small craft—Bilge-pumping systems"] defines the "critical bilge-water level" as the "level at which bilge water

FIGURE 12-3. A copper coin landed on this aluminum tank. With the addition of salt water, it set up a galvanic cell that ate right through the tank!

will contact metallic fuel tanks, couplings, engine pans, nonsubmersible machinery, or nonwatertight electrical circuits and connections, with the craft in the static floating position or in normal operation.")

Copper fittings. Copper-based fittings (commonly used in fuel systems) can be particularly destructive to aluminum (Figure 12-4). When exposed to an electrolyte, the normal galvanic interaction is exacerbated by the fact that copper ions enter the electrolyte and plate out on the aluminum causing small, very active, localized galvanic cells. *Copper-based fittings must always be separated from aluminum tanks* (generally through the use of stainless steel washers and adapters).

Installation issues. Careful installation will eliminate many of the causes of corrosion, so among other things, ABYC and ISO standards call for the following:

- Metallic components used in a fuel system must be selected and assembled to minimize galvanic interaction.

- In particular, copper-based alloy components (e.g., many tank fittings) must be separated from contact with aluminum tanks by a galvanic barrier such as 300 series stainless steel adapters and washers.

- All nonintegral tank supports (i.e., not welded to the tank), chocks, or hangers must be separated from tank surfaces by a nonmetallic, non-moisture-absorbent, nonabrasive material such as neoprene, Teflon, or high-density plastic.

- Self-wicking material, such as carpet pile, must not be in contact with a metallic tank.

- Tanks must be designed and installed to allow water drainage from all surfaces when the boat is in its static floating position.

- Any tank installed above a flat surface must be separated from the surface by at least a ¼-inch (ABYC)/5 mm (ISO) air space, and the surface must not trap water.

- Tanks must be installed where they *cannot be reached by normal accumulations of bilge water* in the static floating position. (The ISO requires the bottom of the tank to be "no less than 25 mm above the top of the bilge pump inlet or the bilge pump automatic float switch.")

- *It should be possible to remove a metal tank without tearing the boat apart.*

The preferred method of installing metal tanks is to use flanges on the tank, or welded-on

FIGURE 12-4. Copper-based fittings should always be isolated from aluminum tanks. These are not, which is asking for trouble.

tabs, so that no part of the tank itself is in contact with any mounting surface. This way, moisture will not be trapped against any tank surface, and any corrosion that does take place will tend to be concentrated under the flanges or tabs and will not threaten the integrity of the tank itself. For such an approach to work, the flanges or tabs and any associated welds clearly must be strong enough to withstand all stresses the tank will be subjected to. Repair or replacement of the flange or tab should be possible without tearing the boat apart.

Eventual failure. Regardless of the method used to mount the tank, it will still be impossible to eliminate all sources of moisture contact with tank surfaces. For example, the common practice of filling fuel tanks before leaving a boat leads to moisture formation (the fuel in the tank responds to temperature changes more slowly than the surrounding ambient atmosphere, resulting in condensation on the exterior tank surfaces). The moisture gets under straps and bearers when these are used, and in minute crevices in the metal if the tank is not in contact with other surfaces, and corrosion may start.

From a theoretical point of view, the UL study postulates that 0.090-inch (2.3 mm) plate (the minimum thickness permitted by ABYC for aluminum fuel tank construction) has a service life of 6.5 years in the marine environment; 0.125-inch (3.2 mm) plate (commonly used for more heavily built tanks) has a service life of 17.4 years. In real life, of course, things are not nearly this predictable, but the salient point remains: *You cannot assume aluminum tanks will last the life of today's boats.*

Stainless Steel Tanks

What about stainless steel? Stainless steel tanks are often considered by the buying public to be the mark of superior quality. This is a misconception that can have expensive consequences, for it turns out that many stainless steel tanks are just as susceptible to corrosion as aluminum tanks.

As noted in Chapter 5, stainless steel contains both chromium and nickel. The stainless gets its resistance to corrosion when the chromium in the alloy reacts with oxygen in the atmosphere to form a microscopic surface layer of chromium oxide. Anytime this layer is breached, the underlying metal is at risk of corroding. However, given a continuing supply of oxygen, the chromium oxide layer will "heal" itself, preventing corrosion.

Problems arise when stainless steel gets wet in a deoxygenated environment. Without oxygen, the chromium oxide layer is likely to break down. When this occurs, all it takes to set up a galvanic cell is a little moisture, combined with minute differences in the composition of the stainless alloy. Corrosion can then be quite rapid. Just as with aluminum, typical areas in which corrosion is likely to develop are under hold-down straps or where a tank is resting on its bearers. As a result, the same installation requirements listed above for aluminum tanks also apply to stainless steel tanks.

Acceptable grades of stainless steel. In general, given a specific chromium content, the alloys with higher nickel contents are more corrosion resistant. Of those most commonly used in the marine world, 304 has 18% chromium and 10% nickel, 316 has 17% chromium and 12% nickel, and 317 has 18% chromium and 14% nickel. 316 and 317 also have small amounts of molybdenum (2.5% and 3.5%, respectively), which further enhances corrosion resistance.

In addition to these grades of stainless steel, other more corrosion-resistant grades have become widely available in recent years. These are distinguished both by the incorporation of 6% or more molybdenum in the mix (resulting in the nickname the "6% mollies"), and also typically around 0.2% nitrogen (which has also been found to enhance corrosion resistance; for more on stainless steel, see Chapter 5).

Low-carbon alloys. Most stainless alloys contain traces of carbon. In standard alloys, the carbon content is limited to 0.08% by weight. When the metal is welded, this carbon has a tendency to migrate to the boundaries of the weld and to combine with the chromium in these areas. The carbon effectively *locks up* the chromium, not only disabling it in terms of its corrosion-prevention role, but also creating differences in the composition of the alloy in and around the weld. In the presence of moisture, a galvanic cell is likely to develop, resulting in corrosion (something known as *intergranular corrosion* or *weld decay*).

Heat treatment of welded stainless components will redistribute the carbon and prevent intergranular corrosion, but this is generally impractical with large items such as tanks. The addition of trace amounts of niobium or titanium to an alloy will also neutralize the carbon (yielding types 347 and 321 stainless steel, respectively), resulting in what are known as *stabilized* alloys. Another way to minimize

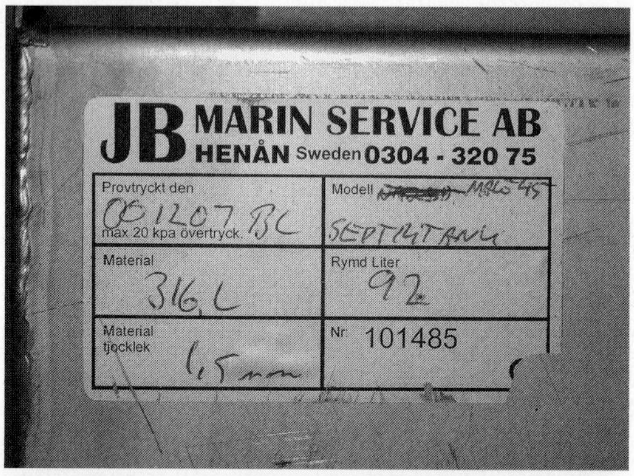

FIGURE 12-5A. The label on a holding tank being installed in our new boat. Note that the tank is 316L stainless steel. Nevertheless, I am not happy with the use of metal tanks . . .

FIGURE 12-5B. . . . especially since the tank is built into the boat and cannot be replaced without major surgery.

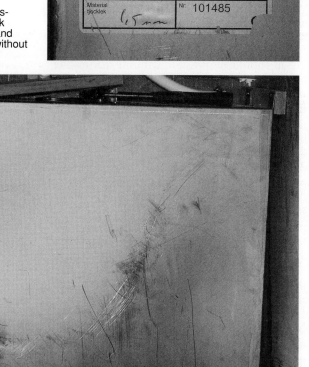

problems is to use specially formulated stainless steels that have a very low carbon content (below 0.03%). Such alloys are often designated by the addition of an "L" after the alloy number; e.g., 304L and 316L (Figure 12-5A).

Making choices. Experience has shown that although they are widely used, especially in off-shore-built boats (primarily from the Far East), *304 and 304L are not suitable for tank construction.* The 316L/317L alloys should be the minimum that are used for boat tanks. The 6% mollies are a better choice. While not immune to corrosion, 6% mollies, along with proper design and fabrication, will produce a tank with a life exceeding that of most small craft. Although more expensive than the 316L/317L alloys, the cost of a tank will be cheaper on a life-cycle cost basis.

As with aluminum tanks, it should be possible to remove a stainless steel tank (whatever the grade of stainless steel) from a boat without having to tear the boat apart (Figures 12-5B and 12-5C).

Construction issues. Unfortunately, until problems start to show up, in most circumstances neither a boatowner nor a marine surveyor can tell a good stainless steel tank from a bad one. As a result, quality control and a reputable manufacturer are very important.

Aside from choosing an appropriate grade of stainless steel for tank construction (including an appropriate filler metal for welding, which is crucial if galvanic corrosion along the weld line is to be avoided), skilled labor is needed for tank assembly. If the tank is to have a trouble-free service life, it is also essential that proper shop procedures are followed during manufacture and installation. Most important is to avoid con-

tamination of the stainless steel (Figure 12-6). If, for example, a weld is cleaned with a steel brush, or a neighboring ferrous item is ground down spattering the stainless steel with ferrous particles, these ferrous particles will start to rust once the tank is in a salt atmosphere, leaving unsightly stains.

Of more significance is the fact that the rusting particles can initiate galvanic corrosion of the underlying stainless steel, which can continue until the tank is perforated. Even something as apparently benign as a grease pencil mark can result in corrosion by creating an anaerobic environment (absence of oxygen) in

FIGURE 12-5C. The main water tank installed in our new boat (center of the picture) with structural beams being installed over the top. Once again, this is a stainless steel tank that will require the boat to be torn apart if it ever needs replacing. The boatbuilder claims never to have had a failed tank, but it still makes me nervous. *(Ulf Mattson)*

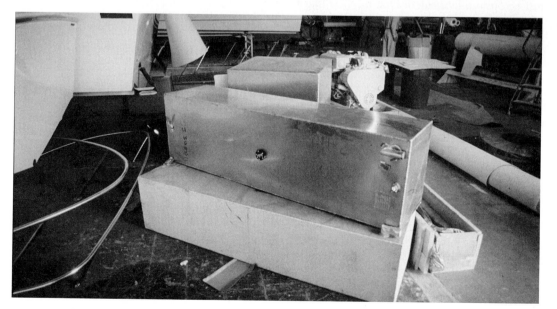

FIGURE 12-6. Stainless and aluminum tanks awaiting installation. There is no telling what surface contaminants are being acquired by these tanks. Add a little salt water, and these contaminants can initiate a galvanic cell.

which a drop of moisture can initiate a galvanic cell (although the higher corrosion resistance of the 6% mollies makes a grease pencil mark a highly unlikely cause of crevice corrosion).

Steel Tanks

Despite its tendency to corrode, particularly when exposed to salt water, steel is not a bad tank material. It is cheap and can be made thick enough to substitute mass for corrosion resistance. In gasoline applications, it should be hot-dip-galvanized both internally and externally. But in diesel applications, galvanizing should never be used on the inside of the tank since the sulfur in the fuel will dissolve the galvanizing, creating a sludge that is damaging to the fuel system. A steel tank that is properly primed and painted with a two-part epoxy will be as resistant to corrosion as most aluminum and stainless steel tanks, but at far less cost.

Similar installation issues apply as with aluminum and stainless steel, and tanks should be removable without tearing the boat apart.

Plastic: Fiberglass, Polyethylene, Polypropylene, and Flexible Tanks

This brings us back to some form of a plastic tank. The two common choices are fiber-reinforced plastic (FRP—fiberglass) and polyethylene (PE).

The UL study of aluminum fuel tanks noted in passing that "fiberglass tanks . . . have been in existence for many years. This type of tank has a good track record and has proven its effectiveness . . ."

Fiberglass. As far as I know, there are no production builders of fiberglass tanks; each tank must be custom-fabricated. One method that I have used for tanks with a capacity of less than 30 gallons is to make a mold from Styrofoam (the mold can be shaped to fit any space), and then cover the mold with a plastic film. This creates a smooth surface over which the tank is laid up, using resin-rich layers on the inside to make the tank impermeable. When the tank is finished, I cut an access hole in the top, and either dig out the foam or dissolve it (gasoline works well, although this creates a disposal problem). Larger tanks require baffles, which necessitates either constructing the tank with the top off so that the baffles can be bonded in place before adding the top or adding antisurge baffling after construction is finished.

Antisurge baffling (safety foam baffling) is a material used in the race car industry to minimize fuel leaks and fires in crashes that rupture fuel tanks. You can buy it in premanufactured sizes to fit a tank under construction before the top goes on, or in blocks that can be added in chunks through a large-enough inspection hatch. It holds the fuel in its open cell structure, providing the same damping action as a baffle. If the tank space is completely occupied by foam, it will take up about 3% of the volume. It is compatible with both gasoline and diesel. The one drawback is that it may start to break down after a number of years (Aero Tec Laboratories, the manufacturer, says 7), clogging fuel filters. For more information, go to www.atlfuelcells.com.

Properly constructed and installed, fiberglass tanks can be expected to last the life of a boat. They would be my preferred option. However, as the UL study notes, "the disadvantage of these tanks is that they are very labor-intensive to produce, making this option time- and cost-prohibitive . . ." The cost is particularly high for gasoline tanks, which by law have to be tested for compliance with Coast Guard and ISO standards. On a production line, the cost of testing a representative sample can be amortized over the entire production run; with custom-building, it must be absorbed by the individual tank.

Polyethylene. Polyethylene is the other commonly available plastic for tank construction. It is amazingly tough and durable. Best of all, of course, is the fact that as with all plastics, polyethylene is immune to corrosion.

Polyethylene comes in two forms—*linear* and *cross linked*. In both cases, the raw material (*resin*) is in the form of a powder that has the consistency of sugar. A given amount of this material is weighed and placed inside a female mold. The mold is slowly rotated *biaxially* (in two axes) while being heated. The powder uniformly coats the inside of the mold, turning into a gel. The mold is then air and water cooled, after which it is opened and the tank popped out. This process, known as *rotational molding*, is computer controlled, which ensures effective quality control.

Quite complex shapes can be produced, including indentations for hold-down devices, reinforcements for fittings, and baffles (partial dams molded into the top and bottom surfaces) on larger tanks. However, there are limitations to what can be done. In particular, the larger the tank, the harder it is to create adequate baffles. As a result, most large tanks are built from aluminum or stainless steel, although antisurge baffling may also be added to a PE tank.

Linear polyethylene. Linear polyethylene is a thermoplastic, meaning it will soften if reheated, and in fact it can be recycled (although recycled material is not as strong as virgin material). The FDA requires the use of virgin linear polyethylene in water tanks, which is where it is principally used (also for holding tanks). Linear polyethylene is not suitable for fuel tanks because hydrocarbons eventually cause it to crack.

Generally linear polyethylene tanks are partially transparent, which the manufacturers tout as an advantage since it enables the liquid level to be determined. When used for holding tanks, this partial transparency allows the tanks to meet an ISO requirement that the level of the contents "shall be observable when the holding tank is ¾ full by volume" (if the tank is not observable, the level must be indicated "by other means"). However, if light is allowed to enter a freshwater system, it encourages the growth of algae. My preference for this application is opaque tanks and tubing.

Note that the ISO requires holding tanks over 40 liters capacity (10 U.S. gallons) to have "an accessible, sealable (i.e., vapour- and liquid-tight) minimum opening of 75 mm diameter or smallest dimension to the holding tank interior for flushing, cleaning, and maintenance" (the ABYC does not have the same requirement). I see numerous installations that are not accessible enough to meet this standard, and in any case do not have an opening of the requisite size.

Cross-linked polyethylene. Cross-linked polyethylene (XLPE) has a peroxygen added that chemically changes the material into a thermoset (i.e., once the melt has hardened, it will not melt again with reheating). Of more importance is the fact that the peroxygen raises the environmental stress crack resistance (ESCR) so long-term use with various fuels does not degrade the material. As a result, cross-linked polyethylene makes an excellent fuel tank material, although it is not acceptable to the FDA for use on potable water systems.

Construction and installation issues. Wall thickness is in many ways the key determinant of a tank's strength and quality. In the case of holding tanks, it is also important in terms of minimizing odor permeation (you should use nothing thinner than ¼ inch/6 mm). Wall thickness should increase with tank size to be able to withstand the strains and stresses the tank will experience (e.g., when full, a 40-gallon tank weighs around 300 pounds/140 kg).

Both linear and cross-linked polyethylene commonly have UV inhibitors added to the mix, which pretty much eliminates problems with age hardening (something that was an issue years ago). In fact, given the properties of today's resins, if the walls are thick enough, modern PE tanks are just about indestructible. Here is a material that should last the life of a boat. When failures do occur, it is mostly around the fittings for water and holding tanks (i.e., linear polyeth-

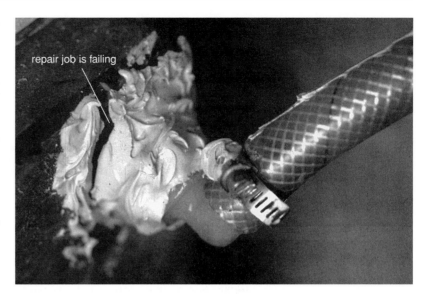

repair job is failing

FIGURE 12-7. This vent fitting on a holding tank broke when stepped on. A repair was attempted with polyurethane sealant, but nothing sticks too well to polyethylene.

ylene tanks, not cross-linked), typically as a result of the following:

- Inadequate wall thickness and strength.
- Improper installation of hose barbs and lines (i.e., too much torque when screwing in threaded components, failure to add a flexible section in attached piping, or inadequate support of hoses and piping).
- Improper stowage of gear.
- Someone accidentally stepping on the fitting when working on the boat (Figure 12-7).
- Leaking seals around inspection ports on holding tanks (a frustratingly common problem caused by molding imperfections and the flexing of tank walls as they fill up).

As far as PE tank installation is concerned, a whole new set of rules apply. Gone are (1) the requirement that the tank be above accumulations of bilge water, (2) the need to inspect the surfaces of the tank for corrosion, and (3) the necessity for the tank to be mounted on a self-draining platform. Instead, there are a few new requirements:

- Manufacturers recommend fully supporting the bottom of a tank (with a surface shaped to match the tank) and adding neoprene padding between the tank and other contact points.
- Whatever method is used to retain the tank, it must not create chafing, cutting, or abrasion.
- A fuel tank must be given room to "grow." After filling a cross-linked PE tank with gasoline or diesel, during the first month or so of use it will expand in all directions by about 2% (approximately ¼ inch per foot/6 mm per 30 cm). After this it stabilizes, regardless of

whether or not it has fuel in it. The installation must allow for this expansion, which means cross-linked PE fuel tanks should never be foamed in place. Nylon webbing works well as a retainer since it is impervious to corrosion and will stretch to accommodate the growth of the tank.

- Once a tank is secured, all connections must be made with properly supported, flexible lines.

A properly built and installed, and suitably protected, polyethylene tank can pretty much be fitted and forgotten. The one drawback to polyethylene is that if there is no stock tank to fit an application, the cost of developing a mold is high unless the mold can subsequently be used for a substantial production run. However, there are literally hundreds of different shapes and sizes of polyethylene tanks that can be bought off the shelf. If necessary, at the design stage of the boat, the interior spaces can be modified to accept a stock tank, which to me seems preferable to using a custom-built metal tank that may fail before the boat reaches the end of its life.

Polypropylene. Like linear polyethylene, polypropylene (PP) is an excellent material for water and holding tanks, but it is not suitable for fuel tanks (note that in the U.S. it may not be FDA approved for potable water systems). The difference is that polypropylene lends itself well to welding, which makes it a good choice for one-off and awkwardly shaped tanks. However, because tanks are individually made, it is much harder to ensure consistent production standards. The keys to a successful tank are once again adequate thickness combined with skilled labor and good quality control—i.e., buying from a reputable manufacturer, especially if the boat is to be built around the tank.

Flexible tanks. Flexible *(bladder)* tanks are formed from a polyester material impregnated with polyurethane (PU). They can be made for water, fuel, or waste. Food-grade polyurethane is used for water tanks, and hydrocarbon-resistant polyurethane is used for fuel tanks. Tanks can be bought in assorted shapes and sizes and also built to order.

Flexible tanks are mostly installed as a retrofit in an area of the boat where it is difficult to install a rigid tank. They are rarely properly secured against movement (which is, in any event, difficult to achieve because the tank expands and collapses as it fills and empties). As a result, the two principal failure modes are rupturing from chafe or abrasion and failure of the fittings and connecting hoses. These issues need

to be addressed at the time of installation, with the installation designed to mitigate the chances of failure; for example:

- Cushion the surrounding area.
- Ensure there are no hard spots.
- Provide adequate supporting surfaces to minimize movement under all conditions.
- Ensure tank connections have whatever flexibility is needed.

Miscellaneous Design Issues

Whatever the tank material, larger tanks need to be baffled at least every 30 inches (75 cm; Figure 12-8). All tanks should be designed and installed with a distinct low spot that will act as a sump from which contaminants can periodically be removed. (Note that drains are not permitted on gasoline tanks—they have to be pumped out from above—but they are permitted on diesel tanks.) Ideally, all other tank openings should be in the top of a tank to minimize the chance of losing the contents if a line fails. (This is not as important with water tanks, is quite important with diesel tanks, and is legally required with gasoline tanks.) Holding tanks typically have the drain line coming from the bottom of the tank, leaving a hose permanently full of effluent. But where possible (it depends on the installation—see later in this chapter), a holding tank would benefit from having this fitting come off the top, with a pipe inside the tank plumbed to near the bottom.

The standard fill hose has a $1\frac{1}{2}$-inch (38 mm) inside diameter (ID); the minimum vent hose has a $\frac{9}{16}$-inch (14 mm) ID (see later in this chapter for more on hoses). Fill fittings, especially on fuel tanks, should be plumbed to within an inch or so of the bottom of a tank to reduce foaming and also effectively seal any vapor in the tank from the fill line until the tank is almost empty.

Fuel tanks. On fuel tanks, fuel lines are sized according to the application. The suction line should be plumbed to within an inch or so (but no closer) of the bottom of the tank to allow sediment and water to settle out beneath it. Diesel engines have a fuel return line. If a boat has more than one tank, it is essential to design and label the suction and return valves so that fuel cannot be withdrawn from one tank and returned to another (which might cause the second tank to overflow). If there are crossover lines between tanks, they should either be fully protected from damage or else be built strongly enough to be stood on. If sight gauges are fitted (permitted on diesel tanks, but not gasoline), there should be a valve at both the top and the

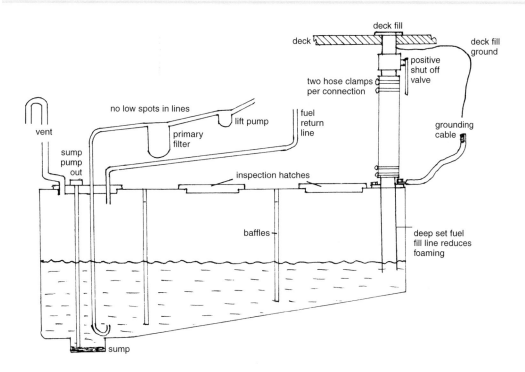

FIGURE 12-8. A proper fuel tank showing baffles.

bottom of the sight glass. Only open the valves to read the level, then close them to avoid the risk of rupturing a glass and draining the tank. (Note that the ISO requires all fuel tanks to have a means of determining the fuel level or quantity; the ABYC only requires this for gasoline tanks.)

I always recommend that fuel tanks have a sampling line run to the lowest point in the tank so a pump can be attached to withdraw fuel samples and periodically cleanse the tank (see Chapter 9).

Longer tank life. In the days when boats were all built of wood, it was axiomatic that all parts of the structure needed to be accessible. As a result, tanks tended to be relatively small and were designed to be removed. Problems with tanks were relatively easy to resolve, if necessary by removing the tank.

Fiberglass introduced many new dimensions to boatbuilding. One of these is that it is no longer necessary to maintain accessibility to all areas of the hull. It is logical that boatbuilders should look at tanks, which are large and awkward and require no regular maintenance, as

items that can be built into inaccessible spaces and forgotten. Given the weight of a tank when full, it is also logical that they should be placed low in a boat, which frequently puts them in contact with bilge water, even if only intermittently.

In such circumstances, it is unfortunate that some of the most commonly used materials in tank construction do not have the same life expectancy as fiberglass hulls! There are an ever-increasing number of boats with tank problems that are both troublesome and expensive to fix.

Many of these problems, particularly those resulting from corrosion, can be avoided with proper installation practices, and in any case are unnecessary. Noncorrosive polyethylene tanks and other plastics have been available for almost 30 years. They have proved their reliability in hard service. It makes sense to use plastic tanks in plastic boats! And just to be safe, a tank should still be installed so that it can be removed without ripping the boat apart. This takes care of all eventualities. However, my inability to persuade the builder of our latest boat to convert to plastic is illustrative of the difficulties facing all but those buying custom boats!

Plumbing

Plumbing can be a bit of a nightmare aboard a boat. To avoid mismatches between equipment and pipes or hoses, and untoward plumbing failures, it is necessary to understand how pipes and

hoses are specified, the suitability of different pipes and hoses for different applications, and proper installation practices.

The *nominal* sizes of most pipes, hoses, and

fittings often do not correspond to their *actual* sizes, either the *outside diameter* (OD) or the *inside diameter* (ID). In addition, there is no universal standard governing sizes. Given two items that are nominally the same size (e.g., ¾ inch/ 20 mm), it is quite likely that neither will actually be this size, and what is more, that they will not be the same size as each other!

Pipes and fittings are commonly copper, other metals, or plastic (*PVC* or *CPVC*). Copper pipe in the United States is subdivided into *water* pipe or tubing and *refrigeration* pipe or tubing (pipe comes in straight lengths, tubing in coils).

Copper Pipe or Tubing

Water pipe (U.S.) has a purely nominal size (Table 12-1). In other words, *its nominal size does not correspond to either its ID or its OD.* Refrigeration pipe or tubing, on the other hand, *is measured by its OD*—½-inch (13 mm) refrigeration tubing really has a ½-inch (13 mm) outside diameter. Copper fittings (connectors, elbows, tees, etc.) *are made mostly to water pipe sizes.* Since water pipe of any given nominal size is actually one size larger than refrigeration pipe of the same nominal size, when buying fittings for use with refrigeration pipe or tubing, *generally you must buy a fitting the next size smaller* (e.g., ⅜-inch/10 mm fittings for ½-inch/13 mm refrigeration pipe or tubing—see Table 12-2).

Copper pipe or tubing is further defined by its wall thickness. In the United States, it is given a K, L, or M rating; K has the thickest wall. Type L

is generally used for household, refrigeration, and liquefied petroleum gas (LPG) plumbing. In the EU, copper pipe and fittings are all standardized according to the OD of the pipe or tubing (8, 10, 15, 22, 28 mm, etc.), with the wall thickness specified separately (e.g., 8 mm tubing with 0.8 mm wall thickness).

Specific refrigeration tubing or pipe should always be bought *for refrigeration purposes*—it is specially cleaned, dehydrated, and capped to keep out moisture. For water systems, you can buy either refrigeration or water tubing or pipe from any hardware store. Tubing has the advantage that it can be worked around the awkward shapes of a boat with very few joints. It generally comes in 50-foot rolls. When making tubing runs, bend the copper as little as possible; with constant flexing it *work-hardens* and then is prone to kinking or cracking. You can resoften hardened tubing by heating it to a cherry-red color with a propane torch, then dousing it with cold water (*annealing*—for some reason copper is annealed the opposite way to other metals, which are heated and then cooled slowly).

Tight bends are liable to flatten out, kink, or both unless made with proper bending tools or springs. Bending springs, which simply slip over the outside of the tubing and are then removed when the bend is complete, are quite cheap and available from plumbing suppliers.

If possible, always cut tubing and pipe with tubing cutters since this is the only way to ensure a smooth and square cut (especially important for making flare connections—see below). To make a cut, clamp the cutters *lightly* around the tube or

TABLE 12-1. Pipe Sizes

Nominal Outside Diameter (inches)	Actual Outside Diameter (inches)					Wall Thickness (copper tubing, in inches)				
	Schedule 40 Pipe			Copper Tubing		Water			Refrigeration	
	Metal[1]	PVC	CPVC	Water	Refrigeration	K	L	M	K	L
⅛ (0.125)	0.405	—	—	¼	N/A[2]	0.032	0.025	0.025	N/A	N/A
¼ (0.250)	0.540	—	—	⅜	N/A	0.035	0.030	0.025	N/A	N/A
⅜ (0.375)	0.675	—	—	½	⅜	0.049	0.035	0.025	0.032	0.032
½ (0.500)	0.840	0.840	⅝	⅝	½	0.049	0.040	0.028	0.049	0.032
⅝ (0.625)	N/A	—	—	¾	⅝	0.049	0.042	0.030	0.049	0.035
¾ (0.750)	1.050	1.050	⅞	⅞	¾	0.065	0.045	0.032	0.049	0.035
⅞ (0.875)	N/A	—	—	N/A	⅞	N/A	N/A	N/A	0.065	0.045
1 (1.0)	1.315	1.315	—	1⅛	N/A	0.065	0.050	0.035	N/A	N/A
1⅛ (1.125)	N/A	—	—	N/A	1⅛	N/A	N/A	N/A	0.065	0.050
1¼ (1.250)	1.660	1.660	—	1⅜	N/A	0.065	0.055	0.042	N/A	N/A
1⅜ (1.375)	N/A	—	—	N/A	1⅜	N/A	N/A	N/A	0.065	0.060
1½ (1.500)	1.900	1.900	—	—	—	—	—	—	—	—
2 (2.0)	2.375	2.375	—	—	—	—	—	—	—	—
2½ (2.500)	2.875	2.875	—	—	—	—	—	—	—	—

1. Metal pipe includes brass, bronze, black, and galvanized.
2. N/A = not applicable.

pipe and make a full turn (Figure 12-9). Tighten the handle a half turn after each turn until the cut is complete. On the back of the cutters will be a hinged arrowhead fitting—use this fitting to clean off any burrs on the inside of the cut.

To join copper pipe and tubing, use compression fittings, flare fittings, and solder fittings.

Compression fittings. Compression fittings are in many ways the easiest to make but the least reliable in service.

1. Slide a nut up the tube or pipe, then slip on a compression ring, or *olive* (Figure 12-10).
2. Fit the tube or pipe into a recess in the compression fitting. The fit must be perfectly square.
3. Slide the nut up onto the fitting and tighten, *keeping the tube or pipe pressed into the recess at all times.*
4. Squeeze the compression ring against the fitting and into the soft metal of the tube or pipe, forming an effective seal.

Flare fittings. Flares are made with a special tool. There are a number of relatively inexpensive flaring kits on the market, and one or two real Cadillacs for around $80. The cheaper kits consist of a clamp that fits around the tube or pipe and has a machined bevel in its face. A horseshoe-shaped bracket with a threaded bolt in its center fits over the clamp. On the base of this bolt is a *spinner*—a block of metal cut to the same taper as the bevel in the clamp. The spinner is screwed into the mouth of the tube or pipe, which forces its sides out against the bevel (Figure 12-11), completing the flare.

Here are some tips:

1. The nut must be put on the line before making the flare! If possible use long-nosed flare nuts (as opposed to the more common short ones), since they provide more support to the joint and reduce the chances of cracking due to vibration.
2. The end of the tube or pipe must be *cut square and cleaned of all burrs inside and out.* Any dirt, trash, or metal filings will especially come back to haunt refrigeration and gas systems.
3. Warming the tube or pipe before screwing down the spinner will help prevent cracking (ideally, the tube should be annealed).
4. Depending on clamp configuration, the tube or pipe may need to protrude above the face of the clamp by one-third to one-half the depth of the bevel to permit an adequate flare. If the pipe is set flush with the face of the

TABLE 12-2. Size Relationships

Nominal Copper Fitting Size (inches)	Fits Refrigeration Tubing with Outside Diameter of (inches)
1/8	1/4
1/4	3/8
3/8	1/2
1/2	5/8
3/4	7/8
1	1 1/8

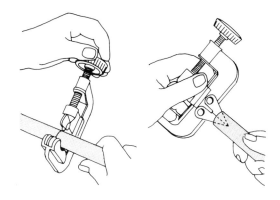

FIGURE 12-9. Using tubing cutters.

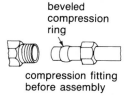

beveled compression ring

compression fitting before assembly

FIGURE 12-10. A compression fitting.

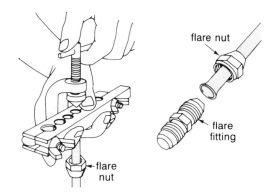

flare nut

flare fitting

flare nut

FIGURE 12-11. Making a flare connection.

clamp, the resulting flare will be skimpy and prone to leaking. When made, the flare should just fit into—but not hang up on—the sides of the flare nut.

5. The spinner should be oiled when making the flare.
6. *The spinner should not be screwed down too tightly*—it will weaken the flare. When the joint is done up, the flare nut will pull the flare snugly onto the flared fitting.

7. If the flare looks uneven or in any other way unsatisfactory, it must be cut off and remade. Doing so right away will be a lot easier than doing so later.

Soldering. Solder fittings (sweat fittings) can be used on both copper tubing and pipe. A wide range of fittings is readily available. Some fittings are presoldered (omit steps 4 and 5 below), but most are not.

1. Clean both surfaces to be soldered with fine (400- to 600-grit) wet-or-dry sandpaper *until the entire surfaces to be soldered are shiny* (Figure 12-12). *Do not use emery cloth*—oils in the cloth backing will spoil the soldering.
2. Apply soldering flux immediately but sparingly to both surfaces. Push the fitting onto the tube or pipe and twist to spread the flux evenly. The flux is there to keep out oxygen and contaminants *once the joint is clean*. Flux is no substitute for cleaning.
3. Heat the joint evenly with a propane torch.
4. Touch solid solder to the joint periodically until the tube or pipe and fittings are hot enough to melt the solder. *The solder itself is not heated by the torch*—if the metal in the joint is not hot enough to melt the solder, the solder will not flow properly.
5. Let solder flow into the joint. Apply only enough heat to keep the solder melting; more will overheat the joint. Generally the flame can be held at some distance or turned away from the joint and passed over it quickly a couple of times.
6. When solder shows all around the fitting, the joint is complete. Remove the heat. Any more solder added to the joint will merely flow out the other side and into the tube or pipe, causing a partial blockage.
7. Keep the joint stationary while it cools—if it is moved, it may result in a weak joint that will be prone to failure. When the joint is cool, clean away the excess flux.

If you experience problems in getting leak-proof joints, the most likely culprit is contamination of the soldering surface on the pipe or in the fitting. To be certain of making successful joints, you can tin the surfaces (i.e., give them a thin film of solder) to be soldered prior to mating them. If the solder does not spread out evenly, the copper is not clean enough. Once tinned, the pipe may not push into the fitting, in which case you need a little heat to melt the solder while seating the pipe.

Steel Pipe

Black pipe is plain steel (technically, *black* metal is *wrought* iron, but today the term is used to describe plain rolled steel); it is used in some commercial boat applications but not on pleasure boats. *Galvanized* pipe is steel pipe coated with zinc to resist corrosion, but even so has only

FIGURE 12-12. Soldering. Refer to the text for a step-by-step description of the process.

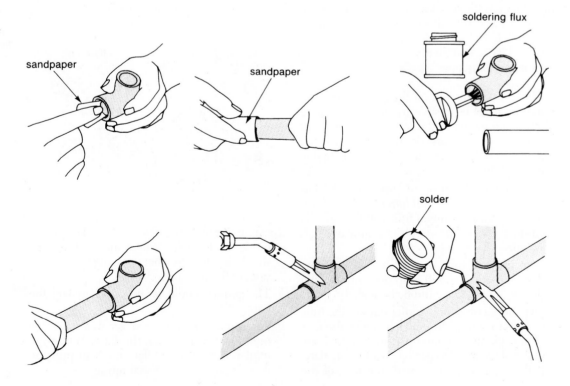

limited applications. It is sometimes found in fuel systems but *should never be used with diesel fuel* since the diesel will dissolve the zinc, which will then clog the fuel system.

Pipe sizes are standardized, but as can be seen in Table 12-1, the actual outside diameter of metal pipe is considerably more than its nominal diameter. The thickness of a pipe is given as its *schedule*. Schedule 20 is thin-wall pipe, unsuitable for boat applications; schedule 40 is standard pipe, suitable for most applications; and schedule 80 is thick-wall pipe, rarely used. The additional thickness is gained by narrowing the inside diameter, so regardless of a pipe's schedule, *a given fitting will fit any pipe of the same nominal size.*

Pipe fittings. Metal pipe is almost invariably joined with threaded fittings; threads are, once again, standardized. Pipe fittings are labeled according to the nominal size of pipe they will accommodate. A 1½-inch (38 mm) fitting, for example, fits a 1½-inch (38 mm) pipe. Since the 1½-inch (38 mm) pipe is actually around 1⅞-inch (48 mm) in diameter, and the fitting must go around the pipe, a 1½-inch (38 mm) fitting will be more than 2 inches (52 mm) in diameter.

Pipe threads are tapered. As a pipe or fitting is screwed up, it becomes progressively harder to turn. A certain amount of experience is required to gauge how tightly to do up differently sized fittings. A threaded pipe joint is rarely water or gas tight without the addition of some kind of a sealant to the joint. Various pastes can be bought for this purpose, but by far the most useful thing to carry on board is several rolls of Teflon (PTFE) tape, which is available at any hardware store. The most useful general-purpose size is ½ inch (12 or 13 mm) wide. Wind the tape around the male fitting *in the opposite direction to which it will be screwed into the female fitting.* Three or four wraps are more than enough. Then stretch the tape until it breaks, and smooth the loose end down. Note that a special variant of Teflon tape is needed for propane systems.

Although it is commonly done, it is not a good idea to screw metal pipes into plastic *adapters* (see below)—hardening of the plastic with age combined with expansion and contraction of the metal are liable to crack the plastic fitting. On the other hand, plastic adapters screwed into metal fittings rarely fail.

Plastic Pipe

PVC (polyvinyl chloride) pipe is commonly used for cold-water applications, while CPVC (chlorinated polyvinyl chloride) pipe is used for hot-water applications. The two are not interchangeable. Nominal and actual dimensions are given in Table 12-1 (standard EU sizes are 10, 15, 22, 28, 35 and 42 mm).

Both types of pipe are joined with glued fittings. It is important to match the type of glue to the type of pipe (best of all is to buy a quality glue suitable for both types of pipe). Adapters are available with a glue-type terminal on one end and a threaded fitting on the other so that it is possible to go from metal pipe and metal pipe fittings to glued pipe and fittings (but note the caveat above). Once again, Teflon tape will be needed on the threads. Various compression-type fittings are also now available for use with plastic pipe.

Plastic pipe, which is available from any hardware store, is excellent for many plumbing jobs on board and as conduit for electrical wires. It is readily cut with a hacksaw, comes with a tremendous range of fittings, and can be glued together in seconds. Also it is easily cut up and glued back together for later modifications.

Prior to gluing, lightly sand the end of the pipe and the inside of the fitting with 400-grit wet-or-dry sandpaper, then clean with a solvent cleaner (available from any hardware store), and finally coat with the cement. *Immediately* press the pipe home, twisting a half turn or so to spread the glue evenly. Hold for about 30 seconds to give the glue a chance to grip; do not subject the joint to pressure for at least half an hour. Once installed, plastic piping is maintenance free.

Note: Solvent cleaners and plastic-pipe glues are highly flammable and evaporate rapidly, giving off toxic fumes. They should be used only in well-ventilated, nonsmoking environments. Read the labels carefully and observe all cautions.

Polyethylene plumbing systems. In recent years, semirigid polyethylene tubing with associated fittings has come to dominate freshwater plumbing on boats (see, for example, Whale Water Systems at www.whalepumps. com). Blue tubing is used for cold water, and red tubing for hot water. The tubing comes in three sizes—12, 15, and 22 mm (½, ⅝, and ⅞ inch)—with a wide range of fittings that are installed simply by pushing them onto the tubing. The system can be disassembled at any time by pushing back on a collet on the fittings and pulling out the tubing (Figure 12-13). The fittings are reusable.

This is an excellent system with great versatility that simplifies installations (all you need is tubing cutters!) and makes disassembly, should it be necessary, a snap. The only criticism I have is that the semitranslucent nature of much of the tubing encourages algae growth in potable water

To assemble:

1. Cut to length by making a straight clean cut.

2. Simply push the tube into the fitting up to the second internal stop.

To disconnect:

3. Push back on the gray collet against the face of the fitting.

4. Hold the collet in and pull out the tube.

systems that are not used for extended periods. Opaque tubing is preferable.

Hoses

Building a quality hose for a specific purpose is more complicated than first meets the eye. On the surface of things, most hoses are round and black with a hole in the middle. But that's where the similarity ends. Even with two hoses that look identical, there may be all kinds of differences in terms of the chemicals that have gone into the *compounding* of the hose, the kind of fabric used in reinforcement, the skill with which the hose has been laid up (much hose is still made by hand), the quality of the adhesion between different layers in the hose, and so on (Figure 12-14).

Manufacturing hoses is a worldwide cottage industry, with factories scattered all the way from the Far East to Turkey, Italy, and the United States. Almost none of the handful of wholesalers or retailers of marine hoses in the United States and Europe actually make their own

hoses. From time to time, some pretty awful hose makes its way into the marketplace. What this means is that the boatbuilder or consumer is very much dependent on the wholesaler or retailer when buying hose. To ensure that you buy only quality hose, it is best to buy from a recognized dealer and ensure that the hose is manufactured to recognized standards (UL, SAE, USCG, and ISO).

Maintenance is important. No matter how carefully hoses are selected and installed, there is always the unforeseeable failure. For example, friends of ours got a rat aboard. The first they knew of it was the night it chewed through the flexible connection to their propane galley stove. Fortunately, since they are safety-conscious cruisers, they always close the tank valve after using the stove, otherwise the rat might have killed them. Once they came face to face with the beast and realized what was going on, they had the foresight to close their seacocks, which was just as well because before they finally cornered it and dispatched it, it had taken bites out of half the hoses on the boat!

By the way, our friends were able to close their seacocks because they regularly maintain them. This is in contrast to so many boatowners who leave crucial seacocks open from one season to the next and never inspect their hoses and hose clamps. After a year or two, the valves are frozen in place and the hose clamps are covered in rust. This situation is an accident waiting to happen—any kind of a below-the-waterline hose failure, for any reason whatsoever, has the potential to sink the boat.

multiple layers of fabric and compound

FIGURE 12-14. There is more to quality hose construction than meets the eye; many include multiple layers of different compounds and fabrics bonded together.

Exhaust hose. In a water-cooled exhaust, beyond the water-injection point quality steam hose can be used to good advantage. In the past, no standards existed governing these hoses. Good hose was invariably labeled as "Type Certified Marine Exhaust Hose" or something similar. The ABYC standard now states that this hose should comply with SAE J2006 or UL 1129 (as far as I know, the ISO does not have a similar standard). These standards contain a number of performance tests that the hose must pass, including the ability to withstand shock, vibration, and various chemicals (oil, diesel, salt water, etc.), and also the ability to withstand a test that simulates 2 minutes of dry operation (no cooling water) *with the engine at full output,* after which the cooling water is restored; to pass, there must be no loss of watertight integrity.

If a hose is not stamped SAE J2006 or UL 1129, it does not comply with the current ABYC standard. From a practical standpoint, as far as I know, no exhaust hose on the market meets UL 1129 (because of a requirement that the hose be able to withstand a prolonged immersion in hot gasoline), whereas there are plenty of hoses that do meet SAE J2006. Those designated SAE J2006-R1 are soft-wall hoses (without wire reinforcement); those designated SAE J2006-R2 have wire reinforcement. Some manufacturers provide three grades of SAE J2006–compliant hose. Standard rubber hose will tolerate continuous temperatures of 250°F/120°C; blue silicon hose is good for 350°F/180°C; while top-of-the-line red silicon hose will withstand 500°F/260°C.

Installation issues. Most manufacturers recommend that exhaust hoses longer than four to six times the inside diameter of the hose (this covers most exhaust hoses), or those with relatively tight curves, be wire reinforced for added support. The objective is to prevent the hose kinking on bends (Figure 12-15A), sagging on long horizontal runs, and *panting* (pulsing) from the constant pressure changes that occur in an exhaust.

However, there are disadvantages to wire reinforcement, including the fact that the wire is formed from spring steel, which will rust if exposed to the atmosphere (Figure 12-15B), weakening the hose. (This is particularly likely if the hose has poor adhesion between its layers; note that J2006 has stringent adhesion requirements.) There have also been cases where the wire became the path for stray currents, causing devastating corrosion, or for short circuits, resulting in a fire. In addition to which the wire is nasty stuff to cut, often leaving a razor-sharp piece of metal sticking out the end of the hose, and if the hose isn't a *perfect* fit on its nipple, the wire makes it difficult to get the hose to seal.

In many situations, if you adequately support a

kinked soft-wall exhaust hose

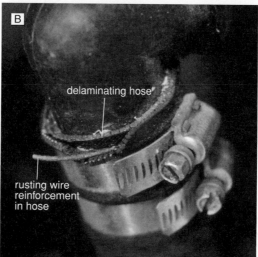

delaminating hose

rusting wire reinforcement in hose

FIGURE 12-15A. Sagging soft-wall exhaust hose. When it gets hot, it sags some more, significantly interfering with the exhaust flow and engine performance at higher engine loads.

FIGURE 12-15B. A combination of a rusting wire reinforcement and a delaminating hose.

hose and avoid tight bends, you can avoid the reinforcement. But in this case, the support is critical. Exhaust hose, particularly soft-wall hose, should not span open spaces or be hung from deck beams because panting will cause chafe at the supports or hangers. If necessary, give the hose a bed to sit on. Another way to avoid hard-wall hose where long exhaust runs are needed (and also to save money) is to splice in lengths of fiberglass marine exhaust tubing (manufactured by Vernay/Centek, www.centekindustries.com; Halyard Marine, www.halyard.eu.com; and others), although this tubing is not as effective as hose at absorbing exhaust noise.

As far as clamping exhaust hose is concerned, the ABYC standard (P-1—"Installation of Exhaust Systems for Propulsion and Auxiliary Engines") calls for double clamping all exhaust hose connections, with a minimum band width (for each clamp) of ½ inch (13 mm). The intention is to minimize the chances of carbon monoxide and water leaks into the boat. The standard also states, "Clamps used for this pur-

FIGURE 12-16. T-bolt clamps on an exhaust. However, the single clamps do not comply with ABYC standards.

T-bolt clamps; there should be two to comply with ABYC standards

the small print says J2006

FIGURE 12-17. J2006 water hose (see the small print in the center of the photo).

others; Figure 12-16) are far more dependable than regular hose clamps. Note, however, that although many industrial T-bolt clamps have stainless steel bands, the bolts are often carbon steel, which rusts in the marine environment.

Engine raw-water hoses. When it comes to engine raw-water hoses, the engine manufacturer installs the hoses from the raw-water pump to the heat exchanger, including any oil coolers in the raw-water circuit, terminating with a hose into the water injection elbow on the exhaust. Here we find heavy-duty fabric-reinforced hoses. But then all too often, the engine installer will use a light-duty rubber or plastic hose (commonly, automotive heater hose) to connect the raw-water seacock to the raw-water pump, to plumb in a siphon break if needed, and to make the connections to a hot-water heater if this has a built-in heat exchanger.

Although heater hose is generally designed to tolerate temperatures to 210°F/100°C and pressures to 60 psi, it is relatively thin walled and soft. In the event that either the raw-water screen on the outside of the boat or the raw-water filter becomes clogged, the vacuum pulled by the raw-water pump will collapse heater hose, and most other non-wire-reinforced hose, starving the engine of water. What is more, primarily because it is thin walled, heater hose has relatively poor abrasion resistance. If the hose is in contact with some part of the engine bed or supporting structures and is not firmly supported (a frequent occurrence), the engine vibrations that are invariably transmitted to the hose may cause it to wear through.

Quality marine water hose, on the other hand, is thicker than heater hose and is reinforced with different synthetic materials (commonly, polyester yarn in two or more layers, or *plies*). Often it is manufactured to the same standards as exhaust hose—i.e., SAE J2006 (Figure 12-17). This kind of hose will handle both vacuums and pumping pressures, tolerate the various chemicals that may be found in the water flow, and resist abrasion.

Below-the-waterline hoses. Similar considerations as those above govern the selection of hoses for below-the-waterline use. In fact, very often the exact same hose that is used for engine raw-water hose is an appropriate choice for cockpit drains, sink drains, toilet suction lines, and associated applications. In other words, what is needed is a hose with a certain minimal strength, a fairly broad tolerance of chemicals, resistance to abrasion, and in the case of bilge-pump and toilet suction hoses, the ability to withstand the maximum suction pressure of the

pose shall be entirely of stainless steel; clamps depending solely on spring tension shall not be used." It would be nice to see this standard extended one step further by requiring that the hose clamps be of all 300 series stainless steel. This would eliminate from consideration the commonly used "all-stainless" hose clamps that have a 400 series stainless steel screw that rusts almost as soon as it comes into contact with salt water (see Chapter 5). For larger-diameter exhaust hoses, T-bolt hose clamps (sold by Shields Marine Hose, www.shieldshose.com; Trident Marine, www.tridentmarine.com; and

pump without collapsing (i.e., fabric-reinforced rubber hose or heavy-duty vinyl [PVC] hose). Instead, what is often found is some variant of a flexible, reinforced, thin-wall rubber or PVC hose that even the manufacturer or wholesaler may label as "not recommended for below-the-waterline use." This is inappropriate. Anything attached to a through-hull is an extension of the hull; therefore, it must have an integrity as close as possible to that of the hull.

If a hose is reinforced, it may be smooth walled on the inside, in which case it can be directly slid over, and fastened to, a suitable smooth pipe stub or hose nipple. But at other times, the inner wall contains a spiral rib that makes it next to impossible to achieve an effective seal without the addition of special adapters (see the Connecting Hoses section below).

Sanitation hose. Toilet discharge hoses require special attention. Even many heavy-duty hoses are minutely porous and in time will give off foul odors. (To test, rub a clean rag up and down the hose jacket, then sniff the rag. For a more thorough test, wrap a hot, damp cloth around the low point in hoses, leave to cool, and then remove and sniff.) Special impermeable hoses are required (generally labeled "Sanitation Hose"). There are two choices: some variant of PVC, or *heavy-wall* rubber sanitation hose. Often the PVC hose is considerably cheaper (less than half the price) but more prone to problems (note, however, that SeaLand has a very high quality, and expensive, PVC hose—Odor-Safe—that has tested better than rubber hoses—see www.sealandtechnology. com).

PVC versus rubber. In order to increase its resistance to moisture absorption, PVC hose for sanitation purposes must be specially formulated *(compounded)* from a high-density material with a greater-than-normal wall thickness. Ultimately, however, any flexible PVC hose that is permanently filled with effluent will absorb enough moisture to begin to smell. The reason for this is that to make the hose flexible it must contain a plasticizer, which creates a larger molecular structure, which in turn is minutely permeable. Rigid PVC pipe (used for household effluent) does not have a plasticizer and so does not suffer from the same problem; as a result it makes an excellent choice when it can be used. However, it is more difficult to run than hose and has a tendency to develop leaks at the joints as a result of the constant flexing that takes place when a boat is at sea. (If used, it may be best to include flexible connections—i.e., lengths of hose—at either end of the rigid piping.)

PVC sanitation hose is relatively stiff. It is essential to make it fit closely to any hose barbs.

If the barb is undersized, the clamping pressure needed to seal the hose to the barb will cut into the hose, causing it to develop microscopic cracks (resulting in hard-to-trace leaks) at the edge of the clamp. On the other hand, if the barb is too big and the hose has to be stretched over it, the hose will harden and once again develop microscopic cracks in the clamping area.

Rubber sanitation hose is more tolerant than PVC hose of poor hose barb fits. It also has greater flexibility. Its resistance to permeation is directly related to wall thickness—with rubber hose, thickness rules!

Installation issues. Ultimately, any hose, whatever its quality, that is filled with standing effluent will start to smell. When installing both PVC and rubber sanitation hoses, avoid low spots that retain effluent. If you cannot, *flush the head sufficiently after each use to clear all the effluent out of the line*. Better yet, substitute rigid PVC pipe for those hose runs that may end up with standing effluent.

Alcohol-based antifreeze, petrochemicals, and most toilet bowl deodorizers must be avoided; all contain chemicals that will destroy the moisture-absorption resistance of the hose (PVC hose will be damaged faster than rubber hose).

Note that rubber-clad stainless steel hose clamps and hangers leave a brown print on PVC hose that goes all the way through the hose and can cause it to crack (this applies to any PVC hose, not just sanitation hose).

Whatever hose is used for sanitation purposes, it should have a smooth wall on the inside (this is an ISO requirement). This will minimize the chances of clogging. Nevertheless, if you use salt water for flushing, the inside of the hose will slowly plug up with calcium deposits. At some point, you may need to remove and replace the hose or beat it on the dock to break the calcium loose (see later in this chapter for other methods of dealing with calcium buildup). If the hose is not built ruggedly enough to take a beating, it is not suitable for the job!

Discharge and vent hoses. The boatbuilding industry's standard is $1\frac{1}{2}$-inch (38 mm) ID hose for toilet discharge lines and pumpout lines to holding tanks (Figure 12-18). The U.S. boatbuilding industry seems to have settled on either $\frac{9}{16}$-inch (14 mm) or $\frac{5}{8}$-inch (16 mm) ID hose as a suitable vent size, but in Europe the ISO standard requires that:

- For holding tanks with a capacity of up to 400 liters (100 U.S. gallons), the minimum vent ID is 19 mm ($\frac{3}{4}$ inch), although 16 mm ($\frac{5}{8}$ inch) can be used if there is an additional manual relief valve in the system.

FIGURE 12-18. An
internationally agreed-
upon standardized
pumpout deck fitting.
The 1½-inch pipe thread
is purely nominal—the
outside diameter is closer
to 1⅞ inch. The 1½-inch
hose diameter is the actual
inside diameter of the
hose.

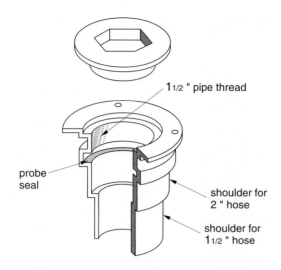

1½ " pipe thread

probe
seal

shoulder for
2 " hose

shoulder for
1½ " hose

FIGURE 12-19A. A
properly labeled fuel hose.

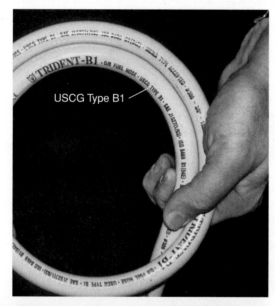

USCG Type B1

this tells us nothing!

FIGURE 12-19B. A fuel
fill hose on a boat. No
matter how good the
hose, without the required
labeling it does not comply
with ABYC, ISO, and
USCG standards.

The reasons for the larger vent size are:

1. To prevent the vent from plugging if the holding tank gets overfilled. Plugging can lead to
bursting of the tank if additional effluent is
pumped in or collapsing of the tank when it is
pumped out.
2. To provide for a sufficient inflow of air when
pumping out the tank, once again to ensure
that the tank does not collapse.

Large vents have another benefit since they
help maintain an oxygenated environment in
the tank, which is key to eliminating odors (see
the Problems Common to All Marine Toilets
section below). Whatever hose you use for the
vent, it should be reinforced to avoid the risk of
its collapsing when the tank is pumped out. If it
collapses, it will seal the vent, which may cause
the tank to implode.

As noted previously, ISO standards require
some means to determine when the tank is three-
quarters full, but there is no similar requirement
in the United States (although it clearly makes a
lot of sense). Various level indicators are available
at a cost of $20 to $60 (one source is Fireboy-
Xintex—www.fireboy-xintex.com).

Fuel-carrying hoses. Fuel hoses are a special
item, particularly on gasoline engines. These are
the only hoses on a boat for which the construction must *by law* comply with certain USCG
and ISO standards regarding the fire resistance
of a hose and its permeability.

Fire resistance is determined by something
known as the *2½-minute burn test*. Hoses that
pass the test are classified as Type A; hoses that
do not pass the test but which comply with permeation and other requirements are classified as
Type B. As far as permeability is concerned,
hoses that pass the most stringent test (which
limits gasoline-vapor migration through the hose
under test conditions to less than 100 grams per
square meter of interior hose surface per 24
hours) are classified as Class 1; those with somewhat higher permeation rates (up to 300 grams
per square meter per 24 hours) are classified as
Class 2.

We end up with four classes of hose refer-
enced in the Coast Guard regulations: USCG
Type A1, USCG Type A2, USCG Type B1, and
USCG Type B2. These correspond with ISO
7840-A1, ISO 7840-A2, ISO 8469-B1, and ISO
8469-B2. To qualify for any of these categories,
the hose designation must be written on the hose
(Figure 12-19A), as well as the date of manufacture and the name of the manufacturer (or a
registered trademark). *If a fuel hose does not carry
a description of its USCG and/or ISO rating to-*

- For holding tanks with a capacity above 400
liters (over 100 U.S. gallons), the minimum
vent ID is 38 mm (1½ inches); or there can be
multiple vents, each with a minimum ID of
19 mm (¾ inch), or there can be a minimum
16 mm ID vent with a manual relief valve.

gether with this other information (Figure 12-19B), it does not comply with the regulations and it is not legal in those systems that must comply with these regulations.

The ABYC standard for gasoline fuel systems (H-24) and diesel fuel systems (H-33), and ISO 10088 ("Small craft—Permanently installed fuel tanks and fuel systems") have a blanket requirement that Type A1 or A2 hoses be used for all fill and vent hoses *inside engine compartments.* Outside engine compartments, B1 and B2 hose can be used. Flexible fuel lines must be Type A1 (for gasoline) or Type A1 or A2 (for diesel).

Installation issues. Fill hoses must have a minimum 1½-inch (38 mm) ID; vent hoses a minimum ⁹⁄₁₆-inch (14 mm) ID. All fill and vent lines must be self-draining (i.e., they must not have low spots that retain fuel). The USCG, ABYC, and ISO standards specify maximum tolerances that are acceptable between fuel line hoses and any nipples to which they are attached (they have to make a close fit). The standards require a bead, a flare, or serrations on the nipple (but do not allow installation of hose over a pipe thread) and a hose clamp that does not "depend solely on the spring tension of the clamp for compressive force" (i.e., some kind of tightening device is required). Double clamps are required on fuel fill pipes, each with a minimum band width of ½ inch (ABYC) or 10 mm (ISO).

Drinking water hoses.

For drinking water in the United States, the ABYC and National Marine Manufacturers Association (NMMA) standards state that the entire system should be plumbed with hose or tubing manufactured with FDA-approved materials, with the hoses or tubing so labeled. The FDA, in its turn, requires PVC hoses to be manufactured from virgin PVC and virgin textile reinforcement (as opposed to recycled). Compliant hoses are stamped "FDA Approved."

Although such hoses are commonly clear plastic, this has never made much sense to me since the light that gets into drinking water promotes algae growth. It is far better to use opaque FDA-approved hose or pipe, and in fact most household PVC water pipe is ideal. If this is combined with opaque water tanks so that no light gets into the system, water will stay clean and drinkable more or less indefinitely. (If PVC pipe from the hardware store is used, it should be noted that most is only rated for cold water; CPVC pipe is required for hot-water systems.)

Connecting hoses.

Hoses are almost always specified by their inside diameter; a 1-inch (25 mm) hose will have a 1-inch (25 mm) ID. Sizes in the United States are almost all multiples of

FIGURE 12-20. Hoses rarely make a clean fit on pipes. If this poorly fitting hose, which leads to a below-the-waterline through-hull, comes loose, it could sink the boat.

⅛ inch or ¼ inch (Europe is comparable in metric sizes). Since the outside diameters of metal pipe and PVC pipe are very rarely multiples of ⅛ inch or ¼ inch, *hoses rarely make a clean fit on pipes*, so adapters are needed (Figure 12-20; the exception is CPVC pipe, which normally has an OD of ⅝ inch or ⅞ inch). Adapters are readily available as either threaded fittings with hose barbs or glued fittings with hose barbs, but sometimes the necessary combination (i.e., the specific pipe size and hose size) cannot be found in a single fitting, in which case the threaded or glued end has to be sized up or down using *bushings.*

Various hoses (water, bilge, and sanitation) can be bought with a spiral *(threaded)* outer casing. On some, the inside is also ribbed, but on others it is smooth (for sanitation use, it should definitely be smooth; this is an ISO requirement). Some hose has a *right-handed* thread, and some a *left-handed* thread. End fittings *(cuffs—*Figures 12-21A and 12-21B) and couplings screw right onto the hose either to make a

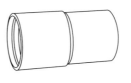

FIGURE 12-21A. A hose cuff.

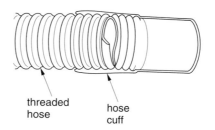

threaded hose

hose cuff

FIGURE 12-21B. A hose cuff screwed onto a hose.

FIGURE 12-22. Adding
sealant to a poorly fitting
hose connection.

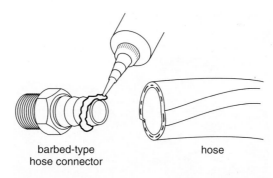

barbed-type   hose
hose connector

connection to a hose barb or else to join two lengths of hose. Clearly, a right-handed hose needs a right-handed fitting, and a left-handed hose needs a left-handed fitting. The end of the hose is liberally coated with plastic pipe cement (the same used for PVC or CPVC pipe) and immediately screwed into the cuff until it bottoms out. This makes a clean and watertight connection. If the cuff is properly matched to the hose barb or pipe it will go on, this too will make a clean and watertight connection.

Making a hose fit. Many times, however, a hose or cuff is not quite the right size for its pipe or hose barb. In certain circumstances (notably exhaust systems and fuel systems), *the ABYC and ISO flatly require that it BE the right size*, but in other instances it is possible to fudge a little. *If the hose is a loose fit,* smear a little caulking (3M 5200 works well) over the surface of the pipe or hose barb (Figure 12-22); it will spread out on the inside of the hose and make a good joint (as long as it is given time to set up). *Do not apply caulking to the inside of the hose* because the pipe or barb will simply push it up the hose and form a blockage. After the caulking has set up, clamp the hose down tightly enough to also produce a mechanical connection—the caulking is simply there to make a seal. (If you do this before the caulking has set up, it will be squeezed out.)

If a hose is a tight fit, a little dishwashing liquid will do wonders as a lubricant. If this is not enough, soften the hose by holding it in a pot of boiling water for a few seconds, then try the dishwashing liquid. (You can also use a heat gun, but you run the risk of melting or damaging the hose.)

Hose clamps. As noted above, all-stainless hose clamps frequently use an inferior grade of stainless (400 series) for the screw that rusts and then corrodes the band inside the screw housing (see Chapter 5). *You can detect these screws with a magnet.* Better-quality screws are made of 300 series stainless (which is nonmagnetic, or almost nonmagnetic; the clamp will be marked "300"). The best clamps have 316 series screws (notably all AWAB hose clamps manufactured by ABA Group).

Many people make a blanket recommendation to place double hose clamps on all below-the-waterline hose connections (I have in the past), but if the connection is watertight, and a quality clamp is used in the first place, this practice adds very little security on smaller hoses. What is more, all too often there is insufficient room to properly space two hose clamps, with the result that one is halfway off the end of the fitting, creating a risk of damaging the hose (it should be in 1/4 inch/6 mm). Larger hoses generally attach to longer nipples or barbs (in addition to which the pressure exerted by a hose clamp is distributed over a larger area), so two clamps will usually fit and are recommended (in which case they should be arranged so the screws are 180 degrees apart). Regardless of opinion, the ABYC and ISO *require* double hose clamps on exhaust connections and fuel fill hoses (these are the only two places where double clamping is required).

At the time of writing, Glacier Bay has introduced heat-shrink hose clamps that are slipped around a hose and shrunk down with a heat gun. Glacier Bay claims they do a better job than regular hose clamps, in particular because they create a more even pressure, but this remains to be seen. There are some applications in which a mechanical clamp is required by the ABYC and ISO, and in which heat-shrink clamps are clearly not appropriate without a change in the standards.

Specialized hoses.

LPG and CNG hoses. Hoses for liquefied petroleum gas (LPG—i.e., propane and butane) or compressed natural gas (CNG) are commonly used for supply lines or to make the flexible connection from a copper supply line to a gimballed galley stove. These hoses are clearly a critical safety item. For LPG systems, the ABYC's A-1 standard ("Marine Liquefied Petroleum Gas [LPG] Systems") states that the hose should be marked as complying with "UL 21 LP Gas Hose," while A-22 ("Marine Compressed Natural Gas [CNG] Systems") states that CNG hose should be marked as complying with "NFPA 52." In both cases, the standards call for end fittings to be permanently attached (for example, by swaging; hose clamps are not acceptable). ISO 10239 ("Small craft—Liquefied petroleum gas [LPG] systems") has the same end-fitting requirement.

Hydraulic hoses. Hydraulic systems, particularly winches and windlasses, may experience pressures of thousands of pounds per square inch. It is essential you use only the specified tubing, hoses, and fittings, and that you assemble them with great care. In addition, most hydraulic systems are supersensitive to dirt; if you have to cut a hose, absolute cleanliness and careful cleanup of all shavings and particles are critical when assembling systems. Always cap hoses when they are not connected, especially if passing them through bulkheads or lockers where they might pick up dirt, and always flush new hoses with hydraulic oil before connecting them to a system.

As a general rule, hydraulic hose should meet one of the following standards: Aeroquip 2651, SAE 100R7, or ISO DIS 3949. Any of these hoses have adequate burst pressures for most pleasure-boat systems (2,000 psi or more in smaller sizes); they all have a rubber outer cover that protects the inner braid (if metal) against corrosion; and perhaps most importantly, they are designed for use with *reusable* (as opposed to *crimp*) fittings, which facilitates repairs in the field. (Note that not all SAE 100R7 hose is suitable for reusable fittings.) Other commonly available rubber-coated hoses suitable for reusable fittings are Aeroquip 2781 and SAE 100R2A, but these hoses have higher burst pressures (5,000 psi in smaller sizes) and are overkill in most situations.

The performance of hydraulic equipment is largely a function of hydraulic pressure and flow rate. To keep both up, it is essential that hose runs offer only minimal resistance. In the kind of low-volume hydraulic systems typically found aboard pleasure boats, unless otherwise speci-

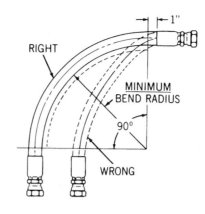

FIGURE 12-23. Right and wrong ways to make a bend in a hydraulic hose.

fied, hose runs of up to 50 feet (16 m) can be ½-inch (13 mm) ID, while those more than 50 feet should be ⅝-inch (15 or 17 mm) ID. On some powerful systems on larger boats, larger hoses will be needed. Hoses should never have tight bends (Figure 12-23) and should be fastened at regular intervals (sudden pressure changes can make them move around).

End fittings. Installing crimp fittings requires specialized equipment; reusable fittings need just a vise and a couple of adjustable wrenches (Figure 12-24). Note that some reusable fittings require a *mandrel* for assembly while others do not. You can fit the mandrel type without using a mandrel, but you run the risk of the fitting cutting into the hose wall—check carefully when

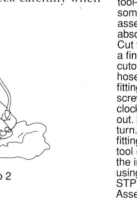

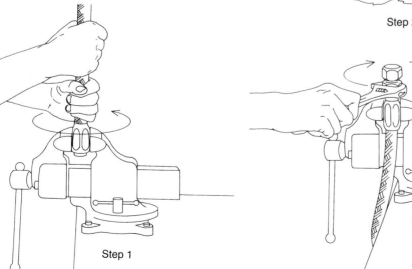

Step 1

Step 2

Step 3

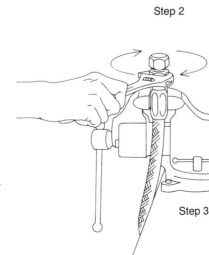

FIGURE 12-24. Adding end fittings to hydraulic hoses. A special assembly tool—a mandrel—is sometimes required for assembly, but is not absolutely necessary. 1. Cut the hose square with a fine-tooth hacksaw or cutoff wheel. Clean the hose bore. Put the end fitting socket in a vise and screw in the hose counter-clockwise until it bottoms out. Back off one-quarter turn. 2. Liberally oil the end fitting nipple, the assembly tool (mandrel) if used, and the inside of the hose, using a heavy oil such as STP or Aeroquip Hose Assembly Lube. 3. Push the assembly tool (if used) into the nipple. Add a few drops of oil, then screw the nipple into the socket and hose clockwise. Tighten the nipple, leaving a clearance of 0.030 to 0.060 inch (0.8 to 1.6 mm) between the nipple hex and the socket. Clean the assembly by blowing out with dry air or washing with warm water. Inspect the hose internally for a cut or bulged tube and general cleanliness. Check for the proper gap between the nut and socket or hex and socket—nuts should swivel freely. Cap the ends to keep the hose clean. *(Jim Sollers)*

done to ensure the hose is undamaged. If using reusable fittings, be careful that shards of rubber (cut from the hose) do not find their way into the hydraulic oil. They can block the valve shuttles with potentially disastrous results, then move elsewhere, creating a problem that is often difficult to locate. Be sure to flush the hoses before putting them into service! The use of crimped fittings avoids these problems.

Various fittings are available with different threads and angles on the seating surfaces. Since there is no international standardization, matching replacement fittings to existing equipment can be a minefield for the unwary cruiser. In the United States, 37-degree flares are the most common, with some 45-degree flares; in Germany and many parts of the world, a 24-degree cone is common; and in the UK, a 60-degree cone is the most common. However, besides these there are at least a dozen other flares and cones with varying thread patterns! Before leaving port, *be sure to lay in a stock of correctly matched reusable end fittings for any critical hydraulic systems.* End fittings can be male or female, swiveling or non-swiveling, threaded or quick-connect. (The latter have a spring-loaded knurled ring that is pulled back while pushing the connector onto its fitting. *Always check a quick-connect for dirt before making a connection, and keep it capped when not in use.*)

Since hydraulic service technicians are few and far between outside Western cities, the voyaging cruiser should carry whatever fittings are needed to splice the hoses in the system, and preferably, sufficient hose to replace the longest run of hydraulic hose or pipe on board.

Marine Toilets (Heads)

U.S. Discharge Regulations

Discharging untreated sewage is illegal anywhere within the United States' 3-mile limit (as it is in many European areas). In the United States, any installed sewage treatment or retention system (*marine sanitation device* or *MSD*) in a vessel *under 65 feet in length* must conform to one of three types:

1. Type I MSDs break up sewage so that no visible floating solids remain. The sewage is treated chemically to kill bacteria and then discharged overboard (see below for more on these devices).

2. Type II MSDs are similar to Type I, but treat sewage according to more exacting standards. They are much bigger and more expensive and draw considerably more power than Type I devices, and so are rarely seen on pleasure boats.

3. Type III MSDs include portable toilets, but more typically store sewage in a holding tank and then discharge it either through a dockside pumpout facility or overboard beyond the 3-mile limit (Figures 12-25A and 12-25B).

Currently it is perfectly legal to have a toilet and holding tank (Type III device) with a Y-valve so that the toilet can be pumped directly overboard (when outside the 3-mile limit—Figures 12-25B and 12-25C) or into the holding tank. However, it is no longer legal for U.S. builders to build boats in this fashion; the toilet discharge must be plumbed directly to the holding tank (Figure 12-25A), after which the discharge can be directed (via a Y-valve) overboard or to a pumpout fitting. The valve must be secured in the holding tank position when in territorial or no-discharge zone (NDZ) waters (see below). Padlocking, removal of the valve handle, or use of a plastic wire tie are all considered adequate methods of securing the valve. Long-term cruisers will want the ability to pump the holding tank at sea as shown in Figure 12-25D (see below for a better way to set up the toilet installation).

Type I and II devices must be properly certified and have a certification label. Holding tanks require no certification provided they store sewage only at ambient temperatures and pressures (usually provided by venting the tank to atmosphere via a through-hull fitting). Vessels longer than 65 feet can use only Type II or III systems.

No-discharge zones (NDZ). There has been increasing concern that (1) the chemicals used to treat the effluent in many Type I and II systems are themselves damaging to the environment; and (2) there is, and can be, no guarantee that the devices are working properly. This is increasingly leading to the designation of no-discharge zones (NDZ), which forbid any overboard discharge, whether treated or not. An unfortunate consequence of this is that by outlawing Type I and II devices while often not providing workable alternatives, these NDZs may lead to an increase in the illegal discharge of raw sewage. Nevertheless, given this changing operating environment, Type III devices are probably the way to go on a new boat, although it has to be recognized that *reliance on a Type III device almost invariably causes cruising sailors to engage in illegal discharges*.

Heading Off Toilet Problems

Proper installations. Almost all marine toilets use a ¾ inch (19 mm) ID suction hose (supplying water for flushing) and a 1½-inch (38 mm) ID discharge hose. Suction hoses must be non-

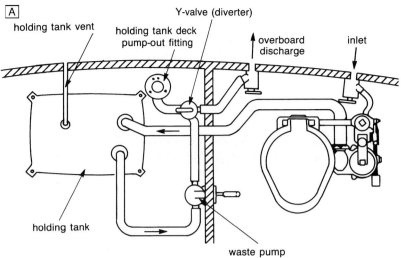

FIGURE 12-25A. A typical arrangement of an onboard waste disposal system with a holding tank and overboard discharge. In this configuration, all effluent first passes through the holding tank before being pumped overboard (which is how boats are now required to be built in the U.S.). The inlet and discharge lines should be looped above the waterline and fitted with vented loops. *(Simpson Lawrence)*

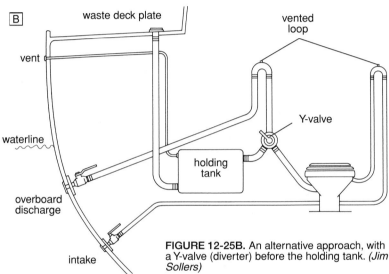

FIGURE 12-25B. An alternative approach, with a Y-valve (diverter) before the holding tank. *(Jim Sollers)*

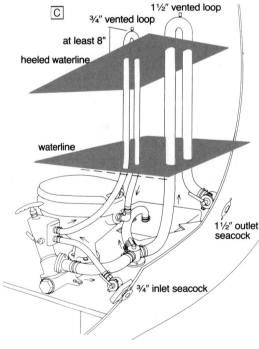

FIGURE 12-25C. What the schematic drawing in Figure 12-25B might look like in actuality. *(ITT/Jabsco)*

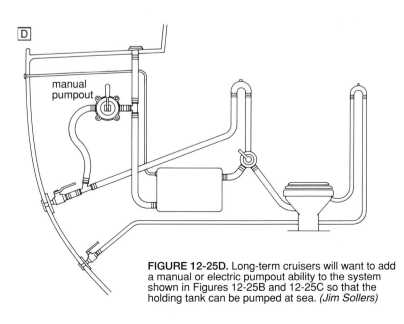

FIGURE 12-25D. Long-term cruisers will want to add a manual or electric pumpout ability to the system shown in Figures 12-25B and 12-25C so that the holding tank can be pumped at sea. *(Jim Sollers)*

FIGURE 12-26. First-class hoses and chafe protection on our old Pacific Seacraft 40.

siphon water into the toilet, eventually sinking the boat if it is not discovered in time. A number of boats have sunk this way. If there is any chance of a siphon developing, *it is absolutely essential to fit some form of a siphon break on both suction and discharge lines* (Figures 12-25C and 12-28).

A siphon break is formed by looping the line above the water level and installing a valve at the high point of the loop that allows air to be drawn into the line. This valve must be above the water level *at all angles of heel*. The usual configuration consists of an upside-down U-bend with a small tee containing a rubber flap at the top of the bend. Several problems may arise:

- The vent will sometimes plug, notably with salt crystals in the suction line, rendering the loop inoperative. Periodically unscrew the vent valve and wash it in warm fresh water.

- Air can be drawn into a suction pump through a vented loop. This will reduce the water flow to the toilet, and in extreme cases can lead to a loss of prime and subsequent air-locking of the suction pump. The installation of a U-trap in the suction line close to the toilet will retain some water and keep the pump wetted. However this simple measure may not suffice for some electric pumps; in this case, install a solenoid valve on the vent so that the solenoid closes when the toilet is flushed and opens when flushing is completed (a normally open solenoid valve).

- A vented loop in the discharge line may allow foul odors into the boat. It is best to attach a small hose to the vent and run this overboard. Be sure its exit is above the waterline at *all angles of heel*, or it may siphon into the boat and negate the purpose of the vented loop. Better yet is to eliminate the need for the vented loop (see below).

collapsible—any good-quality, reasonably firm water hose will do. Discharge hoses must be proper sanitation hose (see above). Hoses must be run without sharp bends (which may cause kinking and encourage blockages) and with adequate chafe protection where they pass through bulkheads (Figure 12-26). As noted previously, discharge hoses should not contain standing effluent (Figure 12-27). If this is likely, replace them with rigid PVC pipe where possible.

Y-valves. Most toilet installations include at least one Y-valve, and some have two or more. The seals on the shafts (to which the handles attach) are prone to leaking and are a frequent source of odors on boats. All too often, in one position or another, the Y-valve traps standing effluent in a hose. It pays to install quality Y-valves, and to design the installation so that in normal circumstances the valve and its associated hoses are filled with clean water and not standing effluent. Better yet is to eliminate the valves (see below).

Vented loops. Almost all sailboat toilets, and many powerboat toilets, are installed below the waterline. The toilets have valves on both the suction and discharge sides, but even so, any leakage past a suction or discharge valve can

FIGURE 12-27. Way too many boats have long hose runs that remain filled with standing effluent, as in this illustration. This is an invitation for obnoxious odors. *(Jim Sollers and SeaLand Technology)*

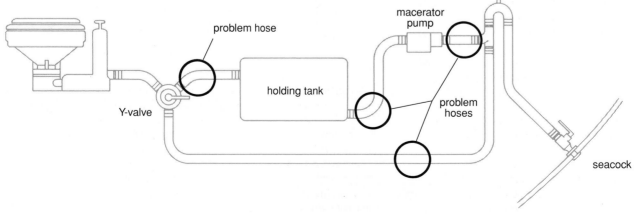

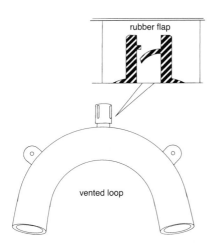

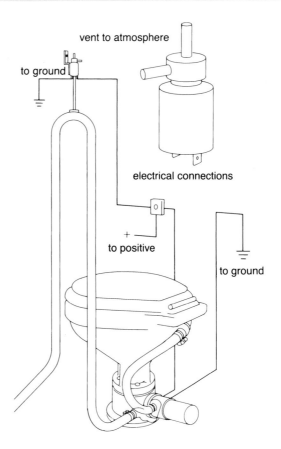

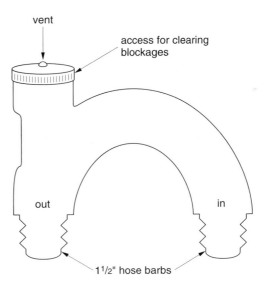

Some vented loops for discharge lines incorporate a cleanout fixture—a useful addition to any system.

Macerator pumps. Macerator pumps are used to break up and pump out the waste from many holding tanks. The macerating device is a metal blade; the pumpout device is almost always a rubber impeller pump (see Chapter 13). Macerator pumps may be inside or on top of a holding tank, or they may be mounted separately.

Macerator pumps have a high failure rate relative to their infrequent and intermittent use. Common problems are failed impellers (chemicals in the effluent swell the rubber vanes and cause them to jam in the pump housing and tear off) and a leaking seal around the drive shaft (the latter only matters on pumps external to the tank).

Never run a macerator pump dry; on most, the seal and impeller will burn up. Never run it continuously; the motor will burn up (motors are rated for intermittent use—2 to 15 minutes, depending on the make of the pump). It is best to fit only momentary-type switches—i.e., spring-loaded buttons or switches that must be held in the ON position.

In the event of a problem, try to run the pump. If the macerator part makes a loud whirring noise but nothing is being discharged, the rubber impeller has probably failed. If a pump mounted above a holding tank spins but fails to pump, before pulling it apart disconnect the discharge hose and pour in some water to make sure it is primed. It may just be air-bound. If the pump makes no noise, make all the usual voltage and electric motor tests at the pump (see Chapters 4 and 7).

I prefer to use a manual diaphragm–type pump rather than an electric macerator pump. Better yet is to design the installation so that a discharge pump is not needed (see below).

Modified installation. When looking at new construction or when modifying an existing toilet system, just about all of the issues raised above in connection with Y-valves, vented loops, and macerator/discharge pumps can be avoided by installing the holding tank high enough to get its base *above the boat's heeled waterline* (the easiest way to achieve this is to mount the tank high on the centerline—Figure 12-29).

The toilet discharge can now be plumbed directly to the top of the holding tank. Install a pumpout tube almost to the bottom of the tank and plumb it via a hose to the deck fitting. Plumb the tank discharge via a valve from the base of the tank to a seacock and install the tank's vent as usual. The result—no vented loop, Y-valve, or macerator/discharge pump.

When offshore, open the discharge valve and seacock. Effluent is pumped from the toilet into the tank and flows (via gravity) overboard. The tank vent acts as a vented loop for the system. When in inshore waters, close the discharge valve and seacock, and the tank fills.

Keys to a successful installation and operation are as follows:

- Plumb the toilet discharge to the top of the holding tank and not the bottom (as is commonly done). This is necessary to keep standing effluent out of the discharge line.

- After each use of the toilet, flush sufficient water through the toilet to clear the discharge line between the toilet and holding tank of all effluent. This is the only hose/pipe run likely to contain standing effluent; if possible, use rigid PVC pipe.

- Ensure the tank has a vent large enough to keep it aerated so that aerobic bacteria (not anaerobic) predominate—this will eliminate odors (see below) and will also turn all effluent into a liquid, which will prevent plugging of the discharge line from the holding tank.

- Plumb the drain from the tank to the seacock with a short, straight hose so that if it does clog, it can be cleared by poking something up the through-hull from outside the boat. Install a valve at the tank end of this hose run

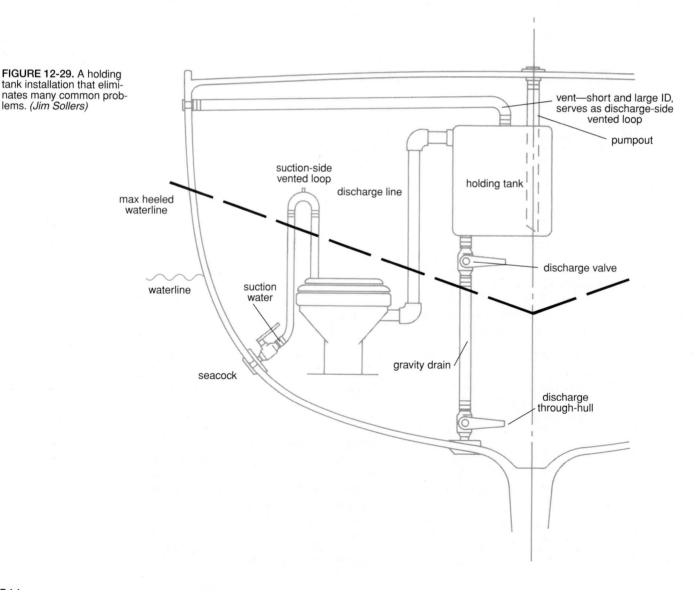

FIGURE 12-29. A holding tank installation that eliminates many common problems. *(Jim Sollers)*

vent—short and large ID, serves as discharge-side vented loop

pumpout

holding tank

suction-side vented loop

discharge line

max heeled waterline

discharge valve

waterline

suction water

gravity drain

seacock

discharge through-hull

so that when the tank is being used as a holding tank and the valve is closed, there will not be standing effluent in the line between the tank and seacock.

Note that such an installation will also work even if the base of the tank is not above the heeled waterline, *as long as the top of the tank together with the inlet from the toilet and also the vent are above the heeled waterline, and the base is above the static waterline when the boat is on an even keel.* Installed like this, on one tack or the other, the tank will partially backflush with seawater when the discharge valves are open (not such a bad idea), but this will not affect the functioning of the system. To fully discharge the tank, the boat will need to be put on an even keel or on the other tack.

Broken seat hinges. When a boat is heeled, if someone sits on the toilet the seat tends to move sideways. This severely stresses the hinges, which frequently break. You can eliminate this problem by fastening a couple of blocks to the underside of the seat so that the blocks fit just inside the toilet bowl rim when the seat is down (Figure 12-30).

General maintenance.
Marine toilets require little maintenance. The single biggest complaint is odors, particularly after a boat has been closed up for a while.

There are two types of bacteria that break down raw sewage—anaerobic (which live in an environment void of oxygen) and aerobic (which require oxygen). Anaerobic bacteria cause odors. Most holding tanks are deprived of oxygen, as is any stagnant effluent trapped in a hose. To improve the air circulation, install the largest, straightest vent fitting possible on the tank, and preferably two (to create cross-ventilation)—this is where the large vents required by the ISO work well. The periodic addition of an aerobic bacteria treatment will help to get the "good" bacteria going and keep them alive (treatments are available from Microphor, www.microphor. com; Raritan Engineering, www.raritaneng. com; and others). To hinder the growth of anaerobic bacteria, always flush the toilet sufficiently to clear all effluent out of the discharge line.

Avoid using antibacterial toilet bowl cleaners, drain cleaners, bleaches, or deodorants. These all kill aerobic bacteria, in addition to which many attack and swell up rubber parts.

Periodically check all wire terminals on electric toilets for corrosion, and clean when necessary. Keep a sharp eye out for external signs of leaking pump seals on macerator pumps, since these are a major cause of pump failures.

Winterizing. Improper winterization is a signif-

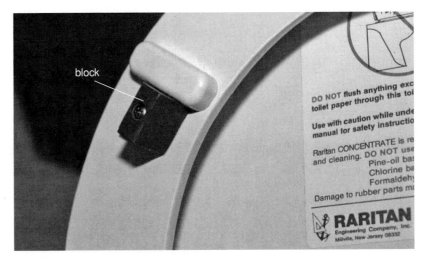

FIGURE 12-30. A block added to the underside of a toilet seat to keep it from sliding sideways and breaking the seat's hinges.

icant cause of toilet failure. It is not enough just to pump the toilet dry and leave it. Water remains trapped in low spots in both the suction and discharge lines as well as in the toilet's pump housings and any macerator or other discharge pump. To winterize properly:

1. Close the suction seacock, disconnect the hose, and dip it in a can of antifreeze. Use propylene glycol available from hardware stores and chandleries for winterizing freshwater systems. (Ethylene glycol, the usual antifreeze, is harmful to the environment and so should not be flushed overboard; alcohol, which is sometimes used as an antifreeze, will swell up rubber parts.) Pump the toilet until the antifreeze washes down the bowl sides and flows out the discharge. The toilet can either be pumped dry or left with the antifreeze in it.
2. Close the discharge seacock.
3. Drain and winterize holding tanks and treatment systems—if present—separately (this is important). Some specialized types (such as Raritan's LectraSan) should be disconnected *before* antifreeze is put in the system, since the antifreeze will cause problems.

Problems common to all marine toilets.
Regardless of type, all toilets will at some time smell, get clogged, and slowly plug up with calcium (if flushed with salt water).

Odors. As noted above, the primary cause of odors is a lack of fresh air in the system. Given this anaerobic environment, the obvious source of odors is a leak. Less obvious are the following:

- Permeable hose. Rub a cloth on the hose and sniff it. If the cloth smells, the hose is permeable and should be replaced with proper sanitation hose.
- Marine life, especially eelgrass, in the flushing

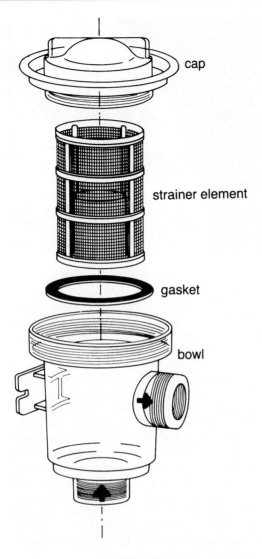

cap

strainer element

gasket

bowl

water. This gets caught on the underside of the toilet bowl rim and gives off a rotten-egg smell. Where this is a constant problem, you may need a strainer on the suction line seacock (Figure 12-31).

- The discharge line vented loop. Attach a piece of hose to the vent and lead it outside cabin areas; make sure the hose is never underwater at any angle of heel.

- Clogged vent on the holding tank. This generally results from overfilling the tank and driving solid waste up the vent.

- Low spots in the holding tank vent lines. These may fill with liquid and act as a U-trap, effectively plugging the vent.

- Defective discharge valve on the toilet (generally a "joker" valve; see below). The result can be that raw sewage backs up into the toilet bowl, a problem that may not be obvious since the water in the bowl may appear clean. However, the bacteria present will cause the

bowl to stain rapidly—overnight in warm climates.

- Worn O-ring or piston rings on a manual toilet with a double-acting piston (see below). This will allow raw sewage to work up past the piston into the flushing side of the pump. The pump must be dismantled and rebuilt.

Clogging. Marine toilets use little water (commonly as little as 1 quart per flush) and contain pumps, impellers, and valves that cannot handle solid objects. Clogging is an ever-present problem, so much so that some experienced cruising sailors keep a separate receptacle for waste toilet paper and put *only* human waste down the toilet (this, however, is not necessary with a proper installation).

There are special short-fiber toilet papers on the market for use on boats. These break down quickly, reducing the risk of clogging. But the key is to keep paper usage to a minimum. No fibrous substances (e.g., rags, sanitary napkins) should ever be put down a marine toilet. In fact, aside from toilet paper, nothing that hasn't been eaten first should be put down the head.

Never combat a blockage with drain cleaners; these will attack sensitive parts in the toilet. The best bet is to add water to the toilet bowl and leave it overnight. Usually the waste will break down enough to pump out the following morning.

Sooner or later, however, we all have to face a clogged toilet that won't clear (such as when our daughter threw a piece of coconut down the toilet!). There is nothing to be done but take it apart.

Calcium buildup. In time, calcium deposits, similar to the deposits in a tea kettle, build up in all toilets that use salt water for flushing, primarily on discharge valves, lines, and seacocks (Figure 12-32A). In extreme cases, the calcium can pretty well plug a toilet. If a toilet has become progressively harder to flush over a period of time, with an ever-increasing tendency to clog, or if its discharge line is constantly leaking back into the bowl, calcium is a likely culprit.

A good dose of vinegar (acetic acid) left overnight on a regular basis—say once a month—will go a long way toward keeping things free (Figures 12-32B and 12-32C), but if the lines begin to clog, you need a stronger treatment. Muriatic (hydrochloric) acid, obtainable from many boat chandleries and hardware stores, dissolves the calcium, but it will also attack metal parts in the toilet, albeit at a much slower rate. Place a 10% solution in the bowl, observing all the warnings on the bottle (in particular, when diluting concentrated muriatic acid, *always add the acid to water and **not** the*

calcium starting to build up

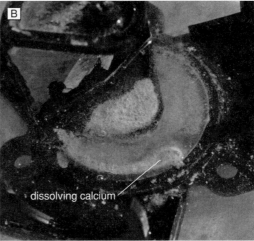

dissolving calcium

FIGURE 12-32A. Calcium is beginning to form in this Y-valve, making it difficult to operate (the handle broke!). Left long enough, calcium can completely plug a hose.

FIGURE 12-32B. Calcium dissolves in undiluted vinegar. Stronger stuff (e.g., muriatic acid) will dissolve it faster.

FIGURE 12-32C. Giving our toilet its regular monthly dose of vinegar.

other way around). The solution will bubble and fizz as it works, until the bowl and its immediate drain are free of calcium.

When the bubbling has ceased, pump the bowl almost dry. This will move the acid solution into the pump and the first part of the discharge line. Wait awhile and then flush the toilet a few strokes more to move the solution farther through the line. Continue in this manner until the entire discharge line has been covered. Thoroughly flush the system to remove all traces of acid.

The acid is used up as it bubbles. In severe cases of calcification, it may be necessary to treat the system several times. Once it is clear, a small dosage at periodic intervals should keep it clear. If the acid treatment fails, the only recourse is to break down the toilet and discharge lines and chip out the calcium. You can beat the hoses on the dockside to break loose the deposits but replacing them is preferable.

Troubleshooting and Repair

There are three types of marine toilets in common use: manual and electrified manual, electric (macerating), and vacuum; there are also some uncommon variants (notably, composting toilets and several waste treatment systems).

Manual and electrified manual toilets. The central component in a manual toilet is a double-acting piston pump, either operated by hand or, in an electrified manual toilet, driven by an electric motor. The suction water is led to the top of the pump cylinder and from there to the toilet bowl rim. The toilet bowl discharges into the bottom of the pump cylinder, then

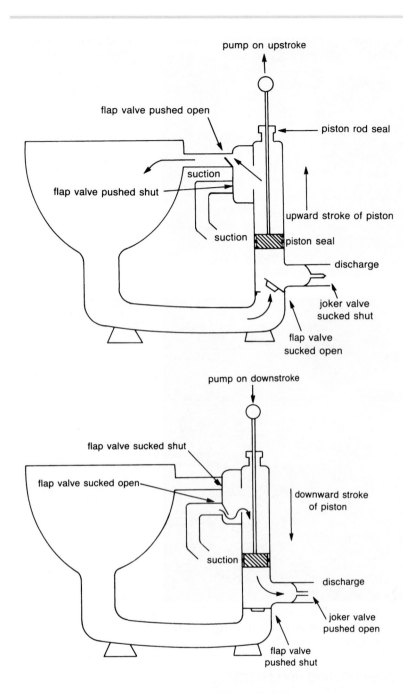

pump on upstroke

flap valve pushed open

piston rod seal

flap valve pushed shut

suction

suction

upward stroke of piston

piston seal

discharge

joker valve sucked shut

flap valve sucked open

pump on downstroke

flap valve sucked shut

flap valve sucked open

downward stroke of piston

suction

discharge

joker valve pushed open

flap valve pushed shut

FIGURE 12-33A. The operation of a double-acting piston toilet.

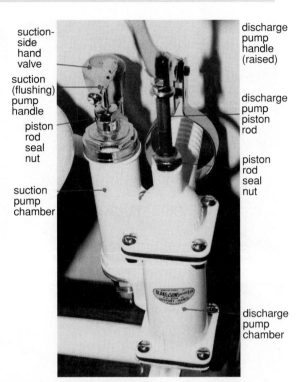

suction-side hand valve

suction (flushing) pump handle

piston rod seal nut

suction pump chamber

discharge pump handle (raised)

discharge pump piston rod

piston rod seal nut

discharge pump chamber

FIGURE 12-33B. A Blakes toilet, with independent flushing and discharge pumps.

either to a holding tank or overboard (Figure 12-33A). There are in and out valves on the suction and discharge sides. (A few toilets—notably Baby Blakes—have separate suction and discharge pumps and pump cylinders [Figure 12-33B], but the majority are as described.)

On the downstroke, the pump piston pulls flushing water into the top of the cylinder while driving effluent out the bottom end. On the upstroke, the piston forces the flushing water into the toilet while sucking effluent into the base of the cylinder.

Since the piston rod is attached to the top of the piston and therefore passes through the flush-water end of the pump cylinder, the flushing-side volume is less than the waste discharge–side volume by the amount of space occupied by the piston rod. In theory the pump will always pump out more than it sucks in, thus keeping the bowl dry. To make sure, a manual valve is invariably fitted on the suction side, enabling the flushing water to be turned off while the bowl is evacuated.

Internal suction and discharge valves may be one of three types: spring-loaded ball valves, flapper valves, or joker (*duckbill*) valves.

Ball valves are held against a seat by a weak spring. Pressure from the opposite side of the seat lifts the ball off the seat, allowing water to flow past; pressure from the other direction combines with the spring pressure to push the ball against the seat and hold the valve closed. A *flapper* valve is nothing more than a weighted flap resting on a base plate (Figure 12-33C). Fluid can flow one way, lifting it off its seat; flow in the other direction forces the flap down onto its seat. A *joker* valve is a slit rubber hemisphere, to the convex surface of which is attached a rubber sleeve (the duck's bill). Fluid pushing through the base of the hemisphere opens the slit and sleeve; fluid approaching the hemisphere from the other side collapses and closes it (the discharge valve in Figure 12-33D).

Leaking seals. Where the piston rod exits the top of its cylinder on a manual toilet there is a

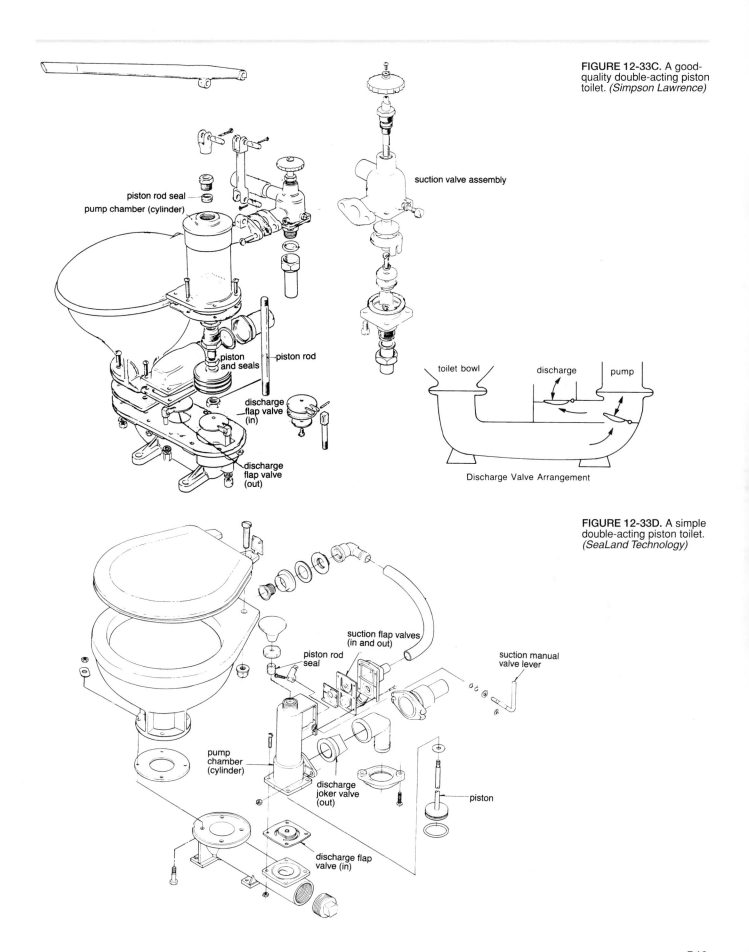

FIGURE 12-33C. A good-quality double-acting piston toilet. *(Simpson Lawrence)*

piston rod seal
pump chamber (cylinder)

suction valve assembly

piston and seals

piston rod

discharge flap valve (in)

discharge flap valve (out)

toilet bowl

discharge

pump

Discharge Valve Arrangement

FIGURE 12-33D. A simple double-acting piston toilet. *(SeaLand Technology)*

suction flap valves (in and out)

suction manual valve lever

piston rod seal

pump chamber (cylinder)

discharge joker valve (out)

piston

discharge flap valve (in)

FIGURE 12-34. To replace an external piston-rod seal, remove the pump handle (1); remove the yoke (2) from the piston rod (2A); remove the star washer or packing nut (3); and replace the seal (4). To access the discharge valve and the piston seal (6), remove the cylinder retaining screws (5) and the hoses; check the piston O-ring (6) and the discharge valve (7). To check the suction valves, remove the two covers (8) to provide access to the springs and ball valves (9). *(Raritan Engineering)*

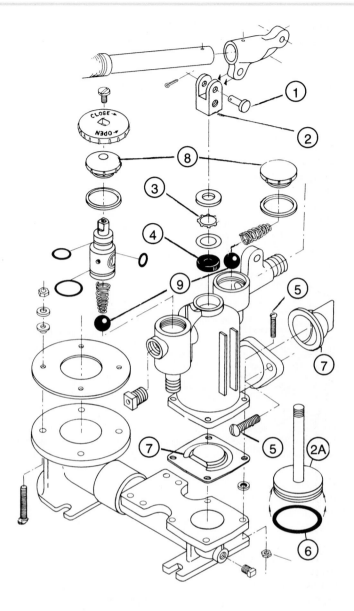

seal—the familiar grease-type seal consisting of a metal case and a rubber lip to grip the rod. Sooner or later, these seals always seem to start leaking and have to be replaced. Note that what is leaking is clean water, not effluent; a minor leak is annoying but can safely be left until a repair is convenient.

Most seals are accessible from the outside, but some can be reached only by dismantling the pump, which is a very poor design and extremely aggravating. When buying, avoid these toilets.

External seals. To replace, close the seacocks. Lift the pump handle, wrap the piston rod with tape, and grip gently with Vise-Grips (mole wrench). Unscrew the handle, knob, or yoke (depending on the make and type of pump

action—Figure 12-34), *taking great care not to let go of the rod, since it may drop down inside the pump!* Unscrew the seal assembly (or remove the retaining snap ring or circlip) and slide the assembly off the piston rod, temporarily removing the Vise-Grips to let the assembly past. Before installing a new seal, lightly tape the threads on the top of the piston rod to avoid damaging the seal when it slides over. The lip of the seal, if present, faces toward the pump cylinder (i.e., down).

Internal seals. Remove the pump body from the toilet by unscrewing it from its base and disconnecting the suction and discharge hoses (Figure 12-35). Wrap a piece of tape around the piston rod, gently grip the rod with Vise-Grips, and unscrew the handle or knob. The piston and rod can then be knocked out of the bottom of the pump (after removing any calcium deposits as described above).

The seal fits into a recess at the top of the pump housing and must be pried out, which is frequently a time-consuming and frustrating business. Straighten a piece of stiff wire (such as a coat hanger), file a point on its end, and bend the last ¼ inch (6 mm) in at 90 degrees. Poke this through the top of the piston housing and try to force it between the seal and its seat. Once the seal starts to work loose, it is important to work it from side to side, or it will get cockeyed and jam.

Tape the threads at the top of the piston rod and slide on a new seal with its lip facing down (toward the piston). Put the piston rod back in the pump housing and use the piston to push the new seal gently into place.

In time, the plastic bore around the piston rod (at the top of the cylinder) wears, and the rod action becomes sloppy. Once this happens, the seal fails more quickly. One solution is to add a small length of hose to the top of the pump housing and clamp a second seal into this to form a flexible stuffing box (packing gland). It may be necessary to file down the top of the housing to get the hose to fit. The pump stroke (and therefore capacity) will be reduced by the length of the hose, and the toilet therefore will require a little more pumping. You can extend the life of this second seal by fabricating a spacer out of a piece of plastic and inserting it as shown in Figure 12-35. If you drill the plastic to make a reasonably close fit around the pump shaft, it will act as a kind of Cutless bearing, maintaining the alignment between the shaft and the seal.

Bowl fills faster than it drains. As noted, pumps are designed to empty the bowl faster than it fills. If the reverse happens, it is almost always because a discharge flapper or joker valve is stuck partially open. Vigorous pumping will generally clear it unless the problem is a result of scale buildup or valve failure. Try the muriatic acid treatment. If all else fails, dismantle the toilet and replace the valves (see below).

Bowl fills when not in use. Either the suction or the discharge valve(s) are leaking. Close first one seacock, then the other, observing the bowl level to find out on which side the problem lies. You will have to dismantle the toilet to check the valves. In addition to the internal suction valve, many toilets have a handwheel-type manual valve on the suction line (e.g., Blakes). These often seem to leak after a few years; however, they are not repairable and must be replaced.

Handle is pumped but nothing happens. If you feel strong resistance, check that the seacocks are open and the inlet valve is in the correct position. Check also that the holding tank is not full. If you

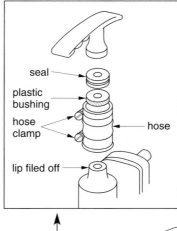

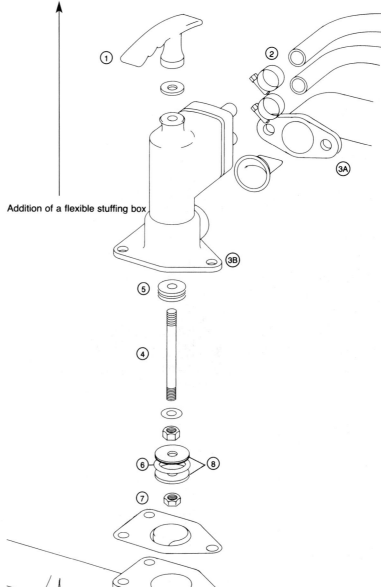

FIGURE 12-35. To replace an internal piston-rod seal, remove the pump handle or knob (1), remove the suction (2) and discharge (3A) hoses, remove the pump cylinder retaining screws and cylinder (3B), knock the piston rod (4) out of the base of the cylinder, then pick out the old seal (5) and put in a new one. If necessary, replace the piston seal O-ring (6) by taking off the piston retaining nut (7) and separating the two halves of the piston (8). Inset: Alleviate leakage due to wear-induced slop in the piston rod by adding a flexible stuffing box. *(Jim Sollers)*

seal
plastic bushing
hose clamp
hose
lip filed off

Addition of a flexible stuffing box

still feel resistance, the discharge line is probably clogged. As noted above, adding water to the bowl and exercising patience (leave it overnight) may give the blockage time to break down.

Some pumps use an O-ring to seal the piston in the cylinder. A damaged cylinder wall or swollen O-ring can make the pump action really stiff. Lubricate the pump by adding vegetable or baby oil to the toilet and flushing it through the system; note that if a holding tank is in use, the oil will settle out on the surface of the effluent, blocking oxygen and thus encouraging anaerobic (odor-producing) bacteria.

If you feel little or no resistance, the piston nut has probably fallen off, allowing the piston to drop off its shaft. The pump will need dismantling.

Electric pump operates slowly or not at all. First check the voltage *at the motor, while it is running* (see Chapters 4 and 7). If there is no voltage (it will not be running!), check all fuses, breakers, connections, etc. If the voltage is low, check the ship's battery and recharge as necessary. If the battery is OK, there must be excessive voltage drop between the battery and the motor (no more than 10% is permissible). Refer to Chapter 4.

Because of the heavy electrical loads and long wiring runs, some pumps use a solenoid *(relay)* to close the motor circuit, with a remotely operated switch at the toilet. The principle is the same as that of an engine-starting circuit. Check the solenoid for voltage drop (see pages 318–20 for troubleshooting this type of circuit).

If the voltage is adequate and the motor appears to be spinning, disconnect the electric drive (normally one bolt—Figures 12-36A and 12-36B) and operate the toilet manually. If it works normally, check the electric drive gears (normally a worm-gear arrangement) and linkage for binding.

Repairing valves and pistons. Disassembly and reassembly are simple. Two to four screws remove the pump from its base; two or more screws undo the discharge manifold; and suction hoses are generally held with hose clamps.

Inspect flapper valves for damage, swelling, or dirt and calcium buildup, any of which could prevent them from seating properly. Inspect joker valves for obstructions in the sleeve (duckbill). Break up calcium deposits by flexing the rubber or putting the valves in a 10% muriatic acid solution (observe all cautions on the acid bottle). Check ball-valve springs for corrosion and adequate tension, and the balls and their seats for trash and pitting.

Flapper valves are replaced with the weight uppermost. Make sure the side of the valve that hinges is matched to the belled side of its housing; otherwise the valve will fail to open or will hang up in operation.

Joker valves are fitted with the sleeve or duckbill facing *away* from the toilet, *toward* the holding tank and seacock.

Pistons generally consist of two dished washers trapping an O-ring and held to the end of the piston rod with a nut. If the O-ring needs replacing, simply undo the nut and separate the washers. Make sure the new O-ring is mounted

FIGURES 12-36A AND 12-36B. An electrified toilet and drive mechanism. To disconnect the drive (12-36B), remove the drive bolt (4) and operate the toilet manually. Check the connecting rod (3) and worm gears (2A and 2B) for binding. Test the motor (1) for voltage drop and shorts. *(Raritan Engineering)*

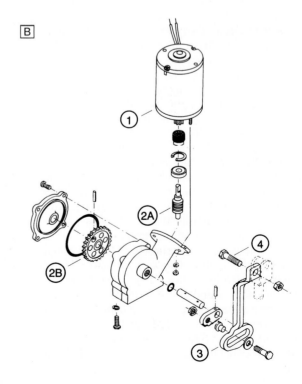

squarely, and be sure the piston retaining nut is adequately locked to its shaft with a lock washer or liquid adhesive (such as Loctite) or by peening (hammering) the shaft threads over once the nut is on. Grease the cylinder wall with Vaseline before replacing the piston.

Scrupulously clean all mating surfaces before reassembly; otherwise leaks are almost certain. Do not overtighten screws, especially on plastic toilets. A little silicone gasket cement or sealing compound smeared on mating surfaces before reassembly will prevent most minor leaks.

Electric (macerating) toilets. At the base of these toilets is a multipurpose pump (Figure 12-37A), usually comprising the following components mounted on a common shaft: a small rubber impeller pump (supplies flushing water to the toilet bowl); a macerator pump (breaks up the sewage into tiny particles); and a good-sized rubber impeller or centrifugal pump to discharge the waste (Figures 12-37B and 12-37C).

FIGURE 12-37A. A typical electric toilet. *(Raritan Engineering)*

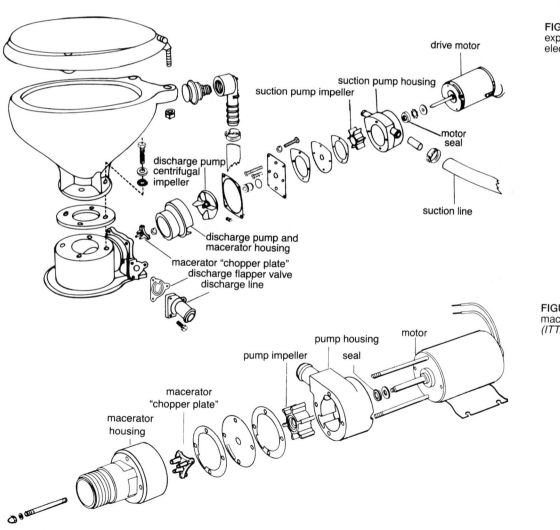

FIGURE 12-37B. An exploded view of an electric toilet. *(ITT/Jabsco)*

FIGURE 12-37C. A macerator pump. *(ITT/Jabsco)*

Macerating toilets use more water than any other type of toilet (typically 1 to 3 gallons to achieve a full flush) and as such will rapidly load up a Type I, II or III (holding tank) MSD. Insufficient flushing, which leaves effluent in the unit, will shorten the unit's life; the effluent attacks metal parts in the macerator and swells up rubber impellers and seals. Seal leaks often result in motor failures.

A somewhat different approach is used in Jett Head toilets (Raritan Engineering), the Royal Flush (Headhunter, www.headhunterinc.com), and similar products. These use a high-capacity centrifugal pump to direct a powerful jet of water into the toilet bowl, breaking up waste and flushing it away. Power consumption is high, but for a very short time, resulting in a relatively small overall drain (on a 12-volt system, the Royal Flush pulls 57 amps but for just 10 to 20 seconds, resulting in a drain of 0.15 to 0.3 Ah per flush). These toilets use far more water than conventional marine toilets (1.0 to 1.5 gallons per flush) and as such are not suitable for use with typical holding tanks. They are rarely found on anything other than large yachts and powerboats, and for this reason, they are not covered in this book.

Bowl fills faster than it drains. Waste is probably caught in the discharge valves. Close the inlet, pump down, open the inlet, and flush through to clear the discharge lines. If the problem persists, check the discharge pump impeller, valves, and lines for wear, obstructions, or calcification.

Inadequate flushing. The pump may be running slowly because of a variety of electrical problems that usually involve low voltage; the suction pump impeller may be worn; or the pump may be sucking air through a loose connection or the vented loop (see page 542). The suction seacock may even be coming out of the water when the boat is heeled.

Motor runs but either suction or discharge fails to operate. The pump impeller, particularly if it is the rubber-impeller type, is probably stripped. *Most pumps cannot tolerate being run dry for more than a few seconds without damage.* But before pulling the pump apart, check that all valves and seacocks are open and the pump is primed. Note that when a pump is run dry, the impeller(s) and the seal(s) are likely to be damaged.

Motor repeatedly blows fuses. This is especially likely at the start of a new season. During the winter, rubber impellers frequently get stuck to their pump housings; they then overload the motor and fuse on start-up. Try lubricating the pump (pour some water in the bowl and suction lines) and, if possible, turn it by hand. The other common problem is the swelling of pump impellers caused by inappropriate chemicals

(e.g., toilet bowl cleaners, deodorants, drain openers) being put down the toilet. In this case you will need to dismantle the pump and replace the impeller.

Loud noises from the pump. There may be a solid object jammed in the macerator, or the motor bearings may be worn out. The latter generally happens because leaking seals allow water into the bearings. In either case, the pump needs disassembling (see below).

Water leaks around pump housings. One of the pump seals is leaking (some pumps have one seal; others have a central motor with pumps on both ends of the shaft, in which case there is a seal at both ends). *Any defective seal needs immediate corrective action. Seal leaks are one of the principal causes of bearing and motor failures.*

Motor operates sluggishly or erratically. Check for low voltage at the motor. If the voltage is OK, the pumps may be partially plugged, or the motor brushes may be worn or hanging up in their holders. The brushes should be accessible after a couple of covers are removed. Check the brush springs and the free movement of the brushes in their holders. While the brushes are out, check the commutator for excessive carbon and signs of arcing and burning (Chapter 7).

Motor burnout. The principal causes of burned-out motors are:

- Seal leaks into the motor causing a short circuit.

- Overheating as a result of low voltage, pump clogging, or *extended running*. Motors are rated for intermittent use—some as little as 2 minutes at a time, some as long as 15 minutes. Motors should have momentary-type switches —switches that must be held "on" against a spring pressure—to guard against their accidentally being left on.

Overhauling the pump and motor. Disassembly is usually reasonably obvious and straightforward. There will be one or more flap and/or joker valves on the discharge side. The first unit encountered is generally the macerator, with the discharge pump behind it (the latter may be either a centrifugal pump or a rubber-impeller pump). PAR toilets have the suction pump mounted behind this, followed by a seal and the motor. Raritan toilets have a double-ended motor shaft, with the suction pump on one end and the macerator and discharge pump on the opposite end. In this case both ends of the motor shaft have a seal.

Nearly all suction pumps are the rubber-impeller type. Inspect the vanes for wear on their outer edges (they should be rounded and not flat) and for adequate flexibility with no signs of distortion or cracking.

Seal replacement. Pry and push out old seals with bent coat hangers, screwdrivers, etc., taking care not to score the seal housing, then scrupulously clean the housing. Press new seals into position with equal care; this is the most important part of any rebuilding job. If the seal is at all cockeyed, bent, or distorted, it will leak and the motor will fail in a short time.

Place new seals in their housings with the lip that encloses the motor shaft facing *toward* the pump chamber that is being sealed. Use a piece of dowel or a socket of the same diameter as the seal to push the seal home; use the minimum pressure and keep the seal square to the housing at all times.

Testing the motor. Motors are the universal type (Chapter 7). Older motors usually have field windings; newer motors are the permanent-magnet type. The various tests outlined in Chapter 7 may be applied to armatures, commutators, field windings, and brushes. The armature should be flexed and spun to check the bearings and to make sure it is not rubbing on the field winding shoes or magnets.

If there is any problem with the armature, field windings, or bearings, it is better to replace the entire motor than to disassemble it. Motors are constructed to very close tolerances to eliminate vibration and shaft seal leaks. It is impossible to meet these standards without specialized bench equipment.

When refitting pumps, be sure to get the positive and negative wires the right way around. Polarity is not necessarily critical on motors with field windings, but it is critical on the more common permanent-magnet types. The usual color coding on DC motors comprises a red or orange wire for the positive and a black (or maybe yellow) wire for the negative. On AC motors, a black wire is normally hot (ungrounded); a white wire, neutral; and a green wire, ground (U.S. color codes; see Chapter 4 for EU equivalents).

Vacuum toilets. The only manual vacuum toilet I know of is the Lavac (made by Blakes Lavac Taylors, www.blakes-lavac-taylors.co.uk), and the only powered version is the VacuFlush (SeaLand Technology).

Lavac toilets. Lavacs are elegantly simple. The toilet lid is designed to make a seal with the bowl. When the waste is pumped out (with the lid down), a vacuum is created in the bowl, which sucks in the flushing water (Figures 12-38A and 12-38B). No inlet pump or valves are needed. There is almost nothing to go wrong. Lavacs use diaphragm pumps on the discharge (Chapter 13), which are far less troublesome

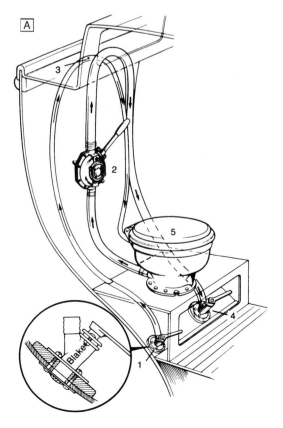

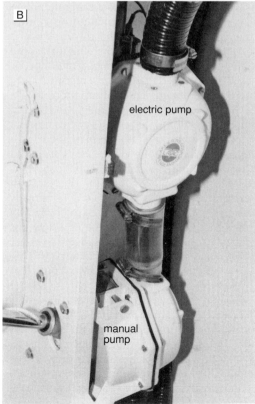

FIGURE 12-38A. A Lavac toilet. As the waste is pumped overboard (or to the holding tank—not shown) the resulting vacuum draws in flushing water through the inlet. Inlet seacock (1); diaphragm discharge pump (2); air bleed valve (3), a simple plastic plug with a hole drilled in it (the size of the hole controls the level of water remaining in the bowl; the larger the hole, the less the water); discharge seacock (4); bowl (5). *(Blakes Lavac Taylors)*

FIGURE 12-38B. A Lavac toilet with electric and manual diaphragm pumps in series.

than piston pumps. Where an electric diaphragm pump is fitted, it is advisable to install a manual diaphragm pump *in series* with it as a backup (Figure 12-38B). This is the same pump minus the motor drive, so only one set of spare pump valves and diaphragm is needed. The suction line has no valves—merely a vented loop. If it starts siphoning into the bowl, it means the vented loop is plugged and needs cleaning. The bowl can always be pumped dry with the lid open.

The most likely problem is a loss of vacuum in the bowl, leading to a reduction or complete loss of the flushing water. Older Lavacs have plastic-coated aluminum bowls. Once they start to corrode, and the seal fails between the bowl and the lid, the bowl will need replacing with one of the newer (post-1981) porcelain bowls.

If the bowl is OK, check the sealing face on the underside of the lid. If this is sound, check all the suction hose connections for an air leak. For diaphragm pump repair, see Chapter 13.

VacuFlush toilets. VacuFlush toilets utilize a vacuum pump and a vacuum chamber (Figure 12-39). Depressing a foot pedal in the base of the toilet opens a ball valve. The waste is sucked out and passed to a holding tank or overboard. The vacuum pump then kicks in and pulls down the vacuum chamber ready for the next flush. Water for rinsing the bowl is normally taken from the boat's *pressurized freshwater* supply (1 to 3 pints per flush) although seawater can be used (but this would considerably increase maintenance and would require an additional pump to pressurize the water supply). The rinsing valve is connected to the foot pedal, opening just before the main ball valve and closing just after it.

Less water is used than in most marine toilets, which means holding tanks fill up more slowly. The use of fresh water for flushing also tends to reduce odors (although it obviously eats into the freshwater supply; if this is replenished via a watermaker, the cost of making the water should be factored into the overall cost equation).

It takes 60 to 90 seconds for the vacuum pump to pull down the vacuum chamber ready for use. The pump will then kick in after every flush (15 to 45 seconds). Because of a slow loss of vacuum, the pump can be expected to come on as often as once every 2 hours even if the toilet is not flushed. At 12 volts, the pump pulls 4 to 6 amps, which comes to around 0.03 to 0.1 Ah per flush, with an additional drain of around 1 Ah a day to maintain the vacuum.

If the pump runs longer than 90 seconds or more frequently than once every 2 hours between flushes, a more serious vacuum leak is present. Likely sources include faulty hose connections, poor seals on the main ball valve, and leaking check valves. (There are several joker-type valves in the system.) Tighten all hose clamps. Pour a little water in the bowl; if it is sucked away, the seals are leaking. In this case, try tightening the main clamp ring, but beware of overtightening, which will jam the valve or prevent it from closing properly. If check valves are suspected, try repeated flushings. If this fails, add muriatic acid to dissolve calcium deposits (pages 546–47). If all else fails, take the valves apart and inspect.

A lack of flushing water will arise from low pressure on the freshwater system, a plugged freshwater valve (there is a filter screen on the inlet), or a defective water valve. If the water will not turn off, the valve may be stuck open due to a bent operating lever or dirt on the valve seat, or the valve itself may be defective.

The various rubber parts need replacing every 3 to 4 years with freshwater use; perhaps as often as annually with seawater use. The pump is a bellows or diaphragm type (covered in Chapter 13).

Biological digesters. Human waste contains bacteria that, if left to do their job and given fresh air, will break solids down in an odorless manner. This is the principle that underlies composting toilets for off-the-grid homes. Typically, the solids are separated from the liquids, and the liquids are evaporated by a fan and/or heater. The bacteria break down the solids into an odorless substance that looks like soil. It is removed once in a while (generally, a drawer pulls out from the base of the toilet) and disposed of.

The typical composting toilet is too bulky for a boat, but there are a couple of derivatives that are sometimes used.

Microphor toilets. The Microphor system has been around in one form or another for decades. Unlike a true composting toilet, it uses flushing toilets (manual or some electric types). The effluent flows through a series of filter columns that strain out the solids. The liquids are treated with chlorine to kill bacteria and discharged overboard (these are classified as Type I or II MSDs). The solids are broken down by bacterial action and converted to liquids; then they join the liquid waste stream.

Traditionally, the filter columns have been formed from the bark of redwood trees, but in recent years, synthetic materials have been introduced that have a longer life, are less susceptible to damage, and are easier to clean should this become necessary (see below). Clearly, the filter columns need to have sufficient surface area to keep up with the maximum amount of solids entering the system. If not, they will become plugged. As a result, Microphor units tend to be large and heavy; the unit recommended for a crew of four is over 2 feet (60 cm) wide and high,

TANKS, PLUMBING, TOILETS, AND THROUGH-HULL FITTINGS

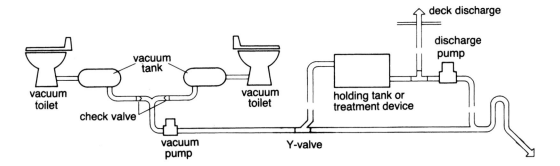

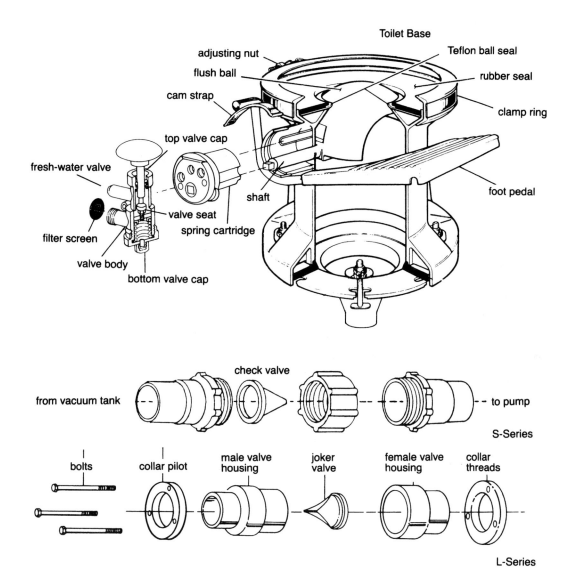

FIGURE 12-39. A VacuFlush toilet. **Top:** A central vacuum pump is used to transfer waste to the holding tank or treatment device. **Middle:** The main foot-operated valve and freshwater rinsing valve. **Bottom:** In-line check valves. *(SeaLand Technology)*

3 feet (90 cm) long, and weighs 360 pounds (164 kg). In addition, there are other requirements that complicate the installation on the typical pleasure boat.

Any such system cannot tolerate the use of antibacterial sanitizers (such as Lysol, Pine-Sol, and ammonia-based cleaners); these kill the bac-

terial action, causing the system to fill with solids and plug up. Bacterial action is also slowed in colder weather; below 60°F/15°C problems may occur. You can boost bacterial action by the addition of bacteria in solids or liquid form (Microphor sells a product called MicroCulture for this purpose and a microbial cleaning agent for toilet bowls called MicroScrub; these will enhance the aerobic bacterial action in any holding tank). Should the system stop working and get plugged up, it may need to be opened and flushed, in particular flushing the filter columns until they are clean. The traditional redwood bark will, in any case, need replacing every few years; the newer, synthetic media lasts longer (it is guaranteed for 5 years).

Air Head toilet. The Air Head Dry Toilet (Eos Design, www.airheadtoilet.com), a recent introduction to the marine marketplace, is a true composting toilet in a size compact enough to fit comfortably on a boat. It uses no flushing water. It is designed to separate urine, which is drained into a separate container, from solids, which are deposited in a paper filter (a coffee filter) and dumped into the base. The urine is periodically disposed of (if desired, the urine can be plumbed to a conventional holding tank and disposed of at sea or through a pumpout facility; because no water is used for flushing, the holding tank will take a long time to fill).

The base of the toilet has a small fan (150 mA at 12 volts = 3.6 Ah per day) that is exhausted outside the boat via a vent fitting. The fan is left on when the boat is unattended; a small solar panel is recommended to keep up with its needs. The constant airflow dries any residual moisture in the solids and promotes aerobic action (which is also initiated by the addition of peat moss). Periodically, the base is removed and its soil-like contents are dumped.

On the positive side, the system should be odorless. It requires minimal installation (the vent for the fan); takes up no more space than a traditional toilet; and does not need a holding tank or any of the hoses, valves and through-hulls associated with a traditional installation. Its storage capacity will last a cruising couple for several weeks, enabling the solids to be dumped periodically when offshore. The overall cost is no more than the cheapest toilet-cum-holding-tank installation and is considerably less than most. The Air Head has received a number of favorable reviews. It may well be the solution to toilet problems in many NDZs, especially those with poor pumpout facilities, and is sufficiently hassle free to be an attractive proposition for wider use.

On the negative side, the Air Head is something that takes a little getting used to! It remains to be seen whether the idea will catch on. If successful, it may spawn similar products.

Type I MSDs. Some Type I MSDs treat one flush at a time and immediately discharge it overboard. As noted, the areas in which this can be done are narrowing. Other Type I MSDs store a number of flushes in a holding tank, then treat the entire batch at one time (and as such combine a Type III MSD with a Type I). The most popular of the former kind is Raritan's LectraSan. The Mansfield TDX (later the SeaLand TDX, then the SeaLand SanX) and Groco's Thermopure (www.groco.net) are examples of the latter.

LectraSan. With the LectraSan, waste is pumped into a small holding tank that has up to a four-flush capacity. In the holding tank, the waste is chopped up by a macerator pump in one chamber and stirred by a mixer in another chamber. In between, through an electrolytic process, two electrodes immersed in the suspension manufacture hypochlorous acid from the seawater, which is used for flushing (Figure 12-40). This is done without adding chemicals. The acid kills the bacteria and further toilet flushes push the treated waste out of the tank and overboard.

The LectraSan system must be used *every time the toilet is flushed*. Failure to do so will overload the macerator and clog the system. This makes it inappropriate for use in a NDZ. The unit goes through a pretreatment cycle of approximately 30 seconds, then a treatment cycle of 2 minutes. The unit must be turned on *before flushing*; it must be flushed *during the pretreatment cycle*; and it must *not* be flushed, or flushed again, during the treatment cycle. In other words, once the toilet is flushed, the unit must be allowed to complete the cycle before reflushing.

LectraSans have a high current draw (45 amps on 12 volts) but for only 2 to 3 minutes—on a 12-volt system this comes to 1.5 to 2.25 Ah per flush. However, with a boatload of guests this can add up! Between flushes there is no current drain. In the event of a problem, perform all the usual voltage drop tests *at the unit while in operation*. See above for macerator pump and electric motor tests.

The control unit has a meter indicating low, normal, and high treatment levels. Treatment levels are related to battery voltage, water salinity, and temperature—the higher the voltage, salinity, and temperature, the higher the meter reading. In fresh or brackish water, salt must be added to maintain salinity, either manually when flushing or via a special tank. If meter readings are low, check first for voltage drop during operation. If the voltage is OK, try adding salt. If meter readings are too high, it's likely too much salt has been added.

The holding tank and electrodes may become encrusted with calcium in time. Flush muriatic acid through the unit as described previously. Rinse well before reusing. If more extensive inspection and cleaning are needed, lift off the whole top and lift out the electrode pack.

Never put toilet bowl cleaners, drain openers,

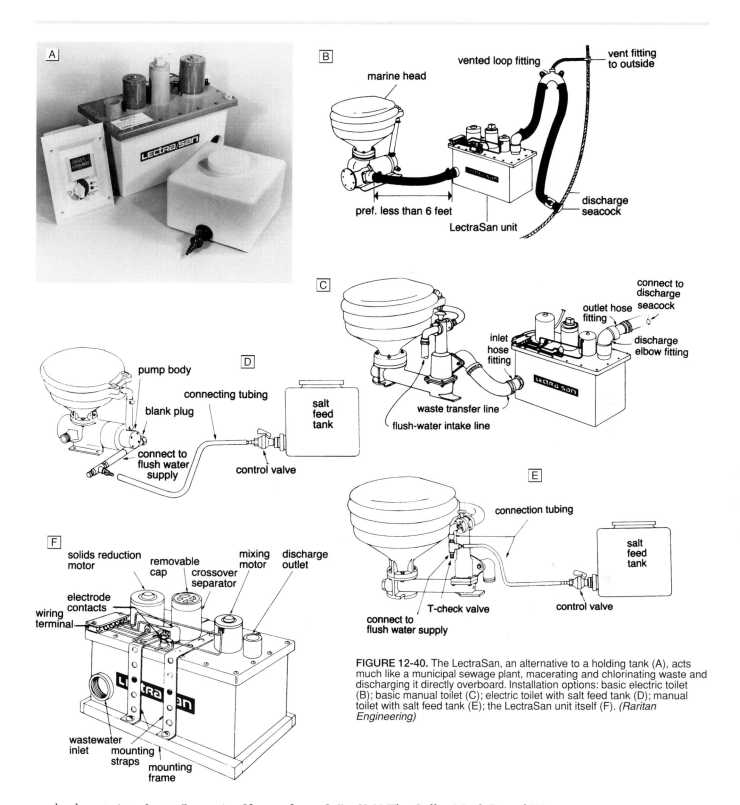

FIGURE 12-40. The LectraSan, an alternative to a holding tank (A), acts much like a municipal sewage plant, macerating and chlorinating waste and discharging it directly overboard. Installation options: basic electric toilet (B); basic manual toilet (C); electric toilet with salt feed tank (D); manual toilet with salt feed tank (E); the LectraSan unit itself (F). (Raritan Engineering)

or deodorants into LectraSan units. If any of these chemicals should enter a unit, flush the toilet repeatedly before turning on the LectraSan again. Otherwise, it is likely that damaging chemical reactions will occur with the hypochlorous acid formed during LectraSan operation.

Galley Maid. The Galley Maid Central Waste Treatment System (www.galleymaid. com) is a batch treatment system that breaks up solids, then treats them via an injection of chlorine before discharging them overboard. It pulls 60 amps at 12 volts, but only for 12 seconds per batch, resulting in a 0.2 Ah drain. It is not common on the boats covered by this book and so is not given further consideration.

SanX. The SeaLand SanX has a 10-gallon tank with an internal macerator and chemical pump, which also has a pumpout fitting. Sewage can be held until an appropriate time to treat and discharge or else until pumped out (at dockside) without treatment. However, the tank is too small to serve as an effective Type III MSD in most applications.

The treat-and-discharge mode uses no power until activated, then it runs for 20 minutes. It first injects a chemical (TDX—which must be bought from the manufacturer), then mixes and liquefies the tank's contents with the macerator pump, after which the contents are pumped overboard (via an electric or manual pump).

TDX costs $15 to $20 a gallon, so chemical costs for operating the system can get quite high. What is more, the chief ingredient is formaldehyde, which is environmentally very unfriendly. The use of this device is likely to be outlawed in many areas.

SeaLand discontinued production of the SanX in 2002, although spare parts will be available for a few years.

Thermopure. Thermopure units come with a 10- or 20-gallon holding tank. Heat, either from AC power (run off shore power, an AC generator, or an inverter) or from a heat exchanger plumbed into the engine's cooling circuit (used when the engine is running) is used to kill bacteria. When the tank is 10% filled, the unit turns on, which is to say that if AC power or engine heat is available it will use either (or both) to heat the tank. When the temperature reaches 167°F/75°C, the contents of the tank are discharged overboard. Treatment time (and energy requirements) vary with flush-water temperature and volume.

If no heat source is available, the tank continues to fill. At the 75% full level, an alarm is activated, telling the operator it is time to provide a heat source or quit flushing the toilet until the system has had time to reach the discharge temperature.

The Thermopure has *significant* power demands. Below 10% full, the unit draws just milliamps (150 mA), but at 10%, various relays close, ramping up the power demands. The AC heating element pulls 15 amps at 110 volts; the discharge pump pulls 17 amps at 12 volts. This is not a device for a power-starved or energy-conscious cruising boat, but it may work well in many powerboat applications and aboard larger sailboats with extended generator running hours.

The Thermopure must not be allowed to freeze. In cold climates, you must either winterize it or pump antifreeze (polyethylene glycol, NOT ethylene) through it at each flush.

Through-Hulls and Seacocks

As installed, a vast number of through-hulls do not comply with the limited ABYC and ISO standards that apply in this field. To make matters worse, boatyard personnel and marine surveyors estimate that 40% to 50% of the seacocks they inspect are seized (mostly in the open position), and 15% are subsequently found to be corroded to the point of being nonrepairable. Of the through-hulls and seacocks that are repaired or replaced, 25% can be reached only with difficulty, and 5% to 10% are totally inaccessible.

Given the huge amounts of water that a failed through-hull or seacock can allow into a boat (see Chapter 13), these are pretty scary statistics, and in fact through-hull and seacock failures are one of the primary causes of boat sinkings. You should *track down all the through-hulls and seacocks on board* to ensure that (1) all are *marine-grade fittings installed to marine standards*, and (2) they are both *accessible and operative*.

Definitions

Both the ABYC and ISO define a *through-hull* as a device that allows the passage of liquids or gases through a hull, while a *seacock* is a valve fitted to the inboard side of a through-hull or directly to the hull. The ABYC definition of a seacock goes further by stating that it "is operated by *a lever-type handle usually operating through a 90-degree arc* giving a clear indication

FIGURE 12-41. A row of plastic through-hulls just above the waterline, none of which have seacocks.

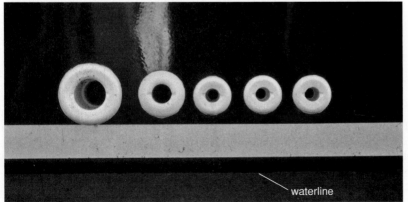

waterline

of whether it is open or shut" (ABYC H-27; emphasis added).

Heeled waterline. The ABYC standard requires that: "All piping, tubing, or hose lines penetrating the hull below the maximum heeled waterline and under all normal conditions of trim shall be equipped with a seacock to stop the admission of water in the event of a failure of pipes, tubing or hose." In other words, if the through-hull is ever likely to be underwater, it has to have an attached seacock (the ABYC does allow one or two exceptions, including cockpit drains that discharge overboard above the static waterline). This is an obvious safety requirement that is, however, not required by ISO standards, and in fact many European boats that I have tested in recent years (including our new Malo 45) have cockpit drains that are bonded into the hull below the waterline without seacocks, and as such, when imported into the United States, do not comply with ABYC standards. (For my own peace of mind, I took a section of the fiberglass pipe that Malo bonds into their boats, filled it with water, capped the ends, and put it in the freezer; it did not burst!)

The ABYC and ISO define the *maximum heeled waterline* on powerboats as a 7-degree angle of heel (it used to be 14 degrees). On sailboats the *maximum heeled waterline* is considered to be the waterline when the boat is heeled to the point at which the midships sheerline is down to the surface of the water. On most sailboats, this puts much of the hull below the heeled waterline, meaning that *almost all through-hulls should have an attached seacock.* A quick look at most boats will reveal through-hulls that don't meet this standard (Figure 12-41). A glance at marine catalogs will show that the industry itself has not grasped the significance of this standard. I have several catalogs that contain comments to the effect that through-hulls without seacocks should not be installed below the waterline "as per ABYC H-27." In my admittedly incomplete survey, I haven't seen a single catalog that refers to the *heeled* waterline!

Defining characteristics of seacocks. Turning now to the definition of a seacock, the ABYC wording that I italicized above, which was only added in recent years, is quite significant. A "lever-type handle" eliminates all gate and globe valves from consideration as seacocks (gate and globe valves are operated by handwheels requiring multiple turns to open and close; see below and Figure 12-42). This makes sound sense. Despite their widespread use, gate and globe valves have four design flaws in seacock applications:

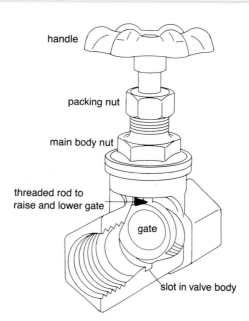

FIGURE 12-42. A gate valve. *(Jim Sollers)*

handle

packing nut

main body nut

threaded rod to raise and lower gate

gate

slot in valve body

1. The valve operating stems have a narrow cross section and as such can be relatively easily sheared. Given the fact that seacocks are often obstructed by marine growth and calcium, and as a result are hard to operate, these valves are especially prone to failure.

2. If any marine growth or other obstruction occurs on the seat of the valve, it is next to impossible to clean this off without valve disassembly, and next to impossible to get the valve to seat properly until it is cleaned off (as opposed to other types of valves that are wiped clean in operation).

3. The mechanism is indirect (the handle turns a gear that operates the valve), which makes it less reliable than the direct mechanism of a seacock (the handle turns the drum or ball).

4. It is not possible to tell by looking at the valve handle whether the valve is open or closed.

The last point relates to the other part of the italicized ABYC definition that calls for the operating handle to move through a 90-degree arc. This requirement is normally met by having the handle line up with the body of the valve when the valve is open, and at right angles to the body of the valve when the valve is closed. A quick visual inspection is all that you need to see if the valve is open or closed (Figure 12-43). Positive stops limit the movement in both directions.

The ISO achieves much the same result as the ABYC by requiring seacocks to be designed so as to permit "a visual check of the open and closed position" (thus ruling out all handwheel-type valves).

FIGURE 12-43. Proper seacocks—the position of the handle immediately shows whether they are open or closed. Note the wide load-bearing flange on one but not the other. Given that this is a relatively lightweight wooden hull, the seacock without a flange may put undue stress on the hull if ever struck hard.

poorly supported seacock

well-supported seacock

Metal Versus Plastic

There is a wide range of metal and plastic through-hulls and seacocks on the market. The fundamental advantage of metal is that it is stronger and will not melt in a fire; the fundamental advantage of plastic is that it does not corrode.

Corrosion. As far as metal through-hulls and seacocks are concerned, both the ABYC and ISO require all materials to be corrosion resistant and galvanically compatible in the marine environment and with respect to the fluids passing through them.

Widespread problems have occurred through the use of brass valves as opposed to bronze. As noted in Chapter 5, brass is an alloy of copper and zinc. If these two metals are electrically interconnected (which occurs automatically in an alloy) and are then immersed in an electrolyte (salt water and all but the purest fresh water), a galvanic cell is established that results in the dissolution of the zinc, leaving a soft and porous casting (often identifiable by its reddish hue). Most gate and globe valves are brass rather than bronze (another reason for not using them). Even those that have bronze bodies may have brass internal components.

Among the bronzes, there are many different alloys, some of which also contain zinc and as a result are more susceptible to corrosion than nonzinc alloys. Clearly, buyers such as you and I are not able to make metallurgical tests to determine the suitability of the alloy in a valve or through-hull for marine use. Our best guarantee of a quality fitting is to buy only recognized marine brand names, which in the United States should be UL listed (the relevant UL standard is 1121; fittings that meet this standard are also available in the EU). To try and cut costs by buying cheaper industrial products, or those of unknown origin, seems to me the height of foolishness.

The internal parts of a valve have to be gal-vanically compatible, or nonreactive, with its body. The traditional tapered plug–type seacock has a plug machined from the same stock as the body. Ball-type valves mostly have chrome-plated bronze balls riding in Teflon seals, with the chrome providing corrosion resistance and the plastic seals electrically insulating the ball from the bronze body (note that some have stainless steel balls that are susceptible to pitting corrosion). Then there is the rubber-plug type of valve in which the rubber eliminates all galvanic interaction between the plug and its body.

Other materials that have been used in metal seacocks are stainless steel and aluminum. However, most grades of stainless steel are not suitable in any permanently wet application. When stainless steel is submerged in stagnant water (precisely the conditions inside many seacocks), it will lose its stainless quality and corrode much like regular steel. Even when used for such items as handles, unless a high-quality (and expensive) grade of stainless steel is used, it will corrode in time (especially if coated with plastic).

Aluminum is often used for welded through-hulls on aluminum boats and sometimes for sea-cocks. The key consideration here is to use only a high-quality marine-grade aluminum, making sure that it is galvanically compatible with the hull (i.e., the same, or a similar, grade of material).

Bonding. The question then arises as to whether metal through-hulls and seacocks should be given cathodic protection. Aluminum fittings, if welded to the hull, will automatically be included in the hull's protection system. The debate centers on whether or not to connect bronze fittings in wood, fiberglass, and composite hulls to the boat's bonding system and zincs. In general, the answer is no, for a couple of reasons:

1. Bronze will almost certainly be the most noble metal on board. As such, bronze through-hulls and seacocks are not likely to suffer from galvanic corrosion. If wired into the bonding circuit, and therefore electrically connected to other less noble metals on the boat, the through-hulls and seacocks will simply accelerate the rate of consumption of the boat's zincs. If the zincs are neglected, the bronze will accelerate corrosion of other metals.

2. The added galvanic activity caused by wiring the bronze into the bonding circuit will generate alkaline hydroxides in the vicinity of the bronze that will blister paint and destroy the wooden backing blocks in fiberglass boats and the hull planking on wooden boats (see Chapter 5).

This opposition to bonding bronze through-hulls and seacocks is based on the assumption that in the absence of a bonding connection, the through-hull or seacock will be electrically isolated, which is almost always the case, particularly if the inboard connection is made with a rubber hose. However, if there is any chance of the through-hull or seacock being part of a path for stray currents (for example, installation below the normal accumulation of bilge water, or a hard metal connection from a bilge pump to a through-hull), the fitting should be bonded.

If through-hulls or seacocks in fiberglass or wooden hulls are bonded for any reason, the vessel is going to need a proper lightning-protection system (it should have one anyway), containing a separate immersed ground plate of at least 1 square foot in surface area (an external keel will serve this purpose). Without such a ground plate, the bonded through-hulls may become the path to ground for a lightning strike. Lacking adequate surface area to safely dissipate a strike, they may heat up to the point at which they will melt, burn, or explode out of the hull (see Chapter 5).

Plastic through-hulls and seacocks. The corrosion and corrosion-prevention problems associated with metal through-hulls and seacocks make plastic an attractive alternative. Plastic fittings are totally noncorrosive and require no corrosion-prevention strategies. In addition, they are lighter, frequently easier (and therefore cheaper) to install, and usually cheaper to buy in the first place. Of course, they have drawbacks, including reduced physical strength when compared to metal, less abrasion resistance, susceptibility to damage from ultraviolet degradation and chemicals, a limited ability to tolerate temperature extremes (Figure 12-44), and embrittlement with age.

When looking at these drawbacks, it is possible to distinguish two somewhat different sets of issues:

1. The suitability of different plastics for use in the manufacture of through-hulls and seacocks.
2. Ensuring that the fittings, as manufactured, will withstand the rigors of through-hull and seacock service.

Suitable plastics. Considering the widespread use of plastic through-hulls and seacocks, it is remarkable how little has been written about the suitability of different plastics in this application (ABYC, ISO, and UL standards are silent on the subject).

A suitable plastic needs:

- Impact resistance. From time to time, boats experience violent motion. Externally, there will be impacts from crashing into waves; internally there may be severe shocks from loosely stowed objects or falling bodies.

- Flexibility, tensile strength, and good "memory." A boat's hull is constantly flexing while machinery and other sources cause vibration. Any fittings attached to the hull must be able to absorb this flexing and vibration without damage or permanent distortion in shape.

- Abrasion resistance, both in normal situations (such as sand and other particles in cooling water and bilge water) and abnormal situations (such as groundings).

- Tolerance of temperature extremes, from the high temperatures associated with engine manifolds and hot fluids to subzero conditions.

- Resistance to a broad range of household chemicals, hydrocarbons, effluent, and the by-products of various forms of marine growth.

- No ultraviolet degradation.

- Continuous freedom of movement, meaning the plastics in the various internal components must not bond together or otherwise cause the valve to seize up if a seacock is left undisturbed in one position for a long period of time.

- The ability to be drilled, threaded, and otherwise machined without developing internal stresses that may result in later failure.

One study concluded that the only plastics suitable for through-hulls and seacocks are nylons, acetals, and PBTs (polybutylene terephthalate), and that these are only suitable when reinforced with between 20% and 33% fiberglass and UV inhibited. The study specifically ruled out PVC, CPVC, and ABS (acrylonitrile butadiene styrene), which from time to time are all found in through-hull fittings (note that these

FIGURE 12-44. Even fire-retardant plastic through-hulls will burn if enough heat is applied.

FIGURE 12-45. A broken plastic Y-valve handle.

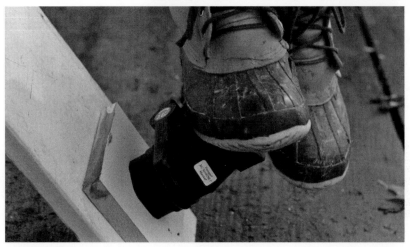

FIGURE 12-46. Simulating a static load test in my barn (no, Terrie, my wife, does not weigh 500 pounds!).

materials may be suitable for less-demanding situations, but not for through-hulls and seacocks).

The well-known Marelon line of fiber-reinforced nylon through-hulls and seacocks from Forespar (www.forespar.com) have 13% fiber reinforcement in the through-hulls, and 33% in the seacocks. Forespar has been selling these fittings for many years without experiencing problems with the material (although there have been some design glitches—see below).

There is a great deal of anecdotal evidence to support the position that other non-fiber-reinforced and non-UV-inhibited plastics are NOT suitable for through-hulls and seacocks! This evidence includes numerous boat sinkings caused by fittings that failed from UV degradation; embrittlement with age; inability to withstand temperature extremes; and inadequate resistance to shock, fatigue, and abrasion.

Design issues. It is one thing to find a plastic that is acceptable for through-hull and seacock use; it is quite another to design a fitting suitable for such use. The most conspicuous design and manufacturing weakness with plastic seacocks has been the operating handles (Figure 12-45); failures are common.

I have been told that handles only break when

valves freeze up from a lack of use (all seacocks—both metal and plastic—should be "exercised" at least once or twice a season) and a lack of lubrication. This is probably true. Given this lack of maintenance, the explanation continues, the handle, as the weak link, is protecting the valve from being overstressed. I find this attitude unacceptable. If I have a failed hose with water flooding into my boat, and the handle breaks off the seacock, it will be small consolation to know that the broken handle is protecting the valve from damage! It is significant that most manufacturers have beefed up their handles over the years, but even so I still get nervous around a tight plastic seacock (as opposed to the old tapered bronze ones that you can whack with a mallet to loosen up).

Many plastic valves sometimes used as seacocks are bonded together, as opposed to bolted, making disassembly and repair impossible. They also have unacceptably short hose attachment stubs that lack barbs. This violates both ABYC and ISO standards (the hose barbs are required to have sufficient length for two hose clamps).

Other ABYC and ISO performance standards are that any threaded components must have at least five full-thread engagements, the valve position once set (open or closed) must not be altered by shock or vibration, the valve must still operate with marine growth inside it, and it must have a drain (unless it can withstand the pressure of freezing water without suffering damage).

Testing Through-Hulls and Seacocks

In order to establish quantifiable standards, UL has devised a number of tests that any through-hull or seacock (metal or plastic) must pass to receive UL certification. These tests include subjecting a fitting to temperature extremes, then seeing if it still operates (a seacock with no drain plug is filled with water and frozen hard). There is a special shock and vibration machine, and also an abrasion test in which a fitting is driven through 2 feet of dry sand 10,000 times. The operation of seacocks is tested both dry and saturated (some plastics swell up and seize when wet). Both through-hulls and seacocks are submerged in hydrocarbons, bleach, ammonia, and salt water. Plastics are subjected to an accelerated UV test, then tested for retention of at least 70% of their original strength. And there's the static load test, otherwise known as the 500-pound-man test (the 1,500 Newton test in ISO 9093-2).

Static load test. The static load test consists of mounting a through-hull or seacock in a simulated hull section and then applying a static load of 500 pounds to its inboard end (this is done by hanging a 500-pound weight from the fitting; Figure 12-46). The fitting must be able to support the weight for 30 seconds without suffering damage or deformation that impairs its performance (with seacocks, the test is followed by a leak test to see if the valve still seals properly).

The static load test is the ultimate test of plastic through-hulls and seacocks, and even of smaller sizes of bronze fittings (some ½-inch/13 mm and ¾-inch/19 mm bronze fittings fail). The smaller (½-inch/13 mm and ¾-inch/19 mm) sizes of the Marelon fittings as originally designed (the old series) could not pass this test. Forespar had to redesign and retool the fittings, changing the original (tapered) pipe threads on the fittings to a buttress thread (an untapered thread, as found on bolts). The company now produces a series of through-hulls and valves, which is UL tested and listed, alongside the old series, which is not UL listed. The UL listed series is sold primarily to boatbuilders; the old series is sold to the aftermarket (marine chandleries and catalogs).

As far as I know, there are no other plastic through-hulls and seacocks that are UL listed, although there may be some that the manufacturer describes as "meeting the UL standard." The distinction here is that in the first instance, UL has not only done the requisite testing but has also established a factory-inspection program to ensure that the manufacturing facility will reliably produce products that meet the standard; in the second instance, the manufacturer has either itself or through an outside laboratory tested its own products to see if they will pass the UL tests (UL has in no way validated the results or established a factory-inspection program).

Common Seacock Types

Traditional seacocks. A traditional seacock has a tapered plug, bored for the passage of fluids, in a tapered seat. It takes just a quarter turn on the handle to open or close, and it is instantly obvious whether it is open or shut. When open, the handle lines up with the tailpiece; when shut, the handle is at a right angle to the tailpiece. Construction is simple, rugged, and more or less chemical proof (Figure 12-47).

The tapered plug and seat have a large surface area with the potential for considerable friction. A traditional seacock needs regreasing annually, and the keeper nuts or plug-retaining nut should be tightened only enough to stop the seacock from leaking. Overtightening will squeeze out the grease, and the resulting metal-to-metal contact will lead to accelerated wear and seizure.

Generally you can free a seized plug by tap-

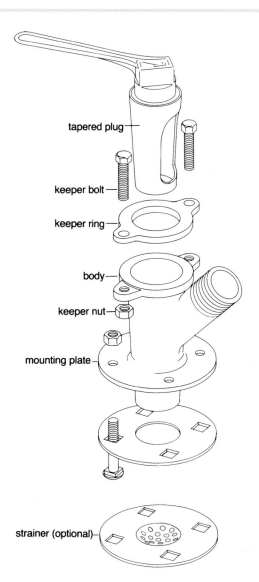

FIGURE 12-47. A traditional, tapered-plug bronze seacock. *(Jim Sollers)*

tapered plug

keeper bolt

keeper ring

body

keeper nut

mounting plate

strainer (optional)

ping on the handle with a mallet. Many plugs are installed across the barrel of the seacock. In this case, after loosening the plug-retaining nut, tap the plug from the base to jar it loose in its barrel.

In time, the plug tends to become wasp waisted, allowing water to leak around the plug sides, and the seacock fails to hold. Overtightening keeper nuts or the plug-retaining nut will not solve this problem but merely create others. Remove the plug, smear it with grinding paste (available from automotive stores), and work it around and around in its seat until a smooth metal-to-metal contact is reestablished on all surfaces. Clean away all traces of the grinding paste, then regrease the plug.

If the plug and its seat are worn beyond restoration, a new seacock is called for. Dezincification as a result of galvanic corrosion (Chapter 5) also sometimes occurs with manganese bronze fittings, in which case the fitting will take on a pink-

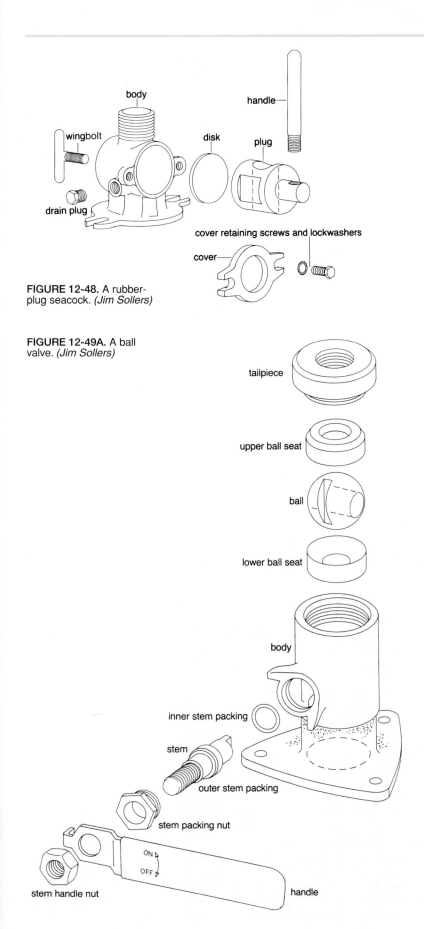

FIGURE 12-48. A rubber-plug seacock. *(Jim Sollers)*

FIGURE 12-49A. A ball valve. *(Jim Sollers)*

ish blush and you will need to replace it. Plugs and seats come in matched pairs; generally it is not possible to replace one without the other.

Rubber-plug seacocks. The popular rubber-plug seacocks are manufactured by Groco, among others. A solid rubber bung replaces the tapered plug of a conventional seacock, through which is a metal-lined hole. The bung seats on a metal plate, or disc. A threaded locking handle (wing bolt) is set into the body of the seacock. When the handle is tightened, it forces the metal plate against the bung, which compresses the rubber, squeezing it against the sides of the seacock and sealing it (Figure 12-48).

To operate the seacock, loosen the locking handle until the seacock can be turned, then tighten it just until the seacock stops dripping from around its plug-retaining (*keeper*) ring (also simply called a *cover*). Overtightening will deform the rubber, especially when the seacock is closed, forcing the sides of the bung up into the seacock inlet and discharge ports.

FIGURE 12-49B. This interesting Groco ball valve incorporates a quick-release plug. If the seacock is used on the raw-water intake to an engine cooling circuit, removal of the plug and its replacement with a special adapter allows the seacock to be rapidly converted to an emergency bilge pump (using the engine's raw-water pump). The quick-release fitting can also be used to simplify engine winterizing procedures. *(Groco)*

These seacocks are not suitable for applications where chemicals may be present (e.g., toilets and sinks). The rubber will swell, jamming the bung and making it next to impossible to turn. Maintenance involves annual regreasing. You can salvage a bung that has swelled into the ports by filing down the excess rubber with a coarse wood file (or belt sander).

Gate and globe valves. Gate valves have a metal disc (the *gate*) that moves in a slot in the body of the valve. The gate rides on a threaded rod; turning the rod via a handle raises and lowers the gate (refer back to Figure 12-42A). Globe valves are similar, but on the end of the threaded rod, they have a disc that screws down against a seat.

As noted above, despite their widespread use, gate and globe valves have no place on boats. Most are made of brass and will dezincify in time, falling apart. Even when the body is made of bronze, they suffer from several drawbacks: the interior parts may not be bronze; it is not possible to tell by looking at the handle whether the valve is open or shut; trash is easily trapped under the gate or disc, keeping the valve from sealing; the threaded rod the gate or disc rides on is relatively thin and easily sheared if the valve jams; and lacking a mounting flange, the valve cannot be independently fastened to the hull (see installation below).

If you have these valves and are unwilling to replace them, at least get into the habit when opening the valve of fully opening it *and then turning the handle back half a turn so that it is free* (this is an old oil-field trick). There will likely be less confusion as to whether the valve is open or shut (when closed, the handle will be tight; when open, loose) and less chance of forcing the handle the wrong way and shearing the stem.

It is advisable to disassemble gate and globe valves annually, inspect them closely for corrosion, and regrease the stems and threads. To do this, unscrew the main housing nut on the valve body. When reassembling the valve, screw the gate partially up before tightening the main housing nut, otherwise the gate or disc may bottom out in its slot and suffer damage. The small nut around the stem is a packing nut; tighten it gently if the stem leaks and repack if necessary.

Ball valves. A ball valve has a ball with a hole through it. This fits into a spherical seat with inlet and discharge ports. Turned one way, the hole in the ball lines up with the ports and allows flow; turned the other way, it closes the ports (Figures 12-49A and 12-49B).

Ball valves are efficient and effective. The metal versions generally have bronze bodies with chrome-plated bronze balls riding in Teflon seals, although some have stainless steel balls (not recommended; the stainless is likely to suffer from pitting corrosion within a year or two). Plastic ones have reinforced plastic bodies and balls, again riding in Teflon seals.

To disassemble a ball valve, undo the main body nut. The balls, whether plastic or bronze, should be greased annually. In my experience, the plastic stems on many plastic valves are the weak spot, tending to harden and become brittle with age. *Do not force them, or they will break.*

Through-Hull and Seacock Installation

Even if a product is UL listed, this is still no guarantee that it will be installed correctly or in a safe manner. Key issues here are protecting the hull in the way of the fitting, maintaining watertight integrity at all times, providing adequate fastening, making sure the fitting as installed (as opposed to on the test bench) will withstand the static load test, and placing all seacocks in readily accessible locations.

Hull issues. Particularly in fiberglass hulls, through-hulls and seacocks need some kind of a backing block, faired to the shape of the hull and providing a level surface on its inboard side on which to seat the retaining nut or seacock (Figures 12-50A and 12-50B). This helps distribute the inevitable shocks, stresses, and vibrations experienced by the fitting to a larger area of the hull. Clearly the through-hull needs to be bedded or bonded in place so that it will not develop leaks over time. This is most essential in cored hulls, where even a small leak can do extensive, and expensive, damage to the core (ideally, the core will be removed and the two skins bonded together in the area of the through-hull). Threaded fittings should be wrapped with Teflon tape.

At one time the ABYC required seacocks to have flanges that could be securely (i.e., independently) fastened to the hull. This is no longer part of any standard, although many bronze seacocks are still installed in this manner. In this case, the fasteners must be galvanically compatible with, and at least as noble as, the seacock itself (otherwise the fasteners will soon suffer from galvanic corrosion). If installed in a cored hull, it is essential to remove the core and replace it with a solid bung or laminate where the fasteners go through (Figure 12-50C). If this is not done, sooner or later the fasteners will become a path for water migration into the core.

Plastic seacocks are almost always held in place by the through-hull fitting, with maybe

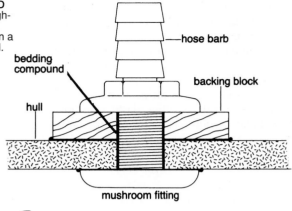

FIGURES 12-50A AND 12-50B. Proper through-hull (top) and seacock (bottom) installations in a wood or fiberglass hull. *(Jim Sollers)*

hose barb

bedding compound

backing block

hull

mushroom fitting

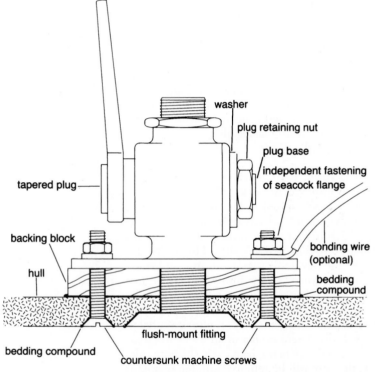

washer

plug retaining nut

plug base

independent fastening of seacock flange

tapered plug

backing block

hull

bonding wire (optional)

bedding compound

bedding compound

flush-mount fitting

countersunk machine screws

FIGURE 12-50C. An excellent through-hull installation in a cored hull (a Pacific Seacraft 40). The core has been removed and replaced with a solid fiberglass plug with an additional backing plate to level the hull. However, the double hose clamps are overkill, and I do not like the relatively lightweight ribbed PVC hose on one through-hull—it is not really appropriate for below-the-waterline use.

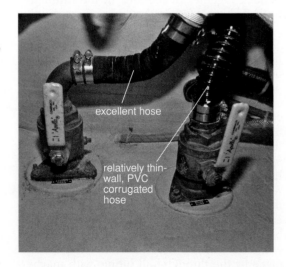

excellent hose

relatively thin-wall, PVC corrugated hose

some additional bonding inside the hull. With the integrity of the installation riding solely on the through-hull, it is essential to have a properly qualified through-hull (preferably UL listed, but at a minimum fiber reinforced). In other words, it should not be vulnerable to external damage (for example, being broken off if the boat bangs against a dock or pylon); should have at least five full threads engaged with its seacock or retaining nut; and be properly installed with the seacock or retaining nut bedded to a backing block.

Static load test. To meet ABYC and ISO standards, a seacock as installed must pass the relevant static load test (the UL standard is a test-bench standard; ABYC and ISO standards are "in-the-boat" standards). If a seacock is supplied with an integral through-hull, and the entire assembly is UL listed, then it will automatically pass the static load test if it is properly installed (as per the manufacturer's instructions). However, problems arise when through-hulls and seacocks are mixed and matched. Even if the individual components are UL listed, a specific combination of through-hull and seacock may not pass the static load test (notably when an unsupported seacock, or seacock and raw-water filter, is screwed onto the end of a through-hull extending some way into a boat—Figure 12-51).

Because it is next to impossible to rig up the static load test inside a boat, an installation generally cannot be tested for compliance with the standards. For this reason, it is best to ensure that the through-hull and seacock are a matched pair. If not, a certain amount of common sense is needed with through-hull and seacock installations, viewing each one from the perspective of "Will it hold if a heavy person, or a loose battery or toolbox, is thrown violently against it?"

Metal hulls. With metal hulls, properly constructed and reinforced plastic through-hulls and seacocks can be installed as above. *Most metal through-hulls and seacocks must be insulated from the hull to prevent galvanic interaction.* The seacock must then be electrically isolated from the piping attached to it by means of an intervening length of rubber hose (Figure 12-52).

Hose attachments. Make hose attachments using properly matched adapters, hose barbs, or tailpieces. Use *all 300 series stainless steel* hose clamps (make sure the screws are 300 series stainless and not 400 series—see Chapter 5). Check all hoses and clamps at least once a year. Undo the clamps for inspection, since they frequently rust and fail inside the worm screw housing where the rust is not visible.

Accessibility. Finally, the last installation requirement in the standards, which would be too obvious to state were it not for the fact that it is routinely ignored, is to make sure that all seacocks are readily accessible. A seacock is nothing more than an insurance policy designed to protect against the failure of the hose that is attached to it. However, if a hose fails and you can't get at the seacock to close it, the seacock won't do a bit of good and might just as well not have been there in the first place. Accessibility is also necessary for maintenance and to drain the seacock when winterizing the boat (make sure the drain is on the lower side!).

Keep one or two fids (tapered softwood plugs) on board of a suitable size to (1) ram into seacocks, and (2) ram into hull openings occupied by seacocks. In the event of a catastrophic failure of the hose or seacock, or the complete loss of a seacock, you can rapidly plug the hole.

Keeping the Water Out

In days gone by, there was only one choice when it came to a "proper" through-hull and seacock installation—bronze. Today, with plastic fittings proven over many years of service, there seems to be a bewildering array of choices. However, a closer inspection reveals that very few of these choices meet even the limited standards (UL, ABYC, and ISO) that pertain to these products. As a result, the choices are still fairly limited—basically either bronze or glass-reinforced nylon. Given that there is not much of a cost difference between the two, the choice of which to use is largely a matter of the brute strength of bronze as opposed to the lighter weight and freedom from corrosion that comes with plastic. Either makes an excellent choice, as long as the through-hull and seacock are properly installed.

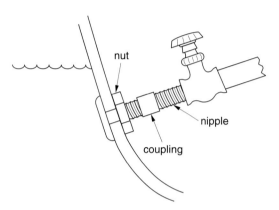

FIGURE 12-51. How *not* to install a through-hull or seacock! There is no backing block; the valve should be connected directly to the through-hull fitting to reduce potential stresses (for example, someone stepping on the valve); this is a gate or globe valve, which is not suitable for marine use; and the valve has no independent mounting flange.

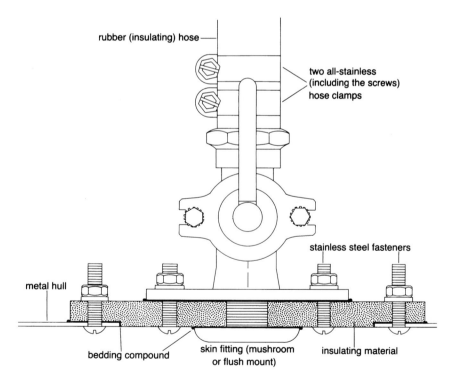

FIGURE 12-52. Seacock installation on a metal hull. *(Jim Sollers)*

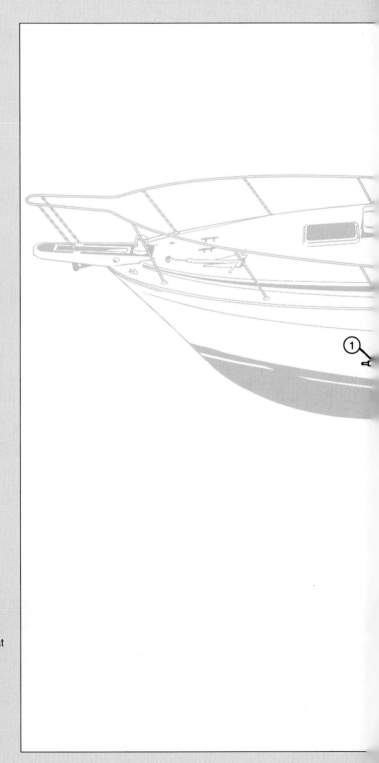

CHAPTER 13

FIGURE 13-1. A thorough understanding of pumps and their repair could someday keep your vessel afloat in an emergency. *(Jim Sollers)*

(1) toilet pump
(2) bilge pump
(3) macerator pump
(4) collection box
(5) foot pump
(6) engine cooling pump
(7) freshwater pump
(8) watermaker

Pumps and Watermakers

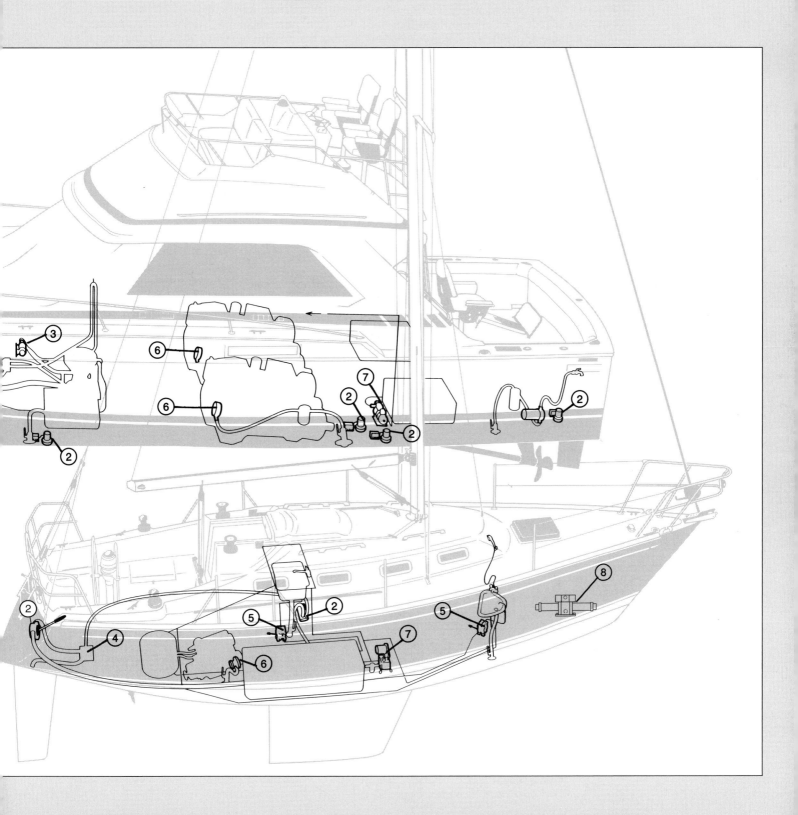

Pumps

This chapter deals with the mechanical (pumping) end of pumps and with watermakers (which depend on powerful pumps). If you are experiencing problems with electric motors, refer to Chapter 7, bearing in mind that most old motors are *wound-field-coil universal motors*, while most new ones are *permanent-magnet universal motors*.

How They Work

Pumps on boats fall into three broad categories (these are my categories): variable-volume impeller, centrifugal, and positive displacement.

Variable-volume impeller pumps. The principle behind variable-volume impeller pumps is a change in the displaced volume of the impeller from one side of a pump chamber to another. The most common variety has a flexible impeller turning in a pump body that has one side flattened by screwing a blanking piece (a *cam*) into the body. As the vanes on the impeller reach the cam, they are squeezed down, expelling any fluid trapped between them. As the vanes pass the cam, they spring back up, drawing in more fluid (Figure 13-2).

Less common variations on the same theme are vane and rotary pumps. On vane pumps, the drive shaft is permanently offset in the pump housing so that the impeller *(rotor)* is always closer to the pump body at some points than at others. Hard vanes are set in slots in the rotor and held against the pump body. As the rotor spins, the vanes move in and out of their slots, thus maintaining contact with the pump body. The

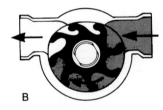  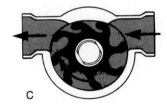

FIGURE 13-2. Operation of a variable-volume flexible-impeller pump. Upon leaving the offset cam, the flexible impeller blades expand, creating a vacuum that draws liquid into the pump body (A). As the impeller rotates, each successive blade draws in liquid and carries it to the outlet port (B). The liquid is expelled when the flexible impeller blades are again compressed by the offset cam, creating a continuous, uniform flow (C). *(ITT/Jabsco)*

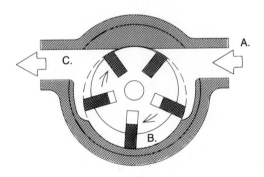

FIGURE 13-3. Operation of a variable-volume vane pump. Upon leaving the eccentric portion of the pump body's liner, the vanes create a partial vacuum, which draws in fluid (A). As the rotor rotates, each successive vane draws in liquid and carries it to the discharge port (B). When the vanes again contact the eccentric portion of the liner, they force liquid out the discharge port (C). *(Jim Sollers)*

FIGURE 13-4. Operation of a rotary pump. The pump at rest (A). The impeller oscillates over and down, opening a space between the impeller and impeller guide, which draws in fluid through the inlet port (B). Suction-side volume increases steadily, drawing in more fluid. At the same time, the discharge-side volume decreases, expelling fluid (C). Discharge-side volume is near minimum; most fluid is expelled. Suction-side volume is still increasing, drawing in more fluid (D). *(Jim Sollers)*

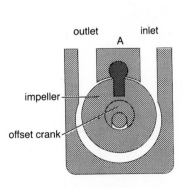 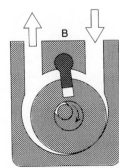 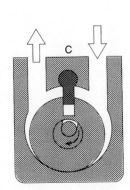 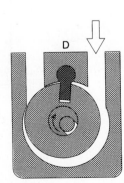

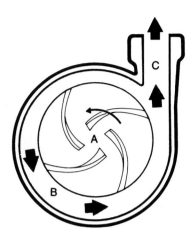

FIGURE 13-5. Operation of a centrifugal pump. Liquid enters the inlet port in the center of the pump (A). The level of liquid must be high enough above the pump for gravity to push it into the pump, or the pump must receive initial priming. Centrifugal force generated by the rotating and curved impeller forces the fluid to the periphery of the pump casing, and from there toward the discharge port (B). The velocity of fluid discharge translates into hydraulic pressure in the system downstream from the pump (C). The flow rate is dependent upon restrictions in the inlet and outlet piping and the height that the liquid must be lifted. (ITT/Jabsco)

changing volume between the vanes alternately draws in and expels fluid in much the same manner as the vane action in a flexible impeller pump (Figure 13-3).

The impeller does not actually rotate in a rotary pump! Instead it is mounted on but not keyed to an *eccentric* shaft. The shaft is centered in the pump housing but with an offset section where it passes through the impeller bearing. The impeller is kept from spinning by an impeller guide (Figure 13-4) held in the pump body and fitted in a slot in the impeller. As the shaft turns, the impeller oscillates in a circular pattern but without actually turning, pulling in and expelling fluid as it goes.

Finally we have gear pumps, in which fluid is trapped between the teeth of two gear wheels and then driven out at the point where the gear teeth mesh. Gear pumps are used primarily as oil pumps on engines and hydraulic systems; they are capable of pumping to very high pressures.

Centrifugal pumps. A centrifugal pump has an impeller with vanes and is designed so that fluid drawn into the center of the impeller is thrown out by centrifugal force (Figure 13-5). The momentum generated in the fluid keeps it moving and makes the pump work. A less common variation on the same principle is a *turbine* pump, which has a somewhat different vane arrangement on the impeller but is otherwise the same.

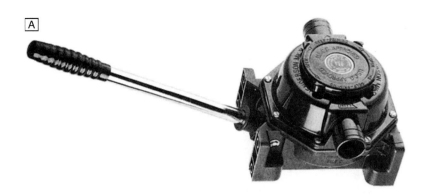

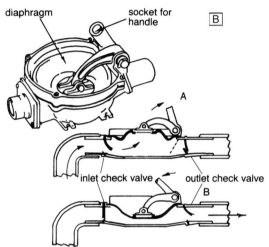

diaphragm — socket for handle

inlet check valve — outlet check valve

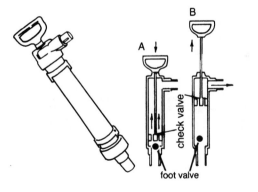

check valve

foot valve

FIGURE 13-6A. A manual diaphragm pump. *(Whale)*

FIGURE 13-6B. Operation of a manual diaphragm pump. As the handle is pulled back, the flexible diaphragm expands, creating a vacuum that pulls back the inlet check valve and draws fluid into the pump chamber (A). When the handle is pushed down, hydraulic pressure forces the inlet check valve to close, at the same time opening the outlet check valve and expelling the fluid (B).

FIGURE 13-7. Operation of a piston pump. The handle is depressed. Fluid is trapped between the base of the piston and the foot valve and forced up into the pump body through the check valve in the base of the piston (A). As the handle is lifted, the check valve closes and fluid is lifted to the outlet. At the same time, a vacuum is formed below the check valve, which draws more fluid into the pump chamber through the foot valve (B).

Positive-displacement pumps. A positive-displacement pump moves a diaphragm, bellows, or piston in and out of a pump chamber, alternately increasing and decreasing its volume (Figures 13-6A, 13-6B, and 13-7). These pumps, unlike the others, can only work with a set of valves—one valve lets the fluid into the chamber and traps it; another lets it out and stops it from being sucked back in. Since there is no impeller, there is no shaft entering the pump chamber and therefore no shaft seal and associated leaks (except on some piston pumps; see the Piston Pumps section later in the chapter).

Pros and Cons

The most important factors when choosing a pump for a given application are:

- Its ability to self-prime.
- The effect of head pressure on its performance.
- Its tolerance for solids, chemicals, and running dry.
- With electric pumps, the duty rating must also be taken into consideration.

Self-priming or not. All pumps except centrifugal pumps are self-priming—in other words, they have the capability to draw up fluid to themselves. *Centrifugal pumps have no self-priming capability whatsoever* and will not hold a prime after being shut down if they are installed above the level of the liquid they are pumping. They must always be installed below the liquid level, *at all angles of heel.* (Note: The addition of a check valve in the suction piping to a centrifugal pump will retain fluid in the pump when it is shut down, thus maintaining its prime. Installed like this, a pump can be placed above the liquid it is pumping, but should the check valve leak back when the pump is shut down, the pump will lose its prime and will have to be hand-primed in some manner—generally by disconnecting the discharge line at some point above the pump and pouring fluid into the line.)

When shut down, a centrifugal pump offers little to no resistance to liquid flowing through it. For this reason, *centrifugal pumps should not share a supply line with another pump.* To illustrate why this is so, consider a centrifugal refrigeration cooling pump sharing the same raw-water inlet as an engine raw-water pump that has a rubber impeller. If the inlet becomes even partially obstructed, the engine pump will suck back through the refrigeration pump, causing both to run dry.

The effect of head pressure. Head pressure refers to the resistance to flow that a pump must overcome to move fluid from one place to another. I deal with it in depth below (see the Head Pressure and Centrifugal Pump Installations section). For now, it is worth noting the following general points:

Centrifugal pumps. Centrifugal pumps are very sensitive to head pressure. This has a dramatic impact on a pump's output, sometimes stalling it out altogether. Head-pressure calculations are especially important in connection with bilge pumping applications.

Variable-volume impeller pumps. These are far less sensitive than centrifugal pumps to head pressure. They suffer little loss of performance until the head pressure begins to exceed 10 to 20 feet, then the loss is gradual rather than sudden (most are, in any case, rated at 10 feet of head as opposed to the open flow rating—i.e., zero head pressure—used with many centrifugal pumps). As head pressure rises, flexible-impeller pumps will suffer a loss of capacity a little faster than the vane or rotary type. With rising head pressure, the motor will steadily draw more current. Beyond a certain point something will burn out or break (see below).

Positive-displacement pumps. These suffer almost no loss of pumping ability as head pressure rises. With rising head pressure, the motor will once again steadily draw more current. Beyond a certain point something will burn out or break (see below).

Blockage of the discharge. The more restricted the discharge, the higher the head pressure. A centrifugal pump responds by moving less fluid until it simply spins to no effect; the less the flow, the less work the pump is doing and the less its power requirements (less amp draw if electrically driven). All other types of pumps operate in a completely opposite fashion—the higher the head pressure, the harder the pump works and the more energy it draws, until eventually something fails (fuses blow, motors burn out, or hoses burst).

Any variable-volume impeller pump or positive-displacement pump used in a system where the flow gets cut off while the pump is running (e.g., a freshwater system or a saltwater washdown system with a garden hose–type shutoff nozzle) must have some form of built-in pressure switch to protect the system.

Passing solids. Centrifugal pumps have a moderate tolerance for solids, depending largely on the size of the pump—the particles simply get flushed along in the fluid stream. Variable-volume impeller pumps (all types), on the other hand, have little tolerance for solids—anything stuck between a vane and a pump body will cause a loss of performance and likely damage the impeller or the body. Positive-displacement pumps have a very variable tolerance for solids— the valves on the smaller diaphragm and piston pumps are easily put out of action, whereas the flap valves on many larger pumps have the greatest tolerance for solids of all the pump types.

Running dry. *Diaphragm pumps can run dry indefinitely without damage.* Piston pumps are less tolerant, generally depending on the nature of the piston seals. On all other pumps there are two considerations—the impeller, and the pump shaft seals.

No *flexible-impeller or vane pump can run dry for more than a few seconds without damage*—the fluid pumped is critical for lubrication. (Globe, www.globerubberworks.com, has developed a flexible impeller that will run dry for up to 15 minutes; it's considerably more expensive, but well worth the price.) All centrifugal pump impellers can run dry indefinitely. Most rotary pumps fall somewhere between these two extremes.

However, even when an impeller can tolerate running dry, the shaft seal probably cannot. No lip-type seal can run dry for very long without heating up its shaft and damaging the seal. Carbon-ceramic seals are more tolerant, but again there are very definite limits (see below for more information on seals).

If a pump is likely to run dry, a diaphragm or bellows pump or a centrifugal pump that is rated for dry running must be used.

Chemical tolerance. This is an important consideration in many applications even if it is not obvious at first. Galley sinks and shower drains handle many kinds of soap, detergents, and bleach; bilges contain traces of oil and diesel; effluent systems have to handle urine, which is acidic, and are frequently subjected to powerful toilet bowl cleaners, drain openers, deodorants, and bleaches (though they most definitely should *not* be—see Chapter 12); and even freshwater systems handle traces of chlorine and other chemicals.

Flexible impellers are the most susceptible to chemical damage—they swell up and bind in their pump housings. Fuses blow and/or vanes strip off. The standard impeller is normally made of neoprene (which is generally the worst choice!), but nitrile, polyurethane, and Viton are all available for special applications (Table 13-1). Positive-displacement pumps also have diaphragms and valves that are susceptible to chemical damage. Centrifugal pumps and many vane and rotary pumps have relatively inert bronze or plastic (phenolic or epoxy) impellers and vanes; however, they may still have chemical tolerance problems with lip-type shaft seals. (Note: Carbon-ceramic seals are far more chemical tolerant, but generally they are sealed in pump housings and on shafts with rubber boots and O-rings that may not be tolerant.)

The duty cycle. Most pump motors are designed for *intermittent* use only—sometimes as little as 2 minutes at a time. After this you must allow the motor to cool down or it may burn up. Other motors can run indefinitely without damage. Check the manuals that come with your pump to ascertain its limitations.

Choosing a pump. The five most common uses for a pump aboard a boat are for engine cooling, refrigeration and air-conditioning cooling, freshwater systems, bilge and shower pumping, and deck washdown (Table 13-2).

Engine cooling pumps are specified by the manufacturer—the user rarely has to make a choice. Refrigeration cooling pumps are about evenly split between centrifugal pumps and flexible-impeller pumps. A centrifugal pump has the edge in terms of being less prone to breakdown and requiring less maintenance. However, *it must be installed below the waterline at all angles of heel*—if this is not possible, a flexible-impeller pump is needed.

A freshwater system almost always uses an electrically driven diaphragm pump, which is ideal. The pumps are reliable, relatively quiet, and can tolerate dry running if the tank should run dry but the pump fails to turn off. The most likely source of trouble is the pressure switch; fortunately, these tend to fail in the open (OFF) position rather than the closed (ON) position, since the latter situation results in something else breaking (a pipe bursts or the motor burns out).

The same electric diaphragm pumps are frequently used for gray water (i.e., shower and sink drains) and bilge pumping applications, *for which they are not so well suited*. On the one hand, they are self-priming, can be mounted in a dry area (which protects the electrical side of things), and can be run dry, but on the other hand, *quite small solids, hairs, and other detritus can disable the valves*. As a result, these pumps must be protected with a relatively fine mesh strainer. These strainers, however, plug easily and are especially prone to plugging when the pump is most needed (on a wild night when the boat is shipping water, and the motion has shaken all kinds of debris into the bilge).

Submersible centrifugal pumps offer the best overall bilge pumping capability, *as long as the pump is powerful enough to compensate for the losses generated by the head pressure on the system* (see the next section). A centrifugal pump can be used with a relatively coarse and easily cleaned strainer (strum box), is reliable, requires little maintenance, and can be run dry. When it comes to *manual* bilge pumps, *a high-capacity diaphragm pump* (preferably a *double-diaphragm* pump) *is unbeatable*.

Just about any pump will do for a deck washdown as long as it can generate a flow of 3 or 4 gallons a minute at a reasonable pressure (say, 30 psi—this will exclude most centrifugal pumps). Diaphragm-type pumps in general are more trouble free than variable-volume impeller pumps. With all but centrifugal pumps, the system will

TABLE 13-1. Chemical Compatibility for Impellers

Chemical or Compound	Bronze	316 Stainless	Phenolic	Epoxy	Polypropylene	Neoprene[1]	Nitrile	Viton
Acetone	1	1	1	3	1	3	3	3
Alcohol								
ethyl	1	1	1	1	1	1	2	2
isopropyl	1	1	1	1	1	1	2	1
methyl	1	1	1	1	1	2	3	3
Ammonia	3	1	1	1	1	1	2	3
Antifreeze								
most brands	1	1	1	1	1	1	1	1
Prestone	1	1	1	1	1	3	1	2
Valvoline	1	1	1	1	1	2	2	—
Beer	1	1	1	1	3	1	—	—
Butter	3	1	3	1	1	2	1	1
Carbolic acid	1	1	3	1	1	2	—	—
Citric acid (lemon juice, etc.)	2	1	1	1	1	1	2	—
Clorox (bleach)	1	1	3	1	1	1	2	2
Corn oil	2	1	1	1	—	2	1	1
Cottonseed oil	1	1	1	1	1	2	1	1
Deodorants, some	1	1	1	1	1	3	3	—
Detergents	1	1	—	1	1	1	1	—
Diesel fuel	1	1	—	1	2	3	2	1
Disinfectant deodorant	1	1	1	1	—	2	1	1
Gasoline	1	1	1	1	2	3	3	1
Grease	1	1	2	1	—	3	3	1
Horseradish	—	—	—	1	—	1	3	—
Hydraulic oil	1	1	3	1	3	3	2	1
Hydrogen peroxide	3	2	3	1	1	3	1	—
Kerosene, paraffin	1	1	1	1	1	3	2	1
Ketchup	2	1	3	1	—	2	1	1
Lard	1	1	3	1	1	2	1	—
Lemon oil	—	1	1	1	—	2	—	1
Linseed oil	1	1	3	1	—	3	1	—
Mayonnaise	3	1	—	1	—	1	2	1
Mineral oil	1	1	1	1	1	2	1	1
Muriatic acid	2	3	1	1	2	1	2	1
Phosphoric acid	2	1	3	1	2	1	1	1
Pine oil	3	1	2	1	—	3	3	1
Propylene glycol	1	1	1	1	1	2	1	—
Rapeseed oil	1	1	—	1	—	2	—	1
Refrigeration gases								
R-12	1	3	—	1	1	2	2	2
R-22	1	2	—	1	1	2	2	3
Sesame seed oil	1	1	—	1	1	2	1	1
Soap solutions	2	1	1	1	1	2	1	1
Soybean oil	1	1	3	1	1	3	1	1
Starch	1	1	1	1	1	1	2	1
Toothpaste	1	1	3	1	—	2	1	1
Turpentine	2	1	—	1	2	3	1	1
Urine	2	1	1	1	1	3	1	—
Varnish	1	1	1	1	1	3	2	—
Vegetable juice	2	2	1	1	1	2	2	—
Vegetable oil	1	1	2	1	1	2	1	1
Vinegar	2	1	—	1	1	2	2	3

1. Note how poorly neoprene performs, and yet this is the standard flexible pump impeller material!
Key: 1 = OK; 2 = proceed with caution—flush after use; 3 = rapid deterioration; — = no information.

TABLE 13-2. Pump Types and Common Applications

Common Application	Flexible Impeller	Vane	Rotary	Centrifugal[1]	Electric Diaphragm	Manual Diaphragm	Piston
Engine cooling							
raw water	X	—	—	X	—	—	—
fresh water	—	—	—	X	—	—	—
Refrigeration condensers and air conditioners	X	—	—	X	—	—	—
Deck washdown	X	—	—	X	—	—	—
Bilge							
electric	—	—	—	X	X	—	—
manual	—	—	—	—	—	X	X
Sink discharge	—	—	—	—	X	X	—
Toilets							
electric	X	—	—	X	—	—	—
manual	—	—	—	—	—	X	X
Showers	—	—	—	—	X	—	—
Fresh water							
pressurized	X	—	—	—	X	—	—
manual	—	—	—	—	—	X	X
Fuel transfer[2]	—	X	X	—	—	—	—

1. Must be installed below the waterline.
2. Must be compatible with diesel.

need a pressure cutoff switch to protect the pump and its plumbing.

Head Pressure and Centrifugal Pump Installations

As noted above, head pressure refers to the resistance to flow that a pump must overcome. Head pressure includes (1) the vertical height the fluid must be lifted (from the suction intake to the discharge point), and (2) *the effect of resistance within the piping or tubing runs.* This latter aspect is frequently ignored but can in fact cause more resistance than the vertical lift itself.

Vertical lift. Vertical lift is easy to measure. It is simply the difference in the height of the suction and discharge points. One foot of vertical lift is equal to 0.433 psi of back pressure, which is to say that 2.3 feet of lift results in approximately 1 psi of pressure. When thinking about vertical lift, it is important to remember the effects of heeling. Let's say we have a submersible bilge pump mounted on the centerline of a boat with a 14-foot beam. The discharge fitting is 5 feet above the pump, in the side of the boat. If the boat is heeled 30 degrees, this vertical lift will decrease to 1.5 feet on one tack, *but will increase to 8.5 feet on the other tack.* (Note that if the discharge line is looped up under the deck, the vertical lift will be the height to the *top of the loop* rather than to the discharge point in the side of the hull.)

Conversion Factors

My apologies! As elsewhere in this book, it was my intention to include metric measurements alongside Imperial throughout this section, but it makes it hard to read. The following are the relevant conversion factors:

Inches to centimeters, multiply by 2.54

Centimeters to inches, divide by 2.54

Feet to centimeters, multiply by 30.5

Centimeters to feet, divide by 30.5

U.S. gallons to Imperial gallons (UK), divide by 1.2

Imperial gallons (UK) to U.S. gallons, multiply by 1.2

U.S. gallons to liters, multiply by 3.785

Liters to U.S. gallons, divide by 3.785

The resistance effect of piping and tubing runs. The resistance effect of piping and tubing runs is harder to measure than vertical lift. I have made some gross simplifications in Tables 13-3 and 13-4 to arrive at approximate figures. The tables are based on the resistance of schedule 40 pipe, the inside diameter of which, rather conveniently, is only marginally larger than its nominal size (Chapter 12), so *these tables can also be used for smooth hose of the same size with reasonable accuracy* (note that corrugated hose may have up to 40% more resistance).

To calculate the resistance of a piping run, we must first determine its nominal size (for pipe) or ID (for hose), then note all the bends and elbows and any seacock or other valves. Table 13-3 is used to determine what length of pipe or hose would generate the same amount of resistance as the bends, elbows, and fittings. For example, consider a submersible bilge pump that has a 1½-inch discharge hose containing three long bends, culminating in a 180-degree bend (or vented loop) under the deck. Table 13-3 tells us that each of the three 1½-inch bends has the same resistance as 2.2 feet of 1½-inch pipe (giving a total of 6.6 feet of pipe) and the 180-degree bend has the resistance of 6.0 feet of pipe. The bends have a total resistance equal to that of 12.6 feet of pipe. Next we measure the actual length of the discharge hose and find it is 12 feet, so we have a combined resistance equal to that of 24.6 feet of pipe (12.0 + 12.6 = 24.6).

The second step in determining the resistance

TABLE 13-3. Resistance of Various Common Fittings (expressed as feet of pipe)

| Fitting | Pipe Size (nominal schedule 40 pipe) | | | | |
	¾ in.	1 in.	1¼ in	1½ in.	2 in.
In-line seacock (fully open)	0.4	0.5	0.7	0.9	1.2
90-degree seacock (fully open)	5.0	7.0	10.0	12.0	15.0
45-degree elbow (bend)	0.8	1.0	1.4	1.7	2.4
90-degree elbow (bend)	1.4	1.8	2.5	3.0	4.2
Long elbow or bend (90 degrees)	1.0	1.3	1.8	2.2	3.0
180-degree bend or vented loop	2.5	3.5	5.0	6.0	8.0

Notes:
1. For any fitting of a given pipe or hose size read off its approximate resistance in "feet of pipe" of the same size. For example, three long bends and a vented loop in the 1½-inch discharge hose from a bilge pump have the same resistance as: [(3 x 2.2) + 6.0] = 12.6 feet of 1½-inch hose.
2. Intuitively, this table seems wrong, since in reality the larger a pipe size, the less the resistance for a given rate of flow, but this table shows that the larger the fitting, the greater the equivalent length of pipe. In fact, this makes sense since the larger the pipe, the lower its resistance and therefore the longer it must be to produce a given resistance. When the length of pipe that is extracted from this table is multiplied by the factors in the next table it all works out!

TABLE 13-4. Resistance per Foot of (Old) Pipe (expressed as feet of head) as a Function of Pipe Size and Water Flow Rate

| Gallons (U.S.) per Minute | Pipe Size (nominal schedule 40 pipe) | | | | |
	¾ in.	1 in.	1¼ in.	1½ in.	2 in.
5	0.105	0.033	0.008	0.004	0.002
10	0.380	0.117	0.030	0.014	0.005
15	0.800	0.250	0.065	0.030	0.010
20	1.360	0.420	0.111	0.052	0.018
25		0.640	0.166	0.078	0.027
30		0.890	0.230	0.110	0.038
35		1.190	0.312	0.147	0.051
40		1.520	0.400	0.188	0.066
50			0.600	0.284	0.099
60			0.850	0.396	0.139
70			1.130	0.530	0.184

Notes:
1. For any given flow rate and pipe or hose size, read from the body of the table the resistance in feet of head per foot of pipe length. Multiply this by the length of the pipe or hose to find total resistance in feet of head. For example, 24.6 feet of 1½-inch hose at 3,000 gph = 50 gpm. The factor is 0.284. Total resistance is 24.6 x 0.284 = 6.986 feet of head. *(Source: Caterpillar Engine Installation and Service Handbook)*
2. To convert Imperial gallons to U.S. gallons (for reading this table), multiply by 1.2.

TABLE 13-5. Total Head Pressure

Flow Rate (U.S. gph)	Even-Keel Head (feet)	Maximum Heel Head (feet)	Effect of Tubing (feet)	Total Head (feet) Even keel	Total Head (feet) Heeled
600	5.0	8.5	0.3	5.3	8.8
1,200	5.0	8.5	1.3	6.3	9.8
1,800	5.0	8.5	2.7	7.7	11.2
2,400	5.0	8.5	4.6	9.6	12.9
3,000	5.0	8.5	7.0	12.0	15.5

effect of piping and tubing is to relate the size of the pipe or tube to the rate of flow through it. Our bilge pump is rated at 3,000 gallons per hour (gph), which is 50 gallons per minute (gpm). From Table 13-4, reading across the 50 gpm column (remember, these are U.S. gallons) to the 1½-inch-pipe column, we find that the resistance of every foot of pipe at these rates of flow is equal to 0.284 feet of vertical head. Multiplying our 24.6 feet of pipe by 0.284, we discover our 12-foot tubing run with its bends has the same resistance as 7.0 feet of vertical head!

Adding the vertical lift and the effect of resistance in the tubing run, we find that on the tack that already has 8.5 feet of vertical lift, the total head pressure is 15.5 feet (8.5 + 7.0), while even with an even keel with a 3,000 gph rate of flow, the total head pressure is 12.0 feet (5.0 + 7.0). We now have to see what effect this has on different types of pumps.

Centrifugal bilge pumps. To determine the performance of a pump, especially a centrifugal bilge pump, we have to go one step further. The above calculations are based on the *rated* flow of the bilge pump (3,000 gph). Almost all submersible bilge pumps are centrifugal pumps. These are rated under what are known as *open-bucket* or *open-flow* conditions, which means the pump has no discharge piping connected to it and is not lifting the water at all. *These are totally unrealistic conditions.* As soon as a discharge line is added to the pump and some lift is factored in, *output drops dramatically.* Some smaller centrifugal pumps stall out entirely with just 4 or 5 feet of head pressure!

All pump manufacturers have graphs that show pump output as a function of head pressure (Figure 13-8A). We need to superimpose on such a graph *the total head pressure of our system at different rates of flow.* Referring back to Table 13-4, we find that at 10 gpm (600 gph), resistance to flow *per foot of 1½-inch hose* is equal to 0.014 feet of head. With the equivalent of a 24.6-foot tubing run, this gives us a total of 0.344 feet of head (24.6 × 0.014 = 0.344); at 20 gpm (1,200 gph), the resistance factor is 0.052, for a total of 1.3 feet of head (24.6 × 0.052 = 1.3); at 30 gpm (1,800 gph), the resistance factor is 0.110, for a

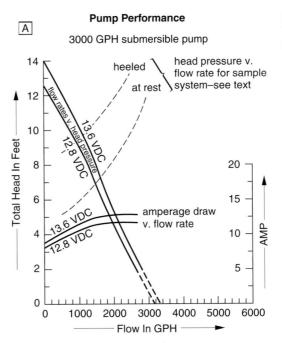

Pump Performance
3000 GPH submersible pump

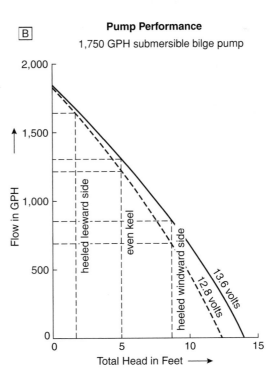

Pump Performance
1,750 GPH submersible bilge pump

FIGURES 13-8A AND 13-8B. Typical centrifugal pump performance curves.

Notes:
1. Assuming a 5-foot head pressure, at 13.6 volts the pump's rated output is 1,300 gph; at 12.8 volts the rated output is 1,200 gph.
2. With a 30-degree heel on a boat with a 12-foot beam, the output on one tack rises to 1,650 gph, but on the other tack falls to 850 gph at 13.6 volts, and just 700 gph at 12.8 volts.
3. At a more realistic 11.0 to 12.0 volts, all output figures will be further reduced.

total of 2.7 feet of head; and at 40 gpm (2,400 gph), the resistance factor is 0.188, for a total of 4.6 feet of head. If we add these figures to the even-keel head of 5 feet and the maximum heeled head of 8.5 feet, we get the results in Table 13-5.

If we plot these results on the graph of pump output (the dashed lines in Figure 13-8A), *the point at which the dashed line crosses the performance curves gives us the pump capability when the boat is at rest and also heeled 30 degrees.* As can be seen, *output is related to voltage:* if the engine is running so the alternator has the battery voltage well up, the 3,000 gph pump *in this installation* will have an output of 1,750 gph on an even keel and 1,250 gph when heeled; if the engine is shut down but the batteries are fully charged and there is no voltage drop in the pump circuit (impossible to attain), output will fall to 1,450 gph on an even keel and 980 gph when heeled. Interpolating a little, we can see that if the voltage at the pump is down around 12.0 volts (very typical on a sailboat with some voltage drop in the wiring even with a fully charged battery), the pump output will be down to little more than 1,250 gph on an even keel and 700 gph when heeled.

Figure 13-8B gives the performance numbers for a submersible bilge pump rated at 1,750 gph installed in a boat with a 12-foot beam. On one tack, the ouptut is likely to drop below 700 gph.

Note that electric bilge pumps are invariably rated at an unrealistic 13.6 volts (for a 12-volt system); there is a 10% to 12% reduction in rated output if this voltage is lowered to a more realistic 12.0 volts.

These figures are for a high-capacity bilge pump with a reasonably well-charged battery in a rather typical installation; imagine what a pitiful stream of water a small pump with a half-dead battery would be moving! Figure 13-9 gives the published specifications for a popular pump rated at 630 gph. Its maximum flow rate at 12.0 volts and 3 feet of head is 345 gph, while at 12.0 volts its maximum lift is just 6.0 feet (at which point flow rate is down to 0 gph). *These specifications are derived from a new pump in ideal test conditions. Add a bit of wear, and a couple of hairs wrapped around the impeller, and the pump will be virtually useless in many applications.* It's a little shocking, isn't it? When buying pumps, it is important to look closely at these output tables because two similar-looking pumps with similar open-flow ratings may have dissimilar capabilities when subjected to real-life operating conditions (Figure 13-10). (Table 13-6 in the Flooding Rates sidebar gives the flooding rate, in gallons *per minute,* of different-sized holes at different depths in a hull. It gives some sense of how large a pump is needed to deal with even small holes.)

Minimizing head pressure. *The single greatest improvement in the performance of centrifugal pumps will come from reducing the head pressure.* Given that the vertical lift component is more or less fixed by the physical dimensions of a boat, the only component of head pressure that we can readily reduce is the piping run. Clearly we need to use the largest size of hose possible, keep the hose run as short and direct as possible, and avoid any additional resistance, such as that imposed by check valves or dirty suction filters. Within this overall framework, the discharge hose must maintain a steady rise at all angles of heel up to its through-hull or vented loop. Otherwise, every time the pump stops, the low spots will trap water. When the pump restarts, the trapped water may act as a plug, air-locking the pump and effectively stalling it out.

To minimize friction, hoses should have a smooth interior wall. Unfortunately, many of the most popular bilge pumps on the market have a 1⅛-inch OD discharge nipple. As far as I know, the only hoses that are manufactured to fit this nipple size are corrugated hoses, some of which have a smooth internal bore, but many of which do not. Internal corrugations in a hose wall will significantly increase the head pressure created

FIGURE 13-9 (right). Published pump data for a popular submersible bilge pump.

FIGURE 13-10 (below). Two popular small submersible bilge pumps that look very similar, with the same rated output. Note the considerably larger motor in the Rule pump (right), resulting in improved performance in real-life situations.

Rated flow: 630 gph
Open flow (13.6 volts) 630 gph
Open flow (12.0 volts) 570 gph
3′ head at 13.6 volts 450 gph
3′ head at 12.0 volts 345 gph
Maximum head at 13.6 volts 7′ 8″
Maximum head at 12.0 volts 6′ 0″

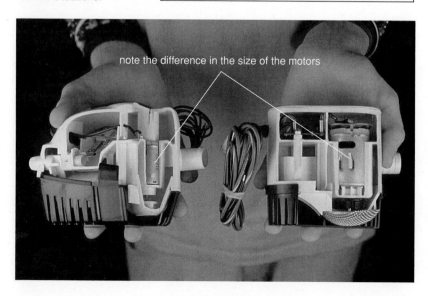

note the difference in the size of the motors

Flooding Rates

Calculating flooding rates through holes of different sizes is complicated. It is affected by obvious things (such as the size of the hole and how far it is below the waterline), not so obvious things (such as whether the hole is round or square, smooth or jagged), and really obscure things (such as the acceleration of gravity, which varies according to latitude). The formula that is commonly used is $Q = K \times 2D \times \sqrt{H}$, where Q is the flooding rate in *U.S. gallons*, K is a constant, D is the diameter of the hole, and H is the depth below the waterline.

If the diameter (D) and depth (H) are expressed in inches, K = 5.67. If the diameter (D) is expressed in inches and the depth (H) in feet, K = 19.63. If the diameter (D) and depth (H) are expressed in centimeters, K = 1.40.

Table 13-6 has been developed using this formula, and rounds the results to the nearest (U.S.) gallon.

When you compare these flooding rates to published bilge pump flow rates, you will discover that once a hole in a boat gets up around 2 inches in diameter, with even a minimal head pressure of 1 foot the predicted flow rate of 79 gpm (4,740 gph) exceeds the rated capacity, let alone the actual capacity, of any popular bilge pump on the market. This is a sobering thought. Out of curiosity, I have done some kitchen sink experiments at home, replicating a 1-inch hole in a hull (Figure 13-11). The results confirmed the decidedly catastrophic-looking numbers in the table.

What happens if a hose that is attached to a seacock fails? In this case, the seacock and hose add some resistance to flow, slowing the rate of water ingress. Table 13-7 illustrates the effect of a seacock with 1 foot of attached hose; it cuts the flow rate in half.

FIGURE 13-11. Kitchen sink flow rate experiments through a 1-foot length of 1-inch ID hose. It confirmed the flow rate numbers in the *U.S. Navy Salvor's Handbook.*

TABLE 13-6. Flooding Rate (gpm) of Various Size Openings at Various Depths

Depth of Hole (feet)	Diameter of Opening in Hull (inches)							
	1	1.5	2	2.5	3	3.5	4	6
1	20	44	79	123	177	241	314	707
2	28	62	111	174	250	340	444	1,000
3	34	77	136	213	306	417	544	1,224
4	39	88	157	245	353	481	628	1,414
5	44	99	176	274	395	538	702	1,581
6	48	108	192	301	433	589	770	1,731
7	52	117	208	325	468	636	831	1,870
8	56	125	222	347	500	680	889	1,999
9	59	133	236	368	530	722	942	2,121
10	62	140	248	388	559	761	993	2,235

(Based on a formula in the U.S. Navy Salvor's Handbook)

TABLE 13-7. Flooding Rates (gpm) of Various Size Openings at Various Depths, Assuming a Seacock with a 1-Foot Hose in Place

Depth of Hole (feet)	Inside Diameter of Pipe (inches)							
	1	1.5	2	2.5	3	3.5	4	5
1	9.0	20.3	36.0	56.3	81.0	110.3	144.0	225.0
2	12.7	28.6	50.9	79.6	114.6	155.9	203.7	318.2
3	15.6	35.1	62.4	97.4	140.3	191.0	249.4	389.8
4	18.0	40.5	72.0	112.5	162.0	220.5	288.0	450.1
5	20.1	45.3	80.5	125.8	181.1	246.6	322.0	503.2
6	22.0	49.5	88.2	137.8	198.4	270.1	352.8	551.2

by a given length of hose (by up to 40%) and so should be avoided. In any case, such hoses are often extremely thin walled, and as a result, easily damaged—not the kind of stuff I want on my boat in such an important application. Once pump nipple sizes get above $1\frac{1}{8}$ inches, they come in standard hose sizes so any high-quality smooth-bore hose can be used.

Check valves. Check valves are another problem in bilge pumping applications. Sailboats, in particular, are liable to have a centralized bilge sump. The shortest path overboard for bilge water is to the side of the vessel. But when well heeled on one tack or the other, any discharge fitting is likely to be underwater. This creates the potential for water to siphon back into the boat, which has resulted in many floodings, including one on one of our own boats! The response is often to fit a check valve in the line (we installed one). But not only do check valves have an equivalent resistance of many feet of pipe or hose, they are also prone to both plugging (in which case the pump is inoperative) and getting jammed in the open position (in which case they will not stop water from siphoning into the boat). In any event, ABYC standards *prohibit the use of a check valve if the bilge pump discharge through-hull exits the boat below the maximum heeled waterline*. In other words, *a check valve is not considered an acceptable means of keeping a pump from siphoning back*; the standards call for installing a vented loop.

If a check valve is installed, it is advantageous to mount the pump on a small pedestal. Heavier sediments will then settle out below the level of the pump, from where they can be periodically cleaned out manually. In addition, whenever the pump is shut down, the water column below the check valve in the discharge hose will return to the bilge, backflushing the system. With the pedestal, contaminants will be washed clear of the pump. Even so, be sure any check valve you install can be disassembled and place it in a readily accessible position so that you can service it when necessary (Plastimo—www.plastimo.com—manufactures an excellent, easily disassembled check valve).

A much better way to prevent a siphon from forming is to dispense with the check valve altogether, raise the discharge hose from the pump above the highest possible heeled waterline level, and fit a siphon break at the top of the loop. You will have to factor the extra static head into the bilge pump flow rate calculations, but even so the result will be substantially less than the head pressure created by a check valve.

Electrical considerations. *The second greatest improvement in bilge pumping performance will come from wiring a pump with cables sized to minimize voltage drop.* Typically, there is a relatively long cable run from the distribution panel or battery to a bilge pump. For a given cable size, the longer the cable run, the greater the cumulative voltage drop. All too often, cables are not sized to take this into consideration, and voltage drop ends up at around 10% or even higher. This means that given a battery voltage of 12.0 volts (not uncommon), the pump will only be seeing 10.8 volts, which, as we have seen, will drop the pump's rated output by *as much as 20%*.

Although it is sometimes considered acceptable to wire pumps with cables sized according to the ABYC and ISO 10% voltage drop tables, you will significantly improve pump performance by using the 3% voltage drop tables (see Chapter 4). In addition, given the inhospitable environment in a bilge, you should use tinned cable in preference to plain copper and seal all connections with glue-type heat-shrink tubing to make them as waterproof as possible.

Something that is often overlooked by do-it-yourself installers when wiring a pump is the importance of ensuring that the pump switch is installed in the positive feed to the pump. The pump itself will work just as well with the switch in the negative side of the circuit; however, if you install the switch in the negative side, the circuit as far as the pump will be energized at all times. If any internal electrical leaks to ground develop within the pump, notably through the accumulation of carbon dust (as a consequence of brush wear) or as a result of current tracking through moisture in the pump, the boat's batteries will attempt to feed current into the bilge water via this path. When the pump switch is in the OFF position, there will be no direct path back to battery ground for such stray currents. If another path is found—say through the bilge water to an immersed metal through-hull, and then through the water outside the boat to the propeller shaft, the transmission, and the engine block—*any metal in this circuit that is discharging the current into the water (in this case, metal components in the bilge pump and the through-hull itself) will suffer from potentially devastating stray-current corrosion* (see Chapter 5).

Something very similar happens when the seals on even a correctly installed submersible switch fail. As soon as the water provides an internal path from the battery side of the switch to the pump side of the switch, anytime the switch is in the OFF position, low levels of battery current will track through the water from one side of the switch to the other. The terminal that is discharging the current into the water (the battery side) will corrode until the cable falls off the switch terminal, at which point the switch is inoperative. If the boat has an unattended leak, it will sink. There is no simple way to guard against this, other than buying a high-quality switch in the first place and routinely checking its operation (I check ours every time we leave the boat), or else using a nonsubmersible switch (see below).

Overcurrent protection and locked rotors. One other electrical issue that has to be addressed is overcurrent protection. As with all other circuits on a boat, a bilge pump circuit should be protected at its source—which is generally a battery but is sometimes a bus bar wired back to the battery—with an overcurrent protection device (a fuse or breaker). My preference is for a fuse rather than a breaker because this creates less of an opportunity to accidentally turn off the bilge pump when leaving the boat. This fuse should have a rating that does not exceed the current-carrying capability (the *ampacity*) of the smallest cables in the circuit (as often as not, the cables that come attached to the pump or its float switch).

Properly sized, the fuse will prevent the pump wiring from melting down in the event of a serious short circuit. However, with bilge pumps there is always the risk of a piece of debris jamming the pump impeller and creating a locked-rotor state. Given a locked rotor, the current draw of a pump rises dramatically but not necessarily enough to blow the fuse. The pump may then get hot enough to start a fire. *This is especially likely to happen if the wiring to the pump is somewhat undersized*; the cumulative resistance of the undersized cables may be enough to limit the current flow on the circuit to a level at which the fuse will not blow. Using a lower-rated fuse is not the way to deal with this problem, since this may result in nuisance blowing with the normal inrush current (which is several times higher than operating current) to the pump. The correct solution is to upgrade the cabling. Then, given a locked rotor, the cables will pass a current flow that is high enough to blow the fuse, shutting down the circuit.

Given this bilge pump meltdown potential, the ABYC requires that all motors and motor circuits be designed and protected so that they can withstand a locked-rotor condition for 7 hours without creating a fire hazard. This doesn't necessarily mean that the motor itself must be able to withstand a locked rotor for 7 hours. It does mean that in a locked-rotor situation, either the circuit must be designed to shut off power to the motor, or the motor must be able to withstand the locked-rotor condition for 7 hours without creating a fire hazard—one or the other.

The ABYC also requires that a bilge pump be able to operate dry for 7 hours without creating a fire hazard, and that if it cannot do this, it must have an *integral* means of shutting itself off (i.e., an external fuse or breaker will not suffice; in any case, these will not provide protection because there is no overcurrent situation). Typically, if the pump cannot run dry for the

---

A Case History

An owner of a new powerboat with two large diesels had the yard launch his boat at the beginning of the season. He proceeded to take it out for a cruise. After a while he smelled burning rubber. He shut down the engines to investigate and found that the raw-water seacocks were closed (he assumed the yard had opened them when launching). The burning smell was from the exhaust hose, which was being deprived of cooling water. He radioed the yard to seek advice. They suggested he open the seacocks, restart his engines, and see if he had coolant flow from the exhaust. As luck would have it, he did. He assumed (correctly) that the raw-water pump impellers were still functional, and that it was therefore OK to proceed.

A short while later, he glanced below and saw water over the cabin sole. A quick investigation showed that the earlier lack of cooling water had caused the hot exhaust gases to burn through the exhaust hose. He had been pumping much of his cooling water into the boat at a rate that had overwhelmed the limited capability of the bilge pump. He shut down the engines to give the bilge pump time to catch up, but the water kept rising. Unfortunately, the weight of water in the boat had now depressed his exhaust outlets below the waterline. Water was flooding into the boat through the 6-inch exhaust through-hulls and out of the damaged hose at an alarming rate. He fired up the engines and headed for shore, but the boat was clearly going to sink before he could reach it so he beached in shoal water.

In retrospect, we can see that a better course of action would have been to shut down the engines and plug the exhaust through-hulls. As with most serious leaks, the only realistic way to save a boat is to slow the influx of water, rather than rely on the bilge pump to keep up with the flow while other measures are taken.

required 7 hours without getting dangerously hot, the manufacturer builds a heat-sensitive (thermal) trip into the case.

Maintenance, Troubleshooting, and Repair

Flexible-impeller pumps (Figure 13-12). The principal causes of failure are impeller damage from solids, running dry, and chemicals.

Flexible-impeller pumps like to be used often. If left for long periods without running (e.g., over the winter), the impeller vanes have a tendency to stick to the pump housing. When the pump is restarted, it may blow fuses or strip off its vanes. If this is a constant problem, try fit-

ting an overthick gasket (see below—this technique results in a small loss of pump efficiency). Otherwise loosen the pump cover until the pump starts spinning.

Other common problems are leaking seals (again, quite likely as a result of running dry) and worn or corroded bearings. Apart from normal wear, bearings will be damaged by water (from leaking seals), improper belt tension (too tight), and misalignment of drive pulleys or couplings. Optimum belt tension permits the longest stretch of a belt to be depressed $\frac{1}{3}$ to $\frac{1}{2}$ inch with moderate finger pressure. Check pulley alignment by removing the belt and placing a rod in the groove of the two pulleys; any misalignment will be clearly visible.

Winterizing. Loosen the end cover to drain the pump. It is best to leave the cover loose in case any more fluid finds its way in. Withdraw the impeller, grease it lightly (with petroleum jelly or Teflon-based waterproof grease), and put it back. This will keep the impeller from sticking to the pump body and aid in priming the pump the next time it is run.

Impeller removal and inspection. Despite the thousands of different flexible-impeller pumps, most share many construction similarities (Figure 13-13). Removal of the end cover (four to six screws) will expose the impeller. For difficult-to-access covers, you can make the removal and replacement process a lot easier, and with little

FIGURE 13-12. A typical flexible-impeller pump. (ITT/Jabsco)

Leaving a Boat Unattended

I read somewhere that more boats sink at their moorings or in their slips than at sea. It certainly seems quite plausible. A slow drip from a stern gland will, over an extended period of time, allow large amounts of water into a boat. This in turn—if the battery is not regularly charged—will cause the bilge pump to flatten the battery until the pump no longer operates, and the boat will go down. Even with adequate provisions for battery charging, there are numerous ways in which the bilge pump may be put out of action, including a failed level switch, a jammed pump impeller, or a failed electrical circuit (e.g., corrosion in a fuse holder causes the fuse to overheat and blow).

When leaving a boat unattended, it is foolhardy to place undue reliance on the bilge pump. Instead, stop the ingress of water into the boat, primarily by ensuring that the propeller shaft seals and rudder shaft seals are not leaking. *If the seals can't be made drip-free, there is a problem that needs attention.* Routinely close all but the cockpit-drain sea-

cocks. Flush the bilges, pump them dry, and *clean out all debris.* Closely inspect the bilge pump wiring circuit for any signs of corrosion or damage. And there must be some means of keeping the batteries charged, particularly wet-type batteries, which, in hot climates, will discharge to the point of being useless in just a few months.

Finally, consider adding a high-level alarm circuit to the bilge pump circuit. This can take the form of a separate level switch or sensor mounted above the regular level switch or sensor or, in the case of some of the electronic switches (see below), a built-in timer that activates a secondary alarm circuit if the pump remains on for more than a set period of time (e.g., 5 minutes). Depending on the complexity of the system and the current-carrying capability of the alarm circuit, it may be possible to wire a secondary backup pump into this circuit. If the boat is kept in a marina or some other public place, it would also be a good idea to include an external alarm light or bell.

Bilge Pumping Efficiency and Life Expectancy

Given the importance of bilge pumps to boats, surprisingly little objective data is available by which to compare one pump to another when making choices. The data that is available has mostly been developed by manufacturers. The following information is derived from tests conducted by Imanna Laboratory (an independent testing facility—www.imanna.com) in 2002. These tests were financed by Rule Industries (www.rule-industries.com). Imanna used six off-the-shelf samples of a number of pumps from three different manufacturers to compare their performance at different head pressures, using both smooth-bore and corrugated-bore hoses. The results given in Table 13-8 are the averages of the six pumps in each sample.

Another interesting test, also financed by Rule (back in 1997), is a simple endurance test—i.e., how many hours a pump will run before failure. In this case, the pumps were tested at 13.6 volts in an open-flow condition (no head pressure). Three pumps were tested for each model. The average life is shown in Table 13-9.

What stands out in both sets of tests is the significant variation between rated performance and real-life performance, and the even greater variation in pump life from one pump to another (although this has to be treated with caution given the small size of the samples). Rule, an industry leader, comes out of these tests extremely well. This is not just a function of the fact that Rule financed the tests, but is also a function of the way in which they build pumps (refer back to Figure 13-10)!

TABLE 13-9. Average Pump Life

Model	Average Life (hours) for Three Samples
Rule 800	1,473
Mayfair 750	496
Attwood V750	372
Rule 500	1,537
Mayfair 500	1,313
Attwood V450	249
Mayfair 360	887
Rule 360	1,609

TABLE 13-8. Flow Rate (gph) at Specified Head Pressure, with Smooth-Bore and Corrugated-Bore Hoses

		Feet of Head							
		3		5		7		9	
Manufacturer	Rated Output	Smooth	Corrugated	Smooth	Corrugated	Smooth	Corrugated	Smooth	Corrugated
Johnson	2,200	821	684	712	599	583	487	424	349
Rule	2,000	1,052	880	945	798	843	714	728	622
Attwood	2,000	911	788	777	680	612	535	416	391
Attwood	1,250	702	566	578	458	403	289	144	90
Johnson	1,250	574	479	482	392	369	286	183	137
Rule	1,100	682	530	562	424	402	280	255	132
Johnson	1,000	467	274	414	221	334	161	212	125
Attwood	900	611	493	493	389	359	262	102	77
Johnson	500	325	233	229	161	92	58	0	0
Rule	500	316	262	253	222	182	168	111	117
Attwood	500	302	242	224	179	116	96	19	24

risk of losing the screws in the bilge, by installing a Speedseal cover (www.speedseal.com).

Almost all impellers are a sliding fit on the drive shaft (either with splines, square keys, Woodruff keys, one or two flats on the shaft, or a slotted shaft). Using a pair of needle-nose pliers or Vise-Grips (mole wrench), grip the impeller and pull it out. If it is not possible to get at the impeller with pliers, an impeller puller may do the trick (approximately $50 from West Marine and others; for more on removing impellers, see pages 397–98).

Note that some impellers are sealed to their shafts with O-rings; most are not. If the impeller will not come loose, it may be one of the few locked in place with a setscrew (Allen screw; in particular, some Volvo, Atomic Four, and Universal engines). If the screw is inaccessible, you must disassemble the drive side of the impeller and knock the impeller out on its shaft.

The impeller vanes should have rounded tips (not worn flat), with no signs of swelling, distortion, or cracking of the vanes, or any kind of a *set* (bend). If in doubt, replace the impeller. If an

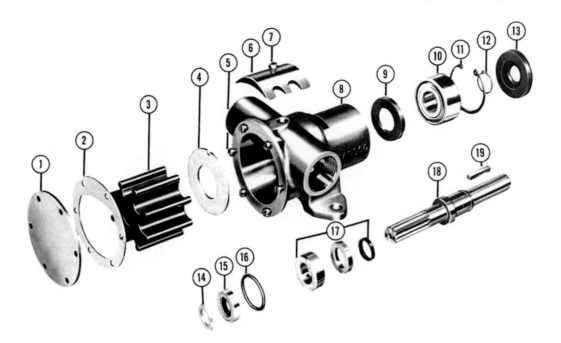

FIGURE 13-13. An exploded view of the pump shown in Figure 13-12. Pump cover (1). Gasket (2). Impeller (splined type; 3). Wear plate (4). Pump cover retaining screws (5). Cam (mounted inside pump body; 6). Cam retaining screw (7). Pump body (8). Slinger (to deflect any leaks away from the bearing; 9). Bearing (10). Bearing-retaining circlip (11). Shaft-retaining circlip (12). Outer seal (13). Inner seal assembly, lip type (14, 15, 16), or inner seal assembly, carbon-ceramic type (17). Pump shaft (18). Drive key (19). *(ITT/Jabsco)*

O-ring is fitted to the shaft, check it for damage. If the impeller has a tapered metal sleeve on its inner end (*extended insert* impellers), inspect the sleeve and discard the impeller if there is any sign of a step where the sleeve slides into the shaft seal.

Wear plate and seal removal. If it is necessary to remove the cam (e.g., to replace a *wear plate*—see next paragraph), loosen the cam retaining screw, tap the screw until the cam breaks loose, and remove the screw and cam. Clean all surfaces of sealing compound.

Some impellers have a wear plate at the back of the pump chamber. If fitted, you can hook out the plate with a piece of bent wire. Note the notch in its top; this aligns with a dowel in the pump body. If the wear plate is grooved or scored, replace it.

There are three types of shaft seals:

1. Lip-type seals, which press into the pump housing and have a rubber lip that grips the shaft.

2. Carbon-ceramic seals, in which a ceramic disc with a smooth face seats in a rubber boot in the pump housing. A spring-loaded carbon disc, also with a smooth face, is sealed to the pump shaft with a rubber sleeve or O-ring. The spring holds the carbon disc against the ceramic disc, and the extremely smooth faces of the two provide a seal.

3. An external stuffing box (packing gland), which is the same as a propeller-shaft stuffing box. These are not very common. For care and maintenance, see pages 442–45.

Although it is possible to hook out and replace some carbon-ceramic seals with the shaft still in place (this cannot be done with lip-type seals), in most cases the shaft must be taken out to replace a seal. To do this, take apart the drive end of the shaft. First unbolt the pump from its engine or remove the drive pulley (if it is belt driven); then proceed as follows:

If the pump has a seal at the drive end of the shaft (number 13 in Figure 13-13), hook it out. When removing any seals, *be extremely careful not to scratch the seal seat*. You will usually find a bearing-retaining circlip behind the seal in the body of the pump (pumps bolted directly to an engine housing may not have one). Remove the circlip, flexing it the minimum amount necessary to get it out. If it gets bent, it should be replaced, not straightened and reused.

Support the pump body on a couple of blocks of wood and tap out the shaft, hitting it on its *impeller* end (Figure 13-14; the exception is pumps with impellers fastened to the shaft—these must be driven out the other way). Do not hit the shaft hard; be especially careful not to burr or flatten the end of the shaft. It is best to use a block of wood between the hammer and the shaft rather than hit the shaft directly.

If the shaft won't move, take another look for a bearing-retaining circlip. If there truly is none, try hitting a little harder. If the shaft remains stuck, try heating the pump body in the area of the bearings with hot water or the gentle use of a propane torch. The shaft will come out complete with bearings.

The main shaft seal can now be picked out from the impeller side of the body with a piece of bent wire. There may well be another bearing seal on the drive side and quite probably a *slinger* washer between the two. If the washer drops down inside the body, retrieve it through the drain slot.

Bearing removal and replacement. To remove the bearings from the shaft, take the small bearing-retaining circlip off the shaft, support the assembly with a couple of blocks of wood placed *under the inner bearing race*, and tap out the shaft, hitting it on its drive end (Figure 13-15).

Inspect the shaft for any signs of wear, especially in the area of the shaft seal. Spin the bearings and discard them if they are rough and uneven, or if the outer race is loose. Scrupulously clean the pump body, paying special attention to all seals and bearing seats. Do not scratch any bearing, seal, or seating surfaces.

To fit new bearings to a shaft, support the inner race of the bearing and tap the shaft home. To make the job easier, first heat the bearing (e.g., in an oven to around 200°F/93°C but no more) and cool the shaft (in the icebox). The shaft should just about drop into place. Replace the bearing-retaining circlip, with the flat side toward the bearing.

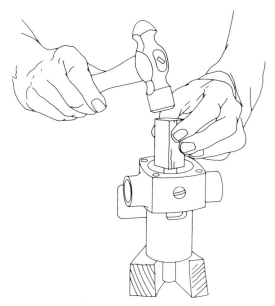

FIGURE 13-14. Removing a pump shaft. Remove the end cover and impeller. Support the pump body with a couple of blocks of wood, impeller end up. Protect the end of the impeller shaft with a block of wood and lightly tap the shaft free. (*Jim Sollers*)

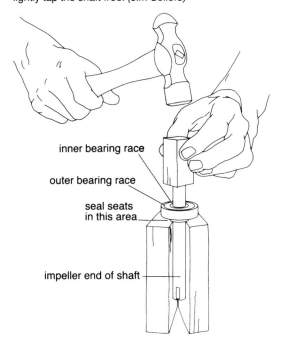

inner bearing race

outer bearing race

seal seats in this area

impeller end of shaft

FIGURE 13-15. Removing a bearing from the pump shaft. Remove the bearing-retaining circlip from the shaft. Support the bearing with a couple of blocks of wood placed under the inner bearing race. Protect the shaft end with a block of wood and lightly tap the shaft free from the bearing. (*Jim Sollers*)

Troubleshooting Chart 13-1. Flexible Impeller, Vane, and Rotary Pump Problems: No Flow	
If the pump is belt driven, is the pump pulley turning? **YES**	**NO** Tighten or replace the drive belt.
If a clutch is fitted, is it working? (The center of the pulley will be turning with the pulley itself.) **YES**	**NO** Adjust or replace the clutch.
For gear-driven pumps, and for belt-driven pumps on which the pulley is turning, proceed as follows:	
Remove the pump cover; are the impeller vanes intact? **YES**	**NO** Replace the impeller and track down any missing vanes. The pump probably ran dry; find out why. Check for a closed seacock, plugged filter, collapsed suction hose, or excessive heeling that causes the suction line on a raw-water pump to come out of the water. Less likely is a blockage on the discharge side causing the pump to overload.
Are the vanes making good contact with the pump body? **YES**	**NO** The impeller is badly worn and needs replacing. On vane and rotary pumps the vanes may be jammed in the impeller and just need cleaning.
Does the impeller turn when the pump drive gear or pulley turns? **YES**	**NO** The impeller, drive gear, or pulley is slipping on its shaft, or the clutch (if fitted) is inoperative. Repair as necessary.
If the impeller turns, the pump may just need priming. Otherwise the suction or discharge line must be blocked. Check for a closed seacock, plugged filter, collapsed suction hose, or excessive heeling that causes the suction line on a raw-water pump to come out of the water.	

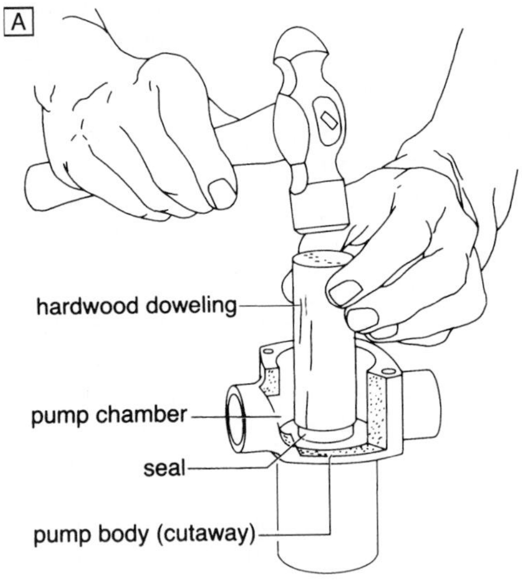

FIGURE 13-16A.
Replacing a pump seal.
Seat the seal squarely in
its housing. Using very soft
hammer taps and
a piece of hardwood
doweling the same or
larger diameter as the
seal, push the seal down
until flush with the pump
chamber. *(Jim Sollers)*

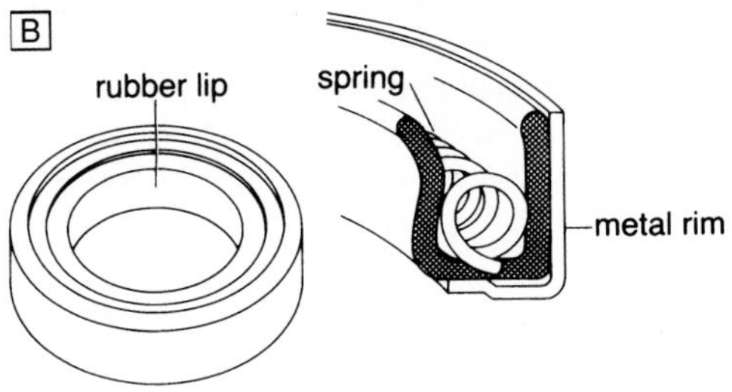

FIGURE 13-16B. When
replacing a pump seal,
make sure the hardwood
doweling seats on the
seal's metal rim and not
the rubber lip. The seal
goes in with the rubber lip
toward the pump chamber.
(Jim Sollers)

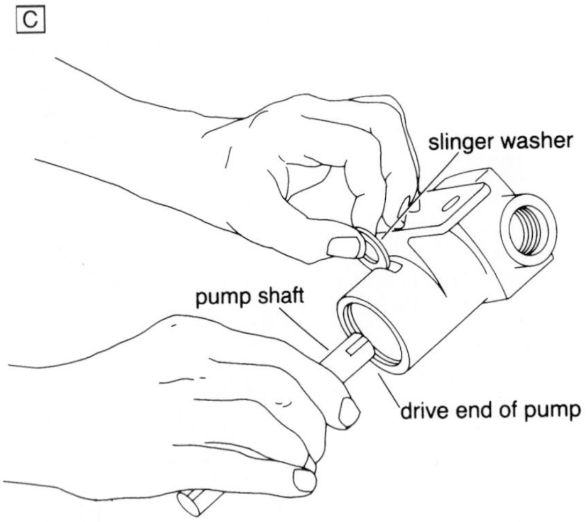

FIGURE 13-16C.
Replacing a slinger
washer. Push the washer
up through its slot in the
pump body, threading the
shaft through it and into
the shaft seal.
(Jim Sollers)

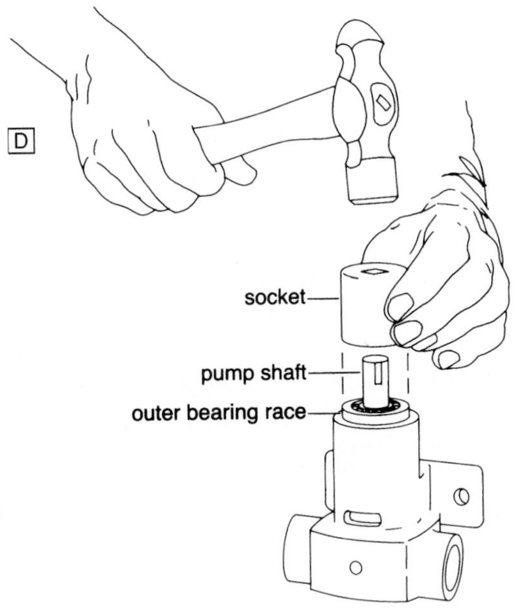

FIGURE 13-16D. Driving
home a bearing. Use a
ratchet drive–type socket
with a diameter slightly
smaller than the outer
bearing race.
(Jim Sollers)

A

hardwood doweling

pump chamber

seal

pump body (cutaway)

B

rubber lip

spring

metal rim

C

slinger washer

pump shaft

drive end of pump

D

socket

pump shaft

outer bearing race

FIGURE 13-16E. There
are two basic types of
carbon-ceramic pump
shaft seals—wave-washer
seals (uncommon) and
coil-spring seals. In either
case, the ceramic seal and
rubber boot are pressed
into place in the pump
body, and the carbon-ring
seal and retainer are fitted
to the pump shaft.
(ITT/Jabsco)

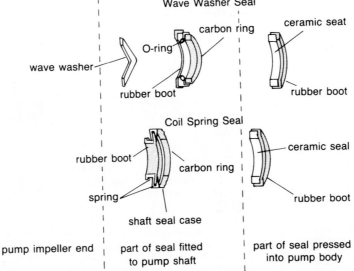

Wave Washer Seal

wave washer — O-ring — carbon ring — ceramic seat

rubber boot — rubber boot

Coil Spring Seal

rubber boot — carbon ring

spring — ceramic seal

shaft seal case — rubber boot

pump impeller end | part of seal fitted to pump shaft | part of seal pressed into pump body

Seal and shaft replacement. Now is the time to put the new shaft seal in the pump body—also the inner bearing seal (if fitted). Lip-type seals have the lip *toward the impeller*. Carbon-ceramic seals have the ceramic part in the pump body, set in its rubber boot with the shiny surface facing the impeller.

A lip-type seal is lightly greased (with petroleum jelly or a Teflon-based waterproof grease), but a *carbon-ceramic seal must not be greased.* The seal faces must be wiped spotlessly clean—even finger grease must be kept off them—and the seal lubricated with water.

All seals must be centered squarely and pushed in evenly. If the seal is bent, distorted, or cock-eyed in any way, it is sure to leak. A piece of hardwood doweling the same diameter as, or a little bigger than, the seal makes a good drift (Figures 13-16A and 13-16B). Push the seal down until it is flush with the pump chamber.

If the pump has a slinger washer, slide it up through the body drain and maneuver the shaft in from the drive side of the body (Figure 13-16C), easing it through the slinger and into the shaft seal. Pass the shaft through any seals very carefully.

Seat the bearings squarely in the pump housing, support the pump body, and drive the bearings home evenly, applying pressure to the *outer* race (Figure 13-16D; a socket with a diameter just a little smaller than the bearing works well). Once again, heating the pump body and cooling bearings will help tremendously. Refit the bearing-retaining ring (circlip) with the flat side to the bearing and press home the outer bearing seal (if fitted), with the lip side toward the pump impeller.

Turn now to the pump end (refer back to Figure 13-13). If the pump has a carbon-ceramic seal, clean the seal face, lubricate it with water, and slide the carbon part up the pump shaft, with the smooth face toward the ceramic seat.

Some seals use *wave* washers to maintain tension between the carbon seal and seat; most use springs (Figure 13-16E; if the seal has both, discard the wave washer).

Wear plate, cam, and impeller replacement. Replace the wear plate, locating its notch on the dowel pin. Lightly apply some sealing compound (e.g., Permatex) to the back of the cam and to its retaining screw. *Loosely* fit the cam. Lightly grease the impeller with petroleum jelly, a Teflon-based grease, or dishwashing liquid, then push it home, bending down the vanes in the opposite direction to pump rotation. Replace the gasket and pump cover. Tighten the cam screw.

The correct gasket is important—too thin, and the impeller will bind; too thick, and pumping efficiency is lost. Most pump gaskets are 0.010 inch (ten-thousandths of an inch) thick, but on larger pumps they may be 0.015 inch. As noted previously, some impellers on intermittently used pumps have a tendency to stick in their housings and, if electrically driven, blow fuses when the pump is started. To stop this, loosen the pump cover on initial start-up, then tighten it back down. (You can achieve this same result, with only a small loss in pumping efficiency and without loosening the cover screws, by fitting an overthick gasket.)

When refitting a flanged pump to an engine, be sure the slot in the pump shaft, or the drive gear, correctly engages the tang or gear on the engine. Also make sure the pump flange seats squarely *without pressure.* Some pumps have spacers or adapters that go between the end of the pump shaft and the engine drive shaft. Pulley-driven pumps must be properly aligned with their drive pulleys, and the belt must be correctly tensioned.

Manual clutches. Some pump pulleys are turned on and off via manually operated clutches (Figure 13-17). The pulley spins on a bearing

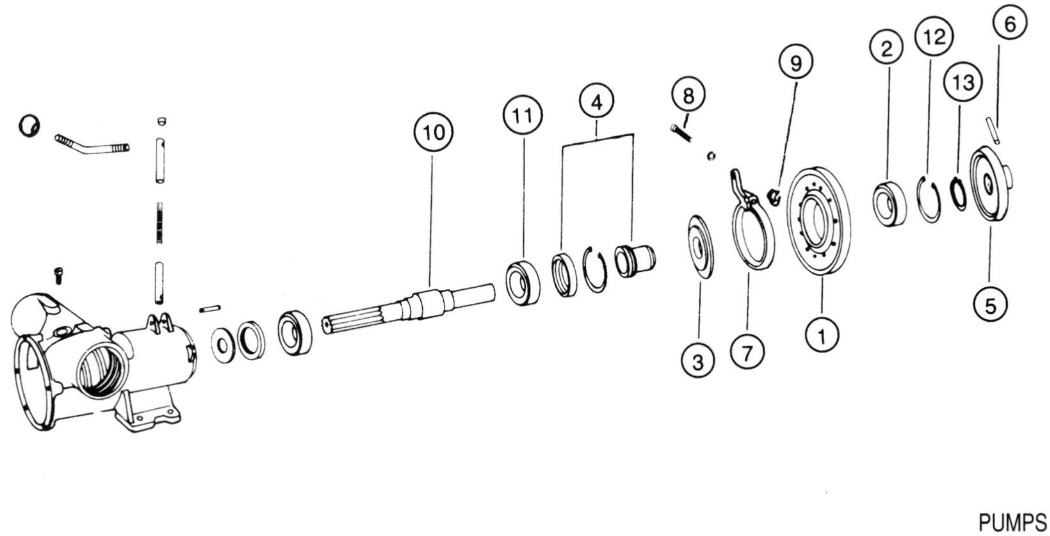

FIGURE 13-17. An exploded view of a manual clutch for a pump. Pulley (1). Pulley bearing (2). Adapter ring (3). Body plug and engaging sleeve (4). Clutch cone (5). Clutch-cone locking pin (6). Clutch-operating ring (7). Clutch-operating-ring securing bolt (8). Clutch-operating-ring securing nut (9). Pump shaft (10). Bearing (11). Pulley-to-bearing retaining ring (12). Engaging-sleeve-to-bearing retaining ring (13). To adjust this type of clutch: A. Engage the clutch. B. Loosen nut (9) and the clutch-operating-ring securing bolt (8). C. Open up the slot in the operating ring by prying with a screwdriver. D. Hold the adapter ring (3) stationary and rotate the clutch-operating ring backward 20 degrees. E. Retighten the operating ring nut and bolt. *(ITT/Jabsco)*

mounted on an *adapter ring*. The adapter ring in turn fits on an assembly known as a *body plug and engaging sleeve*. The engaging sleeve is threaded (screwed) onto the body plug. On the back of the pulley, a tapered friction surface fits loosely inside a tapered housing, the *clutch cone*, which is locked to the pump shaft. The pulley freewheels, and the pump remains stationary until the clutch lever is operated. Then the operating lever turns the adapter ring, which in turn *backs out* the engaging sleeve on the threaded body plug, forcing the pulley's tapered friction surface into contact with the clutch cone; this locks up the whole assembly and the pump turns.

In time the clutch wears and begins to slip. It can be adjusted by unscrewing the engaging sleeve a little more from the body plug, but this solution is limited by the number of threads between plug and sleeve. If the engaging sleeve (and therefore the pulley) is unscrewed too much, it will start to wobble, accelerating wear.

Adjust the clutch by first engaging the clutch and then loosening the clutch-operating ring (also called the *lever ring* or the *engaging clamp ring*) where it fits around the adapter ring. Jam the adapter ring in place with a screwdriver and rotate the operating ring backward around the

FIGURE 13-18. An exploded view of a pump with an electromagnetic clutch. *(ITT/Jabsco)*

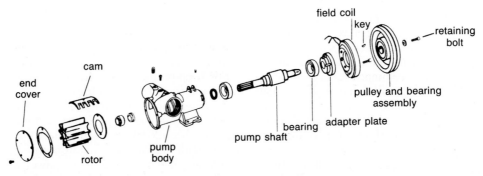

FIGURE 13-19. An exploded view of a vane pump. *(ITT/Jabsco)*

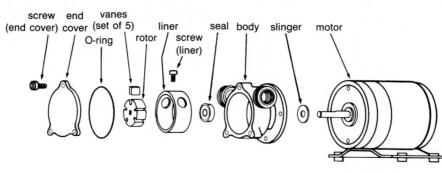

FIGURE 13-20. An exploded view of a rotary pump. This one has twin impellers. *(Groco)*

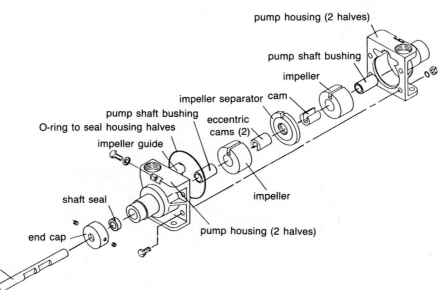

adapter ring (it may be necessary to wedge open the slit in the operating ring with a second screwdriver). Move the operating ring 20 degrees or so, retighten its securing bolt, and try the clutch. Repeat if necessary; if the ring has to be moved more than a total of 45 degrees, the clutch is badly worn and needs replacing.

Clutch kits contain the body plug and engaging sleeve assembly, pulley, bearing, adapter ring, and instructions for fitting. Note that the body plug and engaging sleeve are a matched set and should always be replaced together.

Electric clutches.
With electric clutches, the device that locks a pulley to its shaft is a *field coil* (Figure 13-18), which is energized electrically and locks a freewheeling pulley to its hub by electromagnetic force. An electric clutch cannot be adjusted—it either works or it doesn't. If it fails, first check that there is full voltage at the coil and it is grounded properly.

To replace either a pulley and bearing assembly or the field coil, remove the pulley. Undo its center retaining bolt (it will probably be necessary to remove the pump cover and hold the impeller to stop the shaft from turning). If the bolt proves tough to break loose, place a correctly sized wrench (spanner) on it and hit the wrench smartly with a hammer—the shock should do the trick.

The end of the pump shaft, where the pulley fits on, is tapered. Between the shaft and the pulley is a key. Tap the pulley loose with a soft-faced mallet or a hammer and a block of wood. Watch out for the key—don't let it fall into the bilges! The field coil is unbolted from either an adapter or the pump body. To reassemble the clutch, reverse these steps—be sure to put the key back.

Rotary and vane pumps.
In most cases removing an end cover provides access to the impeller, which will slide off its shaft (Figures 13-19 and 13-20). The vanes on vane pumps tend to fall out of the rotor. Since it is best to put them back in the same slots and the same way around, slip a rubber band around the rotor when it is halfway out; this will hold the vanes in place.

Besides the usual seal, shaft, and bearing inspections, check old vanes against a new vane (always carry spares on board) for signs of wear. If any are worn down more than one-third of their original length, replace the whole set. If the new vanes have a radiused edge, this faces out (toward the pump wall). Some vane pumps have removable liners; replace the liner if the one in place is excessively scored.

Seal and bearing replacement for vane and rotary pumps is similar to the procedure for flexible-impeller pumps.

Centrifugal pumps.
The most common problem is loss of prime, which can generally be restored by removing the discharge hose and pouring in a cup of water.

Gradual wear of the impeller blades increases clearances between the impeller and its housing, resulting in a slow loss of pumping efficiency. If the pump is installed in a pressurized system, it will run for longer periods until finally its output pressure cannot reach the cutout point of the pressure switch; the pump then stays on all the time. Wear will cause centrifugal bilge pumps

Troubleshooting Chart 13-2. Centrifugal Pump Problems: No Flow or Reduced Flow	
Is the pump refusing to spin? **TEST:** Check the voltage at electric motors while switched on, or the drive mechanism on other pumps (gears, belt, pulley, clutch); check for trash jammed in the impeller on a bilge pump.	**FIX:** Remove trash. Repair or replace belt, or refer to Chapter 7 for problems with electric motors. (Note: Most old motors are wound-field-coil universal motors; newer ones are permanent-magnet universal motors.)
Has the pump lost its prime? **TEST:** Prime the pump by disconnecting a discharge line and pouring in fluid to fill the pump chamber. Run the unit again. If there is flow, the pump is OK.	**FIX:** 1. Check that the pump is below the waterline (including when the boat is heeled) or, if above the waterline, that it has a check valve in the suction line. If the valve is fitted, check that it is not leaking back. 2. Check that the suction line is not kinked or blocked (by a closed seacock or a plugged filter, for example). 3. Check that the suction line makes a continuous run up to the pump with no U-bends that can trap air. 4. Check that all suction line connections are tight and not sucking air.
Are there obstructions in the discharge line? **TEST:** Check for common obstructions in the discharge line, such as a kinked hose or closed seacock.	**FIX:** Straighten hose or open seacock and try running the unit again. If there is flow, the pump is OK.
Is the head pressure too high? **TEST:** Disconnect the discharge line at its overboard discharge, lower it in relation to the pump, and try running the unit again.	**FIX:** Reduce the head or get a more powerful pump. If the pump has previously worked as installed, the loss of pumping ability is likely due to a worn impeller. Replace the impeller.

FIGURE 13-21A. An exploded view of a centrifugal pump with a turbine impeller. *(Groco)*

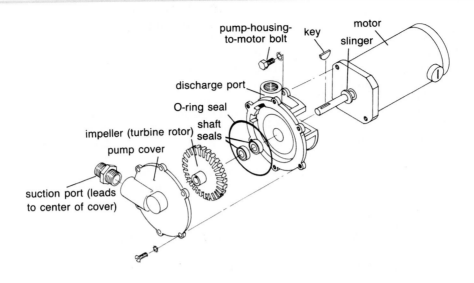

pump-housing-to-motor bolt key motor slinger

discharge port

O-ring seal

impeller (turbine rotor) shaft seals

pump cover

suction port (leads to center of cover)

FIGURE 13-21B. A spiral-vane centrifugal pump. *(ITT/Jabsco)*

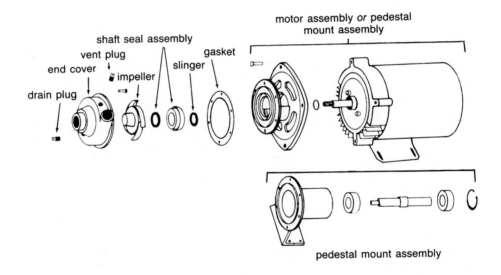

shaft seal assembly

vent plug

end cover impeller slinger gasket

drain plug

motor assembly *or* pedestal mount assembly

pedestal mount assembly

with a considerable lift to pump at a slower and slower rate.

Removal of the end housing gives access to the pump impeller (Figures 13-21A and 13-21B). Some impellers are held on with setscrews (Allen screws); others are screwed onto their shafts. To undo the latter, tape the drive shaft and grip it with Vise-Grips; unscrew the impeller (generally counterclockwise when viewed from the impeller end).

The procedure for seal and bearing replacement for centrifugal pumps is similar to that for flexible-impeller pumps.

Piston pumps. A piston fits in a cylinder, with a valve on the base of the piston and one in the cylinder (or else "in" and "out" valves in the cylinder). When the piston is pulled up, it draws fluid into the cylinder. When it is pushed down,

the valve in the cylinder (the inlet valve) closes, and the trapped fluid pushes past the valve in the piston or out of a second valve in the cylinder (the discharge valve). If the fluid has moved past the piston into the upper side of the cylinder, the next upward stroke of the piston drives it out of the discharge port. On this type of pump, the piston rod must be sealed where it enters the cylinder to prevent leaks (Figures 13-22A and 13-22B).

Many different valve types are used on both pistons and cylinders. Older pistons may have a dished leather washer screwed to the lower end. As the piston descends its cylinder, trapped fluid in the cylinder pushes in the sides of the washer and forces its way up past the piston. When the piston is withdrawn, the fluid pressure pushes the sides of the washer out against the cylinder wall to form a seal. Modern pistons of this type

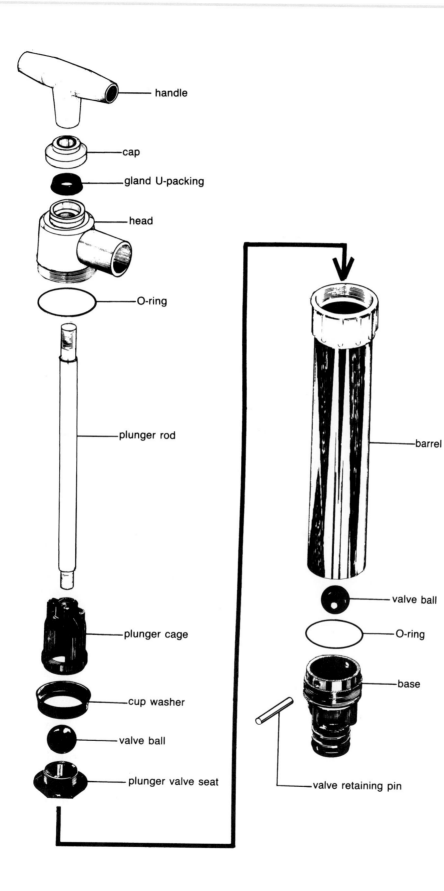

FIGURE 13-22A. A piston pump with ball valves. *(Whale)*

handle

cap

gland U-packing

head

O-ring

plunger rod

plunger cage

cup washer

valve ball

plunger valve seat

barrel

valve ball

O-ring

base

valve retaining pin

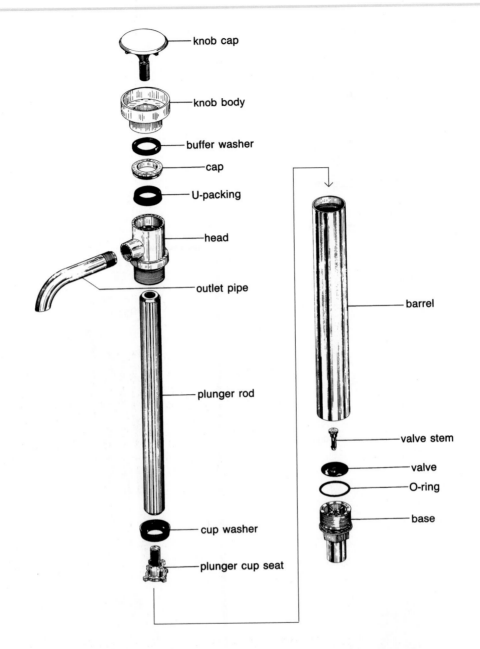

knob cap

knob body

buffer washer

cap

U-packing

head

outlet pipe

plunger rod

cup washer

plunger cup seat

barrel

valve stem

valve

O-ring

base

are sealed with a neoprene cup washer. Another approach is to use an O-ring to seal the piston in its cylinder and fit a ball or flapper valve into the piston's base.

Cylinder valves may be simple rubber or metal flaps, balls, or a rubber disc with a central retaining valve stem. As fluid is sucked in, the valves, regardless of type, are lifted off their seats. When fluid is discharged, the valves are forced down against their seats.

Foot-operated piston-type galley pumps have spring-loaded pistons. Foot pressure pushes the piston in; the spring brings it back out.

Problems. The most common piston-pump problem is trash in valve seats; this causes a loss of prime and the ability to pump. A failure of a piston's dished washer or O-ring will have the same result. Before blaming the pump, check for air leaks in the suction line. Vigorous pumping will sometimes restore prime and clear valves.

The piston-rod seals will leak eventually, especially after a winter shutdown. Most have a cap, which you can tighten to improve the seal.

Overhaul and repair. Most pistons are withdrawn by unscrewing the piston-rod seal from the top of the cylinder. Replace damaged dished washers with a piece of thin leather (e.g., from an old wallet) if no spares are available. Cut the washer a little larger in diameter than the cylinder bore, screw it to the piston, and lubricate with water. Form the edges up around the base of the piston until the washer fits the cylinder.

Cylinder valves generally unscrew from the base of the cylinder, although on cheaper pumps they are housed in a rubber boot that simply pushes on and pulls off. If the valve consists of a rubber disc, inspect it closely for small tears and nicks, which might not be immediately apparent. Look for and remove pieces of trash between all valves and seats.

Manual diaphragm pumps. On a manual diaphragm pump, a handle moves a lever (rocker arm or *fork*) that arcs backward and forward around a pivot point or fulcrum. Attached to the lever is a diaphragm. As the diaphragm moves out, it draws fluid into a pump chamber; as it moves in, it expels the fluid (Figures 13-23A and 13-23B). Simple flap or joker valves (Chapter 12) on the inlet and outlet allow the fluid in and out.

A double-diaphragm pump has a diaphragm and pump chamber on both sides of the lever; as one diaphragm moves in, the other moves out, and vice versa (Figure 13-24A). Each pump chamber has its own inlet and outlet valves; the two suction and discharge ports feed into common suction and discharge manifolds. Some double-diaphragm pumps have a spring in one chamber to return the operating handle unfailingly to the same position. Foot-operated diaphragm pumps have a spring-loaded plunger instead of an operating handle and lever (Figure 13-24B). Standing on the plunger moves the diaphragm in; the spring brings it back out.

All of these pumps can be modified to be driven by an electric motor (Figure 13-25).

Problems. There is almost nothing to go wrong with a diaphragm pump. If the pump fails to prime, suspect an air leak in the suction hose or improperly seated valves. A less likely possibility is a ruptured diaphragm.

Valve problems generally arise as a result of pieces of trash lodging in the valves and holding them open. Chemicals also swell up the rubber flaps, which either fail to seat properly or hang up in the open position on the side of the valve housing. In some applications, calcium builds up on

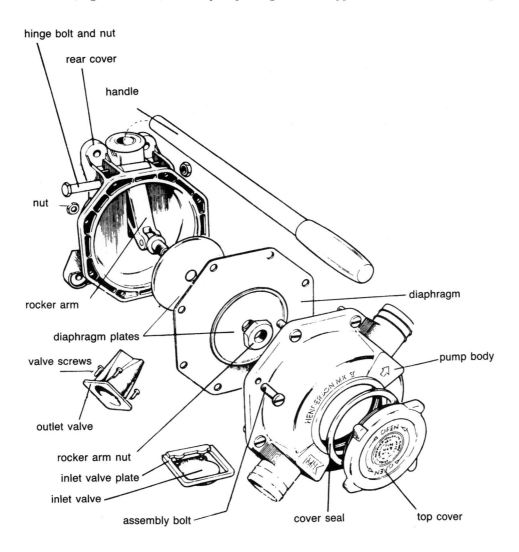

hinge bolt and nut
rear cover
handle
nut
rocker arm
diaphragm plates
valve screws
outlet valve
rocker arm nut
inlet valve plate
inlet valve
assembly bolt
diaphragm
pump body
cover seal
top cover

FIGURE 13-23A. A manual diaphragm pump with an internally mounted handle. *(Whale)*

FIGURE 13-23B. A manual
diaphragm pump with an
externally mounted handle.
(Whale)

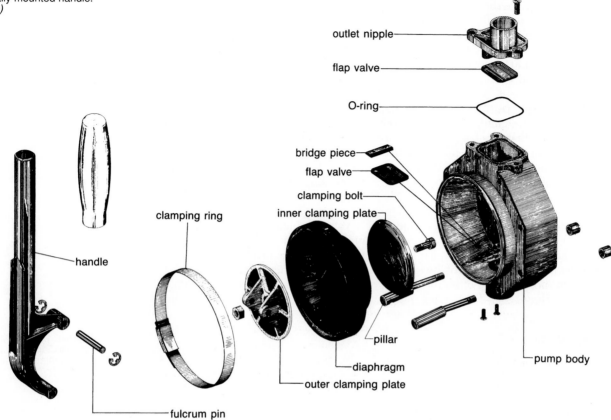

outlet nipple

flap valve

O-ring

bridge piece

flap valve

clamping bolt

inner clamping plate

clamping ring

handle

pillar

diaphragm

outer clamping plate

pump body

fulcrum pin

FIGURE 13-24A. A foot-
operated double-
diaphragm pump. (Whale)

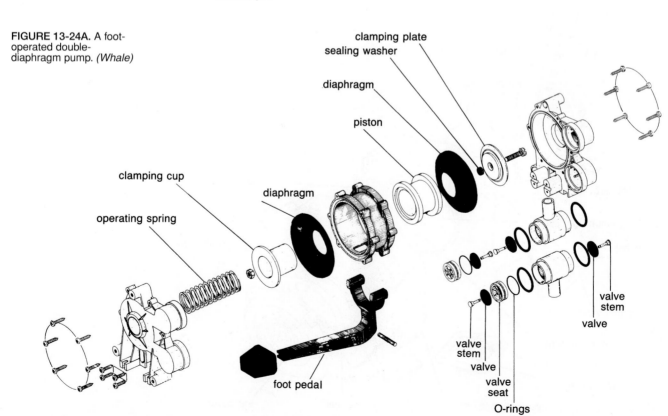

clamping plate

sealing washer

diaphragm

piston

clamping cup

diaphragm

operating spring

foot pedal

valve
stem

valve

valve
stem

valve

valve
seat

O-rings

valve seats (Chapter 12). Eventually fatigue will cause the flaps to tear and come loose.

Diaphragms are constructed of several layers of fabric. Before a complete failure occurs, the layers may delaminate, trapping fluid in between. Complete failure is close. Rarely, one of the diaphragm plates (on each side of the diaphragm) will fracture, and the broken pieces will punch a hole in the diaphragm.

Many pump housings and levers are cast aluminum while hinge pins are stainless steel. Galvanic corrosion and seizure may occur, especially if the pump is rarely used. On some models, pump handles have a nasty habit of collapsing and breaking where they slot into or over the rocker arm (lever arm). Always carry a spare handle.

Overhaul and repair. Almost all diaphragm pumps are simple to dismantle and reassemble. The greatest problems arise with stainless steel fasteners frozen in aluminum housings; they often shear off when you try to undo them (see Appendix B, Freeing Frozen Parts and Fasteners).

Diaphragms are variously retained by screwed-in retaining plates, slotted clamping rings, and large hose clamps (Jubilee clips). On either side of a diaphragm is a plate, held together with one central bolt or with several screws. Two things are important when fitting a new diaphragm: (1) make sure that all seating surfaces are spotlessly clean; and (2) properly line up the lever (fork) pivot point on the outer plate with the lever (fork) before tightening down the diaphragm-retaining device. Where a diaphragm is held with a retaining ring and a number of screws, tighten the screws evenly, alternating side to side.

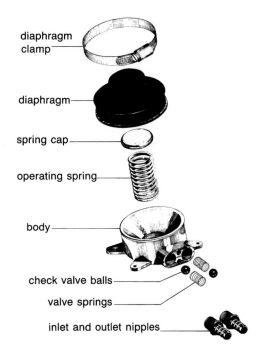

FIGURE 13-24B. A foot-operated single-diaphragm pump. *(Whale)*

diaphragm clamp

diaphragm

spring cap

operating spring

body

check valve balls

valve springs

inlet and outlet nipples

Some valves are changed by unscrewing the valve ports from the outside of the pump body (the hoses must first come off); access to others is from inside the pump body (the diaphragm normally must be removed). Valves are variously retained by valve plates, *bridge pieces*, and clips. Remember, the key points are: (1) scrupulously clean all mating surfaces; (2) make sure the valves are inserted the *right way up* (inlet valves flapping inward; outlet valves outward; joker valves on the discharge side with the duckbill

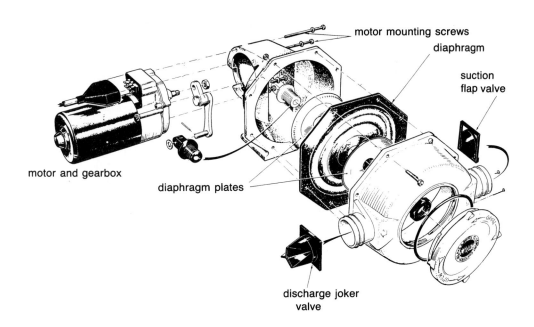

motor mounting screws

diaphragm

suction flap valve

motor and gearbox

diaphragm plates

discharge joker valve

FIGURE 13-25. An electrified manual diaphragm pump. This is the same pump as shown in Figure 13-23A, with the exception of a modified rocker arm and a rear housing adapted to take a motor. *(Blakes Lavac Taylors)*

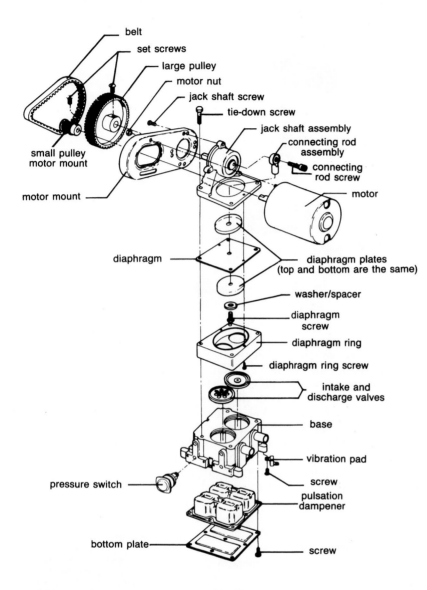

Belt-Driven Pump

- belt
- set screws
- large pulley
- motor nut
- jack shaft screw
- tie-down screw
- jack shaft assembly
- connecting rod assembly
- connecting rod screw
- motor
- small pulley
- motor mount
- motor mount
- diaphragm
- diaphragm plates (top and bottom are the same)
- washer/spacer
- diaphragm screw
- diaphragm ring
- diaphragm ring screw
- intake and discharge valves
- base
- vibration pad
- screw
- pulsation dampener
- pressure switch
- bottom plate
- screw

FIGURE 13-26A. Exploded views of typical PAR diaphragm pumps—belt driven and directly driven. (ITT/Jabsco)

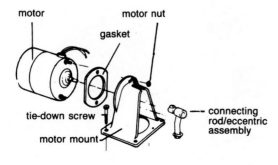

Direct Drive Pump

- motor
- motor nut
- gasket
- tie-down screw
- connecting rod/eccentric assembly
- motor mount

facing *away* from the pump); and (3) make sure the valves are in the *right way around* (some valve housings are asymmetrical—if the valves are inserted improperly, they either will not open or will hang up on the valve housing).

Electric diaphragm pumps. These pumps are widely used in pressurized freshwater and saltwater washdown systems (Figures 13-26A, 13-26B, and 13-26C) and sometimes as bilge, shower, and effluent pumps. In a pressurized water system, the pump is likely to be fitted with a check valve on the discharge side, a pressure switch, an accumulator tank, and possibly a low-tank-level switch. (Note that the latest generation of freshwater pumps has no accumulator. Instead, the speed of the pump motor is regulated to maintain a constant pressure.) None of these is likely in other applications. The following troubleshooting sections refer specifically to pressurized freshwater systems, but cover most other situations.

Pump fails to operate. Check the voltage at the motor (Chapter 4). If there is no voltage, bypass the pressure switch (see the High-Pressure Switches section below). If the pump now runs, the switch is defective. Since these are mostly sealed units, the switch will need replacing (if not sealed, check the points for pitting, burning, or corrosion). If the pressure switch is OK, there may be a low-tank-level switch that has cut out. If the voltage at the motor is OK, check the motor itself (Chapter 7). Some motors have a high-temperature switch that may have tripped—if so, push the reset button, which will be somewhere on the motor housing.

Pump operates but no water flows. First check to see if the motor, if externally mounted, is turning the pump—the drive belt or coupling may be broken, the connecting rod may be loose, etc. If the pump itself is operating, open all faucets to reduce any back pressure on the pump. Check the water tank level, especially if the boat is heeled. If the pump has a suction strainer, inspect it. In some situations, the suction line may have an in-line check valve or foot valve—make sure it is not plugged or stuck shut. The suction hose may be kinked or plugged. Any air leaks (loose connections) will stop the pump from priming. Finally, there may be problems with the pump itself—most probably trash stuck under the valves, but perhaps a hole in the diaphragm (see the Dismantling and Repairing section below). Break loose the discharge line and try blowing back through the pump. If this can be done, there is definitely a problem with the valves or diaphragm.

Pump operates roughly, noisily, and vibrates. The suction line may be kinked, plugged, or too

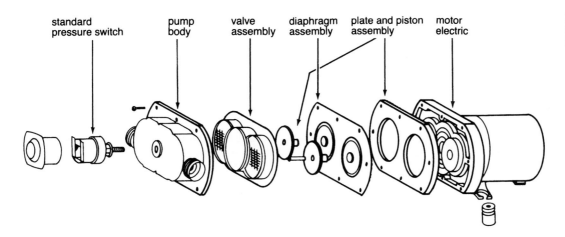

FIGURE 13-26B. An in-line electric double-diaphragm pump. *(ITT/Jabsco)*

standard pressure switch

pump body

valve assembly

diaphragm assembly

plate and piston assembly

motor electric

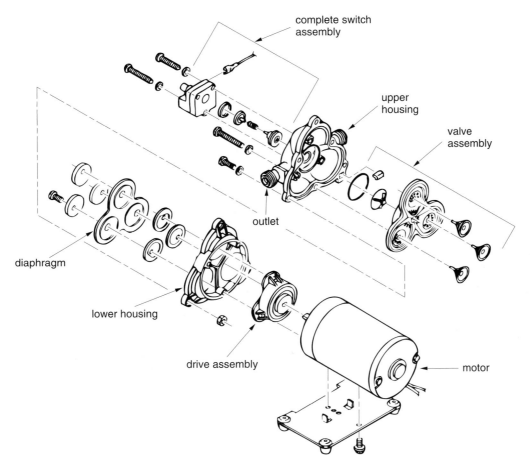

complete switch assembly

upper housing

valve assembly

outlet

diaphragm

lower housing

drive assembly

motor

FIGURE 13-26C. A triple-diaphragm pump. Inside the lower housing is a wobble plate that oscillates when the motor is running. The oscillating plate drives three separate sections of the diaphragm backward and forward, pulling water in and out of three separate chambers in the upper housing, each with its own valves. The chambers are supplied by a common inlet and discharge into a common outlet. The same principles can be used with any number of cylinders (four-cylinder pumps are quite common). *(Shurflo)*

small, thus restricting flow, but more likely the pump itself is the problem. The pump must be securely mounted with vibration-absorbing pads. Loose drive pulleys and/or excessive play in the connecting rod and various bearings on pumps with external motors could be causing the noisy vibration; check them and tighten if necessary. Some pumps have a rubber *pulsation dampener*, or a *surge chamber*, designed to smooth out flow through the pump; as a last resort, take the bottom plate off the pump and check this dampener to see if it is deformed or ruptured (see the Pulsation Dampener Replacement section below).

Pump fails to cut off when faucets (taps) are closed. Check the water tank; it is probably empty! If not, the pump may be air-bound. Open a faucet, allow enough water to flow through so that the pump is primed, and close the faucet. The pressure switch may be stuck "on"—make sure its points are open (if accessible). Last, check the voltage at the motor—a low

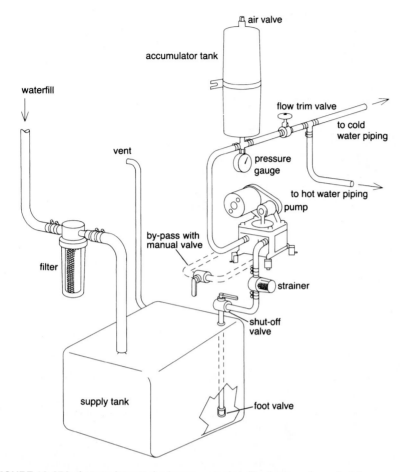

FIGURE 13-27A. Accumulator tanks (pressure tanks), like the one shown in this schematic of a typical onboard pressurized water system, serve as a water reservoir, providing pressurized water between pump cycles and reducing the frequency with which the pump must run. These tanks are susceptible to waterlogging—a reduction in tank air volume as the initial charge of air dissolves into the water. This increases pump cycling and can lead to system damage. *(Jim Sollers)*

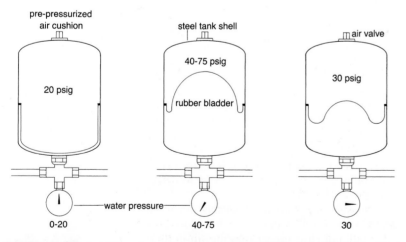

FIGURE 13-27B. A captive-air, or prepressurized, accumulator tank. When the pump starts, water enters the reservoir. At maximum preset pressure, the system is filled, and the pump shuts off. When water is used, pressure in the chamber forces water into the system. The pump stays off until the minimum pressure setting is reached; then the pump turns on. By isolating the water within a rubber bladder, waterlogging is largely eliminated. The air charge is readily renewed with a bicycle pump. *(ITT/Jabsco)*

voltage will cause the pump to operate slowly and perhaps not come to pressure. The motor will be in danger of burning up.

Pump cycles on and off when faucets are closed. Water may be leaking from a loose connection, an open faucet, or perhaps a toilet if freshwater is used for flushing (e.g., a VacuFlush). Otherwise pressure is bleeding off the system *back through the pump*—the discharge check valve (if fitted) or valves are leaking (see below).

Pump cycles rapidly on and off in use; water knocks in the piping. Most pressurized water systems use an *accumulator* tank (Figures 13-27A and 13-27B; some modern pumps do not—see the note on page 598). This is an air-filled tank that tees into the discharge side of the pump. As the pump operates, it fills the tank with water, compressing the air within it until the pressure reaches the cutout setting on the pump pressure switch. When a faucet is opened, the compressed air forces water back out of the tank and through the faucet until the pressure has fallen to the cut-in point on the pump pressure switch. The pump then kicks in and recharges the accumulator tank. The net effect is to reduce the amount of cycling on and off that the pump does, which reduces wear on both the pump and the pressure switch points.

Two types of accumulator tank are in use. The first is just a simple tank. The second has a built-in rubber diaphragm with a tire valve on the outside of the tank. Air is pumped in through the valve to pressurize the tank (generally to around 20 psi; the pressure should be approximately the same as the *cut-in pressure setting* on the pressure switch). Water enters the tank on the other side of the diaphragm, forcing the diaphragm in against the air cushion.

Both tanks can become *waterlogged*. The simple tank becomes so when the initial tankful of air is slowly dissolved and carried away by the water entering and leaving the tank; the diaphragm tank is affected if the pressure bleeds off the air side of the diaphragm or the diaphragm ruptures. In either case, the pump will cycle on and off at shorter and shorter intervals. This causes sudden pressure changes in the plumbing, which in turn not only damages pumps but can produce some surprisingly loud knocks (sometimes called *water hammer*).

Turn off the pump and *open a faucet to bleed all pressure off the system*. The simple tank must be completely drained to renew the air charge; if it has no drain plug, it may be necessary to break the connection loose at its base. The diaphragm type is pumped back up again, generally with a bicycle pump.

Excessive pressure. Some shoreside hookups have pressures that will damage valves and diaphragms. Most pumps are protected with a built-in check valve in the discharge fitting. Even so, always fit a pressure regulator (to around 35 psi) on the shoreside connection.

Dismantling and repairing. Turn off the power and bleed down the system through the faucets.

Pumps with external motors: Removing four screws allows the complete drive and diaphragm assembly to be lifted off, providing access to the valves. Inspect new valves carefully—if one has a small hole in it, this is the intake valve. Be sure to put in new valves the same way up as the old ones.

Disconnect the diaphragm by undoing the screws in the diaphragm-retaining ring and pulling off the ring, which provides access to the central bolt or screw holding the diaphragm and its plates together. If fitting anything other than a circular diaphragm, take care to align it properly so that it does not get twisted. When replacing the diaphragm assembly, make sure the surfaces are clean, and tighten the screws evenly.

The discharge fitting in some pumps has a check valve, which generally cannot be repaired. In the event of failure, the whole fitting must be replaced. Remove the old fitting, carefully noting its orientation so that you will put in the new one the right way around!

Pumps with internal motors: The motor is generally held to the pump head with three or four screws, while another three or four screws hold the cover on the pump. Removing either is easy. Take off the cover for valve and diaphragm access and replacement.

Pulsation dampener replacement (pumps with external motors). Mark the base plate(s) and pump body so that they can be put back properly. Remove all the screws from the base plate(s). Pull out the rubber pulsation dampener(s) and check for deformation, ruptures, or cuts. When replacing the base-plate screws, first tighten the center screws on each side and then work out toward the corners. Do not overtighten.

Winterizing. Pumps with pulsation dampeners generally can freeze without damage, but the rest of the water system cannot, so winterize the whole system. Either drain the pump and all its piping, or disconnect the suction line from the tank and pump *propylene glycol* antifreeze through it.

Note: Automotive antifreeze is made from ethylene glycol and is poisonous—*do not use it in freshwater systems.* Propylene glycol has almost identical antifreeze properties and is safe to use. Flush the system at the start of the new season. It can take quite a bit of flushing to get the taste of antifreeze out of the system; instead of adding antifreeze, it's preferable to fully drain the system, if you can do so without the risk of pockets of water freezing and doing damage.

Pump Switches

Pressure Switches

High-pressure switches. High-pressure switches are used in freshwater systems and on washdown pumps. The switch opens the electric circuit to a pump at a preset pressure, then closes it once the pressure falls by a certain amount. Increasingly these switches are sealed units either screwed or built into the body of a pump. They are not user serviceable or repairable—a failed switch is simply replaced.

To determine if a switch has failed, you must access and bypass its wiring so that the pump is connected directly to the electrical supply. A pump can be run with its switch bypassed, but a failure to turn it off just one time after use will result in a blown-out system or a burned-out pump motor.

WARNING: If the pump is AC powered, turn off the power before accessing the switch terminals. REMEMBER, AC POWER CAN KILL. If you are at all unsure about what you are doing, don't do it!

Older and larger pumps tend to have adjustable switches. A central retaining screw allows you to lift off the cover, exposing the points and two adjusting screws. Dirty, pitted, and/or corroded points are a frequent source of trouble; inspect them and all wiring terminals closely. Clean the points with a fine grade of wet-or-dry sandpaper (400 grit). Check the operation of the points by prying them apart and pushing them together with a screwdriver. There may be a small spark; a large spark indicates a problem with the points or the pump motor (it may be shorted). If the points close but the pump fails to come on, bridge the wire terminals with a jumper wire to see if the switch is defective (observe all necessary safety precautions with AC-powered pumps).

The two adjusting screws control the pump cut-in and cutout pressures. Generally, turning down one screw increases both pressures; turning down the other raises the cutout pressure without altering the cut-in pressure. The adjustment procedure, therefore, is to set the cut-in pressure with the first screw and fine-tune the cutout pressure with the second screw.

Low-pressure switches. Low-pressure switches are mechanically similar to high-pressure switches, although their function is different. They are mounted on the discharge side of a pump. They break the circuit when pressures are abnormally low, as would happen if a tank ran dry (e.g., 6 psi on a system set to maintain 20 to 40 psi). A low-pressure shutdown switch may well be built into the same unit as a pressure-regulating switch. Adjustment and points maintenance follow high-pressure switch procedures. Once tripped, or on initial start-up of a system (before pressure has built up), some have to be reset manually.

Level Switches

Level switches are used primarily in bilge pumping circuits but also for some shower sumps and similar applications. There is much to be said for having a manual switch on bilge circuits, since it forces you to regularly check the state of the bilge. But in practice the boating public demands an automatic switch that is generally backed up with a manual override (this override is, in any case, a requirement of the ABYC standards for small craft, which also require that automatic switches have a visual means—generally an LED—of indicating when they are turned on).

By far the most common switch for bilge pumps is a float switch; in addition there are switches operated by air pressure, and at least three forms of electronic switches. The variety of switches is testimony to the fact that no one type has been found to be universally satisfactory in bilge pumping applications. It is instructive to see why this is the case, starting with float switches.

Float switches. The concept of a float switch is simple. A rising water level lifts a float, which is used to turn on a switch. A falling level drops the float, which turns off the switch. Most of these switches have the float on a hinge. In many, there is a sealed vial that contains a drop of mercury (a highly conductive liquid metal). When the float rises, the mercury runs to one end of the vial, closing a circuit between two terminals to turn on the pump. When the float drops, the mercury runs the other way, opening the circuit (Figure 13-28).

Mercury switches are environmentally unfriendly and can develop problems if the drop of mercury breaks up, reducing its current-carrying capability. The switch heats up, melting the insulation on nearby wiring, which may cause stray-current leaks into the bilge water and, in any case, will cause the insulation to go hard, reducing its flexibility. So instead of mercury, some switches use a rolling ball that mechanically triggers the switch (the ball itself is not part of the electrical circuit). With either type, it is important to match the current rating (ampacity) of the switch to the pump in question. Many lightweight switches are simply not rated to carry the current drawn by higher-capacity pumps, in which case the switch becomes the weak link in the system, and this is before taking into account the effects of a locked-rotor situation.

The problem with any switch in which the wires are carried into the float is that the wires constantly flex or twist as the float moves up and down, with an obvious risk of eventual failure, especially if the insulation has become hard. One way around this is to mount the switch in the fixed part of the unit with a sealed diaphragm over the switch. As the hinged float moves up

FIGURE 13-28. How mercury float switches work. A rise in fluid level causes the buoyant end of the switch to rise. The electrically conductive mercury contained in the switch cavity (A) flows to the bottom of the switch, where it bridges two terminals, completing the circuit (B) and turning on the pump. *(Jim Sollers)*

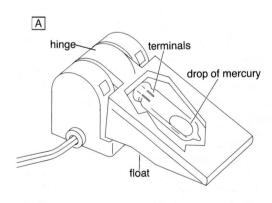

hinge
terminals
drop of mercury
float

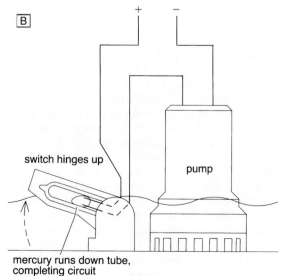

switch hinges up
pump
mercury runs down tube, completing circuit

and down with changing fluid levels, a lever on its base operates the switch. The wires themselves remain static. But this still leaves a hinge, which in itself is vulnerable. As we, and many others, have found, a relatively small piece of trash caught in the hinge can jam the switch in either the OFF or ON position. Some switches include a cover to keep debris away from the switch, but since the cover must have holes to allow the free flow of water, this is only a partial solution to the problem.

A more foolproof approach to float switch construction, used in the Ultra Pumpswitches manufactured by Ultra Safety Systems (www.ultrasafetysystems.com), is to have the float riding on a vertical shaft inside a plastic tube with holes that allow water in and out. There is no hinge, and the switch itself is at the top of the tube, above normal water levels and enclosed in a watertight housing. It is triggered magnetically anytime the float rises up the tube.

Switch location. The location of a switch in relation to its pump is important. If a switch is mounted in a position where it is offset from its pump, when the boat is heeled on one tack the switch will not respond until considerably more water is in the bilge than is needed for a level-state response. While on the other tack, there is a very real danger that the switch will stay energized after the pump has sucked itself dry, causing the pump to run continuously, which creates a heavy drain on the batteries and risks pump failure. To minimize these problems, always mount a float switch as close to its pump as possible and in the same fore-and-aft plane. In practice, many are simply clipped into the base of the pump, but in this case, it is essential to ensure that the switch is aligned fore and aft. If it is set to one side of the pump, the pump will definitely run dry on one tack or the other.

The very nature of a float switch is such that the change in water level between turning on and off is only 1 or 2 inches at best. Even if a switch is mounted in the same fore-and-aft plane as its pump, when the boat is pounding into a head sea or rolling from side to side, the action of a small amount of water surging backward and forward in the bilge can flick the switch on and off until eventually something fails (the wiring, the switch points or motor, or the hinge on the switch). This situation also creates an unnecessary drain on the batteries.

A similar but even more annoying condition occurs when the bilge pump and switch are installed in a deep, narrow sump, with a moderately long discharge hose from the pump to the overboard through-hull. Every time the pump is shut down, the water in the hose will flow back down into the bilge, raising the level of the bilge

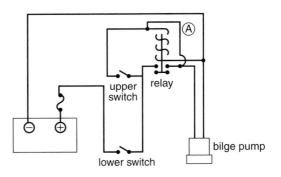

FIGURE 13-29. A bilge pump circuit that will eliminate short-cycling.

water—sometimes to the point at which the pump kicks back on (short-cycles). The pump keeps on cycling until the battery is dead. You can alleviate this condition in several different ways:

- Put a check valve in the discharge hose. As noted previously, these valves are prone to failure, so this is the least desirable way to solve the short-cycling problem.

- The Ultra Pumpswitches come with a series of operating differentials from as small as ¾ inch up to 2½ inches, with greater differentials (up to 1 to 2 feet) available as a special-order item. The greater the operating differential, the less the likelihood of short-cycling.

- Rule's Rule-Mate pumps include what Rule calls a "spongeability" feature. Essentially, the pump is kept running for 15 seconds after the float switch would normally shut it down, which drives the last of the water out of the bilge. This feature is especially useful on modern boats with flat bilges since it helps ensure a drier bilge, which results in less water flowing up the sides of the boat when it is heeled.

- A reader (unfortunately, I have lost his or her name) suggests wiring two float switches as shown in Figure 13-29. A rising water level closes the lower switch but does not start the pump because the circuit is broken by the (open) relay. When the level gets a little higher, the second switch closes, completing the circuit to the pump and also energizing the relay, which completes the circuit for the lower switch. When the level drops low enough to open the upper switch, the wire labeled "A" maintains power to the relay, keeping the relay energized and the lower switch circuit closed. The circuit to the pump is not broken until the level falls low enough to open the lower switch. At this point, the pump discharge drains back and the lower switch closes once again, but the pump remains off until the level rises enough to close the upper switch. The relative positions of the two switches can be adjusted to ensure that short-cycling does not occur.

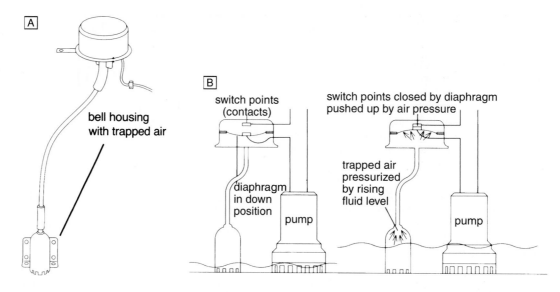

FIGURE 13-30. How pneumatic level switches work. When the fluid level rises, air trapped in the bell housing (A) is pressurized and pushes in the diaphragm. This closes the switch points and completes the circuit (B), turning on the pump. *(Jim Sollers)*

bell housing with trapped air

switch points (contacts)

diaphragm in down position

pump

switch points closed by diaphragm pushed up by air pressure

trapped air pressurized by rising fluid level

pump

Air switches. These sorts of difficulties with float switches have led to the development of other kinds of switches. An air switch has a bell housing, which is installed with the open end facing down. A length of tubing connects the top of the housing to a diaphragm within a separate switch housing (Figure 13-30). Rising water in the bilge first closes off the bottom of the bell housing, trapping air within it, then raises the air pressure within the housing. This in turn moves the diaphragm to operate the switch (this is the same mechanism used for a level switch on a washing machine).

The clear advantages of such an approach are that there is no electric wiring in the bilge, and there are no moving parts in the bilge to jam or break. But there are drawbacks. Once again, the range between "on" and "off" is quite narrow (less than 2 inches), and the unit must be installed on the same fore-and-aft axis as the pump. In turbulent conditions, water sloshing around the bilge can displace the air in the bell housing, with the result that the switch is not activated until the water level is higher than normal. If the tubing from the bell housing to the switch has *any dips at any angle of heel*, water can gather at the low spot, effectively blocking the action of the switch. And if the tubing gets kinked, crushed, or holed, the switch will fail to operate.

Electronic switches. An electronic switch avoids these problems but introduces new ones!

Conductivity sensors. The traditional electronic switch has two stainless steel sensors mounted a small distance apart. If the water level rises to the level of the sensors, it forms a circuit between them that activates the bilge pump switch. When the water level falls below the sensors, the circuit is broken, opening the

switch. This seems straightforward enough, but in real life the conductivity of the liquids the sensors are likely to encounter varies widely, which causes difficulties. Fresh water, particularly clean rainwater or condensate water from air-conditioning units, has a very low conductivity, whereas salt water, especially dirty salt water, is highly conductive. Oil is nonconductive, whereas some bilge cleaners are not only quite conductive but will also form a slimy film across the sensors.

If the sensor circuitry is set to react to fresh water, the switch may well end up staying "on" permanently when coated with bilge cleaner. On the other hand, if the sensitivity is reduced, a coating of oil may add enough resistance to cause the switch to stay off permanently. (Note that the different conductivity of oil enables some sophisticated sensors to differentiate between bilge water and petroleum products, turning off the pump if hydrocarbons are encountered and thus avoiding a potential oil discharge.) A Teflon coating on some sensors helps reduce the extent to which various contaminants can adhere to the sensors, improving reliability. But even so, a balancing act still has to be struck in terms of sensitivity settings. If the sensors are not kept reasonably clean, the switch may malfunction.

Light-activated switches. Instead of measuring conductivity, some electronic sensors use a beam of light to detect the presence of fluids. In a typical unit, the sensor emits a short pulse of light at timed intervals (for example, every 30 seconds). In the absence of fluid, the light is reflected back by a special lens, and the system remains quiescent. When the lens is covered by fluid, the light is refracted through the fluid, which triggers the control unit into activating the pump. These sensors will work in just about any fluid, including heavily contaminated oil. Depending on the complexity of a system, multiple sensors can be used to operate more than one pump, to sound a high-bilge-level alarm, and so on.

Time delays. Assuming functioning electronic sensors, it is no good having the pump come on the second the sensors detect fluid. For one thing, the level would immediately drop, turning the pump back off and causing the pump to short-cycle; for another, any surging of the water in the bilge would cause the switch to repeatedly flick on and off. Some sort of a built-in delay is needed. This can be achieved with sensors at different heights, with the higher one activating the circuit and the lower one breaking it. The other way is to program the unit so that a single sensor must be *continuously* immersed for a certain length of time (e.g., 12 seconds) before the switch is activated, with the switch remaining activated for a certain length of time (e.g., 12 seconds once again) after the sensor is no longer immersed.

Load-sensing switches. Load-sensing switches are a variant of electronic switches. They track fluid levels through the current draw of the bilge pump motor. The sensing unit and switch are built into the pump itself. A timer turns the pump on at preset intervals (every 2½ minutes in the case of Rule's Automatic pumps). If there is water in the bilge, the pump will have to work harder than if there is no water, in which case the motor's current draw will be higher than in a no-load situation. The sensing unit measures the current draw to determine whether to keep the pump running or not. Once it senses a no-load condition, it shuts down the pump.

These automatic bilge pumps have certain obvious advantages. Since the sensing unit and switch are built into the pump itself, there is no need for any external switching device, which makes installation simpler and immediately solves all problems with offset switches and fluctuating (surging) water levels. The principal disadvantage is that the pump is cycling on and off repeatedly whether there is a leak into the bilge or not (every 2½ minutes is 24 times an hour, 576 times a day, 4,032 times a week, 17,472 times a month, and 209,664 times a year!). This is bound to accelerate pump and switch wear, as well as impose an unnecessary drain on the batteries (albeit a small one—for a 12-volt, 1,100 gph pump, Rule claims a 0.25 Ah drain per day). A less obvious but perhaps more serious problem is that if the pump impeller develops an increased resistance to movement (such as might happen with pet hairs wrapped around the impeller or some other obstruction), the sensor

FIGURE 13-31. A load-sensing circuit in a Rule pump.

will interpret this as water in the bilge and keep the pump running constantly. It won't take long to flatten a battery.

Rule's Platinum pumps have a similar load-sensing circuit but with more sophisticated electronics (Figure 13-31). If no load (water) is detected for five consecutive cycles, instead of being activated every 2 minutes, the pump is activated every 10 minutes. The pump itself is initially activated at reduced power and only switches to full power if a load is detected. The circuitry has built-in overload protection.

Hybrid switches. The Rule-Mate pumps already mentioned have an internal float switch that turns the pump on but does not turn it off. The OFF function is controlled by a load-sensing circuit with a built-in 15-second time delay (hence the spongeability function; Figure 13-32). This is a useful set of characteristics, but in common with all load-sensing circuits, if the impeller gets fouled, there is a risk of the pump staying on until the battery is flat.

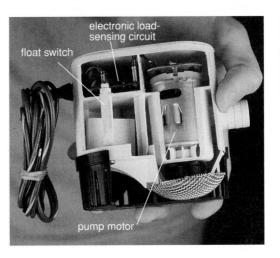

FIGURE 13-32. A Rule pump with a float switch to turn it on (lower left of the pump) and an electronic load-sensing circuit to turn it off (in the watertight chamber above the float switch).

"Smart" circuit breakers. Modern solid-state circuit breakers can track current (amperage) flows and can have programmable capabilities. By the time this edition is published, we will have the first generation of bilge pump circuit breakers that turn on periodically and measure the current flow, as with automatic bilge pumps. If the current flow is above a certain level, the pump will be kept on until the current flow drops (indicating a dry bilge). If the current level goes too high, indicating a jammed impeller, the pump will be turned off. The circuit breaker will have a memory chip that stores how often the pump is turned on and off, and for how long, so that the operator can display this information elsewhere and get a sense of how much water is coming into the boat. There will be various programmable alarms (e.g., jammed impeller, pump stays on longer than normal, etc.). The circuit breaker itself will be well above the bilge water, eliminating all existing problems with water penetration of switch seals and electronic circuits.

Choosing a switch. All of the above just goes to show that no matter the quality of a bilge pump installation and the ingenuity of pump and switch designers there are still plenty of failure modes! So at this point it would be nice to tie things together by laying down some prescriptions concerning which pumps and switches are best to use in which applications.

The truth is, properly installed, they all work in most situations, although generally with nowhere near the anticipated pumping capacity. In terms of the installation, the keys to remember are:

- Make sure the pump discharge is siphon proof.
- Keep all hoses as short and straight as possible.
- Use the largest-diameter hose feasible on the discharge side.
- Size the wiring and switches for the maximum current rating of the pump.
- Properly fuse the circuit.
- Keep all electrical connections above the highest water level.
- Position switches so that they work properly at all conceivable angles of heel.

One general point is clear: *Putting an expensive boat in the hands of a cheap float switch is fool-hardy.*

Beyond this, it is important to understand the potential weaknesses of a given installation so that you don't become overreliant on it. Fundamental aspects of housekeeping and seamanship must

---

A Personal Experience

For years we had nothing more than a couple of manual diaphragm pumps to empty the bilge. It was part of our ship routine to check the bilge each watch and to report any water to the captain. We would be immediately aware of leaks and could take steps to find and fix them. When we laid up the boat afloat, I tightened down the stuffing box to eliminate all drips. We would come back after a protracted absence to find dust in the bilges.

But then one year we decided to leave *Nada* for an indefinite period anchored out in a secluded bay on the island of Culebra. I began to think of all those "what ifs . . ." What if the packing began to drip? What if rainwater somehow found its way belowdecks? What if the cockpit drain hoses sprang a leak? And so on. So I bought and installed a 12-volt submersible bilge pump and float switch.

We returned after three months to find dust in the bilges as usual. The pump had clearly not kicked on even one time. We resumed our cruise. For a while we left the pump turned off and continued to check the bilges each watch. If water was present, instead of pumping manually, we simply flicked the pump switch. After a month or two we got lazy and put the switch to automatic. Then we began to get lazy about checking the bilge each watch . . .

Then there came a dark and dirty night, when we were beating into a stiff wind and uncomfortable seas with the side decks constantly awash. I swung down the companionway hatch to check the chart and went flying as my feet shot out from under me, skidding across a cabin sole awash and made as slippery as an ice rink by a slick of dirty engine oil.

I picked myself up and began cranking the manual pump. The water receded rapidly—wherever it was coming from, it was not a serious leak. With the bilge dry, I found that the float switch was jammed in the OFF position, with water siphoning in through the pump discharge hose, which, although it vented at the level of the gunwales, was submerged due to our extreme angle of heel.

Ours is not an unusual story. If you hang around any marina for any length of time, you are certain to hear of some electric bilge pump failure. We were left with a clinging, greasy film of dirty engine oil to clean up but no other damage. Many others are not so lucky.

---

still be stressed. The bilge must be kept clean, objects must be properly stowed, and above all, it should be a part of your ship routine to check the bilge on every watch. In the sidebar opposite I describe a fairly typical bilge pump failure of ours. Had I followed my own advice, we would have discovered this failure well before it caused any problems!

Watermakers

In previous editions of this book I deliberately omitted watermakers because I felt the cost per gallon of water produced (when amortized over the life of a watermaker), the energy required to make water, and the amount of maintenance involved was out of proportion to the benefit accruing to sailors. Over the past decade, all three things have changed:

- The cost of water in many parts of the world has gone up, sometimes considerably, making watermakers more cost effective.
- With some watermakers, the energy needed to make water has been dramatically reduced.
- The amount of maintenance associated with watermakers has gone down considerably.

Given these changes I am putting a watermaker on our new boat.

Benefits of Watermakers

A watermaker has the following benefits:

- It frees you from relying on sometimes dubious sources of shoreside supply. The nature of the watermaking process is such that the *product* water (what goes into a boat's water tank) is purer than that from most municipal water supplies. In particular, an undamaged watermaker membrane will strain out all bacteria and almost all viruses. Additional health protection can be provided with UV sterilizers.
- As long as sufficient water is carried to support the crew on a boat's longest passage (as a backup if the watermaker breaks down), considerably less water needs to be carried on board, which reduces both the volume occupied by tanks and the weight.
- A watermaker almost always results in valued lifestyle improvements, notably the ability to take long freshwater showers. It is one of those devices whose results are somewhat addictive (like pressurized hot water and refrigeration); once experienced, there is no going back!
- For many boatowners, the ability to rinse the boat down with fresh water is much appreci-

ated and also unquestionably extends the life of both the gelcoat finish and much deck equipment.

How They Work

In essence, a watermaker is a very simple device. The core component is a membrane that has a microscopic pore structure large enough to allow water molecules to pass through it, but small enough to block salt, minerals, bacteria, viruses, etc. In order to force water through such a membrane, a great deal of pressure is required, generally on the order of 600 to 800 psi (42 to 56 kg per cm^2). Manufacturing pumps that can generate this kind of pressure is relatively simple, but it has taken space-age technology to create membranes with the requisite consistency in the pore structure and to assemble them in a manner that will withstand the necessary pressure in the system over time without fouling.

Given the microscopic size of the pores in the membranes, fouling is an ever-present possibility. In order to prevent this, all watermakers have a prefiltration step for the *source* water (incoming seawater). Only a small percentage of the source water is converted to product water, with the rest (known as *brine*) used to flush the surface of the membrane and keep it clean. The brine is then discharged overboard.

Membranes. Worldwide, there are only a handful of membrane manufacturers. Most of those found in the marine marketplace are manufactured by FilmTec (www.filmtec.com), a subsidiary of Dow Chemical. Membranes are designed to work at a certain flow rate and pressure. Significant deviations from these design parameters will result in lower-quality product water (higher levels of dissolved solids) and shortened membrane life (increased fouling).

With a traditional watermaker (but not low-energy pumps—see below), a number of things can affect the flow rate through a membrane and the pressure in the system, notably the salinity of the source water and its temperature. At any given pressure, the lower the salinity, the greater the percentage of the source water that will be converted to product water. If the pressure is not adjusted

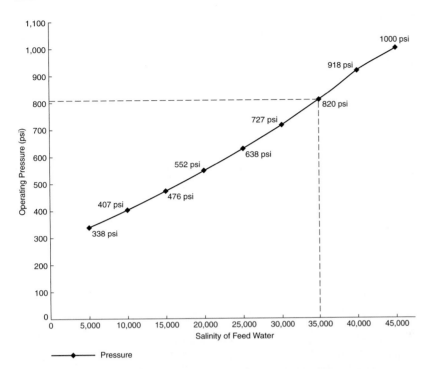

FIGURE 13-33A. Operating pressure as a function of salinity, assuming the standard seawater temperature (77°F/25°C). The curved line represents rated output. The standard test salinity is 35,000 parts per million (ppm) of total dissolved solids. At this salinity, it takes an operating pressure of 820 psi to achieve rated output. As the salinity falls, so too does the pressure required to achieve rated output (e.g., at 15,000 ppm total dissolved solids, the pressure only needs to be 476 psi). As the salinity rises, so too does the pressure needed to maintain rated output (e.g., at 45,000 ppm total dissolved solids, the pressure must be 1,000 psi). *(Sea Recovery)*

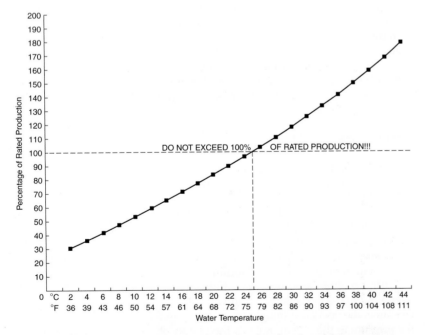

FIGURE 13-33B. Conventional watermaker output as a function of the seawater temperature at the standard operating pressure (820 psi). The standard seawater rating temperature is 77°F/25°C. At higher water temperatures and the standard operating pressure, the output will rise above the rated output. The operating pressure needs to be dropped to keep the output down to 100% of rated output. *(Sea Recovery)*

downward to lower the ratio of product water to brine, inadequate membrane flushing occurs, and membrane life is shortened. Warmer source water also increases the ratio of product water to brine, while lower temperatures decrease it. Once again, adjustments in the pressure are necessary if an optimal ratio is to be maintained (Figures 13-33A, 13-33B, and 13-33C).

Aside from changes in salinity and temperature, any kind of fouling of the membrane will clearly impair its performance. Fouling may take the form of fine particles of silt, oil, and chemicals, which make their way through the filtration system, or biofouling. Biofouling is especially likely if a watermaker is left unused for more than a week.

Filtration. From the above, it is clear that effective filtration of the source water is a key component of any watermaker. The extent of the filtration process varies markedly from one watermaker to another. At its most basic, it may consist of a raw-water strainer and a single 20-micron filter with a replaceable pleated synthetic element. At its most complete, it is likely to include the raw-water strainer, maybe a plankton filter, two or more particle filters (with the final one having a mesh size as low as 5 microns), and an oil-water separator.

In most systems that have more than minimal filtration, a booster pump is needed to draw the source water into the system and pump it through the filters to the main pump. Without a booster pump, the main pump will be drawing in water under a vacuum and may suck in air, in which case it will cavitate. This can be quite damaging (tiny steam bubbles form and implode, eroding the internal pump surfaces). However, a booster pump adds to the overall energy load.

Better systems have a low-side pressure gauge for detecting when the filters are beginning to plug and a low-pressure shutdown circuit.

The higher the capacity of a unit, the better the filtration and protection circuits are likely to be, and the more tolerant the unit will be of less-than-ideal source water. On the other hand, many of the smaller, energy-efficient watermakers have somewhat marginal filtration and little in the way of protective shutdown circuits. In this case, it behooves the owner to not use these units in silty, contaminated, or brackish water. In fact, many seasoned cruisers restrict watermaker usage to the open ocean.

Z-Guard. The Z-Guard system consists of a filter housing containing an electrode that generates a powerful electrostatic field. The theory is that this puts a positive charge on any particles (mineral or bacterial) in the source water entering the watermaker. This positive charge is said to keep the particles from binding together and sticking to surfaces in the system, including the membrane. In this way, biofouling and scale formation are minimized. Spectra, the manufacturer (www.spectrawatermakers.com), claims that this eliminates the need for pickling watermakers (see below) when they are not in use. Others in the industry believe that the effect of the electrostatic field is short lived, after which the water reverts to its natural state, rendering the system ineffective. (At the time of writing, I don't have enough data to give an opinion on whether or not, and how well, the Z-Guard works.) The units run on 12 volts, pulling 150 mA (3.6 Ah over 24 hours).

Low-energy pumps. All the water passing through a watermaker has to be raised to the necessary operating pressure (600 to 900 psi/42 to 63 kg per cm^2), but the brine is discharged overboard at atmospheric pressure. The pump needed to generate the high operating pressure is the principal energy consumer in the system (in some cases, the only energy consumer). The higher the ratio of product water to source water, the more efficient the process in terms of energy usage, but the greater the risk of membrane fouling. Typically, around 10% of the source water is turned into product water, with the other 90% discharged overboard, although this ratio may be increased to as much as 30% product water and 70% brine.

In a traditional watermaker, the 70% to 90% of source water discharged as brine represents a substantial energy loss since the water has been raised to pressure and is then dumped overboard. A few manufacturers (notably Spectra, Sea Recovery—www.searecovery.com, and Horizon Reverse Osmosis [HRO]—www.hrosystems.com

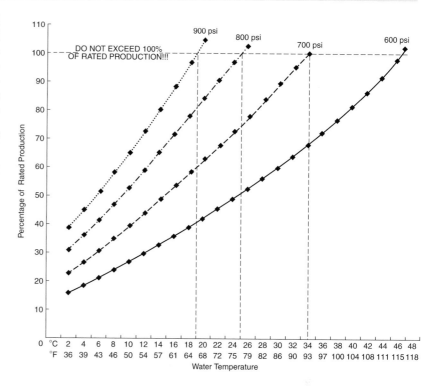

[now owned by Sea Recovery]) have patented processes that capture a considerable amount of the energy contained in the brine, and as a result reduce the overall energy required per gallon of product water produced. In the case of Spectra (all its watermakers), Sea Recovery (the Ultra Whisper watermakers), and HRO (the Seafari Escape watermakers), the energy requirements are as little as *one-third* that of a traditional watermaker.

The technology that makes Spectra and HRO/Sea Recovery watermakers so efficient is very similar (Figures 13-34A, 13-34B, and 13-34C). All systems use a relatively low-pressure

FIGURE 13-33C. Watermaker output as a function of pressure and seawater temperature. Given water of standard salinity, at the standard seawater temperature (77°F/25°C), a pressure of around 800 psi will produce the watermaker's rated output. If the seawater temperature falls to 66°F/19°C, the pressure must rise to 900 psi if the rated output is to be sustained; at a seawater temperature of 93°F/34°C, the pressure must be dropped to 700 psi to keep the output down to rated output. *(Sea Recovery)*

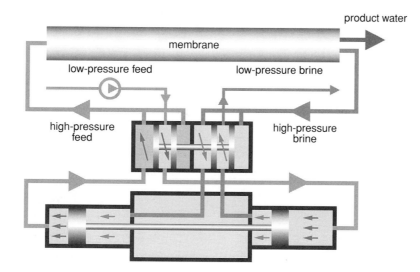

FIGURE 13-34A. An HRO/Sea Recovery Energy Transfer Device (ETD). *(Sea Recovery)*

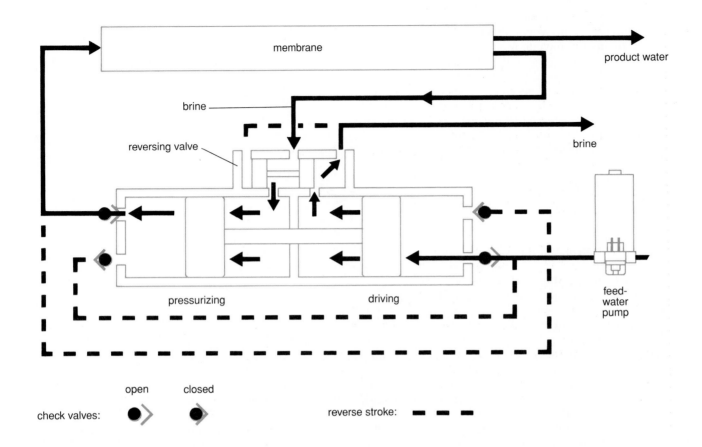

membrane

product water

brine

brine

reversing valve

feed-
water
pump

pressurizing

driving

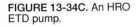

check valves: open   closed   reverse stroke: ▬ ▬ ▬

FIGURE 13-34B. A Spectra Clark Pump (pressure intensifier). *(Jim Sollers, adapted from a drawing courtesy Spectra)*

feed pump (around 100 psi/7 kg per cm²) to pump water into one of two opposed cylinders, each of which contains a piston connected by a common rod. The water entering the first cylinder moves both pistons. Water in the second cylinder is driven into the membrane housing, then from there to the backside of the piston in the second cylinder. When the pistons reach the limit of their travel, the pump output is directed to the second cylinder, driving both pistons back the other way, with the discharge from the membrane housing now switched to the backside of the piston in the first cylinder.

Because of the rod connecting the two cylinders, there is not as much volume on the backsides of the pistons as on the driven sides. This

FIGURE 13-34C. An HRO ETD pump.

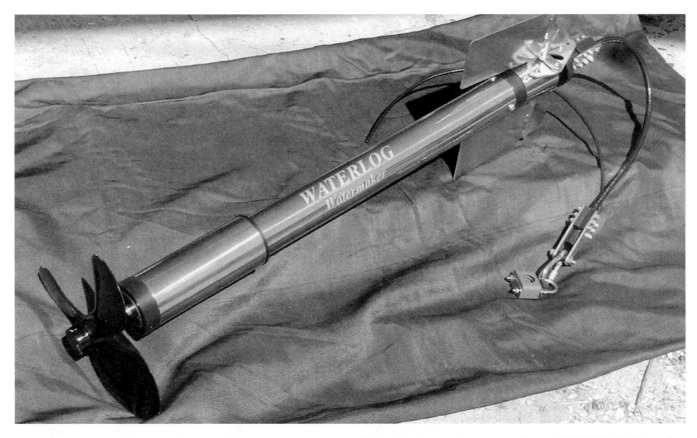

FIGURE 13-35. A towed watermaker. At the time of writing, the jury is still out on whether this is a realistic approach to making water. *(Waterlog)*

loss of volume is equal to ±10% of the volume of the cylinders fed by the pump (it varies from system to system, from as low as 7.5% to as high as 20%). Water is incompressible, so the "extra" ±10% that comes out of the cylinders must go somewhere; it is forced through the membrane to become product water. The pressure needed to do this is generated by the fact that the driving surface of the pistons is plus or minus ten times as great as the surface area of the rod. The net result is that, allowing for some inefficiencies, 100 psi/7 kg per cm^2 of inlet pressure is geared up to around 800 psi/60 kg per cm^2 of discharge pressure.

The device that makes all this possible is a shuttle valve. The shuttle valve takes the brine coming out of the membrane housing (at this point in the process, the brine is at full system pressure) and feeds it to the backside of one or the other piston in a manner that recaptures much of the energy used to pressurize the water in the first place. Only after this has been done is the brine discharged overboard at atmospheric pressure. This is some clever technology that really works, especially for an energy-conscious boat. A spin-off benefit is that it is extremely quiet, in contrast to conventional watermakers, which can be quite noisy.

Note: There are also towed watermakers, which use the boat's speed through the water to spin a propeller that drives the watermaker pump (Figure 13-35). These require no energy from the boat's systems. I have to say that I am skeptical about these. I find it hard to believe the necessary filtration can be achieved with such a minimalist device; if it is not, the membrane will have a relatively short life.

Filtration. Since the primary goal of low-energy watermakers is to minimize energy consumption, all of them dispense with the booster pump on the downstream side of the filters (a booster pump would eat up much of the saved energy). The feed pump becomes the only pump in the system. As such, it must either draw or push the source water through whatever filters are installed. To some extent, this limits the degree to which the source water can be filtered; there may be just a strainer and one 20-micron filter (although Spectra filters to 5 microns, in combination with monitoring the pressure drop across the filter to ensure it does not impose an undue restriction—Figure 13-36). The owner of such a system needs to be especially careful not to run it in visibly fouled or contaminated water.

Command and control. Given that the ratio of product water to source water in a low-energy system is determined by the ratio of the volume of the piston rod to the volume of the cylinders, the ratio cannot be varied to adjust for such things as changes in salinity and temperature. To

FIGURE 13-36. Spectra schematic. Note the single prefilter after the feed pump and ahead of the Clark Pump. This system is manually backflushed (by changing the position of the relevant valves). Many newer systems are automatically backflushed (see Figure 13-38B). *(Jim Sollers, adapted from a drawing courtesy Spectra)*

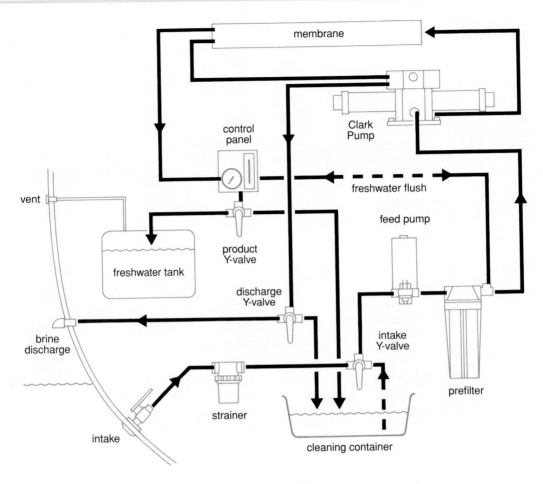

some extent, this can be seen as an advantage as there is not the loss of product water at lower temperatures that occurs with most traditional watermakers. Added to this, the units are very simple to operate, requiring little or no user interaction. However, to some extent it is also a disadvantage, since the system cannot be fine-tuned to secure the maximum life expectancy from the membrane.

Selecting and Installing a Watermaker

Regardless of watermaker type, there are a number of issues you must address when selecting and installing a watermaker. First and foremost—and inseparably linked—are the desired volume of product water, the overall capacity of the watermaker (rated in gallons or liters per hour [gph or lph] or gallons or liters per day [gpd or lpd]), and the power source.

Watermaker capacity. In many situations, the ideal is to have a watermaker that does not require running a fossil-fueled engine simply to power the watermaker. This, in turn, is a signifi-

cant factor in determining what size watermaker to install, since *the total water need must be met during those periods when the necessary energy sources are available.* The watermaker must be sized to meet this need (e.g., if the need is 15 gpd, and the energy source is only available for 1 hour, a unit with a minimum $15 \times 24 = 360$ gpd [1,400 lpd] capacity is needed).

Whenever estimating water needs, it is important to make generous allowance for the extra water that will inevitably be consumed by a more extravagant lifestyle, and also to take into account such things as freshwater deck washes. (People invariably underestimate the extent to which they will use more water than they have in the past; in general, double your previous consumption figures.) If a watermaker will be run intermittently or the boat will be left unattended without pickling the system, you also need to include the water that will be needed for periodic freshwater flushes (see below)—maybe as much as 5 to 7 gallons every 5 to 7 days.

Over time, the output of a watermaker will decline as the membrane ages or as a result of partial fouling of filters. When making capacity calculations, downgrade the rated output of a

Choosing a Watermaker

The key choice is whether or not to use a low-energy watermaker. The energy savings represent an excellent payback for an energy-conscious cruising sailor who has relatively low water needs. But if energy is not such an issue (e.g., most boats with onboard AC generators) or higher water outputs are wanted, a traditional watermaker may be a more reliable and effective investment.

If you want a low-energy model, at the time of writing, the choice is between Spectra models and those from HRO/Sea Recovery (Seafari Escape and Ultra Whisper, respectively). The technology, energy consumption, capacity, and pricing are similar. All offer similar options (such as automatic flushing). Spectra has considerably more experience and real-world testing than HRO/Sea Recovery, but HRO/Sea Recovery are larger companies with a strong, worldwide dealer network.

When comparing traditional watermakers, for a fair comparison it is important to compare the same rated outputs and options. Watermakers can vary from bare-bones models to highly sophisticated ones. The key differences are:

• The degree of filtration of the source water.

• Whether there is a booster pump, and the quality of this pump.
• The extent of the instrumentation and the sophistication of the control circuits, including whether or not there is (are):

1. Automatic salinity sampling and automatic diversion of the product water overboard if the salinity is too high.
2. Automatic pressure adjustment to compensate for changes in salinity and temperature.
3. Automated membrane flushing system.
4. High- and low-pressure shutdowns.

• Whether there is additional treatment of the product water, such as an activated charcoal filter and/or a UV sterilizer.
• Whether there is an activated charcoal filter on the membrane *flushing* circuit (in addition to any filter on the *product* water circuit). With a filter, flushing water can be drawn from the boat's tanks; without one, a separate flushing tank should be installed.
• The cost of filters and other parts needed for routine maintenance.

---

watermaker by 10% to 20% to allow for this. If you will be operating a *traditional* watermaker in areas with water temperatures significantly below the standard rating temperature of 77°F/25°C, downgrade the rated output some more (by as much as 35% if the water temperature is down to 50°F/10°C; refer back to Figure 13-33A). Note that high-efficiency units do not suffer the same decline in output in colder water.

Energy source. Almost all large-capacity watermakers require an AC power source—i.e., an onboard AC generator. For lower capacities, AC, DC, and engine-driven units can all be used.

AC watermakers. On a boat with a continuously operating AC generator, a relatively small AC watermaker can be run long enough to meet the demand. This helps keep down the overall load on the generator, minimizing the size of generator needed as well as the size and weight of the watermaker. When a generator is only run intermittently, the watermaker needs to have the capacity to meet the demand in the restricted running hours. This may result in a larger watermaker, which then requires a larger generator to run it. Longer generator running hours may

have to be accepted in order to downsize the watermaker and generator. Alternatively, it may be possible to employ load-sharing technology to run a larger watermaker from a relatively small generator by managing the other AC loads on board.

DC watermakers. DC watermakers run off the batteries. Typically the demands of the watermaker are low enough and the capacity of the battery bank is large enough to be able to run a relatively small watermaker long enough to meet the boat's needs. The batteries are then recharged during normal charging periods. (Note that most DC watermakers will have a somewhat higher output when batteries are being charged because of the higher voltage on the DC system; it often pays to include battery-charging periods in the watermaker run time.) The net result is a relatively small and lightweight installation that can meet a substantial water need. The precondition is a DC system that has the capacity to handle the demands of the watermaker (see Chapter 1).

Engine-driven watermakers. Although watermaker pumps can be driven off a boat's main propulsion engine, it is not generally recommended. The variable engine speeds when the

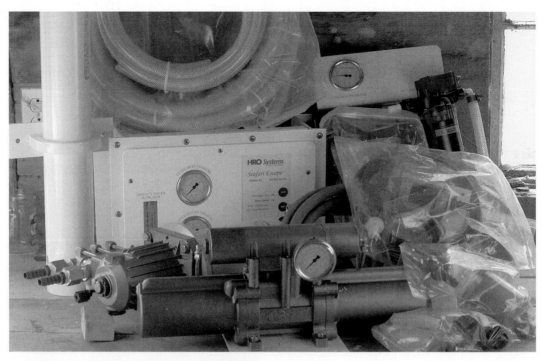

FIGURE 13-37A. All the components for a modular watermaker. This gives some sense of the large number of pieces, hose connections, etc.

FIGURE 13-37B. A modular system installed in a boat.

boat is underway may cause problems, and in any case, most times you don't want to have to run the main engine at anchor to make water (any more than you want to run it to refrigerate). If your boat has an AC or DC generator (both of which typically run at fairly constant speeds), you may be able to configure the system to directly drive the watermaker pump. However, it generally makes just as much sense, and is a more versatile installation, to use an AC- or DC-powered watermaker. In any event, if you decide to use an engine-driven watermaker, you must size it to provide the necessary output during normal engine-running hours.

Installing a watermaker. Watermakers can be bought as an integrated unit mounted on a common base plate (compact unit) or as component parts that are mounted individually in the boat (a modular unit—Figures 13-37A and 13-37B). Generally there is little difference in the purchase price, although there will often be a significant difference in the installation cost because of the added work required by the modular units. The choice of which to use will be driven by the available spaces on the boat, bearing in mind that:

- The raw-water intake must be as low in the boat as possible (to ensure that the system receives a constant supply of water with no air entering the feed line). It must be located well away from toilet discharges and sink, shower, and bilge pump drains. Flat hull inlets should be avoided because they can cause a vacuum; a forward-facing scoop is recommended. The through-hull inlet should be dedicated to the watermaker alone to avoid the risk of air entering from another system and to ensure adequate flow to the watermaker.

- Hose runs should be kept as short as possible, with as few restrictions (e.g., bends) as possible, to minimize friction in the system. This is especially important on low-energy systems, where every extra foot of hose or additional bend absorbs pump energy and lowers performance.
- It is a good idea to place the through-hull for the brine discharge above the waterline so that the discharge can be monitored.
- All components, especially filters, need to be readily accessible.
- Some salt water will inevitably be lost when changing filters, so filters need to be placed where the water will not drip on sensitive equipment.
- The high-pressure circuits may develop a drip. All connections need to be located so that water will not drip on sensitive equipment at any angle of heel.
- Traditional watermakers are noisier than the low-energy models so they need to be located where they will not disturb the crew.

Following installation, it is an excellent idea to log as much benchmark data on the performance of the unit as can be measured with the available instrumentation. This data will provide valuable reference points for future monitoring and troubleshooting (in particular, giving you early warning of filter and membrane fouling). Include such notations as:

- Source water (seawater) temperature.
- Feed-water pressure (if there is a booster pump) or vacuum (if there is no booster pump) upstream of the filters (on the inlet side of the main pump).
- Operating pressure on the system (at the membrane housing).
- Product water flow rate. If no gauge is available, measure flow rate by diverting the flow to a bucket and timing how long it takes to collect a measured amount.
- Salinity of the product water (if there is a salinity meter).
- Brine flow rate. Again, this can be measured by holding a bucket below the discharge through-hull and timing how long it takes to collect a measured amount.
- Amp draw on a DC system.

Maintenance

Filters and membranes are the two principal maintenance items with watermakers. In addition, most high-pressure pumps and some booster pumps have an oil-filled sump that needs checking from time to time. Then there is winterizing.

Filter maintenance. The addition of a monitoring device (such as a pressure gauge on the suction side of the main pump) that will warn when filters start to plug is recommended. More sophisticated watermakers also have an automatic shutdown circuit that will not allow the watermaker to run with plugged filters.

As with an engine raw-water strainer, you must clean the raw-water strainer in your watermaker—most have a removable basket that you wash out in seawater.

Additional filtration generally consists of some kind of a removable pleated filter. Often you can clean these by careful flushing of the filter surface. Each hosing will yield approximately an additional 50% life expectancy (e.g., if the new filter runs 100 hours, after the first hosing, it will go another 50 hours; after the second, another 25 hours, etc.). At the first sign of damage, discard the filter (some manufacturers recommend cleaning no more than once, then discarding it).

Membrane maintenance. Depending on how the watermaker is used, membrane care can be the major part of the needed maintenance. The extent of the work involved varies markedly from unit to unit, principally as a function of the quality of the source water filtration, regularity of use, and the existence of an automatic flushing circuit.

Flushing a membrane. As noted previously, if a membrane is left unused for more than a week, it will be susceptible to bacterial fouling. The best way to minimize watermaker maintenance is to use it often. In other words, *do not* fill the tanks and then shut the watermaker down for two weeks; instead, *top off the tanks at least every 3 days*. If the unit will not be used for more than a week, either put it into storage mode (see below) or else flush it with fresh water at least once a week.

Note that long-distance passagemakers confronted with an approaching storm may find it advantageous to top off the tanks before the storm hits. That way there will be plenty of water on board, and the system will not need to be run, flushed, or maintained in any way for several days.

Typically, the water used for flushing (somewhere between 5 and 7 gallons) is drawn from

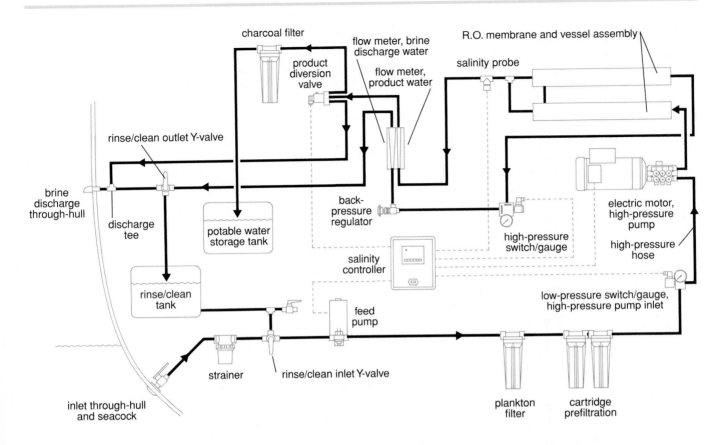

charcoal filter

flow meter, brine
discharge water

R.O. membrane and vessel assembly

product
diversion
valve

flow meter,
product water

salinity probe

rinse/clean outlet Y-valve

brine
discharge
through-hull

discharge
tee

potable water
storage tank

back-
pressure
regulator

salinity
controller

rinse/clean
tank

feed
pump

high-pressure
switch/gauge

electric motor,
high-pressure
pump

high-pressure
hose

low-pressure switch/gauge,
high-pressure pump inlet

strainer

rinse/clean inlet Y-valve

plankton
filter

cartridge
prefiltration

inlet through-hull
and seacock

FIGURE 13-38A. A system with a separate freshwater flushing tank and manual flushing valves. *(Jim Sollers, adapted from a drawing courtesy Sea Recovery)*

the boat's water tanks. However, *traces of chlorine will do permanent damage to membranes.* For this reason, some installations include a separate tank into which product water is diverted and held for flushing purposes (see Figures 13-36 and 13-38A), while others include an activated charcoal filter between the water tanks and the flushing circuit (Figures 13-38B and 13-38C). The charcoal filter removes any traces of chlorine. Note that once wetted, charcoal filters only last about 6 months.

Bare-bones systems have to be flushed manually, which is done by switching a couple of valves on the inlet and discharge sides of the watermaker and turning it on (Figures 13-36 and 13-38A). Sophisticated systems have automatic flushing controls powering solenoid-operated valves (Figures 13-38B and 13-38C). The flush interval can be set by the user. This enables a watermaker to be left idle for some time without the need to pickle the membrane (as long as the unit does not run out of flushing water).

On some units, the flushing water also passes through the feed pump; on others it does not, which leaves salt water standing in the pump. If the pump is made of plastic (e.g., the Shurflo pump used by Spectra and others), this is not a problem, but if it is made of stainless steel, it may lead to corrosion.

Pickling a membrane. Special biocides are used for pickling a membrane. These are mixed with product water and then pumped through the system, leaving the membrane cylinder full of the biocide solution. When it comes time to put the unit back in service, the biocide is flushed out by running the unit in an unpressurized state (to achieve maximum flow through it, with no product water production) for some time (generally 15 to 20 minutes) before restoring pressure and production. The initial product water will still be high in dissolved solids, and so must be discharged overboard via a bypass line (this is the case anytime a watermaker is first started). On cheaper units, this is done manually; on more sophisticated units, a salinity meter controls an automated bypass circuit.

Note that some watermakers (notably Spectra's) include parts that are degraded by some pickling agents. It is essential to only use the pickling agent recommended by the manufacturer.

Winterizing takes the form of pickling the membrane (it must never be left dry), draining the filters and the rest of the plumbing (filters should not be left wet), and in some cases, adding potable antifreeze (propylene glycol, like that sold for winterizing RVs and trailers) to the high-pressure pump. (Low-energy pumps, in particular, can trap water that is hard to drain;

this can crack the pump in a hard freeze.) Spectra also recommends pickling the membrane with propylene glycol; it suggests propylene glycol for pickling in general because "this seems to do less damage to the membranes than other storage compounds."

During a relatively short-term layup, it is generally better to backflush the system every week, if this can be done, rather than pickle it.

Cleaning a membrane. Over time, a membrane inevitably becomes fouled. The watermaker exhibits higher than normal pressures and lower than normal product water flow rates. However, given those symptoms, *before assuming the membrane is to blame, check the feed salinity, feed temperature, operating pressures, and filters.* Also, check the operating voltage (DC or AC) at the pump under load. DC systems, in particu-lar, will be significantly affected by low voltage.

On average, membranes need cleaning once every 2 years (the average membrane life is 5 years). There are two types of membrane clean-ers—alkali and acid. The alkali cleaner is most effective on biofouling and is generally used first (although Spectra recommends using the acid first). The acid cleaner is effective on mineral fouling (e.g., calcium), but it is generally only used if the alkali fails to restore product water flow rates.

To clean a membrane, first flush it with clean water (see above), then mix the alkali solution with clean water in a bucket (preferably hot water because this will improve the performance of the cleaning agents). Depressurize the unit and divert the suction, product water, and dis-charge lines into a bucket. Run the unit for an

FIGURE 13-38B. A system with automatic back-flushing. Note the fresh-water flush charcoal filter to prevent membrane dam-age from chlorine that may be in the water tank. *(Jim Sollers, adapted from a drawing courtesy Sea Recovery)*

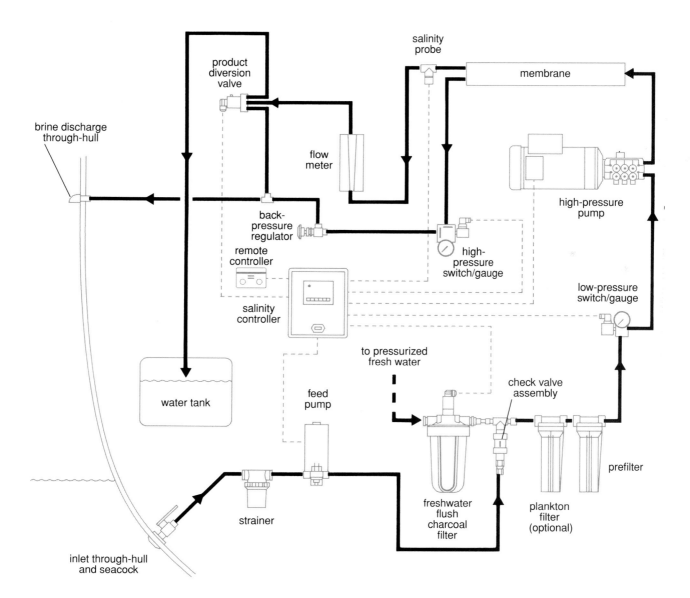

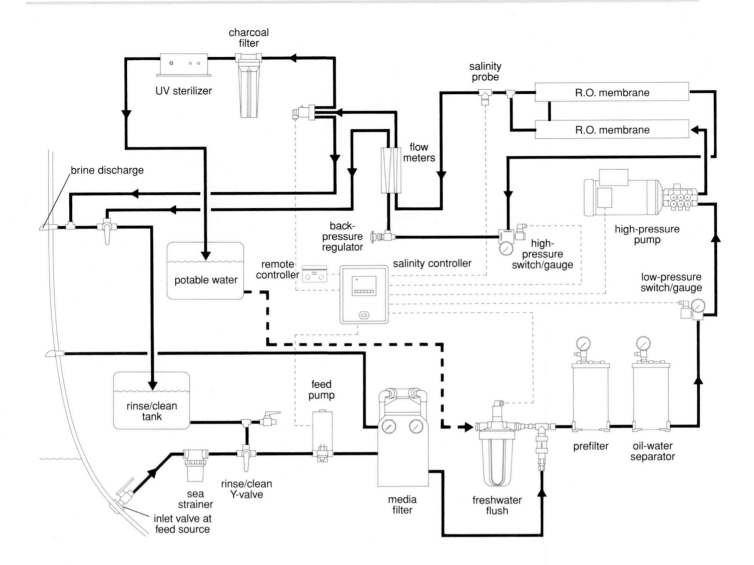

FIGURE 13-38C. An industrial-quality water-maker with commensurate filtration, controls, and complexity. *(Jim Sollers, adapted from a drawing courtesy Sea Recovery)*

hour or so to circulate the solution through the membrane, allow it to rest for an hour or so, and run it again for 15 minutes or so. After this, put the system back into service, unpressurized, and run it for 15 minutes or so to clear out the cleaning solution, then return it to regular service. Once again, discharge the initial product water overboard, either manually or automatically.

If performance is still poor, repeat the same procedure with the acid cleaning solution. Cleaning membranes is hard on them, and something of a crapshoot. Only do it when other measures do not restore output or operating pressures.

Pump maintenance. When operated with properly filtered source water, traditional water-maker high-pressure pumps need valves and seals replaced approximately every 2,000 hours of use; manufacturers provide rebuild kits and instructions. Booster pumps and the feed pumps

on low-energy systems need an overhaul at similar intervals. Those pumps that have an oil-filled crankcase need an oil change every 500 hours.

Troubleshooting

Properly installed and run watermakers are pretty reliable and trouble free. The following are some of the more common problems:

System will not start. The problem is probably electrical. Check for voltage at the motor. If not present, check all fuses and breakers (see Chapter 4) and any shutdown circuits (the unit may have shut down because of high or low pressure). If there is voltage at the motor, refer to Chapter 7 for motor tests.

System starts but shuts down after a while. The high- or low-pressure protection devices are sensing plugged filters or abnormally high operating pressures.

Pump is operating but there is no product water. Check the high-pressure gauge to ensure that the system is operating at the required pressure. Make sure the through-hull is open, all valves are in the correct position (you may be sucking from a flushing intake or discharging the product water overboard), and the pressure relief valve is closed.

Reduced product water. A traditional watermaker operating in cold water will experience a substantial drop in its product water output. Otherwise, suspect a fouled membrane (the membrane housing pressure will be unusually high on a low-energy system, but may not be on a traditional unit; the amp draw will be high on a low-energy system). On a low-energy system, plugged filters may also cause a reduced output (check the inlet pressure/vacuum to the main pump to see if it is low), as will low voltage at the pump when operating.

The pressure relief valve may be partly open or leaking past its seat. There may be leaks in the high-pressure hoses. If none of these is the case, the high-pressure pump cylinders may be leaking past the pistons. In all such cases, the amp draw on a low-energy system will be lower than normal.

Normal water production but with high pressure. The seawater is colder than normal and/or the membrane is fouled.

Normal water production but with low pressure. The seawater is warmer than normal, or the salinity is lower than normal.

Water production is high but poor quality. The membrane or an O-ring in the membrane housing has failed.

Low-energy watermaker exhibits uneven pressure and flow readings. One of the seals in the shuttle valve, on the piston rod, or in the cylinders is leaking, or one of the cylinders is scored and leaking.

Low-energy pump locks up. The shuttle valve is broken. The pump may, in fact, run when unpressurized but lock up under pressure. (On some of the earlier Spectra models, you can repair this by drilling a hole through the shuttle valve and screwing the pieces back together.)

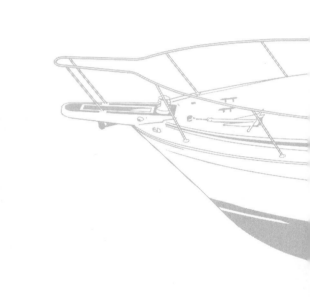

CHAPTER 14

FIGURE 14-1. Types of steering and self-steering systems are as diverse as types of boats, but all follow logical installation and maintenance procedures. *(Jim Sollers)*

(1) wind vane self-steering
(2) rudder
(3) pedestal
(4) wheel
(5) autopilot
(6) hydraulic steering station with integral pump
(7) check valve
(8) hydraulic reservoir
(9) steering cylinder

Steering Systems, Autopilots, and Wind Vanes

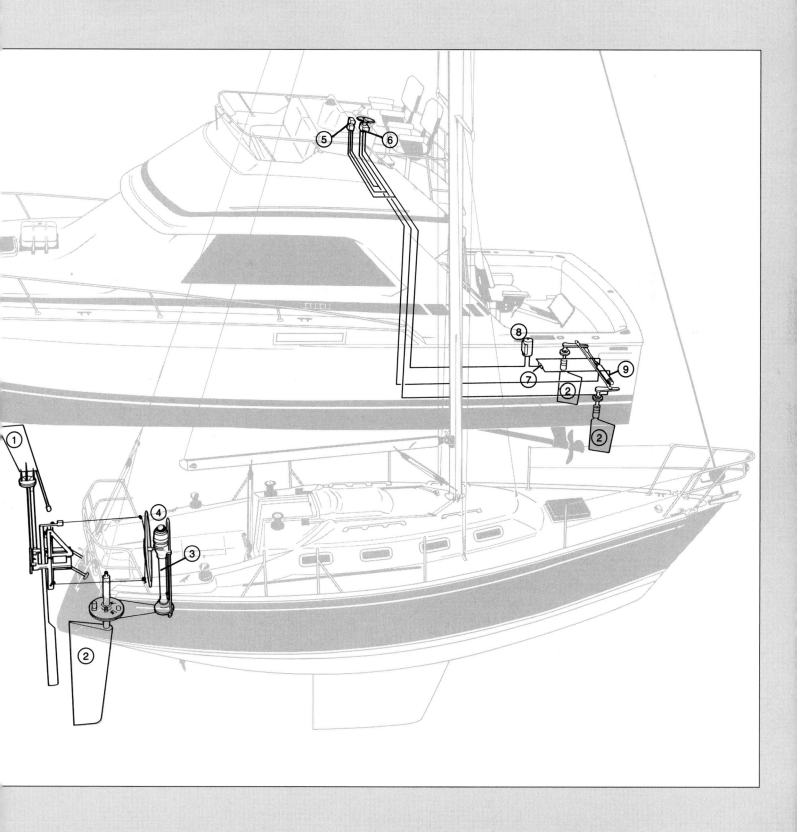

Types of Steering

Traditionally, rudders have been hinged either to the stern of a boat and a full-length keel (aft-hung rudders; Figure 14-2A) or else underneath the boat to the trailing edge of a shorter keel or separate skeg (Figure 14-2B). The hinge used is known as a *gudgeon* (the strap part or socket) and *pintle* (the hinge pin; Figure 14-2C). At the base of the rudder is a *heel* bearing to support the weight of the rudder (Figure 14-2D).

A rudder hinged in this manner on its forward edge is *unbalanced*. When it is turned, the force of the water acting on it is all in one direction. Pivoting a rudder at a point set back from its forward edge counterbalances the forces and makes the rudder much easier to turn. Such *semibalanced* and *balanced* rudders now predominate. A semibalanced rudder is commonly hung from a partial skeg (Figure 14-2E) with the upper part of the rudder unbalanced and the lower part balanced. Balanced rudders are commonly used without any skeg—the rudder, a *spade* rudder, is simply suspended beneath the boat (Figure 14-2F)—with a fin keel that is set well forward.

Most aft-hung rudders are extended above deck level with a reinforcing pad on either side (*cheek blocks*) and a tiller slotted between the

FIGURE 14-2A. A transom-mounted (outboard) rudder.

FIGURE 14-2B. A full-skeg rudder.

FIGURE 14-2C. A gudgeon and pintle.

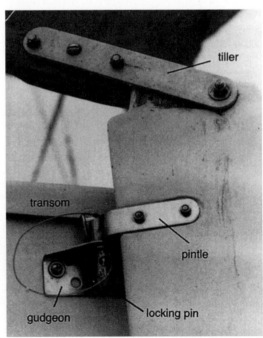

FIGURE 14-2D. A heel bearing arrangement.

FIGURE 14-2E. A half-skeg rudder.

pads. Most other rudders have a hollow or solid pipe (the *rudderstock* or *rudderpost*), with a framework welded or bonded to it (the *web*), around which the rudder is built.

There is a bearing where a rudderstock enters a boat and another one at the top of the stock. In order to prevent the entry of seawater around the stock, either a seal is placed on top of the lower bearing or the bearing and stock are contained inside a pipe (the *bearing tube*), which is sealed into the bottom of the boat. This bearing tube generally rises above water level to the second bearing. There may or may not be a seal on top of the second bearing, depending on its relationship to the boat's waterline.

There are a number of different methods used to turn rudders; some of the most popular are:

Tiller steering. A piece of wood slots in between the cheek blocks on aft-hung rudders or between two metal straps attached to the head of the rudderstock (Figure 14-3). For maximum strength, it is important that the tiller be constructed of straight-grained wood, or better still, a laminate of several thin layers of wood.

All other steering configurations use a wheel.

Geared steering. Over the years, a number of means have been found to directly couple the force generated by a steering wheel to the tiller arm on a rudderstock. All such systems involve some kind of gearing.

Worm-drive steering. Worm-drive steering is rarely seen these days. The drive shaft has a *worm*

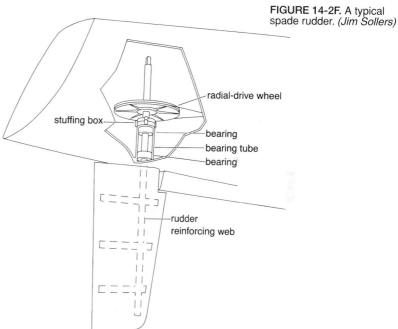

FIGURE 14-2F. A typical spade rudder. *(Jim Sollers)*

radial-drive wheel

stuffing box

bearing

bearing tube

bearing

rudder reinforcing web

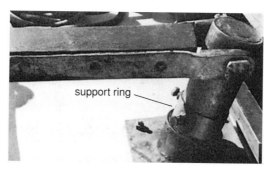

support ring

FIGURE 14-3. There are even more ways to control rudders than there are types of rudders. This tiller installation shows a support ring to accept the weight of the rudder.

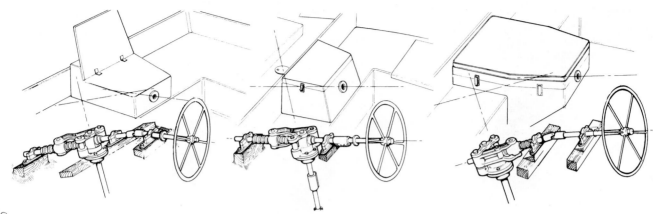

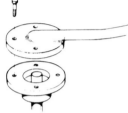

emergency steering tiller

FIGURE 14-4 (above).
Three different configurations of a worm-drive pedestal-steering mechanism. The unit can be adapted to a variety of boats by the use of U-joints. Should the worm seize in operation, the steerer can be unbolted from the rudderhead and an emergency tiller substituted. *(Edson International)*

FIGURE 14-5 (right).
Mechanical-linkage wheel steerers, although not inexpensive, are easily maintained and provide positive steering action. Shown here is rack-and-pinion steering.

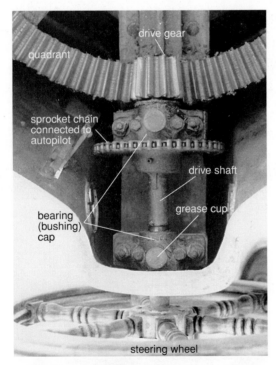

quadrant · drive gear

sprocket chain connected to autopilot

drive shaft

bearing (bushing) cap

grease cup

steering wheel

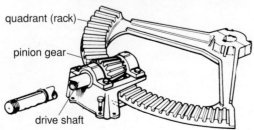

quadrant (rack)

pinion gear

drive shaft

gear fastened along it. A *traversing nut* rides up and down the worm gear, connected to the rudderhead by various linkages (Figure 14-4). Moving the traversing nut turns the rudder.

Traditional rack-and-pinion steering. Traditional rack-and-pinion steering has the steering wheel keyed to a shaft (the drive shaft) on the other end of which is a beveled gear (the *pinion*). This gear engages a circular bevel-geared *quadrant* (the *rack*), which is fastened to the rudderstock and turns the rudder (Figure 14-5). There is generally a universal joint between the wheel and the pinion gear. Traditional rack-and-pinion steering has to be set up close to, and at roughly the same height as, the rudderhead, which makes it impossible to use a steering pedestal. It, too, is rarely seen these days.

Pedestal-based rack-and-pinion steering. To use rack-and-pinion steering in the context of the steering pedestal seen on almost all modern boats, another *dummy* rudder shaft must be set up in the pedestal. The steering wheel, drive shaft, and rack-and-pinion gear are mounted to the top of this dummy shaft just as in a traditional rack-and-pinion setup. An output lever keyed to the bottom of the dummy shaft is connected by a solid rod (the *drag link*) to a second lever (the *tiller arm* or *lever*) on the rudder shaft (Figures 14-6A, 14-6B, and 14-6C). Such a system provides instant rudder feedback and is more or less maintenance free. It now dominates the marketplace for new aft cockpit boats (see Whitlock Steering Systems, www.lewmar.com/whitlock; Jefa Steering, www.jefa.com/steering/steering.htm; and Edson, www.edsonmarine.com).

Another type of rack-and-pinion pedestal assembly is sometimes used that has a non-beveled pinion and a straight, rather than circular, rack. The wheel turns a sprocket that drives an *endless* roller chain (i.e., joined at both ends like a bicycle chain). The chain turns a second sprocket in the base of the unit. This sprocket drives the pinion gear, moving the rack. The rack turns the rudder via a solid link and lever arm.

Bevelhead and gearbox options. On many boats, notably those with center cockpits and inside steering stations, the location of the steering wheel is such that a direct connection cannot be made from the wheel, or the base of the pedestal

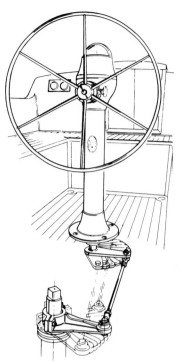

FIGURE 14-6A. Rack-and-pinion pedestal-drive steering. The photo shows a similar pedestal arrangement. *(Whitlock and Tim Sylvia, Edson International)*

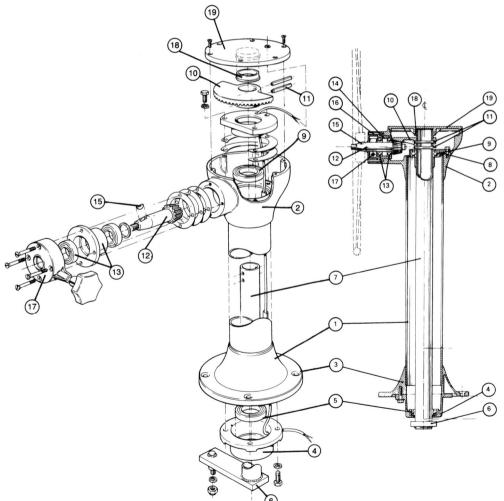

FIGURE 14-6B. An exploded view of the steering pedestal from a rack-and-pinion steering system. Pedestal tube (1). Pedestal bowl (2). Pedestal base (3). Lower bearing housing (4). Sealed ball bearing (5). Output lever (6). Downtube assembly (7). Output socket (8). Sealed ball bearing (9). Gear quadrant (10). Pin (11). Input pinion (12). Sealed ball bearing (13). Input socket (14). Woodruff key (15). Brake cover (16). Brake clamp assembly (17). Top cover bearing (18). Top cover (19). *(Whitlock)*

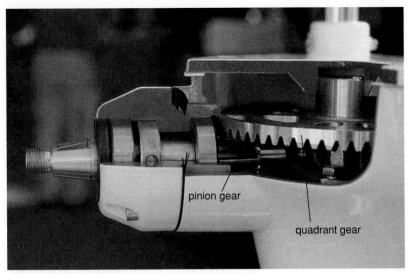

FIGURE 14-6C. A close-up of the rack and pinion in a rack-and-pinion pedestal steerer.

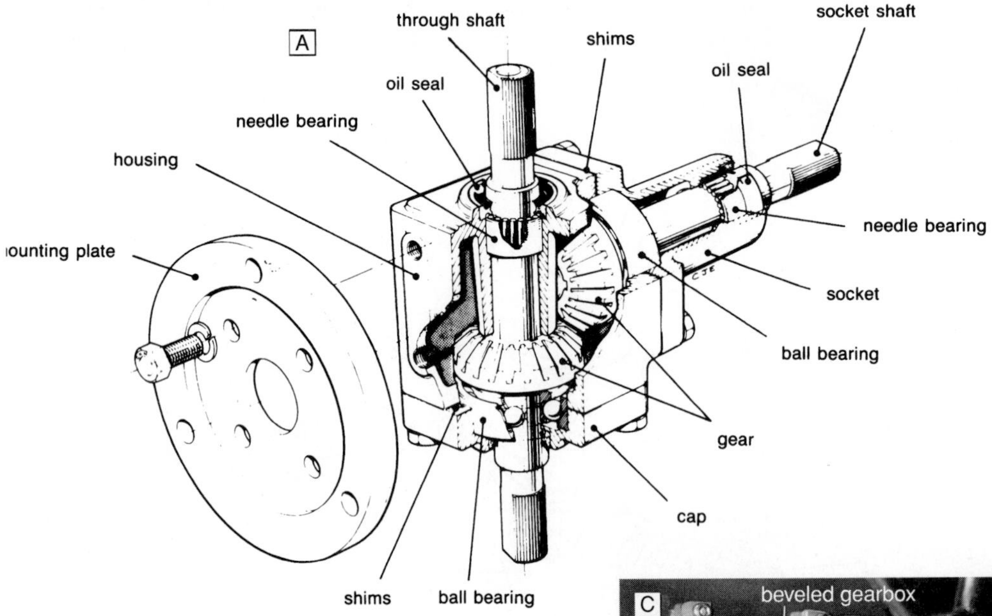

FIGURE 14-7A. For large boats and boats with power-assisted steering, a bevel box such as this often replaces the rack-and-pinion pedestal shown in Figure 14-6B. *(Whitlock)*

FIGURE 14-7B. The Mamba system. *(Whitlock)*

FIGURE 14-7C. Two right-angle bevel boxes and a set of universal joints in a Mamba system.

on which the wheel is mounted, to the tiller arm. This makes it impossible to install pedestal-type rack-and-pinion steering. If some sort of rigid-link steering system is wanted (as opposed to a system using cables—see below), a series of beveled gears and shafts with universal joints is needed (the most popular system is the Mamba system from Whitlock—Figures 14-7A, 14-7B, and 14-7C).

The beveled gears provide a means of taking the turning force imparted by a steering wheel and changing its direction, typically through 90 degrees. This force is then transmitted via solid rods, normally with universal joints that will tolerate some degree of misalignment or change of direction between the rods, to as many additional beveled gears as are needed to work around the boat's internal spaces. This culmi-

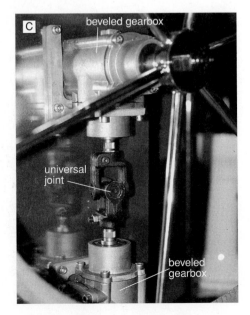

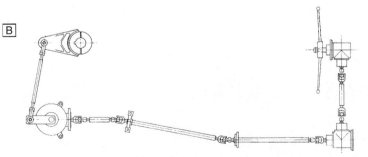

Bevelheads are used for 90-degree changes of direction and universal joints are used for up to 25-degree misalignment. Torque tubes are made to customers' requirements and adjustable by ±20 mm on assembly. Self-aligning bearings are used to support the series of torque tubes.

nates in a reduction gearbox with a tiller arm that is connected via a drag link to the tiller arm on the rudderstock.

Gearboxes can be given two or more input shafts, enabling more than one steering station and/or an autopilot to be connected into the system. The result is a rigid-link system with excellent rudder feedback that enables the steering wheel to be installed just about anywhere, and that is once again more or less maintenance free.

Cable steering. With all forms of cable steering, the wheel turns a sprocket, which drives a length of roller chain that has wire cables attached at each end (Figure 14-8A). There are two methods of running these cables to the rudderhead: *open-cable* steering that uses a series of sheaves (pulley blocks—Figures 14-8B and 14-8C), and *pull-pull* steering that uses enclosed cable conduits (Figures 14-8D and 14-8E). Some systems combine both. Open-cable steering is best where there is a clear cable run from the pedestal to the rudderhead (e.g., aft-cockpit boats); pull-pull works better where there are complex routing problems (e.g., center-cockpit boats). On smaller boats the two cables of a pull-pull system are sometimes replaced with a single *push-pull* cable.

At the rudderhead the cables are attached either to a circular fitting (*radial* or *disc-drive steering*—Figure 14-8B) or to a quadrant (Figures 14-8C, 14-8D, and 14-8E). Determining

which to use is largely a matter of space and accessibility.

Note that radial steering on an aft-cockpit boat eliminates the outboard sheaves that are necessary with the more traditional quadrant steering. This greatly simplifies installation and removes a couple of potential problem areas.

Hydraulic steering. The wheel turns a hydraulic pump, which sends oil under pressure to a hydraulic piston at the rudderhead. This piston

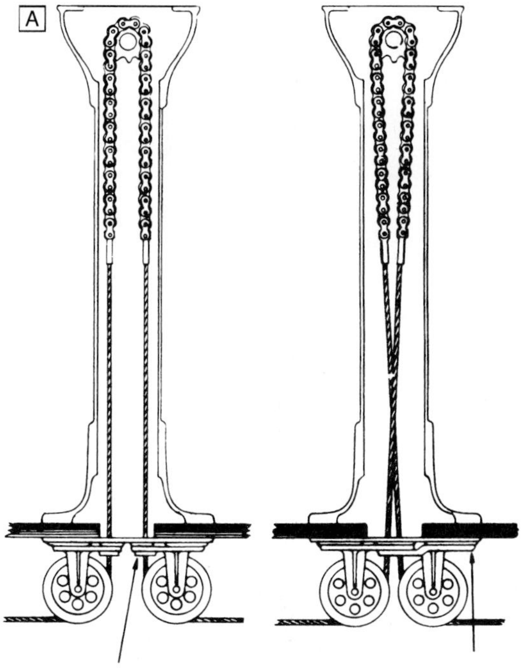

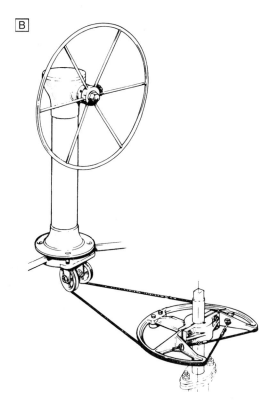

FIGURE 14-8B. Cable steering using a radial (disc) drive at the rudderhead. *(Whitlock)*

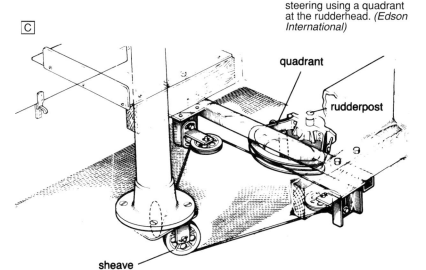

FIGURE 14-8C. Cable steering using a quadrant at the rudderhead. *(Edson International)*

quadrant

rudderpost

sheave

FIGURE 14-8A. Pedestal arrangements with cable steering.

FIGURE 14-8D. Pull-pull cable steering via a quadrant mounted on the rudderhead. *(Whitlock)*

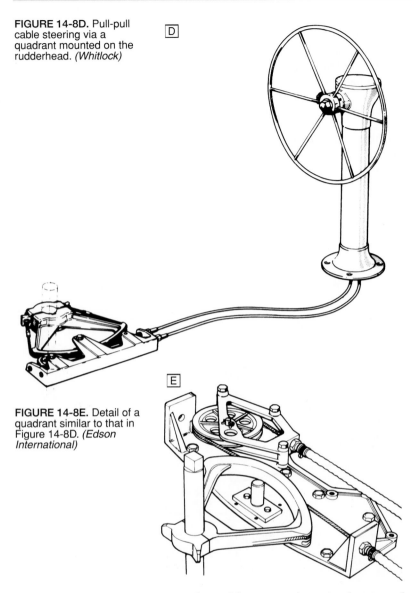

FIGURE 14-8E. Detail of a quadrant similar to that in Figure 14-8D. *(Edson International)*

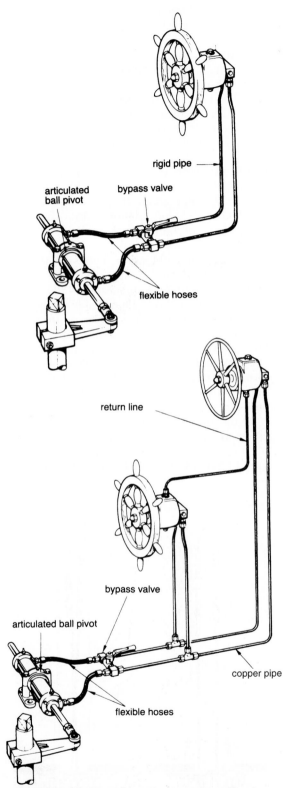

turns the rudder via an operating lever on the rudderstock (Figures 14-9A and 14-9B). Sometimes the drive shaft on the pump is coupled directly to the steering wheel. At other times, the steering wheel turns a sprocket, and an endless (circular) roller chain connects this sprocket to another one on the pump drive shaft. The steering wheel can be mounted pretty much anywhere, and the hydraulic hoses are easy to run through spaces that might prove difficult with other systems. More than one steering station and/or an autopilot can be added to the system.

Twin rudders and/or twin steering wheels. An increasing number of modern high-performance boats have either twin rudders with a single steering wheel (Figures 14-10A and 14-10B) or twin steering wheels with a single rudder (Figures 14-10C and 14-10D), or twin

FIGURE 14-9A. Powerboats, and not a few sailboats, increasingly rely on hydraulic steering. The steering wheel powers a hydraulic pump connected via high-pressure tubing to a hydraulic cylinder, or ram, mounted at the rudderhead. Shown here are a typical single-station hydraulic steering assembly (top) and a representative dual-station assembly (bottom). *(Whitlock)*

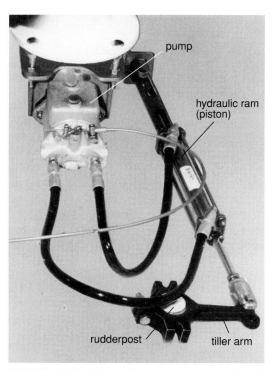

pump

hydraulic ram
(piston)

rudderpost

tiller arm

FIGURE 14-9B. A hydraulic steering system designed for use with pedestal steering.

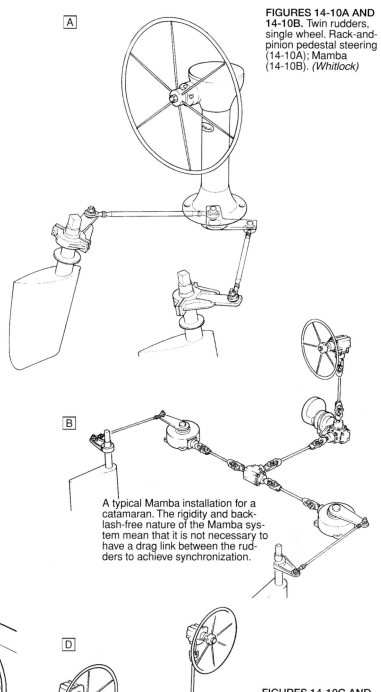

A

B

FIGURES 14-10A AND 14-10B. Twin rudders, single wheel. Rack-and-pinion pedestal steering (14-10A); Mamba (14-10B). *(Whitlock)*

A typical Mamba installation for a catamaran. The rigidity and back-lash-free nature of the Mamba system mean that it is not necessary to have a drag link between the rudders to achieve synchronization.

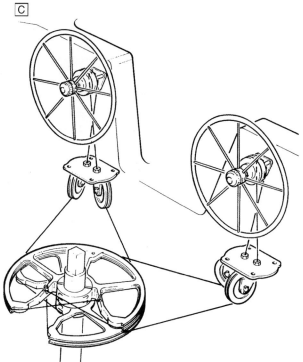

C

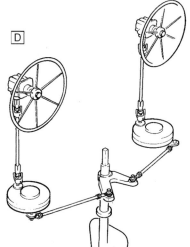

D

FIGURES 14-10C AND 14-10D. Single rudder, twin wheels. Radial steering (14-10C); Mamba (14-10D). *(Whitlock)*

steering wheels and rudders. Regardless of the combination, the pieces will be similar to what has already been described.

Maintenance and Troubleshooting

Gudgeons and pintles. At every annual haulout, check for wear and loose fasteners by flexing the rudder up and down and from side to side. If the rudder is fastened with stainless steel gudgeons, *remove the rudder and inspect the pintles closely for signs of crevice corrosion* (Chapter 5). Many gudgeons ride on Delrin washers—these too need checking and replacing if worn.

Loose fasteners can be a problem with both wood and fiberglass rudders. With wood, if the surrounding area is damaged or rotted, it is best to remove the gudgeon or pintle, drill an oversized hole to undamaged wood, plug this with epoxy, and refit the gudgeon or pintle, drilling a new hole for the fastener through the epoxy plug. See Figure 17-5 on page 734 for details.

Most fiberglass rudders have a foam, balsa, or wood core. Water entry into this core through loose or improperly bedded fasteners, or around loose shafts, can lead to various problems, including delamination, cracking along mold lines, and corrosion of any internal web. If the rudder has become waterlogged, it will be necessary to drill a hole in its base and leave it to drain until there is no sign of moisture around the drain hole (this may take weeks) before sealing up the hole and rebedding the fasteners

properly with polyurethane caulking (e.g., 3M 5200).

When refitting a rudder be sure to secure it properly. Some have a cotter pin (split pin) through a pintle; others have a threaded pintle with a retaining nut. On a few, one pintle is reversed and must be unbolted to remove and replace the rudder. Be especially careful to lock off nuts. Although you can do this by tightening two nuts against each other or by using a Nylok nut, it is preferable to drill through the pintle and insert a cotter pin.

Rudderstocks and rudders. Many rudderstocks are hollow. Most are not built to withstand any kind of a serious grounding—a spade rudder with a hollow stock is especially liable to bend at the point where the stock enters the base of the hull (Figure 14-11). *Bent hollow-stock rudders should be replaced, not straightened.* Any straightening reduces the strength of the most highly stressed point of the rudder. If the rudder cannot be replaced, straighten it and insert a second tube down into the stock to reinforce it at the point of the bend. Mildly bent solid stocks can be straightened.

Core issues. Most modern rudders are laminated around a stainless steel or aluminum rudderstock to which a *web*—a series of internal plates—is welded. Typically, the rudder is made in two halves that are bonded together. The rudder may be a solid laminate, but as often as not, it has a core of plywood or foam (Figure 14-12).

FIGURE 14-11. Bent (left) and broken (right) spade rudders. Their unsupported heels and unprotected leading edges make this type of rudder particularly susceptible to damage.

A number of poorly constructed rudders have either inadequate or improperly fastened internal webs. Under a severe load, the rudderstock will break loose from the web causing a complete failure of the rudder. Before this happens, the stock may start to twist inside the rudder; failure is imminent. Whenever a boat is hauled, tie off the wheel or tiller and flex the rudder as hard as possible. *If there is any movement between the rudder and rudderstock, the rudder must be replaced immediately.*

With cored rudders, it is next to impossible to prevent water entering the core (notably around the rudderstock where it exits the top of the rudder). If the core material is foam, it will slowly become saturated; if it is wood, it may rot and also swell, cracking the seam where the two rudder halves are joined. On older boats, it is not a bad idea to drill a hole in the base of the rudder and see if water runs out. If it does, you should ideally try to find some means of drying it out (this is not easy). In any event, carefully check the seam area for any cracking. If found, grind back the seam and apply new laminate.

Corrosion. Anytime water penetrates a rudder with a stainless steel or aluminum stock and internal web, given the deoxygenated atmosphere inside the rudder, corrosion is likely to occur—see Chapter 5; sooner or later the web will fail. With aluminum rudderstocks, if the small section of the rudderstock between the top of the rudder and the underside of the boat is immersed (as it normally is), and if it is in any way electrically connected to the boat's DC ground (as it will be if bonded for any reason—see Chapter 5), it will be especially prone to corrosion. Anytime the boat's zincs become depleted, the rudderstock will become the next sacrificial metal in the galvanic series. It can be destroyed quite rapidly.

Because of the corrosion potential with rudderstocks, Jefa Rudder, a major rudderstock manufacturer (www.jefa.com/rudder.htm), strongly recommends keeping rudderstocks completely electrically isolated from the rest of the boat (i.e., not included in any bonding or lightning-protection system). This, however, can be quite difficult to accomplish, since the rudderstock will be electrically connected via the tiller arm and steering system to the steering pedestal, which in turn may be electrically connected to the DC ground via an autopilot, and/or the compass lighting circuit, and/or various electronic instruments mounted on the binnacle, and/or the engine controls. Jefa manufactures insulated *rose joints* (the fitting that goes on the end of the drag link in rigid steering systems and on autopilot rams). They recommend insulating the engine controls from the pedestal, as well as ensuring

FIGURE 14-12. A foam-core spade rudder breaking apart where the rudderstock enters the rudder (the boat hit a reef).

foam core

that all wiring in the pedestal is isolated from the pedestal. A test is then made with an ohmmeter (R × 1 scale on an analog meter) checking for an open circuit (infinite resistance) between the rudderstock and DC ground.

However, even if initially a rudder is successfully electrically isolated, it is difficult to maintain this condition. Such things as carbon dust from brush wear in autopilot motors, modifications made to the boat's equipment, or even gear lying against components in the steering system can bypass the isolation, added to which electrical isolation makes it impossible to include the binnacle and steering wheel in the lightning-protection system. It may be better to bond and simply ensure that the zincs are renewed in a timely manner. This is especially important on boats moving from cooler climates (such as northern Europe) to warmer ones (such as the Mediterranean or Caribbean), because zinc consumption may be dramatically accelerated—initially, the zincs will need checking far more frequently.

If you install an electrically isolated rudder, periodically check its isolation with an ohmmeter.

Bearings, tubes, and seals. The vast majority of rudders are installed through the bottom of the boat, with the rudderstock riding in two bearings set in a tube, the top end of which may or may not have some kind of a seal (depending on its relationship to the waterline).

Bearings. Rudder bearings on smaller boats generally consist of a plastic bushing (Delrin, etc.). On larger boats various roller bearings are used. Over the past decade, self-aligning bearings have become common (Tides Marine—www.tidesmarine.com, Jefa, Edson, and others). These have an outer case, which is

FIGURE 14-13A. A rigid bearing bonded into the bottom of a boat.

FIGURE 14-13B. Under a load, all rudderstocks bend. Rigid bearings then tend to bind in their housings. *(Jim Sollers)*

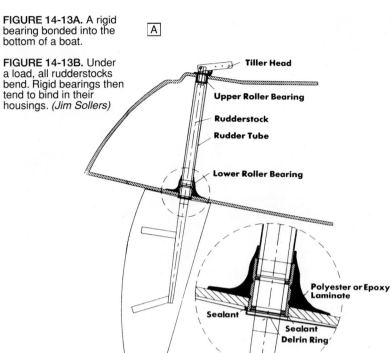

A

Tiller Head

Upper Roller Bearing

Rudderstock

Rudder Tube

Lower Roller Bearing

Polyester or Epoxy Laminate

Sealant

Sealant
Delrin Ring

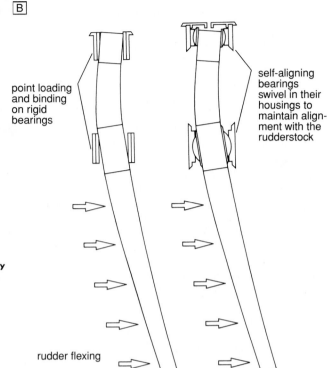

B

point loading and binding on rigid bearings

self-aligning bearings swivel in their housings to maintain alignment with the rudderstock

rudder flexing

FIGURE 14-13C. A self-aligning bearing. The bearing is contained in a housing that has a conical surface. This housing seats in a corresponding convex surface in the bearing's outer shell, which is bonded into the boat. Under a load, when the rudderstock flexes, the bearing housing can swivel a few degrees inside the outer shell, maintaining correct bearing alignment and support.

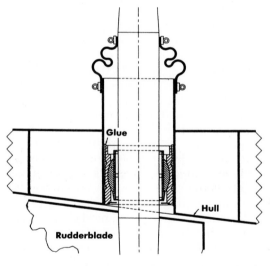

Glue

Hull

Rudderblade

fastened to the boat, with a spherical concavity cut into its inner surface. The bearing (which may be either a solid plastic bearing or a bearing case containing roller bearings) has a spherical, convex outside surface that fits inside the concave surface of the housing. The rudderstock rides inside the bearing. The bearing assembly is free to rotate a few degrees in any direction inside the bearing housing (Figures 14-13A to 14-13D). This is a highly desirable feature that will accommodate both minor rudder misalignment at the time of installation and also flexing of the rudderstock under a load. With some designs (notably from Jefa and Edson), it also

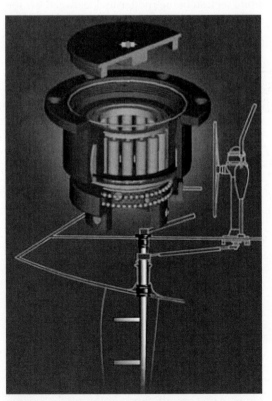

FIGURE 14-13D. Anatomy of a self-aligning bearing. *(Jefa)*

permits easy replacement of the bearings without the use of any tools (after the rudder and its stock have been removed).

During a haulout, if the rudder flexing described above reveals more than minimal play, *the bearings need replacing.* (If they are left as is and they fail in a seaway, the rudder will start banging around quite violently and do a considerable amount of damage. If this cracks or breaks the bearing tube, it could even sink the boat.) Note that bearings consisting of plastic bushings generally require a little more clearance around the rudderstock than those with roller bearings, and as a result will exhibit more play.

Some plastics, notably nylon, swell in salt water. Dimensional changes of up to 6% can result in seized or tight steering. If the steering on a new boat becomes stiff, *break the cables loose at the rudderhead and turn the rudder. If it is binding, the bearings probably need reaming out.*

Two materials that have zero water absorption are PTFE (Teflon) and UHMWPE (ultrahigh-molecular-weight polyethylene). PTFE is far too soft for bearing use and has a very low compressive strength in its natural state; therefore, it is normally combined with copper or fiberglass. UHMWPE is readily available from plastics distributors, has a very low coefficient of friction, and a high compressive strength, making it one of the best materials for bearing use. Delrin is another widely used plastic (it absorbs some water, but swells by less than 0.1%).

Bearing tubes. Most rudder tubes are fiberglass pipes bonded into the base of the hull. The lower bearing is sometimes built into the rudder tube; otherwise, it is pushed up from below and held with either a couple of setscrews or a bead of sealing compound *around its base* (3M 5200 caulk or similar). Do not put caulking up *inside*

the bearing tube as it will make later bearing removal very difficult. The bearing tube may terminate in a seal (Figure 14-14A) or be carried up and bonded to the underside of the deck (Figure 14-14B).

The upper bearing not only absorbs sideways loading but also holds the weight of the rudder in spade rudder installations (Figure 14-14B again). Either a collar or the rudderhead fitting (quadrant, radial-drive wheel or disc, or tiller strap fitting) rests on the bearing and keeps the rudder in the boat. *Note that loosening this fitting may allow the rudder to fall out of the bottom of the boat, so be warned!*

The bearing-tube-to-hull joint is critical. If it should fail, the boat is in danger of sinking. Bearing tubes in fiberglass hulls are bonded fiberglass; in steel and aluminum hulls, they are welded pipes. Inspect the joint annually for any signs of cracking.

If you need to repair a fiberglass tube, follow these steps:

1. Clean and abrade the hull for 4 to 6 inches (100 to 150 mm) around the bearing tube and up its sides. Be sure to remove all traces of paint, gelcoat, and dirt. Abrade the surface of the fiberglass with a coarse sander. Liberally swab the area with acetone. (Note: Acetone fumes are powerful; if working in confined spaces, ensure adequate ventilation. Spilled acetone will dissolve some hoses, so take care not to spill it!)

2. If the tube-to-hull joint has a tight radius, this is probably the reason it is cracking. Fair it out with a paste made from catalyzed polyester or epoxy resin and a filler such as microballoons or talc. (Prefilled putties are available from chandleries.) In a pinch, use talcum powder

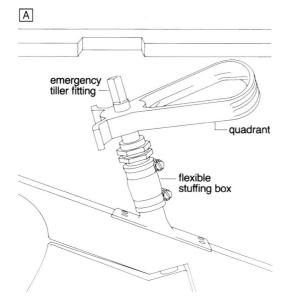

A

emergency
tiller fitting

quadrant

flexible
stuffing box

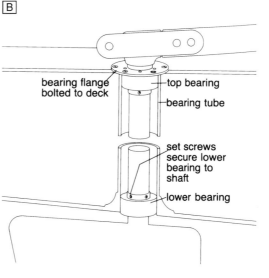

B

bearing flange
bolted to deck

top bearing

bearing tube

set screws
secure lower
bearing to
shaft

lower bearing

FIGURE 14-14A. A typical arrangement for wheel steering without a top bearing on the rudderstock. The flexible stuffing box keeps water out of the boat. *(Jim Sollers)*

FIGURE 14-14B. Typical support bearings for a rudderstock with a top bearing. The top of the bearing tube is sealed to the deck. *(Jim Sollers)*

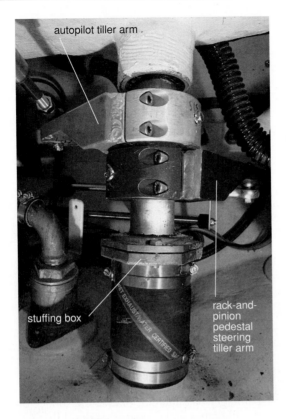

autopilot tiller arm

stuffing box

rack-and-pinion pedestal steering tiller arm

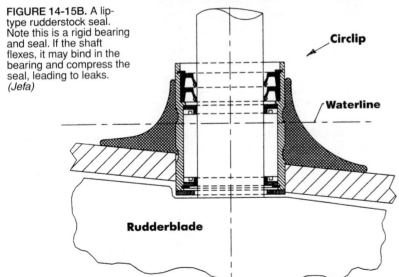

Circlip

Waterline

Rudderblade

ter bond with the existing laminate. Cut the mat and cloth into manageable strips (say, 3 inches wide by 8 inches long/75 mm by 200 mm). When laying up the strips, use a disposable brush to apply the resin. Make sure you *saturate the mat or cloth*; you can mop up any excess later. The fiberglass becomes completely transparent when fully saturated.

4. Try to lay up successive layers of fiberglass before earlier layers have completely gelled. Stagger all joints to avoid any *hard* edges, which will concentrate stresses. If you lay up more than one layer, use alternate layers of mat and cloth. Cut the successive layers longer so that the top layer of cloth makes a smooth transition to the hull and tube sides.

Note that polyester resin is normally used on fiberglass because it does the job and is relatively cheap. Various epoxies, however, will provide a better bond to old fiberglass, making a stronger and more flexible repair.

Seals. Unless the top of the rudder tube is well above the maximum heeled waterline, it will need a seal. Note that the most critical condition for the majority of rudder installations is when powering at hull speed. The stern wave often maintains a consistently high water level, which creates a greater likelihood of water entering the boat than the intermittent surging effect of waves moving past the boat. For boats with twin rudders, the leeward rudder can be deeply submerged, creating quite a bit of pressure in its rudder tube. To minimize the chances of water ingress, rudder tubes should be made as long as possible to keep them above the waterline at all angles of heel. If this is not possible, take special care to ensure an effective seal.

In terms of seals, the same seals used on propeller shafts are often used for rudder tubes—i.e., a traditional stuffing box (packing gland), a mechanical seal, or a lip-type seal. In all instances, installation and maintenance issues are the same as with propeller shaft seals (see Chapter 10).

In spite of its widespread use, a traditional rigid stuffing box does not make a good rudder shaft seal. First of all, there is some friction. Second, under load, the shaft will flex in its bearings, compressing the packing in the shaft seal, which then increases the chance of subsequent leaks. Better choices are a flexible stuffing box (Figure 14-15A) or mechanical or lip-type seals (Figure 14-15B).

If the space between the top of the rudder tube and the quadrant or tiller arm allows it, clamp a rubber bellows (a *gaiter*) to the top of the tube and also to the rudder shaft (Figures 14-15C and 14-15D). The bellows is sufficiently

for a filler. Cut a piece of stiff cardboard to the desired curvature (in profile) and use this to shave off the excess putty and impart a smooth finish. Practice on a scrap piece before applying the putty to the boat.

3. Fiberglass cloth is easier to work into compound curves than either mat or woven rovings, and pound for pound it is also stronger. However, it is best laid up over a layer of mat, which holds more resin. This helps to fill in any air spaces in the cloth and provides a bet-

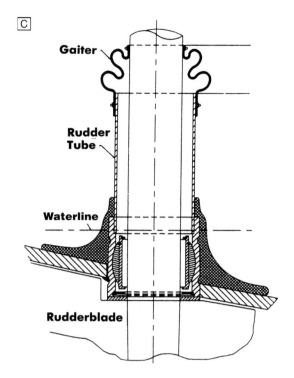

Gaiter

Rudder
Tube

Waterline

Rudderblade

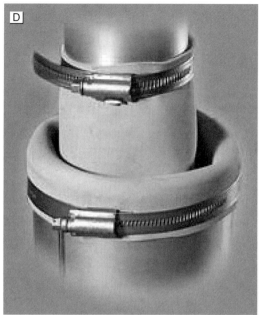

FIGURE 14-15C. A gaiter-type rudderstock seal. (Jefa)

FIGURE 14-15D. A gaiter installed on a rudder tube and rudder shaft.

flexible to allow the rudder to turn from side to side without stressing or damaging the bellows. In this case there is no maintenance, other than periodically checking to make sure the bellows is undamaged. Such a bellows can also be added to lip-type seals as a backup.

All seals should be readily accessible (few are). Every year, I get several e-mails from people who experienced near-catastrophic leaks from rudder shaft seals, which took some time to track down or access.

Rudderhead fittings. The rudderhead fitting is subjected to tremendous loads from time to time, notably when the rudder is slammed around in heavy seas. Should any play develop between the rudderhead fitting and rudderstock, the movement of the rudder will ceaselessly work away at this weakness until something fails. At the annual haulout, when flexing the rudder with the tiller or wheel tied off, check closely for any play. *Any play at all is unacceptable.*

Rudderhead fittings are clamped to rudderstocks and locked with keys, setscrews, or through-bolts. A key is a length of square metal that fits into matching slots machined in the rudderstock and rudderhead clamp (Figure 14-16A).

FIGURE 14-16A. Variations on a rudderhead fitting theme. **Left:** Keyway machined into rudderstock and quadrant. **Middle:** Through-bolted, using a high-tensile bolt. **Right:** Drilled and pinned, using a high-tensile peg. Because of the potential for extreme point loading at the end of the peg, this method is not recommended. (Whitlock)

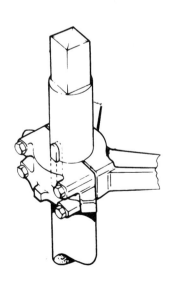
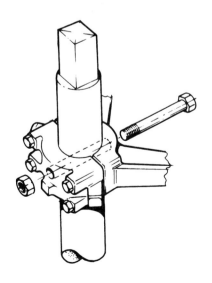
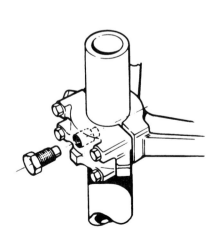

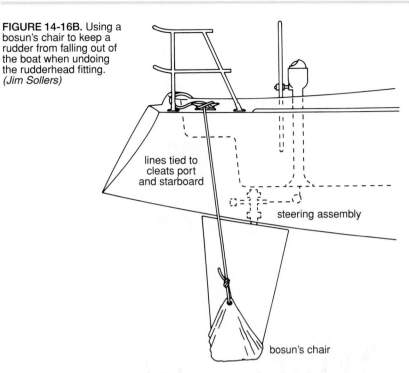

lines tied to cleats port and starboard

steering assembly

bosun's chair

Keys both here and elsewhere in the steering system *must be stainless steel and not brass*, since brass will not only dezincify and fail, but will also cause galvanic corrosion on aluminum quadrants and discs (radial-drive wheels), causing them to fail. (Note that aluminum rudderhead fittings should be used only on aluminum and stainless steel rudder shafts—never on bronze.) Setscrews are frequently threaded into the rudderhead clamp and seated in dimples in the shaft. This is not adequate. It is far better to drill out and tap (thread) the seat in the shaft so that the setscrew will positively screw into the shaft. This way the screws cannot slip. Be sure to use some locking compound on the screws so that they cannot work their way out (e.g., Loctite).

Many rudderhead fittings on hollow stocks are through-bolted. If the bolt holes become stretched (elongated), allowing movement of the bolt, drill out the holes and fit a larger-diameter bolt. However, do not take this too far since the loss of metal will weaken the clamp and shaft.

Tighten a loose rudderhead clamp either by wrapping a thin piece of galvanically compatible metal (a *shim*) around the shaft beneath the clamp or by filing a small amount off the clamp faces so that the clamp pulls up tighter.

Once again, remember that the rudderhead clamp may be the only thing holding a spade rudder in the boat. Before loosening it, *secure the rudder!* (One way to keep a rudder in the boat is to position a bosun's chair in the water under the rudder, with a couple of lines coming up over the stern quarters to cleats or winches—Figure 14-16B. If there is room to fit a hose

clamp around the shaft somewhere else, do so as a security measure in case the rudderhead fitting ever slips.)

Rack-and-pinion steering (mounted on rudderstock). Rack-and-pinion steering is just about foolproof. The critical factors are to keep the drive shaft at 90 degrees to the quadrant and to keep the quadrant and pinion gears closed up so that the teeth cannot jump. Where the wheel is not mounted at a right angle to the quadrant, a universal joint will be fitted to the shaft.

The pinion gear is generally supported in a couple of bronze bushings, which will need lubricating two or three times a season. Some have grease cups or fittings for this purpose (use Teflon-based waterproof grease); if not, engine oil will do. The gears and rack need greasing.

Often you can adjust the pinion-gear-to-quadrant clearance by loosening the quadrant clamps on the rudderstock and moving the quadrant slightly up and down its keyway (this *cannot* be done with setscrews or through-bolts on hollow shafts). If the pinion gear–mounting bracket has a *contact arm* the quadrant rests on, you can temporarily close up worn pinion and quadrant gears by *shimming* the contact arm (sliding a piece of thin metal between it and the quadrant).

The mounting bracket for the pinion gear takes *all* the steering loads—check its fasteners carefully at the annual inspection. Lubricate any universal joint and check for play in the joint, its keyways, or the pins locking it to its shafts. Note that many universal joints are steel, not stainless steel. Cover these with a grease-filled rubber boot (obtainable from large tool supply houses). In the absence of a boot, grease the universal joint and wrap a length of inner tubing around it, securing the tubing with two stainless steel hose clamps.

Rack-and-pinion steering (pedestal type). On some models, the top plate and input socket screws (refer back to Figure 14-6B) tend to freeze if not removed annually, cleaned, and refitted, preferably with an antiseize compound (Tef-Gel and Duralac are two good brands).

The fit of the popular Whitlock Cobra rack-and-pinion gear system is adjusted at the factory by placing shims (thin metal or plastic spacers) under the face of the pedestal input and output sockets. Remove any wear that takes place by taking away a shim *from the input socket only*. This will close up the gears, eliminating play. To do this:

- Remove the brake wheel (in the center of the steering wheel), steering wheel, and steering wheel shaft key.

- Remove the four input socket screws.
- Replace the wheel on its shaft and use it to pull out the input socket assembly (you may need to put a block of wood behind the steering wheel hub and hit it with a hammer to jar the assembly loose).
- Remove one shim and reassemble.

Some (older) pedestals use needle bearings (Figure 14-6B again) on the output shaft. They will need annual greasing, and even when properly maintained, have been found to lead to premature wear of the shaft and bearing. Other (newer) pedestals use sealed carbon steel ball bearings, which are essentially maintenance free. Although these bearings are liberally coated at assembly with water-repellent grease to prevent corrosion, they should still be inspected annually for any signs of rust, which, if present, should occasion cleaning and recoating.

If the unit ever needs to be disassembled, disconnect the drag link, undo the mounting bolts, and remove the entire unit from the boat. The output lever on the Cobra system is welded in place; if it needs to be taken off, the welds will have to be ground off (first mark the lever and down tube so that it can be put back in the same relationship). On Jefa and Edson units, the output lever is bolted in place.

Wide-angle geometry. On all rack-and-pinion pedestal steerers, the tiller lever on the rudder shaft is longer than the output lever on the pedestal (generally, approximately $1\frac{1}{2}$ times longer). This provides very direct steering near amidships, but the farther the rudder moves from amidships, the more the wheel must be turned for a given change in rudder action. In other words, the steering is increasingly *geared down* to compensate for the anticipated higher steering loads.

When the rudder is amidships, the tiller arm and output lever need to be parallel to one another, with the drag link at a right angle to both of them. To accomplish this, if the two were the same length, the tiller arm and output lever would need to be set up at right angles to the centerline of the boat, and the drag link would then be at right angles to both. However, the more the tiller arm and output lever differ in length, and the closer together they are (i.e., the shorter the drag link between them), the more their angle with the centerline must deviate from a right angle to keep the drag link at a right angle (Figures 14-17A and 14-17B). The offset angle from the centerline will be given in the literature that came with the unit.

If the tiller arm and/or output lever are disturbed at any time, it is important to check this geometry. If it is incorrect, in a worst-case situation, the drag link may *cam over* center, in which case the steering reverses! This results in excessive loads on the pedestal, rudder bearings, and the linkage. A lack of rudderstops (see the Rudderstops section below) or a failure of the rudderstops can produce the same result (and will void any warranty on the unit).

Check to see that *with the rudder straight ahead, the pinion is centered on the rack, and the output lever and tiller arm are offset from a right angle to the centerline by the specified amount.*

Troubleshooting Chart 14-1. Wheel Steering Failures: Rack-and-Pinion	
Does the drive shaft turn when the wheel is turned? **YES**	**NO** Check for a disengaged clutch or slipping wheel (loose and/or sheared-off key).
Does the rack-and-pinion gear turn when the shaft turns? **YES**	**NO** Check for a sheared pin locking the rack-and-pinion gear to its shaft, or a slipping universal joint (if fitted). Repair as necessary.
Does the quadrant turn when the gear turns? **YES**	**NO** Check for a jumping or stripped gear. Close up the clearance between the gear and the quadrant.
Does the rudderstock turn when the quadrant turns? **YES**	**NO** The quadrant clamp is slipping on the rudderstock. Tighten or replace bolts and setscrews, or shim as necessary.
The internal webs in the rudder itself have sheared. Rig a jury rudder. On sailboats, balance the rig.	

Troubleshooting Chart 14-2. Wheel Steering Failures: Cable and Pull-Pull	
Do the cables at the base of the pedestal move when the wheel is turned? **YES**	**NO** Check for a disengaged clutch, slipping wheel or sprocket, stripped sprocket teeth, or a jumped chain. Repair as necessary.
Does the quadrant (or wheel) turn at the rudderhead when the steering wheel is turned? **YES**	**NO** Check for broken or jumped cables between the pedestal and rudderhead.
Does the rudderstock turn when the quadrant (or wheel) turns? **YES**	**NO** The quadrant clamp is slipping on the rudderstock. Tighten or replace bolts and setscrews or shim as necessary.
The internal webs in the rudder itself have sheared. Rig a jury rudder. On sailboats, balance the rig.	

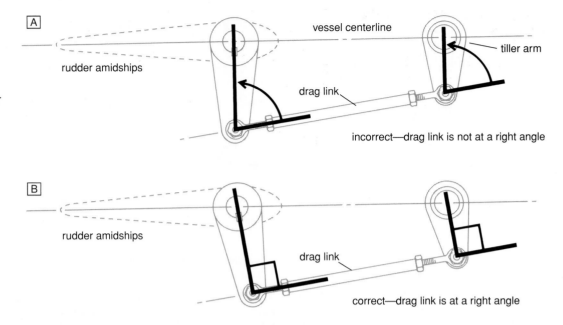

FIGURES 14-17A (incorrect) AND 14-17B (correct). The more the tiller arm and output lever differ in length, and the closer together they are, the more they must be offset from a right angle with the centerline in order to keep the drag link at a right angle with them. *(Jim Sollers)*

Labels in figure A: vessel centerline; tiller arm; rudder amidships; drag link; incorrect—drag link is not at a right angle

Labels in figure B: rudder amidships; drag link; correct—drag link is at a right angle

Operate the wheel from hard over to hard over and ensure that *the rudderstops come into play well before the drag link can cam over center.*

Worm-drive steering. The wheel must be at 90 degrees to the rudderhead, or else a universal joint is needed. The worm gear and traversing nut need greasing two or three times a year. Worm gears are frequently steel (not bronze). Without adequate and regular greasing, they will freeze solid when not in use and prove very hard to free up. There are also a number of links, hinge pins, and clevis pins, all of which need lubricating (with engine oil), and probably a central grease fitting on the top of the shaft assembly.

In time, wear between the worm gear and traversing nut and in the various hinges will allow the rudder to rock ceaselessly from side to side, especially at anchor, accelerating the rate of wear. The traversing nut normally has relatively soft threads of babbitt metal (the white metal found in many bearings) and is designed to wear, thus protecting the worm gear. The threads are renewable at the factory. The various links and clevis pins will need rebushing and renewing as necessary.

Correct alignment on a worm steerer is critical to smooth operation and long life. Once a year, separate the two coupling halves at the rudderhead and check the alignment just as for a propeller shaft (Chapter 10).

Cable steering. Galvanized, brass, bronze, aluminum, and plastic sheaves are all in use on cable steering systems. The metal sheaves gener-

ally have bronze bushings running on stainless steel or brass shafts, though some have stainless steel needle bearings. There is an obvious potential for galvanic interaction; thus it is important to keep the sheaves clean and lubricated. Use engine oil two to three times a season and at the winter haulout.

Plastic sheaves have plastic bearings; the better ones also incorporate extra ball races to absorb side loading. These bearings do not corrode and need no lubrication, although they will attract dirt and thus need flushing with fresh water periodically.

Once a year slack off the cables and check all sheaves to make sure they are spinning freely without excessive play. Replace sheaves and shafts as necessary.

Mounting and aligning sheaves. Sheaves are sometimes subjected to tremendous loads. All sheaves must be rigidly mounted so that no movement that causes loss of cable tension or alignment can occur. *Screws are not acceptable;* the sheave mounting plate should always be through-bolted. Annually, or before a trip, check all fasteners to make sure they are tight and that the bolt holes are not elongating.

The two final sheaves leading the cables onto a steering quadrant take the highest loads of all. These are normally incorporated into one solid fixture, but if they are mounted independently on either side of the quadrant, a rigid brace should be placed between the two bulkheads to which they are fastened (Figure 14-18A).

Accurate alignment of sheaves, rudderhead fittings, and the final lead-in of push-pull and pull-pull cables to a rudderhead fitting is essential to minimize binding, cable wear, and the risk that a cable will jump off a sheave. Most sheaves have adjustable bases (Figures 14-18A and 14-18B); some are self-aligning. As an alignment check, a length of doweling placed in one sheave groove should drop cleanly into the next. When the system is all set up, put the wheel hard over from port to starboard, observing all sheaves, etc. Sometimes with angled rudderstocks and sheaves, some surprising and unexpected changes in alignment can occur. Take the boat out under full engine power and have someone observe all the sheaves and other system components while the rudder is thrown hard over and back a few times. This should reveal any weaknesses.

Cables. Stainless steel 7 × 19 cables are used on most systems (although modern racing boats may use synthetic fibers); 1 × 19 cable is not flexible enough to withstand the constant bending around sheaves, discs, quadrants, etc. Cables need lubricating—when oiling the sheaves (two or three times a season), soak a rag in the same oil (engine oil) and rub it along the whole length of the cables. If you find even one *fishhook* (a broken strand of wire), *replace the cables*. You should, in any case, routinely replace them every few years and keep a spare set—perhaps an old set taken out of service—on board.

Wear on cables is greatly accelerated if they are forced through too tight a radius. For example, ³⁄₁₆-inch (approximately 4 mm) cable should have sheaves with a *minimum* diameter of 4 inches (10 cm); ¼-inch (6 mm) cable, 6 inches (15 cm). This gives a ratio of cable diameter to sheave diameter of a little over *1 to 20*. Push-pull and pull-pull cable conduit should never be turned through a radius of less than *8 inches (20 cm). The fewest possible number of bends and sheaves should be used in routing cables.* If a sheave ever freezes, inspect the cable closely where it has been dragging over the sheave.

Tension. Regularly check cable tension. How frequently depends on the type of steering (open-cable or pull-pull), the length of the steering run, and the amount of boat usage. Six to twelve times a season would not be unreasonable on heavily used open-cable systems. If tension is loose, the steering will be sloppy, with a risk of cables jumping off sheaves and rudderhead fittings; too tight, and the steering will be stiff, with accelerated wear.

With the wheel tied off, it should not be possible to turn the rudderhead fitting by grasping it and applying torque. As a general rule of thumb for an open-cable system, with moderate finger pressure it should be possible to depress the cable between sheaves 1 inch per foot of

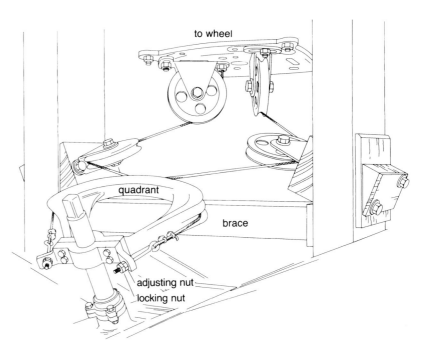

FIGURE 14-18A. To provide trouble-free service, open-cable steering must be designed carefully. The sheaves must be mounted rigidly and aligned accurately with one another. Alignment can be checked by laying a thin steel rod in the grooves of two connecting sheaves; the rod should lie absolutely fair. A solid brace should be used between the last pair of sheaves before the rudderhead. The tremendous forces generated can easily collapse sheave-bearing bulkheads in heavy-weather conditions. *(Jim Sollers)*

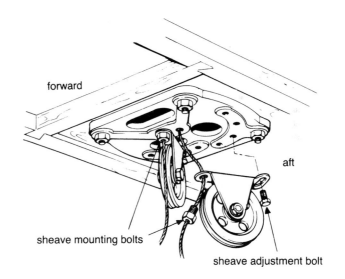

FIGURE 14-18B. An open-cable pedestal steerer viewed from the underside of the cockpit sole. The sheaves are readily adjustable for angle. *(Whitlock)*

cable run, but no more. Because of the inherent friction between cable and conduit in pull-pull systems, cables are kept looser than in open-cable systems; cable tensioners should be only hand-tight. A certain amount of slack in the feel of the steering is unavoidable.

Make cable adjustments at the rudderhead by tightening a tensioning nut on each cable (Figure 14-18A again), but first center the chain in the pedestal on its sprocket with the rudder

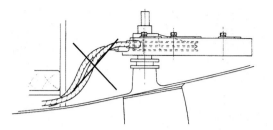 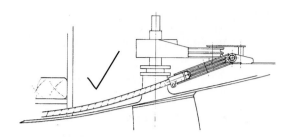

FIGURE 14-19A. Incorrect (left) and correct (right) conduit lead onto the rudderhead fitting. *(Whitlock)*

pointing dead ahead. This is hard to check without taking the compass off the top of the binnacle, which should be done in any event once a year to lubricate the pedestal bearings, so this may be a good time to do both.

Before removing a compass, make a mark on the compass and pedestal so that the two can be exactly realigned. Two or three pieces of masking tape stuck across the joint and then slit works well. The compass should be *swung* by a compass adjuster after it is put back since its characteristics may have changed. (This too should be done annually.)

Some chains have a removable link in the center. If not present, determine the central link and identify it with a piece of string. Line this up on the center of the sprocket and tie off the wheel. Now adjust the cable tensioners so that the rudderhead fitting is also centered in the boat. Be sure to lock off the cable adjusting nuts when finished. Finally, run the wheel from hard over port to hard over starboard, and ensure that the rudder comes up against its stops well before the ends of the chain run off the sprocket.

Cables in conduits. Pay particular attention to the point where the cables exit the conduits; any misalignment will result in cable and conduit wear (Figure 14-19A). Inspect the conduits closely for any signs of cracking in the jacket,

cuts, burned or melted spots, kinks, corrosion under the jacket, or separation of the end fittings from the jacket (Chapter 10). Cables and conduits are not repairable; if any problems exist, replace them both.

Turn the wheel hard over from port to starboard. If you feel any binding, jerking, or stickiness, break the cables loose at the rudderhead and try again. If operation is still rough, the cables probably need replacing (unless there are problems in the pedestal or bulkhead steering; see the Wheels, Pedestals, and Bulkhead Stations section below).

Once a year remove the cables from their conduits and inspect them closely (Figure 14-19B). Refit with a liberal smearing of Teflon-based grease.

Cable-end fittings. Almost all cables terminate in a thimble and two clamps at the rudderhead. Check that there is no wear in the area of the thimble bearing on the cable tensioner; that the cable is snugged up tight around the thimble; that the *saddle* of the cable clamp is over the *standing* part of the cable, and the U-bolts are over the bitter end (Figures 14-20A and 14-20B); and that the cable clamps are tight.

A variety of fittings can be used at the wheel end for joining cables and chains (Nicopress or Talurit sleeves around thimbles, swaged termi-

FIGURE 14-19B. An end fitting used with cables in conduit, commonly used in pull-pull or push-pull steering systems. Less common are in-line conduit greasers, which greatly extend cable life. *(Edson International)*

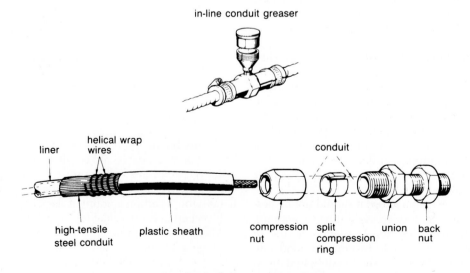

in-line conduit greaser

liner
helical wrap wires
conduit

high-tensile steel conduit
plastic sheath
compression nut
split compression ring
union
back nut

Conduit-end Compression Fitting

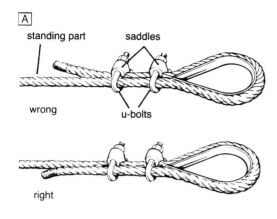

standing part   saddles

wrong

u-bolts

right

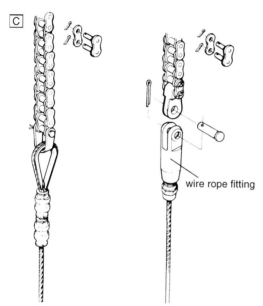

wire rope fitting

FIGURE 14-20A. Cable clamps (Bulldog clamps) are less elegant, but strong and easily adjusted and repaired end fittings. Make sure the clamp's saddle rests on the standing part of the cable. *(Whitlock)*

FIGURE 14-20B. Double cable clamps snugged up to the thimble to stop the cable from working loose. Note the locknut on the adjustment for the eye bolt to keep it from working loose.

FIGURE 14-20C. Chain-to-cable connections. On the left, a thimble retained by two compression sleeves (Nicopress, Talurit); on the right, a mechanical end fitting (Norseman, Sta-Lok). *(Edson International)*

nals, etc—Figure 14-20C). The Standing Rigging section in Chapter 17 gives points to look for. Remove clevis pins and check for wear; be sure to refit the cotter pins (split pins).

Wheels, pedestals, and bulkhead stations.
Wheels are keyed to drive shafts and retained with a wheel nut. In some instances, where wheel and shaft do not match, a brass adapter will be fitted between the two. The wheel may or may not have both a clutch and a brake (Figure 14-21).

Clutch units employ a sliding coupling keyed to the drive shaft that can be pushed in and out of engagement with the wheel hub and locked in place with a spring-loaded pin. The wheel is disengaged when certain types of autopilots or a second steering station are in use.

Older brakes consist of a friction band that clamps around the drive shaft. Newer brakes are almost always operated by a small handwheel in

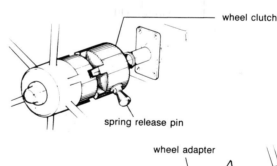

wheel clutch

spring release pin

FIGURE 14-21. A wheel clutch disengages a wheel from the shaft when an autopilot or another wheel (two-station steering) is in use. Adapters make it possible to install wheels on otherwise incompatible shafts. *(Edson International)*

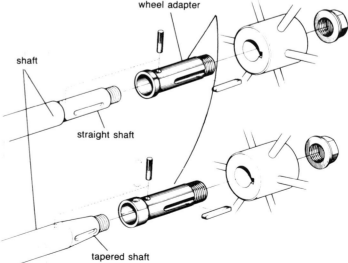

wheel adapter

shaft

straight shaft

tapered shaft

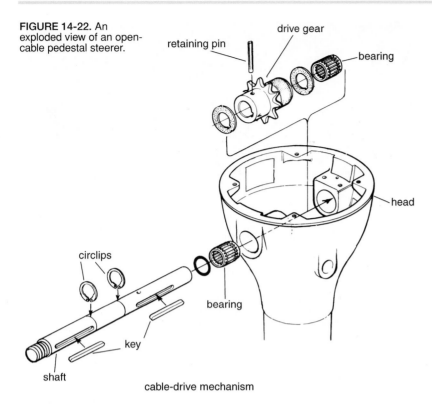

FIGURE 14-22. An exploded view of an open-cable pedestal steerer.

drive gear

retaining pin

bearing

head

circlips

bearing

key

shaft

cable-drive mechanism

FIGURE 14-23. A pedestal should be tied into the boat's bonding and lightning-protection system to reduce corrosion and lightning-strike hazards. *(Whitlock)*

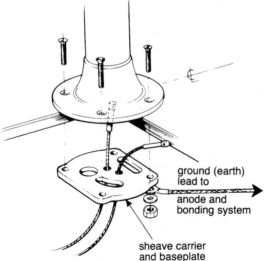

ground (earth) lead to anode and bonding system

sheave carrier and baseplate

the center of the steering wheel that is threaded into the end of the wheel shaft; screwing in the handwheel tightens the brake.

Drive shafts run in bronze bushings or needle bearings (Figure 14-22). The latter are either stainless steel or plastic. A brass or bronze (much preferred) sprocket is keyed to the drive shaft turning a stainless steel chain, except on rack-and-pinion pedestal steering (see previous section).

Clutch hubs, pedestal bearings, and chains all need lubricating at least annually, preferably two or three times a season. The compass will need to be removed from the binnacle (see the Tension section above). Engine oil is fine for the clutch at the point where it slides on the drive shaft and for bronze bushings and chain. Do *not* use grease on the chain since it merely sits on the surface of the links collecting dirt. It *is* used, however, on stainless steel needle bearings (Teflon-based waterproof grease, such as Lubriplate Marine-Lube "A"). Plastic roller bearings need no lubrication but will benefit from a shot of Teflon spray.

Pedestals are made from various grades of aluminum with different surface treatments (anodizing, painting, etc.). They merely need washing and waxing; wax with a good-quality boat or car polish. Pedestals should be tied into the boat's bonding and lightning-protection systems to reduce corrosion and lightning strike hazards (Figure 14-23; note that this conflicts with advice given by Jefa—see above).

Trouble spots. Apart from routine wear of all components, galvanic interaction sometimes occurs between stainless steel bearings and aluminum pedestals, causing corrosion and blistering of painted surfaces.

If a bulkhead steerer starts to stiffen up, check the shaft where it passes through the bulkhead; the problem may be nothing more than damp wood swelling and binding on the shaft. In this case, the hole will just need enlarging.

If a rudder is not fitted with rudderstops (see the Rudderstops section below), or if the rudderstops fail, there is a danger of chain-to-wire adapters running up onto sprockets, breaking teeth, damaging adapters, and possibly throwing the chain off the sprocket. Units that have an endless chain driving a second sprocket must be kept tensioned and aligned to stop the chain from jumping off the sprockets; the lower unit will be adjustable.

Pedestal overhaul. Remove the compass, wheel nut, wheel, and clutch (if fitted). Slack off the cables at the rudderhead, lift the chain off the sprocket, and tie it off out of the way. Place some rags in the pedestal to catch any dropped fittings. In most instances, the drive shaft is retained in the pedestal solely by the locking pin through the sprocket. Drive this pin out with a hammer and punch (carefully—it may come out only one way). Place a nut back on the shaft and use a block of wood behind the nut to drive the shaft assembly out of the pedestal. Replace worn or broken parts at this time. Reassembly is the reversal of disassembly.

Hydraulic steering. A simple hydraulic system has a single helm station pumping hydraulic fluid to a single steering cylinder. The piston in the cylinder moves a tiller arm that is fastened to the rudderstock. Sometimes a single helm pump is installed without check valves. In this case, if the rudder is turned (e.g., by a wave hitting it), the wheel will turn. Most pumps, however, incorporate check valves, which prevent the rudder from turning the wheel. Where two or more helm stations or an autopilot are teed into the same hydraulic circuit, check valves are essential to prevent one helm station from *motoring* another, rather than turning the rudder.

A typical check valve assembly's operation is illustrated in Figure 14-24A. *All hydraulic steering systems with built-in check valves should have either a manually operated or a solenoid-operated bypass valve*, as shown in Figure 14-24B. In the event of a steering failure, the bypass valve is opened, allowing oil to pass freely from one side of the steering cylinder to the other. An emergency tiller can then be installed on the rudderpost and used to steer the boat. (In reality, many systems do not have this bypass valve; in this case, at the very least *the pin that connects the hydraulic cylinder to the rudder arm should be both accessible and of a type that can be released quickly, freeing up the rudder.*)

Routine maintenance. If the pump is chain driven, check the alignment and tension on the chain every three or four months. Raise or lower the pump on its mount to adjust tension. Pumps are best installed with chain sprockets in a vertical plane; if they are not, loose chains tend to work their way off.

The oil level in pump reservoirs should also be checked every three or four months and topped off as necessary. *Hydraulic systems are extremely sensitive to dirt; before removing any filler plugs, scrupulously clean the external surfaces of the pump.* If any oil has been lost, check all connections, seals, hoses, and lines. Make sure there is no chafing where hoses and lines pass through bulkheads.

Where two or more helm stations (or an autopilot) are teed into the same hydraulic circuit, the normal practice is to tie all the pump reservoirs together. A line is run from the fill plug on the lowest pump to the drain plug on the next highest, etc. The whole system is topped off via *the fill plug on the highest pump.*

When topping off, use only the specified hydraulic oil; *never use engine oil or brake fluid.* Table 14-1 gives a list of hydraulic oils obtainable worldwide and suitable for most systems. Once a year drain a sample of oil *from the lowest pump* and check for any signs of contamination such as water or dirt. (Moisture can form from condensation in reservoirs—it will cause rust on sensitive valves and spools, leading to failure.) If any

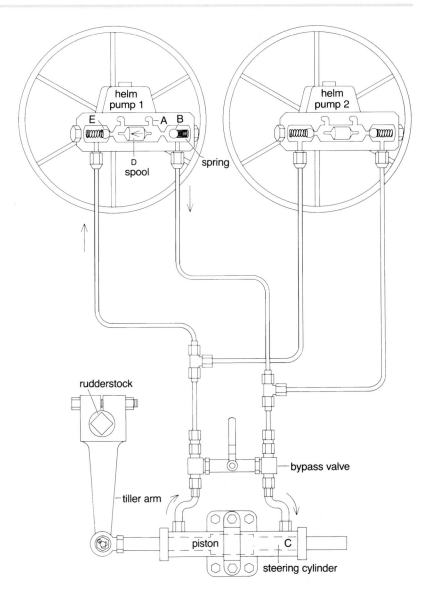

FIGURE 14-24A. The operation of hydraulic steering systems. Imagine the wheel on helm pump 1 is turned clockwise. Oil is pushed down line A; the oil pressure lifts ball valve B off its seat against its spring pressure and sends oil to piston C. At the same time, the oil pressure moves piston D—the spool—to the left, and the pin on the end of this spool pushes the second ball valve, E, off its seat. This allows return oil from the other side of the steering cylinder back into the helm pump reservoir. The oil pressure pushes both ball valves in the check valve at helm pump 2 against their seats so that no oil flows through the auxiliary steering station. *(Jim Sollers)*

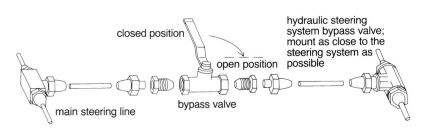

FIGURE 14-24B. Detail of a hydraulic steering bypass valve assembly, which is essential for fitting an emergency tiller (see pages 646–47). *(Wagner Marine)*

TABLE 14-1. Hydraulic Oil Recommendations

Manufacturer	Hydraulic Oil
Agip	OSO 32
Aral	Vitam GF 32, Vitam DE 32
Avia	Avilub RSL 32
BP	Energol HLP 32, Energol HLP-D 32
Castrol	Hyspin AWS 32
Chevron	EP Hydraulic Oil 32
Defrol	HLP 22
Esso	Nuto H 32
Fina	Hydran 32
Fuchs	Renolin MR 10, Renolin B 10
Mobil	DTE 24, Hydraulic Oil HLPD 32
OMV	HLP 32
Optimol	Hydro 5035
Shell	Tellus Oil 32
Texaco	Rando Oil HD A-32
Valvoline	ETC 25

moisture or dirt is present, drain the system until only clean oil comes out, then refill and bleed as necessary (see the following section).

Bleeding a hydraulic system. Oil leaks are the main cause of problems on hydraulic systems. Small leaks can be handled by regularly topping off the reservoir until repairs can be made. However, if any air gets into the system it will cause the steering to feel spongy or even to fail altogether. To test for air, put the wheel hard over in both directions; if it bounces back when released, that's a pretty good indication of trapped air. To remove the air, or after draining and refilling a system, use the following procedure:

1. Fill all pump reservoirs, starting at the lowest (if there is more than one pump) and working to the highest. Replace the fill plugs on the lower reservoirs but leave the upper (or only) one open. Find a length of tubing that will screw into the upper reservoir fill fitting and a clean funnel that will jam in the tubing. *Maintain a good oil level in the funnel at all times.*

2. Fit two lengths of clear plastic tubing to the bleed nipples on the steering cylinder(s) (Figure 14-25) and place the free ends in a container with a little oil in it. Keep the tubing immersed in the oil to prevent air from being sucked up the lines. (Note that pistons must be installed with the bleed nipples facing up.)

3. Close any cylinder bypass lines. Determine which side of a cylinder will be pressurized when the wheel is turned clockwise, and open the bleed screw on that side.

4. Turn the wheel (the highest wheel, if there is more than one) clockwise slowly. Air and oil will be vented from the cylinder bleed screw. *Keep the funnel topped off.* When no more air

is vented, tighten the bleed screw, open the bleed screw on the other end of the cylinder, and turn the wheel counterclockwise slowly until all air is expelled.

5. If the system has more than one wheel, repeat the procedure at each helm station while keeping the funnel on the highest reservoir filled with oil. If the system has twin steering cylinders, open the bleed screws on the same side of both cylinders at the same time, and close each when all the air is vented.

6. The steering may still be spongy due to residual air. This should work its way up into the top reservoir over time. Check its level periodically. If the sponginess persists, repeat the bleeding procedure.

Tests at the annual haulout. In time—especially if dirt has entered and scored pumps and cylinders—wear on pumps, check valves, and steering cylinders will lead to hydraulic *creep* or *slip*; the rudder will slowly turn independently of the wheel, or it will be possible to keep turning the wheel slowly when the rudder is hard over. This poses no immediate problem, but the unit will need rebuilding at the next haulout.

To determine where the problem lies, close any bypass valves (but not any valves on lines to helm stations), fit the emergency tiller (this will be good practice!) or grasp the rudderhead by hand if there is no emergency tiller, and push the rudder hard in both directions.

1. If the rudder moves but the wheel(s) remains stationary, fluid is seeping down the sides of the piston in the steering cylinder; the steering cylinder needs rebuilding.

2. If the rudder and steering wheel(s) both move, the check valves in the helm pump are leaking and need rebuilding. (In a single-pump installation with no check valves the wheel will turn; this is OK.)

Amateurs should not attempt pump and piston disassembly; pumps, check valves, and steering cylinders are built to very close tolerances. Seek professional help.

Troubleshooting. As long as the oil is kept clean and the system is properly installed, hydraulic steering is very reliable. The following are the most common problems:

Wheel is stiff. Disconnect the steering cylinder from the tiller arm at the rudderpost and try again. If this eliminates the stiffness, the problem is in the rudder installation (see previous sections) and not the steering system. If the stiffness persists, check the wheel itself for binding (maybe the brake is on!). Other potential sources

Hydraulic Pistons (Rams)

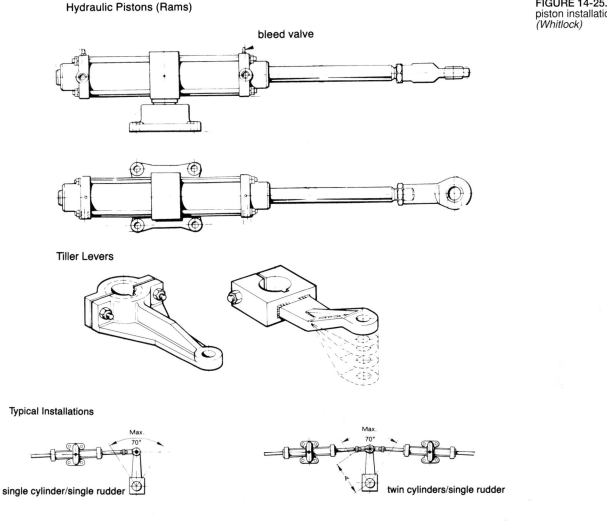

bleed valve

Tiller Levers

Typical Installations

Max. 70°

single cylinder/single rudder

Max. 70°

twin cylinders/single rudder

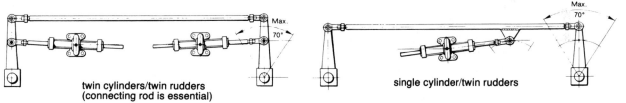

Max. 70°

twin cylinders/twin rudders
(connecting rod is essential)

Max. 70°

single cylinder/twin rudders

FIGURE 14-25. Hydraulic piston installations. *(Whitlock)*

of trouble are the wrong oil in the system (too viscous) or undersized piping.

Wheel turns but rudder does not respond. Check first to see that a cylinder bypass valve is not open. Check for a mechanical failure (tiller arm slipping on rudderpost, etc.) or a loss of hydraulic oil. If the system has more than one helm station, check to see whether the other wheel (or autopilot motor) is turning. If so, its check valves are defective.

If none of these checks reveals a problem, break the steering cylinder loose at the tiller arm and try moving the cylinder rod in and out by hand. If you can move it, the internal piston seals have gone and the cylinder needs rebuild-ing. If the cylinder checks out OK, then the helm pump itself may have failed, though this is uncommon. In any event, ship an emergency tiller (see the Emergency Steering section below) and seek professional help.

Hydraulic plumbing. Refer to Chapter 12.

Rudderstops. Good, strong rudderstops capa-ble of absorbing sudden heavy shock loads (such as when a rudder is slammed over by a following wave, or someone lets go of the tiller or wheel when moving backward) are essential to protect both the rudder and the steering system (Whit-lock recommends that rudderstops be able to absorb 150% of the maximum rated rudder

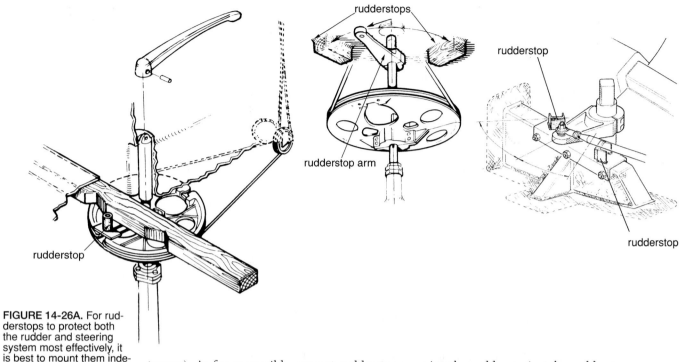

 runderstops

ruderstop arm

runderstop

runderstop

ruderstop

FIGURE 14-26A. For rudderstops to protect both
the rudder and steering
system most effectively, it
is best to mount them independently of the rest of the
steering system. In the
illustration at left, the rud-
derstop is mounted on a
radial-drive wheel; in the
middle and right illustrations, the ruderstops are
mounted independently.
(Edson International)

torque). As far as possible, mount ruderstops
independently of the rest of the steering system,
rather than building them into quadrants and
radial-drive wheels and discs (Figures 14-26A
and 14-26B).

At a marina or at anchor, always tie off the
steering so that there is no risk of waves slam-

ming the rudder against the ruderstops.

Annually, check that the ruderstops are
secure and they engage the relevant fitting on
the rudderstock cleanly and fully.

Emergency steering. All wheel-steered boats
must have some form of emergency tiller that
can be installed readily if the steering fails (Figure 14-27). What is almost as important is that
the skipper and crew practice fitting it *before* an
emergency to avoid surprises.

A solid rudderstock is usually squared off to
accept the emergency tiller. Hollow shafts with
through-bolted rudderhead fittings take a slotted
tiller fitting over the bolt. Since the wheel

Troubleshooting Chart 14-3. Wheel Steering Failures: Hydraulic	
Does the hydraulic pump drive shaft turn when the wheel is turned? **YES**	**NO** Check for disengaged clutch; slipping wheel or sprockets; or broken or jumped clutch, if fitted.
Does the pump have oil? (Check the reservoir.) **YES**	**NO** If the oil is low, fill and bleed (see page 644). Check all connections, hoses, and seals for leaks.
Does the piston at the rudderhead move when the wheel is turned? **YES**	**NO** Make sure no bypass valve or solenoid is open. Double-check the oil level and bleed again. If this fails to restore steering, the piston and/or pump or the check valves (if fitted) need rebuilding.
Does the rudderstock turn when the piston moves the tiller arm? **YES**	**NO** The tiller arm clamp is slipping on the rudderstock. Tighten or replace bolts and setscrews or shim as necessary (see pages 635–36).
The internal webs in the rudder itself have sheared. Rig a jury rudder. On sailboats, balance the rig.	

FIGURE 14-26B. Ruderstops on the base of a rack-
and-pinion pedestal-type steerer. *(Jefa)*

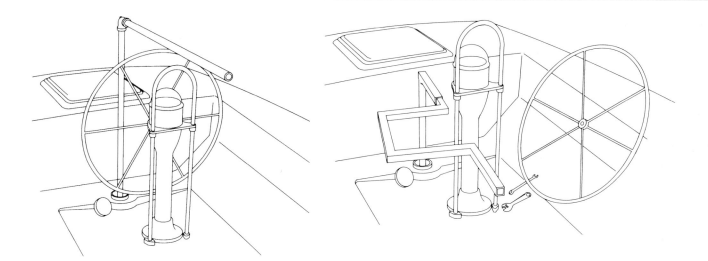

pedestal is frequently in the way of the tiller, four approaches can be taken to get around it:

1. A very short tiller, which will be of little use in large seas.
2. A very tall tiller coming over the top of the pedestal, which will be hard to control, with a serious tendency to bend sideways.
3. A curved tiller bending around the pedestal, which is the preferred solution.
4. A tiller installed facing aft, which will "reverse" the steering.

It is extremely hard to fit a long tiller to a rudderstock when the seas are causing the rudder to weave around. It is far better to have a tiller in two sections: a short stub to be fitted to the rudder to bring it under control, and the main tiller slotting onto the stub to provide leverage for effective steering. Note that any tiller passing close to a compass should be nonmagnetic.

If the hydraulic steering has internal check valves and no bypass valve, you will have to disconnect the drive cylinder actuating arm from the tiller arm before using an emergency tiller (unless the hydraulic circuit has failed). With worm-drive steering, you will have to unbolt the whole steering assembly from the rudderstock flange and bolt on a separate, flanged tiller.

Autopilots

Autopilots are now considered a necessity by most cruising sailors and are finding their way onto ever-smaller boats. On long journeys, once freedom from the helm has been experienced, there's no going back to hand steering!

How They Work

The boat's course is set on a compass. Two types of compasses are used: *fluxgate* compasses (by far the most common), which operate electronically, and *photo-optic* compasses, which utilize a light beam to read the compass.

Any deviation from the preset course is transmitted to a central processing unit (CPU), a minicomputer. This unit then switches power to an electric motor that drives an actuator to effect a course correction. The control unit's sophisticated circuitry smoothes out rhythmical fluctuations in the course, such as those that arise from following seas. There may also be a rudder control, which alters the degree of response to any change in the boat's heading: a low rudder control setting will result in small rudder movements; a high setting causes large rudder movements. Some units have a sea-state or deadband control. This simply determines how far off course the boat may wander before the autopilot responds with a course correction. Newer units may include a *rate gyro*—a solid-state device that responds to acceleration. This can be used to fine-tune the steering response when a boat is being thrown about by the waves. In short, the electronics packages are becoming increasingly sophisticated, resulting in autopilots that can hold ever-more consistent headings, even in difficult sea states.

All autopilots use an electric motor to move

the rudder and make course corrections. Some motors drive a belt or chain (rotary autopilots); others move an arm in and out (linear). This may be done mechanically (via a set of gears) or hydraulically (via a pump and hydraulic piston or *ram*). Almost all motors are geared down: the reduction box may be a *worm* type or a *planetary* type. Mechanical linear drive units must also convert rotary motion to an in-and-out motion; this is generally done via a gear mounted on a worm shaft similar to the worm-drive steering already covered in this chapter, though obviously on a much more compact scale.

Cockpit-mounted units are either rotary, using a belt to turn the boat's steering wheel, or mechanical linear, using an arm to move the tiller backward and forward (Figures 14-28A to 14-28D). Below-deck units may be rotary, mechanical linear, or hydraulic linear. Below-deck rotary units use a chain to drive another sprocket and chain linked into existing cable steering, or else operate a completely independent cable system with its own quadrant on the rudder shaft. Mechanical linear and hydraulic units either turn the existing quadrant via an operating arm or else are connected to an independent tiller arm mounted on the rudder shaft (Figures 14-29A and 14-29B).

An autopilot linked to a GPS and electronic navigation can be set up to steer a route with multiple course changes. If linked to a wind direction sensor, in the *wind mode* it will hold a course with respect to the wind direction (i.e., operate in similar fashion to a wind vane—see below), rather than holding a compass course.

Below-deck hookups. All autopilots using existing steering systems suffer from a major

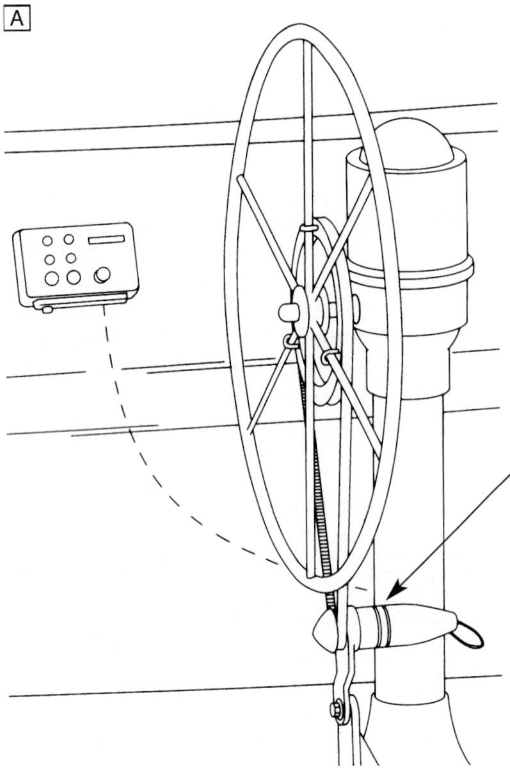

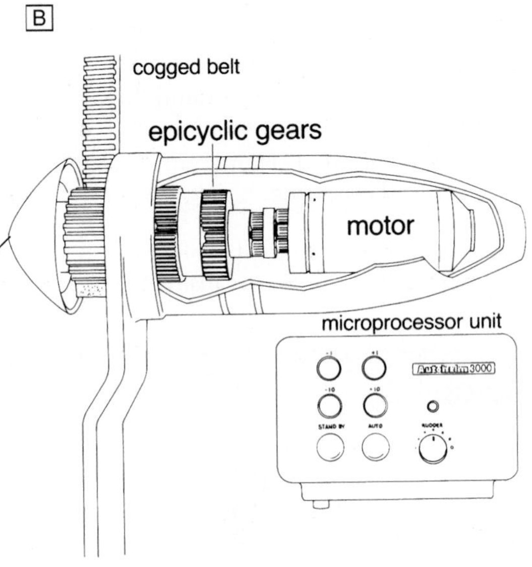

FIGURES 14-28A AND 14-28B. This wheel-mounted autopilot utilizes an epicyclic (planetary) reduction gearbox to rotate the wheel via a cogged belt. *(Jim Sollers)*

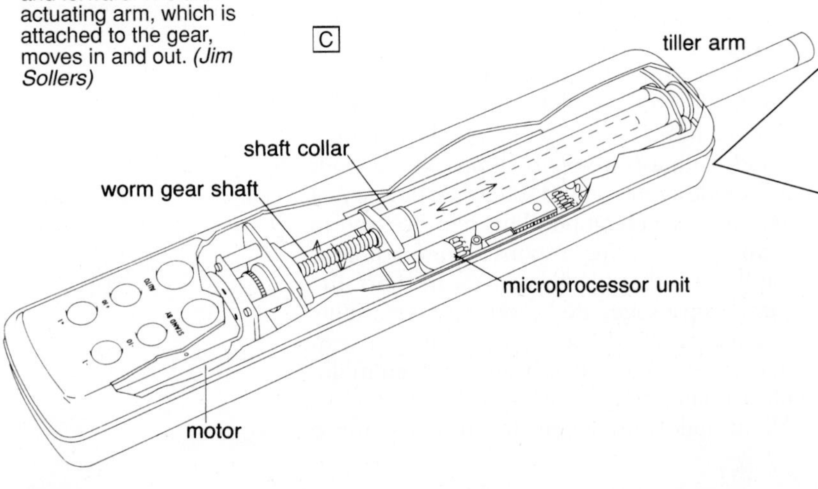

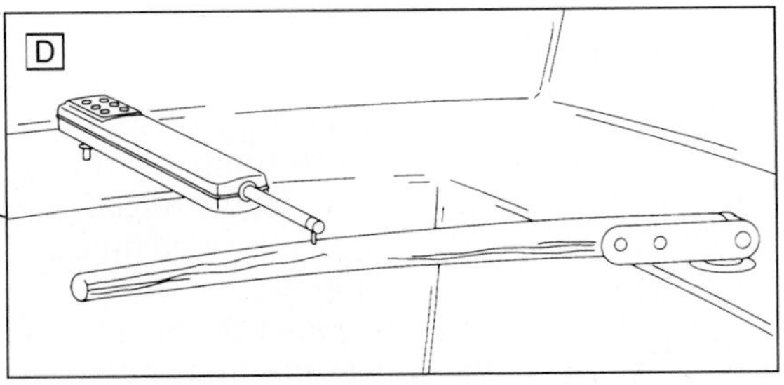

cogged belt

epicyclic gears

motor

microprocessor unit

FIGURES 14-28C AND 14-28D. Worm-gear autopilot. This tiller-mounted unit has a gear running on a worm-geared shaft. As the shaft turns, the gear moves backward and forward. The tiller actuating arm, which is attached to the gear, moves in and out. *(Jim Sollers)*

tiller arm

shaft collar

worm gear shaft

microprocessor unit

motor

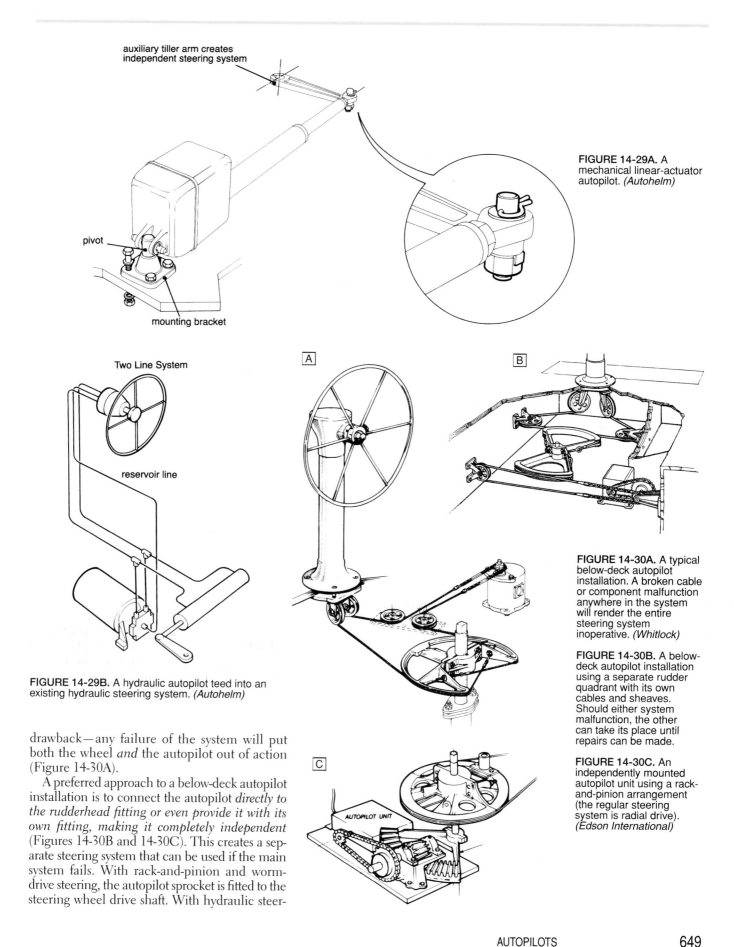

auxiliary tiller arm creates
independent steering system

pivot

mounting bracket

FIGURE 14-29A. A mechanical linear-actuator autopilot. *(Autohelm)*

Two Line System

reservoir line

FIGURE 14-29B. A hydraulic autopilot teed into an existing hydraulic steering system. *(Autohelm)*

A

B

C

AUTOPILOT UNIT

FIGURE 14-30A. A typical below-deck autopilot installation. A broken cable or component malfunction anywhere in the system will render the entire steering system inoperative. *(Whitlock)*

FIGURE 14-30B. A below-deck autopilot installation using a separate rudder quadrant with its own cables and sheaves. Should either system malfunction, the other can take its place until repairs can be made.

FIGURE 14-30C. An independently mounted autopilot unit using a rack-and-pinion arrangement (the regular steering system is radial drive). *(Edson International)*

drawback—any failure of the system will put both the wheel *and* the autopilot out of action (Figure 14-30A).

A preferred approach to a below-deck autopilot installation is to connect the autopilot *directly to the rudderhead fitting or even provide it with its own fitting, making it completely independent* (Figures 14-30B and 14-30C). This creates a separate steering system that can be used if the main system fails. With rack-and-pinion and worm-drive steering, the autopilot sprocket is fitted to the steering wheel drive shaft. With hydraulic steering, the main circuit will need a bypass valve, and the autopilot itself will need a bypass valve for when it is not in use (see Figure 14-33 below).

Problems with Autopilots

Regardless of its size, an autopilot has a limited power output. The more the wind and seas build, the harder an autopilot will work (as opposed to a wind vane self-steerer, which tends to work better in strong winds—see below). If a boat is not well balanced, the autopilot will have trouble steering. In fact, as a general rule, if the helmsperson is having trouble holding a course for any reason, the autopilot will too. An autopilot is not a fix for a boat that does not steer well!

Problems common to all autopilots. There are certain recurrent themes with all autopilots:

The boat slowly veers off to one side. There is insufficient rudder reaction to course changes. Increase the rudder setting.

The boat oversteers and follows an S-course. There is too much rudder reaction to course changes. Decrease the rudder setting.

Course corrections are delayed. The boat continually wanders off course before the autopilot reacts. The deadband (sea-state) setting is too high (this may not be adjustable). There may be too much slack in the steering cables, loose linkages, or air in a hydraulic unit (the rudder is weaving independently of the steering system). This will be more pronounced in calm conditions. Tighten cables as necessary. Check the oil level on hydraulic circuits and bleed all air from the circuits. Find out where the oil is going. In particular, check the shaft seals on hydraulic rams.

The boat heads onto a different course or turns in circles. This is almost certainly the result of *electrical interference* from such things as a noisy alternator or an SSB (especially when transmitting; see Chapter 8). If it happens only when the engine is running, it is almost certainly the alternator or its regulator. It could also be the result of interaction between the autopilot compass and the boat's compass. They should be at least 39 inches (1 m) apart; try moving one. Perhaps someone has just placed a radio or other source of magnetic interference close to the autopilot's compass.

The autopilot trips off. This is likely to be the result of either low voltage or voltage spikes (high-voltage transients). In either case the CPU trips. Does it happen only when a large load kicks in, such as when cranking the engine or using an electric winch? Check for voltage drop at the CPU and at the autopilot drive motor when the motor is in operation (Chapter 4).

Check all wiring connections, especially terminals and plugs on cockpit-mounted units. It may be necessary to move the CPU power leads to their own battery and/or increase the size of the leads to combat voltage drop. Voltage spikes can be generated by alternators, especially if batteries are in poor shape, or they can occur when large loads kick off.

The autopilot fails to work at all. Check for voltage *at the* CPU and at the autopilot drive motor. If present, check the polarity (Chapter 4); reverse polarity may have done irreparable damage. If the unit has power and correct polarity, disconnect the leads to the drive motor, set a course, turn the boat, and check to see if there is any output voltage from the CPU. If not, it has an internal problem.

If the CPU is producing output voltage, connect a 12-volt battery (or 24 volts on a 24-volt system) directly to the motor and see if it spins. Reverse the leads; the motor should reverse. Larger motors have a solenoid-operated clutch; if the motor fails to work, identify the solenoid and jump it out to see which item is defective (see the Starter Motor Circuits section in Chapter 7). If the motor still fails to work, *disconnect it from any actuating mechanism* (since this may be seized) and try again. If the motor is bad, conduct the various motor tests outlined in Chapter 7 in the Permanent-Magnet Motors section.

The autopilot operates sluggishly. Check for low voltage at the drive motor *when it is operating.* Check for binding in the parts of the steering system driven by the motor, such as a wheel brake accidentally left engaged. If necessary, disconnect the motor to check its no-load operation; while doing this, check the free movement of all relevant linkages in the steering system.

The unit operates backward. The power leads from the CPU to the motor are crossed; reverse them. Some units have an internal changeover switch that effectively reverses the leads.

The autopilot exhibits a lack of power. This is a perennial problem on sailboats. The only answer is to *balance* the sails, even at the expense of performance. For tiller autopilots, see below.

Cockpit-mounted units. Salt water, in one way or another, is the big problem with all cockpit-mounted equipment.

Water in the CPU. All cockpit-mounted units are susceptible to water in the electronics. Many are only spray proof. A good dunking in green water—such as when pooped—may penetrate the seals. Do not mount CPUs in wet locations and be sure to store them in a dry place.

Water in the drive motor. The most likely point of ingress is through the cable gland. If the unit is likely to be subjected to a lot of spray or solid water, check this seal before use and improve it as necessary—with 3M 5200 caulking, for example.

Corrosion in the power supply socket. Another likely source of trouble! Keep the pins and plugs liberally coated with petroleum jelly. I have found that even when clean, some plugs make a poor contact with the pins; knocking or twisting the plug slightly will break the power supply and cause the CPU to trip off. A bit of judicious bending of pins or plug sockets generally solves the problem.

Cockpit wheel steerers. *Wheel drum centering and motor alignment.* Wheel drums are bolted to the center of steering wheels. If the drum is not centered exactly, it will alternately tighten and loosen belt tension as the wheel turns. If not bolted squarely to the wheel, or if the motor is not mounted *directly in line with and square to* the wheel drum, alignment will be out, stressing belts and tending to throw them off (Figure 14-31). Motor mounting must be solid and inflexible.

Slipping belts. Most belts are toothed (i.e., have ridges across them); the teeth mate with a spline on the end of the motor drive shaft. While some have good-sized teeth, others do not; the latter are especially prone to slip when wet, when under a load, or whenever the drum is not properly centered or aligned. Beware of overtightening belts to stop slipping; this will lead to premature bearing failure in the motor. Tension of small-toothed belts should be sufficient to prevent slipping when the steering wheel is turned by hand with the clutch engaged; when the clutch is disengaged, however, the steering wheel should spin freely with no belt drag. If an old belt is glued around the drum with its splines facing out, it will greatly increase traction, but this in turn may lead to the destruction of the gears instead of slipping of the belt!

Broken belts. Like paper, belts are strong in tension but tear easily if nicked or damaged. Rough spots on wheel drums and poor alignment will shorten belt life.

Stripped drive gears. Most units incorporate a planetary-type reduction gearbox, which will allow the motor to be turned over by the wheel and so absorb some shock loads from the rudder. Nevertheless, a good number of gears are plastic and will strip off under heavy loads.

Some units, however, incorporate larger motors and worm gearing. The motors *cannot* be turned over by the steering wheel (the worm gears exert too much braking action). In this case, the drive pulley will be installed with shear pins, and if overloaded, the pins will give. If the motor shaft turns but the pulley does not, check the shear pins.

It seems that most small autopilots are made for the weekend market and not designed for

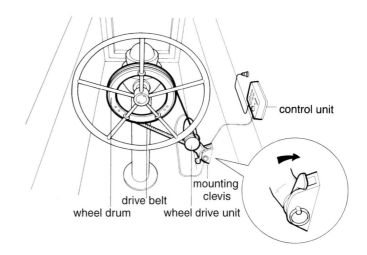

drive belt
wheel drum
mounting clevis
wheel drive unit
control unit

FIGURE 14-31. An autopilot drive arrangement on a cockpit-mounted wheel steerer. To work properly, the wheel drum must be centered exactly in relation to the wheel's axis, and the drum must be in line with and square to the wheel drive unit. *(Autohelm)*

continuous cruising. Manufacturers accept a small percentage of failures from heavy use to hold down the cost for the majority of the marketplace. For offshore cruising, an oversized autopilot is strongly recommended.

Tiller steerers. *Seizure of the operating arm.* All units use a gear traveling up and down a worm-geared shaft to move the actuating arm in and out through a seal. Many units, such as old Autohelms (prior to the 1990s; www.raymarine.com), use a *steel* gear, which is likely to rust if not properly lubricated and kept dry.

When the actuating arm moves in and out, minor pressure changes occur inside the unit that can draw in humid, salt-laden air. (Some units have a pressure compensation chamber to reduce this effect.) If salt-laden air does penetrate the seals, and the unit is then left unused for an extended period, it may seize. If this happens, remove the motor and check motor operation and actuator movement independently of each other to confirm that the actuator is at fault.

It may be possible to free a frozen actuator with liberal doses of penetrating fluid (e.g., WD-40 or Boeshield), perhaps some heat from a propane torch, and a judicious application of force! Clean all threads and bearings, grease with a high-quality marine grease such as Lubriplate Spray Lube "A," and *regrease every time the unit is put away for more than a day or two.* Better get a spare; this actuator won't last long.

Autopilot is overpowered by the waves. If the actuating unit is continually overpowered, with the arm being driven in and out against its end stops, sooner or later something will give. The unit had better be unshipped.

Two boats ago we had a heavy-displacement (30,000 pounds), 39-foot ketch, steered by a tiller. Our Autohelm 2000 was repeatedly overwhelmed, and the mounting units at both ends broke at different times. We solved the problem by installing a trim tab on the trailing edge of the rudder with an operating arm at the rudderhead (Figure 14-32). Two cables came forward to a *dummy* operating arm on the tiller. The autopilot actuating unit was mounted on a stainless steel pipe and hooked onto the dummy operating arm. The pipe slotted into a hole drilled through the tiller and was locked in place at a right angle to the tiller by a pin pushed down through the tiller and the pipe. The autopilot steered the boat *via the trim tab*, which took minimal effort—never more than a pound or two of thrust—and used minimal power.

Every time a wave hit the rudder, the whole unit was free to swing and go with the flow; the autopilot was *never* stressed. It did thousands of miles in all kinds of conditions. It even held a pretty fair course in sizable quartering and following seas. I understand that 20 years later it is still working fine! Given the right size trim tab, this setup can be used to control tiller-steered boats *of any size*. Note that anytime the actuating unit is mounted on the tiller and moves with it, *the CPU must be mounted independently of the actuating unit*. If the CPU is built into the actuator (as many are), every time the tiller moves, it will confuse the CPU!

A similar system can be used on any wind vane self-steerer (see below) by connecting a small tiller-type autopilot in place of the vane and using the rest of the system to steer the boat. Once again, the load on the autopilot is minimal; large boats can be steered by small autopilots, with a power drain well below that of a traditionally installed autopilot.

Below-deck linear actuators (mechanical and hydraulic).

Quadrant failures. Many times a linear actuator is attached to an existing quadrant by simply drilling a hole in the quadrant and through-bolting. Most quadrants, especially lightweight ones, are not designed for this kind of point loading. If the actuator must be attached to the quadrant, *a plate of the same material as the quadrant* should be bolted firmly to the quadrant, and the actuator should be bolted to the plate to spread the stresses. The preferred system has an independent tiller arm bolted to the rudder shaft; this provides a completely independent steering system if the main system fails.

Reduction gear failure (mechanical actuators). In all instances a rudder installation must be designed so that the rudder hits its stops before the autopilot actuator is driven into its stops. Otherwise, powerful following seas, or letting go of the wheel when moving backward, can slam the rudder over and destroy the actuator.

Actuator jams. Check all mounting bolts. Full steering loads taken by the actuator require it to be mounted as solidly as any other part of the steering system. Note that unless the quadrant or tiller arm on the rudderpost and the actuator are

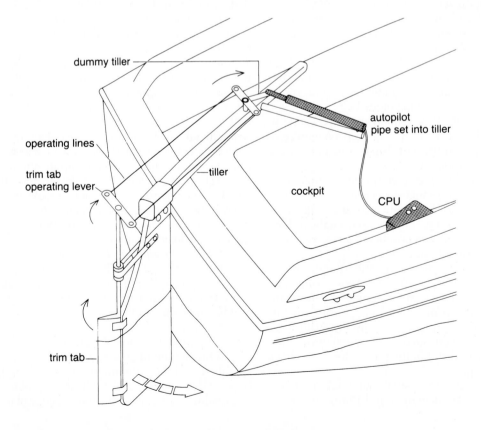

FIGURE 14-32. Autopilot performance on a tiller-steered boat can be improved by the use of a trim tab. The autopilot is tiller-mounted and controls the trim tab through a dummy tiller and bell crank assembly. *(Jim Sollers)*

dummy tiller

autopilot pipe set into tiller

operating lines

trim tab operating lever

tiller

cockpit

CPU

trim tab

in the same plane (mounted at the same angle), their angle to one another will change as the rudder turns. *The actuator installation must accommodate this changing angle.* If it does not, the unit will jam and/or the actuator will be bent or torn from its mounting.

Hydraulic creep. Hydraulic steering may have a pump teed into an existing hydraulic circuit, or it may have a separate pump, reservoir, and actuator operating an independent tiller arm at the rudderpost (the latter is preferred; see the Below-Deck Hookups section above).

When an autopilot (teed into an existing circuit) is in use, check valves on the steering wheel–mounted pump prevent flow through that pump (Figure 14-33); when the steering wheel is in use, check valves on the autopilot pump close off the autopilot circuit. If any of the check valves fail to seat properly, the steering will creep (i.e., the rudder will move slowly even when the wheel is locked).

Creep may also result from fluid that bleeds down the sides of the piston that drives the actuating arm. This can happen in both teed units and independently mounted units.

Hydraulic emergency override. When an *independently mounted* hydraulic unit is in operation, *it is almost impossible to override it.* Such units should have an emergency bypass solenoid remotely controlled from the steering station so that at the push of a button the hydraulic pump can be bypassed, restoring full control to the steering wheel (Figure 14-33 again). The solenoid should be the *normally open* type so that any power failure (and therefore autopilot failure) will *automatically* open the circuit.

Below-deck rotary autopilots.
Alignment, tension, and mounting. As in other installations, full steering loads are taken by the motor. It must be rigidly bolted down, with its chain sprocket correctly aligned and chain tension maintained. Any flex in the motor mounts will accelerate chain wear and run the risk of driving the chain off a sprocket.

Centering of chains and rudderstops. In cases

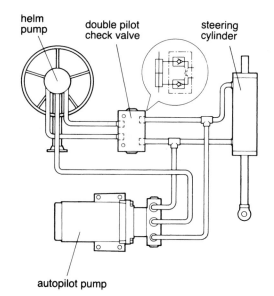

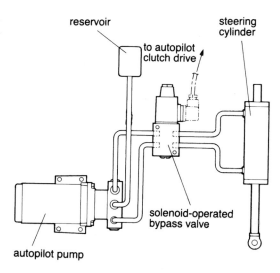

FIGURE 14-33. Typical hydraulic autopilot circuits. An autopilot teed into existing steering system (left). Most helm pumps have built-in check valves, but if these are not fitted, the double check-valve unit shown will have to be installed to enable the wheel to override the autopilot pump. An independent hydraulic autopilot (below). The solenoid bypass valve allows the wheel to override the autopilot, either on command by the helmsperson or if power fails. (Wagner Marine)

where the autopilot drives a length of chain fitted into a cable system, it is obviously essential that the chain be centered over the motor sprocket when the rudder is centered, and that the rudder hit its stops before the sprocket runs onto the chain-to-wire-rope adapters.

Wind Vane Self-Steering

Wind vane self-steering holds a boat on a certain course *in relation to the wind.* If the wind direction changes, the course will change to maintain the same relationship. The lighter the apparent wind, the less effective wind vane self-steering is; the stronger the wind, the more effective it tends to be (this is the opposite of autopilots—in some ways, the two are complementary).

How It Works

A small wind vane is aligned with the wind. When the boat veers off course, the wind continues to hold the vane in alignment—in other words, the boat turns in relation to the vane. This movement is used to correct the steering. There are two significant problems with this

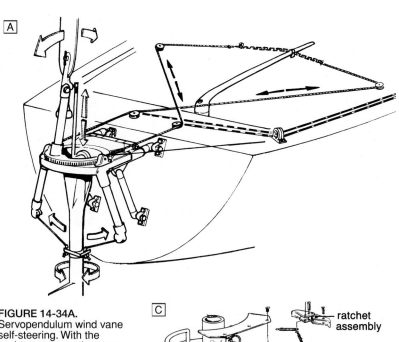

FIGURE 14-34A.
Servopendulum wind vane self-steering. With the yacht on course, the vane is feathered into the wind. When the yacht goes off course, wind pressure on one face of the vane forces it down around a horizontal axis. This motion is transmitted through a linkage that twists the servo-rudder around its vertical axis, away from its normal position in line with the boat's keel. Pressure from the passing water forces the servo-rudder to swing sideways on its top bearings, and this in turn pulls the steering lines that operate the tiller. (Marine Vane Gears Ltd.)

FIGURE 14-34B. A Monitor wind vane, the most popular of today's servopendulum types. (Scanmar)

FIGURES 14-34C AND 14-34D. Controlling and adjusting wind vanes—gear-type clutch. The course adjusting line disengages the ratchet, allowing the vane to align with the wind (14-34C). Fine-tuning the system is done where the control lines attach to the tiller or wheel drum (14-34D). (Marine Vane Gears Ltd.)

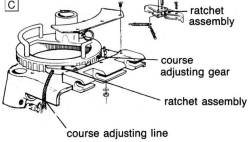

ratchet assembly

course adjusting gear

ratchet assembly

course adjusting line

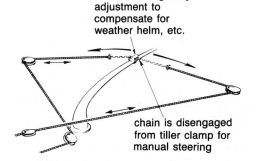

chain joins control lines, allowing easy adjustment to compensate for weather helm, etc.

chain is disengaged from tiller clamp for manual steering

system that must be overcome:

- If the vane pivots around a vertical axis (as all did in the early days of development), at best the angle of the vane to the boat will only change by the extent that the boat is off course, which limits the amount of vane movement available to achieve course corrections. Thus a boat tends to get well off course before the vane reacts enough to provide a course correction. This problem is resolved by having the vane pivot around a horizontal axis, with the leading edge of the vane facing

directly into the wind—anytime the boat gets off course, the wind catches one or the other side of the vane, knocking it flat, and thus producing a substantial vane movement for even a small course deviation. (In practice, the axis of the vane is up to 20 degrees from horizontal, which effectively dampens the vane's motion, reducing yawing and producing more consistent steering.) Many manufacturers produce two vane sizes—a large one for light air, and a small one for heavy air.

- Unless it is extremely large, a vane, whether pivoted vertically or horizontally, can only develop a very limited amount of force with which to achieve a course correction. This force needs amplifying. Three approaches are used: *servopendulums, auxiliary rudders,* and *trim tabs.*

Servopendulum units. Servopendulum wind vanes are by far the most popular, including the Aries (www.selfsteering.dk), Cape Horn (www.capehorn.com), Fleming (www.flemingselfsteering.com), Monitor (www.selfsteer.com), Sailomat (www.sailomat.com), and Windpilot Pacific Light and Pacific (www.windpilot.com). All have the wind vane pivoting around a *horizontal* axis (Figures 14-34A and 14-34B). The vane itself is generally a piece of thin plywood (as opposed to a small sail), aluminum, or reinforced plastic. A counterweight is suspended below the vane's pivot point so that it barely remains vertical when aligned to the wind and is easy to knock down when off the wind.

The boat is put on its chosen course and the thin, leading edge of the vane is aligned with the wind. A clutch is engaged, connecting the vane with a balanced or semibalanced (i.e., it requires very little effort to turn it) airfoil-shaped *servo-rudder* in the water (Figures 14-34C and 14-34D). This rudder is not much larger than the blade of an oar. It has its leading edge lined up with the flow of water past the boat (i.e., more or less fore and aft).

If the boat veers off course, the wind vane is brought increasingly broadside to the wind; the wind blows it down around its pivot point. The base of the vane is connected via a linkage to the shaft holding the servo-rudder. As the wind vane is knocked down, this linkage rotates the servo-rudder away from its alignment with the water flow. As the rudder rotates, its airfoil shape creates lift on one side and pressure on the other, causing it to swing sideways with considerable force—the faster the boat is moving, the greater the force generated. (A minimum of 2 to 2.5 knots of boat speed is generally required for the system to operate. Once boat speed is up to 4 to 5 knots, most servopendulum self-steering devices will create more force than a helmsperson can override.) Lines attached to the servo-rudder are fastened either to the tiller or to a drum on the steering wheel. When the servo-rudder swings, these lines turn the boat's own rudder and correct the course.

Auxiliary rudders. Auxiliary rudder systems have a completely separate rudder installed behind the boat. To use the device, the main rudder is locked off and the auxiliary rudder is used for steering and controlled by a wind vane. With some systems, the auxiliary rudder is balanced (e.g., Hydrovane—www.hydrovane.com) and thus requires very little effort to turn it—the wind vane directly turns the rudder—whereas with others the rudder is unbalanced, requiring more effort to turn than can be directly generated by the wind vane. To generate this effort, the Windpilot Pacific Plus has a servopendulum device mounted on the auxiliary rudder while the Auto-Helm (www.selfsteer.com) has a trim tab (see Figure 14-35 and below).

Trim tabs. Trim tabs can also be added to the trailing edge of the boat's main rudder, coupled to a wind vane, and used to steer the boat. Trim tabs are once again balanced or semibalanced so that little effort is needed to turn them. The larger the trim tab, and/or the farther it is set back from the trailing edge of its rudder, the greater the force it will exert. The Auto-Helm (Figure 14-36A) has a trim tab attached directly to the back of a transom-hung rudder (it can only be used with transom-hung rudders). The Saye's Rig (www.selfsteer.com; Figure 14-36B) is somewhat unusual since it has a vertical axis wind vane (not horizontal) that operates a servopendulum blade, which is connected via a forked rod to the back of the main rudder. When the servopenulum blade swings sideways, it directly turns the rudder (as opposed to turning it via a system of blocks and lines attached to the tiller or wheel). The greater the distance between the servopendulum and the rudder, the more leverage the Saye's Rig exerts, and the better it tends to amplify the low-powered signal generated by the vertical axis vane.

What Vane to Use?

There is almost too much choice in the wind vane market! However, choices may be limited by the physical configuration of your boat or existing steering system. For example, the complex steering linkages often associated with center cockpit boats make it difficult to fit a servopendulum unit, and servopendulums do not work well with hydraulic steering except when the control lines can be led directly to a quadrant or tiller arm on the rudderstock (the exception in both cases is the Cape Horn, which is designed to operate just such a quadrant). Servopendulums also do not work well on wheel-steered boats with more than three or four turns of the wheel from lock to lock (hard over port to hard over starboard). In all these cases, an auxiliary rudder type is generally the best choice (because it does not have to interact with the existing steering).

Beyond this, there are numerous differences, large and small, between the units that may affect your choice. These include:

- Auxiliary rudders result in a second permanently installed rudder, providing a degree of steering redundancy.
- However, because of their permanent installation, auxiliary rudders permanently add drag,

even when not needed (as opposed to servopendulums that can be lifted out of the water), and create another permanent in-the-water obstruction that can foul fishing lines, lobster-pot warps, etc.

- Servopendulums require the addition of blocks and lines (which can obstruct the cockpit) to connect to the tiller or wheel, whereas auxiliary rudders do not.
- These blocks and lines can cause stretch and slack in the system as well as friction, all of which impair steering performance (especially in light winds).
- On the other hand, servopendulums typically create greater steering forces that compensate for any additional friction, and which are adequate to steer even relatively unbalanced boats.
- Set against this, if your boat is unbalanced, with an auxiliary rudder type you can lock off the main rudder so as to compensate for the imbalance (however, you may need to alter the rudder position every time sail trim is changed or with changes in wind strength).
- The physical space required varies from unit to unit and may be a determining factor in working around such things as swim platforms, davits, radar arches, overhanging mizzen and yawl booms, etc.
- Some units can be mounted off-center, and some cannot.
- There is a considerable difference in the amount of work it takes to install one unit over another.

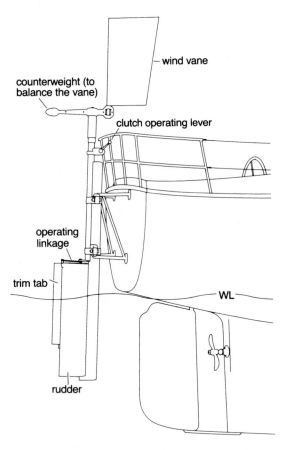

FIGURE 14-35. The operation of trim tab–type wind vane self-steering. *(Jim Sollers)*

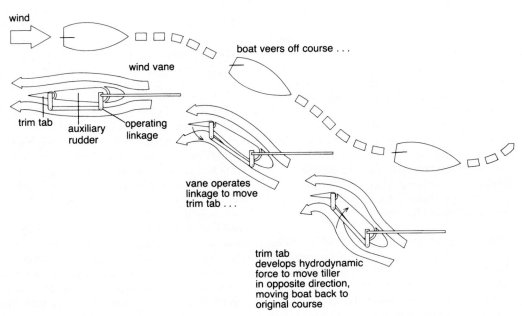

STEERING SYSTEMS, AUTOPILOTS, AND WIND VANES

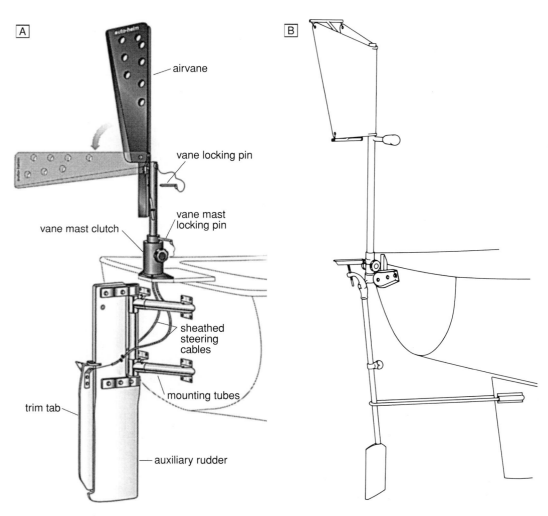

FIGURE 14-36A. An Auto-Helm wind vane. *(Scanmar)*

FIGURE 14-36B. A Saye's Rig wind vane. *(Jim Sollers and Scanmar)*

A — airvane, vane locking pin, vane mast locking pin, vane mast clutch, sheathed steering cables, mounting tubes, trim tab, auxiliary rudder

The following issues should be considered no matter which unit you eventually choose:

- The ease and safety with which course adjustments can be made (on some, it can be done from inside the cockpit; on others you have to hang over the stern).

- The ease and safety with which the wind vanes can be changed (if there is more than one size of vane).

- The ease and speed with which the system can be disconnected at those times when it is necessary to recover manual steering in a hurry (auxiliary rudders can generally be overridden with the main rudder; servopendulums must be disconnected).

- The impact of the unit when maneuvering, especially going astern (if an auxiliary rudder or trim tab is off-center, it can take the boat in an unintended direction).

- The ease with which the steering blade on a servopendulum unit can be pulled out of the water, set back down, and locked in place. (On some, it is difficult to get the blade to go into position if the boat is moving at more than a knot or two, in which case you end up hanging over the stern of the boat trying to set it.)

- Whether or not the entire unit can be removed from the transom (e.g., Sailomat and Windpilot), and if so how hard it is to do this.

- Whether or not the auxiliary rudder or servopendulum blade is protected against shock-loading, and if so, the nature of this protection. (Of those that are protected, some will trip out of the way and are easily reset, some will break shear pins that then need replacing, and some will break a tube that has to be replaced.)

Adding an autopilot. Given the ability of a wind vane self-steering system to translate a relatively small energy input from the wind vane into a powerful steering force, almost all wind vanes can be readily adapted to operate as an autopilot using a fraction of the power drain

FIGURE 14-37. Hydrovane adjustments. Course adjustments are made via the line from the worm gear (1) to the helm or by pointing the vane into the wind using a simple friction clamp (2). Both provide infinite adjustment. The vane axis is adjusted via the knob (3), which enables the vane to be tilted from the vertical for less sensitivity in strong winds. The rudder ratio is adjusted at (4) by varying the amount of rudder movement that will occur as a result of any given vane movement, and in so doing, varying the degree of steering correction that will occur. *(Hydrovane)*

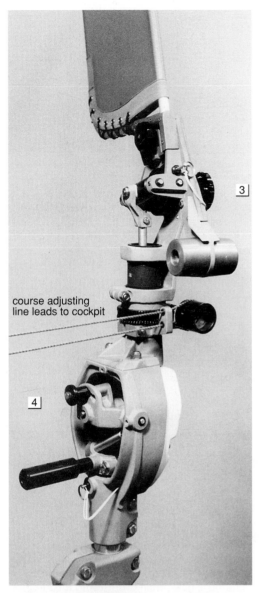

course adjusting line leads to cockpit

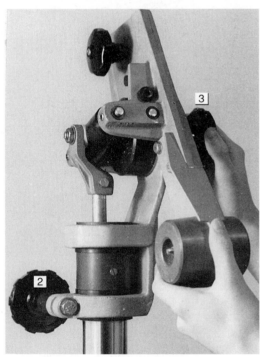

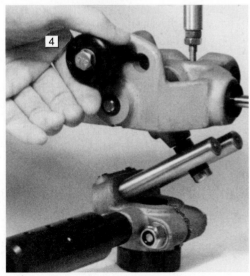

associated with a normal autopilot. The way this is done is to remove the vane and to attach a cockpit-style tiller-type autopilot in place of the vane, with the autopilot providing the steering.

Control and adjustment. On many self-steerers, the wind vane shaft pivots on a bearing with a toothed gear keyed to the shaft (refer back to Figure 14-34C). When the clutch is disengaged, the vane turns to align with the wind. When the clutch is engaged, a ratchet engages the gear and locks the vane to the trim tab or servo-rudder. The principal disadvantage of such a system is that course corrections cannot be made in less than 5- to 10-degree increments, since this is the effect of moving from one gear tooth to the next. Finer adjustments are generally made where the control lines attach to the tiller or wheel drum (refer back to Figure 14-34D).

More-accurate course adjustments can be made when a *worm gear* is used on the wind vane (Figure 14-37). The gear is disengaged to allow the vane to line up with the wind, then fine-tuned by rotating the gears; infinite corrections are possible.

A somewhat different approach, which also allows infinite adjustment of the vane's *angle of attack* (its alignment with the wind), is to use a *cone clutch*. The vane shaft has a tapered seat attached to it. A tapered friction pad is keyed to the output shaft. The vane is allowed to free-wheel around the output shaft until it aligns with the wind. The tapered friction pad is then pushed into the tapered seat on the vane shaft, locking the vane to its trim tab or servo-rudder.

Regardless of clutch or adjustment type, the mechanism needs to be kept clean and lubricated. *It is a matter of basic safety to be able to disengage the wind vane quickly and without difficulty in emergency situations.* Although the forces generated by a vane are quite small, on a boat traveling at speed, the forces that can be developed by a trim tab or servo-rudder (especially the latter) can be quite astounding (far exceeding the strength of a helmsperson). (Note that any wind vane assembly must be *extremely rigidly* mounted to its transom.)

Maintenance and Troubleshooting

Friction. The initial force developed by a wind vane on any system is quite small. Before this force can be amplified, it must be transmitted to the trim tab or servo-rudder. *Any friction or sloppiness in the linkage between vane and trim tab or servo-rudder will dramatically lessen the unit's performance.* The gear's exposed location ensures the accumulation of salt crystals in bearings and linkages, and if poorly chosen materials

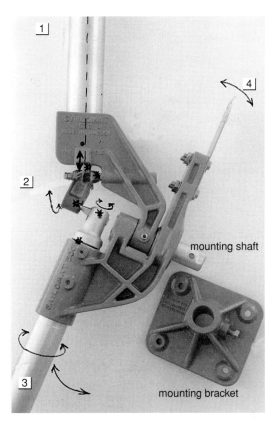

mounting shaft

mounting bracket

FIGURE 14-38. Critical maintenance points on wind vane self-steerers. Friction at any of these points will greatly reduce system performance. Linkage inside this shaft (1) connects to the base of the wind vane. When the vane is blown over around its axis, this linkage moves up or down. The linkage is connected at (2) to an offset cam, causing this lever to push from side to side around its axis. This in turn rotates the servo-rudder shaft as shown (3), causing the rudder to swing sideways. Control lines attached at (4), and through blocks to the rudder or wheel, translate the sideways swing of the servo-rudder into a pull on the helm.

are used in construction, corrosion is inevitable. *Regularly clean the linkage of dirt or corrosion and check often for free movement* (Figure 14-38). Sloppy movement will allow the boat to wander around the course line before any correction is made. Where adjustment is possible, take out any sloppiness, but stop the adjustment just short of the point at which friction and binding set in.

Damage control. A self-steerer's exposed location renders it vulnerable to damage from both large waves and collision, such as when docking. Fishing lines can snarl the auxiliary rudder or servo-rudder. Most vanes rely on a combination of brute strength and designed-in weak links to deal with these situations (Figure 14-39).

Wind vanes are mostly thin plywood, aluminum, or plastic, and are easily replaced. *Always carry spares.* Auxiliary rudders are permanent installations and take all the steering loads: *They must be built as strongly as the boat's main rudder.* Servo-rudders will sometimes be thrown violently sideways. Some—such as from Sailomat, Fleming, and the Windpilot Pacific Plus—can pivot 90 degrees from the vertical without damage, but others can't. Whatever happens, the shock loads must not be thrown on the delicate control linkage. As noted, the unit may have shear pins or breakaway tubes to relieve stress. If so, carry spares. In any event, think about these things before leaving the dock. Be prepared.

FIGURE 14-39.
Breakaway tubes and
other designed-in weak
links protect vulnerable
and expensive wind vanes
from collision damage.
Shock-loading shears the
breakaway tube and
allows the main frame
to pivot safely out of the
way of flotsam.

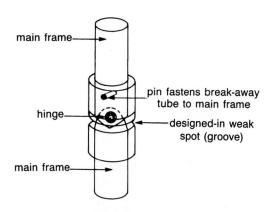

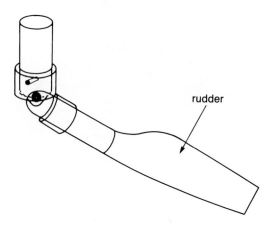

In the past there have been problems with fiberglass auxiliary rudders and trim tabs delaminating (they are generally built in two halves, and the halves will sometimes separate). Watch for telltale cracks in the gelcoat. Many newer rudders—Hydrovane, for example—are built of nylon and are virtually indestructible.

Finally, perhaps the greatest problem comes from installing too small a unit for a given boat in order to cut costs. Not only will performance be unsatisfactory, but the unit will be overstressed and likely to fail. It is far better to err on the conservative side, especially if contemplating ocean crossings.

Balancing a boat. Despite the dramatic force amplification achieved by all wind vanes, in light winds and at slow boat speeds, the end forces generated by self-steerers are not that powerful. *No self-steering apparatus will operate effectively unless the boat is balanced first.* This is largely a matter of sail trim, although where an auxiliary rudder and trim tab are used, the main rudder can be tied off so as to correct for helm imbalance (e.g., weather helm).

Some boats will self-steer hard on the wind without a self-steerer. But as the boat comes off the wind, balance is harder and harder to achieve. Few boats can be balanced on a beam

reach, and it may be necessary to sacrifice optimum sail trim (e.g., by letting the mainsail luff somewhat or dropping it altogether) in order not to overpower the self-steerer.

When a boat is broad-reaching and running, the more the center of effort can be concentrated in the headsails, the easier the boat will be to control. Perhaps the ideal situation on a downwind run is to drop the main (and mizzen) altogether and set two poled-out jibs (what is known as a *trade-wind rig*). Since *apparent* wind speed is much reduced when a boat is running, the wind vane exerts less force than on any other point of sail. Combine this with the fact that sea conditions are generally at their most difficult to handle when the boat is headed downwind, and it is easy to see that the self-steerer will need all the help it can get. Downwind sailing in light air and ocean swells is the acid test of any self-steerer.

Yawing. A self-steerer *reacts* to a change in course and can never *anticipate* wind shifts or wave action. It has, therefore, a built-in tendency to cause the boat to yaw from side to side around the course line. The farther the boat is off the wind, the greater the tendency to yaw. Better steerers have a degree of yaw-damping capability; the unit is designed so that as the auxiliary rudder or boat's rudder turns in response to instructions from the wind vane, trim tab, or servo-rudder, the force exerted is lessened (*dampened*). This helps to reduce violent rudder movements and sharp course changes. But even so, no self-steerer will hold a downwind course in following or quartering seas without a fair degree of yawing—just as no helmsperson can. The best that can be hoped for with self-steering is to approximate the performance of a helmsperson.

Long-Distance Cruising

Although the design of wind vane self-steering devices is quite sophisticated, from a mechanical point of view they are simple, rugged, mostly trouble free, and long lived; if problems do arise, they are generally fixable at sea. This makes them particularly attractive to long-distance cruisers. This attractiveness is amplified by the fact that they require no onboard energy to operate, as opposed to an autopilot, which is typically one of the higher energy consumers when passagemaking (and one of the devices most prone to failure).

A wind vane self-steerer has less of an application for coastal cruising, especially in relatively confined waters, primarily because it will not follow a compass course, but instead causes the boat to change course with every wind shift. However, as noted above, most can, in fact, be adapted to function as an autopilot—following a compass course and not the wind—by the addition of a (relatively cheap) cockpit-style tiller-type autopilot. Even on a boat that has an inboard autopilot installation, this is a worthwhile addition, providing a backup to the main autopilot. On a boat that does not have an autopilot, it is often possible to install a wind vane self-steerer with an autopilot addition for no more money, and maybe less money, than an inboard autopilot would cost.

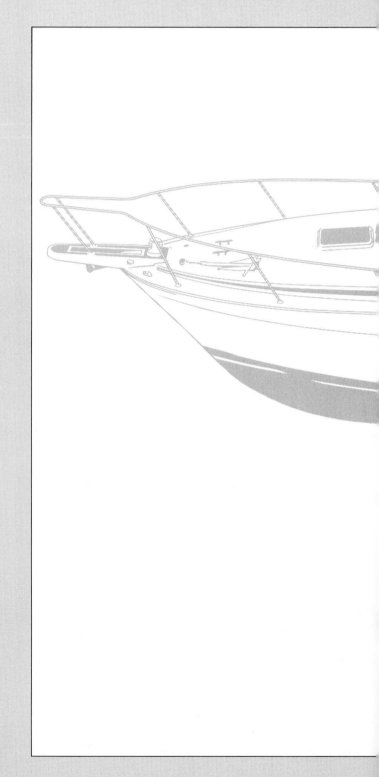

CHAPTER 15

FIGURE 15-1. Properly maintained, appliances such as these make life aboard a pleasure; poorly maintained, they can have quite the opposite effect. *(Jim Sollers)*

(1) range
(2) water heater
(3) propane tank
(4) propane stove
(5) propane cabin heater
(6) kerosene lantern

Stoves, Cabin Heaters, Gas-Powered Water Heaters, and Lanterns

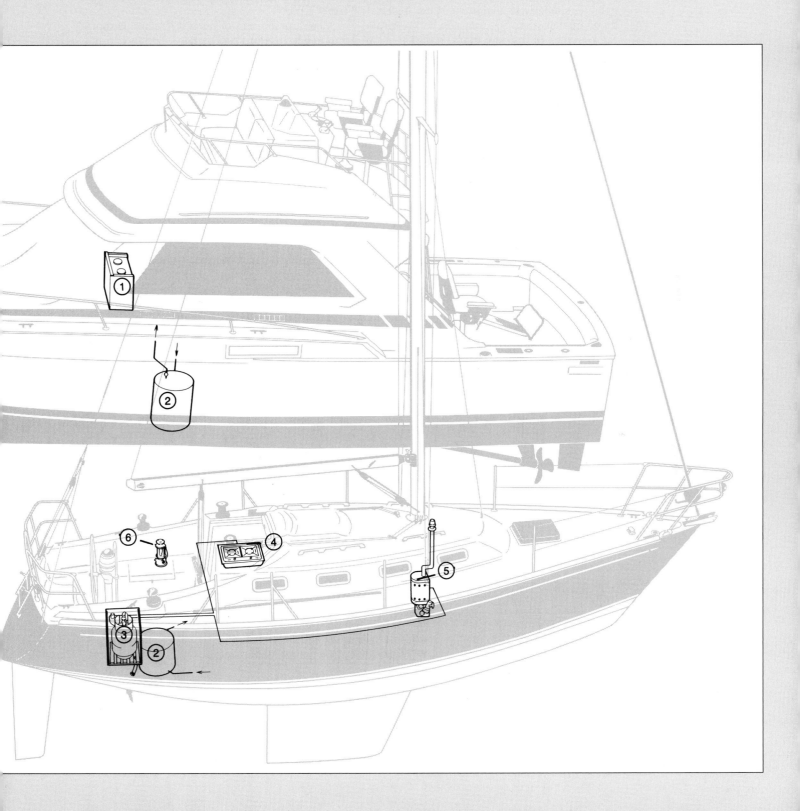

This chapter deals with various appliances that operate by burning fuel of some sort. The method of burning any given fuel—whether it be LPG, kerosene/paraffin, or some other—is more or less the same regardless of the appliance to which a burner is fitted. A kerosene stove operates similarly to a kerosene water heater. It therefore makes sense to focus on fuel types and the methods of burning them, rather than on specific appliances.

Any fuel that produces a flame consumes oxygen when burning and gives off carbon dioxide (CO_2) and water vapor. Boat interiors have little volume, and cabin spaces are well sealed (they must be to be watertight); therefore, the available oxygen in a closed cabin can be consumed quite rapidly. Insufficient oxygen makes the fuel burn improperly, and instead of producing carbon dioxide, it begins to form deadly carbon monoxide (CO).

The combination of oxygen loss and carbon monoxide buildup can be fatal—it has caused numerous deaths over the years. I address this issue in detail at the end of the chapter. I urge all readers to study this section.

Gas

Properties of LPG and CNG

The three types of gas in widespread use are propane, butane, and compressed natural gas (CNG). The first two are broadly interchangeable and are generally lumped together as liquefied petroleum gas (LPG).

LPG and CNG are not interchangeable without modification of appliance burners. LPG has a much higher heat output (approximately 21,000 Btu per pound as opposed to approximately 9,000 Btu per pound). Its burners therefore have much smaller orifices than those used with CNG. CNG used in LPG burners will produce less than half the designed output; LPG used in CNG burners will cause high flames and dangerous overheating.

Butane and propane both liquefy at low pressures and temperatures—at 100°F/37.8°C propane liquefies at 177 psi; butane at 37.5 psi (Table 15-1). When gas is pumped into a cylinder at ambient temperatures, these pressures are reached quickly. Then, as more gas is pumped in, it liquefies—with the temperature and pressure remaining relatively stable. When a full cylinder is rocked from side to side, the liquid can be heard sloshing around. In higher ambient temperatures, pressure in an LPG cylinder will increase somewhat, but never beyond 250 psi for propane and 60 psi for butane; in lower temperatures, it will decrease (for a fuller explanation of these phenomena, see Chapter 11, Refrigeration and Air-Conditioning).

As long as an LPG cylinder is kept upright, there will always be gas at the top, liquid at the bottom, and stable pressures—until the cylinder is almost empty. At this point, the pressure begins to fall as the last of the liquid evaporates.

The principal difference between butane and propane is that the former liquefies at higher temperatures and lower pressures than the latter. In extremely cold weather, liquid butane's rate of evaporation from a cylinder can slow to the point at which appliances fail to work properly. In these conditions propane should be substituted.

Compressed natural gas liquefies only at very high pressures that are not found in boat applications. CNG is just that—compressed gas. Consequently, as gas is pumped into a cylinder, pressures rise continuously—a full cylinder at 100°F/37.8°C has a pressure of 2,400 psi. As gas is used, the pressure declines steadily.

TABLE 15-1. LPG Cylinder Pressures in PSI as a Function of Ambient Temperature and Gas Composition

Gas Composition	Ambient Temperature (°F/°C)														
	−30/−34.4	−20/−28.9	−10/−23.3	0/−17.8	10/−12.2	20/−6.7	30/−1.1	40/4.4	50/10	60/15.6	70/21.1	80/26.7	90/32.2	100/37.8	110/43.3
100% propane	6.8	11.5	17.5	24.5	34	42	53	65	78	93	110	128	150	177	204
70% propane, 30% butane	—	4.7	9	15	20.5	28	36.5	46	56	68	82	96	114	134	158
50% propane, 50% butane	—	—	3.5	7.6	12.3	17.8	24.5	32.4	41	50	61	74	88	104	122
30% propane, 70% butane	—	—	—	2.3	5.9	10.2	15.4	21.5	28.5	36.5	45	54	66	79	93
100% butane	—	—	—	—	—	—	—	3.1	6.9	11.5	17	23	30	38	47

STOVES, CABIN HEATERS, GAS-POWERED WATER HEATERS, AND LANTERNS

Safety Precautions

LPG and CNG both form dangerously explosive mixtures when combined with oxygen in the air. LPG is considerably heavier than air—gas leaks sink to the bilges; CNG is lighter—leaks rise to the cabin top. A popular fallacy holds that since CNG rises, leaks will dissipate safely through hatches and ventilators. I am living proof that this is not so: I still bear the scars from second-degree burns to my face and hands incurred when I was engulfed by a natural gas explosion on an oil platform. Nevertheless, CNG has an excellent safety record.

LPG leaks are particularly dangerous on boats since small leaks can remain undetected in deep bilges. A tiny spark (which can be generated by static electricity on any boat) can blow the boat apart.

Boatowners with gas on board would be well advised to invest in a good-quality *sniffer*—a device that will detect small concentrations of gas (well below the explosion point) and sound an alarm (available from suppliers such as Trident Marine, www.tridentmarine.com, and Fireboy-Xintex, www.fireboy-xintex.com). Be sure that the sniffer is totally enclosed, and that it and all its associated wiring and switches are spark proof. I know of one boat that blew up when the sniffer was switched on for a safety check!

Both LPG and CNG are odorless in their natural state but have smelly gases added for resale. When you are refilling cylinders in foreign countries, *if the gas does not smell, it is not safe to have on board*. Regardless of safety devices, gas sniffers, and so on, the boatowner with gas on board should regularly stick his or her nose into all potential gas-trapping spaces and take a good sniff or two.

Warning! The ABYC requires that "all appliances shall have flame failure devices on all burners, and pilot lights, that will prevent gas from flowing to the burner if flame is not present." Nevertheless, many older propane stoves, especially the grills in these stoves, and many barbecues do not have a flame failure device. In the event that (1) the gas is turned off via the remotely operated solenoid when the grill or barbecue is lit, (2) the cylinder runs out, or (3) the burner goes out for any other reason, turning the gas back on at the cylinder will cause gas to flow unchecked out of the unlit burners.

Over time in the marine environment, burners also tend to corrode, and this can create gas leaks. In particular, the underside of the burners may develop pinholes that can only be seen by removing the burner. On older boats, it is recommended to periodically remove the burners and give them a thorough inspection. Be sure to clean out any debris from corrosion because this can affect combustion in a way that leads to carbon monoxide formation.

The Problem of Refills

CNG is virtually unobtainable outside the United States and is even hard to find in some parts of the United States. *For this reason, if no other, it is not suitable as a fuel on a cruising boat* (in addition to which, it is considerably more expensive per Btu of output than LPG).

As far as LPG is concerned, there is no worldwide standardization of gas usage, gas cylinders, or gas valves and fittings. This also causes problems for cruising sailors, but these are not insurmountable. The predominant LPG in the United States, the Caribbean islands, Australia, New Zealand, and Scandinavia is propane; in the UK, the Mediterranean, and many tropical countries (including Brazil, Venezuela, and many South Pacific islands), it is butane.

Although most LPG devices will work on both propane and butane, *propane cannot be stored in a butane cylinder*—propane has much higher cylinder pressures, which will blow the safety valve on a butane cylinder. Butane, however, *can be stored in a propane cylinder*, so *for worldwide cruising start out with propane cylinders*. (Note that if devices designed for propane are used with butane, the higher heat output may lead to overheating and damage; it is advisable to not turn the device to its full heat.)

There are numerous different threads and fittings (both male and female) on LPG cylinders. There are two ways to deal with this when overseas:

1. Connect the boat's gas regulator (see below) to its gas cylinder using fittings that will take *LPG-approved high-pressure hose (ordinary hose will NOT do since LPG attacks rubber and similar materials)*. Then, if you cannot get the gas cylinder refilled, buy a local cylinder with a discharge fitting that accepts a hose and simply connect the hose to this fitting.

2. Keep a cylinder-to-hose adapter, with a length of high-pressure hose, on board. When in a foreign country, find a suitable local adapter that fits the other end of this hose so you can refill your cylinder from the available supplies.

A cautious sailor would follow both approaches. For a U.S. boat going to Europe, note that Trident Marine sells an adapter that will allow the popular blue disposable Campingaz cylinders (www.campingaz.com) sold all over Europe to be screwed onto a U.S.-style propane cylinder fitting, in which case no other modification to the system is needed. (However, Campingaz cylinders are a relatively expensive way to buy propane.)

In some countries (particularly in Europe), it is not possible to get anything other than locally approved cylinders refilled, in which case if you're not using Campingaz or other disposable cylinders, you will have to buy or rent new cylinders. A U.S. propane fitting will fit a UK propane cylinder, although in point of fact the threads are marginally smaller, so *this is not recommended*; a UK propane fitting *will not fit a U.S. cylinder.*

When refilling cylinders, *it is essential that they are not refilled beyond 80% of their capacity* (70% in hot climates). If a cylinder is completely filled with liquid and the ambient temperature then rises, *the expanding liquid can generate enough pressure to rupture the cylinder.* Another problem is that overfilling cylinders increases the possibility of *liquid carryover into the regulator and the low-pressure lines* to the appliances, which can result in a dangerous *seventyfold* increase in pressure on this side of the system (and can also, even if it does no other damage, destroy the thermostat on a thermostatically controlled oven).

Many cylinders (in the U.S. and Europe) are designed so that they begin to vent once they are 80% filled, but others do not have this important safety device. Every cylinder should be stamped with both its *tare* (empty) weight and the weight of LPG it is designed to hold (*net fill* weight). A full cylinder can be weighed; if its weight exceeds the tare weight plus the net fill weight, it is overcharged, and some of the contents should be carefully vented.

In the United States, a new style of cylinder fitting was introduced in the 1990s that keeps a cylinder from being overfilled—an OPD (overfill protection device). These fittings have "OPD" stamped on the body of the valve just below the valve handle. OPD fittings also accept a new-style hand-tightened connector—a quick-closing coupling (QCC)—that makes changing cylinders easier than in the past (Figure 15-2). In addition to the fact that these cylinders are more convenient to use than the old-style ones, it is no longer legal to have the old style refilled.

In the United States, LPG cylinders are typically steel, painted white, or bare aluminum. No cylinder should ever be painted a dark color: in direct sunlight, a cylinder could absorb enough heat to burst. (In some states, it is illegal to paint a cylinder anything other than its original color.) In the United States, tanks are required by law to be recertified every 12 years by a qualified testing facility; in the UK, every 15 years.

Refilling from another cylinder. One LPG cylinder can be refilled from another as long as the relevant cylinder fittings are available. The procedure is as follows (Figure 15-3):

1. Place the cylinder to be filled upright (with its valve closed) below the refilling cylinder.

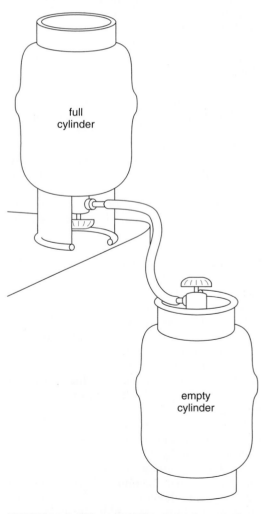

FIGURE 15-3. Filling one LPG cylinder from another (see the text for an explanation).

FIGURE 15-2. A U.S.-style cylinder with a quick-connect coupling. Note the OPD label below the valve handle.

2. Screw the connecting hose to the refilling cylinder; invert the refilling cylinder (with its valve closed) above the cylinder to be refilled.

3. Loosely attach the connecting hose to the cylinder being refilled, and *crack* the valve on the full cylinder just enough to blow off a little gas at the loose connection, then snug it up (this purges the hose of air).

4. Open both cylinder valves wide. Since the liquid in the full cylinder will be at the valve end, this liquid will flow down to the lower cylinder. The rate of flow will be slow (depending on the size of the fill hose among other things)—it will probably take several hours to get even a moderately full cylinder. The process can be speeded up if the full cylinder is warmer than the cylinder being refilled (this will raise the pressure in the full cylinder); one way to do this is to place the full

cylinder in the sun and the cylinder being refilled in the shade. In addition, I have wrapped both cylinders in towels, dribbling hot water over one and cold water over the other.

5. To disconnect, close the valve on the upper cylinder first, allow a few minutes for the hose to drain down, then close the lower valve. *Crack* the fitting at either cylinder, allowing the hose to bleed off, and remove.

LPG Installations

Gas locker requirements. LPG cylinders, both in use and in storage, must be kept well secured in compartments that are sealed from all machinery and living spaces and are vented overboard (Figures 15-4A to 15-4D). Cylinders must be secured in an upright position; if LPG

FIGURE 15-4A. A typical U.S.-style LPG installation. Two-tank installations are connected by a selector/ shutoff valve, but are otherwise similar. Note: If the regulator is mounted on the bulkhead and connected to the cylinder with a length of hose, it will make it easier to connect to different cylinders when overseas (see the text). *(Jim Sollers)*

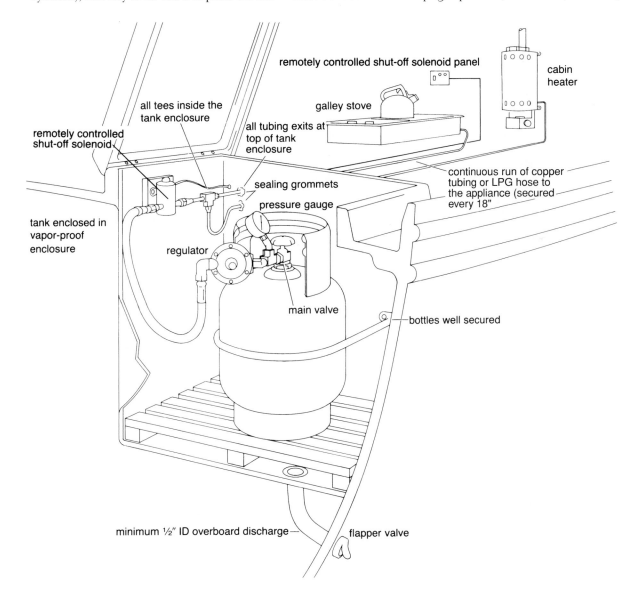

FIGURE 15-4B. An ABYC-compliant propane locker in the side deck of a boat. The one problem is that it is at the low spot of the side deck; as a result salt water tends to get into it, corroding the fittings.

FIGURE 15-4C. This homemade locker does not comply with the requirement to have a gasketed lid, but that is OK since it is installed outside the boat on the deck (in which case no locker is required; the locker is there to protect the cylinders and fittings from the weather).

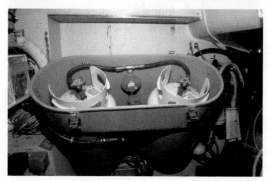

FIGURE 15-4D. An ABYC-compliant, commercially made propane locker for retrofitting boats with propane.

cylinders tip over, *liquid*, instead of gas, will come out, with potentially dangerous results.

LPG compartments need to be vented *from the base*. The ABYC requires a minimum ½-inch (13 mm) inside diameter (ID) vent; the ISO requires a minimum 19 mm (¾-inch) ID vent. The vent must *slope continuously downward so that no water can form a U-trap, and it must exit the hull above the waterline at all angles of heel* (the ISO requires a minimum of 75 mm/3 inches above the at-rest waterline in the fully loaded condition). All gas vents must exit well clear of engine exhausts, ventilators, and air intakes. The ABYC requires an LPG compartment to:

- Open from the top only.
- Have a lid that is gasketed and latched tightly.
- Be openable without the use of tools.
- Be reserved for LPG stowage only.

Pressure gauge. The ABYC requires a pressure gauge immediately *downstream* of the main cylinder valve and *before* the gas regulator (the valve that reduces cylinder pressure to operating pressure). The gauge will then be measuring *cylinder* pressure—a 300 psi (20 bar) gauge is needed on LPG (a 3,000 psi/200 bar gauge on CNG). The gauge is an essential leak-testing tool (see the Periodic Testing section below).

European boats tend not to have pressure gauges. Some may have a bubbler device installed downstream of the regulator that will show any leak, but these have a relatively low throughput and so cannot be used with systems with higher rates of consumption. Another device sometimes seen is a high/low automatic cutoff valve, which detects both excessive pressure and loss of pressure and cuts off the gas supply. Such devices have to be reset manually.

Step-down regulator. Install regulators with the vent port *facing down* so that water cannot collect in the vent and enter the system. Different gases are regulated to different pressures. Measurements are made on the low (downstream) side of the regulator in *inches of water column* using a manometer (barometric pressure is used in Europe—multiply inches of water by 2.49 to find *millibars*, which is abbreviated as *mbar*).

You can construct a manometer quite simply (Figure 15-5). Take a board 2 feet long and a few inches wide. Mark it off in inches. Attach a U-shaped piece of ¼-inch (6 mm) or larger (the size is irrelevant) clear plastic tubing. This is a manometer. To use it, set it on end, fill it half full of water, and connect one end to the gas line being tested, leaving the other end open to atmosphere. Open the gas valve.

The gas pressure will push the water up the other side of the manometer. The difference in inches between the two columns of water is the pressure of the gas, given in inches of water.

Most LPG appliances are designed to run with a pressure of around 11 inches *water gauge* (WG; also called *water column* [WC]), which equals 27 mbar. Propane can be run a little higher than butane, sometimes up to 15 inches WG (37 mbar). *Pressures should never exceed 18 inches* WG (45 mbar; ABYC specifications limit LPG systems to 12 inches = 0.433 psi = 30 mbar). *CNG operates at much lower pressures*—6.5 inches WG is normal (16 mbar).

Note that most regulators are made of die-cast aluminum, which can deteriorate rapidly in the marine environment, particularly if left exposed on deck (corrosion is evidenced by a heavy whitish coating), while cylinder valves are made of brass, which can dezincify (see Chapter 5). Corroded valves will sometimes fail without warning. Replace regulators and valves at the

clear plastic tubing

flexible tubing

copper pipe

water

gas line

inches

12" WG

backboard

first sign of significant corrosion; buy regulators from suppliers used to dealing with boats.

Master shutoff valve. The ABYC states that it must be possible to shut off the main gas flow from the vicinity of the appliance without reaching over an open flame. Given that the cylinder valve is almost never readily accessible from a stove or other appliance, this condition is met by installing a (normally closed) solenoid-operated master shutoff valve in the cylinder compartment, wired to a remote switch close to the appliance using the gas. The remote switch makes it possible to close off the cylinder (without having to get at it) anytime the appliance is not in use. The ABYC requires that this switch have a light to indicate when the solenoid is open. The cylinder valve should still be closed manually when leaving the boat. However, tripping the battery isolation switch will close the master shutoff valve and provide a fair measure of safety for those who forget to close the cylinder valve manually.

Although some stove manufacturers suggest installing the master shutoff valve upstream of the regulator (i.e., in the high-pressure section of line between the cylinder and regulator), most are designed to be installed *downstream* of the regulator (such as the popular Trident devices; Fireboy-Xintex has a solenoid valve that can go on either side of the regulator). If the valve is to be installed upstream, first make sure it is suitable (i.e., rated for the pressure).

The smaller of the two Trident valves is too small ($\frac{1}{4}$ inch/6 mm) for larger stoves (three or more burners with an oven). If you use it in such an installation, you will need to plumb two valves and wire them in parallel (Figures 15-6A and 15-6B). This has a side benefit since if one

solenoid fails the other will still supply gas to the appliances. Trident has a larger valve ($\frac{3}{8}$ inch/ 10 mm) that is adequate for four-burner stoves with an oven. The Trident switch panel has built-in circuitry to add a gas detector if desired (an excellent idea).

A solenoid-operated master shutoff valve is the single most likely piece of equipment to fail in a properly installed propane system. Long-distance cruisers are advised to carry a spare and also a length of hose with the appropriate fittings, so that if necessary the solenoid valve can be removed from the system and replaced with the hose.

Note that European boats rarely have a remotely operated shutoff valve, and as such, when imported into the United States, they may not comply with the ABYC requirement to have a readily accessible means of shutting off the supply *from the vicinity of the appliance.*

Tee fittings. ABYC standards state that every appliance should be served by a continuous (no connections) fuel line from the gas cylinder regulator to the appliance (or, in the case of gimballed stoves, to a length of flexible hose connecting to the appliance). In other words, if a boat has more than one gas appliance, it is not acceptable to run a common supply line and tee off this line to the devices. *Any connections or tees have to be made inside the gas cylinder locker.* This will keep any leaks from the connections or tees out of the boat. For LPG systems, run *unbroken* (without fittings) soft copper tubing or LPG hose to each appliance.

The ISO standard is a little different. If the supply line is a hose, it must also be a single, continuous run (and must not be run through an engine room), but if the line is pipe, connections

FIGURE 15-6A. Solenoid installations. The top illustration shows a single solenoid; the bottom shows two solenoids plumbed and wired in parallel to increase system capacity. In both cases, a manually operated selector valve upstream of the regulator determines which cylinder is online. *(Ocean Navigator)*

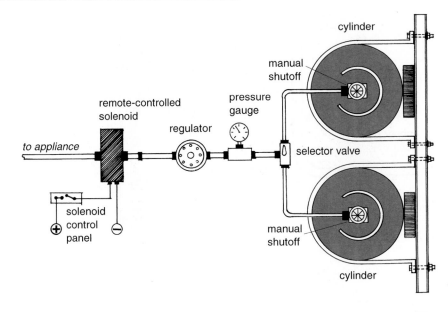

FIGURE 15-6B (below). A common two-cylinder installation without a selector valve. To change cylinders, the regulator must be moved from one cylinder to the other. These are old-style (non-OPD) U.S. cylinders that can no longer be legally filled in the United States. The tight installation is putting an excessive bend on the hose and making it vulnerable to chafe. This is the same installation shown in Figure 15-4B (in the side deck of a boat). Salt water has been dribbling over the solenoid (top center) and its wiring, causing corrosion. This is an installation guaranteed to give trouble at some point in the future simply because of its poor location on the boat!

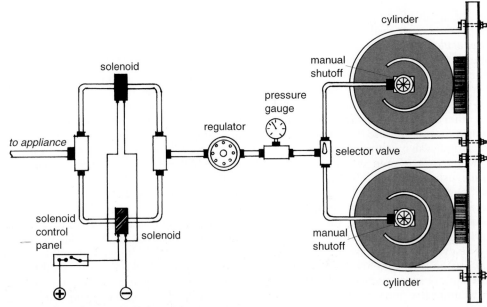

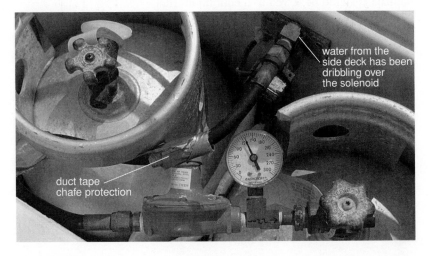

and joints are acceptable (except in engine rooms). The ABYC requirement for continuous hose or pipe runs precludes valves in the line *at the appliance* (because these would require connections outside the gas locker), whereas the ISO permits such valves, and in fact requires them if there is no remotely operated shutoff valve. (Valves at the appliance are routinely fitted on European boats, and as such, are not compliant with the ABYC standards when these boats are imported into the U.S.)

Tubing or hose runs. For copper tubing, clean refrigeration or water tubing is used (Type K or L in the U.S., to ASTM standards B88-75a or B280; in Europe, a minimum wall thickness

TABLE 15-2. Propane Flow[1] as a Function of Tubing Length and Diameter

Tubing Length (ft.)	Type L Refrigeration Tubing Outside Diameter (in.)			
	3/8	1/2	5/8	3/4
10	39	92	199	329
20	26	62	131	216
30	21	50	107	181
40	19	41	90	145
50	18	37	79	131
60	16	35	72	121

1. Output in thousands of Btu per hour; maximum output at 11 inches WC, based on a 1/2-inch WC pressure drop in the tubing.

Notes: To determine the tubing size needed, measure the distance from the tank to the appliance farthest from it. Add up the total Btu requirements of all the appliances hooked into the system. (With galley stoves, add all the burners and oven together.) For example, if the tubing run is 30 feet and the appliances use 25,000 Btu, use 1/2-inch OD tubing. Note that some safety shut-off solenoids have only 1/4-inch ports. When fitted downstream from the regulator, regardless of tubing size, the entire system essentially has been downgraded to 1/4-inch, about one-third the figures given for 3/8-inch tubing. Two solenoids plumbed in parallel will double the capacity (see the text).

of 0.8 mm for tubing under 12 mm in diameter, and 1.5 mm for tubing over 12 mm in diameter). Tubing sizes are given in Table 15-2. In general, 1/4-inch (6 mm) *refrigeration* tubing (i.e., with an outside diameter the same as its nominal diameter) is adequate for two-burner stoves and small cabin heaters, but 3/8-inch (10 mm) tubing will be needed on larger stoves (three or more burners with an oven).

Connections at the regulator end and the appliance should be made with flare fittings. (The ABYC does not accept compression fittings—refer to the Plumbing section in Chapter 12 for more information on these fittings; the ISO accepts compression fittings.) Long-nut flare fittings are preferred over the short-nut type typically used in refrigeration (the long nut lessens the chance of fatigue failure from vibration). Flexible connections to gimballed stoves should be made with LPG-approved hose that is no more than 36 inches in length and that has permanently attached end fittings (no hose clamps).

Some installers prefer hose to copper supply line tubing because it won't corrode or develop stress or fatigue cracks, and it is much easier to install. If hose is used, both the ABYC and ISO require permanently attached end fittings, such as swaged terminals. In the United States, the hose should be labeled as compliant with "UL 21 LP Gas Hose"; in Europe it must meet EN1763-1 and EN1763-2, Class 2 and 3. Companies such as Trident will supply preassembled hoses (with female flare fittings already installed

on each end) in standard lengths from 5 to 50 feet and custom-made lengths above this.

The ISO requires LPG supply lines to be run at least 30 mm (12 inches) away from electrical conductors, except when the supply line is in a joint-free conduit, or when the cables are sheathed or in a conduit or trunking. (In practice, the outer sheath on duplex and triplex cables counts as sheathing, so most cable used in boats automatically complies with the sheathing requirement.)

Securing tubing runs. Securely fasten all tubing runs at least every 18 inches (50 cm) and ensure they are protected from abrasion, flexing, pinching, or knocks where equipment may bounce around in lockers. Seal all holes where tubing passes through bulkheads or decks.

Periodic testing. Test the system at least every two weeks as follows:

1. Close all appliance valves.
2. Open the cylinder valve and master solenoid valve.
3. Observe the pressure on the cylinder gauge and let it stabilize. Make a note of the pressure.
4. Close the cylinder valve, but not the solenoid valve, and wait 3 minutes.
5. Check the cylinder gauge. *If the pressure has fallen at all, there is a leak somewhere.*

FIGURE 15-7. An ABYC-recommended warning label for LPG systems. (ABYC)

⚠ **WARNING**

Liquefied propane gas (LPG) is flammable and explosive. Follow these instructions to avoid injury or death from fire or explosion.

- This system is designed for use with liquefied petroleum gas (LPG/butane/propane) only. Do not connect compressed natural gas (CNG) to this system.
- Keep LPG cylinder and/or solenoid valve(s) closed when the boat is unattended, and when appliances are not in use.
- Close cylinder valves immediately in any emergency.
- Keep empty cylinders tightly closed.
- Close all appliance valves before opening cylinder valve.
- Apply ignition source to burner before opening appliance valve.
- Test the system for leakage in accordance with the instructions required to be posted in the vicinity of the cylinder each time the supply valve is opened for appliance use. Never use flame to check for leaks!

Never use a flame for leak testing! Mix a 50-50 solution of dishwashing liquid and water; brush this liberally onto all connections between the cylinder valve and the appliance. Any leak will cause the solution to form a mass of tiny bubbles. However, *never use detergents that contain ammonia for leak testing (check the detergent label)—ammonia could cause brass fittings to develop cracks and leaks in a matter of months.*

Troubleshooting Gas Appliances

Gas odors.

- Immediately extinguish all open flames and smoking materials.
- Close the manual and solenoid cylinder valves and shut down any engines.
- Check to see that all appliance valves are closed.
- Thoroughly ventilate all interior compartments, especially the bilges if LPG is used; do not use any blowers that are not spark proof (ignition protected). LPG can be *bailed* with a bucket or pumped out with a manual bilge pump if the pump is sucking air.
- When the boat is free of gas odors, perform a leak test as outlined above and fix any leaks.

No gas at an appliance. Make sure the cylinder valve is wide open (turn counterclockwise) and check the pressure on the cylinder gauge. If a new cylinder has just been put on, air may have entered the line—purge the line by leaving an appliance valve open. Keep a match or light on the burner so that when the gas starts to come through, it will burn and not collect in the boat. *Many burners have a safety device that must be overridden when you light the burner* (the most common requirement is to hold in a stove knob against a spring until the burner is lit and hot). Perhaps the safety device is not being overridden; this is one of the most common reasons for not being able to get a burner to light!

Check the voltage at the master solenoid valve. If you have a DC systems monitor, you can also check for amp draw (it should be around 1 amp at 12 volts). Have someone turn the solenoid on and off—you should be able to hear it click each time. If the voltage is OK but the solenoid doesn't appear to be working, close the solenoid, loosen its downstream connection, reopen the solenoid, and check for gas coming out of the loosened connection. If there is no gas, the solenoid is defective and needs replacing. After tightening, test the connection for leaks.

FIGURE 15-8A. A gas stove burner, showing the thermocouple and spark igniter.

FIGURE 15-8B. The same burner with the burner cap removed to show the spark igniter, which works (and looks) just like a spark plug. The burner nipple is at the bottom of the center hole.

The line may be kinked or crushed. Inspect its entire length.

The burner may be plugged, especially if something has boiled over on the stove. Remove the burner cap (Figures 15-8A and 15-8B) and unscrew the nipple in the center of the burner (use a deep socket). It may be necessary to remove the burner from the appliance to get at the nipple. Clean out the nipple orifice with a sewing needle or a fine piece of wire (see also Figures 15-12A to 15-12G below).

On stovetops with multiple burners but only one central pilot light, if the thermocouple fails (see the Thermocouples section below), none of the burners will light.

Some of the newer gas appliances have sophisticated electronic controls that may operate another solenoid valve at the appliance. For example, on-demand water heaters operate when a faucet (tap) is turned on. On older models with a constantly burning pilot light, a flow switch on the waterline opens a solenoid on the gas line; on newer models with no pilot light, the flow switch initiates an electronic cycle—first an igniter of some sort is activated, then the gas solenoid valve is opened. Consult any available manuals. Things to look for are power to the solenoid valve/electronic panel and correct polarity. With an on-demand water heater, check the water flow by opening a faucet; the flow switch may be plugged. Even if the flow is adequate, try jumping out the switch—it may be defective. If the heater has just been installed and has never worked, make sure the hot- and cold-water lines are hooked up properly.

Igniter fails to work. Light the burner with a match to make sure there is gas flow. If the flame is low, inadequate flow may be the problem (see the Unit Ignites Improperly section below).

Three types of igniter are in common use: constantly burning pilot lights, spark *(Piezo)* igniters, and filament (glow wire) igniters. Pilot lights themselves may be lit with spark igniters or filaments.

Pilot lights. These are generally lit by holding in a button and operating a spark igniter. If the pilot fails to light, try a match. If it still fails, check the gas supply. The pilot light orifice may be plugged and need cleaning.

If the pilot lights, but fails to ignite the main burner when it is turned on, check for obstructions between the pilot light and burner. If the pilot light is some distance away, there is often a small tube along which the flame must travel or a hole in the burner surround through which it must pass (Figure 15-9). This may be incorrectly aligned. A low flame height also may be the cause of this problem. To increase the pilot flame height, trace the pilot line to the main valve. There will probably be a screw underneath a cap on this valve; adjust the screw and check flame height. Both procedures (alignment and adjustment) may be necessary.

(Note: *Current ABYC regulations ban this type of continuously lit pilot light* except for an oven pilot that operates only when the oven is lit, or for a pilot light in a sealed combustion chamber. In spite of this, there are many, many pilot lights still in service that are not covered by these exceptions.)

Spark (Piezo) igniters. A spark (Piezo) igniter works by pressing a button that moves a magnet rapidly between coils, generating a spark. Some units have a battery; others do not. If fitted, check the battery voltage and connections. The unit may have a remote spark plug with an ignition lead from the sparker. If there is no spark, inspect the lead and its connection. At the pilot light or burner end, there may be a rigid spark plug (Figure 15-10) or flexible terminals. If there is a spark plug, the plug head should be approximately 1/16 to 1/8 inch (1.5 to 3.0 mm) from the burner rim to which the spark jumps; it may be

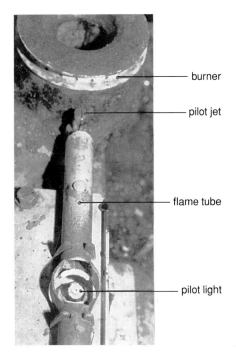

FIGURE 15-9. A constantly burning pilot light. When the burner is turned on, gas is directed into the flame tube and ignites.

burner

pilot jet

flame tube

pilot light

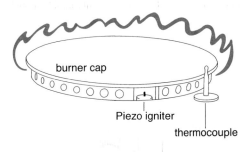

FIGURE 15-10. A Piezo spark plug and thermocouple. *(Jim Sollers)*

burner cap

Piezo igniter

thermocouple

necessary to adjust its position. If the terminals are flexible, bending the sparker more directly into the gas path may provide more consistent ignition. Note that grease buildup in the area of a sparker will stop it from working.

Filament igniters. With filament igniters, a short length of high-resistance wire—the filament—glows red hot, igniting the burner. An external power source is needed, sometimes provided by a flashlight (torch) battery and sometimes by the ship's battery (if the unit is electronically controlled). If the igniter fails to work, check the battery voltage and connections. To check the filament, *turn off the gas,* remove any covers to provide a view of the igniter, and activate it—it must glow brightly. If the filament is heating up but still fails to ignite the burner, check its position in relation to the gas flow and bend it gently into a better position if necessary. Filaments wear out and should be replaced every one or two seasons.

Unit ignites improperly. Delayed ignition is accompanied by a *pop* and a flare-up; excess gas is collecting due to the delayed ignition, then exploding.

Gas flow over the igniter may be inadequate (see the Inadequate Heat or Flame section below). Alternatively, the pilot light flame, igniter spark, or filament heat may be weak or improperly placed (see the Igniter Fails to Work section above).

Once lit, unit fails to stay on. All units for marine use should have some kind of safety device that closes the gas valve if the flame goes out. By far the most common cutout is a thermocouple (Figure 15-11), but some electronically controlled units use an optical sensor instead.

Thermocouples. A thermocouple is a device incorporating two dissimilar metals that when heated generate a very small amount of electricity (on the order of $1\frac{1}{2}$ millivolts). This power is used to open a solenoid valve. If the burner goes out, the thermocouple cools and stops generating electricity; the solenoid valve closes.

A thermocouple must get hot before it works, thus the need to hold the gas valve open manually for up to 30 seconds after a unit lights, giving the thermocouple time to heat up and take over. If, after this, the unit goes out when the manual override is released, the thermocouple is defective.

Check first that the tip of the thermocouple (a small bulblike protrusion) is in the center of the pilot light or burner flame. Two wires from the thermocouple terminate in a fitting screwed into the solenoid valve; check that this fitting is not loose. However, do not overtighten it; this will short-circuit the wires and necessitate a new thermocouple. If the valve still fails to open, unscrew the wire fitting and clean the terminals with very fine sandpaper (400- to 600-grit wet-or-dry). If the unit still will not stay online, replace the thermocouple.

Optical sensors. An optical sensor detects the burner or pilot light flame. Loss of the light from the flame causes the sensor to close a solenoid valve. If the unit will not stay online, make sure that the optical sensor is clean. Some manufacturers that formerly used optical sensors have found them to be unreliable and no longer use them. Before buying an appliance with this type of cutout, *check its reliability record in actual boat use.*

Inadequate heat or flame. Make sure the cylinder valve is wide open and check the cylinder pressure. Inspect the gas lines for kinking or crushing. If the problem occurs on initial start-up of new equipment, the gas lines are probably undersized; check the pressure *at the appliance* with a manometer (refer back to Figure 15-5) *with all burners turned on.*

Check the burners for blockages. On stoves, remove the burner caps and check for rust or corrosion that may be plugging either the gas orifice or the air ducts—clean the caps with a wire brush, and use a needle, straightened paper clip, or something similar to clean out orifices (Figures 15-12A to 15-12G). Note that rust in burner caps often builds up over time with a slow degradation of heating performance that goes unnoticed by the boatowner. Aside from the loss of performance, combustion may now be incomplete, leading to carbon monoxide formation. It is a good idea to periodically closely inspect and clean out all stove burners and caps as shown. On other appliances, make sure any air vents or chimneys are not obstructed.

In extremely cold weather, switch from butane to propane. Make sure CNG has not inadvertently been connected to an LPG system. Use a manometer to check the regulator pressure.

FIGURE 15-11. A mouse's-eye view of the burner assembly on a cabin heater. *(Jim Sollers)*

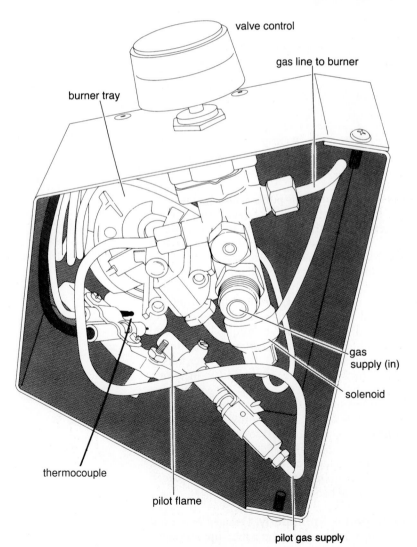

valve control

gas line to burner

burner tray

gas supply (in)

solenoid

thermocouple

pilot flame

pilot gas supply

STOVES, CABIN HEATERS, GAS-POWERED WATER HEATERS, AND LANTERNS

Additional safety devices. Various appliances have safety devices in addition to those already mentioned—an oven-temperature cutout or an oxygen-depletion cutout, for example. Almost all are self-resetting when a problem is resolved (i.e., the unit cools down or oxygen levels recover). Consult the manuals.

FIGURES 15-12A TO 15-12G. A burner with steadily deteriorating performance (a 3-year-old boat; 15-12A). Something has also recently boiled over on the stove top! To clean it, lift off the burner cap (15-12B). Rod out the air holes in the cap with an ice pick (15-12C). Unscrew the burner nipple/gas orifice (15-12D). Clean the orifice by poking a strand of a brass-bristle brush through it (a straightened paper clip, needle, or any other fine metal object will do just as well; 15-12E). The cleaned orifice. There is still a little crud on the nipple (15-12F). The burner is now putting out more heat than it has in a year or two (15-12G), and is less likely to cause carbon monoxide formation.

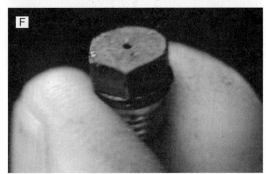

Alcohol, Kerosene, and Diesel Appliances

Fuel Quality

The vast majority of problems with alcohol, kerosene (paraffin), and diesel-fueled appliances can be traced to improper or dirty fuel. The orifices in the burners are very small and easily plugged. There are thus two requirements of a fuel:

- It must be spotlessly clean.
- It must contain no contaminants that can form carbon or other deposits in the burner.

We ran a kerosene stove for 7 years *without a single blockage* until we ran out of kerosene in Venezuela. We were forced to buy inferior fuel, and within weeks all our burners were plugged. I was cleaning them once a week, then once a day, and finally once every 10 minutes! Then they failed completely and left us without a stove.

Alcohol. There are a number of different types of alcohol on the market, notably butyl alcohol (butanol), methyl alcohol (methanol or wood alcohol), ethyl alcohol (grain alcohol), and isopropyl alcohol (a synthetic alcohol from petroleum gases, not a fermentation product). *Alcohol stoves are designed to run on ethyl alcohol. Both butanol and methanol have low heat production and impurities that clog burners.*

Unfortunately for boat users, the taxation of alcohol in drinks is a major source of revenue for all governments, and it is ethyl alcohol that is being taxed. In order to free ethyl alcohol, which is available for sale in other applications, of excise duties, it must be rendered unfit for human consumption—a process known as *denaturing*. In the United States, there are currently about 600 recognized ways of doing this, many of which introduce impurities that will plug up stove burners! (Note: Alcohol in liquor also contains impurities and cannot be substituted for fuel.)

Straight ethyl alcohol is best as stove fuel, but it is illegal almost everywhere! The common way to denature ethyl alcohol is to add 5% methyl alcohol (which forms *methylated spirits*), but then other trace elements are put in. Alcohol stove fuel available at marine stores is 95% ethyl alcohol that has been denatured using a process to make it compatible with alcohol burners. Various shellac thinners commonly available in hardware stores are made from denatured alcohol; many of these thinners will also work well in alcohol stoves.

You can do a simple alcohol purity test by pouring some in an open dish and lighting it. If there is *any* residue after the fuel has burned away, it is not suitable for use as a fuel.

Isopropyl alcohol—the solvent, not the rubbing alcohol—is not readily available but also works well as a stove fuel. It burns hotter than ethyl alcohol, is slightly smokier, and must be a minimum 91% concentration to work properly. Rubbing alcohol (surgical spirits) cannot be used as fuel because it contains various oils (which will clog burners) and frequently quite a bit of water.

For preheating kerosene (paraffin) burners, any 95% denatured ethyl alcohol or 91% isopropyl alcohol will work fine. In the absence of alcohol, a small propane torch played over the burner for 30 to 40 seconds works well.

Kerosene (paraffin) and diesel. The *yellower* the kerosene, the higher its carbon content, and the worse it will be as a stove fuel. Ideally, kerosene should be colorless (except where artificial colors have been added, as in Esso Blue). (Note that in a number of Spanish-speaking countries *kerosena* is diesel, while kerosene is *gasolina blanca*, which translates to *white gas*).

In the United States, any good-quality, colorless kerosene is OK. In the UK, both *pink* and *blue* paraffin are suitable; in Europe and Scandinavia, Esso Blue and Esso Exsol D 60.

For diesel stoves, buy the clearest diesel possible. Number 1 diesel is a cold-weather formulation; it is better for stove use year-round. Number 2 diesel (what is typically sold in the U.S. in all but cold climate regions in the wintertime) will tend to foul up burners. If Number 2 is all that is available, it is better to use home heating oil or kerosene (which will be much more expensive). If the diesel for heating purposes is currently drawn from the engine fuel tank, using home heating oil or kerosene may necessitate establishing a separate tank.

Cleanliness. Old fuel will collect a certain amount of water. Periodically empty all tanks and start again. Isopropyl alcohol (3% to 5% of the total fuel) added to kerosene tanks will take care of any residual moisture.

At low temperatures (below 5°F/–15°C) kerosene or diesel may separate out, producing a wax that will plug lines, filters, and burners. The addition of 3% to 5% isopropyl alcohol will help prevent this. If blockage occurs, run neat alcohol through the circuit—without lighting it—to flush out the wax.

Some cruisers add various carburetor cleaning solutions to their kerosene, believing that it prevents carbon formation. Whether it does or not I cannot say, but I certainly know from bitter experience that no amounts of additives will handle truly low-grade fuel. *The only way to have a trouble-free kerosene stove is to use clean fuel.*

All fuel taken on board needs to be scrupulously filtered through a very fine mesh. In the absence of a suitable filter, use a pair of pantyhose.

Troubleshooting

In the past, the majority of alcohol, kerosene, and diesel burners have had a tank in which fuel is pressurized. Pressurization is achieved by pumping manually with a bicycle pump or small hand pump built into the tank (Figure 15-13). The pressurized fuel is led to channels set in the burner head. When the burner is primed, the fuel in the burner is heated and vaporizes (Figure 15-14). The burner is then lit, and the fuel *vapor* is burned. In what follows, I look at this type of system first.

Some alcohol stoves do away with the pressure pump and priming. The small tank (enough fuel to burn for 1 hour) is built into the stove pan. A wick in the center of the burner is lit and heats alcohol in the burner. When this boils, the pressure generated forces vaporized alcohol into the burner where it is ignited by the burning wick. Heat produced by the burner keeps the process going.

Diesel drip-pot stoves and heaters rely on a gravity feed (see below) or a small pump.

More recently, there have been an increasing number of devices (notably, kerosene- and diesel-powered heating systems, but also some stoves) with an electric pump (12 or 24 volts) that supplies fuel to the burner and maintains fuel pressure. A glow wire or some other device on the burner generates the heat to produce initial vaporization.

Pressurized fuel tanks. Kerosene tanks are pressurized up to 15 psi, alcohol tanks to 6 or 7 psi, by pumping air (fifteen to twenty-five strokes on most tanks and pumps). Tanks that use bicycle pumps have a check valve built into the tank to which the pump attaches. Tanks with integral pumps have a bicycle-type pump built in, with a check valve at its base (Figure 15-15).

If a pump handle bounces back when pumped, or if the pump handle is pushed all the way back out after a stroke, *the check valve is not holding.*

The check valve is usually a spring-loaded ball. On tanks with external (bicycle) pumps, it is simply unscrewed from the tank. On tanks with integral pumps, the check valve is at the base of the pump cylinder—the piston must be taken out to gain access, and a special long-handled wrench is needed to unscrew the valve (Figure 15-16). *This is an essential tool.*

Examine the valve for dirt on its seat. Clean with a lint-free rag and/or replace as necessary.

FIGURE 15-13. Pumping up a kerosene tank.

FIGURE 15-14. A little alcohol in the cup around the burner is used to preheat the burner, vaporizing the fuel in its internal channels.

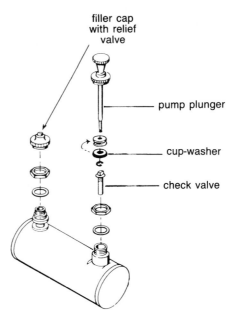

filler cap with relief valve

pump plunger

cup-washer

check valve

FIGURE 15-15. A pressure tank for an alcohol or kerosene stove. *(Kenyon Marine)*

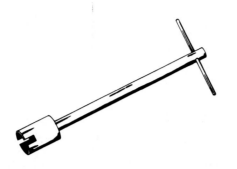

Pump cup washer. If the pump requires an excessive amount of stroking to build up pressure, but the tank then holds this pressure, the pump cup washer needs lubricating or replacing.

To get at the pump cup washer, unscrew the top of the pump and pull the piston straight out. On the bottom, held with a nut and washer, is a dish-shaped leather or neoprene washer, which is the cup washer. When the pump handle is raised, air is pulled down the sides of this washer. When the pump is stroked, the washer's sides push out and seal on the cylinder wall. The cup washer needs periodic lubrication with a little silicone spray or something similar (cooking oil does fine!). Keep a spare on board.

Install the new washer with the sides facing down into the cylinder. In a pinch, you can make a new one from a piece of thin leather cut a little larger than the cylinder bore; screw it to the end of the pump rod, lubricate it, and work it down over the lower washer until it can be slid into the cylinder.

Tank filler cap. If the tank loses pressure and needs continual pumping but the pump handle stays in, the seals around the filler cap or the pump unit are leaking. Some filler caps incorporate a pressure relief valve (safety valve)—this too may be leaking. If the valve can be disassembled, check any seals and make sure the valve seat is clean. If the leak continues, replace the valve.

Traditional (Primus-type) burners. Alcohol, kerosene, and diesel burners all behave in much the same fashion and exhibit the same sorts of problems.

No fuel at the burner. Check for fuel in the tank, for tank pressure, and that any valve fitted in the fuel line is open. Alcohol burners have filters in the burner, which may plug up; kerosene and diesel burners have no filters but some may have a restrictor fitting and/or an in-line fuel filter, both of which can plug up.

Yellow smoky flame on start-up. Inadequate preheating is one cause. Shut off the burner, let it cool down, and start again. If the burner is difficult to preheat because of drafts, remove both ends of a 3- to 4-inch-diameter (7.5 to 10 cm) can and place this can around the burner to contain the heat while preheating.

Extremely fierce flames when lit, which then die. The unit has a tank valve that was closed while the tank and fuel line were under pressure. The tank valve has not been reopened. The priming process vaporized fuel in the burner and generated high pressures that could not bleed off back into the tank. This pressure caused the initial fierce flame, but then the fuel in the line ran out.

Priming a pressurized burner with a closed tank valve can build up enough force to blow up the burner. For this reason some manufacturers will not fit a tank valve (although the ABYC requires one on all *remotely mounted* tanks, but not integral tanks). If a valve is fitted, it is still better to bleed pressure off the tank after use and before closing the valve.

Some yellow flames occur during operation. This is a result of improper combustion, either from a lack of oxygen (air) or excess fuel.

On alcohol burners, hold the burner flange with a pair of pliers and rotate it slightly to adjust the air-to-fuel ratio (Figure 15-17). On all burners check for obstructions to the air supply (or exhaust on vented burners); if found, remove them.

Let the burners cool down and check the outer and inner caps for proper seating—misalignment will impede the airflow. While doing this, inspect the caps for any carbon deposits and clean as necessary.

A lack of pressure, blockage in the fuel lines, or excessive restriction of flow with the control knob makes a burner run cool, which can cause improper vaporization of the incoming fuel. Then slugs of unvaporized fuel cause spurts of yellow flame. Problems are exacerbated by colder, draftier conditions.

If the orifice in the nipple is enlarged by improper cleaning, too much fuel comes through

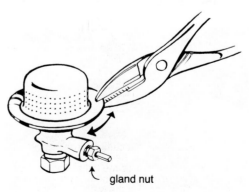

gland nut

FIGURE 15-17. Adjusting the air-to-fuel ratio of an alcohol stove by turning the burner flange. *(Kenyon Marine)*

and combustion is incomplete. Replace the nipple.

The flame burns correctly but dances away from the burner. This signifies too much oxygen (air). Check the outer and inner caps for proper seating. If they are fine, file three or four notches around the bottom edge of the outer cap. The notches allow some air to bypass the combustion process.

Flame gets progressively smaller. Check the pressure; if it is adequate, carbon is plugging the fuel passages, the needle valve, and/or the nipple orifice. Use a screwdriver or a wrench to tap the body of the burner while it is lit, turning the control knob backward and forward. This may well dislodge the carbon, generating a shower of sparks. If the burner has a built-in cleaning needle (or pricker), push it *gently* into the orifice a couple of times. Do not force it: cleaning needles tend to expand, jam up, and break off in hot burners. In general, use the cleaning needle only on a cold burner. (Note that carbon builds up more quickly when burners are run on a low light—run the burners as hot as possible.)

At the first opportunity, dump the fuel and refill the tank with a clean, clear replacement.

Eventually carbon in the fuel passages will plug a burner completely and no amount of normal stripping down and cleaning will clear it out. Generally, the burners must be junked (but see Figure 15-18 for how to salvage a carboned-up burner).

The flame surges. The burner is too far from the tank and pressure surges are occurring in the fuel line. Fit a surge restrictor in the base of the

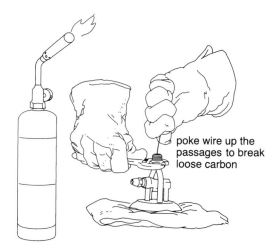

FIGURE 15-18. Salvaging a carboned-up burner. Remove the old burner and heat it to a dull red on a working burner or with a propane torch. Don't overdo it—burners are silver soldered and brazed together, and excessive heat will melt the welds. Let the burner cool slowly, then poke a piece of wire up all the passages. The carbon should break loose and can be shaken out. (*Jim Sollers*)

burner. Note: Some stoves, such as Shipmates, have a built-in pulsation dampener. This is nothing more than a cushion of air trapped in the stove's fuel manifold. It acts like an accumulator tank on a water system (Chapter 13), and just like an accumulator tank, the manifold can lose its air cushion. To replace it, if the fuel tank is above the stove, maintain tank pressure and use the oven until the tank runs out of fuel; if the fuel tank is below the stove, shut off all burners, release the pressure on the tank, and open the oven burner. The fuel will siphon back to the tank and restore the air cushion.

A small flame burns around the control knob. The packing on the handle stem is leaking. Tighten the packing nut. If this fails, replace the packing (see the Burner Removal and Replacement section below).

Burner leaks fuel when not in use. If the knob turns 180 degrees or more, the cleaning needle is incorrectly installed (see the Burner Reassembly section below). Otherwise the knob is in the clean position (needle up) rather than closed, or the needle valve is not seated properly and needs replacing (see the Burner Removal and Replacement section). Never attempt to stop a leak by forcing the control knob; this will simply damage the valve or its seat (which may be why it is leaking in the first place).

Burner removal and replacement. Kerosene and diesel burners are basically the same (Figure 15-19A), and alcohol burners are very similar (Figure 15-19B). Before working on any burner, release all tank pressure. If the burner is above the fuel tank, open the burner control knob and allow the fuel line to bleed back into the tank. If the burner is below the fuel tank, close the tank outlet valve (if fitted) or drain the tank, then break the fuel line loose at the burner and drain it.

Most burners are factory installed with a high-temperature thread-sealing compound—the burners can prove quite difficult to undo and even harder to seal up again when put back. Since very few problems require burner removal to solve, *remove a burner only when absolutely necessary.* If you must remove a burner, place a wrench on the flat at the burner base; never apply force to the burner top.

When refitting burners, it helps to have a supply of soft—or *annealed*—copper washers. These can be obtained from Force 10 (www.force10.com), to name just one source. Most diesel engine fuel injection shops will also have a selection of soft copper washers, since they are used for many sealing applications on fuel injection systems. Finally, you can anneal existing hardened copper washers by heating them to a cherry-red color (with a propane torch or another burner) and dropping them into cold water (although annealing is generally done by heating and cooling *slowly*, copper has unique properties and requires rapid cooling).

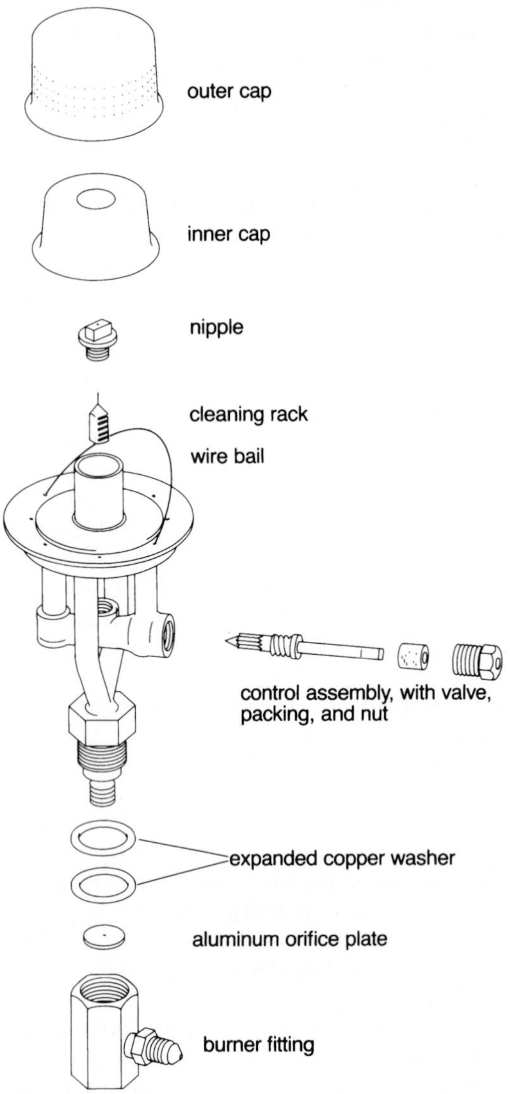

If the burner has a priming cup, fit a washer on it and one on the adapter for the incoming fuel line.

Burner disassembly. Remove the burner's outer and inner steel caps—they pull off (the outer cap may have a retaining wire). You may need to twist the cap around until two small retaining tags on the burner body line up with flat spots on the rim of the cap.

Unscrew the nipple (jet). This requires a special wrench (refer back to Figure 15-16). A piece of masking tape stuck in the end of the wrench will grip the nipple and make it easier to lift out.

Open the control knob. This raises the cleaning needle into the nipple opening. Using a pencil with an eraser on its end, push the eraser down onto the cleaning needle. Continue to open the control knob, lifting gently on the pencil, until the cleaning needle comes free. (You may also be able to pull the needle out with a pair of tweezers.)

Take out the spring clip that holds the control knob stem and remove the control knob. Undo the packing nut from the valve stem. Replace the control knob and continue undoing the valve until the valve threads disengage from the burner body. Pull the valve out (if the packing is tight, it may need a pretty good pull). The packing will come with the valve.

Clean all parts and inspect the tapered end of the valve for any *step*. This is where it seats in the

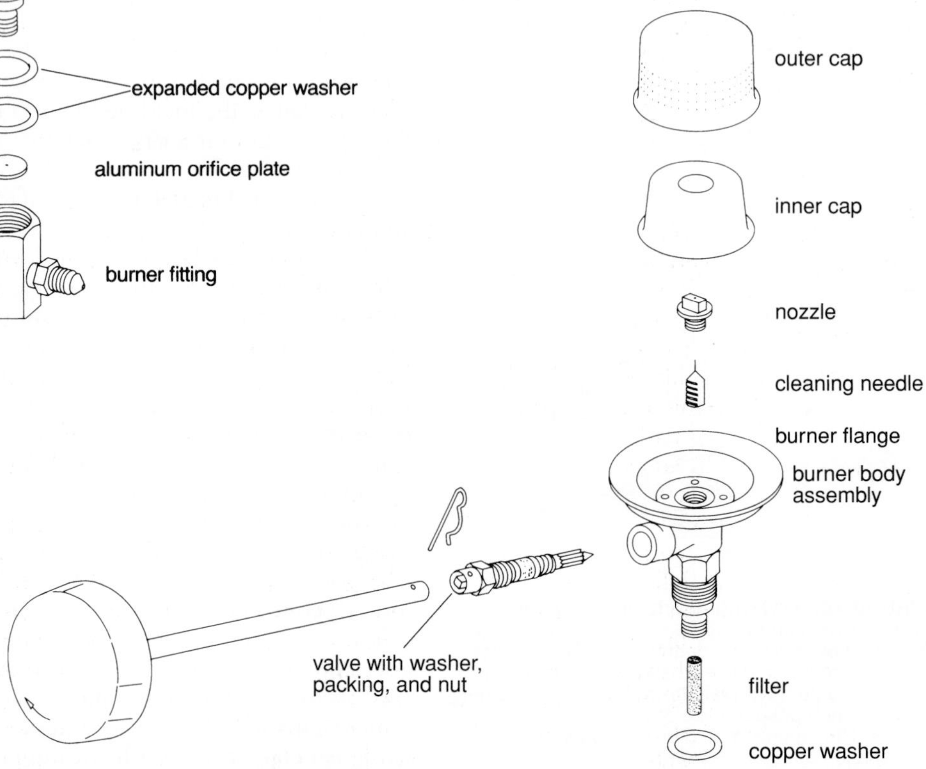

FIGURE 15-19A. An exploded view of a kerosene burner. *(Jim Sollers)*

outer cap

inner cap

nipple

cleaning rack
wire bail

control assembly, with valve, packing, and nut

expanded copper washer

aluminum orifice plate

burner fitting

FIGURE 15-19B. An exploded view of an alcohol burner. *(Kenyon Marine and Jim Sollers)*

outer cap

inner cap

nozzle

cleaning needle

burner flange
burner body assembly

valve with washer, packing, and nut

filter

copper washer

burner body. If the burner has been leaking when turned off, damage to the valve face or seat is a likely cause. Valve faces and seats are not repairable; when they are damaged, the entire burner must be replaced.

A heavily carboned burner may be salvaged as shown in Figure 15-18. Another suggestion from a reader: Make up a strong solution of caustic soda by mixing drain cleaner with water in a glass jar with a plastic lid. Store the burner in this solution for an extended period (weeks if necessary). I am told it will loosen the carbon. In any event, *be sure to observe all cautions on the drain-opener container and place the jar in a safe place!* Yet another reader tells me that some carburetor cleaners (the OMC brand was mentioned) will also soften carbon, and another writes that many fuel injection repair shops have ultrasonic cleaning machines that they use on injectors, and which will get the carbon out of burners. (You can tell by the amount of feedback I have gotten on this over the years that these burners can be a pain in the butt!)

Filters. Kerosene and diesel burners do not incorporate filters, but most alcohol burners do. The filter is likely to be at the base of the burner on the incoming fuel line. Quite possibly another filter is up inside the body of the burner.

You can pull some filters out with tweezers or needle-nose pliers. Others are composed of a sintered bronze material that is jammed in the burner. These may prove impossible to pull out, so you will have to drill out the filter using great care—it will be soft. The drill bit is liable to pass straight through the filter and damage the burner. It is best to drill a little and have another go at tugging and pulling out the rest of the filter. Select a drill bit slightly smaller than the filter so as not to damage any threads in the burner.

Burner reassembly. As far as I know, all stove manufacturers use burners made by Optimus (www.optimus.usa.com) or, in the past, Hipolito (from Portugal). Quality is about the same, and burners are broadly interchangeable. However, the gearing on the valve spindles and cleaning needle (pricker) units is different, and the nipples (nozzles) and cleaning needles may be different. So, when mixing parts, keep the valve spindles, cleaning needle units, and nozzles as matched sets. When replacing these parts, stay with the same manufacturer.

Thoroughly clean all passages, using compressed air if available. Install any filters; sintered bronze filters are wrapped in braid to make a tight fit. Screw the valve assembly in until it bottoms out in the burner. Push in the valve stem packing, washers, and packing gland nut. Put the control knob back on the valve stem and replace the spring clip. Tighten the packing nut while rotating the control knob backward and forward until the packing begins to bind on the valve stem. Screw the control knob back in until it is closed.

Look through the hole in the top of the burner and locate the valve gear on one side. Skewer a cleaning needle with the eraser on a pencil and lower it into the burner, its teeth facing the valve gear teeth, until the cleaning needle bottoms out on the gear. Press down lightly on the pencil while slowly undoing the control knob. You'll feel the valve gear teeth bounce on the cleaning needle gear teeth; count four distinct *clicks* (Kenyon stoves have five clicks—www.kenyonmarine.com).

Slowly screw the control knob back in. It will draw the cleaning needle down into the burner. If it jams, start again. Close the valve all the way and screw the nipple (jet) back on with the special wrench.

Open the valve all the way, noting how much the control knob rotates from fully closed to fully open. The cleaning needle should come up through the jet. If the knob rotates only 90 degrees, the cleaning needle is probably not down far enough into the burner—start again. If the knob rotates more than 135 degrees (180 degrees on Kenyon stoves), the cleaning needle is probably in too far and liable to bottom out before the valve closes, causing the burner to leak when turned off. To check, pump the tank up to pressure and see if the valve leaks. If it does, reassemble it, only this time set the cleaning needle in one less *click*.

Diesel Drip-Pot Stoves

A valve allows a metered amount of fuel into an open combustion chamber, where it is ignited. Air is provided by natural draft or a fan. The burning fuel heats the combustion chamber until incoming fuel is vaporized. At this point the stove functions similarly to a kerosene or alcohol stove, but without the pressurized tank.

The heart of this kind of burner is the fuel-metering valve—a simple device set up in line and level with the combustion chamber. The fuel level in the valve determines the (unlit) fuel level in the burner (Figure 15-20).

Because incoming fuel vaporizes upon entry into the combustion chamber, the fuel level in the burner is lower than that in the valve. A knob regulates the valve level and therefore the rate of flow (and heat output of the burner). Raising the valve level increases the differential with the combustion chamber and speeds up the rate of flow.

In a boat, *the combustion chamber and the valve must be in line fore and aft*; if not, every time the boat heels the valve will either be higher than the combustion chamber, causing flooding, or lower, causing fuel starvation.

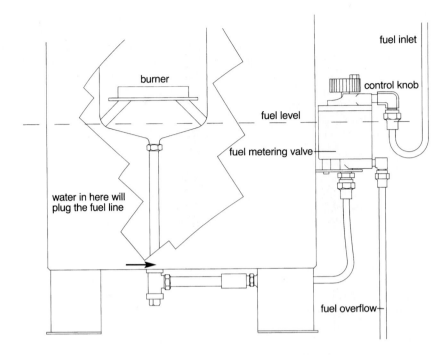

FIGURE 15-20. The components of a diesel drip-pot burner. *(Jim Sollers)*

Labels in figure:
burner
fuel inlet
control knob
fuel level
fuel metering valve
water in here will plug the fuel line
fuel overflow

Valves are designed to operate with a simple gravity feed from a tank. A fuel pump can be used instead, but its output pressure must be low (less than 3.5 psi on Dickinson stoves and heaters—www.dickinsonmarine.com), or it will overwhelm the valve and cause flooding.

Given sufficient draft, drip-pot stoves burn cleanly (no black smoke or soot). The stack (flue or chimney) must be large enough, long enough, and straight up—any bends can cause problems.

One problem I have experienced is that water finds its way down a chimney into the combustion chamber. Since water is heavier than diesel, even a few drops sitting in the fuel inlet will act as a plug and prevent diesel from entering the chamber—the stove will not light. Soak up the water with pieces of tissue paper or suck it out with a vacuum cleaner.

Diesel and Kerosene Heating Systems

Central heat is becoming an increasingly popular option on larger cruising boats. The best recognized brands are Eberspächer/Espar (www.espar.com); Wallas (www.wallas.fi; distributed in the U.S. by Scan Marine—www.scanmarine usa.com); Webasto (www.webasto.us; a good source in the U.S. is Sure Marine—www.sure marine.com); and Ardic (available in the U.S. from Scan Marine). The fuel is generally drawn from the boat's diesel tank by a small pump. A blower pumps air into the combustion chamber (the combustion air is generally drawn from inside the boat, but can be ducted in from outside). The fuel-air mixture is ignited by some kind of a spark plug or glow wire. The exhaust gases are vented overboard (Figure 15-21). At a minimum, flame sensors and overheat sensors maintain safe operation (there may be other sensors/shutdowns). Either air or water is passed over the outside surface of the combustion chamber and used to heat the boat.

Hot-air systems have air ducts to the cabins. A single thermostat (generally in the saloon) turns the system on and off. A hot-water system (a *hydronic* system) can be plumbed to panel radiators throughout the boat (as in a house) or (where space is limited, as it is on most boats) to small automotive-style radiators with a fan blowing air through them. The water lines take up far less room and are often easier to install than the air ducts for a hot-air system.

A hydronic system can have individual thermostats for each outlet. It can also be plumbed into a heat exchanger in the water heater (a separate heat exchanger will be needed from the engine coolant–heat exchanger) and even into the engine-cooling circuit to assist engine starting in very cold climates. If antifreeze (nontoxic propylene glycol) is added to the water circuit, it will not be at risk of freezing and will not need winterizing.

Hot-air systems typically run from 5,000 to 50,000 Btu; hydronic systems from 10,000 to well over 100,000 Btu. Fuel consumption is clearly a function of heat output, varying from less than $\frac{1}{10}$ of a gallon per hour up to closer to 1 gallon

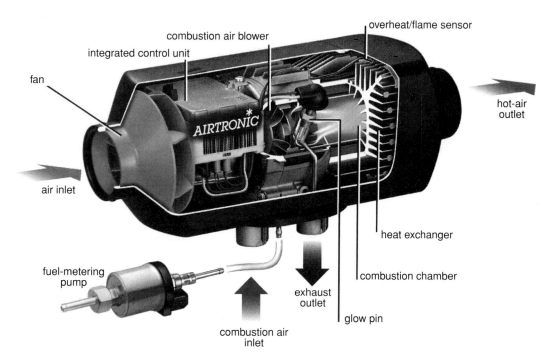

FIGURE 15-21. A diesel central heating system. *(Espar)*

combustion air blower

integrated control unit

overheat/flame sensor

fan

AIRTRONIC*

hot-air outlet

air inlet

heat exchanger

fuel-metering pump

combustion chamber

exhaust outlet

glow pin

combustion air inlet

per hour for 120,000 Btu of heat output. Electric consumption (12 or 24 volts) is a function of unit size and hours of use, and it can be significant (on high power, it will be around 2 amps at 12 volts on small systems, rising to 5 amps at 24 volts on large hydronic systems).

Installation issues. The unit needs to be sized properly. Very often, a decision is made to heat only one cabin, and a small heater is installed. This then ends up trying to heat the entire boat, runs continuously at full output, and fails prematurely. Make an accurate assessment of heating needs, and size the heater to keep its *duty cycle* (the time it is on) down to around 50%.

An unobstructed supply of clean fuel is key to trouble-free operation. Although the fuel supply for a heater is commonly teed off the supply for the boat's engine or a generator, it is much better to plumb it with its own supply line direct from the fuel tank. This is because the fuel pump on all systems is a small solenoid pump that will not have the capacity to "fight" other fuel pumps on the system in the event there is some minor restriction in the fuel supply (such as a plugged filter). A loss of supply, or air getting into the system, will cause it to shut down or run erratically. Because of the small pump size, keep the fuel suction lines reasonably short (see the manual).

It is also important to have an unobstructed exhaust. Keep the exhaust short with no excessive bends. On hot-air systems, you also need to keep the ducting to the cabins reasonably short

if heat is to get to the end of the system (once again, see the manual). Make sure the exhaust is adequately insulated.

Size the electrical wiring to keep voltage drop down to 3% (see Chapter 4). All too often, undersized wiring is run back to the DC distribution panel. Cumulative voltage drops from the battery to the panel, and from the panel to the heater, impair performance, especially ignition (resulting in excessive carbon formation).

Many systems (especially older systems) come with a rheostat for setting the output of the unit. Once the boat is warm, the rheostat is set to maintain a low output. However, continuous low-load operation can lead to excessive carbon formation. The heater will perform better if it is set to run at high output and connected to a thermostat so that it is either on or off.

An ABYC requirement is that hot-air systems must not draw the air supply for cabin heat from the engine room, and any ducting that passes through engine rooms must be fully sealed. This is to minimize the chance of picking up carbon monoxide (see the end of this chapter) and transferring it to living spaces.

Maintenance. As with other diesel-powered burners, the quality of the fuel greatly affects the amount of maintenance that is needed. In general, European diesel is better suited to diesel heaters than U.S., notably U.S. Number 2 diesel. With the latter, you can minimize maintenance by setting up the system to run hot when it is running.

On all heaters, the addition of small amounts of isopropyl alcohol will absorb moisture in the diesel, enabling it to pass through the system and get burned off. Run heaters at full heat for a minimum of 20 minutes at least once a month. This will burn off most carbon deposits and ensure that the fuel pump is kept lubricated with clean fuel.

Set up properly, very little maintenance is needed other than checking the glow plug (older models) or the ceramic igniter/glow pin (on newer models) every few years, and maybe cleaning the mat in the combustion chamber of carbon deposits. (Take it out and soak it overnight in kerosene or a carburetor cleaner; be sure to also clean the air vent hole in the vicinity of the glow plug/igniter.) Periodically replace glow plugs (maybe every 2 years); ceramic igniters/glow pins last for many years. You may also need to periodically replace the atomizer screen (where the fuel gets injected into the combustion chamber).

Troubleshooting. The most likely failures are electrical. In the event a heater is not working properly, check for voltage drop at the control box (which may be external to the heater or mounted inside it) with the unit running and the rest of the boat's DC circuits loaded up (see Chapter 4). If the supply voltage is adequate—generally, above 12.6 volts on a 12-volt system—check the voltage at the fuel pump, blower, and glow plug or igniter (once again, with the unit operating and the circuit under a load).

If there is no voltage at the pump, blower, or ignition device, check for a blown fuse in the control box. If this is OK, first check the thermostat (or rheostat)—you may simply have the unit turned off! If it is on, one of the safety shutdowns may have tripped the circuit. There will be, at a minimum, a flame sensor and an over-temperature device (and a low-water shutdown on hydronic systems). Track these down, reset if tripped (note that if a flame failure device trips the system, the ABYC requires operator intervention to restart it—i.e., it cannot be restarted automatically) or bypass it (with a jumper wire; also bypass the thermostat/rheostat in case it is faulty). If this restores voltage, then either the circuit has tripped because of a fault, or the shutdown device is faulty.

Given functioning electrical circuits, break the fuel line loose from the pump to ensure it is supplying fuel. If fuel flows, check for a plugged filter at the appliance.

Still not working? Inspect the ignition device and combustion chamber, and while you're at it, check to make sure the inlet air and exhaust are unobstructed.

Carbon Monoxide Poisoning

All forms of heating (except electric heat) and engine combustion involve burning a fuel, which converts oxygen from the air to carbon dioxide. If the air that is consumed comes from cabin spaces, oxygen levels may be steadily depleted. In itself, this is potentially hazardous. If combustion is at all incomplete, as it almost always is, carbon monoxide will also be created, as opposed to carbon dioxide. Carbon monoxide can be deadly.

Carbon monoxide poisoning is the leading cause of death by poisoning in the United States (I don't have the equivalent figures for Europe). Boatowners are particularly at risk because (1) boats contain a small volume of air; (2) boats are necessarily tightly sealed (to keep the water out); and (3) within these small, sealed spaces, there are generally several appliances capable of producing carbon monoxide (e.g., a galley stove, the main engine, an AC generator, a nonelectric cabin heater, and maybe a gas- or diesel-powered water heater).

How It Happens

What makes carbon monoxide such an insidious killer is the fact that it is odorless, colorless, tasteless, and more or less the same weight as air (just a little lighter), so that it tends to hang around. When present in the air, it is inhaled into the lungs. From the lungs, carbon monoxide enters the bloodstream, where it binds with blood hemoglobin (red blood cells), replacing critical oxygen molecules and forming something known as *carboxyhemoglobin* (COHb). As a result, the body is deprived of oxygen.

Carbon monoxide binds to blood hemoglobin far more readily than oxygen does, even if oxygen is available. *The mere presence of carbon monoxide is dangerous, with or without plenty of fresh air.* Once attached to the hemoglobin, carbon monoxide is relatively stable. As a result, very low levels can progressively poison people.

Permissible limits, as set by various U.S. regulatory agencies, range from 35 to 50 parts per

Kerosene and White-Gas Lanterns

Principles for lantern burners are the same as for other pressurized burners. The vapor is burned inside a mesh "sock" or bag called a *mantle*, which becomes white hot, giving off light. Mantles are extremely delicate—the slightest touch will cause them to fall apart.

Mantle replacement is straightforward (Figure 15-22). Remove all traces of the old mantle, including the string that was used to tie it on. The new mantle can be handled until first lit. Slide the open end over the ceramic tube in the lantern and tie it on with its string. Arrange the mantle uniformly around the tube and make sure it is hanging evenly with no major creases (A).

Set the mantle on fire (B). It will smolder slowly, shrinking and giving off unpleasant fumes as a coating on it burns off (C). When all the coating is burned off, the mantle will assume its finished size and shape, and the lantern is ready to use.

After lighting (D), a mantle is extremely fragile. Any sudden knocks—even the slightest touch–will cause it to disintegrate (E). Although a mantle with just a hole in its side will still give off light, it should not be lit. A hot jet of flame will shoot out of the hole, quite likely cracking the lantern glass.

FIGURE 15-22.
Replacing a mantle on kerosene and white-gas lanterns.

  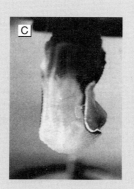  

million (ppm) if sustained for an 8-hour period. To put this in perspective, 1 ppm is the equivalent of one drop of food coloring in 13.2 gallons (50 liters) of water. As little as 0.2% carbon monoxide in the air (2,000 ppm) binds up red blood cells (i.e., forms carboxyhemoglobin) at the rate of 1% (of the body's red blood cells) per minute. If the person is doing work, the rate can double to over 2% per minute. Within 45 minutes, 75% of the red blood cells are taken up with carbon monoxide, resulting in a lethal concentration. At the other end of the scale, high doses of carbon monoxide can be lethal in a matter of minutes (Table 15-3). If a victim escapes death, there may still be permanent brain damage.

The symptoms. Typically, carbon monoxide poisoning produces a range of symptoms, beginning with watery and itchy eyes and a flushed appearance, then progressing through an inability to think coherently, headaches, drowsiness, nausea, dizziness, fatigue, vomiting, collapse, coma, and death. Note that many of the early

TABLE 15-3. Carbon Monoxide Poisoning Symptoms

CO Amount (ppm)[1]	Symptoms
200	Slight headache within 2 to 3 hours.
400	Frontal (migraine-type) headache within 1 to 2 hours.
800	Dizziness, nausea, and convulsions within 45 minutes. Insensible within 2 hours.
1,600	Headache, dizziness, and nausea within 20 minutes. Death within 60 minutes.
3,200	Headache, dizziness, and nausea in 5 to 10 minutes. Death within 30 minutes.
6,400	Headache and dizziness in 1 to 2 minutes. Death in less than 15 minutes.
12,800	Death in less than 3 minutes.

1. PPM = parts per million carbon monoxide in the atmosphere; 1,000 ppm = 0.1% carbon monoxide in the atmosphere.

(Courtesy Fireboy-Xintex)

symptoms are similar to those of seasickness, flu, or food poisoning—all too often people suffering from carbon monoxide poisoning fail to recognize the problem. Note also that the poisoning creeps up on people; it dulls the senses, causing a failure to recognize the problem, which enables the fatal punch to be delivered. BoatU.S. quotes an example of a family of three on a large sailboat with a washing machine and a propane-fueled water heater. The washing machine malfunctioned, causing the water heater to stay lit. The heater produced carbon monoxide. The son fell, tried to get up, and fell again. Hearing the loud thump, the wife got up, was overcome, and collapsed.

"My husband saw me go down and thought I had fainted because of seeing our son (whose lip was bleeding). He stepped over me to assist our son, and looking back, he noticed the cat lying beside me. It clicked—I might faint, but not the cat. He picked up the phone and pushed a preprogrammed button to call our neighbors and let them know we were in trouble. He tried to pull us out, but he, too, was going down." All three were rescued by the local fire department and regained consciousness.

What is particularly interesting about this case is that the boat's hatches were wide open with a 10-knot wind blowing outside. I have other similar accounts on file. The question is, what can be done to prevent such incidents?

Minimizing Carbon Monoxide Formation

Engine installations. All engine exhausts contain carbon monoxide; *gasoline engines produce far higher levels than diesels.* (For this reason, Onan, a major generator manufacturer, stopped selling gasoline-powered AC generators in the marine market and conducted an extensive advertising campaign warning of the dangers of carbon monoxide poisoning.) Cold, poorly tuned, and overloaded engines produce more carbon monoxide than warm, properly tuned, and load-matched engines. So the first task in minimizing the potential for carbon monoxide formation is to ensure that the engine is properly matched to its task, and as far as possible, will be operated as designed. There is always, however, the cruising sailor who uses the engine more for battery charging at anchor than for propulsion, which results in the engine running long, underloaded hours below its designed temperature; there is not much that can be done about this, other than to make sure that the carbon monoxide is gotten out of the boat.

In recent decades, the drive to make engines increasingly quiet has led to ever-tighter, better-insulated engine boxes and engine rooms. On the exhaust side, the near-universal use of water lift–type silencers adds a measure of back pressure to the system. Both of these design trends increase the probability of restricting the airflow through an engine, and as such, increase the likelihood of carbon monoxide formation.

To keep carbon monoxide out of accommodation spaces, it is crucial to have an exhaust system that is gas-tight to the hull. This in turn requires adequate support and strain relief built into the exhaust system (to absorb engine vibration without failure), the use of galvanically compatible materials (to lessen corrosion), proper marine exhaust hose in wet exhaust systems, and double-clamping of all hose connections with *all*-stainless-steel hose clamps (see Chapter 5). Each engine on a boat must have its own dedicated exhaust system, with nothing teed into this exhaust (with the sole exception of a cooling-water injection line on a water-cooled exhaust).

Regardless of the quality of the initial exhaust installation, *an exhaust system is a regular maintenance item.* Leaking gasoline exhausts on boats are far and away the leading cause of death from carbon monoxide poisoning. At least annually, inspect the entire system for any signs of corrosion or leaks. Warning signs are discoloration or stains around joints, water leaks, rusting around the screws on hose clamps, corrosion of the manifold discharge elbow on water-cooled engines, and carbon buildup within the exhaust (which will increase the back pressure, the production of carbon monoxide, and the probability of leaks). To check a discharge elbow, remove the exhaust hose, which will also enable you to check for carbon buildup.

Fuel-burning appliances. When it comes to fuel-burning appliances, which are almost always in the accommodation spaces themselves, certain other protective measures need to be taken. The optimum situation is one in which the appliance has its combustion air ducted in from outside the accommodation spaces, with combustion occurring inside a sealed chamber, which then exhausts through an external flue (this setup is known as a *sealed combustion system*). As long as the combustion chamber does not corrode through, such an appliance cannot cause oxygen depletion, nor can it emit carbon monoxide directly into accommodation spaces.

Some cabin heaters are built in this fashion, although commonly the inlet air is drawn from within the boat, with the exhaust plumbed outside the boat. In this case, as long as there is no back draft down the flue (a matter of proper design, although there may be situations in which the airflow off sails will cause back-drafting with just about any flue), and as long as the flue is not obstructed (primarily a matter of design once again, in particular ensuring that the flue cannot trap water), even in a situation of oxygen depletion and carbon monoxide formation, the carbon monoxide will be vented outside accommodation spaces.

However, note that the nature of ventilation on boats is such that it is sometimes possible to create a *negative* pressure (with respect to the outside air pressure) inside the boat. This occurs, for example, when the hatches, ventilators, openings, and canvas structures (such as dodgers) are lined up with respect to the wind so that air is sucked out of the cabin rather than driven in (this is not hard to do). In such a situation, any combustion chamber that draws its inlet air from inside the boat has the potential to feed carbon monoxide into the boat (Figure 15-23). Over the years, this has been the cause of a number of deaths.

With or without ducted inlet air, check a combustion chamber as part of your regular maintenance schedule to ensure that there is no damage or corrosion. Also inspect inlet and exhaust ducting to make sure it is gas-tight.

Safety can be enhanced by the addition of an *oxygen depletion sensor* wired so that it automatically cuts off the fuel supply to an appliance in the event of oxygen depletion (this is an ABYC requirement on all systems that do not have sealed combustion chambers). It should be noted, however, that in a situation where carbon monoxide is produced but there is still a good airflow through the cabin, the oxygen depletion sensor will do nothing to protect the occupants.

Unvented appliances. Then there are all those appliances that not only draw their air from accommodation spaces but also exhaust the combustion gases into the same atmosphere. These include all nonelectric galley stoves and also some cabin heaters and water heaters. These appliances are potentially the most lethal of all; boatowners need to think long and hard before using them. It is essential to understand that these appliances:

- Should *never* be used when *unattended* or when *sleeping* (carbon monoxide is especially dangerous when sleeping since victims don't feel any side effects and may simply not wake up).

- Should *only* be used in conjunction with *adequate ventilation*. In particular, *galley stoves should not be used for cabin heat* (which is easier said than done if you have no other source of cabin heat; I have to confess that we have used our stove from time to time, but never unattended, and never when sleeping).

User education. This leaves certain potentially lethal situations that cannot be eliminated at the equipment design and installation phase. Examples include running an engine with the boat up against a dock so that the exhaust is deflected back into accommodation spaces (Figure 15-24A) or running the engine when rafted to another boat, with similar results (Figure 15-24B). The operation of AC generators in such situations is of particular concern, especially if they are run at night when people are sleeping, which is commonly done to keep an air conditioner going. Boats with a lot of canvas aft (dodgers, biminis, and cockpit enclosures) can create what is known as the *station wagon effect* (Figure 15-24C). This is more likely on a power-boat at speed, but can also occur on sailboats.

And then there is always the cruising sailor who decides to save the wear and tear on the

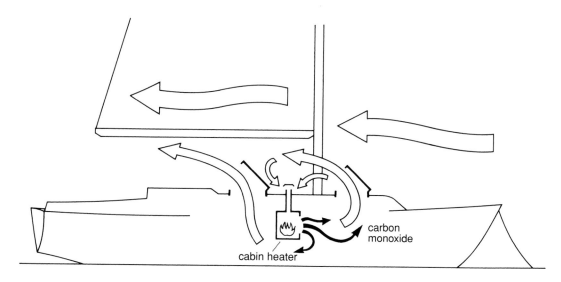

FIGURE 15-23. A boat at anchor with its hatches opening on their forward faces. Wind blowing over the hatches will create a negative pressure inside the boat, which has the potential to cause any externally vented, fuel-burning appliance to back-draft down the chimney, putting carbon monoxide in the boat. *(Jim Sollers)*

cabin heater

carbon monoxide

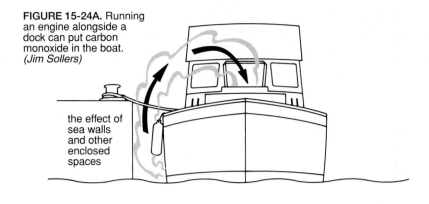

FIGURE 15-24A. Running an engine alongside a dock can put carbon monoxide in the boat. *(Jim Sollers)*

the effect of sea walls and other enclosed spaces

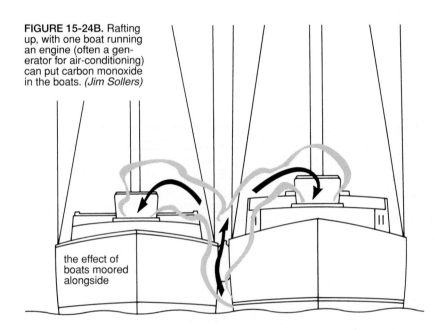

FIGURE 15-24B. Rafting up, with one boat running an engine (often a generator for air-conditioning) can put carbon monoxide in the boats. *(Jim Sollers)*

the effect of boats moored alongside

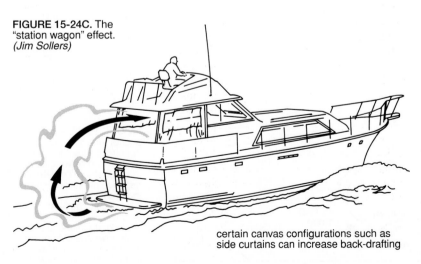

FIGURE 15-24C. The "station wagon" effect. *(Jim Sollers)*

certain canvas configurations such as side curtains can increase back-drafting

main engine when battery charging at anchor by buying an inexpensive portable gasoline generator, which is placed on the foredeck for an hour a day and run with the exhaust blowing down the hatch! These kinds of hazards can only be mitigated through a process of public education and the use of effective carbon monoxide alarms.

Carbon Monoxide Alarms

The design of an effective carbon monoxide alarm is a complicated business. This is because relatively low levels of carbon monoxide over an extended period of time can be just as lethal as high doses over a short period of time. Conversely, relatively high levels over a short period of time are not necessarily harmful (Figure 15-25). It is not unusual for there to be relatively high levels from time to time that rapidly disperse (for example, when an engine is first cranked at dockside, or when a boat in close proximity to other boats fires up its engine or generator, with the exhaust drifting across the other boats). If an alarm is designed simply to respond to a given threshold level of carbon monoxide, the threshold must be set at a very low level to protect against long-term low-level contamination. However, this will cause the alarm to be triggered by any short-term rise in carbon monoxide levels, resulting in many nuisance alarms (which almost invariably results in the alarm being disconnected or bypassed by the boat operator, at which point the alarm is effectively useless). If, on the other hand, an alarm is set to respond to a higher threshold, it will provide no protection against low levels of carbon monoxide contamination sustained over long periods of time.

Time-weighted average. An effective carbon monoxide alarm must have the ability to track carbon monoxide levels over time and to monitor in some fashion the likely impact on carboxyhemoglobin levels. This is a complicated process, particularly since carbon monoxide concentrations, when present, will almost certainly be constantly changing. Newer devices incorporate microprocessors that enable them to keep track of carbon monoxide concentrations over a set period of time (known as a *time-weighted average*—TWA), and to calculate the corresponding carboxyhemoglobin levels in the blood. This would filter out most nuisance alarms if it were not for the fact that it has proven extremely difficult to find affordable sensors that react solely to carbon monoxide (as opposed to styrene emissions from fiberglass and all kinds of other emissions commonly found on new boats).

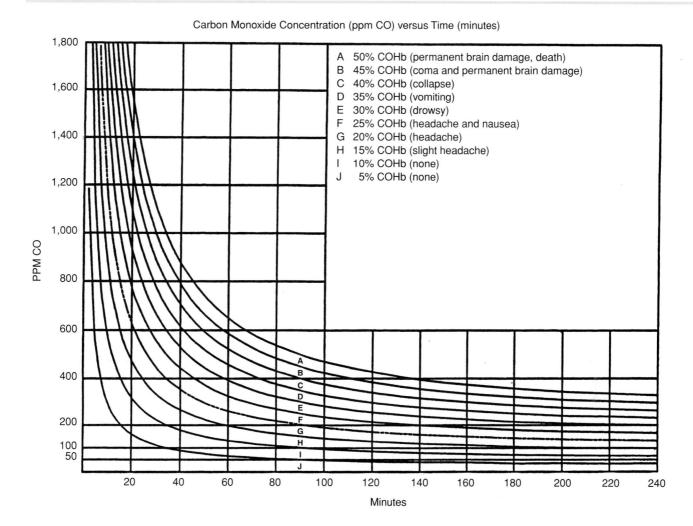

Carbon Monoxide Concentration (ppm CO) versus Time (minutes)

A 50% COHb (permanent brain damage, death)
B 45% COHb (coma and permanent brain damage)
C 40% COHb (collapse)
D 35% COHb (vomiting)
E 30% COHb (drowsy)
F 25% COHb (headache and nausea)
G 20% COHb (headache)
H 15% COHb (slight headache)
I 10% COHb (none)
J 5% COHb (none)

Cell phones and other communications devices in the 866 to 910 MHz band have also caused nuisance alarms. As a result, carbon monoxide alarms will still sometimes falsely alarm.

In the United States, UL has a standard for carbon monoxide detectors in boats (the latest version at the time of writing is UL 2034-2003; it requires the elimination of nuisance alarms caused by new-boat gases and cell phones). It is incorporated in the ABYC standard. These standards require an alarm to sound if the TWA reaches 10% carboxyhemoglobin levels, with an additional requirement that it sound after a maximum of 3 minutes if CO levels exceed 1,200 ppm, and that it not sound at concentrations up to 30 ppm (Figure 15-26). European standards are similar. Some sources are MTI Industries (www.mtiindustries.com), Fireboy-Xintex, Fyrnetics (www.fyrnetics.com), and SF Detection (www.sfdetection.com).

Alarm override. Aside from sensitivity issues, once many carbon monoxide alarms go off, they may continue to sound for some time, which can be annoying to the boat operator who has taken steps to deal with the carbon monoxide problem but must still listen to the alarm. The alarm continues to sound because the internal microprocessor is simulating the carboxyhemoglobin levels in the blood. As noted previously, once attached to hemoglobin, carbon monoxide is relatively stable. Even if the atmosphere is cleared of all carbon monoxide (or other contaminants), the simulated carboxyhemoglobin levels will only reduce slowly; it may take 15 or 20 minutes for an alarm to clear (many alarms will not clear until CO levels are below 70 ppm).

Newer alarms (in the U.S.) include a push button that can be used to silence an alarm for up to 6 minutes (this is the limit allowed by the UL standards), after which—if the device still records dangerous levels of carbon monoxide—it will start alarming again, with no additional override allowed. In combination with the kinds of adjustments to microprocessor logic already mentioned, this has resolved many past problems.

FIGURE 15-25. Carboxyhemoglobin levels in the blood stream as a function of carbon monoxide concentrations in the atmosphere and length of exposure. Note that relatively low concentrations over long periods of time can do as much damage as high concentrations over short periods of time (e.g., 200 ppm CO for 240 minutes results in the same carboxyhemoglobin level—30%—as 1,600 ppm for 10 minutes). (ABYC)

FIGURE 15-26. UL 2034-
2003 alarm thresholds.

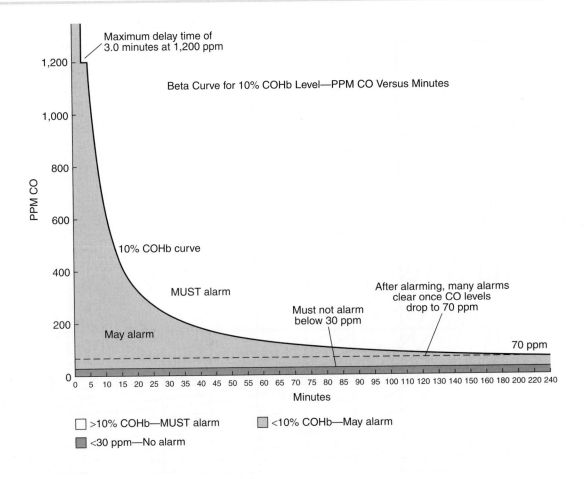

Installation issues. Beyond the manufacturing issues with carbon monoxide detectors, there are installation issues. Ideally, there should be a detector in all sleeping areas. Detectors need to be located away from corners and other dead-air areas that do not experience the natural circulation of air through the boat; on the other hand, they should not be in the airstream from ventilators or air-conditioning ducts that may dilute any concentrations of carbon monoxide in a cabin. In other words, a detector needs to be located somewhere where it receives a representative sample of air. This location needs to be protected from spray and out of the way of likely physical abuse. To minimize nuisance alarms, it should also be at least 5 feet from any galley stove (particularly alcohol stoves, since alcohol is another substance that will trigger most alarms). The detector should be at eye level to make it easy to monitor.

The detector should be wired so that anytime the boat's batteries are in service (i.e., the battery isolation switch is on), the detector is in service. Some boat manufacturers go a step further and wire carbon monoxide detectors to the *battery side* of the isolation switch so that they are in continuous service. The one disadvantage to this is the fact that many detectors draw 90 to 240 mA at 12 volts. This amounts to a 2 to 6 Ah battery drain per day, which may be enough to kill a Group 27 battery (approximately 100 Ah capacity) stone dead over a period of a month if the boat is not in use and not plugged into shore power or other charging sources. However, some detectors now draw as little as 60 mA, which amounts to less than 1.5 Ah a day in continuous use, or 40 Ah per month (the ESL SafeAir from GE Interlogix draws 8 mA, but I don't know if it complies with the marine standards; in general, the power drain of detectors is constantly being lowered). Given a moderately powerful DC system, it is practicable to leave these on permanently.

Many CO detectors for homes are relatively cheap and operate on their own battery, which is good for 5 years or more. Although they may not be tested for compliance with marine standards, one of these will be better than nothing!

Install an alarm! The bottom line is that although carbon monoxide alarms have had something of a bad reputation in the past for nuisance alarming, the latest generation has resolved most problems. *They should be standard equipment on any boat with a gasoline engine (including a portable AC generator), any boat that leaves an AC generator (diesel or gasoline) running when crew members are sleeping, and any boat that has a heating system that will operate when people are sleeping.* They are recommended on all other cruising boats.

If an alarm is triggered or carbon monoxide poisoning is suspected for any reason, *the absolute first priority is to get all affected people out into fresh air*, and then shut down all potential sources of carbon monoxide formation. With mild cases of poisoning, fresh, uncontaminated air is all that is needed for recovery. If poisoning symptoms are pronounced, seek medical help.

CHAPTER 16

FIGURE 16-1. These are other high-repair-cost items that can remain virtually trouble free through the application of proper maintenance procedures. *(Jim Sollers)*

(1) bow thrusters
(2) anchor windlass
(3) boom vang
(4) turning block
(5) line stopper
(6) winch
(7) mainsheet
(8) genoa track

Blocks, Winches, Windlasses, and Bow Thrusters

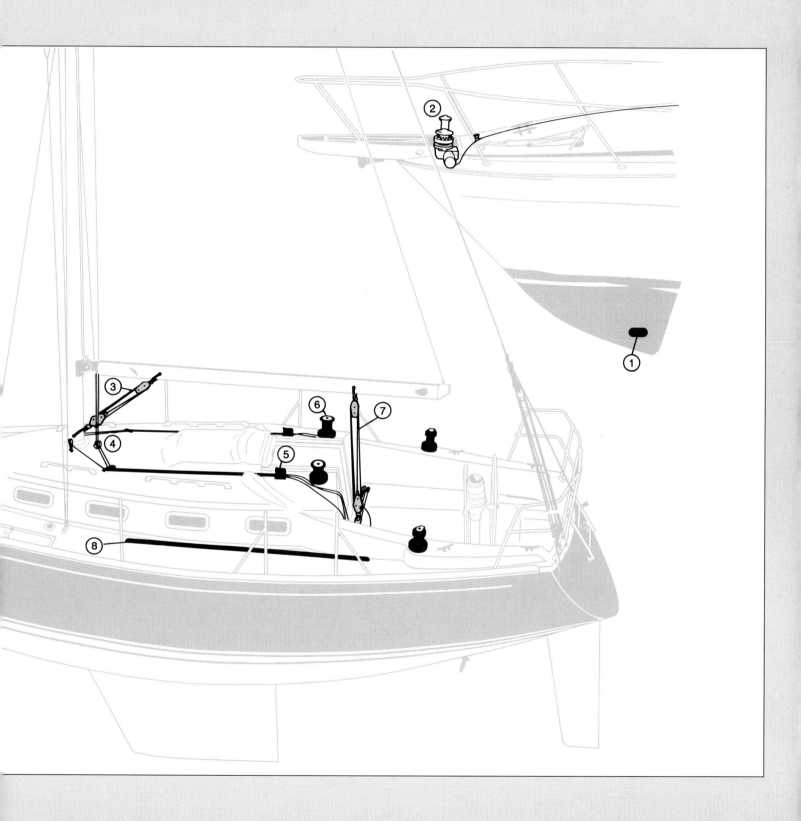

Blocks

Terminology and Loading Factors

First, some nomenclature. The basic unit of running rigging, around which ropes and wires are turned, is a *block*. The wire or rope is led around a *sheave*, which is the part that turns within the block. This sheave spins on either a *bushing* (sleeve) or a *bearing*. Bearings consist of either a number of balls set in a machined groove (a *race*) or *rollers* (pins set on end). On either side of the sheave is a *cheek plate* (*side plate* or *shell*). The cheek plates are frequently reinforced by *straps* through which pass the fasteners that hold the block together and the fastening for the block *head assembly*—the means by which it is attached to the boat (Figures 16-2A, 16-2B, and 16-2C).

Sheaves may be plastic or aluminum; bushings may be bronze or plastic; and ball bearings are generally plastic (I am using *plastic* to cover some widely varying materials). Rollers may be bronze, stainless steel, or plastic. Cheek plates may be plastic, aluminum, or stainless steel. Straps are always stainless steel except in a few expensive racing blocks where titanium is used.

Sheave selection. Three factors are important in sheave selection: the overall diameter of the sheave, the shape of its groove, and the material from which it is constructed.

Diameter. Pulling any wire or rope around a sheave deforms the lay of the line or wire; the tighter the curve, the greater the distortion.

Groove shape. The groove in a sheave must match the shape of the line or wire passing over it if it is to provide maximum support and minimum distortion. A groove suitable for ½-inch (13 mm) Dacron line will provide poor support for ¼-inch (6 mm) 7 × 19 stainless steel wire rope. Different kinds of line use different groove shapes—Kevlar uses a flatter groove than Dacron (Figure 16-3). Grooves for wire rope are frequently scored to match the lay of the outer strands of the rope.

Materials. Sheaves for synthetic line are generally plastic while those for wire rope are almost always aluminum to withstand the greater abrasion. Wire would soon tear up plastic sheaves.

Loading factors. Blocks are designed to take a direct pull on the sheave with only minimal sideways loading. Numerous head fittings are available to ensure the correct alignment of block and line (straight shackles, *upset* shackles,

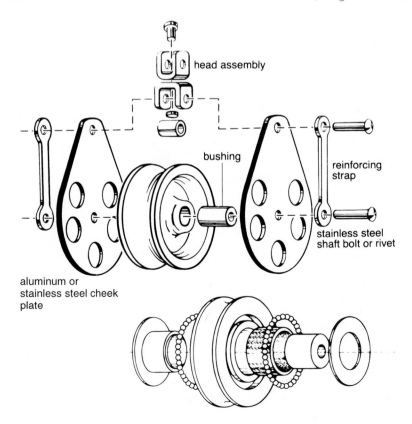

FIGURE 16-2A. Basic block construction. *(Schaefer Marine)*

head assembly

bushing

reinforcing strap

stainless steel shaft bolt or rivet

aluminum or stainless steel cheek plate

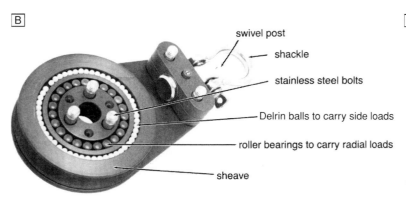

B

swivel post

shackle

stainless steel bolts

Delrin balls to carry side loads

roller bearings to carry radial loads

sheave

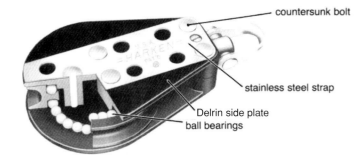

countersunk bolt

stainless steel strap

Delrin side plate
ball bearings

C

cam cleat

FIGURE 16-2B. Bearing-type block construction. *(Harken)*

FIGURE 16-2C. Use of bearings in a cam cleat and in the pedestal of a swivel block. *(Harken)*

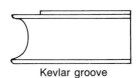

wire/rope groove   Kevlar groove

FIGURE 16-3. Block sheaves are available for use with different types of rope or wire. Use of an incorrect sheave can lead to early failure of the rope. *(Harken)*

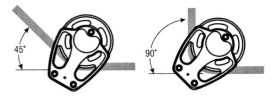

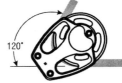

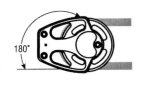

FIGURE 16-4A. Block loading factors. The load on a block depends on the tension of the line passing through the block and the turning angle involved. *(Schaefer Marine)*

swiveling heads, spring-loaded bases, and now *soft shackles*, using high-tech line such as Spectra). Blocks are rated at their *safe working load*, which is generally 50% of the breaking strength of the hardware.

Loads on blocks are directly related to the angle through which a line is turned. For example, a block that does not turn a line at all is subjected to no load, while one that turns a line through 180 degrees is subjected to a load of *double* the pull on the line. Figure 16-4A and Table 16-1 illustrate block loading factors.

The loads imposed on headsail sheets can be approximately calculated using the following formula: sheet load = $SA \times V^2 \times K$.

To derive the sheet load in pounds, SA = sail area in square feet, V = the wind speed in knots, and $K = 0.00431$.

To derive the sheet load in kilograms, SA = sail area in square meters, V = the wind speed in knots, and $K = 0.02104$.

TABLE 16-1. Block Loading as a Function of Turning Angle

Turning Angle	Block Loading Relative to Load	Block Load (based on 100 lbs./ 45 kg line tension)
0°	0%	0 lb./0 kg
30°	52%	52 lbs./23.5 kg
45°	77%	77 lbs./34.9 kg
60°	100%	100 lbs./45.4 kg
90°	141%	141 lbs./64.3 kg
120°	173%	173 lbs./78.7 kg
135°	185%	185 lbs./83.9 kg
150°	193%	193 lbs./87.8 kg
180°	200%	200 lbs./90.9 kg

Note that because the wind speed is squared, it is the most important factor in this calculation. The maximum (worst-case) wind speed should be used. The relevant wind speed is the apparent wind speed, not the true wind speed. The load on the blocks in the sheeting system is then deter-

**FIGURES 16-4B AND
16-4C.** Headsail sheet
loads. The headsail sheet
leads onto the car at 45
degrees (16-4B). The load
on the adjusting tackle is
approximately one-third
that of the load on the
block. The headsail sheet
leads onto the car at 60
degrees (16-4C). The load
on the adjusting tackle is
approximately one-half
that of the load on the
block. *(Jim Sollers)*

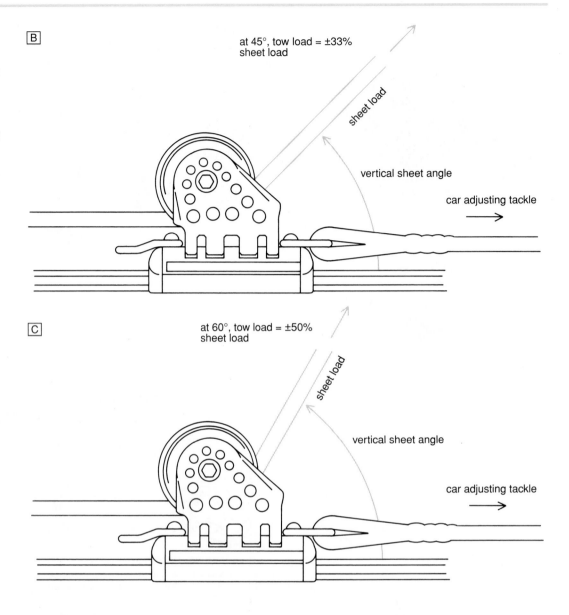

mined by the angle formed by the sheet (see above). If the sheet is fed onto an adjustable sheet lead car, the load on the adjusting tackle is a function of the angle at which the sheet comes onto the car. At an angle of 45 degrees, the load will be about one-third that of the load on the block; at 60 degrees, it will be about one-half that of the load on the block (Figures 16-4B and 16-4C, and Table 16-2; Figure 16-4D provides a rapid method for estimating approximate sheet loads).

Schaefer Marine has a formula for calculating the load on mainsheets that it notes is "not as widely accepted as that for headsail sheets" (Figure 16-4E): mainsheet load = $(E^2 \times P^2 \times V^2 \times K)/(\sqrt{[P^2 + E^2]} \times [E - X])$.

To derive the load in pounds, E = mainsail foot length in feet, P = mainsail luff length in

TABLE 16-2. Loads on the Adjusting Tackle for Headsail Cars

Sheet Angle	Load as Percent of Sheet Load
70°	65%
60°	50%
50°	35%
40°	25%

feet, V = wind speed in knots, X = the distance in feet from the aft end of the boom to the point at which the mainsheet is attached to the boom, and K = 0.00431.

To derive the load in kilograms, E = mainsail foot length in meters, P = mainsail luff length in meters, V = wind speed in knots, X = the distance in meters from the aft end of the boom to

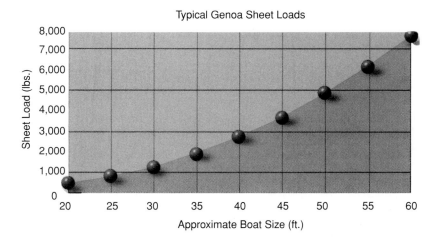

Typical Genoa Sheet Loads

FIGURE 16-4D. A graph for rapidly establishing the approximate sheet loads on a genoa sheet. *(Schaefer Marine)*

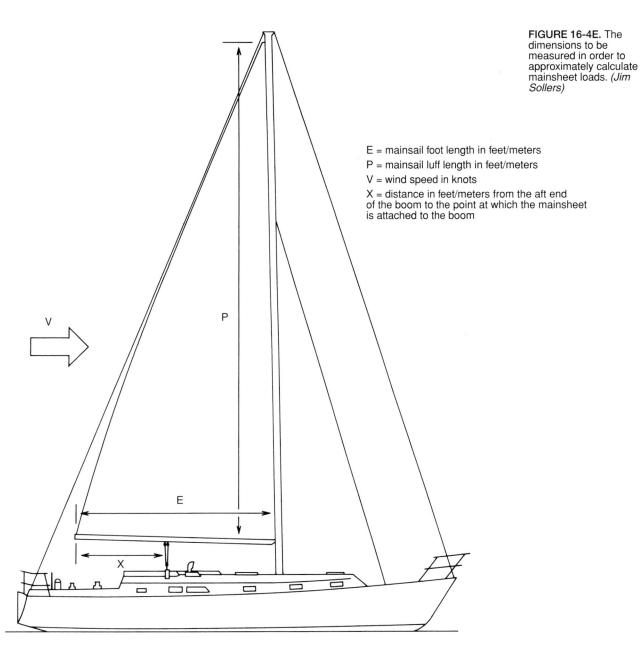

FIGURE 16-4E. The dimensions to be measured in order to approximately calculate mainsheet loads. *(Jim Sollers)*

E = mainsail foot length in feet/meters

P = mainsail luff length in feet/meters

V = wind speed in knots

X = distance in feet/meters from the aft end of the boom to the point at which the mainsheet is attached to the boom

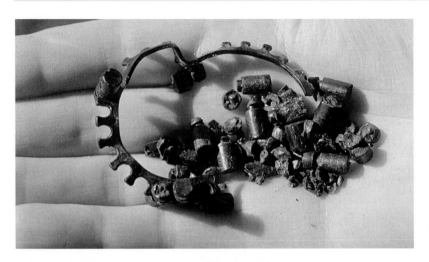

FIGURE 16-4F. A disintegrated turning block. The plastic bearings were not up to the task! This particular block was subsequently redesigned with higher-strength plastic (Torlon) bearings.

the point at which the mainsheet is attached to the boom, and K = 0.02104.

The loads on the traveler car adjuster tackle are considered to be one-fifth the load on the sheet.

If blocks are subjected to greater loads than they are designed for, or to more than minimal sideways loading through improper alignment, the sheaves, bushing, and/or bearing will deform and friction will build up rapidly. Even correctly rated blocks may start to deform if left permanently loaded (as far as possible, leave a block in an unloaded state when you are not sailing). Sometimes deformed plastic bearings and sheaves will recover their proper shape after a period of rest, but frequently damage is permanent. In cases of extreme overloading, blocks will *explode* (disintegrate) without warning, creating a serious safety hazard (Figure 16-4F).

Line loads. Line loads may be calculated as above for headsails and mainsheets but must then be adjusted for any system that employs blocks to increase the purchase of the system (Figure 16-4G). If there were no friction, then every time a purchase was doubled, the line load would be halved. But in practice there is, of course, some additional friction load.

Maintenance

Cleaning. Every time a block gets wet and dries out, salt crystals are left behind. In time the accumulation of salt in the bearings increases friction. This in turn increases wear on the moving parts, or else it freezes up the block completely—especially common with infrequently used blocks and those that have bushings as opposed to bearings.

Flush all blocks with fresh water several times a season to wash out salt crystals, dirt, and any byproducts of corrosion. Particularly stubborn deposits will generally succumb to *hot* water. If

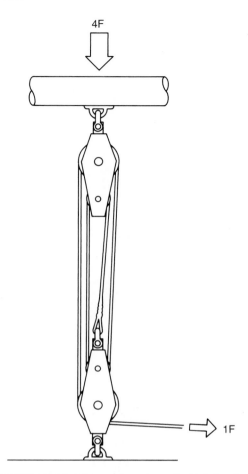

FIGURE 16-4G. A four-part purchase (tackle). A pull of 1F on the line exerts a downward force of 4F (minus the friction losses in the system). *(Jim Sollers)*

not, use plain white (clear) vinegar but rinse after flushing. In general do not use detergents on anodized aluminum, since some contain chemicals (ammonia) that will attack anodizing. Remove stains on stainless steel with metal polish, copper scouring pads, or a bronze wire brush (not steel wire wool, since tiny flecks of steel left behind will rust and leave more stains).

Spin sheaves to ensure free turning without excessive play. No lubrication is needed, but a shot of WD-40 or some silicone spray will do no harm.

Combating corrosion. Almost all blocks incorporate two or more galvanically incompatible metals, so sooner or later corrosion is inevitable. Aluminum sheaves and cheek plates, being the least noble metal involved, get eaten away. Stainless steel shafts suffer from crevice corrosion. The buildup of aluminum oxides in a block, together with salt and dirt, helps freeze it up. (It should be noted that aluminum cheek plates are primarily a weight-saving measure intended for racing boats. Since the blocks will

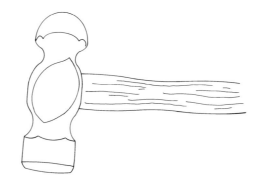

FIGURE 16-5. Removing a corroded-in-place sheave bolt. *(Jim Sollers)*

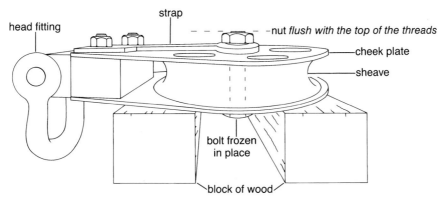

head fitting

strap

nut *flush with the top of the threads*

cheek plate

sheave

bolt frozen in place

block of wood

be replaced every few seasons, corrosion will be minimal. Unfortunately, these blocks have also been widely used by manufacturers of cruising boats. Here the blocks need to hold up for many years, and corrosion frequently becomes a problem. *Cruising sailors should specify blocks with stainless steel or plastic cheek plates.*)

Disassembly. Smaller, cheaper blocks are riveted together and so cannot be disassembled. If cleaning and lubrication do not return a block to service, you will have to discard it. Larger and more-expensive blocks are bolted together, and thus can be disassembled when necessary.

Frequently, through-bolts become corroded in place. Remove the nuts, flush with hot water and white vinegar, and spray with penetrating fluid. Grip the bolt head and try working it backward and forward to free it up. If this fails, put the nut back on and screw it down until just flush with the top of the threads on the bolt, support the block on the other side, and hit the nut smartly with a hammer (Figure 16-5). This should jar things loose. Then go back to twisting the bolt back and forth.

Sheaves that ride on bearings (as opposed to bushings) often have a retaining plate to hold the balls or rollers in place. The bearings come out complete with the sheave and are then accessible by removing the retaining plates. Other bearings are such that once the block (or mainsheet traveler or whatever) is partially disassembled, all the balls start to roll out! It is always a good idea to disassemble any block somewhere where balls cannot go down drains or bounce overboard (plastic ball bearings bounce surprisingly well!).

Inspect the bearing races for any indentations and the balls for flat spots. In either case, replace. Note that widely differing grades of plastic are used in bearings, some of which will deform and crumble under relatively moderate loads. If a bearing collapses, check with the manufacturer to see if a stronger plastic is available for this application.

Winches

Winches can be operated with a handle inserted in the top *(top acting)* or the bottom *(bottom acting)*. In the case of larger winches on racing boats, they may be set up with handles on both sides of a pedestal *(coffee grinders)*. Most are designed so that the drum turns in only one direction and locks in the other. The exception is halyard winches, which have a brake. When

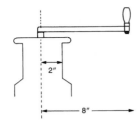

FIGURE 16-6. How winches work. The line pull of the winch equals four times the turning force on the handle.

FIGURE 16-7. A single-speed, direct-drive, top-acting winch. *(Lewmar)*

the brake is released the drum is free to rotate in reverse.

Regardless of individual differences, the operating principles remain the same. There is a high degree of similarity among different types of winches and also among similar winches from one manufacturer to another. The following text focuses on top-acting winches, since these constitute the overwhelming majority.

How They Work

If a vertical handle were to be fitted to the outer rim of a winch drum, any turning force exerted on the handle would be the same as the pull of the winch (assuming no friction losses, etc.). But if the handle is lengthened until it is four times as long as the distance from the center of the drum to its outer rim, the same force on the handle will produce four times the pull at the winch (Figure 16-6). The trade-off is that the handle is now moving through four times the distance that it was before. If it is turned at the same speed as before, only one-quarter as much line will be

pulled in for the same period of time; in effect, we have a 4:1 gear ratio.

This relationship between the distance of a winch handle and drum rim from the center of the drum is what imparts power to small, simple winches. The actual mechanism is as follows:

The winch handle turns a shaft *(spindle)* with a gear on it (Figure 16-7). The body of the winch (the drum) contains hinged, spring-loaded metal pieces called *pawls*, which bear against this gear. When the spindle is turned in one direction, the pawls engage the spindle gear, locking the drum to the spindle so that the drum and spindle turn as one. When the spindle is turned in the other direction, the pawls hinge inward against their springs and disengage the spindle gear, allowing the drum to remain stationary (*ratcheting* or *freewheeling*).

At this point we have the ability to turn the drum, but when we let go of the winch handle, there is nothing to stop the drum from spinning in reverse when under a load. Another set of spring-loaded pawls in the drum, operating in the opposite direction to the first set, engages a second gear on the winch mounting plate (winch base). This gear is forever locked in one place. Cranking on the winch handle turns the drum, which ratchets around the base-plate gear. When the winch handle is released, the second set of pawls engages the base-plate gear and prevents the drum from spinning in reverse.

What I have just described is a single-speed, direct-drive, top-acting winch: *single-speed* because there is always the same gear ratio between the spindle (i.e., winch handle) and the drum; *direct-drive* because the spindle directly engages the drum; and *top-acting* because the winch handle is inserted in the top of the drum.

Halyard winches. A *reel-type* halyard winch is essentially the same, with the exception that the base-plate gear is itself free to rotate but has a brake band around it, which is fastened to the base plate (Figure 16-8). When the brake band is tightened, it locks the base-plate gear to the base plate, and the winch operates as above. When the brake band is loosened, the base-plate gear is free to rotate and the drum unwinds. But note that as it unwinds, the drum pawls engaging the spindle gear will lock the drum and spindle together and spin the spindle with the drum. Thus, if the winch handle is left in the winch, it too will spin, and herein lies the cause of many a broken finger and wrist. *Never release the brake on a halyard winch with the handle in place.* (Note that the same situation arises with a regular winch if the pawls engaging the base-plate gear fail for any reason—*never leave handles in winches!*)

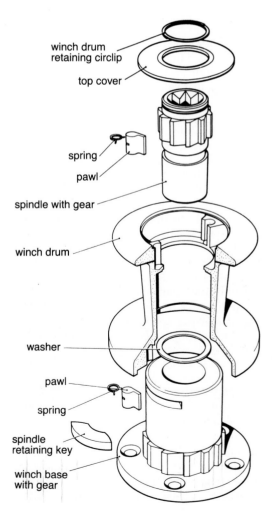

winch drum retaining circlip

top cover

spring

pawl

spindle with gear

winch drum

washer

pawl

spring

spindle retaining key

winch base with gear

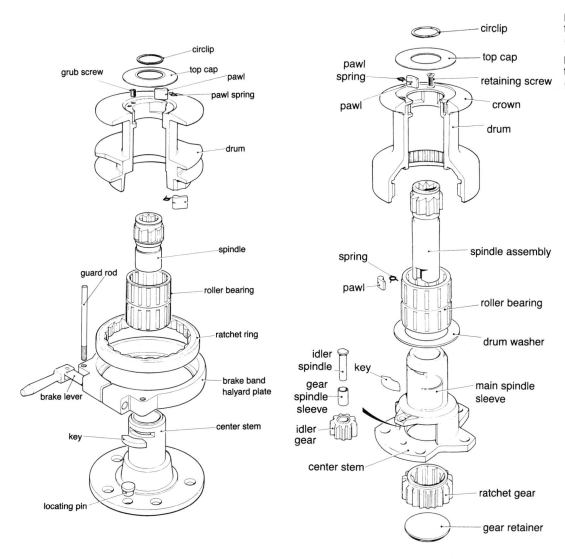

circlip
grub screw
top cap
pawl
pawl spring
drum
spindle
guard rod
roller bearing
ratchet ring
brake band halyard plate
brake lever
center stem
key
locating pin

circlip
pawl spring
top cap
retaining screw
pawl
crown
drum
spindle assembly
spring
pawl
roller bearing
drum washer
idler spindle
key
gear spindle sleeve
main spindle sleeve
idler gear
center stem
ratchet gear
gear retainer

FIGURE 16-8 (left). A reel-type halyard winch. *(Lewmar)*

FIGURE 16-9 (right). A two-speed winch. *(Lewmar)*

Multiple-speed winches. When the winch handle is turned on a single-speed winch, it engages the drum in only one direction and freewheels (ratchets) in the other. On a two-speed winch, the handle also engages the drum in the second direction but at a different gear ratio (i.e., given the same winch handle speed, the drum turns at a different speed). This is achieved as follows:

There is the usual single-speed gear machined onto the spindle. The spindle also fits inside a second gear. Pawls on the spindle ratchet inside this second gear when the winch handle is cranked in the first (single-speed) direction. The pawls engage the inside of this second gear when the winch handle is turned in reverse (the single-speed gear itself is ratcheting at this point). The spindle and second gear are now turning in reverse. Obviously, to be of any use the drum itself must continue to turn in the single-speed direction; otherwise it would just

oscillate backward and forward as the handle was cranked backward and forward. An *idler gear* is fitted between the second spindle gear and the drum; this converts the backward spindle movement into forward drum movement (Figure 16-9).

With this arrangement, although it is a little hard to visualize, any load on the drum (e.g., line pull) tries to turn the spindle in one direction via the first (single-speed) gear and the opposite direction via the second gear. Since the spindle cannot rotate in two directions at once, the winch is effectively locked in place by these counterposed forces. When the drum is spun the other way (freewheeled), both gears ratchet, allowing it to turn.

In order to make a winch more powerful, the gear ratio between the handle and the drum must be increased. This could be done by increasing the length of the winch handle, but this is clearly impractical. Instead, what is done

FIGURE 16-10. Larger winches—with higher gear ratios to handle higher loads—are more complex than simple winches. *(Lewmar)*

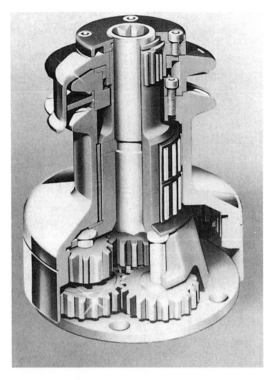

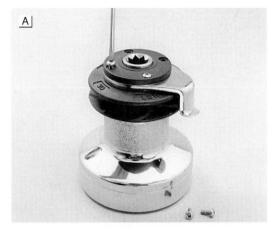

FIGURES 16-11A TO 16-11I. Step-by-step winch disassembly for cleaning and maintenance. Remove screws (16-11A), circlip (16-11B), or unscrew the winch top (not shown). If the winch is self-tailing, pull out retaining collets (16-11C). On a halyard winch, the halyard must be released from the drum, accomplished here by undoing the two "grub" (Allen) screws (16-11D). Lift off the drum and bearings (16-11E), and oil the top drum pawls (16-11F). Remove the spindle. The plastic key, which fits into a groove in the spindle, and is itself retained by the bearings fitted around the winch stem, holds the spindle in place (16-11G). You can pry loose a spindle or gear shaft (16-11H). Finally, remove the gears (16-11I). *(Lewmar)*

is to fit more gears into the winch and play with the relative gear sizes (Figure 16-10). The net result is that a large three-speed winch can look quite complicated, but the principles remain the same as for simpler winches.

Servicing and Overhaul

Given the ease and speed with which a winch can be serviced, *it is a shame that so many boat-owners go from one year to the next without paying the slightest attention to their winches.* If servicing is left until a noticeable problem has developed (extreme stiffness, drum freewheels in both directions, etc.), the winch is likely to have suffered unnecessary and permanent damage (primarily from corrosion).

Disassembly. The pawls and pawl springs are very small, easily lost, and absolutely indispensable to winch operation. *Before dismantling a winch, clear the area around it and plug any nearby drains*—sometimes the pawls and springs hang up and fly out at unexpected moments. Even better, keep spares on board in case any do get lost or broken. One way to keep from losing parts is to cut a hole in the bottom of a cardboard box and then place the box—open side up—over the winch during disassembly.

On many newer winches, undoing a screw down inside the socket the winch handle goes into releases the complete drum assembly, which can then be lifted off.

On many older winches, the top of the winch

BLOCKS, WINCHES, WINDLASSES, AND BOW THRUSTERS

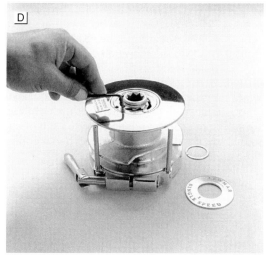

groove in
spindle

winch stem

key

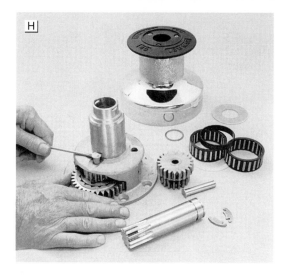

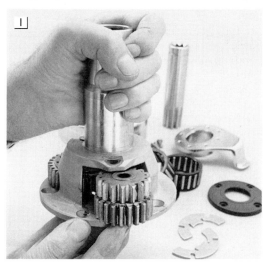

must be removed (Figure 16-11A) in order to get the rest apart. On some the top plate unscrews; others are variously retained with machine screws, socket-head screws, or spring clips (*circlips*—Figure 16-11B). Beneath the top cover may be a couple of *collets* fitted into slots in the spindle (Figure 16-11C). Removal should be self-evident. If the winch has a self-tailing mechanism, take it off next. First *note the position of the stripper arm in relation to the boat so that you can put it back in the same place.* Some self-tailers have a number of springs—lift off the top plate carefully to prevent the springs from flying out. (Note that unless there is a specific reason to disassemble a self-tailing mechanism, you can normally lift it off in one piece with the drum, in which case ignore this step.) The halyard will need to be released from a halyard winch (Figure 16-11D). Now you can lift off the winch drum (Figure 16-11E)—this is where you must take care to watch out for loose pawls, especially any fitted in the base of the drum. Either now or on reassembly, the pawls need to be lightly oiled (Figure 16-11F).

On all but the largest winches, all of the bearings and gears are now accessible. The main bearings (for the drum) should be retained in a *cage* and may be inside the drum or on the center stem. With the bearings removed, somewhere in the center stem, there may be a key or collets, which you must gently pry out to release the spindle (Figure 16-11G).

If any corrosion is present, the spindle itself may be a little hard to remove. Give it a good spraying with penetrating fluid to help it along, then use a winch handle that is locked in place to work the spindle out. Any gears will be retained by shafts (also called spindles) that simply lift out

(Figure 16-11H), enabling the gears to be removed (Figure 16-11I). Larger winches have replaceable sleeves around the gear shafts, or the gears themselves ride on small roller bearings.

Gear shafts, sleeves, and/or bearings should all go back in the same place. As you disassemble a winch, it is best to lay everything out on a clean work surface, with the various parts the right way up and in the correct relationship to each other, so that there will be no confusion when it comes time for reassembly.

Thoroughly clean everything—kerosene (paraffin), diesel, and mineral spirits all work well—and dry with a lint-free rag. Inspect the gears for worn, chipped, or stepped teeth; the stainless steel shafts for crevice corrosion; the bearings for corrosion or flat spots; the center stem and inside of the drum for corrosion; above all the pawls for any signs of wear or chipping; and the pawl springs for corrosion and loss of tension. Anodized aluminum self-tailing mechanisms retained by stainless steel fasteners are especially susceptible to corrosion around the fasteners (Figure 16-12). A little Tef-Gel, Duralac, or the like on the fastener threads will help keep this at bay.

Figures 16-13A to 16-13N illustrate the disassembly of another winch (a Barient). Figure

FIGURE 16-12. Galvanic corrosion around a stainless steel fastener in an aluminum self-tailing mechanism.

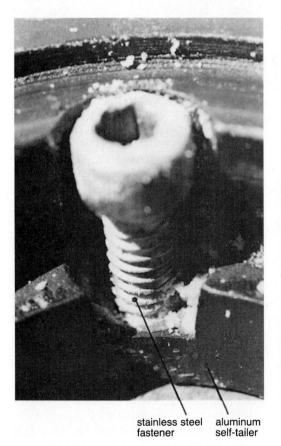

stainless steel fastener   aluminum self-tailer

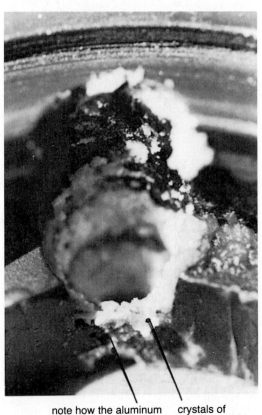

note how the aluminum is eaten away   crystals of aluminum oxide and salt

FIGURES 16-13A TO 16-13N. Disassembling a Barient winch. Use a deck-plate key to unscrew the top of the winch (16-13A). Remove the top plate (16-13B), allowing the stripper arm to be lifted off (16-13C). Next comes the drum (16-13D). The drum bearings are a little grungy (16-13E). The center stem above the surface on which they seat is some-what corroded, but this will not affect winch perfor-mance (nothing seats on this part of the surface). Lift off the drum bearings (16-13F). Use a winch handle locked in place to pull out the spindle (16-13G; be careful as the last of it comes out—there may be spring-loaded pawls in its base). Un-screw the center stem (16-13H). Remove the center stem to expose the gears (16-13I). The gears and pawls (16-13J). A pawl in good condition (16-13K). The pawl spring (the narrow wire) can be seen behind the pawl (the rest of the spring is buried in a groove in the pawl). Re-move the remaining gears to expose their bearings (16-13L). Cleanup time (16-13M). Add a light coating of the recom-mended lubricant on reassembly (16-13N).

(photos continued on next page)

spring

BARIENT
BARLUBE

BLOCKS, WINCHES, WINDLASSES, AND BOW THRUSTERS

16-14 gives a sense of the number of components in larger winches. Note the sheet hanging from the lifelines to prevent any pawls and springs from flying overboard!

Reassembly. Reassembly is the reverse of disassembly (Figures 16-15A to 16-15E). Pay special attention to those all-important pawls and springs, which should be lightly oiled (3-In-One Oil, Marvel Mystery Oil). Make sure that ratchet gears are *right side up* (Figures 16-15D and 16-15E) and the parts properly seated. *Do not grease the pawls*—the grease is likely to attract dirt and salt until eventually the pawls bind in their housings and fail to operate. However, *lightly* grease gears and bearings with a Teflon-based marine grease (Lubriplate Marine-Lube "A," etc.; some winch manufacturers have proprietary greases).

Never apply oil or grease to the brake band or mechanism on any halyard winch—doing so can create a serious safety hazard.

Note that gear shafts fit into holes in the base plate. During cleaning operations, particles of dirt are liable to fall into these holes. They must

FIGURE 16-14. Disassembling a moderately large two-speed winch. All the parts are laid out in order, making it easier to remember where they go back. The sheet on the lifelines is to prevent pawls and springs from flying overboard. The cockpit and deck drains have been plugged for the same reason.

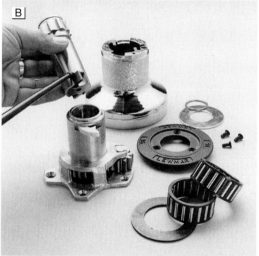

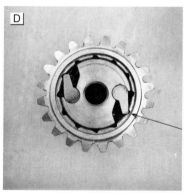

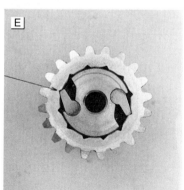

FIGURES 16-15A TO 16-15E. A large three-speed winch disassembled (16-15A). You'd better keep all the parts organized and the right way up! Oil the pawls (16-15B). Lightly grease the spindles and bearings (16-15C). Where there is a choice, make sure that ratchet gears are the right way up. Those shown in 16-15D are wrong—the pawls are not seated properly; those shown in 16-15E are correct—the pawls are fully seated. *(Lewmar)*

FIGURE 16-16A. A self-tailing winch. *(Lewmar)*

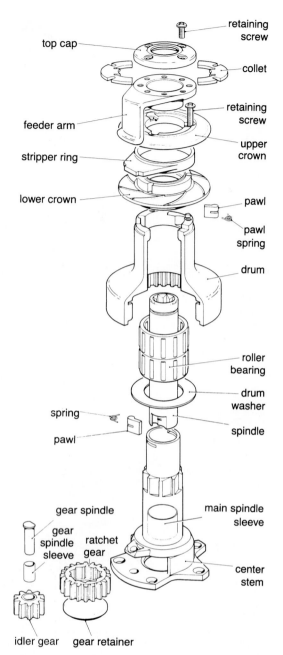

retaining screw

top cap

collet

feeder arm

retaining screw

upper crown

stripper ring

lower crown

pawl

pawl spring

drum

roller bearing

drum washer

spring

spindle

pawl

gear spindle

main spindle sleeve

gear spindle sleeve

ratchet gear

center stem

idler gear   gear retainer

FIGURE 16-16B. Reassembling a self-tailing mechanism. Note the stripper arm being lined up to fit under the feeder arm.

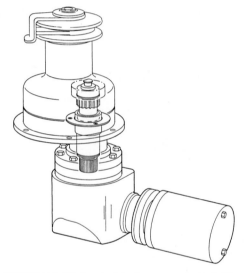

FIGURE 16-17. An electrically powered winch. The winch is essentially the same as a manual winch with the exception of some minor modifications to take the motor drive. *(Lewmar)*

be scrupulously cleaned out, or the shafts will not seat properly. The shafts themselves have odd-shaped heads fitting into machined recesses and *must be properly seated.* The spindle key (if present) fits into a machined groove in the spindle. If it won't go in, *don't force it* (in fact, *nothing* on a winch needs forcing). Lock a winch handle in place to raise or lower the spindle a fraction until the key is an easy fit.

Refitting a self-tailing mechanism. If it has a separate stripper ring (Figures 16-16A and 16-16B), make sure to place it under the stripper arm (it fits in a slot) and put the stripper arm back in the necessary relationship to the boat to make the sheet fall in the correct place. Any fasteners just need to be hand-tightened and then pinched up a little more—don't overtighten, especially where plastic housings are involved.

Powered Winches

Powered winches are becoming increasingly popular. They can be powered either with electric motors or with sophisticated hydraulic systems (e.g., Lewmar's Commander system—www.lewmar.com). In any event, the winch end of things is the same as a manual winch, except for some minor modifications to the spindle to allow a motor (electric or hydraulic) to be geared in from below (Figure 16-17).

The motor end of an electrically powered winch is the same as for an electric windlass—see the Electric Windlasses section later in this chapter. Two- and three-speed electrically powered winches may have electronic devices linked to a central microprocessor that sense the load and reverse the motor at a certain point. This has the same effect as reversing the direction of cranking on a winch handle—it engages another gear. At higher loads an electromagnet is tripped to engage a third gear (where fitted).

If a two-speed winch operates only at one speed, try reversing the power leads *from* the control unit *to* the motor (*not* the power leads *to* the control unit—that would probably wreck the control unit).

Faced with a motor failure, run all the usual voltage tests (Chapter 4); jump the motor directly from the battery to make sure it really is at fault. Check the brushes, brush springs, and commutator; run the motor tests outlined in Chapter 7.

Windlasses

Anchor windlasses can be horizontal or vertical, with some differences between them:

- On a horizontal windlass, the drum (for rope) and *wildcat* (*gypsy*, for chain) stick out the sides; on the vertical windlass, they are set one on top of the other.

- A horizontal windlass provides only a 90-degree wrap for an anchor chain around the wildcat, whereas a vertical anchor provides a 180-degree wrap. There is less risk of the chain skipping over the wildcat with the vertical windlass.

- The chain drops directly off a horizontal windlass, which helps it come off cleanly, whereas the chain has to be fed off a vertical windlass, which requires a minimum vertical drop of a foot or so (about 30 cm) beneath the windlass to provide the necessary weight to keep it moving without jamming.

- To avoid problems, the bow roller on a horizontal windlass installation must be directly lined up with the wildcat, whereas it can be off a degree or two with a vertical windlass.

- In terms of handling a rope rode, it is easier to tail a line off a horizontal drum than a vertical drum, but the line pull can only be in one direction (from the bow roller), whereas with the vertical drum, the line pull can be from any direction. (This can be handy for warping into a dock, kedging off, etc.)

- If two anchors are to be handled with one winch (as they are on most offshore cruising boats), a horizontal windlass is easier to use.

Anchor locker design is critical to trouble-free windlass operation. With a chain rode, the locker must be deep enough for the entire rode to be able to pile up without fouling the chain pipe or underside of the windlass. (Without this depth, the chain will jam the windlass, and someone will have to get into the anchor locker to knock down the chain pile.) For rope rodes, ideally there will be a rope locker with an opening hatch positioned so that the rode can be tailed off the warping drum and dropped into the locker (Figures 16-18A, 16-18B, and 16-18C). In all cases, with a powered windlass, if the windlass motor is bolted to the underside of the windlass (as most are), hanging down into the anchor locker, it needs protection from chain flailing around in a seaway and water splashing off the rodes (Figure 16-18D).

Windlasses can be manually operated, although most are now powered; the majority of the latter have electric motors (although some are hydraulically driven). As the load increases

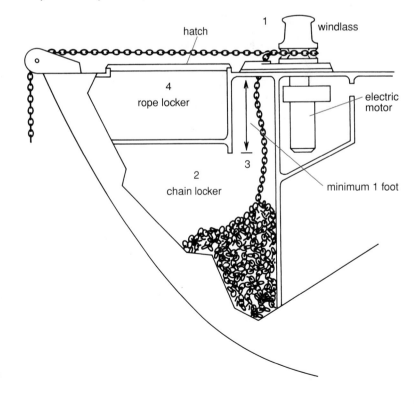

FIGURE 16-18A. A good ground tackle setup. The windlass is set well aft in order to get it over the deepest part of the chain locker (1). The chain locker is deep and narrow (2), which keeps the chain from fouling the underside of the chain pipe. There is a drop of a foot or so from the windlass (3), so that the weight of the chain hanging down will keep it feeding cleanly off the windlass. There is a relatively shallow deck locker for a rope rode positioned so that the rode can be tailed off the windlass and dropped into it (4). *(Jim Sollers)*

FIGURE 16-18B. The ground tackle setup being constructed on our new Malo 45. The windlass seats in a shallow well with drains on either side. Any mud that comes aboard with the rodes will be caught in this well and not go down the side decks. The chain pipe in this photo is not centered over the chain locker, so I subsequently had the builder cut it out and move it over! The chain locker itself is deep and narrow. The locker we are looking into is a sail locker (for the asymmetric spinnaker and storm jib). On the left-hand side is a locker for a rope rode positioned so that the rode can be tailed directly into it.

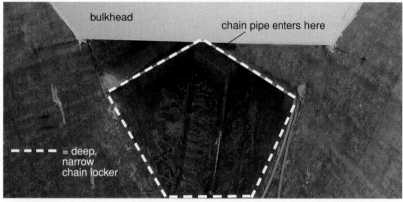

FIGURE 16-18C. The chain locker under construction. Once the chain pipe was moved, the chain dropped into the deepest part of the locker. Note the sloped topsides; because of the way chain piles up, much of the volume in the top of a traditional chain locker is never used and is wasted space.

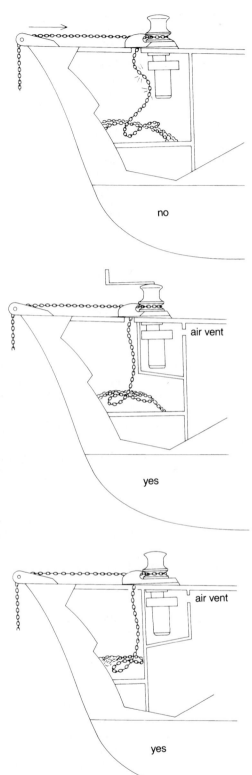

on an electric windlass, its power consumption goes up and the rate of rode retrieval (the chain or rope speed) goes down. Hydraulic windlasses run at a constant speed.

The rated maximum pulling capacity *(stall load)* of an electric anchor windlass should be *at least* three times the total weight of the ground tackle (anchor + chain + any rope rode) that will be attached to it. Typically, the rated working load is one-third of the stall load—it is the load the windlass will be handling once the anchor is off the bottom.

Problems Common to All Windlasses

Corrosion. Anchor windlasses occupy one of the most exposed positions on any boat, and are subject to constant saltwater drenchings. Since most incorporate dissimilar metals (notably aluminum, bronze, steel, and stainless steel), there is

FIGURE 16-18D. Proper windlass installation. The unprotected windlass motor (top) is subjected to salt corrosion and can be shorted out by the chain. Enclosing the motor (middle) solves both of these problems. The best solution is to mount the windlass assembly outside the chain locker (bottom). *(Simpson Lawrence and Jim Sollers)*

FIGURE 16-19. A windlass shaft sheared by snubbing loads.

an obvious potential for galvanic interaction. Windlasses will benefit from a periodic washing down with fresh water. Luckily, most external corrosion problems tend to be cosmetic or peripheral to the main functioning of the windlass (e.g., blistering of paintwork on aluminum windlasses, and oxidizing of aluminum housings and base plates around stainless steel fasteners). To reduce problems, coat all fasteners with a corrosion inhibitor. External corrosion can be irritating and make disassembly and overhaul difficult, but it rarely interferes with the basic functioning of a windlass.

Far more damaging is internal corrosion, which leads to seizure. Corrosion from condensation alone can seize up an unused windlass. Windlasses in anchor wells, even though closed off and protected, are sometimes more prone to corrosion than those on foredecks—the anchor well produces a wonderfully warm and humid environment!

It is essential to ensure that no water enters the windlass case, and to turn a windlass over regularly in case water does get in; this will maintain oil and grease coatings on internal parts, and hold seizure at bay.

Snubbing loads. The majority of operating problems arise from overloading a windlass through excessive snubbing loads. When an anchored boat is lying to an all-chain rode in choppy seas, the foredeck can pitch up and down through many feet, gaining considerable momentum in the process. If the anchor is well buried, as it should be, the anchor windlass is subjected to repeated shock-loading when the bow comes up, which will open up deck seals and may tear the windlass loose from the foredeck or shear a shaft (Figure 16-19).

Anchor windlasses are not designed to handle heavy snubbing loads; consequently, they should always be protected against shock loads. This is done as follows:

1. Drop the anchor, pay out adequate scope (at least 4:1 on chain), and set the anchor (make sure it is dug in).
2. Attach a length of *nylon* line (the snubbing line) to the anchor chain at the bow roller, leave a few feet to dangle, and firmly cleat off the other end to a mooring cleat or samson post (Figure 16-20).
3. Pay out some more chain until the snubbing line is taking all the anchoring loads, then feed out a foot or two more of chain and lock off the windlass.
4. If breaking out a deeply buried anchor, *snub the rode up to a samson post or cleat and use the engine to break the anchor loose, not the*

FIGURE 16-20. Relieve the load on windlasses with a snubbing line. On boats with bowsprits and bobstays, lead the snubbing line through the bulwark chock. The boat will lie slightly off the wind and the bobstay will not "saw" on the snubbing line and anchor chain. *(Jim Sollers)*

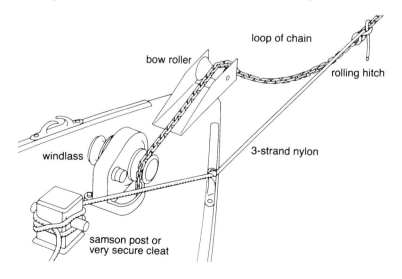

windlass (if there is any kind of wave action, snub the rode up short and use the pitching of the boat to break out the anchor). With electric windlasses, running the engine has the added advantage that the alternator will keep the battery voltage up, reducing the voltage drop at the windlass.

It is important to use nylon rope for a snubbing line, since it will stretch and act as a shock absorber. Three-strand nylon is better in this respect than plaited (braided) types. The size of the line will depend on the boat's weight and the sea conditions—too heavy a line will not stretch; too light will break. Three-eighths-inch (10 mm) works well on most boats to around 25,000 pounds (11,000 kg); ½-inch (13 mm) up to 40,000 pounds (18,000 kg); ⅝-inch (16 mm) thereafter. Only a few feet are required—certainly no more than 15 feet (5 m) need be let out in most conditions. The amount of chain left dangling (note loop in Figure 16-20) should be about one-quarter the length of the snubbing line. In a strong blow, the line will stretch tight, allowing the chain and windlass to take some of the load. Nylon will tolerate repeated stretching to 125% of its original length without failure.

Many people use chain hooks to attach a snubbing line to the chain. Having lost several of these in the past, for years I have used a rolling hitch and have never had a snubber either slip or prove too difficult to undo (see Figure 16-20 again).

Should the snubbing line part, the windlass will be subjected to a sudden shock load that may break the shaft or (on a horizontal windlass) simply cause the chain to jump up on the wildcat and start running out. Once a chain starts to do this, it very often will not reseat itself. *It is essential to have at least one more line of defense against loosing all the chain.* A very strong attachment point for the bitter end of the chain is obviously called for, but *it would be better to have an additional chain stopper on deck or to place a loop of chain around a samson post.* If all the chain runs out, and the boat comes up short on its bitter-end attachment point, there may well be an enormous shock load that simply rips the bitter end loose.

Chain difficulties. Sometimes chain will jump off a wildcat, especially a horizontal wildcat. This can be the result of an improper match between the chain and the wildcat, but it can also arise through improper chain leads and twisted chains.

Chain sizing and related issues. The big difficulty in matching chain to a wildcat is that there are no universally accepted international standards for chain sizes. Even within individual countries, chain manufacturers still tend to be small-shop operations, and variations in chain of nominally the same size are common. *The only sure way to match the chain and the wildcat is to take the wildcat to the chain.* Better still, order chain from the windlass manufacturer when you purchase the windlass.

The nominal size of chain is a measure of the diameter of the metal *(wire)* in the links. In Europe, nominal and actual diameters coincide, but in the United States, it is customary to use wire that is ¹⁄₃₂-inch larger in diameter than the nominal size of the chain!

Chain comes as long (or regular) link, short link, and studded. The link length is called *pitch.* Long link is not suitable for anchoring (the most common form of long-link chain found in marine catalogs is *proof coil* chain). Short link is used in most applications except for really large boats (superyachts), which may use studded-link chain (the links have a bar through the center that keeps them from deforming when overloaded). Two common short-link chains used for anchoring are *BBB* and *high test.*

Steel (galvanized) anchor chain is designated by a grade system. The grade is related to the strength of the alloy used to manufacture the chain. BBB and proof coil, sometimes referred to as *G3* or *System 3*, are made from the same material, which is between grades 28 and 30 (the higher the number, the stronger the alloy). High test (*G4* or *System 4*) is made from material that is between grades 40 and 43. Table 16-3 summarizes chain statistics.

The advantage of a higher-grade chain is that a smaller, lighter chain can be used to achieve the same strength as a larger, lower-grade chain. The smaller chain link size either enables the weight of the rode to be reduced, or it enables a greater length of chain to be stowed in a given space. Higher grades than high test are available and are sometimes recommended for additional weight savings. But in practice there is little benefit to buying them because the inside diameter of the links for a given strength becomes too small to be able to fit a similarly rated shackle (this can, however, be overcome by having an oversized link welded into the end of the chain). In most situations, high test represents the optimum choice and is often recommended by windlass manufacturers.

Typically, *safe working loads* (generally referred to as *working load limits* or simply *working loads*) are normally (but not always—read the fine print) defined as 25% of the breaking load *under a straight, even pull* (Table 16-3 again—note that because of this "straight, even pull" assumption, the actual breaking load in many service conditions, particularly when sub-

TABLE 16-3. Approximate Chain Dimensions (U.S.)[1]

Type of Chain	Trade Size (in.)	Wire Size (in.)	Working Load Limit (lbs.)	Pitch (in.)	Nominal Inside Width (in.)	Maximum Length 100 Links (in.)	Links per Foot	Weight per 100 Feet (lbs.)
BBB	$5/16$	$11/32$	1,950	1.00	0.50	104	12	120
	$3/8$	$13/32$	2,750	1.09	0.62	113	11	173
	$7/16$	$15/32$	3,625	1.21	0.68	126	$9^{3/4}$	232
	$1/2$	$17/32$	4,750	1.34	0.75	139	9	307
Proof coil	$5/16$	$11/32$	1,900	1.10	0.50	114	11	106
	$3/8$	$13/32$	2,650	1.23	0.62	128	$9^{3/4}$	155
	$7/16$	$15/32$	3,500	1.37	0.75	142	$8^{3/4}$	217
	$1/2$	$17/32$	4,500	1.54	0.79	156	$7^{3/4}$	270
High test	$5/16$	$11/32$	3,900	1.01	0.48	105	$12^{1/4}$	110
	$3/8$	$13/32$	5,400	1.15	0.58	121	$10^{1/2}$	160
	$7/16$	$15/32$	7,200	1.29	0.67	134	$9^{1/8}$	216
	$1/2$	$17/32$	9,200	1.43	0.76	148	$8^{1/2}$	280

1. Working load must not be exceeded. European chain is measured in millimeters, but there are differences in measurements from one country to another.

jected to snubbing loads, will be considerably less than four times the working load limit).

In recent years, stainless steel BBB chain from Asia (manufactured by Suncor) and Germany (WASI) has become widely available. It has a working load limit somewhere between that of galvanized BBB and high test—at approximately three times the price (it can sometimes be bought for a fraction of its normal price). Its big advantages are that (1) it does not need regalvanizing every few years (see below), and (2) it is much more "slippery" than galvanized chain. As a result it does not build up a chain "pyramid" in the chain locker and so is less likely to foul the windlass.

Chain lead. On a horizontal windlass, the wildcat must be at least as high as the bow roller so that the chain feeds *at least horizontally and preferably up* to the wildcat (Figure 16-21). This ensures proper engagement of the chain and wildcat (if the wildcat is below the bow roller, there will be less than a 90-degree chain engagement, and a real risk of the chain skipping). On the other side of the wildcat, the chain ideally should have a free fall of a foot or two so that its weight maintains a little pull on the wildcat. With vertical windlasses, the free fall is even more important; without it, it is sometimes necessary to have someone tail the chain from below (i.e., maintain pressure on it). If this is not done, the chain can get jammed between the stripper and the deck opening.

Twisting of chain. If a boat repeatedly swings around its anchor, the chain can twist up. The same thing can happen when a combination three-strand nylon line and chain rode is put under a heavy load—the nylon may partially unlay and twist the chain. When the anchor is weighed, twisted chain has a tendency to sit on the surface of a wildcat rather than seat in it. The

chain can then skip back out. Swivels fitted between the chain and the anchor will help eliminate the twist in the chain, but having looked at a few and used one or two, I suspect that most swivels form *the* weak link in an anchor system. It is a rare occasion indeed when twisted chain is anything more than a minor irritation, and I prefer to live with it.

If a swivel is fitted, it is essential to attach it to the anchor shank with a shackle, rather than fasten it directly to the shank (as is commonly done). Without the shackle, if the boat swings at anchor, a severe side load can be put on the swivel, which it is not designed for. This can lead to a failure, at which point the boat drifts free.

Galvanizing. With the exception of stainless steel chain, all anchor chain is galvanized (coated with zinc to protect against corrosion). When buying anchor chain, *hot-dipped chain is preferable to electroplated*; the former will resist corrosion longer.

In time, the galvanizing will strip off anchor chains. In certain instances, this can happen quite rapidly, such as when a boat anchors on top of a steel wreck—galvanic interaction can strip the zinc off the anchor chain in a matter of days! The chain should be turned end for end

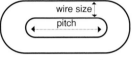

Note: Pitch and wire size can be used to determine the exact type of an unknown chain. For accuracy, they should be measured with calipers.

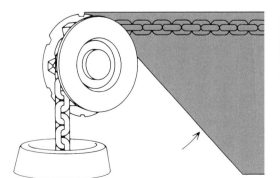

FIGURE 16-21. Chain must be horizontal or slope up to a wildcat (i.e., be within the shaded area). *(Simpson Lawrence and Jim Sollers)*

each year, and regalvanized when it starts to rust. Turning the chain also ensures that all connections and links (shackles, swivels, chain-to-rope splices, and the fastening on the bitter end) get undone and inspected at least once a year. Be sure to properly seize all shackles with stainless steel wire after doing them back up.

General Maintenance

Windlasses are generally low-maintenance, trouble-free items. The most essential part of preventive maintenance is to periodically wash down the exterior surfaces with fresh water. Open-gear (nonlubricated) windlasses should be flushed out at the same time.

Many windlasses run in an oil or grease bath. Infrequent use causes the lubricant to settle out. Take a sample annually from the base of the gearbox to check for salt water or emulsification. If you find either, flush the gearbox and add fresh lubricant. (To clean out a grease-filled box, unbolt the windlass and remove the base plate.)

Sometimes special greases are used that coat and adhere to the internal parts better than a normal grease. Refer to the manual.

In addition to maintaining oil or grease levels, *periodically crank a windlass to distribute lubricant around the gears*. Many gears, sprockets, and chains, especially on older windlasses, are steel—a failure to turn the windlass over from time to time will lead to rusting and seizure.

Some clutch cones and brake linings need annual lubrication; the manual will specify the type of lubricant. Undo the clutch nut and slip off the wildcat to gain access to the clutch or brake pad. Where the windlass has a *plated steel* shaft (as opposed to bronze or stainless steel), be sure to remove the rope drum annually and grease the shaft, or the two will seize together and be *impossible* to separate.

Horizontal Manual Windlasses

How they work. Although most new windlasses are powered, there are many older manual

FIGURE 16-22A. The spur-geared manual windlass revealed. This is the popular SL555 from Simpson Lawrence. *(Simpson Lawrence and Jim Sollers)*

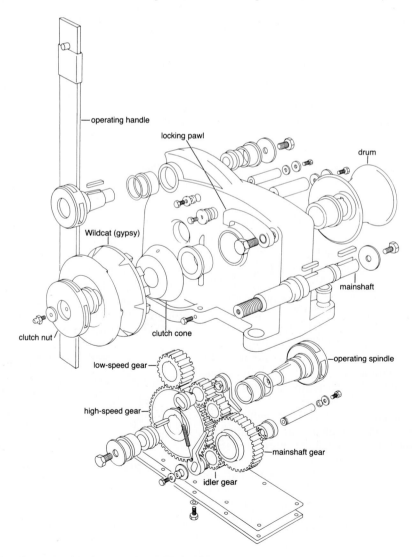

operating handle

locking pawl

drum

Wildcat (gypsy)

mainshaft

clutch nut

clutch cone

operating spindle

low-speed gear

high-speed gear

mainshaft gear

idler gear

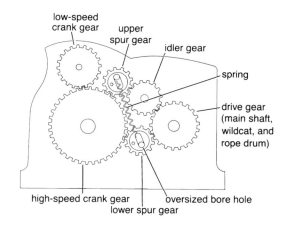

low-speed crank gear

upper spur gear

idler gear

spring

drive gear (main shaft, wildcat, and rope drum)

high-speed crank gear

lower spur gear

oversized bore hole

FIGURE 16-22B. The operation of a spur-geared manual horizontal anchor windlass. Pulling back and pushing forward on the winch handle both rotate the wildcat and rope drum in the same direction (A and B). A load on the wildcat forces both spur gears against the crank gear, locking the windlass (C). *(Jim Sollers)*

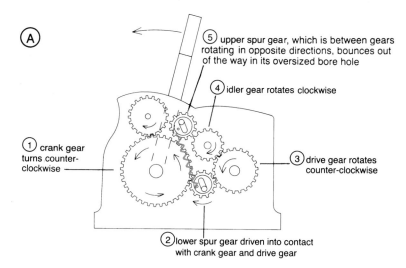

(A)

⑤ upper spur gear, which is between gears rotating in opposite directions, bounces out of the way in its oversized bore hole

④ idler gear rotates clockwise

① crank gear turns counter-clockwise

③ drive gear rotates counter-clockwise

② lower spur gear driven into contact with crank gear and drive gear

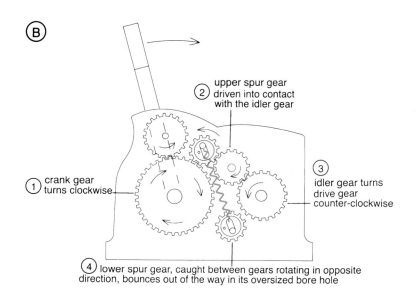

(B)

② upper spur gear driven into contact with the idler gear

① crank gear turns clockwise

③ idler gear turns drive gear counter-clockwise

④ lower spur gear, caught between gears rotating in opposite direction, bounces out of the way in its oversized bore hole

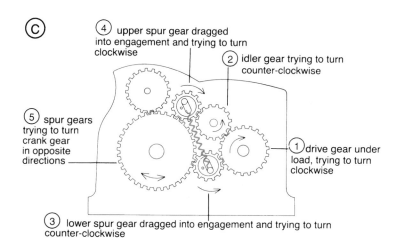

(C)

④ upper spur gear dragged into engagement and trying to turn clockwise

② idler gear trying to turn counter-clockwise

⑤ spur gears trying to turn crank gear in opposite directions

① drive gear under load, trying to turn clockwise

③ lower spur gear dragged into engagement and trying to turn counter-clockwise

windlasses still to be found on boats. With almost all of them, the engineering problem that must be overcome is how to convert back-and-forth (reciprocal) motion of the operating lever into a constant rotation at the main shaft. Two approaches are followed, which I call *spur gearing* and *ratchet gearing*.

Spur gearing. A gear (the *crank* gear) is keyed to the same shaft that the crank handle turns backward and forward. Two smaller gears (*spur* gears) are placed in contact with the crank gear. These spur gears have oversized bore holes that allow them to flop back out of contact with the crank gear. A spring between the two spur gears holds them up against the crank gear. One spur gear also contacts a gear (the drive gear) keyed to the output shaft; the other spur gear contacts an idler gear, which in turn is permanently engaged with the drive gear (Figures 16-22A and 16-22B).

When the crank handle is moved in one direction (counterclockwise—part A of Figure 16-22B), the crank gear traps the lower spur gear between itself and the drive gear, turning the drive gear. The drive gear not only turns the main shaft and wildcat but at the same time turns the idler gear. The second (upper) spur gear finds itself between the idler gear and the crank gear, which are turning in opposite directions. It is bounced out of the way against the spring pressure.

When the crank handle is moved in the other direction (clockwise—part B of Figure 16-22B), the crank gear traps the upper spur gear between itself and the idler gear. This turns the idler gear, which reverses the direction of rotation and so imparts the same rotation as before to the drive gear and the output shaft. The lower spur gear

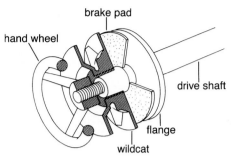

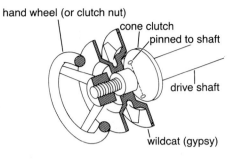

Brake Pad

Cone Clutch

FIGURE 16-24. The operation of a ratchet-geared windlass. **Left:** 1. The handle cranked as shown; the pawl engages the drive gear and turns it counterclockwise. 2. The intermediate gears reverse rotation and the counterdrive gear freewheels around the output shaft; the pawl bounces out of engagement. **Middle:** 1. The handle is cranked as shown; the pawl engages the counterdrive shaft and turns it clockwise. 2. The intermediate gears turn the drive gear counterclockwise. 3. The drive gear pawl bounces off the gear. **Right:** 1. A load on the windlass tries to turn the drive gear clockwise, locking it into its pawl. 2. The intermediate gears attempt to turn the counterdrive gear counterclockwise, locking it into its pawl. 3. The two gears, *locked in opposite directions*, lock up the windlass. *(Jim Sollers)*

finds itself between the drive gear and the crank gear, which are moving in opposite directions. It is bounced out of the way against the spring pressure.

When the wildcat (gypsy) is under a load, both spur gears are forced down into contact with the crank gear, but in *opposite* directions of rotation (part C of Figure 16-22B). The counterposed forces lock up the windlass and prevent the wildcat from letting out chain. Some means is needed to release the wildcat in order to drop the anchor.

The wildcat itself is not keyed to the drive shaft. Either it is tapered on its inner face and sits on a tapered friction pad (a *cone clutch*, which is locked to the shaft), or the wildcat is trapped between a flange on the drive shaft and a friction (brake) pad or lining. In both cases a handwheel or clutch nut, threaded to the end of the main shaft, can be tightened to trap the wildcat and lock it to the shaft or loosened to let the wildcat freewheel (Figure 16-23). Tension on the handwheel or clutch nut acts as a brake to control the rate of release of chain.

A second (low) speed is easily added to this windlass by placing another small (low-speed) crank gear in contact with the primary (high-speed) crank gear. When the operating lever is used to crank the low-speed gear backward and forward, this gear turns the high-speed gear, but at a greatly reduced rate. From there on everything is the same as above.

Ratchet gearing. The crank handle rotates around the output (wildcat) shaft with a gear on either side of the handle (Figure 16-24). One gear (the *direct-drive* gear) is keyed to the output shaft; the other (the *counterdrive* gear) floats (i.e., is free to rotate around the shaft). On either side of the crank handle assembly are pawls, which are counterposed (i.e., face in opposite directions) to each other.

When the crank handle is moved one way, one pawl engages the direct-drive gear, turning it and also the output shaft. The other pawl bounces over the counterdrive gear. When the handle reverses, the direct-drive pawl bounces free while the counterdrive pawl engages and turns the counterdrive gear.

The counterdrive gear meshes with an intermediate gear. This in turn meshes with a second intermediate gear, which also engages the direct-drive gear. When the counterdrive gear turns

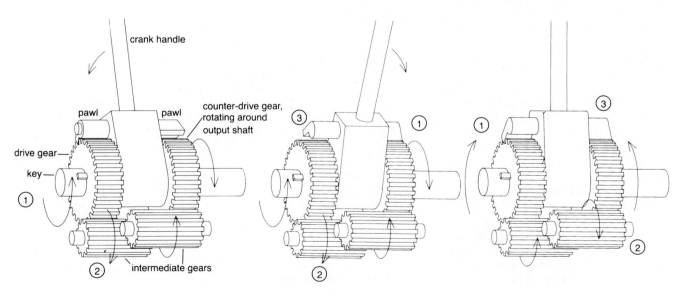

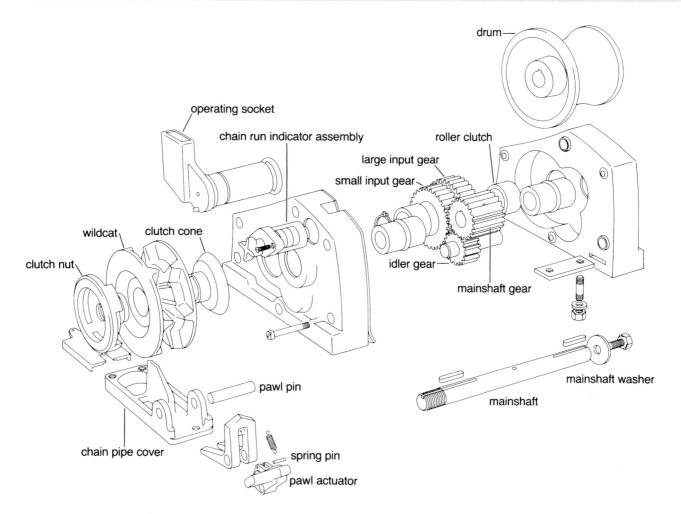

operating socket

chain run indicator assembly

drum

roller clutch

large input gear

small input gear

wildcat

clutch cone

clutch nut

idler gear

mainshaft gear

mainshaft washer

mainshaft

pawl pin

chain pipe cover

spring pin

pawl actuator

one way, the direct-drive gear turns the other way (i.e., the same way as before).

When a load is applied to the wildcat, and through it to the direct-drive gear, the reverse rotation brings *both* the direct-drive and the counterdrive gears up against their pawls but from opposite directions. The counterposed forces effectively lock up the windlass. The wildcat can be released only via a cone clutch or brake, just as on a spur gear–type winch.

A variation on the same theme keys the crank handle to an auxiliary shaft with two gears on it (Figure 16-25A). Both gears are mounted on roller clutches so that they freewheel (ratchet) in one direction and grip in the other. The clutches are installed in opposite directions (i.e., one locks one way, the other the opposite way). One gear directly engages an output gear on the main shaft, while the other engages the output gear via an idler gear (on an idler shaft). Operation is then as in Figure 16-24.

Yet another variation on the same theme is the old Simpson Lawrence Hyspeed (510) windlass, which has two bicycle sprockets mounted on the main shaft on opposing ratchets (Figure 16-25B).

The operating lever drives two chains backward and forward, turning the sprockets. One chain drives its sprocket directly; the other chain is fed around rollers to reverse the direction of drive. When the handle is cranked one way, one sprocket turns the shaft while the other freewheels; cranking the other way engages the second sprocket while the first freewheels.

Dismantling and repair. While the windlass is still securely fastened to the foredeck remove the clutch nut or handwheel and the rope-drum retaining bolt. Pull off the drum and the wildcat.

Wildcats will jam on clutch cones when ungreased and unused—loosen the clutch nut and then lever the wildcat free. (A stubborn wildcat can be broken loose by jamming the anchor against the stemhead, loosening the clutch nut, and operating the windlass.) Plated steel shafts will corrode to rope drums and may not come free, even with a 10-ton press! In that case the output shaft must be hacksawed through, obviously necessitating subsequent replacement.

Now remove the windlass from the foredeck (generally four bolts). Some windlasses use no

FIGURE 16-25A. The ratchet-geared windlass exposed. *(Simpson Lawrence and Jim Sollers)*

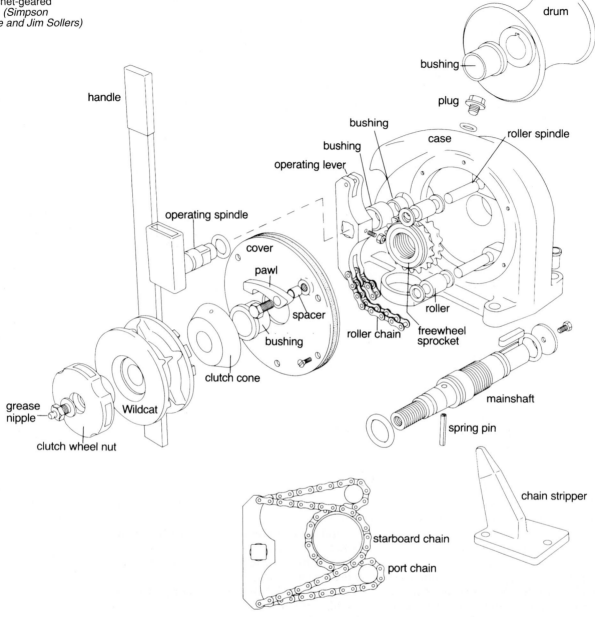

FIGURE 16-25B. A chain-drive ratchet-geared windlass. *(Simpson Lawrence and Jim Sollers)*

drum

bushing

plug

bushing

bushing

case

roller spindle

operating lever

handle

operating spindle

cover

pawl

spacer

bushing

clutch cone

roller chain

roller

freewheel sprocket

grease nipple

Wildcat

clutch wheel nut

mainshaft

spring pin

chain stripper

starboard chain

port chain

lubrication and have an open base. Others are filled with oil or grease and have a plate that must be removed.

With the base open, tap out the main shaft; in some cases it may come out either side of the windlass, but if the holes in the sides of the windlass casing differ in size, it will have to come out the side with the largest hole. The drive gear or sprockets, and any other gears and parts mounted on the shaft, will all come loose and can be retrieved through the base of the windlass. Watch out for keys locking gears to shafts—they are easily lost and hard to replace.

Any other gears are removed the same way. The various shafts will have retaining screws,

seals, and/or plates; once these are undone, the shaft is knocked out and the gear falls into the windlass.

Inspect the gears for broken or chipped teeth or steps in the teeth; inspect the shafts for ridges; slide the gears back on their shafts and check for play; and slip the shafts into the windlass housing and check for play again. Most shafts fit into removable bushings. If these need replacing, they can generally be knocked out with a suitably sized *drift*; a socket with an outside diameter a little less than the diameter of the bushing works well. The important thing is to exert an even pressure over the whole bushing.

Fitting new bushings will be greatly facilitated by pouring boiling water over the housing to expand it. But first, warm the *entire* housing to avoid any sudden localized heating, which could cause castings to crack. Knock in the new bushing using a piece of hardwood as a drift.

Windlasses frequently use only a small portion of their gears (e.g., the main crank gear on a spur-geared windlass generally moves back and forth through 90 degrees), and loads are concentrated on only one side of shafts and bushings. Faced with some breakdowns and no spare parts, it may be possible to get by temporarily by turning bushings and gears through 90 or 180 degrees and reassembling.

Vertical Manual Windlasses

A vertical manual windlass has a winch handle socket in the top of its drum. A winch handle is used to turn the drum and the wildcat, winching in the anchor. Ratchets on the windlass pedestal engage the drum to keep it from unwinding. Between the drum and the wildcat is a friction pad or surface (Figure 16-26). Turning the winch handle in reverse unscrews a clutch nut, allowing the wildcat to freewheel and let out chain.

Unscrewing the clutch nut completely allows the drum and wildcat to be lifted off, exposing any clutch cones (friction pads) if fitted, as well as pawls and springs. Inspect the clutch cones (or friction surfaces between the drum, wildcat, and winch base if no clutch cones are fitted) for excessive wear or scoring. Pay particular attention to the pawls and pawl springs (see the relevant sections on winches earlier in this chapter).

Electric Windlasses

How they work. A large electric motor drives the windlass through a reduction gearbox. Three types of gears are commonly used: offset (spur), worm, and epicyclic (planetary). Motors are reversible by switching the power leads, although in many installations the motor is used only for hauling in the anchor; the anchor is then let out as in manual installations (i.e., by loosening the clutch nut). In most cases the wildcat and drum are ratcheted so that they can be operated manually, independent of the motor and gearing, in the event of windlass failure. However, manual operation is often direct drive (no gearing), in which case it provides very little power (this is not always the case).

Offset (spur) gears. Offset gears (Figure 16-27) are more efficient than worm gears, which typically absorb up to 45% of motor output, dissipating it as heat. Because of the efficiency of

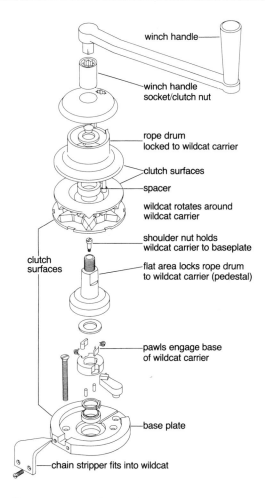

winch handle

winch handle socket/clutch nut

rope drum locked to wildcat carrier

clutch surfaces

spacer

wildcat rotates around wildcat carrier

shoulder nut holds wildcat carrier to baseplate

flat area locks rope drum to wildcat carrier (pedestal)

clutch surfaces

pawls engage base of wildcat carrier

base plate

chain stripper fits into wildcat

FIGURE 16-26. Vertical manual windlasses are gearless; the length of the winch handle provides the only leverage. Cranking tightens the clutch nut, trapping the wildcat between the clutch friction surfaces. Continued cranking rotates the drum, ratcheting in the anchor rode. The pawls prevent it from unwinding. Reversing the winch handle's direction loosens the clutch nut and allows chain or warp to veer out. Note: The clutch surfaces are metal to metal. Trapped particles of dirt will lead to scoring. To compensate, some units have renewable friction pads. *(Simpson Lawrence and Jim Sollers)*

offset gearing, when a load is placed on the windlass, the gears can spin the motor in reverse, allowing the windlass to let out chain or line. This type of electric windlass has to incorporate a braking device; typically a clutch locks the gears when the windlass is not in use but is electrically released via a solenoid as soon as the motor is energized.

Worm gears. Worm gears (Figures 16-28A, 16-28B, and 16-28C) provide a tremendous amount of resistance to being driven backward by a load on the windlass. No separate clutch/brake is needed. However, they are, as noted, inefficient. The main rationale for their use is that they tend to be cheaper, and they enable a more compact installation to be made (the motor on most units is horizontal rather than vertical), which interferes less with headroom in the boat. There are, of course, fewer parts to break down, so reliability is higher. (Given the small amount of use that most windlasses see, reliability is more important than efficiency.)

Lewmar employs a very fine toothed modified worm gear (called a *spiroid gear*) in a number of its powered winches and windlasses.

(continued on page 722)

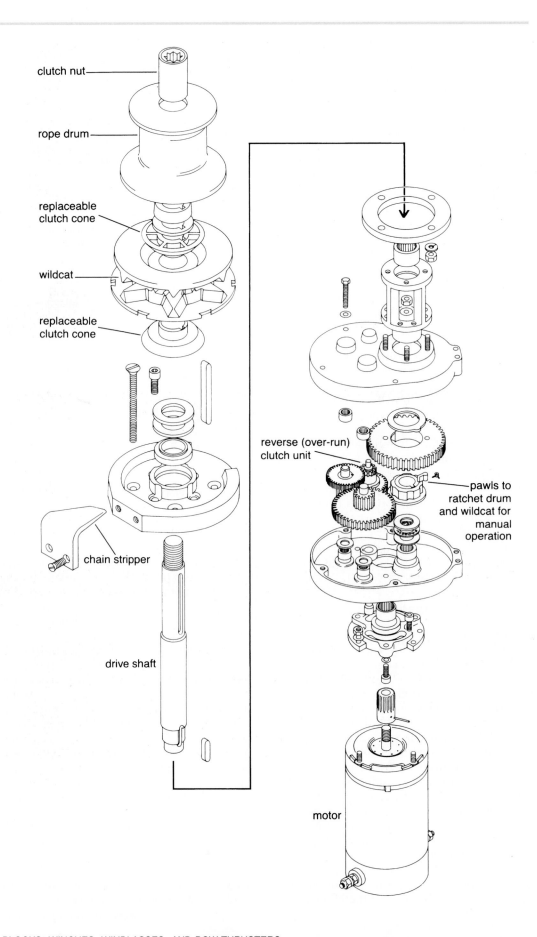

FIGURE 16-27. An electric windlass with offset gears. *(Simpson Lawrence and Jim Sollers)*

clutch nut

rope drum

replaceable clutch cone

wildcat

replaceable clutch cone

chain stripper

drive shaft

reverse (over-run) clutch unit

pawls to ratchet drum and wildcat for manual operation

motor

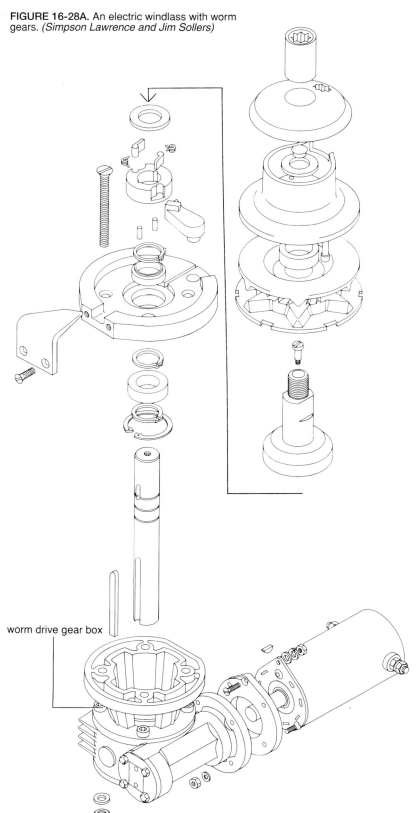

FIGURE 16-28A. An electric windlass with worm gears. *(Simpson Lawrence and Jim Sollers)*

worm drive gear box

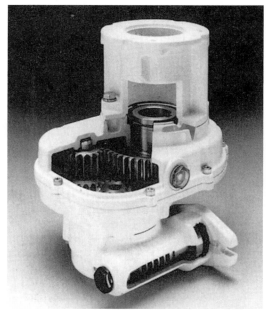

FIGURE 16-28B. The arrangement of the gears in a vertical windlass. *(Maxwell)*

FIGURE 16-28C. A cutaway of a worm-geared horizontal windlass. *(Lighthouse Manufacturing Co.)*

(continued from page 719)

Epicyclic (planetary) gearing. This type operates on the same principles as a planetary actuator on an autopilot (Chapter 14).

Installation.
Trouble-free operation of an electric windlass is largely dependent upon the quality of its installation.

Electrical considerations. A typical 12-volt windlass will draw from 60 to 100 amps at its *working load* (note that *working load* is an ill-defined concept that varies from manufacturer to manufacturer). However, put that same windlass under a near-stalling load, and *its current draw can easily jump to 300 to 400 amps* (Table 16-4).

A windlass will commonly have a 30- to 40-foot (9 to 12 m) cable run between it and the batteries that are powering it. When pulling 300 amps, if voltage drop is to be limited to 10% over a 30-foot (9 m) cable run (in each direction), a 3/0 cable (90 mm²) is needed on a 12-volt circuit (Table 16-5 and Chapter 4). At higher loads and over longer distances, considerably larger cables are needed. These cable sizes are, in most situations, impractically large—the upper size of cables in boat use is generally 2/0 (70 mm²). What this means is that even with the largest practicable cable size, many windlasses suffer from a greater than 10% voltage drop when under maximum load. This causes a loss of power when it is needed most and a tendency to stall, which in turn can lead to overheating and burnout. About the best that can be done is to fit the largest practicable cables, and to ensure that they at least supply the working load with minimal voltage drop.

It is sometimes suggested that long, heavy cable runs can be avoided by having a separate windlass battery in the forepeak with short connections to the windlass. But anytime this battery is well discharged, it will pull an alternator's full output. If the boat has a high-output alternator, this may amount to 100 amps or more, necessitating heavy charging cables, and bringing us back to where we started.

The positive cable to a windlass is generally fastened to the boat side of a battery isolation switch or to a positive distribution post or bus bar (Figure 16-29); the negative cable should be fastened to the boat's main negative bus bar (see Chapter 5). Note, however, that if a shunt-type ammeter is wired into the negative battery circuit (Chapter 1) between the common ground point and the battery negative(s), and if the stall load on the windlass *exceeds the rating of the shunt*, the windlass negative must be wired to the *battery* side of the shunt so that the windlass current does not flow through the shunt. Wired like this, the ammeter will not measure the current draw of the windlass, but since windlass use is infrequent and for short periods of time, its effect will not be significant in terms of the overall DC load (bow thrusters, which draw even more current, should be installed the same way).

A windlass must have some sort of overload protection device as close to its batteries as possible. Should the windlass ever stall (locked rotor state) or get stuck "on" (which can happen with a defective switch), its current draw will rise sharply to the point at which it may melt down wiring (especially if the cables are undersized) and start a fire. It will also burn up. Overload protection can take the form of either a suitably sized fuse (relatively cheap) or a circuit breaker (expensive).

TABLE 16-4. Windlass Current Draw Versus Load[1]

Load (lbs.)	Current Draw (amps)	Speed of Recovery (ft./m per min.)
500	110	28.2/8.6
1,000	170	23.6/7.2
1,500	230	19.0/5.8
2,000	290	14.1/4.3
2,500	350	9.5/2.9
3,000	410	4.9/1.5

1. These data are based on a Lewmar 2000 (12 volts), which takes a working load of 1,000 pounds and a maximum load of 2,000 pounds.

TABLE 16-5. Conductor Sizes for 10% Voltage Drop at 12 Volts

Current Draw (amps)	Length of Conductor from Battery to Windlass and Back (ft.)						
	10	20	30	40	50	60	
100	10 (6)	6 (16)	4 (20)	4 (20)	2 (35)	2 (35)	AWG (mm²) Cable Size
125	8 (10)	6 (16)	4 (20)	2 (35)	2 (35)	1 (40)	
150	8 (10)	4 (20)	2 (35)	2 (35)	2 (35)	1 (40)	
175	6 (16)	4 (20)	2 (35)	2 (35)	1 (40)	1/0 (50)	
200	6 (16)	4 (20)	2 (35)	1 (40)	1/0 (50)	2/0 (70)	
250	6 (16)	2 (35)	1 (40)	1/0 (50)	2/0 (70)	3/0 (95)	
300	4 (20)	2 (35)	1/0 (50)	2/0 (70)	3/0 (95)	4/0 (110)	
350	4 (20)	2 (35)	1/0 (50)	2/0 (70)	3/0 (95)	4/0 (110)	
400	4 (20)	1/0 (50)	2/0 (70)	3/0 (95)	4/0 (110)	—	

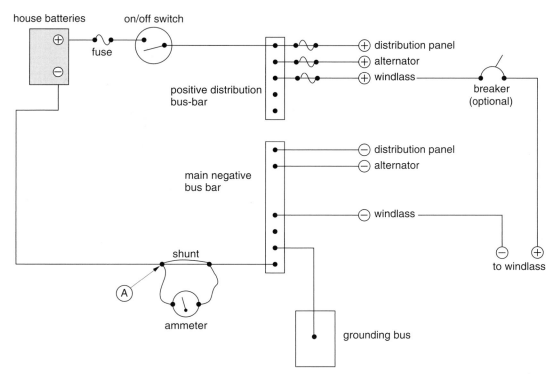

FIGURE 16-29. Wiring a windlass into the boat's DC circuits. Note: If the full-load current of the windlass (when combined with the other loads) exceeds the rating of the shunt, wire the windlass negative to point A.

The circuit to a windlass is closed by a solenoid, which in turn is energized by another circuit that passes through a foot switch or some other remotely operated switch. *Any such control circuit should have its own isolation switch that is kept in the OFF position except when the windlass is actually in use* (Figures 16-30A and 16-30B). This is a matter of basic safety. As long as this switch is off, there is no chance that someone will accidentally activate the windlass (e.g., by inadvertently standing on a foot switch). Since the wiring in the control circuit is relatively lightweight (18 to 12 AWG/1 to 4 mm^2), the switch need be no more than a simple toggle switch.

The main solenoid terminals carry the full operating current of a windlass. When a solenoid closes, and then when it opens once again, there is a tendency for arcing to occur across the points as the circuit is made and broken. *For a long, trouble-free life, the solenoids need to have a rating equal to the full-load draw of the windlass.* Also the solenoid must be in a dry location (not, for example, in an anchor well—if the drain plugs, and the well floods, the solenoid will short out). If a solenoid does short, or stick in the ON position, *the windlass will operate continuously and uncontrollably.* The only way to stop it will be to turn off the main isolation switch or to trip the main breaker.

Mechanical considerations. A windlass needs to be solidly mounted to an inflexible base. This is important for several reasons. First of all, the

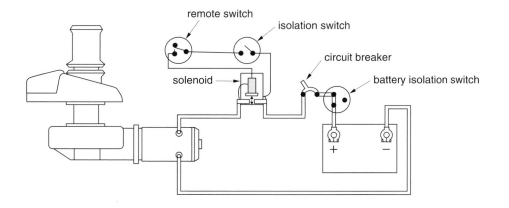

FIGURE 16-30A. A wiring diagram for a nonreversing electric windlass. (Lewmar)

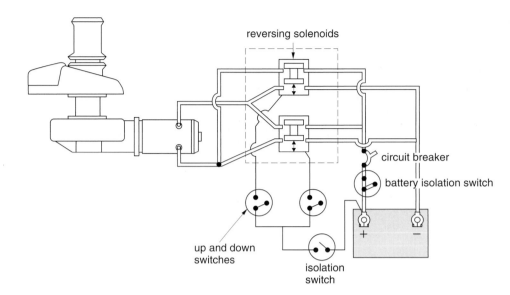

FIGURE 16-30B. A wiring diagram for a reversing electric windlass. Note that with this kind of arrangement, operating both switches simultaneously will put a dead short across the batteries. Some other reversing installations are protected against such an eventuality. *(Lewmar)*

reversing solenoids

circuit breaker

battery isolation switch

up and down switches

isolation switch

windlass mount must obviously be capable of withstanding all the loads that may be imposed on the windlass, including occasional severe snubbing loads. Second, if the windlass flexes, the seal between the windlass base and the deck will open up, allowing water to find its way below, perhaps onto sensitive electrical components. Third, many electric windlasses have a vertical capstan with the motor mounted belowdecks, and a spacer between the capstan and motor unit (Figure 16-31). The drive shaft runs from the motor through the spacer unit and into the capstan. Flexing of the deck is likely to throw out the alignment between the motor and the capstan unit, leading to increased friction, a

loss of performance, premature bearing damage, and perhaps motor damage.

Belowdecks, the windlass motor and all associated wiring must be protected from any potential drips and from the chain as it flails around in a seaway (refer back to Figure 16-18D).

Operation. The majority of electric motors fitted to older windlasses are modified starter motors, or industrial motors, with series-wound field coils (Chapter 7); some newer windlasses have permanent-magnet motors, which significantly improve the duty cycle. In all cases, the motors are designed for intermittent use only—in automotive use for no more than 30 seconds at a time. They do not incorporate cooling fins or fans of any kind. If run for longer periods of time, especially under heavy loads, they will rapidly heat up; sustained high-load usage will cause the motor to burn up.

A correctly sized circuit breaker will provide limited protection from damage to the motor that might arise from an excessive current (amperage) draw or a short circuit. It will not provide protection from excessive heat buildup as a result of prolonged operation or repeated high-load operation. Even if the windlass has a sophisticated electronic overload protection unit (OPU, or similar designation), *if the unit is repeatedly tripped and reset, motor damage will result.* In the final analysis, regardless of protection devices, an operator without a sense of the limits of tolerance of a windlass motor can destroy just about any motor.

Maintenance and troubleshooting. Most problems with electric windlasses are electrical in nature. A typical unidirectional (up-only) circuit is shown in Figure 16-32—it is basically the

FIGURE 16-31. A vertical windlass with a spacer. For trouble-free operation, the deck must be rigid enough to prevent flexing between the capstan and the below-deck installation. *(Maxwell)*

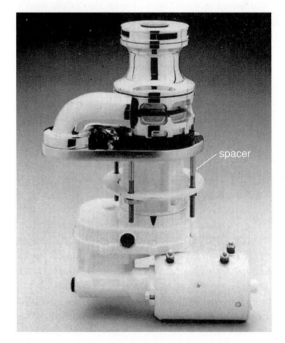

spacer

same as a starter motor circuit; the same tests can be made (Chapter 7). (A circuit with both "up" and "down" functions is shown in Figure 16-30B.)

Safety. Before working on an electric windlass:

1. *Turn off the battery isolation switch before disconnecting the main cables from any part of a windlass circuit.* If a live cable is accidentally shorted to a ground, very high amperages will flow that can cause serious burns and damage.

2. Always isolate any circuits before working on them so that the windlass is not accidentally set in motion.

3. When performing tests on a windlass, remove the anchor chain from the wildcat beforehand so that the anchor is not accidentally dragged into the stemhead, stalling the windlass and perhaps damaging the stemhead. However, *always tie up an anchor before taking its chain off the wildcat!* This will stop the anchor from slipping overboard and the chain from running out uncontrollably.

Annual maintenance. At least once a year, inspect all terminals and connections, and if any corrosion is present, clean them. Then spray the terminals with an appropriate sealer, such as CRC 2043 PlastiCote 70, CRC 3013 Soft Seal, or CRC 2049 Clear Urethane Seal Coat. If the windlass has seen much active service, the motor brushes need inspecting; replace them if they are worn down to the point where they are approaching half the length of new brushes (you should have a set of new brushes on hand). At this time, blow out any carbon dust and wipe the surface of the commutator clean (Chapter 7), taking particular care to get the carbon out of the insulated grooves between the copper bars. If the commutator is seriously contaminated with carbon, spray it with an appropriate cleaner, such as CRC 2018 Lectra Clean.

Failure to operate at all. Check for voltage at the inputs to the solenoids and foot switches (point 1, Figure 16-32). If no voltage is present, the battery isolation switch or control-circuit isolation switch is off, the breaker (if fitted) is tripped, or a fuse is blown. If voltage is present, have someone operate a foot or other switch and test for voltage at the positive foot-switch terminal on the solenoid (point 2, Figure 16-32).

If no voltage is present, the foot switch is defective. If voltage is present, keep the switch depressed and check for voltage at the main solenoid output terminal or motor input terminal (point 3, Figure 16-32). If no voltage is present, check the solenoid coil ground circuit for a break—if it is intact, the solenoid is defective (refer to Chapter 7).

If voltage is present at the main output from the solenoid, the motor itself is open-circuited. Take a close look at the motor wiring and wiring connections, particularly those on the ground side. If any signs of corrosion are present on any terminals, remove the cables and clean the terminals. If the problem still can't be found, take a look at the brushes inside the motor to see if any are hung up in their brush holders. If the brushes are in good shape and making a firm contact with their commutator, the motor is likely burned up (open or short circuit).

Bellows switches. Lewmar has an optional *air bellows* in place of switches. A small air chamber with a diaphragm is connected via PVC tubing to another chamber and diaphragm attached to the solenoid switch. Depressing the first diaphragm causes air pressure to move the second diaphragm, which operates the switch. There are no external switches on deck likely to get wet and corrode.

If the air switch appears to have failed, jump out the main solenoid terminals. If the motor now runs, check for air leaks on the PVC tubing connections, collapsed or damaged tubing, or holes in the switch diaphragms.

Note that with older switches a potentially dangerous situation can arise with long tubing runs in hot areas (e.g., engine rooms, or under teak decks, which soak up the sun). The air in the tube can expand enough to trip the switch and set off the motor! If this should happen, bleed off some air pressure and see about shortening, or rerouting, the tubing (newer switches

have a built-in safety bleed). (Lewmar recommends that the maximum length of the air tube between a bellows and the switch it operates should be no longer than 6 feet/2 m.)

Breaker trips every time the battery isolation switch is turned on. There is a short in the circuit, most likely as a result of a burned-out motor. However, first check the entire circuit for other possibilities—a piece of equipment may have fallen against a hot terminal and shorted it to a ground. If any of the circuitry is exposed in the anchor well (it shouldn't be, but sometimes it is), the drain may have plugged, flooding the well and shorting the cables. If the motor is at fault, refer to Chapter 7. Note that if the anchor is up against the stemhead, and the "up" switch has shorted, whenever the battery isolation switch is turned on the windlass will kick into action under a stall load and trip its breaker.

Sluggish operation. *Do not continue to use a windlass that operates sluggishly*—it may burn up. If the windlass is overloaded, ease the load (e.g., by motoring up to the anchor, or tying off the rode and using the boat's engine to break out the anchor). Make sure the alternator is charging the batteries and that the voltage is well up.

If operation is still sluggish, check the voltage across the windlass motor terminals *while someone operates the windlass* (point 3, Figure 16-32). *There should be at least 11.0 volts* (on a 12-volt system). If the voltage is low, there is a severe voltage drop in the circuit—check for undersized cables, poor or corroded connections, or resistance across the battery isolation switch or solenoid (feel them to see if they are heating up). If voltage is above 11.0 volts and the anchor is not fouled, the motor is seizing mechanically (check the alignment of the motor and the windlass on through-deck installations) or burning up.

Dismantling and repair. The top (above-deck) end is similar to a winch and generally simplicity itself to take apart. Motor removal is also very straightforward—taking out two or three bolts should allow it to be pulled off.

Tackle gearboxes carefully, paying close attention to where *and which way around* everything goes. Note in particular that Lewmar's spiroid gearboxes are built to close tolerances. *Extreme precision* is required on reassembly to ensure correct meshing of the gears. It is best not to delve into gearboxes unless absolutely necessary.

Hydraulic Windlasses

A separate pump supplies hydraulic oil at high pressure (typically up to 2,000 psi) to a hydraulic motor on the base of the windlass. Reversing oil

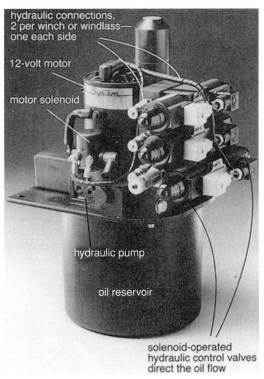

FIGURE 16-33. A hydraulic windlass (left) and an electrically powered hydraulic power pack (right). Solenoid-operated hydraulic control valves (upper right on the power pack) direct oil to the winch through the connectors (two per winch; one each side). *(Lewmar)*

flow reverses winch operation. Cutting off oil flow locks the winch. (Sometimes there is *creep* as a result of oil escaping past the hydraulic motor vanes. In this case, fit a pilot-operated check valve—POCV—into the circuit. This valve is often also needed on hydraulic sail reefing devices for the same reason.) As with all windlasses, a manual clutch/wildcat release for letting out chain is provided, and the wildcat is ratcheted for manual operation in the event of motor failure. Oil pressure can be supplied by either an engine-driven pump or an electric pump (e.g., Lewmar Commander systems—Figure 16-33).

Problems. Hydraulic windlasses are generally very rugged and trouble free. Most difficulties arise as a result of one of the following:

Leaks. Leaks, as ever, are the bane of any hydraulic system. Leaks lead to air in the system, and then pumps can become air-bound. If the hydraulic pump is working but the windlass fails to turn, check the oil level in the system; top off and purge (bleed) as necessary. Also find out where the lost oil is going. For hydraulic oil recommendations, see Table 14-1 (page 644).

Dirt and moisture. The next most common causes of hydraulic problems are dirt and moisture—hydraulic systems must be *scrupulously* clean. Pumps and motors are built to *very close* tolerances. Valves will not seat with even a speck of dirt on them. Pistons and cylinders will score.

When installing hydraulic hoses, be very careful not to get sawdust in them as you push them through holes in bulkheads, and watch out for dirt in quick-connect fittings. All units should have a filter on the return line to the hydraulic tank.

Moisture can arise from condensation in hydraulic oil tanks; periodically drain a sample of oil from the base of the tank and check for contamination. If not removed, moisture will cause rust on all kinds of sensitive parts and lead to expensive damage. (Lewmar recommends changing the hydraulic oil and filter element after every 1,000 hours of operation, and sooner if the oil becomes contaminated or emulsified by water.)

Undersized hydraulic lines. Hydraulic lines that are too small for the system they are serving create pressure drops, overheated pumps, and loss of performance (just as undersized wiring causes voltage drop and overheated motors). Anchor windlasses (and bow thrusters—see below) are frequently at the end of long hose runs, so make sure the hoses are adequate, keep bends to a minimum, and avoid tight radiuses. Hydraulic plumbing is covered in more detail in Chapter 12.

Electrical problems. Most hydraulic systems have an electrically powered hydraulic pump, with the system operated via electric solenoid valves, remote switches, etc. (Figure 16-34). Although hydraulic systems are conceptually quite simple, in practice the electrical side can

FIGURE 16-34. A Lewmar hydraulic system as installed. The solenoid valves that direct hydraulic oil to various hydraulic motors are on the left; the two pumps and the oil reservoir are on the right.

get quite complicated by the time you add in the circuits for the switches, remote operating stations, the solenoid-operated control valves (which control the hydraulic fluid flow), and various safety shutdowns.

In the event the system does not work, first ensure that all breakers are turned on and all fuses are intact. Then check for power at the hydraulic pump. If present, and the pump is not running, check the electric motor (see Chapter 7; note that the motor will have a high-temperature cutout that may have tripped). If there is no power at the pump, check for power into the control box. If there is no power at the control box, go back and check the breakers and fuses again!

Assuming power at the control box but not at the motor, you will need to trace the various switch and safety shutdown circuits to see if one of them is causing the problem. They are, in essence, similar to a starter motor circuit (see Chapter 7) since remote switches trigger solenoids that then operate the control valves in the hydraulic system. If no problem is found, consult the manufacturer; there may be a problem with the electronics (the central processing unit—CPU).

Hydraulic component failure. Aside from the

CPU, very little in a hydraulic system is custom-built for the marine marketplace. All the hydraulic components (pumps, valves, etc.) and electrical components (solenoids, etc.) are standard industrial parts—spare parts are typically available worldwide. A boatowner with a hydraulic system should carry information on the sources of all the component parts so that in the event of a component failure, the part can be sourced from the original component manufacturer, rather than having to go back through the manufacturer of the hydraulic system for the boat.

Dismantling and repair. As with an electric windlass, the top (above-deck) end is similar to a winch and generally simple to take apart. The motor and a reduction gearbox will be belowdecks. Hydraulic motors and gearboxes are built to close tolerances and should be left alone (especially since spare parts are unlikely to be on board). About the only thing you might try is to unbolt the motor to see if it is spinning when the windlass is turned on. If not, the problem lies in the pump, plumbing, or electrical circuits, and not in the motor itself. While the motor is out, try to operate the windlass manually, just to make sure it is not frozen up.

Bow Thrusters

As more and more boats are sold and pressure on limited mooring and docking spaces grows, close-quarters maneuvering is an increasing component of sailing activities. Bow thrusters provide unparalleled control over a boat in difficult situations; for good reasons, they are becoming popular and are now found on boats down to 40 feet (12 m) in length.

There is not a lot to a bow thruster—an electric or hydraulic motor drives a propeller in a tunnel. Perhaps the most significant issue is the huge energy drain this typically creates—a thruster for a 50-foot boat will be rated at somewhere between 4 to 8 hp (3 to 6 kW). If powered by an electric motor, this translates to 300 to 600 amps at 12 volts, or 150 to 300 amps at 24 volts. DC-powered bow thrusters are available with outputs up to 15 hp (10 kW), which translates to an astonishing 650 amp drain at 24 volts.

These kinds of loads, even though sustained for only a few seconds in most circumstances, require huge cables to keep voltage drop down, and perfect electrical connections (including holes in cable terminals that are exactly matched to terminal studs, and connecting nuts that are carefully torqued down). Any accidental resistance in a circuit will generate a great deal of heat, and the potential to start a fire. It may be impractical to install large-enough cables to directly power a bow thruster from batteries located aft in the boat, in which case a substantial buffer battery will have to be located close to the bow thruster, with large charging cables run aft. This battery will need a cold cranking amps rating (see Chapter 1) that is at least as high as the maximum rated current draw of the bow thruster.

Hydraulic bow thrusters often require greater hydraulic flows than can be maintained by DC-powered hydraulic pumps. In this case, an auxiliary hydraulic pump has to be added to the boat's main engine or a generator engine.

Propellers on bow thrusters generally have a protective zinc that needs to be monitored for zinc loss and replaced at the annual haulout, or sooner if necessary.

Troubleshooting

Note that when troubleshooting, a bow thruster should *never* be run with the boat out of the water (the thruster will overspeed, damaging its seals).

Electric bow thrusters. Electric bow thrusters have circuits similar to those of starter motors and electric windlasses, but with a few more safety functions built in. The operating switches (which may be in the form of buttons or a joystick) supply power to a solenoid mounted at or close to the bow thruster motor. This solenoid closes the circuit to the motor. There will be two circuits—one for port, and one for starboard. There is likely to be an over-temperature shutdown and maybe a time-out function (which prevents the thruster from being used for more than a certain length of time).

In the event of a failure to operate at all, check the voltage in the solenoid circuit and also the main circuit to determine at what point the circuit has failed. If there is no voltage at the motor, check the protection circuits (the unit may have shut down for good reason). If there is voltage at the motor and it is not operating, it has failed (check the brushes and see Chapter 7 for motor tests).

In the event the bow thruster runs sluggishly, check for voltage drop at the motor while it is running (on a 12-volt system, the minimum voltage should be 10 volts; on a 24-volt system, 21 volts).

Hydraulic bow thrusters. See the section on hydraulic windlasses (pages 726–28).

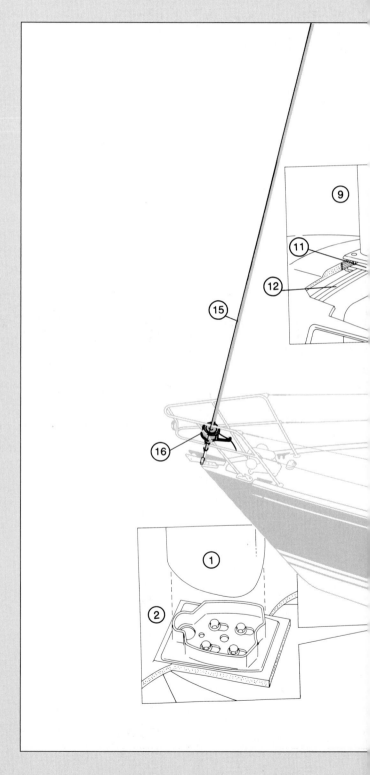

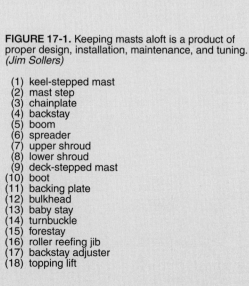

CHAPTER 17

FIGURE 17-1. Keeping masts aloft is a product of proper design, installation, maintenance, and tuning. *(Jim Sollers)*

(1) keel-stepped mast
(2) mast step
(3) chainplate
(4) backstay
(5) boom
(6) spreader
(7) upper shroud
(8) lower shroud
(9) deck-stepped mast
(10) boot
(11) backing plate
(12) bulkhead
(13) baby stay
(14) turnbuckle
(15) forestay
(16) roller reefing jib
(17) backstay adjuster
(18) topping lift

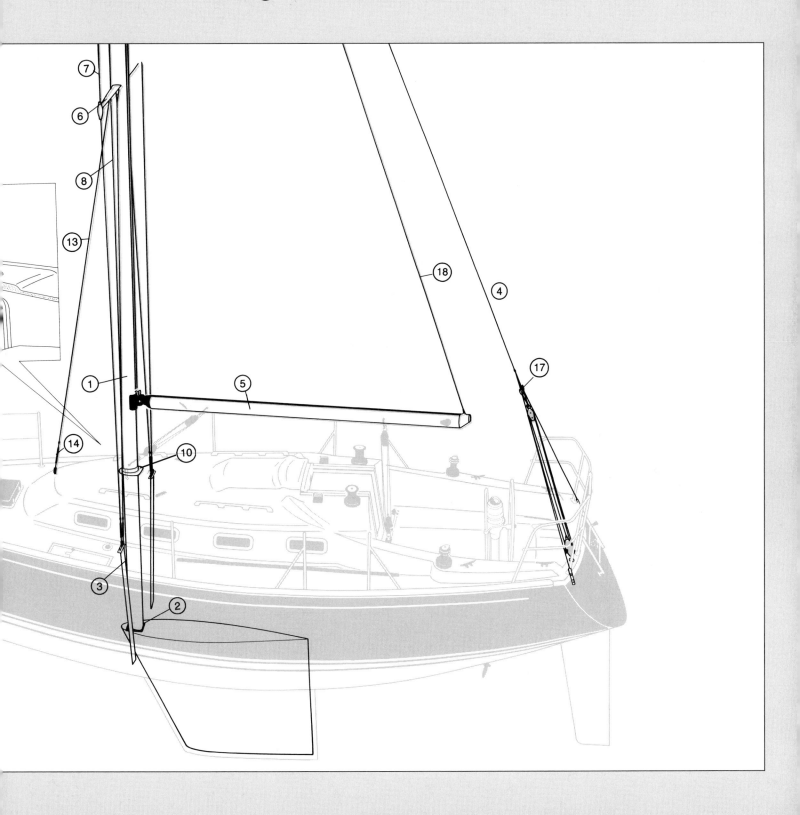

This is the one chapter in this book that is exclusively for sailboat owners! It addresses issues concerning masts, standing rigging, and various headsail and mainsail reefing devices.

Spars

Wooden Spars and Spreaders

Wooden spars, especially when varnished, are a high-maintenance item. All masts, booms, and spreaders need regular, close inspection for telltale signs of delamination and rot, and they will need repainting or revarnishing at least every few years (probably every year if varnished and kept in the tropics).

Construction. In the days when labor was cheap, very fine round and oval spars were constructed. The procedure was to laminate a hexagon or octagon, then round out the corners. Nowadays wooden spars are almost invariably a box section, which is much less labor intensive and far easier to clamp up. The occasional mast will incorporate a double-box section, with the outer box laminated to the inner one (Figure 17-2).

Since no planks will be long enough to run the complete length of a mast side, several planks must be joined together. The usual joint is a simple *scarf*, in which a taper is cut in both boards and the two are glued together (Figure 17-3A, left). The taper should have a ratio of at least 1:8; i.e., with a board 1 inch (25 mm) thick, the taper should extend over a length of 8 inches (20 cm). The feather edge of the taper is weak and susceptible to damage until it is glued up; sometimes it is squared off (Figure 17-3A, right), but this is a more-difficult and time-consuming joint to execute properly and is not often done. In the finished box spar, the scarf joints in the four sides must be staggered up and down the length of the spar so that no two are in close proximity. The exterior tapers should be pointing down so that water cannot work into the joint.

Some spars are hollow from top to bottom, with just a blocking piece at the head to keep water out of the masthead fittings. Such a spar tends to distribute loads evenly over its whole length. Many spars include additional internal reinforcement (blocking) at the spreader-attachment points and the base (Figure 17-3B). In any

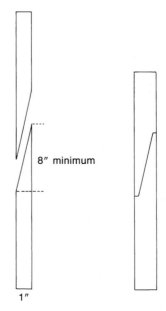

8″ minimum

1″

FIGURE 17-3A. **Left:** A simple 1:8 scarf joint. **Right:** A squared-off scarf joint.

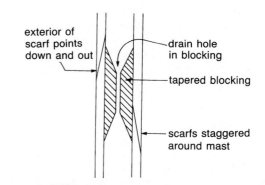

exterior of scarf points down and out

drain hole in blocking

tapered blocking

scarfs staggered around mast

FIGURE 17-3B. Details of proper wooden mast construction.

FIGURE 17-2. Wooden mast construction.

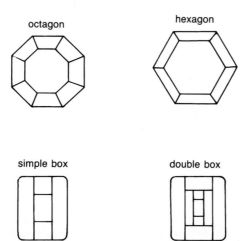

octagon

hexagon

simple box

double box

SPARS, STANDING RIGGING, AND ROLLER REEFING

event, such blocking should always be tapered at the top and bottom to eliminate *hard* spots that would tend to concentrate stresses. The blocking also must provide a free passage for water to drain out.

Plastic resin, resorcinol, and epoxy glues are all used to glue up masts. To be effective, the first two require very close fits in all the joints—they have no gap-filling properties. Epoxies are more tolerant. Resorcinol leaves an unsightly dark purple glue line at joints. For making repairs, a suitable epoxy (e.g., West System, www.westsystem.com, and System Three, www.systemthree.com) is probably the best bet.

All wood spars should be treated internally with fungicide. While external rot can usually be found and repaired before a failure occurs, internal rot is an undetectable time bomb waiting to bring the rig down. If in doubt, the next time the mast is unstepped, pour a gallon of a rot-proofing agent (e.g., a copper naphthenate–based solution) into it and slosh the fluid gently from end to end, rotating the spar periodically until the wood is thoroughly saturated.

Paint or varnish. Varnished spars on a traditional boat look beautiful, but they require a lot of work, especially in hotter climates. Even the most expensive varnishes with ultraviolet blockers will hold up no more than 2 years in the tropics, normally only 1. The topsides of spreaders will *never* go more than a year, and are frequently cracking and peeling within a few months. This admits moisture, which is then trapped by the intact varnish on the undersides and inboard ends of the spreaders, causing rapid rotting. A strong case can be made for painting rather than varnishing the upper spreader surfaces.

Aside from looks, varnish does have one advantage over paint—any water that penetrates the varnish is immediately apparent as a dark stain in the wood below. Failures with painted surfaces are far less obvious—the paint generally has to blister or the wood become spongy (in which case rot is well advanced) before problems are noticed. Painted spars will, however, hold up for as long as 5 years between coats, especially with many of the newer paints.

The main problem with varnish is the time required for its upkeep. On our old boat, we developed a quick and dirty method for laying on a substantial thickness of varnish very quickly. We unstepped the masts and laid them out horizontally. We washed them, lightly abraded them with a palm sander, put plastic bags on the winches, taped off other fittings, and then picked a hot day to varnish. I loaded up an airless sprayer and then sprayed the whole length of one side of the mast at walking speed, getting half of the upper side at the same time. An airless sprayer really pumps out the varnish. There were runs and drips everywhere, so someone else walked behind with a large paintbrush, working out the runs and dribbles. Once I got to the end of the mast, I grabbed another brush and started at the beginning, working on the runs. We kept this up until the varnish tacked up (that's why we picked a hot day—it tacked up in 10 to 15 minutes), then sprayed the other side and the other half of the upper side. The next day we rolled the mast and did the underside. *With just two coats we could lay on as much varnish as we used to in seven coats of hand brushing, and in a total time of around 2 hours!* It didn't look as pretty close up, but from 10 feet away it looked the same, and it lasted 2 years (just) in the tropics.

Danger areas. The following are the most likely areas for rot to get started:

Fasteners. Any fastener, even when properly bedded but especially when improperly bedded, is a potential source of water ingress and thus rot. The loads that modern rigs impose on fittings, combined with undersized or insufficient fasteners, frequently will cause the fasteners to crush surrounding woodwork. The fastener loosens, bedding compounds pull free, and water wicks in (Figure 17-4). Loose hardware is a sure sign of trouble, but the wood surrounding even securely fastened hardware should be inspected closely, at least annually, for signs of deterioration.

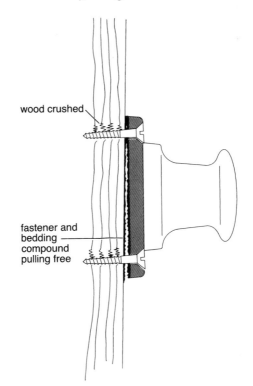

FIGURE 17-4. Fasteners subjected to excessive loads, such as those holding this halyard winch, can crush the wood surrounding them, allowing fasteners to loosen further and water to penetrate. *(Jim Sollers)*

wood crushed

fastener and bedding compound pulling free

Where problems are being experienced with excessive loads on the wood, the Gougeon Brothers (manufacturers of West System epoxies; www.gougeon.com) have shown that an effective answer is to drill an oversized hole, fill this with epoxy, and set the fastener in this epoxy plug. The epoxy penetrates and bonds to the surrounding wood and, with a considerably larger surface area than the original fastener, dissipates the loads on the fastener over a much greater area.

After ripping a couple of cleats off our mast and an outhaul track off a boom, we rebedded all the hardware using the Gougeon Brothers' techniques and had no more failures.

The specific procedure is as follows (see Figure 17-5):

1. Drill a pilot hole to the depth of the fastener.

2. Drill the oversized hole to a little *less* than the depth of the fastener.

3. Fill the hole with epoxy and top off as the wood soaks it up. On vertical surfaces, first wet out the hole (a pipe cleaner works well), then thicken the epoxy with microballoons or talc—as much as needed to stop the glue from draining out. In a pinch, talcum powder works well as a thickening agent.

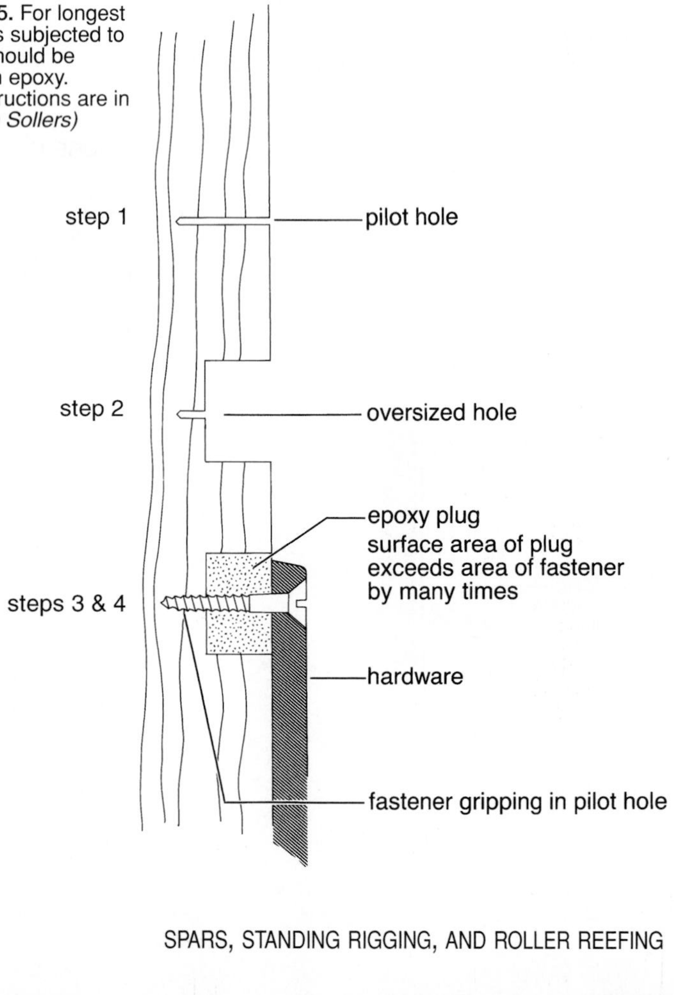

FIGURE 17-5. For longest life, fasteners subjected to high loads should be embedded in epoxy. Detailed instructions are in the text. *(Jim Sollers)*

step 1 —— pilot hole

step 2 —— oversized hole

steps 3 & 4 —— epoxy plug
surface area of plug exceeds area of fastener by many times

—— hardware

—— fastener gripping in pilot hole

4. Clean the fastener (acetone works well) and install it when the epoxy begins to gel. The section of fastener that runs down into the pilot hole (at the bottom of the oversized hole) should provide just enough grip to snug up the fastener until the glue sets.

Interestingly enough, the Gougeon Brothers also have shown convincingly that on most applications a stainless steel machine screw makes a much stronger fastener than either a regular wood screw or a self-tapping screw. Their book, *The Gougeon Brothers on Boat Construction*, is a gold mine of useful information for anyone with extensive woodwork.

Exit holes. *Any* exit holes for electric cables or halyards are likely to let in water sooner or later. The worst case is where a cable runs down into a mast, providing a perfect path for water to trickle in. All cables should have drip loops where they exit the mast, and the exit holes should be angled downward (refer to Figure 17-11 below).

Base of spreaders. As noted previously, the upper faces of wooden spreaders are notorious for letting in water, which drains down into the spreader bases (due to the angle of the spreaders) and becomes trapped. Another common source of spreader problems is the holes through the spreaders for mounting pins (Figure 17-6). As often as not, the spreader hardware consists of a stainless steel plate fastened on the top and bottom sides with two clevis pins passing through both the plates and the spreader. Water can run down the pins and into the spreader.

This problem with spreader-mounting holes is easily cured in one of two ways: (1) Remove one of the plates, drill oversized holes in the spreader, fill with epoxy, and allow to set. Then replace the plate and drill through the epoxy plug for the clevis pins (Figure 17-7, top). (2) Design the spreader-mounting bracket so that the wood does not protrude into the area of the clevis pins (Figure 17-7, bottom).

Base of the mast. With both deck-stepped and keel-stepped masts, the heel fitting is a notorious source of dampness and rot. It must be designed to allow any water running down either inside or outside the spar to drain away and also to provide a free flow of air around the heel. The heel fitting needs regular close inspection.

Mast partners. On keel-stepped masts, *mast partners* (the blocking where a mast passes through the deck) can be the source of problems for similar reasons as above—dampness and poor air circulation.

Masthead. Problems can develop on uncapped masts, or masts with improperly sealed head boxes. On many traditional rigs, the stays and

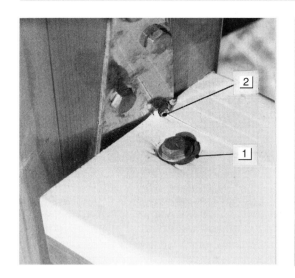

FIGURE 17-6. How *not* to install a spreader. These are top and bottom views of a spreader installation on a *brand-new* mast. No upper spreader plate (1). The wood is crushed already and is sure to soak up water and rot. Any up-or-down loading on the spreader will bend the mounting bolt and crush the wood further. The single bolt has allowed the spreader to rotate and crush its inner face (2). Note the split in the grain, already extending up the spreader. As the bolt works against the upper spreader face, it will embed itself and loosen (3). The lock washer will exert no tension. The nylon locking ring of the Nylok nut engages no threads and therefore will not lock (4). This spreader is likely to fail before long, bringing the mast down with it.

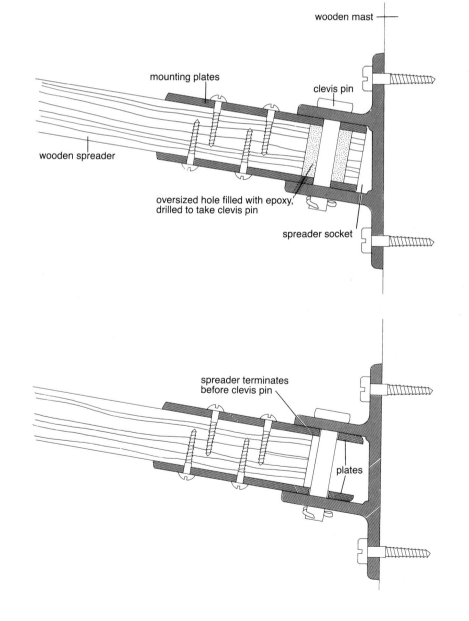

wooden mast

mounting plates

clevis pin

wooden spreader

oversized hole filled with epoxy, drilled to take clevis pin

spreader socket

spreader terminates before clevis pin

plates

FIGURE 17-7. Two superior approaches to spreader base fittings. Contrast these with the example shown in Figure 17-6. **Top:** A clevis pin mounted through an epoxy plug. **Bottom:** Top and bottom spreader plates extended past wooden spreader. *(Jim Sollers)*

FIGURE 17-8. Traditional masthead attachments. *(Jim Sollers)*

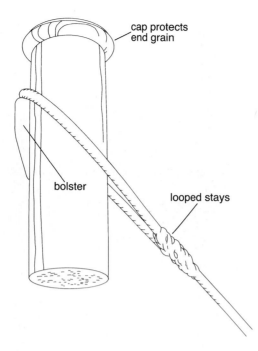

cap protects
end grain

bolster

looped stays

cap shrouds are looped around the masthead
and supported by blocks of wood on the mast
side (Figure 17-8). The masthead itself is bare.
The end grain *must* be properly capped, a function traditionally served by sheet copper or a
wooden disc. Even if the rest of the spar is varnished, paint the top few feet for added protection—it will look perfectly shipshape.

Other spars have masthead boxes incorporat-

FIGURE 17-9. A wooden
spar with external
masthead hardware.

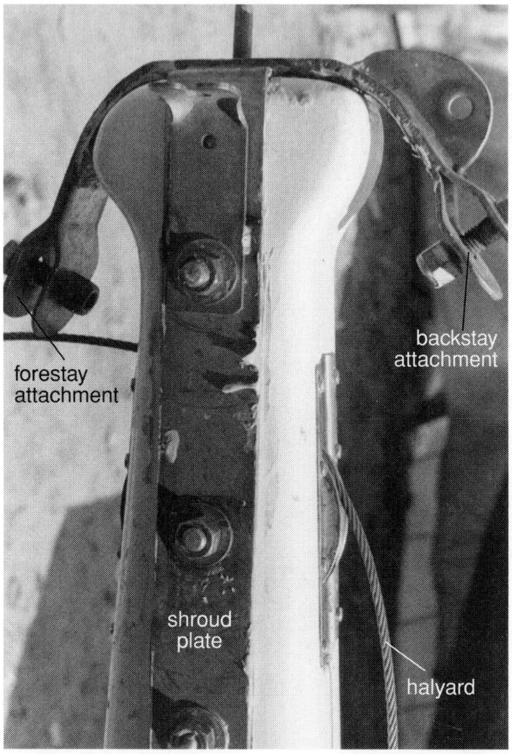

forestay
attachment

backstay
attachment

shroud
plate

halyard

ing halyard sheaves and attachment points for
stays and shrouds. Older designs are often let
into and attached to the sides of the spar, leaving
exposed woodwork (Figures 17-9 and 17-10).
Newer spars sometimes have an all-purpose
head box, which simply drops over the top of the
mast (Figure 17-11). In the latter case, the head
box must be sealed (i.e., welded shut with a
plate) below the sheaves so that no water can
ever make its way down into the spar. Electric
cables that are run internally in the mast can exit
the spar below the head box and run up its outside rather than upset its watertight integrity. For
maintenance and overhaul of head boxes, see
the Masthead Boxes section later in this chapter.

Sprung seams. Over time the constant flexing
of a mast as it works may weaken and eventually
crack some of the glue lines. This is more likely
if the mast is improperly tuned (e.g., excessive
mast bend, slack rigging—see the Tuning a Rig
section at the end of this chapter). A lightning
strike may also open up seams.

Bowsprits. These are prone to rotting in three
distinct areas:

1. At the tip where the *cranse iron* (the bobstay
   and headstay hardware) attaches.
2. At the bow of the boat where there is generally
   another collar of sorts.
3. At the butt block or bitts.

It is essential to remove all the hardware periodically (every few years) and closely inspect the
wood beneath. The loss of a bowsprit endangers
the whole rig; it is not worth taking chances.

Repairs. One of the principal advantages of
wooden spars is that they can be repaired, generally being returned to as-good-as-new condition.

Anytime the protective paint or varnish layer
is damaged, patch it up as soon as possible (as
long as the underlying wood is dry). Lin and
Larry Pardey, widely published cruising sailors,
carry a fingernail polish jar (the kind with the
brush attached to the underside of the lid) filled
with varnish. Whenever they have a minor
scratch, they can paint over it immediately, without the fuss of digging out varnish cans, brushes,
and brush cleaner. Since the brush is kept in the
jar, it doesn't need cleaning. This is an excellent
idea.

Treat small areas of damage to spars by chisel-
ing out the affected area and cutting an insert to
fit. Preferably you should make the insert, or
Dutchman, of the same kind of wood with the
grain running in the same direction.

Cut back large areas of rot or damage to clean
wood, then fit in fresh planks. As often as not the
hardest part of a major repair is finding an ade-

FIGURE 17-10. How *not* to fit masthead sheaves. This is the same mast shown in Figure 17-6. Note the gaps for rainwater entry (1) and the split-out grain (2).

quate bench to support the spar and enough clamps to fit the new pieces (which should be clamped at least every 12 inches).

The important steps to remember are:

1. Keep the scarf-joint ratios at or above 8:1.
2. Stagger the joints around the spar.
3. Have the outsides of joints pointing down.
4. Treat interior surfaces with an antirot solution.
5. Taper all internal blocking.
6. Find out what caused the problem in the first place and fix it!

Aluminum Spars and Spreaders

When set up right, modern aluminum spars are long lived and almost maintenance free. However, failing to carry out the little maintenance required, or to spot and rectify danger signals from just one fixture, can result in the loss of a whole rig.

Construction. Aluminum spars are *extruded*—that is to say molten aluminum is pushed through a mold, cooling and gelling as it goes. The interior parts of the mold are held in place by metal rods attached to the exterior parts of the mold. The aluminum has to flow around these retaining rods and re-form on the other side.

The extrusion is tempered, or hardened, in the process. (Tempering of metals, with the

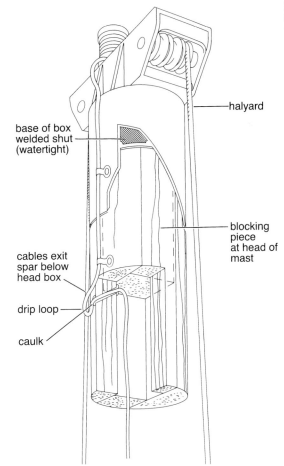

FIGURE 17-11. A wooden spar with a head box. *(Jim Sollers)*

base of box welded shut (watertight)

halyard

cables exit spar below head box

blocking piece at head of mast

drip loop

caulk

exception of copper, which behaves in reverse of most metals, is done by raising the metal to a high heat and then cooling it rapidly.) Then the upper section of most masts is progressively tapered. This is done by cutting a section out of the extrusion, bringing the halves together, and welding them back up. However, the welding process reheats the metal around the weld and then allows it to cool relatively slowly. This effectively undoes the tempering in the area of the weld, softening the metal. (This process is known as annealing.) The degree of softening, and its impact on spar strength, depends on a number of factors, including the kind of welding gun used (MIG welding requires less heat than other methods) and the amount of metal in the weld area (some walls are thickened on the sides and forward face to add strength). Some quality spars are retempered *after* the tapering.

Many masts have various fixtures welded in place, such as the head box, spreader sockets, winch bases, and halyard exit boxes. This can make the mast soft in these areas, and so is not favored by some manufacturers; on the other hand, there are none of the corrosion problems that can develop around the fasteners on non-welded fittings. The mast is next *anodized* or painted.

Anodizing or painting. Aluminum is notoriously hard to coat. The surface oxidizes very rapidly (which gives it that typical gray appearance of untreated metal), and surface coatings will not adhere to the oxidized metal.

Once the initial oxidation has occurred, the surface becomes relatively stable. Apart from its unsightliness and the fact that it leaves gray deposits on sails and halyards, untreated aluminum works fine for spars (many European aluminum boat builders leave their hulls bare). Surface coatings are therefore largely cosmetic.

Anodizing electrochemically builds up a hard protective coating both *within* the surface metal of the aluminum and on it (as opposed to paint, which only sits on the surface). With anodizing, the *inside* of the mast is also treated, though not to the same extent as the outside. Should an anodized surface become scratched or damaged it cannot be reanodized—the best thing to do is clean the bare metal and then polish it with a good-quality liquid-silicone polish (for cars or boats).

In order to get paint to key to aluminum, the surface must first be cleaned and microscopically roughened to improve the adhesion of the paint. This can be done with sanders, but generally it is done by treating the aluminum with phosphoric acid, which eats into—*etches*—the surface of the metal, removing the oxidation in

the process. The acid is washed off, and the bare metal is immediately treated with a zinc chromate primer, which inhibits fresh oxidation. The paint is applied as soon after this treatment as possible to seal the surface—usually with a primer of two-part epoxy followed by one of the two-part linear polyurethane top coats (e.g., Awlgrip—www.awlgrip.com, Imron—www.dupont. com, or Interthane Plus—www.yachtpaint.com).

Damaged painted areas can be restored by the owner using the same steps. Various companies (e.g., the Gougeon Brothers) market aluminum *prebonding kits* with the necessary acid for etching, zinc chromate primer, and instructions for use. Some of the linear polyurethanes also are available for application by brush. (Observe all safety warnings—these paints are hazardous!) The resulting touch-up job will not match an original sprayed finish, but it can come close.

In any event, painted masts will need repainting sooner or later, whereas anodizing generally lasts for the life of the spar. Another advantage to anodizing is that it will show stress areas (the anodizing takes on a crazed pattern or goes dull white) more clearly than painted masts (Figure 17-12A). Few mast builders, however, have an anodizing bath that is long enough to handle large spars, so these tend to be painted (unless built in sections—Figure 17-12B).

Danger areas. Periodic, quick inspections will discover most problems before they get out of hand.

Welds. As stated, during the extrusion process aluminum spars are hardened. Any welding causes localized softening (annealing) of the extrusion. Vertical welds up and down a spar (e.g., for tapering) present no great problems, but any welds *around* the spar produce a weak section prone to buckling. Notable in this respect are welded spreader sockets, especially where the sockets wrap a good way around the spar.

Any clustering of welded fittings, winch bases, or the like around one area of the mast will produce a weak section. Welding shroud tangs can soften the tangs; flexing of the shrouds will lead to fatigue and failure. Excessive heat when welding head boxes will sometimes soften the metal where the forestay and backstay toggles attach, and thus lead to failure.

Inspect all welded fixtures regularly and carefully for any signs of cracks around the welds or deformation of the fixture or mast wall.

Hardware and fasteners. Aluminum is fairly well down the list in the galvanic series table (Chapter 5). Most hardware and fasteners are well up the list (e.g., bronze and stainless steel). As noted earlier, add a little salt water, and you

FIGURE 17-12A. Stress patterns show up clearly on an anodized aluminum mast.

FIGURE 17-12B. Longer anodized masts must be built of sections riveted together.

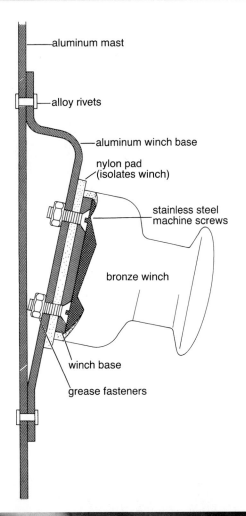

aluminum mast

alloy rivets

aluminum winch base

nylon pad (isolates winch)

stainless steel machine screws

bronze winch

winch base

grease fasteners

FIGURE 17-13A. Dissimilar metals used to mount hardware can cause galvanic corrosion problems on aluminum masts. Fasteners must be coated with a corrosion inhibitor, such as Tef-Gel or Duralac. *(Jim Sollers)*

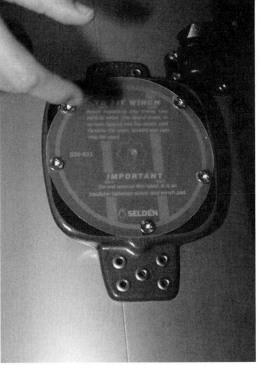

FIGURE 17-13B. A winch pad on a Selden mast. It comes with a galvanic insulator already installed.

have excellent conditions for galvanic interaction!

It is important to insulate larger hardware items from the spar with a nylon or similarly electrically inert pad (Figures 17-13A and 17-13B). Where this is impractical, apply a zinc chromate paste between the hardware and the mast wall to help protect the aluminum, serving the same function as a sacrificial zinc anode.

Fasteners present special problems. Aluminum alloy rivets are compatible with aluminum but will be eaten away rapidly if in contact with more noble metals. They work well for

FIGURE 17-14. Aluminum mast repairs. This boat fell over in the yard, crushing the mast at the spreaders. The ruined section of mast was cut out and a new section spliced in.

fastening aluminum spreader brackets, winch bases, exit boxes, and so on, but cannot be used on stainless or bronze hardware. These items are generally attached with Monel rivets or stainless steel self-tapping and machine screws.

Stainless steel fasteners should be coated with a corrosion inhibitor (such as Tef-Gel or

Duralac), but essentially nothing will permanently stop corrosion. Sooner or later oxidized aluminum will build up around the fastener and freeze it in place—attempts to remove it will likely just shear off the head of the fastener. Since aluminum oxide has a greater volume than the original aluminum, sometimes enough pressure is generated to break fasteners without any outside help!

If it is ever likely that the fittings held in place with stainless steel fasteners will need to be removed (e.g., boom ends with internal lines and fittings), pull the fasteners annually and recoat with a corrosion inhibitor to prevent them from becoming locked in place.

Spreaders and spreader sockets. Spreaders are either round tubes or they have an airfoil (*streamlined*) cross section. The former are designed for compression loads only and must not be forced backward and forward or up and down (Figure 17-14). The latter will take some fore-and-aft loading and are used where bends are induced in the mast to improve sailing performance, but once again, they will take very little up-and-down loading.

Some spreaders (normally tubular ones) are *flexibly* mounted with a limited swing fore and aft to relieve stresses created by flexing masts and rigging. Most spreaders, however—particularly airfoil-section spreaders—are rigidly mounted. Unfair loads can be generated by excessive mast bend, the pumping action of slack lee-side rigging, or allowing a mainsail to bear against the spreaders when running downwind.

The most excessive fore-and-aft loads generally arise as a result of cranking down on a backstay adjuster, causing the mast to flex forward at the spreaders. The spreader sockets try to pull free of the mast wall on the forward edge and to compress the mast on the aft edge (Figure 17-15). Look for cracked welds or loose rivets on the front face and dented mast walls to the rear. Any damage is going to require a specialist's attention.

Semiflexible tubular spreaders frequently bear on a hardened rubber pad in the base of the spreader socket. If excessive play is evident, check this pad and replace it if it is damaged or destroyed.

Many older masts have spreader sockets designed to spread loads over a substantial area of the mast wall (Figure 17-16A). Newer masts usually have *spreader bars* that pass clean through the mast, or some sort of similar reinforcement inside the mast (Figure 17-16B). The loads from opposing spreaders tend to cancel out, reducing the load on the mast wall.

Cutouts. Aluminum spars inevitably have a number of holes cut into them for various fittings

FIGURE 17-15. The effect of excessive mast bend on spreaders. *(Jim Sollers)*

spreader pulling back

rivets on spreader bracket pulled loose forward

mast dented aft

spreader tip held in original alignment by shroud

mast bends forward at spreaders

backstay over-tensioned

FIGURE 17-16A. This excellent type of spreader socket distributes the spreader's loads over a substantial area of the mast.

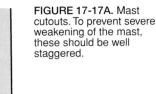

FIGURE 17-16B. A spreader bar arrangement. (Selden)

(e.g., exit boxes) and access hatches. These holes must never be concentrated in any one area or severe weakening of the spar will result. Most important is not to have exit holes horizontally opposed to one another. All cutouts should have rounded corners to reduce stress concentration. If cracks start to radiate out from corners, you can temporarily halt them by drilling a small hole (up to ¼ inch/6 mm) at the point of the farthest extension of the crack (Figures 17-17A and 17-17B). Keep loads on the rig down.

Mast heels. Mast heels are particularly susceptible to corrosion. Keel-stepped masts are in the (generally damp) bilges, while deck-stepped masts are subject to constant saltwater spray. Keep the mast step drained and ventilated (make sure the mast step has a drain—some don't—and that the drain is clear). Periodically wash off salt to slow down corrosion. Annually pull stainless fasteners and treat them with a corrosion inhibitor.

Maintenance and overhaul. Aluminum spars require very little attention, but do check:

Masthead boxes. Modern masthead boxes integrate halyard and topping-lift sheaves, spinnaker halyard leads, masthead electrical equipment mounts, forestay and backstay attachment points, and maybe cap shroud tangs into one neat and seaworthy package.

On aluminum spars the head box is open at its base to allow electric cables and halyards to be run inside the mast. On wooden spars, the box

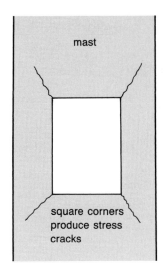

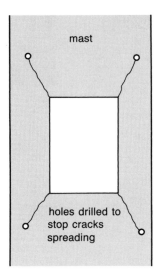

FIGURE 17-17A. Mast cutouts. To prevent severe weakening of the mast, these should be well staggered.

mast

square corners produce stress cracks

mast

holes drilled to stop cracks spreading

mast

rounded mast cut-out produces less stress concentration

FIGURE 17-17B. A mast under construction. Notice the rounded stress-relieving corners on the cutouts.

FIGURE 17-18A. A removable head box makes sheave maintenance much easier than on many older masts. *(Selden)*

should be sealed below the sheaves to keep water out of the mast.

If halyards become recalcitrant, it is important to go aloft and find out why as soon as possible. Salt crystals will plug masthead sheaves just as they will freeze up deck-level blocks. Attempts to free a sheave by dragging a halyard over it will only score the sheave and abrade the halyard. Slack off all the halyards. Once aloft, check all the sheaves for free movement. Flex the sheaves up and down; there should be no binding or any undue play.

Removal of sheaves. This is straightforward enough, but there is always the risk of dropping parts down inside the mast. The first step, therefore, is to tape a piece of line to each sheave, turn the sheave until the line can be pulled out the other side, then tie off the sheave securely. Access the sheaves by removing either a plate from the top of the mast or the plate that separates sheaves from one another, which will allow them to be lifted out. Or, remove a couple of cotter pins or small plates screwed to the box on either side (Figures 17-18A and 17-18B). After these plates or cotter pins are removed, drive out the sheave pin, using a punch and hammer if necessary. Once done, you can then withdraw the sheaves with the lines already tied around them. Clean and inspect the sheaves and pins. Before replacing, lubricate them with a light machine oil or penetrating fluid (WD-40, etc.).

Replacing halyards. It is important to maintain a free fall inside the mast and avoid tangles with other lines. First set up all other halyards tightly to hold them in their normal alignment; next attach a short length of light chain (bicycle chain works well) as a weight to a messenger line and feed it over the appropriate sheave at the masthead. Feed the messenger line down into

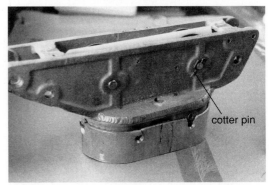

cotter pin

FIGURE 17-18B. A removable head box. To remove sheaves, pull out the cotter pin (split pin) and knock out the clevis pin. Be sure to tie a lanyard around the sheaves to prevent them from falling into the mast. This mast got tangled up in a drawbridge as the bridge was opening. The boat was picked up by the mast-head, which tore the head box from the mast. This is not a recommended method for removing the head box.

FIGURE 17-19. Selden's in-mast car for a fully battened mainsail. *(Selden)*

the mast and retrieve the chain at the base through the appropriate exit hole using a piece of bent coat hanger. Tie the messenger line to the halyard and use it to pull the halyard up through the mast. Use the same technique for running electric cables inside the internal conduit. Note: When not in use, secure halyards so they don't continually slap on the mast. Apart from the noise irritation, sooner or later this action will wear through the anodizing or paint. (Some masts—e.g., some from Selden, www.seldenmast.com—have an internal foam lining for sound insulation.)

Spinnaker halyards. These are led through blocks suspended at the masthead. Many blocks swivel to accommodate changing spinnaker positions while providing a constantly fair lead for the halyards to the masthead sheaves, thus eliminating undue friction. However, some spinnaker halyards are run straight off the masthead sheaves past fairing pads fastened to the exit point from the head box. In the latter case, whenever the pull of the spinnaker halyard is off to one side, it drags over these pads. This leads to wear of the pads and halyards, and sometimes considerable friction when raising and lowering the spinnaker. If you use this kind of rig, regularly inspect the fairing pads and halyards.

Sail track and slides. Only nylon sail slides should be used on aluminum spars, since metal will score the track and generate galvanic corrosion. Periodically flush salt crystals out of the slides and track, then lubricate them with sili-

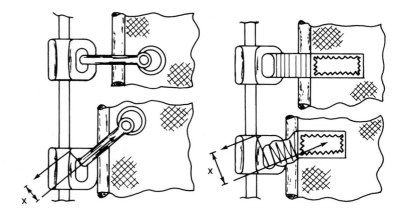

cone car or boat polish or with Vaseline (it works fine). Masts with a luff groove (as opposed to a track) will accept either special sail slides or a boltrope. The latest generation of Selden masts have an enlarged slot that will accept a car for a full-battened mainsail—an excellent way to handle this kind of sail (Figure 17-19).

If the sail slides are correctly matched to the track or groove and everything is clean and polished, but the sail tends to jam, the problem most likely lies in the method of attaching the slides to the sail rather than in the mast and slides (Figure 17-20).

End of season. When a mast is unstepped at the end of the sailing season, it and all its rigging should be washed free of salt crystals and the inside of the mast hosed out. Pay particular attention to hard-to-reach areas and the mast heel. Do not use detergents since some can cause corrosion. (If detergents *are* used, be sure to rinse well.)

Check all moving parts for free operation or undue wear and lubricate lightly with a penetrating fluid such as WD-40. Remove and treat with a corrosion inhibitor any stainless steel fasteners that must not be allowed to freeze up. Inspect all welds and fasteners for cracks and movement, particularly spreader sockets. Check the mast wall around the spreader sockets and shroud tangs or *ball sockets* (see below) for distortion (Figure 17-21). Inspect the forestay- and backstay-mounting holes in the head box for signs of elongation.

Before storing a mast, *dry it well*. It is excellent practice to apply a coat of silicone boat or car polish. Support the mast evenly at several points along its length so that no section is sagging. Don't store stainless steel rigging against aluminum spars, since corrosion is likely.

Carbon Fiber Spars

Carbon fiber spars cost about twice as much as comparable aluminum spars, so why would any-

FIGURE 17-20. Attaching slides to a sail. Use a round shackle (left) that can move freely in the slide. Keep the distance marked X small; this will allow the slide to run freely. At right, the slide is attached by a fabric band; distance X is too great and the slide will jam. *(David Potter, The Care of Alloy Spars and Rigging, Adlard Coles Ltd.)*

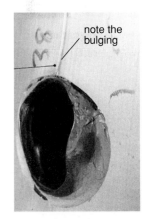

note the bulging

FIGURE 17-21. Check for these trouble spots around the shroud socket area of a mast wall: mast wall distorted by T-ball shroud socket (top), and mast wall cracked by shroud socket (bottom).

one buy carbon fiber? The answer is weight. A carbon fiber spar often weighs half as much as a comparable aluminum one.

This sounds great, and often it is. However, aside from the cost aspect of carbon fiber, there are other issues that modify this rosy picture to some extent.

Added fittings. The weight most often quoted when comparing carbon fiber to aluminum is the *bare pole* weight. In the case of aluminum, this is the weight of the extrusion; in the case of carbon fiber, it is likely to be the weight when the pole comes off the tool (either the male mandrel or the female mold). All the fittings then have to be attached to the spar (head boxes, spreader brackets, etc.). In the case of a carbon fiber spar, these can also be made of carbon fiber, but only at considerable expense. More typically, aluminum or stainless steel are used. The weight added in installing the fittings is likely to be similar to that added to the aluminum extrusion.

Then there are the spreaders, the boom, and the rig. Because of the cost of producing carbon fiber spreaders and booms, it is common to use aluminum, as with an aluminum spar. The rig itself will also be the same for both carbon fiber and aluminum, with the same weight in the wire or rod as well as in the terminals. When all of this is added to the spar weight, the savings on the gross rig weight will be nowhere near as dramatic as those on the bare tube weight. In other words, although a carbon fiber mast can save as much as 50% over the bare tube weight of an equivalent aluminum spar, the savings on the total rig weight are likely to be only 10% to 20%, depending on whether carbon spreaders and other fittings are used.

Engineering and materials. The picture is complicated by the fact that these weight savings are highly dependent on the individual manufacturer and the methodology used to produce the spar. Unlike aluminum masts, which are extruded from the same raw material with predictable engineering properties, carbon fiber spars are hand-constructed from varying grades of carbon fibers, with the result that every single one has slightly different engineering properties.

The higher (stronger) grades of carbon fiber are dramatically more expensive than other grades (up to ten times more expensive). Since even with standard grades of carbon fiber, the raw material is around one-quarter to one-third the cost of the finished product, this has a big impact on the overall cost of a spar. As a result, in practice, most spar manufacturers use stan-dard modulus (T-300) material or something very similar, rather than more exotic and expensive fibers. However, when it comes to high performance racing masts, such as those for the America's Cup, T-800 (intermediate modulus material) is used. This is approximately 20% stiffer than T-300, but two-and-a-half to three times more expensive.

Manufacturing methods. Assuming basically the same raw material from one manufacturer to another, there are a number of different ways in which this material can be laminated into the finished product, including layup with a male or female mold, unidirectional prepreg or braided construction, vacuum-bag or pull-tape debulking, and vacuum-bag or autoclave curing (Figures 17-22A and 17-22B). This is not the place to get into these things. However, the point I want to bring home is that a carbon spar is significantly a handmade, one-off product in which quality control is critical. If the engineering or production is at all screwed up, the mast may either end up grossly overweight or come down around the ears of the buyer (it may do both). Before going to the considerable expense of investing in a carbon fiber spar, it would be wise to study the technology and make sure that what you are getting will meet your needs and expectations.

Lightning and other survival issues. Carbon is a good electrical conductor, whereas the glue in a carbon fiber laminate is not. If the carbon fibers in a mast were to be fused into an electrically tight connection, the mast would in all likelihood be able to conduct the high currents of a lightning strike to ground without damage. However, in the event of a strike any resistance (such as that caused by the glue) will result in localized heating that will soften or melt the resin and potentially cause irreparable damage to the mast. As a result, carbon fiber mast manufacturers commonly recommend installing a lightning grounding system. If this meets ABYC standards (see Chapter 5), it will have a masthead lightning rod connected by a 4 AWG (20 mm^2) stranded copper cable to an immersed ground plate.

Even with such a lightning-protection system, there is no guarantee that there won't be localized damage due to heating around the base of a lightning terminal and in other areas. Given the small number of carbon fiber masts in use, and the even smaller number of known lightning strikes, almost no baseline data exist with which to assess the impact of such damage.

This raises a more general point. Given the

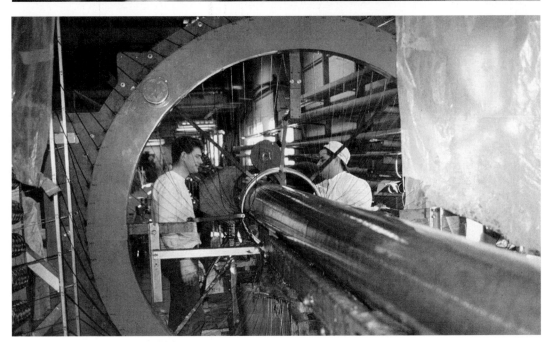

FIGURES 17-22A AND
17-22B. Carbon spars are
substantially handmade.
The top photo shows a
hand layup using prepreg
fibers, a very labor intensive and lightweight
approach; the bottom
photo shows a spar being
woven, a less labor intensive and not as lightweight
approach.

limited experience accumulated with carbon fiber spars, we still do not have a good, practical understanding of how the laminates will stand up over time in real-life—as opposed to labora-tory—applications. Fatigue is one unknown. In addition there are other issues: How do you keep an eye on the spar over its lifetime? What main-tenance items and warning signs indicate impending failure? What happens if you want to move a winch, add another one, or change the position of an exit hole? What will be the effect of a loose shackle or halyard beating against the mast? And so on.

Only time will tell.

Downwind, Whisker, and Spinnaker Poles

All poles used for winging out sheets and sails are designed for *compression loading only*—that is to say, the poles must be set up so that all loads are transmitted directly along the length of the pole to the heel fitting (generally mounted on the mast). In this respect poles are very like spread-ers—flexing loads (such as wrapping the pole around a shroud) are likely to cause a pole to buckle.

As far as possible a pole must be set up at a right angle to the mast. The more a pole deviates

TABLE 17-1. Spar Maintenance Checklist

| Item or Aspect | Spar Material | | |
---	Wood	Aluminum	Carbon Fiber
Finish	Check for bare spots, blistering, peeling, cracking, and delaminating. Remove and replace all rotted areas. Refinish.	If spars are anodized, clean and polish any bare spots. If spars are painted, clean, acid-etch, and repaint bare spots.	Clean
Fasteners	Check for separation of wood and fasteners, water ingress, and rot. Repair and rebed as necessary.	Check for stress patterns, looseness, cracks, and corrosion. Remove any fasteners that must come out periodically; clean, coat with a corrosion inhibitor, and replace.	Check for looseness and signs of stress in the surrounding laminate, such as unusual coloration or distorted fibers.
Spreaders	Pay particular attention to spreader tops and the attachment points to the mast.	Check spreader sockets for cracks (especially if welded), mast deformation, and loose rivets. Check any rubber pads in semiflexible spreader sockets.	As above.
Spreader angles	Make sure all spreaders bisect their shrouds.	Same as for wooden spars.	Same as for wooden spars.
Heel fitting	Check for water and rot.	Check for corrosion.	Check for any evidence of crushed fibers.
Masthead	Check that sheaves spin freely, and check for wear; where sheaves are set in the mast, check for water ingress into the masthead.	Check that sheaves spin freely, and for wear.	Same as for aluminum spars.
Mast track	Check all of the mast track for loose fasteners and misaligned joints.	Same as for wooden spars, if there is an external track.	Same as for wooden spars, if there is an external track.
Storage	Wash off all salt, dry, and store in a cool, dry place with adequate support.	Same as for wooden spars. Prevent all rigging from contacting the spars.	Same as for wooden spars.

FIGURE 17-23. A typical arrangement of pole end fittings. Salt deposits in the cylinder that inhibit the free operation of the piston can be removed by judicious applications of hot water and vinegar. *(Jim Sollers)*

from a right angle, the more likely it is to be driven up or down the mast, suffering damage in the process.

There are dozens of different end fittings for poles. Almost all include an anodized aluminum casting together with some form of spring-loaded pin (a piston). Poles are subject to a lot of saltwater spray. Galvanic interaction between the stainless steel spring and piston and the aluminum housing is common, more so on poles that are rarely used. Since the pistons are a close fit in their housings, they frequently freeze up.

Telescoping poles and end fittings need frequent flushing with fresh water. Where excessive salt builds up, white vinegar will dissolve it. Avoid using detergents; some attack anodized aluminum.

Even if not used, *exercise* pole fittings frequently. Lack of use is the biggest problem in the life of poles and end fittings. Lightly lubricate end fittings with Teflon-based grease to inhibit corrosion.

Where an end fitting does freeze up, it can generally be easily restored to service, often as follows (Figure 17-23):

The spring-loaded piston is held in place by a cotter pin. Remove this pin and slide the piston and spring out of their cylinder (it will be neces-

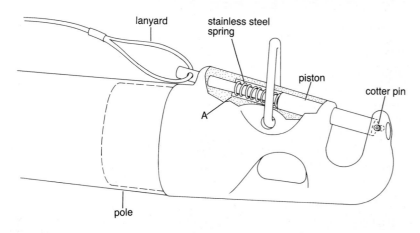

lanyard
stainless steel spring
piston
cotter pin
A
pole

Going Aloft

Having been at a masthead for several hours at a time on more than one occasion, let me tell you that comfort (or, at the least, minimizing *dis*comfort) is a prime consideration. I advise sailboat owners to get one of those deep-sided canvas bosun's chairs with lots of pockets all the way around. Just one point—the pockets tend to sag and do not retain tools securely, so it is worth putting Velcro tape on the larger pockets to close them off.

Safety

- *Do not* hook a bosun's chair to a snap-shackle on the halyard. Use a screw shackle or a bowline.

- *Do not* use a wire halyard with a rope tail. If this must be done, first check the rope-to-wire splice *very closely*.

- *Do not* use a winch directly below the mast to go aloft—any dropped tool will land on the winch operator, who will probably let go of the rope tail, and down you will come. Rig a block and take the line to a cockpit winch.

- *Do not* use electric winches—it is all too easy for the winch operator to run the bosun's chair up into the head box and tear the halyard loose from the bosun's chair.

- *Do* set up another external halyard or taut line so that you have something to hang onto and help pull yourself up. In the event of a riding turn on the winch (which can create quite a dangerous situation as it is unwrapped), you can take the weight off the hoisting line.

- *Do* place a safety line or strap around the mast as you go aloft. Should the hoisting line fail or come loose, the safety strap will hold you. It will have to be undone and reset at each spreader.

- *Do* tie off once up. This is a most basic safety precaution. It also frees up both hands for working. A good strong belt will be more comfortable than a piece of line. Have the winch operator *cleat off the hoisting line* even if using a self-tailing winch.

The most difficult work aloft is repairing things *on top of* the mast—for example, masthead lights. The bosun's chair most likely will

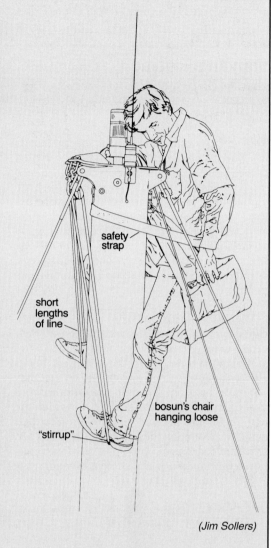

safety strap

short lengths of line

"stirrup"

bosun's chair hanging loose

(Jim Sollers)

not get you high enough. It is well worth having a couple of mast steps installed at the masthead, one higher than the other, so that the lower one puts your chest at masthead level (with a straight leg), and the other (about a foot higher) allows you to push yourself up a little more if necessary. Otherwise, a couple of short lengths of line can be hung from the masthead as "stirrups," serving the same purpose.

sary to remove the lanyard). If the piston is frozen, use hot water and vinegar to remove deposits, then knock the piston out with a punch, hitting it at the end where the lanyard attaches. Be sure to use a good-sized punch and hit it squarely—if the top of the piston gets burred over, it is not going to pass through the narrow part of the cylinder bore. In serious cases of corrosion, the spring and cylinder bore will be completely plugged with aluminum oxide, so you will need quite a bit of force to free things up.

After repeated freeze-ups, several years ago we drilled out our cylinders by running an oversized drill in from the cotter pin end (we opened the cylinders up by an extra $\frac{1}{32}$ inch). We have not had a problem since. (Note: This will destroy any anodizing, but since it was completely corroded anyway we weren't worried.) *It is absolutely vital to drill no farther than point* A *in Figure 17-23—if the drill goes all the way through, the piston spring will have nothing to seat on and the fitting will be ruined.*

Standing Rigging

Wire Rope

Rod rigging (see the Rod Rigging section below) has won acceptance on performance-oriented cruising boats, but nevertheless most rigging is still done with stainless steel wire rope. First, the terminology. The basic unit of construction is a *wire*. A straight length of wire is used as a *center wire*, and then a number of other wires are *laid up* around the center wire to form a *strand*. One strand is used as a *core cable* and other strands, or individual wires, are laid up around this core to form the finished cable, known as *wire rope* (Figure 17-24).

When forming strands and cables, the individual wires or strands are *not* bent around their center wires or cores. All of the individual wires are manufactured with the required bends already built in (called *preforming*) so that they naturally take up the right position without stress. Depending on the direction in which the wires or strands are laid up in relation to their center wire or core, they are *right lay* or *left lay*. Under a load, a cable laid up in only one direction tends to unravel and stretch; therefore, the outer layers of wire rope are laid up in a direction opposite to that of the inner layers—any tendencies to unravel or stretch cancel out. Norseman has a line of wire rope called Dyform in which the strands are not only preformed but also shaped to eliminate the air spaces that occur around circular strands—Figure 17-25A. This results in a considerably stronger and slightly heavier rope for a given diameter or, put another way, in a smaller and lighter rope for a given strength. To quote Norsemen: "the next best thing to rod, but with all the advantages of wire."

The fewer the wires and strands in the construction of a cable, the greater its strength and the less its stretch; the ultimate is a cable of only one solid strand—rod rigging. However, the fewer the wires and strands, the less the flexibility and therefore the greater the tendency for the cable to fatigue and fail.

Almost all standing rigging uses 1 × 19 wire rope. This consists of an inner strand (the core) that has six preformed wires laid up around one straight center wire (giving a total of seven

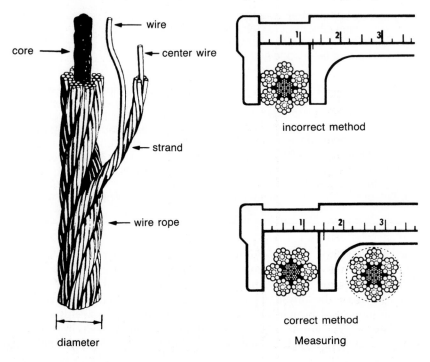

FIGURE 17-24. Wire rope construction and terminology. Wire rope is measured as shown at right. *(Loos and Co.)*

core

wire

center wire

strand

wire rope

diameter

incorrect method

correct method

Measuring

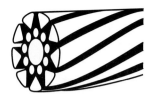

FIGURE 17-25A. Norseman Dyform wire rope. *(Norseman)*

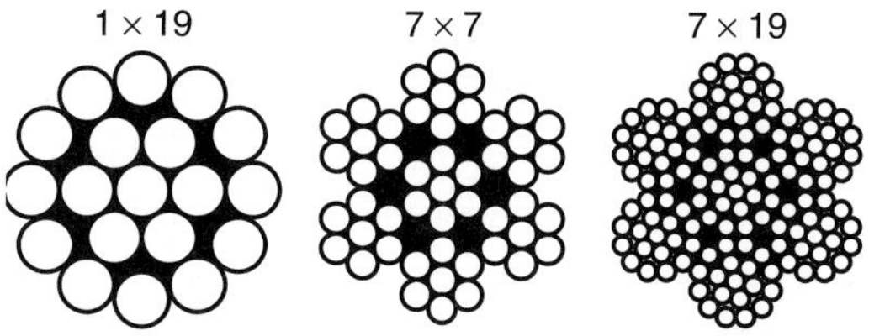

1 × 19   7 × 7   7 × 19

FIGURE 17-25B. Strand arrangement of the most commonly seen types of wire rope. *(Norseman)*

wires). Twelve more individual preformed wires are laid up around this core. The designation "1 × 19" refers to the fact that there is one strand (the core) and a total of nineteen individual wires (Figure 17-25B).

Where greater flexibility is required, 7 × 7 and 7 × 19 cable is used. A 7 × 7 cable has seven strands with seven wires each (the strands are the same as the core in 1 × 19 wire rope); 7 × 19 wire has seven strands with nineteen wires each (each strand is the same as 1 × 19 wire rope). The 7 × 19 wire—the most flexible—is commonly used for steering cables and halyards.

Wire rope is rated at a breaking strength, which is just that—the load under which it breaks. Industrial practice, where lives are frequently at stake, is to establish a *safe working load* of 20% to 25% of the breaking strength. In marine use, a safe working load of up to 50% of the breaking strength is frequently used (it cuts cost as well as weight aloft). The argument is that the rigging is always in *column* (i.e., straight), and the rope is less likely to fatigue. This doesn't take into account the constant flexing that can rapidly build up a very high number of fatigue cycles. When rigging or rerigging a boat, it is far better to use the safer industrial practice—establish a safe working load of no more than 25% of breaking strength (Table 17-2).

Stainless steel wire rope is made from many different grades of stainless steel. *Nothing but 316 should be used on boats.*

Fitting end connections (terminals) to wire rope.

Eye terminals using thimbles. At one time, when galvanized wire rope was the norm, almost all rigging was formed into an eye around a

TABLE 17-2. Breaking Loads for Stainless Steel Wire Rope[1]

Nominal Diameter (strand size)		1 x 19 Minimum Breaking Load		7 x 7 Minimum Breaking Load		7 x 19 Minimum Breaking Load	
Inches	MM	Pounds	Kilograms	Pounds	Kilograms	Pounds	Kilograms
—	2	704	320	532	242	—	—
—	2.5	1,100	500	—	—	—	—
1/8	3	1,584	720	1,199	545	1,122	510
5/32	4	2,816	1,280	2,130	968	2,134	970
3/16	4.76	3,960	1,800	—	—	2,827	1,285
—	5	4,400	2,000	3,322	1,510	3,124	1,420
7/32	5.56	5,295	2,470	—	—	3,857	1,753
—	6	6,336	2,880	4,796	2,180	4,488	2,040
1/4	6.35	7,084	3,220	—	—	5,031	2,287
9/32	7	7,810	3,550	6,534	2,970	6,116	2,780
5/16	8	10,208	4,640	8,514	3,870	7,986	3,630
—	9	12,914	5,870	—	—	—	—
3/8	9.53	14,476	6,580	—	—	11,330	5,150
—	10	15,950	7,250	13,310	6,050	12,474	5,670
7/16	11	19,294	8,770	—	—	—	—
—	12	22,880	10,400	19,162	8,710	17,952	8,160
1/2	12.7	25,630	11,650	—	—	20,123	9,147
9/16	14	31,196	14,180	26,180	11,900	24,420	11,100
5/8	16	40,832	18,560	—	—	—	—
3/4	19	47,564	21,620	—	—	—	—
7/8	22	63,954	29,070	—	—	—	—
1	26	89,320	40,600	—	—	—	—

1. The loads given are based on Norseman figures. Each company gives slightly different figures.

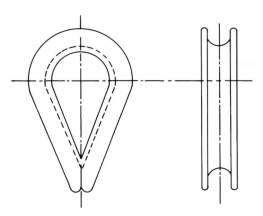

FIGURE 17-26. Although rigging eyes spliced in wire rope around thimbles are seldom seen these days, eyes retained by cable clamps or Nicopress (Talurit) sleeves are a common sight. They are just as secure as a splice, and far easier to make. Be sure to use the proper size thimble and the proper tool for crimping the sleeve, such as the portable Nicopress tool shown top right. If using cable clamps, be sure the saddle rests on the *standing* part of the wire rope (bottom right). *(Norseman)*

u-bolt   saddle

thimble and then spliced back into itself. Today wire splices have been almost completely superseded by cable clamps and Nicopress (Talurit) sleeves.

Cable clamps (Crosby or Bulldog clamps) have a U-bolt and a *saddle*. The saddle is scored with grooves to match the lay of the external wires in the rope it goes around. When using cable clamps, *the saddle always goes over the standing (loaded) part of the cable* and the U-bolt over the bitter end, since the U-bolt tends to crush and weaken the rope (Figure 17-26).

Two, and preferably three, clamps should be used, spaced 2 to 3 inches (50 to 75 mm) apart and snugged tight. Galvanized cable clamps in sizes below ³⁄₈ inch (10 mm) have a tendency to shear off when tightened; stainless clamps are much stronger.

Nicopress (Talurit) fittings consist of a copper sleeve that is slid up the cable. The bitter end of the cable is wrapped around a thimble and fed back through the sleeve alongside the standing part. The sleeve is crimped (swaged) with a special tool. The finished eye splice is both strong and neat, but inevitably some deformation of the

wire occurs, reducing its strength. A Nicopress kit (the swaging tool and a collection of different-size thimbles and sleeves) is a useful item in any emergency rigging kit.

All wire terminals using thimbles suffer from a number of problems:

1. Unless impractically large thimbles are used, 1 × 19 wire, especially in sizes over ¼ inch (6 mm), cannot be wrapped around a thimble without deforming the wire's lay (and therefore weakening the wire). Both 7 × 7 and 7 × 19 wire are more tolerant, and for this reason, thimbles and cable clamps are used extensively as wire terminals in steering systems.

2. Almost all thimbles are relatively light weight and open at the base. Under a load the thimbles tend to pinch, slacking the fit of the cable, or even collapse. It is preferable to use thimbles with the base welded shut or, best of all, thimbles machined from solid metal (hard to find and expensive; Edson—www.edson marine.com—manufactures one or two sizes).

3. Cosmetically speaking, cables terminated in thimbles are nowhere near as attractive as most other terminations.

Swages. Swaged terminals are manufactured to make a close fit over the end of the wire rope for which they are designed (Figure 17-27). The section of the terminal around the rope is then passed through a set of rollers and subjected to enormous pressure. The metal of the terminal is squeezed down into the lay of the cable and effectively cold-welded to the cable.

With the right equipment and skilled opera-

FIGURE 17-27. Swaged terminals look so nice when new, but unless done by skilled professionals, they have a relatively high rate of failure. *(Gibb)*

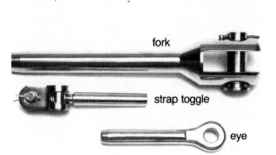

fork

strap toggle

eye

tors, swaging produces fast, neat, low-profile bonds exceeding the breaking strength of the wire rope, and is therefore popular with boat manufacturers and riggers alike. However, it must be done right.

All swaging tends to work-harden the metal involved. The use of incorrect swaging pressures and/or the repeated rolling of fittings will make the terminal brittle and prone to develop hairline cracks. It is not uncommon for improperly swaged fittings to fail within 2 years.

Unfortunately it is generally not possible to tell from a visual inspection whether swaging has been done correctly (unless a terminal is obviously banana shaped, in which case it should be discarded immediately). If having swaging done, take it to a reputable rigging loft. (Check the swaging machine—the best swages are made by hydraulic *one-time-pass-through* machines; manual boatyard machines generally have twin rotary dies through which the fitting must be passed twice, which frequently results in a banana shape; and the worst machines are rotary hammers, which will work-harden a terminal, resulting in premature failure.)

Compression fittings. There are a number of compression-type (swageless) fittings on the market, the best known being those made by Norseman (www.navtec.net) and Sta-Lok (www.stalok.com) (Figures 17-28A and 17-28B). In 2003 Petersen Stainless Rigging, a British company (www.petersen-stainless.co.uk), introduced Hi-Mod, a line of swageless fittings that has some advantages over conventional designs (distributed in the U.S. by Hayn Marine, www.hayn.com).

All swageless fittings work on the same principle. A belled sleeve, tapered and threaded toward its lower end, is slid up the cable. The outer wires or strands of the cable are unlaid and a tapered wedge or cone is slid up over the core. The outer wires or strands are then re-formed around the wedge or cone, the sleeve is slid down over the top, and the terminal itself is

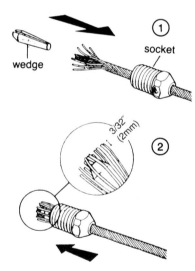

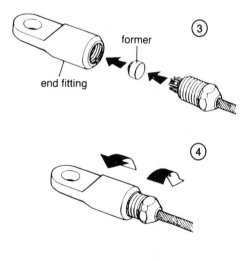

FIGURE 17-28A. Alternatives to swaged terminals, such as Sta-Lok, Norseman, or Castlok rigging terminals, are fully as secure as swages and can be installed relatively easily by the boatowner—even at sea. Sta-Lok terminals are designed for use with preformed 1 x 19, 7 x 7, and 7 x 19 wire rope. The 1 x 19 wedge is plain, but the wedge for 7 x 7 and 7 x 19 rope has a castellated ring with six gates to take the strands. These are not interchangeable. 1. Cut the cable cleanly. (There should be no protruding wires.) Slip the socket over the end of the cable, and unlay the outer wires or strands to expose a section of the center core equal in length to the wedge. 2. Slip the wedge over the center core of the cable (narrow end first), leaving about $3/32$ inch (2 mm) of core and outer wires protruding beyond the wide end of the wedge. Re-lay the outer wires or strands around the wedge, taking care to retain the wedge in its correct position. Carefully pull the socket into position over the wedge to prevent the wires or strands from unlaying. Check the assembly to ensure that the outer wires are spaced evenly around the top of the wedge, and that none of the wires has slipped into the slot in the wedge. Each of the six outer strands of seven-strand ropes should lie in the "gates" provided (not shown). 3. Insert the *former* into the threaded hole in the end fitting. Screw the end fitting onto the already assembled unit and tighten with a wrench. Too much force can damage the threads; use no more than can be applied with one hand. 4. To waterproof the fitting, unscrew the two parts and insert a raisin-size blob of silicone caulking on the former, inside the bottom of the end fitting. Apply two or three drops of Loctite on the male thread of the socket; screw both parts together again and tighten. The end fitting may be unscrewed whenever required for inspection or rewiring. When rewiring, cut off and discard the end of the cable and the old wedge. Always use a new wedge when rewiring. The remainder of the terminal parts may be reused a number of times if undamaged. (Sta-Lok)

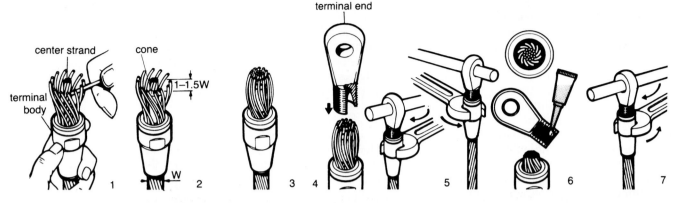

center strand

cone

terminal end

terminal body

1–1.5W

W

1   2   3   4   5   6   7

FIGURE 17-28B. To assemble Norseman terminal fittings: 1. Slide the terminal body over the wire rope, and unlay the outer strands from the center strands. 2. Slide the cone down over the center strand, leaving exposed a length equal to 1½ times the full diameter of the rope. 3. Re-lay the outer wires or strands, spaced evenly around the cone. 4. Fit all the protruding wires into the blind recess of the terminal end fitting (eye, fork, stud, etc.), and start threading the body and end fitting together. 5. Complete the assembly, turning the appropriate component in the direction of the lay of the rope, as shown. Tighten until the resistance indicates that the cone is being compressed into the body of the terminal. Do not overtighten; you may damage the threads. 6. Unscrew the fitting to inspect and ensure that the wires are evenly spaced and closed neatly over the cone. Apply a thread-locking adhesive, such as Loctite, to the threads. 7. Insert a blob of marine sealant, such as 3M 5200, into the end fitting's blind hole and retighten the assembly. Repeat if necessary until the sealant oozes from the body end. Wipe clean. *(Norseman)*

FIGURE 17-28C. A cutaway of a Sta-Lok fitting. *(Sta-Lok)*

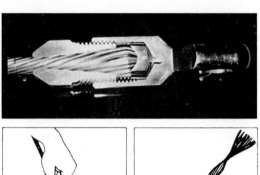

FIGURE 17-28D. To install Castlok fittings: 1. Thoroughly degrease the end of the cable with a solvent such as acetone. 2. Push the cable through the narrow end of the sleeve and expose 2 to 3 inches of wire beyond the end. Unlay the strands for approximately ¾ turn. 3. Retract the cable partially into the sleeve, leaving the end of the cable just exposed. Unlay all the wires in the center strand (1 x 19 wire rope) or in each strand (7 x 7 and 7 x 19 wire rope). 4. Retract the cable back into the sleeve until the end is at the bottom of the threads. 5. Read the manufacturer's instructions on the preparation and use of resin thoroughly. Inject the resin into the threaded opening until the sleeve is filled to the top of the threads. 6. Screw the stud into the sleeve to the end of the threads. This forces the resin into and around the cable and seals the juncture of wire and sleeve, as well as locking the threads of the stud into place. Allow the assembly to cure for 24 hours before using. *(Castlok)*

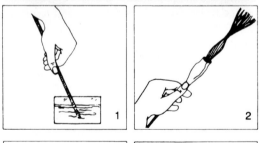

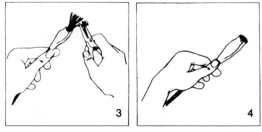

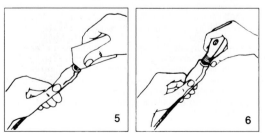

screwed into the sleeve. The individual wires or strands of the cable are sandwiched between the sleeve and the wedge or cone and held firmly (Figure 17-28C). In all instances the bond is stronger than the cable itself. Castlok fittings are a variation on the same theme, but in this instance, epoxy glue is used to form the wedge in place of a metal cone (Figure 17-28D). The glue sets up, forming a solid, incompressible plug, which serves much the same function as the cone (which is why I have included these terminals here).

This type of fitting (particularly Castlok) causes less deformation of, and places less stress on, the wire rope than any other. Corrosion resistance is also unequaled—in the case of Norseman and Sta-Lok fittings, a blob of sealant placed in the terminal prevents moisture from entering; with Castlok, glue completely fills the terminal and squeezes out and up the lay of the rope, where it emerges from the sleeve. Swageless terminals can be relatively easily fitted in the field with basic tools and are reusable. (Although melting the glue out of an old Castlok fitting requires careful use of a propane torch, and the mechanical swageless terminals may need new cones. In some cases, the cable may need cutting back.)

Petersen manufactures a range of compression extenders that enable a defective swage-type terminal to be cut off existing rigging, a swageless terminal to be added, and the rig extended to compensate for the loss of the length that is cut off. This is a great addition to any emergency repair kit. Petersen also has a backstay insulator (to convert a backstay into a SSB antenna) that is designed in a fail-safe manner and will maintain the mechanical integrity of the rig even if the (plastic) insulating components fail. (With most backstay insulators, if the insulator fails the backstay itself also fails.)

Rod Rigging

From its introduction 30 years ago until recently, rod rigging has been the only choice for high-tech racing boats. It never, however, found anywhere near the same acceptance in the cruising community. It is now being supplanted in the racing community by various forms of fiber rigging (Kevlar, PBO, and carbon).

The reluctance on the part of many cruisers to use rod rigging was fueled by well-publicized early failures. Many of these were the result of the racing community's drive to push their boats to the limit. Whereas a cruising rig is typically designed with a 4:1 safety margin between the anticipated rig load and its ultimate breaking strength, a racing boat may be designed with as little as a 2:1 ratio, sometimes even less. But even taking this into account, there has been a lingering suspicion in many cruisers' minds that rod rigging is more susceptible to failure.

Compounding this suspicion have been other perceived disadvantages of rod, as opposed to wire, in a cruising environment, particularly the facts that:

- When it fails it tends to do so without warning, resulting in catastrophic losses, whereas it is argued that wire rope will begin to strand prior to failure, providing advance notice in time to take remedial action.
- Rod rigging is carried and can be fitted by only a limited number of yards around the world.
- It is extremely difficult to find space for spare lengths of rod on board.
- Rod is more expensive than wire rigging (of course).

Avoiding failures. Today's rod rigging is made from Nitronic 50, the most corrosion-resistant material in day-to-day rig use, which is then generally terminated with fittings also machined from Nitronic 50 or else 316 stainless steel. The rod itself is smooth, without crevices to trap and hold water (Figure 17-29), in contrast to wire rope which wicks salt water down the lay of the rope into end terminals, particularly lower terminals. While corrosion-induced failures at lower terminals are one of the primary causes of rig failures on wire rope rigs, particularly if

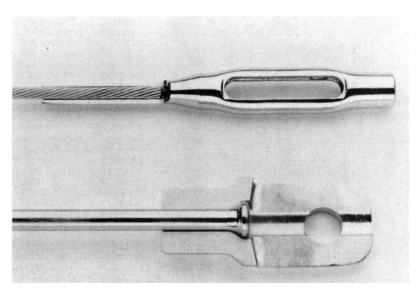

FIGURE 17-29. Comparison of rod and wire rigging terminals. The rod is smooth, without crevices to trap water. *(Navtec)*

swaged-on terminals are used in warm environments, they are not generally a problem with rod rigging. Properly installed, today's rod rigging is every bit as reliable as wire rigging.

Although less susceptible than wire rigging to corrosion, rod rigging is more prone to suffer from fatigue-induced failures. Two areas are of particular concern: the points at which a rod emerges from its end terminals, and the bend that a shroud has to make over a spreader tip. Over the years a considerable amount of research has been carried out to find ways of alleviating the stresses at these points.

End terminals. *Proper toggling of end terminals is critical.* To ease stresses, rods are generally terminated with a tapered sleeve that threads into the relevant end fitting, holding the rod in place. The taper spreads bending loads along the rod, rather than concentrating them at one point. Navtec's *fatigue-indicating* fittings extend the sleeve and then groove it toward its end (Figure 17-30). If the rod is subjected to excessive bending, before it fails the tip of the sleeve will crack and break off. This has two purposes: first of all, it serves as advance warning that the rod is being

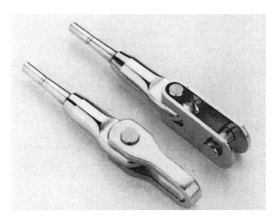

FIGURE 17-30. Fatigue-indicating rod rigging terminals. If the fitting is subjected to undue stress, the upper portion of the sleeve (above the groove) will break away to give early warning of a possible failure. *(Navtec)*

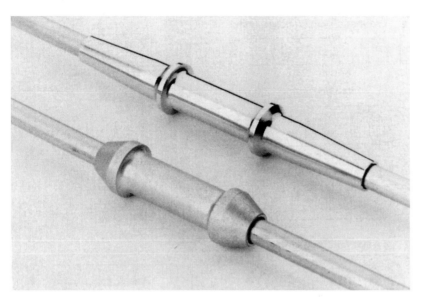

FIGURE 17-31A. Spreader bends relieve the stress of rod rigging where it bends around the tip of a spreader. *(Navtec)*

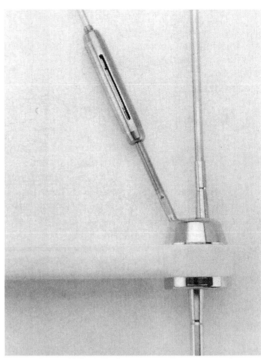

FIGURE 17-31B. Discontinuous rod rigging eliminates the bending stress at the spreader tip. *(Navtec)*

overstressed and is in danger of failing; second, in breaking off it moves the point of maximum stress concentration to a different section of the rod, which extends the life of the rod, providing time to make a repair.

In recent years, T-hook and stemball terminals have become increasingly popular. However, under flexing and cyclic loads, they do not provide the same degree of stress relief as traditional toggles and eyes.

Spreader fittings. Historically, *the point at which a shroud bends over a spreader has been another area of failure.* Here, too, solutions have been found, and two different approaches have been widely adopted. The first is to enclose the shroud (rod) in a sleeve (a *spreader bend*) that is pre-bent to precisely the correct spreader-tip angle (±1 degree—Figure 17-31A) prior to installation; the second is to terminate the shrouds at the spreader tip, fitting separate rods from the mast to the spreader tip, and from the spreader tip to the chainplate (*discontinuous rigging*), thus eliminating the bend altogether (Figure 17-31B). Spreader bends have been found to work well with rigid masts and spreaders, but they are not such a good choice with the fore-and-aft movement that occurs with bendy masts and flexible spreaders. In this case, discontinuous rigging is recommended. Due to its greater inherent reliability, *discontinuous rigging is recommended for any kind of a distance-cruising boat.*

Dealing with failures. Should repairs at sea or in some foreign port become necessary, a temporary length of wire rope can be used. To facilitate such a substitution, *cruising boats should terminate individual shrouds and stays at both ends with eye fittings.* A coil of wire rope, as long as the longest stay on the boat and with one eye already fastened, can then be cut to length; fitted with a Norseman, Sta-Lok, or Hi-Mod eye at the other end; and used to replace any suspect length of rod.

In the end the choice between rod and wire rigging boils down to a matter of cost versus performance. There is no question that rod is more expensive, quite a bit more so in many cases. However, rod rigging manufacturers claim that today's rod rigging will outlast a comparable wire rig. If you intend to keep your boat for many years, rod rigging may turn out to be the cheapest long-term option, with its performance benefits simply thrown in as an added bonus!

Fiber Rigging

Kevlar rigging is now commonplace on racing boats, and on some performance-oriented cruising catamarans. PBO rigging is also becoming more widespread on racing boats. At the time of writing, the first generation of carbon fiber standing rigging is being tested (under license to Southern Spars—www.southernspars.com). We can expect rapid development over the next few years, with some of this technology filtering down to performance-oriented cruising boats (in much the same way that rod rigging and carbon fiber spars have filtered down).

Fiber rigging raises different concerns than stainless rigging (for example, UV degradation of the fibers may be a major concern, and getting

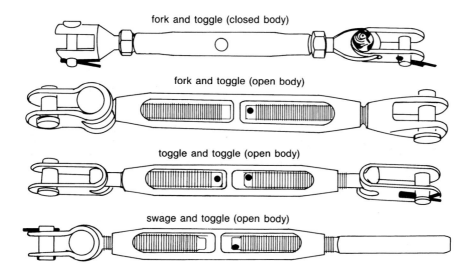

fork and toggle (closed body)

fork and toggle (open body)

toggle and toggle (open body)

swage and toggle (open body)

FIGURE 17-32.
Turnbuckles come with a variety of end fittings to tailor them to different situations aboard. *(Gibb)*

end fittings to adhere to the rig with adequate strength can be a problem), but in general the issues for cruisers are the usual ones of cost, longevity, the ability to detect impending failures, and the ease of replacement in the field. It will take time to see how fiber rigging pans out in the cruising world.

Fitting Rigging to a Boat

All boats use *chainplates* to fasten stays and shrouds to the boat (stays run in a fore-and-aft direction, shrouds run athwartships). Chainplates are generally nothing more than heavy metal straps fastened securely to the hull, or else a U-bolt, which goes through the deck and is fastened from below with either a substantial backing plate or some means of spreading the load to the hull, generally a *tie bar* of some sort. (Racing boats have carbon fiber chainplates bonded to the hull.) A chainplate has a hole in its top to take a clevis pin. Unfortunately there is no inter-

national standardization of pin sizes, which often makes the matching of chainplates, clevis pins, and end fittings a matter of trial and error.

Next come *turnbuckles* (rigging screws) to tension the rig (Figure 17-32). A turnbuckle is a hollow sleeve, threaded at both ends but with one thread being right-handed (normal) and the other left-handed (reverse thread). The right-handed thread should be uppermost. A threaded stud goes in each end—one right-handed, one left-handed. Turning the turnbuckle one way pulls both studs in, tightening the rig; turning it the other way pushes both studs out, loosening the rig.

Various means are used to make the connections from chainplates to turnbuckles, and from turnbuckles to wire rope or rod rigging terminals. The most common are solid toggles, strap toggles, forks, eyes, and straight-threaded terminals. However the connections are made, *the lower ends of all stays and shrouds must be free to flex in all directions* (Figure 17-33). This movement is generally provided by a strap toggle.

toggles allow flexing in either direction

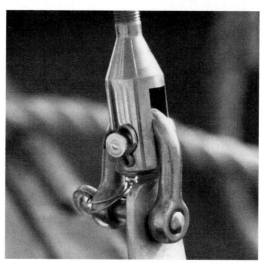

FIGURE 17-33. Stays are subject to considerable flexing and therefore must have toggles—top and bottom—to prevent early rigging failure. **Left:** Toggles allow flexing in either direction. **Right:** Using a shackle as a temporary toggle. The shackle pin has been lashed correctly with seizing wire.

FIGURE 17-34. The ball-and-socket shroud terminal, increasingly popular on aluminum masts, allows a certain amount of flexing in all directions. *(Gibb)*

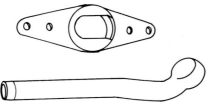

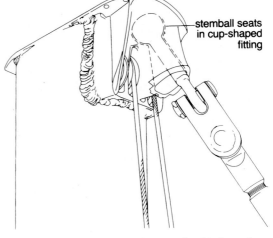

stemball seats in cup-shaped fitting

FIGURE 17-36. Stemball fittings, as fitted to Isomat spars, act much like a toggle. In this instance, the forestay is fully toggled below the stemball to absorb the stresses of a roller reefing rig. *(Jim Sollers)*

Where the upper ends of shrouds attach to a mast, the most common practice in the past was to terminate the wire rope with an eye fitting, which slips between two metal plates (tangs) fastened to the mast. A clevis pin passing through the tangs and the eye is secured with a *cotter pin* (split pin). This allows fore-and-aft flexing but no athwartships play.

A second method of attaching shrouds and stays, now popular, is to fasten a slotted ball socket inside the mast wall, into the base of spreaders and spreader bars, or in the masthead fitting (a *stemball* fitting—see below). The shroud is terminated in a T-terminal or ball (Figure 17-34). The curved face of the tee end or ball rests in the ball socket and is free to flex a limited amount in all directions. Note that this does not generally provide the same strain relief as a traditional toggle and eye fitting.

Stays, especially headstays, are subjected to considerable flexing in all directions and *must have a toggle at the head as well as the foot.* A typ-

ical arrangement is to run a clevis pin between two plates welded to the head box. A strap toggle is hung from the clevis pin (Figure 17-35). Where the head box has a single, central mounting plate, a slotted strap toggle fits up either side of the plate. Otherwise the installation is the same.

As noted, many newer spars have what is called a stemball fitting as the upper terminal on the stays and shrouds. Stemballs once again are free to flex a limited amount in all directions. When a stemball is used on a headstay, this flexing is adequate to handle the loads of a hanked-on sail, but may not be adequate to handle the additional flexing imposed by a roller reefing headsail. Where a roller reefer is fitted, the stemball may need adapting so that it is fully toggled (Figure 17-36).

If a backstay is used as an antenna (aerial) for an SSB (single-sideband) or ham radio, insulators are fitted at the top and bottom of the stay (though the bottom insulator may not be necessary—Chapter 8). For wire rope, these insulators come with both swaged and compression-type terminals. Many rigs also incorporate a backstay tension adjuster, which may be an arrangement of blocks with a tackle, an oversize turnbuckle with handles attached to the barrel, or a hydraulically operated cylinder.

Inspection and Maintenance

Wire rope. *Rigging is designed for direct in-line loading only. Any flexing fatigues the wire rope.* Without toggles, the stress is concentrated at the exit points from the wire rope terminals; with toggles, it is distributed through the cable as a whole. *The use of toggles is essential to reduce*

FIGURE 17-35. A typical arrangement of a masthead toggle. Note that the swaged eye terminal was run through the swaging machine at different angles. There is likely to be localized stress damage at this point.

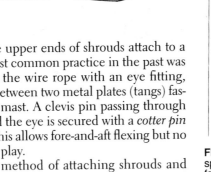

clevis pin

strap toggle

swaged eye terminal

marks from swaging machine

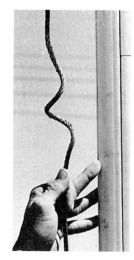

stress, but eventually the *fatigue cycles* will still build up to the point at which the rigging fails.

Given the inevitability of failure, when should properly installed and maintained rigging be routinely replaced? Norseman recommends replacement after any of the following: sailing around the world once, three heavy races such as the transatlantic or Round Britain, 5 to 8 years of seasonal ocean racing, 10 years around the buoys, and possibly 12 to 15 years of summer cruising. In the meantime, give rigging a close annual inspection for any of the following danger signs:

Stranded wire rope. Wire rope rarely breaks without some warning. Usually before total failure, one or two individual wires fracture and stick out, forming nasty *fishhooks*. The most likely places are where the rope enters terminal fittings (Figure 17-37). *There is no acceptable number of broken wires in a rope.* Even if only *one* has failed, the cable has been severely overstressed and needs immediate replacement.

Deformed wire rope. When a wire rope is dragged through too sharp a turn (e.g., undersized sheaves, spinnaker halyards dragging around masthead fairing pads, or roller reefing halyards wrapping around the forestay), the rope will be permanently deformed (it generally forms a spiral when not under tension). *It cannot be straightened again*, which would merely compound the problem by putting the rope through more severe stresses. It will fail sooner rather than later and needs replacing.

Stress points on hardware. Pay attention to the following:

1. Chainplates must be lined up exactly with the shroud or stay that they support.

2. If tangs or chainplates incorporate any bends or welds (most do), the bends and welds are the most likely points of failure (Figure 17-38). At the first sign of cracks or pinholes, replace them. A magnifying glass helps in inspection, but better yet is periodic use of one of the proprietary crack-detection sets on the market (e.g., Spotcheck, Magnaflux—www.magnaflux.com). You can also detect cracks by scrubbing a fitting with an iodine solution and bronze wool.

3. Stainless steel attachment bolts on external chainplates and the through-deck bolts on U-bolt chainplates will eventually succumb

FIGURE 17-37. Left: Stranded wire rope. **Middle:** Fractured strands sticking out. Remember: "There is no acceptable number of broken wires in a rope." **Right:** This deformed wire rope is the result of halyard wrap on a roller reefing unit (see later in this chapter).

TABLE 17-3. Rigging Checklist

Part or Aspect	Procedure
Cable terminals	Check all clevis pins, toggles, forks, and eyes for elongation, wear, and spreading of toggles or forks.
Cable clamps	Make sure cables are wrapped tightly around thimbles. Check thimbles for distortion. Make sure that clamps are tight.
Swages	Discard any banana-shaped swages and swages with signs of cracking or repeated rolling.
Turnbuckles	Undo all turnbuckles; clean, regrease, and reinstall.
Ball-and-socket terminals	Check the socket and mast for any signs of deformation.
Shroud tangs	Remove the mounting bolt and check for crevice corrosion.
Alignment	Check all chainplates and rigging terminals for alignment. Pay particular attention to the correct placement of toggles and to even loading on fork terminals.

FIGURE 17-38. Stress points on hardware.

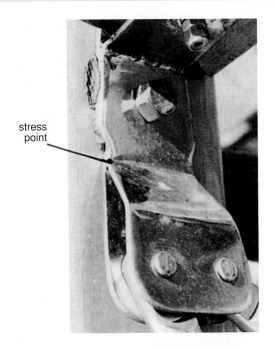

stress point

chain plate   stress point

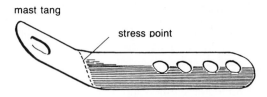

mast tang   stress point

FIGURE 17-39. Even professionally done swages are hard to check for hidden flaws. Corrosion in the socket is a particular problem. The swages on the left are banana shaped as well as cracked.

note the crack

a second crack is just developing at this point

to crevice corrosion. These should be withdrawn and inspected every few years, especially if there is *any* sign of moisture ingress via the fastener.

4. Swages are especially prone to cracking down the body of the swage (Figure 17-39). Ideally, they should be crack-tested every year or two (see above). No cracks are acceptable! If a swage is at all curved (banana shaped), it also needs replacing—it has been improperly swaged and may fail without warning.

5. T-terminals on shrouds will develop small cracks on the inside of the radius as they fatigue. The mast-reinforcement plates may develop elongated slots or loose rivets, or distort the mast wall.

6. Thimbles will start to collapse (elongate), work loose in their cable eyes, and wear through at the point of pressure on the thimble. Cable clamps need retightening periodically.

7. If any fork terminal is unevenly stressed, sooner or later the loaded side is likely to crack and break off (Figure 17-40). Eye terminals are inherently stronger and alignment is not so critical.

8. Turnbuckles of *all*-stainless-steel construction have a bad habit of *galling*, a process of cold-welding that destroys the threads and makes it impossible to screw or unscrew them. *The cause is almost always dirt in the threads.* If at any time a turnbuckle (or any other threaded fitting, for that matter) becomes hard to turn,

FIGURE 17-40. Broken fork terminal (left) and cracked turnbuckle (right).

don't force it. Spray it with penetrating fluid, give the threads time to cool down (a surprising amount of heat is generated), screw it back the other way, lubricate again, and then keep working it backward and forward, and hope it frees up. Bronze turnbuckles, and stainless turnbuckles with bronze thread inserts or bronze studs, are far less prone to galling than all-stainless-steel ones.

9. Every clevis pin should be withdrawn annually and inspected for wear on the pin itself, elongation of the holes, and/or cracks around the holes through which it passes. Stainless steel will tolerate a certain amount of elongation without serious loss of strength, but *aluminum will not.* If the mounting holes in aluminum brackets are stretching, the bracket is being overloaded and failure is not far off.

10. Clevis pins, eyes, and strap toggles must be closely matched with only small clearances. Overly long clevis pins will allow toggles to spread and the pins to bend; oversized eyes will allow the clevis pin to bend. In both cases, the pin is likely to fail (Figure 17-41).

11. Cotter pins (split pins) need to be opened out 20 to 30 degrees and should be taped to avoid snagging sheets and other lines.

12. Many shroud tangs (and some other items of hardware) are held with a bolt through the mast. These bolts can suffer from hidden crevice corrosion and should be withdrawn and inspected periodically. When replacing, be sure to securely lock the retaining nut either with a cotter pin or by peening over the threads on the end of the bolt. If a Nylok nut is used—one with a nylon insert that stops it from working loose—replace the nut.

Corrosion. Stainless steel is corrosion resistant as long as it has a free flow of air (oxygen) over its surface. Remove this oxygen, add a little stagnant water, and it can corrode quite rapidly (Chapter 5). *These are exactly the conditions found in many lower wire terminals and closed-body turnbuckles, around some clevis pins* (particularly those passing through wooden spread-

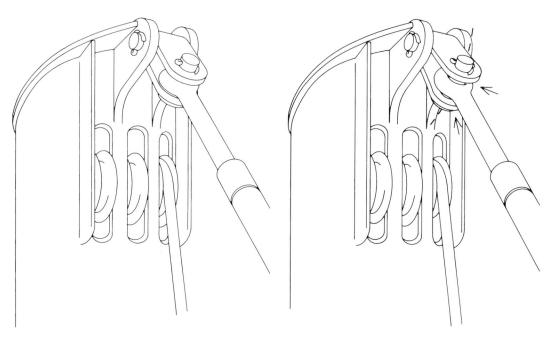

FIGURE 17-41. To prevent clevis pin failure, ensure that the strap toggles match their eye fittings. The clevis pin on the left fits correctly; the one on the right has excessive clearance and will bind and ultimately fail under load. *(Jim Sollers)*

FIGURES 17-42A TO 17-42D. Anatomy of a rigging failure. The below-deck backing plate and tie-rod arrangement for a U-bolt chainplate (17-42A). Note that although the hardware looks perfectly clean, the locknuts are barely engaging the threads of the U-bolt. During the 10-year working life of this rig, water has found its way down the U-bolts into the main retaining nuts (17-42B). Unseen crevice corrosion has weakened the nuts to the point that some have cracked. In 15 knots of wind, and 3- to 4-foot swells, the main retaining nuts on a shroud chainplate broke up. The chainplate jerked up a half inch. The sudden shock load on the barely engaged locknuts stripped the threads off the chainplate U-bolt, allowing it to pull out of the deck (17-42C). With the loss of the shroud, the load transferred to the cap shroud. The retaining nuts burst on its chainplate, and the rig went over the side. The rig had to be cut loose and sank in 8,000 feet of water. It took a year and over $20,000 to replace it. Here's another fine mess (17-42D)! The stainless steel shackle has caused extensive galvanic corrosion of the iron centerboard; the shackle pin and shackle plate are both deformed with the pin about to pull out of the cheek plate; the thimble is deformed; and the wire rope is seriously abraded. The centerboard could let go at any time.

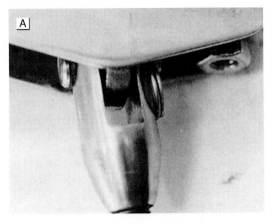

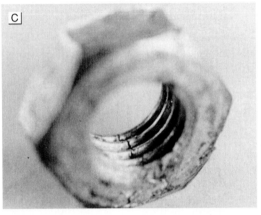

ers) *and chainplate attachment bolts,* and also where inboard chainplates pass through a deck. Crevice and pinhole corrosion in these fittings is often virtually undetectable and can lead to a serious rigging failure without warning (Figures 17-42A to 17-42D).

Wherever possible all lower terminals should be filled with something to keep water out. Sta-Loks and Norsemans are made up with a sealant; Castloks are automatically filled with glue. Swages present a special problem and are notorious for sudden failure in the tropics. When terminals are new, and before their first soaking in salt water, lower swage terminals can be heated *gently* until beeswax or anhydrous lanolin flows down into the lay of the cable to fill any air spaces.

Once a year inspect all turnbuckles and any other fittings with threaded studs: Remove any rigging tape, completely undo them, and check the body and threads for corrosion. After a thorough cleaning, grease lightly or coat with a corrosion inhibitor before reassembly. Every few years, withdraw and inspect any chainplate or chainplate fastener that may have gotten damp.

Annual maintenance. In addition to the above recommendations, wash all dirt and salt from the rigging before a winter layup. Remove boots or tapes on spreader tips for cleaning and inspection. If you leave the rigging attached to aluminum spars, make sure the stainless wire is not resting on the aluminum; corrosion will be the likely result.

A review of insurance claims shows that most mast failures at sea occur in relatively benign conditions not gales, and that in almost all instances there were telltale warning signs of impending failure (e.g., signs of corrosion around rigging terminals) that the owners ignored. A thorough annual rig inspection will go a long way toward preventing unpleasant surprises.

Tuning a Rig

Regardless of sea states and weather conditions, for a boat to be sailed to best effect, its rig must be properly tuned. The prerequisite for tuning a rig on a sailboat is a solid platform for the rig—i.e., a well-built and properly engineered boat. Without this, all efforts are doomed to failure. Given such a platform, basic rig tuning is a straightforward business that just about any owner can undertake. (I'm not talking about fancy racing rigs here, but typical cruising rigs.)

The idea is to keep the mast centered in the boat, vertical (except for maybe a degree or two of rake aft), and supported in such a way that the head doesn't flop off to leeward when the boat is hard pressed and the mast doesn't buckle out of column. (For a more detailed look at tuning a rig, go to www.seldenmast.com, click on "Manuals," then select "Hints and advice" under "General information.")

Preparatory measurements. Getting the masthead centered in the boat is the first order of business. If starting from scratch with an unknown boat, measure the mast step (on a deck-stepped mast) or the aperture in the deck (keel-stepped mast) to be sure it is centered athwartship in the boat (this is by no means guaranteed). Then check the shroud chainplates to make sure that counterposed port and starboard plates are equidistant from the mast, equidistant from the bow of the boat, and protruding the same distance above the deck (once again, by no means guaranteed). Next, measure the cap shrouds to ensure they are exactly equal in length (this step assumes the mast is off the boat; if not, see below).

If the shrouds are not the same length, before stepping the mast, adjust the rigging screws so as to produce shrouds of equal length; make the same adjustments with any other shrouds and also with the backstays if the boat has twin backstays (in which case, also check the backstay chainplates for equidistant placement from the mast).

Static tuning—masthead rig. Most cruising boats have masthead rigs—the forestay comes to the top of the mast—as opposed to a fractional rig, on which the forestay is attached below the masthead (for tuning a fractional rig, see below). Given a masthead rig, after the mast is stepped, loosely tension it (by hand) using the forestay, the backstay(s), and the cap shrouds. If the shrouds have been equalized in length, as described above, as long as the same number of turns, in the same direction, are made to the rigging screws on the cap shrouds (and the backstays, if twin backstays are used), simple geometry tells us the masthead will be centered athwartships above the mast step (Figure 17-43).

If it has not been possible to check the shroud lengths with the mast off the boat, or there is some disparity in chainplate placement, in the past I recommended using a halyard to check the athwartship centering of the mast. The halyard is cleated off so that it just touches the cap rail at right angles to the base of the mast on one side of the boat. It is then taken across the boat

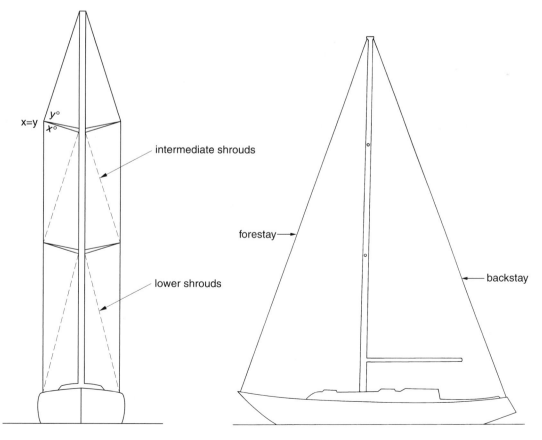

$x = y$

$y°$

$x°$

intermediate shrouds

lower shrouds

forestay

backstay

FIGURE 17-43. Static rig tensioning. **Left:** Center the mast athwartships with the cap (upper) shrouds set up tight. **Right:** Set the *rake* with the forestays and backstay(s) set up tight. Pull the mast into a straight column athwartships using first the intermediate, then the lower shrouds. Use little more than hand tension. *(Jim Sollers)*

FIGURE 17-44A. A common sight. The angle made by the shrouds with these spreaders is not equal on the top and bottom sides of the spreaders (the spreader tips are too low). Under load, the spreader tips will want to slide down the shrouds, potentially bringing the mast down.

to the other cap rail, which it should also just touch (this requires a halyard that comes off a sheave that is centered in the masthead). However, I've come to the conclusion that even a shift of several inches at the masthead produces a minimal change in halyard length, which would be hard to distinguish from stretch. I think I do better by simply maneuvering the boat into a position where I can eyeball the athwartship mast trim from the dock. If the boat is trimmed so that it is level in the water (the finicky can use a spirit level on the cabin sole), it is normally possible to detect even small mast deviations from the vertical.

While eyeballing the athwartship trim, also inspect the cap shrouds to make sure that where they pass over the (upper) spreaders, the angle the shrouds make with the spreaders is the same on the top and bottom sides of the spreader. This rule is frequently violated. A spreader is designed to take a compression load (straight into the mast). The more the top and bottom shroud angles differ, the greater the bending moment on the spreader, and the more likely it is to fail (either by buckling or as a result of its tip sliding up or down the shroud—Figure 17-44A). With continuous rigging, there needs to be some means of locking a spreader tip in place (it may have to be lashed); with discontinuous rigging, the rigging itself holds it in place (Figure 17-44B).

With the masthead centered athwartships, lightly tension the rest of the shrouds, eyeballing the mast to make sure that it is not pulled out of column. You can accurately double-check this by sighting up the mast track (with the mainsail slides removed)—any sideways curvature will be immediately apparent. If the boat has intermediate shrouds, once again it is important to ensure that the angles the shrouds make with their

spreader end cap for
continuous rigging

spreader end cap for
linked rigging

spreader end cap for rod
Tip Cup

FIGURE 17-44B. Spreader tip arrangements. **Top:** A mechanism for locking continuous wire rigging in place. **Middle:** Discontinuous wire rigging using swaged terminals. **Bottom:** Discontinuous rod rigging with stemball fittings. *(Selden)*

spreaders are equal on the top and bottom sides of the spreaders.

Next maneuver the boat so that it is lying alongside the dock. Establish the fore-and-aft rake (if any) by tensioning the forestay and backstay(s) and eyeballing the rig from the dock. If the boat is leveled fore and aft in the water (use the waterline as a gauge or a spirit level on the cabin sole), a weight hung from the mainsail halyard will act as a plumb bob for those who want accurate measurements. Rake should not exceed 1% of the mast height (e.g., 6 inches on a 50-foot mast).

Now you can tighten the forestay, backstay(s), and cap shrouds to close to their final tension. For most of us, this is a bit of a guessing game. You can buy various tension gauges, and look up in tables the breaking strain of different cable sizes, and do all of this scientifically. But I have to confess that I generally just tweak the cables to see that they are taut, and that they all flex about the same amount under the same kind of tweaking load.

Scientific rig tension. A more scientific approach to tensioning rigging is to measure exactly 2 meters up from the top of the turnbuckle (rigging screw) after a shroud or stay has first been tensioned by hand and put a piece of tape around the wire at this point. Better yet, open a folding rule to 2 meters (or cut a length of wood to precisely 2 meters), place one end against the top of the turnbuckle, and tape the other end to the shroud or stay. Measure the gap that forms between its base and the turnbuckle as the rig is tensioned (Figure 17-45).

Stainless steel wire rope will stretch approximately 1 mm over a 2-meter length when loaded to 5% of its breaking strength. Given that it is desirable to preload cap shrouds by 15% to 25% of their breaking strength, they should be tightened until each cable has stretched by 3 to 5 mm over the measured 2-meter length. If you count how many turns it takes to achieve 15% stretch, and then divide this by 3, you have what it takes for a 5% stretch, which is useful to know if you ever want to tighten another 5%. The forestay and backstay are given more tension (±25% of breaking strength).

For shrouds, tape the rule or piece of wood to one shroud, tension this until a 1.5 to 2.5 mm gap develops, then tension the opposite shroud by the same amount. There is no need to move the rule or piece of wood, and you can continue to measure the widening gap on the first shroud, *because tensioning one shroud affects its opposite one to the same extent. With a masthead rig, the gap can be measured at the backstay with the proviso that because the backstay makes a wider angle with the masthead, increasing its tension*

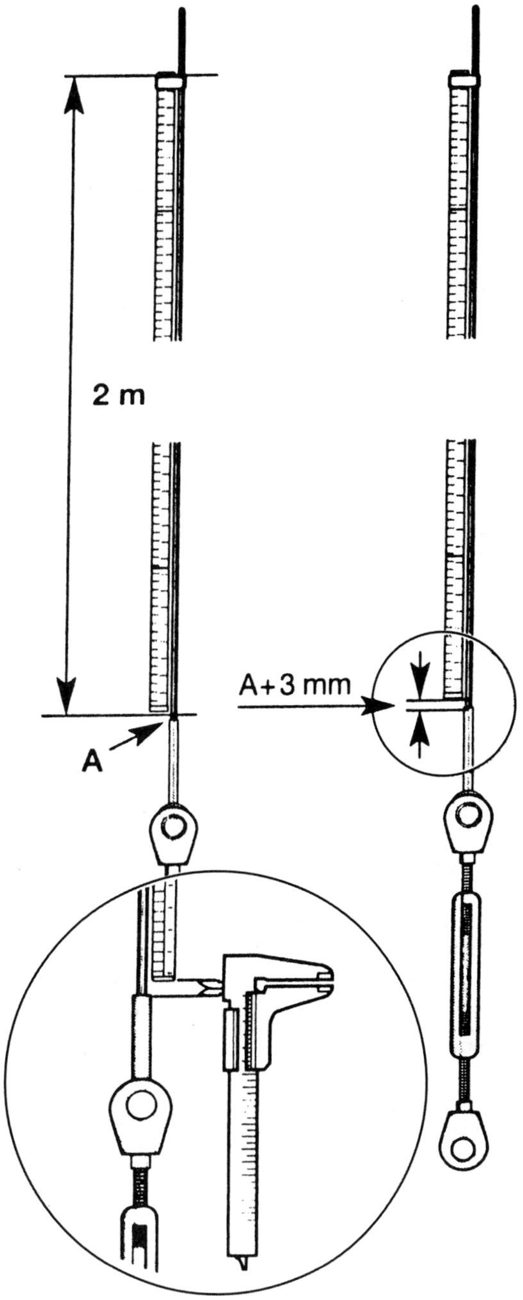

FIGURE 17-45. A moderately scientific way to measure the tension in standing rigging. Once a rig is hand-tightened, a stretch of 3 mm over 2 meters represents a tension of approximately 15% of its breaking strength, with each additional millimeter of stretch representing another 5% tension. *(Selden)*

2 m

A+3 mm

A

Hint! Count how many turns on the rigging screw corresponds to 1 mm elongation (5% of the breaking load). Make a note of it. This is useful to know if you ever need to tension "another 5%."

has a disproportionate effect on the forestay—a backstay tensioned to 20% of its breaking strength will tension the forestay to between 25% and 30% of its breaking strength (assuming they use the same-sized wire).

If the boat has an inner forestay, it is generally desirable to induce a small bend aft in the head of the mast. This is done primarily by tightening the inner forestay and the backstay(s). You can eyeball the degree of bend from dockside or sight up the side of the mast. Finally, tighten the lower (and intermediate, if fitted) shrouds, making equal adjustments to counterposed shrouds, and sight up the mast track after each pair of adjustments to see that the mast is still in column. Do not tension intermediate shrouds quite as much as cap shrouds; tension lower shrouds about the same as cap shrouds.

Use the same approach with Dyform and rod rigging, except that the stretch over 2 meters per 5% of rig tension is 0.95 mm for Dyform and 0.7 mm for rod.

Static tuning—fractional rig. A fractional rig is treated a little differently than a masthead rig. On most, the spreaders are swept back, bringing the cap shrouds aft of the mast. The cap shrouds provide most of the forestay tension (rather than the backstay). At the same time, pre-bend is forced into the mast by tightening the cap shrouds until the mast bends forward in the middle. The lower shrouds are used to control the amount of pre-bend. When sailing, the backstay is used to control the mainsail shape with additional mast bend.

Set up the rig by tightening the cap shrouds and forestay at the same time, generally to higher loadings than are used on a masthead rig. Then tension the intermediate shrouds (if present) and the lower shrouds to keep the mast centered athwartships and to control the mast bend. Finally tension the backstay.

The high rig loads will cause some initial deformation on all fiberglass hulls (after which

the hull should stabilize). It is important to check the tension under sail (see below), making sure the leeward shroud is never loose, and to periodically recheck the tension.

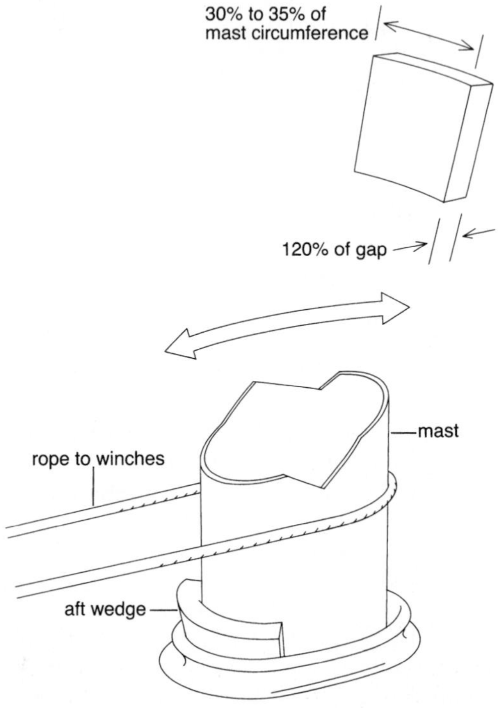

B & R rig. The B & R rig is increasingly popular because it dispenses with both running backstays and the backstay. This is achieved by angling the spreaders well aft (around 30 degrees) and installing discontinuous reverse diagonals (they run from the spreader tips downward to the mast) between the mast and the spreaders. These are used to induce pre-bend into the rig, stiffening the mast sections.

Before installing the mast, lay it on trestles with the sail track facing down. Tighten the reverse diagonals until the mast curves forward uniformly. Then install it in the boat and tension the rig in a similar fashion to a fractional rig.

Mast chocking. With keel-stepped masts, install wedges (chocking) at the partners (the reinforcement around the hole in the deck). You can use wood on wood spars, but always use hard rubber on aluminum—one pad in front and one to the rear. The total thickness of the pads should be 120% to 125% of the total gap between the mast and partners. The total length of the pads should add up to 30% to 40% of the total circumference of the mast. Do not place pads at the mast sides. The pads will be easier to slip in if soaked in dishwashing liquid. If you put the aft ones in place first, you can run a line from a cockpit winch around the front of the mast and back to another winch (Figure 17-46). Cranking in the line will pull the mast aft, compressing the aft wedges and allowing the forward ones to be slipped in. (The latest Selden mast rings incorporate tapered pads that are exceptionally easy to install.)

An alternative to chocking is Spartite (www.spartite.com, and similar products), a two-part solution that sets to a hard, rubber-like consistency. After completing the static tuning at dockside, seal the mast aperture from below, grease the aperture with Vaseline (so the Spartite will not adhere to it), then pour in the solution. It forms a near-watertight seal. Any time the mast is removed, the ring of Spartite comes out with it.

At sea—dynamic tuning. To test a rig tune, take the boat out in a stiff breeze (Force 4 to 5—10 to 20 knots), and put it hard on the wind on both tacks (Figure 17-47). At about a 20-degree angle of heel, the lee shrouds on a masthead rig should lose tension but should not be slack; on a fractional rig, the shrouds should never go loose. If the shrouds are loose, take up the slack on the rigging screws, adjusting coun-

FIGURE 17-46. For keel-stepped masts, set the fore-and-aft wedges in place. Compress the first pad by running a line passed around the mast to the sheet winches, then slip in the second pad. *(Jim Sollers)*

30% to 35% of mast circumference

120% of gap

mast

rope to winches

aft wedge

FIGURE 17-47. Testing the leeward shrouds for tension when close hauled in 10 knots of wind.

terposed (port and starboard) shrouds equally, until the slackness is gone. (Note: Only tighten a rigging screw when it is on the leeward side; attempting to adjust it under tension may cause it to seize up.)

Sighting up the mast track will show if the mast is remaining in column (Figure 17-48). The masthead will, in fact, probably sag off slightly to leeward. If this sag looks excessive, tighten the cap shrouds a little (tighten port and starboard shrouds equally). If the masthead is centered in the boat, but the mast is out of column (i.e., the center section curves to windward or leeward), you can pull it back into column using the intermediate (if fitted) and lower shrouds. However, if the dockside work was done correctly, this should not be necessary.

Sighting up the mast from the side will show if it is bending aft or forward, or not at all. Under sailing loads, the headstay tension will likely take out most of any aft bend induced in the head of the mast by the static tuning, but the mast should *never* be curving forward. If it is, the backstay(s) needs tightening.

At this point the rig will be adequately tensioned for cruising purposes. It should, of course, be rechecked at regular intervals, especially if the rig is new (wire rope stretches somewhat when first put in service, and fiberglass hulls deform to some extent but should then stabilize). If a rig will not hold its tension in stronger winds, but it regains tension when the load is taken off, most likely the hull is flexing; nothing can be done to the rig that will resolve this problem. Even worse, if the rig repeatedly slackens up and no amount of adjustment of the rigging screws will restore tension for long, the hull is likely continuously deforming. In either case, it is time to call in the professionals.

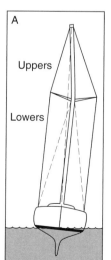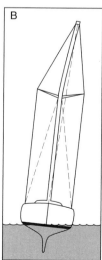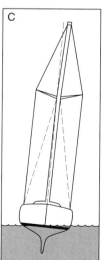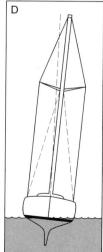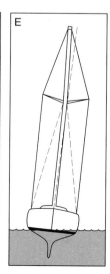

A | B | C | D | E

Uppers

Lowers

FIGURE 17-48. Tuning under sail. The windward lower shrouds on the rig at (A) are too loose. The masthead is correctly positioned, but the spreaders are out of column. The rig at (B) has its windward lowers too tight. The masthead is correctly positioned, but the spreaders are out of column. The rig at (C) has its upper shrouds too slack. The spreaders are in column, but the masthead is sagging off. The rig at (D) has both its uppers and lowers too slack, and the mast is sagging off along its entire length. The rig at (E) has its uppers too tight, and the masthead is dragged up to windward.

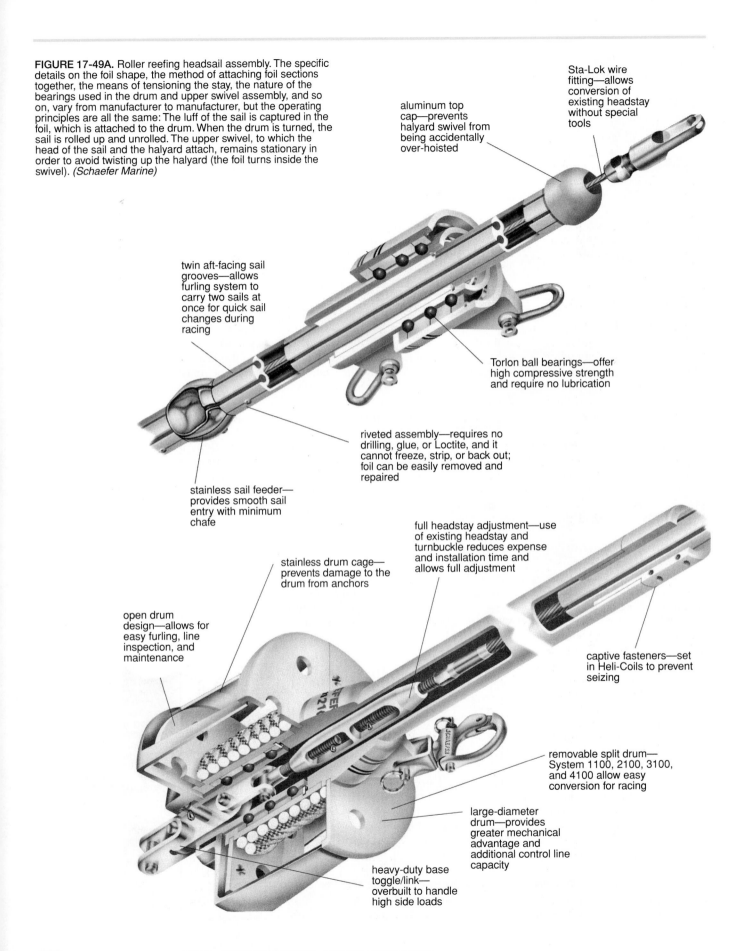

FIGURE 17-49A. Roller reefing headsail assembly. The specific details on the foil shape, the method of attaching foil sections together, the means of tensioning the stay, the nature of the bearings used in the drum and upper swivel assembly, and so on, vary from manufacturer to manufacturer, but the operating principles are all the same: The luff of the sail is captured in the foil, which is attached to the stay. When the drum is turned, the sail is rolled up and unrolled. The upper swivel, to which the head of the sail and the halyard attach, remains stationary in order to avoid twisting up the halyard (the foil turns inside the swivel). *(Schaefer Marine)*

aluminum top cap—prevents halyard swivel from being accidentally over-hoisted

Sta-Lok wire fitting—allows conversion of existing headstay without special tools

twin aft-facing sail grooves—allows furling system to carry two sails at once for quick sail changes during racing

Torlon ball bearings—offer high compressive strength and require no lubrication

riveted assembly—requires no drilling, glue, or Loctite, and it cannot freeze, strip, or back out; foil can be easily removed and repaired

stainless sail feeder—provides smooth sail entry with minimum chafe

full headstay adjustment—use of existing headstay and turnbuckle reduces expense and installation time and allows full adjustment

captive fasteners—set in Heli-Coils to prevent seizing

stainless drum cage—prevents damage to the drum from anchors

open drum design—allows for easy furling, line inspection, and maintenance

removable split drum—System 1100, 2100, 3100, and 4100 allow easy conversion for racing

large-diameter drum—provides greater mechanical advantage and additional control line capacity

heavy-duty base toggle/link—overbuilt to handle high side loads

Roller Reefing and Furling

Roller reefing and furling are now in near-universal use on headsails and on many mainsails (either in-mast furling, or else in-boom furling). Roller reefers can, as implied by their name, be used with the sail partially reefed. Roller furlers, which have become increasingly popular for lightweight headsails in recent years, can only be used with the sail fully unrolled. Both have been refined to the point that, *assuming proper installation*, they are not only reliable but also long lived.

Roller Reefing Headsails

A roller *reefing* headsail (as opposed to a roller *furler*—see below) employs a *foil*—an aluminum or plastic extrusion into which the luff tape of a sail slides. This foil is fitted around the headstay. (On a few units, the foil *is* the headstay.) An upper swivel fits around the foil and attaches to the halyard and the head of the sail; a lower drum grips the foil (Figures 17-49A and 17-49B). When the drum is turned, the foil rotates and wraps the sail around itself. Since the foil is rigid and grips the sail along its whole length (more or less), the sail is rolled up evenly (there is no twist between the tack and the head). For this reason, these rigs can be used for reefing (whereas a roller furler cannot).

The principal disadvantage of a roller reefer is that it is incorporated in the standing rigging. Failure can, in certain instances, lead to the loss of the headstay and so jeopardize the mast. Aside from this, the roller reefer cannot be put up and taken down without disconnecting the headstay. This means that many problems (for example, with a foil section) are just about irreparable at sea and may render the headsail unusable. Unless an auxiliary headstay is fitted (few are) and standby hanked-on headsails kept on board (this too is rare), the boat is left without its principal sail.

A secondary problem is the difficulty of making sail changes—for example, shortening sail in a blow. A conventional sail can be dropped and gasketed (tied off to make it manageable) and then unhanked. A roller reefer has to be pulled out of its luff groove in the foil. In order to do this, the whole sail must be unfurled and the sheets eased. In any kind of a wind, the sail left in the foil will be flogging around while the loose sail will be billowing up on the foredeck and trying to take off.

Taking down roller reefing headsails can be tough—but setting the new sail is even worse. It has to be fed into the luff groove just right and

FIGURE 17-49B. Another view of the drum unit in Figure 17-49A. *(Schaefer Marine)*

eased on up with the halyard. The portion of sail set will be banging around; the sail still to be set will be billowing all over the deck. No matter what claims are made for various *prefeeders*, headsail changes on roller reefers are no fun, especially for the shorthanded!

In practice, the majority of cruising sailors use a single headsail on a roller reefer (generally a genoa) and never change it. This means the sail has to be overbuilt for light weather to stand the stresses of being reefed down in heavier air, and most likely it will not be optimized for any condition. This is the price that has to be paid for the convenience of roller reefing.

FIGURE 17-50A. These
roller reefing installations
are likely to cause trouble.
The arrangement at left
only allows sideways
flexing, that at right only
fore-and-aft flexing. Both
could result in a failure of
the forestay and loss of the
mast.

 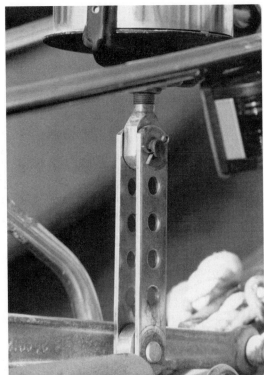

Headstay failure. Although headstay failure
in general is not common, it is more common
on rigs with roller reefers than without. Since it
is potentially so catastrophic, it deserves special
attention.

A hanked-on headsail has its tack attached at
the deck. A roller reefed sail is tacked to the top
of the furling drum. With a hanked-on sail, sideways loading (which generates headsail sag) is
spread uniformly from the tack up through the
stay; on a roller reefer there is a concentration of
stress at the drum. *Whatever method is used to
mount the drum, it must be properly toggled to
relieve this stress.* Many are not. If the drum is fastened to the stemhead with metal straps, a toggle
needs to be placed between the straps and the
stemhead (Figure 17-50A).

Many roller reefing drums are fastened to a
turnbuckle (rigging screw) rather than the stemhead (Figure 17-50B). In this case, a specially
designed turnbuckle with a beefed-up lower stud
is needed to carry the extra side loading.

Fastening the drum to a turnbuckle (rather
than to the stemhead) has a couple of potential
disadvantages. If the bearings become stiff, or
when reefing and unfurling under a load, the
sail can generate fairly high twisting (torsional)
loads on the turnbuckle. These can undo the
lower turnbuckle stud, or occasionally lead to a
complete failure of the lower portion of the turnbuckle or its mounting hardware. Alternatively,
the torsional stresses can *unlay the headstay,*

FIGURE 17-50B. A fully toggled roller reefing drum.

leading to wire fatigue and failure. This is very hard to detect since the stay is completely covered by drum and foil.

If the turnbuckle fails, since the drum is not independently fastened to the deck in any way, the whole headstay, foil, sail, and drum assembly will break loose and start flogging around. The masthead is left with no support, and the mast is in imminent danger of collapse. To get things back under control, the sail must be taken down; but to do this, it must be taken out of its groove; and to do this, *it must be completely unfurled*, compounding your problems!

A variation on this disaster sometimes occurs when a turnbuckle-mounted drum is raised off the deck with a distance piece of some sort. Such distance pieces must be designed to withstand high torsional loads—rod rigging and wire rope are out of the question. Heavy metal straps should be used and properly toggled.

Not only must a drum be properly mounted and toggled, it is also vital to *fully toggle the headstay at the masthead*. A hanked-on headsail is dropped when not in use; a roller reefing headsail stays on the headstay. The combined weight of the foil, sail, and swivels is considerable. Anytime the boat is pounding or rolling (e.g., motoring into a head sea), the whole shooting match flexes all over the place. (Try placing a hand well up any rolled-up sail to see just how much it can be bounced around, no matter how tightly the rig is set up.) The headstay is subjected to severe additional flexing on top of normal sideways loading. *Masthead toggles are essential* (see pages 755–56).

More and more boats have a stemball fitting on the forestay at the masthead (Figure 17-51). A *stemball will not provide adequate toggle action for a roller reefing headsail*. An adapter and toggle should be set in place as shown.

Bearings. Swivel and drum bearings have variously been made of carbon steel, stainless steel, plastic, or a combination of stainless steel and plastic. The multiplicity of bearing types is a reflection of the problems that have been experienced in the search for bearings that will hold up in roller reefing applications. Today most bearings are made of an ultra-high-strength plastic called Torlon, which seems to do extremely well, although some bearings (notably those in Profurl units—www.profurl.com) are still carbon steel.

Point loading. The loads on bearings can be high, especially if attempts are made to reef or furl a sail under tension using a cockpit winch on the reefing line (something that most manufacturers say should *not* be done, but which is done routinely by many sailors, often with

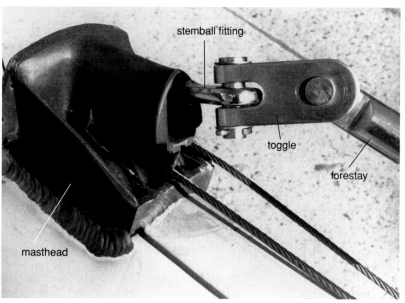

FIGURE 17-51. A stemball-mounted stay modified to include a toggle so as to absorb the flexing of a roller reefer.

FIGURE 17-52A. Off-center point loading places high demands on the bearings of roller reefing systems. (*Jim Sollers*)

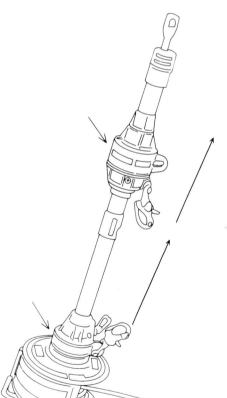

destructive results). These loads are not spread uniformly around a bearing since the tack and head of the sail, as well as the halyard, must all be attached off-center to clear the foil and headstay (Figure 17-52A). This generates *point loading*—pressure concentrated on only a small area

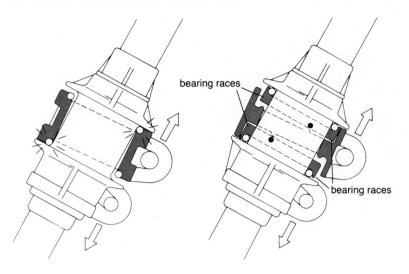

bearing races

bearing races

FIGURE 17-52B. The Furlex lash compensator is a means of solving the problem in Figure 17-52A. The off-center load gets concentrated at the two points marked. The lash compensator spreads these loads over the bearing races as a whole. (*Jim Sollers*)

of the bearings and bearing housings (races)—which tends to jam bearings. (This problem does not arise with roller furling rigs—see below—since there is no foil or headstay to contend with and all attachments are made to the center of the various swivels.)

Selden's Furlex system solves some of these problems by incorporating a patented *lash compensator* in the swivels. The lash compensator cancels out the off-center pull of the sail and halyard and reduces point loading (Figure 17-52B). Other manufacturers spread the bearings, which has the effect of spreading the load.

Bearing materials. Carbon steel bearings are the hardest and will therefore consistently withstand abuse and unfair point loading better than stainless steel and plastic. But any kind of steel, of course, is terribly susceptible to rust in a salt atmosphere. Carbon steel bearings (earlier Schaefer roller furling rigs, Profurl) must be greased for life (special greases are used) and *sealed*. The bearing seal is probably the most important part of the unit over the long run!

Because of problems with grease seals, most roller reefers used stainless steel bearings for a time. Stainless steel bearings have balls made of 316 stainless steel running in races of 304. In the presence of salt, corrosion between the two can occur. Even more likely is a galvanic interaction where the stainless races fit into their aluminum housings.

The bearings are almost always open so that they can periodically be flushed clean with fresh water. But very few owners flush the bearings more than once a season, and certainly few cruising sailors are going to pour a bucket of precious fresh water down the roller reefer after every sail! So inevitably, salt and dirt accumulate in the majority of units.

Another problem with these open stainless steel bearings is that stainless steel is hard, but

not that hard. If the rig is left heavily loaded in one position for long periods of time, the balls can deform and the races can indent, especially if corrosion occurs at the point of contact between the balls and the races. The bearing begins to run roughly, friction builds up, and all kinds of other problems develop, with the most extreme cases leading to *galling*, also called *cold-welding*—a process in which molecules on the surface of one part transfer to the surface of the other, rendering the bearing useless.

By alternating stainless and plastic ball bearings (the races are still stainless) the chances of galling can be significantly reduced, though not eliminated, and friction is lessened. Hood (www.pompanette.com/hood) and Plastimo (www.plastimo.com), among others, have used this approach. However, the plastic, being softer, carries very little of the bearing load, thus effectively reducing the load-bearing portion of the bearings.

Today, *all*-plastic (Torlon) balls are more commonly used, notably by Harken (www. harken. com) and Schaefer (www.schaefermarine.com). The balls run in an inner race of nickel-plated silicon bronze and an outer race of specially coated and hardened aluminum. To compensate for the loss of hardness, the bearings are increased in size and number and are carefully engineered to spread the loads; otherwise ball deformation is inevitable.

Friction. Once friction begins to develop in any bearing, the drum-mounting shaft and the halyard swivel tend to turn with the foil during furling and unfurling operations, exerting torsional stresses on the drum-mounting hardware and pulling the halyard around the forestay. (Halyard wrap is probably *the* most common problem with roller reefers and is dealt with in the Halyard Wrap section below.) The greater the bearing friction, the more the torsional stresses. Sooner or later something will give—the drum mount or turnbuckle, the halyard, or the stay.

Because of potential bearing problems, almost all manufacturers recommend slacking the halyard before reefing or unfurling, as well as easing the sheets and allowing the sail to luff, though not to flog. These measures lessen friction and point loading on the bearings. However, many halyard winches and halyard cleats are mounted on the mainmast. One of the principal reasons for having a roller reefer in the first place is to avoid having to go forward when the wind begins to pipe up and it is time to shorten sail. In practice, very few sailors slacken the halyard from one month to the next, let alone every time they use the reefing gear. (Note that if a backstay is tensioned *after* the halyard has been tensioned, as the masthead moves aft the halyard is tensioned further, frequently putting excessive loads on roller reefing bearings. First tension a backstay; only then, tension a halyard.)

Regardless of your normal operating practices, never force a roller reefer if it is becoming hard to operate. The use of cockpit winches, and worse still, powered winches (since these give no feel for what is going on), is a strict no-no! Go forward and find out what the problem is before something expensive gets broken.

Extrusions and extrusion bearings. The aluminum extrusions used for foils vary greatly in strength, shape, and the means used to join individual sections together. All are critical to a smoothly operating, long-lived roller reefer.

Since the reefing drum turns only the lower end of an extrusion, if a sail is rolled up under a load, the extrusion is subjected to strong torsional (twisting) forces. *Many lightweight extrusions cannot handle these stresses*—the extrusion buckles and/or the joints deform.

Foil extrusions come in numerous shapes (Figure 17-53). A round extrusion requires a uniform pressure to furl or unfurl the sail even when the sail is loaded and the extrusion sags off to leeward. It will turn smoothly and wrap tightly. In contrast, oval-shaped extrusions may work well at

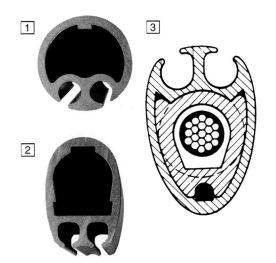

FIGURE 17-53. Roller reefing extrusions. A round extrusion turns smoothly and wraps tightly but creates more windage (1). A more streamlined extrusion with twin luff grooves (2). A streamlined oval extrusion with twin luff grooves—preferred for racing (3). *(Profurl)*

the dock, but under a load and the inevitable headstay sag, they tend to rotate unevenly and jerkily, increasing stresses on the extrusion and its joints. Inadequate headstay tension will exacerbate this situation.

Most joints are made with extruded sections *(splice pieces, sleeves)*, which make a close fit inside the sections of foil being connected (Figure 17-54). Inside the splice, a plastic bearing is fitted around the headstay. This centers the foil

FIGURE 17-54. Extrusion joints. *(Profurl)*

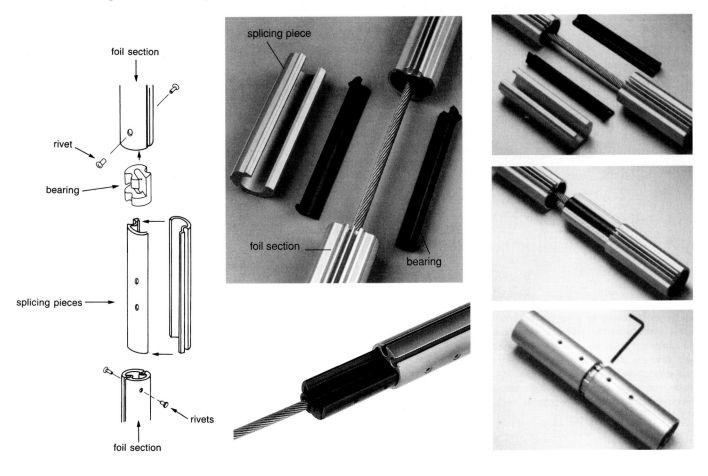

on the headstay and reduces friction during furling and unfurling operations.

The foil sections and splice pieces are variously held together with pins, setscrews, spring-loaded buttons, pieces of wire, silicone caulking, and glue. In time, torsional stresses loosen all but the best joints. Loose joints lead to luff groove misalignment, and then the sail starts to hang up in the joints when being raised or lowered. Luff tapes jam, making it impossible to take sails up and down, and sails get torn. There is normally no solution to this problem short of new foils and connections.

One or two units incorporate full-length PVC inserts around the headstay, which act as a bearing and keep the stainless steel stay insulated from the aluminum foil. However, other manufacturers claim that when the headstay and foil sag under a load, this setup increases friction unacceptably. In any event, PVC absorbs chlorine, which attacks stainless steel.

Instead of a full-length headstay liner, most units have bearing inserts that are placed around the headstay at each joint in the foil. The idea is to use only as many inserts as are strictly necessary to keep the foil centered on the headstay (and out of contact with the stay itself), even under conditions of maximum headstay and foil sag. This reduces friction to a minimum while keeping the foil and the stay apart.

Halyard wrap. Halyard wrap occurs when the upper half of the halyard swivel turns with the lower half, wrapping the halyard around the forestay. Wire halyards become permanently deformed, and rope halyards can be seriously abraded and weakened. The foil may be damaged if the swivel is too low (see following paragraphs). If excessive pressure is applied (e.g., winching in the reefing line), the halyard will part (Figure 17-55), or the headstay or its end terminal and hardware may be damaged, endangering the mast.

By far the most common cause of halyard wrap is improper installation in the first place, even by factory-authorized rigging lofts. There are three common, and interrelated, faults:

1. The angle the halyard makes with the headstay is too small.
2. The swivel is too low.
3. The swivel is too high.

Halyard angle. When a sail is hoisted, the halyard should angle away from the headstay by 10 to 30 degrees (Figure 17-56A, top). If the halyard runs parallel to—or worse still, angles into—the headstay, there is very little to stop it from wrap-

FIGURE 17-55. This wire halyard wrapped around the forestay, which sawed through it. Down came the sail. The disappointed owner (this was the second offense) complained that it had spoiled his day's sailing. He should look on the bright side. The halyard could just as easily have sawed through the forestay and brought the mast down! For a look at what caused this problem, see Figure 17-56A, bottom.

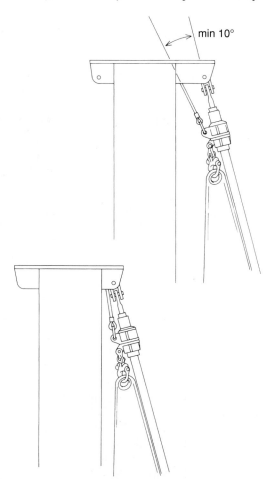

FIGURE 17-56A. Preventing halyard wrap. The angle shown at top is good. The halyard shown at bottom angles into the headstay and is sure to wrap sooner or later. (Jim Sollers)

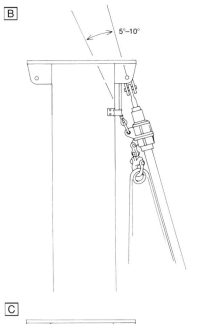

B

5°–10°

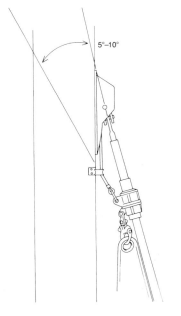

5°–10°

FIGURE 17-56B. A halyard fairlead can establish the correct angle (left) even when the swivel is too low (right).

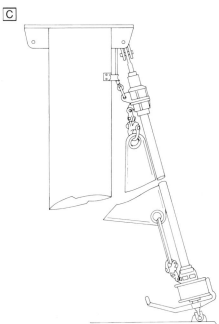

C

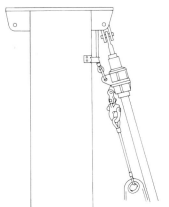

FIGURE 17-56C. A superior solution to a low swivel and fairlead (as shown in Figure 17-56B, above right) is to add a pendant to the tack (left) or the head (right) of the sail. *(Jim Sollers)*

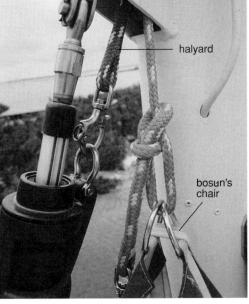

halyard

bosun's chair

FIGURE 17-56D. This halyard makes a closer-than-desirable angle to the headstay. It works in this situation because the exposed length of halyard is not long enough to wrap around the stay, but if the sail did not hoist as high as it does it could lead to trouble.

ping around the stay (Figure 17-56A, bottom); the slightest friction in the upper swivel (such as is almost sure to develop over time) will cause halyard wrap. If necessary, the halyard must be led through a fairlead fastened to the front of the mast to provide the correct lead angle (Figure 17-56B).

The lower the swivel on the foil, the longer the exposed length of halyard, the smaller the halyard angle, and the greater the chance of halyard wrap. When a sail is hoisted and winched up to its maximum halyard tension, the swivel should be almost at the top of the foil. *If not, a pendant must be fitted to either the head or the tack of the sail to allow the swivel to come up this far* (Figures 17-56C and 17-56D). If you intend

FIGURE 17-57. Left: The off-center loading of this rig wore the nylon bushing in the halyard swivel to the point that it hung up at the point indicated (note the excessively large clearance worn into the opposite side; this was a warning sign missed by the owner). **Middle:** The halyard then wrapped around and ultimately destroyed the foil (note that the swivel was also mounted too low; the sail needed a pendant). **Right:** The wire halyard was also permanently deformed.

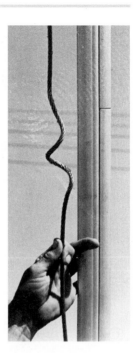

to use more than one sail on the same roller reefer, *supply each sail with a pendant so that the upper swivel always hoists to the same position.*

However, it is equally important that no pendant allows the swivel to come even partially off the top of the foil. If this happens, the off-center loads on the swivel will cause it to cock to one side, jamming on and damaging the foil.

Most swivels slide up and down the foil on nylon pads (inserts or bushings). In time the off-center loads on the swivel cause these pads to wear down on opposite sides at the top and bot-

FIGURES 17-58A AND 17-58B. Halyard antiwrap devices. Profurl's Multitop device (17-58A), which uses a halyard-deflecting ring to prevent halyard wrap, and a mast-mounted sheave from Harken (17-58B). *(Profurl, Harken)*

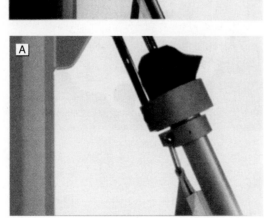

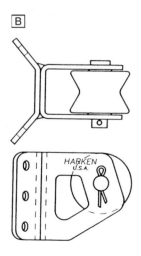

tom (this problem is most likely with oval foils). The swivel cocks a little to one side (Figure 17-57). In some cases, as the foil turns in reefing and unreefing operations, it catches on the upper (halyard) half of the swivel, dragging the swivel around with it and wrapping the halyard around the headstay. New pads are needed.

Antiwrap devices. One or two roller reefing units incorporate specific antiwrap devices (Figures 17-58A and 17-58B)—generally a *deflector ring* fitted around the headstay above the foil to hold halyards off the headstay. The Profurl unit has a solid metal strap between the top of the upper swivel and the halyard. If the swivel turns, this strap comes up against a protrusion on the deflector ring (which Profurl calls Multitop), and the swivel then turns no farther, thus providing a positive lock against halyard wrap. Harken has a mast-mounted sheave performing the same function as the fairlead in Figure 17-56B but with less friction.

Riding turns on the reefing drum. Riding turns on the reefing drum are another common problem (Figure 17-59A). The causes are just the same as for riding turns on winches—inadequate tension and incorrect sheet lead angles. If the reefing drum does not include an integral sheet lead, a suitable pad eye or block must be set up on deck to ensure that the reefing line runs onto the drum *at an angle of 90 degrees to the headstay* (Figures 17-59B and 17-59C). During reefing and unfurling operations, always maintain a moderate tension on the reefing line to keep it from jumping around. In addition to maintaining a fair lead onto the drum for the

FIGURE 17-59A. A riding turn on a drum as a result of the reefing line not being fed onto the drum at 90 degrees.

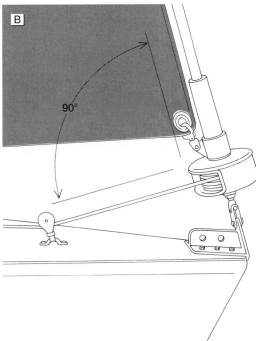

FIGURES 17-59B AND 17-59C. A block, or pad eye, set up to ensure the reefing line enters the reefing drum at the correct angle. *(Jim Sollers)*

FIGURE 17-60. A stanchion-mounted reefing block that maintains low friction in the reefing system. *(Schaefer Marine)*

reefing line, *the line must be led back to the cockpit through a series of blocks that ensure minimal friction* (Figure 17-60). When the sail is partially reefed, the load on the sail will cause this line to work backward and forward. If the line is dragging across a hard surface at any point, sooner or later it will part, allowing the entire sail to unroll uncontrollably. Since the sail is only likely to be reefed in heavy conditions, this too will only occur in heavy conditions, which will make the situation very difficult to handle. The largest line size that will fit on the drum should be used. This will not only provide the maximum strength, but also make for the greatest ease of handling (in practice, ⅜-inch line is often the largest that can be accommodated; ½-inch line, if it fits, is much easier on the hands).

Sail damage. Headsail damage is more prevalent with roller reefers than with hanked-on headsails. Generally the genoa is set up as the primary (and frequently, the only) sail for the roller reefer. When the wind pipes up, either there is no smaller sail to set or, rather than setting it, the genoa is steadily reefed down. Sooner or later the sail encounters wind strengths for which it was not designed and blows out. Correct sail design will help alleviate stresses (generally radial or vertical panels), as will the use of heavier sailcloth in the panels closest to the leech—those still operational when the sail is reefed.

When reefing down, if the halyard and sheets are eased too far, the sail rolls up loosely. In a gale of wind, the poorly furled head of the sail will flog around and eventually tear. Gentle pressure must be maintained on the sheets while reefing so that the sail rolls up tightly. Once the sail is completely rolled up, continue turning it a few more times to wrap the sheets around it.

Even when furled, the outer wraps of a sail are still exposed to the sun's UV rays. To prevent degradation of the sailcloth, sew a sacrificial strip of material to the leech of the sail. All too often you can see roller reefing sails with torn and tattered UV covers—slowly and steadily, sunlight will literally be eating up the outer wrap of the sail. The next time it is put to a test, it is likely to fail; once a tear starts, it will run clear across the sail.

Summary: dos and don'ts.

Do:
• Install the unit properly, with:

1. The halyard swivel at the top of the foil as close to the masthead sheave as possible.
2. The halyard angled away from the swivel by at least 10 degrees.
3. All the sails to be used fitted with suitable pendants to ensure that the swivel is hoisted to the same height with each one.

• Keep the headstay tight to avoid foil sag.
• Slack off the halyard, ease the sheets, and luff up when reefing.
• Retain *moderate* tension on sheets and reefing line at all times to avoid loose wraps and riding turns on the reefing drum.
• Flush stainless and plastic bearings at regular intervals with fresh water.
• Slack the halyard at all times when the sail is furled to avoid prolonged point loading on the bearings.
• Install adequate toggles at both ends of the headstay and on the drum mount (where appropriate).
• Check the lower turnbuckle terminal on turnbuckle-mounted units to make sure that it is not backing off.

Don't:
• Try to reef the sail against full sheet tension.
• Reef with a highly tensioned halyard.
• Tension the backstay after tensioning the halyard.

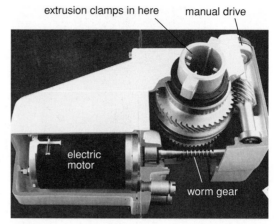

FIGURE 17-61. Worm gearing on an electrically powered headsail reefer. *(Profurl)*

• Leave the halyard tensioned when the sail is not in use.
• Force the reefing line. If it jams or there is unusual resistance, *find out why:* check for halyard wrap, a riding turn on the reefing drum, or rough bearings.
• Let the sail flog when reefing—uneven tension on the reefing line is likely to cause a riding turn.
• Force a sail up or down its luff groove.
• Use reefed sails in wind conditions stronger than the sailcloth is designed to tolerate.

Powered headsail reefers. Some larger rigs are driven by electric and hydraulic motors (Figure 17-61). Older hydraulic units tend to have a direct drive from the hydraulic motor and rely on the motor check valves to maintain oil pressure and keep the sail in position. Any pump, check valve, or seal leaks result in creep and in the slow unwinding of the sail.

Some units also have adapted industrial hydraulic equipment with *steel* interiors. Water in the hydraulic oil (such as from condensation in oil reservoirs) leads to rusting of sensitive parts and thus all kinds of problems. For other problem areas and troubleshooting, see the sections in Chapter 16 on hydraulic windlasses.

Newer hydraulic drive units use worm gearing (which acts as an effective brake against the sail's unwinding) and all-stainless-steel construction. Electrically driven units are very similar (on the motor and control side) to electrically powered windlasses—refer to the relevant section in Chapter 16 for troubleshooting.

Maintenance

Some roller reefers are advertised as *maintenance free.* It is a foolish owner who takes this too

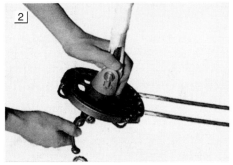

literally! All roller reefers incorporate dissimilar metals in the drum assemblies, foil joints, and upper swivels. The drum assemblies in particular are subjected to a great deal of saltwater spray and therefore are prone to galvanic corrosion. At the very least, this unit needs a thorough flushing with fresh water several times a season and before a winter layup.

If the drum and swivel have open bearings, they should be rotated while being flushed. This helps wash out all the salt and dirt. Plastic and stainless steel bearings will benefit from a good shot of WD-40. At the end of the season, after stainless steel bearings have been thoroughly washed out, pump in a little Teflon-based waterproof grease and spin the units to spread the grease around the balls and races.

Before winter layup, wash the foil. (As noted earlier, do not use detergents containing ammo-

nia on anodized aluminum.) After washing, rinse well, and liberally coat all aluminum surfaces with a silicone car or boat polish.

Roller Furling Headsails

In recent years roller furling headsails have been popularized by single-handed round-the-world racers (with all kinds of fancy names such as Code Zero sails, Screachers, gennakers, etc.). As with a roller reefer, a furler has an upper swivel and lower drum, but it has no foil to which the sail attaches and no stay. Instead, the sail itself has the equivalent of a foil and stay built into its luff (generally in the form of a Kevlar tape) that has sufficient rigidity to enable the sail to be rolled up around its own luff (Figures 17-62A and 17-62B). This luff tape, however, is not rigid enough to permit the sail to be rolled up under

FIGURE 17-62A. Anatomy of a modern roller furler. The tack of the sail is attached directly to the drum (1), which is fastened to a pad eye on the boat (in this case with a snapshackle for easy installation and removal—2). The luff of the sail contains a Kevlar or similar high-tech tape that resists twisting (3). The head of the sail is fastened to a swivel, to which the halyard attaches. Pulling the "endless" (i.e., it forms a continuous loop) furling line turns the drum, which turns the luff tape, rolling the sail up around itself. This cannot be done under any kind of a load because the luff tape would twist. As a result the sail can only be used fully unfurled (not reefed). *(Profurl)*

FIGURE 17-62B. A similar rig as in Figure 17-62A, but this time using a furling drum. *(Schaefer Marine)*

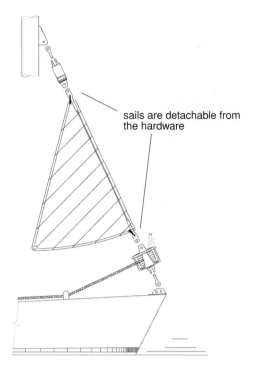

FIGURE 17-63. Some roller furlers are designed such that they allow the use of more than one sail with the same furling hardware. *(Schaefer Marine)*

sails are detachable from the hardware

a load, nor will it allow the sail to be used partially rolled up (i.e., reefed). The sail must be unloaded to be furled, and it must be either rolled up all the way or let out all the way—hence the designation of these units as roller *furlers*, not roller *reefers*.

The lower side of the drum on a roller furler is tacked down to the end of some kind of a sprit, or to the equivalent of a chainplate on the foredeck, and the halyard is attached to the upper half of the upper swivel. As noted, the sail's luff tape serves as a stay. Commonly, the drums have a single, endless line (i.e., one big loop) around them; pulling on the line turns the drum to unwind the sail or wind it back up (some use a conventional roller reefing–style drum). Because the line does not get wound up on the drum, there is no risk of a riding turn.

When not needed, a roller furling sail can be taken down and stowed as with any other sail. On some, the drum and swivel remain attached, but on others, the sail is detached from the drum and swivel, which can then be used for other roller furling sails (Figure 17-63). Another variant, used by Profurl, is to install the equivalent of the luff tape permanently to the drum and swivel, then *zipper* the luffs of different sails around this rig. One way or another these sails are easy to use and the various rigs quite versatile, hence their increasing popularity beyond the racing circuit for both large off-the-wind sails and also for small stormsails.

In-Mast and Behind-the-Mast Reefing

The success of roller reefing headsails has resulted in the adaptation of the same hardware to furling and reefing applications for mainsails and mizzens. In almost all instances, existing headsail reefing equipment, with minor modifications, is installed either inside a specially built mast (for new builds) or just behind the mast (some retrofits).

Exactly the same principles apply as for headsail reefing. The sail feeds into a slot in a foil. The head of the sail is attached to a swivel, which fits around the foil, and is hoisted by the halyard; the tack of the sail attaches to a furling drum or some other fitting attached to the foil. The foil is rotated to wind up the sail (Figures 17-64A, 17-64B, and 17-64C).

Now for some minor variations. The foil on a *behind-the-mast* reefer must be set up on the equivalent of a substitute headstay, and this stay must be kept tensioned to prevent sail sag (Figure 17-64D). Generally a rod is fitted between a bracket at the masthead and a fixed gooseneck, then tensioned by tightening a nut on the underside of the gooseneck mount. The foil rotates around the rod.

In-mast reefers, which have a narrow slot in the mast, are not subject to sail sag—the slot in the mast provides support along the length of the sail. As long as the sail is tensioned (via its halyard), there is no need for any tension on the foil or on any rod around which it rotates. In fact, there is not even a need for the rod at all—the foil can simply be set up in bearings attached to the inside of the mast. However, with wider mast slots, inadequate rod or foil tension can allow the foil to sag into the slot and jam.

Foils can be turned (Figure 17-65) by a conventional reefing drum, a line driver, a motor, or by cranking with a winch handle (in the event of motor failure). A line driver resembles the jaws on a self-tailing winch. An endless line feeds through the jaws, around various blocks, and back to a similar unit in the cockpit. A winch handle is used to turn the cockpit driver, cranking the sail in or out. Line drivers are either installed directly on a foil or set in the aft face of the mast, turning the foil via a set of bevel gears.

Problems and answers. Much of the information in the section on roller reefing is applicable here, especially that relating to bearings, foil extrusions, halyard wrap, and maintenance. In addition, certain other points need to be noted.

Mast bend. In-mast reefers cannot accommodate mast bend—the foil extrusion and sail will

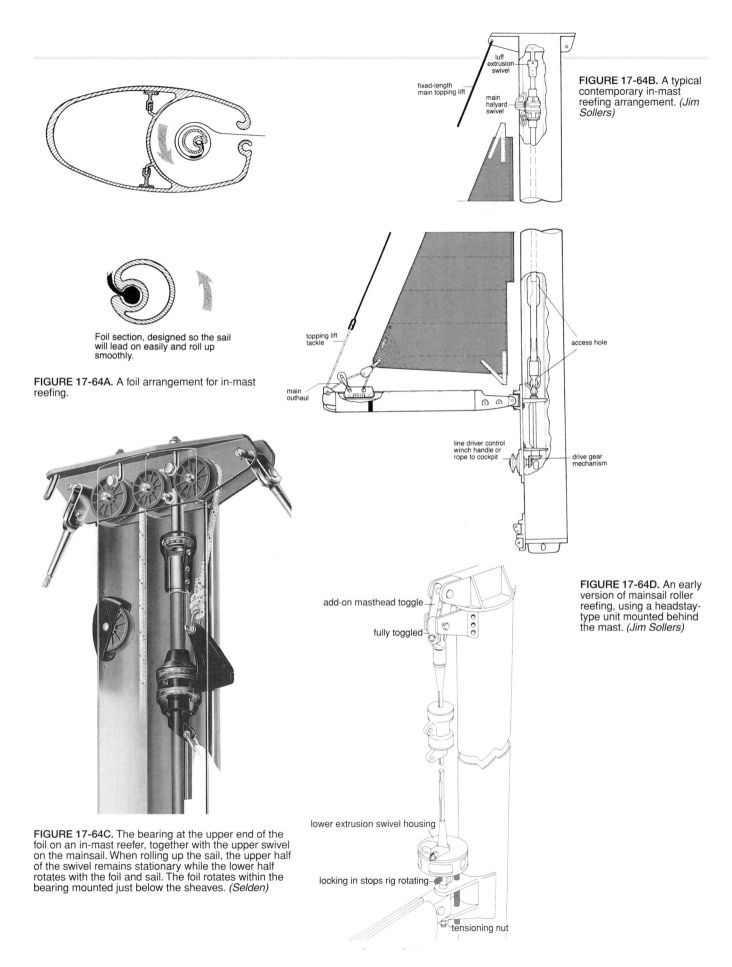

Foil section, designed so the sail will lead on easily and roll up smoothly.

FIGURE 17-64A. A foil arrangement for in-mast reefing.

luff extrusion swivel

fixed-length main topping lift

main halyard swivel

FIGURE 17-64B. A typical contemporary in-mast reefing arrangement. *(Jim Sollers)*

topping lift tackle

main outhaul

access hole

line driver control winch handle or rope to cockpit

drive gear mechanism

FIGURE 17-64C. The bearing at the upper end of the foil on an in-mast reefer, together with the upper swivel on the mainsail. When rolling up the sail, the upper half of the swivel remains stationary while the lower half rotates with the foil and sail. The foil rotates within the bearing mounted just below the sheaves. *(Selden)*

add-on masthead toggle

fully toggled

lower extrusion swivel housing

locking in stops rig rotating

tensioning nut

FIGURE 17-64D. An early version of mainsail roller reefing, using a headstay-type unit mounted behind the mast. *(Jim Sollers)*

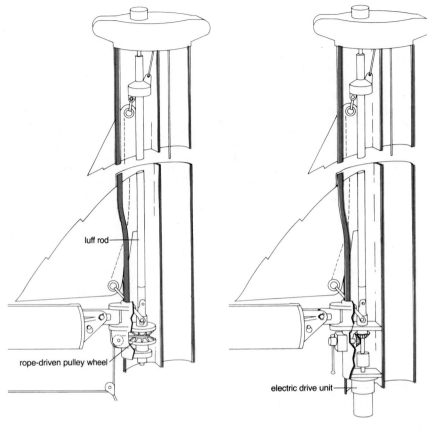

AFIGURE 17-65. In-mast reefing drive options. Many feature a rope-driven pulley with the furling line led aft to the cockpit. Larger units incorporate an electric or hydraulic motor. *(Jim Sollers)*

luff rod

rope-driven pulley wheel

electric drive unit

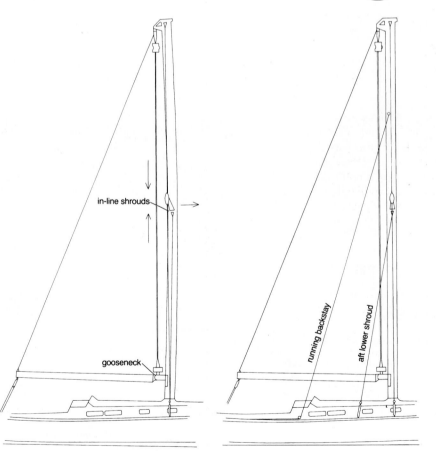

FIGURE 17-66. Behind-the-mast reefers impose severe strains on the mast, which must receive additional support. *(Jim Sollers)*

in-line shrouds

gooseneck

running backstay

aft lower shroud

hang up on the mast. Early-style behind-the-mast reefers suffer from changing rod tension with changes in mast shape. Note that *behind-the-mast reefers should be fully toggled at the top and bottom to accommodate sail sag* (see the Powered Headsail Reefers section above). Some retrofitted behind-the-mast reefers can impose severe bending stresses on masts (rather like the string on a bow—Figure 17-66), in which case, *aft* lower shrouds are a necessity to keep the mast in column (straight)—*in-line* shrouds will not work. Running backstays may be needed to keep the mast from pumping in heavy seas. Some masts still may not be able to take the added strain. In-mast reefing does not suffer from the same problems since the mast loading is all in direct compression.

Tension. Moderate tension must be maintained at all times on the clew of the sail when reefing and unfurling. If this is not done, the sail will wrap and unwrap loosely, jamming inside the mast or mast slot. Some first-generation units jammed up so badly that the sails had to be cut out! This has been largely eliminated by improving the ratio of foil sizes to slots.

In-mast rod tension. Where an *in-mast* foil is mounted on a rod, excessive tension on the rod will merely distort mounting brackets, damage bearings, wear out bevel gears, etc. As mentioned previously, tensioning *in-mast* mounting rods will do nothing to improve sail shape or performance.

Motor failures. See the relevant sections on powered windlasses in Chapter 16—motor installations are very similar (both electric and hydraulic).

Fluting. Anytime a boat with a slotted mast is berthed, the sail is rolled up, and the wind moves aft of the beam, the wind will make a moaning noise as it blows across the slot (just like blowing across the top of a bottle). This is easily stopped by hoisting a strip of sailcloth (an antivibration strip or *flute stopper*) up the slot. The problem does not occur at anchor since the boat will stay head to wind.

Roller Reefing Booms

After an absence of 30 years or more, roller reefing booms have made a comeback in a new incarnation. The modern variant was first popularized by Forespar's Leisure Furl (www.forespar.com), and subsequently adapted by Profurl, Schaefer, and others (Figures 17-67A and 17-67B). It is easier to reef than the traditional roller reefing boom and results in a far better sail shape. Fully battened mainsails with as much

furls any mainsail, even modern, high-performance, full-batten mains

Torlon bearings are set in angular contact races to absorb high compression loads and minimize friction

Torlon ball bearings reduce friction to facilitate hoisting, reefing, or furling

aft drum aligns track with gooseneck for easy furling and reefing on all points of sail

solid vang with stainless spring and vang shaft for correct alignment and boom support

roach as wanted can be accommodated. The weight of the reefed sail is kept as low as possible. If the gear fails, the sail can be dropped in the conventional manner (by releasing the halyard).

Early "teething" problems have been largely overcome. Roller reefing booms are proving their worth, but are relatively expensive and do require some skill to operate—it is easy to get in a mess with them. Perhaps the single most important consideration is an installation that in all weather conditions and sea states, and in daylight and darkness, enables the boat operator to easily set and hold the boom at precisely the angle required for smooth furling. This will eliminate most reefing problems.

FIGURE 17-67A. Schaefer's entry into the in-boom reefing marketplace. It is unusual since the reefing device is at the back of the boom rather than at the gooseneck. *(Schaefer Marine)*

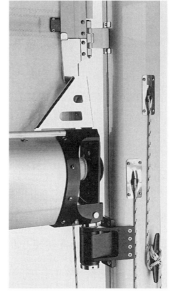

FIGURE 17-67B. Detail shots of Schaefer's in-boom reefing. *(Schaefer Marine)*

Glossary

Accumulator: An air-filled tank used to smooth out pressure in a freshwater system; also a tank used in a refrigeration system to hold liquid refrigerant that might otherwise damage the compressor.

Aerial. See *antenna*.

Alignment: Bringing together of two coupling halves in near-perfect horizontal and vertical agreement.

Alternating current (AC): An electrical current reversing its direction at regular intervals. Each repetition of these changes is a cycle, and the number of cycles that take place in 1 second is the frequency (measured in Hertz).

Alternator: A machine for generating electricity by spinning a magnet inside a series of coils. The resulting power output is alternating current. In DC systems, this output is rectified via silicon diodes.

Ambient conditions: The surrounding temperature or pressure, or both.

Ammeter: An instrument for measuring current flow.

Ampere (amp): A measure of the rate of electric current flow.

Ampere-hour (Ah): A measure of the amount of electricity stored in a battery.

Annealing: A process of softening metals.

Anode: The negative terminal of a battery or cell.

Antenna/aerial: A conductor that radiates or collects radio waves.

Antenna gain: The measure of the effectiveness of an antenna.

Antisiphon valve: A valve that admits air to a line and prevents siphonic action.

Aqualift: An engine exhaust and silencing system in which cooling water is injected into the exhaust and carried out by the exhaust gases.

Area effect: The influence on the rate of corrosion of the relative areas of an anode and a cathode when connected in a galvanic cell.

Armature: The rotating windings in a generator (AC or DC).

Atmospheric pressure: The pressure of the air at the surface of the earth, conventionally taken to be 14.7 psi.

Atomizer. See *injector*.

Babbitt: A soft white metal alloy frequently used to line replaceable shell-type engine bearings; also used in the traversing nut on worm steering.

Back pressure: A buildup of pressure in an exhaust system.

Backstay: A wire rope or rod giving aft support to a mast.

Ball valve: Either a valve with a spring-loaded ball or one with a ball rotating in a spherical seat.

Battery: *Automotive*—A lead-acid battery with many thin plates and low-density active material.

    Deep-cycle—A lead-acid battery with thicker, stronger plates and high-density active material.

    Wet-cell—A conventional lead-acid battery with liquid electrolyte.

    Gel-cell—A lead-acid battery in which the electrolyte is trapped in a gel.

    Absorbed glass mat (AGM)—A lead-acid battery in which the electrolyte is held in fiberglass plate separators.

    No-maintenance—Either a sealed gel-cell or AGM battery or a sealed, conventional wet battery with excess electrolyte.

Battery isolation switch: A switch installed next to the battery and carrying full battery output, used to isolate the battery from all circuits.

Battery sensed: A voltage regulator that senses system voltage at the battery (as opposed to at the alternator).

Bearing: A device for supporting a rotating shaft with minimum friction. It may take the form of a metal sleeve (a bushing), a set of ball bearings (a roller bearing), or a set of pins around the shaft (a needle bearing).

Bearing race: The outer cage within which a set of balls rotates in a roller bearing.

Bendix: The drive gear (pinion) arrangement on a starter motor.

Bevel gear: A means of transmitting drive through a 90-degree angle.

Binnacle: A housing for a compass.

Bleeding: The process of purging air from a fuel or hydraulic system.

Block: The general term for a rigging pulley.

Blocking diode: A diode used to permit charging of more than one battery from one power source without paralleling the battery outputs. Also known as a "battery isolation diode."

Blowby: The escape of gases past piston rings or closed valves.

Bobstay: A stay from the tip of a bowsprit to the waterline.

Bonding: The process of electrically tying together all major fixed metal items on a boat.

Bosun's chair (a corruption of boatswain's chair): A canvas seat used for hoisting someone up a mast.

Bottle screw. See *turnbuckle*.

Bridge rectifier: An arrangement of diodes for converting alternating current (AC) to direct current (DC).

Brush: A carbon or carbon-composite spring-loaded rod used to conduct current to or from commutators or slip rings.

Btu (British thermal unit): A unit used to measure quantities of heat.

Bulldog clamp. See *cable clamp*.

Bus bar: A heavy copper strap used in breaker boxes and circuit panel boxes for carrying high currents and making multiple connections.

Bushing. See *bearing*.

Cable clamp: A U-shaped bolt with a saddle used to join or to make loops in wire rope.

Cam: An elliptical protrusion on a shaft.

Cam cleat: A cleat with two spring-loaded, toothed jaws that trap and hold a line.

Capacitor: A device for storing electric energy. A capacitor blocks the flow of DC but lets AC through (analogous to a flexible membrane that will oscillate but not allow flow through it).

Cap shroud. See *shroud.*

Cathode: The positive terminal of a cell or battery.

Caulking: Various semiflexible compounds used to seal seams. Sometimes applied with less precision to sealing and bedding compounds.

Cell: A single unit that makes electricity through chemical energy. A group of cells makes a battery.

Centrifugal action: The process of imparting velocity to a liquid through a spinning impeller that drives the liquid from the center of a pump housing to its periphery.

Chainplates: The metal or carbon fiber straps bolted to a hull to which standing rigging attaches.

Check valve: An electrical or mechanical valve that allows flow in only one direction.

Cheek plates: The plates that enclose the sheave on a block.

Choke. See *inductor.*

Circlip. See *snap ring.*

Circuit: The path of electric current. A *closed* circuit has a complete path. An *open* circuit has a broken or disconnected path. A *short* circuit has an unintentional direct path bypassing the equipment (appliance, resistance) in the circuit.

Circuit breaker: A load-sensitive switch that trips (opens a circuit) if a threshold-exceeding current flows through it.

Clevis pin: A metal pin with a flattened head at one end and a hole for a cotter pin (split pin) at the other. It is used to fasten rigging together.

Clew: The lower, aft corner of a sail.

Clutch: A device used to couple and uncouple a power source from a piece of equipment. It may be manually, hydraulically, or electromagnetically operated. A *cone* clutch forces a tapered seat onto a tapered friction pad. A *brake-band* clutch tightens a friction band around a smooth face on a gear. A *disc* clutch holds alternating metal and friction plates together.

CNG (compressed natural gas): Liquefies only at very high pressures that are not found in boat applications.

Coaxial cable: A cable enclosed in an insulating sleeve (or dielectric), then a metal braided sleeve, and finally another insulating sleeve.

Cold cranking amps (CCA): The number of amps a battery at 0°F/–17.8°C can deliver for 30 seconds and maintain a voltage of 1.2 volts per cell or more.

Cold plate. See *holding plate.*

Cold-welding: The transfer of a metal from one threaded part to another that sometimes occurs as a result of friction generated by dirt or corrosion. It is almost exclusively confined to stainless steel. See also *galling.*

Collet: A metal chip designed to hold winch spindles and engine valves in place.

Common ground point: A central stud, normally connected to the earth's ground via a through-hull fitting, to which are attached AC and DC grounding circuits, any bonding circuit, various radio and lightning grounds, and any cathodic protection system.

Commutator: The copper segments that are arranged around the end of an armature and on which the brushes ride.

Compression ratio: The volume of a combustion chamber with the piston at the top of its stroke as a proportion of the total volume of the cylinder with the piston at the bottom of its stroke.

Compressor: A device used to compress refrigeration gases. A *reciprocal* compressor has two pistons attached to a rotating crankshaft as in a conventional engine. A *swash-plate (wobble plate)* compressor has five or six pistons attached to a plate that oscillates, driven by a rotating cam.

Condenser: A unit designed to remove sufficient heat from a compressed refrigeration gas to make the gas condense into a liquid.

Conditioning. See *equalization.*

Conductance: A measure of the ability to conduct electricity.

Conduit: A pipe in which electric cables are run; also a reinforced sheathing used with steering and engine control cables.

Cone clutch. See *clutch.*

Constant-current voltage regulation. See *voltage regulation.*

Continuity: A complete path or circuit through which current can flow.

Controllable-pitch propeller: One in which the pitch of the blades is adjustable.

Corrosion: A process that leads to the destruction of metals. *Galvanic* corrosion arises when dissimilar, electrically connected metals are immersed in an electrolyte (e.g., salt water). A current is generated, leading to the destruction of the *anode* (*less noble* metal) and the protection of the *cathode* (*more noble* metal). *Pinhole* and *crevice* corrosion are the results of galvanic corrosion occurring in just one piece of metal due to differences in the composition of the metal. *Stray-current* corrosion is the result of external current leakage through metal fittings in contact with an electrolyte, such as salt water. Massive corrosion can occur where the current leaves a fitting. The term "electrolysis" refers to the passage of electricity through the electrolyte.

Cotter pin: A pin with two legs. With legs together, the pin is placed through the hole in a clevis pin. The legs are then opened outward to prevent the cotter pin from backing out of the hole. The cotter pin, in turn, prevents the load-bearing clevis pin from backing out of its retaining hole.

Creep: The slow seepage of hydraulic fluid down the sides of a piston or ram, or through check valves, leading to gradual movement of the rudder or steering wheel.

Crosby clamp. See *cable clamp.*

Cup washer: A dished leather or neoprene washer fitted to the rod end in some piston-style pumps.

Current: The rate of flow of electricity (measured in amps).

Cutless bearing: A ribbed rubber sleeve in a metal tube used to support a propeller shaft.

CVJ (constant velocity joint): A type of propeller shaft coupling that permits considerable engine misalignment.

Cycles. See *alternating current*.

Deep-cycle battery. See *battery*.

Diaphragm: A reinforced rubber membrane that moves in and out in certain pumps.

Dielectric: An insulating material. See also *coaxial cable*.

Diffusion: The process by which the acid in a battery electrolyte permeates the active material in the plates.

Diode: An electronic check valve.

Direct current (DC): An electric current that flows in one direction only.

Disc-drive steering. See *radial-drive steering*.

Double-pole switch: A switch that makes or breaks two separate connections at the same time.

Dowel: A round metal or wooden pin.

Drier: A cylinder containing hygroscopic (water-absorbing) material used to remove moisture from refrigeration circuits.

Drift: Any suitably sized round metal bar used to knock out bushings, clevis pins, and the like.

Drip loop: A deliberately induced low spot in a run of electrical cable designed to keep moisture out of terminal boxes, etc.

Drive ratio: The ratio between the radius of a driven pulley and the radius of the driving pulley.

Duckbill valve: A hemispherical rubber valve with a slit in it and protruding rubber lips. Internal pressure forces the lips apart, opening the valve; external pressure closes the lips, sealing the valve.

Earth: The reference point (*ground potential*) for AC circuits.

Earth leak. See *ground fault*.

Electric motor: A device for converting electromagnetic force into rotary motion. *Universal* motors operate on both AC and DC currents. *Permanent-magnet* motors also run on both currents. *Induction* motors operate on AC only.

Electrolysis. See *corrosion*.

Electrolyte: A liquid conductor of electricity; the solution in a battery.

Electromagnet: A magnetic force induced by passing a direct current through a coil wrapped around an iron core (shoe).

Electromagnetic compatibility (EMC): The ability of electronic equipment to operate in proximity with other electrical and electronic equipment without suffering from, or causing, impaired performance.

Electromagnetic clutch: A cone clutch in which the driving and driven halves are pulled together by an electromagnet.

Electromagnetic interference (EMI): Electromagnetic or electrical disturbances that result in undesirable responses, or impede the performance of other electrical or electronic equipment.

Equalization: The process of driving a liquid electrolyte (wet) lead-acid battery up to its highest natural voltage in order to reconvert sulfated plate material back into active material.

Eutectic: A particular level of a salt solution at which the whole solution freezes at one specific temperature (as opposed to progressively freezing through a process of ice crystallizing as temperatures lower).

Evaporator: The unit in which liquid refrigerant converts back into a gas, absorbing latent heat in the process.

Excitation: The initial magnetism induced in a field winding in order to initiate alternator or generator output.

Excitation windings: A separate set of coils built into the stator on brushless AC alternators. It is used to induce field current in the rotor.

Expansion valve: A valve with a minute, adjustable orifice used to separate the high- and low-pressure sides of a refrigeration system, and through which the liquid refrigerant sprays into the evaporator.

Extrusion: A complex metal (normally aluminum) shape produced in continuous lengths.

Fail-safe diode: A diode set to block current flow at normal voltages but to open with abnormally high voltage. Used to protect alternator diodes against accidental open-circuiting.

Fast fuse: Used to protect alternator diodes against accidental reverse polarity.

Feed pump. See *lift pump*.

Feeler gauge: Thin strips of metal machined to precise thicknesses and used for measuring small gaps.

Fid: A softwood plug to hammer up and block off a through-hull fitting or hull opening below the waterline in the event of a failure of the through-hull.

Field windings: Electromagnetic coils used to create magnetic fields in alternators, generators, and electric motors.

Filament: A very fine piece of high-resistance wire that glows red (or white) hot when a current is passed through it.

Filter: An electrical device for screening out unwanted interference; also a device for screening out impurities in fuel, air, or water.

Filter-drier. See *drier*.

Flap valve: A simple rubber flap, sometimes weighted. Fluid pressure opens it in one direction and closes it in the other.

Flashing the field: The use of an external DC source to supply momentary excitation to alternator or generator field coils.

Flax: A natural fiber used in packing.

Flexible-impeller pump: A pump with a rubber impeller and a cam on one side of the pump chamber. As the impeller passes the cam, its vanes are squeezed down, expelling fluids trapped between them. The vanes then spring back, sucking in more fluid.

Float charge: The current required to maintain a battery at full charge without overcharging.

Forestay: A wire rope or rod that gives forward support to a mast.

Frequency. See *alternating current*.

Fuse: A protective device designed to break a circuit by melting if the current goes above a certain level.

Gain. See *antenna gain*.

Galling: A process of *cold-welding* that can completely seize up stainless steel fasteners, particularly when their threads are dirty or damaged.

Galvanic corrosion. See *corrosion*.

Galvanic isolator: A device that blocks galvanic currents but closes a circuit when faced with higher voltages.

Gasket: A piece of material placed between two parts to seal them against leaks.

Gassing: A process in which battery electrolyte breaks down, giving off hydrogen and oxygen.

Gate valve: A valve in which a flat metal plate (gate) screws down to block off flow.

Gauge set: A pair of gauges mounted on a manifold that can be connected to a refrigeration unit to measure high and low pressures and to vacuum down and charge the unit.

Gear ratio: The relative size of two gears. If the gears are in contact, their relative speed of rotation will be given by the gear ratio. Example: If the gear ratio is 8:1, the smaller gear will rotate eight times faster than the larger gear.

Generator: A machine for generating electricity by spinning a series of coils inside a magnet. The resulting power output is alternating current. In DC systems, this output is rectified via a commutator and brushes.

Glow plug: A heating element installed in a diesel engine precombustion chamber to aid in cold-starting.

Gooseneck: A swivel fitting that holds a boom to a mast.

Governor: A device for maintaining an engine or electric motor at a constant speed, regardless of load.

Grid: A lead-alloy framework that supports the active material of a battery plate and conducts current.

Ground: A connection between an electric circuit and the earth, or some conducting body serving in place of the earth.

Grounded conductor: A normally current-carrying AC conductor maintained at earth's potential (i.e., the neutral wire).

Ground fault: A current leak to ground bypassing proper circuits.

Ground fault circuit interrupter (GFCI): A safety device that breaks an AC circuit anytime a short to ground occurs; also known as a "ground fault circuit breaker (GFCB)," a "residual current circuit breaker (RCCB)," or a "residual current device (RCD)."

Grounding conductor: A normally non-current-carrying AC conductor maintained at the earth's potential (i.e., the ground wire). Also used to refer to bonding wires attached to DC equipment.

Ground point. See *common ground point.*

Gudgeon: One-half of a rudder hinge (the other half is the pintle).

Gypsy: A wheel on a windlass notched for chain (also called a "wildcat").

Halyard: A wire rope or synthetic rope used to raise a sail.

Halyard wrap: The twisting of a headsail halyard around the forestay.

Head: A marine toilet.

Head box: The assembly of sheaves and wire rope attachments at the top of a mast.

Header tank: A small tank set above an engine on heat exchanger–cooled systems. The header tank serves as an expansion chamber, coolant reservoir, and pressure regulator (via a pressure cap).

Heat exchanger: A vessel containing a number of small tubes through which cooling water is passed, while raw water is circulated around the outside of the tubes to carry off heat from the cooling water.

Heat-shrink tape and tubing: Insulating tape that shrinks and melts when heated, forming an effective seal. Also known as "self-amalgamating tape."

Heat sink: A mounting for an electronic component designed to dissipate heat to the atmosphere.

Hemp. See *flax.*

Hertz (Hz): The unit of frequency of an alternating current. One Hertz equals one cycle per second.

Holding plate: A refrigerator or freezer tank containing an evaporator coil and a solution with a freezing point below that of water.

Hose adapter: A standard plumbing fitting on one end with a suitable hose connection on the other.

Hose barb: A tapered and ridged fitting that slides up inside a hose.

Hose clamp: An adjustable stainless steel band for clamping hoses. Also known as a "Jubilee clip" in the UK.

Hunting: A rhythmic cycling up and down in speed of a governed engine.

Hydraulic steering: Steering that uses a manual hydraulic pump driven by the steering wheel and operates a hydraulic piston (ram), which turns the rudder via a tiller arm.

Hydrometer: A float-type instrument used to determine the state of charge of a battery by measuring the specific gravity of the electrolyte (i.e., the amount of sulfuric acid in the electrolyte).

Impedance: A kind of alternating current resistance; the ratio of voltage to current.

Impeller: The rotating fitting that imparts motion to a fluid in a rotating pump.

Impressed-current cathodic protection: A means of protecting underwater hardware by pushing controlled amounts of current into the water.

Incandescent light: A light with filaments.

Inches of mercury ("Hg): A scale for measuring small pressure changes, particularly those below atmospheric pressure (vacuums).

Inductance: A property of a conductor or coil that determines how much voltage will be induced in it by a change of current.

Induction motor: An AC motor in which the stator coils generate a rotating magnetic field that drags the rotor around.

Inductor: A coil designed so that it filters out unwanted radio frequency noise.

In-mast reefing: Roller reefing for mains and mizzens installed inside specially extruded masts.

Injection pump: A pump designed to meter out precisely controlled amounts of diesel fuel and then raise it to injection pressures at precisely controlled moments in an engine cycle.

Injector: A device for atomizing diesel fuel and spraying it into a cylinder.

Injector nut: The nut that holds a fuel line to an injector.

Insulated return: A circuit in which both the outgoing and returning conductors are insulated.

Interference: Undesired radio wavelengths. See also *electromagnetic interference*.

Inverter: A device for changing DC to AC.

Isolation transformer: A transformer that transfers power from one winding to another magnetically and without any direct connection.

Joker valve. See *duckbill valve*.

Jubilee clip. See *hose clamp*.

Kilo: 1,000, as in *kilowatt* or *kilohertz*.

Latent heat: Heat absorbed or given up during changes of state with no change of temperature.

Life cycles: The number of times before failing that a battery can be pulled down to a certain level of discharge and then recharged.

Lift pump: A low-pressure pump in a fuel injection system supplying fuel from the tank to the injection pump.

Line driver: A winch with a set of jaws that grips an endless line (a continuous loop).

Lip-type seal: A seal, using automotive-style oil seals, that is used in place of a stuffing box.

Liquid slugging: Liquid refrigerant entering a compressor as a result of excess refrigerant being fed into the evaporator.

Live: A circuit energized with electricity.

Loading coil: A coil placed in series with an antenna and used to tune it.

Load testing: The use of a high load for a short period of time to test a battery and check its ability to perform under actual engine starting conditions.

Lower shroud. See *shroud*.

LPG (liquefied petroleum gas): Petroleum gases, principally propane and butane, that liquefy at relatively low pressures (below 200 psi).

Macerator: A specially designed impeller for breaking up solids prior to pumping.

Machine screw: A countersunk, slotted screw with machined threads such as are found on bolts.

Machine sensed: A voltage regulator that senses system voltage at the alternator (as opposed to at the battery).

Main down conductor: The cable from a lightning rod to an immersed ground plate or ground (such as an external ballast keel).

Manifold: A pipe assembly, attached to an engine, that conducts air into the engine or exhaust gases out of it; any pipe assembly with more than one fitting screwed into it, for example, a gauge set manifold.

Manometer: A U-shaped, water-filled tube used for measuring very low pressures (commonly from 0 to 1 psi).

Mechanical seal: A spring-loaded seal used in place of a stuffing box on a propeller shaft. Also known as "rotary seals" or "face seals."

Mega: 1,000,000, as in *megawatt* and *megahertz*.

Microfarad (μF): One-millionth of a farad; a measure of capacity.

Milliamp/millivolt: One-thousandth of an amp or volt.

Mole wrench: Vise-Grips.

MOV (metal oxide varistor): One kind of transient voltage suppressor. MOVs have an open circuit until hit by a high voltage (a voltage spike or surge), then they conduct to ground to short out the spike (surge).

Needle bearing. See *bearing*.

Noble metal: A metal high on the galvanic table. Noble metals are likely to form a cathode in any cases of galvanic corrosion and therefore are unlikely to corrode.

Noise: A general expression for electrical interference.

Offset gear: An arrangement of gears in which one gear engages another on the same plane (i.e., the gears are in line with one another).

Ohm: The standard unit of measurement of resistance.

Ohmmeter: An instrument for measuring resistance. Usually incorporated as one function of a multimeter.

Open circuit. See *circuit*.

Open-circuit voltage: The voltage of a rested battery that is not receiving or delivering power.

Orifice: A very fine opening in a nozzle.

Outhaul: A device for tensioning the foot of a main or mizzen sail.

Overcharging: Forcing excessive current into a battery, which causes the battery to heat up and start to gas.

Packing: Square, grease-impregnated, natural fiber rope, usually hemp (flax), used to seal stuffing boxes.

Packing gland. See *stuffing box*.

Parallel connection: Connecting battery positive terminals together and negative terminals together to increase system capacity without increasing voltage.

Parallel paths: Paths to ground, other than that provided by the main down conductor, taken by a lightning strike.

Pawl: A spring-loaded metal piece used in winch ratchets.

Pedestal: The column on which a steering wheel and various engine controls are mounted; generally topped with a binnacle and compass.

Pilot light: A constantly burning small flame used to ignite main burners on a gas appliance.

Pinion: A small gear designed to mesh with a large gear (for example, a starter-motor drive gear).

Pintle: One-half of a rudder hinge (the other half is the gudgeon).

Pitch: The total distance a propeller would travel in one revolution, as determined by the amount of deflection of its blades, if there were no losses as it turned.

Planetary gears: An arrangement of small gears around a central drive gear, with a large ring gear around the outside of the small gears.

Point loading: Uneven loading on a bearing, which throws all the pressure on one part of the bearing instead of distributing it evenly over the whole bearing.

Points: The metal pieces that make and break the circuit in various switching devices, such as pressure switches, solenoids, circuit breakers, ordinary switches, etc.

Polarity: The distinction between positive and negative conductors in a DC system; the opposite magnetic poles in an alternator, a generator, or an electric motor.

Polarity indicating light: A test light on AC circuits to check that the neutral wire is the grounded conductor and not the hot wire.

Polarized circuit: An AC system in which the grounded (neutral) and ungrounded (hot) conductors are connected in the same relationship to all terminals and loads.

Potentiometer: A variable resistance used for adjusting some voltage regulators.

Primary winding: The incoming side of a transformer.

PSI (pounds per square inch): Pressure measurement. *Psia* (pounds per square inch absolute) measures actual pressure with no allowance for atmospheric pressure. *Psig* (pounds per square inch gauge) measures pressure with the gauge set to zero (0) at atmospheric pressure (14.7 psia). In other words psig = psia – 14.7. Unless otherwise stated, psi always refers to psig.

Purging: The process of removing all air from a refrigeration gauge set before connecting to a refrigeration system. Also, bleeding a diesel engine fuel system or hydraulic system.

Pyrometer: A gauge for measuring exhaust temperatures.

Quadrant: A type of rudderhead fitting to which the steering cables are attached.

Quartz halogen: A special type of bulb element that gives off more light per watt consumed than conventional incandescent filaments.

Race: The inner and outer cases on a bearing between which the balls are trapped.

Rack-and-pinion steering: Traditionally a geared quadrant attached to the rudderpost is driven by a small pinion on the steering wheel drive shaft. A more modern version has the steering wheel driving a beveled gear in the pedestal with the output transmitted by solid rods to a tiller arm attached to the rudderpost.

Radial-drive steering: A large pulley wheel attached to the rudderpost is turned via cables driven by the steering wheel.

Radio frequency interference (RFI): Impaired performance of electronic equipment as a result of conducted or radiated radio frequency signals.

Ratchet: A gear designed so that spring-loaded pawls lock it in one direction but allow it to rotate, or ratchet, in the other.

Raw water: The seawater side of cooling systems.

Reciprocal: Up-and-down motion.

Rectifier: A *bridge rectifier* is an arrangement of diodes to convert AC to DC. See also *diode*.

Refrigerant: The gas used in refrigeration and air-conditioning systems (formerly R-12 or R-22 in boat use; sometimes referred to as Freon-12 and Freon-22, which are trade names of DuPont, but now also including HFC-134a and various blends and other substances).

Relay: An electromechanical switch activated by a small current in its coil.

Reserve capacity: The time in minutes that a battery will deliver 25 amps before dying.

Residual magnetism: Magnetism remaining in field winding shoes after all current has been cut off to the field windings.

Resistance: The opposition an appliance or wire offers to the flow of electric current, measured in ohms.

Reverse polarity: Connecting a battery backward, i.e., connecting the positive terminal to the negative cable and the negative terminal to the positive cable.

RFD (receiver-filter-drier). See *drier*.

Rheostat: A variable resistance.

Riding turn: The result of one turn on a winch "riding" up over another, effectively locking it up.

Rigging screw. See *turnbuckle*.

Ripple: Undesired alternating current superimposed on a direct current power supply.

Roller bearings. See *bearings*.

Roller chain: Bicycle-type chain, generally made of stainless steel, used primarily in steering systems, but also in some windlasses.

Roller furling: Furling a sail by rolling it around its own luff wire. The sail can be used only fully unfurled. This is not a reefing system.

Roller reefing: Furling a sail by rolling it around a solid luff extrusion. Sails can be used partially furled (i.e., reefed).

Rosin-core solder: A type of solder for electrical work with rosin-type flux set in a hollow tube.

Rotor: The name given to the rotating field winding arrangement in an alternator.

Rotary seal. See *mechanical seal*.

Rudderpost, pipe, or stock: The metal post around which a rudder is constructed and to which a tiller arm or quadrant is attached.

Rudderstops: Solid stops that limit the turning radius of a rudder. They must always stop the rudder before the limits of the steering system are reached.

Rudder tube: The hollow tube in which rudderpost bearings are set. It frequently terminates in a stuffing box or some other form of shaft seal.

Running backstays: Intermediate backstays set up on quick-release levers.

Running rigging: Rigging used to hoist and control sails.

Sacrificial anodes: Anodes of a less noble metal (generally zinc) electrically connected to underwater hardware and designed to corrode, thereby protecting the rest of the hardware.

Samson post: A strong post in the foredeck.

Screening: The placing of electronic equipment in grounded metal boxes to reduce interference.

Secondary winding: The output winding of a transformer.

Self-amalgamating tape. See *heat-shrink tape*.

Self-discharge: The gradual loss of capacity by a battery when standing idle.

Self-limiting: A built-in feature of some stator

windings that limits alternator output to a certain maximum regardless of speed of rotation.

Self-steering: An apparatus that holds a sailboat on a set course in relation to the wind.

Separators: The material used to divide one battery plate from another.

Series connection: A circuit with only one path for the current to flow. Batteries or appliances are connected one after another; in the case of batteries, negative to positive. Batteries in series deliver greater voltage but no greater capacity than a single battery.

Series-wound motors: A DC motor in which the field winding is connected in series with the armature. If unloaded, series-wound motors run away and can self-destruct.

Servopendulum: The principle underlying many self-steering devices.

Sheave: The pulley within a block.

Shielding: The placing of electric cables within grounded, braid-covered sheaths (or copper tubing) to reduce interference.

Shim: A specially cut piece of shim stock used as a spacer in specific applications, generally engine alignment.

Shim stock: Very thin, accurately machined pieces of metal.

Short circuit. See *circuit*.

Shroud: Wire rope or rod supporting a mast in an athwartships direction. *Cap* shrouds (*upper* shrouds) run to the masthead, *intermediate* shrouds to the upper spreaders (if fitted), and *lower* shrouds to the lower spreaders.

Shunt: A special low-resistance connection in a circuit enabling an ammeter to be connected in parallel with the circuit.

Shunt-wound motors: Motors in which the field windings and armature are connected in parallel.

Sine wave: The wave made by alternating current when voltage is charted against time.

Siphon: The ability of a liquid to flow through a hose if one end is lower than the liquid level, even if the hose is looped above the liquid level.

Siphon break. See *antisiphon valve*.

Skeg: A small keel aft used to support a rudder.

Slinger: A washer on an electric pump shaft designed to deflect any leakage past the shaft seals away from the motor.

Slip rings: Insulated metal discs on a rotor or armature shaft through which current is fed, via brushes, to or from armature or rotor windings.

Slow blow fuse: A fuse with delayed action for use with motors with high starting loads.

Snap ring: A spring-tensioned ring that fits into a groove on the inside of a hollow shaft or around the outside of a shaft.

Snap ring pliers: Special pliers for installing and removing snap rings.

SNR (signal-to-noise ratio): The ratio of the desired signal to the background noise.

Snubber. See *fail-safe diode*.

Solenoid: A powerful relay.

Spade rudder: A rudder with no support beneath the hull.

Spanner: British term for a wrench.

Specific gravity (sg): A measure of the density of the electrolyte in a battery, i.e., the strength of the acid and therefore the battery's state of charge.

Spike: A sudden high-voltage peak superimposed on a DC system.

Spindle: A shaft in a winch.

Spiroid gear: A particular type of worm gear.

Split-charging: Charging two or more batteries independently from one charging source.

Split pin. See *cotter pin*.

Spreader: A strut on a mast to improve the angle of shrouds and stiffen the mast panels.

Spreader socket: The means of attaching a spreader to a mast.

Spur gears: A variation of offset gears.

Standing rigging: Permanently attached rigging supporting a mast.

Standpipe: A variation of an Aqualift exhaust.

Stator: The stationary armature on an alternator within which the rotor spins.

Stays: Devices to provide fore-and-aft support for a mast.

Stray-current corrosion. See *corrosion*.

Stuffing box: A device for making a watertight seal around a propeller shaft at the point where it exits the boat.

Sulfation: The normal chemical transformation of battery plates when a battery discharges. If a battery is left in a discharged state, the sulfates crystallize, causing a permanent loss of capacity.

Sun gears. See *planetary gears*.

Supercharger: A blower mechanically driven by an engine and used to pressurize the inlet air.

Superheat: An adjustment of an expansion valve in a refrigeration system designed to produce maximum efficiency while providing a margin of safety against liquid slugging at the compressor.

Suppressor: A resistor put in series with a spark plug lead to reduce ignition-radiated interference.

Surge. See *spike*.

Surge protector. See *fail-safe diode*.

Swage (swedge): A wire rope terminal in which the terminal is cold-welded to the rope by extreme pressure.

Swash plate. See *compressor*.

Tack: The lower forward corner of a sail.

Tailpiece: A hose adapter that screws onto a through-hull or seacock.

Tang: A fitting on a mast to which rigging attaches.

Thermistor: A resistor that changes in value with changes in temperature.

Thermocouple: A device containing two dissimilar metals that generates a very small voltage when heated. It is used to open a solenoid on gas appliances; if the flame fails, the solenoid closes.

Thermostat: A heat-sensitive device used to control the flow of coolant through an engine; a heat-sensitive switch used to turn a water-heating element, refrigeration unit, or air conditioner off and on.

Thickness gauge. See *feeler gauge*.

Thimble: A grooved metal fitting around which loops in wire rope are formed.

Tinning: The process of getting solder to adhere to a soldering iron, wire end, or fitting.

Tiller arm: A short lever arm bolted to a rudderpost.

Toggle: A swivel joint used in rigging.

Topping lift: A line used to hold a boom off the deck.

Transformer: An AC device consisting of two or more coils used to magnetically couple one circuit to another. Depending on how the coils are wound, it can be used to lower or raise voltage. See also *isolation transformer*.

Transient voltage suppressor. See *fail-safe diode*.

Traversing nut: The nut that rides up and down the worm gear in worm steering.

Trickle charge: A continuous low-current charge.

Trim tab: A small rudder hinged to the trailing edge of a main or auxiliary rudder.

Turbocharger: A blower driven by engine exhaust gas and used to pressurize the inlet air.

Turnbuckle: An adjustable fitting used to tension standing rigging.

Two-pole switch (or breaker). See *double-pole switch*.

Tywraps. Plastic cable ties used for bundling up cables and/or fastening them to a hull side.

Ungrounded conductor. A current-carrying conductor in an AC circuit that is completely insulated from ground (a hot conductor).

Upper shroud. See *shroud*.

Vacuum: Pressure below atmospheric pressure.

Vacuum pump: A pump to suck a refrigeration system into an almost complete vacuum.

Valve: A device to allow gases in and out of a cylinder at precise moments; a means of controlling the flow of liquids, such as a ball valve, a gate valve, etc.

Valve clearance: The gap between a valve stem and its rocker arm when the valve is fully closed.

Valve cover: The housing of an engine bolted over the valve mechanism.

Vane pumps: Pumps with hard plastic blades (vanes) slotted into a central rotating hub.

Varistor: A resistor that changes in value with changes in voltage.

Vented loop. See *antisiphon valve*.

Vise-Grips: Mole wrench.

Volt: A unit of measurement of the "pressure" in an electrical system.

Voltage drop: The loss in "pressure" in wiring, switches, and connections due to unwanted resistance.

Voltage regulation: The process of controlling the output of an alternator or a generator. The output is normally matched to the battery's state of charge, tapering down as the battery comes up to full charge; this is *constant-potential* regulation. Alternatively, output can be maintained at a certain level regardless of state of charge; this is *constant-current* regulation.

Watt: A unit of electrical power.

Wavelength: The distance between successive crests of a wave (radio, sound, or water).

Wear plate: A replaceable plate found in some pumps.

Wildcat. See *gypsy*.

Windings: Coils in a motor or transformer.

Worm gear: A particular type of high-reduction gear used to redirect a drive force or torque through a 90-degree angle.

Worm steering: The application of worm gearing to a steering unit.

Wrench: Spanner.

Yaw: The characteristic of a boat, particularly a sailboat running downwind, to wander rhythmically either side of a course line.

Zone of security: The "protected" area beneath a lightning rod.

Appendix A: Checklist of Winterizing Procedures

The following is a very complete list of winterizing procedures. Not all of them will be needed at every haulout; the individual boatowner will have to make some decisions about how thorough to be.

It is far better to perform most routine maintenance at the end of the season when laying up rather than when recommissioning for the next season. Engines, in particular, will benefit from clean oil. Problem areas will be identified while you have plenty of time to fix them.

Note: Whenever using antifreeze, remember that ethylene glycol (automotive antifreeze) is poisonous, so do not put it in freshwater systems. Use propylene glycol, which is nontoxic.

Laying Up

Engine and gear train.

- Change the engine and transmission oil at the beginning of the winter. The old oil will contain all kinds of harmful acids and contaminants, which should not be left to work on the engine and transmission all winter long.
- Change the antifreeze on freshwater-cooled engines. The antifreeze itself does not wear out, but it has various corrosion-fighting additives that do.
- Drain the raw-water system, taking particular care to empty all low spots. Remove rubber pump impellers, lightly grease with petroleum jelly, and replace. Leave the pump cover screws loose so that the impeller won't stick in the pump housing. Run the engine for a *few seconds* to drive any remaining water out of the exhaust. Wash salt crystals out of any vented loops.
- Check the primary fuel filter and fuel tank for water and sediment; clean as necessary. Keeping the tank full will cut down on condensation.
- Squirt some oil or WD-40 into the inlet manifold and turn the engine over a few times (without starting it) to spread the oil over the cylinder walls.
- Grease all grease points.
- Remove the inner wires of engine control cables from their outer sheaths; clean, inspect, grease, and replace. Check the sheathing as outlined in Chapter 10.
- Seal all openings into the engine (e.g., air inlet, exhaust) and the fuel tank vent. *Put a conspicuous notice somewhere that you have done this so that you remember to unseal everything at the start of the next season.*
- Inspect all flexible feet and couplings for signs of softening (generally from oil and fuel leaks) and replace as necessary.
- Inspect all hoses for signs of softening, cracking, and/or bulging, especially hoses on the hot side of the cooling and exhaust systems.
- Check the propeller shaft–coupling setscrews or through-bolt.
- If hauling out: Check for propeller blade misalignment; flex the propeller and propeller shaft to check for Cutless bearing wear; tighten any strut mounting bolts; and inspect a stainless steel propeller shaft for any signs of crevice corrosion.

Batteries. Bring batteries to a full charge. Equalize wet-cell deep-cycle batteries. Top off. Clean the battery tops. Unless the batteries are being properly float-charged (via a solar panel or battery charger with *float* regulation), remove them from the boat and store in a cool, dry place. Bring wet-cell batteries to a full charge once a month.

Generators and electric motors. Clean and spray with a moisture-dispelling aerosol such as WD-40. Brush springs, in particular, will benefit from a shot of spray. Where generators have grease or oil fittings, give one shot or put in a drop. Pay particular attention to starter motor pinions.

Electrical circuits. Clean corrosion off all terminals and connections and protect with petroleum jelly or a shot of WD-40 or other moisture-dispelling aerosol. Pay particular attention to all external outlets, especially the AC shore-power inlet. Open up all coaxial connections if there is any possibility of water ingress; clean, repair as necessary, and reseal.

Electronic equipment. Remove electronic equipment to a warm, dry place.

Refrigeration and air-conditioning units. Drain condenser raw-water circuits. If loops in the circuits make this impossible, pump 30% to 50% antifreeze solution through the unit. Spray a compressor clutch with WD-40.

Toilets. Drain and/or pump a 30% to 50% antifreeze solution through the system. (Note: Specialized holding tanks, such as Raritan's

LectraSan, must be winterized according to the manufacturer's instructions.) Break loose the discharge hose and check for calcification. Wash out all vented loops.

Pumps. Drain and/or pump through a 30% to 50% antifreeze solution. Remove flexible impellers, lightly grease with a Teflon-based grease, and put back. Leave pump covers loose; tighten down only when recommissioning. Inspect all vanes, impellers, etc., for wear; check for shaft seal leaks. If wintering in the water, check the bilge pump float switch, wiring, switch, and the state of charge of the battery.

Freshwater systems. Pump out the tanks and drain the system. Clean the tanks. If antifreeze is used in any pumps, make sure it is *propylene glycol*. Lightly oil connecting rod bearings (if fitted) on freshwater pumps.

Stuffing boxes. If hauling out, repack. If wintering in the water, tighten down to stop any drip. *Be sure to loosen before reusing the propeller or the shaft will overheat* (post a note in a prominent place).

Seacocks. If hauling out, pull and grease all seacock plugs where possible. Dismantle and grease gate valves. If wintering in the water, close all seacocks (except cockpit drains) and make a close inspection of cockpit drain hoses and clamps.

Hydraulic systems. Drain a little oil and check for water or contaminants. Top off as necessary. Check all seals and hoses for signs of leaks; check hoses for damage.

Water heaters. Drain all water. *Leave a conspicuous notice somewhere so that you will be sure to refill before turning electric heaters back on.*

Stoves. Drain a little fuel from kerosene and/or alcohol tanks to check for water or contaminants. Close LPG or CNG gas valves *at the cylinder*. It is a good idea to renew filaments on filament-type igniters at least every 2 years.

Steering. Lightly oil cables, and oil or grease sheave and pedestal bearings as called for. Pay particular attention to the worm gear (if fitted) and other steel parts that might seize up. Remove cables from conduits; clean, inspect, grease, and replace. Check all sheave mountings, bracing, and rudderstops. Check the rudderhead and tension the cables. With pedestal-type rack-and-pinion steering, remove the top plate and input socket screws; clean, grease, and replace.

Running rigging. Wash all blocks. Disassemble and clean where possible. Use hot water and vinegar on stubborn salt deposits. Lubricate and reassemble. Wash all synthetic lines in a warm detergent solution. Adding a little bleach will do no harm.

Spars and standing rigging.

- *Wooden spars and spreaders:* Wash and inspect closely for any signs of rot (e.g., softening or discoloration), especially on spreaders and around fasteners and exit holes. Seal bare spots even if you are not varnishing or painting at this time.
- *Aluminum spars:* Wash and inspect for signs of corrosion, distortion of mast walls (especially around spreader sockets), crazing of anodizing, and hairline cracks (especially around welds and cutouts). Remove and grease any fasteners that must be prevented from freezing up. Wax the spar before storing.
- *Carbon fiber spars:* Clean and inspect all attachment points for signs of delamination or other damage.
- *All spars:* Withdraw mast tang bolts and check for crevice corrosion. Remove boots or covers from spreader tips. Remove head box sheaves and inspect shafts and sheaves. Lubricate and replace. Remove turnbuckle boots, tape, etc. Undo all turnbuckles; clean, inspect, and grease. Pay close attention to clevis pins; when replacing, tape over the ends of cotter pins (split pins). Inspect swages for hairline cracks. Wash all rigging. Do not store stainless against aluminum spars.

Winches, windlasses, and deck hardware. Strip down, clean, grease, and oil all winches. Pay particular attention to pawls and pawl springs. Check the lubricant in windlasses for water and change as necessary. Crank windlasses over to spread lubricant around the internal parts. Remove the rope drum and wildcat (gypsy) and grease clutches and shafts. Check fasteners on all deck hardware; check carefully for flaws in the bedding (caulking) that might cause deck leaks.

Roller reefing gear. Thoroughly flush all open bearings with warm fresh water. Regrease or lubricate as called for by the manufacturer, spinning the bearings to spread the lubricant around. Wash extrusions and apply wax. Pay close attention to all joints. Do not leave the sail up; it should be stowed for the winter.

Sacrificial anodes. Inspect and change all zincs

as necessary (hull, rudder, propeller shaft, engine cooling system, refrigeration condenser, etc.).

Recommissioning

1. Check the layup list and complete those jobs that weren't done.
2. *Observe and obey all conspicuous notes*; envision areas that should have such notes but do not (plugged-off engine air inlets and exhausts, overtightened packing nut, empty hot-water tank, etc.).
3. Check all hoses and through-hull connections (hose clamps: *undo the clamps a turn or two to check for corrosion of the band inside the screw housing*).

4. Check the refrigerant charge on refrigeration systems—engine-driven compressor seals are especially prone to drying out and leaking during long periods of shutdown.
5. "Exercise" (i.e., switch on and off a few times) all switches—this helps clean surface corrosion off terminals. Open and close seacocks; spin blocks and windlasses. Turn the steering wheel from side to side and check for any stiff spots or binding. Spin the drum and halyard swivels on roller reefers.
6. Tighten down all flexible-impeller pump covers; prime centrifugal pumps.
7. Once the boat is in the water, allow the hull to stabilize (this takes a few days on wooden hulls), then check the engine alignment.

Appendix B: Freeing Frozen Parts and Fasteners

Problems with frozen fasteners are inevitable on boats. One or more of the following techniques may free things up.

Lubrication

- Clean everything with a wire brush (preferably one with brass or stainless steel bristles), douse liberally with penetrating oil, and wait. Find something else to do for an hour or two, overnight if possible, before having another go. Be patient.
- Clevis pins: After lubricating and waiting, grip the large end of the pin with Vise-Grips (mole wrench) and turn the pin in its socket to free it. If the pin is the type with a cotter pin in both ends, remove one of the cotter pins, grip the clevis pin, and turn. Since the Vise-Grips will probably mar the surface of the pin, it should be knocked out from the other end.

Shock Treatment

An impact wrench is a handy tool to have around. These take a variety of end fittings (e.g., screwdriver bits and sockets) to match different fasteners. Hit the wrench hard with a hammer and hopefully it will jar the fastener loose. If an impact wrench is not available or does not work, apply other forms of shock but with an acute sense of the breaking point of the fastener and adjacent engine castings, etc. Unfortunately this sense is generally acquired only after a lifetime of breaking things! Depending on the problem, shock treatment may take different forms:

- A bolt stuck in an engine block: Put a sizable punch squarely on the head of the bolt and give it a good knock into the block. Now try undoing it.
- A pulley on a tapered shaft, a propeller, or an outboard motor flywheel: Back out the retaining nut *until its face is flush with the end of the shaft* (this is important to avoid damage to the threads on the nut or shaft). Apply pressure behind the pulley, propeller, or flywheel as if trying to pull it off, then hit the end of the retaining nut or shaft smartly. The shock will frequently break things loose without the need for a specialized puller.
- A large nut with limited room around it or one on a shaft that wants to turn (for example, a crankshaft pulley nut): Put a short-handled wrench on the nut, hold the wrench to prevent it from jumping off, and hit it hard.
- If all else fails, use a cold chisel to cut a slot in the side of the offending nut or the head of the bolt, place a punch in the slot at a tangential angle to the nut or bolt, and hit it smartly.

Leverage

- Screws: With a square-bladed screwdriver, put a crescent (adjustable) wrench on the blade, bear down hard on the screw, and turn the screwdriver with the wrench. If the screwdriver has a round blade, clamp a pair of Vise-Grips to the base of the handle and do the same thing.
- Nuts and bolts: If using wrenches with one box end and one open end, put the box end of the

appropriate wrench on the fastener and hook the box end of the next size up into the free open end of the wrench. This will double the length of the handle and thus the leverage.

- Cheater pipe: Slip a length of pipe over the handle of the wrench to increase its leverage.

Heat

Heat expands metal, but for this treatment to be effective, frozen fasteners must often be raised to cherry-red temperatures, which will upset tempering in hardened steel. Uneven heating of surrounding castings may cause them to crack. Heat must be applied carefully.

Heat applied to a frozen nut will expand it outward, and it can then be broken loose. But equally, heat applied to the bolt will expand it within the nut, generating all kinds of pressure that helps to break the grip of rust, etc. When the fixture cools it will frequently come apart quite easily.

Broken Fasteners

- Rounded-off heads: Sometimes there is not enough head left on a fastener to grip with Vise-Grips or pipe (stillson) wrenches, but there is enough to accept a slot made by a hacksaw. A screwdriver can then be inserted and turned as above.

- If a head breaks off, it is often possible to remove whatever it was holding, thus exposing part of the shaft of the fastener. It can then be lubricated, gripped with Vise-Grips, and backed out.

- Drilling out: It is very important to drill down the center of a broken fastener. Use a center punch and take some time putting an accurate "dimple" at this point before attempting to drill. Next, use a small drill to make a pilot hole to the desired depth. If Ezy-Outs or screw extractors (hardened, tapered steel screws with reversed threads—available from tool supply houses) are on hand, drill the correctly sized hole for the appropriate Ezy-Out and try extracting the stud. Otherwise drill out the stud *up to the insides of its threads but no farther*, or you will do irreparable damage to the threads in the casting. The remaining bits of fastener thread in the casting can be picked out with judicious use of a small screwdriver or some pointed instrument. If a tap is available to clean up the threads, so much the better.

- Pipe fittings: If you can get a hacksaw blade inside the relevant fittings (which can often be done using duct tape to make a handle on the blade), cut a slit in the fitting along its length, then place a punch on the outside, alongside the cut. Hit it, and collapse it inward. Do the same on the other side of the cut. The fitting should now come out easily.

Miscellaneous

- Stainless steel: Stainless-to-stainless fasteners (for example, many turnbuckles) have a bad habit of *galling* when being done up or undone, especially if there is any dirt in the threads to cause friction. Galling (also known as *cold-welding*) is a process in which molecules on the surface of one part of the fastener transfer to the other part. Everything seizes up for good. Galled stainless fastenings cannot be salvaged—they almost always end up shearing off. When doing up or undoing a stainless fastener, if any sudden or unusual friction develops, *stop immediately*, let it cool off, lubricate thoroughly, work the fastener backward and forward to spread the lubrication around, go back the other way, clean the threads, and start again.

- Aluminum: Aluminum oxidizes to form a dense white powder. Aluminum oxide is more voluminous than the original aluminum and so generates a lot of pressure around any fasteners passing through aluminum fixtures—sometimes enough pressure to shear off the heads of fasteners. Once oxidation around a stainless or bronze fastener has reached a certain point, it is virtually impossible to remove the fastener without breaking it. (One reader has written me to say that if corroded aluminum parts are immersed in fresh water for 7 to 14 days, the aluminum oxide precipitates out, allowing fasteners to be undone.)

- Damaged threads: If all else fails, and a fastener must be drilled out, the threads in the casting may be damaged. There are two options:

  1. Drill and tap for the next-larger fastener.
  2. Install a Heli-Coil insert. A Heli-Coil is a new thread. An oversized hole is drilled and tapped with a special tap, and the Heli-Coil insert (the new thread) is screwed into the hole with a special tool. You end up with the original size hole and threads. Any good machine shop will have the relevant tools and inserts.

Appendix C: Tools and Spare Parts

The following tool and spare parts lists may cause some people to accuse me of letting my imagination run wild. Let me assure you we have had all of this and more (including oxyacetylene, rolls of copper tubing, and a complete controllable-pitch propeller unit) on board at various times, and we have used almost everything at one time or another on our boat or someone else's. (Note: When ordering spares, always include the model number and the serial number of the equipment the spares are for, in case there have been changes within a model range.)

However, nowadays, given a newer boat and expanded worldwide delivery services (FedEx, UPS, DHL, etc.), and given a greater focus on performance and weight reduction, I carry something closer to a bare-bones tool kit and spare parts inventory.

There is a continuum here between trying to carry everything and carrying almost nothing. Where you fall on this continuum will depend on the age and condition of your boat, how far off the beaten track you intend to sail, and your personal level of paranoia!

Mechanic's Toolbox

Screwdrivers—Phillips head and slotted—a selection. Especially useful is a short-handled version of each for awkward corners.

Open end/box end wrench (spanner) set—$\frac{1}{4}$″ to 1″ (or metric equivalent, or both if you have a mixture of U.S. Standard and metric nuts and bolts)

$\frac{3}{8}$″ drive socket set, $\frac{1}{4}$″ to 1″ (or metric, as above). The $\frac{3}{8}$″ is much easier to handle in tight spaces than a $\frac{1}{2}$″ drive, but with the larger-sized sockets (over $\frac{3}{4}$″), it will get severely stressed, so buy only top-quality ratchets and extensions.

6″ and 10″ crescent (adjustable) wrench

6″ and 10″ Vise-Grips (mole wrench)

12″ and 18″ pipe wrench—preferably aluminum, which is much lighter and won't rust nearly as badly (although aluminum wrenches still have steel jaws)

Side-cutting needle-nose pliers

Ball-peen hammer

Set of Allen wrenches (keys)

Set of feeler (thickness) gauges—inches or metric, as appropriate

Aligning punches—these taper to a reasonably fine head

Straight punches—for knocking out recalcitrant clevis pins, etc.

Cold chisels

Files—flat, half round, and round

Scrapers—for removing old gaskets

Brass or stainless steel bristle wire brush—steel bristles leave flecks of rust

Emery cloth

Fine and medium grinding paste

Hacksaw and blades—buy one in which the end fittings are captured—i.e., cannot fall out when the blade breaks—or they are sure to get lost

Snap ring (circlip) pliers—both inside (internal) and outside (external)

Pulley puller—very useful on occasion

Set of taps and dies—U.S. Standard, metric, or both

Propane torch

Small vise—if it can be accommodated (some very neat ones clip into a standard winch socket)

Engine and Mechanical Supplies

Engine and transmission (gearbox) oil

Oil filter (and sealing rings) and an oil-filter wrench

Fuel filters and a fuel-filter wrench (where needed)

Filter funnel for taking on fuel

Grease gun

Grease

Oil squirt can

Silicone spray

WD-40

Valve cover gasket

Injector sealing washers (if fitted)

Injector

Set of injector lines (injection pump to injectors)

Lift pump (feed pump) diaphragm

Pump overhaul kits for all cooling-water pumps (impellers/diaphragms, seals, and bearings)

Gasket cement

Thermostat

Hoses (including oil cooler hoses)

O-ring kit (an assortment)

All belts

Packing

Wrench (spanner) for packing nut

Packing removal tool

$\frac{1}{4}''$, $\frac{5}{16}''$, $\frac{3}{8}''$, and $\frac{1}{2}''$ stainless steel threaded rod

Stainless steel nuts and lock washers for the above

Length of $\frac{1}{4}''$ and $\frac{3}{8}''$ keystock

Flare tubing kit (if there is any flared copper tubing on board)

Tubing cutters

Zincs (world cruisers might consider carrying a spare heat exchanger and oil cooler)

Electrical Tool Kit

Different sizes of multistranded and tinned copper cable

Wire strippers/crimpers

Appropriate crimp-on terminals

Heat-shrink (self-amalgamating) tape and tubing

Electrician's putty

Insulating (electrician's) tape

Soldering iron, solder, and flux (rosin type)

Spare coaxial end fittings and connectors

Hydrometer for battery testing

Battery terminal puller

Multimeter

Test light(s)

Amprobe for measuring AC amps (if the boat has a lot of AC equipment)

Ground fault tester for checking dockside power

Flashlight batteries

Fuses

Petroleum jelly—for greasing terminals

Spare alternator and voltage regulator

Lightbulbs (especially quartz halogen navigation bulbs—note that boats with higher voltage regulator settings will blow bulbs faster than those with lower settings)

Ballast units for fluorescent lights

Woodworking Tool Kit (choose to suit)

Crosscut saw

Chisels

Wood bits (drill bits)

Plug cutters

Set square

Framing square

Bar clamps

Doweling

Epoxy glue and thickeners

Plastic resin glue (e.g., Weldwood)

Tenon (back) saw

Mallet

Countersink

Tape measure

Bevel square

C-clamps

Plane

Sandpaper—wet-or-dry, #80 grit to #400

Power Tools (where appropriate)

Electric drill—$\frac{1}{2}''$ chuck

Set of drill bits—$\frac{1}{16}''$ to $\frac{1}{2}''$

Set of holesaws—very useful, buy good quality

Jigsaw

Circular saw

Palm (block) sander

Router and bits

General Supplies

Paint, varnish, and brushes

Paint scrapers

Thinners

Acetone (ensure it cannot spill)

Fiberglass cloth, mat, and disposable brushes

Fasteners—bronze threaded nails, bronze or stainless steel screws, stainless steel nuts and bolts

Duct tape

Masking tape

Teflon tape—very useful

Bedding (caulking)—polyurethane adhesive such as 3M 5200, polysulfide adhesive sealant such as Boatlife or Thiokol, silicone sealant

Old inner tube—when cut up in strips and wrapped tightly around ruptured hoses, it seals very effectively

Selection of all-stainless-steel hose clamps (Jubilee clips)—be sure to check the screws for nonmagnetism, indicating a 300-grade stainless steel

Copper pipe and fittings—where appropriate

PVC pipe, fittings, and glue—check the glue annually and replace as necessary; it may dry out

Sail repair kit

Selection of hoses and hose adapters (hose barbs, etc.)

Antifreeze—ethylene glycol for general purpose; *propylene glycol for freshwater systems*

Rigging Kit

Length of cable as long as the longest stay on the boat—preferably 7 × 19, which is more flexible than 1 × 19 and can be used in steering repairs

End fittings for the above—e.g., Sta-Lok or Norseman. If using 7 × 19 wire be sure to get the correct inserts if they differ from those used on 1 × 19 wire.

Turnbuckles, toggles, forks, and eyes—e.g., Sta-Lok or Norseman

Bolt cutters

Nicopress (Talurit) kit

Cable clamps (Crosby clamps, Bulldog clamps) —matched to cable sizes

Thimbles—matched to cable sizes

Shackles

Seizing wire

Complete chain and wire rope assembly for wheel steering

Selection of clevis pins and cotter pins (split pins)

One or two spare blocks

Specific Supplies

Pump overhaul kit—impeller/diaphragm/vanes/ cup washers, seals, bearings, and any valves for every pump on board

Spare DC motors for electric pumps, especially vital ones (e.g., an electric toilet or refrigeration condenser pump)

Brushes for universal or permanent-magnet motors

Freshwater pump overhaul kit and pressure switch

Manual toilet overhaul kit—valves, piston cup washers or O-rings, piston rod seal (get extra spares)

Baby (mineral) oil

Muriatic acid

Winch pawls and springs

Generator brushes and capacitors

AC electric motor capacitors

Wind generator vanes (blades) and brushes— where appropriate

Self-steering wind vanes

Autopilot belts—where appropriate

Electric water heater element and thermostat

Gas stove and appliance thermocouples and/or optical sensors

Burner and pressure tank repair kit where appropriate—kerosene or alcohol stove nipple (orifice) wrench, 10 mm wrench (spanner) for the valve stem packing, an eraser-tipped pencil (for removing cleaning needles), and cup washers for the fuel tank pump

Spare burners and burner parts (valve stems, cleaning needles, and nipples), sealing washers

Mantles for pressurized kerosene (white-gas) lanterns or gas lanterns

Refrigeration supplies:

Refrigerant—R-12, HFC-134a, R-22, or whatever is used in the boat

Stem-type valve wrench

Gauge set

Leak detection kit—to fit the propane torch in the mechanic's tool kit

Refrigeration oil

Receiver-filter-drier (or filters and sight glass if the unit has individual components)

Compressor clutch coil for engine-driven compressor

Special tools for removing the compressor pulley

Condenser water pump overhaul kit

Expansion valve

Sacrificial zinc anodes

Multifunction "key" for undoing fuel and water fill caps and deck plates—very useful little item

Softwood fids—to fit all seacocks and hull openings below the waterline

One or two plywood blanks—to fit portholes, with some means of quickly securing them, in case a porthole gets stove in

Hydraulic systems:

Length of hydraulic hose as long as the longest hose run on the boat

Sufficient fittings to be able to use hose length to replace any hose run

Hydraulic oil—a good reserve supply

Spare filter

Appendix D: Useful Tables

TABLE D-1. Fraction, Decimal, and Metric Equivalents

Fractions	Decimal In.	Metric mm.	Fractions	Decimal In.	Metric mm.
1/64	.015625	.397	33/64	.515625	13.097
1/32	.03125	.794	17/32	.53125	13.494
3/64	.046875	1.191	35/64	.546875	13.891
1/16	.0625	1.588	9/16	.5625	14.288
5/64	.078125	1.984	37/64	.578125	14.684
3/32	.09375	2.381	19/32	.59375	15.081
7/64	.109375	2.778	39/64	.609375	15.478
1/8	.125	3.175	5/8	.625	15.875
9/64	.140625	3.572	41/64	.640625	16.272
5/32	.15625	3.969	21/32	.65625	16.669
11/64	.171875	4.366	43/64	.671875	17.066
3/16	.1875	4.763	11/16	.6875	17.463
13/64	.203125	5.159	45/64	.703125	17.859
7/32	.21875	5.556	23/32	.71875	18.256
15/64	.234375	5.953	47/64	.734375	18.653
1/4	.250	6.35	3/4	.750	19.05
17/64	.265625	6.747	49/64	.765625	19.447
9/32	.28125	7.144	25/32	.78125	19.844
19/64	.296875	7.54	51/64	.796875	20.241
5/16	.3125	7.938	13/16	.8125	20.638
21/64	.328125	8.334	53/64	.828125	21.034
11/32	.34375	8.731	27/32	.84375	21.431
23/64	.359375	9.128	55/64	.859375	21.828
3/8	.375	9.525	7/8	.875	22.225
25/64	.390625	9.922	57/64	.890625	22.622
13/32	.40625	10.319	29/32	.90625	23.019
27/64	.421875	10.716	59/64	.921875	23.416
7/16	.4375	11.113	15/16	.9375	23.813
29/64	.453125	11.509	61/64	.953125	24.209
15/32	.46875	11.906	31/32	.96875	24.606
31/64	.484375	12.303	63/64	.984375	25.003
1/2	.500	12.7	1	1.00	25.4

TABLE D-2. Inches to Millimeters Conversion Table

Inches	Millimeters	Inches	Millimeters	Inches	Millimeters
0.001	0.0254	0.010	0.2540	0.019	0.4826
0.002	0.0508	0.011	0.2794	0.020	0.5080
0.003	0.0762	0.012	0.3048	0.021	0.5334
0.004	0.1016	0.013	0.3302	0.022	0.5588
0.005	0.1270	0.014	0.3556	0.023	0.5842
0.006	0.1524	0.015	0.3810	0.024	0.6096
0.007	0.1778	0.016	0.4064	0.025	0.6350
0.008	0.2032	0.017	0.4318		
0.009	0.2286	0.018	0.4572		

TABLE D-3. Torque Conversion Table, Pound Feet to Newton Meters

Pound-Feet (lb.-ft.)	Newton Metres (Nm)	Newton Metres (Nm)	Pound-Feet (lb.-ft.)
1	1.356	1	0.7376
2	2.7	2	1.5
3	4.0	3	2.2
4	5.4	4	3.0
5	6.8	5	3.7
6	8.1	6	4.4
7	9.5	7	5.2
8	10.8	8	5.9
9	12.2	9	6.6
10	13.6	10	7.4
15	20.3	15	11.1
20	27.1	20	14.8
25	33.9	25	18.4
30	40.7	30	22.1
35	47.5	35	25.8
40	54.2	40	29.5
45	61.0	50	36.9
50	67.8	60	44.3
55	74.6	70	51.6
60	81.4	80	59.0
65	88.1	90	66.4
70	94.9	100	73.8
75	101.7	110	81.1
80	108.5	120	88.5
90	122.0	130	95.9
100	135.6	140	103.3
110	149.1	150	110.6
120	162.7	160	118.0
130	176.3	170	125.4
140	189.8	180	132.8
150	203.4	190	140.1
160	216.9	200	147.5
170	230.5	225	166.0
180	244.0	250	184.4

TABLE D-4. Feet to Meters Conversion Table

Feet — metres 1 foot = 0.3048 m			
ft.	met.	ft.	met.
1	0,305	31	9,449
2	**0,610**	**32**	**9,754**
3	0,914	33	10,058
4	**1,219**	**34**	**10,363**
5	1,524	35	10,668
6	**1,829**	**36**	**10,973**
7	2,134	37	11,278
8	**2,438**	**38**	**11,582**
9	2,743	39	11,887
10	**3,048**	**40**	**12,192**
11	3,353	41	12,497
12	**3,658**	**42**	**12,802**
13	3,962	43	13,106
14	**4,267**	**44**	**13,441**
15	4,572	45	13,716
16	**4,877**	**46**	**14,021**
17	5,182	47	14,326
18	**5,486**	**48**	**14,630**
19	5,791	49	14,935
20	**6,096**	**50**	**15,240**
21	6,401	51	15,545
22	**6,706**	**52**	**15,850**
23	7,010	53	16,154
24	**7,315**	**54**	**16,459**
25	7,620	55	16,764
26	**7,925**	**56**	**17,069**
27	8,230	57	17,374
28	**8,534**	**58**	**17,678**
29	8,839	59	17,983
30	**9,144**	**60**	**18,288**

TABLE D-5. Meters to Feet Conversion Table

Metres — Feet 1 metre = 3.2808 feet	
met.	feet
1	3,28
2	**6,56**
3	9,84
4	**13,12**
5	16,40
6	**19,69**
7	22,97
8	**26,25**
9	29,53
10	**32,81**
11	36,09
12	**39,37**
13	42,65
14	**45,93**
15	49,21
16	**52,49**
17	55,77
18	**59,06**
19	62,34
20	**65,62**

TABLE D-6. Inches to Centimeters Conversion Table

Inches — centimetres 1 inch = 2.54 cm	
inches	cm
1	2,54
2	**5,08**
3	7,62
4	**10,16**
5	12,70
6	**15,24**
7	17,78
8	**20,32**
9	22,86
10	**25,40**
11	27,94
12	**30,48**

°F	°C	°F	°C	°F	°C	°F	°C	°F	°C	°F	°C	°F	°C	°F	°C
-454	-270	-31	-35	19.4	-7	70	21.1	120.2	49	171	77.2	225	107.2	660	348.9
-450	-268	-30	34.4	20	-6.7	71	21.7	121	49.4	172	77.8	230	110	662	350
-440	-262	-29.2	-34	21	-6.1	71.6	22	122	50	172.4	78	235	112.8	670	354.4
-436	-260	-29	-33.9	21.2	-6	72	22.2	123	50.6	173	78.3	239	115	680	360
-430	-257	-28	-33.3	22	-5.6	73	22.8	123.8	51	174	78.9	240	115.6	690	365.6
-420	-251	-27.4	-33	23	-5	73.4	23	124	51.1	174.2	79	245	118.3	693	370
-418	-250	-27	-32.8	24	-4.4	74	23.3	125	51.7	175	79.4	248	120	700	371.1
-410	-246	-26	-32.2	24.8	-4	75	23.9	125.6	52	176	80	250	121.1	710	377
-400	-240	-25.6	-32	25	-3.9	75.2	24	126	52.2	177	80.6	255	123.9	716	380
-390	-234	-25	-31.7	26	-3.3	76	24.4	127	52.8	177.8	81	257	125	720	382
-382	-230	-24	-31.1	26.6	-3	77	25	127.4	53	178	81.1	260	125.7	730	388
-380	-229	-23.8	-31	27	-2.8	78	25.6	128	53.3	179	81.7	265	129.4	734	390
-370	-223	-23	-30.6	28	-2.2	78.8	26	129	53.9	179.6	82	266	130	740	393
-364	-220	-22	-30	28.4	-2	79	26.1	129.2	54	180	82.2	270	132.2	750	399
-360	-218	-21	-29.4	29	-1.7	80	26.7	130	54.4	181	82.8	275	135	752	400
-350	-212	-20.2	-29	30	-1.1	80.6	27	131	55	181.4	83	280	137.8	760	404
-346	-210	-20	-28.9	30.2	-1	81	27.2	132	55.6	182	83.3	284	140	770	410
-340	-207	-19	-28.3	31	-0.6	82	27.8	132.8	56	183	83.9	285	140.6	780	416
-330	-201	-18.4	-28	32	0	82.4	28	133	56.1	183.2	84	290	143.3	788	420
-328	-200	-18	-27.8	33	0.6	83	28.3	134	56.7	184	84.4	293	145	790	421
-320	-196	-17	-27.2	33.8	1	84	28.9	134.6	57	185	85	295	146.1	800	427
-310	-190	-16.6	-27	34	1.1	84.2	29	135	57.2	186	85.6	300	148.9	806	430
-300	-184	-16	-26.7	35	1.7	85	29.4	136	57.8	186.8	86	302	150	810	432
-292	-180	-15	-26.1	35.6	2	86	30	136.4	58	187	86.1	310	154.4	820	438
-290	-179	-14.8	-26	36	2.2	87	30.6	137	58.3	188	86.7	320	160	824	440
-280	-173	-14	-25.6	37	2.8	87.8	31	138	58.9	188.6	87	330	165.6	830	443
-274	-170	-13	-25	37.4	3	88	31.1	138.2	59	189	87.2	338	170	840	449
-270	-168	-12	-24.4	38	3.3	89	31.7	139	59.4	190	87.8	340	171.1	842	450
-260	-162	-11.2	-24	39	3.9	89.6	32	140	60	190.4	88	350	176.7	850	454
-256	-160	-11	-23.9	39.2	4	90	32.2	141	60.6	191	88.3	356	180	860	460
-250	-157	-10	-23.3	40	4.4	91	32.8	141.8	61	192	88.9	360	182.2	870	466
-240	-151	-9.4	-23	41	5	91.4	33	142	61.1	192.2	89	370	187.8	878	470
-238	-150	-9	-22.8	42	5.5	92	33.3	143	61.7	193	89.4	374	190	880	471
-230	-146	-8	-22.2	42.8	6	93	33.9	143.6	62	194	90	380	193.3	890	477
-220	-140	-7.6	-22	43	6.1	93.2	34	144	62.2	195	90.6	390	198.9	896	480
-210	-134	-7	-21.7	44	6.7	94	34.4	145	62.8	195.8	91	392	200	900	482
-202	-130	-6	-21.1	44.6	7	95	35	145.4	63	196	91.1	400	204.4	910	488
-200	-129	-5.8	-21	45	7.2	96	35.6	146	63.3	197	91.7	410	210	914	490
-190	-123	-5	-20.6	46	7.8	96.8	36	147	63.9	197.6	92	420	215.6	920	493
-184	-120	-4	-20	46.4	8	97	36.1	147.2	64	198	92.2	428	220	930	499
-180	-118	-3	-19.4	47	8.3	98	36.7	148	64.4	199	92.8	430	221.1	932	500
-170	-112	-2.2	-19	48	8.9	98.6	37	149	65	199.4	93	440	226.7	940	504
-166	-110	-2	-18.9	48.2	9	99	37.2	150	65.6	200	93.3	446	230	950	510
-160	-107	-1	-18.3	49	9.4	100	37.8	150.8	66	201	93.9	450	232.2	960	516
-150	-101	-0.4	-18	50	10	100.4	38	151	66.1	201.2	94	460	237.8	968	520
-148	-100	0	-17.8	51	10.6	101	38.3	152	66.7	202	94.4	464	240	970	521
-140	-96	1	-17.2	51.8	11	102	38.9	152.6	67	203	95	470	243.3	980	527
-130	-90	1.4	-17	52	11.1	102.2	39	153	67.2	204	95.6	480	248.9	986	530
-120	-84	2	-16.7	53	11.7	103	39.4	154	67.8	204.8	96	482	250	990	532
-112	-80	3	-16.1	53.6	12	104	40	154.4	68	205	96.1	490	254.4	1000	538
-110	-79	3.2	-16	54	12.2	105	40.6	155	68.3	206	96.7	500	260	1004	540
-100	-73.3	4	-15.6	55	12.8	105.8	41	156	68.9	206.6	97	510	265.6	1022	550
-94	-70	5	-15	55.4	13	106	41.1	156.2	69	207	97.2	518	270	1050	566
-90	-67.8	6	-14.4	56	13.3	107	41.7	157	69.4	208	97.8	520	271.1	1100	593
-80	-62.2	6.8	-14	57	13.9	107.6	42	158	70	208.4	98	530	276.7	1112	600
-76	-60	7	-13.9	57.2	14	108	42.2	159	70.6	209	98.3	536	280	1150	621
-70	-56.7	8	-13.3	58	14.4	109	42.8	159.8	71	210	98.9	540	282.2	1200	649
-60	-51.1	8.6	-13	59	15	109.4	43	160	71.1	210.2	99	554	290	1202	650
-58	-50	9	-12.8	60	15.6	110	43.3	161	71.7	211	99.4	560	293.3	1250	677
-50	-45.6	10	-12.2	60.8	16	111	43.9	161.6	72	212	100	570	298.9	1292	700
-40	-40	10.4	-12	61	16.1	111.2	44	162	72.2	213	100.6	572	300	1300	704
-39	-39.4	11	-11.7	62	16.7	112	44.4	163	72.8	213.8	101	580	304.4	1350	732
-38.2	-39	12	-11.1	62.6	17	113	45	163.4	73	214	101.1	590	310	1382	750
-38	-38.9	12.2	-11	63	17.2	114	45.6	164	73.3	215	101.7	600	315.6	1400	760
-37	-38.3	13	-10.6	64	17.8	114.8	46	165	73.9	215.6	102	608	320	1450	788
-36.4	-38	14	-10	64.4	18	115	46.1	165.2	74	216	102.2	610	321.0	1472	800
-36	-37.8	15	-9.4	65	18.3	116	46.7	166	74.4	217	102.8	620	326.7	1500	816
-35	-37.2	15.8	-9	66	18.9	116.6	47	167	75	217.4	103	626	330		
-34.6	-37	16	-8.9	66.2	19	117	47.2	168	75.6	218	103.3	630	332.2		
-34	-36.7	17	-8.3	67	19.4	118	47.8	168.8	76	219	103.9	640	337.8		
-33	-36.1	17.6	-8	68	20	118.4	48	169	76.1	219.2	104	644	340		
-32.8	-36	18	-7.8	69	20.6	119	48.3	170	76.7	220	104.4	650	343.3		
-32	-35.6	19	-7.2	69.8	21	120	48.9	170.6	77	221	105				

TABLE D-8. Nautical Miles to Kilometers Conversion Table

1 Nautical Mile = 1.8520 Kilometres
(identical conversion for Knots – Kilometres/hour)

nm	0	1	2	3	4	5	6	7	8	9	nm
0	0	1,85	3,70	5,56	7,41	9,26	11,11	12,96	14,82	16,67	0
10	18,52	20,37	22,22	24,08	25,93	27,78	29,63	31,48	33,34	35,19	10
20	37,04	38,89	40,74	42,60	44,45	46,30	48,15	50,00	51,86	53,71	20
30	55,56	57,41	59,26	61,12	62,97	64,82	66,67	68,52	70,38	72,23	30
40	74,08	75,93	77,78	79,64	81,49	83,34	85,19	87,04	88,90	90,75	40
50	92,60	94,45	96,30	98,16	100,01	101,86	103,71	105,56	107,42	109,27	50
60	111,12	112,97	114,82	116,68	118,53	120,38	122,23	124,08	125,94	127,79	60
70	129,64	131,49	133,34	135,20	137,05	138,90	140,75	142,60	144,46	146,31	70
80	148,16	150,01	151,86	153,72	155,57	157,42	159,27	161,12	162,98	164,83	80
90	166,68	168,53	170,38	172,24	174,09	175,94	177,79	179,64	181,50	183,35	90
100	185,20	187,05	188,90	190,76	192,61	194,46	196,31	198,16	200,02	201,87	100

Kilometres – Nautical Miles
1 Kilometre = 0.5400 Nautical Miles
(identical conversion for Kilometres/hour into Knots)

km	0	1	2	3	4	5	6	7	8	9	km
0	0	0,54	1,08	1,62	2,16	2,70	3,24	3,78	4,32	4,86	0
10	5,40	5,94	6,48	7,02	7,56	8,10	8,64	9,18	9,72	10,26	10
20	10,80	11,34	11,88	12,42	12,96	13,50	14,04	14,58	15,12	15,66	20
30	16,20	16,74	17,28	17,82	18,36	18,90	19,44	19,98	20,52	21,06	30
40	21,60	22,14	22,68	23,22	23,76	24,30	24,84	25,38	25,92	26,46	40
50	27,00	27,54	28,08	28,62	29,16	29,70	30,24	30,78	31,32	31,86	50
60	32,40	32,94	33,48	34,02	34,56	35,10	35,64	36,18	36,72	37,26	60
70	37,80	38,34	38,88	39,42	39,96	40,50	41,04	41,58	42,12	42,66	70
80	43,20	43,74	44,28	44,82	45,36	45,90	46,44	46,98	47,52	48,06	80
90	48,60	49,14	49,68	50,22	50,76	51,30	51,84	52,38	52,92	53,46	90
100	54,00	54,54	55,08	55,62	56,16	56,70	57,24	57,78	58,32	58,86	100

This is how it works!
Example 43 nm = ?? km
Go down the first column until you come to 40, then move across to 3.
The result is where the two rows meet (79.64 km)
For values of over 100, the decimal point should be adjusted.
Conversely: 43 km = ?? nm
43 km = 23.22 nm

TABLE D-9. Kilowatts to Horsepower Conversion Table

Kilowatts (kW) into Horsepower (HP)
1 kW = 1.3596 HP

kW	0	1	2	3	4	5	6	7	8	9	kW
0	0	1,3596	2,72	4,08	5,44	6,80	8,16	9,52	10,88	12,24	0
10	13,60	14,96	16,32	17,67	19,03	20,39	21,75	23,11	24,47	25,83	10
20	27,19	28,55	29,91	31,27	32,63	33,99	35,35	36,71	38,07	39,43	20
30	40,79	42,15	43,51	44,87	46,23	47,59	48,95	50,31	51,66	53,02	30
40	54,38	55,74	57,10	58,46	59,82	61,18	62,54	63,90	65,26	66,62	40
50	67,98	69,34	70,70	72,06	73,42	74,78	76,14	77,50	78,86	80,22	50
60.	81,58	82,94	84,30	85,65	87,01	88,37	89,73	91,09	92,45	93,81	60
70	95,17	96,53	97,89	99,25	100,61	101,97	103,33	104,69	106,05	107,41	70
80	108,77	110,13	111,49	112,85	114,21	115,57	116,93	118,29	119,64	121,00	80
90	122,36	123,72	125,08	126,44	127,80	129,16	130,52	131,88	133,24	134,60	90
100	135,96	137,32	138,68	140,04	141,40	142,76	144,12	145,48	146,84	148,20	100

Horsepower (HP) into Kilowatts
1 HP = 0.7355 kW

HP	0	1	2	3	4	5	6	7	8	9	HP
0	0	0,7355	1,47	2,21	2,94	3,68	4,41	5,15	5,88	6,62	0
10	7,36	8,09	8,83	9,56	10,30	11,03	11,77	12,50	13,24	13,97	10
20	14,71	15,45	16,18	16,92	17,65	18,39	19,12	19,86	20,59	21,33	20
30	22,07	22,80	23,54	24,27	25,01	25,74	26,48	27,21	27,95	28,68	30
40	29,42	30,16	30,89	31,63	32,36	33,10	33,83	34,57	35,30	36,04	40
50	36,78	37,51	38,25	38,98	39,72	40,45	41,19	41,92	42,66	43,39	50
60	44,13	44,87	45,60	46,34	47,07	47,81	48,54	49,28	50,01	50,75	60
70	51,49	52,22	52,96	53,69	54,43	55,16	55,90	56,63	57,37	58,10	70
80	58,84	59,58	60,31	61,05	61,78	62,52	63,25	63,99	64,72	65,46	80
90	66,20	66,93	67,67	68,40	69,14	69,87	70,61	71,34	72,08	72,81	90
100	73,55	74,29	75,02	75,76	76,49	77,23	77,96	78,70	79,43	80,17	100

This table is very simple to use. Read off the tens in the vertical scale and the units in the horizontal scale. The answer is where the two lines meet.

Example (above): convert 63 kW into HP. Go down the first column until you find 60 and the across until you come to 3. The result is where the two rows join.
63 kW = 85.65 HP.
For values of over 100, the decimal point should be adjusted.

Example (below): Convert 65 HP into kW. Go down the first column until you find 60 and then across until you come to 3. The result is where the two rows join.
63 HP = 46.34 kW.
For values of over 100, the decimal point should be adjusted.

TABLE D-10. Pounds per Square Inch to Kilograms per Square Centimeter Conversion Table

lb. per sq. inch	0 kg per sq. cm	1 kg per sq. cm	2 kg per sq. cm	3 kg per sq. cm	4 kg per sq. cm	5 kg per sq. cm	6 kg per sq. cm	7 kg per sq. cm	8 kg per sq. cm	9 kg per sq. cm
0	..	0.0703	0.1406	0.2109	0.2812	0.3515	0.4218	0.4922	0.5625	0.6328
10	0.7031	0.7734	0.8437	0.9140	0.9843	1.0546	1.1249	1.1952	1.2655	1.3358
20	1.4061	1.4765	1.5468	1.6171	1.6874	1.7577	1.8280	1.8983	1.9686	2.0389
30	2.1092	2.1795	2.2498	2.3201	2.3904	2.4607	2.5311	2.6014	2.6717	2.7420
40	2.8123	2.8826	2.9529	3.0232	3.0935	3.1638	3.2341	3.3044	3.3747	3.4450
50	3.5154	3.5857	3.6560	3.7263	3.7966	3.8669	3.9372	4.0075	4.0778	4.1481
60	4.2184	4.2887	4.3590	4.4293	4.4997	4.5700	4.6403	4.7106	4.7809	4.8512
70	4.9215	4.9918	5.0621	5.1324	5.2027	5.2730	5.3433	5.4136	5.4839	5.5543
80	5.6246	5.6949	5.7652	5.8355	5.9058	5.9761	6.0464	6.1167	6.1870	6.2573
90	6.3276	6.3980	6.4682	6.5386	6.6089	6.6792	6.7495	6.8198	6.8901	6.9604
100	7.0307	7.1010	7.1713	7.2416	7.3120	7.3822	7.4525	7.5228	7.5932	7.6635

kg per sq. cm	0 lb. per sq. in.	1 lb. per sq. in.	2 lb. per sq. in.	3 lb. per sq. in.	4 lb. per sq. in.	5 lb. per sq. in.	6 lb. per sq. in.	7 lb. per sq. in.	8 lb. per sq. in.	9 lb. per sq. in.
0	..	14.22	28.45	42.67	56.89	71.12	85.34	99.56	113.79	128.01
10	142.23	156.46	170.68	184.90	199.13	213.35	227.57	241.80	256.02	270.24
20	284.47	298.69	312.91	327.14	341.36	355.58	369.81	384.03	398.25	412.48
30	426.70	440.92	455.15	469.37	483.59	497.82	512.04	526.26	540.49	554.71
40	568.93	583.16	597.38	611.60	625.83	640.05	654.27	668.50	682.72	696.94
50	711.17	725.39	739.61	753.84	768.06	782.28	796.51	810.73	824.95	839.18
60	853.40	867.62	881.85	896.07	910.29	924.52	938.74	952.96	967.19	981.41
70	995.63	1009.9	1024.1	1038.3	1052.5	1066.8	1081.0	1095.2	1109.4	1123.6
80	1137.9	1152.1	1166.3	1180.5	1194.8	1209.0	1223.2	1237.4	1251.7	1265.9
90	1280.1	1294.3	1308.6	1322.8	1337.0	1351.2	1365.4	1379.7	1393.9	1408.1
100	1422.3	1436.6	1450.8	1465.0	1479.2	1493.4	1507.7	1521.9	1536.1	1550.3

TABLE D-11. Pound Feet to Kilogram Meters Conversion Table

lb./ft.	0 kg metre	1 kg metre	2 kg metre	3 kg metre	4 kg metre	5 kg metre	6 kg metre	7 kg metre	8 kg metre	9 kg metre
0	..	0.138	0.277	0.415	0.553	0.691	0.830	0.968	1.106	1.244
10	1.383	1.521	1.659	1.797	1.936	2.074	2.212	2.350	2.489	2.627
20	2.765	2.903	3.041	3.180	3.318	3.456	3.595	3.733	3.871	4.009
30	4.148	4.286	4.424	4.562	4.701	4.839	4.977	5.115	5.254	5.392
40	5.530	5.669	5.807	5.945	6.083	6.222	6.360	6.498	6.636	6.775
50	6.913	7.051	7.189	7.328	7.466	7.604	7.742	7.881	8.019	8.157
60	8.295	8.434	8.572	8.710	8.848	8.987	9.125	9.263	9.401	9.540
70	9.678	9.816	9.954	10.093	10.231	10.369	10.507	10.646	10.784	10.922
80	11.060	11.199	11.337	11.475	11.613	11.752	11.890	12.028	12.166	12.305
90	12.443	12.581	12.719	12.858	12.996	13.134	13.272	13.411	13.549	13.687
100	13.826	13.964	14.102	14.240	14.379	14.517	14.655	14.793	14.932	15.070

kg/m	0 lb. ft.	1 lb. ft.	2 lb. ft.	3 lb. ft.	4 lb. ft.	5 lb. ft.	6 lb. ft.	7 lb. ft.	8 lb. ft.	9 lb. ft.
0	..	7.23	14.47	21.70	28.93	36.17	43.40	50.63	57.87	65.10
10	72.33	79.56	86.80	94.03	101.26	108.50	115.73	122.96	130.20	137.43
20	144.66	151.89	159.13	166.36	173.59	180.83	188.06	195.29	202.52	209.76
30	216.99	224.22	231.46	238.69	245.92	253.16	260.39	267.62	274.86	282.09
40	289.32	296.55	303.79	311.02	318.25	325.49	332.72	339.95	347.19	354.42
50	361.65	368.88	376.12	383.35	390.58	397.82	405.05	412.28	419.52	426.75
60	433.98	441.21	448.45	455.68	462.91	470.15	477.38	484.61	491.85	499.08
70	506.31	513.54	520.78	528.01	535.24	542.48	549.71	556.94	564.18	571.41
80	578.64	585.87	593.11	600.34	607.57	614.81	622.04	629.27	636.51	643.74
90	650.97	658.23	665.44	672.67	679.90	687.14	694.37	701.60	708.84	716.07
100	723.30	730.53	737.77	745.00	752.23	759.47	766.70	773.93	781.17	788.40

TABLE D-12. Comparative Sheet Metal Thicknesses

Gauge No.	Uncoated Steel and Stainless Steel*	Aluminum, Brass, and Copper
28	0.015" (1/64")	0.012"
26	0.018"	0.016" (1/64")
24	0.024"	0.020"
22	0.030"	0.025"
20	0.036" (1/32")	0.032" (1/32")
18	0.048" (3/64")	0.040"
16	0.060" (1/16")	0.051"
14	0.075" (5/64")	0.064" (1/16")
12	0.105" (7/64")	0.081" (5/64")

*Galvanized steel is slightly thicker than uncoated or stainless steel.

Table D-13. Equivalencies

Square Measure Equivalents

1 square yard = 0.836 square meter
1 square foot = 0.0929 square meter = 929 square centimeters
1 square inch = 6.452 square centimeters = 645.2 square millimeters

1 square meter = 10.764 square feet = 1.196 square yards
1 square centimeter = 0.155 square inch
1 square millimeter = 0.00155 square inch

Cubic Measure Equivalents

1 cubic inch = 16.38706 cubic centimeters
100 cubic inches = 1.64 liters
1 Imperial gallon = 4.546 liters
1 Imperial quart = 1.136 liters
1 US gallon = 3.785 liters
1 US quart = 0.946 liter

1 cubic centimeter = 0.061 cubic inch
1 liter (cubic decimeter) = 0.0353 cubic foot = 61.023 cubic inches
1 liter = 0.2642 US gallon = 1.0567 US quarts = 0.2200 Imperial gallon

Weight Equivalents

1 Imperial ton (UK) = 2240 pounds (long ton)
1 short ton (USA) = 2000 pounds
1 ton (of 2000 pounds) = 0.9072 metric ton
1 ton (of 2240 pounds) = 1.016 metric tons = 1016 kilograms
1 pound = 0.4536 kilogram = 453.6 grams

1 metric ton = 2204.6 pounds
1 kilogram = 2.2046 pounds

Miscellaneous Equivalents

1 Imperial gallon (UK) = 1.2 gallons (US)
1 h.p. = 2,544 Btus
1 kw = 3,413 Btus
1 watt = 3.413 Btus

Index

Numbers in **bold** refer to pages with illustrations

A

absorbed glass mat batteries. *See* AGM (absorbed glass mat) batteries
absorption phase, 29–30, 32–33
ABYC. *See* American Boat and Yacht Council (ABYC)
AC circuits, **2–3**, 133–56; color codes, 145–46; galvanic corrosion and, 135, 137, 200; galvanic isolation, **137–39**, **141**, **143**–44; grounding circuits, **134–37**, 141, **142**, **144**, 232; leaks, 138–39, 152, **153**, 208, 218; loads, **49**–50, 258–**59**, 260; polarity testers, 149–**50**; receptacles, 150–**51**; ship-to-shore transfer switch, **151**; single-phase circuits, 145–**51**; testing, 151–**54**, 156. *See also* circuit breakers
AC compressors, **475**, 499
accumulator tanks, **606**
AC current, 85, **238**
AC generators, **290–305**; battery chargers and, 242; cogeneration, 53–**54**; features, **294**; maintenance, 294–95, 303; operational principles, **290**–94; setup, **133**, **134**; troubleshooting, 295–303, **297**, **298**, **299**, **300**, **301**, **302**; types of, **291**–94; use of, 48–**49**, 51, 67; variable-speed technology, 303–5
AC refrigeration, 472, **475**–76
AC ripple voltage, **97**, 241
AC watermakers, 613
Adaptive Energy Optimizer (Danfoss), 481–**82**, 486
aerials. *See* antennas
aft-hung rudders, **622**–23
AGM (absorbed glass mat) batteries, **8**, 14–**16**; charging, 239, 241, 245; problems with, 9, 84, 85; reliability of, 12, 257; temperature and, 75
AGS (automatic generator start) devices, 56–57
Ah (amp-hours), 4, **13**
AIC (ampere interrupting capacity), 181–82
air-conditioning systems: installation, **288–89**, 458–59, 490–91, **662–63**; maintenance, **495–96**; operational principles, 493, 495; options, 488–89; power demand of, **67**; pressures, **498**; sizing, 489–**90**
air-conditioning system troubleshooting and repair, 496–509; clutch replacement, **501**–4; cooling-water differentials, 496–97; failure to run, 498–504; leak detection, 498; pressures, 497–**98**; sight glass, 496; super-heat adjustments, **507**–9; unit cuts an and off, 504; unit fails to cool, 504–7, **506**
air-cooled condensers, 484–85, 497, 505
Air Head toilets, 558
air switches, **604**
alcohol, 676
alcohol appliances: burners, **678**–81; carbon monoxide formation, 686–**87**; stoves, **677–78**
alloys, 200–203
Alston, Kevin, 467
alternating current. *See* AC entries
alternators, 4, 45, 86–**87**; belts, 26, 27–28, 89–91, **90**; charging battery banks, **37–41**; construction, **86**, **88**; diode testing, **97**–99; dual-voltage DC systems, 62–**64**; horse-power requirements, 26; ignition-protected alternators, 24, 87; installation, 24, 25–**26**, **37**, **38**, **72–73**, 88–**91**; interference, 355, 358–**59**; isolated-ground alternators, 87; maintenance, 88–**91**; operational principles, 85–**88**; output, **23**–24, **25**, 26, 104–**5**; overcurrent protection, 190; pulleys, 24–25, 27–28, 89–**90**; repairing, 99–**104**; speed of rotation, 24–**25**
alternators, troubleshooting: no output, **94**–99; over-charging, 94; undercharging, 91–**93**
aluminum, 199, 201, 205–6
aluminum hulls, 215, 216, 217, 568–**69**
aluminum seacocks, 562
aluminum spars and spreaders, 737–**43**, 746
aluminum tanks, **520–21**, **523**
American Boat and Yacht Council (ABYC) standards, **536**; batteries, 35; battery chargers, **243**; battery isolation switch, 42; bearings, 450; cables, electrical, 157–**58**, 159, 161, 162–63, 175, **178**; capacitors, 139; carbon monoxide alarms, 689; circuit breakers, 149, 184, 193–94; connectors and terminals, 170, 178–79, 181; corrosion protection, 215, 217; distribution panels, 179, **180**; electrical circuits, 70, 233; electric motors, 184–85; electro-magnetic compatibility, 340; fuel hoses, 537; gal-vanic isolation, 139, 143–44; gas appliances, 665, **668**, 669, 670, 671, 673, 678, 684; graphite packing tape, 444; ground fault circuit breakers, 140; grounding circuits, **144**; heating systems, 683; hoses, 533, 538; isolation transformers, **144**, 146; lightning protection, 219, 223–**24**, 226; motors, 583; overcurrent protection, 188–**90**; receptacles, 151; reverse polarity indicating device, 150; seacocks, 560–61, 564; shaft seals, 442, 443; shore power, 146, **147**; switches, 602; tanks, 518, 520, 521, 525, 527; voltage drop tables, 164, 165, 168
American Petroleum Institute (API), 366–67
American Wire Gauge (AWG), 164, 166
ammeters, 17, 42, **43**, 116, **310**
ampacity of cables, 161–64, 184
amperage (amps), 85; amps-to-watts conversion, 17; measuring, 116, 118, 119–20, 310–11, 321; shore power choices, 149; water system analogy, 114–16
ampere interrupting capacity (AIC), 181–82

bosun's chair, **636**
bowsprits, 736
bow thrusters, 41, 729
brake band, **425**
brass, 186, 199, 201, 205–6, 562
bridge rectifiers, **87**, **88**, **292**, **297**
British Marine Electronics Association (BMEA), 353
bronze, 186, **198**, 204, 205–6, **207**, **216**, **218**, 562, 569
Brunton Autoprop, **457**
brushes, **86**, 103; maintenance, **91**; repairing, 100–**102**
brushless AC generators, **292**–93, 300–303, **301**, **302**
brushless alternators, 86
brushless DC (BLDC) motors, **66**–**68**, 70–71
brush spring, **91**
bulk charge, 29–30, 31–32, 33, **240**, 245
burners: alcohol, kerosene, and diesel, **677**, **678**–81; gas appliances, **672**–**75**
bus bars, **180**–**81**, **185**, 186, 187, **263**
butane. *See* gas
bypass valves, **643**

C
cabin heaters: carbon monoxide formation, 686–**87**; diesel and kerosene, 677, 682–84, **683**; gas, **674**; installation, **662**–**63**
cable clamps, **641**, **750**, 757
cables, electrical, **157**–**68**; ABYC standards, 157–**58**, 159, 161, 162–63, 175, **178**; ampacity, 161–64, 184; color codes, 160; construction, **157**–**58**, 160, **166**; cost, 57–58, 64; data, 193; equalizer vs. converter installation, 59–60; European cable-sizing procedures, 167, 168; installation, 175–79, **176**, **177**, **178**, 185; ISO standards, 157–**58**, 159, 161, 162–63, **178**; labeling, **158**, 159; size, 57–58, 160–61, 166; three-cable boat, 192–95; UL standards, 158, 159, 166; U.S. Coast Guard standards, 159; voltage drop and, 164–68; weight, 57–58, 64
cable steering, **627**, **628**, 637, 638–**41**

calcium buildup, 546–**47**
cam cleat, **695**
Campingaz cylinders, 665–66
capacitive coupling, 117–18
capacitors, 138–**39**, **298**–**99**, 499
capacitor-start motors, 308
capacity testing, 82
capillary tubes, 486, 506
cap shrouds, **736**, **761**, **762**, 763, 764, 765
captive-air accumulator tanks, **606**
carbon-ceramic seals, 575, **588**, 589
carbon dioxide, 462, 664
carbon fiber spars, 226–27, 743–**45**, 746
carbon monoxide, 664
carbon monoxide alarms, 688–91, **690**
carbon monoxide poisoning, 684–**88**, **689**
carbon-silica aerogel core material, **466**, **467**
Castlok terminals, **751**, **752**
catamarans, 232, **629**
cathodic disbondment, 217
cathodic protection, **214**–19
CE (Conformité Européene)-marked equipment, 228, 245, 340, 342
central bonding straps, **233**
centrifugal pumps: applications, 577; chemical compatibility, 575; installation, 490–91, 574, 577–84; operational principles, **573**; performance, **579**, **580**; troubleshooting, 591–**92**
CFCs (chlorofluorocarbons), **460**, 461–62
chain, 712–14, **713**
chain lockers, **709**, **710**
chainplates, **730**–**31**, 757–**58**, **760**
charge acceptance rate, 19, 23, 29, **31**, 33, 51
charge-divert regulators, 271–**72**, 273
chart lights, **333**
check valves, 582, **643**, **677**
check valve wrench, 677, **678**
chemical compatibility, 575, 576
chilled-water circuits, 491
chlorinated polyvinyl chloride (CPVC) pipe, 531
chlorofluorocarbons (CFCs), **460**, 461–62
chromium, 199, 202, 203, 522

circuit breakers: ABYC standards, 149, 184, 193–94; ampere interrupting capacity (AIC), 181–82; electronic, 194; ground fault circuit breakers, 140; installation, 180, **181**; ISO standards, 149, 192; performance, **191**–92; remotely operated, 192–94; size, 183–**84**; smart, 194, 606; two-pole breakers, **149**
clamping voltage, 228
Clark Pump (Spectra), 609, **610**, 611, **612**
Clean Air Act (1990), 461
clevis pins, **759**
Climate Control compressors, 501, **504**
clutches: adjustments, 429, **430**–31, 432; Blissfield, 501, **504**; Climate Control, 501, **504**; forward, 424, **425**, **426**; Hurth adjustments, 432; installation, **422**–**23**; maintenance and troubleshooting, **589**–91; replacement, **501**–**4**; reverse, 424, **425**, **426**; Sanden, **501**–**4**; Sanden clutch, **500**; slipping, 433; wheel clutch, **641**, 642
CNG (compressed natural gas), 538, 664–65, 674
coaxial cable, **157**, 346–**51**
Code of Federal Regulations (CFR), 518
Code of Practice for Electrical and Electronics Installations in Boats (BMEA), 353
coffee-grinder winches, 699
cogeneration, 53–55, **54**, **256**
coil-spring seals, **588**, 589
cold cranking amps (CCA), 11, **13**, 42
common ground point, 232–**33**
commutator: construction, **306**; electronic commutator, **66**, 71; maintenance, 311–**14**, **323**, **324**, **325**
compasses, 231, 354, 640
compressed natural gas (CNG), 538, 664–65, 674
compression fittings, **529**, **751**–53
compressors: installation, **458**–**59**; refrigeration cycle, 492–94, **493**; speed, 480, **481**–**82**, 486; troubleshooting, 505–**6**; vacuuming a unit, 514–15

F

fasteners: in aluminum, 738–40, **741**; stainless steel, **704**, 740; in wood, **733–34**

FCC Rule 15, Part B, 245, 340, 342

feathering propellers, 453, **455–56, 457**

ferritic stainless steel, **202**–3

ferro-resonant chargers, 238, **239, 240**, 244, **249**

fiberglass hulls, 216, 217, 562–63, 567, **568**

fiberglass marine exhaust tubing, 533

fiberglass rudders, 630

fiberglass tanks, 518, 524, 527

fiber rigging, 754–55

field winding, 85, **86**

filament igniters, 673, **714–19**

filtering techniques, 356–58, **357**

Fischer Panda generator, **56, 294**

fishhook, 639

fixed-pitch propellers, 452

flame primers, **384**

flapper valves, 548, **549**, 551, 552

flare fittings, **529**–30

flashing the field, **96**, 97, 297–98, 302–3

flexible-impeller pumps. *See* variable-volume impeller pumps

flexible tanks, 526

Flex-O-Fold propellers, **454–55**

float charge, **33**, 34, **240**, 244, 245, 285

float switches, **208–9, 602–3, 605**, 606

flooded electrolyte batteries, 6–7

flooding rates, **581**, 583

fluorescent lights, 326, 327, **329–32**, 359, **662–63**

flute stopper, 781

fluxgate compasses, 231, 647

folding propellers, 453–55, **454**, 456–57

forestays, **730–31**, 763, **768–69**

fork terminals, 758, **759**

four-part purchase, **698**

Fourwinds generators, **269**

fractional rig tuning, 764

freezers, **458–59**, 479, 480, 497

Freon-12, 460–61, 462–63

Freon-22, 460, 490

frequency, 85, 238

freshwater pumps, 575, 577

freshwater tanks, **516–17**

Frigoboat: couplings and tubing, **481**; evaporator plates, 478–**79**; keel cooler, **484**–85, 495; Smart Speed Control, **481**–82, 486

fuel, 676–77. *See also specific fuels*

fuel-burning appliances, 686–**87**. *See also* alcohol appliances; diesel appliances; gas appliances; kerosene appliances

fuel cells, 65–66

fuel filters, 677, 681

fuel injection pumps, **388**–95

fuel pumps, 577

fuel tanks and systems, 214, **677–78**; hoses, **536–37**; ISO standards, 214, 524, 527; pipe, 531; tanks, 518, 519, 521, 524, 525–**27**; U.S. Coast Guard standards, 214, 524

full-skeg rudders, **622**

fuses, 183–**84**, 189

G

gain, 343–45, **344**

gaiter-type rudderstock seals, 634–**35**

Galley Maid Central Waste Treatment System, 559–60

galvanic cells, 199–**200**

galvanic corrosion: AC circuits and, 135, 137, 200; conditions for, 203, 205; electrolytes and, **198**–201, 203, **205**, 206, 215; galvanic cells, 199–**200**; galvanic series, **198**–203; prevention, 53, 203–**7**

galvanic isolators: ABYC standards, 139, 143–44; converters used for, 61–62; corrosion and, 200, 219; location, **139, 141**; operational principles, **137–39**, 145; testing, **143**

galvanic series of metals, **198**–203

galvanized chain, 713–14

galvanized pipe, 530–31

gas: cylinder types, 665–66; hoses, 538; pressure measurement, 668, **669**; refilling cylinders, 665–67, **666**; safety precautions, 665; types of, 664

gas appliances: ABYC stan-

dards, 665, **668**, 669, 670, 671, 673, 678, 684; gas lockers, **667–68**; installation, **667**–72; ISO standards, 668, 669–70, 671; troubleshooting, **672–75**

gasoline engines, 358

gasoline tanks, 518, 524, 525–27, 526

gassing of batteries, 7, 9, 14, 15, 31

gassing voltage, 33

gate valves, **561**, 567

gauge sets, 463, **510**, 511–15

geared steering, 623–27, **624, 625, 626**, 636–**38**

gears, 719–**21**

gear-type lift pumps, **394**

gel-cell batteries, **7**–8, **14**–15; charging, 239, 241, 245; problems with, 9, 84, 85; reliability of, 12, 257; temperature and, 75, **76**, 78

generators, **236–37**; BLDC motors and, **66–68**, 70–71; limitations of, 303; use of, 18

generators, types of: belt-driven VST generators, 304, 305; DC generators, 53, 55–57, **56**, 68, 190, **305**; permanent-magnet generators, **68**; prop-shaft generators, 267; VST, 303–5; water generators, 266, 267. *See also* AC generators; wind generators

genoa sheet loads, **697**

Glacier Bay: holding plates, **477**; hose clamps, 538; insulation, **467, 472, 473**, 474–75; insulation tests, 465; Micro Blast Chiller, 488; Micro HPS system, **487**–88

globe valves, 561, 567

glow plugs, **384–85**

going aloft, **747**

golf-cart batteries, 15

Gori three-bladed folding propeller, 456–57

The Gougeon Brothers on Boat Construction, 734

governors, **309**

graphite packing tape, 444

Groco ball valve, **566**

grounded circuits, 231–32

ground fault circuit breakers (GFCBs), 140

ground fault circuit interruptors (GFCIs), 140, 150

ground faults, **130–32**, 152, **153**

refrigeration systems, types of: AC units, 472, **475**–76; constant-cycling AC units, 472; constant-cycling DC units, 464, **478–81**, 483, **484**–87, **499**–501; DC units, 476; engine-driven units, 476–78, **499**, **501**–4, **510**; high-capacity holding-plate DC units, 483, 485–86, 487; holding-plate AC units, 472, **475**–76; holding-plate DC units, **483**, 485–86, 489, **499**, **500**; holding-plate units, **476**–78, 509; hybrid systems, **487**–88

refrigeration system troubleshooting and repair, 496–509; clutch replacement, **501**–4; cooling-water differentials, 496–97; failure to run, 498–504; leak detection, 498; pressures, 497–**98**; sight glass, 496; superheat adjustments, **507**–9; unit cuts an and off, 504; unit fails to cool, 504–7, **506**

relays, battery paralleling, 39–**40**, **43**, 45, 62, **63**, 64

remotely operated circuit breakers (ROCBs), 193

remotely operated switches, 192–94

reserve capacity, **13**

residual current circuit breakers (RCCBs), 140

residual current devices (RCDs), 140

resistance, 114, **115–16**, 117, **120–21**

resistance effect, 578–79

resistance tests, 311

reverse-avalanche silicon diodes, 88–**89**

reverse polarity indicating device, 149–**50**

rheostats, **309**

rigging. *See* standing rigging

ripple voltage, **97**, 241

rod rigging, 748, **753**–54, **762**

roller reefing and furling, **766–81**; bearings, **769**–72; behind-the-mast reefing, 778–81, **779**, **780**; booms, **781**; extrusions, **771**–72; halyard wrap, **772**–74; headsails, **766–76**, **777–78**; in-mast reefing, 778–81, **779**, **780**; installation, **730–31**; maintenance, 776–77; powered

headsail reefers, **776**; riding turns on the reefing drum, 774–**75**; sail damage, 775–76; tips, 776

rolling ball concept, **223**

rope lockers, **709**, **710**

rotary pumps: applications, 577; chemical compatibility, 575, 576; operational principles, **572**–73; troubleshooting, 587, **590**, 591

rotational molding, 524

Rotolock valves, 505–**6**, **511**–14

rotors, 85, **86**, **103**–4, **305**

rotor windings, **292**, 301–2

Royal Flush toilets, 554

rubber-plug seacocks, **566**–67

rubber sanitation hoses, 535

rubber sleeve bearings, **422–23**, 424, **449–51**

rudder bearings, 631–**33**

rudderhead fittings, **635–36**, **640**

rudders: auxiliary, 655, 656; construction, 630–**31**; installation, **620–21**; maintenance and troubleshooting, **630–31**; twin installation, 628–30, **629**; wide-angle geometry, 637–**38**

rudder shaft seals, 449, 584, **634–35**

rudderstocks, 623, 630–**31**, **632**, 634–**35**

rudderstops, 645–**46**

Rule Industries, **580**

Rule pumps, 603, **605**

S

sacrificial anodes. *See* zinc anodes

SAE (Society of Automotive Engineers), 164, 166

sailboats: antennas, **345**–46; lightning protection, **222–23**, 232; stainless steel corrosion, 204; struts, 449

saildrives, 424, **428**

sail locker, **710**

sails. *See* headsails; mainsails

sail tracks and slides, **743**

saltwater intrusion, 360–61

Sanden clutch, **500**, **501**–4

Sanden compressors, **501**–4

sanitation hoses, 535–**36**, **542**

sanitation systems, **516–17**, 535–**36**, **541**, **542**, **544**, 558–60, **559**

SanX MSD (Sealand), 560

scarf joints, **732**, 737

Schaefer in-boom reefing, **781**

Schrader-type valves, 506, **511–14**

scientific rig tensioning, **763**–64

sealed valve regulated (SVR) batteries. *See* gel-cell batteries.

SCR (silicon-controlled rectifier), 86–**87**, **88**, **238**, **240**

seacocks, 560–**69**; ABYC standards, 560–61, 564; galvanic isolation, **207**; handles, 561, **562**; installation, 490–91, 567–**69**; ISO standards, 561, 564; maintenance, 532; materials, **562–64**, 567–68; resistance, 578; testing, **564**–65, 568; types of, **561**, 562, **565**–67

Sea Frost holding plate, **477**

SeaLand SanX MSD, 560

sealed combustion chamber, 686

Sea Recovery Energy Transfer Device, **609**–11

self-aligning bearings, **632**

self-steering. *See* wind vane self-steering

self-tailing winches, 703–4, **708**

series regulators, 40, **41**, 45

series-wound motors, **306**–7, 308–**9**, 311, 314–15

servopendulum wind vane self-steering, **654**, 655, 656

setscrew, 437, **438**

shaded-pole induction motors, **308**

shaft brakes, 435–**37**

shaft log, **446**, **447**, 449

shaft seals: ABYC standards, 442, 443; carbon-ceramic seals, 575; engine alignment and, 448–49; externally driven compressors, 495, **496**; leaks, 584; lip-type seals, 424, **447–48**, 449, 575, **588**, 589, **634**, 635; mechanical seals, 445–47, **446**, 449; replacement, **588**–89; rudder shaft seals, 449, 584, **634–35**; stuffing boxes, **422–23**, 424, **442–45**, 449, 633, 634

sheaves, **627**, 638–**39**

shedding (battery failure), **8**–9, 19

shielding techniques, **356**